GREAT POLITICAL THINKERS

PLATO TO THE PRESENT

SIXTH EDITION

GREAT POLITICAL THINKERS

PLATO TO THE PRESENT

SIXTH EDITION

William Ebenstein
(1910–1976)

*University of Wisconsin at Madison, Princeton University,
and University of California at Santa Barbara*

Alan Ebenstein

Harcourt College Publishers

Fort Worth   Philadelphia   San Diego   New York   Orlando   Austin
San Antonio   Toronto   Montreal   London   Sydney   Tokyo

Publisher	Earl McPeek
Executive Editor	David Tatom
Market Strategist	Laura M. Brennan
Project Editor	Laura Therese Miley
Art Director	Burl Sloan
Production Manager	Diane Gray

Cover Image © PhotoDisc

ISBN: 0-15-507889-5
Library of Congress Catalog Card Number: 99-61321

Address for Domestic Orders
Harcourt College Publishers, 6277 Sea Harbor Drive, Orlando, FL 32887-6777
800-782-4479

Address for International Orders
International Customer Service
Harcourt, Inc., 6277 Sea Harbor Drive, Orlando, FL 32887-6777
407-345-3800
(fax) 407-345-4060
(e-mail) hbintl@harcourtbrace.com

Address for Editorial Correspondence
Harcourt College Publishers, 301 Commerce Street, Suite 3700, Fort Worth, TX 76102

Web Site Address
http://www.harcourtcollege.com

Printed in the United States of America

9 0 1 2 3 4 5 6 7 8   039   9 8 7 6 5 4 3 2

Harcourt College Publishers

To Ruth

W. E.

Works by WILLIAM EBENSTEIN

FASCISM AT WORK

REINE RECHTSLEHRE

FASCIST ITALY

THE LAW OF PUBLIC HOUSING

THE NAZI STATE

THE GERMAN RECORD
A Political Portrait

THE PURE THEORY OF LAW

MAN AND THE STATE
Modern Political Ideas

GREAT POLITICAL THINKERS
Plato to the Present, Sixth Edition (co-author)

INTRODUCTION TO POLITICAL PHILOSOPHY

MODERN POLITICAL THOUGHT
The Great Issues, Second Edition

TODAY'S ISMS
Socialism, Capitalism, Fascism, Communism, Libertarianism, Tenth Edition (co-author)

POLITICAL THOUGHT IN PERSPECTIVE

CHURCH AND STATE IN FRANCO SPAIN

TWO WAYS OF LIFE
The Communist Challenge to Democracy, Second Edition

TOTALITARIANISM
New Perspectives

COMMUNISM IN THEORY AND PRACTICE

AMERICAN GOVERNMENT IN THE TWENTIETH CENTURY
Third Edition (co-author)

AMERICAN DEMOCRACY IN WORLD PERSPECTIVE
Fifth Edition (co-author)

INTRODUCTION TO POLITICAL THINKERS
(co-author)

Works by ALAN EBENSTEIN

THE GREATEST HAPPINESS PRINCIPLE
An Examination of Utilitarianism

GREAT POLITICAL THINKERS
Plato to the Present, Sixth Edition (co-author)

INTRODUCTION TO POLITICAL THINKERS
(co-author)

TODAY'S ISMS
Socialism, Capitalism, Fascism, Communism, Libertarianism, Tenth Edition (co-author)

EDWIN CANNAN
Liberal Doyen

FRIEDRICH HAYEK
The Road to Libertarianism

PREFACE

PREFACE TO THE SIXTH EDITION

This 2000 edition of *Great Political Thinkers* marks the fiftieth publication year of this best-selling textbook of the history of political philosophy. Political theory has changed since 1951. Rawls was not on the scene yet, Berlin barely was a presence, and Hayek was author of a recent anti-planning work. Topical thinkers included those who are not so considered now. Communism was a much larger presence—to say the least. Fascism was a recent force.

For the sixth edition, *Great Political Thinkers* features a tripartite division. I have written a new Christianity section, incorporating material from my father, and retitled the chapter including the section "The Jewish Belief in One God, and Christian Love," closer to my father's original titles. I have revised the Hegel chapter and added new reading selections to it and the chapter on Kant. Tocqueville and Mill now are in separate chapters from the single "The Dilemma of Democracy: Liberty and Equality" chapter comprising both of them in previous editions, and I have added to the Mill chapter. A Mill reading from the first four editions of *Great Political Thinkers* has been returned to this edition. The Nietzsche section has been separated into a chapter.

The chapters on liberalism, socialism, and the welfare state have been reworked—the chapters most revised over the half-century. Keynes and Myrdal have been moved from the chapter now titled "From Classical Liberalism to Democratic Socialism," and Thomas Hill Green and Harold Laski (of whom my father was a student) have been added in their places. Keynes and Myrdal, together with William Beveridge (also, with Green and Laski, new to this edition), now compromise the following chapter, "The Welfare State." I almost entirely have rewritten the Keynes section introductory essay. In place of the fifth edition chapter on Hayek, the chapter "Libertarianism," incorporating a new introductory essay on Hayek and Milton Friedman (who is new to this edition), is substituted. The chapter on Isaiah Berlin is new and I have rewritten the Rawls chapter.

Bill Herms prepared new bibliographical entries and provided general advice, significantly contributing to this edition. I again should like to thank Larry Adams, Tom Schrock, and Gordon Baker for their advice, encouragement, and assistance. Bill, Larry, and Rob Ebenstein read new introductory essay drafts. Finally, I especially should like to thank David Tatom for having given me the opportunity to revise the fifth edition of *Great Political Thinkers,* making this edition and my other related work possible.

Alan Ebenstein
Santa Barbara, California
1999

ORIGINAL PREFACE

The purpose of this book is to present the major turning points of western political thought from Plato to the present. The best way to understand these vital and trailblazing ideas is to read the great writers themselves rather than works about them. There is room for commentary and critical analysis, but neither can take the place of the original sources. Political philosophy, like all philosophy, is not always easy and unambiguous, and the reproduction of the original statements familiarizes the reader most faithfully with the intention of the writer. Moreover, the great works of political literature have attained the rank of classics not only because they reveal philosophical depth and penetration but because they are perennially fresh and exciting as pieces of literature, providing aesthetic pleasure and enjoyment as well as intellectual challenge and stimulation. The presentation of carefully selected portions from original writings is most likely to attain both objectives.

The original materials from the great political writings are supplemented in this book in two ways. First, each chapter is prefaced by an introductory essay that seeks to place thinkers and issues in the proper historical setting and perspective. Second, the Bibliographical Notes at the end of the book contain explanatory and critical data and comments designed to help the student in his research on a particular author or problem. The customary listing of mere titles for further reading is of little use to the student who desires to broaden the range and scope of his knowledge, and it is hoped that the more detailed Bibliographical Notes in this book will aid him in discovering and exploring the vast territories of political philosophy. In general, the emphasis is on books and articles in English, but consideration is also given to bibliographical resources in other languages.

The problem of selecting important political writers for a book of this sort is not without its difficulties. Some authors are obvious musts, others are less imperative. With regard to American political thought, the field has grown so immensely that I hope to prepare a separate volume on it which will give due scope to its importance. Also, the question arises whether each author should be presented by means of a comparatively lengthy selection from his major work or by several briefer excerpts from several of his works. Most chapters in this book deal with only one writer, and the selection is usually limited to his single most important work. Such a method makes it possible for the reader to concentrate on fewer authors and to familiarize himself more thoroughly with the outstanding political classics of world literature and philosophy. The purpose of providing portions of great works in the original is to whet the reader's appetite to read them in their entirety, and it is hoped that this book will contribute to that end.

Whether all authors included deserve to be called "great" is open to question. Particularly regarding the more recent writers, history alone will tell how important they are from a long-term viewpoint. In some instances writers have been included, not necessarily because they are great thinkers, but because they have had considerable influence on politics, and because their statements typify an entire school of thought that is of direct and vital concern today. Similarly, not all the authors included fall, strictly speaking, into the domain of traditional political science. But it is hoped that a great economist, like Keynes, or a great psychologist, like Freud, will awaken in the student of politics the awareness that our political wisdom will grow in proportion to our ability to draw on new sources of knowledge and insight.

William Ebenstein
Princeton, New Jersey
1950

PREFACE TO THE SECOND EDITION

The friendly and generous reception accorded the first edition by both students and teachers has encouraged publication of a second edition. A new chapter on The Welfare State has been added, emphasizing its philosophical, political, and economic aspects. I hope that the usefulness of the book will thus be considerably enhanced, since the problem of the welfare state is inevitably emerging as one of the major issues of contemporary political thought.

W. E., *1956*

PREFACE TO THE THIRD EDITION

In addition to many minor changes, this new edition contains two major ones: Chapter 12 on the Protestant Reformation has been greatly expanded by the inclusion of Luther and Calvin, and the Bibliographical Notes have been completely revised and brought up-to-date.

W. E., *1960*

PREFACE TO THE FOURTH EDITION

The continuously friendly and generous reception accorded to the previous three editions by both students and teachers of political ideas has encouraged publication of a fourth edition, completely revised and reset. The introductory essays have been rewritten and in numerous cases substantially expanded, and some readings have been added and others removed. Thus, Chapter Twenty-three, "Revolutionary Communism," now includes selections from Marx's *Economic and Philosophical Manuscripts* of 1844, an essay of the young Marx long neglected and only recently translated into English. Chapter Twenty-four on "Democratic Socialism" and Chapter Twenty-five on "The Welfare State" have been combined into a new Chapter Twenty-four, "Democratic Socialism and the Welfare State," because welfare state policies have become such a central concern of democratic socialist parties and governments. In this new Chapter Twenty-four, Hugh Gaitskell, the late leader of the British Labour Party, presents new approaches to socialism in general and to nationalization in particular, while Gunnar Myrdal, the great Swedish social scientist, discusses the basic reasons for the growth of economic planning and social welfare and their intimate connection with democratic socialism. In addition to the substantial changes in the introductory essays and selected readings, the Bibliographical Notes have been completely revised and considerably increased in length.

W. E., Santa Barbara, California, *1969*

PREFACE TO THE FIFTH EDITION

Over the forty years since its first edition appeared in 1951, *Great Political Thinkers: Plato to the Present* has established itself as one of the all-time best sellers in the area of the history of political theory. The purpose of the fifth edition is to update the material presented. The method of this edition remains what it has always been: introductory essays on the greatest political thinkers—placing them in their historical contexts and providing some analytic apparatus—followed by key selections from the thinkers' greatest works. This approach combines the strengths of original readings and of commentary. In addition, comprehensive "Bibliographical Notes" are provided at the end of the book.

Extensive market research was performed in advance of this edition. Surveys were sent to existing users of *Great Political Thinkers,* and personal interviews were conducted. As a result, three thinkers have been excluded—Clement Attlee, Lord Lindsay of Birker, and Hugh Gaitskell—and eight thinkers have been added—John Rawls, Friedrich Hayek, Mohandas Gandhi, Friedrich Nietzsche, Adam Smith, Immanuel Kant, David Hume, and Epicurus. Further, at his death, William Ebenstein was working on a book to be titled *The Roots of the West,* the purpose of which would have been to trace the beginnings of western political thought to Greek rationalism, Jewish monotheism, and Christian love. His chapter drafts on these subjects have been incorporated here to give a more interpretive account.

Existing users of *Great Political Thinkers* will find that, with the exception of the chapter "Democratic Socialism and the Welfare State" (including Attlee, Lord Lindsay, and Gaitskell), the fifth edition retains almost all of the fourth. All chapters, both introductory essays and readings, have, however, been reviewed and updated where necessary. Other significant changes are placing Hegel in a chapter of his own, adding selections from John Stuart Mill's *The Subjection of Women* to the chapter including him, rearranging the order of several chapters, and moving Gunnar Myrdal to the chapter that was comprised of Herbert Spencer and John Maynard Keynes.

For their advice, assistance, encouragement, and support on the fifth edition of *Great Political Thinkers,* I should like to thank three good friends of my father's and mine—Professors Larry Adams, Tom Schrock, and Gordon Baker—and my brother Rob.

A. O. E., Santa Barbara, California, *1990*

CONTENTS

GREAT POLITICAL THINKERS

PLATO TO THE PRESENT

SIXTH EDITION

PART I

ANCIENT AND MEDIEVAL

CHAPTER ONE

ROOTS OF
THE WEST

The purpose of this work is to present key ideas that have shaped the western world. The book does not attempt to give a history of western civilization in a nutshell, but seeks to show main ideas that have gone into the making of the west, and still are its main sources of its inspiration. The assumption of the book is that the west is more than a haphazard conglomeration of individual countries and more than a sequence of loosely connected historical periods. Beyond the differences of individual countries and historical eras, there is a core of fundamental ideas.

Western civilization is not a geographical concept. Its birthplace is the Mediterranean—Greece, Palestine, and Italy. From there, it spread throughout Europe and the Middle East. A penetration into Asia and Africa lasted for several centuries. Egypt, for example, was a Christian country before the advent of Islam. But it was in Europe that Greco-Judeo-Christian civilization thrived, and it was Europe that transplanted this civilization to other continents over the last five hundred years. Spain and Portugal created a new world in South and Central America; England transplanted its language, customs, law, and religion to North America and Australia; the French recreated their own civilization in Quebec.

The spread of the west should not be confused with mere colonial expansion. Where Europeans did the dirty work of clearing the forest and plowing the soil, western civilization, generally, was most fully transplanted. Where, on the other hand, Europeans remained a small minority—a master race exploiting subjected indigenous majorities—western civilization has often been only a veneer over an enduring, non-western civilization.

Less than two hundred fifty years old, the United States is now the center of gravity of western civilization in terms of economics, politics, culture, and military power. Assuming that this civilization continues to exist, it is easily conceivable that the center of western civilization will someday be elsewhere. In antiquity, Athens, Jerusalem, and Rome were the leading points. During the Dark Ages, Byzantium (not Rome) was the most important site of cultural, literary, and administrative leadership. In the seventeenth and eighteenth centuries, Paris was the undisputed cultural capital of the west. In the nineteenth century, London inherited that place. New York became the leading artistic, scientific, and intellectual clearing-house in the world during the twentieth

3

century, and its place in the year 2000 is being taken, in terms of cultural influence by Los Angeles and the west coast, demonstrating the geographical mobility of western civilization.

Western civilization is not a fixed geographical entity largely because it revolves around potentially universal ideas rather than a more limited core of racial or ethnic links. The supra-national and supra-racial quality of western civilization at its best is the distinctive feature that has made it so adaptable, dynamic, and enduring: Western civilization is not tied to a particular race, nation, or geographical area. Its center of gravity has shifted, throughout its evolution from the Eastern Mediterranean through Europe to a community of nations in both the eastern and western hemispheres. Not all European nations have consistently demonstrated a western outlook. Nazi Germany provides the most glaring example of a European nation's intentional renunciation of western values.

Over the last five hundred years, hardly a corner of the world, from the tropical jungles to the frozen Arctic, has not felt the impact of western civilization. In terms of space and time, there has never been a civilization of such scope and magnitude. Technological and scientific impact are undisputed, and the more controversial issue of spiritual and intellectual influence is not much different. Asian and African societies only gained independence after they developed a class of leaders trained in the west or according to western methods. The revolt of non-western societies against their western overlords occurred following their indoctrination by the west in the concept of individuals' rights to happiness and dignity: Asians and Africans did not revolt against the west, but against its failure to practice its own teachings in dealing with non-western peoples.

Communism, although often a perversion and distortion of western ideas and ideals, was western in origin. As Lenin cogently observed, Marx derived his economic ideas from British economics, his political ideas from French revolutionary politics, and his philosophy from German thinkers. To some non-westerners, communism appeared the quickest way to modernization and westernization.

The questions we have to answer are, what is so essential in the structure of western civilization that, were it removed, the whole building would either collapse or at least require overall reconstruction rather than patchwork repairs; and, on what principles are its ethical, legal, economic, social, and political structures founded? It is difficult to know what is fundamental, because every aspect calls for attention. We shall find the roots of western civilization and its political theories when, in going back into the past, we reach a point beyond which it is either impossible or impractical to inquire. This process will allow us to sift the enduring from the ephemeral, the essential from the incidental, and the fundamental from the decorative.

We know that reason, the *belief in reason,* and the use of reason are not inventions of the twentieth century. Immediately, one recalls the great Age of Reason or Enlightenment which reached a peak in seventeenth- and eighteenth-century France and irradiated throughout the entire western world. Yet, we know France did not invent the cult of reason—rationalism as a way of life—and so we go back and back until we finally find the origin: sixth-century B.C. Greece.

It is true, of course, that the Greeks did not start from scratch—various Oriental peoples influenced them. Nevertheless, Greek civilization, as it imprinted itself on much of the world, was original; it was not derived from any earlier people in the same direct way in which other peoples borrowed some of their basic ideas from the Greeks.

The second root of the west is the Jewish *belief in one God* (monotheism), with the resulting concepts of the brotherhood of mankind (all men and women being children of the same Father) and of one world ruled by a higher law which is above human whim and arbitrariness. Again, it can be shown that some other nations "came close" to the concept of one God before the Jews did. But just as the Greeks were the first to assign to reason a place in thought and conduct such as no society had done before, the Jews were the first to build their whole life around their belief in one God, and to base their thought, ethics, law, and government on this belief.

The practical expression of thought in action is central in classical Judaism. Had the Jewish contribution been confined to an original discovery in religion as a philosophical exercise, its impact on western civilization would have been temporary. But Jewish belief in one God was reflected in a moral code that remains the foundation of western law and ethics. Whereas the supreme Greek ideal was to *think clearly,* the supreme Jewish aspiration was to *act justly.*

The third western root is the Christian *conception of love.* Christianity incorporated Greek rationalism and absorbed Jewish monotheistic ethics, and added a new dimension that went beyond both: the principle of love as the basis of people's relation with God, and, more importantly, each other.

Once again, the point can be made that Greek thought and life put a great value on "sympathy" (a Greek word meaning "to feel with") and friendship, the latter considered by Aristotle, for example, to be the basis of all social and political organizations. The Greeks were intensely interested in love; Plato's dialogue *Symposium* is one of the great conversations on love in world literature. Yet love in the *Symposium* is primarily the mutual embrace of two souls soaring together to the heights of perfection in the life of reason. On a lower level, love was seen by the Greeks as a fierce demon, something approaching madness. Similarly, classical Jewish thought emphasizes compassion and charity, and admonishes its adherents to "love thy neighbor as thyself." But neither the Greek nor the Jewish conception of love has the unconditional, universal character of Christian love. In Christian thought, love is not in the periphery of life, in the rare moments of ecstasy, but in the center of life: Love is life itself.

The three roots of western life—Greek rationalism, Jewish monotheism, and Christian love—are so encompassing that it is difficult, if not impossible, to derive specific social, economic, or political systems from them. Both the Old and New Testaments have been invoked to justify slavery and human freedom, obedience to government and revolution, democracy and monarchy, and capitalism and socialism, to mention but a few. Similarly, Greek rationalism has been appealed to in support of authoritarianism and liberalism, the planned economy and free enterprise, censorship and freedom of thought, and many other contradictory political and philosophical systems.

These contradictions have two causes. First, the conceptions of Greek rationalism, Jewish monotheism, and Christian love have never fully been lived up to in the western world. They have served as guiding ideals, but practice has often lagged behind the ideals. Second (and a reason which often is overlooked), these three sources of western thought are not completely complementary. There has always been a tension—though not irreconcilable—between the three elements, a pressure which has been both painful and fruitful. In antiquity itself, for example, Greeks and Jews were not overly fond of one another. To the ancient Greek, the ancient Jew was a fanatical puritan, living by a strict code that knew of no concessions to human frailty or levity. To the Jew, the Greek—with all his theorizing and endless philosophizing—was an ethical barbarian, whose gods indulged in debaucheries worse than would be tolerated among the lowest sinners in Israel.

Similarly, there is the tension between Christianity on the one side and Greek and Jewish ideals on the other. Christianity is not the mechanical merger of Greek and Jewish ideals, but an attempt to transcend them with something new and different; this process of "going beyond" Greek and Jewish ideals inevitably produced spiritual distances, gaps, stresses. At their worst, these tensions resulted in the burning of "pagan" Greek and Roman books by Christian priests and zealots in the early Middle Ages, or in Christian persecutions of Jews at various times. At their best, tensions between Christianity and its Greek and Jewish antecedents have been harmonized in exceptional persons like Albert Schweitzer. His example testifies that it is possible to unite in one life the three Greco-Judeo-Christian ideals of reason, ethics, and love. As a scholar-philosopher-artist, he would have been completely at home if he had been suddenly transported to fifth-century Athens; his conviction that moral belief must be expressed here and now in action that knows no allegiance other than God places him in the central tradition of Judaism; his choice to work among the poorest of humanity places him among the great Christians of all time.

CHAPTER TWO

THE GREEK DISCOVERY OF REASON IN NATURE

The essence of both Judaism and Christianity can be grasped, albeit imperfectly and incompletely, from the study of a few sources: The Old Testament and the Prophets, combined with the post-Biblical Talmudic literature (commentaries on the Bible), convey an adequate understanding of the essence of classical Judaism. The New Testament, supplemented perhaps by Augustine, Thomas Aquinas, Luther, and Calvin, enables one to intellectually understand the inner meaning of Christianity. This relative simplicity in fixing the roots and essence of Judaism and Christianity arises because both are religious in outlook, and therefore authoritarian to a degree. Authority makes for simplicity.

By contrast, Greek thought is predominantly rational and secular in orientation; there is, therefore, no Bible, no book of authority, no one single source that sums up the essence of Greek thought. The source of Greek thought is Greek life over eight centuries, from the sixth century B.C. to the end of the second century of the Christian era. There is no Moses, as in Judaism, and no Jesus, as in Christianity.

Looking for knowledge, understanding, wisdom, and illumination in the exploration of nature and man, Greek thought was marked in its progress by diversity, contradictions, and lack of definitiveness. Each generation seems to start all over again, incorporating some ideas of its predecessors, rejecting others, and trying to interpret the world in the light of its own experience and its own style of thinking.

The birth of western science and philosophy occurred in the sixth century B.C. The place was not mainland Greece, but the Ionian settlements on the west coast of Asia Minor and on the islands off the coast. These settlements had been formed by emigrants from mainland Greece many centuries before. In the Greek communities on the mainland, the ties of tribal unity were strong. Conversely, the migrants to the Ionian settlements came from various parts of Greece, and thus were relatively free of tribal beliefs and taboos, allowing them to look at the world from a less traditional perspective, both scientifically and politically. They were the first to organize city-states and learn self-government. Since the coastal strip of Asia Minor where they settled was narrow, and land therefore limited, they early took to navigation and commerce, exploring and doing business in the Mediterranean from its eastern shores in Egypt to the western shores of southern France. Undoubtedly these travels also facilitated their progress.

It is hard to overstate the originality and genius of ancient Greece, which continue to shine brightly and inspire after more than two thousand years. Never before or since have so many brilliant minds been clustered in such a small part of time and space. Their sudden rise in civilization—to heights never before imagined, much less ascended—distinguishes the Greeks. Seemingly instantaneously, scientific theories and political philosophies emerged fully grown, as did Athena (the goddess of wisdom for whom Athens was named) from the head of Zeus in Greek mythology.

The men who discovered this knowledge were obviously not "modern" in the sense in which we now use this term (to designate the period roughly from 1500 to the present), but they surely were the absolute moderns of their day, which is why we continue to remember and discuss them in our time. Their concepts and contributions in mathematics, science, philosophy, literature, politics, and the arts continue to be examples of excellence.

Sixth-century B.C. Ionian thought marks the beginning of western science, aptly described as "the Greek way of thinking about the world." The most important Ionian city was Miletus, a rich port and commercial center, the first bourgeois civilization in the west, and the birthplace of the first three great Greek thinkers, Thales, Anaximander, and Anaximenes, the founders of the "Milesian School."

The literary fate of these early giants of Greek science and philosophy illustrates, and explains, at least one of the reasons why pre-Socratic thought is sometimes falsely seen as merely a prelude to Plato and Aristotle rather than as the greatest period of Greek originality, compared with which Plato and Aristotle mark the beginning of the end, rather than the peak, of Greek creative genius. Of Thales, we do not even know whether he ever wrote a book. If he did, no single authentic fragment survives. The only reason we know approximately when he lived is because he predicted an eclipse, which astronomy tells us took place in 585 B.C. About a dozen lines survive of Anaximander. We know that Anaximenes wrote one book: A single sentence has come down to us.

Compared to the majestic fullness of the works of Plato and Aristotle, the extant pieces of pre-Socratic Greek thought are thin indeed. Yet, the nature and influence of pre-Socratic Greek thinkers can be analyzed through the reactions of their contemporaries and, more often, of later writers still close enough to give us an authentic reflection of pre-Socratic thought.

A second reason, in addition to mere paucity of sources, that pre-Socratic thought has not received the attention it deserves is the influence of Christianity. In many respects, Christianity is the synthesis of Greek and Jewish thought. Yet, the Greek elements in Christianity are primarily Platonic and Aristotelian. There is not a single element of pre-Socratic Greek thought in Christianity. The main ideas of the pre-Socratics, from the sixth-century Ionian scientists and philosophers to the fifth-century sophists, are either opposed or at least indifferent to the main tenets of Christian philosophy. The lack of sympathy felt by the early Christian theologians with respect to pre-Socratic Greek thought was inherited from Plato, as were so many other of his preferences and animosities.

The main interest of the Ionian scientists and philosophers was the rational exploration of nature. The very concept of "nature" *(physis)* is itself a Greek intellectual discovery and invention. There is no word for "nature" in the Old Testament. In the pre-Greek, nonscientific world there is no concept of nature as a system of universal laws and regularities graspable by reason. Primitive man is aware only of *individual* things and events in the outside world, primarily from the viewpoint of their utility or harmfulness to himself. The primitive outlook of the world is animistic; it sees a demon, spirit, or divinity in every rock or tree. This leads to a world view that is irrational and dominated by the supernatural and mythical.

Thus, the Greek discovery of nature is one of the few great intellectual revolutions of all time, as it freed reason. From Thales onward, Greek thinkers were firmly convinced that nature could be understood. The modern distinction between scientist and philosopher was, incidentally, unknown to the Greeks. "Philosophy" means in Greek "love of knowledge" or "love of wisdom." It was not, as it is today, a branch of learning, but the process of learning itself. Philosophy implied the searching for knowledge in all areas—scientific, metaphysical, and social. The emphasis, further, was on the activity of searching for knowledge and understanding, regardless of what the results might be.

From the idea that nature can be understood, early Greek thinkers stepped to the still bolder idea that *all* of nature can be understood; this step in turn led to the conclusion that everything was part of nature, and subject to its laws. This conclusion denied the existence of the supernatural, governed by arbitrary whims of gods or demons. There is only one kind of phenomenon: nature. Everything is subject to its laws, which human feelings and desires cannot influence, and from which even the gods are not exempt. Whereas primitive man sought—by prayer or sacrifice—to *influence* external phenomena or objects, the Greeks were the first to *observe* and *understand* them, realizing that there was no other way to master the universe.

Greek religious conceptions were intimately connected with the rational comprehension of nature. As early as Homer, no sharp separation between God and nature exists, and the miracle—an event running counter to natural law because so willed by God—plays a very small part. Whereas in the Judeo-Christian view God is *above* nature, changing its regularities when He sees fit, the Greek religious view sees the divine *in* nature: the laws of nature express the divine *reason*. The Judeo-Christian miracles, on the other hand, express the divine *will*. For the Jew and Christian, a miracle takes place when divine intervention changes the expected regularities of nature; for the Greek, the greatest miracle of all is the orderly regularity in which natural events occur. In later Hellenistic thought, the identification of God and nature become virtually complete, culminating in the Stoic religious philosophy of pantheism, according to which the whole universe is a manifestation of divine rationality, a view Thales may have expressed centuries earlier in a statement attributed to him, "all things are full of gods."

It is a tribute to the Greeks' sense of realism—so clearly expressed in their literature and art—that they first tackled the rational understanding of physical nature before taking on the much more complex job of rational mastery: man. The Greeks were the first people in history in which laymen, not a priestly class, carried on intellectual activities of a higher order. The *intellectual* as a distinct social type, whether he be a thinker, scientist, writer, lecturer, or teacher—the individual whose sole business it is to think, asking new questions and proposing new answers to old questions—is a phenomenon in the western world that goes back to the Greeks.

The spread of Ionian scientific observation and philosophical speculation challenged traditional modes of thought. The first to attack traditional Greek religious beliefs was Xenophanes, whose early ties with Ionian philosophy stimulated him to describe the processes of nature as the result of natural laws which one can clearly read by careful observation of natural phenomena. In the field of religion, Xenophanes put forward a view from which all study of comparative religion has since drawn sustenance: that *man creates God in his own image* (rather than the other way around, as the Bible puts it). Xenophanes attacked Homer and Hesiod, the two greatest Greek poets, for "attributing to the gods all things that are a shame and a disgrace among men: theft, adultery, and deception." He also ridiculed the current images of the gods as being created by birth like humans, wearing garments, and possessing bodies and voices like humans. He noted that the Ethiopians visualized their gods black, whereas the Thracians (in Greece) imagined their gods to have blue eyes and red hair. To drive home his point, Xenophanes then makes one of the most famous statements in the history of the study of religion: "If oxen or horses could draw and make statues as men do, oxen would draw the pictures of gods like oxen, and horses like horses."

The critical and empirical tendency in Xenophanes is also reflected in his attitude toward truth and knowledge. Certain truth is impossible, he says, particularly when it comes to the ultimate questions about man or the gods. Conjecture or probability is all that man can attain in his search for truth: "The gods have not revealed all things to men from the beginning; but by long seeking men discover what is better." Xenophanes thus suggests that the road to truth is long and endless, and that there is no shortcut through revelation.

Protagoras (480–411 B.C.), the first of the sophists, expresses a similar view about the nature and limitations of human knowledge: "Concerning the gods, I am unable to know whether they exist or not, nor what form they have; many things prevent this knowledge: the obscurity of the problem and the brevity of man's life."

Protagoras' famous saying that "man is the measure of all things" expresses a similar viewpoint. It does not mean that each individual can set up, in a completely anarchical and irresponsible way, his standards of knowledge and ignorance, truth and error, virtue and vice. What Protagoras tried to say is that, unless we claim to have divinely revealed truth (which he denied), we can only mobilize our human resources in trying to discover knowledge about mankind and nature.

This *belief in man* is the source of all subsequent tendencies in western civilization that go under the name of humanism. Greek humanism did not, as has often been alleged, worship man as the "Lord of Creation," nor did it worship any other idol. The greatness of pre-Platonic humanism consisted precisely in accepting, for the first time in history, the limitations as well as the potentialities of human intelligence and creativity.

In this humanistic view, man was neither a worm of no value and significance (as in the Oriental despotisms of Egypt and Babylonia), nor was he a demigod. The story of Prometheus, as dramatized by Aeschylus, clearly illustrates Greek humanism. Prometheus arouses the anger of Zeus for having taught men the art of fire: Zeus punishes him by chaining him to a mountain rock and orders a vulture to gnaw away at his liver. Prometheus defies Zeus and even dares to curse him. Peace is finally made between Zeus and Prometheus, neither coming out as victor. Prometheus does not meekly submit in the end (as does Job, for example, in a similar Biblical story of a just man receiving undeserved misfortune from God), nor, though, does he triumph over God—as he would have done had the Greeks been human-worshippers.

Protagoras and Democritus, who was an originator of the atomic theory, adhered to the philosophy of empiricism, holding that knowledge derives solely from experience (and not from revelation), and that knowledge is therefore subject to constant change and improvement. Both Protagoras and Democritus also favored liberal democracy in politics: The parallelism between philosophical empiricism and political liberalism has often been repeated in western thought, as can be seen from the later examples of Locke, Mill, Jefferson, John Dewey, and Bertrand Russell.

Plato in the *Laws* reversed Protagoras' saying of man being the measure of all things into the statement that "God ought to be the measure of all things, and not man." This anti-empirical and anti-humanist view of Plato is reflected in his political philosophy. Knowledge of truth and error—of right and wrong—is certain because it ultimately derives from a mystic vision of God. But only a few are capable of attaining, after a long preparatory education, such absolute certainty; these are to rule as philosopher-kings. Absolute political authority of the few is based in Plato on the assumption that only a few have the capacity to reach certain knowledge.

Since the ancient Greeks, those who have held that truth is certain have also generally held the parallel view that only a few are capable of reaching that truth. On the other hand, those who have held that truth is never final, that it can never be more infallible than fallible man himself, have more often taken the view that everyone has the capacity to reach the imperfect truth that exists in the world as it is constituted.

The philosophy of the early Greek thinkers was both practical and speculative. The Babylonians were skilled in observing the stars, but their primary interest was astrology, not astronomy. The Egyptians were skilled in some measurements, but they did not push mathematics further. Christian writers of the early Christian era rejected the rare harmony between theory and practice of the Greeks; for them, philosophy assumes a different meaning—a life of meditation, contemplation, withdrawal, and self-denial. Plato passed this conception of philosophy on to Christianity, another illustration of how Plato differed from typical and representative Greek thinking.

The philosophical origins of democracy in ancient Greece are not based, as is often mistakenly asserted, on the shallow rationalistic ground of the perfectibility of mankind. On the contrary, the pre-Socratic thinkers saw the imperfection and fallibility of human judgment and knowledge. They therefore concluded that all men are in the same boat of doubt and uncertainty. There is no aristocracy of those who know (as Plato thought). Therefore (and here philosophy merges with politics), if there is no absolute standard of right and wrong, the opinions of the majority are to decide. After all, the only alternative to this position is for the minority to decide what is best for the majority—which is even less satisfying than the democratic solution. The philosophy of empiricism maintains a middle position between skepticism (according to which no knowledge is possible) and metaphysical idealism (according to which truth is absolutely certain). Political democracy similarly holds the middle ground between anarchy (no government) and authoritarianism or totalitarianism (all-pervasive government).

The sophists' great period was the century of 450–350 B.C. Because of the Platonic caricature of the sophists, the term has acquired a derogatory meaning in modern western languages: Sophistry is now considered a method of reasoning which perverts truth by captious and cunning logic, bordering on dishonesty. "Sophist" originally meant in Greek a skilled craftsman and, more generally, a wise or prudent man.

The sophists travelled from city to city lecturing and teaching. Unlike pre-sophistic teaching in special disciplines or vocations, the sophists were the first to undertake the education of the whole man, particularly the political man: man as a citizen and, above all, as a political leader. In the Platonic dialogue named for him, Protagoras is represented as saying he does not wish to instruct pupils in special fields like arithmetic, geometry, music, or astronomy. Instead he wants to teach "the art of politics"—managing one's own affairs prudently and effectively, and speaking and acting for the best in the affairs of the state.

The revolutionary new educational concept of the sophists was largely a response to the change of Greek civilization from an aristocratic society to a bourgeois (middle-class) one. In the old aristocratic society, character and political ability were not formally acquired, but were inherited through ties of blood, social "atmosphere," and in-bred customs revered and cultivated in the few privileged families of the aristocracy. But in the democratic city-states, such as Athens, everybody was held to possess the potential ability to participate in public affairs.

If political leadership no longer depended on inherited virtues, then only one alternative was open—educating citizens in those spiritual and intellectual qualities that enable them to play their roles as citizens and leaders in a democratic society. From the beginning, the emphasis was on *education for leadership.* The sophists charged fees which only the well-to-do could afford. However, the citizens of the democratic city-states understood that democracy, like any other form of state or society, could not maintain itself against internal or external threats without imaginative and competent political leaders.

Since the democratic city-states produced rival political parties and factions, the art of persuasion (or "rhetoric") included both the content and form of political oratory. Later, the term "rhetoric" increasingly stood for the form rather than the content of political or legal oratory. The question of the intrinsic merit of a political program became subordinated to the desire to sell it to as many people as possible. It was at this later stage that the sophists were attacked as teachers of political propaganda, advertising, and salesmanship rather than of political character and high-minded statesmanship.

The teachings of the sophists shocked many because they emphasized *what social reality is* rather than what it should be. At all times, realistic political analysis has produced the charge that it leads to moral cynicism. This charge has, in fact, also often been levelled against artists and writers who present life as it is rather than as it should be. Those who benefit from the *status quo* prefer to see it presented as universal truth and justice, and they may therefore resent anyone who presents social reality in political philosophy or in fictional literature.

The sophist doctrine of the origin of social and political institutions shocked many of their more conservative contemporaries. The sophists were the original progenitors of the *social contract.* They held that social and political institutions are not the product of superhuman, divine forces, endowed with absolute truth and justice: Laws and institutions, the sophists argued, are nothing other than social conventions, agreed upon by men for utilitarian reasons. What might be useful and right under one set of circumstances, in one society, might be harmful and wrong under different circumstances or in a different society. The sophists thus denied that laws and governments could ever base their claim for allegiance on absolute or divine truth, just as the later social contract theory of the seventeenth and eighteenth centuries denied the doctrine of the "divine right of kings."

If convenience and utility became the sole foundation of social and political institutions, obedience to government could be based only on consent, since no one would freely consent to government that is oppressive or harmful to him, if it were not divinely established. The sophist doctrine of the social contract (as its revival in the last three centuries) thus inevitably led to the liberal and democratic conception of *government by consent.* The most famous description of Greek democracy at its best is contained in Pericles' funeral address (430 B.C.) in honor of the Athenians who gave their lives in the war with Sparta. While most of the Athenians of Pericles' day were not citizens, for those who were, his words had real meaning:

> Our government is called a democracy because it is in the hands of the many and not of the few. Our laws secure equal justice for all in their private disputes, and our public opinion welcomes and honors talent in every kind of achievement, not for any sectional reason, but on grounds of excellence alone. And as we give free play to all in our public life, so we carry the same spirit into our daily relations with one another. We are not angry with our neighbor if he does what he likes, nor do we put on our sour looks at him which, though harmless, are unpleasant. Open and friendly in our private relations, in our public acts we keep strictly within the law. We recognize the restraint of reverence; we are obedient to officials and laws,

especially to the laws that protect the oppressed and to the unwritten laws whose violation brings admitted shame.

Yet ours is no work-a-day city only. No other provides so many recreations for the spirit—contests and sacrifices all year round, and beauty in our public buildings to cheer the heart and delight the eye day by day. Moreover, this city is so large and powerful that the wealth of all the world flows into her, so that our own products seem no more homelike to us than those of other nations.

Our military training is different from that of our opponents. Our city is thrown open to the world, and we never expel a foreigner or prevent him from seeing or learning anything which might be useful to an enemy. For our trust is not in the devices of material equipment, but in our own good spirits for battle. In education, our enemies laboriously cultivate courage from early youth, while we live at ease, and yet are equally ready to face danger when it arises. If we choose to face danger with an easy mind rather than after a rigorous training, and to trust in native manliness rather than in state-made courage, the advantage lies with us; for we are spared all the weariness of practicing for future hardships, and when the hour of danger comes we are as brave as our plodding rivals. Our city thus sets an example in peace as in war.

We love beauty without extravagance, and wisdom without unmanliness. We employ wealth, not as a means to vanity and ostentation, but as an opportunity for service. To acknowledge poverty is no disgrace; the true disgrace is in making no effort to overcome it. An Athenian citizen does not neglect public affairs because he takes care of his private business; we regard a person who takes no interest in public affairs, not as "quiet" but as useless. If few of us are originators, we are all sound judges of a policy. The great impediment to action is, in our opinion, not discussion, but the lack of full information which is gained by discussion prior to action.

To sum up: Athens is the school of all Greece, and Athenians yield to none in independence of spirit, versatility of accomplishment, and complete self-reliance in limbs and brain. This is no passing and idle word, but truth and fact verified by the position to which these qualities have raised the state. No other city faces her ordeal greater than men ever dreamed; no other is so powerful that the invading enemy feels no bitterness at being repulsed, and her subject cities feel no shame at the indignity of their dependence.

There is a striking similarity between Pericles' funeral address and Abraham Lincoln's Gettysburg Address—two of the most famous statements about democracy, uttered on similar occasions to honor those who had given their lives defending freedom.

The most memorable creation of Athenian civilization, of all of Greek antiquity, is not this or that idea, this or that sculpture or drama, but a person: Socrates (born in 469 B.C. and executed in 399 B.C.). Like Jesus, he never wrote a line, yet his influence on western thought, directly and indirectly through Plato, is second to none. One of the great teachers of all time, Socrates said of himself, "I have never set myself up as any man's teacher." He was ready at all times to converse with anyone who wished to do so, and "to answer questions for rich and poor alike."

In his youth he was strongly impressed with the philosophical and scientific ideas then current and generally accepted by the intellectuals throughout Greece. As he grew older, his interest shifted—like that of Greek thought generally—from the understanding of the outer world to the inner world of man. What was important (in fact, the only important thing) was the understanding and mastery of the inner life of individuals and their relations with others. He felt that just as knowledge unravelled the mysteries of physical nature, so it could lead to mankind's moral mastery. But this knowledge was not the specialized knowledge of the craftsman or expert in a particular field, but the knowledge of moral principles by which all are to be governed.

The method he used in the process of discovering these principles was not one of dogmatically laying down the truth in advance, followed by arguments in support. Socrates' method—and this is what makes him a teacher second to none—was to proceed by question and answer, helping the other person to use his own mind in finding answers to those questions that must be answered if life is to have meaning. Socrates liked to think of himself as merely fulfilling the function of an intellectual midwife, facilitating the birth of ideas already conceived in the mind of the other person.

The questions he asked were those that every person encounters in everyday living: What are the meanings of justice, courage, beauty, the good? By adducing practical examples of these abstract concepts, Socrates helped his fellow-debaters or interlocutors to gradually arrive at a general definition. Yet, he did not state he had final answers. He said that the only difference between himself and others was that, whereas they thought they knew, he at least knew he did not. If the moral life depends on knowledge, then virtue, or doing the good, and philosophy, or knowing the good, become identical. Living the right kind of life thus leads to an endless search for the knowledge of the right principles of living. Humankind's salvation from confusion and conflict lies, therefore, Socrates teaches, in a lifelong quest for philosophical—and, consequently, moral—self-mastery. Humanity is saved, not (as in Christianity) by outside divine grace, but by inner rational and moral forces, provided these are mobilized and utilized properly.

Socrates was a profoundly religious man; yet his religion knew of no rewards and punishments, as in the Judeo-Christian theology. His innermost desire was to transcend the material temptations of life and to achieve a life of pure spirit on earth—to "practice immortality" in this life. He was not sure whether there was a life after death, but he faced death with equanimity whether death meant complete annihilation or the migration of the soul to another world.

Socrates was tried in 399 B.C., ostensibly on the charge of corrupting the minds of the young and of believing in deities of his own invention. In fact, the trial was political. The Pelopennesian War between the two alliances of states—one led by Athens, the other by Sparta—had started in 431 B.C., and ended in 404 B.C. with the defeat of Athens, a defeat from which neither Athens nor Greece ever recovered. As a result of this defeat, an antidemocratic regime, led by Critias, a disciple of Socrates, was set up, and it committed many crimes of violence and tyranny. In 403 B.C. this unpopular tyranny was overthrown and democracy was restored.

Socrates was known as the spiritual guide and mentor of many of the antidemocratic faction and therefore something had to be done against him. In addition to this obvious political cause of the trial, there was also a deeper motivation: the fear of independent, unorthodox thinking. This was a fear not peculiar to democracy in ancient Athens. Had he asked for mercy or pity, there is little doubt Socrates would have received them from his judges. He also had the opportunity of escaping from his jail after he was sentenced to death. Yet Socrates used his trial (as described in Plato's *Apology*) not as means of saving his own life but as his last opportunity of serving his fellow citizens in the only way which he knew and thought was right, telling them again what his life was all about, what he believed in, and what it means to be a human. Possibly the most succinct summary of Socrates' thought, expressing both his intellectual and moral beliefs, is one brief statement during his trial: *"The unexamined life is not worth living."*

The balance between rationalism and mysticism in Socrates was profoundly altered in favor of mysticism in his greatest disciple, Plato, who was born shortly after the Pelopennesian War broke out and saw Athens' final defeat in 404 B.C. Born into one of the oldest aristocratic families in Athens, and closely related, by family ties or personal friendship, to the most antidemocratic elements in Athens, Plato's hostility to democracy became implacable after the trial and execution of Socrates.

In Sparta, the first rigidly planned totalitarian state, Plato saw the model of the ideal political community as elaborated—in a mixture of rational philosophy and visionary poetry—in the *Republic.* Next to the Old and New Testaments, the *Republic* has been the most influential book in western intellectual history, and Plato therefore the most influential philosopher in western civilization. Plato wrote his works in the form of dialogues with Socrates as the main speaker. It is not always easy, however, to know where Socrates ends and where Plato begins.

As mentioned earlier, far from being the culmination of Greek civilization, Plato is the beginning of the end. Gone is the faith in man and in his capacity to think for himself, to rule himself; instead, we find in Plato a pessimism, atypical of the Greek tradition, that is all-pervasive. Rigid thought control and censorship, as outlined in the *Republic,* must protect humanity from its weaknesses. Even the lie is justified in protecting people's minds against the unuseful truth: Plato limits the use of the lie to circumstances where it is important to the health of the body politic, but even a "noble lie" or "medicinal lie" is still a lie.

Powerful as Plato's explicit opposition to democracy is, his implicit opposition to democratic humanism is even more serious, because less easily detected. Plato rejects the traditional Greek this-worldly outlook—of the worth of life in this world and advocates the pessimistic philosophy that humans can find true self-realization, the discovery of truth, only after their souls are liberated from the "folly of the body" by death.

As long as the soul dwells in the body, it can never attain pure knowledge: The soul comes closest to knowledge by avoiding as much as possible all contact or association with the body. Plato considers the body a disease of the soul, and believes humans can attain final purification and deliverance only in death. All of these thoughts affected Christianity. Yet, the body is not only the source of intellectual evil and disease; it is also the source of moral evil: "Wars and revolutions and battles are due simply and exclusively to the body and its desires. All wars are undertaken for the acquisition of wealth, and the reason why we have to acquire wealth is the body, for we are slaves in its service." Intellectual and (therefore) moral perfection—the two are in Plato's thought identical—are thus divorced from man's life in this world and relegated to the after-life.

Plato's deep distrust in the world as it is leads him to idolize the future life of the soul in the next world. From this idolization stems his contempt for empirical science as a means of obtaining knowledge. Observations of facts, according to Plato, can only lead to uncertain opinions, because facts are fleeting phenomena, far removed from reality. Reality is Idea, Form—only imperfectly reflected in tangible objects.

The Platonic Idea or Form is not idea or thought in our minds, but is the object of thought; it exists in another world of changeless eternity and can but imperfectly be reflected in this world. Just as the human body distorts the perfection of the soul temporarily inhabiting it, the physical properties of any object distort the perfection of its Idea or Form. This applies to the Good or Justice. No human act or institution can be perfectly just, for which reason the ideal community of the *Republic* can never exist in reality. Perfect Justice exists as an absolute reality outside the world of empirical fact, and it can only be approximated in just acts or institutions. This absolute reality of Idea, Form, or Justice can be apprehended only by the mind after it has freed itself from the necessary imperfections of physical fact and empirical observation.

Plato assumes that Truth (with a capital "T") is eternal and unchanging and that only a few can contemplate it after years of systematic and rigorous training. He nowhere defines the nature of Idea, Form, or the Good in rational or verifiable terms. It is a secret, "something beyond truth and knowledge." In his *Seventh Letter* (which, while some hold it a forgery, still would reflect the spirit of his thought), he writes, "The truths of philosophy cannot be expressed in words as other subjects can, but after personal assistance in these studies from a guide, after living for some time with that guide, suddenly a flash of understanding, as it were, is kindled by a spark that leaps across, and once it has come into being within the soul it proceeds to nourish itself."

This is closer to a description of a mystical vision, a miracle, than any other Greek writer ever put forward. Familiar as the concept of miracle or mystical vision is in Christian religious tradition, it was alien to the Greeks. Plato was the first to express the thought that mystical, unverifiable intuition, and not empirical, rational knowledge, is the key to the discovery of reality.

The Platonic concept of Truth is challenged (since Bacon, Hume, and Locke) by the more modern view (going back in time to the pre-Socratic Ionian scientists and philosophers) of truth (with a small "t") as something tentative, hypothetical, and changeable, subject to constant checking, verification, modification, or rejection. It is an endless process of testing old and new hypotheses against new experience: it is not discovered in the sudden Platonic flash of mystical insight and intuition, but pieced together, step by step, in the process of observing. The modern view does not regard truth as a mountain peak that will eventually be conquered. Each new discovery of knowledge opens up new areas of ignorance: the more we find out about nature and reality, the more we are aware of what we do not know—truth is not the visible peak of the mountain (high as it may be), but no more than a way-station in an endless journey on an endless road.

Neither Plato nor his great student, Aristotle—who expressed the empirical more than his teacher—understood the Greek political decline that was going on before their eyes. The traditional city-state was doomed to failure, and with it, political freedom and independence. In 338 B.C., Greece became subject to the Macedonian monarchy, and in 146 B.C. it became a province of the Roman Empire. Yet, the end of Greek political independence was not synonymous with the failure or death of Greek civilization. Through the work of the Macedonian monarchs and Rome, Greek civilization became a root of western civilization.

In the first century A.D., a Greek-speaking commercial traveler could travel from Spain to India, either along the northern or southern shores of the Mediterranean, and find everywhere either Greek settlers or Greek-speaking persons of all nationalities who considered Hellenism their first civilization, whatever their original mother-tongue might have been. The Hellenistic period lasted about five centuries (from about 300 B.C. to about 200 A.D.). Yet, as its very name suggests, Hellenism was no longer exclusively Greek, but a mixture of Greek and non-Greek. Hellenization was the process of transmitting Greek ideas and the Greek style of thought to non-Greeks, and was also characterized by the continuous entry of non-Greeks into Greek life. Gradually, Greece ceased to be the source, and instead became the universal clearing-house, of new ideas.

The most influential school of thought of the Hellenistic period was Stoicism. In its classical era, Stoicism was a moral, rather than a political, philosophy. It appealed to the individual as a man rather than as a citizen. Reflecting the loss of individual liberty in the new imperial structure of Rome, Stoicism taught individuals to disregard passions, emotions, desires, or worldly possessions. The emphasis was on reason, the most characteristically human of traits. A rational faculty common to all humanity, the Stoics argued, also implies the existence of universal law and justice. This concept of a natural law became, in the seventeenth and eighteenth centuries, one of the leading political doctrines.

Stoicism never became deeply rooted in the masses, because it emphasized rational self-discipline, passionless austerity, and personal responsibility. Its religious appeal was also limited to a small, though influential, minority: Stoicism neither threatened penalties nor promised rewards, as most religions do, but asked individuals *to do good solely because it was good,* as is vividly expressed in the famous Stoic definition of God: "God is man's helping of man."

Stoicism has had its greatest appeal in those ages or circumstances in which persons find themselves facing the world alone. Under enemy occupation, after great natural catastrophes, or faced with the reality of death, individuals often find that wealth, possessions, and glory count for little, and that in the end moral integrity and selfhood are all that one has or needs. Stoicism thus often became a philosophy of consolation, and in this it was true to its own origins.

The legacy of the Greeks to the western world can be briefly summarized. They invented the idea of a *secular civilization.* All members of the community *have* the opportunity to contribute to the intellectual and moral progress of society; there is no concept of a privileged priestly class morally and intellectually superior to the rest. The United States was the first modern country to separate church and state, thus denying any church or priesthood the right to set itself up as the moral or intellectual master of society. Philosophy and science—the insatiable curiosities about the nature of the world, about things as they really are—are other permanent Greek legacies. They could only have been born in a secular civilization and are based on the daring assumption that man is able to discover the meaning of physical and human phenomena, provided he is not afraid of where knowledge will lead him.

Knowledge is often painful: *The source of knowledge* is therefore *not only intellectual curiosity, but also moral courage.* Only a few centuries ago, scientists were persecuted because they held theologically wrong views about physical nature; today, churches no longer interfere with free scientific research in the physical sciences. Yet, fear can impede the results of free investigation and the progress of knowledge in social and humanistic studies. Now, it is no longer the churches that stand in the way of free thought, but vested social interests.

Implied in the Greek inventions of philosophy and science was the belief in free thought to be expressed in free speech. The Romans had in their law the principle of *audiatur et altera pars* ("the other side, too, must be heard"). For the Greeks, this principle applied to all spheres of human relations, not only to the narrow field of law. Drama is more than an important artistic invention of the Greeks; it has an equally important philosophical message: Truth and justice—between man and God or between man and man—are not simple matters settled once and for all in a few sacred formulas. Truth and justice are as uncertain and elusive as human life itself. Because truth has many facets, even an authoritarian thinker like Plato used the dialogue in his philosophy.

In public affairs, too, the dialogue takes its proper place in the search for truth and justice. The Greek invention of government by popular assemblies recognizes the fundamental belief that truth is complex, and that it is more than a choice between black and white. There are many ways of seeing and experiencing the world, and all must be heard before a decision is made. This concept of the dialogue also implies that free speech is the proper instrument of adjusting human relations, and not despotic force. If one recognizes the philosophical principle that no one person possesses infallible truth, then one must also recognize the implication that free thought and free speech are the only ways of eliciting as many opinions as possible, The Greeks held that, if reason was humanity's most characteristic attribute, free speech was the only way of utilizing the rational faculty.

As its very name suggests, politics is a Greek discovery. The inventiveness of the Greeks in this field is shown both in theory and in practice. There has been little advance in politics since them. Although Greece was small by any standards, ancient or modern, the Greek political practice covered a whole range of systems from the extreme totalitarianism of Sparta to the liberal democracy (for its citizens) of Athens. Political theories in Greek thought ranged from the liberal democratic views of Democritus or Protagoras to the rational authoritarianism of Plato.

The dominance of Greek over European thought lasted until the seventeenth century. Two philosophies competed: Materialism, which was founded by the pre-Socratic philosopher-scientists, and idealism, which was founded by Plato. In the seventeenth and eighteenth centuries, a new major philosophical school of philosophical empiricism, founded by Locke and Hume, gained importance. Yet, even this newest and currently most influential school in western philosophy can be traced to the pre-Socratics.

The history of Christianity provides another illustration of Greek dominance. In its beginnings, Christianity was under the sway of Plato, the "most Christian of the pagan philosophers," as St. Augustine called him. In the thirteenth century, St. Thomas Aquinas, a devotee of Aristotle, successfully challenged the dominant Platonic-Augustinian trend. Through St. Augustine and St. Thomas Aquinas, the two greatest leaders of Christian theology in its history, Plato and Aristotle continued to dominate the philosophical aspects of Christianity. In the sixteenth century an Augustinian monk, Martin Luther, challenged the predominance of the Aristotelian-Thomistic tradition, and urged what he regarded as a return to the original and authentic Christian tradition of Plato and St. Augustine, thereby starting the Protestant Reformation.

Greek thought has provided us, in whatever language we employ, with common logical tools and categories (such as "form and substance," "appearance and reality," "particulars and universals," "cause and effect"). As long as there continues a tradition in the west that honors the courage of pursuing truth, of seeing things as they really are, and at the same time cherishes the stirring of our imagination through the arts, the Greek experience will not have been in vain.

CHAPTER THREE

PLATO

The imperishable contribution of the Greeks to western civilization lies in the taming of man and nature through reason. In the pre-Greek world, advanced peoples had learned to live with nature by wresting from it, through patient observation, some of its secrets, and by applying them to gainful purposes. But such practical knowledge never lost its close association with demons and myths, fears and hopes, punishments and rewards; and the pre-Greek conception of nature viewed physical phenomena as essentially individual, unique, and incalculable rather than as general, universal, and predictable. The Greeks were not the first to think about recurrent regularities of inanimate events; but they were the first to develop—going beyond observation and knowledge—the *scientific attitude,* a new approach to the world that constitutes to this day one of the distinctive elements of western life.

In the field of human relations, too, Greek inventiveness and originality lay, not in this or that political theory, but in the discovery of the scientific study of politics. The Greeks were not the first to think about the problem of a well-ordered society. But pre-Greek political thought had been a mixture of legend, myth, theology, and allegory, and if there was an element of independent reasoning, it served as a means to a higher end, usually to be found in the tenets of a supernatural system, such as religion. Thus the contribution of Jewish thought to the political heritage of the world has been seminal: The idea of the brotherhood of man, of "one world," is deeply rooted in the conception of monotheism as transmitted through the Bible. By contrast, polytheism made it difficult for the Greeks to see the basic oneness of mankind, and their religious pluralism reflected their inability to transcend, intellectually and institutionally, the confines of the city-state.

From a social viewpoint, the Bible was opposed to slavery on principle—a unique phenomenon in antiquity—established a weekly day of rest (still unknown in some parts of the earth), and contained a host of protective rules in favor of workers, debtors, women, children, and the poor. The concept of "covenant," first appearing in the agreement between God and Abraham, is a frequent theme in the Bible whenever momentous decisions are to be made; it becomes again an inspiration centuries later when the Puritans attempt to build a new religion and civil society, or, still later, when President Wilson, a devout Presbyterian, names the constitution of the League of Nations a "Covenant." But, significant as these contributions to western civilization have been, they never were, nor were they meant to be, political science. They were political and social *ethics* rather than science, and as such constitute one of the three chief tributaries to the mainstream of western civilization, the other two being the Christian principle of *love* and the Greek principle of *rationalism.*

The first work that deserves to be called political science, in that it applies systematic reasoning and critical inquiry to political ideas and institutions, is Plato's *Republic.* After almost twenty-four hundred years it is still matchless as an introduction to the basic issues that confront human beings as citizens. No other writer on politics has equaled Plato (427–347 B.C.) in combining penetrating and dialectical reasoning with poetic imagery and symbolism.

One of the main (and most revolutionary) assumptions of the *Republic* is that the right kind of government and politics can be the legitimate object of rigorous, rational analysis, rather than the inevitable product of muddling through fear and faith, indolence and improvisation. This Platonic assumption of the applicability of reason to social relations is as hotly debated in the twentieth century as it was in Plato's own time, and it is one of the key elements that go into the making of our political outlook and temperament. To the extent that we believe in the possibility of applying reason and critical analysis to the solution of political and social issues we are all Plato's spiritual heirs, although we may heartily disagree with any or all of his specific teachings. By seeking to disprove Plato on a point of political doctrine or practice, the anti-Platonist has already conceded to Plato the most important single point: that political and social issues can be clarified by argument rather than by force and dogma.

Socrates, Plato's teacher and the chief figure in the *Republic,* has been contemptuously called the "first Social Democrat" by some modern totalitarians; what they hate in him above all is his irritating habit of endlessly searching, through argument, for the reason that lies behind accepted ideas and institutions. Other totalitarians, penetrating less deeply into Plato's thought, have usurped him as their first intellectual ancestor because there is so much in the *Republic* that is explicitly undemocratic, or outright antidemocratic. Yet, implicit in Plato's and Socrates' rationalism is the assumption, incompatible with the cult of violence, that man's intellect can discover the nature of the good life and the means of attaining it by philosophical inquiry.

In one basic point, modern political analysis would gain in insight and understanding if it followed Plato more closely: Plato never starts out with the hypothesis of a *homo politicus,* an abstract "political man" unrelated to the richness and complexity of individual selves or of society as a whole. Today Plato's psychology may seem naive in its analogies and presumed facts, but what is of timeless significance is his conviction that no theory of politics can be sound unless based on the study of man. Modern psychology has taught us enough about neurotic persons to make us realize that a healthy society cannot be composed of men and women who are haunted by fear and insecurity.

Plato's political thought also introduced the concept of the "public" as distinct from the "private" in the context of governmental relations. As a Greek, Plato could not be clearly aware of the opposing ideas of the individual and (or, sometimes, versus) the state because the city-state was a spiritual and religious unity, as well as a social, economic, and political one. The Jewish and Christian religions separated man's soul from his quality as a citizen and established the notion of an inalienable and indestructible human spirit outside the domain and jurisdiction of government, a philosophy that was unknown and unknowable to Plato. In the polytheistic religions of the city-states, the gods were community gods, and there could be no question of the individual's being in one respect a member of his community, and in another not. Yet, if Plato was unaware of the opposition of the individual versus the state—since the seventeenth century the dominant leitmotiv of western political speculation—he was keenly aware of the *res publica,* the "common thing" in the mutual relations of human beings.

Before Greek experience and analysis, the only major dichotomy known to man, consciously or unconsciously, was that between the "sacred" and the profane." Its evolution into that of "public" and "private" is part of western secularism that goes back directly to Greek life and thought. Medieval feudalism abandoned the distinction between private and public relations in political and economic institutions; from the king downward there was no clear-cut division between the private and public property or authority of the lords and their vassals. In such a system the color and intensity of personal relations between the ruler and the ruled make rational discussion of political issues and true constitutionalism difficult; this fact can still be observed today in countries in which (as in some parts of the third world) impersonal government is an ideal rather than a reality.

Even when the concept of the modern sovereign state first developed in sixteenth-century Italy, *lo stato* meant essentially the ruler and the "machine" that he had built up for himself, and it was a long time before "the state" assumed the anonymous and impersonal character with which it was later endowed. In some modern authoritarian and totalitarian regimes, rulers tend again to mingle inextricably the domains of the public and the private, "borrowing" castles and picture galleries that belong to the state, "acquiring" vast industrial empires for their brothers and nephews, and building up private, and often personal, military forces competing with those of the state. The inevitable growth of corruption in such regimes is the price paid for the dissolution of the clear separation between public and private authority.

One of the hallmarks of genius is that it can enrich each generation anew. In the heyday of *laissez faire,* Plato's ideal of a highly trained administrative and political class, dedicated to public service without consideration of personal happiness or financial gain, exercised relatively less appeal because society was assumed to be an automatic and self-regulating piece of machinery, and political wisdom could well be summarized in the succinct formula of "the less government, the better." Plato's conception of government as the highest moral and practical task to which men of knowledge and virtue ought to devote themselves seemed out of date in the days in which doing nothing was deemed to be the noblest function of a political association. The force of circumstances, accelerated by wars and depressions, has necessarily enlarged, in recent times, the scope and function of government, and in Plato we rediscover the ideal of public service as second to none. Democrats are bound to reject Plato's own solution of this problem, the rule of those who know over those who do not, regardless of the latter's consent, but they will have to grasp, if democracy is to survive in a tough and dangerous world of competing skills, that there is no substitute for high-minded and efficient government in solving tensions and conflicts within and between nations.

We also increasingly practice Plato's teaching that the road to better government and public service is through an appropriately conceived system of education. In fact, the ultramodern and rapidly growing realization of education as a never-ending process, embracing adults as well as the young, goes back directly to Plato: he clearly saw that education was more than the acquiring of basic facts and ideas in one's childhood and adolescence, and he was the first to propose an elaborate system of adult training and education.

Democrats differ with Plato's system of education on two scores: first, Plato reserved educational opportunities of prolonged duration and intensity for future rulers only, whereas the democrat looks on education as a means to the good life that should be available to all. Second, Plato believed that the selection of rulers could best be made through the prolonged training of men and women, generally those born into the ruling class or picked, in exceptional situations, from the lower classes of the workers, farmers, and merchants. Democrats reject such a scheme and insist that political rulers be selected by popular voting. This democratic theory is valid as long as voters have enough judgment and discrimination to elect the best to public office. When they freely choose to put knaves and fools into high positions of public trust and authority, the democratic theory of selecting rulers is quickly swept away by demagogues and dictators. Whereas democracy will continue to reject Plato's scheme of training an elite of political *rulers,* it will view more sympathetically the possibility and desirability of training *public servants.* On that point, democracies are more and more abandoning the older doctrine that the spoils system, or government by crony, can be a substitute for honest and efficient administration.

One of the main causes of Plato's pervasive and persuasive influence throughout history is that he is the ablest exponent of the aristocracy theory of the state, and the acutest critic of the democratic way of life. In the evolution of mankind the extent of democratic experience is infinitesimally small, compared with its ignorance of democratic living, and putting the one on top of the other is like putting a postage stamp on top of a tall skyscraper. If history has been largely the history of inequality, it is no wonder that Plato's philosophy of inequality, mellowed by the accretion of prestige and sweetened by the reasonableness of its argument, should have been the most venerated and idealized political philosophy of the ages. Its relative moderation has immensely added to the influence of the *Republic.* Though in general in favor of a hierarchical society that, once set up, is closed rather than open, the *Republic* must seem repugnant to some conservatives on several grounds: The idea of rational inquiry into the foundations of society, that is, going to the roots of social institutions, must seem too radical, because the conservative likes to behold them as a product of natural growth with which one must not willfully, by intelligence or other means, interfere.

In describing the "first city," before the "feverish condition" sets in that necessitates the formation of the two classes of the rulers (guardians) and soldier-administrators (auxiliaries), Plato portrays a pattern of natural growth of social institutions, untampered by conscious reason, that would appeal to the conservative. But the first city, whose sole *raison d'être* lies in the satisfaction of material wants through the principle of the division of labor, is, as Glaucon puts it, a "community of pigs," lacking as yet the conscious direction of a ruling class whose specific excellence is reason. The growth of the simple first city into a condition of fever is caused, according to Plato, by the expansion and refinement of human wants, that is, by luxury. The inability of the community to fill the newly developing luxurious needs out of the existing resources (land, labor, skills) is the cause of war, either aggressive or defensive war.

The feverish condition is, however, not limited to the threat of external war but also implies the possibility of the disruption or dissolution of the health and balance of the first city through internal unrest. In order to safeguard or, rather, restore the original balance of the community, a special class of fighters is needed. Yet, if the new fighting class is not to degenerate into a class of praetorians, drunk with power and quarreling continuously among themselves and with the members of the producing class, it must receive a training that will make its members "gentle to their own people and dangerous only to enemies," instill them with courage to defend the city against internal and external enemies, and at the same time imbue them with an understanding of the principles that make the city worth defending.

The class of the fighters (auxiliaries) thus makes the existence of a still higher class necessary, the guardians, or rulers, who pick and train the auxiliaries as well as the future guardians. The characteristic quality of the rulers is *wisdom,* just as *courage* (tempered by understanding) is the characteristic quality of the fighters and *appetite* (or the desire to satisfy material wants) is the distinctive trait of the working population (workers, farmers, merchants, doctors, nurses, actors). Just as the first city was the product of unconscious growth, the "second," or "ideal," city of the *Republic* is the product of rational direction.

The Platonic community is the first example of a planned state; but it must be borne in mind that the planned sector of this state applies only to the guardians and auxiliaries, whereas the producing class is left to itself as far as its economic activities go. Plato was an aristocrat who exhibited the bias against labor and business so characteristic of aristocrats in all ages, and the lack of regulations of the economic order of the producing class in the *Republic* indicates the contempt of the nobleman for the prosaic existence of those who must work for a living.

The life of the guardians and auxiliaries excludes individual interests, whether in property, love, or the family, but this community of absolute sharing is not socialism. The outlook of socialism is hedonistic: Its objective is the increase of human happiness through the abolition of want and misery. The goal of socialism is not the realization of a preconceived just ideal of society but the attainment of maximum *happiness* for the maximum number of people *here and now.* The sharing of the guardians and auxiliaries in the *Republic* is based on a principle that is almost diametrically opposed to that of socialism: the principle of *austerity,* which puts little, if any, value on material wants and their satisfaction. Not happiness of human beings with varying and unique personalities, but the realization of a predetermined social ideal of justice is the purpose of the political community as described in the *Republic.*

Though the analogy to the communal life of the guardians and auxiliaries is not to be found in the socialist state (in which all citizens share in the amenities of life) nor in socialist communities within a nonsocialist state, it can be found in armies, monastic orders, and the clergy of churches who are denied marriage or private property. In all such groups the ruling class shares with the Platonic guardians the certainty of knowing what is best for the ruled, without asking for their consent, as well as the relative disregard for property, sex, family, or other forms of personal happiness. Plato's "socialism" of the guardians was authoritarian service rather than the sharing of happiness and enjoyment, and as such the exact antithesis of western socialism.

The *Republic* is opposed to democracy on two levels of argument: a more obvious explicit level and a less obvious implicit level. The explicit opposition of the *Republic* to democracy rests on the threefold division of the population into rulers, fighters, and producers (farmers, artisans, traders). A numerically small aristocracy of rulers, in command of a well-trained body of soldiers and administrators, governs the third class, or producers, which constitutes four-fifths or more of the total population. Plato claims that the threefold class division of the second city is but an extension of the principle of the division of labor, characteristic of the first city. Ruling or defending a state, Plato argues, is just as much a *specialized craft* as shoemaking; and if the principle of the division of labor forbids the shoemaker from making furniture, he is equally excluded from ruling, or defending and administering, the city—functions that constitute special, and specialized, crafts.

There is one objection to Plato's reasoning here (and this objection is fundamental to the whole edifice of the *Republic*): If the nature of ruling and administering a state is a specialized craft no different from shoemaking or farming, it is difficult to see why he does not simply add the two new crafts of the second city to the already existing number of crafts of the first city. In it, we may recall, there were no special crafts of ruling and administering, because the harmony of society was maintained naturally, growing out of the division of labor and without conscious guidance or rule. If, for example, the number of crafts in the first city was one hundred, the addition of two new crafts of ruling and fighting in the second city should produce one hundred and two crafts, if the second city were still based, as before, on the principle of division of labor. Instead, Plato presents us with the concept of *three classes* in the second city: first, the class of rulers (guardians in the narrower sense); second, the class of military and civilian executive aides (auxiliaries); third, the class of producers or handworkers. This last class composed, in the first city, the entire population, organized on the principle of division of labor; now, in the second city, the working part makes up only from eighty to ninety percent.

The principle of the division of labor can produce only more and more specialized crafts, as the needs and skills of society proliferate, but it can never lead to a class system based on hierarchical values. If Plato nevertheless introduces the concept of the threefold class division into the second city, a new principle, different from that of the division of labor, must be found to distinguish the functions of ruling and administering the state from all other crafts. The main difference between the ruler-philosophers and the producers in the *Republic* is the difference between *political wisdom* and *technical knowledge.* Only the philosophers have insight into *human* problems, insight that is more than highly specialized learning. The craftsman, by contrast, has no all-comprehensive understanding of the phenomena of nature and society of which he is a part, only *limited* knowledge of a *technical* nature. Even where such knowledge, as in medicine, applies to human beings, it is still only technical knowledge and not higher philosophical understanding and insight, because the physician is interested in human beings as parts of the psychophysical world, and not of the world of values and ideas.

The Platonic craftsman is thus inferior, in two ways, to the philosopher: First, his material is limited and finite, and subject to causal or esthetical laws, the knowledge of which is relatively easy, compared with the material of the philosopher—mankind and the cosmos, the laws of which are most difficult to discover and grasp. Second, the knowledge of the craftsman never attains the height of wisdom and understanding that the philosopher reaches in his study of ultimate values, intrinsic forms, and cosmic laws. The knowledge of the craftsman is only an intermediary stage, raw material that goes into the process of learning and acquiring wisdom to which the philosopher is subjected in the *Republic.*

The democratic theory of politics challenges Plato not only in his basic assumption that the capacity to govern is possessed by only a small class, but that such capacity can be transmitted, in general (Plato admits occasional exceptions), by selective breeding. This Platonic concept of a hereditary aristocratic ruling class, not too hermetically closed to talent from below, is rejected by the democratic theory of man and the state on grounds of historical evidence and rational reflection. The democratic view of man is less pessimistic than Plato's and assumes hopefully that wisdom and understanding may be found in the most unexpected places, in log cabins as well as in stately mansions.

If the explicit opposition of the *Republic* to the democratic way of life is serious enough, the implicit opposition is even more fundamental and irreconcilable. Plato assumes (in the *Republic* as in his other writings) that Truth is something eternal, unchanging and unchangeable, and that it can be made accessible to a select few through an ingeniously devised training reserved for the future fighters and rulers. The preparation of the rulers begins before they are born, as the very pairing of the parents is arranged by a preconceived plan that is to insure the highest physical and mental qualities of the offspring to be bred. Nothing is left to personal whim or accident from infancy on, and the process of education, both theoretical and practical, continues until the age of fifty. Literature, music, physical and military instruction, elementary and advanced mathematics, philosophy and metaphysics, and subordinate military and civilian-service assignments are the stages of the planned program of training philosopher-rulers:

> Then when they are fifty, those who have come safely through and proved the best in all points in action and in study must be brought at last to the goal. They must lift up the eye of the soul to gaze on that which sheds light on all things; and when they have seen the Good itself, take it as a pattern for the right ordering of the state and the individual, themselves included. For the rest of their lives, most of their time will be spent in study; but they will all take their turn at the troublesome duties of public life and act as Rulers for their country's sake, not regarding it as a distinction but as an unavoidable task.

Plato thus regarded the training in literary, mathematical, and philosophical knowledge as a mere preparation for the "ascent to the vision of Goodness," the "highest object of knowledge," which final stage cannot be mastered by mere rational instruction or comprehension, but partakes of the nature of *revelation,* a mystical and socially incommunicable experience.

Plato nowhere defines the nature of the Good in verifiable or rational terms; it is a secret, "something beyond truth and knowledge, and, precious as these both are, of still higher worth," as he says in the *Republic.* The only approach to it is through vision and revelation, and few are blessed with the capacity to "climb the ascent" to such visions. The Platonic philosopher-ruler thus bases his rule over the people, not on superior character and rational knowledge alone, as it might appear from a hasty reading of the *Republic,* but on a personal and unique innermost experience that is mystical and incommunicable in rational terms. To know is to "contemplate the realities themselves as they are for ever in the same unchanging state," and because the ruler *knows,* as the result of his vision of the Good, he has the right to rule the people; they can never hope to attain similar summits of insight and vision and can only *believe* in, but not rationally understand, a social order built on intuitions that are, in the ultimate, mysterious and inaccessible to common-sense experience.

The nature and scope of the authority of the rulers in the *Republic* are intimately related to its foundation. Just as the knowledge of the rulers that gives them title to rule is directed to the absolute, so is their authority, which is morally based on their training and wisdom, absolute and unconditional. The rulers have the moral right to constrain the ruled if they show any sign of defection from the established order. Plato assumes that, in general, such compulsion will not be necessary. The people will be brought up to believe in the existing class system by means of myths and allegories, because they are incapable of rigorous scientific and philosophical thinking.

But if the use of force in the *Republic* raises serious critical considerations, the recommended use of censorship and the "medicinal lie" for the upbringing of the ruling and military-executive classes is no less alarming. Plato often compares the rulers to doctors, and the ruled to patients, and he says that "for a private person to mislead the Rulers we shall declare to be a worse offense than for a patient to mislead his doctor"; and he goes on to attack such crimes as "fatal" and "subversive" in a state. Though the ruled are under no circumstances permitted to deviate from truth, particularly in their relations with the rulers, the latter may lie "in the way of a medicine." Just as a medicine may be handled only by a doctor, "if anyone, then, is to practice deception, either on the country's enemies or on its citizens, it must be the Rulers of the commonwealth, acting for its benefit; no one else may meddle with this privilege."

An illustration of such a "medicinal lie" is the fable of the origins of the class system, according to which God put gold into those who are fit to rule, silver into the auxiliaries, and iron and brass into the farmers and craftsmen. "I shall try to convince," Socrates says, "first the Rulers and the soldiers, and then the whole community," and if they accept this fable, all three classes will think of each other as "brothers born of the same soil" and will be ready to defend their land, which they will eventually think of as "mother and nurse." It is significant that Plato's example of a "medicinal lie" relates, not to a matter of subordinate expediency and convenience, but to the root of his ideal political community, namely, the inequality of the threefold class system.

As to censorship, Plato frequently expresses in the *Republic* hostility toward artists. His hostility arises from his apprehension that art appeals to feeling and passion rather than to reason and intellect. Specifically, poets must write in a way that will further the objectives of the future rulers' training (it may be recalled that only the rulers and the military-executive, but not the ruled population, are to be educated). Negatively, the poet must not, for example, present the gods in an unattractive and "all-too-human" light; if he does, "we shall be angry and refuse him the means to produce his play." Positively, the poets will be told by the rulers what elements to stress in their stories and "the limits beyond which they must not be allowed to go." The main, perhaps only, value of art is moral education, particularly self-control: "And for the mass of mankind that chiefly means obeying their governors, and themselves governing their appetite for the pleasure of eating and drinking and sex."

Plato finds Homer, Hesiod, and the other masters of Greek literature opprobrious and corrupting. Toward the end of the *Republic* the conclusion is presented that "all poetry, from Homer onwards, consists in representing a semblance of its subject, whatever it may be, including any kind of human excellence, with no grasp of the reality." In fact, the artist is assigned a place below the shoemaker or smith, because the latter have at least a limited *direct* knowledge of reality, that of their craft, whereas the artist "knows nothing worth mentioning, about the subjects he represents"; art, therefore, "is a form of play, not to be taken seriously." Because the poet, by appealing to sentiment rather than reason, "sets up a vicious form of government" in the individual soul, "We shall be justified in not admitting him into a well-ordered commonwealth." Like Plato, modern authoritarian rulers are also keenly aware that poetry, fiction, and other kinds of imaginative literature can be more dangerous than factual historical, political, or economic analyses. In the twentieth century, four of the most influential books against totalitarian government have been novels: Arthur Koestler's *Darkness at Noon,* George Orwell's *1984,* Bores Pasternak's *Dr. Zhivago,* and Aleksandr Solzhenitsyn's *One Day in the Life of Ivan Denisovich.*

In accepting the "medicinal lie" and the regulation, positive and negative, of the arts, Plato started a line of thought that has been enthusiastically accepted by those who base their right to rule on superior and exclusive knowledge rather than on the freely expressed consent of the ruled. Those who adhere to the creed of certainty are eventually driven to use, as a means of governing, medicinal lies, censorship, thought control, and physical compulsion.

The Platonic conception of Truth is challenged by the modern view. Modern philosophers insist that truth is intimately, related to experience, that it can never be fully grasped, that it is an *endless process* of testing new hypotheses against new experiences, that it is not something that exists prior to man, but that it is constantly made and remade in *doing,* rather than discovered in intellectual speculation or in a flash of mystical insight. Plato's concept of Truth is more *absolute* and *individual-aristocratic:* Truth is eternally the same and unchangeable, and it can be perceived by the use of the speculative and intuitive faculties of the philosophical person, who therefore has the right to rule those who do not possess these capacities. The modern view of truth is more *relative, empirical,* and *social-cooperative:* Truth is not eternally the same, is changeable and changing, is never attainable more than in a proximate and practical way, and—what is perhaps most important of all—it is not the product of brilliant individual intellects but of the cooperative effort of many individuals and social groups.

To take a practical illustration, according to Plato the concept of social justice is one that can be discovered and defined through illuminated reasoning. The more modern empirical and relative view holds that social justice is not a preexisting reality logically or intuitively *discovered* by speculation or revelation, but that *temporary approximations* to justice can be worked out in a socially satisfactory fashion through negotiation and bargaining of interested groups and classes. This *dynamic* concept of truth is more modest than the *static* one of Plato, inasmuch as it appreciates the limitations of human capacity and disinterestedness in the face of a constantly, changing world of circumstances; but at the same time, it is also more optimistic than Plato's concept, because it holds that the process of working out approximations to truth is *open to all,* and that, in fact, such approximations are likely to be more accurate if related to the widest possible range of ascertainable experience. By contrast, Plato's view of the possibility of finding truth is more pessimistic in the sense that it is conceived as a form of intellectual insight that is open, because of its final and absolute value, to only a *few select* minds. If antidemocratic and authoritarian political systems throughout history have looked back sympathetically to Plato, the reason has been less the explicit opposition of the *Republic* to democracy than the implicit view of the world in which truth—social, philosophical, metaphysical, religious—is the prerogative of a small elect class, endowed with special and exclusive capacities to apprehend it in a regime of formal training, and enabled to translate it into reality in a preconceived framework of society in which the few govern and the many obey and conform.

Yet even more deeply than Plato's conception of Truth, his conception of an is not compatible with democracy. In Plato's three-class society, the rulers have the right, and duty, to rule all because they possess the highest quality—rational wisdom. The class of civilian-military administrators (auxiliaries) is characterized by courage, or the ability to face reality, to serve as an intermediary between the ruling class and the third, lowest, class, the mass of the people whose dominant psychological trait is the desire to satisfy their crude material and instinctual desires. According to Plato, this threefold division of society merely reflects the threefold division of the individual soul: It, too, is made up of three elements: the *rational,* which is the highest; the *spirited,* which has the capacity to follow and assert the claims of reason; and the *appetitive,* the lowest in rank, which harbors man's desires and emotions. Plato assumes that in these three elements of the soul, the rational is the highest and has the duty to keep the other two elements in line. In society, too, the class that is characterized by superior rational endowment is therefore the natural ruler over the other two subordinate classes. The case against Plato's three-class society in which one small superior class rules over the rest can thus be greatly strengthened if his psychological premise is wrong or at least open to serious challenge.

Modern psychological thought often divides the human mind into several components. Freud, for example, divides the human mind into three elements which bear a striking resemblance to Plato's three parts of the soul: First, there is, according to Freud, the *id*—the seat of man's undirected and unconscious instinctual drives. Then, there is the *ego,* which is in the conscious level of the mind and adjusts *id* drives and primitive desires to reality, that is, to the rules of morals and society. Finally, there is in the human mind the *superego,* the civilized rational conscience which directs the *ego* in dealing with the claims of the *id.* However, in Freud's view—and this is a fundamental rejection of Plato—the three elements of the mind are not ranked hierarchically as superior and inferior, but are coordinate. In particular, Freud pointed to the psychic dangers of repressing *id* drives too harshly rather than channeling them off for purposes that cause no harm to either the individual or society.

Following Freud's pioneering work, modern psychological thinking holds that mental health and stability depends on the balance between intellectual and emotional interests and activities, and that neither are inferior or superior to the other. In modern psychological thought, repression of the so-called lower emotional elements of the mind by the so-called higher intellectual element has been largely replaced by the concept of balance and integration, in which each element of the human personality has its rightful place. Following Plato's example and projecting the relations of the different elements of the mind on the larger social canvas, the modern conception of the human personality would seem to lead to a democratic conception of society in which each group and class has a rightful place of recognition and respect, being neither naturally superior or inferior to any other group or class.

The *Republic* is not a utopia but the work of a thinker passionately interested in practical politics. Rejecting the doctrine that man must fatally and inextricably remain a prisoner of natural or social circumstances, Plato has faith in man's ability to create a community that will correspond to the ideal of knowledge and, therefore, justice. If philosophy and the vision of the Good are the highest forms of human activity, "there can be no rest from troubles" for states or for all mankind, "unless either philosophers become kings in their countries or those who are now called kings and rulers come to be sufficiently inspired with a genuine desire for wisdom; unless, that is to say, political power and philosophy meet together." This passage, probably the most famous in the *Republic,* summarizes Plato's conception of a society in which the best rule, and it makes little difference to him whether this rule is monarchy ("when there is one man who stands out above the rest of the rulers") or aristocracy ("when there are more than one"). The plan of such a perfect constitution and of a "perfect man" might be difficult, "but not impossible."

Nevertheless, Plato anticipated the eventual decline of the best state and its degeneration into progressively lower types of constitution. The first of these forms of state is timocracy, based on ambition and love of honor and war, as represented by Crete and Sparta, "so commonly admired." The second is oligarchy or plutocracy, the rule of the wealthy; the third is democracy, the rule of the people; the fourth, and most imperfect, is despotism, which develops inevitably out of the anarchy of the democratic state. In each instance, Plato correlates a type of human character with the form of government in which it is most commonly reflected: "Constitutions cannot come out of sticks and stones; they must result from the preponderance of certain characters which draw the rest of the community in their wake."

This penetrating insight of Plato, that government is more than a piece of machinery, that its essence is ultimately determined by the quality of the men and women who compose it, is still not fully grasped today. The twentieth century, in particular, has been strewn with the wreckage of constitutions that failed dismally, not because they were imperfect in themselves, but because they were not suited to the "preponderant characters" in the societies for which they were devised, whether these individuals were the rulers or the ruled.

In his classification of forms of state, Plato considered democracy the second worst type of government. His description of life in a democratic society may be overdrawn, but it remains to this day the most incisive critique of democracy. Unless democrats assume that democracy is an exception to all human creations, and thus free from imperfections, they must be aware of its intrinsic as well as its incidental weaknesses. If Plato maintains that democracy is "an agreeable form of anarchy with plenty and variety and an equality of a peculiar kind for equals and unequals alike," who can say that his thesis is completely wrong? The buoyant diversity and creative pluralism of the democratic society are its glory, but they are often the path to dissolution and disintegration when its members forget that they are not merely individuals with rights and liberties but also social beings with duties and obligations. Similarly, the unwillingness of democratic citizens to be led is one of the mainsprings of democratic vitality; but if carried too far, if the honest and able leaders are prevented from governing, the dishonest demagogues will take their place.

The fate of democracies in the twentieth century, in particular, has demonstrated that Plato's critique of democracy and the democratic man, far from being an unrealistic caricature of democratic life, is full of sound warnings that no democrat should miss. Nazi, fascist, and communist criticisms of democracy were and are relatively ephemeral and superficial, compared with the enduring and fundamental objections that Plato raises. The answer to Plato's apprehensions about the possibility of democracy lies not in the arguments of democrats but in their lives. The experience of history is harder to disprove than a theoretical argument. If Plato makes democrats more keenly conscious how difficult the life of freedom and fellowship is, he has, perhaps unwittingly, performed a major service to the cause of democracy.

The literary form of the *Republic* is the dialogue, in which Socrates is both the narrator and chief figure. In fact, as the dialogue proceeds, it becomes virtually a monologue, for the other participants increasingly confine their dialectical contributions to nods, monosyllabic expressions of consent, and brief rhetorical assertions that merely give Socrates a cue to go on with his argument. The conversation starts in the house of Cephalus, a retired wealthy businessman. The company includes Cephalus' son, Polemarchus, Plato's two elder brothers, Glaucon and Adeimantus, and a sophist, Thrasymachus, who is represented as a cynic. The discussion soon turns to the central question in the *Republic,* What is justice? In the discussion of justice, all elements of Plato's political philosophy are contained. In his theory of justice the relations of man to nature, to the *polis,* and to his fellow men form an architectonic whole.

Cephalus states the view, based on a long life of practical experience, that justice means honesty and rendering what is due to gods and men. Socrates sees some merit in this approach but is not satisfied with it. Polemarchus next suggests that justice means helping one's friends and harming one's enemies. Socrates is again not satisfied, as such a definition befits more the moral standards of a despot than those of a just man. At this point Thrasymachus breaks into the discussion and puts forward the view that "just" or "right" means nothing but "what is to the interest of the stronger party."

PLATO

*The Republic**

JUSTICE AS THE INTEREST
OF THE STRONGER

All this time Thrasymachus had been trying more than once to break in upon our conversation; but his neighbours had restrained him, wishing to hear the argument to the end. In the pause after my last words he could keep quiet no longer; but gathering himself up like a wild beast he sprang at us as if he would tear us in pieces. Polemarchus and I were frightened out of our wits, when he burst out to the whole company:

What is the matter with you two, Socrates? Why do you go on in this imbecile way, politely deferring to each other's nonsense? If you really want to know what justice means, stop asking questions and scoring off the answers you get. You know very well it is easier to ask questions than to answer them. Answer yourself, and tell us what you think justice means. I won't have you telling us it is the same as what is obligatory or useful or advantageous or profitable or expedient; I want a clear and precise statement; I won't put up with that sort of verbiage.

I was amazed by this onslaught and looked at him in terror. If I had not seen this wolf before he saw me, I really believe I should have been struck dumb;[1] but fortunately I had looked at him earlier, when he was beginning to get exasperated with our argument; so I was able to reply, though rather tremulously:

---

*From *The Republic of Plato* (trans. F. M. Cornford, Oxford University Press, 1945). By permission.

[1] A popular superstition, that if a wolf sees you first, you become dumb.

Don't be hard on us, Thrasymachus. If Polemarchus and I have gone astray in our search, you may be quite sure the mistake was not intentional. If we had been looking for a piece of gold, we should never have deliberately allowed politeness to spoil our chance of finding it; and now when we are looking for justice, a thing much more precious than gold, you cannot imagine we should defer to each other in that foolish way and not do our best to bring it to light. You must believe we are in earnest, my friend; but I am afraid the task is beyond our powers, and we might expect a man of your ability to pity us instead of being so severe.

Thrasymachus replied with a burst of sardonic laughter.

Good Lord, he said; Socrates at his old trick of shamming ignorance! I knew it; I told the others you would refuse to commit yourself and do anything sooner than answer a question.

Yes, Thrasymachus, I replied; because you are clever enough to know that if you asked someone what are the factors of the number twelve, and at the same time warned him: "Look here, you are not to tell me that 12 is twice 6, or 3 times 4, or 6 times 2, or 4 times 3; I won't put up with any such nonsense"—you must surely see that no one would answer a question put like that. He would say: "What do you mean, Thrasymachus? Am I forbidden to give any of these answers, even if one happens to be right? Do you want me to give a wrong one?" What would you say to that?

Humph! said he. As if that were a fair analogy!

I don't see why it is not, said I; but in any case, do you suppose our barring a certain answer would prevent the man from giving it, if he thought it was the truth?

Do you mean that you are going to give me one of those answers I barred?

I should not be surprised, if it seemed to me true, on reflection.

And what if I give you another definition of justice, better than any of those? What penalty are you prepared to pay?[2]

The penalty deserved by ignorance, which must surely be to receive instruction from the wise. So I would suggest that as a suitable punishment.

I like your notion of a penalty! he said; but you must pay the costs as well.

I will, when I have any money.

That will be all right, said Glaucon; we will all subscribe for Socrates. So let us have your definition, Thrasymachus.

Oh yes, he said; so that Socrates may play the old game of questioning and refuting someone else, instead of giving an answer himself!

But really, I protested, what can you expect from a man who does not know the answer or profess to know it, and, besides that, has been forbidden by no mean authority to put forward any notions he may have? Surely the definition should naturally come from you, who say you do know the answer and can tell it us. Please do not disappoint us. I should take it as a kindness, and I hope you will not be chary of giving Glaucon and the rest of us the advantage of your instruction.

Glaucon and the others added their entreaties to mine. Thrasymachus was evidently longing to win credit, for he was sure he had an admirable answer ready, though he made a show of insisting that I should be the one to reply. In the end he gave way and exclaimed:

So this is what Socrates' wisdom comes to! He refuses to teach, and goes about learning from others without offering so much as thanks in return.

I do learn from others, Thrasymachus; that is quite true; but you are wrong to call me ungrateful. I give in return all I can—praise; for I have no money. And how ready I am to applaud any idea that seems to me sound, you will see in a moment, when you have stated your own; for I am sure that will be sound.

Listen then, Thrasymachus began. What I say is that "just" or "right" means nothing but what is to the interest of the stronger party. Well, where is your applause? You don't mean to give it me.

I will, as soon as I understand, I said. I don't see yet what you mean by right being the interest of the stronger party. For instance, Polydamas, the athlete, is stronger than we are, and it is to his interest to eat beef for the sake of his muscles; but surely you don't mean that the same diet would be good for weaker men and therefore be right for us?

You are trying to be funny, Socrates. It's a low trick to take my words in the sense you think will be most damaging.

No, no, I protested; but you must explain.

Don't you know, then, that a state may be ruled by a despot, or a democracy, or an aristocracy?

Of course.

And that the ruling element is always the strongest?

Yes.

Well then, in every case the laws are made by the ruling party in its own interest; a democracy makes democratic laws, a despot autocratic ones, and so on. By making these laws they define as "right" for their subjects whatever is for their own interest, and they call anyone who breaks them a "wrongdoer" and punish him accordingly. That is what I mean: in all states alike "right" has the same meaning, namely what is for the interest of the party established in power, and that is the strongest. So the sound conclusion is that what is "right" is the same everywhere: the interest of the stronger party.

Now I see what you mean, said I; whether it is true or not, I must try to make out. When you define right in terms of interest, you are yourself giving one of those answers you forbade to me; though, to be sure, you add "to the stronger party."

---

[2] In certain lawsuits the defendant, if found guilty, was allowed to propose a penalty alternative to that demanded by the prosecution. The judges then decided which should be inflicted. The "costs" here means the fee which the sophist, unlike Socrates, expected from his pupils.

An insignificant addition, perhaps!

Its importance is not clear yet; what is clear is that we must find out whether your definition is true. I agree myself that right is in a sense a matter of interest; but when you add "to the stronger party," I don't know about that. I must consider.

Go ahead, then.

I will. Tell me this. No doubt you also think it is right to obey the men in power?

I do.

Are they infallible in every type of state, or can they sometimes make a mistake?

Of course they can make a mistake.

In framing laws, then, they may do their work well or badly?

No doubt.

Well, that is to say, when the laws they make are to their own interest; badly, when they are not?

Yes.

But the subjects are to obey any law they lay down, and they will then be doing right?

Of course.

If so, by your account, it will be right to do what is not to the interest of the stronger party, as well as what is so.

What's that you are saying?

Just what you said, I believe; but let us look again. Haven't you admitted that the rulers, when they enjoin certain acts on their subjects, sometimes mistake their own best interests, and at the same time that it is right for the subjects to obey, whatever they may enjoin?

Yes, I suppose so.

Well, that amounts to admitting that it is right to do what is not to the interest of the rulers or the stronger party. They may unwittingly enjoin what is to their own disadvantage; and you say it is right for the others to do as they are told. In that case, their duty must be the opposite of what you said, because the weaker will have been ordered to do what is against the interest of the stronger. You with your intelligence must see how that follows.

Yes, Socrates, said Polemarchus, that is undeniable.

No doubt, Cleitophon broke in, if you are to be a witness on Socrates' side.

No witness is needed, replied Polemarchus; Thrasymachus himself admits that rulers sometimes ordain acts that are to their own disadvantage, and that it is the subjects' duty to do them.

That is because Thrasymachus said it was right to do what you are told by the men in power.

Yes, but he also said that what is to the interest of the stronger party is right; and, after making both these assertions, he admitted that the stronger sometimes command the weaker subjects to act against their interests. From all which it follows that what is in the stronger's interest is no more right than what is not.

No, said Cleitophon; he meant whatever the stronger *believes* to be in his own interest. That is what the subject must do, and what Thrasymachus meant to define as right.

That was not what he said, rejoined Polemarchus.

No matter, Polemarchus, said I; if Thrasymachus says so now, let us take him in that sense. Now, Thrasymachus, tell me, was that what you intended to say—that right means what the stronger thinks is to his interest, whether it really is so or not?

Most certainly not, he replied. Do you suppose I should speak of a man as "stronger" or "superior" at the very moment when he is making a mistake?

I did think you said as much when you admitted that rulers are not always infallible.

That is because you are a quibbler, Socrates. Would you say a man deserves to be called a physician at the moment when he makes a mistake in treating his patient and just in respect of that mistake; or a mathematician, when he does a sum wrong and just in so far as he gets a wrong result? Of course we do commonly speak of a physician or a mathematician or a scholar having made a mistake; but really none of these, I should say, is ever mistaken, in so far as he is worthy of the name we give him. So strictly speaking—and you are all for being precise—no one who practises a craft makes mistakes. A man is mistaken when his knowledge fails him; and at that moment he is no craftsman. And what is true of craftsmanship or any sort of skill is true of the ruler: he is never mistaken so long as he is acting as a ruler; though anyone might speak of a ruler making a mistake, just as he might of a physician. You must understand that I was talking in that loose way when I answered your question just now; but the precise statement is this. The ruler, in so far as he is acting as a ruler, makes no mistakes and consequently enjoins what is best for himself; and that is what the subject is to do. So, as I said at first, "right" means doing what is to the interest of the stronger.

Very well, Thrasymachus, said I. So you think I am quibbling?

I am sure you are.

You believe my questions were maliciously designed to damage your position?

I know it. But you will gain nothing by that. You cannot outwit me by cunning, and you are not the man to crush me in the open.

Bless your soul, I answered, I should not think of trying. But, to prevent any more misunderstanding, when you speak of that ruler or stronger party whose interest the weaker ought to serve, please make it clear whether you are using the words in the ordinary way or in that strict sense you have just defined.

I mean a ruler in the strictest possible sense. Now quibble away and be as malicious as you can. I want no mercy. But you are no match for me.

Do you think me mad enough to beard a lion or try to outwit a Thrasymachus?

You did try just now, he retorted, but it wasn't a success.

RULING AS AN ART

Enough of this, said I Now tell me about the physician in that strict sense you spoke of: is it his business to earn money or to treat his patients? Remember, I mean your physician who is worthy of the name.

To treat his patients.

And what of the ship's captain in the true sense? Is he a mere seaman or the commander of the crew?

The commander.

Yes, we shall not speak of him as a seaman just because he is on board a ship. That is not the point. He is called captain because of his skill and authority over the crew.

Quite true.

And each of these people has some special interest?[3]

---

[3] All the persons mentioned have some interest. The craftsman *qua* craftsman has an interest

No doubt.

And the craft in question exists for the very purpose of discovering that interest and providing for it?

Yes.

Can it equally be said of any craft that it has an interest, other than its own greatest possible perfection?

What do you mean by that?

Here is an illustration. If you ask me whether it is sufficient for the human body just to be itself, with no need of help from without, I should say, Certainly not; it has weaknesses and defects, and its condition is not all that it might be. That is precisely why the art of medicine was invented: it was designed to help the body and provide for its interests. Would not that be true?

It would.

But now take the art of medicine itself. Has that any defects or weaknesses? Does any art stand in need of some further perfection, as the eye would be imperfect without the power of vision or the ear without hearing, so that in their case an art is required that will study their interests and provide for their carrying out those functions? Has the art itself any corresponding need of some further art to remedy its defects and look after its interests; and will that further art require yet another, and so on for ever? Or will every art look after its own interests? Or, finally, is it not true that no art needs to have its weaknesses remedied or its interests studied either by another art or by itself, because no art has in itself any weakness or fault, and the only interest it is required to serve is that of its subject-matter? In itself, an art is sound and flawless, so long as it is entirely true to its own nature as an art in the strictest sense—and it is the strict sense that I want you to keep in view. Is not that true?

So it appears.

Then, said I, the art of medicine does not study its own interest, but the needs of the body, just as a groom shows his skill by caring for horses, not for the art of grooming.

---

in doing his work as well as possible, which is the same thing as serving the interest of the subjects on whom his craft is exercised; and the subjects have their interest, which the craftsman is there to promote.

And so every art seeks, not its own advantage—for it has no deficiencies—but the interest of the subject on which it is exercised.

It appears so.

But surely, Thrasymachus, every art has authority and superior power over its subject.

To this be agreed, though very reluctantly.

So far as arts are concerned, then, no art ever studies or enjoins the interest of the superior or stronger party, but always that of the weaker over which it has authority.

Thrasymachus assented to this at last, though he tried to put up a fight. I then went on:

So the physician, as such, studies only the patient's interest, not his own. For as we agreed the business of the physician, in the strict sense, is not to make money for himself, but to exercise his power over the patient's body; and the ship's captain, again, considered strictly as no mere sailor, but in command of the crew, will study and enjoin the interest of his subordinates, not his own.

He agreed reluctantly.

And so with government of any kind: no ruler, in so far as he is acting as ruler, will study or enjoin what is for his own interest. All that he says and does will be said and done with a view to what is good and proper for the subject for whom he practises his art.

At this point, when everyone could see that Thrasymachus' definition of justice had been turned inside out, instead of making any reply, he said:

Socrates, have you a nurse?

Why do you ask such a question as that? I said. Wouldn't it be better to answer mine?

Because she lets you go about sniffling like a child whose nose wants wiping. She hasn't even taught you to know a shepherd when you see one, or his sheep either.

What makes you say that?

Why, you imagine that a herdsman studies the interests of his flocks or cattle, tending and fattening them up with some other end in view than his master's profit or his own: and so you don't see that, in politics, the genuine ruler regards his subjects exactly like sheep, and thinks of nothing else, night and day, but the good he can get out of them for himself. You are so far out in your notions of right and wrong, justice and injustice, as not to know that "right" actually means what is good for someone else, and to

be "just" means serving the interest of the stronger who rules, at the cost of the subject who obeys; whereas injustice is just the reverse, asserting its authority over those innocents who are called just, so that they minister solely to their master's advantage and happiness, and not in the least degree to their own. Innocent as you are yourself, Socrates, you must see that a just man always has the worst of it. Take a private business: when a partnership is wound up, you will never find that the more honest of two partners comes off with the larger share; and in their relations to the state, when there are taxes to be paid, the honest man will pay more than the other on the same amount of property; or if there is money to be distributed, the dishonest will get it all. When either of them hold some public office, even if the just man loses in no other way, his private affairs at any rate will suffer from neglect, while his principles will not allow him to help himself from the public funds; not to mention the offence he will give to his friends and relations by refusing to sacrifice those principles to do them a good turn. Injustice has all the opposite advantages. I am speaking of the type I described just now, the man who can get the better of other people on a large scale: you must fix your eye on him, if you want to judge how much it is to one's own interest not to be just. You can see that best in the most consummate form of injustice, which rewards wrongdoing with supreme welfare and happiness and reduces its victims, if they won't retaliate in kind, to misery. That form is despotism, which uses force or fraud to plunder the goods of others, public or private, sacred or profane, and to do it in a wholesale way. If you are caught committing any one of these crimes on a small scale, you are punished and disgraced; they call it sacrilege, kidnapping, burglary, theft and brigandage. But if, besides taking their property, you turn all your countrymen into slaves, you will hear no more of those ugly names; your countrymen themselves will call you the happiest of men and bless your name, and so will everyone who hears of such a complete triumph of injustice; for when people denounce injustice, it is because they are afraid of suffering wrong, not of doing it. So true is it, Socrates, that injustice, on a grand enough scale, is superior to justice in strength and freedom and autocratic power; and "right," as I said at first, means simply what serves the interest of the stronger party; "wrong" means what is for the interest and profit of oneself.

Having deluged our ears with this torrent of words, as the man at the baths might empty a bucket over one's head, Thrasymachus meant to take himself off; but the company obliged him to stay and defend his position. I was specially urgent in my entreaties.

My good Thrasymachus, said I, do you propose to fling a doctrine like that at our heads and then go away without explaining it properly or letting us point out to you whether it is true or not? Is it so small a matter in your eyes to determine the whole course of conduct which every one of us must follow to get the best of life?

Don't I realize it is a serious matter? he retorted.

Apparently not, said I; or else you have no consideration for us, and do not care whether we shall lead better or worse lives for being ignorant of this truth you profess to know. Do take the trouble to let us into your secret; if you treat us handsomely, you may be sure it will be a good investment; there are so many of us to show our gratitude. I will make no secret of my own conviction, which is that injustice is not more profitable than justice, even when left free to work its will unchecked. No; let your unjust man have full power to do wrong, whether by successful violence or by escaping detection; all the same he will not convince me that he will gain more than he would by being just. There may be others here who feel as I do, and set justice above injustice. It is for you to convince us that we are not well advised.

How can I he replied. If you are not convinced by what I have just said, what more can I do for you? Do you want to be fed with my ideas out of a spoon?

God forbid! I exclaimed; not that. But I do want you to stand by your own words; or, if you shift your ground, shift it openly and stop trying to hoodwink us as you are doing now. You see, Thrasymachus, to go back to your earlier argument, in speaking of the shepherd you did not think it necessary to keep to that strict sense you laid down when you defined the genuine physician. You represent him, in his character of shepherd, as feeding up his flock, not for their own sake but for the table or the market, as if he were out to make money as a caterer or a cattledealer, rather than a shepherd. Surely the sole concern of the shepherd's art is to do the best for the charges put under its care; its own best interest is sufficiently provided for, so long as it does not fall short of all that shepherding should imply. On that principle it followed, I thought, that any kind of authority, in the state or in private life, must, in its character of authority consider solely what is best for those under its care. Now what is your opinion? Do you think that the men who govern states—I mean rulers in the strict sense—have no reluctance to hold office?

I don't think so, he replied; I know it.

Well, but haven't you noticed, Thrasymachus, that in other positions of authority no one is willing to act unless he is paid wages, which he demands on the assumption that all the benefit of his action will go to his charges? Tell me: Don't we always distinguish one form of skill from another by its power to effect some particular result? Do say what you really think, so that we may get on.

Yes, that is the distinction.

And also each brings us some benefit that is peculiar to it: medicine gives health, for example; the art of navigation, safety at sea; and so on.

Yes.

And wage-earning brings us wages; that is its distinctive product. Now, speaking with that precision which you proposed, you would not say that the art of navigation is the same as the art of medicine, merely on the ground that a ship's captain regained his health on a voyage, because the sea air was good for him. No more would you identify the practice of medicine with wage-earning because a man may keep his health while earning wages, or a physician attending a case may receive a fee.

No.

And, since we agreed that the benefit obtained by each form of skill is peculiar to it, any common benefit enjoyed alike by all these practitioners must come from some further practice common to them all?

It would seem so.

Yes, we must say that if they all earn wages, they get that benefit in so far as they are engaged in wage-earning as well as in practising their several arts.

He agreed reluctantly.

This benefit, then—the receipt of wages—does not come to a man from his special art. If we are to speak strictly, the physician, as such, produces health; the builder, a house; and then each, in his further capacity of wage-earner, gets his pay. Thus every art has its own function and benefits its proper subject. But suppose the practitioner is not paid; does he then get any benefit from his art?

Clearly not.

And is he doing no good to anyone either, when he works for nothing?

No, I suppose he does some good.

Well then, Thrasymachus, it is now clear that no form of skill or authority provides for its own benefit. As we were saying some time ago, it always studies and prescribes what is good for its subject—the interest of the weaker party, not of the stronger. And that, my friend, is why I said that no one is willing to be in a position of authority and undertake to set straight other men's troubles, without demanding to be paid; because, if he is to do his work well, he will never, in his capacity of ruler, do, or command others to do, what is best for himself, but only what is best for the subject For that reason, if he is to consent, he must have his recompense, in the shape of money or honour, or of punishment in case of refusal.

What do you mean, Socrates? asked Glaucon. I recognize two of your three kinds of reward; but I don't understand what you mean by speaking of punishment as a recompense.

Then you don't understand the recompense required by the best type of men, or their motive for accepting authority when they do consent. You surely know that a passion for honours or for money is rightly regarded as something to be ashamed of.

Yes, I do.

For that reason, I said, good men are unwilling to rule, either for money's sake or for honour. They have no wish to be called mercenary for demanding to be paid, or thieves for making a secret profit out of their office; nor yet will honours tempt them, for they are not ambitious. So they must be forced to consent under threat of penalty; that may be why a readiness to accept power under no such constraint is thought discreditable. And the heaviest penalty for declining to rule is to be ruled by someone inferior to yourself. That is the fear, I believe, that makes decent people accept power; and when they do, they face the prospect of authority with no idea that they are coming into the enjoyment of a comfortable berth; it is forced upon them because they can find no one better than themselves, or even as good, to be entrusted with power. If there could ever be a society of perfect men, there might well be as much competition to evade office as there now is to gain it; and it would then be clearly seen that the genuine ruler's nature is to seek only the advantage of the subject, with the consequence that any man of understanding would sooner have another to do the best for him than be at the pains to do the best for that other himself. On this point, then, I entirely disagree with Thrasymachus' doctrine that right means what is to the interest of the stronger.

THE RUDIMENTS OF
SOCIAL ORGANIZATION

I was delighted with these speeches from Glaucon and Adeimantus, whose gifts I had always admired. How right, I exclaimed, was Glaucon's lover to begin that poem of his on your exploits at the battle of Megara by describing you two as the

sons divine
of Ariston's noble line!

Like father, like sons: there must indeed be some divine quality in your nature, if you can plead the cause of injustice so eloquently and still not be convinced yourselves that it is better than justice. That you are not really convinced I am sure from all I know of your dispositions, though your words might well have left me in doubt. But the more I trust you, the harder I find it to reply. How can I come to the rescue? I have no faith in my own powers, when I remember that you were not satisfied with the proof I thought I had given to Thrasymachus that it is better to be just. And yet I cannot stand by and hear justice reviled without lifting a finger. I am afraid to commit a sin by holding aloof while I have breath and strength to say a word in its defence. So there is nothing for it but to do the best I can.

Glaucon and the others begged me to step into the breach and carry through our inquiry into the real nature of justice and injustice, and the truth about their respective advantages. So I told them what I thought. This is a very obscure question, I said, and we shall need keen sight to see our way. Now, as we are not remarkably clever, I will make a suggestion as to how we should proceed. Imagine a rather short-sighted person told to read an inscription in small letters from some way off. He would think it a godsend if someone pointed out that the same inscription was written up elsewhere on a bigger scale, so that he could first read the larger characters and then make out whether the smaller ones were the same.

No doubt, said Adeimantus; but what analogy do you see in that to our inquiry?

I will tell you. We think of justice as a quality that may exist in a whole community as well as in an individual, and the community is the bigger of the two. Possibly, then, we may find justice there in larger proportions, easier to make out. So I suggest that we should begin by inquiring what justice means in a state. Then we can go on to look for its counterpart on a smaller scale in the individual.

That seems a good plan, he agreed.

Well then, I continued, suppose we imagine a state coming into being before our eyes. We might then be able to watch the growth of justice or of injustice within it. When that is done, we may hope it will be easier to find what we are looking for.

Much easier.

Shall we try, then, to carry out this scheme? I fancy it will be no light undertaking; so you had better think twice.

No need for that, said Adeimantus. Don't waste any more time.

My notion is, said I, that a state comes into existence because no individual is self-sufficing; we all have many needs. But perhaps you can suggest some different origin for the foundation of a community?

No, I agree with you.

So, having all these needs, we call in one another's help to satisfy our various requirements; and when we have collected a number of helpers and associates to live together in one place, we call that settlement a state.

Yes.

So if one man gives another what he has to give in exchange for what he can get, it is because each finds that to do so is for his own advantage.

Certainly.

Very well, said I. Now let us build up our imaginary state from the beginning. Apparently, it will owe its existence to our needs, the first and greatest need being the provision of food to keep us alive. Next we shall want a house; and thirdly, such things as clothing.

True.

How will our state be able to supply all these demands? We shall need at least one man to be a farmer, another a builder, and a third a weaver. Will that do, or shall we add a shoemaker and one or two more to provide for our personal wants?

By all means.

The minimum state, then, will consist of four or five men.

Apparently.

Now here is a further point. Is each one of them to bring the product of his work into a common stock? Should our one farmer, for example, provide food enough for four people and spend the whole of his working time in producing corn, so as to share with the rest; or should he take no notice of them and spend only a quarter of his time on growing just enough corn for himself, and divide the other three-quarters between building his house, weaving his clothes, and making his shoes, so as to save the trouble of sharing with others and attend himself to all his own concerns?

The first plan might be the easier, replied Adeimantus.

That may very well be so, said I; for, as you spoke, it occurred to me, for one thing, that no two people are born exactly alike. There are innate differences which fit them for different occupations.

I agree.

And will a man do better working at many trades, or keeping to one only?

Keeping to one.

And there is another point: obviously work may be ruined, if you let the right time go by. The workman must wait upon the work; it will not wait upon his leisure and allow itself to be done in a spare moment. So the conclusion is that more things will be produced and the work be more easily and better done, when every man is set free from all other occupations to do, at the right time, the one thing for which he is naturally fitted.

That is certainly true.

We shall need more than four citizens, then, to supply all those necessaries we mentioned. You see, Adeimantus, if the farmer is to have a good plough and spade and other tools, he will not make them himself. No more will the builder and weaver and shoemaker make all the many implements they need. So quite a number of carpenters and smiths and other craftsmen must be enlisted. Our miniature state is beginning to grow.

It is.

Still, it will not be very large, even when we have added cowherds and shepherds to provide the farmers with oxen for the plough, and the builders as well as the farmers with draught-animals, and the weavers and shoemakers with wool and leather.

No; but it will not be so very small either.

And yet, again, it will be next to impossible to plant our city in a territory where it will need no imports. So there will have to be still another set of people, to fetch what it needs from other countries.

There will.

Moreover, if these agents take with them nothing that those other countries require in exchange, they will return as empty-handed as they went. So, besides everything wanted for consumption at home, we must produce enough goods of the right kind for the foreigners whom we depend on to supply us. That will mean increasing the number of farmers and craftsmen.

Yes.

And then, there are these agents who are to import and export all kinds of goods—merchants, as we call them. We must have them; and if they are to do business overseas, we shall need quite a number of shipowners and others who know about that branch of trading.

We shall.

Again, in the city itself how are the various sets of producers to exchange their products? That was our object, you will remember, in forming a community and so laying the foundation of our state.

Obviously, they must buy and sell.

That will mean having a market-place, and a currency to serve as a token for purposes of exchange.

Certainly.

Now suppose a farmer, or an artisan, brings some of his produce to market at a time when no one is there who wants to exchange with him. Is he to sit there idle, when he might be at work?

No, he replied; there are people who have seen an opening here for their services. In well-ordered communities they are generally men not strong enough to be of use in any other occupation. They have to stay where they are in the market-place and take goods for money from those who want to sell, and money for goods from those who want to buy.

That, then, is the reason why our city must include a class of shopkeepers—so we call these people who sit still in the market-place to buy and sell, in contrast with merchants who travel to other countries.

Quite so.

There are also the services of yet another class, who have the physical strength for heavy work, though on intellectual grounds they are hardly worth including in our society—hired labourers, as we call them, because they sell the use of their strength for wages. They will go to make up our population.

Yes.

Well, Adeimantus, has our state now grown to its full size?

Perhaps.

Then, where in it shall we find justice or injustice? If they have come in with one of the elements we have been considering, can you say with which one?

I have no idea, Socrates; unless it be somewhere in their dealings with one another.

You may be right, I answered. Anyhow, it is a question which we shall have to face.

THE LUXURIOUS STATE

Let us begin, then, with a picture of our citizens' manner of life, with the provision we have made for them. They will be producing corn and wine, and making clothes and shoes. When they have built their houses, they will mostly work without their coats or shoes in summer, and in winter be well shod and clothed. For their food, they will prepare flour and barley-meal for kneading and baking, and set out a grand spread of loaves and cakes on rushes or fresh leaves. Then they will lie on beds of myrtle-boughs and byrony and make merry with their children, drinking their wine after the feast with garlands on their beads and singing the praises of the gods. So they will live pleasantly together; and a prudent fear of poverty or war will keep them from begetting children beyond their means.

Here Glaucon interrupted me: You seem to expect your citizens to feast on dry bread.

True, I said; I forgot that they will have something to give it a relish, salt, no doubt, and olives, and cheese, and country stews of roots and vegetables. And for dessert we will give them figs and peas and beans; and they shall roast myrtle-berries and acorns at the fire, while they sip their wine. Leading such a healthy life in peace, they will naturally come to a good old age, and leave their children to live after them in the same manner.

That is just the sort of provender you would supply, Socrates, if you were founding a community of pigs.

Well, how are they to live, then, Glaucon?

With the ordinary comforts. Let them lie on couches and dine off tables on such dishes and sweets as we have nowadays.

Ah, I see, said I; we are to study the growth, not just of a state, but of a luxurious one. Well, there may be no harm in that; the consideration of luxury may help us to discover how justice and injustice take root in society. The community I have described seems to me the ideal one, in sound health as it were: but if you want to see one suffering from inflammation, there is nothing to hinder us. So some people, it seems, will not be satisfied to live in this simple way; they must have couches and tables and furniture of all sorts; and delicacies too, perfumes, unguents, courtesans, sweetmeats, all in plentiful variety. And besides, we must not limit ourselves now to those bare necessaries of house and clothes and shoes; we shall have to set going the arts of embroidery and painting, and collect rich materials, like gold and ivory.

Yes.

Then we must once more enlarge our community. The healthy one will not be big enough now; it must be swollen up with a whole multitude of callings not ministering to any bare necessity: hunters and fishermen, for instance; artists in sculpture, painting, and music; poets with their attendant train of professional reciters, actors, dancers, producers; and makers of all sorts of household gear, including everything for women's adornment. And we shall want more servants: children's nurses and attendants, lady's maids, barbers, cooks and confectioners. And then swineherds—there was no need for them in our original state, but we shall want them now; and a great quantity of sheep and cattle too, if people are going to live on meat.

Of course.

And with this manner of life physicians will be in much greater request.

No doubt.

The country, too, which was large enough to support the original inhabitants, will now be too small. If we are to have enough pasture and plough land, we shall have to cut off a slice of our neighbours' territory; and if they too are not content with necessaries, but give themselves up to getting unlimited wealth, they will want a slice of ours.

That is inevitable, Socrates.

So the next thing will be, Glaucon, that we shall be at war.

No doubt.

We need not say yet whether war does good or harm, but only that we have discovered its origin in desires which are the most fruitful source of evils both to individuals and to states.[4]

Quite true.

This will mean a considerable addition to our community—a whole army, to go out to battle with any invader, in defence of all this property and of the citizens we have been describing.

Why so? Can't they defend themselves?

Not if the principle was right, which we all accepted in framing our society. You remember we agreed that no one man can practice many trades or arts satisfactorily.

True.

Well, is not the conduct of war an art, quite as important as shoemaking?

Yes.

---

[4] "All wars are made for the sake of getting money," *Phaedo* 66 c.

But we would not allow our shoemaker to try to be also a farmer or weaver or builder, because we wanted our shoes well made. We gave each man one trade, for which he was naturally fitted; he would do good work, if he confined himself to that all his life, never letting the right moment slip by. Now in no form of work is efficiency so important as in war; and fighting is not so easy a business that a man can follow another trade, such as farming or shoemaking, and also be an efficient soldier. Why, even a game like draughts or dice must be studied from childhood; no one can become a fine player in his spare moments. Just taking up a shield or other weapon will not make a man capable of fighting that very day in any sort of warfare, any more than taking up a tool or implement of some kind will make a man a craftsman or an athlete, if he does not understand its use and has never been properly trained to handle it.

No; if that were so, tools would indeed be worth having

These guardians of our state, then, inasmuch as their work is the most important of all, will need the most complete freedom from other occupations and the greatest amount of skill and practice.

I quite agree.

And also a native aptitude for their calling.

Certainly.

So it is our business to define, if we can, the natural gifts that fit men to be guardians of a commonwealth, and to select them accordingly. It will certainly be a formidable task; but we must grapple with it to the best of our power.

Yes.

THE GUARDIANS' TEMPERAMENT

Don't you think then, said I, that, for the purpose of keeping guard, a young man should have much the same temperament and qualities as a well-bred watch-dog? I mean, for instance, that both must have quick sense to detect an enemy, swiftness in pursuing him, and strength, if they have to fight when they have caught him.

Yes, they will need all those qualities.

And also courage, if they are to fight well.

Of course.

And courage, in dog or horse or any other creature, implies a spirited disposition. You must have noticed that a high spirit is unconquerable. Every soul possessed of it is fearless and indomitable in the face of any danger.

Yes, I have noticed that.

So now we know what physical qualities our Guardian must have, and also that he must be of a spirited temper.

Yes.

Then, Glaucon, how are men of that natural disposition to be kept from behaving pugnaciously to one another and to the rest of their countrymen?

It is not at all easy to see.

And yet they must be gentle to their own people and dangerous only to enemies; otherwise they will destroy themselves without waiting till others destroy them.

True.

What are we to do, then? If gentleness and a higher temper are contraries, where shall we find a character to combine them? Both are necessary to make a good Guardian, but it seems they are incompatible. So we shall never have a good Guardian.

It looks like it.

Here I was perplexed, but on thinking over what we had been saying, I remarked that we deserved to be puzzled, because we had not followed up the comparison we had just drawn.

What do you mean? he asked.

We never noticed that, after all, there are natures in which these contraries are combined. They are to be found in animals, and not least in the kind we compared to our Guardian. Well-bred dogs, as you know, are by instinct perfectly gentle to people whom they know and are accustomed to, and fierce to strangers. So the combination of qualities we require for our Guardian is, after all, possible and not against nature.

Evidently.

Do you further agree that, besides this spirited temper, he must have a philosophical element in his nature?

I don't see what you mean.

This is another trait you will see in the dog. It is really remarkable how the creature gets angry at the mere sight of a stranger and welcomes anyone he knows, though he may never have been treated unkindly by the one or kindly by the other. Did that never strike you as curious?

I had not thought of it before; but that certainly is how a dog behaves.

Well, but that shows a fine instinct, which is philosophic in the true sense.

How so?

Because the only mark by which he distinguishes a friendly and an unfriendly face is that he knows the one and does not know the other; and if a creature makes that the test of what it finds congenial or otherwise, how can you deny that it has a passion for knowledge and understanding?

Of course, I cannot.

And that passion is the same thing as philosophy—the love of wisdom.[5]

Yes.

Shall we boldly say, then, that the same is true of human beings? If a man is to be gentle towards his own people whom he knows, he must have an instinctive love of wisdom and understanding.

Agreed.

So the nature required to make a really noble Guardian of our commonwealth will be swift and strong, spirited, and philosophic.

Quite so.

Given those natural qualities, then, how are these Guardians to be brought up and educated? First, will the answer to that question help the purpose of our whole inquiry, which is to make out how justice and injustice grow up in a state? We want to be thorough, but not to draw out this discussion to a needless length.

Glaucon's brother answered: I certainly think it will help.

If so, I said, we must not think of dropping it, though it may be rather a long business.

I agree.

Come on then. We will take our time and educate our imaginary citizens.

Yes, let us do so.

---

[5] The ascription of a philosophic element to dogs is not seriously meant. We might regard man's love of knowledge as rooted in an instinct of curiosity to be found in animals; but curiosity has no connexion with gentleness, and for Plato reason is an independent faculty, existing only in man and not developed from any animal instinct.

PRIMARY EDUCATION OF THE GUARDIANS: CENSORSHIP OF LITERATURE

What is this education to be, then? Perhaps we shall hardly invent a system better than the one which long experience has worked out, with its two branches for the cultivation of the mind and of the body. And I suppose we shall begin with the mind, before we start physical training.

Naturally.

Under that head will come stories,[6] and of these there are two kinds: some are true, others fictitious. Both must come in, but we shall begin our education with the fictitious kind.

I don't understand, he said.

Don't you understand, I replied, that we begin by telling children stories, which, taken as a whole, are fiction, though they contain some truth? Such story-telling begins at an earlier age than physical training; that is why I said we should start with the mind.

You are right.

And the beginning, as you know, is always the most important part, especially in dealing with anything young and tender. That is the time when the character is being moulded and easily takes any impress one may wish to stamp on it.

Quite true.

Then shall we simply allow our children to listen to any stories that anyone happens to make up, and so receive into their minds ideas often the very opposite of those we shall think they ought to have when they are grown up?

No, certainly not.

It seems, then, our first business will be to supervise the making of fables and legends, rejecting all which are unsatisfactory; and we shall induce nurses and mothers to tell their children only those which we have approved, and to think more of moulding their souls with these stories than they now do of rubbing their limbs to make them strong and shapely. Most of the stories now in use must be discarded.

What kind do you mean?

---

[6] In a wide sense, tales, legends, myths, narratives in poetry or prose.

If we take the great ones, we shall see in them the pattern of all the rest, which are bound to be of the same stamp and to have the same effect.

No doubt; but which do you mean by the great ones?

The stories in Hesiod and Homer and the poets in general, who have at all times composed fictitious tales and told them to mankind.

Which kind are you thinking of, and what fault do you find in them?

The worst of all faults, especially if the story is ugly and immoral as well as false—misrepresenting the nature of gods and heroes, like an artist whose picture is utterly unlike the object he sets out to draw.

That is certainly a serious fault; but give me an example.

A single instance of false invention about the highest matters is that foul story, which Hesiod repeats, of the deeds of Uranus and the vengeance of Cronos;[7] and then there is the tale of Cronos's doings and of his son's treatment of him. Even if such tales were true, I should not have supposed they should be lightly told to thoughtless young people. If they cannot be altogether suppressed, they should only be revealed in a mystery, to which access should be as far as possible restricted by requiring the sacrifice, not of a pig, but of some victim such as very few could afford.[8]

It is true: those stories are objectionable.

Yes, and not to be repeated in our commonwealth, Adeimantus. We shall not tell a child that, if he commits the foulest crimes or goes to any length in punishing his father's misdeeds, he will be doing nothing out of the way, but only what the first and greatest of the gods have done before him.

I agree; such stories are not fit to be repeated.

Nor yet any tales of warfare and intrigues and battles of gods against gods, which are equally untrue. If our future Guardians are to think it a disgrace to quarrel lightly with one another, we shall not let them embroider robes with the Battle of the Giants[9] or tell them of all the other feuds of gods and heroes with their kith and kin. If by any means we can make them believe that no one has ever had a quarrel with a fellow citizen and it is a sin to have one, that is the sort of thing our old men and women should tell children from the first; and as they grow older, we must make the poets write for them in the same strain. Stories like those of Hera being bound by her son, or of Hephaestus flung from heaven by his father for taking his mother's part when she was beaten, and all those battles of the gods in Homer, must not be admitted into our state, whether they be allegorical or not. A child cannot distinguish the allegorical sense from the literal, and the ideas he takes in at that age are likely to become indelibly fixed; hence the great importance of seeing that the first stories he hears shall be designed to produce the best possible effect on his character.

Yes, that is reasonable. But if we were asked which of these stories in particular are of the right quality, what should we answer?

I replied: You and I, Adeimantus, are not, for the moment, poets, but founders of a commonwealth. As such, it is not our business to invent stories ourselves, but only to be clear as to the main outlines to be followed by the poets in making their stories and the limits beyond which they must not be allowed to go.

True; but what are these outlines for any account they may give of the gods?

Of this sort, said I. A poet, whether he is writing epic, lyric, or drama, surely ought always to represent the divine nature as it really is. And the truth is that that nature is good and must be described as such.

Unquestionably.

Well, nothing that is good can be harmful; and if it cannot do harm, it can do no evil; and so it cannot be responsible for any evil.

---

[7] Hesiod, *Theogony,* 154 ff. A primitive myth of the forcing apart of Sky (Uranus) and Earth (Gaia) by their son Cronos, who mutilated his father. Zeus, again, took vengeance on his father Cronos for trying to destroy his children. These stories were sometimes cited to justify ill-treatment of parents.

[8] The usual sacrifice at the Eleusinian Mysteries was a pig, which was cheap. In a mystery unedifying legends might be given an allegorical interpretation, a method which had been applied to Homer since the end of the sixth century B.C.

---

[9] Such a robe was woven by maidens for the statue of Athena at the Great Panathenaea.

I agree.

Again, goodness is beneficent, and hence the cause of well-being.

Yes.

Goodness, then, is not responsible for everything, but only for what is as it should be. It is not responsible for evil.

Quite true.

It follows, then, that the divine, being good, is not, as most people say, responsible for everything that happens to mankind, but only for a small part; for the good things in human life are far fewer than the evil, and, whereas the good must be ascribed to heaven only, we must look elsewhere for the cause of evils.

I think that is perfectly true.

So we shall condemn as a foolish error Homer's description of Zeus as the "dispenser of both good and ill." We shall disapprove when Pandarus' violation of oaths and treaties it said to be the work of Zeus and Athena, or when Themis and Zeus are said to have caused strife among the gods. Nor must we allow our young people to be told by Aeschylus that "Heaven implants guilt in man, when his will is to destroy a house utterly." If a poet writes of the sorrows of Niobe or the calamities of the house of Pelops or of the Trojan war, either he must not speak of them as the work of a god, or, if he does so, he must devise some such explanation as we are now requiring: he must say that what the god did was just and good, and the sufferers were the better for being chastised. One who pays a just penalty must not be called miserable, and his misery then laid at heaven's door. The poet will only be allowed to say that the wicked were miserable because they needed chastisement, and the punishment of heaven did them good. If our commonwealth is to be well-ordered, we must fight to the last against any member of it being suffered to speak of the divine, which is good, being responsible for evil. Neither young nor old must listen to such tales, in prose or verse. Such doctrine would be impious, self-contradictory, and disastrous to our commonwealth.

I agree, he said, and I would vote for a law to that effect.

Well then, that shall be one of our laws about religion. The first principle to which all must conform in speech or writing is that heaven is not responsible for everything, but only for what is good.

I am quite satisfied.

If anyone, then, is to practise deception, either on the country's enemies or on its citizens, it must be the Rulers of the commonwealth, acting for its benefit; no one else may meddle with this privilege. For a private person to mislead such Rulers we shall declare to be a worse offence than for a patient to mislead his doctor or an athlete his trainer about his bodily condition, or for a seaman to misinform his captain about the state of the ship or of the crew. So, if anyone else in our commonwealth "of all that practise crafts, physician, seer, or carpenter," is caught not telling the truth, the Rulers will punish him for introducing a practice as fatal and subversive in a state as it would be in a ship.

SELECTION OF RULERS: THE GUARDIANS' MANNER OF LIVING

Good, said I; and what is the next point to he settled? Is it not the question, which of these Guardians are to be rulers and which are to obey?

No doubt.

Well, it is obvious that the elder must have authority over the young, and that the rulers must be the best.

Yes.

And as among farmers the best are those with a natural turn for farming, so, if we want the best among our Guardians, we must take those naturally fitted to watch over a commonwealth. They must have the right sort of intelligence and ability; and also they must look upon the commonwealth as their special concern—the sort of concern that is felt for something so closely bound up with oneself that its interests and fortunes, for good or ill, are held to be identical with one's own.

Exactly.

So the kind of men we must choose from among the Guardians will be those who, when we look at the whole course of their lives, are found to be full of zeal to do whatever they believe is for the good of the commonwealth and never willing to act against its interest.

Yes, they will be the men we want.

We must watch them, I think, at every age and see whether they are capable of preserving this conviction that they must do what is best for the community, never forgetting it or allowing themselves to be either forced or bewitched into throwing it over.

How does this throwing over come about?

I will explain. When a belief passes out of the mind, a man may be willing to part with it, if it is false and he has learnt better, or unwilling, if it is true.

I see how he might be willing to let it go; but you must explain how he can be unwilling.

Where is your difficulty? Don't you agree that men are unwilling to be deprived of good, though ready enough to part with evil? Or that to be deceived about the truth is evil, to possess it good? Or don't you think that possessing truth means thinking of things as they really are?

You are right. I do agree that men are unwilling to be robbed of a true belief.

When that happens to them, then, it must be by theft, or violence, or bewitchment.

Again I do not understand.

Perhaps my metaphors are too high-flown. I call it theft when one is persuaded out of one's belief or forgets it. Argument in the one case, and time in the other, steal it away without one's knowing what is happening. You understand now?

Yes.

And by violence I mean being driven to change one's mind by pain or suffering.

That too I understand, and you are right.

And bewitchment, as I think you would agree, occurs when a man is beguiled out of his opinion by the allurements of pleasure or scared out of it under the spell of panic.

Yes, all delusions are like a sort of bewitchment.

As I said just now, then, we must find out who are the best guardians of this inward conviction that they must always do what they believe to be best for the commonwealth. We shall have to watch them from earliest childhood and set them tasks in which they would be most likely to forget or to be beguiled out of this duty. We shall then choose only those whose memory holds firm and who are proof against delusion.

Yes.

We must also subject them to ordeals of toil and pain and watch for the same qualities there. And we must observe them when exposed to the test of yet a third kind of bewitchment. As people lead colts up to alarming noises to see whether they are timid, so these young men must be brought into terrifying situations and then into scenes of pleasure, which will put them to severer proof than gold tried in the furnace. If we find one bearing himself well in all these trials and resisting every enchantment, a true guardian of himself, preserving always that perfect rhythm and harmony of being which he has acquired from his training in music and poetry, such a one will be of the greatest service to the commonwealth as well as to himself. Whenever we find one who has come unscathed through every test in childhood, youth, and manhood, we shall set him as a Ruler to watch over the commonwealth; he will be honoured in life, and after death receive the highest tribute of funeral rites and other memorials. All who do not reach this standard we must reject. And that, I think, my dear Glaucon, may be taken as an outline of the way in which we shall select Guardians to be set in authority as Rulers.

I am very much of your mind.

These, then, may properly be called Guardians in the fullest sense, who will ensure that neither foes without shall have the power, nor friends within the wish, to do harm. Those young men whom up to now we have been speaking of as Guardians, will be better described as Auxiliaries, who will enforce the decisions of the Rulers.

I agree.

Now, said I, can we devise something in the way of those convenient fictions we spoke of earlier, a single bold flight of invention,[10] which we may induce the community in general, and if possible the Rulers themselves, to accept?

What kind of fiction?

Nothing new; something like an Eastern tale of what, according to the poets, has

[10] This phrase is commonly rendered by "noble lie" a self-contradictory expression no more applicable to Plato's harmless allegory than to a New Testament parable or the Pilgrim's Progress, and liable to suggest that he would countenance the lies, for the most part ignoble, now called propaganda.

happened before now in more than one part of the world. The poets have been believed; but the thing has not happened in our day, and it would be hard to persuade anyone that it could ever happen again.

You seem rather shy of telling this story of yours.

With good reason, as you will see when I have told it.

Out with it; don't be afraid.

Well, here it is; though I hardly know how to find the courage or the words to express it. I shall try to convince, first the Rulers and the soldiers,[11] and then the whole community, that all that nurture and education which we gave them was only something they seemed to experience as it were in a dream. In reality they were the whole time down inside the earth, being moulded and fostered while their arms and all their equipment were being fashioned also; and at last, when they were complete, the earth sent them up from her womb into the light of day. So now they must think of the land they dwell in as a mother and nurse, whom they must take thought for and defend against any attack, and of their fellow citizens as brothers born of the same soil.

You might well be bashful about coming out with your fiction.

No doubt; but still you must hear the rest of the story. It is true, we shall tell our people in this fable, that all of you in this land are brothers; but the god who fashioned you mixed gold in the composition of those among you who are fit to rule, so that they are of the most precious quality; and he put silver in the Auxiliaries, and iron and brass in the farmers and craftsmen. Now, since you are all of one stock, although your children will generally be like their parents, sometimes a golden parent may have a silver child or a silver parent a golden one, and so on with all the other combinations. So the first and chief injunction laid by heaven upon the Rulers is that, among all the things of which they must show themselves good guardians, there is none that needs to be so carefully watched as the mixture of metals in the souls of the children. If a child of their own is born with an alloy of iron or brass, they must, without the smallest pity, assign him the station proper to his nature and thrust him out among the craftsmen or the farmers. If, on the contrary, these classes produce a child with gold or silver in his composition, they will promote him, according to his value, to be a Guardian or an Auxiliary. They will appeal to a prophecy that ruin will come upon the state when it passes into the keeping of a man of iron or brass. Such is the story; can you think of any device to make them believe it?

Not in the first generation; but their sons and descendants might believe it, and finally the rest of mankind.[12]

Well, said I, even so it might have a good effect in making them care more for the commonwealth and for one another; for I think I see what you mean.

So, I continued, we will leave the success of our story to the care of popular tradition; and now let us arm these sons of Earth and lead them, under the command of their Rulers, to the site of our city. There let them look round for the best place to fix their camp, from which they will be able to control any rebellion against the laws from within and to beat off enemies who may come from without like wolves to attack the fold. When they have pitched their camp and offered sacrifice to the proper divinities, they must arrange their sleeping quarters; and these must be sufficient to shelter them from winter cold and summer heat.

Naturally. You mean they are going to live there?

Yes, said I; but live like soldiers, not like men of business.

What is the difference?

I will try to explain. It would be very strange if a shepherd were to disgrace himself by keeping, for the protection of his flock, dogs who were so ill-bred and badly trained that hunger or unruliness or some bad habit or other would set them worrying the sheep and behaving no better than wolves. We must take every precaution against our

---

[11] Note that the Guardians themselves are to accept this allegory, if possible. It is not "propaganda" foisted on the masses by the Rulers.

[12] Just as the tradition that the Athenians were "autochthonous" in a literal sense was popularly believed, though Plato would suppose it to have been originally invented by some myth-making poet.

Auxiliaries treating the citizens in any such way and, because they are stronger, turning into savage tyrants instead of friendly allies; and they will have been furnished with the best of safeguards, if they have really been educated in the right way.

But surely there is nothing wrong with their education.

We must not be too positive about that, my dear Glaucon; but we can be sure of what we said not long ago, that if they are to have the best chance of being gentle and humane to one another and to their charges, they must have the right education, whatever that may be.

We were certainly right there.

Then besides that education, it is only common sense to say that the dwellings and other belongings provided for them must be such as will neither make them less perfect Guardians nor encourage them to maltreat their fellow citizens.

True.

With that end in view, let us consider how they should live and be housed. First, none of them must possess any private property beyond the barest necessaries. Next, no one is to have any dwelling or store-house that is not open for all to enter at will. Their food, in the quantities required by men of temperance and courage who are in training for war, they will receive from the other citizens as the wages of their guardianship, fixed so that there shall be just enough for the year with nothing over; and they will have meals in common and all live together like soldiers in a camp. Gold and silver, we shall tell them, they will not need, having the divine counterparts of those metals always in their souls as a god-given possession, whose purity it is not lawful to sully by the acquisition of that mortal dross, current among mankind, which has been the occasion of so many unholy deeds. They alone of all the citizens are forbidden to touch and handle silver or gold, or to come under the same roof with them, or wear them as ornaments, or drink from vessels made of them. This manner of life will be their salvation and make them the saviours of the commonwealth. If ever they should come to possess land of their own and houses and money, they will give up their guardianship for the management of their farms and

households and become tyrants at enmity with their fellow citizens instead of allies. And so they will pass all their lives in hating and being hated, plotting and being plotted against, in much greater fear of their enemies at home than of any foreign foe, and fast heading for the destruction that will soon overwhelm their country with themselves. For all these reasons let us say that this is how our Guardians are to be housed and otherwise provided for, and let us make laws accordingly.

By all means, said Glaucon.

Here Adeimantus interposed. Socrates, he said, how would you meet the objection that you are not making these people particularly happy? it is their own fault too, if they are not; for they are really masters of the state, and yet they get no good out of it as other rulers do, who own lands, build themselves fine houses with handsome furniture, offer private sacrifices to the gods, and entertain visitors from abroad; who possess, in fact, that gold and silver you spoke of, with everything else that is usually thought necessary for happiness. These people seem like nothing so much as a garrison of mercenaries posted in the city and perpetually mounting guard.

Yes, I said, and what is more they will serve for their food only without getting a mercenary's pay, so that they will not be able to travel on their own account or to make presents to a mistress or to spend as they please in other ways, like the people who are commonly thought happy. You have forgotten to include these counts in your indictment, and many more to the same effect.

Well, take them as included now.

And you want to hear the answer?

Yes.

We shall find one, I think, by keeping to the line we have followed so far. We shall say that, though it would not be surprising if even these people were perfectly happy under such conditions, our aim in founding the commonwealth was not to make any one class specially happy, but to secure the greatest possible happiness for the community as a whole. We thought we should have the best chance of finding justice in a state so constituted, just as we should find injustice where the constitution was of the worst possible type; we could then decide the question which has been before us all this time. For the moment, we are constructing, as we believe, the state which will be happy as a whole, not trying to secure the well-being of a select few; we shall study a state of the opposite kind presently. It is as if we were colouring a statue and someone came up and blamed us for not putting the most beautiful colours on the noblest parts of the figure; the eyes, for instance, should be painted crimson, but we had made them black. We should think it a fair answer to say: Really, you must not expect us to paint eyes so handsome as not to look like eyes at all. This applies to all the parts: the question is whether, by giving each its proper colour, we make the whole beautiful. So too, in the present case, you must not press us to endow our Guardians with a happiness that will make them anything rather than guardians. We could quite easily clothe our farmers in gorgeous robes, crown them with gold, and invite them to till the soil at their pleasure; or we might set our potters to lie on couches by their fire, passing round the wine and making merry, with their wheel at hand to work at whenever they felt so inclined. We could make all the rest happy in the same sort of way, and so spread this well-being through the whole community. But you must not put that idea into our heads; if we take your advice, the farmer will be no farmer, the potter no longer a potter; none of the elements that make up the community will keep its character. In many cases this does not matter so much: if a cobbler goes to the bad and pretends to be what he is not, he is not a danger to the state; but, as you must surely see, men who make only a vain show of being guardians of the laws and of the commonwealth bring the whole state to utter ruin, just as, on the other hand, its good government and well-being depend entirely on them. We, in fact, are making genuine Guardians who will be the last to bring harm upon the commonwealth; if our critic aims rather at producing a happiness like that of a party of peasants feasting at a fair, what he has in mind is something other than a civic community. So we must consider whether our aim in establishing Guardians is to secure the greatest possible happiness for them, or

happiness is something of which we should watch the development in the whole commonwealth. If so, we must compel these Guardians and Auxiliaries of ours to second our efforts; and they, and all the rest with them, must be induced to make themselves perfect masters each of his own craft. In that way, as the community grows into a well-ordered whole, the several classes may be allowed such measure of happiness as their nature will compass.

I think that is an admirable reply.

THE VIRTUES IN THE STATE

So now at last, son of Ariston, said I, your commonwealth is established. The next thing is to bring to bear upon it all the light you can get from any quarter, with the help of your brother and Polemarchus and all the rest, in the hope that we may see where justice is to be found in it and where injustice, how they differ, and which of the two will bring happiness to its possessor, no matter whether gods and men see that he has it or not.

Nonsense, said Glaucon; you promised to conduct the search yourself, because it would be a sin not to uphold justice by every means in your power.

That is true; I must do as you say, but you must all help.

We will.

I suspect, then, we may find what we are looking for in this way. I take it that our state, having been founded and built up on the right lines, is good in the complete sense of the word.

It must be.

Obviously, then, it is wise, brave, temperate, and just.

Obviously.

Then if we find some of these qualities in it, the remainder will be the one we have not found. It is as if we were looking somewhere for one of any four things: if we detected that one immediately, we should be satisfied; whereas if we recognized the other three first, that would be enough to indicate the thing we wanted; it could only be the remaining one. So here we have four qualities. Had we not better follow that method in looking for the one we want?

Surely.

To begin then: the first quality to come into view in our state seems to be its wisdom; and there appears to be something odd about this quality.[13]

What is there odd about it?

I think the state we have described really has wisdom; for it will be prudent in counsel, won't it?

Yes.

And prudence in counsel is clearly a form of knowledge; good counsel cannot be due to ignorance and stupidity.

Clearly.

But there are many various kinds of knowledge in our commonwealth. There is the knowledge possessed by the carpenters or the smiths, and the knowledge how to raise crops. Are we to call the state wise and prudent on the strength of these forms of skill?

No; they would only make it good at furniture-making or working in copper or agriculture.

Well then, is there any form of knowledge, possessed by some among the citizens of our new-founded commonwealth, which will enable it to take thought, not for some particular interest, but for the best possible conduct of the state as a whole in its internal and external relations?

Yes, there is.

What is it, and where does it reside?

It is precisely that art of guardianship which resides in those Rulers whom we just called Guardians in the full sense.

And what would you call the state on the strength of that knowledge?

Prudent and truly wise.

And do you think there will be more or fewer of these genuine Guardians in our state than there will be smiths?

Far fewer.

Fewer, in fact, than any of those other groups who are called after the kind of skill they possess?

Much fewer.

So, if a state is constituted on natural principles, the wisdom it possesses as a whole will be due to the knowledge residing in the smallest part, the one which takes the lead and governs the rest. Such knowledge is the only kind that deserves the name of wis-dom, and it appears to be ordained by nature that the class privileged to possess it should be the smallest of all.

Quite true.

Here then we have more or less made out one of our four qualities and its scat in the structure of the commonwealth.

To my satisfaction, at any rate.

Next there is courage. It is not hard to discern that quality or the part of the community in which it resides so as to entitle the whole to be called brave.

Why do you say so?

Because anyone who speaks of a state as either brave or cowardly can only be thinking of that part of it which takes the field and fight in its defence; the reason being, I imagine, that the character of the state is not determined by the bravery or cowardice of the other parts.

No.

Courage, then, is another quality which a community owes to a certain part of itself. And its being brave will mean that, in this part, it possesses the power of preserving, in all circumstances, a conviction about the sort of things that it is right to be afraid of— the conviction implanted by the education which the law-giver has established. Is not that what you mean by courage?

I do not quite understand. Will you say it again?

I am saying that courage means preserving something.

Yes, but what?

The conviction, inculcated by lawfully established education, about the sort of things which may rightly be feared. When I added "in all circumstances," I meant preserving it always and never abandoning it, whether under the influence of pain or of pleasure, of desire or of fear. If you like, I will give an illustration.

Please do.

You know how dyers who want wool to take a purple dye, first select the white wool from among all the other colours, next treat it very carefully to make it take the dye in its full brilliance, and only then dip it in the vat. Dyed in that way, wool gets a fast colour, which no washing, even with soap, will rob of its brilliance; whereas if they choose wool of any colour but white, or if they neglect to prepare it, you know what happens.

---

[13] Because the wisdom of the whole resides in the smallest part, as explained below.

Yes, it looks washed-out and ridiculous.

That illustrates the result we were doing our best to achieve when we were choosing our fighting men and training their minds and bodies. Our only purpose was to contrive influences whereby they might take the colour of our institutions like a dye, so that, in virtue of having both the right temperament and the right education, their convictions about what ought to be feared and on all other subjects might be indelibly fixed, never to be washed out by pleasure and pain, desire and fear, solvents more terribly effective than all the soap and fuller's earth in the world. Such a power of constantly preserving, in accordance with our institutions, the right conviction about the things which ought, or ought not to be feared, is what I call courage. That is my position, unless you have some objection to make.

None at all, he replied; if the belief were such as might be found in a slave or an animal—correct, but not produced by education—you would hardly describe it as in accordance with our institutions, and you would give it some other name than courage.

Quite true.

Then I accept your account of courage.

You will do well to accept it, at any rate as applying to the courage of the ordinary citizen;[14] if you like we will go into it more fully some other time. At present we are in search of justice, rather than of courage; and for that purpose we have said enough.

I quite agree.

Two qualities, I went on, still remain to be made out in our state, temperance and the object of our whole inquiry, justice. Can we discover justice without troubling ourselves further about temperance?

I do not know, and I would rather not have justice come to light first, if that means that we should not go on to consider temperance. So if you want to please me, take temperance first.

Of course I have every wish to please you.

Do go on then.

I will. At first sight, temperance seems more like some sort of concord or harmony than the other qualities did.

How so?

Temperance surely means a kind of orderliness, a control of certain pleasures and appetites. People use the expression, "master of oneself," whatever that means, and various other phrases that point the same way.

Quite true.

Is not "master of oneself" an absurd expression? A man who was master of himself would presumably be also subject to himself, and the subject would be master; for all these terms apply to the same person.

No doubt.

I think, however, the phrase means that within the man himself, in his soul, there is a better part and a worse; and that he is his own master when the part which is better by nature has the worse under its control. It is certainly a term of praise; whereas it is considered a disgrace, when, through bad breeding or bad company, the better part is overwhelmed by the worse, like a small force outnumbered by a multitude. A man in that condition is called a slave to himself and intemperate.

Probably that is what is meant.

Then now look at our newly founded state and you will find one of these two conditions realized there. You will agree that it deserves to be called master of itself, if temperance and self-mastery exist where the better part rules the worse.

Yes, I can see that is true.

It is also true that the great mass of multifarious appetites and pleasures and pains will be found to occur chiefly in children and women and slaves, and, among free men so called, in the inferior multitude; whereas the simple and moderate desires which, with the aid of reason and right belief, are guided by reflection, you will find only in a few, and those with the best inborn dispositions and the best educated.

Yes, certainly.

Do you see that this state of things will exist in your commonwealth, where the desires of the inferior multitude will be controlled by the desires and wisdom of the superior few? Hence, if any society can be called master of itself and in control of pleasures and desires, it will be ours.

---

[14] As distinct from the perfect courage of the philosophic Ruler, based on immediate knowledge of values.

Quite so.

On all these grounds, then, we may describe it as temperate. Furthermore, in our state, if anywhere, the governors and the governed will share the same conviction on the question who ought to rule. Don't you think so?

I am quite sure of it.

Then, if that is their state of mind, in which of the two classes of citizens will temperance reside—in the governors or in the governed?

In both, I suppose.

So we were not wrong in divining a resemblance between temperance and some kind of harmony. Temperance is not like courage and wisdom, which made the state wise and brave by residing each in one particular part. Temperance works in a different way; it extends throughout the whole gamut of the state, producing a consonance of all its elements from the weakest to the strongest as measured by any standard you like to take—wisdom, bodily strength, numbers, or wealth. So we are entirely justified in identifying with temperance this unanimity or harmonious agreement between the naturally superior and inferior elements on the question which of the two should govern, whether in the state or in the individual.

I fully agree.

Good, said I. We have discovered in our commonwealth three out of our four qualities, to the best of our present judgment. What is the remaining one, required to make up its full complement of goodness? For clearly this will be justice.

Clearly.

Now is the moment, then, Glaucon, for us to keep the closest watch, like huntsmen standing round a covert, to make sure that justice does not slip through and vanish undetected. It must certainly be somewhere hereabouts; so keep your eyes open for a view of the quarry, and if you see it first, give me the alert.

I wish I could, he answered; but you will do better to give me a lead and not count on me for more than eyes to see what you show me.

Pray for luck, then, and follow me.

I will, if you will lead on.

The thicket looks rather impenetrable, said I; too dark for it to be easy to start up the game. However, we must push on.

Of course we must.

Here I gave the cry halloo. Glaucon, I exclaimed, I believe we are on the track and the quarry is not going to escape us altogether.

That is good news.

Really, I said, we have been extremely stupid. All this time the thing has been under our very noses from the start, and we never saw it. We have been as absurd as a person who hunts for something be has all the time got in his hand. Instead of looking at the thing, we have been staring into the distance. No doubt that is why it escaped us.

What do you mean?

I believe we have been talking about the thing all this while without ever understanding that we were giving some sort of account of it.

Do come to the point. I am all ears.

Listen, then, and judge whether I am right. You remember how, when we first began to establish our commonwealth and several times since, we have laid down, as a universal principle, that everyone ought to perform the one function in the community for which his nature best suited him. Well. I believe that that principle, or some form of it, is justice.

We certainly laid that down.

Yes, and surely we have often heard people say that justice means minding one's own business and not meddling with other men's concerns; and we have often said so ourselves.

We have.

Well, my friend, it may be that this minding of one's own business, when it takes a certain form, is actually the same thing as justice. Do you know what makes me think so?

No, tell me.

I think that this quality which makes it possible for the three we have already considered, wisdom, courage, and temperance, to take their place in the commonwealth, and so long as it remains present secures their continuance, must be the remaining one. And we said that, when three of the four were found, the one left over would be justice.

It must be so.

Well now, if we had to decide which of these qualities will contribute most to the excellence of our commonwealth, it would be hard to say whether it was the unanimity of rulers and subjects, or the soldier's fidelity to the established conviction about what is, or is not, to be feared, or the watchful intelligence of the Rulers; or whether its excellence were not above all due to the observance by everyone, child or woman, slave or freeman or artisan, ruler or ruled, of this principle that each one should do his own proper work without interfering with others.

It would be hard to decide, no doubt.

It seems, then, that this principle can at any rate claim to rival wisdom, temperance, and courage as conducing to the excellence of a state. And would you not say that the only possible competitor of these qualities must be justice?

Yes, undoubtedly.

Here is another thing which points to the same conclusion. The judging of lawsuits is a duty that you will lay upon your Rulers, isn't it?

Of course.

And the chief aim of their decisions will be that neither party shall have what belongs to another or be deprived of what is his own.

Yes.

Because that is just?

Yes.

So here again justice admittedly means that a man should possess and concern himself with what properly belongs to him.

True.

Again, do you agree with me that no great harm would be done to the community by a general interchange of most forms of work, the carpenter and the cobbler exchanging their positions and their tools and taking on each other's jobs, or even the same man undertaking both?

Yes, there would not be much harm in that.

But I think you will also agree that another kind of interchange would be disastrous. Suppose, for instance, someone whom nature designed to be an artisan or tradesman should be emboldened by some advantage, such as wealth or command of votes or bodily strength, to try to enter the order of fighting men; or some member of that order should aspire, beyond his merits, to a seat in the council-chamber of the Guardians. Such interference and exchange of social positions and tools, or the attempt to combine all these forms of work in the same person, would be fatal to the commonwealth.

Most certainly.

Where there are three orders, then, any plurality of functions or shifting from one order to another is not merely utterly harmful to the community, but one might fairly call it the extreme of wrongdoing. And you will agree that to do the greatest of wrongs to one's own community is injustice.

Surely.

This, then, is injustice. And, conversely, let us repeat that when each order—tradesman, Auxiliary, Guardian—keeps to its own proper business in the commonwealth and does its own work, that is justice and what makes a just society.

I entirely agree,

THE THREE PARTS
OF THE SOUL

We must not be too positive yet, said I. If we find that this same quality when it exists in the individual can equally be identified with justice, then we can at once give our assent; there will be no more to be said; otherwise, we shall have to look further. For the moment, we had better finish the inquiry which we began with the idea that it would be easier to make out the nature of justice in the individual if we first tried to study it in something on a larger scale. That larger thing we took to be a state, and so we set about constructing the best one we could, being sure of finding justice in a state that was good. The discovery we made there must now be applied to the individual. If it is confirmed, all will be well; but if we find that justice in the individual is something different, we must go back to the state and test our new result. Perhaps if we brought the two cases into contact like flint and steel, we might strike out between them the spark of justice, and in its light confirm the conception in our own minds.

A good method. Let us follow it.

Now, I continued, if two things, one large, the other small, are called by the same name, they will be alike in that respect to which the common name applies. Accordingly, in so far as the quality of justice is concerned, there will be no difference between a just man and a just society.

No.

Well, but we decided that a society was just when each of the three types of human character it contained performed its own function; and again, it was temperate and brave and wise by virtue of certain other affections and states of mind of those same types.

True.

Accordingly, my friend, if we are to be justified in attributing those same virtues to the individual, we shall expect to find that the individual soul contains the same three elements and that they are affected in the same way as are the corresponding types in society.

That follows.

Here, then, we have stumbled upon another little problem: Does the soul contain these three elements or not?

Not such a very little one, I think. It may be a true saying, Socrates, that what is worth while is seldom easy.

Apparently; and let me tell you, Glaucon, it is my belief that we shall never reach the exact truth in this matter by following our present methods of discussion; the road leading to that goal is longer and more laborious. However, perhaps we can find an answer that will be up to the standard we have so far maintained in our speculations.

Is not that enough? I should be satisfied for the moment.

Well, it will more than satisfy me, I replied.

Don't be disheartened, then, but go on.

Surely, I began, we must admit that the same elements and characters that appear in the state must exist in every one of us; where else could they have come from? It would be absurd to imagine that among peoples with a reputation for a high-spirited character, like the Thracians and Scythians and northerners generally, the states have not derived that character from their individual members; or that it is otherwise with the love of knowledge, which would be ascribed chiefly to our own part of the world, or with the love of money, which one would specially connect with Phoenicia and Egypt.

Certainly.

So far, then, we have a fact which is easily recognized. But here the difficulty begins. Are we using the same part of ourselves in all these three experiences, or a different part in each? Do we gain knowledge with one part, feel anger with another, and with yet a third desire the pleasures of food, sex, and so on? Or is the whole soul at work in every impulse and in all these forms of behaviour? The difficulty is to answer that question satisfactorily.

I quite agree.

Let us approach the problem whether these elements are distinct or identical in this way. It is clear that the same thing cannot act in two opposite ways or be in two opposite states at the same time, with respect to the same part of itself, and in relation to the same object. So if we find such contradictory actions or states among the elements concerned, we shall know that more than one must have been involved.

Very well.

Consider this proposition of mine, then. Can the same thing, at the same time and with respect to the same part of itself, be at rest and in motion?

Certainly not.

We had better state this principle in still more precise terms, to guard against misunderstanding later on. Suppose a man is standing still, but moving his head and arms. We should not allow anyone to say that the same man was both at rest and in motion at the same time, but only that part of him was at rest, part in motion. Isn't that so?

Yes.

An ingenious objector might refine still further and argue that a peg-top, spinning with its peg fixed at the same spot, or indeed any body that revolves in the same place, is both at rest and in motion as a whole. But we should not agree, because the parts in respect of which such a body is moving and at rest are not the same. It contains an axis and a circumference; and in respect of the axis it is at rest inasmuch as the axis is not inclined in any direction, while in respect of the circumference it revolves; and if, while it is spinning, the axis does lean out of the perpendicular in all directions, then it is in no way at rest.

That is true.

No objection of that sort, then, will disconcert us or make us believe that the same thing can ever act or be acted upon in two opposite ways, or be two opposite things, at the same time, in respect of the same part of itself, and in relation to the same object.

I can answer for myself at any rate.

Well, anyhow, as we do not want to spend time in reviewing all such objections to make sure that they are unsound, let us proceed on this assumption, with the understanding that, if we ever come to think otherwise, all the consequences based upon it will fall to the ground.

Yes, that is a good plan.

Now, would you class such things as assent and dissent, striving after something and refusing it, attraction and repulsion, as pairs of opposite actions or states of mind—no matter which?

Yes, they are opposites.

And would you not class all appetites such as hunger and thirst, and again willing and wishing, with the affirmative members of those pairs I have just mentioned? For instance, you would say that the soul of a man who desires something is striving after it, or trying to draw to itself the thing it wishes to possess, or again, in so far as it is willing to have its want satisfied, it is giving its assent to its own longing, as if to an inward question.

Yes.

And, on the other hand, disinclination, unwillingness, and dislike, we should class on the negative side with acts of rejection or repulsion.

Of course.

That being so, shall we say that appetites form one class, the most conspicuous being those we call thirst and hunger?

Yes.

Thirst being desire for drink; hunger, for food?

Yes.

Now, is thirst, just in so far as it is thirst, a desire in the soul for anything more than simply drink? Is it, for instance, thirst for hot drink or for cold, for much drink or for little, or in a word for drink of any particular kind? Is it not rather true that you will have a desire for cold drink only if you are feeling hot as well as thirsty, and for hot drink only if you are feeling cold; and if you want much drink or little, that will be because your thirst is a great thirst or a little one? But, just in itself, thirst or hunger is a desire for nothing more than its natural object, drink or food, pure and simple.

Yes, he agreed, each desire, just in itself, is simply for its own natural object. When the object is of such and such a particular kind, the desire will be correspondingly qualified.[15]

We must be careful here, or we might be troubled by the objection that no one desires mere food and drink, but always wholesome food and drink. We shall be told that what we desire is always something that is good; so if thirst is a desire, its object must be, like that of any other desire, something—drink or whatever it may be—that will be good for one.[16]

Yes, there might seem to be something in that objection.

But surely, wherever you have two correlative terms, if one is qualified, the other must always be qualified too; whereas if one is unqualified, so is the other.

I don't understand.

Well, "greater" is a relative term; and the greater is greater than the less; if it is much greater, then the less is much less; if it is greater at some moment, past or future, then the less is less at that same moment. The same principle applies to all such correlatives, like "more" and "fewer," "double" and "half"; and again to terms like "heavier" and "lighter," "quicker" and "slower," and to things like hot and cold.

Yes.

---

[15] The object of the following subtle argument about relative terms is to distinguish thirst as a mere blind craving for drink from a more complex desire whose object includes the pleasure or health expected to result from drinking. We thus forestall the objection that all desires have "the good" (apparent or real) for their object and include an intellectual or rational element, so that the conflict of motives might be reduced to an intellectual debate, in the same "part" of the soul, on the comparative values of two incompatible ends.

[16] If this objection were admitted, it would follow that the desire would always be correspondingly qualified. It is necessary to insist that we do experience blind cravings which can be isolated from any judgment about the goodness of their object.

Or take the various branches of knowledge: is it not the same there? The object of knowledge pure and simple is the knowable—if that is the right word—without any qualification; whereas a particular kind of knowledge has an object of a particular kind. For example, as soon as men learnt how to build houses, their craft was distinguished from others under the name of architecture, because it had a unique character, which was itself due to the character of its object; and all other branches of craft and knowledge were distinguished in the same way.

True.

This, then, if you understand me now, is what I meant by saying that, where there are two correlatives, the one is qualified if, and only if, the other is so. I am not saying that the one must have the same quality as the other—that the science of health and disease is itself healthy and diseased, or the knowledge of good and evil is itself good and evil—but only that, as soon as you have a knowledge that is restricted to a particular kind of object, namely health and disease, the knowledge itself becomes a particular kind of knowledge. Hence we no longer call it merely knowledge, which would have for its object whatever can be known, but we add the qualification and call it medical science.

I understand now and I agree.

Now, to go back to thirst: is not that one of these relative terms? It is essentially thirst for something.

Yes, for drink.

And if the drink desired is of a certain kind, the thirst will be correspondingly qualified. But thirst which is just simply thirst is not for drink of any particular sort—much or little, good or bad—but for drink pure and simple.

Quite so.

We conclude, then, that the soul of a thirsty man, just in so far as he is thirsty, has no other wish than to drink. That is the object of its craving, and towards that it is impelled.

That is clear.

Now if there is ever something which at the same time pulls it the opposite way, that something must be an element in the soul other than the one which is thirsting and driving it like a beast to drink; in accordance with our principle that the same thing cannot behave in two opposite ways at the same time and towards the same object with the same part of itself. It is like an archer drawing the bow: it is not accurate to say that his hands are at the same time both pushing and pulling it. One hand does the pushing, the other the pulling.

Exactly.

Now, is it sometimes true that people are thirsty and yet unwilling to drink?

Yes, often.

What, then, can one say of them, if not that their soul contains something which urges them to drink and something which holds them back, and that this latter is a distinct thing and overpowers the other?

I agree.

And is it not true that the intervention of this inhibiting principle in such cases always has its origin in reflection; whereas the impulses driving and dragging the soul are engendered by external influences and abnormal conditions?[17]

Evidently.

We shall have good reason, then, to assert that they are two distinct principles. We may call that part of the soul whereby it reflects, rational; and the other, with which it feels hunger and thirst and is distracted by sexual passion and all the other desires, we will call irrational appetite, associated with pleasure in the replenishment of certain wants.

Yes, there is good ground for that view.

Let us take it, then, that we have now distinguished two elements in the soul. What of that passionate element which makes us feel angry and indignant? Is that a third, or identical in nature with one of those two?

It might perhaps be identified with appetite.

I am more inclined to put my faith in a story I once heard about Leontius, son of Aglaion. On his way up from the Piraeus outside the north wall, he noticed the bodies of some criminals lying on the ground, with the executioner standing by them. He wanted to go and look at them, but at the same time he was disgusted and tried to turn away. He struggled for some time and

---

[17] Some of the most intense bodily desires are due to morbid conditions, e.g. thirst in fever, and even milder desires are caused by a departure from the normal state, which demands "replenishment."

covered his eyes, but at last the desire was too much for him. Opening his eyes wide, he ran up to the bodies and cried, "There you are, curse you; feast yourselves on this lovely sight!"

Yes, I have heard that story too.

The point of it surely is that anger is sometimes in conflict with appetite, as if they were two distinct principles. Do we not often find a man whose desires would force him to go against his reason, reviling himself and indignant with this part of his nature which is trying to put constraint on him? It is like a struggle between two factions, in which indignation takes the side of reason. But I believe you have never observed, in yourself or anyone else, indignation make common cause with appetite in behaviour which reason decides to be wrong.

No, I am sure I have not.

Again, take a man who feels he is in the wrong. The more generous his nature, the less can he be indignant at any suffering, such as hunger and cold, inflicted by the man he has injured. He recognizes such treatment as just, and, as I say, his spirit refuses to be roused against it.

That is true.

But now contrast one who thinks it is he that is being wronged. His spirit boils with resentment and sides with the right as he conceives it. Persevering all the more for the hunger and cold and other pains he suffers, it triumphs and will not give in until its gallant struggle has ended in success or death; or until the restraining voice of reason, like a shepherd calling off his dog, makes it relent.

An apt comparison, he said; and in fact it fits the relation of our Auxiliaries to the Rulers: they were to be like watchdogs obeying the shepherds of the commonwealth.

Yes, you understand very well what I have in mind. But do you see how we have changed our view? A moment ago we were supposing this spirited element to be something of the nature of appetite; but now it appears that, when the soul is divided into factions, it is far more ready to be up in arms on the side of reason.

Quite true.

Is it, then, distinct from the rational element or only a particular form of it, so that the soul will contain no more than two elements, reason and appetite? Or is the soul like the state, which had three orders to hold it together, traders, Auxiliaries, and counsellors? Does the spirited element make a third, the natural auxiliary of reason, when not corrupted by bad upbringing?

It must be a third.

Yes, I said, provided it can be shown to be distinct from reason, as we saw it was from appetite.

That is easily proved. You can see that much in children: they are full of passionate feelings from their birth; but some, I should say, never become rational, and most of them only late in life.

A very sound observation, said I, the truth of which may also be seen in animals. And besides, there is the witness of Homer in that line I quoted before: "He smote his breast and spoke, chiding his heart." The poet is plainly thinking of the two elements as distinct, when he makes the one which has chosen the better course after reflection rebuke the other for its unreasoning passion.

I entirely agree.

THE VIRTUES
IN THE INDIVIDUAL

And so, after a stormy passage, we have reached the land. We are fairly agreed that the same three elements exist alike in the state and in the individual soul.

That is so.

Does it not follow at once that state and individual will be wise or brave by virtue of the same element in each and in the same way? Both will possess in the same manner any quality that makes for excellence.

That must be true.

Then it applies to justice: we shall conclude that a man is just in the same way that a state was just. And we have surely not forgotten that justice in the state meant that each of the three orders in it was doing its own proper work. So we may henceforth bear in mind that each one of us likewise will be a just person, fulfilling his proper function, only if the several parts of our nature fulfil theirs.

Certainly.

And it will be the business of reason to rule with wisdom and forethought on behalf of the entire soul; while the spirited element ought to act as its subordinate and ally. The two will be brought into accord, as we said earlier, by that combination of mental and bodily training which will tune up one string of the instrument and relax the other, nourishing the reasoning part on the study of noble literature and allaying the other's wildness by harmony and rhythm. When both have been thus nurtured and trained to know their own true functions, they must be set in command over the appetites, which form the greater part of each man's soul and are by nature insatiably covetous. They must keep watch lest this part, by battening on the pleasures that are called bodily, should grow so great and powerful that it will no longer keep to its own work, but will try to enslave the others and usurp a dominion to which it has no right, thus turning the whole of life upside down. At the same time, those two together will be the best of guardians for the entire soul and for the body against all enemies from without: the one will take counsel, while the other will do battle, following its ruler's commands and by its own bravery giving effect to the ruler's designs.

Yes, that is all true.

And so we call an individual brave in virtue of this spirited part of his nature, when, in spite of pain or pleasure, it holds fast to the injunctions of reason about what he ought or ought not to be afraid of.

True.

And wise in virtue of that small part which rules and issues these injunctions, possessing as it does the knowledge of what is good for each of the three elements and for all of them in common.

Certainly.

And, again, temperate by reason of the unanimity and concord of all three, when there is no internal conflict between the ruling element and its two subjects, but all are agreed that reason should be ruler.

Yes, that is an exact account of temperance, whether in the state or in the individual.

Finally, a man will be just by observing the principle we have so often stated.

Necessarily.

Now is there any indistinctness in our vision of justice, that might make it seem somehow different from what we found it to be in the state?

I don't think so.

Because, if we have any lingering doubt, we might make sure by comparing it with some commonplace notions. Suppose, for instance, that a sum of money were entrusted to our state or to an individual of corresponding character and training, would anyone imagine that such a person would be specially likely to embezzle it?

No.

And would he not be incapable of sacrilege and theft, or of treachery to friend or country; never false to an oath or any other compact; the last to be guilty of adultery or of neglecting parents or the due service of the gods?

Yes.

And the reason for all this is that each part of his nature is exercising its proper function, of ruling or of being ruled.

Yes, exactly.

Are you satisfied, then, that justice is the power which produces states or individuals of whom that is true, or must we look further?

There is no need; I am quite satisfied.

And so our dream has come true—I mean the inkling we had that, by some happy chance, we had lighted upon a rudimentary form of justice from the very moment when we set about founding our commonwealth. Our principle that the born shoemaker or carpenter had better stick to his trade turns out to have been an adumbration of justice; and that is why it has helped us. But in reality justice, though evidently analogous to this principle, is not a matter of external behaviour, but of the inward self and of attending to all that is, in the fullest sense, a man's proper concern. The just man does not allow the several elements in his soul to usurp one another's functions; he is indeed one who sets his house in order, by self-mastery and discipline coming to be at peace with himself, and bringing into tune those three parts, like the terms in the proportion of a musical scale, the highest and lowest notes and the mean between them, with all the intermediate intervals. Only when he has linked these parts together in well-tempered harmony and has made himself one man instead of many, will he be ready to go about whatever he may have to do, whether it be making money and satisfying bodily wants, or business transactions, or the affairs of state. In all these fields when he speaks of just and honourable conduct, he will mean the behaviour that helps to produce and to preserve this habit of mind; and by wisdom he will mean the knowledge which presides over such conduct. Any action which tends to break down this habit will be for him unjust; and the notions governing it he will call ignorance and folly.

That is perfectly true, Socrates.

Good, said I. I believe we should not be thought altogether mistaken, if we claimed to have discovered the just man and the just state, and wherein their justice consists.

Indeed we should not.

Shall we make that claim, then?

Yes, we will.

So be it, said I. Next, I suppose, we have to consider injustice.

Evidently.

This must surely be a sort of civil strife among the three elements, whereby they usurp and encroach upon one another's functions and some one part of the soul rises up in rebellion against the whole, claiming a supremacy to which it has no right because its nature fits it only to be the servant of the ruling principle. Such turmoil and aberration we shall, I think, identify with injustice, intemperance, cowardice, ignorance, and in a word with all wickedness.

Exactly.

And now that we know the nature of justice and injustice, we can be equally clear about what is meant by acting justly and again by unjust action and wrongdoing.

How do you mean?

Plainly, they are exactly analogous to those wholesome and unwholesome activities which respectively produce a healthy or unhealthy condition in the body; in the same way just and unjust conduct produce a just or unjust character. Justice is produced in the soul, like health in the body, by establishing the elements concerned in their natural relations of control and subordination, whereas injustice is like disease and means that this natural order is inverted.

Quite so.

It appears, then, that virtue is as it were the health and comeliness and well-being of the soul, as wickedness is disease, deformity, and weakness.

True.

And also that virtue and wickedness are brought about by one's way of life, honourable or disgraceful.

That follows.

So now it only remains to consider which is the more profitable course: to do right and live honourably and be just, whether or not anyone knows what manner of man you are, or to do wrong and be unjust, provided that you can escape the chastisement which might make you a better man.

But really, Socrates, it seems to me ridiculous to ask that question now that the nature of justice and injustice has been brought to light. People think that all the luxury and wealth and power in the world cannot make life worth living when the bodily constitution is going to rack and ruin; and are we to believe that, when the very principle whereby we live is deranged and corrupted, life will be worth living so long as a man can do as he will, and wills to do anything rather than to free himself from vice and wrongdoing and to win justice and virtue?

Yes, I replied, it is a ridiculous question.

EQUALITY OF WOMEN

We must go back, then, to a subject which ought, perhaps, to have been treated earlier in its proper place; though, after all, it may be suitable that the women should have their turn on the stage when the men have quite finished their performance, especially since you are so insistent. In my judgment, then, the question under what conditions people born and educated as we have described should possess wives and children, and how they should treat them, can be rightly settled only by keeping to the course on which we started them at the outset. We undertook to put these men in the position of watch-dogs guarding a flock. Suppose we follow up the analogy and imagine them bred and reared in the same sort of way. We can then see if that plan will suit our purpose.

How will that be?

In this way. Which do we think right for watch-dogs: should the females guard the flock and hunt with the males and take a share in all they do, or should they be kept within doors as fit for no more than bearing and feeding their puppies, while all the hard work of looking after the flock is left to the males?

They are expected to take their full share, except that we treat them as not quite so strong.

Can you employ any creature for the same work as another, if you do not give them both the same upbringing and education?

No.

Then, if we are to set women to the same tasks as men, we must teach them the same things. They must have the same two branches of training for mind and body and also be taught the art of war, and they must receive the same treatment.

That seems to follow.

Possibly, if these proposals were carried out, they might be ridiculed as involving a good many breaches of custom.

They might indeed.

The most ridiculous—don't you think? — being the notion of women exercising naked along with the men in the wrestling-schools; some of them elderly women too, like the old men who still have a passion for exercise when they are wrinkled and not very agreeable to look at.

Yes, that would be thought laughable, according to our present notions.

Now we have started on this subject, we must not be frightened of the many witticisms that might be aimed at such a revolution, not only in the matter of bodily exercise but in the training of women's minds, and not least when it comes to their bearing arms and riding on horseback. Having begun upon these rules, we must not draw back from the harsher provisions. The wits may be asked to stop being witty and try to be serious; and we may remind them that it is not so long since the Greeks, like most foreign nations of the present day, thought it ridiculous and shameful for men to be seen naked. When gymnastic exercises were first introduced in Crete and later at Sparta, the humorists had their chance to make fun of them; but when experience had shown that nakedness is better uncovered than muffled up, the laughter died down and a practice which the reason approved ceased to look ridiculous to the eye. This shows how idle it is to think anything ludicrous but what is base. One who tries to raise a laugh at any spectacle save that of baseness and folly will also, in his serious moments, set before himself some other standard than goodness of what deserves to be held in honour.

Most assuredly.

The first thing to be settled, then, is whether these proposals are feasible; and it must be open to anyone, whether a humorist or serious-minded, to raise the question whether, in the case of mankind, the feminine nature is capable of taking part with the other sex in all occupations, or in none at all, or in some only; and in particular under which of these heads this business of military service falls. Well begun is half done, and would not this be the best way to begin?

Yes.

Shall we take the other side in this debate and argue against ourselves? We do not want the adversary's position to be taken by storm for lack of defenders.

I have no objection.

Let us state his case for him. "Socrates and Glaucon," he will say, "there is no need for others to dispute your position; you yourselves, at the very outset of founding your commonwealth, agreed that everyone should do the one work for which nature fits him." Yes, of course; I suppose we did. "And isn't there a very great difference in nature between man and woman?" Yes, surely. "Does not that natural difference imply a corresponding difference in the work to be given to each?" Yes. "But if so, surely you must be mistaken now and contradicting yourselves when you say that men and women, having such widely divergent natures, should do the same things?" What is your answer to that, my ingenious friend?

It is not easy to find one at the moment. I can only appeal to you to state the case on our own side, whatever it may be.

This, Glaucon, is one of many alarming objections which I foresaw some time ago. That is why I shrank from touching upon these laws concerning the possession of wives and the rearing of children.

It looks like anything but an easy problem.

True, I said; but whether a man tumbles into a swimming-pool or into mid-ocean, he has to swim all the time. So must we, and try if we can reach the shore, hoping for some Arion's dolphin or other miraculous deliverance to bring us safe to land.[18]

I suppose so.

Come then, let us see if we can find the way out. We did agree that different natures should have different occupations, and that the natures of man and woman are different; and yet we are now saying that these different natures are to have the same occupations. Is that the charge against us?

Exactly.

It is extraordinary, Glaucon, what an effect the practice of debating has upon people.

Why do you say that?

Because they often seem to fall unconsciously into mere disputes which they mistake for reasonable argument, through being unable to draw the distinctions proper to their subject; and so, instead of a philosophical exchange of ideas, they go off in chase of contradictions which are purely verbal.

I know that happens to many people; but does it apply to us at this moment?

Absolutely. At least I am afraid we are slipping unconsciously into a dispute about words. We have been strenuously insisting on the letter of our principle that different natures should not have the same occupations, as if we were scoring a point in a debate; but we have altogether neglected to consider what sort of sameness or difference we meant and in what respect these natures and occupations were to be defined as different or the same. Consequently, we might very well be asking one another whether there is not an opposition in nature between bald and long-haired men, and, when that was admitted, forbid one set to be shoemakers, if the other were following that trade.

That would be absurd.

Yes, but only because we never meant any and every sort of sameness or difference in nature, but the sort that was relevant to the occupations in question. We meant, for instance, that a man and a woman have the same nature if both have a talent for medicine; whereas two men have different

natures if one is a born physician, the other a born carpenter.

Yes, of course.

If, then, we find that either the male sex or the female is specially qualified for any particular form of occupation, then that occupation, we shall say, ought to be assigned to one sex or the other. But if the only difference appears to be that the male begets and the female brings forth, we shall conclude that no difference between man and woman has yet been produced that is relevant to our purpose. We shall continue to think it proper for our Guardians and their wives to share in the same pursuits.

And quite rightly.

The next thing will be to ask our opponent to name any profession or occupation in civic life for the purposes of which woman's nature is different from man's.

That is a fair question.

He might reply, as you did just now, that it is not easy to find a satisfactory answer on the spur of the moment, but that there would be no difficulty after a little reflection.

Perhaps.

Suppose, then, we invite him to follow us and see if we can convince him that there is no occupation concerned with the management of social affairs that is peculiar to women. We will confront him with a question: When you speak of a man having a natural talent for something, do you mean that he finds it easy to learn, and after a little instruction can find out much more for himself; whereas a man who is not so gifted learns with difficulty and no amount of instruction and practice will make him even remember what he has been taught? Is the talented man one whose bodily powers are readily at the service of his mind, instead of being a hindrance? Are not these the marks by which you distinguish the presence of a natural gift for any pursuit?

Yes, precisely.

Now do you know of any human occupation in which the male sex is not superior to the female in all these respects? Need I waste time over exceptions like weaving and watching over saucepans and batches of cakes, though women are supposed to be good at such things and get laughed at when a man does them better?

---

[18] The musician Arion, to escape the treachery of Corinthian sailors, leapt into the sea and was carried ashore at Taenarum by a dolphin, Herodotus, i. 24.

It is true, he replied, in almost everything one sex is easily beaten by the other. No doubt many women are better at many things than many men; but taking the sexes as a whole, it is as you say.

To conclude, then, there is no occupation concerned with the management of social affairs which belongs either to woman or to man, as such. Natural gifts are to be found here and there in both creatures alike; and every occupation is open to both, so far as their natures are concerned, though woman is for all purposes the weaker.

Certainly.

Is that a reason for making over all occupations to men only?

Of course not.

No, because one woman may have a natural gift for medicine or for music; another may not.

Surely.

Is it not also true that a woman may, or may not, be warlike or athletic?

I think so.

And again, one may love knowledge; another, hate it; one may be high-spirited; another, spiritless?

True again.

It follows that one woman will be fitted by nature to be a Guardian; another will not, because these were the qualities for which we selected our men Guardians. So for the purpose of keeping watch over the commonwealth, woman has the same nature as man, save in so far as she is weaker.

So it appears.

It follows that women of this type must be selected to share the life and duties of Guardians with men of the same type, since they are competent and of a like nature, and the same natures must be allowed the same pursuits.

Yes.

We come round, then, to our former position, that there is nothing contrary to nature in giving our Guardians' wives the same training for mind and body. The practice we proposed to establish was not impossible or visionary, since it was in accordance with nature. Rather, the contrary practice which now prevails turns out to be unnatural.

So it appears.

Well, we set out to inquire whether the plan we proposed was feasible and also the best. That it is feasible is now agreed; we must next settle whether it is the best.

Obviously.

Now, for the purpose of producing a woman fit to be a Guardian, we shall not have one education for men and another for women, precisely because the nature to be taken in hand is the same.

True.

What is your opinion on the question of one man being better than another? Do you think there is no such difference?

Certainly I do not.

And in this commonwealth of ours which will prove the better men—the Guardians who have received the education we described, or the shoemakers who have been trained to make shoes?

It is absurd to ask such a question.

Very well. So these Guardians will be the best of all the citizens?

By far.

And these women the best of all the women?

Yes.

Can anything be better for a commonwealth than to produce in it men and women of the best possible type?

No.

And that result will be brought about by such a system of mental and bodily training as we have described?

Surely.

We may conclude that the institution we proposed was not only practicable, but also the best for the commonwealth.

Yes.

The wives of our Guardians, then, must strip for exercise, since they will be clothed with virtue, and they must take their share in war and in the other social duties of guardianship. They are to have no other occupation; and in these duties the lighter part must fall to the women, because of the weakness of their sex. The man who laughs at naked women, exercising their bodies for the best of reasons, is like one that "gathers fruit unripe," for he does not know what it is that he is laughing at or what he is doing. There will never be a finer saying than the one which declares that whatever does good should be held in honour, and the only shame is in doing harm.

That is perfectly true.

ABOLITION OF THE FAMILY
FOR THE GUARDIANS

So far, then, in regulating the position of women, we may claim to have come safely through with one hazardous proposal, that male and female Guardians shall have all occupations in common. The consistency of the argument is an assurance that the plan is a good one and also feasible. We are like swimmers who have breasted the first wave without being swallowed up.

Not such a small wave either.

You will not call it large when you see the next.

Let me have a look at the next one, then.

Here it is: a law which follows from that principle and all that has gone before, namely that, of these Guardians, no one man and one woman are to set up house together privately: wives are to be held in common by all; so too are the children, and no parent is to know his own child, nor any child his parent.

It will be much harder to convince people that that is either a feasible plan or a good one.

As to its being a good plan, I imagine no one would deny the immense advantage of wives and children being held in common, provided it can be done. I should expect dispute to arise chiefly over the question whether it is possible.

There may well be a good deal of dispute over both points.

You mean, I must meet attacks on two fronts. I was hoping to escape one by running away: if you agreed it was a good plan, then I should only have had to inquire whether it was feasible.

No, we have seen through that manœvre. You will have to defend both positions.

Well, I must pay the penalty for my cowardice. But grant me one favour. Let me indulge my fancy, like one who entertains himself with idle day-dreams on a solitary walk. Before he has any notion how his desires can be realized, he will set aside that question, to save himself the trouble of reckoning what may or may not be possible. He will assume that his wish has come true, and amuse himself with settling all the details of what he means to do then. So a lazy mind encourages itself to

be lazier than ever; and I am giving way to the same weakness myself. I want to put off till later that question, how the thing can be done. For the moment, with your leave, I shall assume it to be possible, and ask how the Rulers will work out the details in practice; and I shall argue that the plan, once carried into effect, would be the best thing in the world for our commonwealth and for its Guardians. That is what I shall now try to make out with your help, if you will allow me to postpone the other question.

Very good; I have no objection.

Well, if our Rulers are worthy of the name, and their Auxiliaries likewise, these latter will be ready to do what they are told, and the Rulers, in giving their commands, will themselves obey our laws and will be faithful to their spirit in any details we leave to their discretion.

No doubt.

It is for you, then, as their lawgiver, who have already selected the men, to select for association with them women who are so far as possible of the same natural capacity. Now since none of them will have any private home of his own, but they will share the same dwelling and eat at common tables, the two sexes will be together; and meeting without restriction for exercise and all through their upbringing, they will surely be drawn towards union with one another by a necessity of their nature—necessity is not too strong a word, I think?

Not too strong for the constraint of love, which for the mass of mankind is more persuasive and compelling than even the necessity of mathematical proof.

Exactly. But in the next place, Glaucon, anything like unregulated unions would be a profanation in a state whose citizens lead the good life. The Rulers will not allow such a thing.

No, it would not be right.

Clearly, then, we must have marriages, as sacred as we can make them; and this sanctity will attach to those which yield the best results.

Certainly.

How are we to get the best results? You must tell me, Glaucon, because I see you keep sporting dogs and a great many game birds at your house; and there is something about their mating and breeding that you must have noticed.

What is that?

In the first place, though they may all be of good stock, are there not some that turn out to be better than the rest?

There are.

And do you breed from all indiscriminately? Are you not careful to breed from the best so far as you can?

Yes.

And from those in their prime, rather than the very young or the very old?

Yes.

Otherwise, the stock of your birds or dogs would deteriorate very much, wouldn't it?

It would.

And the same is true of horses or of any animal?

It would be very strange if it were not.

Dear me, said I; we shall need consummate skill in our Rulers, if it is also true of the human race.

Well, it is true. But why must they be so skilful?

Because they will have to administer a large dose of that medicine we spoke of earlier. An ordinary doctor is thought good enough for a patient who will submit to be dieted and can do without medicine; but he must be much more of a man if drugs are required.

True, but how does that apply?

It applies to our Rulers: it seems they will have to give their subjects a considerable dose of imposition and deception for their good. We said, if you remember, that such expedients would be useful as a sort of medicine.

Yes, a very sound principle.

Well, it looks as if this sound principle will play no small part in this matter of marriage and child-bearing.

How so?

It follows from what we have just said that, if we are to keep our flock at the highest pitch of excellence, there should be as many unions of the best of both sexes, and as few of the inferior, as possible, and that only the offspring of the better unions should be kept.[19] And again, no one but the

Rulers must know how all this is being effected; otherwise our herd of Guardians may become rebellious.

Quite true.

We must, then, institute certain festivals at which we shall bring together the brides and bridegrooms. There will be sacrifices, and our poets will write songs befitting the occasion. The number of marriages we shall leave to the Rulers' discretion. They will aim at keeping the number of the citizens as constant as possible, having regard to losses caused by war, epidemics, and so on; and they must do their best to see that our state does not become either great or small.[20]

Very good.

I think they will have to invent some ingenious system of drawing lots, so that, at each pairing off, the inferior candidate may blame his luck rather than the Rulers.

Yes, certainly.

Moreover, young men who acquit themselves well in war and other duties, should be given, among other rewards and privileges, more liberal opportunities to sleep

---

[19] That is, "kept *as Guardians*." The inferior children of Guardians were to be "thrust out among the craftsmen and farmers." A breeder of

racehorses would *keep* the best foals, but not kill the rest.

[20] Plato seems to forget that these rules apply only to Guardians. If the much larger third class is to breed without restriction, a substantial rise in their numbers might entail suspension of all childbirth among Guardians, with a dysgenic effect. Plato, however, feared a decline, rather than a rise, in the birth-rate. (The state described in the *Laws* is always to have 5040 citizens, each holding one inalienable lot of land.)

The "number of marriages" may include both the number of candidates admitted at each festival and the frequency of the festivals. But it is perhaps likely that the festivals are to be annual, so that women who had borne children since the last festival would be re-marriageable. If so, at each festival a fresh group will be called up, consisting of all who have reached the age of 25 for men or 20 for women since the previous festival. Some or all of these will be paired with one another or with members of older groups. The couples will cohabit during the festival, which might last (say) for a month. The marriages will then be dissolved and the partners remain celibate until the next festival at earliest. This follows from the statement that the resulting batch of children will all be born between 7 and 10 months after the festival.

with a wife,[21] for the further purpose that, with good excuse, as many as possible of the children may be begotten of such fathers.

Yes.

As soon as children are born, they will be taken in charge by officers appointed for the purpose, who may be men or women or both, since offices are to be shared by both sexes. The children of the better parents they will carry to the creche to be reared in the care of nurses living apart in a certain quarter of the city. Those of the inferior parents and any children of the rest that are born defective will be hidden away, in some appropriate manner that must be kept secret.[22]

They must be, if the breed of our Guardians is to be kept pure.

These officers will also superintend the nursing of the children. They will bring the mothers to the crèche when their breasts are full, while taking every precaution that no mother shall know her own child; and if the mothers have not enough milk, they will provide wetnurses. They will limit the time during which the mothers will suckle their children, and hand over all the hard work and sitting up at night to nurses and attendants.

That will make child-bearing an easy business for the Guardians' wives.

So it should be. To go on with our scheme: we said that children should be born from parents in the prime of life. Do you agree that this lasts about twenty years for a woman, and thirty for a man? A woman should bear children for the commonwealth from her twentieth to her fortieth year; a man should begin to beget them when he has passed "the racer's prime in swiftness," and continue till he is fifty-five.

Those are certainly the years in which both the bodily and the mental powers of man and woman are at their best.

If a man either above or below this age meddles with the begetting of children for the commonwealth, we shall hold it an offence against divine and human law. He will be begetting for his country a child conceived in darkness and dire incontinence, whose birth, if it escape detection, will not have been sanctioned by the sacrifices and prayers offered at each marriage festival, when priests and priestesses join with the whole community in praying that the children to be born may be even better and more useful citizens than their parents.

You are right.

The same law will apply to any man within the prescribed limits who touches a woman also of marriageable age when the Ruler has not paired them. We shall say that he is foisting on the commonwealth a bastard, unsanctioned by law or by religion.

Perfectly right.

As soon, however, as the men and the women have passed the age prescribed for producing children, we shall leave them free to form a connexion with whom they will, except that a man shall not take his daughter or daughter's daughter or mother or mother's mother, nor a woman her son or father or her son's son or father's father; and all this only after we have exhorted them to see that no child, if any be conceived, shall be brought to light, or, if they cannot prevent its birth, to dispose of it on the understanding that no such child can be reared.[23]

That too is reasonable. But how are they to distinguish fathers and daughters and those other relations you mentioned?

They will not, said I. But, reckoning from the day when he becomes a bridegroom, a man will call all children born in the tenth

---

[21] Not to have several wives at once, but to be admitted at more frequent intervals to the periodic marriage festivals, not necessarily with a different wife each time.

[22] Infanticide of defective children was practiced at Sparta; but the vague expression used does not imply that all children of inferior Guardians are to be destroyed. Those not defective would be relegated to the third class. Promotion of children from that class was provided for above.

[23] The unofficial unions might be permanent. The only unions barred as incestuous are between parents and children, or grandparents and grandchildren (all such are included, since, if a woman cannot marry her father's father, a man cannot marry his son's daughter). It seems to follow that Plato did not regard the much more probable connexions of brothers and sisters as incestuous; and if so, he would see no reason against legal marriage of real brothers and sisters, who would not know they were so related. Such unions were regular in Egypt; and some modern authorities deny that they are dysgenic. Greek law allowed marriage between brother and half-sister by a different mother.

or the seventh month sons and daughters, and they will call him father. Their children he will call grandchildren, and they will call his group grandfathers and grandmothers; and all who are born within the period during which their mothers and fathers were having children will be called brothers and sisters. This will provide for those restrictions on unions that we mentioned; but the law will allow brothers and sisters to live together, if the lot so falls out and the Delphic oracle also approves.[24]

Very good.

This, then, Glaucon, is the manner in which the Guardians of your commonwealth are to hold their wives and children in common. Must we not next find arguments to establish that it is consistent with our other institutions and also by far the best plan?

Yes, surely.

We had better begin by asking what is the greatest good at which the lawgiver should aim in laying down the constitution of a state, and what is the worst evil. We can then consider whether our proposals are in keeping with that good and irreconcilable with the evil.

By all means.

Does not the worst evil for a state arise from anything that tends to rend it asunder and destroy its unity, while nothing does it more good than whatever tends to bind it together and make it one?

That is true.

And are not citizens bound together by sharing in the same pleasures and pains, all feeling glad or grieved on the same occasions of gain or loss; whereas the bond is broken when such feelings are no longer universal, but any event of public or personal concern fills some with joy and others with distress?

Certainly.

And this disunion comes about when the words "mine" and "not mine," another's" and "not another's" are not applied to the same things throughout the community. The best ordered state will be the one in which the largest number of persons use these terms in the same sense, and which

accordingly most nearly resembles a single person. When one of us hurts his finger, the whole extent of those bodily connexions which are gathered up in the soul and unified by its ruling element is made aware and it all shares as a whole in the pain of the suffering part; hence we say that the man has a pain in his finger. The same thing is true of the pain or pleasure felt when any other part of the person suffers or is relieved.

Yes; I agree that the best organized community comes nearest to that condition.

And so it will recognize as a part of itself the individual citizen to whom good or evil happens, and will share as a whole in his joy or sorrow.

It must, if the constitution is sound.

It is time now to go back to our own commonwealth and see whether these conclusions apply to it more than to any other type of state. In all alike there are rulers and common people, all of whom will call one another fellow citizens.

Yes.

But in other states the people have another name as well for their rulers, haven't they?

Yes; in most they call them masters; in democracies, simply the government.

And in ours?

The people will look upon their rulers as preservers and protectors.

And how will our rulers regard the people?

As those who maintain them and pay them wages.

And elsewhere?

As slaves.

And what do rulers elsewhere call one another?

Colleagues.

And ours?

Fellow Guardians.

And in other states may not a ruler regard one colleague as a friend in whom he has an interest, and another as a stranger with whom he has nothing in common?

Yes, that often happens.

But that could not be so with your Guardians? None of them could ever treat a fellow Guardian as a stranger.

Certainly not. He must regard everyone whom he meets as brother or sister, father or mother, son or daughter, grandchild or grandparent.

---

[24] This last speech deals with two distinct questions: (1) avoidance of incestuous union as above defined; (2) legal marriage of brothers and sisters.

Very good; but here is a further point. Will you not require them, not merely to use these family terms, but to behave as a real family? Must they not show towards all whom they call "father" the customary reverence, care, and obedience due to a parent, if they look for any favour from gods or men, since to act otherwise is contrary to divine and human law? Should not all the citizens constantly reiterate in the hearing of the children from their earliest years such traditional maxims of conduct towards those whom they are taught to call father and their other kindred?

They should. It would be absurd that terms of kinship should be on their lips without any action to correspond.

In our community, then, above all others, when things go well or ill with any individual everyone will use that word "mine" in the same sense and say that all is going well or ill with him and his.

Quite true.

And, as we said, this way of speaking and thinking goes with fellow-feeling; so that our citizens, sharing as they do in a common interest which each will call his own, will have all their feelings of pleasure or pain in common.

Assuredly.

A result that will be due to our institutions, and in particular to our Guardians' holding their wives and children in common.

Very much so.

But you will remember how, when we compared a well-ordered community to the body which shares in the pleasures and pains of any member, we saw in this unity the greatest good that a state can enjoy. So the conclusion is that our commonwealth owes to this sharing of wives and children by its protectors its enjoyment of the greatest of all goods.

Yes, that follows.

Moreover, this agrees with our principle that they were not to have houses or lands or any property of their own, but to receive sustenance from the other citizens, as wages for their guardianship, and to consume it in common. Only so will they keep to their true character; and our present proposals will do still more to make them genuine Guardians. They will not rend the community asunder by each applying that word "mine" to different things and dragging off whatever he can get for himself into a private home, where he will have his separate family, forming a centre of exclusive joys and sorrows. Rather they will all, so far as may be, feel together and aim at the same ends, because they are convinced that all their interests are identical.

Quite so.

Again, if a man's person is his only private possession, lawsuits and prosecutions will all but vanish, and they will be free of those quarrels that arise from ownership of property and from having family ties. Nor would they be justified even in bringing actions for assault and outrage; for we shall pronounce it right and honourable for a man to defend himself against an assailant of his own age, and in that way they will be compelled to keep themselves fit.

That would be a sound law.

And it would also have the advantage that, if a man's anger can be satisfied in this way, a fit of passion is less likely to grow into a serious quarrel.

True.

But an older man will be given authority over all younger persons and power to correct them; whereas the younger will, naturally, not dare to strike the elder or do him any violence, except by command of a Ruler. He will not show him any sort of disrespect. Two guardian spirits, fear and reverence, will be enough to restrain him—reverence forbidding him to lay hands on a parent, and fear of all those others who as sons or brothers or fathers would come to the rescue.

Yes, that will be the result.

So our laws will secure that these men will live in complete peace with one another; and if they never quarrel among themselves, there is no fear of the rest of the community being divided either against them or against itself.

No.

There are other evils they will escape, so mean and petty that I hardly like to mention them: the poor man's flattery of the rich, and all the embarrassments and vexations of rearing a family and earning just enough to maintain a household; now borrowing and now refusing to repay, and by any and every means scraping together money to be handed over to wife and servants to spend. These sordid troubles are familiar and not worth describing.

Only too familiar.

Rid of all these cares, they will live a more enviable life than the Olympic victor, who is counted happy on the strength of far fewer blessings than our Guardians will enjoy. Their victory is the nobler, since by their success the whole commonwealth is preserved; and their reward of maintenance at the public cost is more complete, since their prize is to have every need of life supplied for themselves and for their children; their country honours them while they live, and when they die they receive a worthy burial.

Yes, they will be nobly rewarded.

Do you remember, then, how someone who shall be nameless reproached us for not making our Guardians happy: they were to possess nothing, though all the wealth of their fellow citizens was within their grasp? We replied, I believe, that we would consider that objection later, if it came in our way: for the moment we were bent on making our Guardians real guardians, and moulding our commonwealth with a view to the greatest happiness, not of one section of it, but of the whole.

Yes, I remember.

Well, it appears now that these protectors of our state will have a life better and more honourable than that of any Olympic victor; and we can hardly rank it on a level with the life of a shoemaker or other artisan or of a farmer.

I should think not.

However, it is right to repeat what I said at the time: if ever a Guardian tries to make himself happy in such a way that he will be a guardian no longer; if, not content with the moderation and security of this way of living which we think the best, he becomes possessed with some silly and childish notion of happiness, impelling him to make his power a means to appropriate all the citizens' wealth, then he will learn the wisdom of Hesiod's saying that the half is more than the whole.

My advice would certainly be that he should keep to his own way of living.

You do agree, then, that women are to take their full share with men in education, in the care of children, and in the guardianship of the other citizens; whether they stay at home or go out to war, they will be like watch-dogs which take their part either in guarding the fold or in hunting and share in every task so far as their strength allows. Such conduct will not be unwomanly, but all for the best and in accordance with the natural partnership of the sexes.

Yes, I agree.

THE PARADOX: PHILOSOPHERS MUST BE KINGS

But really, Socrates, Glaucon continued, if you are allowed to go on like this, I am afraid you will forget all about the question you thrust aside some time ago: whether a society so constituted can ever come into existence, and if so, how. No doubt, if it did exist, all manner of good things would come about. I can even add some that you have passed over. Men who acknowledged one another as fathers, sons, or brothers and always used those names among themselves would never desert one another; so they would fight with unequalled bravery. And if their womenfolk went out with them to war, either in the ranks or drawn up in the rear to intimidate the enemy and act as a reserve in case of need, I am sure all this would make them invincible. At home, too, I can see many advantages you have not mentioned. But, since I admit that our commonwealth would have all these merits and any number more, if once it came into existence, you need not describe it in further detail. All we have now to do is to convince ourselves that it can be brought into being and how.

This is a very sudden onslaught, said I; you have no mercy on my shilly-shallying. Perhaps you do not realize that, after I have barely escaped the first two waves, the third, which you are now bringing down upon me, is the most formidable of all. When you have seen what it is like and heard my reply, you will be ready to excuse the very natural fears which made me shrink from putting forward such a paradox for discussion.

The more you talk like that, he said, the less we shall be willing to let you off from telling us how this constitution can come into existence; so you had better waste no more time.

Well, said I, let me begin by reminding you that what brought us to this point was our inquiry into the nature of justice and injustice.

True; but what of that?

Merely this: suppose we do find out what justice is, are we going to demand that a man who is just shall have a character which exactly corresponds in every respect to the ideal of justice? Or shall we be satisfied if he comes as near to the ideal as possible and has in him a larger measure of that quality than the rest of the world?

That will satisfy me.

If so, when we set out to discover the essential nature of justice and injustice and what a perfectly just and a perfectly unjust man would be like, supposing them to exist, our purpose was to use them as ideal patterns: we were to observe the degree of happiness or unhappiness that each exhibited, and to draw the necessary inference that our own destiny would be like that of the one we most resembled. We did not set out to show that these ideals could exist in fact.

That is true.

Then suppose a painter had drawn an ideally beautiful figure complete to the last touch, would you think any the worse of him, if he could not show that a person as beautiful as that could exist?

No, I should not.

Well, we have been constructing in discourse the pattern of an ideal state. Is our theory any the worse, if we cannot prove it possible that a state so organized should be actually founded?

Surely not.

That, then, is the truth of the matter. But if, for your satisfaction, I am to do my best to show under what conditions our ideal would have the best chance of being realized, I must ask you once more to admit that the same principle applies here. Can theory ever be fully realized in practice? Is it not in the nature of things that action should come less close to truth than thought? People may not think so; but do you agree or not?

I do.

Then you must not insist upon my showing that this construction we have traced in thought could be reproduced in fact down to the last detail. You must admit that we shall have found a way to meet your demand for realization, if we can discover how a state might be constituted in the closest accordance with our description. Will not that content you? It would be enough for me.

And for me too.

Then our next attempt, it seems, must be to point out what defect in the working of existing states prevents them from being so organized, and what is the least change that would effect a transformation into this type of government—a single change if possible, or perhaps two; at any rate let us make the changes as few and insignificant as may be.

By all means.

Well, there is one change which, as I believe we can show, would bring about this revolution—not a small change, certainly, nor an easy one, but possible.

What is it?

I have now to confront what we called the third and greatest wave. But I must state my paradox, even though the wave should break in laughter over my head and drown me in ignominy. Now mark what I am going to say.

Go on.

Unless either philosophers become kings in their countries or those who are now called kings and rulers come to be sufficiently inspired with a genuine desire for wisdom; unless, that is to say, political power and philosophy meet together, while the many natures who now go their several ways in the one or the other direction are forcibly debarred from doing so, there can be no rest from troubles, my dear Glaucon, for states, nor yet, as I believe, for all mankind; nor can this commonwealth which we have imagined ever till then see the light of day and grow to its full stature. This it was that I have so long hung back from saying; I knew what a paradox it would be, because it is hard to see that there is no other way of happiness either for the state or for the individual.

Socrates, exclaimed Glaucon, after delivering yourself of such a pronouncement as that, you must expect a whole multitude of by no means contemptible assailants to fling off their coats, snatch up the handiest weapon, and make a rush at you, breathing fire and slaughter. If you cannot find arguments to beat them off and make your escape, you will learn what it means to be the target of scorn and derision.

Well, it was you who got me into this trouble.

Yes, and a good thing too. However, I will not leave you in the lurch. You shall have my friendly encouragement for what it is worth; and perhaps you may find me more complaisant than some would be in answering your questions. With such backing you must try to convince the unbelievers.

I will, now that I have such a powerful ally.

THE ALLEGORY OF THE CAVE

Next, said I, here is a parable to illustrate the degrees in which our nature may be enlightened or unenlightened. Imagine the condition of men living in a sort of cavernous chamber underground, with an entrance open to the light and a long passage all down the cave.[25] Here they have been from childhood chained by the leg and also by the neck, so that they cannot move and can see only what is in front of them, because the chains will not let them turn their heads. At some distance higher up is the light of a fire burning behind them; and between the prisoners and the fire is a track[26] with a parapet built along it, like the screen at a puppet-show, which hides the performers while they show their puppets over the top.

I see, said he.

Now behind this parapet imagine persons carrying along various artificial objects, including figures of men and animals in wood or stone or other materials, which project above the parapet. Naturally, some of these persons will be talking, others silent.[27]

It is a strange picture, he said, and a strange sort of prisoners.

Like ourselves, I replied; for in the first place prisoners so confined would have seen nothing of themselves or of one another, except the shadows thrown by the fire-light on the wall of the Cave facing them, would they?

Not if all their lives they had been prevented from moving their heads.

And they would have seen as little of the objects carried past.

Of course.

Now, if they could talk to one another, would they not suppose that their words referred only to those passing shadows which they saw?[28]

Necessarily.

And suppose their prison had an echo from the wall facing them? When one of the people crossing behind them spoke, they could only suppose that the sound came from the shadow passing before their eyes.

No doubt.

In every way, then, such prisoners would recognize as reality nothing but the shadows of those artificial objects.

Inevitably.

Now consider what would happen if their release from the chains and the healing of their unwisdom should come about in this way. Suppose one of them set free and forced suddenly to stand up, turn his head, and walk with eyes lifted to the light; all these movements would be painful, and he would be too dazzled to make out the objects whose shadows he had been used to see. What do you think he would say, if someone told him that what he had formerly seen was meaningless illusion, but now, being somewhat nearer to reality and turned towards more real objects, he was getting a truer view? Suppose further that he were shown the various objects being carried by and were made to say, in reply to questions, what each of them was. Would he not be perplexed and believe the objects now shown him to be not so real as what he formerly saw?

Yes, not nearly so real.

And if he were forced to look at the fire-light itself, would not his eyes ache, so that he would try to escape and turn back to the things which he could see distinctly, convinced that they really were clearer than these other objects now being shown to him?

---

[25] The *length* of the "way in" (*eisodos*) to the chamber where the prisoners sit is an essential feature, explaining why no daylight reaches them.

[26] The track crosses the passage into the cave at right angles, and is *above* the parapet built along it.

[27] A modem Plato would compare his Cave to an underground cinema, where the audience watch the play of shadows thrown by the film passing before a light at their backs. The film itself is only an image of "real" things and events in the world outside the cinema. For the film Plato has to substitute the clumsier apparatus of a procession of artificial objects carried on their heads by persons who are merely part of the machinery, providing for the movement of the objects and the sounds whose echo the prisoners hear. The parapet prevents these persons' shadows from being cast on the wall of the Cave.

[28] Adam's text and interpretation. The prisoners, having seen nothing but shadows, cannot think their words refer to the objects carried past behind their backs. For them shadows (images) are the only realities.

Yes.

And suppose someone were to drag him away forcibly up the steep and rugged ascent and not let him go until he had hauled him out into the sunlight, would he not suffer pain and vexation at such treatment, and, when he had come out into the light, find his eyes so full of its radiance that he could not see a single one of the things that he was now told were real?

Certainly he would not see them all at once.

He would need, then, to grow accustomed before he could see things in that upper world. At first it would be easiest to make out shadows, and then the images of men and things reflected in water, and later on the things themselves. After that, it would be easier to watch the heavenly bodies and the sky itself by night, looking at the light of the moon and stars rather than the Sun and the Sun's light in the day-time.

Yes, surely.

Last of all, he would be able to look at the Sun and contemplate its nature, not as it appears when reflected in water or any alien medium, but as it is in itself in its own domain.

No doubt.

And now he would begin to draw the conclusion that it is the Sun that produces the seasons and the course of the year and controls everything in the visible world, and moreover is in a way the cause of all that he and his companions used to see.

Clearly he would come at last to that conclusion.

Then if he called to mind his fellow prisoners and what passed for wisdom in his former dwelling-place, he would surely think himself happy in the change and be sorry for them. They may have had a practice of honouring and commending one another, with prizes for the man who had the keenest eye for the passing shadows and the best memory for the order in which they followed or accompanied one another, so that he could make a good guess as to which was going to come next.[29] Would our released prisoner be likely to covet those prizes or to envy the men exalted to honour and power in the Cave? Would he not feel like Homer's Achilles, that he would far sooner "be on earth as a hired servant in the house of a landless man" or endure anything rather than go back to his old beliefs and live in the old way?

Yes, he would prefer any fate to such a life.

Now imagine what would happen if he went down again to take his former seat in the Cave. Coming suddenly out of the sunlight, his eyes would be filled with darkness. He might be required once more to deliver his opinion on those shadows, in competition with the prisoners who had never been released, while his eyesight was still dim and unsteady; and it might take some time to become used to the darkness. They would laugh at him and say that he had gone up only to come back with his sight ruined; it was worth no one's while even to attempt the ascent. If they could lay hands on the man who was trying to set them free and lead them up, they would kill him.[30]

Yes, they would.

Every feature in this parable, my dear Glaucon, is meant to fit our earlier analysis. The prison dwelling corresponds to the region revealed to us through the sense of sight, and the firelight within it to the power of the Sun. The ascent to see the things in the upper world you may take as standing for the upward journey of the soul into the region of the intelligible; then you will be in possession of what I surmise, since that is what you wish to be told. Heaven knows whether it is true; but this, at any rate, is how it appears to me. In the world of knowledge, the last thing to be perceived and only with great difficulty is the essential Form of Goodness. Once it is perceived, the conclusion must follow that, for all things, this is the cause of whatever is right and good; in the visible world it gives birth to light and to the lord of light, while it is itself sovereign in the intelligible world and the parent of intelligence and truth. Without having had a vision of this Form no one can act with wisdom, either in his own life or in matters of state.

---

[29] The empirical politician, with no philosophic insight, but only a "knack of remembering what usually happens" (*Gorg.* 501 A). He has *eikasia* = conjecture as to what is likely *(eikos)*.

---

[30] An allusion to the fate of Socrates.

So far as I can understand, I share your belief.

Then you may also agree that it is no wonder if those who have reached this height are reluctant to manage the affairs of men. Their souls long to spend all their time in that upper world—naturally enough, if here once more our parable holds true. Nor, again, is it at all strange that one who comes from the contemplation of divine things to the miseries of human life should appear awkward and ridiculous when, with eyes still dazed and not yet accustomed to the darkness, he is compelled, in a law-court or elsewhere, to dispute about the shadows of justice or the images that cast those shadows, and to wrangle over the notions of what is right in the minds of men who have never beheld Justice itself.

It is not at all strange.

No; a sensible man will remember that the eyes may be confused in two ways—by a change from light to darkness or from darkness to light; and he will recognize that the same thing happens to the soul. When he sees it troubled and unable to discern anything clearly, instead of laughing thoughtlessly, he will ask whether, coming from a brighter existence, its unaccustomed vision is obscured by the darkness, in which case he will think its condition enviable and its life a happy one; or whether, emerging from the depths of ignorance, it is dazzled by excess of light. If so, he will rather feel sorry for it; or, if he were inclined to laugh, that would be less ridiculous than to laugh at the soul which has come down from the light.

That is a fair statement.

If this is true, then, we must conclude that education is not what it is said to be by some, who profess to put knowledge into a soul which does not possess it, as if they could put sight into blind eyes. On the contrary, our own account signifies that the soul of every man does possess the power of learning the truth and the organ to see it with; and that, just as one might have to turn the whole body round in order that the eye should see light instead of darkness, so the entire soul must be turned away from this changing world, until its eye can bear to contemplate reality and that supreme splendour which we have called the Good. Hence there may well be an art whose aim would

be to effect this very thing, the conversion of the soul, in the readiest way; not to put the power of sight into the soul's eye, which already has it, but to ensure that, instead of looking in the wrong direction, it is turned the way it ought to be.

Yes, it may well be so.

It looks, then, as though wisdom were different from those ordinary virtues, as they are caned, which are not far removed from bodily qualities, in that they can be produced by habituation and exercise in a soul which has not possessed them from the first. Wisdom, it seems, is certainly the virtue of some diviner faculty, which never loses its power, though its use for good or harm depends on the direction towards which it is turned. You must have noticed in dishonest men with a reputation for sagacity the shrewd glance of a narrow intelligence piercing the objects to which it is directed. There is nothing wrong with their power of vision, but it has been forced into the service of evil, so that the keener its sight, the more harm it works.

Quite true.

And yet if the growth of a nature like this had been pruned from earliest childhood, cleared of those clinging overgrowths which come of gluttony and all luxurious pleasure and, like leaden weights charged with affinity to this mortal world, hang upon the soul, bending its vision downwards; if, freed from these, the soul were turned round towards true reality, then this same power in these very men would see the truth as keenly as the objects it is turned to now.

Yes, very likely.

Is it not also likely, or indeed certain after what has been said, that a state can never be properly governed either by the uneducated who know nothing of truth or by men who are allowed to spend all their days in the pursuit of culture? The ignorant have no single mark before their eyes at which they must aim in all the conduct of their own lives and of affairs of state; and the others will not engage in action if they can help it, dreaming that, while still alive, they have been translated to the Islands of the Blest.

Quite true.

It is for us, then, as founders of a commonwealth, to bring compulsion to bear on the noblest natures. They must be made to climb the ascent to the vision of Goodness, which we called the highest object of knowledge; and, when they have looked upon it long enough, they must not be allowed, as they now are, to remain on the heights, refusing to come down again to the prisoners or to take any part in their labours and rewards, however much or little these may be worth.

Shall we not be doing them an injustice, if we force on them a worse life than they might have?

You have forgotten again, my friend, that the law is not concerned to make any one class specially happy, but to ensure the welfare of the commonwealth as a whole. By persuasion or constraint it will unite the citizens in harmony, making them share whatever benefits each class can contribute to the common good; and its purpose in forming men of that spirit was not that each should be left to go his own way, but that they should be instrumental in binding the community into one.

True, I had forgotten.

You will see, then, Glaucon, that there will be no real injustice in compelling our philosophers to watch over and care for the other citizens. We can fairly tell them that their compeers in other states may quite reasonably refuse to collaborate: there they have sprung up, like a self-sown plant, in despite of their country's institutions; no one has fostered their growth, and they cannot be expected to show gratitude for a care they have never received. "But," we shall say, "it is not so with you. We have brought you into existence for your country's sake as well as for your own, to be like leaders and king-bees in a hive; you have been better and more thoroughly educated than those others and hence you are more capable of playing your part both as men of thought and as men of action. You must go down, then, each in his turn, to live with the rest and let your eyes grow accustomed to the darkness. You will then see a thousand times better than those who live there always; you will recognize every image for what it is and know what it represents, because you have seen justice, beauty, and goodness in their reality; and so you and we shall find life in our commonwealth no mere dream, as it is in most existing states, where men live fighting one another about shadows

and quarrelling for power, as if that were a great prize; whereas in truth government can be at its best and free from dissension only where the destined rulers are least desirous of holding office."

Quite true.

Then will our pupils refuse to listen and to take their turns at sharing in the work of the community, though they may live together for most of their time in a purer air?

No; it is a fair demand, and they are fair-minded men. No doubt, unlike any ruler of the present day, they will think of holding power as an unavoidable necessity.

Yes, my friend; for the truth is that you can have a well-governed society only if you can discover for your future rulers a better way of life than being in office; then only will power be in the hands of men who are rich, not in gold, but in the wealth that brings happiness, a good and wise life. All goes wrong when, starved for lack of anything good in their own lives, men turn to public affairs hoping to snatch from thence the happiness they hunger for. They set about fighting for power, and this internecine conflict ruins them and their country. The life of true philosophy is the only one that looks down upon offices of state; and access to power must be confined to men who are not in love with it; otherwise rivals will start fighting. So whom else can you compel to undertake the guardianship of the commonwealth, if not those who, besides understanding best the principles of government, enjoy a nobler life than the politician's and look for rewards of a different kind?

There is indeed no other choice,

DEMOCRACY AND THE DEMOCRATIC MAN

Democracy, I suppose, should come next. A study of its rise and character should help us to recognize the democratic type of man and set him beside the others for judgment.

Certainly that course would fit in with our plan.

If the aim of life in an oligarchy is to become as rich as possible, that insatiable craving would bring about the transition to democracy. In this way: since the power of the ruling class is due to its wealth, they will not want to have laws restraining prodigal young men from ruining themselves by extravagance. They will hope to lend these spendthrifts money on their property and buy it up, so as to become richer and more influential than ever. We can see at once that a society cannot hold wealth in honour and at the same time establish a proper self-control in its citizens. One or the other must be sacrificed.

Yes, that is fairly obvious.

In an oligarchy, then, this neglect to curb riotous living sometimes reduces to poverty men of a not ungenerous nature. They settle down in idleness, some of them burdened with debt, some disfranchised, some both at once; and these drones are armed and can sting. Hating the men who have acquired their property and conspiring against them and the rest of society, they long for a revolution. Meanwhile the usurers, intent upon their own business, seem unaware of their existence; they are too busy planting their own stings into any fresh victim who offers them an opening to inject the poison of their money; and while they multiply their capital by usury, they are also multiplying the drones and the paupers. When the danger threatens to break out, they will do nothing to quench the flames, either in the way we mentioned, by forbidding a man to do what he likes with his own, or by the next best remedy, which would be a law enforcing a respect for right conduct. If it were enacted that, in general, voluntary contracts for a loan should be made at the lender's risk, there would be less of this shameless pursuit of wealth and a scantier crop of those evils I have just described.

Quite true.

But, as things are, this is the plight to which the rulers of an oligarchy, for all these reasons, reduce their subjects. As for themselves, luxurious indolence of body and mind makes their young men too lazy and effeminate to resist pleasure or to endure pain; and the fathers, neglecting everything but money, have no higher ideals in life than the poor. Such being the condition of rulers and subjects, what will happen when they are thrown together, perhaps as fellow-travellers by sea or land to some festival or on a campaign, and can observe one another's demeanour in a moment of danger? The rich will have no chance to feel superior to the poor. On the contrary, the poor man, lean and sunburnt, may find himself posted in battle beside one who, thanks to his wealth and indoor life, is panting under his burden of fat and showing every mark of distress. "Such men," he will think, "are rich because we are cowards"; and when he and his friends meet in private, the word will go round: "These men are no good: they are at our mercy."

Yes, that is sure to happen.

This state, then, is in the same precarious condition as a person so unhealthy that the least shock from outside will upset the balance or even without that, internal disorder will break out. It falls sick and is at war with itself on the slightest occasion, as soon as one party or the other calls in allies from a neighbouring oligarchy or democracy; and sometimes civil war begins with no help from without.

Quite true.

And when the poor win, the result is a democracy. They kill some of the opposite party, banish others, and grant the rest an equal share in civil rights and government, officials being usually appointed by lot.

Yes, that is how a democracy comes to be established, whether by force of arms or because the other party is terrorized into giving way.

Now what is the character of this new régime? Obviously the way they govern themselves will throw light on the democratic type of man.

No doubt.

First of all, they are free. Liberty and free speech are rife everywhere; anyone is allowed to do what he likes.

Yes, so we are told.

That being so, every man will arrange his own manner of life to suit his pleasure. The result will be a greater variety of individuals than under any other constitution. So it may be the finest of all, with its variegated pattern of all sorts of characters. Many people may think it the best, just as women and children might admire a mixture of colours of every shade in the pattern of a dress. At any rate if we are in search of a constitution, here is a good place to look for one. A democracy is so free that it contains a sample of every kind; and perhaps anyone who intends to found a state, as we have been doing, ought first to visit this emporium of constitutions and choose the model he likes best.

He will find plenty to choose from.

Here, too, you are not obliged to be in authority, however competent you may be, or to submit to authority, if you do not like it; you need not fight when your fellow citizens are at war, nor remain at peace when they do, unless you want peace; and though you may have no legal right to hold office or sit on juries, you will do so all the same if the fancy takes you. A wonderfully pleasant life, surely, for the moment.

For the moment, no doubt.

There is a charm, too, in the forgiving spirit shown by some who have been sentenced by the courts. In a democracy you must have seen how men condemned to death or exile stay on and go about in public, and no one takes any more notice than he would of a spirit that walked invisible. There is so much tolerance and superiority to petty considerations; such a contempt for all those fine principles we laid down in founding our commonwealth, as when we said that only a very exceptional nature could turn out a good man, if he had not played as a child among things of beauty and given himself only to creditable pursuits. A democracy tramples all such notions under foot; with a magnificent indifference to the sort of life a man has led before he enters politics, it will promote to honour anyone who merely calls himself the people's friend.

Magnificent indeed.

These then, and such as these, are the features of a democracy, an agreeable form of anarchy with plenty of variety and an equality of a peculiar kind for equals and unequals alike.

All that is notoriously true.

Now consider the corresponding individual character. Or shall we take his origin first, as we did in the case of the constitution?

Yes.

I imagine him as the son of our miserly oligarch, brought up under his father's eye and in his father's ways. So he too will enforce a firm control over all such pleasures as lead to expense rather than profit—unnecessary pleasures, as they have been called. But, before going farther, shall we draw the distinction between necessary and unnecessary appetites, so as not to argue in the dark?[31]

Please do so.

There are appetites which cannot be got rid of, and there are all those which it does us good to fulfil. Our nature cannot help seeking to satisfy both these kinds; so they may fairly be described as necessary. On the other hand, "unnecessary" would be the right name for all appetites which can be got rid of by early training and which do us no good and in some cases do harm. Let us take an example of each kind, so as to form a general idea of them. The desire to eat enough plain food—just bread and meat—to keep in health and good condition may be called necessary. In the case of bread the necessity is twofold, since it not only does us good but is indispensable to life; whereas meat is only necessary in so far as it helps to keep us in good condition. Beyond these simple needs the desire for a whole variety of luxuries is unnecessary. Most people can get rid of it by early discipline and education; and it is as prejudicial to intelligence and self-control as it is to bodily health. Further, these unnecessary appetites might be called expensive, whereas the necessary ones are rather profitable, as helping a man to do his work. The same distinctions could be drawn in the case of sexual appetite and all the rest.

Yes.

Now, when we were speaking just now of drones, we meant the sort of man who is under the sway of a host of unnecessary pleasures and appetites, in contrast with our miserly oligarch, over whom the necessary desires are in control. Accordingly, we can now go back to describe how the democratic type develops from the oligarchical. I imagine it usually happens in this way. When a young man, bred, as we were saying, in a stingy and uncultivated home, has once tasted the honey of the drones and keeps company with those dangerous and cunning creatures, who know how to purvey pleasures in all their multitudinous variety, then the oligarchical constitution of his

---

[31] A classification of appetites is needed because oligarchy, democracy, and despotism are based on the supremacy of three sorts of appetite: (1) the necessary, (2) the unnecessary and spendthrift, and (3) the lawless.

soul begins to turn into a democracy. The corresponding revolution was effected in the state by one of the two factions calling in the help of partisans from outside. In the same way one of the conflicting sets of desires in the soul of this youth will be reinforced from without by a group of kindred passions; and if the resistance of the oligarchical faction in him is strengthened by remonstrances and reproaches coming from his father, perhaps, or his friends, the opposing parties will soon be battling within him. In some cases the democratic interest yields to the oligarchical: a sense of shame gains a footing in the young man's soul, and some appetites are crushed, others banished, until order is restored.

Yes, that happens sometimes.

But then again, perhaps, owing to the father's having no idea how to bring up his son, another brood of desires, akin to those which were banished, are secretly nursed up until they become numerous and strong. These draw the young man back into clandestine commerce with his old associates, and between them they breed a whole multitude. In the end, they seize the citadel of the young man's soul, finding it unguarded by the trusty sentinels which keep watch over the minds of men favoured by heaven. Knowledge, right principles, true thoughts, are not at their post; and the place lies open to the assault of false and presumptuous notions. So he turns again to those lotus-eaters and now throws in his lot with them openly. If his family send reinforcements to the support of his thrifty instincts, the impostors who have seized the royal fortress shut the gates upon them, and will not even come to parley with the fatherly counsels of individual friends. In the internal conflict they gain the day; modesty and self-control, dishonoured and insulted as the weaknesses of an unmanly fool, are thrust out into exile; and the whole crew of unprofitable desires take a hand in banishing moderation and frugality, which, as they will have it, are nothing but churlish meanness. So they take possession of the soul which they have swept clean, as if purified for initiation into higher mysteries; and nothing remains but to marshal the great procession bringing home Insolence, Anarchy, Waste, and Impudence, those resplendent divinities crowned with garlands, whose praises they sing under flattering names: Insolence they call good breeding, Anarchy, freedom; Waste, magnificence; and Impudence, a manly spirit. Is not that a fair account of the revolution which gives free rein to unnecessary and harmful pleasures in a young man brought up in the satisfaction only of the necessary desires?

Yes, it is a vivid description.

In his life thenceforward he spends as much time and pains and money on his superfluous pleasures as on the necessary ones. If he is lucky enough not to be carried beyond all bounds, the tumult may begin to subside as he grows older. Then perhaps he may recall some of the banished virtues and cease to give himself up entirely to the passions which ousted them; and now he will set all his pleasures on a footing of equality, denying to none its equal rights and maintenance, and allowing each in turn, as it presents itself, to succeed, as if by the chance of the lot, to the government of his soul until it is satisfied. When he is told that some pleasures should be sought and valued as arising from desires of a higher order, others chastised and enslaved because the desires are base, he will shut the gates of the citadel against the messengers of truth, shaking his head and declaring that one appetite is as good as another and all must have their equal rights. So he spends his days indulging the pleasure of the moment, now intoxicated with wine and music, and then taking to a spare diet and drinking nothing but water; one day in hard training, the next doing nothing at all, the third apparently immersed in study. Every now and then he takes a part in politics, leaping to his feet to say or do whatever comes into his head. Or he will set out to rival someone he admires, a soldier it may be, or, if the fancy takes him, a man of business. His life is subject to no order or restraint, and he has no wish to change an existence which he calls pleasant, free, and happy.

That well describes the life of one whose motto is liberty and equality.

Yes, and his character contains the same fine variety of pattern that we found in the democratic state; it is as multifarious as that epitome of all types of constitution. Many a man, and many a woman too, will find in it something to envy. So we may see in him the counterpart of democracy, and call him the democratic man.

CHAPTER FOUR

ARISTOTLE

Plato's strength and weakness lay in his gift to confront social reality with what *ought* to be. If that is utopian, every critic and reformer is a utopian. The *Republic* is not a work of abstract contemplation by an aloof philosopher addressed to no one in particular, but the impassioned plea of an Athenian old-family aristocrat. Opposing popular government, Plato recommended to his fellow citizens a constitution and way of life that in many respects, though not in all, resembled those of Sparta, a military and aristocratic state whose distinctive marks were discipline, unity, and complete subordination of the individual to the state. Deeply concerned about practical affairs as he was, Plato nevertheless often went beyond the analysis of what does happen, or is likely to happen, and let himself be carried off into the realm of the Ought. Looking into what may or ought to develop in the future, one is more likely to think in terms of the absolute and perfect, because the imagination of the future is pure idea, unmodified by that relentless relativist and compromiser—experience.

Plato found the corrective to his thinking in his own student, Aristotle (384–322 B.C.), not an Athenian, but a native of Stagira, a Greek colonial town on the Macedonia coast. Reared on the fringe of Greek civilization, Aristotle early acquired some of the worldly wisdom, detachment, and tolerance that were generally characteristic of colonial Greeks in constant touch with other peoples and cultures. Unlike Plato, Aristotle came from an upper-middle-class family, his father being a physician. At the age of seventeen, Aristotle went to Athens, the intellectual center of Greece, entered Plato's Academy, and studied under Plato for twenty years, until his master's death. During the subsequent twelve years, he traveled widely and spent several years at the Court of Philip of Macedon as tutor to his son, Alexander.

In 335 B.C. Aristotle returned to Athens and set up a school of his own, the Lyceum, whose teaching and research program included every branch of knowledge. In 323 B.C. Alexander suddenly died, and the national-democratic forces in Athens quickly rose against the Macedonian overlordship and its lieutenants and spokesmen in Greece. Aristotle, widely known for his intimate associations with the Macedonian monarchy and Alexander, was suspected of pro-Macedonian sentiments and indicted. However, Aristotle preferred exile to a court trial and possible sentence; he died the following year (322 B.C.) in Chalcis, a stronghold of Macedonian influence that gave him generous refuge during the last months of his life.

In the history of political philosophy no one has surpassed Aristotle in encyclopedic interest and accomplishment. From his father he inherited a flair for medical and biological subjects, and he may have practiced medicine for a time. This interest drew him into zoology, physics, and the natural sciences in general, and fostered in him the habit of observing and weighing data before expressing any general formulas and hypotheses. In philosophy proper, logic and metaphysics were his two main branches of study and writing; he also contributed to esthetics and rhetoric and wrote the first book on psychology; and his *Ethics* and *Politics* are the first systematic treatises in their respective fields. The *Politics* lacks the fire and poetic imagery of the *Republic,* but it is more systematic and analytical, and after twenty-three hundred years it is still an introductory textbook to the entire field of political science. It cannot easily be surpassed in clarity of thought, sobriety of expression, range of topics, and undogmatic openness of mind, for Aristotle prefers beings occasionally self-contradictory to being always right.

Aristotle opens the *Politics* with two important ideas: (1) that the state is a community, and (2) that it is the highest of all communities, "which embraces all the rest, aims at good in a greater degree than any other, and at the highest good." The first thesis came naturally to a Greek of the classical period: his *polis* was a city-state with a small area and population; lacking the impersonal anonymity of ancient empires or modern national states, it combined within itself the active citizenship of an early New England or modern Swiss community and the warmth and fellowship of a religious congregation, all deepened by a joint sharing in the arts and pleasures of life.

Aristotle may not have been the first to consider the state a community, but he was the first to define it clearly as such, and thus he laid the foundation for the *organic* conception of the state, one of the two major types into which all political theories of the state may roughly be divided. According to him, the state is a natural community, an organism with all the attributes of a living being. The other major type views the state as an instrument, a mechanism, a piece of machinery to be used for purposes and ends higher than itself. This type, called the *instrumentalist* view of the state, is actually older, having been propounded by the Sophists a century before Aristotle; however, it was rejected by Plato and revived only in modern times by Hobbes, Locke, and John Dewey.

Aristotle conceives of the state as "natural" in two ways. First, he briefly delineates the evolution of social institutions from the family through the village to the city-state; in this historical sense, the state is the natural and final stage in the growth of human relations. The state is also considered by Aristotle to be natural in a logical and philosophical sense: "The state is by nature clearly prior to the family and the individual, since the whole is of necessity prior to the part." Similarly, Aristotle says that "man is by nature a political animal," and that only gods or beasts can exist without the confines of the sheltering city.

But Aristotle maintains not only that the state is a community but that it is the *highest community* aiming at the highest good. The family is the first form of association, lowest in the chain of social evolution, and lowest on the rung of values, because it is established by nature "for the supply of men's everyday wants." The village is the second form of association, genetically more complex than the family, and aiming "at something more than the supply of daily needs," meeting at least some rudimentary and primitive cultural wants that the family cannot satisfy. The third and highest form of association is the city-state, highest in terms of social evolution and highest in terms of value and purpose; whereas family and village exist essentially for the preservation of life and the comforts of companionship, the "state exists for the sake of a good life, and not for the sake of life only," and "political society exists for the sake of noble actions, and not of mere companionship."

Unlike Plato, who conceives of reality in terms of unchanging and unchanging static essences and Ideas, Aristotle identifies the nature of a thing with the end toward which it is developing; at each unfinished stage, the thing is partly realizing its own nature and is fully itself when its end is wholly realized. Aristotle's biological, scientific, and historical interests enabled him to view the philosophical problem of reality from a more dynamic and relative standpoint than Plato's, and Aristotle's conception of the state therefore encompasses a wider range of forms of state, varying blends of idea and circumstance, of the perfect and the imperfect.

The state is the highest form of association, not only in terms of the social and institutional, or objective, values, but in terms of man's own nature. In the family, man reproduces himself; in the village, he satisfies elementary wants of human companionship; in the state alone, he realizes his entire self, and particularly the highest part of himself. Man thus represents a compound of qualities that are reflected in corresponding forms of association: his *material* appetites and biological urges, the lowest on the scale of values, are reflected in the family; his *social* sentiment, his desire for companionship and community, is expressed in the village; his *moral* nature, the quality that makes him most specifically human, is fulfilled in the state.

In modern thought, especially in the social sciences, a sharper distinction is drawn between the individual, social groups and associations, and, finally, the state. Aristotle sees all three as organically connected with one another. Man cannot be conceived as being apart from, or superior to, the state because, as was explained earlier, Aristotle considers that "the whole is of necessity prior to the part." Only a "beast or a god" is unable to live in society, or has no need for it. Man can realize himself, that which is most human in him, in society alone. Similarly, Aristotle recognizes no basic difference between social and political associations. To him, all associations are political, inasmuch as they aim at a common good through joint action; the state differs from other associations in that it aims at the highest good, the general advantage of all.

Since the seventeenth century the state has been sharply distinguished from all other organizations because it alone possesses sovereignty, or the highest authority in a politically organized community, and the legal monopoly of enforcing such authority in its territory. Aristotle knows not of the conceptual distinction, or contrast, between individual and society, nor can he visualize the later conflict between society (conceived as the sphere of unhindered and spontaneous activity) and the state (conceived as the sphere of regulated and compelled behavior). If Aristotle were to think at all of the state as sovereign, he would think of the *highest purpose* of the state rather than of its supreme authority over its citizens. His is a conception of *moral sovereignty* rather than of *legal sovereignty.* Nurtured in the tradition of the small city-state, Aristotle could still say that "the will to live together is friendship," and he would have abhorred the conception that the state is held together, not by personal bonds of fellowship and friendship, but by impersonal and anonymous rules of law, uniformly applying to vast territories and populations, as in modern states and empires.

In his organic view of the state Aristotle expresses more clearly what is implicit, and to some extent explicit, in Plato, but he is unwilling to go as far as his teacher. Unity became for Plato an ideal to which almost anything else was to be sacrificed, the happiness of the rulers as well as the ruled. By contrast, Aristotle warns against the dangers of excessive unity in the state; even if it could be attained, it ought to be rejected, "for it would be the destruction of the state." Moreover, Aristotle is doubtful whether such perfect unity is attainable, and he likens the guardian-rulers of the *Republic* to a "mere occupying garrison," with the result that Plato's ideally united state actually contains "two states in one, each hostile to the other."

Whereas Plato saw only a few basic differences of individuals, such as the differences between members of the three classes of the ideal state, Aristotle is aware of many more differences, and he expresses a truth that is as provocative today as ever, that "a state is not made up only of so many men, but of different kinds of men," and that "the nature of a state is to be a plurality." The danger of all organic theories of the state is that they tend to stress communal unity over individual differences and to sub-ordinate the individual to the state. Plato's conception of the state carried the idea of unity, implicit in all organic theories, to the excess of self-destruction; Aristotle found the counterweight to such an extreme and perfectionist view in the elements of his thinking that pointed toward relativism and pluralism.

Aristotle's organic conception of the state has been used more eagerly and more fre-quently by conservatives and antidemocrats than by democratic political writers. Yet as time went on, the awareness grew that the state must be more than an instrument or piece of machinery and that the democratic state in particular should aim at becoming a community, not only of law, but of fellowship. Underlying the modern development of the welfare state is the notion that society must have no outcasts, that its inequalities must be reduced, and that the basic amenities of civilized life must be accessible to all.

The second basic doctrine of Aristotle, that the state is the highest community, is less likely to be accepted by democrats. Two objections can be raised: first, democrats are unwilling to concede that any institution per se is entitled to claim primary and exclu-sive loyalty. Man feels attached to various, and often conflicting, religious, social, eco-nomic, and political groups, and his conscience has to decide in each instance of conflict which loyalty comes first. In one instance he may put his church above his country; in another, his country above his economic interest, but there is no way of telling a priori that any institution is entitled to first allegiance under all circum-stances. As a Greek, Aristotle would have felt little sympathy for such a conception of the state, which is implicit in all democratic political doctrines, because the small city-state with its intimate social life was church and state at the same time, and no sharp distinction was felt between socioeconomic and political institutions.

The second objection against the conception of the state as the highest community can be made by democrats on the ground, originally stated by the Sophists and later reem-phasized by the Stoics, that man's loyalty is to mankind as a whole rather than to any particular fraction. This faith was given added force by the Judeo-Christian religious tradition, in which the oneness of God inspires the belief in the oneness of mankind.

By studying virtually all then-known constitutions and political systems, Aristotle laid the foundations of an important branch of political science: *comparative govern-ment and politics.* Of 158 such studies made by him, only one survives, the *Constitution of Athens,* discovered in 1890. The study of comparative political institutions is of in-terest to the political scientist as well as to the practicing statesman, who must know the varieties of political experience if he is to be able to remedy the defects of exist-ing constitutions.

In considering the general problem of the various forms of government, Aristotle says, in an obvious reference to Plato, that "there are some who would have none but the most perfect." The knowledge of the best state may have some value as a norm and standard, but, on the other hand, "the best is often unattainable, and therefore the true legislator and statesman ought to be acquainted, not only with (1) that which is best in the abstract, but also with (2) that which is best relatively to circumstances." Where the attention to Plato, in the *Republic* at least, is centered on the desirable kind of state, Aristotle holds that we "should consider, not only what form of government is best, but also what is possible and what is easily attainable by all."

In classifying the forms of state, Aristotle distinguishes governments that are carried on "with a view to the common interest" from those that serve private interests, whether of one, of few, or of many. Of true governments, there are three: kingship, aristocracy, and constitutional government. Each form has its perversion, of which there are also three: tyranny, oligarchy, and democracy (the rule of the poor).

Of the three forms, Aristotle holds monarchy to be the most ideal kind of government. If a man "preeminent in virtue" can be found, who surpasses in virtue and political capacity "all the rest," he cannot be regarded as a part of the state, subject to the law like everybody else: "Such an one may truly be deemed a God among men." Since there is no law for men of preeminent virtue, monarchs "are themselves a law." Their superior virtue and political capacity give them the right to "practise compulsion and still live in harmony with their cities, if their own government is for the interest of the state."

Like Plato, Aristotle puts virtue of the rulers above consent of the ruled, although both would prefer to have the ruled submit voluntarily to their rulers, to avoid the necessity of compulsion. If a man of preeminent virtue be the monarch, Aristotle argues, "all should joyfully obey such a ruler, according to what seems to be the order of nature." Monarchy can be justified, however, by another consideration: that "a king is the resource of the better classes against the people," and that "the idea of a king is to be a protector of the rich against unjust treatment, of the people against insult and oppression."

Aristotle's deep sympathy for monarchy, as expressed in the *Politics* in so many passages, is to be understood in the light of his relations with the rising Macedonian monarchy. His father had been the royal physician at the Macedonian court, and Aristotle himself the tutor of Alexander. Both Philip and Alexander sought to conquer Greece intellectually as well as politically and militarily; just as in the struggle between Sparta and Athens class loyalties often came before patriotism, and each city had its (antidemocratic) Spartan and (prodemocratic) Athenian party, so the Macedonian effort to annex Greece to its rule was accompanied by the growth of pro-Macedonian groups in the major Greek city-states. In Athens, the national and democratic movement was led by Demosthenes, to whom all monarchy, good or bad, was "un-Athenian"; the conservative classes, anxious above all to maintain their privileged social-economic position, received their intellectual support from Aristotle's school of philosophy and Plato's Academy, and they were therefore generally pro-Macedonian.

Aristocracy is nowhere described in the *Politics* systematically, perhaps because the problem of aristocracy and democracy (particularly in relation to Athenian self-government) was not of such practical importance as that of monarchy (particularly in relation to the Macedonian kingdom). Aristotle defines aristocracy as a "government formed of the best men absolutely," and not merely of men who are good relatively, that is, in relation to changing circumstances and constitutions. But Aristotle admits that, in addition to such a pure form of aristocracy, which is based on merit and virtue only, there is a type of aristocracy that also takes into account the elements of wealth. Generally, however, Aristotle speaks of monarchy and aristocracy as "the perfect state," the government of the best, both forms aiming at the general good; the main difference between the two consists in the fact that in monarchy virtue is centered in one "preeminent" man, whereas in aristocracy virtue is diffused among several men. The deteriorated form of aristocracy is oligarchy, in which government by the wealthy is carried on for their own benefit rather than for that of the whole state. Whereas merit and virtue are the distinctive qualities to be considered in selecting the rulers in an aristocracy, wealth is the basis of selection in an oligarchy.

The third of the true forms of state is constitutional government ("polity"). Aristotle defines it as the state that the citizens at large administer for the common interest. Constitutional government is a compromise between the two principles of freedom and wealth, the attempt to "unite the freedom of the poor and the wealth of the rich," without

giving either principle exclusive predominance. Aristotle concedes that the doctrine of
the multitude being supreme rather than the few best, "though not free from difficulty,
yet seems to contain an element of truth." When many ordinary persons meet together,
their collective wisdom and experience may be superior to that of the few good, "just as
a feast to which many contribute is better than a dinner provided out of a single purse."
Aristotle suggests the general analogy of the user of a thing being a better judge than its
producer, and that, returning to culinary similes, "the guest will judge better of a feast
than the cook."

Thinking realistically of the stability of the state, Aristotle holds that the freedom of
the poor must be given some consideration, "for a state in which many poor men are excluded from office will necessarily be full of enemies." Aristotle never abandons the
ideal state (monarchy or aristocracy, that is, the rule of the best) as an "aspiration," but
he realizes that it assumes a standard of virtue "which is above ordinary persons"; in
practice, therefore, constitutional government, based on limited suffrage, turns out to
be "the best constitution for most states, and the best life for most men."

By relating forms of political organization to the social milieu that conditions them,
Aristotle anticipated some of the main doctrines of Montesquieu and, still more recently, the sociological approach to the study of politics. He saw the danger that would
arise if any principle singly and exclusively dominated the constitution, and he therefore advocated, for reasons of stability and practicability, *mixed constitutions,* such as
"polity" (constitutional government), based on the two principles of wealth and numbers. However, he realized that a mixed political system could exist in the long run only
if backed by a stable society without extremes of wealth and poverty.

Although many persons in the twentieth century find the cause of revolution in conspiracies of evil men, and its remedy in intimidation by investigatory committees or in
repression by antirevolutionary legislation, Aristotle states that "poverty is the parent
of revolution and crime," and that "when there is no middle class, and the poor greatly
exceed in number, troubles arise, and the state soon comes to an end." Because he realized that political stability depends on an equitable social and economic order, he was
opposed to selfish class rule by either an excessively wealthy plutocracy (called by him
"oligarchy") or by a propertyless proletariat (called by him "democracy"): "Thus it is
manifest that the best political community is formed by citizens of the middle class,
and that those states are likely to be well-administered, in which the middle class is
large, and stronger if possible than both the other classes, or at any rate than either
singly." The middle classes thus provided for Aristotle the balance and equilibrium
without which no constitution can endure.

The degenerate form of constitutional government (or "polity") is called by Aristotle
"democracy," and defined as a system in which "the poor rule." It is government by the
poor, and for the poor only, just as tyranny is government by one for his own benefit,
and oligarchy government by the wealthy few for their class benefit. But of the degenerate forms, government of the poor for the benefit of the poor ("democracy") is "the
most tolerable of the three." Aristotle names popular sovereignty and individual liberty
the two characteristic principles of democracy, and he condemns them, in language
similar to that of Plato, as incompatible with the stability of the existing moral and political order: "Men think that what is just is equal; and that equality is the supremacy of
the popular will; and that freedom means the doing what a man likes. In such democracies every one lives as he pleases."

Though Aristotle was more appreciative than Plato of the common sense and collective wisdom of the people, he was nevertheless afraid of government in which the democratic principle of popular sovereignty was allowed to operate without the modifying

influence of other principles, particularly wealth. In this fear of the sovereignty of the majority, Aristotle is conservative rather than antidemocratic, and the godfather of all conservatives in history who have tried to harmonize respect for constitutional government with social and economic inequality.

Aristotle's conservative viewpoint is also clearly expressed in his conception of *citizenship*. He defines a citizen as follows: "he who has the power to take part in the deliberative or judicial administration of any state." Representative government was unknown to Aristotle because the Greek city-state was governed directly by its citizens, with but few representative elements. Aristotle could not have foreseen the modern concept of the citizen whose main (and often sole) political act is to vote (and frequently he neglects to do that) every few years in an election, and otherwise to leave the actual functions of government to professional legislators, judges, and civil servants. Within the small city-state, all slaves and the majority of the free were excluded from citizenship; to be a citizen meant to participate directly in the legislative and executive functions of government.

Aristotle's idea of citizenship is that of the economically independent gentleman who has enough experience, education, and leisure to devote himself to *active* citizenship, for "citizens must not lead the life of mechanics or tradesmen, for such life is ignoble, and inimical to virtue. Neither must they be husbandmen, since leisure is necessary both for the development of virtue and the performance of political duties." Stressing even more clearly the relation between property and virtue, Aristotle maintains that "the ruling class should be the owners of property, for they are citizens, and the citizens of a state should be in good circumstances; whereas mechanics or any other class which is not a producer of virtue have no share in the state."

Aristotle makes an important distinction between the "parts" of the state and its "necessary conditions." Only those who actively share, or have the means and leisure to share, in the government of the state are its component or integral parts. All the others are merely the "necessary condition" who provide the material environment within which the active citizens, freed from menial tasks, can function. Aristotle finds it "no more absurd" to exclude "the lower class" from citizenship than to exclude "slaves and freedmen," none of whom are resident aliens or foreigners; what the "lower class" has in common with slaves and freedmen is the fact that all its members are "necessary to the existence of the state" but not parts of the state. Aristotle even notes that in ancient times, the "artisan class *were* slaves or foreigners, and therefore the majority of them are so now." Although mechanics and laborers are not legally aliens, morally and politically they are, because "he who is excluded from the honors of the state is not better than an alien."

In comparing the propertied citizens with the propertyless mechanics and laborers, Aristotle draws the analogy between ends and means, the latter existing for the sake of the former. Aristotle was unaware of the idea, expressed in religious terms by the Judeo-Christian teachings in antiquity, and in philosophical terms by Kant in modern times, that every man is, by virtue of being human, an end in himself, and must not be reduced to a means.

If free artisans and laborers are to be treated as means rather than ends, it is none too difficult for Aristotle to defend the institution of *slavery*. Whereas artisans and laborers are to be viewed as means in relation to the state only, slaves are means in every aspect of their existence; they belong "wholly" to their masters. Aristotle assumes that nature is universally ruled by the contrast of the superior and inferior: man is superior to the animals, the male to the female, the soul to the body, reason to passion. In all these divisions, it is just that the superior rule over the inferior, and such a rule is to the advantage of both. Among men, there are those "whose business is to use their body, and who can do nothing better," and they are by nature slaves. Just as it is fair to hunt against wild animals, so it is "against men who, though intended by nature to be governed, will not submit." Because the question of who is intended by nature to govern, or to be governed, is likely to be decided by the conquerors of a defeated nation rather than by an impartial, third-party court of appeal, Aristotle—in his doctrine of just wars of conquest and enslavement—anticipates Hegel's dictum that "world history is the world court."

Aristotle concedes to slaves the mental ability of apprehending the rational actions and orders of their masters but denies them the ability of acting rationally on their own initiative. The slave is a possession, a live tool; comparing slaves to tame animals. Aristotle notes the difference that the latter cannot even apprehend reason, whereas slaves do, but "the use made of slaves and of tame animals is not very different; for both with their bodies minister to the needs of life." Untouched by the monotheistic doctrine of the divinity and uniqueness of every human soul, Aristotle expresses the pagan view that "from the hour of their birth, some are marked out for subjection; others, for rule."

Aristotle was realistic enough to see that many were slaves by law rather than nature, particularly those who were reduced to slavery by conquest, a custom widely practiced in the wars of antiquity. Feeling strongly about the cultural unity (and superiority) of the Greeks, Aristotle was particularly disturbed by slavery in Greece, and said that "Hellenes do not like to call Hellenes slaves, but confine the term to barbarians." Just as Plato had urged that Greeks conduct war against one another with a higher set of standards than against "barbarians," Aristotle looked on the mastery-slavery relation as not befitting superior Greeks, because "some are slaves everywhere, others nowhere."

This difference, however, was not a fact to be observed, but a wish to be expressed, because Greeks did enslave one another, and some of those who were slaves were by nature (and often, by birth) free. Aristotle did not resolve the dilemma between his general theory of slavery, which was based on moral and rational superiority, and the slavery of his time, which was based on force, custom, and utility, and had little to do with moral superiority.

All in all, Aristotle's view of slavery was not too extreme for his time. By reminding the master that his rule over the slave must be based on moral excellence and that abuse of his authority was injurious to both, by allowing the possibility of friendship between them, by conceding to slaves the faculty of apprehending reason, Aristotle prepared the ground for more searching ideas. Yet his general acceptance of slavery shows how even a wise and great philosopher is captive of the institutions of his time, and of the prejudices that rationalize them.

Aristotle's views on *property* are developed in direct reference to Plato, but they are of more general bearing and constitute to this day the ablest defense of private property. In his polemic against Plato, Aristotle attributes to him the advocacy of a communist property scheme in the *Republic*. In fact, Plato proposed nothing of the sort: the workers, artisans, and farmers in the *Republic* live in a system of private ownership and management of property; as to the rulers, they own no means of production of any kind, and their only economic activity consists in consuming what they derive from the farming and working population as tribute befitting an austere yet noble style of living. Although Plato did not advocate economic communism, he nevertheless outlawed private property for the rulers as a possible menace to their sense of unity and their devotion to the state.

By contrast, Aristotle denies that private property is, in itself, a threat to moral perfection, and he defends his view on four grounds. First, he adduces the *incentive and progress* argument: when "every one has a distinct interest, men will not complain of one another, and they will make more progress, because every one will be attending to his own business." Thus, Aristotle links the idea of self-interest with that of social progress through greater individual effort and competence, whereas under a communist system, "those who labor much and get little will necessarily complain to those who labor little and receive or consume much." The collapse of Communist states in 1989 can in large part be traced to their nonrecognition of the profit motive in spurring individual initiative.

Aristotle's second argument in support of private property is the *pleasure* that the ownership of property gives, "for all, or almost all, men love money and other such objects in a measure." Aristotle sharply distinguishes such love of property from selfishness and miserliness, and considers it rather from the viewpoint of self-respect and material self-realization.

The third argument is that of *liberality*. Under common ownership, no one can afford to practice generosity and liberality because of the excessive equalization of property; it takes a system of private property, with at least some wealth and inequality, to "set an example of liberality or do any liberal action; for liberality consists in the use which is made of property."

Aristotle's fourth argument has a distinctly Burkean flavor: there must be something deeply and enduringly human in the idea of private property, if it has *existed* for such a *long time,* and "we should not disregard the experience of ages." As to communist practices, "in the multitude of years these things, if they were good, would certainly not have been unknown."

Aristotle is aware of the evils that befall men in a system of private property, but he says that they "are due to a very different cause—the wickedness of human nature." The cure for social imperfections is not equality of property but the moral improvement of man, and "the beginning of reform is not so much to equalize property as to train the nobler sort of natures not to desire more, and to prevent the lower from getting more; that is to say, they must be kept down, but not ill-treated." As a matter of public policy, the legislator ought to aim at equitable, rather than equal, distribution of property; what seems most important to Aristotle is *not who owns property but how property is used,* and that is an essentially moral question, not one of political economy.

Aristotle nevertheless realizes that excessive inequalities of wealth are dangerous to the balance and harmony of the state, and for this reason he praises with deep feeling the advantages of a society in which the middle classes are strongest. By contrast, where "some possess much, and the others nothing," constitutional government is impossible to maintain, and the state will be ruled by one of two extremes: either a plutocratic regime (oligarchy) for the exclusive benefit of the wealthy, or a proletarian regime (democracy) for the benefit of the urban poor, and "a tyranny may grow out of either extreme."

Unlike Plato, who searched for perfect justice, Aristotle understood that the basic issue is between the *rule of law* and the *rule of men.* Conceding that manmade law can never attain perfect justice, Aristotle nevertheless stresses that "the rule of the law is preferable to that of any individual," and that magistrates should regulate only matters on which the law is silent, because a general rule or principle cannot embrace all particulars. Whereas government based on law cannot be perfectly just, it is at least the lesser evil, when contrasted with the arbitrariness and passion inherent in government based on the rule of men.

The Aristotelian concept of the rule of law became one of the dominant political ideas to come forth from the Middle Ages—when interest in Aristotle revived—though during which political relations were still largely based on custom. In modern times the concept of the rule of law has become one of the pillars of the constitutional edifice of the United States and elsewhere. The constitutional state is perhaps the most important legacy Aristotle has bequeathed to posterity. In nondemocratic political systems still today, the strength or weakness of the rule of law is one of the clearest indications of the direction in which a particular state is moving. Historically, the rule of law has generally preceded democracy rather than been created by it. In ancient Greece, for example, the word "isonomia" (equality before the law) was coined before "demokratia" (rule of the people).

Aristotle's specific ideas, beliefs, and proposals are often conservative, even for his own time. But running through all his works, and implicit in his temper and personality, is a spirit that is wise and gentle, moderate, broad in outlook, open to new ideas, averse to dogmatism, conscious of the intricacy and complexity of human affairs, and imbued with sympathy that illuminates and enriches philosophical enquiry. Though explicitly conservative, Aristotle's thinking was suffused with qualities that characterize the liberal temper and the open mind.

ARISTOTLE

*Politics**

NATURE AND ORIGIN OF THE STATE

Every state is a community of some kind, and every community is established with a view to some good; for mankind always act in order to obtain that which they think good. But, if all communities aim at some good, the state or political community, which is the highest of all, and which embraces all the rest, aims at good in a greater degree than any other, and at the highest good.

Some people think that the qualifications of a statesman, king, householder, and master are the same, and that they differ, not in kind, but only in the number of their subjects. For example, the ruler over a few is called a master; over more, the manager of a household; over a still larger number, a statesman or king, as if there were no difference between a great household and a small state. The distinction which is made between the king and the statesman is as follows: When the government is personal, the ruler is a king; when, according to the rules of the political science, the citizens rule and are ruled in turn, then he is called a statesman.

But all this is a mistake; for governments differ in kind, as will be evident to any one who considers the matter according to the method which has hitherto guided us. As in other departments of science, so in politics, the compound should always be resolved into the simple elements or least parts of the whole. We must therefore look at the elements of which the state is composed, in order that we may see in what the different kinds of rule differ from one another, and whether any scientific result can be attained about each one of them.

He who thus considers things in their first growth and origin, whether a state or anything else, will obtain the clearest view of them. In the first place there must be a union of those who cannot exist without each other; namely, of male and female, that the race may continue (and this is a union which is formed, not of deliberate purpose, but because, in common with other animals and with plants, mankind have a natural desire to leave behind them an image of themselves), and of natural ruler and subject, that both may be preserved. For that which can foresee by the exercise of mind is by nature intended to be lord and master, and that which can with its body give effect to such foresight is a subject, and by nature a slave; hence master and slave have the same interest. Now nature has distinguished between the female and the slave. For she is not niggardly, like the smith who fashions the Delphian knife for many uses; she makes each thing for a single use, and every instrument is best made when intended for one and not for many uses. But among barbarians no distinction is made between women and slaves, because there is no natural ruler among them: they are a community of slaves, male and female.

Wherefore the poets say—

It is meet that Hellenes should rule over barbarians;

as if they thought that the barbarian and the slave were by nature one.

*From Aristotle, *Politics* (trans. Benjamin Jowett, Oxford University Press). By permission.

Out of these two relationships between man and woman, master and slave, the first thing to arise is the family, and Hesiod is right when he says—

First house and wife and an ox for the plough,

for the ox is the poor man's slave. The family is the association established by nature for the supply of men's everyday wants, and the members of it are called by Charondas "companions of the cupboard," and by Epimenides the Cretan, "companions of the manger." But when several families are united, and the association aims at something more than the supply of daily needs, the first society to be formed is the village. And the most natural form of the village appears to be that of a colony from the family, composed of the children and grandchildren, who are said to be suckled "with the same milk." And this is the reason why Hellenic states were originally governed by kings; because the Hellenes were under royal rule before they came together, as the barbarians still are. Every family is ruled by the eldest, and therefore in the colonies of the family the kingly form of government prevailed because they were of the same blood. As Homer says:

Each one gives law to his children and to his wives.

For they lived dispersedly, as was the manner in ancient times. Wherefore men say that the Gods have a king, because they themselves either are or were in ancient times under the rule of a king. For they imagine, not only the forms of the Gods, but their ways of life to be like their own.

When several villages are united in a single complete community, large enough to be nearly or quite self-sufficing, the state comes into existence, originating in the bare needs of life, and continuing in existence for the sake of a good life. And therefore, if the earlier forms of society are natural, so is the state, for it is the end of them, and the nature of a thing is its end. For what each thing is when fully developed, we call its nature, whether we are speaking of a man, a horse, or a family. Besides, the final cause and end of a thing is the best, and to be self-sufficing is the end and the best.

Hence it is evident that the state is a creation of nature, and that man is by nature a political animal. And he who by nature and not by mere accident is without a state, is either a bad man or above humanity; he is like the

Tribeless, lawless, heartless one,

whom Homer denounces—the natural outcast is forthwith a lover of war; he may be compared to an isolated piece at draughts.

Now, that man is more of a political animal than bees or any other gregarious animals is evident. Nature, as we often say, makes nothing in vain, and man is the only animal whom she has endowed with the gift of speech. And whereas mere voice is but an indication of pleasure or pain, and is therefore found in other animals (for their nature attains to the perception of pleasure and pain and the intimation of them to one another, and no further), the power of speech is intended to set forth the expedient and inexpedient, and therefore likewise the just and the unjust. And it is a characteristic of man that he alone has any sense of good and evil, of just and unjust, and the like, and the association of living beings who have this sense makes a family and a state.

Further, the state is by nature clearly prior to the family and to the individual, since the whole is of necessity prior to the part; for example, if the whole body be destroyed, there will be no foot or hand, except in an equivocal sense, as we might speak of a stone hand; for when destroyed the hand will be no better than that. But things are defined by their working and power; and we ought not to say that they are the same when they no longer have their proper quality, but only that they have the same name. The proof that the state is a creation of nature and prior to the individual is that the individual, when isolated, is not self-sufficing; and therefore he is like a part in relation to the whole. But he who is unable to live in society, or who has no need because he is sufficient for himself, must be either a beast or a god: he is no part of a state. A social instinct is implanted in all men by nature, and yet he who first founded the state was the greatest of benefactors. For man, when perfected, is the best of animals, but, when separated from law and justice, he is the worst of all; since armed injustice is the more dangerous, and he is equipped at birth with arms, meant to be used by intelligence and virtue, which he may use for the worst ends. Wherefore, if he have not virtue, he is the most unholy and the most savage of animals, and the most full of lust and gluttony. But justice is the bond of men in states, for the administration of justice, which is the determination of what is just, is the principle of order in political society.

SLAVERY

But is there any one thus intended by nature to be a slave, and for whom such a condition is expedient and right, or rather is not all slavery a violation of nature?

There is no difficulty in answering this question, on grounds both of reason and of fact. For that some should rule and others be ruled is a thing not only necessary, but expedient; from the hour of their birth, some are marked out for subjection, others for rule.

And there are many kinds both of rulers and subjects (and that rule is the better which is exercised over better subjects—for example, to rule over men is better than to rule over wild beasts; for the work is better which is executed by better workmen, and where one man rules and another is ruled, they may be said to have a work); for in all things which form a composite whole and which are made up of parts, whether continuous or discrete, a distinction between the ruling and the subject element comes to light. Such a duality exists in living creatures, but not in them only; it originates in the constitution of the universe; even in things which have no life there is a ruling principle, as in a musical mode. But we are wandering from the subject. We will therefore restrict ourselves to the living creature, which, in the first place, consists of soul and body: and of these two, the one is by nature the ruler, and the other the subject. But then we must look for the intentions of nature in things which retain their nature, and not in things which are corrupted. And therefore we must study the man who is in the most perfect state both of body and soul, for in him we shall see the true relation of the two; although in bad or corrupted natures the body will often appear to rule

over the soul, because they are in an evil and unnatural condition. At all events we may firstly observe in living creatures both a despotical and a constitutional rule; for the soul rules the body with a despotical rule, whereas the intellect rules the appetites with a constitutional and royal rule. And it is clear that the rule of the soul over the body, and of the mind and the rational element over the passionate, is natural and expedient; whereas the equality of the two or the rule of the inferior is always hurtful. The same holds good of animals in relation to men; for tame animals have a better nature than wild, and all tame animals are better off when they are ruled by man; for then they are preserved. Again, the male is by nature superior, and the female inferior; and the one rules, and the other is ruled; this principle, of necessity, extends to all mankind. Where then there is such a difference as that between soul and body, or between men and animals (as in the case of those whose business is to use their body, and who can do nothing better), the lower sort are by nature slaves, and it is better for them as for all inferiors that they should be under the rule of a master. For he who can be, and therefore is, another's, and he who participates in rational principle enough to apprehend, but not to have, such a principle, is a slave by nature. Whereas the lower animals cannot even apprehend a principle, they obey their instincts. And indeed the use made of slaves and of tame animals is not very different; for both with their bodies minister to the needs of life. Nature would like to distinguish between the bodies of freemen and slaves, making the one strong for servile labour, the other upright, and although useless for such services, useful for political life in the arts both of war and peace. But the opposite often happens—that some have the souls and others have the bodies of freemen. And doubtless if men differed from one another in the mere forms of their bodies as much as the statues of the Gods do from men, all would acknowledge that the inferior class should be slaves of the superior. And if this is true of the body, how much more just that a similar distinction should exist in the soul? but the beauty of the body is seen, whereas the beauty of the soul is not seen. It is clear, then, that some men are by nature free, and others slaves, and that for these latter slavery is both expedient and right.

But that those who take the opposite view have in a certain way right on their side, may be easily seen. For the words slavery and slave are used in two senses. There is a slave or slavery by law as well as by nature. The law of which I speak is a sort of convention—the law by which whatever is taken in war is supposed to belong to the victors. But this right many jurists impeach, as they would an orator who brought forward an unconstitutional measure: they detest the notion that, because one man has the power of doing violence and is superior in brute strength, another shall be his slave and subject. Even among philosophers there is a difference of opinion. The origin of the dispute, and what makes the views invade each other's territory, is as follows: in some sense virtue, when furnished with means, has actually the greatest power of exercising force: and as superior power is only found where there is superior excellence of some kind, power seems to imply virtue, and the dispute to be simply one about justice (for it is due to one party identifying justice with goodwill, while the other identifies it with the mere rule of the stronger). If these views are thus set out separately, the other views have no force or plausibility against the view that the superior in virtue ought to rule, or be master. Others, clinging, as they think, simply to a principle of justice (for law and custom are a sort of justice), assume that slavery in accordance with the custom of war is justified by law, but at the same moment they deny this. For what if the cause of the war be unjust? And again, no one would ever say that he is a slave who is unworthy to be a slave. Were this the case, men of the highest rank would be slaves and the children of slaves if they or their parents chance to have been taken captive and sold. Wherefore Hellenes do not like to call Hellenes slaves, but confine the term to barbarians. Yet, in using this language, they really mean the natural slave of whom we spoke at first; for it must be admitted that some are slaves everywhere, others nowhere. The same principle applies to nobility. Hellenes regard themselves as noble everywhere, and not only in their own country, but they deem the barbarians noble only when at home, thereby implying that there are two sorts of nobility and freedom, the one absolute, the other relative. The Helen of Theodectes says:

Who would presume to call me servant who am on both sides sprung from the stem of the Gods?

What does this mean but that they distinguish freedom and slavery, noble and humble birth, by the two principles of good and evil? They think that as men and animals beget men and animals, so from good men a good man springs. But this is what nature, though she may intend it, cannot always accomplish.

We see then that there is some foundation for this difference of opinion, and that all are not either slaves by nature or freemen by nature, and also that there is in some cases a marked distinction between the two classes, rendering it expedient and right for the one to be slaves and the others to be masters: the one practising obedience, the others exercising the authority and lordship which nature intended them to have. The abuse of this authority is injurious to both; for the interests of part and whole, of body and soul, are the same, and the slave is a part of the master, a living but separated part of his bodily frame. Hence, where the relation of master and slave between them is natural they are friends and have a common interest, but where it rests merely on law and force the reverse is true.

CRITIQUE OF PLATO'S
REPUBLIC

Our purpose is to consider what form of political community is best of all for those who are most able to realize their ideal of life. We must therefore examine not only this but other constitutions, both such as actually exist in well-governed states, and any theoretical forms which are held in esteem; that what is good and useful may be brought to light. And let no one suppose that in seeking for something beyond them we are anxious to make a sophistical display at any cost; we only undertake this inquiry because all the constitutions with which we are acquainted are faulty.

We will begin with the natural beginning of the subject. Three alternatives are conceivable: The members of a state must either have (1) all things or (2) nothing in common, or (3) some things in common and some not. That they should have nothing in common is clearly impossible, for the constitution is a community, and must at any rate have a common place—one city will be in one place, and the citizens are those who share in that one city. But should a well-ordered state have all things, as far as may be, in common, or some only and not others? For the citizens might conceivably have wives and children and property in common, as Socrates proposes in the *Republic* of Plato. Which is better, our present condition, or the proposed new order of society?

There are many difficulties in the community of women. And the principle on which Socrates rests the necessity of such an institution evidently is not established by his arguments. Further, as a means to the end which he ascribes to the state, the scheme, taken literally, is impracticable, and how we are to interpret it is nowhere precisely stated. I am speaking of the premiss from which the argument of Socrates proceeds, "that the greater the unity of the state the better." Is it not obvious that a state may at length attain such a degree of unity as to be no longer a state?—since the nature of a state is to be a plurality, and in tending to greater unity, from being a state, it becomes a family, and from being a family, an individual; for the family may be said to be more than the state, and the individual than the family. So that we ought not to attain this greatest unity even if we could, for it would be the destruction of the state. Again, a state is not made up only of so many men, but of different kinds of men; for similars do not constitute a state. It is not like a military alliance. The usefulness of the latter depends upon its quantity even where there is no difference in quality (for mutual protection is the end aimed at), just as a greater weight of anything is more useful than a less (in like manner, a state differs from a nation, when the nation has not its population organized in villages, but lives an Arcadian sort of life); but the elements out of which a unity is to be formed differ in kind. Wherefore the principle of

compensation, as I have already remarked in the *Ethics,* is the salvation of states. Even among freemen and equals this is a principle which must be maintained, for they cannot all rule together, but must change at the end of a year or some other period of time or in some order of succession. The result is that upon this plan they all govern; just as if shoemakers and carpenters were to exchange their occupations, and the same persons did not always continue shoemakers and carpenters. And since it is better that this should be so in politics as well, it is clear that while there should be continuance of the same persons in power where this is possible, yet where this is not possible by reason of the natural equality of the citizens, and at the same time it is just that all should share in the government (whether to govern be a good thing or a bad), an approximation to this is that equals should in turn retire from office and should, apart from official position, be treated alike. Thus the one party rule and the others are ruled in turn, as if they were no longer the same persons. In like manner when they hold office there is a variety in the offices held. Hence it is evident that a city is not by nature one in that sense which some persons affirm; and that what is said to be the greatest good of cities is in reality their destruction; but surely the good of things must be that which preserves them. Again, in another point of view, this extreme unification of the state is clearly not good; for a family is more self-sufficing than an individual, and a city than a family, and a city only comes into being when the community is large enough to be self-sufficing. If then self-sufficiency is to be desired, the lesser degree of unity is more desirable than the greater.

PROPERTY: EQUALITY OR INEQUALITY?

Next let us consider what should be our arrangements about property: should the citizens of the perfect state have their possessions in common or not? This question may be discussed separately from the enactments about women and children. Even supposing that the women and children belong to individuals, according to the custom which is at present universal, may there not be an advantage in having and using possessions in common? Three cases are possible: (1) the soil may be appropriated, but the produce may be thrown for consumption into the common stock; and this is the practice of some nations. Or (2), the soil may be common, and may be cultivated in common, but the produce divided among individuals for their private use; this is a form of common property which is said to exist among certain barbarians. Or (3), the soil and the produce may be alike common.

When the husbandmen are not the owners, the case will be different and easier to deal with; but when they till the ground for themselves the question of ownership will give a world of trouble. If they do not share equally in enjoyments and toils, those who labour much and get little will necessarily complain of those who labour little and receive or consume much. But indeed there is always a difficulty in men living together and having all human relations in common, but especially in their having common property. The partnerships of fellow-travelers are an example to the point; for they generally fall out over everyday matters and quarrel about any trifle which turns up. So with servants: we are most liable to take offense at those with whom we most frequently come into contact in daily life.

These are only some of the disadvantages which attend the community of property; the present arrangement, if improved as it might be by good customs and laws, would be far better, and would have the advantages of both systems. Property should be in a certain sense common, but, as a general rule, private; for, when every one has a distinct interest, men will not complain of one another, and they will make more progress, because every one will be attending to his own business. And yet by reason of goodness, and in respect of use, "Friends," as the proverb says, "will have all things common." Even now there are traces of such a principle, showing that it is not impracticable, but, in well-ordered states, exists already to a certain extent and may be carried further. For, although every man has his own property, some things he will place at the disposal of his friends, while of others he shares the use with them. The Lacedaemonians, for example, use one another's slaves, and horses, and dogs, as if they were their own; and when they lack provisions on

a journey, they appropriate what they find in the fields throughout the country. It is clearly better that property should be private, but the use of it common; and the special business of the legislator is to create in men this benevolent disposition. Again, how immeasurably greater is the pleasure, when a man feels a thing to be his own; for surely the love of self is a feeling implanted by nature and not given in vain, although selfishness is rightly censured; this, however, is not the mere love of self, but the love of self in excess, like the miser's love of money; for all, or almost all, men love money and other such objects in a measure. And further, there is the greatest pleasure in doing a kindness or service to friends or guests or companions, which can only be rendered when a man has private property. These advantages are lost by excessive unification of the state. The exhibition of two virtues, besides, is visibly annihilated in such a state: first, temperance towards women (for it is an honourable action to abstain from another's wife for temperance sake); secondly, liberality in the matter of property. No one, when men have all things in common, will any longer set an example of liberality or do any liberal action; for liberality consists in the use which is made of property.

Such legislation may have a specious appearance of benevolence; men readily listen to it, and are easily induced to believe that in some wonderful manner everybody will become everybody's friend, especially when some one is heard denouncing the evils now existing in states, suits about contracts, convictions for perjury, flatteries of rich men and the like, which are said to arise out of the possession of private property. These evils, however, are due to a very different cause—the wickedness of human nature. Indeed, we see that there is much more quarrelling among those who have all things in common, though there are not many of them when compared with the vast numbers who have private property.

Again, we ought to reckon, not only the evils from which the citizens will be saved, but also the advantages which they will lose. The life which they are to lead appears to be quite impracticable. The error of Socrates must be attributed to the false notion of unity from which he starts. Unity there should be, both of the family and of the state, but in some respects only. For there is a point at which a state may attain such a degree of unity as to be no longer a state, or at which, without actually ceasing to exist, it will become an inferior state, like harmony passing into unison, or rhythm which has been reduced to a single foot. The state, as I was saying, is a plurality, which should be united and made into a community by education; and it is strange that the author of a system of education which he thinks will make the state virtuous should expect to improve his citizens by regulations of this sort, and not by philosophy or by customs and laws, like those which prevail at Sparta and Crete respecting common meals, whereby the legislator has made property common. Let us remember that we should not disregard the experience of ages; in the multitude of years these things, if they were good, would certainly not have been unknown; for almost everything has been found out, although sometimes they are not put together; in other cases men do not use the knowledge which they have. Great light would be thrown on this subject if we could see such a form of government in the actual process of construction; for the legislator could not form a state at all without distributing and dividing its constituents into associations for common meals, and into phratries and tribes. But all this legislation ends only in forbidding agriculture to the guardians, a prohibition which the Lacedaemonians try to enforce already.

But, indeed, Socrates has not said, nor is it easy to decide, what in such a community will be the general form of the state. The citizens who are not guardians are the majority, and about them nothing has been determined: are the husbandmen, too, to have their property in common? Or is each individual to have his own? and are the wives and children to be individual or common? If, like the guardians, they are to have all things in common, in what do they differ from them, or what will they gain by submitting to their government? Or, upon what principle would they submit, unless indeed the governing class adopt the ingenious policy of the Cretans, who give their slaves the same institutions as their own, but forbid them gymnastic exercises and the possession of arms. If, on the other hand, the infe-

rior classes are to be like other cities in respect of marriage and property, what will be the form of the community? Must it not contain two states in one, each hostile to the other? He makes the guardians into a mere occupying garrison, while the husbandmen and artisans and the rest are the real citizens. But if so the suits and quarrels, and all the evils which Socrates affirms to exist in other states, will exist equally among them. He says indeed that, having so good an education, the citizens will not need many laws, for example laws about the city or about the markets; but then he confines his education to the guardians. Again, he makes the husbandmen owners of the property upon condition of their paying a tribute. But in that case they are likely to be much more unmanageable and conceited than the Helots, or Penestae, or slaves in general. And whether community of wives and property be necessary for the lower equally with the higher class or not, and the questions akin to this, what will be the education, form of government, laws of the lower class, Socrates has nowhere determined: neither is it easy to discover this, nor is their character of small importance if the common life of the guardians is to be maintained.

Again, if Socrates makes the women common, and retains private property, the men will see to the fields, but who will see to the house? And who will do so if the agricultural class have both their property and their wives in common? Once more: it is absurd to argue, from the analogy of the animals, that men and women should follow the same pursuits, for animals have not to manage a household. The government, too, as constituted by Socrates, contains elements of danger; for he makes the same persons always rule. And if this is often a cause of disturbance among the meaner sort, how much more among high-spirited warriors? But that the persons whom he makes rulers must be the same is evident; for the gold which the God mingles in the souls of men is not at one time given to one, at another time to another, but always to the same: as he says, "God mingles gold in some, and silver in others, from their very birth; but brass and iron in those who are meant to be artisans and husbandmen." Again, he deprives the guardians even of happiness, and says that the legislator ought to make the whole state happy. But the whole cannot be happy unless most, or all, or some of its parts enjoy happiness. In this respect happiness is not like the even principle in numbers, which may exist only in the whole, but in neither of the parts; not so happiness. And if the guardians are not happy, who are? Surely not the artisans, or the common people. The Republic of which Socrates discourses has all these difficulties, and others quite as great.

There is another point: Should not the amount of property be defined in some way which differs from this by being clearer? For Socrates says that a man should have so much property as will enable him to live temperately, which is only a way of saying "to live well"; this is too general a conception. Further, a man may live temperately and yet miserably. A better definition would be that a man must have so much property as will enable him to live not only temperately but liberally; if the two are parted, liberality will combine with luxury; temperance will be associated with toil. For liberality and temperance are the only eligible qualities which have to do with the use of property. A man cannot use property with mildness or courage, but temperately and liberally he may; and therefore the practice of these virtues is inseparable from property. There is an inconsistency, too, in equalizing the property and not regulating the number of the citizens; the population is to remain unlimited, and he thinks that it will be sufficiently equalized by a certain number of marriages being unfruitful, however many are born to others, because he finds this to be the case in existing states. But greater care will be required than now; for among ourselves, whatever may be the number of citizens, the property is always distributed among them, and therefore no one is in want; but, if the property were incapable of division as in the *Laws,* the supernumeraries, whether few or many, would get nothing. One would have thought that it was even more necessary to limit population than property; and that the limit should be fixed by calculating the chances of mortality in the children, and of sterility in married persons. The neglect of this subject, which in existing states is so common, is a never-failing cause of poverty among the citizens; and poverty is the parent of revolution and crime. Pheidon the Corinthian, who was one of the most ancient legislators, thought that the families and the number of citizens ought to remain the same, although originally all the lots may have been of different sizes: but in the *Laws* the opposite principle is maintained. What in our opinion is the right arrangement will have to be explained hereafter.

Other constitutions have been proposed; some by private persons, others by philosophers and statesmen, which all come nearer to established or existing ones than either of Plato's. No one else has introduced such novelties as the community of women and children, or public tables for women: other legislators begin with what is necessary. In the opinion of some, the regulation of property is the chief point of all, that being the question upon which all revolutions turn. This danger was recognized by Phaleas of Chalcedon, who was the first to affirm that the citizens of a state ought to have equal possessions. He thought that in a new colony the equalization might be accomplished without difficulty, not so easily when a state was already established; and that then the shortest way of compassing the desired end would be for the rich to give and not to receive marriage portions, and for the poor not to give but to receive them.

Plato in the *Laws* was of opinion that, to a certain extent, accumulation should be allowed, forbidding, as I have already observed, any citizen to possess more than five times the minimum qualification. But those who make such laws should remember what they are apt to forget—that the legislator who fixes the amount of property should also fix the number of children; for, if the children are too many for the property, the law must be broken. And, besides the violation of the law, it is a bad thing that many from being rich should become poor; for men of ruined fortunes are sure to stir up revolutions. That the equilization of property exercises an influence on political society was clearly understood even by some of the old legislators. Laws were made by Solon and others prohibiting an individual from possessing as much land as he pleased; and there are other laws in states which forbid the sale of property: among the Locrians, for example, there is a law that a man is not to sell his property unless he can prove unmistakably that some misfortune has befallen him. Again, there have been laws which enjoin the preservation of the original lots. Such a law existed in the island of Leucas, and the abrogation of it made the constitution too democratic, for the rulers no longer had the prescribed qualification. Again, where there is equality of property, the amount may be either too large or too small, and the possessor may be living either in luxury or penury. Clearly, then, the legislator ought not only to aim at the equalization of properties, but at moderation in their amount. Further, if he prescribe this moderate amount equally to all, he will be no nearer the mark; for it is not the possessions but the desires of mankind which require to be equalized, and this is impossible, unless a sufficient education is provided by the laws. But Phaleas will probably reply that this is precisely what he means; and that, in his opinion, there ought to be in states, not only equal property, but equal education. Still he should tell precisely what he means; and what, in his opinion, there ought to be in having one and the same for all, if it is of a sort that predisposes men to avarice, or ambition, or both. Moreover, civil troubles arise, not only out of the inequality of property, but out of the inequality of honour, though in opposite ways. For the common people quarrel about the inequality of property, the higher class about the equality of honour; as the poet says—

The bad and good alike in honour share.

There are crimes of which the motive is want; and for these Phaleas expects to find a cure in the equalization of property, which will take away from a man the temptation to be a highwayman, because he is hungry or cold. But want is not the sole incentive to crime; men also wish to enjoy themselves and not to be in a state of desire—they wish to cure some desire, going beyond the necessities of life, which preys upon them; nay, this is not the only reason—they may desire superfluities in order to enjoy pleasures unaccompanied with pain, and therefore they commit crimes.

Now what is the cure of these three disorders? Of the first, moderate possessions and

occupation; of the second, habits of temperance; as to the third, if any desire pleasures which depend on themselves, they will find the satisfaction of their desires nowhere but in philosophy; for all other pleasures we are dependent on others. The fact is that the greatest crimes are caused by excess and not by necessity. Men do not become tyrants in order that they may not suffer cold; and hence great is the honour bestowed, not on him who kills a thief, but on him who kills a tyrant. Thus we see that the institutions of Phaleas avail only against petty crimes.

There is another objection to them. They are chiefly designed to promote the internal welfare of the state. But the legislator should consider also its relation to neighbouring nations, and to all who are outside of it. The government must be organized with a view to military strength; and of this he has said not a word. And so with respect to property: there should not only be enough to supply the internal wants of the state, but also to meet dangers coming from without. The property of the state should not be so large that more powerful neighbours may be tempted by it, while the owners are unable to repel the invaders; nor yet so small that the state is unable to maintain a war even against states of equal power, and of the same character. Phaleas has not laid down any rule; but we should bear in mind that abundance of wealth is an advantage. The best limit will probably be, that a more powerful neighbour must have no inducement to go to war with you by reason of the excess of your wealth, but only such as he would have had if you had possessed less. There is a story that Eubulus, when Autophradates was going to besiege Atarneus, told him to consider how long the operation would take, and then reckon up the cost which would be incurred in the time. "For," said he, "I am willing for a smaller sum than that to leave Atarneus at once." These words of Eubulus made an impression on Autophradates, and he desisted from the siege.

The equalization of property is one of the things that tend to prevent the citizens from quarrelling. Not that the gain in this direction is very great. For the nobles will be dissatisfied because they think themselves worthy of more than an equal share of honours; and this is often found to be a cause of sedition and revolution. And the avarice of mankind is insatiable; at one time two obols was pay enough; but now, when this sum has become customary, men always want more and more without end; for it is of the nature of desire not to be satisfied, and most men live only for the gratification of it. The beginning of reform is not so much to equalize property as to train the nobler sort of natures not to desire more, and to prevent the lower from getting more; that is to say, they must be kept down, but not ill-treated. Besides, the equalization proposed by Phaleas is imperfect; for he only equalizes land, whereas a man may be rich also in slaves, and cattle, and money, and in the abundance of what are called his movables. Now either all these things must be equalized, or some limit must be imposed on them, or they must all be let alone. It would appear that Phaleas is legislating for a small city only, if, as he supposes, all the artisans are to be public slaves and not to form a supplementary part of the body of citizens. But if there is a law that artisans are to be public slaves, it should only apply to those engaged on public works, as at Epidamnus, or at Athens on the plan which Diophantus once introduced.

From these observations any one may judge how far Phaleas was wrong or right in his ideas.

CITIZENSHIP

He who would inquire into the essence and attributes of various kinds of governments must first of all determine "What is a state?" At present this is a disputed question. Some say that the state has done a certain act; others, no, not the state, but the oligarchy or the tyrant. And the legislator or statesman is concerned entirely with the state; a constitution or government being an arrangement of the inhabitants of a state. But a state is composite, like any other whole made up of many parts;—these are the citizens, who compose it. It is evident, therefore, that we must begin by asking, "Who is the citizen," and what is the meaning of the term? For here again there may be a difference of opinion. He who is a citizen in a democracy will often not be a citizen in an oligarchy. Leaving out of consideration those who have been made citizens, or who have obtained the name of citizen in any

other accidental manner, we may say, first that a citizen is not a citizen because he lives in a certain place, for resident aliens and slaves share in the place; nor is he a citizen who has no legal right except that of suing and being sued; for this right may be enjoyed under the provisions of a treaty. Nay, resident aliens in many places do not possess even such rights completely, for they are obliged to have a patron, so that they do but imperfectly participate in citizenship, and we call them citizens only in a qualified sense, as we might apply the term to children who are too young to be on the register, or to old men who have been relieved from state duties. Of these we do not say quite simply that they are citizens, but add in the one case that they are not of age, and in the other, that they are past the age, or something of that sort; the precise expression is immaterial, for our meaning is clear. Similar difficulties to those which I have mentioned may be raised and answered about deprived citizens and about exiles. But the citizen whom we are seeking to define is a citizen in the strictest sense, against whom no such exception can be taken, and his special characteristic is that he shares in the administration of justice, and in offices. Now of offices some are discontinuous, and the same persons are not allowed to hold them twice, or can only hold them after a fixed interval; others have no limit of time—for example, the office of dicast or ecclesiast.[1] It may, indeed, be argued that these are not magistrates at all, and that their functions give them no share in the government. But surely it is ridiculous to say that those who have the supreme power do not govern. Let us not dwell further upon this, which is a purely verbal question; what we want is a common term including both dicast and ecclesiast. Let us, for the sake of distinction, call it "indefinite office," and we will assume that those who share in such office are citizens. This is the most comprehensive definition of a citizen, and best suits all those who are generally so called.

But we must not forget that things of which the underlying principles differ in

---

[1] "Dicast" = juryman and judge in one: "ecclesiast" = member of the ecclesia or assembly of the citizens.

kind, one of them being first, another second, another third, have, when regarded in this relation, nothing, or hardly anything, worth mentioning in common. Now we see that governments differ in kind, and that some of them are prior and that others are posterior; those which are faulty or perverted are necessarily posterior to those which are perfect. (What we mean by perversion will be hereafter explained.) The citizen then of necessity differs under each form of government; and our definition is best adapted to the citizen of a democracy; but not necessarily to other states. For in some states the people are not acknowledged, nor have they any regular assembly, but only extraordinary ones; and suits are distributed by sections among the magistrates. At Lacedaemon, for instance, the Ephors determine suits about contracts, which they distribute among themselves, while the elders are judges of homicide, and other causes are decided by other magistrates. A similar principle prevails at Carthage; there certain magistrates decide all causes. We may, indeed, modify our definition of the citizen so as to include these states. In them it is the holder of a definite, not of an indefinite office, who legislates and judges, and to some or all such holders of definite offices is reserved the right of deliberating or judging about some things or about all things. The conception of the citizen now begins to clear up.

He who has the power to take part in the deliberative or judicial administration of any state is said by us to be a citizen of that state; and, speaking generally, a state is a body of citizens sufficing for the purposes of life.

There is a point nearly allied to the preceding: Whether the virtue of a good man and a good citizen is the same or not. But, before entering on this discussion, we must certainly first obtain some general notion of the virtue of the citizen. Like the sailor, the citizen is a member of a community. Now, sailors have different functions, for one of them is a rower, another a pilot, and a third a look-out man, a fourth is described by some similar term, and while the precise definition of each individual's virtue applies exclusively to him, there is, at the same time, a common definition applicable to them all. For they have all of them a common object, which is safety in navigation. Similarly, one citizen differs from another, but the salvation of the community is the common business of them all. This community is the constitution; the virtue of the citizen must therefore be relative to the constitution of which he is a member. If, then, there are many forms of government, it is evident that there is not one single virtue of the good citizen which is perfect virtue. But we say that the good man is he who has one single virtue which is perfect virtue. Hence it is evident that the good citizen need not of necessity possess the virtue which makes a good man.

The same question may also be approached by another road, from a consideration of the best constitution. If the state cannot be entirely composed of good men, and yet each citizen is expected to do his own business well, and must therefore have virtue, still, inasmuch as all the citizens cannot be alike, the virtue of the citizen and of the good man cannot coincide. All must have the virtue of the good citizen—thus, and thus only, can the state be perfect; but they will not have the virtue of a good man, unless we assume that in the good state all the citizens must be good.

Again, the state, as composed of unlikes, may be compared to the living being: as the first elements into which a living being is resolved are soul and body, as soul is made up of rational principle and appetite, the family of husband and wife, property of master and slave, so of all these, as well as other dissimilar elements, the state is composed; and, therefore, the virtue of all the citizens cannot possibly be the same, any more than the excellence of the leader of a chorus is the same as that of the performer who stands by his side. I have said enough to show why the two kinds of virtue cannot be absolutely and always the same.

But will there then be no case in which the virtue of the good citizen and the virtue of the good man coincide? To this we answer that the good *ruler* is a good and wise man, and that he who would be a statesman must be a wise man. And some persons say that even the education of the ruler should be of a special kind; for are not the children of kings instructed in riding and military exercises? As Euripides says:

No subtle arts for me, but what the state requires.

As though there were a special education needed by a ruler. If then the virtue of a good ruler is the same as that of a good man, and we assume further that the subject is a citizen as well as the ruler, the virtue of the good citizen and the virtue of the good man cannot be absolutely the same, although in some cases they may; for the virtue of a ruler differs from that of a citizen. It was the sense of this difference which made Jason say that "he felt hungry when he was not a tyrant," meaning that he could not endure to live in a private station. But, on the other hand, it may be argued that men are praised for knowing both how to rule and how to obey, and he is said to be a citizen of approved virtue who is able to do both. Now if we suppose the virtue of a good man to be that which rules, and the virtue of the citizen to include ruling and obeying, it cannot be said that they are equally worthy of praise. Since, then, it is sometimes thought that the ruler and the ruled must learn different things and not the same, but that the citizen must know and share in them both, the inference is obvious. There is, indeed, the rule of a master, which is concerned with menial offices—the master need not know how to perform these, but may employ others, in the execution of them: the other would be degrading; and by the other I mean the power actually to do menial duties, which vary much in character and are executed by various classes of slaves, such, for example, as handicraftsmen, who, as their name signifies, live by the labour of their hands:—under these the mechanic is included. Hence in ancient times, and among some nations, the working classes had no share in the government—a privilege which they only acquired under the extreme democracy. Certainly the good man and the statesman and the good citizen ought not to learn the crafts of inferiors except for their own occasional use; if they habitually practice them, there will cease to be a distinction between master and slave.

This is not the rule of which we are speaking; but there is a rule of another kind, which is exercised over freemen and equals by birth—a constitutional rule, which the ruler must learn by obeying, as he would learn the duties of a general of cavalry by being under the orders of a general of cavalry, or the duties of a general of infantry by being under the orders of a general of infantry, and by having had the command of a regiment and of a company. It has been well said that "he who has never learned to obey cannot be a good commander." The two are not the same, but the good citizen ought to be capable of both; he should know how to govern like a freeman, and how to obey like a freeman—these are the virtues of a citizen. And, although the temperance and justice of a ruler are distinct from those of a subject, the virtue of a good man will include both; for the virtue of the good man who is free and also a subject, e.g. his justice, will not be one but will comprise distinct kinds, the one qualifying him to rule, the other to obey, and differing as the temperance and courage of men and women differ. For a man would be thought a coward if he had no more courage than a courageous woman, and a woman would be thought loquacious if she imposed no more restraint on her conversation than the good man; and indeed their part in the management of the household is different, for the duty of the one is to acquire, and of the other to preserve. Practical wisdom only is characteristic of the ruler: it would seem that all other virtues must equally belong to ruler and subject. The virtue of the subject is certainly not wisdom, but only true opinion; he may be compared to the maker of the flute, while his master is like the flute-player or user of the flute.

From these considerations may be gathered the answer to the question, whether the virtue of the good man is the same as that of the good citizen, or different, and how far the same, and how far different.

There still remains one more question about the citizen: Is he only a true citizen who has a share of office, or is the mechanic to be included? If they who hold no office are to be deemed citizens, not every citizen can have this virtue of ruling and obeying; for this man is a citizen. And if none of the lower class are citizens, in which part of the state are they to be placed? For they are not resident aliens, and they are not foreigners. May we not reply, that as far as this objection goes there is no more absurdity in excluding them than in excluding slaves and freedmen from any of the above-mentioned classes? It must be admitted that we cannot consider all those to be citizens who are necessary to the existence of the state; for example, children are not citizens equally with grown-up men, who are citizens absolutely, but children, not being grown up, are only citizens on a certain assumption. Nay, in ancient times, and among some nations, the artisan class *were* slaves or foreigners, and therefore the majority of them are so now. The best form of state will not admit them to citizenship; but if they are admitted, then our definition of the virtue of a citizen will not apply to every citizen, not to every free man as such, but only to those who are freed from necessary services. The necessary people are either slaves who minister to the wants of individuals, or mechanics and labourers who are the servants of the community. These reflections carried a little further will explain their position; and indeed what has been said already is of itself, when understood, explanation enough.

Since there are many forms of government there must be many varieties of citizens, and especially of citizens who are subjects; so that under some governments the mechanic and the labourer will be citizens, but not in others, as, for example, in aristocracy or the so-called government of the best (if there be such an one), in which honours are given according to virtue and merit; for no man can practise virtue who is living the life of a mechanic or labourer. In oligarchies the qualification for office is high, and therefore no labourer can ever be a citizen; but a mechanic may, for an actual majority of them are rich. At Thebes there was a law that no man could hold office who had not retired from business for ten years. But in many states the law goes to the length of admitting aliens; for in some democracies a man is a citizen though his mother only be a citizen; and a similar principle is applied to illegitimate children; the law is relaxed when there is a dearth of population. But when the number of citizens increases, first the children of a male or a female slave are excluded; then those whose mothers only are citizens; and at last the right of citizenship is confined to those whose fathers and mothers are both citizens.

Hence, as is evident, there are different kinds of citizens; and he is a citizen in the highest sense who shares in the honours of the state. Compare Homer's words "like some dishonoured stranger"; he who is excluded from the honours of the state is no better than an alien. But when this exclusion is concealed, then the object is that the privileged class may deceive their fellow inhabitants.

As to the question whether the virtue of the good man is the same as that of the good citizen, the considerations already adduced prove that in some states the good man and the good citizen are the same, and in others different. When they are the same it is not every citizen who is a good man, but only the statesman and those who have or may have, alone or in conjunction with others, the conduct of public affairs.

As in other natural compounds the conditions of a composite whole are not necessarily organic parts of it, so in a state or in any other combination forming a unity not everything is a part, which is a necessary condition. The members of an association have necessarily some one thing the same and common to all, in which they share equally or unequally; for example, food or land or any other thing. But where there are two things of which one is a means and the other an end, they have nothing in common except that the one receives what the other produces. Such, for example, is the relation in which workmen and tools stand to their work; the house and the builder have nothing in common, but the art of the builder is for the sake of the house. And so states require property, but property, even though living beings are included in it, is no part of a state; for a state is not a community of living beings only, but a community of equals, aiming at the best life possible. Now, whereas happiness is the highest good, being a realization and perfect practice of virtue, which some can attain, while others have little or none of it, the various qualities of men are clearly the reason why there are various kinds of states and many forms of government; for different men seek after happiness in different ways and by different means, and so make for themselves different modes of life and forms of government. We must see also how many things are indispensable to the existence of a state, for what we call the parts of a state will be found among the indispensables. Let us then enumerate the functions of a state, and we shall easily elicit what we want:

First, there must be food; secondly, arts, for life requires many instruments; thirdly, there must be arms, for the members of a community have need of them, and in their own hands, too, in order to maintain authority both against disobedient subjects and against external assailants; fourthly, there must be a certain amount of revenue, both for internal needs, and for the purposes of war; fifthly, or rather first, there must be a care of religion, which is commonly called worship; sixthly, and most necessary of all, there must be a power of deciding what is for the public interest, and what is just in men's dealings with one another.

These are the services which every state may be said to need. For a state is not a mere aggregate of persons, but a union of them sufficing for the purposes of life; and if any of these things be wanting, it is as we maintain impossible that the community can be absolutely self-sufficing. A state then should be framed with a view to the fulfilment of these functions. There must be husbandmen to procure food, and artisans, and a warlike and a wealthy class, and priests, and judges to decide what is necessary and expedient.

Having determined these points, we have in the next place to consider whether all ought to share in every sort of occupation. Shall every man be at once husbandman, artisan, councillor, judge, or shall we suppose the several occupations just mentioned assigned to different persons? or, thirdly, shall some employments be assigned to individuals and others common to all? The same arrangement, however, does not occur in every constitution; as we were saying, all may be shared by all, or not all by all, but only by some; and hence arise the differences of constitutions, for in democracies all share in all, in oligarchies the opposite practice prevails. Now, since we are here speaking of the best form of government, i.e. that under which the state will be most happy (and happiness, as has been already said, cannot exist without virtue), it clearly follows that in the state which is best governed and possesses men who are just

absolutely, and not merely relatively to the principle of the constitution, the citizens must not lead the life of mechanics or tradesmen, for such a life is ignoble, and inimical to virtue. Neither must they be husbandmen, since leisure is necessary both for the development of virtue and the performance of political duties.

Again, there is in a state a class of warriors, and another of councillors, who advise about the expedient and determine matters of law, and these seem in an especial manner parts of a state. Now, should these two classes be distinguished, or are both functions to be assigned to the same persons? Here again there is no difficulty in seeing that both functions will in one way belong to the same, in another, to different persons. To different persons in so far as these employments are suited to different primes of life, for the one requires wisdom and the other strength. But on the other hand, since it is an impossible thing that those who are able to use or to resist force should be willing to remain always in subjection, from this point of view the persons are the same; for those who carry arms can always determine the fate of the constitution. It remains therefore that both functions should be entrusted by the ideal constitution to the same persons, not, however, at the same time, but in the order prescribed by nature, who has given to young men strength and to older men wisdom. Such a distribution of duties will be expedient and also just, and is founded upon a principle of conformity to merit. Besides, the ruling class should be the owners of property, for they are citizens, and the citizens of a state should be in good circumstances; whereas mechanics or any other class which is not a producer of virtue have no share in the state. This follows from our first principle, for happiness cannot exist without virtue, and a city is not to be termed happy in regard to a portion of the citizens, but in regard to them all. And clearly property should be in their hands, since the husbandmen will of necessity be slaves or barbarian Perioeci.

Of the classes enumerated there remain only the priests, and the manner in which their office is to be regulated is obvious. No husbandman or mechanic should be appointed to it; for the Gods should receive honour from the citizens only. Now since the body of the citizens is divided into two classes, the warriors and the councillors, and it is beseeming that the worship of the Gods should be duly performed, and also a rest provided in their service for those who from age have given up active life, to the old men of these two classes should be assigned the duties of the priesthood.

We have shown what are the necessary conditions, and what the parts of a state: husbandmen, craftsmen, and labourers of all kinds are necessary to the existence of states, but the parts of the state are the warriors and councillors. And these are distinguished severally from one another, the distinction being in some cases permanent, in others not.

Since every political society is composed of rulers and subjects let us consider whether the relations of one to the other should interchange or be permanent. For the education of the citizens will necessarily vary with the answer given to this question. Now, if some men excelled others in the same degree in which gods and heroes are supposed to excel mankind in general (having in the first place a great advantage even in their bodies, and secondly in their minds), so that the superiority of the governors was undisputed and patent to their subjects, it would clearly be better that once for all the one class should rule and the others serve. But since this is unattainable, and kings have no marked superiority over their subjects, such as Scylax affirms to be found among the Indians, it is obviously necessary on many grounds that all the citizens alike should take their turn of governing and being governed. Equality consists in the same treatment of similar persons, and no government can stand which is not founded upon justice. For if the government be unjust every one in the country unites with the governed in the desire to have a revolution, and it is an impossibility that the members of the government can be so numerous as to be stronger than all their enemies put together. Yet that governors should excel their subjects is undeniable. How all this is to be effected, and in what way they will respectively share in the government, the legislator has to consider. The subject has been already mentioned. Nature herself has provided the distinction when she made a difference between old and young within the same species, of whom she fitted the one to govern and the other to be governed. No one takes offence at being governed when he is young, nor does he think himself better than his governors, especially if he will enjoy the same privilege when he reaches the required age.

We conclude that from one point of view governors and governed are identical, and from another different. And therefore their education must be the same and also different. For he who would learn to command well must, as men say, first of all learn to obey. As I observed in the first part of this treatise, there is one rule which is for the sake of the rulers and another rule which is for the sake of the ruled; the former is a despotic, the latter a free government. Some commands differ not in the thing commanded, but in the intention with which they are imposed. Wherefore, many apparently menial offices are an honour to the free youth by whom they are performed; for actions do not differ as honourable or dishonourable in themselves so much as in the end and intention of them. But since we say that the virtue of the citizen and ruler is the same as that of the good man, and that the same person must first be a subject and then a ruler, the legislator has to see that they become good men, and by what means this may be accomplished, and what is the end of the perfect life.

Now the soul of man is divided into two parts, one of which has a rational principle in itself, and the other, not having a rational principle in itself, is able to obey such a principle. And we call a man in any way good because he has the virtues of these two parts. In which of them the end is more likely to be found is no matter of doubt to those who adopt our division; for in the world both of nature and of art the inferior always exists for the sake of the better or superior, and the better or superior is that which has a rational principle. This principle, too, in our ordinary way of speaking, is divided into two kinds, for there is a practical and a speculative principle. This part, then, must evidently be similarly divided. And there must be a corresponding division of actions; the actions of the naturally better part are to be preferred by those who have it in their power to attain to two out of the three or to all, for that is always to every one the most eligible which is the highest attainable by him. The whole of life is further divided into two parts, business and leisure, war and peace, and of actions some aim at what is necessary and useful, and some at what is honourable. And the preference given to one or the other class of actions must necessarily be like the preference given to one or other part of the soul and its actions over the other; there must be war for the sake of peace, business for the sake of leisure, things useful and necessary for the sake of things honourable. All these points the statesman should keep in view when he frames his laws; he should consider the parts of the soul and their functions, and above all the better and the end; he should also remember the diversities of human lives and actions. For men must be able to engage in business and go to war, but leisure and peace are better; they must do what is necessary and indeed what is useful, but what is honourable is better. On such principles children and persons of every age which requires education should be trained. Whereas even the Hellenes of the present day who are reputed to be best governed, and the legislators who gave them their constitutions, do not appear to have framed their governments with a regard to the best end, or to have given them laws and education with a view to all the virtues, but in a vulgar spirit have fallen back on those which promised to be more useful and profitable. Many modern writers have taken a similar view: they commend the Lacedaemonian constitution, and praise the legislator for making conquest and war his sole aim, a doctrine which may be refuted by argument and has long ago been refuted by facts. For most men desire empire in the hope of accumulating the goods of fortune; and on this ground Thibron and all those who have written about the Lacedaemonian constitution have praised their legislator, because the Lacedaemonians, by being trained to meet dangers, gained great power. But surely they are not a happy people now that their empire has passed away, nor was their legislator right. How ridiculous is the result, if, while they are continuing in the

observance of his laws and no one interferes with them, they have lost the better part of life! These writers further err about the sort of government which the legislator should approve, for the government of freemen is nobler and implies more virtue than despotic government. Neither is a city to be deemed happy or a legislator to be praised because he trains his citizens to conquer and obtain dominion over their neighbours, for there is great evil in this. On a similar principle any citizen who could, should obviously try to obtain the power in his own state—the crime which the Lacedaemonians accuse king Pausanias of attempting, although he had so great honour already. No such principle and no law having this object is either statesmanlike or useful or right. For the same things are best both for individuals and for states, and these are the things which the legislator ought to implant in the minds of his citizens. Neither should men study war with a view to the enslavement of those who do not deserve to be enslaved; but first of all they should provide against their own enslavement, and in the second place obtain empire for the good of the governed, and not for the sake of exercising a general despotism, and in the third place they should seek to be masters only over those who deserve to be slaves. Facts, as well as arguments, prove that the legislator should direct all his military and other measures to the provision of leisure and the establishment of peace. For most of these military states are safe only while they are at war, but fall when they have acquired their empire; like unused iron they lose their temper in time of peace. And for this the legislator is to blame, he never having taught them how to lead the life of peace.

POLITICAL SYSTEMS

Having determined these questions, we have next to consider whether there is only one form of government or many, and if many, what they are, and how many, and what are the differences between them.

A constitution is the arrangement of magistracies in a state, especially of the highest of all. The government is everywhere sovereign in the state, and the constitution is in fact the government. For example, in democracies the people are supreme, but in oligarchies, the few; and, therefore, we say that these two forms of government also are different: and so in other cases.

First, let us consider what is the purpose of a state, and how many forms of government there are by which human society is regulated. We have already said, in the first part of this treatise, when discussing household management and the rule of a master, that man is by nature a political animal. And therefore, men, even when they do not require one another's help, desire to live together; not but that they are also brought together by their common interests in proportion as they severally attain to any measure of well-being. This is certainly the chief end, both of individuals and of states. And also for the sake of mere life (in which there is possibly some noble element so long as the evils of existence do not greatly overbalance the good) mankind meet together and maintain the political community. And we all see that men cling to life even at the cost of enduring great misfortune, seeming to find in life a natural sweetness and happiness.

There is no difficulty in distinguishing the various kinds of authority; they have been often defined already in discussions outside the school. The rule of a master, although the slave by nature and the master by nature have in reality the same interests, is nevertheless exercised primarily with a view to the interest of the master, but accidentally considers the slave, since, if the slave perish, the rule of the master perishes with him. On the other hand, the government of a wife and children and of a household, which we have called household management, is exercised in the first instance for the good of the governed or for the common good of both parties, but essentially for the good of the governed, as we see to be the case in medicine, gymnastic, and the arts in general, which are only accidentally concerned with the good of the artists themselves. For there is no reason why the trainer may not sometimes practise gymnastics, and the helmsman is always one of the crew. The trainer or the helmsman considers the good of those committed to his care. But, when he is one of the persons taken care of, he accidentally participates in the advantage, for the helmsman is also a sailor, and the trainer becomes one of those in training. And so in politics: when the

state is framed upon the principle of equality and likeness, the citizens think that they ought to hold office by turns. Formerly, as is natural, every one would take his turn of service; and then again, somebody else would look after his interest, just as he, while in office, had looked after theirs. But nowadays, for the sake of the advantage which is to be gained from the public revenues and from office, men want to be always in office. One might imagine that the rulers, being sickly, were only kept in health while they continued in office; in that case we may be sure that they would be hunting after places. The conclusion is evident: that governments which have a regard to the common interest are constituted in accordance with strict principles of justice, and are therefore true forms; but those which regard only the interest of the rulers are all defective and perverted forms, for they are despotic, whereas a state is a community of freemen.

Having determined these points, we have next to consider how many forms of government there are, and what they are; and in the first place what are the true forms, for when they are determined the perversions of them will at once be apparent. The words constitution and government have the same meaning, and the government, which is the supreme authority in states, must be in the hands of one, or of a few, or of the many. The true forms of government, therefore, are those in which the one, or the few, or the many, govern with a view to the common interest; but governments which rule with a view to the private interest, whether of the one, or of the few, or of the many, are perversions. For the members of a state, if they are truly citizens, ought to participate in its advantages. Of forms of government in which one rules, we call that which regards the common interests, kingship or royalty; that in which more than one, but not many, rule, aristocracy; and it is so called, either because the rulers are the best men, or because they have at heart the best interests of the state and of the citizens. But when the citizens at large administer the state for the common interest, the government is called by the generic name—a constitution. And there is a reason for this use of language. One man or a few may excel in virtue; but as the number increases it becomes more difficult for them to attain perfection in every kind of virtue, though they may in military virtue, for this is found in the masses. Hence in a constitutional government the fighting-men have the supreme power, and those who possess arms are the citizens.

Of the above-mentioned forms, the perversions are as follows:—of royalty, tryanny; of aristocracy, oligarchy; of constitutional government, democracy. For tyranny is a kind of monarchy which has in view the interest of the monarch only; oligarchy has in view the interest of the wealthy; democracy, of the needy: none of them the common good of all.

DEMOCRACY AND OLIGARCHY

Let us begin by considering the common definitions of oligarchy and democracy, and what is justice oligarchical and democratical. For all men cling to justice of some kind, but their conceptions are imperfect and they do not express the whole idea. For example, justice is thought by them to be, and is, equality, not, however, for all, but only for equals. And inequality is thought to be, and is, justice; neither is this for all, but only for unequals. When the persons are omitted, then men judge erroneously. The reason is that they are passing judgment on themselves, and most people are bad judges in their own case. And whereas justice implies a relation to persons as well as to things, and a just distribution, as I have already said in the *Ethics,* implies the same ratio between the persons and between the things, they agree about the equality of the things, but dispute about the equality of the persons, chiefly for the reason which I have just given—because they are bad judges in their own affairs; and secondly, because both the parties to the argument are speaking of a limited and partial justice, but imagine themselves to be speaking of absolute justice. For the one party, if they are unequal in one respect, for example wealth, consider themselves to be unequal in all; and the other party, if they are equal in one respect, for example free birth, consider themselves to be equal in all. But they leave out the capital point. For if men met and associated out of regard to wealth only, their share in the state would be proportioned to their property, and the oligarchical doctrine would then seem to carry the day. It would not be just that he who paid one mina should have the same share of a hundred minae, whether of the principal or of the profits, as he who paid the remaining ninety-nine. But a state exists for the sake of a good life, and not for the sake of life only: if life only were the object, slaves and brute animals might form a state, but they cannot, for they have no share in happiness or in a life of free choice. Nor does a state exist for the sake of alliance and security from injustice, nor yet for the sake of exchange and mutual intercourse; for then the Tyrrhenians and the Carthaginians, and all who have commercial treaties with one another, would be the citizens of one state. True, they have agreements about imports, and engagements that they will do no wrong to one another, and written articles of alliance. But there are no magistracies common to the contracting parties who will enforce their engagements; different states have each their own magistracies. Nor does one state take care that the citizens of the other are such as they ought to be, nor see that those who come under the terms of the treaty do no wrong or wickedness at all, but only that they do no injustice to one another. Whereas, those who care for good government take into consideration virtue and vice in states. Whence it may be further inferred that virtue must be the care of a state which is truly so called, and not merely enjoys the name: for without this end the community becomes a mere alliance which differs only in place from alliances of which the members live apart; and law is only a convention, "a surety to one another of justice," as the sophist Lycophron says, and has no real power to make the citizens good and just.

This is obvious; for suppose distinct places, such as Corinth and Megara, to be brought together so that their walls touched, still they would not be one city, not even if the citizens had the right to intermarry, which is one of the rights peculiarly characteristic of states. Again, if men dwelt at a distance from one another, but not so far off as to have no intercourse, and there were laws among them that they should not wrong each other in their exchanges, neither would this be a state. Let us suppose that one man is a carpenter, another a husbandman, another a shoemaker, and so on, and that their number is ten thousand: nevertheless, if they have nothing in common but exchange, alliance, and the like, that would not constitute a state. Why is this? Surely not because they are at a distance from one another: for even supposing that such a community were to meet in one place, but that each man had a house of his own, which was in a manner his state, and that they made alliance with one another, but only against evil-doers; still an accurate thinker would not deem this to be a state, if their intercourse with one another was of the same character after as before their union. It is clear then that a state is not a mere society, having a common place, established for the prevention of mutual crime and for the sake of exchange. These are conditions without which a state cannot exist; but all of them together do not constitute a state, which is a community of families and aggregations of families in well-being, for the sake of a perfect and self-sufficing life. Such a community can only be established among those who live in the same place and intermarry. Hence arise in cities family connexions, brotherhoods, common sacrifices, amusements which draw men together. But these are created by friendship, for the will to live together is friendship. The end of the state is the good life, and these are the means towards it. And the state is the union of families and villages in a perfect and self-sufficing life, by which we mean a happy and honourable life.

Our conclusion, then, is that political society exists for the sake of noble actions, and not of mere companionship. Hence they who contribute most to such a society have a greater share in it than those who have the same or a greater freedom or nobility of birth but are inferior to them in political virtue; or than those who exceed them in wealth but are surpassed by them in virtue.

From what has been said it will be clearly seen that all the partisans of different forms of government speak of a part of justice only.

There is also a doubt as to what is to be the supreme power in the state:—Is it the multitude? Or the wealthy? Or the good? Or the one best man? Or a tyrant? Any of these alternatives seems to involve disagreeable consequences. If the poor, for example, because they are more in number, divide among themselves the property of the rich—is not this unjust? No, by heaven (will be the reply), for the supreme authority justly willed it. But if this is not injustice, pray what is? Again, when in the first division all has been taken, and the majority divide anew the property of the minority, is it not evident, if this goes on, that they will ruin the state? Yet surely, virtue is not the ruin of those who possess her, nor is justice destructive of a state; and therefore this law of confiscation clearly cannot be just. If it were, all the acts of a tyrant must of necessity be just; for he only coerces other men by superior power, just as the multitude coerce the rich. But is it just then that the few and the wealthy should be the rulers? And what if they, in like manner, rob and plunder the people—is this just? If so, the other case will likewise be just. But there can be no doubt that all these things are wrong and unjust.

Then ought the good to rule and have supreme power? But in that case everybody else, being excluded from power, will be dishonoured. For the offices of a state are posts of honour; and if one set of men always hold them, the rest must be deprived of them. Then will it be well that the one best man should rule? Nay, that is still more oligarchical, for the number of those who are dishonoured is thereby increased. Some one may say that it is bad in any case for a man, subject as he is to all the accidents of human passion, to have the supreme power, rather than the law. But what if the law itself be democratical or oligarchical, how will that help us out of our difficulties? Not at all; the same consequences will follow.

Most of these questions may be reserved for another occasion. The principle that the multitude ought to be supreme rather than the few best is one that is maintained, and, though not free from difficulty, yet seems to contain an element of truth. For the many, of whom each individual is but an ordinary person, when they meet together may very likely be better than the few good, if regarded not individually but collectively, just as a feast to which many contribute is better than a dinner provided out of a single purse. For each individual among the many has a share of virtue and prudence, and when they meet together, they become in a manner one man, who has many feet, and hands, and senses; that is a figure of their mind and disposition. Hence the many are better judges than a single man of music and poetry; for some understand one part, and some another, and among them they understand the whole. There is a similar combination of qualities in good men, who differ from any individual of the many, as the beautiful are said to differ from those who are not beautiful, and works of art from realities, because in them the scattered elements are combined, although, if taken separately, the eye of one person or some other feature in another person would be fairer than in the picture. Whether this principle can apply to every democracy, and to all bodies of men, is not clear. Or rather, by heaven, in some cases it is impossible of application; for the argument would equally hold about brutes; and wherein, it will be asked, do some men differ from brutes? But there may be bodies of men about whom our statement is nevertheless true. And if so, the difficulty which has been already raised, and also another which is akin to it—viz. what power should be assigned to the mass of freemen and citizens, who are not rich and have no personal merit—are both solved. There is still a danger in allowing them to share the great offices of state, for their folly will lead them into error, and their dishonesty into crime. But there is a danger also in not letting them share, for a state in which many poor men are excluded from office will necessarily be full of enemies. The only way of escape is to assign to them some deliberative and judicial functions. For this reason Solon and certain other legislators give them the power of electing to offices, and of calling the magistrates to account, but they do not allow them to hold office singly. When they meet together their perceptions are quite good enough, and combined with the better class they are useful to the state (just as impure food when mixed with what is pure sometimes makes the entire mass more wholesome than a small quantity of the pure would be), but each individual, left to himself, forms an imperfect judgment. On the other hand, the popular form of government involves certain difficulties. In the first

place, it might be objected that he who can judge of the healing of a sick man would be one who could himself heal his disease, and make him whole—that is, in other words, the physician; and so in all professions and arts. As, then, the physician ought to be called to account by physicians, so ought men in general to be called to account by their peers. But physicians are of three kinds:—there is the ordinary practitioner, and there is the physician of the higher class, and thirdly the intelligent man who has studied the art: in all arts there is such a class; and we attribute the power of judging to them quite as much as to professors of the art. Secondly, does not the same principle apply to elections? For a right election can only be made by those who have knowledge; those who know geometry, for example, will choose a geometrician rightly, and those who know how to steer, a pilot; and, even if there be some occupations and arts in which private persons share in the ability to choose, they certainly cannot choose better than those who know. So that, according to this argument, neither the election of magistrates, nor the calling of them to account, should be entrusted to the many. Yet possibly these objections are to a great extent met by our old answer, that if the people are not utterly degraded, although individually they may be worse judges than those who have special knowledge—as a body they are as good or better. Moreover, there are some arts whose products are not judged of solely, or best, by the artists themselves, namely those arts whose products are recognized even by those who do not possess the art; for example, the knowledge of the house is not limited to the builder only; the user, or, in other words, the master, of the house will be even a better judge than the builder, just as the pilot will judge better of a rudder than the carpenter, and the guest will judge better of a feast than the cook.

This difficulty seems now to be sufficiently answered, but there is another akin to it. That inferior persons should have authority in greater matters than the good would appear to be a strange thing, yet the election and calling to account of the magistrates is the greatest of all. And these, as I was saying, are functions which in some states are assigned to the people, for the assembly is supreme in all such matters. Yet persons of any age, and having but a small property qualification, sit in the assembly and deliberate and judge, although for the great officers of state, such as treasurers and generals, a high qualification is required. This difficulty may be solved in the same manner as the preceding, and the present practice of democracies may be really defensible. For the power does not reside in the dicast, or senator, or ecclesiast, but in the court, and the senate, and the assembly, of which individual senators, or ecclesiasts, or dicasts, are only parts or members. And for this reason the many may claim to have a higher authority than the few; for the people, and the senate, and the courts consist of many persons, and their property collectively is greater than the property of one or of a few individuals holding great offices. But enough of this.

The discussion of the first question shows nothing so clearly as that laws, when good, should be supreme; and that the magistrate or magistrates should regulate those matters only on which the laws are unable to speak with precision owing to the difficulty of any general principle embracing all particulars. But what are good laws has not yet been clearly explained; the old difficulty remains. The goodness or badness, justice or injustice, of laws varies of necessity with the constitutions of states. This, however, is clear, that the laws must be adapted to the constitutions. But if so, true forms of government will of necessity have just laws, and perverted forms of government will have unjust laws.

MONARCHY

If, however, there be some one person, or more than one, although not enough to make up the full complement of a state, whose virtue is so preeminent that the virtues or the political capacity of all the rest admit of no comparison with his or theirs, he or they can be no longer regarded as part of a state; for justice will not be done to the superior, if he is reckoned only as the equal of those who are so far inferior to him in virtue and in political capacity. Such an one may truly be deemed a God among men. Hence we see that legislation is necessarily concerned only with those who are equal in birth and in capacity; and that for men of preeminent

virtue there is no law—they are themselves a law. Any one would be ridiculous who attempted to make laws for them: they would probably retort what, in the fable of Antisthenes, the lions said to the hares, when in the council of the beasts the latter began haranguing and claiming equality for all. And for this reason democratic states have instituted ostracism; equality is above all things their aim, and therefore they ostracized and banished from the city for a time those who seemed to predominate too much through their wealth, or the number of their friends, or through any other political influence. Mythology tells us that the Argonauts left Heracles behind for a similar reason; the ship Argo would not take him because she feared that he would have been too much for the rest of the crew. Wherefore those who denounce tryanny and blame the counsel which Periander gave to Thrasybulus cannot be held altogether just in their censure. The story is that Periander, when the herald was sent to ask counsel of him, said nothing, but only cut off the tallest ears of corn till he had brought the field to a level. The herald did not know the meaning of the action, but came and reported what he had seen to Thrasybulus, who understood that he was to cut off the principal men in the state; and this is a policy not only expedient for tyrants or in practice confined to them, but equally necessary in oligarchies and democracies. Ostracism is a measure of the same kind, which acts by disabling and banishing the most prominent citizens. Great powers do the same to whole cities and nations, as the Athenians did to the Samians, Chians, and Lesbians; no sooner had they obtained a firm grasp of the empire, than they humbled their allies contrary to treaty; and the Persian king has repeatedly crushed the Medes, Babylonians, and other nations, when their spirit has been stirred by the recollection of their former greatness.

The problem is a universal one, and equally concerns all forms of government, true as well as false; for, although perverted forms with a view to their own interests may adopt this policy, those which seek the common interest do so likewise. The same thing may be observed in the arts and sciences; for the painter will not allow the figure to have a foot which, however beautiful, is not in proportion, nor will the ship-builder allow the stern or any other part of the vessel to be unduly large, any more than the chorus-master will allow any one who sings louder or better than all the rest to sing in the choir. Monarchs, too, may practise compulsion and still live in harmony with their cities, if their own government is for the interest of the state. Hence where there is an acknowl-edged superiority the argument in favor of ostracism is based upon a kind of political justice. It would certainly be better that the legislator should from the first so order his state as to have no need of such a remedy. But if the need arises, the next best thing is that he should endeavour to correct the evil by this or some similar measure. The princi-ple, however, has not been fairly applied in states; for, instead of looking to the good of their own constitution, they have used os-tracism for factious purposes. It is true that under perverted forms of government, and from their special point of view, such a mea-sure is just and expedient, but it is also clear that it is not absolutely just. In the perfect state there would be great doubts about the use of it, not when applied to excess in strength, wealth, popularity, or the like, but when used against some one who is preemi-nent in virtue—what is to be done with him? Mankind will not say that such an one is to be expelled and exiled; on the other hand, he ought not to be a subject—that would be as if mankind should claim to rule over Zeus, di-viding his offices among them. The only al-ternative is that all should joyfully obey such a ruler, according to what seems to be the order of nature, and that men like him should be kings in their state for life.

LIBERTY AND EQUALITY

The basis of a democratic state is liberty; which, according to the common opinion of men, can only be enjoyed in such a state;— this they affirm to be the great end of every democracy. One principle of liberty is for all to rule and be ruled in turn, and indeed democratic justice is the application of nu-merical not proportionate equality; whence it follows that the majority must be su-preme, and that whatever the majority ap-prove must be the end and the just. Every citizen, it is said, must have equality, and therefore in a democracy the poor have more power than the rich, because there are

more of them, and the will of the majority is supreme. This, then, is one note of liberty which all democrats affirm to be the princi-ple of their state. Another is that a man should live as he likes. This, they say, is the privilege of a freeman, since, on the other hand, not to live as a man likes is the mark of a slave. This is the second characteristic of democracy, whence has arisen the claim of men to be ruled by none, if possible, or, if this is impossible, to rule and be ruled in turns; and so it contributes to the freedom based upon equality.

Such being our foundation and such the principle from which we start, the charac-teristics of democracy are as follows:—the election of officers by all out of all; and that all should rule over each, and each in his turn over all; that the appointment to all of-fices, or to all but those which require expe-rience and skill, should be made by lot; that no property qualification should be required for offices, or only a very low one; that a man should not hold the same office twice, or not often, or in the case of few except military offices: that the tenure of all of-fices, or of as many as possible, should be brief; that all men should sit in judgment, or that judges selected out of all should judge, in all matters, or in most and in the greatest and most important—such as the scrutiny of accounts, the constitution, and private con-tracts; that the assembly should be supreme over all causes, or at any rate over the most important, and the magistrates over none or only over a very few. Of all magistracies, a council is the most democratic when there is not the means of paying all the citizens, but when they are paid even this is robbed of its power; for the people then draw all cases to themselves, as I said in the previous discus-sion. The next characteristic of democracy is payment for services; assembly, law-courts, magistrates, everybody receives pay, when it is to be had; or when it is not to be had for all, then it is given to the law-courts and to the stated assemblies, to the council and to the magistrates, or at least to any of them who are compelled to have their meals together. And whereas oligarchy is characterized by birth, wealth, and educa-tion, the notes of democracy appear to be the opposite of these—low birth, poverty, mean employment. Another note is that no magistracy is perpetual, but if any such have survived some ancient change in the constitution it should be stripped of its power, and the holders should be elected by lot and no longer by vote. These are the points common to all democracies; but democracy and demos in their truest form are based upon the recognized principle of democratic justice, that all should count equally; for equality implies that the poor should have no more share in the government than the rich, and should not be the only rulers, but that all should rule equally according to their numbers. And in this way men think that they will secure equality and freedom in their state.

Next comes the question, how is this equality to be obtained? Are we to assign to a thousand poor men the property qualifications of five hundred rich men? and shall we give the thousand a power equal to that of the five hundred? or, if this is not to be the mode, ought we, still retaining the same ratio, to take equal numbers from each and give them the control of the elections and of the courts?—Which, according to the democratical notion, is the juster form of the constitution—this or one based on numbers only? Democrats say that justice is that to which the majority agree, oligarchs that to which the wealthier class; in their opinion the decision should be given according to the amount of property. In both principles there is some inequality and injustice. For if justice is the will of the few, any one person who has more wealth than all the rest of the rich put together, ought, upon the oligarchical principle, to have the sole power—but this would be tyranny; or if justice is the will of the majority, as I was before saying, they will unjustly confiscate the property of the wealthy minority. To find a principle of equality in which they both agree we must inquire into their respective ideas of justice.

Now they agree in saying that whatever is decided by the majority of the citizens is to be deemed law. Granted:—but not without some reserve; since there are two classes out of which a state is composed—the poor and the rich—that is to be deemed law, on which both or the greater part of both agree; and if they disagree, that which is approved by the greater number, and by those who have the higher qualification. For example,

suppose that there are ten rich and twenty poor, and some measure is approved by six of the rich and is disapproved by fifteen of the poor, and the remaining four of the rich join with the party of the poor, and the remaining five of the poor with that of the rich; in such a case the will of those whose qualifications, when both sides are added up, are the greatest, should prevail. If they turn out to be equal, there is no greater difficulty than at present, when, if the assembly or the courts are divided, recourse is had to the lot, or to some similar expedient. But, although it may be difficult in theory to know what is just and equal, the practical difficulty of inducing those to forbear who can, if they like, encroach, is far greater, for the weaker are always asking for equality and justice, but the stronger care for none of these things.

THE RULE OF LAW

At this place in the discussion there impends the inquiry respecting the king who acts solely according to his own will; he has now to be considered. The so-called limited monarchy, or kingship according to law, as I have already remarked, is not a distinct form of government, for under all governments, as, for example, in a democracy or aristocracy, there may be a general holding office for life, and one person is often made supreme over the administration of a state. A magistracy of this kind exists at Epidamnus, and also at Opus, but in the latter city has a more limited power. Now, absolute monarchy, or the arbitrary rule of a sovereign over all the citizens, in a city which consists of equals, is thought by some to be quite contrary to nature; it is argued that those who are by nature equals must have the same natural right and worth, and that for unequals to have an equal share, or for equals to have an uneven share, in the offices of state, is as bad as for different bodily constitutions to have the same food and clothing. Wherefore it is thought to be just that among equals every one be ruled as well as rule, and therefore that all should have their turn. We thus arrive at law; for an order of succession implies law. And the rule of the law, it is argued, is preferable to that of any individual. On the same principle, even if it be better for certain individuals to govern, they should be made only guardians and ministers of the law. For magistrates there must be—this is admitted; but then men say that to give authority to any one man when all are equal is unjust. Nay, there may indeed be cases which the law seems unable to determine, but in such cases can a man? Nay, it will be replied, the law trains officers for this express purpose, and appoints them to determine matters which are left undecided by it, to the best of their judgment. Further, it permits them to make any amendment of the existing laws which experience suggests. Therefore he who bids the law rule may be deemed to bid God and Reason alone rule, but he who bids man rule adds an element of the beast; for desire is a wild beast, and passion perverts the minds of rulers, even when they are the best of men. The law is reason unaffected by desire. We are told that a patient should call in a physician; he will not get better if he is doctored out of a book. But the parallel of the arts is clearly not in point; for the physician does nothing contrary to rule from motives of friendship; he only cures a patient and takes a fee; whereas magistrates do many things from spite and partiality. And, indeed, if a man suspected the physician of being in league with his enemies to destroy him for a bribe, he would rather have recourse to the book. But certainly physicians, when they are sick, call in other physicians, and training-masters, when they are in training, other training-masters, as if they could not judge truly about their own case and might be influenced by their feelings. Hence it is evident that in seeking for justice men seek for the mean or neutral, for the law is the mean. Again, customary laws have more weight, and relate to more important matters, than written laws, and a man may be a safer ruler than the written law, but not safer than the customary law.

Again, it is by no means easy for one man to superintend many things; he will have to appoint a number of subordinates, and what difference does it make whether these subordinates always existed or were appointed by him because he needed them? If, as I said before, the good man has a right to rule because he is better, still two good men are better than one: this is the old saying—

two going together,

and the prayer of Agamemnon—

would that I had ten such counsellors!

And at this day there are magistrates, for example judges, who have authority to decide some matters which the law is unable to determine, since no one doubts that the law would command and decide in the best manner whatever it could. But some things can, and other things cannot, be comprehended under the law, and this is the origin of the vexed question whether the best law or the best man should rule. For matters of detail about which men deliberate cannot be included in legislation. Nor does any one deny that the decision of such matters must be left to man, but it is argued that there should be many judges, and not one only. For every ruler who has been trained by the law judges well; and it would surely seem strange that a person should see better with two eyes, or hear better with two ears, or act better with two hands or feet, than many with many; indeed, it is already the practice of kings to make to themselves many eyes and ears and hands and feet. For they make colleagues of those who are the friends of themselves and their governments. They must be friends of the monarch and of his government; if not his friends, they will not do what he wants; but friendship implies likeness and equality; and, therefore, if he thinks that his friends ought to rule, he must think that those who are equal to himself and like himself ought to rule equally with himself. These are the principal controversies relating to monarchy.

CONSTITUTIONAL GOVERNMENT

Polity or constitutional government may be described generally as a fusion of oligarchy and democracy; but the term is usually applied to those forms of government which incline towards democracy, and the term aristocracy to those which incline towards oligarchy, because birth and education are commonly the accompaniments of wealth. Moreover, the rich already possess the external advantages the want of which is a temptation to crime, and hence they are called noblemen and gentlemen. And inasmuch as aristocracy seeks to give predominance to the best of the citizens, people say also of oligarchies that they are composed of noblemen and gentlemen. Now it appears to be an impossible thing that the state which is governed not by the best citizens but by the worst should be well-governed, and equally impossible that the state which is ill-governed should be governed by the best. But we must remember that good laws, if they are not obeyed, do not constitute good government. Hence there are two parts of good government; one is the actual obedience of citizens to the laws, the other part is the goodness of the laws which they obey; they may obey bad laws as well as good. And there may be a further subdivision; they may obey either the best laws which are attainable to them, or the best absolutely.

The distribution of offices according to merit is a special characteristic of aristocracy, for the principle of an aristocracy is virtue, as wealth is of an oligarchy, and freedom of a democracy. In all of them there of course exists the right of the majority, and whatever seems good to the majority of those who share in the government has authority. Now in most states the form called polity exists, for the fusion goes no further than the attempt to unite the freedom of the poor and the wealth of the rich, who commonly take the place of the noble. But as there are three grounds on which men claim an equal share in the government, freedom, wealth, and virtue (for the fourth or good birth is the result of the two last, being only ancient wealth and virtue), it is clear that the admixture of the two elements, that is to say, of the rich and poor, is to be called a polity or constitutional government; and the union of the three is to be called aristocracy or the government of the best, and more than any other form of government, except the true and ideal, has a right to this name.

Thus far I have shown the existence of forms of states other than monarchy, democracy, and oligarchy, and what they are, and in what aristocracies differ from one another, and polities from aristocracies—that the two latter are not very unlike is obvious.

Next we have to consider how by the side of oligarchy and democracy the so-called polity or constitutional government springs up, and how it should be organized. The nature of it will be at once understood from a comparison of oligarchy and democracy; we must ascertain their different characteristics, and taking a portion from each, put the two together, like the parts of an indenture. Now there are three modes in which fusions of government may be affected. In the first mode we must combine the laws made by both governments, say concerning the administration of justice. In oligarchies they impose a fine on the rich if they do not serve as judges, and to the poor they give no pay; but in democracies they give pay to the poor and do not fine the rich. Now (1) the union of these two modes is a common or middle term between them, and is therefore characteristic of a constitutional government, for it is a combination of both. This is one mode of uniting the two elements. Or (2) a mean may be taken between the enactments of the two: thus democracies require no property qualification, or only a small one, from members of the assembly, oligarchies a high one; here neither of these is the common term, but a mean between them. (3) There is a third mode, in which something is borrowed from the oligarchical and something from the democratical principle. For example, the appointment of magistrates by lot is thought to be democratical, and the election of them oligarchical; democratical again when there is no property qualification, oligarchical when there is. In the aristocratical or constitutional state, one element will be taken from each—from oligarchy the principle of electing to offices, from democracy the disregard of qualification. Such are the various modes of combination.

There is a true union of oligarchy and democracy when the same state may be termed either a democracy or an oligarchy; those who use both names evidently feel that the fusion is complete. Such a fusion there is also in the mean; for both extremes appear in it. The Lacedaemonian constitution, for example, is often described as a democracy, because it has many democratical features. In the first place the youth receive a democratical education. For the sons of the poor are brought up with the sons of the rich, who are educated in such a manner as to make it possible for the sons of the poor to be educated like them. A similar equality prevails in the following period of life, and when the citizens are grown up to manhood the same rule is observed; there is no distinction between the rich and poor. In like manner they all have the same food at their public tables, and the rich wear only such clothing as any poor man can afford. Again, the people elect to one of the two greatest offices of state, and in the other they share; for they elect the Senators and share in the Ephoralty. By others the Spartan constitution is said to be an oligarchy, because it has many oligarchical elements. That all offices are filled by election and none by lot, is one of these oligarchical characteristics; that the power of inflicting death or banishment rests with a few persons is another; and there are others. In a well attempered polity there should appear to be both elements and yet neither; also the government should rely on itself, and not on foreign aid, and on itself not through the good will of a majority—they might be equally well-disposed when there is a vicious form of government—but through the general willingness of all classes in the state to maintain the constitution.

Enough of the manner in which a constitutional government, and in which the so-called aristocracies ought to be framed.

THE BEST STATE

In all arts and sciences which embrace the whole of any subject, and do not come into being in a fragmentary way, it is the province of a single art or science to consider all that appertains to a single subject. For example, the art of gymnastic considers not only the suitableness of different modes of training to different bodies (2) but what sort is absolutely the best (1); (for the absolutely best must suit that which is by nature best and best furnished with the means of life), and also what common form of training is adapted to the great majority of men (4). And if a man does not desire the best habit of body, or the greatest skill in gymnastics, which might be attained by him, still the trainer or the teacher of gymnastic should be able to impart any lower

degree of either (3). The same principle equally holds in medicine and ship-building, and the making of clothes, and in the arts generally.

Hence it is obvious that government too is the subject of a single science, which has to consider what government is best and of what sort it must be, to be most in accordance with our aspirations, if there were no external impediment, and also what kind of government is adapted to particular states. For the best is often unattainable, and therefore the true legislator and statesman ought to be acquainted, not only with (1) that which is best in the abstract, but also with (2) that which is best relatively to circumstances. We should be able further to say how a state may be constituted under any given conditions (3); both how it is originally formed and, when formed, how it may be longest preserved; the supposed state being so far from having the best constitution that it is unprovided even with the conditions necessary for the best; neither is it the best under the circumstances, but of an inferior type.

He ought, moreover, to know (4) the form of government which is best suited to states in general; for political writers, although they have excellent ideas, are often unpractical. We should consider, not only what form of government is best, but also what is possible and what is easily attainable by all. There are some who would have none but the most perfect; for this many natural advantages are required. Others, again, speak of a more attainable form, and, although they reject the constitution under which they are living, they extol some one in particular, for example the Lacedaemonian. Any change of government which has to be introduced should be one which men, starting from their existing constitutions, will be both willing and able to adopt, since there is quite as much trouble in the reformation of an old constitution as in the establishment of a new one, just as to unlearn is as hard as to learn. And therefore, in addition to the qualifications of the statesman already mentioned, he should be able to find remedies for the defects of existing constitutions, as has been said before. This he cannot do unless he knows how many forms of government there are. It is often supposed that there is only one kind of democracy and one of oligarchy. But this is a mistake; and, in order to avoid such mistakes, we must ascertain what differences there are in the constitutions of states, and in how many ways they are combined. The same political insight will enable a man to know which laws are the best, and which are suited to different constitutions; for the laws are, and ought to be, relative to the constitution, and not the constitution to the laws. A constitution is the organization of offices in a state, and determines what is to be the governing body, and what is the end of each community. But laws are not to be confounded with the principles of the constitution; they are the rules according to which the magistrates should administer the state, and proceed against offenders. So that we must know the varieties, and the number of varieties, of each form of government, if only with a view to making laws. For the same laws cannot be equally suited to all oligarchies or to all democracies, since there is certainly more than one form both of democracy and of oligarchy.

POLITICAL MODERATION
AND STABILITY:
THE MIDDLE CLASSES

We have now to inquire what is the best constitution for most states, and the best life for most men, neither assuming a standard of virtue which is above ordinary persons, nor an education which is exceptionally favoured by nature and circumstances, nor yet an ideal state which is an aspiration only, but having regard to the life in which the majority are able to share, and to the form of government which states in general can attain. As to those aristocracies, as they are called, of which we were just now speaking, they either lie beyond the possibilities of the greater number of states, or they approximate to the so-called constitutional government, and therefore need no separate discussion. And in fact the conclusion at which we arrive respecting all these forms rests upon the same grounds. For if what was said in the *Ethics* is true, that the happy life is the life according to virtue lived without impediment, and that virtue is a mean, then the life which is in a mean, and

in a mean attainable by every one, must be the best. And the same principles of virtue and vice are characteristic of cities and of constitutions; for the constitution is in a figure the life of the city.

Now in all states there are three elements: one class is very rich, another very poor, and a third in a mean. It is admitted that moderation and the mean are best, and therefore it will clearly be best to possess the gifts of fortune in moderation; for in that condition of life men are most ready to follow rational principle. But he who greatly excels in beauty, strength, birth, or wealth, or on the other hand who is very poor, or very weak, or very much disgraced, finds it difficult to follow rational principle. Of these two the one sort grow into violent and great criminals, the others into rogues and petty rascals. And two sorts of offences correspond to them, the one committed from violence, the other from roguery. Again, the middle class is least likely to shrink from rule, or to be overambitious for it; both of which are injuries to the state. Again, those who have too much of the goods of fortune, strength, wealth, friends, and the like, are neither willing nor able to submit to authority. The evil begins at home; for when they are boys, by reason of the luxury in which they are brought up, they never learn, even at school, the habit of obedience. On the other hand, the very poor, who are in the opposite extreme, are too degraded. So that the one class cannot obey, and can only rule despotically; the other knows not how to command and must be ruled like slaves. Thus arises a city, not of freemen, but of masters and slaves, the one despising, the other envying; and nothing can be more fatal to friendship and good fellowship in states than this: for good fellowship springs from friendship; when men are at enmity with one another, they would rather not even share the same path. But a city ought to be composed, as far as possible, of equals and similars; and these are generally the middle classes. Wherefore the city which is composed of middle-class citizens is necessarily best constituted in respect of the elements of which we say the fabric of the state naturally consists. And this is the class of citizens which is most secure in a state, for they do not, like the poor, covet their neighbours' goods; nor do others covet theirs, as the poor covet the goods of the rich; and as they neither plot against others, nor are themselves plotted against, they pass through life safely. Wisely then did Phocylides pray—"Many things are best in the mean; I desire to be of a middle condition in my city."

Thus it is manifest that the best political community is formed by citizens of the middle class, and that those states are likely to be well-administered, in which the middle class is large, and stronger if possible than both the other classes, or at any rate than either singly; for the addition of the middle class turns the scale, and prevents either of the extremes from being dominant. Great then is the good fortune of a state in which the citizens have a moderate and sufficient property; for where some possess much, and the others nothing, there may arise an extreme democracy, or a pure oligarchy; or a tyranny may grow out of either extreme—either out of the most rampant democracy, or out of an oligarchy; but it is not so likely to arise out of the middle constitutions and those akin to them. I will explain the reason of this hereafter, when I speak of the revolutions of states. The mean condition of states is clearly best, for no other is free from faction; and where the middle class is large, there are least likely to be factions and dissensions. For a similar reason large states are less liable to faction than small ones, because in them the middle class is large; whereas in small states it is easy to divide all the citizens into two classes who are either rich or poor, and to leave nothing in the middle. And democracies are safer and more permanent than oligarchies, because they have a middle class which is more numerous and has a greater share in the government; for when there is no middle class, and the poor greatly exceed in number, troubles arise, and the state soon comes to an end. A proof of the superiority of the middle class is that the best legislators have been of a middle condition; for example, Solon, as his own verses testify; and Lycurgus, for he was not a king; and Charondas, and almost all legislators.

These considerations will help us to understand why most governments are either democratical or oligarchical. The reason is that the middle class is seldom numerous in them, and whichever party, whether the rich or the common people, transgresses the mean and predominates, draws the constitution its own way, and thus arises either oligarchy or democracy. There is another reason—the poor and the rich quarrel with one another, and whichever side gets the better, instead of establishing a just or popular government, regards political supremacy as the prize of victory, and the one party sets up a democracy and the other an oligarchy. Further, both the parties which had the supremacy in Hellas looked only to the interest of their own form of government and established in states, the one, democracies, and the other, oligarchies; they thought of their own advantage, of the public not at all. For these reasons the middle form of government has rarely, if ever, existed, and among a very few only. One man alone of all who ever ruled in Hellas was induced to give this middle constitution to states. But it has now become a habit among the citizens of states, not even to care about equality; all men are seeking for dominion, or, if conquered, are willing to submit.

What then is the best form of government and what makes it the best, is evident; and of other constitutions, since we say that there are many kinds of democracy and many of oligarchy, it is not difficult to see which has the first and which the second or any other place in the order of excellence, now that we have determined which is the best. For that which is nearest to the best must of necessity be better, and that which is furthest from it worse, if we are judging absolutely and not relatively to given conditions: I say "relatively to given conditions," since a particular government may be preferable, but another form may be better for some people.

CAUSES OF REVOLUTION

In considering how dissensions and political revolutions arise, we must first of all ascertain the beginnings and causes of them which affect constitutions generally. They may be said to be three in number; and we have now to given an outline of each. We want to know (1) what is the feeling? (2) what are the motives of those who make them? (3) whence arise political disturbances and quarrels? The universal and chief cause of this revolutionary feeling has been already mentioned; viz. the desire of equality, when men think that they are equal to others who have more than themselves; or, again, the desire of inequality and superiority, when conceiving themselves to be superior they think that they have not more but the same or less than their inferiors; pretensions which may and may not be just. Inferiors revolt in order that they may be equal, and equals that they may be superior. Such is the state of mind which creates revolutions. The motives for making them are the desire of gain and honour, or the fear of dishonour and loss; the authors of them want to divert punishment or dishonour from themselves or their friends. The causes and reasons of revolutions, whereby men are themselves affected in the way described, and about the things which I have mentioned, viewed in one way may be regarded as seven, and in another as more than seven. Two of them have been already noticed; but they act in a different manner, for men are excited against one another by the love of gain and honour—not, as in the case which I have just supposed, in order to obtain them for themselves, but at seeing others, justly or unjustly, engrossing them. Other causes are insolence, fear, excessive predominance, contempt, disproportionate increase in some part of the state; causes of another sort are election intrigues, carelessness, neglect about trifles, dissimilarity of elements.

HOW TO PREVENT REVOLUTION

We have next to consider what means there are of preserving constitutions in general, and in particular cases. In the first place it is evident that if we know the causes which destroy constitutions, we also know the causes which preserve them; for opposites produce opposites, and destruction is the opposite of preservation.

In all well-attempered governments there is nothing which should be more jealously maintained than the spirit of obedience to law, more especially in small matters; for transgression creeps in unperceived and at last ruins the state, just as the constant recurrence of small expenses in time eats up a fortune. The expense does not take place all at once, and therefore is not observed; the mind is deceived, as in the fallacy which says that "if each part is little, then the whole is little." And this is true in one way, but not in another, for the whole and the all are not little, although they are made up of littles.

In the first place, then, men should guard against the beginnings of change, and in the second place they should not rely upon the political devices of which I have already spoken invented only to deceive the people, for they are proved by experience to be useless. Further, we note that oligarchies as well as aristocracies may last not from any inherent stability in such forms of government, but because the rulers are on good terms both with the unenfranchised and with the governing classes, not maltreating any who are excluded from the government, but introducing into it the leading spirits among them. They should never wrong the ambitious in a matter of honour, or the common people in a matter of money; and they should treat one another and their fellow-citizens in a spirit of equality. The equality which the friends of democracy seek to establish for the multitude is not only just but likewise expedient among equals. Hence, if the governing class are numerous, many democratic institutions are useful; for example, the restriction of the tenure of offices to six months, that all those who are of equal rank may share in them. Indeed, equals or peers when they are numerous become a kind of democracy, and therefore demagogues are very likely to arise among them, as I have already remarked. The short tenure of office prevents oligarchies and aristocracies from falling into the hands of families, it is not easy for a person to do any great harm when his tenure of office is short, whereas long possession begets tyranny in oligarchies and democracies. For the aspirants to tyranny are either the principal men of the state, who in democracies are demagogues and in oligarchies members of ruling houses, or those who hold great offices, and have a long tenure of them.

Constitutions are preserved when their destroyers are at a distance, and sometimes also because they are near, for the fear of them makes the government keep in hand the constitution. Wherefore the ruler who has a care of the constitution should invent terrors, and bring distant dangers near, in order that the citizens may be on their guard, and, like sentinels in a night-watch, never relax their attention. He should endeavour too by help of the laws to control the contentions and quarrels of the notables, and to prevent those who have not hitherto taken part in them from catching the spirit of contention. No ordinary man can discern the beginning of evil, but only the true statesman.

As to the change produced in oligarchies and constitutional governments by the alteration of the qualification, when this arises, not out of any variation in the qualification but only out of the increase of money, it is well to compare the general valuation of property with that of past years, annually in those cities in which the census is taken annually, and in larger cities every third or fifth year. If the whole is many times greater or many times less than when the ratings recognized by the constitution were fixed, there should be power given by law to raise or lower the qualification as the amount is greater or less. Where this is not done a constitutional government passes into an oligarchy, and an oligarchy is narrowed to a rule of families; or in the opposite case constitutional government becomes democracy, and oligarchy either constitutional government or democracy.

It is a principle common to democracy, oligarchy, and every other form of government not to allow the disproportionate increase of any citizen, but to give moderate honour for a long time rather than great honour for a short time. For men are easily spoilt; not every one can bear prosperity. But if this rule is not observed, at any rate the honours which are given all at once should be taken away by degrees and not all at once. Especially should the laws provide against any one having too much power, whether derived from friends or money; if he has, he should be sent clean out of the country. And since innovations creep in through the private life of individuals also, there ought to be a magistracy which will have an eye to those whose life is not in harmony with the government, whether oligarchy or democracy or any other. And for a like reason an increase of prosperity in any part of the state should be carefully watched. The proper remedy for this evil is

always to give the management of affairs and offices of state to opposite elements; such opposites are the virtuous and the many, or the rich and the poor. Another way is to combine the poor and the rich in one body, or to increase the middle class: thus an end will be put to the revolutions which arise from inequality.

But above all every state should be so administered and so regulated by law that its magistrates cannot possibly make money. In oligarchies special precautions should be used against this evil. For the people do not take any great offence at being kept out of the government—indeed they are rather pleased than otherwise at having leisure for their private business—but what irritates them is to think that their rulers are stealing the public money; then they are doubly annoyed; for they lose both honour and profit. If office brought no profit, then and then only could democracy and aristocracy be combined; for both notables and people might have their wishes gratified. All would be able to hold office, which is the aim of democracy, and the notables would be magistrates, which is the aim of aristocracy. And this result may be accomplished when there is no possibility of making money out of the offices; for the poor will not want to have them when there is nothing to be gained from them—they would rather be attending to their own concerns; and the rich, who do not want money from the public treasury, will be able to take them; and so the poor will keep to their work and grow rich, and the notables will not he governed by the lower class. In order to avoid peculation of the public money, the transfer of the revenue should be made at a general assembly of the citizens, and duplicates of the accounts deposited with the different brotherhoods, companies, and tribes. And honours should be given by law to magistrates who have the reputation of being incorruptible. In democracies the rich should be spared; not only should their property not be divided, but their incomes also, which in some states are taken from them imperceptibly, should be protected. It is a good thing to prevent the wealthy citizens, even if they are willing, from undertaking expensive and useless public services, such as the giving of choruses, torch-races, and the like. In an oligarchy, on the other hand, great care should be taken of the poor, and lucrative offices should go to them; if any of the wealthy classes insult them, the offender should be punished more severely than if he had wronged one of his own class. Provision should be made that estates pass by inheritance and not by gift, and no person should have more than one inheritance; for in this way properties will be equalized, and more of the poor rise to competency. It is also expedient both in a democracy and in an oligarchy to assign to those who have less share in the government (i.e. to the rich in a democracy and to the poor in an oligarchy) an equality or preference in all but the principal offices of state. The latter should be entrusted chiefly or only to members of the governing class.

CHAPTER FIVE

POLYBIUS

When Greece was politically and militarily subjugated by the Macedonian monarchy, Greek civilization continued to dominate the new and larger horizons of empire; Aristotle's tutoring of Alexander symbolically represented the fact that Greece was still the mistress of the world in the realm of thought, though deprived of independence in the realm of political action. But so difficult was the adaptation of Greeks to the new dimensions of political organization that Aristotle still discussed the city-state as the only imaginable form of state at the very time when it was rapidly becoming a thing of the past. The Greek city-state was never to recover its vitality; the only change during the two centuries following Aristotle was the substitution of Rome for Macedon.

Some Greek statesmen tried to maintain a precarious neutrality in the struggle of Rome and Macedon, but with no success. Shortly after the conquest of Macedon by Rome, one thousand distinguished Greeks were deported to Rome as political prisoners, to await trial against them; no trial was ever held, and after seventeen years the surviving three hundred exiles were finally released.

Among the deported was Polybius (204–122 B.C.), a promising young statesman who had rendered illustrious public service to the Achaean League, a confederation of city-states, and the chief political power in Greece at that time. In Rome, Polybius became acquainted with the leading families; in this and other ways he was able to observe the inner workings of Roman politics at home and abroad. Personal ties of friendship with top political figures, intellectual curiosity concerning the growth of Rome from a small city to the dominant world power, and admiration for Roman civil and military statesmanship turned him into a friend and ally of Rome. He traveled widely on military and diplomatic missions, in Europe as well as in Asia and Africa. His rich practical and scholarly experience is reflected in his *Histories,* written in forty books, of which the first five are fully preserved, and the remaining thirty-five in fragments.

Next to Herodotus and Thucydides, Polybius is recognized as the greatest Greek historian. His work is the first universal history written by a student of politics, for he had the Greek intellectual background of keen observation and philosophical analysis, as well as firsthand experience of world affairs which at that time only long and intimate association with Roman politics and statesmanship could give. His work centers on a relatively short period, the fifty-three years from the Second Punic War (219 B.C.) to the conquest of Macedon by Rome (167 B.C.), but it is the critical period of the rise of Rome from a small state to world hegemony.

Polybius was the first to apply the institutional method to the study of politics and, more particularly, to relate foreign policy to domestic policies and practices. The more he studied the nature and evolution of Roman political institutions, the more he became convinced that Rome's rise to world supremacy was the work, not of a few heroic individuals or of great military leaders, but of the less visible and less dramatic force of high political standards and practices. Whereas Plato and Aristotle had studied political institutions in relation to the good life of the community and the individual—assuming a Greek world in which small, self-sufficient city-states existed side by side without a great deal of mutual interference—Polybius was the first to examine the institutional fabric of a state as the chief determining factor in the formation of national strength.

Polybius thought that the secret of Roman political health lay in the principle of the *mixed constitution.* Aristotle had clearly suggested this principle, but in a more social and economic sense: the mixture was one of social and economic groups and classes, and not of branches of government, and his system of constitutional government (polity) was based on the principles of the wealth of the few and freedom of the many (poor). By contrast, Polybius' idea of the mixed constitution implies a blend of different principles of government authority. Following Aristotle, Polybius saw in monarchy, aristocracy, and democracy the three chief forms of government, and, even more keenly than Aristotle, he was aware that each form carried within itself the seed of its own degeneration, if it were allowed to operate without checks and balances provided by its opposing principles. Monarchy could easily become tyranny, aristocracy sink into oligarchy, and democracy turn into mob rule of force and violence. In the Roman constitution, Polybius believed he found the near-perfect balance among these three principles: the consuls represented the monarchical principle; the senate, the aristocratic one; and the popular assemblies, the democratic.

Polybius describes in detail how the natural tendency of each of the three basic powers of government is to check and balance the two others, so that "none of the three is absolute, but the purpose of one can be counterworked and thwarted by the others," and "any aggressive impulse is sure to be checked."

This system of checks and balances must have appeared to many contemporaries of Polybius—friends and enemies of Roman power—to have an inevitably divisive effect on the internal unity of the state and its capacity to act. Polybius says that, on the contrary, the method of checks and balances "is adequate to all emergencies, so that it is impossible to find a better political system than this." Whenever the menace of a common danger from abroad compels the various branches of government "to act in concord and support each other, so great does the strength of the state become, that nothing which is requisite can be neglected, as all are zealously competing in devising means of meeting the need of the hour, nor can any decision arrived at fail to be executed promptly, as all are cooperating both in public and in private to the accomplishment of the task they have set themselves; and consequently this peculiar form of constitution possesses an irresistible power of attaining every object upon which it is resolved." Despots have lost many wars against constitutionally governed states because they find it difficult, accustomed as they are to the fetish of unity and uniformity, to comprehend the inner reservoirs of strength that lie behind the apparent divisions and quarrels of free peoples.

Polybius knows, however, that no political system can in itself guarantee the growth and vitality of the state, and that ultimately the quality of the people, particularly its leaders and officials, will determine the issue of strength and survival. He compares the lax standards of value in Carthage, where "nothing which results in profit is regarded as disgraceful," with Roman standards, which condemn "unscrupulous gain from forbidden sources." More specifically, "at Carthage candidates for office practise open bribery, whereas at Rome death is the penalty for it." Polybius idealizes perhaps the political morals of his Roman conquerors, but the general principle he states is as valid today as in his own time.

Polybius' influence on Cicero assured him of a popular audience in antiquity, and later on, too, because Cicero was for a long time one of the most widely read ancient authors. In the Middle Ages, Polybius' main ideas are traceable in thinkers as diverse as Marsilio of Padua and St. Thomas of Aquinas, and in the modern era Locke and Montesquieu added new weight to the doctrine of the balance of powers. In the history of the United States, in particular, Polybius played an important intellectual role in the drafting of the Constitution. The political leaders of that formative era, Jefferson, Adams, and many others, were thoroughly familiar with Polybius, and they used his ideas in framing a constitution based on the principle of checks and balances, of liberty through limited government.

POLYBIUS

*The Histories**

THE FORMS OF STATE

In the case of those Greek states which have often risen to greatness and have often experienced a complete change of fortune, it is an easy matter both to describe their past and to pronounce as to their future. For there is no difficulty in reporting the known facts, and it is not hard to foretell the future by inference from the past. But about the Roman state it is neither at all easy to explain the present situation owing to the complicated character of the constitution, nor to foretell the future owing to our ignorance of the peculiar features of public and private life at Rome in the past. Particular attention and study are therefore required if one wishes to attain a clear general view of the distinctive qualities of their constitution.

Most of those whose object it has been to instruct us methodically concerning such matters, distinguish three kinds of constitutions, which they call kingship, aristocracy, and democracy. Now we should, I think, be quite justified in asking them to enlighten us as to whether they represent these three to be the sole varieties or rather to be the best; for in either case my opinion is that they are wrong. For it is evident that we must regard as the best constitution a combination of all these three varieties, since we have had proof of this not only theoretically but by actual experience, Lycurgus having been the first to draw up a constitution—that of Sparta—on this principle. Nor on the other hand can we admit that these are the only three varieties; for we have witnessed monarchical and tyrannical govern-

ments, which while they differ very widely from kingship, yet bear a certain resemblance to it, this being the reason why monarchs in general falsely assume and use, as far as they can, the regal title. There have also been several oligarchical constitutions which seem to bear some likeness to aristocratic ones, though the divergence is, generally, as wide as possible. The same holds good about democracies. The truth of what I say is evident from the following considerations. It is by no means every monarchy which we can call straight off a kingship, but only that which is voluntarily accepted by the subjects and where they are governed rather by an appeal to their reason than by fear and force. Nor again can we style every oligarchy an aristocracy, but only that where the government is in the hands of a selected body of the justest and wisest men. Similarly that is no true democracy in which the whole crowd of citizens is free to do whatever they wish or purpose, but when, in a community where it is traditional and customary to reverence the gods, to honour our parents, to respect our elders, and to obey the laws, the will of the greater number prevails, this is to be called a democracy. We should therefore assert that there are six kinds of governments, the three above mentioned which are in everyone's mouth and the three which are naturally allied to them, I mean monarchy, oligarchy, and mob-rule. Now the first of these to come into being is monarchy, its growth being natural and unaided; and next arises kingship derived from monarchy by the aid of art and by the correction of defects. Monarchy first changes into its vicious allied form, tyranny; and next, the abolishment of both gives birth to aristocracy. Aristocracy by its very nature

---

*From Polybius, *The Histories* (trans. W.R. Paton, Loeb Classical Library, Harvard University Press, 1923), Vol. III. By permission.

degenerates into oligarchy; and when the commons inflamed by anger take vengeance on this government for its unjust rule, democracy comes into being; and in due course the licence and lawlessness of this form of government produces mob-rule to complete the series. The truth of what I have just said will be quite clear to anyone who pays due attention to such beginnings, origins, and changes as are in each case natural. For he alone who has seen how each form naturally arises and develops, will be able to see when, how, and where the growth, perfection, change and end of each are likely to occur again. And it is to the Roman constitution above all that this method, I think, may be successfully applied, since from the outset its formation and growth have been due to natural causes.

THE CAUSES OF
POLITICAL CHANGE

Perhaps this theory of the natural transformations into each other of the different forms of government is more elaborately set forth by Plato and certain other philosophers; but as the arguments are subtle and are stated at great length, they are beyond the reach of all but a few. I therefore will attempt to give a short summary of the theory, as far as I consider it to apply to the actual history of facts and to appeal to the common intelligence of mankind. For if there appear to be certain omissions in my general exposition of it, the detailed discussion which follows will afford the reader ample compensation for any difficulties now left unsolved.

What then are the beginnings I speak of and what is the first origin of political societies? When owing to floods, famines, failure of crops or other such causes there occurs such a destruction of the human race as tradition tells us has more than once happened, and as we must believe will often happen again, all arts and crafts perishing at the same time, then in the course of time, when springing from the survivors as from seeds men have again increased in numbers and just like other animals form herds—it being a matter of course that they too should herd together with those of their kind owing to their natural weakness—it is a necessary consequence that the man who excels in

bodily strength and in courage will lead and rule over the rest. We observe and should regard as a most genuine work of nature this very phenomenon in the case of the other animals which act purely by instinct and among whom the strongest are always indisputably the masters—I speak of bulls, boars, cocks, and the like. It is probable then that at the beginning men lived thus, herding together like animals and following the lead of the strongest and bravest, the ruler's strength being here the sole limit to his power and the name we should give his rule being monarchy.

But when in time feelings of sociability and companionship begin to grow in such gatherings of men, then kingship has struck root; and the notions of goodness, justice, and their opposites begin to arise in men. The manner in which these notions come into being is as follows. Men being all naturally inclined to sexual intercourse, and the consequence of this being the birth of children, whenever one of those who have been reared does not on growing up show gratitude to those who reared him or defend them, but on the contrary takes to speaking ill of them or ill treating them, it is evident that he will displease and offend those who have been familiar with his parents and have witnessed the care and pains they spent on attending to and feeding their children. For seeing that men are distinguished from the other animals by possessing the faculty of reason, it is obviously improbable that such a difference of conduct should escape them, as it escapes the other animals: they will notice the thing and be displeased at what is going on, looking to the future and reflecting that they may all meet with the same treatment. Again when a man who has been helped or succoured when in danger by another does not show gratitude to his preserver, but even goes to the length of attempting to do him injury, it is clear that those who become aware of it will naturally be displeased and offended by such conduct, sharing the resentment of their injured neighbour and imagining themselves in the same situation. From all this there arises in everyone a notion of the meaning and theory of duty, which is the beginning and end of justice. Similarly, again, when any man is foremost in defending his fellows from danger, and braves and awaits the onslaught of the most powerful beasts, it is natural that he should receive marks of favour and honour from the people, while the man who acts in the opposite manner will meet with reprobation and dislike. From this again some idea of what is base and what is noble and of what constitutes the difference is likely to arise among the people; and noble conduct will be admired and imitated because it is advantageous, while base conduct will be avoided. Now when the leading and most powerful man among the people always throws the weight of his authority on the side of the notions on such matters which generally prevail, and when in the opinion of his subjects he apportions rewards and penalties according to desert, they yield obedience to him no longer because they fear his force, but rather because their judgement approves him; and they join in maintaining his rule even if he is quite enfeebled by age, defending him with one consent and battling against those who conspire to overthrow his rule. Thus by insensible degrees the monarch becomes a king, ferocity and force having yielded the supremacy to reason.

Thus is formed naturally among men the first notion of goodness and justice, and their opposites; this is the beginning and birth of true kingship. For the people maintain the supreme power not only in the hands of these men themselves, but in those of their descendants, from the conviction that those born from and reared by such men will also have principles like to theirs. And if they ever are displeased with the descendants, they now choose their kings and rulers no longer for their bodily strength and brute courage, but for the excellency of their judgement and reasoning powers, as they have gained experience from actual facts of the difference between the one class of qualities and the other. In old times, then, those who had once been chosen to the royal office continued to hold it until they grew old, fortifying and enclosing fine strongholds with walls and acquiring lands, in the one case for the sake of the security of their subjects and in the other to provide them with abundance of the necessities of life. And while pursuing these aims, they were exempt from all vituperation or jealousy, as neither in their dress nor in their food and drink did they make any great distinction, but lived very much like everyone else, not keeping apart from the people. But when they received the office by hereditary succession and found their safety now provided for, and more than sufficient provision of food, they gave way to their appetites owing to this superabundance, and came to think that the rulers must be distinguished from their subjects by a peculiar dress, that there should be a peculiar luxury and variety in the dressing and serving of their viands, and that they should meet with no denial in the pursuit of their amours, however lawless. These habits having given rise in the one case to envy and offence and in the other to an outburst of hatred and passionate resentment, the kingship changed into a tyranny; the first steps towards its overthrow were taken by the subjects, and conspiracies began to be formed. These conspiracies were not the work of the worst men, but of the noblest, most high-spirited, and most courageous, because such men are least able to brook the insolence of princes. The people now having got leaders, would combine with them against the ruling powers for the reasons I stated above; kingship and monarchy would be utterly abolished, and in their place aristocracy would begin to grow. For the commons, as if bound to pay at once their debt of gratitude to the abolishers of monarchy, would make them their leaders and entrust their destinies to them. At first these chiefs gladly assumed this charge and regarded nothing as of greater importance than the common interest, administering the private and public affairs of the people with paternal solicitude. But here again when children inherited this position of authority from their fathers, having no experience of misfortune and none at all of civil equality and liberty of speech, and having been brought up from the cradle amid the evidences of the power and high position of their fathers, they abandoned themselves some to greed of gain and unscrupulous money-making, others to indulgence in wine and the convivial excess which accompanies it, and others again to the violation of women and the rape of boys; and thus converting the aristocracy into an oligarchy aroused in the people feelings similar to those of which I just spoke, and in consequence met with the same disastrous end as the tyrant. For whenever anyone who has noticed the jealousy and hatred with which they are regarded by the citizens, has the courage to speak or act against the chiefs of the state he has the whole mass of the people ready to back him. Next, when they have either killed or banished the oligarchs, they no longer venture to set a king over them, as they still remember with terror the injustice they suffered from the former ones, nor can they entrust the government with confidence to a select few, with the evidence before them of their recent error in doing so. Thus the only hope still surviving unimpaired is in themselves, and to this they resort, making the state a democracy instead of an oligarchy and assuming the responsibility for the conduct of affairs. Then as long as some of those survive who experienced the evils of oligarchical dominion, they are well pleased with the present form of government, and set a high value on equality and freedom of speech. But when a new generation arises and the democracy falls into the hands of the grandchildren of its founders, they have become so accustomed to freedom and equality that they no longer value them, and begin to aim at pre-eminence; and it is chiefly those of ample fortune who fall into this error. So when they begin to lust for power and cannot attain it through themselves or their own good qualities, they ruin their estates, tempting and corrupting the people in every possible way. And hence when by their foolish thirst for reputation they have created among the masses an appetite for gifts and the habit of receiving them, democracy in its turn is abolished and changes into a rule of force and violence. For the people, having grown accustomed to feed at the expense of others and to depend for their livelihood on the property of others, as soon as they find a leader who is enterprising but is excluded from the honours of office by his penury, institute the rule of violence; and now uniting their forces massacre, banish, and plunder, until they degenerate again into perfect savages and find once more a master and monarch.

Such is the cycle of political revolution, the course appointed by nature in which constitutions change, disappear, and finally return to the point from which they started. Anyone who clearly perceives this

may indeed in speaking of the future of any state be wrong in his estimate of the time the process will take, but if his judgement is not tainted by animosity or jealousy, he will very seldom be mistaken as to the stage of growth or decline it has reached, and as to the form into which it will change. And especially in the case of the Roman state will this method enable us to arrive at a knowledge of its formation, growth and greatest perfection, and likewise of the change for the worse which is sure to follow some day. For, as I said, this state more than any other, has been formed and has grown naturally, and will undergo a natural decline and change to its contrary.

At present I will give a brief account of the legislation of Lycurgus, a matter not alien to my present purpose. Lycurgus had perfectly well understood that all the above changes take place necessarily and naturally, and had taken into consideration that every variety of constitution which is simple and formed on one principle is precarious, as it is soon perverted into the corrupt form which is proper to it and naturally follows on it. For just as rust in the case of iron and wood-worms and ship-worms in the case of timber are inbred pests, and these substances, even though they escape all external injury, fall a prey to the evils engendered in them, so each constitution has a vice engendered in it and inseparable from it. In kingship it is despotism, in aristocracy oligarchy, and in democracy the savage rule of violence; and it is impossible, as I said above, that each of these should not in course of time change into this vicious form. Lycurgus, then, foreseeing this, did not make his constitution simple and uniform, but united in it all the good and distinctive features of the best governments, so that none of the principles should grow unduly and be perverted into its allied evil, but that, the force of each being neutralized by that of the others, neither of them should prevail and outbalance another, but that the constitution should remain for long in a state of equilibrium like a well-trimmed boat, kingship being guarded from arrogance by the fear of the commons, who were given a sufficient share in the government, and the commons on the other hand not venturing to treat the kings with contempt from fear of the elders, who being selected from the best citizens would be sure all of them to be always on the side of justice; so that that part of the state which was weakest owing to its subservience to traditional custom, acquired power and weight by the support and influence of the elders. The consequence was that by drawing up his constitution thus he preserved liberty at Sparta for a longer period than is recorded elsewhere.

Lycurgus then, foreseeing, by a process of reasoning, whence and how events naturally happen, constructed his constitution untaught by adversity, but the Romans while they have arrived at the same final result as regards their form of government, have not reached it by any process of reasoning, but by the discipline of many struggles and troubles, and always choosing the best by the light of the experience gained in disaster have thus reached the same result as Lycurgus, that is to say, the best of all existing constitutions.

ADVANTAGES OF A MIXED CONSTITUTION

The three kinds of government that I spoke of above all shared in the control of the Roman state. And such fairness and propriety in all respects was shown in the use of these three elements for drawing up the constitution and in its subsequent administration that it was impossible even for a native to pronounce with certainty whether the whole system was aristocratic, democratic, or monarchical. This was indeed only natural. For if one fixed one's eyes on the power of the consuls, the constitution seemed completely monarchical and royal; if on that of the senate, it seemed again to be aristocratic; and when one looked at the power of the masses, it seemed clearly to be a democracy. The parts of the state falling under the control of each element were and with a few modifications still are as follows.

The consuls, previous to leading out their legions, exercise authority in Rome over all public affairs, since all the other magistrates except the tribunes are under them and bound to obey them, and it is they who introduce embassies to the senate. Besides this it is they who consult the senate on matters of urgency, they who carry out in detail the provisions of its decrees. Again

as concerns all affairs of state administered by the people it is their duty to take these under their charge, to summon assemblies, to introduce measures, and to preside over the execution of the popular decrees. As for preparation for war and the general conduct of operations in the field, here their power is almost uncontrolled; for they are empowered to make what demands they choose on the allies, to appoint military tribunes, to levy soldiers and select those who are fittest for service. They also have the right of inflicting, when on active service, punishment on anyone under their command; and they are authorized to spend any sum they decide upon from the public funds, being accompanied by a quaestor who faithfully executes their instructions. So that if one looks at this part of the administration alone, one may reasonably pronounce the constitution to be a pure monarchy or kingship. I may remark that any changes in these matters or in others of which I am about to speak that may be made in present or future times do not in any way affect the truth of the views I here state.

To pass to the senate. In the first place it has the control of the treasury, all revenue and expenditure being regulated by it. For with the exception of payments made to the consuls, the quaestors are not allowed to disburse for any particular object without a decree of the senate. And even the item of expenditure which is far heavier and more important than any other—the outlay every five years by the censors on public works, whether constructions or repairs—is under the control of the senate, which makes a grant to the censors for the purpose. Similarly crimes committed in Italy which require a public investigation, such as treason, conspiracy, poisoning, and assassination, are under the jurisdiction of the senate. Also if any private person or community in Italy is in need of arbitration or indeed claims damages or requires succour or protection, the senate attends to all such matters. It also occupies itself with the dispatch of all embassies sent to countries outside of Italy for the purpose either of settling differences, or of offering friendly advice, or indeed of imposing demands, or of receiving submission, or of declaring war; and in like manner with respect to embassies arriving in Rome it decides what reception and what answer should be given to them. All these matters are in the hands of the senate, nor have the people anything whatever to do with them. So that again to one residing in Rome during the absence of the consuls the constitution appears to be entirely aristocratic; and this is the conviction of many Greek states and many of the kings, as the senate manages all business connected with them.

After this we are naturally inclined to ask what part in the constitution is left for the people, considering that the senate controls all the particular matters I mentioned, and, what is most important, manages all matters of revenue and expenditure, and considering that the consuls again have uncontrolled authority as regards armaments and operations in the field. But nevertheless there is a part and a very important part left for the people. For it is the people which alone has the right to confer honours and inflict punishment, the only bonds by which kingdoms and states and in a word human society in general are held together. For where the distinction between these is overlooked or is observed but ill applied, no affairs can be properly administered. How indeed is this possible when good and evil men are held in equal estimation? It is by the people, then, in many cases that offenses punishable by a fine are tried when the accused have held the highest office; and they are the only court which may try on capital charges. As regards the latter they have a practice which is praiseworthy and should be mentioned. Their usage allows those on trial for their lives when found guilty liberty to depart openly, thus inflicting voluntary exile on themselves, if even only one of the tribes that pronounce the verdict has not yet voted. Such exiles enjoy safety in the territories of Naples, Praeneste, Tibur, and other *civitates foederatae*. Again it is the people who bestow office on the deserving, the noblest reward of virtue in a state; the people have the power of approving or rejecting laws, and what is most important of all, they deliberate on the question of war and peace. Further in the case of alliances, terms of peace, and treaties, it is the people who ratify all these or the reverse. Thus here again one might plausibly say that the people's share in the government is the greatest, and that the constitution is a democratic one.

Having stated how political power is distributed among the different parts of the state, I will now explain how each of the three parts is enabled, if they wish, to counteract or co-operate with the others. The consul, when he leaves with his army invested with the powers I mentioned, appears indeed to have absolute authority in all matters necessary for carrying out his purpose; but in fact he requires the support of the people and the senate, and is not able to bring his operations to a conclusion without them. For it is obvious that the legions require constant supplies, and without the consent of the senate, neither corn, clothing, nor pay can be provided; so that the commander's plans come to nothing, if the senate chooses to be deliberately negligent and obstructive. It also depends on the senate whether or not a general can carry out completely his conceptions and designs, since it has the right of either superseding him when his year's term of office has expired or of retaining him in command. Again it is in its power to celebrate with pomp and to magnify the successes of a general or on the other hand to obscure and belittle them. For the processions they call triumphs, in which the generals bring the actual spectacle of their achievements before the eyes of their fellow-citizens, cannot be properly organized and sometimes even cannot be held at all, unless the senate consents and provides the requisite funds. As for the people it is most indispensable for the consuls to conciliate them, however far away from home they may be; for, as I said, it is the people which ratifies or annuls terms of peace and treaties, and what is most important, on laying down office the consuls are obliged to account for their actions to the people. So that in no respect is it safe for the consuls to neglect keeping in favour with both the senate and the people.

The senate again, which possesses such great power, is obliged in the first place to pay attention to the commons in public affairs and respect the wishes of the people, and it cannot carry out inquiries into the most grave and important offences against the state, punishable with death, and their correction, unless the *senatus consultum* is confirmed by the people. The same is the case in matters which directly affect the senate itself. For if anyone introduces a law meant to deprive the senate of some of its traditional authority, or to abolish the precedence and other distinctions of the senators or even to curtail them of their private fortunes, it is the people alone which has the power of passing or rejecting any such measure. And what is most important is that if a single one of the tribunes interposes, the senate is unable to decide finally about any matter, and cannot even meet and hold sittings; and here it is to be observed that the tribunes are always obliged to act as the people decree and to pay every attention to their wishes. Therefore for all these reasons the senate is afraid of the masses and must pay due attention to the popular will.

Similarly, again, the people must be submissive to the senate and respect its members both in public and in private. Through the whole of Italy a vast number of contracts; which it would not be easy to enumerate, are given out by the censors for the construction and repair of public buildings, and besides this there are many things which are farmed, such as navigable rivers, harbours, gardens, mines, lands, in fact everything that forms part of the Roman dominion. Now all these matters are undertaken by the people, and one may almost say that everyone is interested in these contracts and the work they involve. For certain people are the actual purchasers from the censors of the contracts, others are the partners of these first, others stand surety for them, others pledge their own fortunes to the state for this purpose. Now in all these matters the senate is supreme. It can grant extension of time; it can relieve the contractor if any accident occurs; and if the work proves to be absolutely impossible to carry out it can liberate him from his contract. There are in fact many ways in which the senate can either benefit or injure those who manage public property, as all these matters are referred to it. What is even more important is that the judges in most civil trials, whether public or private, are appointed from its members, where the action involves large interests. So that all citizens being at the mercy of the senate, and looking forward with alarm to the uncertainty of litigation, are very shy of obstructing or resisting its decisions. Similarly everyone is reluctant to oppose the projects of the consuls as all are generally and individually under their authority when in the field.

Such being the power that each part has of hampering the others or co-operating with them, their union is adequate to all emergencies, so that it is impossible to find a better political system than this. For whenever the menace of some common danger from abroad compels them to act in concord and support each other, so great does the strength of the state become, that nothing which is requisite can be neglected, as all are zealously competing in devising means of meeting the need of the hour, nor can any decision arrived at fail to be executed promptly, as all are co-operating both in public and in private to the accomplishment of the task they have set themselves; and consequently this peculiar form of constitution possesses an irresistible power of attaining every object upon which it is resolved. When again they are freed from external menace, and reap the harvest of good fortune and affluence which is the result of their success, and in the enjoyment of this prosperity are corrupted by flattery and idleness and wax insolent and overbearing, as indeed happens often enough, it is then especially that we see the state providing itself a remedy for the evil from which it suffers. For when one part having grown out of proportion to the others aims at supremacy and tends to become too predominant, it is evident that, as for the reasons above given none of the three is absolute, but the purpose of the one can be counterworked and thwarted by the others, none of them will excessively outgrow the others or treat them with contempt. All in fact remains *in statu quo,* on the one hand, because any aggressive impulse is sure to be checked and from the outset each estate stands in dread of being interfered with by the others.

INTEGRITY IN PUBLIC AFFAIRS

The laws and customs relating to the acquisition of wealth are better in Rome than at Carthage. At Carthage nothing which results in profit is regarded as disgraceful; at Rome nothing is considered more so than to accept bribes and seek gain from improper channels. For no less strong than their approval of moneymaking by respectable means is their condemnation of unscrupulous gain from forbidden sources. A proof of this is that at Carthage candidates for office practise open bribery, whereas at Rome death is the penalty for it. Therefore as the rewards offered to merit are the opposite in the two cases, it is natural that the steps taken to gain them should also be dissimilar.

But the quality in which the Roman commonwealth is most distinctly superior is in my opinion the nature of their religious convictions. I believe that it is the very thing which among other peoples is an object of reproach, I mean superstition, which maintains the cohesion of the Roman State. These matters are clothed in such pomp and introduced to such an extent into their public and private life that nothing could exceed it, a fact which will surprise many. My own opinion at least is that they have adopted this course for the sake of the common people. It is a course which perhaps would not have been necessary had it been possible to form a state composed of wise men, but as every multitude is fickle, full of lawless desires, unreasoned passion, and violent anger, the multitude must be held in by invisible terrors and suchlike pageantry. For this reason I think, not that the ancients acted rashly and at haphazard in introducing among the people notions concerning the gods and beliefs in the terrors of hell, but that the moderns are most rash and foolish in banishing such beliefs. The consequence is that among the Greeks, apart from other things, members of the government, if they are entrusted with no more than a talent, though they have ten copyists and as many seals and twice as many witnesses, cannot keep their faith; whereas among the Romans those who as magistrates and legates are dealing with large sums of money maintain correct conduct just because they have pledged their faith by oath. Whereas elsewhere it is a rare thing to find a man who keeps his hands off public money, and whose record is clean in this respect, among the Romans one rarely comes across a man who has been detected in such conduct.

THE DECAY OF POLITICAL GLORY

That all existing things are subject to decay and change is a truth that scarcely needs proof; for the course of nature is sufficient to force this conviction on us. There being two agencies by which every kind of state is liable to decay, the one external and the other a growth of the state itself, we can lay down no fixed rule about the former, but the latter is a regular process. I have already stated what kind of state is the first to come into being, and what the next, and how the one is transformed into the other; so that those who are capable of connecting the opening propositions of this inquiry with its conclusion will now be able to foretell the future unaided. And what will happen is, I think, evident. When a state has weathered many great perils and subsequently attains to supremacy and uncontested sovereignty, it is evident that under the influence of long established prosperity, life will become more extravagant and the citizens more fierce in their rivalry regarding office and other objects than they ought to be. As these defects go on increasing, the beginning of the change for the worse will be due to love of office and the disgrace entailed by obscurity, as well as to extravagance and purse-proud display; and for this change the populace will be responsible when on the one hand they think they have a grievance against certain people who have shown themselves grasping, and when, on the other hand, they are puffed up by the flattery of others who aspire to office. For now, stirred to fury and swayed by passion in all their counsels, they will no longer consent to obey or even to be the equals of the ruling caste, but will demand the lion's share for themselves. When this happens, the state will change its name to the finest sounding of all, freedom and democracy, but will change its nature to the worst thing of all, mob-rule.

CHAPTER SIX

CICERO

Because Roman political thought was not expressed in systematic philosophical works, it has been wrongly assumed by many not to have existed at all. Of political *theory,* expressed in formal treatises by professional thinkers and publicists, there is not much in Roman literature that compares with the brilliant masterpieces of Greek philosophers. But political theory is only one of the sources of political *thought,* its obvious and most directly accessible expression, but not necessarily its most creative one. The political ideas of a nation or an era may, in some instances, have to be culled from less formal and direct sources than systematic treatises by philosophers and political writers. Law, lore, and literature may be important sources for the study of political thinking, though one will find in them more its indirect reflection than its direct statement. But what such sources lack in easy availability and overt presentation, they gain in variety, authenticity, and richness.

This approach to Roman political thought is perhaps not quite so unique as may appear at first sight. If one were to look for some of the most enduring expressions of American political thought in the twentieth century, one could profit as much from an examination of the judicial opinions of jurists like Holmes, Brandeis, Warren, and Scalia as from much of formal theory produced by professional political writers and publicists.

Law and administration are the two great contributions of Rome to the conceptions and practices of government and politics in the western world. The Roman law, constantly adapting itself to changing environments, is still the law of a goodly portion of the globe; its existence to this day as the predominant system on the European Continent, in Latin America, in parts of North America, and in Asia and Africa is proof of a vitality that, enduring for over two thousand years, has been nourished by sources more spiritual than those imposition by armed conquest could have supplied. The flexibility of Roman law, its capacity to adjust itself to changing social and economic conditions, its ability to grow from the law of a city into that of a world empire, its willingness to admit the stranger different in speech and religion into the world-wide community in which the *pax romana* reigned supreme—all this could hardly have been the result of "muddling through"; it was, in fact, the reflection of political wisdom of the highest order. Rome eagerly accepted the universalistic heritage of Hellenistic civilization and passed it on to the western world through institutions rather than through ideas. The marriage between Greek speculative and Roman institutional genius has brought forth much that has become an integral part of the political inheritance of the world.

The only Roman political writer who has exercised enduring influence throughout the ages is Cicero (106–43 B.C.). Characteristically, he was not a professional philosopher and leader of a school or academy of his own, but a lawyer and statesman whose works are reflections on politics rather than on political theory. Like other educated Romans of his class, he owed his philosophical outlook as much to Plato and Aristotle as to Stoicism.

Cicero studied law in Rome, and philosophy in Athens and other Greek centers of learning, and he early acquired wide contacts with other peoples and civilizations. He became the leading lawyer of his time and also rose to the highest offices of state, both in Rome and in the provinces. Yet, his life was not free from sadness; only five years after he had held the highest office in Rome, the consulate, he found himself in exile for a year, and his political fortunes never reached their previous summit.

Rome, unable to solve the growing social and imperial problems in the framework of the traditional institutions of the Republic, incessantly moved toward monarchical government. Cicero thought primarily of political and administrative remedies for the decay of the ancient republican spirit, and he had little understanding of the profound economic issues and cleavages that the rise of a propertyless proletariat in Rome and the other large cities had produced. Instead of looking into the future and accepting as permanent the new social and economic forces in Roman life, he looked back into a past in which these forces had not existed. When confronted with a sweeping popular movement of the poorer classes against the rich, led by Catiline, Cicero suppressed it ruthlessly, and had its leaders executed under circumstances that were hardly legal. Because the aristocrats and wealthy businessmen, Cicero's political friends, understood the revolutionary implications of these social and economic transformations no better than he did, monarchical government, based on considerable popular support, supplanted the proud Republic in which freedom had been nursed to greatness in so many generations.

Cicero fervently believed in moderation, concord, and constitutionalism; such a political faith flourishes best in a time of social stability. When this stability has become seriously undermined by intolerable rifts in society, constitutionalism as a purely political faith offers no solution, unless supplemented by basic social and economic reforms. And when men of moderation and good will fail, demagogues and dictators will take their place and often carry through, albeit in a perverted and distorted fashion, the reforms that, if applied by the conservatives in time, might have saved the traditional fabric of the state.

Realizing the danger too late, Cicero nevertheless showed considerable personal courage in opposing the drift toward dictatorship based on popular support. Caesar was assassinated in 44 B.C., and a year later, in 43 B.C., Cicero was murdered by the henchmen of Antony, a member of the triumvirate set up after Caesar's death. In an age of social revolution, the plea for honest government is not enough.

Cicero's two main works on government are his *Republic* and *Laws,* written in obvious reference to Plato's two works of the same titles. Superficially there is a great deal in Cicero's two works that appears to be a close imitation of Plato and Aristotle. Yet, when it comes to the inner meaning of Cicero's political views, his temper and outlook, there is a remarkable freshness and difference. Most important of all, perhaps, Cicero had a *sense of the world,* whereas Plato and Aristotle were never able to go beyond the conception of the *city-state* as the ultimate in political organization. Both Plato and Aristotle had no place for mankind in their political theories; the world was divided in Greeks and others, who were barbarians and—as Aristotle clearly avowed—inferior to cultured Greeks, who had the right to enslave them. By contrast, Cicero had a more universal outlook, fostered by his political and administrative experience in Rome and the empire, and also fed by the springs of Hellenic Stoicism, which had spread throughout the Mediterranean basin.

Cicero believed in the mission of the Roman empire, but he understood that imperial unity could be attained only through liberty and self-government of the constituent parts, and there was an element of truth in his statement that the Romans "by defending their allies have gained dominion over the whole world." Though every empire profits, in the last analysis, its founders more than its dependent beneficiaries, the Roman empire spread throughout the then-known world and lasted for centuries because the gap between promise and fulfillment was rarely felt to be offensive and intolerable. Cicero believed that the whole universe is "one commonwealth of which both gods and men are members," and that there is a law "valid for all nations and all times." Whereas the general Greek view, as typically expressed by Aristotle, held that some people were superior to others, Cicero said that "there is no human being of any race who, if he finds a guide, cannot attain to virtue."

One of the characteristic assumptions of both Plato's *Republic* and Aristotle's *Politics* is the implicit faith that, once general principles of government are laid down, the process of government can be safely entrusted to the rulers. Philosophy, not law, is the queen of both Plato's and Aristotle's masterpieces. By contrast, Cicero—the Roman, the practicing lawyer, the experienced administrator, the fighting statesman— always speaks of law whenever he discusses the state: in one of his briefest definitions, the state is a "community of law" *(iuris societas)*. The *rule of law* is important to him, and he says that although "we cannot agree to equalize men's wealth, and equality of innate ability is impossible, the legal rights at least of those who are citizens of the same commonwealth ought to be equal."

Cicero derived his faith in law as the basis of civilized life not only from his Roman background and legal training but from his personal creed. The very idea of existence was linked to that of law and government, "without which existence is impossible for a household, a city, a nation, the human race, physical nature, and the universe itself." But Cicero refused to think of law only in terms of formal authority and compulsion: "True law is right reason in agreement with nature." The task of justice is therefore to discover the "nature of things" in a given situation rather than to impose upon it a preconceived solution, supplied either by revelatory insights or logical deductions. By maintaining that man is the only living creature endowed with the faculty of thinking and reasoning, Cicero emphasizes again the oneness of mankind. All men have this faculty in common, and "those who have reason in common must also have right reason in common," that is, common conceptions of law and justice.

There is another note, too, in Cicero that points forward, toward Christianity, rather than backward, to Plato and Aristotle: Cicero's *consciousness of love* as a mighty social bond. Both Plato and Aristotle were more than pure rationalists, and the *Republic* as well as the *Politics* starts out with the hypothesis that man is by nature a social animal, and that the state is the ultimate development of man's need of society. Plato and Aristotle agree that man's social needs and sympathies are the source and starting point of political associations culminating in the state. But the sentiments and instincts of man are, for Plato and Aristotle, no more than the raw material out of which creative reason molds social and political institutions, and it is by their concordance with reason that these institutions can be measured. Affection was, for Plato and Aristotle, a genetic source of the growth of political association, the state, but not a standard by which it could be tested. Cicero sees, by contrast, the foundation of law in "our natural inclination to love our fellow-men."

This aspect of Cicero exercised a profound influence on the early fathers of the church. At the beginning of the Middle Ages he was perhaps more widely read and quoted than any other ancient political writer, as he seemed to pass on a great deal of the best in classical Greek thinking, combined with a new attitude that harmonized with the teachings of Christianity.

In his reflections on the various forms of state, Cicero follows the Aristotelian principle that the distinguishing criterion is the *end* of the state; when its purpose is justice, it makes little difference whether the form is kingship, aristocracy, or democracy. More skeptical than Aristotle, however, Cicero did not advocate any of the three desirable forms of state, because he feared that kingship might develop too easily into tyranny, aristocracy into plutocracy, and democracy into anarchical mob-rule. Cicero therefore considered a "balanced combination" between kingship, aristocracy, and democracy the best constitution; his belief in the virtues of the mixed constitution went back to Aristotle, but it was also a lesson of Roman political history that an astute observer like Cicero could hardly have missed.

Where Cicero goes further than Aristotle is in his stress on popular consent as the foundation of legitimate government, and on liberty: "Liberty has no dwelling-place in any State except that in which the people's power is the greatest, and surely nothing can be sweeter than liberty; but if it is not the same for all, it does not deserve the name of liberty." The principle of popular consent as a source of the law was a commonplace to a Roman lawyer; the conception of the people *(populus)* as a political and legal force in the process of government acquired in Roman constitutional history connotations and undertones similar to those the word "people" has acquired again in modern times in the world-wide struggles for democracy and popular self-government. Plato and Aristotle knew of the *polis,* the city-state, and of social classes, but not of the people. The conception of the "people" in western political thinking is a contribution, not of Roman philosophy, but of Roman public law.

Cicero's influence has been particularly strong in the United States, above all at the time of framing the Constitution. Not only his concept of the mixed constitution appealed to the framers. More fundamentally, his view of the state as a "community of law" seemed to provide the answer for the dilemma the framers had to face: to create one nation out of people who had come to the New World from all parts of the old world, people with very different backgrounds, languages, religions, and customs. The opening words of the brief Preamble to the Constitution read: "We the people of the United States, in order to form a more perfect union, establish justice. . . . " This close linking of national selfhood and unity with justice clearly shows that the framers felt the new nation could not be based on common descent, language, or religion, but on the rule of law.

CICERO

The Republic and *The Laws**

CIVIC RESPONSIBILITY: ITS DUTIES AND REWARDS

[Without active patriotism][1] . . . we could [never] have delivered [our native land] from attack; nor could Gaius Duelius, Aulus Atilius, or Lucius Metellus have freed [Rome] from her fear of Carthage; nor could the two Scipios[2] have extinguished with their blood the rising flames of the Second Punic War; nor, when it broke forth again with greater fury, could Quintus Maximus[3] have reduced it to impotence or Marcus Marcelus have crushed it; nor could Publius Africanus[4] have torn it from the gates of this city and driven it within the enemy's walls.

Marcus Cato again, unknown and of obscure birth—by whom, as by a pattern for our emulation, all of us who are devoted to the same pursuits are drawn to diligence and valour—might surely have remained at Tusculum in the enjoyment of the leisurely life of that healthful spot so near to Rome. But he, a madman as our friends[5] maintain, preferred, though no necessity constrained him, to be tossed by the billows and storms of our public life even to an extreme old age, rather than to live a life of complete happiness in the calm and ease of such retirement. I will not speak of the men, countless in number, who have each been the salvation of this republic; and as their lives do not much antedate the remembrance of the present generation, I will refrain from mentioning their names, lest someone complain of the omission of himself or some member of his family. I will content myself with asserting that Nature has implanted in the human race so great a need of virtue and so great a desire to defend the common safety that the strength thereof has conquered all the allurements of pleasure and ease.

But it is not enough to possess virtue, as if it were an art of some sort, unless you make use of it. Though it is true that an art, even if you never use it, can still remain in your possession by the very fact of your knowledge of it, yet the existence of virtue depends entirely upon its use; and its noblest use is the government of the State, and the realization in fact, not in words, of those very things that the philosophers, in their corners, are continually dinning in our ears. For there is no principle enunciated by the philosophers—at least none that is just and honourable—that has not been discovered and established by those who have drawn up codes of law for States. For whence comes our sense of duty? From whom do we obtain the principles of religion? Whence comes the law of nations, or even that law of ours which is called "civil"? Whence justice, honour, fair-dealing? Whence decency, self-restraint, fear of disgrace, eagerness for praise and honour? Whence comes endurance amid toils and dangers? I say, from those men who, when these things had been

---

*From Cicero, *De re publica, De legibus* (trans. Clinton Walker Keyes, Loeb Classical Library, Harvard University Press, 1928). By permission.

[1] Conjectural restorations of the sense in fragmentary passages are enclosed in brackets.

[2] Publius Cornelius Scipio (consul 218) and his brother Gnaeus Cornelius Scipio Calvus (consul 222).

[3] Quintus Fabius Maximus Cunctator.

[4] Publius Cornelius Scipio Africanus Minor.

[5] The Epicureans, whose ideal of a quiet life free from pain made them discountenance participation in politics.

inculcated by a system of training, either confirmed them by custom or else enforced them by statutes. Indeed Xenocrates, one of the most eminent of philosophers, when asked what his disciples learned, is said to have replied: "To do of their own accord what they are compelled to do by the law." Therefore the citizen who compels all men, by the authority of magistrates and the penalties imposed by law, to follow rules of whose validity philosophers find it hard to convince even a few by their admonitions, must be considered superior even to the teachers who enunciate these principles. For what speech of theirs is excellent enough to be preferred to a State well provided with law and custom? Indeed, just as I think that "cities great and dominant," as Ennius calls them, are to be ranked above small villages and strongholds, so I believe that those who rule such cities by wise counsel and authority are to be deemed far superior, even in wisdom, to those who take no part at all in the business of government. And since we feel a mighty urge to increase the resources of mankind, since we desire to make human life safer and richer by our thought and effort, and are goaded on to the fulfilment of this desire by Nature herself, let us hold to the course which has ever been that of all excellent men, turning deaf ears to those who, in the hope of even recalling those who have already gone ahead, are sounding the retreat.

As their first objection to these arguments, so well founded and so obviously sound, those who attack them plead the severity of the labour that must be performed in the defence of the State—surely a trifling obstacle to the watchful and diligent man, and one that merits only scorn, not merely with reference to matters of such moment, but even in the case of things of only moderate importance, such as a man's studies, or duties, or even his business affairs. Then too they allege the danger to which life is exposed, and confront brave men with a dishonourable fear of death; yet such men are wont to regard it a greater misfortune to be consumed by the processes of Nature and old age, than to be granted the opportunity of surrendering for their country's sake, in preference to all else, that life which in any event must be surrendered to Nature. On this point, however, the objectors

wax wordy and, as they imagine, eloquent, going on to cite the misfortunes of eminent men and the wrongs they have suffered at the hands of their ungrateful fellow-citizens. For at this point they enumerate, first the famous illustrations taken from Greek history—the story of Miltiades, vanquisher and conqueror of the Persians, who, before the wounds had yet healed which he had received full in the front on the occasion of his glorious victory, was cast into chains by his own fellow-countrymen, and at their hands lost the life which the enemy's weapons had spared; and that of Themistocles, who when driven in terror from his country, the land which he had set free, took refuge, not in the harbours of Greece, saved by his prowess, but in the recesses of the barbarian land which he had laid prostrate. Indeed there is no lack of instances of the fickleness and cruelty of Athens toward her most eminent citizens; and this vice, originating and spreading there, has, they say, overflowed even into our own powerful republic. For we are reminded of the exile of Camillus, the disgrace suffered by Ahala, the hatred directed against Nasica, the exile of Laenas, the condemnation of Opimius, the flight of Metellus, the bitter disaster to Gaius Marius, and, a little later, the slaughter and ruin of so many eminent men. In fact they now include my name also, and presumably because they think it was through my counsel and at my risk that their own peaceful life has been preserved to them, they complain even more bitterly and with greater kindness of the treatment I have received. But I find it difficult to say why, when these very men cross the seas merely to gain knowledge and to visit other countries, [they should expect us to be deterred by considerations of danger from the much more important task of defending our native land. For if the philosophers are repaid for the dangers of travel by the knowledge they gain thereby, statesmen surely win a much greater reward in the gratitude of their fellow-citizens. Few may have imagined, in view of all I had suffered, that when,] as I retired from the consulship, I took my oath before an assembly of the people, and the Roman people took the same oath, that the republic was safe [as a result of my efforts alone,] I was amply repaid thereby for all the anxiety and vexation that resulted from the injustice done to me. And yet my sufferings brought me more honour than trouble, more glory than vexation, and the joy I found in the affectionate longing felt for me by good citizens was greater than my grief at the exultation of the wicked. But, as I said before, if it had happened otherwise, how could I complain? For none of the misfortunes that fell to my lot in consequence of my great services was unexpected by me or more serious than I had foreseen. For such was my nature that, although, on account of the manifold pleasures I found in the studies which had engaged me from boyhood, it would have been possible for me, on the one hand, to reap greater profit from a quiet life than other men, or, on the other hand, if any disaster should happen to us all, to suffer no more than my fair share of the common misfortune, yet I could not hesitate to expose myself to the severest storms, and, I might almost say, even to thunderbolts, for the sake of the safety of my fellow-citizens, and to secure, at the cost of my own personal danger, a quiet life for all the rest. For, in truth, our country has not given us birth and education without expecting to receive some sustenance, as it were, from us in return; nor has it been merely to serve our convenience that she has granted to our leisure a safe refuge and for our moments of repose a calm retreat; on the contrary, she has given us these advantages so that she may appropriate to her own use the greater and more important part of our courage, our talents, and our wisdom, leaving to us for our own private uses only so much as may be left after her needs have been satisfied.

Moreover we ought certainly not to listen to the other excuses to which these men resort, that they may be more free to enjoy the quiet life. They say, for example, that is is mostly worthless men who take part in politics, men with whom it is degrading to be compared, while to have conflict with them, especially when the mob is aroused, is a wretched and dangerous task. Therefore, they maintain, a wise man should not attempt to take the reins, as he cannot restrain the insane and untamed fury of the common herd; nor is it proper for a freeman, by contending with vile and wicked opponents, to submit to the scourgings of abuse or expose himself to wrongs which are intolerable to the wise—as if, in the view of good, brave, and high-minded men, there could be any nobler motive for entering public life than the resolution not to be ruled by wicked men and not to allow the republic to be destroyed by them, seeing that the philosophers themselves, even if they should desire to help, would be impotent.

And who in the world can approve of the single exception they make, when they say that no wise man will take any part in public affairs unless some emergency compels him to do so? As if any greater emergency could come upon anyone than that with which I was confronted; and what could I have done in that crisis unless I had been consul at the time? And how could I have been consul unless I had held to a manner of life from my boyhood which led me to the highest office of State in spite of my equestrian birth? Hence it is clear that the opportunity of serving the State, however great the dangers with which it is threatened, does not come suddenly, or when we wish it, unless we are in such a position that it is possible for us to take action. It has always seemed to me that the most amazing of the teachings of learned men is that they deny their own ability to steer when the sea is calm, having never learned the art nor cared to know it, while at the same time they assure us that, when the waves dash highest, they will take the helm. For it is their habit to proclaim openly, and even to make it their great boast, that they have neither learned nor do they teach anything about the principles of the State, either to establish it or to safeguard it, and that they consider the knowledge of such things unsuited to learned or wise men, but better to be left to those who have trained themselves in that business. How can it be reasonable, therefore, for them to promise to aid the State in case they are compelled by an emergency to do so, when they do not know how to rule the State when no emergency threatens it, though this is a much easier task than the other? Indeed, if it be true that the wise man does not, as a general thing, willingly descend from his lofty heights to statecraft, but does not decline the duty if conditions force him to assume it, yet I should think he ought by no means to neglect this science of politics, because it is his duty to acquire in advance all the knowledge that, for aught he knows, it may be necessary for him to use at some future time.

I have treated these matters at considerable length because I have planned and undertaken in this work a discussion of the State; hence, in order that this discussion might not be valueless, I had, in the first place, to remove all grounds for hesitation about taking part in public affairs. Yet if there be any who are influenced by the authority of philosophers, let them for a few moments listen and attend to those whose authority and reputation stand highest among learned men; for even if these have not governed the State themselves, nevertheless, since they have dealt with the State in many investigations and treatises, I consider that they have performed a certain function of their own in the State. And in fact I note that nearly every one of those Seven whom the Greeks called "wise" took an important part in the affairs of government. For there is really no other occupation in which human virtue approaches more closely the august function of the gods than that of founding new States or preserving those already in existence.

THE MAIN TYPES OF STATE

Scipio   Well, then, a commonwealth is the property of a people.[6] But a people is not any collection of human beings brought together in any sort of way, but an assemblage of people in large numbers associated in an agreement with respect to justice and a partnership for the common good. The first cause of such an association is not so much the weakness of the individual as a certain social spirit which nature has implanted in man. For man is not a solitary or unsocial creature, but born with such a nature that not even under conditions of great prosperity of every sort [is he willing to be isolated from his fellow men.] . . .

[About fifteen lines are lost. The following fragment may be part of the missing passage.]

. . . In a short time a scattered and wandering multitude had become a body of citizens by mutual agreement. . . .

---

[6] I.e., *res publica* (public thing or property) is the same as *res populi* (thing or property of a people).

. . . . certain seeds, as we may call them, for [otherwise] no source for the other virtues nor for the State itself could be discovered. Such an assemblage of men, therefore, originating for the reason I have mentioned, established itself in a definite place, at first in order to provide dwellings; and this place being fortified by its natural situation and by their labours, they called such a collection of dwellings a town or city, and provided it with shrines and gathering places which were common property. Therefore every people, which is such a gathering of large numbers as I have described, every city, which is an orderly settlement of a people, every commonwealth, which, as I said, is "the property of a people," must be governed by some deliberative body if it is to be permanent. And this deliberative body must, in the first place, always owe its beginning to the same cause as that which produced the State itself. In the second place, this function must either be granted to one man, or to certain selected citizens, or must be assumed by the whole body of citizens. And so when the supreme authority is in the hands of one man, we call him a king, and the form of this State a kingship. When selected citizens hold this power, we say that the State is ruled by an aristocracy. But a popular government (for so it is called) exists when all the power is in the hands of the people. And any one of these three forms of government (if only the bond which originally joined the citizens together in the partnership of the State holds fast), though not perfect or in my opinion the best, is tolerable, though one of them may be superior to another. For either a just and wise king, or a select number of leading citizens, or even the people itself, though this is the least commendable type, can nevertheless, as it seems, form a government that is not unstable, provided that no elements of injustice or greed are mingled with it.

But in kingships the subjects have too small a share in the administration of justice and in deliberation; and in aristocracies the masses can hardly have their share of liberty, since they are entirely excluded from deliberation for the common weal and from power; and when all the power is in the people's hands, even though they exercise it with justice and moderation, yet the resulting equality itself is inequitable, since it allows no distinctions in rank. Therefore, even though the Persian Cyrus was the most just and wisest of kings, that form of government does not seem to me the most desirable, since "the property of the people" (for that is what a commonwealth is, as I have said) is administered at the nod and caprice of one man; even though the Massilians, now under our protection, are ruled with the greatest justice by a select number of their leading citizens, such a situation is nevertheless to some extent like slavery for a people; and even though the Athenians at certain periods, after they had deprived the Areopagus of its power, succeeded in carrying on all their public business by the resolutions and decrees of the people, their State, because it had no definite distinctions in rank, could not maintain its fair renown.

I am now speaking of these three forms of government, not when they are confused and mingled with one another, but when they retain their appropriate character. All of them are, in the first place, subject each to the faults I have mentioned, and they suffer from other dangerous faults in addition: for before every one of them lies a slippery and precipitous path leading to a certain depraved form that is a close neighbour to it. For underneath the tolerable, or, if you like, the lovable King Cyrus (to cite him as a pre-eminent example) lies the utterly cruel Phalaris, impelling him to an arbitrary change of character; for the absolute rule of one man will easily and quickly degenerate into a tyranny like his. And a close neighbour to the excellent Massilian government, conducted by a few leading citizens, is such a partisan combination of thirty men as once ruled Athens. And as for the absolute power of the Athenian people—not to seek other examples of popular government—when it changed into the fury and licence of a mob . . .

[About fifteen lines are lost. The first two lines of what follows appear to be corrupt, and cannot be translated.]

. . . and likewise some other form usually arises from those I have mentioned, and remarkable indeed are the periodical revolutions and circular courses followed by the constant changes and sequences in governmental forms. A wise man should be acquainted with these changes, but it calls for great citizens and for a man of almost

divine powers to foresee them when they threaten, and, while holding the reins of government, to direct their courses and keep them under his control. Therefore I consider a fourth form of government the most commendable—that form which is a well-regulated mixture of the three which I mentioned at first.

Laelius I know that is your opinion, Africanus, for I have often heard you say so. Nevertheless, if it will not give you too much trouble, I should like to know which you consider the best of the three forms of government of which you have been speaking. For it might help us somewhat to understand . . .

[About fifteen lines are lost. In what follows Scipio is evidently stating the common opinion that liberty is impossible in a monarchy or an aristocracy.]

Scipio . . . and every State is such as its ruler's character and will make it. Hence liberty has no dwelling-place in any State except that in which the people's power is the greatest, and surely nothing can be sweeter than liberty; but if it is not the same for all, it does not deserve the name of liberty. And how can it be the same for all, I will not say in a kingdom, where there is no obscurity or doubt about the slavery of the subject, but even in States where everyone is ostensibly free? I mean States in which the people vote, elect commanders and officials, are canvassed for their votes, and have bills proposed to them, but really grant only what they would have to grant even if they were unwilling to do so, and are asked to give to others what they do not possess themselves. For they have no share in the governing power, in the deliberative function, or in the courts, over which selected judges preside, for those privileges are granted on the basis of birth or wealth. But in a free nation, such as the Rhodians or the Athenians, there is not one of the citizens who [may not hold the offices of State and take an active part in the government.] . . .

[About fifteen lines are lost. In what follows Scipio evidently continues his summing up of the common arguments in favour of democratic government.]

. . . [Our authorities] say [that] when one person or a few stand out from the crowd as richer and more prosperous, then, as a result of the haughty and arrogant behaviour of these, there arises [a government of one or a few], the cowardly and weak giving way and bowing down to the pride of wealth. But if the people would maintain their rights, they say that no form of government would be superior, either in liberty or happiness, for they themselves would be masters of the laws and the courts, of war and peace, of international agreements, and of every citizen's life and property; this government alone, they believe, can rightly be called a commonwealth, that is, "the property of the people." And it is for that reason, they say, that "the property of the people" is often liberated from the domination of kings or senators, while free peoples do not seek kings or the power and wealth of aristocracies. And indeed they claim that this free popular government ought not to be entirely rejected on account of the excesses of an unbridled mob, for, according to them, when a sovereign people is pervaded by a spirit of harmony and tests every measure by the standard of their own safety and liberty, no form of government is less subject to change or more stable. And they insist that harmony is very easily obtainable in a State where the interests of all are the same, for discord arises from conflicting interests, where different measures are advantageous to different citizens. Therefore they maintain that when a senate has been supreme, the State has never had a stable government, and that such stability is less attainable by far in kingdoms, in which, as Ennius says,

No sacred partnership of honour is.

Therefore, since law is the bond which unites the civic association, and the justice enforced by law is the same for all, by what justice can an association of citizens be held together when there is no equality among the citizens? For if we cannot agree to equalize men's wealth, and equality of innate ability is impossible, the legal rights at least of those who are citizens of the same commonwealth ought to be equal. For what is a State except an association or partnership in justice? . . .

[About fifteen lines are lost. There is no change of topic.]

. . . Indeed they think that States of the other kinds have no right at all to the names which they arrogate to themselves. For why should I give the name of king, the title of Jupiter the Best, to a man who is greedy for personal power and absolute authority, a man who lords it over an oppressed people? Should I not rather call him tyrant? For tyrants may be merciful as well as oppressive; so that the only difference between the nations governed by these rulers is that between the slaves of a kind and those of a cruel master; for in any case the subjects must be slaves. And how could Sparta, at the time when the mode of life inculcated by her constitution was considered so excellent, be assured of always having good and just kings, when a person of any sort, if he was born of the royal family, had to be accepted as king? As to aristocrats, who could tolerate men that have claimed the title without the people's acquiescence, but merely by their own will? For how is a man adjudged to be "the best"? On the basis of knowledge, skill, learning, [and similar qualities surely, not because of his own desire to possess the title!] . . .

[About thirty lines are lost. At the end of the gap, Scipio is criticizing the arguments for democracy, and stating those for aristocracy.]

. . . If [the State] leaves [the selection of its rulers] to chance,[7] it will be as quickly overturned as a ship whose pilot should be chosen by lot from among the passengers. But if a free people chooses the men to whom it is to entrust its fortunes, and, since it desires its own safety, chooses the best men, then certainly the safety of the State depends upon the wisdom of its best men, especially since Nature has provided not only that those men who are superior in virtue and in spirit should rule the weaker, but also that the weaker should be willing to obey the stronger.

But they claim that this ideal form of State has been rejected on account of the false notions of men, who, through their ignorance of virtue—for just as virtue is possessed by only a few, so it can be distinguished and perceived by only a few—think

---

[7] *I.e.*, chooses its rulers by lot, as had been done in Athens.

that the best men are those who are rich, prosperous, or born of famous families. For when, on account of this mistaken notion of the common people, the State begins to be ruled by the riches, instead of the virtue, of a few men, these rulers tenaciously retain the title, though they do not possess the character, of the "best." For riches, names, and power, when they lack wisdom and the knowledge of how to live and to rule over others, are full of dishonour and insolent pride, nor is there any more depraved type of State than that in which the richest are accounted the best. But what can be nobler than the government of the State by virtue? For then the man who rules others is not himself a slave to any passion, but has already acquired for himself all those qualities to which he is training and summoning his fellows. Such a man imposes no laws upon the people that he does not obey himself, but puts his own life before his fellow-citizens as their law. If a single individual of this character could order all things properly in a State, there would be no need of more than one ruler; or if the citizens as a body could see what was best and agree upon it, no one would desire a selected group of rulers. It has been the difficulty of formulating policies that has transferred the power from a king to a larger number; and the perversity and rashness of popular assemblies that have transferred it from the many to the few. Thus, between the weakness of a single ruler and the rashness of the many, aristocracies have occupied that intermediate position which represents the utmost moderation; and in a State ruled by its best men, the citizens must necessarily enjoy the greatest happiness, being freed from all cares and worries, when once they have entrusted the preservation of their tranquillity to others, whose duty it is to guard it vigilantly and never to allow the people to think that their interests are being neglected by their rulers. For that equality of legal rights of which free peoples are so fond cannot be maintained (for the people themselves, though free and unrestrained, give very many special powers to many individuals, and create great distinctions among men and the honours granted to them), and what is called equality is really most inequitable. For when equal honour is

given to the highest and the lowest—for men of both types must exist in every nation—then this very "fairness" is most unfair; but this cannot happen in States ruled by their best citizens. These arguments and others like them, Laelius, are approximately those which are advanced by men who consider this form of government the best.

Laelius But what about yourself, Scipio? Which of these three forms do you consider the best?

Scipio You are right to ask which I consider the best of the three, for I do not approve of any of them when employed by itself, and consider the form which is a combination of all them superior to any single one of them. But if I were compelled to approve one single unmixed form, [I might choose] the kingship . . . the name of king seems like that of father to us, since the king provides for the citizens as if they were his own children, and is more eager to protect them than . . . to be sustained by the care of one man who is the most virtuous and most eminent. But here are the aristocrats, with the claim that they can do this more effectively, and that there will be more wisdom in the counsels of several than in those of one man, and an equal amount of fairness and scrupulousness. And here also are the people, shouting with a loud voice that they are willing to obey neither one nor a few, that nothing is sweeter than liberty even to wild beasts, and that all who are slaves, whether to a king or to an aristocracy, are deprived of liberty. Thus kings attract us by our affection for them, aristocracies by their wisdom, and popular governments by their freedom, so that in comparing them it is difficult to say which one prefers.

THE BEST CONSTITUTION

. . . [I consider] the best constitution for a State to be that which is a balanced combination of the three forms mentioned, kingship, aristocracy, and democracy, and does not irritate by punishment a rude and savage heart. . . .

. . . sixty-five years older, for it was founded in the thirty-ninth year before the first Olympiad. And Lycurgus, who lived in very ancient times, had almost the same idea. This equalized system, this combination of three constitutions, is in my opinion common to those nations and to ours. But the unique characteristic of our own commonwealth—the most splendid conceivable—I shall describe more completely and accurately, if I can, because nothing like it is to be found in any other State. For those elements which I have mentioned were combined in our State as it was then, and in those of the Spartans and Carthaginians, in such a way that there was no balance among them whatever. For in a State where there is one official who holds office for life, particularly if he be a king, even if there is a senate, such as existed at Rome under the monarchy and at Sparta under the code of Lycurgus, and even if the people possess some power, as they did under our kings—in spite of these facts the royal power is bound to be supreme, and such a government is inevitably a monarchy and will inevitably be so called. And this form of government is the most liable of all to change, because one man's vices can overthrow it and turn it easily toward utter destruction. For not only is the kingship in itself not at all reprehensible, but I am inclined to consider it by far the best of the simple forms of government—if I could approve any of the simple forms—but only so long as it retains its true character. But it does that only when the safety, equal rights, and tranquillity of the citizens are guarded by the life-long authority, the justice, and the perfect wisdom of a single ruler. To be sure a nation ruled by a king is deprived of many things, and particularly of liberty, which does not consist in serving a just master, but in [serving] no [master at all]. . . .

NATURAL LAW AND THE UNITY OF MANKIND

True law is right reason in agreement with nature; it is of universal application, unchanging and everlasting; it summons to duty by its commands, and averts from wrongdoing by its prohibitions. And it does not lay its commands or prohibitions upon good men in vain, though neither have any effect on the wicked. It is a sin to try to alter this law, nor is it allowable to attempt to repeal any part of it, and it is impossible to abolish it entirely. We cannot be freed from its obligations by senate or people, and we need not look outside ourselves for an expounder or interpreter of it. And there will not be different laws at Rome and at Athens, or different laws now and in the future, but one eternal and unchangeable law will be valid for all nations and all times, and there will be one master and ruler, that is, God, over us all, for he is the author of this law, its promulgator, and its enforcing judge. Whoever is disobedient is fleeing from himself and denying his human nature, and by reason of this very fact he will suffer the worst penalties, even if he escapes what is commonly considered punishment.

That animal which we call man, endowed with foresight and quick intelligence, complex, keen, possessing memory, full of reason and prudence, has been given a certain distinguished status by the supreme God who created him; for he is the only one among so many different kinds and varieties of living beings who has a share in reason and thought, while all the rest are deprived of it. But what is more divine, I will not say in man only, but in all heaven and earth, than reason? And reason, when it is full grown and perfected, is rightly called wisdom. Therefore, since there is nothing better than reason, and since it exists both in man and God, the first common possession of man and God is reason. But those who have reason in common must also have right reason in common. And since right reason is Law, we must believe that men have Law also in common with the gods. Further, those who share Law must also share Justice; and those who share these are to be regarded as members of the same commonwealth. If indeed they obey the same authorities and powers, this is true in a far greater degree; but as a matter of fact they do obey this celestial system, the divine mind, and the God of transcendent power. Hence we must now conceive of this whole universe as one commonwealth of which both gods and men are members.

Out of all the material of the philosophers' discussions, surely there comes nothing more valuable than the full realization that we are born for Justice, and that right is based, not upon men's opinions, but upon

Nature. This fact will immediately be plain if you once get a clear conception of man's fellowship and union with his fellow-men. For no single thing is so like another, so exactly its counterpart, as all of us are to one another. Nay, if bad habits and false beliefs did not twist the weaker minds and turn them in whatever direction they are inclined, no one would be so like his own self as all men would be like all others. And so, however we may define man, a single definition will apply to all. This is a sufficient proof that there is no difference in kind between man and man; for if there were, one definition could not be applicable to all men; and indeed reason, which alone raises us above the level of the beasts and enables us to draw inferences, to prove and disprove, to discuss and solve problems, and to come to conclusions, is certainly common to us all, and, though varying in what it learns, at least in the capacity to learn it is invariable. For the same things are invariably perceived by the senses, and those things which stimulate the senses, stimulate them in the same way in all men; and those rudimentary beginnings of intelligence to which I have referred, which are imprinted on our minds, are imprinted on all minds alike; and speech, the mind's interpreter, though differing in the choice of words, agrees in the sentiments expressed. In fact, there is no human being of any race who, if he finds a guide, cannot attain to virtue.

But the most foolish notion of all is the belief that everything is just which is found in the customs or laws of nations. Would that be true, even if these laws had been enacted by tyrants? If the well-known Thirty had desired to enact a set of laws at Athens, or if the Athenians without exception were delighted by the tyrants' laws, that would not entitle such laws to be regarded as just, would it? No more, in my opinion, should that law be considered just which a Roman interrex proposed, to the effect that a dictator might put to death with impunity any citizen he wished, even without a trial. For Justice is one; it binds all human society, and is based on one Law, which is right reason applied to command and prohibition. Whoever knows not this Law, whether it has been recorded in writing anywhere or not, is without Justice.

But if Justice is conformity to written laws and national customs, and if, as the same persons claim, everything is to be tested by the standard of utility, then anyone who thinks it will be profitable to him will, if he is able, disregard and violate the laws. It follows that Justice does not exist in Nature, and if that form of it which is based on utility can be overthrown by that very utility itself. And if Nature is not to be considered the foundation of Justice, that will mean the destruction [of the virtues on which human society depends]. For where then will there be a place for generosity, or love of country, or loyalty, or the inclination to be of service to others or to show gratitude for favours received? For these virtues originate in our natural inclination to love our fellow-men, and this is the foundation of Justice. Otherwise not merely consideration for men but also rites and pious observances in honour of the gods are done away with; for I think that these ought to be maintained, not through fear, but on account of the close relationship which exists between man and God. But if the principles of Justice were founded on the decrees of peoples, the edicts of princes, or the decisions of judges, then Justice would sanction robbery and adultery and forgery of wills, in case these acts were approved by the votes or decrees of the populace. But if so great a power belongs to the decisions and decrees of fools that the laws of Nature can be changed by their votes, then why do they not ordain that what is bad and baneful shall be considered good and salutary? Or, if a law can make Justice out of Injustice, can it not also make good out of bad? But in fact we can perceive the difference between good laws and bad by referring them to no other standard than Nature; indeed, it is not merely Justice and Injustice which are distinguished by Nature, but also and without exception things which are honourable and dishonourable. For since an intelligence common to us all makes things known to us and formulates them in our minds, honourable actions are ascribed by us to virtue, and dishonourable actions to vice; and only a madman would conclude that these judgments are matters of opinion, and not fixed by Nature.

What of the many deadly, the many pestilential statutes which nations put in force?

These no more deserve to be called laws than the rules a band of robbers might pass in their assembly. For if ignorant and unskilful men have prescribed deadly poisons instead of healing drugs, these cannot possibly be called physicians' prescriptions; neither in a nation can a statute of any sort be called a law, even though the nation, in spite of its being a ruinous regulation, has accepted it. Therefore Law is the distinction between things just and unjust, made in agreement with that primal and most ancient of all things, Nature; and in conformity to Nature's standard are framed those human laws which inflict punishment upon the wicked but defend and protect the good.

The function of a magistrate is to govern, and to give commands which are just and beneficial and in conformity with the law. For as the laws govern the magistrate, so the magistrate governs the people, and it can truly be said that the magistrate is a speaking law, and the law a silent magistrate. Nothing, moreover, is so completely in accordance with the principles of justice and the demands of Nature (and when I use these expressions, I wish it understood that I mean Law) as is government, without which existence is impossible for a household, a city, a nation, the human race, physical nature, and the universe itself. For the universe obeys God; seas and lands obey the universe, and human life is subject to the decrees of supreme Law.

As one and the same Nature holds together and supports the universe, all of whose parts are in harmony with one another, so men are united by Nature; but by reason of their depravity they quarrel, not realizing that they are of one blood and subject to one and the same protecting power. If this fact were understood, surely man would live the life of the gods!

CHAPTER SEVEN

STOICISM AND EPICUREANISM: TWO HELLENISTIC PHILOSOPHIES

Plato and Aristotle failed in one vital point: Neither clearly perceived that the division of Greece into independent sovereign city-states would finally lead to its political end. Both philosophers took the city-state of their age as much for granted as twentieth-century political writers tend to consider the national state the ultimate in political wisdom. When the Greeks were subjugated, first by Macedon and later by Rome, the teachings of Plato and Aristotle, based on their belief that the Greek city-state was superior to the outside "barbarians," seemed inadequate for the new age of empire. The citizen of formerly self-governing small political communities was reduced from an active citizen-ruler to a passive imperial subject.

During the Hellenistic period, what were needed were philosophies of man as an individual in relation to himself and to the world at large. In the small and highly integrated society of the city-state, human relations were essentially aspects of citizenship, as there was no sharp delineation between individual and community. On the one hand, the individual was rarely faced with fundamental challenges affecting him as a person, and, on the other, he was seldom drawn into a collectivity so large as to make his individuality disappear altogether. The fall of the city-state and the rise of the Macedonian and Roman empires were political revolutions that called for new outlooks expressing changed psychological realities. In the new world of empire the old traditional ties of intimate fellowship of the city-state were dissolved; an impersonal and anonymous machinery of government whose object was smooth administrative functioning, and not the good life, took their place.

Deprived of the city-state, the spiritual habitat that had nourished him so long, the individual now found himself tossed between two extremes of existence to which he had to adapt himself. First, he was thrown back on his own inner resources as a person who somehow had to survive in the collapse of traditional political forms and organizations. As his habitual sources of collective support and comfort dwindled, he had to stand on his own feet, derive strength from himself, and learn the lesson that social and political organizations come and go but that individual human beings have to keep on living. This painful discovery of loneliness after centuries of rich communal life must have been a deep shock to the inhabitant of the former city-state, whose traditional values and goals did not seem to fit into the new world.

If the vastness and anonymity of empire forced the citizen to become more consciously aware of himself as an individual, depriving him as they did of the traditional sources of satisfaction that are to be derived from a small society, he was also forced to broaden immensely the range of his outlook and to think in terms of the world. In the new political reality of world empire, the city-state was little more than a small unit of local administration, and the individual had to grow accustomed to the fact that he was part of a motley realm, full of strange and unknown peoples, customs, and ideas. Compared with the citizen of the old city-state, the subject of the new empires had to undergo the double strain of being more intensely *individual* and at the same time more *universal* in outlook than he had ever been before.

Such was the intellectual vitality of Greece even after the loss of her political independence that she continued to lead the world in the realm of intellect and philosophy, as she had done in the heyday of Plato and Aristotle; Alexander himself, when he conquered the ancient empires and states of the East, spread the Greek language throughout the new Greco-oriental, or Hellenistic, world. Although from the viewpoint of narrow Greek patriotism, the Hellenization of "barbarians" might have appeared a falsification and dilution of "pure" Greek culture, from the broader vantage point of world history, Hellenization was the process of transmitting basic values of Greek life and thought to universal civilization. The dilution of tribal purity in the larger stream of hybrid humanity was a relatively small price.

The five centuries from about 300 B.C. to A.D. 200 were predominantly centuries of Hellenistic cultural influence, with Greece proper never failing to play an important part of her own. Even at the peak of Roman political and economic power there was more Hellenization of the Latin world than Romanization of the Hellenistic world. Romanization and Latinization became permanent successes only in areas in which they did not compete with Hellenistic culture. History has never witnessed again such a long hegemony of one civilization; the nearest parallel to it, French cultural leadership in the seventeenth and eighteenth centuries, lasted for about two hundred years, but it was not nearly so expansive and creative, in the sense of entirely transforming existing national societies into an alien pattern of language, art, philosophy, science, and thought.

The Hellenistic period was characterized, however, not only by the impact of Greece on the outside world but also by the continuous entry of non-Greeks into Greek life. Gradually Greece ceased to be the source and instead became the universal clearinghouse of new ideas. In the garb of Greek language and forms, non-Greeks thought, new ideas would be more likely to receive a universal hearing and perhaps acceptance; consequently individual persons and entire families Hellenized their names, adopted the Greek language, studied in Greece or one of the new centers of learning, such as Alexandria, and identified themselves with Hellenistic culture.

The most influential philosophical school of the five centuries from about 300 B.C. to A.D. 200 was *Stoicism*. It was founded by Zeno around 300 B.C., and derived its name from the Painted Porch (or "Stoa") in Athens, in which Zeno used to teach. Zeno was a native of Cyprus, of Hellenized Phoenician origin, and a stranger to Athens. Similarly, nearly all the early leaders of Stoic thought were non-Greeks who came from the fringe of Greek settlements or well beyond them. The geographic variety of Stoicism was matched by its social latitude; it perhaps is symbolic of the personal and universal message of Stoicism that its two most representative figures were a Greek slave and a Roman emperor.

Epictetus (about A.D. 50–120) was a slave from Asia Minor who came to Rome at an early age. His master permitted him to study philosophy and later freed him. Epictetus then set up his own school in Rome; in A.D. 89 Emperor Domitian banished philosophers from Rome, and Epictetus went to Greece to teach philosophy there. Like Socrates, Epictetus never wrote a book; a disciple of his, Flavius Arrian, who was a Roman official, recorded Epictetus' lectures and informal conversations in the *Discourses* and a brief *Manual,* or summary, of his basic ideas.

Epictetus was of poor health and became lame early in life. His master, a freedman at Nero's court, once twisted Epictetus' leg. Epictetus serenely smiled: "You will break it." His master continued, and when the leg was broken, Epictetus merely said: "I told you so." This anecdote vividly reflects one of the qualities that popular imagination has come to regard as particularly characteristic of Stoicism: fortitude of mind under all circumstances, the triumph of mind and will over matter and pain.

The most illustrious philosophical successor to Epictetus was Marcus Aurelius (A.D. 121–180), Roman emperor from A.D. 161–180. Marcus Aurelius was born in Rome of a family that was originally Spanish; he was the nephew of his predecessor on the throne and thus acquainted with public affairs from an early age. He is one of the half-dozen philosopher-kings in history, like those of whom Plato had dreamed in the *Republic,* and he was perhaps more in his element as a philosopher than as the ruler of the Roman empire. Like Epictetus, Marcus Aurelius wrote no books. His *Meditations* are not a book, and were not planned as such by him, but are more in the nature of a journal (as the title has often been rendered), informal notes and observations addressed to himself rather than to the public.

The author, though a Roman emperor, wrote in Greek, which he mastered from early youth. The only other famous ruler who wrote in a foreign language was Frederick the Great of Prussia, who preferred French to German, declaring his own tongue only "fit for horses." During the period of Marcus Aurelius it was not uncommon for non-Greeks to write in Greek, the language of prestige and universal currency, just as during the seventeenth and eighteenth centuries French had no rival among the educated.

Marcus Aurelius was well aware of his general debt to Stoic predecessors in philosophy, but he felt himself under a particular obligation to Epictetus, whom he deeply venerated and whose sayings he often quoted word by word. By identifying himself so closely with a lowly slave, Marcus Aurelius thus practiced the Stoic faith in the equality of all men, regardless of their nationality and station in life.

The Stoics did not think of themselves primarily as political theorists, and Stoicism is not a theory of the state. This fact, however, did not preclude Stoic thought from exercising a considerable influence on government and politics, partly because so many kings and high officials of the Hellenistic and Roman periods were professing, though not always practicing, Stoics. Stoicism appeals to the individual as an individual rather than as a member of an organized community, and in this characteristic lies its strength and weakness. The moral appeal to the individual is not, as in the closely knit city-state of Plato and Aristotle, to idolize and worship the laws and morals of one's community but to live in accordance with nature.

The Stoic concept of nature was different from the earlier view, which presented numerous demons and gods reveling in unpredictable adventures, as it was distinct from the later view, which conceived of nature as a machine, operating according to physical laws. The Stoic conception of nature was less demonistic and less mechanistic than either: nature includes both the process of growth and the goal and principle toward which this process is moving and to which it seeks to give life. Nature, the whole cosmos, is thus pervaded by goal and purpose, and to live according to nature means to work with it to-ward the harmony and orderliness that is inherent in it. The "one principle of action that governs all things" is to be *at one with oneself,* to know oneself, and to act in conformity with one's purposes and rational principles.

Like nature, human beings also are subject to an all-pervading harmonious and ratio-nal ordering, and just as cosmic peace is the expression of such law and harmony, so tranquillity of the individual "is nothing else than the good ordering of the mind." Ac-cording to this Stoic view, man and nature are not opposites; both partake of reason and harmony, which are more important than accidental differences. The *"true self"* of man is therefore, not his "flesh or bones or sinews, but the faculty which uses them," that is, *reason,* the part of man that characterizes him as human, through which he shares in what gives life and purpose to the world as a whole. A person who attains a good ordering of his mind and is at one with himself, also acts and feels responsibly, without blaming others or himself for whatever happens to him. This process of mental health is tersely summed up by Epictetus in three short phrases: "To accuse others for one's own misfortunes is a sign of want of education; to accuse oneself shows that one's education has begun; to accuse neither oneself nor others shows that one's education is complete."

Once he has recognized his rational faculty as his true nature, man can attain com-plete *selfhood,* in other words, if he learns to guide his life in accordance with what is essential, his reason, and if he is not overly impressed by external events that in them-selves are neither good nor bad, productive of neither pain nor pleasure, because what "disturbs men's minds is not events, but their judgments on events." If man can preserve the inner freedom that he possesses as a rational being, no external evil or threat of evil, not even death, can be potent enough to break his freedom, his self, his quality as a ra-tional being. External things, then, are not good or evil in themselves; they are merely "materials for the will, in dealing with which it will find its own good or evil."

Epictetus, in particular, deals with the question of how the isolated individual can preserve himself against the tyrant who is surrounded by sycophantic adulation and who commands irresistible force. The tyrant has power over individuals only to the ex-tent that they fear him, that is, to the extent that they treasure their accidental posses-sions of property and health, their life, more than their inner freedom, their reason, over which no one else can have authority. What maintains a tyrant, therefore, is not his command over external means of compulsion, police and prisons, but the failure of men to preserve their true natures in the face of such external pressures. In other words, it is the control over men's minds rather than their bodies that gives a tyrant his parasitical power; if men began to live in accordance with their natures, their reason and freedom of will, tyrannical power could not long persist. Baruch Spinoza, the seventeenth-century philosopher, expresses this Stoic idea in an even broader form, when he says, "Obedience makes the king." Events in 1989 in Eastern Europe show the validity of this Stoic doctrine, although the revolutions there were also made possible only by the collapse of Soviet control.

Epictetus and Marcus Aurelius express an important idea in saying that "no man can rob us of our free will," and that even death is not frightening, as it involves only the re-turn of the material parts of the body to the elements of which it was made up. More-over, they say, one should be content with death, because it is one of the things that nature wills; one should wait for it as "one of the operations of nature." The Stoic there-fore learns to detach himself from events that are beyond his control, because whatever is "beyond the control of my will, is nothing to me."

Epictetus was aware of the charge that his doctrine of an inalienable rational self, which no tyrant could subjugate, might teach men to "despise the laws." His argument in reply to this charge is ingenious. Stoicism, far from teaching political disobedience, actually makes us obedient to the laws, he says, because it teaches us to give way in regard to "our poor body," property, parents, and children, to "give up everything, resign everything; only our judgments it reserves, and these Zeus willed should be each man's special property."

To the interjection that a man's judgments are "the greatest matters of all," Epictetus retorts in this way: as long as the main concern of rulers is how to live in palaces, enjoy the services of slaves and freedmen, the pleasure of feasts and plays, the power supplied by armies and police forces, and other external matters, men of reason and integrity will cheerfully acknowledge the superiority of their rulers. But how insignificant are such matters when compared with moral selfhood, which cannot be conquered by external force. To influence men's judgment and reason, the rulers ought to busy themselves less with external things, Epictetus says; they should concern themselves more with their own rational selves, if they want to understand those of others. The Stoic is thus willing to give way to the king or tyrant in matters of external force, because there the ruler is superior; "where, on the other hand, I am the better man, it is for you to give way to me, for I have made this my concern, and you have not."

The Stoic doctrine is not free from self-contradiction. If the value of life, property, family, offices, health, and freedom is denigrated, the citizen is more readily inclined to obey the ruler's commands, as long as the latter has the physical means to enforce their compliance. In this sense, Stoicism has had a *conservative* influence throughout the ages, encouraging the individual to submit completely to the powers that be and to realize himself as a person in other realms of thought and action. On the other hand, there is no doubt that the Stoic doctrine of complete individual *moral integrity,* which must not be compromised even at the price of death, has *revolutionary* implications. Some rulers may be satisfied with external, formal obedience. Others will insist on inner adherence and voluntary acceptance, and here Stoicism, fully aware that these are "the greatest matters of all" in human relations, has a distinctly revolutionary flavor. What opposes tyrants and dictators, after all, is not this or that party program but the moral courage of individual human beings, whose integrity and faith in themselves and others, in reason and justice, cannot be broken by any external pressure.

No philosophy before Stoicism, and perhaps none after, has centered its teachings so emphatically on individual responsibility and integrity, and done so without threatening penalties or promising rewards, as some religions are wont to do. The Stoics did not even hold out the immortality of the soul as an ultimate goal to which mortals could hopefully look forward. A philosophical or moral creed has rarely demanded so much of men, and promised so little; as a consequence, Stoicism has never appealed to masses and groups but to individuals in whom the "categorical imperative" (as Kant later puts it) is a living and indomitable force.

Stoicism thus attracted two opposing types of men: *First, the more reflective,* saintly ascetic, who attains full peace of mind and soul by withdrawing from the world completely, to whom love and friendship, pain and pleasure, property and office, mean nothing. He finds his self-realization in contemplation and meditation, which bring him closer to that merging with the Whole of which he is an infinitesimally small part. The second type of Stoic, by contrast, is more active; he seeks his communion with the Whole, not by contemplating it, but by working toward its high purposes and goals, which also encompass his own life.

Epictetus himself, usually considered the more reflective kind of Stoic, nevertheless observes that "it is not arguments that are wanting nowadays," but "the man who will apply his arguments, and bear witness to them by action." Similarly, Marcus Aurelius, who spent a lifetime of hard work in governing a far-flung empire, said: "Not in passivity, but in activity lie the evil and the good of the rational social animal, just as his virtue and his vice lie not in passivity, but in activity." In the beginning of the *Meditations,* in which he analyzes the sources of his moral heritage, Marcus Aurelius also expresses gratitude to his brother who had early taught him a "disposition to do good, and to give to others readily, and to cherish good hopes, and to believe that I am loved by my friends." The ethical ideal of Stoicism was most vividly expressed in a Latin phrase, translated by Pliny from a Greek Stoic: "God is man's helping of man" *(Deus est mortali iuvare mortalem).*

There is a degree of contradiction between the two main Stoic types, based as they are on two not fully reconcilable philosophical conceptions. On the one hand, the world is thought of in terms of Reason, Law, and Harmony, and things and events are predetermined within this realm of cosmic necessity. On the other hand, there are freedom of will and the moral duty to work for that rational ordering of the world toward which it is perpetually moving, and moving more rapidly with the aid of human goodness and reason. This contradiction between the two main types of Stoics is characteristic of most philosophies and religions that try to combine natural law with individual freedom, or the predetermined harmony of the world with its manifest phenomena of discord.

The refusal to promise absolutes prevented Stoicism from becoming a popularly accepted creed; unable to satisfy the quest for certainty that gives mass movements their emotional appeal, Stoicism was taken up by strong personalities who felt themselves equal to its austere demands. According to the Stoic view, no human activity can claim ultimate validity. All that human beings can do is to live and work in accordance with nature, that is, being every activity and thing to the highest level of perfection of which it is capable.

Viewed from the outside, such activities may perhaps appear unimportant in relation to eternal and absolute values. Stoics therefore often compare life to a play: "Remember that you are an actor in a play, and the Playwright chooses the manner of it: if he wants it short, it is short; if long, it is long. If he wants you to act a poor man you must act the part with all your powers; and so if your part be a cripple or a magistrate or a plain man. For your business is to act the character that is given you and act it well; the choice of the cast is Another's." The important thing is therefore, as for an actor in a play, to perform one's task well, regardless of its ultimate value and purpose. Without the promise of heaven and the threat of hell, the Stoic is satisfied with having tried hard, having played his role well, just as the actor is concerned more about the acting of his part than about the character he personifies, or about the success or failure of his doings in the play. The Stoic symbolism of life as a play reflects the contradiction between the two strands in Stoicism that alternatively stress reflection and action, necessity and freedom, predetermined perfection and striving toward perfection. Yet these contradictions in Stoicism possibly reflect, not avoidable imperfections of faulty logic or philosophy, but life itself.

As was pointed out earlier, the decline of the city-state and the rise of empire not only made the individual more conscious of himself as an individual but enlarged his horizon. Here, again, the Stoic philosophy attempted to provide philosophical answers to needs and challenges of restless and changing societies. Zeno, the Hellenized Phoenician, founder of Stoicism, wrote an anti-Platonic *Republic* in which he taught that the ideal state must be a world-state, and that an end should be put to the many individual states, each with its own laws and conceptions of justice. Citizenship would be universal for all men, and there would be one system of law, based on universally accepted reason rather than on local customs and conventions. Zeno also opposed institutions that seemed to him artificial, such as temples, law courts, money, and marriage, and he vigorously condemned the inequality of women, not, as Plato had done, of women who belonged to the ruling class, but of all women. Unlike Aristotle, who assumed that some human beings are by nature slaves, Zeno and the early Stoics insisted that slavery was contrary to natural law, that it was no more than an arbitrary convention based on force and expediency, and that there were no nations or ethnic groups naturally inferior, fit only to serve those who claimed to be superior.

Because the earlier Stoics were Hellenized non-Greeks, they were able to appraise Greek life with a fresh eye. They took nothing for granted, bowed to no sacrosanct taboos, and exposed even the most solidly entrenched practices and prejudices to critical examination. Later on, such radical attacks were toned down, particularly when Rome became the center of Stoicism.

Practical-minded, the Roman Stoics abandoned some of the early denunciations of all conventions and institutions, but they retained the basic Stoic doctrine of *one world.* According to the pantheistic and panrationalistic view of Stoicism, the universe is God, and God is Reason. In this "frame of things," governed by universal reason, "men and God are united," and from this unity, Epictetus says, "come the seeds from which are begotten not only my own father or grandfather, but all things that are begotten and that grow upon earth, and rational creatures in particular—for these alone are by nature fitted to share in the society of God, being connected with Him by the bond of reason— why should he not call himself a citizen of the universe and a son of God?" Epictetus also expresses, in an amazing parallel to Judeo-Christian monotheism, the doctrine of the brotherhood of mankind, inasmuch as all men have "God as maker and father and kinsman."

Marcus Aurelius formulates the idea of universal political and legal unity even more clearly. Because all human beings have mind in common, "the reason also, in respect of which we are rational beings, is common: if this is so, common also is the reason which commands us what to do, and what not to do; if this is so, there is a common law also; if this is so, we are fellow-citizens; if this is so, we are members of some political community; if this is so, the world is in a manner of a state." Marcus Aurelius sees himself both as the emperor of Rome and as a man, a citizen of the world: "But my nature is rational and social; and my city and country, so far as I am Antoninus [his full name included "Antonius"], is Rome, but so far as I am a man, it is the world. The things then which are useful to these cities are alone useful to me."

The Stoics thus consider the faculty to reason the most human quality, one that is shared by all men. The laws of reason prevail independently of, and are above, legal and political rules that owe their acceptance to convenience and expediency rather than to inherent truth. Stressing what unites men rather than what separates them, the Stoics not only attacked narrow tribalism and chauvinism but also pleaded for greater equality of woman and slaves, a revolutionary doctrine at that time, and far from complete realization today.

Once the Stoics clearly understood the unity of mankind (and they were among the first in history to attain this conception on a rational, secular basis), differences of sex, class, social status, and political constitution seemed relatively insignificant. The unity of man was in itself part of a larger world held together by the law of nature, a law whose validity rested on its intrinsic rationality rather than on the fiats of kings and emperors. The Stoic concept of natural law found its practical application in the Roman philosophical idea of *ius naturale* (natural law), as well as in the Roman legal system of *ius gentium* (law of nations); thus it laid the foundations for the later development of international law.

In theory, there was a sharp distinction between the law of nations and natural law; for example, slavery was considered by Roman lawyers to be contrary to natural law but a recognized institution of the law of nations. Yet the sharp theoretical distinction between the law of nations as a set of *rules of positive law and the law of nature as a philosophical system of what the law ought to be* was gradually abandoned under the impact of Stoic ideas, and the two were increasingly identified. Because, as explained earlier, Stoicism stresses what human institutions have in common rather than what separates them—the first being their essence and the second what is accidental, local, and arbitrary in them—natural law and the law of nations became merged into one philosophical conception, according to which, as defined in the *Institutes of Emperor Justinian's Corpus Juris Civilis,* "the law that natural reason has prescribed for all men, is equally observed by all nations, and is called the law of nations, because all nations make use of it" (1.2.1). Thus, wherever the Roman law expanded—and it usually stayed once it had taken root—it carried with it an openness and universality that it owed to the Stoic sense of all men living in "one world."

The Stoic influence on Christianity was no less profound than that on Roman law. When St. Paul stated that there was "neither Jew nor Greek, neither bond nor free," he voiced an ideal that was in complete harmony with the Stoic legacy.

Thrice in modern times have Stoic doctrines played a vitalizing part. First, the development of a new international law from the sixteenth century on was strengthened by the revival of natural law, based on secular or religious foundations. The process is not yet finished, and the Stoic vision of universal government through universal law and justice still awaits its realization. The second impact of Stoic ideas occurred in eighteenth-century France, when the makers of the French Revolution, fired by ideals of liberty, equality, and fraternity, sought to build a new world on purely rational principles, without the burdensome conventions of traditional religion, privilege, or class. Finally, the Stoic idea of a "law above the law" became the fundamental principle of the American constitutional system, jealously guarded by the judiciary and profoundly revered by the American people, who have been unwilling to accept the view that laws of fallible men, exposed to the temptations of passion and interest, are binding under all circumstances.

Every revolution appeals to natural law for justification. Every country, therefore, that has experienced popular revolutions has incorporated some natural law into its heritage. Unlike most other countries, the United States remembers its major revolution, not as one among many phases of its historical experience, but as the source and origin of its very existence. As a result, the tradition of thinking according to natural law, a tradition that goes back directly to Stoic principles, is particularly strong in the United States.

In Epicureanism, another major modern philosophical and political approach is found—utilitarianism. Epicurus (c. 342–270 b.c.) and Zeno, the founder of Stoicism, were contemporaries, and both settled in Athens within a few years of each other and began their schools. Unlike Stoicism, Epicureanism never really developed beyond the teachings of its founder. Regrettably, few of his works survive. Enough is left, however, along with various other ancient sources—including the *Life of Epicurus* by Diogenes Laertius and *On the Nature of Things* by Lucretius—to be able to tell the spirit of his outlook.

Epicurus most commonly is associated with sensual enjoyment. But this association—which both Stoics and many Christians furthered, and which thus came down to modernity as the correct view—does no justice to the man at all. While Epicurus states in his *Principal Doctrines* (which does survive), "No pleasure is a bad thing in itself," his view of pleasure is such as to render his philosophy benign. Like later utilitarians, he does not consider coarse pleasures of bodily indulgence particularly to be pleasures at all. For him, freedom from pain is the principal pleasure. This conception may have been founded upon his own ill health, which frequently confined him to bed, hence the common image of him draped on a couch.

Like so many Greeks, Epicurus was interested both in nature *(physis)* and convention *(nomos)* and he lived, wrote, and thought before the split between science and philosophy. His orientation is more integrated and comprehensive than of most modern writers and thinkers. Although he is a materialist, he is not a determinist. That is, he accepts the atomic theory that reality can be reduced to material atoms (and not some sort of spiritual essence), but does not hold that all of atoms' motions are necessary or programmed. Humans can exercise some control over their actions—will.

Epicurus' hedonism grows out of his materialism. He considers even the soul material and thus perishable. Largely for this reason he later was vilified by Christians (in the *Inferno,* Dante devises a special punishment for Epicureans; because they deny the survival of the soul apart from the body, their souls are to be imprisoned in sealed coffins along with their bodies). Whenever life is held to be transitory in an ultimate sense—that is, there is no afterlife—then a tendency emerges for philosophies to emphasize the worldly, almost *ipso facto* (by this fact). Epicurus's view of divinity scarcely won him more admiration in his day than it subsequently did. "The impious man," he writes, "is not he who denies the gods of the many, but he who attaches to the gods the beliefs of the many." He believes there are immortal gods, but they do not trouble themselves with the affairs of this world. This is a reason for praising them, however, not despising them for at least they do not terrorize (as well as reward) men and women, as many of his contemporaries thought. Humans may be inspired by the gods through contemplation of them and the world they have created.

In his "Letter to Herodotus," Epicurus comments that one should refer "always to the sensations and feelings, for in this way you will obtain the most trustworthy ground of belief." He disapproves of superstitious practices, and resolves all knowledge into what is derived from the senses. He only values knowledge based on sensory data—a most empirical outlook, very similar to his utilitarian successors two-thousand years later—because this allows peace of mind (as it is free of superstitions) and provides contemplative pleasures. His view of death is that it is nothing: Death simply is "deprivation of sensation." When one is deprived of sensation, one is not; therefore there is nothing to worry about in death. The only aspect of Benthamite utilitarianism not present in Epicurus is quantitative valuation of pleasures and pains.

Although believing that all pleasures and pains ultimately are grounded in the senses, Epicurus also feels that non-physical forms of happiness and unhappiness have more worth to individuals than strictly sensory ones. As Diogenes Laertius recorded in the *Life,* in disagreeing with another ancient Greek school—the Cyrenaics—who "thought that bodily pains were worse than those of the soul, . . . Epicurus held that the pains of the soul are worse: for the flesh is only troubled for the moment, but the soul for past, present, and future." Epicurus considers philosophy and friendship to be two chief pleasures, and regarding the physical he advocates a simple diet partially because when one does consume a luxurious item it will give all the more pleasure. Regarding sex he counsels, "Sexual intercourse has never done a man good, and he is lucky if it has not harmed him." In short, Epicurus is no Epicurean at least not as the term has come to be understood.

Epicurus advises withdrawal from the political and active life—there is too great a chance this will lead to personal unhappiness and pain. His was an appropriate response to a changing social order in which residents of city-states had lost control of their destinies. Instead, his followers formed their own communities that lasted throughout the European world for seven centuries. Indeed, of all the Greek philosophies, his is the only one that achieved such a popular following. He himself became considered an ethical progenitor—followers carved likenesses of him in marble, carried his doctrines about in handbooks (pledging to live according to his teachings), and gathered in assemblies on the twentieth of each month to remember him. Some indication of the esteem in which his followers held him is indicated by Lucretius: "Thee [Epicurus] who first was able amid such thick darkness to raise on high a beacon and shed light on the true interests of life, thee I follow, glory of the Greek race." In formal observances, and through their founder's emphases on altruistic hedonism and equality both among individuals and between the sexes, ancient Epicureanism, in addition to Stoicism, prepared the way for European reception of Hebrew monotheism and Christian love.

I EPICTETUS

The Discourses and *The Manual**

WE ARE ALL GOD'S KINSMEN

If these statements of the philosophers are true, that God and men are akin, there is but one course open to men, to do as Socrates did: never to reply to one who asks his country, "I am an Athenian," or "I am a Corinthian," but "I am a citizen of the universe." For why do you say that you are an Athenian, instead of merely a native of the little spot on which your bit of a body was cast forth at birth? Plainly you call yourself Athenian or Corinthian after that more sovereign region which includes not only the very spot where you were born, and all your household, but also generally that region from which the race of your forbears has come down to you. When a man therefore has learnt to understand the government of the universe and has realized that there is nothing so great or sovereign or all-inclusive as this frame of things wherein men and God are united, and that from it come the seeds from which are sprung not only my own father or grandfather, but all things that are begotten and that grow upon earth, and rational creatures in particular—for these alone are by nature fitted to share in the society of God, being connected with Him by the bond of reason—why should he not call himself a citizen of the universe and a son of God? Why should he fear anything that can happen to him among men? When kinship with Caesar or any other of those who are powerful in Rome is sufficient to make men live in security, above all scorn and free from every fear, shall not the fact

that we have God as maker and father and kinsman relieve us from pains and fears?

"And where am I to find food to eat, if I have nothing?" says one.

Well, what do slaves do when they leave their masters, or what do they rely on? Do they rely on fields, or servants, or silver plate? No, on nothing but themselves; nevertheless sustenance does not fail them. And shall our philosopher in his wanderings have to rest his confidence in others, instead of taking care of himself? Is he to be baser and more cowardly than the unreasoning beasts? For each one of them is content with itself, and lacks not its proper sustenance nor the way of life that is naturally suited to it.

I think that the old man who sits here to teach you ought to devote his skill not to save you from being low-minded, and from reasoning about yourselves in a low and ignoble spirit, but rather to prevent young men from arising of the type who, discovering their kinship with the gods, and seeing that we have these fetters attached to us in the shape of the body and its possessions and all that we find necessary for the course and management of our life by reason of the body, may desire to fling all these away as vexatious and useless burdens and so depart to the gods their kindred.

And so your teacher and instructor, if he were a true teacher, should engage in this conflict of argument:

You come saying, "Epictetus, we can bear no longer to be bound with the fetters of this wretched body, giving it meat and drink and rest and purgation, and by reason of the body having to adapt ourselves to this or that set of circumstances. Are not these things indifferent and as nothing to us, and death no evil thing? Are we not kinsmen of

*From Epictetus, *The Discourses and Manual* (trans. P. E. Matheson, Oxford University Press, 1916). By permission.

the gods, from whom we have come hither? Suffer us to depart to the place whence we have come, suffer us to be released from these bonds that are fastened to us and weigh us down. Here are robbers and thieves and law-courts and so-called kings, who by reason of our poor body and its possessions are accounted to have authority over us. Suffer us to show them that they have authority over nothing."

Hereupon I answer: "Men as you are, wait upon God. When He gives the signal and releases you from this service, then you shall depart to Him; but for the present be content to dwell in this country wherein He appointed you to dwell. Short indeed is the time of your dwelling here, and easy for them whose spirit is thus disposed. What manner of tyrant or what thief or what law-courts have any fears for those who have thus set at nought the body and its possessions? Stay where you are, and depart not without reason." Such should be the answer of the teacher to his gifted pupils. How different is what we see! There is no life in your master, and no life in you. When you have had your fill to-day, you sit groaning about the morrow, and how you are to find food. Slave, if you get food, you will have it; if not, you will depart: the door is open. Why do you whine? What room is there for tears any more? What occasion for flattery any more? Why should one envy another? Why should he gaze with wonder on them that are rich or powerful, especially if they be strong and quick to anger? For what will they do with us? We will pay no heed to what they have power to do, what we really care for they cannot touch. Who, I ask you, will be master over one who is of this spirit?

How did Socrates approach these matters? Surely as one should who is convinced of his kinship with the gods. "If you tell me," he says, " 'We acquit you on condition that you discourse no longer as you have done hitherto, and that you do not annoy young or old among us,' I shall answer, 'It is absurd for you to suppose that, while I am bound to maintain and guard any post to which your general appointed me, and should rather die ten thousand times than abandon it, yet if God has appointed us to a certain place and way of life we ought to abandon that.' " [Plato, *Apology*, 29c, 28e]

Here you see a man who is a kinsman of the gods in very truth. But as for us—we think of ourselves as if we were all belly and flesh and animal desire; such are our fears, such our passions; those that can help us to these ends we flatter, and at the same time fear.

Some one has asked me to write for him to Rome, one who, as the world thought, had had misfortunes; he had once been famous and rich, and had now lost everything and was living here. So I wrote for him in a humble tone. And he read my letter and gave it back to me and said, "I wanted your help, not your pity." So, too, Rufus, to try me, used to say, "Your master will do this or that to you"; and when I answered him, "This is the lot of man," "Why then," said he, "do I appeal to your master when I can get everything from you?" for, indeed, it is true that what a man has of himself it is idle and futile for him to receive from another. Am I then, who can get from myself the gift of a noble and lofty spirit, to get from you a field or money or office? Heaven forbid! I will not be so blind to my true possessions. But when a man is mean and cowardly, for him one must needs write letters as for one that is dead. "Make us a present of the corpse of so and so and his miserable quart of blood." For indeed such a one is a mere corpse and a quart of blood and nothing more. If he were anything more, he would have realized that one man cannot make another miserable.

HOW TO BEHAVE TOWARD TYRANTS

If a man possesses some advantage, or thinks he does though he does not, he is bound, if he be uneducated, to be puffed up because of it. The tyrant, for instance, says, "I am mightiest of all men."

Well, and what can you give me? Can you enable me to get what I will to get? How can you? Can you avoid what you will to avoid, independent of circumstances? Is your impulse free from error? How can you claim any such power?

Tell me, on shipboard, do you put confidence in yourself or in the man who knows? And in a chariot? Surely in him who knows. How is it in other arts? Exactly the same. What does your power come to then?

"All men pay me attention."

Yes, and I pay attention to my platter and work it and polish it and I fix up a peg for my oil-flask. Does that mean that these are superior to me? No, but they do me some service, and for this reason I pay them attention. Again: do I not pay attention to my ass? Do I not wash his feet? Do I not curry him? Do you not know that every man pays regard to himself, and to you only as to his ass? For who pays regard to you as a man? Show me. Who wishes to become like you? Who regards you as one like Socrates to admire and follow?

"But I can behead you."

Well said. I forgot, of course, one ought to pay you worship as if you were fever or cholera, and raise an altar to you, like the altar to Fever in Rome.

What is it then which disturbs and confounds the multitude? Is it the tyrant and his guards? Nay, God forbid! It is impossible for that which is free by nature to be disturbed or hindered by anything but itself. It as a man's own judgements which disturb him. For when the tyrant says to a man, "I will chain your leg," he that values his leg says, "Nay, have mercy," but he that values his will says, "If it seems more profitable to you, chain it."

"Do you pay no heed?"

No, I pay no heed.

"I will show you that I am master."

How can you? Zeus gave me my freedom. Or do you think that he was likely to let his own son be enslaved? You are master of my dead body, take it.

"Do you mean that when you approach me, you pay no respect to me?"

No, I only pay respect to myself: if you wish me to say that I pay respect to you too, I tell you that I do so, but only as I pay respect to my water-pot.

This is not mere self-love: for it is natural to man, as to other creatures, to do everything for his own sake; for even the sun does everything for its own sake, and in a word so does Zeus himself. But when he would be called "The Raingiver" and "Fruit-giver" and "Father of men and gods," you see that he cannot win these names or do these works unless he does some good to the world at large: and in general he has so created the nature of the rational animal, that he can attain nothing good for himself, unless he contributes some service to the community. So it turns out that to do everything for his own sake is not unsocial. For what do you expect? Do you expect a man to hold aloof from himself and his own interest? No: we cannot ignore the one principle of action which governs all things—to be at unity with themselves.

What follows? When men's minds harbour wrong opinions on things beyond the will, counting them good and evil, they are bound to pay regard to tyrants. Would that it were only tyrants, and not chamberlains too! How can a man possibly grow wise of a sudden, when Caesar appoints him to the charge of the privy? How is it we straightway say, "Felicio has spoken wisely to me"? I would fain have him deposed from the dung-heap, that he may seem foolish to you again. Epaphroditus had a shoemaker, whom he sold because he was useless: then by some chance he was bought by one of Caesar's officials, and became Caesar's shoemaker. If you could have seen how Epaphroditus honoured him. "How is my good Felicio, I pray you?" Then if someone asked us, "What is your master doing?" the answer was, "He is consulting Felicio about something." What, had he not sold him for useless? Who has suddenly made a wise man of him? This is what comes of honouring anything outside one's will.

He has been honoured with a tribuneship. All who meet him congratulate him; one kisses his eyes, another his neck, his slaves kiss his hands. He comes into his house and finds lamps being lighted. He goes up to the Capitol and offers sacrifice. Who, I ask you, ever offered sacrifice in gratitude for right direction of the will or for impulse in accordance with nature? For we give thanks to the gods for what we think our good!

To-day one spoke to me about the priesthood of Augustus. I told him, "Fellow, leave the thing alone; you will spend a great deal on nothing."

"Well, but those who draw up contracts will record my name."

Can you be there when men read it and say to them, "That is my name," and even supposing you can be there now, what will you do if you die?

"My name will remain."

Write it in a stone and it will remain. But who will remember you outside Nicopolis?

"But I shall wear a golden crown."

If you desire a crown at all, take a crown of roses and wear that: you will look smarter in that.

ON CONSTANCY

The essence of good and of evil lies in an attitude of the will.

What are external things then?

They are materials for the will, in dealing with which it will find its own good or evil.

How will it find its good?

If it does not value over much the things that it deals with. For its judgements on matters presented to it, if they be right, make the will good, and if crooked and perverse make it bad. This law God has ordained and says, "If you want anything good, get it from yourself."

You say, "Not so, but from another."

I say, No, from yourself. So when the tyrant threatens and does not invite me, I say, "What does he threaten?" If he says, "I will bind you," I say, "He threatens my hands and my feet." If he says, "I will behead you," I say, "He threatens my neck." If he says, "I will put you in prison," I say, "He threatens all my poor flesh," and if he threatens banishment, the same.

"Does he then not threaten you at all?"

Not at all, if I feel that these things are nothing to me: but if I fear any of them, he does threaten me. Who is there left for me to fear, and over what has he control? Over what is in my power? No one controls that. Over what is not in my power? I have no concern in that.

"Do you philosophers then teach us to despise kings?"

Heaven forbid! Which of us teaches men to resist them in the matters over which they have authority? Take my bit of a body, take my property, take my good name, take my companions. If I try to persuade any of them to resist, I give him leave to accuse me indeed.

"Yes, but I want to command your judgements."

Who has given you this authority? How can you conquer another's judgement?

"I will conquer him," he says, "by bringing fear to bear on him."

You are not aware that it was the judgement that conquered itself, it was not conquered by another. The will may conquer itself, but nothing else can conquer it. That is the reason too why the noblest and most just law of God is this: "Let the better always be victorious over the worse."

"Ten," you say, "are better than one."

Better for what? To bind, to slay, to carry off where they will, to take away property. Ten conquer one therefore only in so far as they are better.

"In what then are they worse?"

They are worse if the one has right judgements, and the ten have not. I ask you, can they conquer him in this? How can they? If we weigh them in the balance, must not the heavier pull down the scale?

"This is your outcome then, that Socrates should suffer the fate he did at the hands of the Athenians?"

Slave, why do you say, "Socrates"? State the fact as it really is, That Socrates' vile body should be arrested and haled to prison by those who are stronger, and that some one should give hemlock to Socrates' vile body and it should die of chill—does this seem to you marvellous, does this seem unjust, is it for this you accuse God? Did Socrates then get nothing in exchange? In what did his true good consist? Which are we to attend to? To you or to him? Nay, what does Socrates say? "Anytus or Meletus can slay me, but they cannot harm me" [Plato, *Apology,* 30c]: and again, "If God so will, so be it." [Plato, *Crito,* 43d] Prove, I say, that one who has worse judgements gains the mastery over him who is his superior in judgements. You will not prove it: far from it. For the law of nature and of God is this, "Let the better always come out victor over the worse." Victorious in what? In that wherein it is better. One body is stronger than another, the majority are stronger than one, the thief stronger than he who is not a thief. That is why I too lost my lamp, because in the matter of vigilance the thief was a stronger man than I. But he bought his lamp for this price: for a lamp he became a thief, for a lamp he broke his faith, for a lamp be became a brute. This seemed to his judgement to be profitable.

Very well: but now some one has laid hold on my cloak, and drags me into the market, then others raise a clamour against me, "Philosopher, what good have your judgements done you? for, see, you are haled to prison, see, you are about to be beheaded."

And what sort of introduction to philosophy could I have studied, that would save me from being haled off, if a stronger man seizes my cloak, or, if ten men drag me about and cast me into prison, will save me from being cast there? Have I then learnt nothing else? I have learnt to see that everything that happens, if it is beyond the control of my will, is nothing to me. Have you not gained benefit then in this respect? Why do you seek benefit elsewhere than where you learnt that it is to be found?

I sit on then in prison and say, "This person who clamours at me has no ear for the true meaning of things, he does not understand what is said, in a word he has taken no pains to know what philosophers do or say. Let him be."

But the answer comes, "Come out of your prison."

If you have no more need of me in prison, I come out: if you need me again, I will come in. For how long? For as long as reason requires that I should abide by my vile body; but when reason demands it no longer, take it from me and good health to you! Only let me not cast it off without reason or from a faint heart, or for a casual pretext. For again God wills it not: for He has need of a world like this, and of such creatures as ourselves to move upon the earth. But if He give the signal of retreat, as He gave it to Socrates, one must obey His signal as that of the general in command.

"What then? must I say these things to the multitude?"

Why should you? Is it not sufficient to believe them yourself? For when children come up to us and clap their hands and say, "A good Saturnalia to you to-day!" do we say "These things are not good"? Not at all, we clap with them ourselves. So, when you cannot change a man's opinion, recognize that he is a child, clap with him, and if you do not wish to do this, you have only to hold your peace.

These things we must remember, and when called to face a crisis that is to test us we must realize that the moment is come to show whether we have learnt our lesson. For a young man going straight from his studies to face a crisis may be compared to one who has practised the analysis of syllogisms. If some one offers him one that is easy to analyse, he says, "Nay, propound me one

which is cunningly involved, that I may get proper exercise." And so wrestlers are discontented if put to wrestle with young men of light weight: "He cannot lift me," one says. Here is a young man of parts, yet when the crisis calls he must needs weep and say, "I would fain go on learning."

Learning what? If you did not learn your lesson to display it in action, what did you learn it for?

I imagine one of those who are sitting here crying out in the travail of his heart, "Why does not a crisis come to me such as has come to him? Am I to wear my life out idly in a corner, when I might win a crown at Olympia? When will some one bring me news of a contest like that?" Such ought to be the attitude of you all. Why, among Caesar's gladiators there are some who are vexed that no one brings them out or matches them in fight, and they pray to God and go to the managers and implore them to let them fight; and shall no one of you display a like spirit? That is exactly why I should like to take ship for Rome to see how my wrestler puts his lesson into practice.

"I do not want," says he, "an exercise of this sort."

What? is it in your power to take the task you choose? No, a body is given you of such a kind, parents of such a kind, brothers of such a kind, a country of such a kind, a position in it of such a kind: and yet you come to me and say, "Change the task set me." What! have you not resources to deal with what is given you? Instead of saying, "It is yours to set the task, and mine to study it well," you say, "Do not put before me such a syllogism, but such an one: do not impose on me such a conclusion, but such an one." A time will soon come when tragic actors will imagine that they are merely mask and shoes and robe, and nothing else. Man, you have these things given you as your subject and task. Speak your part, that we may know whether you are a tragic actor or a buffoon: for except their speech they have all else in common. Does the tragic actor disappear, if you take away his shoes and mask and bring him on the stage in the bare guise of a ghost, or is he there still? If he has a voice he is there still.

So it is in life: "Take a post of command"; I take it, and taking it show how a philosopher behaves.

"Lay aside the senator's dress, and put on rags and appear in that character." Very well: is it not given me still to display a noble voice?

In what part then do you appear now?

As a witness called by God: "Come and bear witness for me, for I count you worthy to come forward as my witness. Is anything good or evil which lies outside the range of the will? Do I harm any one? Do I put each man's advantage elsewhere than in himself?"

What is the witness you now bear to God?

"I am in danger, O Lord, and in misfortune; no man heeds me, no man gives me anything, all blame me and speak evil of me."

Is this the witness you are going to bear, and so dishonour the calling that he has given you, in that he honoured you thus and counted you worthy to be brought forward to bear such weighty witness?

But suppose that he who has authority pronounces, "I judge you to be godless and unholy," how does this affect you?

"I am judged to be godless and unholy."

Nothing more?

"Nothing."

If he had been giving judgement on a hypothetical proposition and had declared, "I judge the proposition 'if it be day, there is light' to be false," how would it have affected the proposition? Who is judged here? Who is condemned? The proposition or the man who is deluded about it? Who in the world then is this who has authority to pronounce upon you? Does he know what godliness or ungodliness is? Has he made a study of it? Has he learnt it? Where and with what master?

If a musician pays no heed to him when he pronounces that the lowest note is the highest, nor a geometrician when he decides that the lines from the centre of a circle to the circumference are not equal, shall he who is educated in true philosophy pay any heed to an uneducated man when he gives judgement on what is holy and unholy, just and unjust? What a great wrong for philosophers to be guilty of! Is this what you have learnt by coming to school?

Leave other people, persons of no endurance, to argue on these matters to little purpose. Let them sit in a corner and take their paltry fees, or murmur that no one offers them anything, and come forward yourself and practise what you have learnt. For it is not arguments that are wanting nowadays: no, the books of the Stoics are full of them. What then is the one thing wanting? We want the man who will apply his arguments, and bear witness to them by action. This is the character I would have you take up, that we may no longer make use of old examples in the school, but may be able to show an example from our own day.

Whose business then is it to take cognizance of these questions? It is for him that has studied at school; for man is a creature with a faculty of taking cognizance, but it is shameful for him to exercise it in the spirit of runaway slaves. No: one must sit undistracted and listen in turn to tragic actor or harp-player, and not do as the runaways do. At the very moment one of them is attending and praising the actor, he gives a glance all round, and then if some one utters the word "master" he is fluttered and confounded in a moment. It is shameful that philosophers should take cognizance of the works of nature in this spirit. For what does "master" mean? No man is master of another man; his masters are only death and life, pleasure and pain. For, apart from them, you may bring me face to face with Caesar and you shall see what constancy I show. But when he comes in thunder and lightning with these in his train, and I show fear of them, I am only recognizing my master as the runaway does. But so long as I have respite from them I am just like the runaway watching in the theatre: I wash, drink, sing, but do everything in fear and misery. But if I once free myself from my masters, that is from those feelings which make masters formidable, my trouble is past, and I have a master no more.

"Should I then proclaim this to all men?"

No! One should study the weakness of the uninstructed and say to them, "This man advises me what he thinks good for himself, and I excuse him." For Socrates too excused the gaoler who wept when he was going to drink the poison, and said, "How nobly he has wept for us!" Does he say to the gaoler, "That is why we dismissed the women"? No, he says that to his intimate friends, who were fit to hear it, but the gaoler he treats considerately like a child. [Plato, *Phaedo,* 116d]

II MARCUS AURELIUS

*Meditations**

MY SPIRITUAL HERITAGE

1. From my grandfather Verus I learned good morals and the government of my temper.

2. From the reputation and remembrance of my father, modesty and a manly character.

3. From my mother, piety and beneficence, and abstinence, not only from evil deeds, but even from evil thoughts; and further, simplicity in my way of living, far removed from the habits of the rich.

4. From my great-grandfather, not to have frequented public schools, and to have had good teachers at home, and to know that on such things a man should spend liberally.

5. From my governor, to be neither of the green nor of the blue party at the games in the circus, nor a partizan either of the Parmularius or the Scutarius at the gladiators' fights; from him too I learned endurance of labour, and to want little, and to work with my own hands, and not to meddle with other people's affairs, and not to be ready to listen to slander.

6. From Diognetus, not to busy myself about trifling things, and not to give credit to what was said by miracle-workers and jugglers about incantations and the driving away of daemons and such things; and not to breed quails for fighting, nor to give myself up passionately to such things; and to endure freedom of speech; and to have become intimate with philosophy; and to have been a hearer, first of Bacchius, then of Tandasis and Marcianus; and to have written dialogues in my youth; and to have desired a plank bed and skin, and whatever else of the kind belongs to the Grecian discipline.

7. From Rusticus I received the impression that my character required improvement and discipline; and from him I learned not to be led astray to sophistic emulation, nor to writing on speculative matters, nor to delivering little hortatory orations, nor to showing myself off as a man who practises much discipline, or does benevolent acts in order to make a display; and to abstain from rhetoric, and poetry, and fine writing; and not to walk about in the house in my outdoor dress, nor to do other things of the kind; and to write my letters with simplicity, like the letter which Rusticus wrote from Sinuessa to my mother; and with respect to those who have offended me by words, or done me wrong, to be easily disposed to be pacified and reconciled, as soon as they have shown a readiness to be reconciled and to read carefully, and not to be satisfied with a superficial understanding of a book; nor hastily to give my assent to those who talk overmuch; and I am indebted to him for being acquainted with the discourses of Epictetus, which he communicated to me out of his own collection.

8. From Apollonius I learned freedom of will and undeviating steadiness of purpose; and to look to nothing else, not even for a moment, except to reason; and to be always the same, in sharp pains, on the occasion of the loss of a child, and in long illness; and to see clearly in a living example that the same man can be both most resolute and yielding, and not peevish in giving his instruction; and to have had before my eyes a man who clearly considered his experience and his skill in expounding philosophical principles as the smallest of his merits; and

---

*From Marcus Aurelius Antoninus, *Meditations* (trans. George Long, 1862).

from him I learned how to receive from friends what are esteemed favours, without being either humbled by them or letting them pass unnoticed.

9. From Sextus, a benevolent disposition, and the example of a family governed in a fatherly manner, and the idea of living conformably to nature; and gravity without affectation, and to look carefully after the interests of friends, and to tolerate ignorant persons, and those who form opinions without consideration: he had the power of readily accommodating himself to all, so that intercourse with him was more agreeable than any flattery; and at the same time he was most highly venerated by those who associated with him: and he had the faculty both of discovering and ordering, in an intelligent and methodical way, the principles necessary for life; and he never showed anger or any other passion, but was entirely free from passion, and also most affectionate; and he could express approbation without noisy display, and he possessed much knowledge without ostentation.

10. From Alexander the grammarian, to refrain from fault-finding, and not in a reproachful way to chide those who uttered any barbarous or solecistic or strange-sounding expression; but dexterously to introduce the very expression which ought to have been used, and in the way of answer or giving confirmation, or joining in an inquiry about the thing itself, not about the word, or by some other fit suggestion.

11. From Fronto I learned to observe what envy, and duplicity, and hypocrisy are in a tyrant, and that generally those among us who are called Patricians are rather deficient in paternal affection.

12. From Alexander the Platonic, not frequently nor without necessity to say to any one, or to write in a letter, that I have no leisure; nor continually to excuse the neglect of duties required by our relation to those with whom we live, by alleging urgent occupations.

13. From Catulus, not to be indifferent when a friend finds fault, even if he should find fault without reason, but to try to restore him to his usual disposition; and to be ready to speak well of teachers, as it is reported of Domitius and Athenodotus; and to love my children truly.

14. From my brother Severus, to love my kin, and to love truth, and to love justice; and through him I learned to know Thrasea, Helvidius, Cato, Dion, Brutus; and from him I received the idea of a polity in which there is the same law for all, a polity administered with regard to equal rights and equal freedom of speech, and the idea of a kingly government which respects most of all the freedom of the governed; I learned from him also consistency and undeviating steadiness in my regard for philosophy; and a disposition to do good, and to give to others readily, and to cherish good hopes, and to believe that I am loved by my friends; and in him I observed no concealment of his opinions with respect to those whom he condemned, and that his friends had no need to conjecture what he wished or did not wish, but it was quite plain.

15. From Maximus I learned self-government, and not to be led aside by anything; and cheerfulness in all circumstances, as well as in illness; and a just admixture in the moral character of sweetness and dignity, and to do what was set before me without complaining. I observed that everybody believed that he thought as he spoke, and that in all that he did he never had any bad intention; and he never showed amazement and surprise, and was never in a hurry, and never put off doing a thing, nor was perplexed nor dejected, nor did he ever laugh to disguise his vexation, nor, on the other hand, was he ever passionate or suspicious. He was accustomed to do acts of beneficence, and was ready to forgive, and was free from all falsehood; and he presented the appearance of a man who could not be diverted from right rather than of a man who had been improved. I observed, too, that no man could ever think that he was despised by Maximus, or ever venture to think himself a better man. He had also the art of being humorous in an agreeable way.

16. In my father I observed mildness of temper, and unchangeable resolution in the things which he had determined after due deliberation; and no vainglory in those things which men call honours; and a love of labour and perseverance; and a readiness to listen to those who had anything to propose for the common weal; and undeviating firmness in giving to every man according to his

deserts; and a knowledge derived from experience of the occasions for vigorous action and for remission. And I observed that he had overcome all passion for boys; and he considered himself no more than any other citizen; and he released his friends from all obligation to sup with him or to attend him of necessity when he went abroad, and those who had failed to accompany him, by reason of any urgent circumstances, always found him the same. I observed too his habit of careful inquiry in all matters of deliberation, and his persistency, and that he never stopped his investigation through being satisfied with appearances which first present themselves; and that his disposition was to keep his friends, and not be soon tired of them, nor yet to be extravagant in his affection; and to be satisfied on all occasions, and cheerful; and to foresee things a long way off, and to provide for the smallest without display; and to check immediately popular applause and all flattery; and to be ever watchful over the things which were necessary for the administration of the empire, and to be a good manager of the expenditure, and patiently to endure the blame which he got for such conduct; and he was neither superstitious with respect to the gods, nor did he court men by gifts or by trying to please them, or by flattering the populace; but he showed sobriety in all things and firmness, and never any mean thoughts or action, nor love of novelty. And the things which conduce in any way to the commodity of life, and of which fortune gives an abundant supply, he used without arrogance and without excusing himself; so that when he had them, he enjoyed them without affectation, and when he had them not, he did not want them. No one could ever say of him that he was either a sophist or a home-bred flippant slave or a pedant; but every one acknowledged him to be a man ripe, perfect, above flattery, able to manage his own and other men's affairs. Besides this, he honoured those who were true philosophers, and he did not reproach those who pretended to be philosophers, nor yet was he easily led by them. He was also easy in conversation, and he made himself agreeable without any offensive affection. He took a reasonable care of his body's health, not as one who was greatly attached to life,

nor out of regard to personal appearance, nor yet in a careless way, but so that, through his own attention, he very seldom stood in need of the physician's art or of medicine or external applications. He was most ready to give way without envy to those who possessed any particular faculty, such as that of eloquence or knowledge of the law or of morals, or of anything else; and he gave them his help, that each might enjoy reputation according to his deserts; and he always acted conformably to the institutions of his country, without showing any affectation of doing so. Further, he was not fond of change nor unsteady, but he loved to stay in the same places, and to employ himself about the same things; and after his paroxysms of headache he came immediately fresh and vigorous to his usual occupations. His secrets were not many, but very few and very rare, and these only about public matters; and he showed prudence and economy in the exhibition of the public spectacles and the construction of public buildings, his donations to the people, and in such things, for he was a man who looked to what ought to be done, not to the reputation which is got by a man's acts. He did not take the bath at unseasonable hours; he was not fond of building houses, nor curious about what he ate, nor about the texture and colour of his clothes, nor about the beauty of his slaves. His dress came from Lorium, his villa on the coast, and from Lanuvium generally. We know how he behaved to the toll-collector at Tusculum who asked his pardon; and such was all his behaviour. There was in him nothing harsh, nor implacable, nor violent, nor, as one may say, anything carried to the sweating point; but he examined all things severally, as if he had abundance of time, and without confusion, in an orderly way, vigorously and consistently. And that might be applied to him which is recorded of Socrates, that he was able to abstain from, and to enjoy, those things which many are too weak to abstain from, and cannot enjoy without excess. But to be strong enough both to bear the one and to be sober in the other is the mark of a man who has a perfect and invincible soul, such as he showed in the illness of Maximus.

17. To the gods I am indebted for having good grandfathers, good parents, a good

sister, good teachers, good associates, good kinsmen and friends, nearly everything good. Further, I owe it to the gods that I was not hurried into any offence against any of them, though I had a disposition which, if opportunity had offered, might have led me to do something of this kind; but, through their favour, there never was such a concurrence of circumstances as put me to the trial. Further, I am thankful to the gods that I was not longer brought up with my grandfather's concubine, and that I preserved the flower of my youth, and that I did not make proof of my virility before the proper season, but even deferred the time; that I was subjected to a ruler and a father who was able to take away all pride from me, and to bring me to the knowledge that it is possible for a man to live in a palace without wanting either guards or embroidered dresses, or torches and statues, and suchlike show; but that it is in such a man's power to bring himself very near to the fashion of a private person, without being for this reason either meaner in thought, or more remiss in action, with respect to the things which must be done for the public interest in a manner that befits a ruler. I thank the gods for giving me such a brother, who was able by his moral character to rouse me to vigilance over myself, and who, at the same time, pleased me by his respect and affection; that my children have not been stupid nor deformed in body; that I did not make more proficiency in rhetoric, poetry, and the other studies, in which I should perhaps have been completely engaged, if I had seen that I was making progress in them; that I made haste to place those who brought me up in the station of honour, which they seemed to desire, without putting them off with hope of my doing it some time after, because they were then still young; that I knew Apollonius, Rusticus, Maximus; that I received clear and frequent impressions about living according to nature, and what kind of a life that is, so that, so far as depended on the gods, and their gifts, and help, and inspirations, nothing hindered me from forthwith living according to nature, though I still fall short of it through my own fault, and through not observing the admonitions of the gods, and, I may almost say, their direct instructions; that my body has held out so long in such a kind of life; that I never

touched either Benedicta or Theodotus, and that, after having fallen into amatory passions, I was cured; and, though I was often out of humour with Rusticus, I never did anything of which I had occasion to repent; that, though it was my mother's fate to die young, she spent the last years of her life with me; that, whenever I wished to help any man in his need, or on any other occasion, I was never told that I had not the means of doing it; and that to myself the same necessity never happened, to receive anything from another; that I have such a wife, so obedient, and so affectionate, and so simple; that I had abundance of good masters for my children; and that remedies have been shown to me by dreams, both others, and against bloodspitting and giddiness; and that, when I had an inclination to philosophy, I did not fall into the hands of any sophist, and that I did not waste my time on writers of histories, or in the resolution of syllogisms, or occupy myself about the investigation of appearances in the heavens; for all these things require the help of the gods and fortune.

HUMAN REASON
AND ONE WORLD

1. That which rules within, when it is according to nature, is so affected with respect to the events which happen, that it always easily adapts itself to that which is possible and is presented to it. For it requires no definite material, but it moves towards its purpose, under certain conditions however; and it makes a material for itself out of that which opposes it, as fire lays hold of what falls into it, by which a small light would have been extinguished: but when the fire is strong, it soon appropriates to itself the matter which is heaped on it, and consumes it, and rises higher by means of this very material.

2. Let no act be done without a purpose, nor otherwise than according to the perfect principles of art.

3. Men seek retreats for themselves, houses in the country, sea-shores, and mountains; and thou too art wont to desire such things very much. But this is altogether a mark of the most common sort of men, for it is in thy power whenever thou shalt choose to retire into thyself. For nowhere

either with more quiet or more freedom from trouble does a man retire than into his own soul, particularly when he has within him such thoughts that by looking into them he is immediately in perfect tranquillity; and I affirm that tranquillity is nothing else than the good ordering of the mind. Constantly then give to thyself this retreat, and renew thyself; and let thy principles be brief and fundamental, which, as soon as thou shalt recur to them, will be sufficient to cleanse the soul completely, and to send thee back free from all discontent with the things to which thou returnest. For with what art thou discontented? With the badness of men? Recall to thy mind this conclusion, that rational animals exist for one another, and that to endure is a part of justice, and that men do wrong involuntarily; and consider how many already, after mutual enmity, suspicion, hatred, and fighting, have been stretched dead, reduced to ashes; and be quiet at last.—But perhaps thou art dissatisfied with that which is assigned to thee out of the universe.—Recall to thy recollection this alternative; either there is providence or atoms, fortuitous concurrence of things; or remember the arguments by which it has been proved that the world is a kind of political community, and be quiet at last.—But perhaps corporeal things will still fasten upon thee.—Consider then further that the mind mingles not with the breath, whether moving gently or violently, when it has once drawn itself apart and discovered its own power, and think also of all that thou hast heard and assented to about pain and pleasure, and be quiet at last.—But perhaps the desire of the thing called fame will torment thee.—See how soon everything is forgotten, and look at the chaos of infinite time on each side of the present, and the emptiness of applause, and the changeableness and want of judgement in those who pretend to give praise, and the narrowness of the space within which it is circumscribed, and be quiet at last. For the whole earth is a point, and how small a nook in it is this thy dwelling, and how few are there in it, and what kind of people are they who will praise thee.

This then remains: Remember to retire into this little territory of thy own, and above all do not distract or strain thyself, but be free, and look at things as a man, as a human being, as a citizen, as a mortal. But among the things readiest to thy hand to which thou shalt turn, let there be these, which are two. One is that things do not touch the soul, for they are external and remain immovable; but our perturbations come only from the opinion which is within. The other is that all these things, which thou seest, change immediately and will no longer be; and constantly bear in mind how many of these changes thou hast already witnessed. The universe is transformation: life is opinion.

4. If our intellectual part is common, the reason also, in respect of which we are rational beings, is common: if this is so, common also is the reason which commands us what to do, and what not to do; if this is so, there is a common law also; if this is so, we are fellow-citizens; if this is so, we are members of some political community; if this is so, the world is in a manner a state. For of what other common political community will any one say that the whole human race are members? And from thence, from this common political community comes also our very intellectual faculty and reasoning faculty and our capacity for law; or whence do they come? For as my earthly part is a portion given to me from certain earth, and that which is watery from another element, and that which is hot and fiery from some peculiar source (for nothing comes out of that which is nothing, as nothing also returns to nonexistence), so also the intellectual part comes from some source.

5. Death is such as generation is, a mystery of nature; a composition out of the same elements, and a decomposition into the same; and altogether not a thing of which any man should be ashamed, for it is not contrary to the nature of a reasonable animal, and not contrary to the reason of our constitution.

6. It is natural that these things should be done by such persons, it is a matter of necessity; and if a man will not have it so, he will not allow the fig-tree to have juice. But by all means bear this in mind, that within a very short time both thou and he will be dead; and soon not even your names will be left behind.

7. Take away thy opinion, and then there is taken away the complaint, "I have been harmed." Take away the complaint, "I

have been harmed," and the harm is taken away.

8. That which does not make a man worse than he was, also does not make his life worse, nor does it harm him either from without or from within.

9. The nature of that which is universally useful has been compelled to do this.

10. Consider that everything which happens, happens justly, and if thou observest carefully, thou wilt find it to be so. I do not say only with respect to the continuity of the series of things, but with respect to what is just, and as if it were done by one who assigns to each thing its value. Observe then as thou hast begun; and whatever thou doest, do it in conjunction with this, the being good, and in the sense in which a man is properly understood to be good. Keep to this in every action.

11. Do not have such an opinion of things as he has who does thee wrong, or such as he wishes thee to have, but look at them as they are in truth.

12. A man should always have these two rules in readiness; the one, to do only whatever the reason of the ruling and legislating faculty may suggest for the use of men; the other, to change thy opinion, if there is any one at hand who sets thee right and moves thee from any opinion. But this change of opinion must proceed only from a certain persuasion, as of what is just or of common advantage, and the like, not because it appears pleasant or brings reputation.

13. Hast thou reason? I have.—Why then dost not thou use it? For if this does its own work, what else dost thou wish?

ELEMENTS OF STOICISM

1. He who acts unjustly acts impiously. For since the universal nature has made rational animals for the sake of one another to help one another according to their deserts, but in no way to injure one another, he who transgresses her will, is clearly guilty of impiety towards the highest divinity. And he too who lies is guilty of impiety to the same divinity; for the universal nature is the nature of things that are; and things that are have a relation to all things that come into existence. And further, this universal nature is named truth, and is the prime cause of all things that are true. He then who lies

intentionally is guilty of impiety inasmuch as he acts unjustly by deceiving; and he also who lies unintentionally, inasmuch as he is at variance with the universal nature, and inasmuch as he disturbs the order by fighting against the nature of the world; for he fights against it, who is moved of himself to that which is contrary to truth, for he had received powers from nature through the neglect of which he is not able now to distinguish falsehood from truth. And indeed he who pursues pleasure as good, and avoids pain as evil, is guilty of impiety. For of necessity such a man must often find fault with the universal nature, alleging that it assigns things to the bad and the good contrary to their deserts, because frequently the bad are in the enjoyment of pleasure and possess the things which procure pleasure, but the good have pain for their share and the things which cause pain. And further, he who is afraid of pain will sometimes also be afraid of some of the things which will happen in the world, and even this is impiety. And he who pursues pleasure will not abstain from injustice, and this is plainly impiety. Now with respect to the things towards which the universal nature is equally affected—for it would not have made both, unless it was equally affected towards both—towards these they who wish to follow nature should be of the same mind with it, and equally affected. With respect to pain, then, and pleasure, or death and life, or honour and dishonour, which the universal nature employs equally, whoever is not equally affected is manifestly acting impiously. And I say that the universal nature employs them equally, instead of saying that they happen alike to those who are produced in continuous series and to those who come after them by virtue of a certain original movement of Providence, according to which it moved from a certain beginning to this ordering of things, having conceived certain principles of the things which were to be, and having determined powers productive of beings and of changes and of suchlike successions.

2. It would be a man's happiest lot to depart from mankind without having had any taste of lying and hypocrisy and luxury and pride. However to breathe out one's life when a man has had enough of these things is the next best voyage, as the saying is. Hast

thou determined to abide with vice, and has not experience yet induced thee to fly from this pestilence? For the destruction of the understanding is a pestilence, much more indeed than any such corruption and change of this atmosphere which surrounds us. For this corruption is a pestilence of animals so far as they are animals; but the other is a pestilence of men so far as they are men.

3. Do not despise death, but be well content with it, since this too is one of those things which nature wills. For such as it is to be young and to grow old, and to increase and to reach maturity, and to have teeth and beard and grey hairs, and to beget, and to be pregnant and to bring forth, and all the other natural operations which the seasons of thy life bring, such also is dissolution. This, then, is consistent with the character of a reflecting man, to be neither careless nor impatient nor contemptuous with respect to death, but to wait for it as one of the operations of nature. As thou now waitest for the time when the child shall come out of thy wife's womb, so be ready for the time when thy soul shall fall out of this envelope. But if thou requirest also a vulgar kind of comfort which shall reach thy heart, thou wilt be made best reconciled to death by observing the objects from which thou art going to be removed, and the morals of those with whom thy soul will no longer be mingled. For it is no way right to be offended with men, but it is thy duty to care for them and to bear with them gently; and yet to remember that thy departure will be not from men who have the same principles as thyself. For this is the only thing, if there be any, which could draw us the contrary way and attach us to life, to be permitted to live with those who have the same principles as ourselves. But now thou seest how great is the trouble arising from the discordance of those who live together, so that thou mayest say, Come quick, O death, lest perchance I, too, should forget myself.

4. He who does wrong does wrong against himself. He who acts unjustly acts unjustly to himself, because he makes himself bad.

5. He often acts unjustly who does not do a certain thing; not only he who does a certain thing.

6. Thy present opinion founded on understanding, and thy present conduct directed to social good, and thy present disposition of contentment with everything which happens—that is enough.

7. Wipe out imagination: check desire: extinguish appetite: keep the ruling faculty in its own power.

8. Among the animals which have not reason one life is distributed; but among reasonable animals one intelligent soul is distributed: just as there is one earth of all things which are of an earthy nature, and we see by one light, and breathe one air, all of us that have the faculty of vision and all that have life.

9. All things which participate in anything which is common to them all move towards that which is of the same kind with themselves. Everything which is earthy turns towards the earth, everything which is liquid flows together, and everything which is of an aerial kind does the same, so that they require something to keep them asunder, and the application of force. Fire indeed moves upwards on account of the elemental fire, but it is so ready to be kindled together with all the fire which is here, that even every substance which is somewhat dry, is easily ignited, because there is less mingled with it of that which is a hindrance to ignition. Accordingly then everything also which participates in the common intelligent nature moves in like manner towards that which is of the same kind with itself, or moves even more. For so much as it is superior in comparison with all other things, in the same degree also is it more ready to mingle with and to be fused with that which is akin to it. Accordingly among animals devoid of reason we find swarms of bees, and herds of cattle, and the nurture of young birds, and in a manner, loves; for even in animals there are souls, and that power which brings them together is seen to exert itself in the superior degree, and in such a way as never has been observed in plants nor in stones nor in trees. But in rational animals there are political communities and friendships, and families and meetings of people; and in wars, treaties and armistices. But in the things which are still superior, even though they are separated from one another, unity in a manner exists, as in the stars. Thus the ascent to the higher degree is able to produce a sympathy even in things which are separated. See, then, what now

takes place. For only intelligent animals have now forgotten this mutual desire and inclination, and in them alone the property of flowing together is not seen. But still though men strive to avoid this union, they are caught and held by it, for their nature is too strong for them; and thou wilt see what I say, if thou only observest. Sooner, then, will one find anything earthy which comes in contact with no earthy thing than a man altogether separated from other men.

10. Both man and God and the universe produce fruit; at the proper seasons each produces it. But if usage has especially fixed these terms to the vine and like things, this is nothing. Reason produces fruit both for all and for itself, and there are produced from it other things of the same kind as reason itself.

11. If thou art able, correct by teaching those who do wrong; but if thou canst not, remember that indulgence is given to thee for this purpose. And the gods, too, are indulgent to such persons; and for some purposes they even help them to get health, wealth, reputation; so kind they are. And it is in thy power also; or say, who hinders thee?

12. Labour not as one who is wretched, nor yet as one who would be pitied or admired: but direct thy will to one thing only, to put thyself in motion and to check thyself, as the social reason requires.

13. To-day I have got out of all trouble, or rather I have cast out all trouble, for it was not outside, but within and in my opinions.

14. All things are the same, familiar in experience, and ephemeral in time, and worthless in the matter. Everything now is just as it was in the time of those whom we have buried.

15. Things stand outside of us, themselves by themselves, neither knowing aught of themselves, nor expressing any judgement. What is it, then, which does judge about them? The ruling faculty.

16. Not in passivity, but in activity lie the evil and the good of the rational social animal, just as his virtue and his vice lie not in passivity, but in activity.

17. For the stone which has been thrown up it is no evil to come down, nor indeed any good to have been carried up.

18. Penetrate inwards into men's leading principles, and thou wilt see what judges thou art afraid of, and what kind of judges they are of themselves.

19. All things are changing: and thou thyself art in continuous mutation and in a manner in continuous destruction, and the whole universe too.

20. It is thy duty to leave another man's wrongful act there where it is.

21. Termination of activity, cessation from movement and opinion, and in a sense their death, is no evil. Turn thy thoughts now to the consideration of thy life, thy life as a child, as a youth, thy manhood, thy old age, for in these also every change was a death. Is this anything to fear? Turn thy thoughts now to thy life under thy grandfather, then to thy life under thy mother, then to thy life under thy father; and as thou findest many other differences and changes and terminations, ask thyself, Is this anything to fear? In like manner, then, neither are the termination and cessation and change of thy whole life a thing to be afraid of.

22. Hasten to examine thy own ruling faculty and that of the universe and that of thy neighbour: thy own that thou mayest make it just: and that of the universe, that thou mayest remember of what thou art a part; and that of thy neighbour, that thou mayest know whether he has acted ignorantly or with knowledge, and that thou mayest also consider that his ruling faculty is akin to thine.

23. As thou thyself art a component part of a social system, so let every act of thine be a component part of social life. Whatever act of thine then has no reference either immediately or remotely to a social end, this tears asunder thy life, and does not allow it to be one, and it is of the nature of a mutiny, just as when in a popular assembly a man acting by himself stands apart from the general agreement.

24. Quarrels of little children and their sports, and poor spirits carrying about dead bodies, such is everything; and so what is exhibited in the representation of the mansions of the dead strikes our eyes more clearly.

25. Examine into the quality of the form of an object, and detach it altogether from its material part, and then contemplate it;

then determine the time, the longest which a thing of this peculiar form is naturally made to endure.

26. Thou hast endured infinite troubles through not being contented with thy ruling faculty, when it does the things which it is constituted by nature to do. But enough of this.

27. When another blames thee or hates thee, or when men say about thee anything injurious, approach their poor souls, penetrate within, and see what kind of men they are. Thou wilt discover that there is no reason to take any trouble that these men may have this or that opinion about thee. However thou must be well disposed towards them, for by nature they are friends. And the gods too aid them in all ways, by dreams, by signs, towards the attainment of those things on which they set a value.

28. The periodic movements of the universe are the same, up and down from age to age. And either the universal intelligence puts itself in motion for every separate effect, and if this is so, be thou content with that which is the result of its activity; or it puts itself in motion once, and everything else comes by way of sequence in a manner; or indivisible elements are the origin of all things.—In a word, if there is a god, all is well; and if chance rules, do not thou also be governed by it.

Soon will the earth cover us all: then the earth, too, will change, and the things also which result from change will continue to change for ever, and these again for ever. For if a man reflects on the changes and transformations which follow one another like wave after wave and their rapidity, he will despise everything which is perishable.

29. The universal cause is like a winter torrent: it carries everything along with it. But how worthless are all these poor people who are engaged in matters political, and, as they suppose, are playing the philosopher! All drivellers. Well then, man: do what nature now requires. Set thyself in motion, if it is in thy power, and do not look about thee to see if any one will observe it nor yet expect Plato's *Republic:* but be content if the smallest thing goes on well, and consider such an event to be no small matter. For who can change men's opinions? And without a change of opinions what else is

there than the slavery of men who groan while they pretend to obey? Come now and tell me of Alexander and Philip and Demetrius of Phalerum. They themselves shall judge whether they discovered what the common nature required, and trained themselves accordingly. But if they acted like tragedy heroes, no one has condemned me to imitate them. Simple and modest is the work of philosophy. Draw me not aside to indolence and pride.

30. Look down from above on the countless herds of men and their countless solemnities, and the infinitely varied voyagings in storms and calms, and the differences among those who are born, who live together, and die. And consider, too, the life lived by others in olden time, and the life of those who will live after thee, and the life now lived among barbarous nations, and how many know not even thy name, and how many will soon forget it, and how they who perhaps now are praising thee will very soon blame thee, and that neither a posthumous name is of any value, nor reputation, nor anything else.

31. Let there be freedom from perturbations with respect to the things which come from the external cause; and let there be justice in the things done by virtue of the internal cause, that is, let there be movement and action terminating in this, in social acts, for this is according to thy nature.

32. Thou canst remove out of the way many useless things among those which disturb thee, for they lie entirely in thy opinion; and thou wilt then gain for thyself ample space by comprehending the whole universe in thy mind, and by contemplating the eternity of time, and observing the rapid change of every several thing, how short is the time from birth to dissolution, and the illimitable time before birth as well as the equally boundless time after dissolution.

33. All that thou seest will quickly perish, and those who have been spectators of its dissolution will very soon perish too. And he who dies at the extremest old age will be brought into the same condition with him who died prematurely.

34. What are these men's leading principles, and about what kind of things are they busy, and for what kind of reasons do they love and honour? Imagine that thou seest

their poor souls laid bare. When they think that they do harm by their blame or good by their praise, what an idea!

35. Loss is nothing else than change. But the universal nature delights in change, and in obedience to her all things are now done well, and from eternity have been done in like form, and will be such to time without end. What, then, dost thou say? That all things have been and all things always will be bad, and that no power has ever been found in so many gods to rectify these things, but the world has been condemned to be bound in never ceasing evil?

36. The rottenness of the matter which is the foundation of everything! Water, dust, bones, filth: or again, marble rocks, the callosities of the earth; and gold and silver, the sediments; and garments, only bits of hair; and purple dye, blood; and everything else is of the same kind. And that which is of the nature of breath is also another thing of the same kind, changing from this to that.

37. Enough of this wretched life and murmuring and apish tricks. Why art thou disturbed? What is there new in this? What unsettles thee? Is it the form of the thing? Look at it. Or is it the matter? Look at it. But besides these there is nothing. Towards the gods, then, now become at last more simple and better. It is the same whether we examine these things for a hundred years or three.

38. If any man has done wrong, the harm is his own. But perhaps he has not done wrong.

39. Either all things proceed from one intelligent source and come together as in one body, and the part ought not to find fault with what is done for the benefit of the whole; or there are only atoms, and nothing else than mixture and dispersion. Why, then, art thou disturbed? Say to the ruling faculty, Art thou dead, art thou corrupted, art thou playing the hypocrite, art thou become a beast, dost thou herd and feed with the rest?

40. Either the gods have no power or they have power. If then, they have no power, why dost thou pray to them? But if they have power, why dost thou not pray for them to give thee the faculty of not fearing any of the things which thou fearest, or of not desiring any of the things which thou desirest, or not being pained at anything, rather than

pray that any of these things should not happen or happen? for certainly if they can co-operate with men, they can co-operate for these purposes. But perhaps thou wilt say, the gods have placed them in thy power. Well, then, is it not better to use what is in thy power like a free man than to desire in a slavish and abject way what is not in thy power? And who has told thee that the gods do not aid us even in the things which are in our power? Begin, then, to pray for such things, and thou wilt see. One man prays thus: How shall I be able to lie with that woman? Do thou pray thus: How shall I not desire to lie with her? Another prays thus: How shall I be released from this? Another prays: How shall I not desire to be released? Another thus: How shall I not lose my little son? Thou thus: How shall I not be afraid to lose him? In fine, turn thy prayers this way, and see what comes.

41. Epicurus says, In my sickness my conversation was not about my bodily sufferings, nor, says he, did I talk on such subjects to those who visited me; but I continued to discourse on the nature of things as before, keeping to this main point, how the mind, while participating in such movements as go on in the poor flesh, shall be free from perturbations and maintain its proper good. Nor did I, he says, give the physicians an opportunity of putting on solemn looks, as if they were doing something great, but my life went on well and happily. Do, then, the same that he did both in sickness, if thou art sick, and in any other circumstances; for never to desert philosophy in any events that may befall us, nor to hold trifling talk either with an ignorant man or with one unacquainted with nature, is a principle of all schools of philosophy; but to be intent only on that which thou art now doing and on the instrument by which thou doest it.

42. When thou art offended with any man's shameless conduct, immediately ask thyself, Is it possible, then, that shameless men should not be in the world? It is not possible. Do not, then, require what is impossible. For this man also is one of those shameless men who must of necessity be in the world. Let the same considerations be present to thy mind in the case of the knave, and the faithless man, and of every man who does wrong in any way. For at the same time that thou dost remind thyself that it

is impossible that such kind of men should not exist, thou wilt become more kindly disposed towards every one individually. It is useful to perceive this, too, immediately when the occasion arises, what virtue nature has given to man to oppose to every wrongful act. For she has given to man, as an antidote against the stupid man, mildness, and against another kind of man some other power. And in all cases it is possible for thee to correct by teaching the man who is gone astray; for every man who errs misses his object and is gone astray. Besides wherein hast thou been injured? For thou wilt find that no one among those against whom thou art irritated has done anything by which thy mind could be made worse; but that which is evil to thee and harmful has its foundation only in the mind. And what harm is done or what is there strange, if the man who has not been instructed does the acts of an uninstructed man? Consider whether thou shouldst not rather blame thyself, because thou didst not expect such a man to err in such a way. For thou hadst means given thee by thy reason to suppose that it was likely that he would commit this error, and yet thou hast forgotten and art amazed that he has erred. But most of all when thou blamest a man as faithless or ungrateful, turn to thyself. For the fault is manifestly thy own, whether thou didst trust that a man who had such a disposition would keep his promise, or when conferring thy kindness thou didst not confer it absolutely, nor yet in such way as to have received from thy very act all the profit. For what more dost thou want when thou hast done a man a service? Art thou not content that thou hast done something conformable to thy nature, and dost thou seek to be paid for it? Just as if the eye demanded a recompense for seeing or the feet for walking. For as these members are formed for a particular purpose, and by working according to their several constitutions obtain what is their own; so also as man is formed by nature to acts of benevolence, when he has done anything benevolent or in any other way conducive to the common interest, he has acted conformably to his constitution, and he gets what is his own.

III EPICURUS

Letter to Menoeceus and *Principal Doctrines**

EPICURUS TO MENOECEUS

Let no one when young delay to study philosophy, nor when he is old grow weary of his study. For no one can come too early or too late to secure the health of his soul. And the man who says that the age for philosophy has either not yet come or has gone by is like the man who says that the age for happiness is not yet come to him, or has passed away. Wherefore both when young and old a man must study philosophy, that as he grows old he may be young in blessings through the grateful recollection of what has been, and that in youth he may be old as well, since he will know no fear of what is to come. We must then meditate on the things that make our happiness, seeing that when that is with us we have all, but when it is absent we do all to win it.

The things which I used unceasingly to commend to you, these do and practice, considering them to be the first principles of the good life. First of all believe that god is a being immortal and blessed, even as the common idea of a god is engraved on men's minds, and do not assign to him anything alien to his immortality or ill-suited to his blessedness: but believe about him everything that can uphold his blessedness and immortality. For gods there are, since the knowledge of them is by clear vision. But they are not such as the many believe them to be: for indeed they do not consistently represent them as they believe them to be.

And the impious man is not he who denies the gods of the many, but he who attaches to the gods the beliefs of the many. For the statements of the many about the gods are not conceptions derived from sensation, but false suppositions, according to which the greatest misfortunes befall the wicked and the greatest blessings the good by the gift of the gods. For men being accustomed always to their own virtues welcome those like themselves, but regard all that is not of their nature as alien.

Become accustomed to the belief that death is nothing to us. For all good and evil consists in sensation, but death is deprivation of sensation. And therefore a right understanding that death is nothing to us makes the mortality of life enjoyable, not because it adds to it an infinite span of time, but because it takes away the craving for immortality. For there is nothing terrible in life for the man who has truly comprehended that there is nothing terrible in not living. So that the man speaks but idly who says that he fears death not because it will be painful when it comes, but because it is painful in anticipation. For that which gives no trouble when it comes, is but an empty pain in anticipation. So death, the most terrifying of ills, is nothing to us, since so long as we exist, death is not with us; but when death comes, then we do not exist. It does not then concern either the living or the dead, since for the former it is not, and the latter are no more.

But the many at one moment shun death as the greatest of evils, at another yearn for it as a respite from the evils in life. But the wise man neither seeks to escape life nor

* From Epicurus, *The Extant Writings of Epicurus* (trans. C. Bailey, Oxford University Press, 1928). By permission.

fears the cessation of life, for neither does life offend him nor does the absence of life seem to be any evil. And just as with food he does not seek simply the larger share and nothing else, but rather the most pleasant, so he seeks to enjoy not the longest period of time, but the most pleasant.

And he who counsels the young man to live well, but the old man to make a good end, is foolish, not merely because of the desirability of life, but also because it is the same training which teaches to live well and to die well. Yet much worse still is the man who says it is good not to be born, but

'once born make haste to pass the gates of Death.'

[Theognis, 427]

For if he says this from conviction why does he not pass away out of life? For it is open to him to do so, if he had firmly made up his mind to this. But if he speaks in jest, his words are idle among men who cannot receive them.

We must then bear in mind that the future is neither ours, nor yet wholly not ours, so that we may not altogether expect it as sure to come, nor abandon hope of it, as if it will certainly not come.

We must consider that of desires some are natural, others vain, and of the natural some are necessary and others merely natural; and of the necessary some are necessary for happiness, others for the repose of the body, and others for very life. The right understanding of these facts enables us to refer all choice and avoidance to the health of the body and the soul's freedom from disturbance, since this is the aim of the life of blessedness. For it is to obtain this end that we always act, namely, to avoid pain and fear. And when this is once secured for us, all the tempest of the soul is dispersed, since the living creature has not to wander as though in search of something that is missing, and to look for some other thing by which he can fulfil the good of the soul and the good of the body. For it is then that we have need of pleasure, when we feel pain owing to the absence of pleasure; but when we do not feel pain, we no longer need pleasure. And for this cause we call pleasure the beginning and end of the blessed life. For

we recognize pleasure as the first good innate in us, and from pleasure we begin every act of choice and avoidance, and to pleasure we return again, using the feeling as the standard by which we judge every good.

And since pleasure is the first good and natural to us, for this very reason we do not choose every pleasure, but sometimes we pass over many pleasures, when greater discomfort accrues to us as the result of them: And similarly we think many pains better than pleasures, since a greater pleasure comes to us when we have endured pains for a long time. Every pleasure then because of its natural kinship to us is good, yet not every pleasure is to be chosen: Even as every pain also is an evil, yet not all are always of a nature to be avoided. Yet by a scale of comparison and by the consideration of advantages and disadvantages we must form our judgment on all these matters. For the good on certain occasions we treat as bad, and conversely the bad as good.

And again independence of desire we think a great good—not that we may at all times enjoy but a few things, but that, if we do not possess many, we may enjoy the few in the genuine persuasion that those have the sweetest pleasure in luxury who least need it, and that all that is natural is easy to be obtained, but that which is superfluous is hard. And so plain savours bring us a pleasure equal to a luxurious diet, when all the pain due to want is removed; and bread and water produce the highest pleasure, when one who needs them puts them to his lips. To grow accustomed therefore to simple and not luxurious diet gives us health to the full, and makes a man alert for the needful employments of life, and when after long intervals we approach luxuries, disposes us better towards them, and fits us to be fearless of fortune.

When, therefore, we maintain that pleasure is the end, we do not mean the pleasures of profligates and those that consist in sensuality, as is supposed by some who are either ignorant or disagree with us or do not understand, but freedom from pain in the body and from trouble in the mind. For it is not continuous drinkings and revellings, nor the satisfaction of lusts, nor the enjoyment of fish and other luxuries of the wealthy table, which produce a pleasant life, but sober reasoning, searching out the motives for all choice and avoidance, and banishing mere opinions, to which are due the greatest disturbance of the spirit.

Of all this the beginning and the greatest good is prudence. Wherefore prudence is a more precious thing even than philosophy: for from prudence are sprung all the other virtues, and it teaches us that it is not possible to live pleasantly without living prudently and honorably and justly, nor, again, to live a life of prudence, honor, and justice without living pleasantly. For the virtues are by nature bound up with the pleasant life, and the pleasant life is inseparable from them. For indeed who, think you, is a better man than he who holds reverent opinions concerning the gods, and is at all times free from fear of death, and has reasoned out the end ordained by nature? He understands that the limit of good things is easy to fulfil and easy to attain, whereas the course of ills is either short in time or slight in pain: he laughs at destiny, whom some have introduced as the mistress of all things. He thinks that with us lies the chief power in determining events, some of which happen by necessity and some by chance, and some are within our control; for while necessity cannot be called to account, he sees that chance is inconstant, but that which is in our control is subject to no master, and to it are naturally attached praise and blame. For, indeed, it were better to follow the myths about the gods than to become a slave to the destiny of the natural philosophers: For the former suggests a hope of placating the gods by worship, whereas the latter involves a necessity which knows no placation. As to chance, he does not regard it as a god as most men do (for in a god's acts there is no disorder), nor as an uncertain cause of all things: For he does not believe that good and evil are given by chance to man for the framing of a blessed life, but that opportunities for great good and great evil are afforded by it. He therefore thinks it better to be unfortunate in reasonable action than to prosper in unreason. For it is better in a man's actions that what is well chosen should fail, rather than that what is ill chosen should be successful owing to chance.

Meditate therefore on these things and things akin to them night and day by yourself, and with a companion like to yourself, and never shall you be disturbed waking or asleep, but you shall live like a god among men. For a man who lives among immortal blessings is not like to a mortal being.

PRINCIPAL DOCTRINES

I. The blessed and immortal nature knows no trouble itself nor causes trouble to any other, so that it is never constrained by anger or favor. For all such things exist only in the weak.

II. Death is nothing to us: For that which is dissolved is without sensation; and that which lacks sensation is nothing to us.

III. The limit of quantity in pleasures is the removal of all that is painful. Wherever pleasure is present, as long as it is there, there is neither pain of body nor of mind, nor of both at once.

IV. Pain does not last continuously in the flesh, but the acutest pain is there for a very short time, and even that which just exceeds the pleasure in the flesh does not continue for many days at once. But chronic illnesses permit a predominance of pain over pleasure in the flesh.

V. It is not possible to live pleasanty without living prudently and honorably and justly, nor again to live a life of prudence, honor, and justice without living pleasantly. And the man who does not possess the pleasant life, is not living prudently and honorably and justly, and the man who does not possess the virtuous life, cannot possibly live pleasantly.

VI. To secure protection from men anything is a natural good, by which you may be able to attain this end.

VII. Some men wished to become famous and conspicuous, thinking that they would thus win for themselves safety from other men. Wherefore if the life of such men is safe, they have obtained the good which nature craves; But if it is not safe, they do not possess that for which they strove at first by the instinct of nature.

VIII. No pleasure is a bad thing in itself: but the means which produce some pleasures bring with them disturbances many times greater than the pleasures.

IX. If every pleasure could be intensified so that it lasted and influenced the whole organism or the most essential parts of our nature, pleasures would never differ from one another.

X. If the things that produce the pleasures of profligates could dispel the fears of the mind about the phenomena of the sky and death and its pains, and also teach the limits of desires and of pains, we should never have cause to blame them: For they would be filling themselves full with pleasures from every source and never have pain of body or mind, which is the evil of life.

XI. If we were not troubled by our suspicions of the phenomena of the sky and about death, fearing that it concerns us, and also by our failure to grasp the limits of pains and desires, we should have no need of natural science.

XII. A man cannot dispel his fear about the most important matters if he does not know what is the nature of the universe but suspects the truth of some mythical story. So that without natural science it is not possible to attain our pleasures unalloyed.

XIII. There is no profit in securing protection in relation to men, if things above and things beneath the earth and indeed all in the boundless universe remain matters of suspicion.

XIV. The most unalloyed source of protection from men, which is secured to some extent by a certain force of expulsion, is in fact the immunity which results from a quiet life and the retirement from the world.

XV. The wealth demanded by nature is both limited and easily procured; that demanded by idle imaginings stretches on to infinity.

XVI. In but few things chance hinders a wise man, but the greatest and most important matters reason has ordained and throughout the whole period of life does and will ordain.

XVII. The just man is most free from trouble, the unjust most full of trouble.

XVIII. The pleasure in the flesh is not increased, when once the pain due to want is removed, but is only varied: and the limit as regards pleasure in the mind is begotten by the reasoned understanding of these very pleasures and of the emotions akin to them, which used to cause the greatest fear to the mind.

XIX. Infinite time contains no greater pleasure than limited time, if one measures by reason the limits of pleasure.

XX. The flesh perceives the limits of pleasure as unlimited and unlimited time is required to supply it. But the mind, having attained a reasoned understanding of the ultimate good of the flesh and its limits and having dissipated the fears concerning the time to come, supplies us with the complete life, and we have no further need of infinite time: but neither does the mind shun pleasure, nor, when circumstances begin to bring about the departure from life, does it approach its end as though it fell short in any way of the best life.

XXI. He who has learned the limits of life knows that that which removes the pain due to want and makes the whole of life complete is easy to obtain; so that there is no need of actions which involve competition.

XXII. We must consider both the real purpose and all the evidence of direct perception, to which we always refer the conclusions of opinion; otherwise, all will be full of doubt and confusion.

XXIII. If you fight against all sensations, you will have no standard by which to judge even those of them which you say are false.

XXIV. If you reject any single sensation and fail to distinguish between the conclusion of opinion as to the appearance awaiting confirmation and that which is actually given by the sensation or feeling, or each intuitive apprehension of the mind, you will confound all other sensations as well with the same groundless opinion, so that you will reject every standard of judgement. And if among the mental images created by your opinion you affirm both that which awaits confirmation and that which does not, you will not escape error, since you will have preserved the whole cause of doubt in every judgement between what is right and what is wrong.

XXV. If on each occasion instead of referring your actions to the end of nature, you turn to some other nearer standard when you are making a choice or an avoidance, your actions will not be consistent with your principles.

XXVI. Of desires, all that do not lead to a sense of pain, if they are not satisfied, are not necessary, but involve a craving which is easily dispelled, when the object is hard to procure or they seem likely to produce harm.

XXVII. Of all the things which wisdom acquires to produce the blessedness of the

complete life, far the greatest is the possession of friendship.

XXVIII. The same conviction which has
given us confidence that there is nothing
terrible that lasts for ever or even for long,
has also seen the protection of friendship
most fully completed in the limited evils of
this life.

XXIX. Among desires some are natural
and necessary, some natural but not necessary, and others neither natural nor necessary, but due to idle imagination.

XXX. Wherever in the case of desires
which are physical, but do not lead to a
sense of pain, if they are not fulfilled, the
effort is intense, such pleasures are due to
idle imagination, and it is not owing to their
own nature that they fail to be dispelled, but
owing to the empty imaginings of the man.

XXXI. The justice which arises from nature is a pledge of mutual advantage to restrain men from harming one another and
save them from being harmed.

XXXII. For all living things which have
not been able to make compacts not to harm
one another or be harmed, nothing ever is
either just or unjust; and likewise too for all
tribes of men which have been unable or unwilling to make compacts not to harm or be
harmed.

XXXIII. Justice never is anything in itself, but in the dealings of men with one another in any place whatever and at any time
it is a kind of compact not to harm or be
harmed.

XXXIV. Injustice is not an evil in itself,
but only in consequence of the fear which
attaches to the apprehension of being unable
to escape those appointed to punish such
actions.

XXXV. It is not possible for one who acts
in secret contravention of the terms of the
compact not to harm or be harmed, to be
confident that he will escape detection, even
if at present he escapes a thousand times.
For up to the time of death it cannot be certain that he will indeed escape.

XXXVI. In its general aspect justice is
the same for all, for it is a kind of mutual
advantage in the dealings of men with one
another: but with reference to the individual
peculiarities of a country or any other circumstances the same thing does not turn out
to be just for all.

XXXVII. Among actions which are
sanctioned as just by law, that which is
proved on examination to be of advantage
in the requirements of men's dealings with
one another, has the guarantee of justice,
whether it is the same for all or not. But if a
man makes a law and it does not turn out to
lead to advantage in men's dealings with
each other, then it no longer has the essential nature of justice. And even if the advantage in the matter of justice shifts from one
side to the other, but for a while accords
with the general concept, it is none the less
just for that period in the eyes of those who
do not confound themselves with empty
sounds but took to the actual facts.

XXXVIII. Where, provided the circumstances have not been altered, actions which
were considered just, have been shown not
to accord with the general concept in actual
practice, then they are not just. But where,
when circumstances have changed, the same
actions which were sanctioned as just no
longer lead to advantage, there they were
just at the time when they were of advantage
for the dealings of fellow-citizens with one
another; but subsequently they are no longer
just, when no longer of advantage.

XXXIX. The man who has best ordered
the element of disquiet arising from external
circumstances has made those things that he
could akin to himself and the rest at least
not alien: but with all to which he could not
do even this, he has refrained from mixing,
and has expelled from his life all which it
was of advantage to treat thus.

XL. As many as possess the power to
procure complete immunity from their
neighbors, these also live most pleasantly
with one another, since they have the most
certain pledge of security, and after they
have enjoyed the fullest intimacy, they do
not lament the previous departure of a dead
friend, as though he were to be pitied.

CHAPTER EIGHT

THE JEWISH BELIEF IN ONE GOD, AND CHRISTIAN LOVE

In addition to the Greek element of rationalism, the Judeo-Christian religious and moral heritage is the only other major source of western civilization and political thought. The Jewish and Christian contributions to western civilization are immense. From Judaism, the belief in one God and the existence of a firm moral code infused later generations with precepts that shaped their political, legal, and social structures. Christianity consolidated and transcended the Greek and Jewish contributions: Christianity introduced the concept of love as the basis for men and women's relations with each other and with God into world culture.

It is remarkable that the original major sources of western thought and culture derive from small nations, which were not great political, military, or economic powers. The Greeks had to fight for their lives against Persians, Macedonians, and Romans, and were never able to become even a united small power, much less a great power. The Jews, too, were a small nation, inhabiting a small territory, often politically divided, and always surrounded, and often dominated, by big empires—Assyrians, Babylonians, Egyptians, and Romans.

Rome finished both Greeks and Jews as independent nations. But there was a significant difference in the attitude of the vanquished and, therefore, also the victors. When Rome subdued Greece, the Greeks were willing to make spiritual concession to their political master: If the Roman emperor had to be worshipped as a deity in Greek temples, it did not matter too much. In a polytheistic temple, there is always room for one more god. The Greeks were therefore permitted to live in their native land, albeit as political subordinates of Roman imperial government.

But when Rome conquered Judea in A.D. 70, it drove the Jews away from their soil and dispersed them in many lands. The Jews were unwilling to admit more than political or military defeat: There was no room in the Temple of Jerusalem for the statue of the Roman emperor and his worship as a deity. The difference between twelve gods and thirteen is insignificant; the difference between monotheism and polytheism is immense. In the Temple at Jerusalem there was no statue of God; much less could there be one for the worship of a pagan emperor. Rather than compromise their belief in God, the Jews fought to the bitter end, resisting for three years the mighty Roman emperor, until they were punished for their defiance with the cruel fate of exile and dispersion. The Romans sought to destroy not only the Jewish state that had dared to resist its might but also the Jewish nation that had stubbornly, illogically, and unreasonably (from the Roman viewpoint) refused to do what every other conquered people had always done—recognize the Roman emperor as divine.

The Romans were not religious fanatics. They did not care what their subject peoples believed or did not believe. All they wanted was an outward admission of spiritual obeisance to the Roman imperial divinity. They were therefore incensed that the Jews refused "a little thing" like emperor-worship that no other conquered people had ever refused to cooperate in before. Later, Christians, too, would refuse to participate in emperor-worship. The Jewish people's defiance of Rome exemplifies the importance to them of their belief in God.

The Roman era was not the first time that the Jewish people had experienced mass deportations and the end of political independence. In 721 B.C. the Assyrians destroyed the northern kingdom, called Israel, razed its cities, deported the people, and settled the area with outsiders who amalgamated with the few remaining Israelites to form the semi-idolatrous Samaritans. In 586 B.C. the Babylonians conquered the southern kingdom of Judah. After a two-year siege the Babylonians destroyed Jerusalem and many other cities that were never then rebuilt. The Babylonians deported the educated and more well-to-do classes to Babylonia, but many Jews fled to Egypt and Transjordan. Only a small number of "vinedressers and husbandmen" remained in Judah, or Judea, as it became known.

In 540 B.C. Persia defeated Babylonia, and King Cyrus of Persia in 538 B.C. issued the Edict of Liberation, permitting exiled Jews to return to their homeland, rebuild the temple of Jerusalem, and practice their religion freely. Although only a small number returned to Judea, they were active and dedicated individuals. Those who stayed in Babylonia continued to adhere to their faith, and they developed an active Jewish community that eventually became more vigorous—economically, socially, and culturally—than the Jewish community in Palestine itself. In the middle of the 5th century B.C., Ezra moved from Babylonia to Jerusalem. He, more than any other single individual, was instrumental in re-establishing a Jewish commonwealth such as it had existed before the Babylonian captivity.

The Roman conquest of Judea in A.D. 70 had more disastrous effects than either the Assyrian or Babylonian conquests. When the Assyrians destroyed the northern Kingdom of Israel, the southern kingdom of Judah was left. When the Babylonians destroyed Judah and exiled the Jews who were most influential, there was still a Jewish community left behind, although it was leaderless and demoralized.

But when the Romans burned Jerusalem and its temple in A.D. 70, they determined that the Jewish people must never rise again. This goal, however, was not so easy to accomplish. Even before the war was over, the Romans granted permission to establish a center of learning in the coastal town of Yavneh. After the war was over, Yavneh became the religious center of the surviving Jewish community in Palestine. It had no army, police, or any other means of compulsion. The spiritual and religious leaders at Yavneh decided religious issues, but in the Jewish concept, religion also included education, civil and criminal law, and nearly all other aspects of community life. As long as this religious body did not stir up any political trouble, the Roman authorities left it alone.

Emperor Hadrian decided that even religious autonomy for the Jews was too much, and he ordered the erection of a temple to Jupiter on the site of the ruins of the Hebrew Temple. Under the leadership of Simon bar Kochba ("Son of the Star"), the Jews rose in revolt, and fought for three years, until A.D. 135. Hadrian realized, better than his predecessors, that the strength of the Jewish people was the Bible as their source of ethics, learning, and indomitable resistance. He therefore abolished the academy at Yavneh and decreed that henceforth the study of the Bible or its observance would be punished by death. Many preferred martyrdom to the betrayal of their God. Hadrian renamed Jerusalem *Aelia Capitolina,* and the Jews were barred from it.

Yet, even the failure of bar Kochba did not end Jewish life in Palestine. Hadrian's successors relaxed the prohibition against Jewish religion and learning. During the next three centuries, the rabbis (or "teachers") dedicated their main efforts to developing a way of life on the basis of the Bible and the teachings of the prophets that could subsist independently of any outward material or political instrumentalities. This development of Judaism is in many ways the most significant in the religion, because it permitted the existence of the Jewish people without a state for the next eighteen hundred years. This period is, thus, a most important, practical application of the Jewish belief in one God. It also demonstrates the power of this belief and, thus, helps to explain why it has been so influential in the development of western civilization and politics.

In the first five centuries of the Christian era, the rabbis in Palestine and Babylonia developed the *Mishnah* and the *Gemara,* known together as the *Talmud.* The Mishnah ("Repetition") was the first written collection of laws after the Bible. It was a relatively brief compendium of rabbinical oral law and teaching, covering about 250 years (30 B.C. to A.D. 220). This oral teaching of law and ethics was formally compiled around A.D. 220 and was written in Hebrew. The Gemara ("Completion") is a series of commentaries, discussions, and interpretations of the Mishnah. The two together are called *Talmud* ("Study"), compiled in a briefer Palestinian version and in a longer Babylonian version around A.D. 500.

The Babylonian Talmud, running to about 2.5 million words, is over three times longer than the Palestinian Talmud. More importantly, the Babylonian Talmud is the more authoritative of the two. If the Bible is the great and imperishable achievement of the Jewish community in Israel, the Talmud is the enduring monument of the Jewish community in Babylonia, at the time the most important Jewish community "in exile" (*galuth* in Hebrew, or *diaspora* in Greek). Without the Talmud, the religion of the Hebrews based on the Bible and the prophets would very likely have disappeared, as did all other religions which existed at the beginning of the first century of the Christian era in the Roman empire.

Reflecting the work of about two thousand rabbis over a period of eight centuries in Palestine and Babylonia, the Talmud became the third pillar—in addition to the Bible and the prophets—that ensured the survival of the Jewish people as a spiritual and cultural community. Theirs was a nation without the material attribute of a national territory and without the political attribute of national sovereignty. Rabbinical Judaism, which started to evolve even before the destruction of Jerusalem in A.D. 70 and the gradual decimation of Jewish life in Palestine, was not an unconscious anticipatory reaction to threatening disaster: It was a conscious, purposive effort over centuries to make possible the continued existence of the Jewish nation whatever happened in the political world of states and empires. Thus, when the two Jewish wars against the Romans in A.D. 70 and 132–135 ended in catastrophe, rabbinical Judaism had prepared the Jewish communities in Babylonia as well as in the Greco-Roman world to live henceforth without the moral support and inspiration of "the Land of Israel" *(Eretz Yisrael).*

The achievement of the rabbis in ensuring the survival of the Jewish people dispersed in many lands can only be understood if the *Talmud* is understood. The *Talmud* is not "a book" (an English translation runs to 35 volumes). The *Talmud* is also not a legal code, like Justinian's *Corpus Juris.* Further, it is not the Hebrew equivalent of a Plato or of a Platonic Academy: Since only God is presumed to have ultimate authority, the rabbis frequently contradict one another, and no single individual can possibly represent the Talmud. The *Talmud* can best be understood as a collection of discussions by hundreds and hundreds of teacher-scholars over a period of eight hundred years—a series of legal and non-legal discussions and sayings, *obiter dicta,* stories, and allegories as handed down by the rabbis. There is no single, or even primary, focus in the *Talmud.* Virtually every subject is touched on or discussed. From agriculture to zoology, the range of subjects seems limitless—except for one that is hardly dealt with—theology. This is one of the ironies of the *Talmud* as of all Jewish thought. Theology, or the rational study which treats God, his existence and attributes, and his relations to the world and humanity, could only have been first developed by a people such as the Greeks for whom these matters were philosophical problems. But for the Jews, God was no problem: He was simply there. There was no need to philosophize about God's existence, since the existence of everything in the universe was the direct result of God's will and creation.

Classical Jewish thought, as expressed in the *Bible* and the *Talmud,* covers about 1,500 years of organized communal life in Palestine (1000 B.C.–A.D. 500). The Hebrew Bible was started in the tenth century B.C. and finally edited around A.D. 100. The Old Testament of the Bible contains three parts: the Five Books of Moses, called *Torah* (or "Teaching" in Hebrew, but often mistranslated as "Law"); *Prophets* (or "Seers"); and *Writings,* such as Proverbs, Psalms, Job, Song of Songs, Ecclesiastes, and Chronicles. The Bible is called the "Written Teaching," as contrasted with the "Oral Teaching" of the *Talmud.* The three main portions of the Hebrew Bible were not written in consecutive order, but overlap in their dates of original composition. Portions of the five books of Moses date from the ninth century B.C. and were substantially completed within the next five centuries; the books of the prophets were written between the eighth and fourth centuries B.C.; the *Writings* were composed between the fifth and first centuries B.C.

While each statement in the *Talmud* is attributed to a rabbi by name, the Old Testament is an unusual piece of literature that has no known author or authors. There is no Homer, Plato, or Aristotle in the Bible. There is obviously no single author in the five books of Moses, compiled over five centuries. Even in the case of the prophets, the books as we know them today were largely written long after the prophets' deaths, generally based on oral traditions. Thus, the author of the Bible is not a single man or group of men but unknown writers who were interested in preserving, and thus, helping to constantly recreate, a religious tradition centered in God.

From the viewpoint of the anonymous writers and compilers who put in writing the Bible and *Talmud,* God's inspiration was the author of these writings, and not this or that man. Even Moses or Samuel or Jeremiah were no more than vessels through which the voice of God spoke. The Bible is not, in the Jewish conception, a compendium of different and opposing schools of philosophy expressed by numerous individuals, but the expression of God's will. Jews believed that all law comes from God, not man.

The central concept in classical Jewish thought is that of *Torah. Torah* is an old and common Hebrew word, meaning "teaching." After the Jews returned from the Babylonian exile in the sixth century B.C. under the leadership of Ezra, *Torah* increasingly acquired a religious meaning. Ezra understood that the rebuilding of the Second Temple alone would not restore the people of Israel to pre-exilic conditions of normalcy, for the vast majority of Israelites chose to remain in Babylonia. If Israel was to continue to exist, it had to be transformed into a religious community, independent of land, political sovereignty, and even the Temple in Jerusalem. The *Torah* alone could provide the foundation for such a religious community. Tradition credits Ezra with the final decision of determining the text of the Five Books of Moses. In a wider sense, the *Torah* was later understood also to include the *Prophets* and *Writings,* that is, the whole Old Testament. Later still, the *Talmud,* too, was included in the concept of *Torah.* In its widest sense, *Torah* means all teaching relating to Jewish religious (legal or ethical) matters.

Therefore, the common translation of *Torah* as "Law" is much too narrow and misses the much broader meaning of *Torah*—a constant spiritual commitment to a way of life that is centered on God. In the *Septuagint,* the first translation of the Hebrew Bible into Greek in the third century B.C., *Torah* is translated as *Nomos.* Although *Nomos* is broader than Law, it is still narrower than *Torah,* the divinely revealed way of life in its totality, constantly elaborated and interpreted by generations of teachers. The *Torah* helps guide every thought and deed of every individual in each generation who seeks to live by it. The translation of the concept of *Torah* into *Nomos* or *Law* is more than a matter of semantics or literary accuracy or fidelity. The view of Judaism as "arid legalism" became the root of much of the anti-judaic hostility of early Christianity and of later more vehement anti-Jewish attitudes of Christian nations.

It will be helpful to an understanding of Jewish thought to consider some of the differences between it and Greek thought. Such differences also help to underline permanent tensions in western civilization and thought that have imprinted upon them their peculiar vitality and uniqueness. There have been many attempts to reconcile and harmonize these differences, and of such attempts the movement of Christianity is unquestionably the most important. But after two thousand years, one still wonders whether it is possible to harmonize what is fundamentally contradictory. The difference between Jewish and Greek thought can be briefly summarized in several ways. They are all restatements of the same theme: In the Jewish view, God created man; in the Greek mind, man created God.

The Jewish concept therefore challenges man to rise to the closest possible communion with God by living a life of justice. By contrast, the Greek creation of the gods by man brings the gods down to the level of man, depriving him of any standard of perfection toward which mankind can—and must—strive. While in the original Biblical conception of God there are some anthropomorphic traits—such as jealousy, anger, vindictiveness—the later prophetic and rabbinical concept of God becomes purified of anthropomorphisms. In the Greek polytheistic thinking, this progress is lacking. The progress in Greek religious thought is not, as among Jews, from anthropomorphic religion to a more spiritual conception of God, but from anthropomorphic religion to skepticism and loss of faith. The Greeks transformed God (as in Plato) into the abstract idea of the Good or the Ideal, or (as in the Stoics) identified God with nature (pantheism).

The very background of the Greek supreme god, Zeus, would make a Jew of the classical era shudder. Zeus was, according to Greek legends, the son of Kronos and Rhea; thus, he already differs from the Jewish conception of God as the source of all creation, not the product of some other creating agency. Worse still, from the Jewish viewpoint, was the fact that Zeus' parents were brother and sister. Incest was, in the Jewish view, one of the three most horrendous crimes man could commit (the other two being idolatry and murder). But worse was still to come. Kronos devoured all his children as soon as they were born, because he had been told by his parents that he would be overpowered by his own son. When Rhea bore Zeus, she went to the island of Crete, so that Zeus' father would not know of his birth. The prediction about Kronos' fate came true, when Zeus overcame his father by force and cunning, enchained him, and carried him off to the edge of the earth. In the view of the ancient Jews, this sort of thing simply was not done—not even in a low- or middle-class family, and certainly not by a divine being. The Commandments taught to "Honor thy father and thy mother."

The fundamental impulse in Greek religions was to bring the gods down from the heavens to earth, and thus feel comfortable in their company. The fundamental religious passion of the Jew was to rise from the earth to heaven, and tremble in awe in the presence of God. Life thus becomes a ceaseless effort to make man, created in God's image, worthy of his creator. Every moment in man's life is therefore precious, and must be utilized in some practical act that kindles the divine spark in man.

Another basic difference between Jewish and Greek thought is that between the Jewish idea of acting justly and the Greek idea of thinking clearly. Socrates best summarized the essence of Greek thought: "Knowledge is virtue" and "Know thyself." The most typically Jewish view is worlds apart from Socrates and Plato: "The beginning of wisdom is the fear of God." This Jewish view is not a onetime obiter dictum in Psalms, but occurs 17 times in the Book of Proverbs, and numerous times in Job, Ecclesiastes, and other portions of the Bible, not to mention post-Biblical rabbinical literature.

For the Greek, the intellectual activity of reason was the way to perfection. Socrates, Plato, and Aristotle had the certainty that human reason can reach the stage where it can understand and behold reality. The Greek word "theory" derives from the verb *the-atai* (to see), which also appears in the word "theater." The wise man, the philosopher, contemplates reality with complete detachment, interested—like a theater-goer—in understanding what goes on rather than in molding events.

The Jewish approach is fundamentally different on two scores. First, it denies that human reason and wisdom can ever unlock the riddle of existence. The fear of God is the beginning of wisdom, not wisdom itself. The Hebrew word *yirah* means not only "fear," but also "awe." As used in the Bible in some instances, *yirah* means "fear": the fear of man to be punished by God for his sins. In the majority of cases, however, *yirah* means "awe" rather than "fear." Awe expresses the sense of wonder and mystery which draws man nearer to God, the source of all wonders and mysteries. By contrast, in fear we may seek to retreat from the source that inspires us with fear. Whereas fear may lead humanity to despair, awe is more likely to lead to reverence, and reverence is a source of humility without which there can be no wisdom. While awe is no straight path to wisdom as the answer to all riddles of the world, it can be the "beginning of wisdom," as the Psalmist says. But this wisdom is not the intellectual wisdom of the Greeks.

Since understanding reality is the highest ideal for the Greek, those who are most endowed with reason are the most highly esteemed. Plato's *Republic* finds the philosophers—the lovers of knowledge—the only ones fit to rule: Just as knowledge is tantamount to virtue in the Greek view, it is also the basis of political rule. Jewish thought totally rejects this ideal. Only God can rule over man. No man can rise to such perfection of mind and spirit as to make him fit to rule over his fellow-men. Plato idealizes the philosopher even more than appears from the foregoing remarks. In Plato's view, the philosopher is not only good enough to rule over his fellow-men, he is too good. Ideally, the philosopher would desire, according to Plato, to spend his life contemplating reality. Only the harsh facts of civic disorder and class conflict compel the philosophers to descend from the intellectual altitudes of changeless contemplation of the unchanging reality of the perfect Good to the low level of political and social activity. In the Platonic view, human inequality is inevitable.

In his scheme of education for the philosophers, Plato describes how, at the successful conclusion of their education and training, they finally behold Reality, which is Idea, the Form, the Good. It is quite clear in Plato's scheme of human development that in beholding reality as it is man reaches his highest level of perfection. In the Greek mind, Idea is superior to matter, soul to body, and the highest activity of man is therefore mental—to grasp reality as Idea. The activity of beholding such reality is the only appropriate one since, by definition, Idea is changeless, timeless, and spaceless.

By contrast, striving for justice in Jewish thought involves the committment to change reality—not the abstract reality of Idea, divorced from time and space, from matter and body, but the reality of historical man, a mixture of mind and body, of reason and passion, of good and evil. Whereas for the Greek *logos,* or reason, is almost synonymous with God and nature, for the Jew human reason is no better (though no worse) than man himself. The supreme concept for the Jew is not logos, but *tsedakah* (righteousness, justice), both in God and man. To act justly is the supreme Jewish goal, while for the Greek it is to think clearly. Whereas for the Greek knowledge is virtue, the Jew asks, "What does God require of thee, but to do justly, to love mercy, and to walk humbly with thy God?" (Micah 6:8).

The Hebraic roots of Christianity are uncontested. Yet Jesus brought a different message, one that has proven capable of global dissemination. He came, he said (according to the Gospel of Matthew), not "to destroy the law, or the prophets . . . , but to fulfill. For verily I say unto you, Till heaven and earth pass, one jot or one tittle shall in no wise pass from the law, till all be fulfilled."

It now is difficult to know the exact words, sayings, and acts of the historical Jesus for the documentary evidence is not great. The Protestant New Testament of the Bible typically consists of the four gospels Matthew, Mark, Luke, and John; The Acts of the Apostles; 14 letters generally attributed to Paul; 1 letter attributed to James; 2 letters to Peter, 3 letters to John; 1 letter to Jude; and a Revelation attributedly given to John. Apart from these scriptural sources, there are a number of apocryphal and fragmentary writings from the first through fourth centuries A.D. that concern Jesus but are of limited value. The Dead Sea Scrolls provide fascinating insight into Palestinian Judaism at the dawn of the Christian era, but do not mention him.

Mill wrote in *On Liberty* of Jesus that he "left on the memory of those who witnessed his life and conversation, such an impression of his moral grandeur, that eighteen subsequent centuries have done homage to him as the Almighty in person . . ." Whatever one may believe regarding Jesus' divinity, there is no question he has had as great an influence on the world as any other person.

The essential Christian message is to love others. While this always was a part of Jewish teaching, it was not as central within its ethics as within Christianity. Jesus' message of love perhaps is best given in the Gospel of John: "A new commandment I give unto you, that ye love one another; as I have loved you, that ye also love one another. By this shall all men know that ye are my disciples, if ye have love one to another."

For Jesus, love is not a religious or ritualistic practice; it is a way of life. All of a believing Christian's actions and thoughts, attitudes and feelings, hopes and dreams should be directed to loving others, to putting others before oneself. The Christian doctrine of other-directedness is exceptionally strong, and while it is tempered by other injunctions and teachings in the New Testament, there is little question that one of the most distinctive elements of Christianity is the emphasis it places on individuals' ability to love others.

The Christian *principle of love* as the basis of man's relation with God and, more important still, as the basis of man's relations with man, finds its inspiration in Jewish sources. In Greek thought, man's relation to God is that of sympathetic understanding and admiration—the Greek gods generally are little more than slightly oversized human-like heroes: The Greek gods are just like men, only more so.

Socrates came close to the concept of one divine being, but his attitude was not one of love, but of rational and spiritual fusion. As to man's relations with his fellows, the concept of friendship is very common in Greek thought and life, and even pervades Greek social and political thought. Love primarily is known as a dangerous and demonic relation between man and woman, potentially destructive and tragic.

In Jewish thought, there is the admonition in Leviticus in the Old Testament: "Thou shalt love thy neighbor as thyself." But this positive admonition to love one's neighbor is preceded by many "thou shalt nots"; moreover, even the phrase "thou shalt love thy neighbor" immediately is followed by the words of God: "I am the Lord," which makes it sound a little bit like: "You'd better love your neighbor as yourself—or else!" As to the relation of man to God, there is the command in Deuteronomy in the Old Testament: "Thou shalt love the Lord thy God with all thine heart, and with all thy soul, and with all thy might." Yet only a little later in the same chapter of Deuteronomy, we read the command: "Thou shalt fear the Lord thy God," followed by the specific injunction not to go after other gods, or else the Lord who is a "jealous God" will become angry and "destroy thee from off the face of the earth."

This primitive concept of love as expressed in the Old Testament gradually shed the elements of jealousy and fear, and pointed toward the Christian idea of love. In Matthew, Jesus is asked, "which is the great commandment in the law?" Jesus answers as follows: "Thou shalt love the Lord thy God with all thy heart, and with all thy soul, and with all thy mind. This is the first and great commandment. And the second is like unto it, Thou shalt love thy neighbor as thyself." He then adds: "On these two commandments hang all the law and the prophets." In speaking of the love of God and of man, Jesus uses words almost identical with those of the Old Testament, but the spirit is different. Whereas in Jewish thought, the concept of justice is the dominant one, Christianity centers on that of love. Jesus, by emphasizing love as the bond between man and God and man and man, pointed the way to a new way of life different from either the Jewish or Greek way of life and thought.

The Christianity taught by Jesus as recorded in the New Testament is unritualistic. There is little direct teaching by Jesus of formal religious practice. While he prays and fasts, and gathers with followers who want to be near and hear him, there is little description by Jesus of an ecclesiastic structure. Rather, a certain spirit is prescribed—to love others. It also is the case that in the four gospels, there is not as much emphasis placed on Jesus' death and resurrection compared to the number of passages concerning his life. Jesus' primary message was about how to love in this life not about a life to come.

The issue of retribution remains problematic in the different Gospels. Some mention punishment in a life to come. John, on the other hand, more emphasizes that Jesus did not come to judge but to save, and that he will save everyone. All Gospels present Jesus as recommending not to judge. Revelation is consistent with the Gospel of John to the extent that emphasis is placed upon universal salvation and formulaistic ritual is not the way to heaven.

Jesus' message of hope, love, faith, and charity in a better life in this world, and of a world to come, typically is not considered a political doctrine. It instead is an ethical idea and ideal of great animating force. "Render," Jesus taught, "unto Caesar the things which are Caesar's; and unto God the things that are God's." "My kingdom is not of this world . . . " Early and significant contact between Christianity and the preceding pagan world is evident in the writings of St. Augustine.

CHAPTER NINE

ST. AUGUSTINE

The destruction of Roman power in the fifth century was more than a political revolution. The Germanic conquerors from the North swept away an empire that seemed eternal and universal to its inhabitants, and wiped out a civilization and way of life that seemed imperishable. Yet the military helplessness of Rome was not so much the deeper cause of her fall as a symptom of her general decline and disintegration. Military defeat was the end, and not the beginning, of rot and decay.

Rome's decline can be said to have started in the growing betrayal of its pristine civic virtues and in her abandonment of republicanism in favor of despotic, monarchical imperialism. Amid immense material wealth there had been disturbing signs of failure of nerve and loss of faith; above all, unwillingness or inability to solve the social conflicts born of poverty, slavery, and serfdom had contributed to the weakening of the Roman empire and to its final conquest by barbarians emerging from a cultural nowhere—from the dark forests and endless plains beyond the confines of civilization.

The Gothic, Vandal, and Hun warriors could only destroy: they had no civilization of their own that they could substitute for, or mingle with, that of the Roman world. The recorded history of the west knows of no similar catastrophe, when a way of life was so thoroughly destroyed that men forgot what their ancestors had known for centuries, and had to start all over again groping toward a new existence.

It was a long and painful experience, and the process of gradual recovery from a near-mortal illness, the medieval period, fills the ten centuries between the fall of the Roman empire in the fifth century and the revival of ancient thought and learning in the fifteenth. Interest in this period had not been intense until recently, because it was assumed that nothing could henceforth have stopped the march of progress and scientific development, and that history was an unceasing process of liberty unfolding itself all over the world. This optimism, so typical of the eighteenth and nineteenth centuries, was rudely shaken in the twentieth century by World War II, which might have—had the allied nations been defeated—inaugurated a new dark age. The lesson of the fifth century is that an entire civilization can be razed from the earth, and humanity barbarized and decivilized.

When Rome was sacked by the Visigoths in A.D. 410, a popular explanation was that it was the fault of the Christians. Christianity had been officially tolerated in the Roman empire from A.D. 313, and eighty years later it became the official religion of state, paganism being proscribed and prohibited. Because the fall of Rome in A.D. 410 occurred so soon after the triumph of Christianity, many pagans and perhaps even some

181

Christians were inclined to see a connection between the rise of Christianity—so long considered officially a subversive movement—and the weakening of Roman power. From the traditional, pagan, upper-class Roman viewpoint, the Christian qualities of otherworldliness, meekness, pacifism, disregard for public affairs, and contempt for revered national deities had been persistently sapping the strength of Rome. Above all, the Christian refusal to recognize loyalty to Rome as the first loyalty, the dogged perseverance in putting a foreign religion above family, community, and state, must have appeared as a flagrant demonstration of "un-Roman" disloyalty.

Political-minded Romans of the old school were not deeply interested in religions as such, and as long as members of any creed were willing to make a formal gesture of obeisance to the ultimate authority of Rome and its personified imperial divinity, there was no cause for discord and conflict. Few empires and civilizations have, in fact, been as free from religious bigotry and persecution as Rome was, partly because of the moderation and political wisdom of its ruling classes and partly because religion was not taken seriously enough to turn men into tormentors and killers. The very polytheism of paganism ensured a basically tolerant attitude, as all pluralistic viewpoints tend to do. When Rome sought to extirpate Christianity by force in the second half of the third century, the charge was not against Christianity as a religion but against its alleged attempt to build up a state within the state, its boring from within every social class, and its gradual absorption of the Roman empire by infiltration and ideological appeals without overt acts of force.

Neither contempt nor ostracism, nor outright persecution, stopped the march of Christianity. In fact, in the fourth and fifth centuries, when Christianity became the religion of state, the roles were reversed, and paganism was put on the defensive and finally outlawed. The victory of Christianity appeared inevitable and providential to the Christian, because it was the only true religion; but to many pagans the effective extirpation of paganism by Christianity proved only that Christianity was more ruthless than its rival in the contest of persecution, and that the Roman emperors had made the mistake of treating the subversive Christians too leniently, wasting generosity on fanatics who would brook no compromise themselves if put in a position of authority.

When Rome was ravaged in 410, a wave of shock and horror swept through the world. For eight centuries Rome had proudly remained inviolate, growing from a small municipality into the center of a vast empire. The ease and speed with which this empire was broken up took everyone by surprise. The pagans, as we have said, ascribed the catastrophe to the betrayal of the old Roman deities under which Rome had risen to the position of the dominant world power, but Christians, too, were perplexed: it was hard to understand how Rome could be so shamed just after Christianity had become the religion of state, and many Christians began to wonder whether the official alliance of church and empire was such an advantage after all. If Rome was not strong enough to safeguard its own existence against heathen tribes, how could it be the source of worldly power that the church needed in spreading Christianity?

Some Christians who were particularly perturbed about what seemed the end of the world were recent converts; and yet, the strongest reaffirmation of Christian idealism was the work of a convert, St. Augustine (A.D. 354–430), a native and lifelong inhabitant of Roman North Africa. St. Augustine's parents were North Africans; his mother was a devout Christian, but his father never embraced the Christian faith. St. Augustine was baptized in Italy in A.D. 387, after many years of active and more than gay living, led in complete contradiction to Christian standards of morals and belief. But once he was baptized, he rose quickly in the hierarchy of the church; he was made Bishop of

Hippo (the modern port of Buna, in Algeria) in 395, where he stayed until his death in 430.

St. Augustine was moved especially by the pagan attacks that attributed the fall of Rome to the victory of Christianity. He started the *City of God (De Civitate Dei)* in 413, and finished the voluminous work, consisting of twenty-two books, in 426. He set out to answer two main questions. The first concerns the pagan challenge to Christianity. Although from a purely theological viewpoint the issue of paganism is not so intense and controversial in the twentieth century as it was in the fifth, St. Augustine's critique is always vital and timely, if one substitutes for paganism the qualities with which he identified it: contempt for spiritual values, smugness, pride, and injustice.

The rebuttal of paganism, however, is only the more negative part of the *City of God.* Having demonstrated the hollowness and inconsistency of paganism, materialism, and worldly success, Augustine proceeds to his more constructive task: the vision of the heavenly city, as contrasted with the earthly city *(civitas terrena).* St. Augustine's use of the word *civitas,* however, should not be interpreted in a political sense; St. Augustine was not a constitutional lawyer or political theorist but a theologian. He was interested in God, Faith, and Salvation, and not so much in the organization of the state and its political-juridical relations to the church. His heavenly city, or City of God, is therefore not identical with the church, and the earthly city is not the state.

As a theologian and passionate Christian who took his faith seriously, St. Augustine was primarily concerned with *ways of life* and *not* with *organizations of life.* The great struggle in the universe is, then, not between church and state (as later writers mistakenly interpreted St. Augustine for sectarian purposes), but between two opposing ways of life: in the earthly city, the love of self, the lust of power predominate, whereas in the heavenly city the love of God, "even to the contempt of self," is the foundation of order. St. Augustine therefore divides the human race into two parts, "the one consisting of those who live according to man, the other of those who live according to God. And these we also mystically call the two cities, or the two communities of men, of which the one is predestined to reign eternally with God, and the other to suffer eternal punishment with the devil." St. Augustine himself thus emphasizes that the two communities of the heavenly and earthly cities can be called cities only in a mystical or allegorical sense.

Even more explicitly, St. Augustine often speaks of the heavenly city as the eternal kingdom of God that includes the angels preceding the creation of man and the saintly elect *(communio sanctorum);* by contrast, the earthly city is the "society of the impious" *(societas impiorum),* which includes fallen angels as well as human beings who "live after the flesh." Eternal reign with God is the destiny of the heavenly city, whereas eternal punishment with the devil is the doom awaiting the earthly city.

The basic conflict between Good and Evil rages not only in mankind as a whole but in every individual. Just as Plato had stated that the problem of the just society was that of the just individual "writ large," so St. Augustine notes that the struggle between Good and Evil in the world is closely related to, and a reflection of, the conflicts within the individual human being: "For in each individual there is first of all that which is reprobate, that from which we must begin, but in which we need not necessarily remain; afterwards is that which is well approved, to which we may by advancing attain, and in which, when we have reached it, we may abide." In fact, Plato had anticipated the idea of the complex structure of the individual human soul by viewing it as a composite of the three rivaling elements of appetite, courage, and reason, representing three types of men and three ways of living. Justice, or righteousness, is the central concept in Plato's

Republic: an individual is just if the elements of his own soul are rightly ordered and arranged, and consequently he will also act justly in his relations with others by staying in his own station, by living the kind of life he was meant to live. St. Augustine transforms this secular conception of justice into a religious one: the essence of *justice* is the *relation between man and God,* from which right relations between man and man will inevitably follow.

If man is to become worthy of entry into the eternal kingdom of heaven, the City of God, there must be some agency on earth, St. Augustine realizes, that leads in the right direction. Although the central meaning of "heavenly city" is a way of life dedicated to the service of God, St. Augustine also uses this term "mystically," that is, symbolically, for the *church.* It is the part of the heavenly city that "sojourns on earth and lives by faith," and it "lives like a captive and stranger in the earthly city." In inspiring words that recall the Stoic message of universal unity and brotherhood, St. Augustine says that the heavenly city, "while it sojourns on earth, calls citizens out of all nations, and gathers together a society of pilgrims in all languages, not scrupling about diversities in the manners, laws, and institutions whereby earthly peace is secured and maintained," and that these diversities of men ought to be preserved, as long as men are united in God's service.

Yet St. Augustine nowhere clearly defines the church; in one place he calls it the Invisible Church of God's Elect (including some as yet to be converted), and in another, the Visible Church, made up of true believers and of those whose Christianity is little more than formal membership in the church. Because he failed to distinguish sharply the Invisible from the Visible Church, he claimed rights for the one that he would not have claimed for the other, particularly in relation to the state. As a result, his arguments were used later by adherents of papalist doctrines as well as by those who affirmed the sovereignty of mundane rulers over the church.

Just as the heavenly city symbolically represents, but is not identical with, the church, so the earthly city is symbolically reflected in the state. Strictly speaking, the *earthly city* is not identical with any empirical social or political organization but is the *community of the unrighteous,* including sinful members of the church and excluding righteous citizens of the state. Whereas the earthly city, as the incarnation of sin and lust, is the antithesis of any value whatsoever, the state, by contrast, has positive value, through it is not the absolute value inherent in the heavenly city.

The Greco-Roman background of St. Augustine comes out in his assumption that "the life of the wise man must be social," and that there is no man who "does not wish to have peace." The state, therefore, by providing social peace, "has its good in this world"; and St. Augustine recalls Greco-Roman ideas in saying that the state is, "in its own kind, better than all other human good. For it desires earthly peace for the sake of enjoying earthly goods."

At this point St. Augustine parts company with Plato and Cicero, who so strongly influenced him. The peace that the state provides is, according to St. Augustine, not an end in itself, but only a means, a condition that makes the service to God possible. The peace of the state is the temporary tranquillity that enables man to work for the heavenly city, which is "peace never-ending."

Peace is therefore conceived by St. Augustine in terms of justice (that is, the right relation of man and God); it is not merely the absence of social strife and conflict. Without justice there can be no peace, and this moral and religious conception is behind St. Augustine's famous statement: "Justice being taken away, then, what are kingdoms but great robberies?" St. Augustine goes on to say that, viewed from the standpoint of formal, effective authority, robberies (that is, bands of robbers) are but little kingdoms themselves; the difference, therefore, between a state and a band of robbers is qualitative and not quantitative.

St. Augustine thus Christianizes the classical approach to the theory of the state by imbuing the Platonic concept of justice and the Aristotelian notion of the good life with the ideals of Christianity, and his doctrine is firmly anchored in the Greco-Roman and Biblical conceptions of the state in terms of moral purpose rather than formal authority, the monopoly to use force, or sovereignty.

The strong influence of Greco-Roman conceptions and preconceptions on St. Augustine can also be seen in his attitude toward slavery. In essence, it is a Christianized version of Aristotle's rationalization of slavery. Man was created in God's image, to be master of irrational creatures, beasts, but not of fellow men. Slavery is therefore not the result of man's nature, as originally intended by God, but the "result of sin." It is both punishment and remedy for sin, as for Aristotle slavery is the just relation between those who possess virtue and those who do not.

St. Augustine specifically opposes the law of the Old Testament according to which all servitude was to be ended every seventh year, and states that bad slaves are made into good by the example of Christ, and that slaves should not refuse to serve wicked masters. St. Augustine appeals to the slaves to serve their masters "heartily and with good will, so that, if they cannot be freed by their masters, they may themselves make their slavery in some sort free, by serving not in crafty fear, but in faithful love, until all righteousness pass away, and all principality and every human power be brought to nothing, and God be in all." Like Aristotle, St. Augustine also appeals to the masters to act benevolently and responsibly; they "ought to feel their position of authority a greater burden than servants their service."

Yet St. Augustine never examined his theory in the light of empirical evidence: was it really true that slaves were worse sinners than the free? Although he occasionally notes that there are "many wicked masters who have religious men as their slaves," this observation leads him, not to a reexamination of his basic assumption that slavery is the punishment and remedy for sin, but to the more startling conclusion that even such slavery is legitimate because "it is a happier thing to be the slave of a man than of a lust." Weighed carefully, therefore, St. Augustine's theory of slavery, like that of the church in general, probably seemed more reasonable to masters than to slaves, although the institution of slavery was mitigated, in actual use, by the influence of Christianity.

St. Augustine, the greatest of the church Fathers, stood at the turning point of two worlds, that of antiquity and Christianity. The impact of Plato in particular, but also that of Aristotle, Cicero, and the Stoics, is clearly evident in his work, and he helped to transmit the ancient heritage to the new world that was being born. While the Roman empire was breaking up before his eyes, he sought to construe, as a Christian, the vision of a timeless empire in which peace and justice would reign: the City of God.

ST. AUGUSTINE

*The City of God**

JUSTICE—THE FOUNDATION OF THE STATE

Justice being taken away, then, what are kingdoms but great robberies? For what are robberies themselves, but little kingdoms? The band itself is made up of men; it is ruled by the authority of a prince, it is knit together by the pact of the confederacy; the booty is divided by the law agreed on. If, by the admittance of abandoned men, this evil increases to such a degree that it holds places, fixes abodes, takes possession of cities, and subdues peoples, it assumes the more plainly the name of a kingdom, because the reality is now manifestly conferred on it, not by the removal of covetousness, but by the addition of impunity. Indeed, that was an apt and true reply which was given to Alexander the Great by a pirate who had been seized. For when that king had asked the man what he meant by keeping hostile possession of the sea, he answered with bold pride, "What thou meanest by seizing the whole earth; but because I do it with a petty ship, I am called a robber, whilst thou who dost it with a great fleet art styled emperor."[1]

THE TRUE HAPPINESS OF THE RULER

For neither do we say that certain Christian emperors were therefore happy because they ruled a long time, or, dying a peaceful death, left their sons to succeed them in the empire, or subdued the enemies of the republic, or were able both to guard against and to suppress the attempt of hostile citizens rising against them. These and other gifts or comforts of this sorrowful life even certain worshippers of demons have merited to receive, who do not belong to the kingdom of God to which these belong; and this is to be traced to the mercy of God, who would not have those who believe in Him desire such things as the highest good. But we say that they are happy if they rule justly; if they are not lifted up amid the praises of those who pay them sublime honors, and the obsequiousness of those who salute them with an excessive humility, but remember that they are men; if they make their power the handmaid of His majesty by using it for the greatest possible extension of His worship; if they fear, love, worship God; if more than their own they love that kingdom in which they are not afraid to have partners; if they are slow to punish, ready to pardon; if they apply that punishment as necessary to government and defence of the republic, and not in order to gratify their own enmity; if they grant pardon, not that iniquity may go unpunished, but with the hope that the transgressor may amend his ways; if they compensate with the lenity of mercy and the liberality of benevolence for whatever severity they may be compelled to decree; if their luxury is as much restrained as it might have been unrestrained; if they prefer to govern depraved desires rather than any nation whatever; and if they do all these things, not through ardent desire of empty glory, but through love of eternal felicity, not neglecting to offer to the true God, who is their God, for their sins, the sacrifices of humility, contrition, and

* From St. Augustine, *The City of God* (trans. Marcus Dods, in Vol. II of *A Select Library of the Nicene and Post-Nicene Fathers of the Christian Church,* ed. Philip Schaff, Buffalo, 1887).

[1] Cicero, *De Republica,* III.

prayer. Such Christian emperors, we say, are happy in the present time by hope, and are destined to be so in the enjoyment of the reality itself, when that which we wait for shall have arrived.

THE EARTHLY AND THE HEAVENLY CITY

Accordingly, two cities have been formed by two loves: the earthly by the love of self, even to the contempt of God; the heavenly by the love of God, even to the contempt of self. The former, in a word, glories in itself, the latter in the Lord. For the one seeks glory from men; but the greatest glory of the other is God, the witness of conscience. The one lifts up its head in its own glory; the other says to its God, "Thou art my glory, and the lifter up of mine head."[2] In the one, the princes and the nations it subdues are ruled by the love of ruling; in the other, the princes and the subjects serve one another in love, the latter obeying, while the former take thought for all. The one delights in its own strength, represented in the persons of its rulers; the other says to its God, "I will love Thee, O Lord, my strength."[3] And therefore the wise men of the one city, living according to man, have sought for profit to their own bodies or souls, or both, and those who have known God "glorified Him not as God, neither were thankful, but became vain in their imaginations, and their foolish heart was darkened; professing themselves to be wise"—that is, glorying in their own wisdom, and being possessed by pride—"they became fools, and changed the glory of the incorruptible God into an image made like to corruptible man, and to birds, and four-footed beasts, and creeping things." For they were either leaders or followers of the people in adoring images, "and worshipped and served the creature more than the Creator, who is blessed for ever."[4] But in the other city there is no human wisdom, but only godliness, which offers due worship to the true God, and looks for its reward in the society of the saints, of holy angels as well as holy men, that God may be all in all.[5]

THE TWO TYPES OF MAN

Of the bliss of Paradise, of Paradise itself, and of the life of our first parents there, and of their sin and punishment, many have thought much, spoken much, written much. We ourselves, too, have spoken of these things in the foregoing books, and have written either what we read in the Holy Scriptures, or what we could reasonably deduce from them. And were we to enter into a more detailed investigation of these matters, an endless number of endless questions would arise, which would involve us in a larger work than the present occasion admits. We cannot be expected to find room for replying to every question that may be started by unoccupied and captious men, who are ever more ready to ask questions than capable of understanding the answer. Yet I trust we have already done justice to these great and difficult questions regarding the beginning of the world, or of the soul, or of the human race itself. This race we have distributed into two parts, the one consisting of those who live according to man, the other of those who live according to God. And these we also mystically call the two cities, or the two communities of men, of which the one is predestined to reign eternally with God, and the other to suffer eternal punishment with the devil. This, however, is their end, and of it we are to speak afterwards. At present, as we have said enough about their origin, whether among the angels, whose numbers we know not, or in the two first human beings, it seems suitable to attempt an account of their career, from the time when our two first parents began to propagate the race until all human generation shall cease. For this whole time or world-age, in which the dying give place and those who are born succeed, is the career of these two cities concerning which we treat.

Of these two first parents of the human race, then, Cain was the first-born, and he belonged to the city of men; after him was born Abel, who belonged to the city of God. For as in the individual the truth of the apostle's statement is discerned, "that is not first which is spiritual, but that which is natural, and afterward that which is spiritual,"[6] whence it comes to pass that each

---

[2] Ps. iii. 3.
[3] Ps. xviii. 1.
[4] Rom. i. 21–25.
[5] I Cor. xv. 28.

[6] I Cor. xv. 46.

man, being derived from a condemned stock, is first of all born of Adam evil and carnal, and becomes good and spiritual only afterwards, when he is grafted into Christ by regeneration: so was it in the human race as a whole. When these two cities began to run their course by a series of deaths and births, the citizen of this world was the first-born, and after him the stranger in this world, the citizen of the city of God, predestinated by grace, elected by grace, by grace a stranger below, and by grace a citizen above. By grace—for so far as regards himself he is sprung from the same mass, all of which is condemned in its origin: but God, like a potter (for this comparison is introduced by the apostle judiciously, and not without thought), of the same lump made one vessel to honor, another to dishonor.[7] But first the vessel to dishonor was made, and after it another to honor. For in each individual, as I have already said, there is first of all that which is reprobate, that from which we must begin, but in which we need not necessarily remain; afterwards is that which is well-approved, to which we may by advancing attain, and in which, when we have reached it, we may abide. Not, indeed, that every wicked man shall be good, but that no one will be good who was not first of all wicked; but the sooner any one becomes a good man, the more speedily does he receive this title, and abolish the old name in the new. Accordingly, it is recorded of Cain that he built a city,[8] but Abel, being a sojourner, built none. For the city of the saints is above, although here below it begets citizens, in whom it sojourns till the time of its reign arrives, when it shall gather together all in the day of the resurrection; and then shall the promised kingdom be given to them, in which they shall reign with their Prince, the King of the ages, time without end.

CONFLICT AND PEACE IN THE EARTHLY CITY

But the earthly city, which shall not be everlasting (for it will no longer be a city when it has been committed to the extreme penalty), has its good in this world, and rejoices in it

with such joy as such things can afford. But as this is not a good which can discharge its devotees of all distresses, this city is often divided against itself by litigations, wars, quarrels, and such victories as are either life-destroying or short-lived. For each part of it that arms against another part of it seeks to triumph over the nations though itself in bondage to vice. If, when it has conquered, it is inflated with pride, its victory is life-destroying; but if it turns its thoughts upon the common casualties of our mortal condition, and is rather anxious concerning the disasters that may befall it than elated with the successes already achieved, this victory, though of a higher kind, is still only short-lived; for it cannot abidingly rule over those whom it has victoriously subjugated. But the things which this city desires cannot justly be said to be evil, for it is itself, in its own kind, better than all other human good. For it desires earthly peace for the sake of enjoying earthly goods, and it makes war in order to attain to this peace; since, if it has conquered, and there remains no one to resist it, it enjoys a peace which it had not while there were opposing parties who contested for the enjoyment of those things which were too small to satisfy both. This peace is purchased by toilsome wars; it is obtained by what they style a glorious victory. Now, when victory remains with the party which had the juster cause, who hesitates to congratulate the victor, and style it a desirable peace? These things, then, are good things, and without doubt the gifts of God. But if they neglect the better things of the heavenly city, which are secured by eternal victory and peace neverending, and so inordinately covet these present good things that they believe them to be the only desirable things, or love them better than those things which are believed to be better—if this be so, then it is necessary that misery follow and ever increase.

THE LUST FOR POWER IN THE EARTHLY CITY

Thus the founder of the earthly city was a fratricide. Overcome with envy, he slew his own brother, a citizen of the eternal city, and a sojourner on earth. So that we cannot be surprised that this first specimen, or, as the Greeks say, archetype of crime, should,

---

[7] Rom. ix. 21.
[8] Gen. iv. 17.

long afterwards, find a corresponding crime at the foundation of that city which was destined to reign over so many nations, and be the head of this earthly city of which we speak. For of that city also, as one of their poets has mentioned, "the first walls were stained with a brother's blood."[9] or, as Roman history records, Remus was slain by his brother Romulus. And thus there is no difference between the foundation of this city and of the earthly city, unless it be that Romulus and Remus were both citizens of the earthly city. Both desired to have the glory of founding the Roman republic, but both could not have as much glory as if one only claimed it; for he who wished to have the glory of ruling would certainly rule less if his power were shared by a living consort. In order, therefore, that the whole glory might be enjoyed by one, his consort was removed; and by this crime the empire was made larger indeed, but inferior, while otherwise it would have been less, but better. Now these brothers, Cain and Abel, were not both animated by the same earthly desires, nor did the murderer envy the other because he feared that, by both ruling, his own dominion would be curtailed—for Abel was not solicitous to rule in that city which his brother built—he was moved by that diabolical, envious hatred with which the evil regard the good, for no other reason than because they are good while themselves are evil. For the possession of goodness is by no means diminished by being shared with a partner either permanent or temporarily assumed; on the contrary, the possession of goodness is increased in proportion to the concord and charity of each of those who share it. In short, he who is unwilling to share this possession cannot have it; and he who is most willing to admit others to a share of it will have the greatest abundance to himself. The quarrel, then, between Romulus and Remus shows how the earthly city is divided against itself; that which fell out between Cain and Abel illustrated the hatred that subsists between the two cities, that of God and that of men. The wicked war with the wicked; the good also war with the wicked. But with the good, good men, or at least perfectly good men, cannot war; though, while only going on towards perfection, they war to this extent, that every good man resists others in those points in which he resists himself. And in each individual "the flesh lusteth against the spirit, and the spirit against the flesh."[10] This spiritual lusting, therefore, can be at war with the carnal lust of another man; or carnal lust may be at war with the spiritual desires of another, in some such way as good and wicked men are at war; or, still more certainly, the carnal lusts of two men, good but not yet perfect, contend together, just as the wicked contend with the wicked, until the health of those who are under the treatment of grace attains final victory.

LIMITATIONS OF SOCIAL LIFE

We give a much more unlimited approval to their idea that the life of the wise man must be social. For how could the city of God either take a beginning or be developed, or attain its proper destiny, if the life of the saints were not a social life? But who can enumerate all the great grievances with which human society abounds in the misery of this mortal state? Who can weigh them? Hear how one of their comic writers makes one of his characters express the common feelings of all men in this matter: "I am married; this is one misery. Children are born to me; they are additional cares."[11] What shall I say of the miseries of love which Terence also recounts—"slights, suspicions, quarrels, war to-day, peace to-morrow?"[12] Is not human life full of such things? Do they not often occur even in honorable friendships? On all hands we experience these slights, suspicions, quarrels, war, all of which are undoubted evils; while, on the other hand, peace is a doubtful good, because we do not know the heart of our friend, and though we did know it to-day, we should be as ignorant of what it might be to-morrow. Who ought to be, or who are more friendly than those who live in the same family? And yet who can rely even upon this friendship, seeing that secret treachery has often broken it up, and produced enmity as bitter as the amity was sweet, or seemed sweet by the most perfect dissimulation? It is on this account that the words of Cicero

---

[9] Lucan, *Phar.* i. 95.

[10] Gal. v. 17.
[11] Terent. *Adelph.* v. 4.
[12] *Eunuch*, i. 1.

so move the heart of every one, and provoke a sigh: "There are no snares more dangerous than those which lurk under the guise of duty or the name of relationship. For the man who is your declared foe you can easily baffle by precaution; but this hidden, intestine, and domestic danger not merely exists, but overwhelms you before you can foresee and examine it."[13] Is It is also to this that allusion is made by the divine saying, "A man's foes are those of his own household"[14]—words which one cannot hear without pain; for though a man have sufficient fortitude to endure it with equanimity, and sufficient sagacity to baffle the malice of a pretended friend, yet if he himself is a good man, he cannot but be greatly pained at the discovery of the perfidy of wicked men, whether they have always been wicked and merely feigned goodness, or have fallen from a better to a malicious disposition. If, then, home, the natural refuge from the ills of life, is itself not safe, what shall we say of the city, which, as it is larger, is so much the more filled with lawsuits civil and criminal, and is never free from the fear, if sometimes from the actual outbreak, of disturbing and bloody insurrections and civil wars?

SHORTCOMINGS OF HUMAN JUSTICE

What shall I say of these judgments which men pronounce on men, and which are necessary in communities, whatever outward peace they enjoy? Melancholy and lamentable judgments they are, since the judges are men who cannot discern the consciences of those at their bar, and are therefore frequently compelled to put innocent witnesses to the torture to ascertain the truth regarding the crimes of other men. What shall I say of torture applied to the accused himself? He is tortured to discover whether he is guilty, so that, though innocent, he suffers most undoubted punishment for crime that is still doubtful, not because it is proved that he committed it, but because it is not ascertained that he did not commit it. Thus the ignorance of the judge frequently involves an innocent person in suffering. And what is still more unendurable—a thing, indeed, to be bewailed, and, if that were possible, watered with fountains of tears—is this, that when the judge puts the accused to the question, that he may not unwittingly put an innocent man to death, the result of this lamentable ignorance is that this very person, whom he tortured that he might not condemn him if innocent, is condemned to death both tortured and innocent. For if he has chosen, in obedience to the philosophical instructions to the wise man, to quit this life rather than endure any longer such tortures, he declares that he has committed the crime which in fact he has not committed. And when he has been condemned and put to death, the judge is still in ignorance whether he has put to death an innocent or a guilty person, though he put the accused to the torture for the very purpose of saving himself from condemning the innocent; and consequently he has both tortured an innocent man to discover his innocence, and has put him to death without discovering it. If such darkness shrouds social life, will a wise judge take his seat on the bench or no? Beyond question he will. For human society, which he thinks it a wickedness to abandon, constrains him and compels him to this duty. And he thinks it no wickedness that innocent witnesses are tortured regarding the crimes of which other men are accused; or that the accused are put to the torture, so that they are often overcome with anguish, and, though innocent, make false confessions regarding themselves, and are punished; or that, though they be not condemned to die, they often die during, or in consequence of, the torture; or that sometimes the accusers, who perhaps have been prompted by a desire to benefit society by bringing criminals to justice, are themselves condemned through the ignorance of the judge, because they are unable to prove the truth of their accusations though they are true, and because the witnesses lie, and the accused endures the torture without being moved to confession. These numerous and important evils he does not consider sins; for the wise judge does these things, not with any intention of doing harm, but because his ignorance compels him, and because human society claims him as a judge. But though we therefore acquit the judge of malice, we must none the less condemn human life as miserable. And if he is compelled to torture

---

[13] *In Verrem,* ii. I. 15.
[14] Matt. x. 36.

and punish the innocent because his office and his ignorance constrain him, is he a happy as well as a guiltless man? Surely it were proof of more profound considerateness and finer feeling were he to recognize the misery of these necessities, and shrink from his own implication in that misery; and had he any piety about him, he would cry to God "From my necessities deliver Thou me."[15]

THE MISERY OF WAR

After the state or city comes the world, the third circle of human society—the first being the house, and the second the city. And the world, as it is larger, so it is fuller of dangers, as the greater sea is the more dangerous. And here, in the first place, man is separated from man by the difference of languages. For if two men, each ignorant of the other's language, meet, and are not compelled to pass, but, on the contrary, to remain in company, dumb animals, though of different species, would more easily hold intercourse than they, humans though they be. For their common nature is no help to friendliness when they are prevented by diversity of language from conveying their sentiments to one another; so that a man would more readily hold intercourse with his dog than with a foreigner. But the imperial city has endeavored to impose on subject nations not only her yoke, but her language, as a bond of peace, so that interpreters, far from being scarce, are numberless. This is true; but how many great wars, how much slaughter and bloodshed, have provided this unity! And though these are past, the end of these miseries has not yet come. For though there have never been wanting, nor are yet wanting, hostile nations beyond the empire, against whom wars have been and are waged, yet, supposing there were no such nations, the very extent of the empire itself has produced wars of a more obnoxious description—social and civil wars—and with these the whole race has been agitated, either by the actual conflict or the fear of a renewed outbreak. If I attempted to give an adequate description of these manifold disasters, these stern and lasting necessities, though I am quite

unequal to the task, what limit could I set? But, say they, the wise man will wage just wars. As if he would not all the rather lament the necessity of just wars, if he remembers that he is a man; for if they were not just he would not wage them, and would therefore be delivered from all wars. For it is the wrong-doing of the opposing party which compels the wise man to wage just wars; and this wrong-doing, even though it gave rise to no war, would still be matter of grief to man because it is man's wrong-doing. Let every one, then, who thinks with pain on all these great evils, so horrible, so ruthless, acknowledge that this is misery. And if any one either endures or thinks of them without mental pain, this is a more miserable plight still, for he thinks himself happy because he has lost human feeling.

THE OBJECTIVE OF WAR: PEACE

Whoever gives even moderate attention to human affairs and to our common nature, will recognize that if there is no man who does not wish to be joyful, neither is there any one who does not wish to have peace. For even they who make war desire nothing but victory—desire, that is to say, to attain to peace with glory. For what else is victory than the conquest of those who resist us? and when this is done there is peace. It is therefore with the desire for peace that wars are waged, even by those who take pleasure in exercising their warlike nature in command and battle. And hence it is obvious that peace is the end sought for by war. For every man seeks peace by waging war, but no man seeks war by making peace. For even they who intentionally interrupt the peace in which they are living have no hatred of peace, but only wish it changed into a peace that suits them better. They do not, therefore, wish to have no peace, but only one more to their mind. And in the case of sedition, when men have separated themselves from the community, they yet do not effect what they wish, unless they maintain some kind of peace with their fellow-conspirators. And therefore even robbers take care to maintain peace with their comrades, that they may with greater effect and greater safety invade the peace of other men. And if an individual happens to be of

---

[15] Ps. xxv. 17.

such unrivalled strength, and to be so jealous of partnership, that he trusts himself with no comrades, but makes his own plots, and commits depredations and murders on his own account, yet he maintains some shadow of peace with such persons as he is unable to kill, and from whom he wishes to conceal his deeds. In his own home, too, he makes it his aim to be at peace with his wife and children, and any other members of his household; for unquestionably their prompt obedience to his every look is a source of pleasure to him. And if this be not rendered, he is angry, he chides and punishes; and even by this storm he secures the calm peace of his own home, as occasion demands. For he sees that peace cannot be maintained unless all the members of the same domestic circle be subject to one head, such as he himself is in his own house. And therefore if a city or nation offered to submit itself to him, to serve him in the same style as he had made his household serve him, he would no longer lurk in brigand's hiding-places, but lift his head in open day as a king, though the same coveteousness and wickedness should remain in him. And thus all men desire to have peace with their own circle whom they wish to govern as suits themselves. For even those whom they make war against they wish to make their own, and impose on them the laws of their own peace.

But let us suppose a man such as poetry and mythology speak of—a man so unsociable and savage as to be called rather a semi-man than a man.[16] Although, then, his kingdom was the solitude of a dreary cave, and he himself was so singularly bad-hearted that he was named Καχός, which is the Greek word for *bad;* though he had no wife to soothe him with endearing talk, no children to play with, no sons to do his bidding, no friend to enliven him with intercourse, not even his father Vulcan (though in one respect he was happier than his father, not having begotten a monster like himself); although he gave to no man, but took as he wished whatever he could, from whomsoever he could, when he could; yet in that solitary den, the floor of which, as Virgil[17] says, was always reeking with recent slaughter, there was nothing else than peace sought, a peace in which no one should molest him, or disquiet him with any assault or alarm. With his own body he desired to be at peace, and he was satisfied only in proportion as he had this peace. For he ruled his members, and they obeyed him; and for the sake of pacifying his mortal nature, which rebelled when it needed anything, and of allaying the sedition of hunger which threatened to banish the soul from the body, he made forays, slew, and devoured, but used the ferocity and savageness he displayed in these actions only for the preservation of his own life's peace. So that, had he been willing to make with other men the same peace which he made with himself in his own cave, he would neither have been called bad, nor a monster, nor a semi-man. Or if the appearance of his body and his vomiting smoky fires frightened men from having any dealings with him, perhaps his fierce ways arose not from a desire to do mischief, but from the necessity of finding a living. But he may have had no existence, or, at least, he was not such as the poets fancifully describe him, for they had to exalt Hercules, and did so at the expense of Cacus. It is better, then, to believe that such a man or semi-man never existed, and that this, in common with many other fancies of the poets, is mere fiction. For the most savage animals (and he is said to have been almost a wild beast) encompass their own species with a ring of protecting peace. They cohabit, beget, produce, suckle, and bring up their young, though very many of them are not gregarious, but solitary—not like sheep, deer, pigeons, starlings, bees, but such as lions, foxes, eagles, bats. For what tigress does not gently purr over her cubs, and lay aside her ferocity to fondle them? What kite, solitary as he is when circling over his prey, does not seek a mate, build a nest, hatch the eggs, bring up the young birds, and maintain with the mother of his family as peaceful a domestic alliance as he can? How much more powerfully do the laws of man's nature move him to hold fellowship and maintain peace with all men so far as in him lies, since even wicked men wage war to maintain the peace of their own circle, and wish that, if possible, all men belonged to them, that all men and things might serve but one head, and

---

[16] He refers to the giant Cacus.
[17] *Aeneid,* viii. 195.

might, either through love or fear, yield themselves to peace with him! It is thus that pride in its perversity apes God. It abhors equality with other men under Him; but, instead of His rule, it seeks to impose a rule of its own upon its equals. It abhors, that is to say, the just peace of God, and loves its own unjust peace; but it cannot help loving peace of one kind or other. For there is no vice so clean contrary to nature that it obliterates even the faintest traces of nature.

He, then, who prefers what is right to what is wrong, and what is well-ordered to what is perverted, sees that the peace of unjust men is not worthy to be called peace in comparison with the peace of the just. And yet even what is perverted must of necessity be in harmony with, and in dependence on, and in some part of the order of things, for otherwise it would have no existence at all. Suppose a man hangs with his head downwards, this is certainly a perverted attitude of body and arrangement of its members; for that which nature requires to be above is beneath, and *vice versa*. This perversity disturbs the peace of the body, and is therefore painful. Nevertheless the spirit is at peace with its body, and labors for its preservation, and hence the suffering; but if it is banished from the body by its pains, then, so long as the bodily framework holds together, there is in the remains a kind of peace among the members, and hence the body remains suspended. And inasmuch as the earthly body tends towards the earth, and rests on the bond by which it is suspended, it tends thus to its natural peace, and the voice of its own weight demands a place for it to rest; and though now lifeless and without feeling, it does not fall from the peace that is natural to its place in creation, whether it already has it, or is tending towards it. For if you apply embalming preparations to prevent the bodily frame from mouldering and dissolving, a kind of peace still unites part to part, and keeps the whole body in a suitable place on the earth—in other words, in a place that is at peace with the body. If, on the other hand, the body receive no such care, but be left to the natural course, it is disturbed by exhalations that do not harmonize with one another, and that offend our senses; for it is this which is perceived in putrefaction until it is assimilated to the elements of the world, and particle by particle enters into peace with them. Yet throughout this process the laws of the most high Creator and Governor are strictly observed, for it is by Him the peace of the universe is administered. For although minute animals are produced from the carcass of a larger animal, all these little atoms, by the law of the same Creator, serve the animals they belong to in peace. And although the flesh of dead animals be eaten by others, no matter where it be carried, nor what it be brought into contact with, nor what it be converted and changed into, it still is ruled by the same laws which pervade all things for the conservation of every mortal race, and which bring things that fit one another into harmony.

THE TRANQUILLITY OF ORDER IN THE UNIVERSE

The peace of the body then consists in the duly proportioned arrangement of its parts. The peace of the irrational soul is the harmonious repose of the appetites, and that of the rational soul the harmony of knowledge and action. The peace of body and soul is the well-ordered and harmonious life and health of the living creature. Peace between man and God is the well-ordered obedience of faith to eternal law. Peace between man and man is well-ordered concord. Domestic peace is the well-ordered concord between those of the family who rule and those who obey. Civil peace is a similar concord among the citizens. The peace of the celestial city is the perfectly ordered and harmonious enjoyment of God, and of one another in God. The peace of all things is the tranquillity of order. Order is the distribution which allots things equal and unequal, each to its own place. And hence, though the miserable, in so far as they are such, do certainly not enjoy peace, but are severed from that tranquillity of order in which there is no disturbance, nevertheless, inasmuch as they are deservedly and justly miserable, they are by their very misery connected with order. They are not, indeed, conjoined with the blessed, but they are disjoined from them by the law of order. And though they are disquieted, their circumstances are notwithstanding adjusted to them, and consequently they have some tranquillity of order, and therefore some peace. But they are wretched because, although not wholly miserable, they are not in that place where any mixture of misery is impossible. They would, however, be more wretched if they had not that peace which arises from being in harmony with the natural order of things. When they suffer, their peace is in so far disturbed; but their peace continues in so far as they do not suffer, and in so far as their nature continues to exist. As, then, there may be life without pain, while there cannot be pain without some kind of life, so there may be peace without war, but there cannot be war without some kind of peace, because war supposes the existence of some natures to wage it, and these natures cannot exist without peace of one kind or other.

And therefore there is a nature in which evil does not or even cannot exist; but there cannot be a nature in which there is no good. Hence not even the nature of the devil himself is evil, in so far as it is nature, but it was made evil by being perverted. Thus he did not abide in the truth,[18] but could not escape the judgment of the truth; he did not abide in the tranquillity of order, but did not therefore escape the power of the Ordainer. The good imparted by God to his nature did not screen him from the justice of God by which order was preserved in his punishment; neither did God punish the good which He had created, but the evil which the devil had committed. God did not take back all He had imparted to his nature, but something He took and something He left, that there might remain enough to be sensible of the loss of what was taken. And this very sensibility to pain is evidence of the good which has been taken away and the good which has been left. For, were nothing good left, there could be no pain on account of the good which had been lost. For he who sins is still worse if he rejoices in his loss of righteousness. But he who is in pain, if he derives no benefit from it, mourns at least the loss of health. And as righteousness and health are both good things, and as the loss of any good thing is matter of grief, not of joy—if, at least, there is no compensation, as spiritual righteousness may compensate for the loss of bodily health—certainly it is more suitable for a wicked man to grieve in punishment than to rejoice in his fault. As, then,

_____
[18] John viii. 44.

the joy of a sinner who has abandoned what is good is evidence of a bad will, so his grief for the good he has lost when he is punished is evidence of a good nature. For he who laments the peace his nature has lost is stirred to do so by some relics of peace which make his nature friendly to itself. And it is very just that in the final punishment the wicked and godless should in anguish bewail the loss of the natural advantages they enjoyed, and should perceive that they were most justly taken from them by that God whose benign liberality they had despised. God, then, the most wise Creator and most just Ordainer of all natures, who placed the human race upon earth as its greatest ornament, imparted to men some good things adapted to this life, to wit, temporal peace, such as we can enjoy in this life from health and safety and human fellowship, and all things needful for the preservation and recovery of this peace, such as the objects which are accommodated to our outward senses, light, night, the air, and waters suitable for us, and everything the body requires to sustain, shelter, heal, or beautify it: and all under this most equitable condition, that every man who made a good use of these advantages suited to the peace of this mortal condition, should receive ampler and better blessings, namely, the peace of immortality, accompanied by glory and honor in an endless life made fit for the enjoyment of God and of one another in God; but that he who used the present blessings badly should both lose them and should not receive the others.

RULERS AS SERVANTS
OF THE RULED

The whole use, then, of things temporal has a reference to this result of earthly peace in the earthly community, while in the city of God it is connected with eternal peace. And therefore, if we were irrational animals, we should desire nothing beyond the proper arrangement of the parts of the body and the satisfaction of the appetites—nothing, therefore, but bodily comfort and abundance of pleasures, that the peace of the body might contribute to the peace of the soul. For if bodily peace be wanting, a bar is put to the peace even of the irrational soul, since it cannot obtain the gratification of its appetites. And these two together help out the mutual peace of soul and body, the peace of harmonious life and health. For as animals, by shunning pain, show that they love bodily peace, and, by pursuing pleasure to gratify their appetites, show that they love peace of soul, so their shrinking from death is a sufficient indication of their intense love of that peace which binds soul and body in close alliance. But, as man has a rational soul, he subordinates all this which he has in common with the beasts to the peace of his rational soul, that his intellect may have free play and may regulate his actions, and that he may thus enjoy the well-ordered harmony of knowledge and action which constitutes, as we have said, the peace of the rational soul. And for this purpose he must desire to be neither molested by pain, nor disturbed by desire, nor extinguished by death, that he may arrive at some useful knowledge by which he may regulate his life and manners. But, owing to the liability of the human mind to fall into mistakes, this very pursuit of knowledge may be a snare to him unless he has a divine Master, whom he may obey without misgiving, and who may at the same time give him such help as to preserve his own freedom. And because, so long as he is in this mortal body, he is stranger to God, he walks by faith, not by sight; and he therefore refers all peace, bodily or spiritual or both, to that peace which mortal man has with the immortal God, so that he exhibits the well-ordered obedience of faith to eternal law. But as this divine Master inculcates two precepts—the love of God and the love of our neighbor—and as in these precepts a man finds three things he has to love—God, himself, and his neighbor—and that he who loves God loves himself thereby, it follows that he must endeavor to get his neighbor to love God, since he is ordered to love his neighbor as himself. He ought to make this endeavor in behalf of his wife, his children, his household, all within his reach, even as he would wish his neighbor to do the same for him if he needed it; and consequently he will be at peace, or in well-ordered concord, with all men, as far as in him lies. And this is the order of this concord, that a man, in the first place, injure no one, and, in the second, do good to every one he can reach. Primarily, therefore, his own household

are his care, for the law of nature and of society gives him readier access to them and greater opportunity of serving them. And hence the apostle says, "Now, if any provide not for his own, and specially for those of his own house, he hath denied the faith, and is worse than an infidel."[19] This is the origin of domestic peace, or the well-ordered concord of those in the family who rule and those who obey. For they who care for the rest rule—the husband the wife, the parents the children, the masters the servants; and they who are cared for obey—the women their husbands, the children their parents, the servants their masters. But in the family of the just man who lives by faith and is as yet a pilgrim journeying on to the celestial city, even those who rule serve those whom they seem to command; for they rule not from a love of power, but from a sense of the duty they owe to others—not because they are proud of authority, but because they love mercy.

LIBERTY AND SLAVERY

This is prescribed by the order of nature: it is thus that God has created man. For "let them," He says, "have dominion over the fish of the sea, and over the fowl of the air, and over every creeping thing which creepeth on the earth."[20] He did not intend that His rational creature, who was made in His image, should have dominion over anything but the irrational creation—not man over man, but man over the beasts. And hence the righteous men in primitive times were made shepherds of cattle rather than kings of men, God intending thus to teach us what the relative position of the creatures is, and what the desert of sin; for it is with justice, we believe, that the condition of slavery is the result of sin. And this is why we do not find the word "slave" in any part of Scripture until righteous Noah branded the sin of his son with this name. It is a name, therefore, introduced by sin and not by nature. The origin of the Latin word for slave is supposed to be found in the circumstance that those who by the law of war were liable to be killed were sometimes preserved by their victors, and were hence called servants. And

---

[19] I Tim. v. 8.
[20] Gen. i. 26.

these circumstances could never have arisen save through sin. For even when we wage a just war, our adversaries must be sinning; and every victory, even though gained by wicked men, is a result of the first judgment of God, who humbles the vanquished either for the sake of removing or of punishing their sins. Witness that man of God, Daniel, who, when he was in captivity, confessed to God his own sins and the sins of his people, and declared with pious grief that these were the cause of the captivity.[21] The prime cause, then, of slavery is sin, which brings man under the dominion of his fellow—that which does not happen save by the judgment of God, with whom is no unrighteousness, and who knows how to award fit punishments to every variety of offence. But our Master in heaven says, "Every one who doeth sin is the servant of sin."[22] And thus there are many wicked masters who have religious men as their slaves, and who are yet themselves in bondage; "for of whom a man is overcome, of the same is he brought in bondage."[23] And beyond question it is a happier thing to be the slave of a man than of a lust; for even this very lust of ruling, to mention no others, lays waste men's hearts with the most ruthless dominion. Moreover, when men are subjected to one another in a peaceful order, the lowly position does as much good to the servant as the proud position does harm to the master. But by nature, as God first created us, no one is the slave either of man or of sin. This servitude is, however, penal, and is appointed by that law which enjoins the preservation of the natural order and forbids its disturbance; for if nothing had been done in violation of that law, there would have been nothing to restrain by penal servitude. And therefore the apostle admonishes slaves to be subject to their masters, and to serve them heartily and with good-will, so that, if they cannot be freed by their masters, they may themselves make their slavery in some sort free, by serving not in crafty fear, but in faithful love, until all unrighteousness pass away, and all principality and every human power be brought to nothing, and God be all in all.

---

[21] Dan. ix.
[22] John viii. 34.
[23] II Pet. ii. 19.

EQUITABLE RULE

And therefore, although our righteous fathers[24] had slaves, and administered their domestic affairs so as to distinguish between the condition of slaves and the heirship of sons in regard to the blessings of this life, yet in regard to the worship of God, in whom we hope for eternal blessings, they took an equally loving oversight of all the members of their household. And this is so much in accordance with the natural order, that the head of the household was called *paterfamilias;* and this name has been so generally accepted, that even those whose rule is unrighteous are glad to apply it to themselves. But those who are true fathers of their households desire and endeavor that all the members of their household, equally with their own children, should worship and win God, and should come to that heavenly home in which the duty of ruling men is no longer necessary, because the duty of caring for their everlasting happiness has also ceased; but, until they reach that home, masters ought to feel their position of authority a greater burden than servants their service. And if any member of the family interrupts the domestic peace by disobedience, he is corrected either by word or blow, or some kind of just and legitimate punishment, such as society permits, that he may himself be the better for it, and be readjusted to the family harmony from which he had dislocated himself. For as it is not benevolent to give a man help at the expense of some greater benefit he might receive, so it is not innocent to spare a man at the risk of his falling into graver sin. To be innocent, we must not only do harm to no man, but also restrain him from sin or punish his sin, so that either the man himself who is punished may profit by his experience, or others be warned by his example. Since, then, the house ought to be the beginning or element of the city, and every beginning bears reference to some end of its own kind, and every element to the integrity of the whole of which it is an element, it follows plainly enough that domestic peace has a relation to civic peace—in other words, that the well-ordered concord of domestic obedience

---

[24] The patriarchs.

and domestic rule has a relation to the well-ordered concord of civic obedience and civic rule. And therefore it follows, further, that the father of the family ought to frame his domestic rule in accordance with the law of the city, so that the household may be in harmony with the civic order.

THE SUPRANATIONAL CHARACTER OF THE HEAVENLY CITY ON EARTH

But the families which do not live by faith seek their peace in the earthly advantages of this life; while the families which live by faith look for those eternal blessing which are promised, and use as pilgrims such advantages of time and of earth as do not fascinate and divert them from God, but rather aid them to endure with greater ease, and to keep down the number of those burdens of the corruptible body which weigh upon the soul. Thus the things necessary for this mortal life are used by both kinds of men and families alike, but each has its own peculiar and widely different aim in using them. The earthly city, which does not live by faith, seeks an earthly peace, and the end it proposes, in the well-ordered concord of civic obedience and rule, is the combination of men's wills to attain the things which are helpful to this life. The heavenly city, or rather the part of it which sojourns on earth and lives by faith, makes use of this peace only because it must, until this mortal condition which necessitates it shall pass away. Consequently, so long as it lives like a captive and a stranger in the earthly city, though it has already received the promise of redemption, and the gift of the Spirit as the earnest of it, it makes no scruple to obey the laws of the earthly city, whereby the things necessary for the maintenance of this mortal life are administered; and thus, as this life is common to both cities, so there is a harmony between them in regard to what belongs to it. But, as the earthly city has had some philosophers whose doctrine is condemned by the divine teaching, and who, being deceived either by their own conjectures or by demons, supposed that many gods must be invited to take an interest in human affairs, and assigned to each a separate function and a separate department—to one the body, to another the soul; and in the body itself, to one the head, to another the neck, and each of the other members to one of the gods; and in like manner, in the soul, to one god the natural capacity was assigned, to another education, to another anger, to another lust; and so the various affairs of life were assigned—cattle to one, corn to another, wine to another, oil to another, the woods to another, money to another, navigation to another, wars and victories to another, marriages to another, births and fecundity to another, and other things to other gods: and as the celestial city, on the other hand, knew that one God only was to be worshipped, and that to Him alone was due that service which the Greeks call *latreia,* and which can be given only to a god, it has come to pass that the two cities could not have common laws of religion, and that the heavenly city has been compelled in this matter to dissent, and to become obnoxious to those who think differently, and to stand the brunt of their anger and hatred and persecutions, except in so far as the minds of their enemies have been alarmed by the multitude of the Christians, and quelled by the manifest protection of God accorded to them. This heavenly city, then, while it sojourns on earth, calls citizens out of all nations, and gathers together a society of pilgrims of all languages, not scrupling about diversities in the manners, laws, and institutions whereby earthly peace is secured and maintained, but recognizing that, however various these are, they all tend to one and the same end of earthly peace. It therefore is so far from rescinding and abolishing these diversities, that it even preserves and adopts them, so long only as no hindrance to the worship of the one supreme and true God is thus introduced. Even the heavenly city, therefore, while in its state of pilgrimage, avails itself of the peace of earth, and, so far as it can without injuring faith and godliness, desires and maintains a common agreement among men regarding the acquisition of the necessaries of life, and makes this earthly peace bear upon the peace of heaven; for this alone can be truly called and esteemed the peace of the reasonable creatures, consisting as it does in the perfectly ordered and harmonious enjoyment of God and of one another in God. When we shall have reached that peace, this mortal life shall give place to one that is eternal, and our body shall be no more this animal body which by its corruption weighs down the soul, but a spiritual body feeling no want, and in all its members subjected to the will. In its pilgrim state the heavenly city possesses this peace by faith; and by this faith it lives righteously when it refers to the attainment of that peace every good action towards God and man; for the life of the city is a social life.

CHAPTER TEN

JOHN OF SALISBURY

Christianity introduced a revolutionary principle into communal life by destroying the previous equation of personality and citizenship, and by postulating autonomy of a spiritual sphere independent of, and even superior to, political authority. For a time Christianity was on the defensive, and the needs of institutional survival naturally overshadowed the need for theoretical formulas. After Christianity became the official religion of state in the fourth century, and the only permitted creed in the fifth, interest in the theory of the relation of church and state developed more rapidly.

St. Augustine was so deeply concerned with the theological defense of Christianity against paganism and heresy that he did not elaborate a political theory clearly defining the boundaries between political and ecclesiastical power, but toward the close of the fifth century, Pope Gelasius defined the relation between the two authorities (or "two swords," as they were later called). Christ himself was king and priest, but knowing the sinfulness and weakness of human nature, he divided, according to Gelasius, the two offices, assigning to ecclesiastical authority the spiritual and religious welfare of men, and to political authority the care and administration of temporal matters. Both ecclesiastical and political powers derive their authority from God; each is independent, and therefore supreme, in its own sphere, the church in religious matters and the state in political affairs. Yet this independence also implies mutual dependence: because the state is supreme only in its own sphere, the political, it must bow to the supremacy of the church in religious issues. Similarly, the church, because it is supreme only in religious matters, must recognize the authority of the state in mundane government and administration.

Gelasius did not raise, or answer, the question of who is to decide whether a specific issue is predominantly religious or political. In his dualistic conception of authority he assumed that church and state would cooperate in practical tasks rather than engage in bitter jurisdictional disputes: the church needs the state for temporal purposes, and the state needs the church for the attainment of spiritual salvation. The clergy should therefore not interfere with the government's secular business, and the political rulers should keep clear of spiritual matters.

Had Gelasius pressed the issue to its logical conclusions and gone into the question of who is to decide authoritatively, in a given situation, whether the ecclesiastical or

199

temporal interest is predominant, he would have discovered that his dualistic theory was not wholly satisfactory. Under his dualistic doctrine of two coordinate authorities, whoever has the right or power to decide whether a matter at issue is primarily ecclesiastical or temporal, will, in effect, be the first, or, to use a more modern phrase, the sovereign authority. But the formulation of socially significant questions is not a matter of mere logic, and Gelasius may have felt that the cause of peace and the long-term interests of the church would best be served by a doctrine that stressed the possibility of equilibrium rather than of strife. The dualism of ecclesiastical and temporal authority was not conceived to be final: God is the source of both, and in serving God both authorities find their reason for existence.

Nevertheless, Gelasius weighed his doctrine somewhat in favor of the church by mentioning that its burden is heavier than that of the state, because the priest is answerable for the souls of all—subjects, lords, and kings. In Gelasius's own mind, this special position of the church merely involved special responsibilities, inasmuch as the heaviest task of all, spiritual salvation, was assigned to it. Yet the doctrine of the heavier burden—originally a moral ideal of fuller dedication to selfless service—became, from the ninth century on, a positive claim for more dignity and authority in relation to mundane government.

As the conflict between church and empire grew, particularly from the tenth to the twelfth centuries, each side tended to give up the older Gelasian doctrine of two authorities poised in equilibrium. The papalists claimed supreme authority for the church as the representative of the spiritual principle in society and insisted that all authority, ecclesiastical and secular, was originally given to the church; that, retaining the title and exercise of spiritual power, the church then transferred the exercise of secular authority to the state, without, however, abandoning the original title to it. According to the basic papalist theory, the church held its authority directly from God, whereas the state exercised its authority indirectly, having received it from the church as the intermediary between God and society.

In the age of feudalism, social rights and institutions were less well defined and clear-cut than in premedieval or modern times. Thus landed property was not attached to a single owner who had absolute dominion over it, but was broken up into its component elements, so that one person might be the legal owner, whereas many others might share in its uses. Or the owner might retain for himself some forms of the use of his property, and grant other forms of use to his vassals. The papalist doctrine claiming that secular authority was held only as a "fief" (in tenure) by the state, true title resting with the church, was no stranger in construction than was the medieval (and still valid) legal doctrine of "eminent domain" under which the king retains the ultimate title to all property in the land.

In pre- and postfeudal eras the argument of the medieval papalists might logically lead to theocracy, a government in which the priests rule in both ecclesiastical and secular matters. The specific environment of feudalism permitted the formulation of a theory in which even the papalists merely claimed the original title to secular authority but left its exercise to the state. What the papalists demanded was not so much that the pope actually rule and administer the empire but that he control the emperor's action from the viewpoint of Christian values, that he protect the subjects against rulers who strayed from the path of righteousness, and that he have the right to censure and admonish the emperor, and, if necessary, excommunicate and depose him.

By contrast, the representatives of the imperialist position made, in theory at least, more moderate claims. They were willing to concede that neither power was supreme over the other as far as its source and title were concerned, for both powers were handed down directly from God to church and state. Thus, in essence, the moderate imperialist writers were satisfied to restate the Gelasian doctrine of equality and equilibrium between secular and spiritual authorities. As the contest between the papalists and the imperialists sharpened, particularly from the eleventh century on, extreme antipapalists suggested that the office of the king or emperor was, in itself, higher than that of bishop and pope, and that secular authority was supreme in worldly and spiritual matters.

The struggle between papalist and antipapalist doctrines was not only, or even chiefly, an issue of theological disagreement but the expression of vital conflicts of power and control. In particular, the contest was by no means as universal as the phrase "church and empire" would imply. In the first place, the Holy Roman Empire of the Middle Ages (which originated in the coronation of Charlemagne in Rome in 800 and ended in the abdication of the Hapsburg emperor Francis II in 1806) was little more than a German empire, including a great part of Italy but excluding the all-important political areas of England, France, and Spain. Similarly, the church at this time could not speak in the name of all Christendom, but only of those who, especially in the West, were under the jurisdiction of Rome. In 1054 there occurred the final separation between the Eastern Orthodox and Roman Catholic Churches.

Contestants in any dispute often seek to buttress their case by identifying their partial interest with a more general, and possibly universal, one. It was therefore not unnatural for the Catholic Church to represent itself as the guardian of all Christendom, just as it was in the interest of German expansionist monarchs to hug the cloak of the Holy Roman Empire and thus acquire more respectability and universality. Although the Roman empire had been defeated militarily in the fifth century by Germanic invaders streaming into Italy and her possessions from all directions, Roman popes continued, during the Middle Ages, the struggle with expanding German power—a power that the political and military leaders of the old empire had been unable to stem by force. It is to be noted that the papacy also collided with French and English kings, but the principal adversary was the German monarchy, which threatened Italy and the Roman church most directly.

The second aspect of the conflict between church and state was intimately tied to the feudal system. Bishops were, on the one hand, charged with the administration of the church and the care of souls, but at the same time they were feudal holders of land and as such vassals of the king. The feudal link of authority, unlike that of the modern state, was of a highly personal kind, and loyalty of the vassal to the lord was more profound and absorbing than is implied in the modern concept of obeying an impersonal law. The church has always been, and still is, an owner of large landed properties, but the modern concept of ownership is more absolute and does not involve a special kind of allegiance to the government, as was the situation in the feudal era in which landed property was the determining element in the machinery of government.

Another source of conflict lay in the fact that, as the clergy in the Middle Ages for a long time enjoyed a monopoly of literacy and learning, they were entrusted with important administrative positions in the courts and chancelleries of Europe. In theory, perhaps, a bishop could be a faithful representative of the church in spiritual matters and a loyal vassal of the king in economic and political affairs; but this theory was based on the assumption that church and state did not disagree on major policies. When there was disagreement, bishops and priests had to choose which was their first loyalty. The papalists advised them that the church was higher in dignity and authority. The antipapalists insisted that, in secular matters at least, and perhaps in spiritual, too, royal authority was supreme.

The first great conflict between church and empire occurred in the latter part of the eleventh century, when, in 1076, Holy Roman Emperor Henry IV deposed Pope Gregory VII; shortly thereafter, the pope not only deposed the emperor but also excommunicated him and relieved his subjects from their oath of allegiance. From that time until the end of the thirteenth century the conflict between ecclesiastical and secular power dominated the theory as well as the practice of politics.

The most incisive presentation of the papalist viewpoint is the work of an Englishman, John of Salisbury (about 1120–1180). He is considered by many to be the most typical medieval political writer before the discovery and spread of Aristotelianism in the thirteenth century, which gave rise to such divergent and overtowering figures as St. Thomas Aquinas and Marsilio of Padua.

John of Salisbury spent twelve years of his schooling in France, mostly in Paris, then the world center of philosophy and theology, and in Chartres, an important center of humanistic studies. Like other great English political writers later on (Locke, Burke, J.S. Mill), John of Salisbury had wide practical experience in public affairs. At an early age, as the secretary of Archbishop Theobald of Canterbury, he acquired intimate knowledge of government and politics in England, as well as inside penetration into the character and management of the church. He frequently traveled to the papal court in Rome, and was an intimate friend of Adrian IV, the only English pope in history. He also became a friend of Thomas Becket; when the latter succeeded Theobald as Archbishop of Canterbury, John of Salisbury continued as secretary to the new archbishop.

The conflict between ecclesiastical and temporal power in England developed rapidly during this period, and in 1164 John of Salisbury was exiled to France, shortly to be followed by Thomas Becket. Six years later they returned to England, and John of Salisbury was probably with Thomas Becket on the day the latter was murdered in his own cathedral at Canterbury by the henchmen of Henry II, King of England. In 1176 John of Salisbury was asked by the French king, Louis VII, to become bishop of Chartres. John gladly accepted the invitation to return to the city in which he had been introduced, as a youth, to humanistic learning, and in Chartres, where he felt so much at home, he died in 1180.

John of Salisbury's most important work is *The Statesman's Book (Policraticus)*. There is perhaps no single doctrine that he can claim to have discovered first; yet his book is one of the most influential medieval political statements because of the originality with which he combines existing isolated ideas into a new pattern, and because of his style, which has freshness, integrity, and a sense of humor—the latter a particularly rare quality in a medieval writer on politics.

John is best known for his championing of the supremacy of the ecclesiastical over the temporal power. From the ninth century on, this struggle between the two powers periodically erupted. The Gelasian doctrine of equilibrium and cooperation between church and state was constantly modified by the conflicts of power between the popes and the German emperors, and the developing interpretations of church-state relations reflected the strains and tensions of the struggle for hegemony. In the twelfth century, an era of increasing strife between ecclesiastical and mundane authority, the papalists were particularly fortunate in finding John of Salisbury for one of their first spokesmen; he was undisputedly their most effective.

There are no *ifs* and *buts* in his argument: he clearly states that both swords, the material and the spiritual, belong to the church, and that the *prince receives his sword*, or authority, *from the church,* that he is a "minister of the priestly power, and one who exercises that side of the sacred offices which seems unworthy of the hands of the priesthood." As the original and true owner of the temporal sword, the church has the right to depose the prince if he violates the law of God and disregards the precepts of the church, for "he who can lawfully bestow can lawfully take away."

The human body is another symbolic analogy that John of Salisbury employs for proving the superiority of the ecclesiastical over the secular power. John compares the commonwealth to a body, each organ, group, and class representing symbolically parts of the body. Thus farmers and workers correspond to the feet, public-finance officers to the stomach and intestines, officials and soldiers to the hands, and the senate to the heart, while the prince occupies the place of the head. But the church and clergy occupy the highest place of all, as they are likened to the soul in the body, and "the soul is, as it were, the prince of the body, and has rulership over the whole thereof." The secular ruler is therefore subject to God and "to those who exercise His office and represent Him on earth." John of Salisbury was not familiar with Aristotle's *Politics* and its organic conception of the political community; for John, in contrast to Aristotle, the organic theory meant that each organ of state and society had its unchangeable place.

John of Salisbury does not propose that the church actually take over the temporal government and administer it through priests, nor does he recommend that a prince submit every law for prior approval to a supreme court of priests. Yet he makes the extreme claim that "a statute or ordinance *(constitutio)* of the prince is a thing of nought if not in conformity with the teaching *(disciplina)* of the Church." Without proposing the administrative absorption of the state into the church, and unable to think—as a medieval writer—in terms of clearly defined concepts of legal sovereignty, John of Salisbury nevertheless made such an overwhelming case for the moral sovereignty of the church over the secular ruler that later protagonists of the papal cause found it none too difficult to go beyond him and plead for legal supremacy as well.

In his supporting sources, John of Salisbury, like most medieval papalist writers and pampheleteers except St. Augustine, leaned heavily on the Old Testament with its firm bias against temporal rulers, and he quotes frequently from the Hebrew prophets and their struggle against kings and princes. The New Testament emphasized more positively that "the powers that be are ordained of God," and made it possible to interpret the Christian acceptance of mundane power in a manner that would maintain the supremacy of the church. But it was easier to go back to the Old Testament in which the hostility against secular rulers was consistent and unequivocal. Nearly five centuries after John of Salisbury, the English Puritans reverted, in their struggle against secular authority, to the Old Testament as a main source of fighting inspiration.

From the modern secularist viewpoint, the church ought to stay in its place and not contend with the state for temporal power. But John of Salisbury and the papal apologists, in seeking to curb the authoritarian claims of kings and princes, or to gain at least equal authority for the church, were (knowingly or unknowingly) fighting a cause that was larger than their own; the whole issue of human liberty was at stake, and it was a more important issue than the rivalry for power and supremacy that raged between popes and emperors. And though John of Salisbury and the medievalists did not solve this larger issue, neither have the secularists: Is the state, even the democratic state, to have absolute and complete authority, or must there be some competing principles of allegiance that will make it difficult, or impossible, for the state to become an all-absorbing Leviathan? The church can no longer, as in the Middle Ages, play the part of the sole competing source of loyalty and authority, but thus far no other institution or idea is in sight that can be relied on to do the job. The democratic state—precisely because of its popular source of support—has by no means abolished the possibility of tyranny and repression, as was so prophetically foreseen by Tocqueville and J.S. Mill a century ago.

In the liberal orthodoxy of the eighteenth and nineteenth centuries, the struggle for power between state and church in the Middle Ages was unqualifiedly viewed as a struggle between reason and unreason, between progress and reaction. The church was seen to be the main impediment to the development of liberal government, and it was assumed that once the religious influence was eliminated from social and political life, the progress of reason and liberty would be irresistible. Yet this liberal dogma has proved a fallacy to a large extent. It has been disproved by events rather than by argument. The experience of fascist and communist totalitarianism in the twentieth century shows that a community which lacks ideas and institutions that can challenge the state may eventually be devoured by omnipotent despotism.

The conclusion to be drawn from the medieval struggle between state and church is not necessarily that the church alone can be a countervailing or balancing power in limiting the scope of government, but that, unless *some* countervailing ideas and institutions are sufficiently strong in a society, totalitarianism of some sort is that much more likely to develop. In the modern world, such loyalties competing with the loyalty to government may stem from nonreligious, humanist beliefs, or they may still be based on strongly held religious commitments. In any case, the anxiety of twentieth-century man is not that the state has, or will have, too little power, but the fear of too much governmental power. In this perspective, the contemporary democrat is bound to take a different view of the medieval struggle between state and church than was customary in eighteenth- and nineteenth-century liberalism.

John of Salisbury's second main political doctrine, the distinction between king and tyrant, and the justification of tyrannicide, is as provocative today as it was in his own time. The distinction between king and tyrant goes back to Aristotle: the king rules in the interest of the ruled, the tyrant in his own. John of Salisbury states, by contrast, that the *king rules in accordance with the laws,* whereas the *tyrant rules by force.* This distinction is directly related to the Christian and typically medieval respect for law, and it is closer to the modern distinction between legitimate and illegitimate government than is Aristotle's emphasis on interest.

By violating the rule of law, John of Salisbury says, the tyrant assails the grace of God, and "it is God himself who in a sense is challenged to battle." The prince fights for the laws and liberties of the people, and "as the likeness of the Deity, is to be loved, worshipped and cherished; the tyrant, the likeness of wickedness, is generally to be even killed." In one passage John does qualify his general position on tyrannicide by expressing his hope that the most useful and safest way of destroying tyrants is for the oppressed to pray devoutly "that the scourge wherewith they are afflicted may be turned aside from them." But such occasional qualification does not detract from his general view that *tyrants may be lawfully slain.*

In fact, John of Salisbury goes further and asserts that it is not only lawful but even right and just to kill the tyrant, for he who takes the sword shall perish by the sword. The ruler has a special responsibility to obey the law and protect justice. The tyrant usurps power, oppresses justice, and enslaves the law to his arbitrary whims. Of all forms of treason, "none is more deadly than that which is aimed against the very body of justice." In resisting and killing the tyrant, no violation of the law is being committed, as it is the tyrant "who disarms the laws," and it is therefore fitting that "justice arm herself against him." He who does not prosecute and attack the tyrant, sins against himself and against the whole community.

Thus, completely abandoning the Augustinian tradition, John of Salisbury expressed the doctrine of tyrannicide more forcefully and challengingly than any other writer in the Middle Ages; not until the sixteenth century did resistance to tyrants, and their assassination, become again a major theme of political speculation. John Locke expressed the doctrine of revolution and resistance to tyrants in words that bear a striking resemblance to John of Salisbury's. According to Locke, absolute government "is no form of civil government at all," and the absolute prince is in a state of nature, outside the realm of law and justice. The true rebels are the arbitrary and oppressive rulers who violate the law, and resistance to such rulers is the first step toward restoring the law. John of Salisbury thus was one of the first writers to establish the doctrine that obedience to authority is not absolute but conditional, that political authority is ultimately based on justice, and that resistance is a right and duty when peaceful change of a tyrannical regime is impossible.

What made John of Salisbury so convincing as a political writer and papal protagonist was his sense of proportion and his ability to see things in gray rather than black and white. One of the most revealing passages of *The Statesman's Book* is his account of a conversation with Pope Adrian IV on what people thought of the church and of the pope. As John explains, he was "entirely frank" with the pope; he recited a scathing catalogue of sins and vices attributed by many persons to the church and the clergy. He stressed particularly the love of money prevalent among the priests: "They give judgment not for the truth but for money. For money you can get anything done today, and without waiting; but you will not get it done even tomorrow if you do not pay a price."

Next to avarice, John charges the church and priesthood with duplicity and the lust for power, and says they have no compassion for the suffering and misery of the afflicted. Though he was speaking to a pope, John said: "Even the Roman pontiff himself is a grievous and almost intolerable burden to all; the complaint is everywhere made that while the churches which were built by the devotion of the fathers are falling into ruin and collapsing, he has built for himself palaces, and walks abroad not merely in purple but in gold. The palaces of priests dazzle the eye, and meanwhile in their hands the Church of Christ is defiled."

The pope—an Englishman, a friend of John, and a person with a sense of humor—laughed after John had finished, congratulated him for having spoken so frankly, and asked him to report in the future anything unfavorable about the church.

Toward the end of his book, John of Salisbury returns to the subject of ecclesiastical vices and abuses, and attacks, above all, the struggle for power and office within the church; he is shocked by the lack of scruples—even when it comes to murder—among contenders for the papal office: "It is alleged by some, and it is indeed the truth, that the office of Roman pontiff has sometimes, nay rather has often, been contested by ambitious men, and not without the shedding of fraternal blood has the pontiff entered the Holy of Holies." One of the concluding observations of John's is therefore that, as between the temporal and ecclesiastical tyrant, the latter is the worse.

It is precisely because of John of Salisbury's capacity to criticize ruthlessly the abuses of his church that his defense of ecclesiastical supremacy over the temporal power proved so effective. *The Statesman's Book* is not only an important medieval political treatise but also a thoroughly enjoyable piece of literature, modern in its wit, urbanity, learning, balance, and perspective. His papalist viewpoint was not commonly accepted by his countrymen in his own day, and it is less well received today. But his thought and personality point to those qualities in English political philosophy that later assured it a unique position of influence in the world.

JOHN OF SALISBURY

*The Statesman's Book**

THE NATURE AND SOURCE OF ROYAL AUTHORITY

Between a tyrant and a prince there is this single or chief difference, that the latter obeys the law and rules the people by its dictates, accounting himself as but their servant. It is by virtue of the law that he makes good his claim to the foremost and chief place in the management of the affairs of the commonwealth and in the bearing of its burdens; and his elevation over others consists in this, that whereas private men are held responsible only for their private affairs, on the prince fall the burdens of the whole community. Wherefore deservedly there is conferred on him, and gathered together in his hands, the power of all his subjects, to the end that he may be sufficient unto himself in seeking and bringing about the advantage of each individually, and of all; and to the end that the state of the human commonwealth may be ordered in the best possible manner, seeing that each and all are members one of another. Wherein we indeed but follow nature, the best guide of life; for nature has gathered together all the senses of her microcosm or little world, which is man, into the head, and has subjected all the members in obedience to it in such wise that they will all function properly so long as they follow the guidance of the head, and the head remains sane. Therefore the prince stands on a pinnacle which is exalted and made splendid with all the great and high privileges which

he deems necessary for himself. And rightly so, because nothing is more advantageous to the people than that the needs of the prince should be fully satisfied; since it is impossible that his will should be found opposed to justice. Therefore, according to the usual definition, the prince is the public power, and a kind of likeness on earth of the divine majesty. Beyond doubt a large share of the divine power is shown to be in princes by the fact that at their nod men bow their necks and for the most part offer up their heads to the axe to be struck off, and, as by a divine impulse, the prince is feared by each of those over whom he is set as an object of fear. And this I do not think could be, except as a result of the will of God. For all power is from the Lord God, and has been with Him always, and is from everlasting. The power which the prince has is therefore from God, for the power of God is never lost, nor severed from Him, but He merely exercises it through a subordinate hand, making all things teach His mercy or justice. "Who, therefore, resists the ruling power, resists the ordinance of God,"[1] in whose hand is the authority of conferring that power, and when He so desires, of withdrawing it again, or diminishing it. For it is not the ruler's own act when his will is turned to cruelty against his subjects, but it is rather the dispensation of God for His good pleasure to punish or chasten them. Thus during the Hunnish persecution, Attila, on being asked by the reverend bishop of a certain city who he was, replied, "I am Attila, the scourge of God." Whereupon it is written that the bishop adored him as representing the divine majesty. "Welcome," he

*From: *The Statesman's Book* of John of Salisbury (translated by John Dickinson, 1927). Copyright renewed by Lindsay Rogers, 1955. Reprinted by permission of Appleton-Century-Crofts, Division of Meredith Corporation.

[1] Rom. xiii, 2.

said, "is the minister of God," and "Blessed is he that cometh in the name of the Lord," and with sighs and groans he unfastened the barred doors of the church, and admitted the persecutor through whom he attained straightway to the palm of martyrdom. For he dared not shut out the scourge of God, knowing that His beloved Son was scourged, and that the power of this scourge which had come upon himself was as nought except it came from God. If good men thus regard power as worthy of veneration even when it comes as a plague upon the elect, who should not venerate that power which is instituted by God for the punishment of evil-doers and for the reward of good men, and which is promptest in devotion and obedience to the laws? To quote the words of the Emperor, "it is indeed a saying worthy of the majesty of royalty that the prince acknowledges himself bound by the Laws."[2] For the authority of the prince depends upon the authority of justice and law; and truly it is a greater thing than imperial power for the prince to place his government under the laws, so as to deem himself entitled to do nought which is at variance with the equity of justice.

THE RELATION OF THE PRINCE TO AUTHORITY

Princes should not deem that it detracts from their princely dignity to believe that the enactments of their own justice are not to be preferred to the justice of God, whose justice is an everlasting justice, and His law is equity. Now equity, as the learned jurists define it, is a certain fitness of things which compares all things rationally, and seeks to apply like rules of right and wrong to like cases, being impartially disposed toward all persons, and allotting to each that which belongs to him. Of this equity the interpreter is the law, to which the will and intention of equity and justice are known. Therefore Crisippus asserted that the power of the law extends over all things, both divine and human, and that it accordingly presides over all goods and ills, and is the ruler and guide of material things as well as of human beings. To which Papinian, a man most

learned in the law, and Demosthenes, the great orator, seem to assent, subjecting all men to its obedience because all law is, as it were, a discovery, and a gift from God, a precept of wise men, the corrector of excesses of the will, the bond which knits together the fabric of the state, and the banisher of crime;[3] and it is therefore fitting that all men should live according to it who lead their lives in a corporate political body. All are accordingly bound by the necessity of keeping the law, unless perchance there is any who can be thought to have been given the license of wrong-doing. However, it is said that the prince is absolved from the obligations of the law; but this is not true in the sense that it is lawful for him to do unjust acts, but only in the sense that his character should be such as to cause him to practice equity not through fear of the penalties of the law but through love of justice; and should also be such as to cause him from the same motive to promote the advantage of the commonwealth, and in all things to prefer the good of others before his own private will. Who, indeed, in respect of public matters can properly speak of the will of the prince at all, since therein he may not lawfully have any will of his own apart from that which the law or equity enjoins, or the calculation of the common interest requires? For in these matters his will is to have the force of a judgment; and most properly that which pleases him therein has the force of law, because his decision may not be at variance with the intention of equity. "From thy countenance," says the Lord, "let my judgment go forth, let thine eyes look upon equity";[4] for the uncorrupted judge is one whose decision, from assiduous contemplation of equity, is the very likeness thereof. The prince accordingly is the minister of the common interest and the bond-servant of equity, and he bears the public person in the sense that he punishes the wrongs and injuries of all, and all crimes, with even-handed equity. His rod and staff also, administered with wise moderation, restore irregularities and false departures to the straight path of equity, so that deservedly may the Spirit congratulate the power of the prince with the words, "Thy rod and thy

---

[2] Justin. Cod. 1, 14, § 4.

[3] Dig. I. 3, §§· 1–2.
[4] Ps. xvii, 2.

staff, they have comforted me."[5] His shield, too, is strong, but it is a shield for the protection of the weak, and one which wards off powerfully the darts of the wicked from the innocent. Those who derive the greatest advantage from his performance of the duties of his office are those who can do least for themselves, and his power is chiefly exercised against those who desire to do harm. Therefore not without reason he bears a sword, wherewith he sheds blood blamelessly, without becoming thereby a man of blood, and frequently puts men to death without incurring the name or guilt of homicide. For if we believe the great Augustine, David was called a man of blood not because of his wars, but because of Uria. And Samuel is nowhere described as a man of blood or a homicide, although he slew Agag, the fat king of Amalech. Truly the sword of princely power is as the sword of a dove, which contends without gall, smites without wrath, and when it fights, yet conceives no bitterness at all. For as the law pursues guilt without any hatred of persons, so the prince most justly punishes offenders from no motive of wrath but at the behest, and in accordance with the decision, of the passionless law. For although we see that the prince has lictors of his own, we must yet think of him as in reality himself the sole or chief lictor, to whom is granted by the law the privilege of striking by a subordinate hand. If we adopt the opinion of the Stoics, who diligently trace down the reason for particular words, "lictor" means "legis ictor," or "hammer of the law," because the duty of his office is to strike those who the law adjudges shall be struck. Wherefore anciently, when the sword hung over the head of the convicted criminal, the command was wont to be given to the officials by whose hand the judge punishes evil-doers, "Execute the sentence of the law," or "Obey the law," to the end that the misery of the victim might be mitigated by the calm reasonableness of the words.

THE PRINCE SUBORDINATE TO THE PRIESTS

This sword, then, the prince receives from the hand of the Church, although she herself has no sword of blood at all. Nevertheless she has this sword, but she uses it by the hand of the prince, upon whom she confers the power of bodily coercion, retaining to herself authority over spiritual things in the person of the pontiffs. The prince is, then, as it were, a minister of the priestly power, and one who exercises that side of the sacred offices which seems unworthy of the hands of the priesthood. For every office existing under, and concerned with the execution of, the sacred laws is really a religious office, but that is inferior which consists in punishing crimes, and which therefore seems to be typified in the person of the hangman. Wherefore Constantine, most faithful emperor of the Romans, when he had convoked the council of priests at Nicaea, neither dared to take the chief place for himself nor even to sit among the presbyters, but chose the hindmost seat. Moreover, the decrees which he heard approved by them he reverenced as if he had seen them emanate from the judgment-seat of the divine majesty. Even the rolls of petitions containing accusations against priests which they brought to him in a steady stream he took and placed in his bosom without opening them. And after recalling them to charity and harmony, he said that it was not permissible for him, as a man, and one who was subject to the judgment of priests, to examine cases touching gods, who cannot be judged save by God alone. And the petitions which he had received he put into the fire without even looking at them, fearing to give publicity to accusations and censures against the fathers, and thereby incur the curse of Cham, the undutiful son, who did not hide his father's shame. Wherefore he said, as is narrated in the writings of Nicholas the Roman pontiff, "Verily if with mine own eyes I had seen a priest of God, or any of those who wear the monastic garb, sinning, I would spread my cloak and hide him, that he might not be seen of any." Also Theodosius, the great emperor, for a merited fault, though not so grave a one, was suspended by the priest of Milan from the exercise of his regal powers and from the insignia of his imperial office, and patiently and solemnly he performed the penance for homicide which was laid upon him. Again, according to the testimony of the teacher of the gentiles, greater

---

[5] Ps. xxiii, 4.

is he who blesses man than he who is blessed;[6] and so he in whose hands is the authority to confer a dignity excels in honor and the privileges of honor him upon whom the dignity itself is conferred. Further, by the reasoning of the law it is his right to refuse who has the power to grant, and he who can lawfully bestow can lawfully take away.[7] Did not Samuel pass sentence of deposition against Saul by reason of his disobedience, and supersede him on the pinnacle of kingly rule with the lowly son of Ysai?[8] But if one who has been appointed prince has performed duly and faithfully the ministry which he has undertaken, as great honor and reverence are to be shown to him as the head excels in honor all the members of the body. Now he performs his ministry faithfully when he is mindful of his true status, and remembers that he bears the person of the *universitas* of those subject to him; and when he is fully conscious that he owes his life not to himself and his own private ends, but to others, and allots it to them accordingly, with duly ordered charity and affection. Therefore he owes the whole of himself to God, most of himself to his country, much to his relatives and friends, very little to foreigners, but still somewhat. He has duties to the very wise and the very foolish, to little children and to the aged. Supervision over these classes of persons is common to all in authority, both those who have care over spiritual things and those who exercise temporal jurisdiction.

JUSTICE AND MERCY

It should hold true of the prince, as it should hold true of all men, that no one should seek his own interest but that of others. Yet the measure of the affection with which he should embrace his subjects like brethren in the arms of charity must be kept within the bounds of moderation. For his love of his brethren should not prevent him from correcting their errors with proper medicine; he acknowledges the ties of flesh and blood to the end that he may subdue these to the rule of the spirit. It is the practice of

physicians when they cannot heal a disease with poultices and mild medicines to apply stronger remedies such as fire or steel. But they never employ these unless they despair of restoring health by milder means, and so the ruling power when it cannot avail by mild measures to heal the vices of its subjects, rightly resorts, though with grief, to the infliction of sharp punishments, and with pious cruelty vents its rage against wrong-doers to the end that good men may be preserved uninjured. But who was ever strong enough to amputate the members of his own body without grief and pain? Therefore the prince grieves when called upon to inflict the punishment which guilt demands, and yet administers it with reluctant right hand. For the prince has no left hand, and in subjecting to pain the members of the body of which he is the head, he obeys the law in sadness and with groans. Philip once heard that a certain Phicias, who was a good fighting man, had become alienated from him because in his poverty he found difficulty in supporting his three daughters and yet received no aid from the king. When his friends advised him accordingly to beware of the man, "What," said Philip, "if a part of my body were sick, would I cut it off rather than seek to heal it?" Then he sought out this Phicias privately in a friendly way, and provided him with sufficient money which he accepted for the necessities of his private difficulties. And thereby the king made this man better disposed toward him and more faithful than he had been before he supposed himself offended. Accordingly, as Lucius says: "A prince should have an old man's habit of mind, who follows moderate counsels, and should play the part of a physician, who heals diseases sometimes by reducing the diet of the overfed, and again by increasing that of the under-nourished, who allays pain at times by cautery, and at other times by poultices." In addition, he should be affable of speech, and generous in conferring benefits, and in his manners he should preserve the dignity of his authority unimpaired. A pleasant address and a gracious tongue will win for him the reputation of benignity. Kindness will compel the most faithful and constant love from even the sternest, and will increase and confirm the love which it has produced. And the

---

[6] Heb. vii, 7.

[7] Dig. I. 17, § 3.

[8] I.e., Jesse.

reverence of subjects is the fit reward of dignity of manners.

Excellently did Trajan, the best of the pagan emperors, answer his friends when they reproached him with making himself too common toward all men and more so, they thought, than was becoming for an emperor; for he said that he desired to be toward private citizens such an emperor as he had desired to have over him when he was a private citizen himself. And in accordance with this principle, acting on the report of the younger Pliny who at that time with other judges was designated to persecute the Church, he recalled the sword of persecution from the slaughter of the martyrs and moderated his edict. And perchance he would have dealt more gently still with the faithful, had not the laws and examples of his predecessors, and the advice of men who were considered wise counsellors, and the authority of his judges, all urged him to destroy a sect regarded by public opinion as superstitious, and as enemies of true religion. I do not unreservedly and in all respects commend the judgment of a man who knew not Christ, yet I do extenuate the fault of him who broke loose from the pressure of others and followed the instinct of his own natural piety toward kindness and pity, a man whose nature it was to be merciful toward all, though stern toward the few whom it would be sinful to spare; so that in the course of his whole reign only one of the senators or nobles of the city was condemned, although a great number could have been found who had offended grievously against him. And this man was condemned by the Senate without the knowledge of Trajan himself. For it was his habit to say that a man is insane who, having inflamed eyes, prefers to dig them out rather than to cure them. So again he said that the nails, if they are too sharp, should be trimmed and not plucked out. For if a cithern player and other performers on stringed instruments can by diligence find a way to correct the fault of a string which is out of tune and bring it again into accord with the other strings, and so out of discord make the sweetest harmony, not by breaking the strings but by making them tense or slack in due proportions; with how much care should the prince moderate his acts, now with the strictness of justice, and now with the leniency of mercy, to the end that he may make his subjects all be of one mind in one house, and thus as it were out of discordant dispositions bring to pass one great perfect harmony in the service of peace and in the works of charity? This, however, is certain, that it is safer for the cords to be relaxed than to be stretched too tautly. For the tension of slack cords can be corrected by the skill of the artificer so that they will again give forth the proper sweetness of tone; but a string that has once been broken, no artificer can repair.

THE STATE AS AN ORGANISM

A commonwealth, according to Plutarch, is a certain body which is endowed with life by the benefit of divine favor, which acts at the prompting of the highest equity, and is ruled by what may be called the moderating power of reason. Those things which establish and implant in us the practice of religion, and transmit to us the worship of God (here I do not follow Plutarch, who says "of the Gods") fill the place of the soul in the body of the commonwealth. And therefore those who preside over the practice of religion should be looked up to and venerated as the soul of the body. For who doubts that the ministers of God's holiness are His representatives? Furthermore, since the soul is, as it were, the prince of the body, and has rulership over the whole thereof, so those whom our author calls the prefects of religion preside over the entire body. Augustus Cæsar was to such a degree subject to the priestly power of the pontiffs that in order to set himself free from this subjection and have no one at all over him, he caused himself to be created a pontiff of Vesta, and thereafter had himself promoted to be one of the gods during his own life-time. The place of the head in the body of the commonwealth is filled by the prince, who is subject only to God and to those who exercise His office and represent Him on earth, even as in the human body the head is quickened and governed by the soul. The place of the heart is filled by the Senate, from which proceeds the initiation of good works and ill. The duties of eyes, ears, and tongue are claimed by the judges and the governors of provinces. Officials and soldiers correspond to the bands. Those who always attend upon the prince are likened to the sides. Financial officers and keepers (I speak now not of those who are in charge of the prisons, but of those who are keepers of the privy chest) may be compared with the stomach and intestines, which, if they become congested through excessive avidity, and retain too tenaciously their accumulations, generate innumerable and incurable diseases, so that through their ailment the whole body is threatened with destruction. The husbandmen correspond to the feet, which always cleave to the soil, and need the more especially the care and foresight of the head, since while they walk upon the earth doing service with their bodies, they meet the more often with stones of stumbling, and therefore deserve aid and protection all the more justly since it is they who raise, sustain, and move forward the weight of the entire body. Take away the support of the feet from the strongest body, and it cannot move forward by it own power, but must creep painfully and shamefully on its hands, or else be moved by means of brute animals.

THE "FEET" OF THE COMMONWEALTH

Those are called the feet who discharge the humbler offices, and by whose services the members of the whole commonwealth walk upon solid earth. Among these are to be counted the husbandmen, who always cleave to the soil, busied about their ploughlands or vineyards or pastures or flower-gardens. To these must be added the many species of cloth-making, and the mechanic arts, which work in wood, iron, bronze and the different metals; also the menial occupations, and the manifold forms of getting a livelihood and sustaining life, or increasing household property, all of which, while they do not pertain to the authority of the governing power, are yet in the highest degree useful and profitable to the corporate whole of the commonwealth. All these different occupations are so numerous that the commonwealth in the number of its feet exceeds not only the eight-footed crab but even the centipede, and because of their very multitude they cannot be enumerated; for while they are not infinite by nature, they are yet of so many different varieties that no writer on the subject of offices or duties has ever laid down particular precepts for each special

variety. But it applies generally to each and all of them that in their exercise they should not transgress the limits of the law, and should in all things observe constant reference to the public utility. For inferiors owe it to their superiors to provide them with service, just as the superiors in their turn owe it to their inferiors to provide them with all things needful for their protection and succor. Therefore Plutarch says that that course is to be pursued in all things which is of advantage to the humbler classes, that is to say to the multitude; for small numbers always yield to great. Indeed the reason for the institution of magistrates was to the end that subjects might be protected from wrongs, and that the commonwealth itself might be "shod," so to speak, by means of their services. For it is as it were "unshod" when it is exposed to wrongs,—than which there can be no more disgraceful pass of affairs to those who fill the magistracies. For an afflicted people is a sign and proof of the goutiness, so to speak, of the prince. Then and then only will the health of the commonwealth be sound and flourishing when the higher members shield the lower, and the lower respond faithfully and fully in like measure to the just demands of their superiors, so that each and all are as it were members one of another by a sort of reciprocity, and each regards his own interest as best served by that which he knows to be most advantageous for the others.

THE LOVE OF LIBERTY AND FREE SPEECH

Liberty means judging everything freely in accordance with one's individual judgment, and does not hesitate to reprove what it sees opposed to good morals. Nothing but virtue is more splendid than liberty, if indeed liberty can ever properly be severed from virtue. For to all right-thinking men it is clear that true liberty issues from no other source. Wherefore, since all agree that virtue is the highest good in life, and that it alone can strike off the heavy and hateful yoke of slavery, it has been the opinion of philosophers that men should die, if need arose, for the sake of virtue, which is the only reason for living. But virtue can never be fully attained without liberty, and the absence of liberty proves that virtue in its full perfection is wanting. Therefore a man is free in proportion to the measure of his virtues, and the extent to which he is free determines what his virtues can accomplish; while, on the other hand, it is the vices alone which bring about slavery, and subject a man to persons and things in unmeet obedience; and though slavery of the person may seem at times the more to be pitied, in reality slavery to the vices is ever far the more wretched. And so what is more lovely than liberty? And what more agreeable to a man who has any reverence for virtue? We read that it has been the impelling motive of all good princes; and that none ever trod liberty underfoot save the open foes of virtue. The jurists know what good laws were introduced for the sake of liberty, and the testimony of historians has made famous the great deeds done for love of it. Cato drank poison, pierced himself with his sword, and that no delay might prolong life on terms which he deemed ignoble, he thrust in his hand to widen the wound, and poured out his noble blood, that he might not see Cæsar reigning. Brutus set on foot civil wars to save the city from slavery; and that seat of empire preferred rather to bear the wretched afflictions of perpetual war than to endure a lord, though of the mildest character. I pass on to the weaker sex. The wives of the Teutons, because of the value they set upon their chastity, besought Marius after his victory that they might be presented as a gift to the Vestal Virgins, promising that they would abstain from all unchastity; and when their prayers were not heeded, on the following night they ended their lives by strangling themselves in order not to become slaves or suffer loss of their chastity. If I wished to recall individual instances of this kind, time would run out before the examples were exhausted. The practice of liberty is a notable thing and displeasing only to those who have the character of slaves.

Things which are done or spoken freely avoid the fault of timidity on the one hand and of rashness on the other, and so long as the straight and narrow path is followed, merit praise and win affection. But when under the pretext of liberty rashness unleashes the violence of its spirit, it properly incurs reproach, although, as a thing more pleasing in the ears of the vulgar than

convincing to the mind of the wise man, it often finds in the indulgence of others the safety which it does not owe to its own prudence. Nevertheless, it is the part of a good and wise man to give a free rein to the liberty of others and to accept with patience the words of free speaking, whatever they may be. Nor does he oppose himself to its works so long as these do not involve the casting away of virtue. For since each virtue shines by its own proper light, the merit of tolerance is resplendent with a very special glory.

Once a certain man of Privernum, when asked how the captives from his city would keep the peace if they were granted amnesty, replied to the Roman consul: "If you grant them an advantageous peace, they will keep it forever; if a disadvantageous one, they will not keep it long." By these bold words, freely spoken, it came to pass that the citizens of Privernurn obtained not only pardon for their rebellion, but the benefits of Roman citizenship besides, because one man of them had dared to speak out thus boldly in the Senate.

THE DIFFERENCE BETWEEN A TYRANT AND A TRUE PRINCE

Wherein the prince differs from the tyrant has already been set forth above when we were reviewing Plutarch's "Instruction of Trajan"; and the duties of the prince and of the different members of the commonwealth were also carefully explained at that point. Wherefore it will be easier to make known here, and in fewer words, the opposite characteristics of the tyrant. A tyrant, then, as the philosophers have described him, is one who oppresses the people by rulership based upon force, while he who rules in accordance with the laws is a prince. Law is the gift of God, the model of equity, a standard of justice, a likeness of the divine will, the guardian of well-being, a bond of union and solidarity between peoples, a rule defining duties, a barrier against the vices and the destroyer thereof, a punishment of violence and all wrong-doing. The law is assailed by force or by fraud, and, as it were, either wrecked by the fury of the lion or undermined by the wiles of the serpent. In whatever way this comes to pass, it is plain that it is the grace of God which is being assailed, and that it is God himself who in a sense is challenged to battle. The prince fights for the laws and the liberty of the people; the tyrant thinks nothing done unless be brings the laws to nought and reduces the people to slavery. Hence the prince is a kind of likeness of divinity; and the tyrant, on the contrary, a likeness of the boldness of the Adversary, even of the wickedness of Lucifer, imitating him that sought to build his throne to the north and make himself like unto the Most High,[9] with the exception of His goodness. For had he desired to be like unto Him in goodness, he would never have striven to tear from Him the glory of His power and wisdom. What he more likely did aspire to was to be equal with Him in authority to dispense rewards. The prince, as the likeness of the Deity, is to be loved, worshipped and cherished; the tyrant, the likeness of wickedness, is generally to be even killed. The origin of tyranny is iniquity, and springing from a poisonous root, it is a tree which grows and sprouts into a baleful pestilent growth, and to which the axe must by all means be laid.

TYRANNICIDE

It would be a long and tedious task if I wished to bring down to our own times the series of gentile tyrants; a man with only one life will hardly be able to recall the list, for it eludes the mind and overpowers the tongue. My opinions on the subject of tyrants are, however, set forth more fully in my little work entitled "Of the Ends of Tyrants,"[10] a brief manual wherein I have carefully sought to avoid the tedium of prolixity and the obscurity of too great compression. But lest the authority of Roman history be held in small account because it has for the most part been written by infidels concerning infidels, let its lesson be confirmed by examples drawn from sacred and Christian history. For it is everywhere obvious that, in the words of Valerius, only that power is secure in the long run which places bounds to its own exercise. And surely nought is so splendid or so magnificent that it does not need to be tempered by

moderation. The earliest tyrant whom the divine page brings before us is Nembroth, the mighty hunter before the Lord (who is also called Ninus in some histories, although this does not agree with the proper reckoning of dates); and I have already said above that he was a reprobate. For verily he desired to be lord in his own right and not under God, and it was in his time that the attempt to raise a tower to Heaven was made by frail mortality, destined in their blindness to be overthrown and scattered in confusion. Let us, therefore, advance to him who was set over the people by the divine choice, which deserted him when he gave himself up to a wicked desire of ruling rather than of reigning, and in the end he was so utterly overthrown that in the anguish of his suffering he was compelled to put an end to himself. For a right and wholesome assumption of the royal office is of no avail, or only of very little, if the later life of the ruler is at variance therewith, nor does a judge look wholly to the origin of things, but makes his judgment to depend upon their outcome and ending.

The histories teach, however, that none should undertake the death of a tyrant who is bound to him by an oath or by the obligation of fealty. For we read that Sedechias, because be disregarded the sacred obligation of fealty, was led into captivity; and that in the case of another of the kings of Juda whose name escapes my memory, his eyes were plucked out because, falling into faithlessness, he did not keep before his sight God, to whom the oath is taken; since sureties for good behavior are justly given even to a tyrant.

But as for the use of poison, although I see it sometimes wrongfully adopted by infidels, I do not read that it is ever permitted by any law. Not that I do not believe that tyrants ought to be removed from our midst, but it should be done without loss of religion and honor. For David, the best of all kings that I have read of, and who, save in the incident of Urias Etheus, walked blamelessly in all things, although he had to endure the most grievous tyrant, and although he often had an opportunity of destroying him, yet preferred to spare him, trusting in the mercy of God, within whose power it was to set him free without sin. He

---

[9] Isa. xiv, 12–14.

[10] This work of John of Salisbury is not known to be extant.

therefore determined to abide in patience until the tyrant should either suffer a change of heart and be visited by God with return of charity, or else should fall in battle, or otherwise meet his end by the just judgment of God. How great was his patience can be discerned from the fact that when he had cut off the edge of Saul's robe in the cave, and again when, having entered the camp by night, he rebuked the negligence of the sentinels, in both cases he compelled the king to confess that David was acting the juster part. And surely the method of destroying tyrants which is the most useful and the safest, is for those who are oppressed to take refuge humbly in the protection of God's mercy, and lifting up undefiled hands to the Lord, to pray devoutly that the scourge wherewith they are afflicted may be turned aside from them. For the sins of transgressors are the strength of tyrants.

Thus the end of tyrants is confusion, leading to destruction if they persist in malice, to pardon if they return into the way of righteousness. For there is prepared a great fire wherewith to consume the scourge after the Father has employed it for the correction of His children. And it is written, "Acab has humbled himself before my face; therefore will I not bring evil in his days."[11] But Jezebel, who persisted in cruelty, paid the penalty therefore in the merited cruelty of her end, giving her blood to be lapped up by dogs in the place where dogs had lapped up the blood of innocent Naboth. But if the blood of innocent Naboth was thus required at her hands, will not the blood of so many other innocent victims also be required? Her unrighteousness coveted the vineyard of a just man, and as the price thereof she lost her rights to a whole kingdom. Thus wickedness is always punished by the Lord; but sometimes it is His own, and at others it is a human hand, which He employs as a weapon wherewith to administer punishment to the unrighteous.

The emperor Julian, the vile and filthy apostate, persecuted the Christians rather by guile than by the open use of force, yet he did not refrain from force. For under him

arose the most grievous persecution of the Christians, and he sought by his impious attempt to blot out the very name of the Galilean, as he called Him. But while he was leading an ill-fated expedition against the Parthians, and on his return was offering up the slaughter of the Christians as a sacrifice to idols, God took pity upon the prayers of the great Basil and others of the saints, and appointed as his instrument the martyr Mercurius, who, at the command of the Blessed Virgin, pierced the tyrant in his camp with a lance, and compelled the impious wretch as he was dying to confess that the Galilean, namely Christ, whom he persecuted, was victor and had triumphed over him. For when the aforesaid bishop had gathered together the faithful of Cæsarea in the church of the ever Virgin, the Mother of God, to watch out the night in prayer, on that same night the saint recognized the Blessed Virgin herself in a vision and received consolation in this wise: "Call to me," said she, "Mercurius, and he shall depart to slay Julian, who proudly blasphemes against my Son and God."

ECCLESIASTICAL TYRANTS

But grant that it is permissible for men of the flesh to contend for the primacy, still I think that on no account is this ever permissible for churchmen. Yet from the example of men of the flesh, impiety creeps forward under the guise of religion, and priestly power is now not merely contended for, but actually fought for. Of old time men were dragged unwillingly to the seats of honor in the Church although they were eager for martyrdom; but they fled from the chief seats more earnestly than from the prison and the cross. Today priests speak openly to the opposite effect and say that the proverb is a thing of nought. "We do not wish to be martyrs," they say, "but we will not give to another the glory of our thrones." Verily a poor and miserable speech in the mouth of a priest who thus confesses Christ in such wise that he openly admits his unwillingness to follow Him. Can it be doubted whether one dies a true confessor who is not at all times ready to bow his neck to the persecutor should need arise? For Ciprian says, "If a bishop be afraid, all hope for him is gone." But grant him leave to be afraid even;

---

[11] I Kings xxi, 29.

for him not to stand fast in time of need is a thing which is not permissible. A deserter is noxious, infamous.

Yet there is one thing wherein they seem to imitate the steadfastness of martyrs, namely if it becomes needful to fight for their thrones. It is alleged by some, and it is indeed the truth, that the office of Roman pontiff has sometimes, nay rather has often, been contested by ambitious men, and not without the shedding of fraternal blood has the pontiff entered the Holy of Holies. Once more there have been kindled wars more than civil, and priestly conflict has excused Cæsar and Pompey and all the presumption and impious work at Philippi, Leucas, Mutina, or in Egypt or Spain. Are men Christians who thus procure the shedding of blood to the end that they rather than others may be advanced to the office of laying down their lives for their flock, which is the duty of a shepherd? Do they rend the Church asunder and profane the sanctuary, to the end that there may be somewhat to build again and sanctify? Perhaps they wrack the nations with extortion, harry kingdoms, plunder the resources of churches, only to the end that they may create for themselves the opportunity and means of deserving well, only to the end that they may set all things in order and that they may snatch from their competitors the necessity of ministering to and providing for the poor. But if, on the contrary, their object is to procure but a wider license and larger impunity for themselves, to heap up money, to favor, aggrandize and corrupt their flesh and blood, to ennoble their family, if in short they seek their own glory in the Church, lording it haughtily over their flocks rather than being an example unto them, then although with their lips they pretend to assume the pastoral office, they are more rightly to be numbered among tyrants than among princes. The philosophers say, and I think truly, that there is nothing in human affairs better nor more useful than man, and among men themselves nothing better nor more useful than a prince, whether ecclesiastical or temporal; on the contrary there is nothing more hurtful to man than man, and among them the temporal or ecclesiastical tyrant is more hurtful than any other. But certainly of the two kinds, the ecclesiastical is worse that the temporal.

I remember that I once journeyed to Apulia to visit the pontiff, Lord Adrian the Fourth, who had admitted me to his closest friendship, and I sojourned with him at Beneventum for almost three months. We often conversed in the way of friends concerning many things, and he asked me confidentially and earnestly how men felt concerning himself and the Roman Church. I was entirely frank with him, and explained without reserve the abuses which I had heard of in the different provinces. For it was said by many that the Roman Church, which is the mother of all the churches, shows herself to be not so much a mother to the rest as a very stepmother. Scribes and Pharisees sit in her seats, and place on the shoulders of men unbearable burdens which they themselves do not deign to touch with even the tip of their finger. They lord it over the clergy instead of making their own lives an example to lead the flock to life by the straight and narrow path; they pile up costly furniture, they load their tables with gold and silver, sparing themselves overmuch even out of their own avarice. A poor man is seldom or never admitted to their number, and then rather as a result of his own vainglorious ambition than for the love of Christ. They oppress the churches with extortion, stir up strife, bring the clergy and people into conflict, never take compassion on the sufferings and misery of the afflicted, rejoice in the spoils of churches, and count all gain as godliness. They give judgment not for the truth but for money. For money you can get anything done today, and without waiting; but you will not get it done even tomorrow if you do not pay a price. Too often they commit injury, and imitate the demons in thinking that they are doing good when they merely refrain from doing evil; except a few of them who fulfill the name and duties of a shepherd. Even the Roman pontiff himself is a grievous and almost intolerable burden to all; the complaint is everywhere made that while the churches which were built by the devotion of the fathers are failing into ruin and collapsing, he has built for himself palaces, and walks abroad not merely in purple but in gold. The palaces of priests dazzle the eye, and meanwhile in their hands the Church of Christ is defiled. They rend apart the spoils of the provinces as if they strove to refill the treasuries of Cresus. But the

Most High deals justly with them, for they are delivered into the hands of others, and often the vilest of men, to be plundered in their own turn. And while they thus wander in the wilderness, the scourge of God will, I think, never fail to scourge them. Truly the mouth of God has promised that by what judgment they have judged, they shall themselves be judged, and that with their own good measure it shall be meted out to them again. The Ancient of Days cannot lie.

"These are the things, father, which the people are saying," I told him, "since you wish me to bring their opinions to your knowledge." "And you, yourself," he asked, "what do you think?" "There are difficulties," I answered, "about anything that I might say. I fear that I shall be branded with the reproach of falsehood or flattery if I venture by myself alone to contradict the people; but on the other hand, if I do not, then I fear that I shall be charged with *lèse majesté,* and, like one who has set his mouth against Heaven, shall seem to deserve a cross. Nevertheless, since Guido Dens, the cardinal presbyter of St. Potentiana, adds his testimony to that of the people, I shall not presume so far as to contradict him. For he asserts that in the Roman Church there inheres a certain root of duplicity and stimulant of avarice which is the source and root of all evils. Nor did he speak this in a corner, but, while all his brethren sat round about and Holy Eugenius was presiding, he made this public charge when at Florence he blazed out gratuitously against my own innocence. But one thing I will boldly affirm with my conscience as my witness, and this is that I have never anywhere seen more honest clerics than in the Roman church, or ones who hold avarice in greater abhorrence. Who can help admiring Bernard of Redon, cardinal deacon of Saints Cosmas and Damian, for his self-restraint and utter scorn of lucre? The man is not born from whom he accepted a gift, but what was offered for a pure and honest reason by the fellowship of his brethren he was sometimes persuaded to accept. Who does not marvel at the bishop of Praeneste, who, fearing the scruple of conscience, abstained even from sharing in the common goods? Of many others so great is the modesty, so great the austerity, that they will be found not inferior to Fabricius, whom they excel in all respects

for the added reason that they know the way of salvation. But since you urge and press and command me, and since it is certain that it is not lawful to lie to the Holy Spirit, I admit that what you enjoin must be done, although not all of you are to be imitated in all your works. For whoever dissents from the teaching of you of the Roman Church is either a heretic or schismatic. But, thanks to the favor of God, there are some who do not imitate the works of all of you. For the contamination of a few sullies the pure with a stain, and brings infamy upon the Church Universal; and in my opinion the reason why they die so fast is to prevent their corrupting the entire Church. But sometimes the good are likewise snatched away, to the end that they may not be infected with wickedness and turned to evil, and because corrupt Rome is found unworthy of them in the sight of God. Do you, therefore, since it is a part of the duty of your office, seek out and bring in to you men who are humble and despisers of vainglory and money. But I fear lest if you go on asking what you wish, you will hear from an imprudent friend things which you do not wish. What is it, father, to criticize the life of others and not probe searchingly into your own? All men applaud you, you are called father and lord of all, and upon your head is poured all the oil of the sinner.[12] If, therefore, you are father, why do you extort gifts and payments from your children? If you are lord why do you not strike terror into your Romans, and repressing their insolence, call them back to the way of loyalty? But you may answer that you wish to preserve the city to the Church by means of the gifts which you receive. Did Silvester originally acquire it by means of gifts? Father, you are wandering in the trackless wilderness and have strayed from the true way. It must be preserved by means of the same gifts by which it was acquired. What you received without a price, see that you bestow without a price. Justice is the queen of the virtues and blushes to be bartered for a price. If she is to be gracious, she must be gratuitous. It is vain to seek to prostitute for a price her who cannot be corrupted; for she is pure and ever incorrupt. While you oppress others, you will yourself be even more grievously oppressed."

---

[12] Ps. cxl, 5.

The pontiff laughed and congratulated me upon having spoken with such frankness, enjoining me as often as anything unfavorable concerning him came to my ears, to inform him thereof without delay. And, after urging many things in his favor as well as much against himself by way of reply, he finally put before me an apology after this kind: Once upon a time all the members of the body conspired together against the stomach, as against that which by its greediness devoured utterly the labors of all the rest. The eye is never sated with seeing, the ear with hearing, the hands go on laboring, the feet become callous from walking, and the tongue itself alternates advantageously between speech and silence. In fine, all the members provide watchfully for the common advantage of all; and in the midst of such care and toil on the part of all, only the stomach is idle, yet it alone devours and consumes all the fruits of their manifold labors. What remains to be said? They swore to abstain from work and to starve that idle public enemy. Thus passed one day; that which followed was more irksome. The third was so fatal that almost all commenced to be faint. Then, under the pressure of necessity, the brothers again gathered together to take action concerning their own welfare and the state of the public enemy. When all were present, the eyes were found to be dim, the foot failed to sustain the weight of the body, the arms were numb, and the tongue itself, cleaving to the feeble palate, did not make bold to state the common cause. Accordingly all took refuge in the counsel of the heart and after deliberation there, it became plain that these ills were all due to that which had before been denounced as the public enemy. Because the tribute which they paid it was cut off, like a public rationer it withdrew the sustenance of all. And since no one can perform military service without wages, when the wages are no longer forthcoming the soldier becomes faint and weak. Nor could the blame be cast back upon the rationer, since what he had not received he could not pay out to others. Far more beneficial would it be that he should be supplied with somewhat to distribute than that through his starvation all the other members should go hungry. And so it was done; persuaded by reason, they filled the stomach, the members were revived, and the peace of all was restored. And so the stomach was acquitted, which, although it is voracious and greedy of that which does not belong to it, yet seeks not for itself but for the others, who cannot be nourished if it is empty. "And so it is, brother," he said, "if you will but observe closely, in the body of the commonwealth, wherein, though the magistrates are most grasping, yet they accumulate not so much for themselves as for others. For if they are starved, there is nought to be distributed among the members. For the stomach in the body and the prince in the commonwealth perform the same office, according to the well-known passage of Quintus Serenus:

Those who contend that the stomach is king of
    the whole body,
Seem to have truth and reason with them in
    their claim;
For upon its soundness depends the strength of
    all the members
And, contrariwise, all are enfeebled if it be
    sick;
Nay rather, if care is not taken, it is said to harm
The brain and pervert the senses from their
    soundness.[13]

Do not therefore seek to measure our oppressiveness or that of temporal princes, but attend rather to the common utility of all."

---

[13] Serenus, *Lib. Medecin.* 11. 300–305.

CHAPTER ELEVEN

ST. THOMAS AQUINAS

One of the most paradoxical aspects of medieval life is the contradiction between the extreme pluralism of its institutions and the deep yearning for unity in its religious and philosophical ideas. The typical institute of the Middle Ages, the feudal system, represents the hallmark of diversity and decentralization that the western world has experienced. By contrast, medieval thinking on religious and secular matters took the *principle of unity* for granted: the oneness of God, of divine law and reason, permeated the whole universe, the heavens, nature, and society. Mankind was conceived as one community, subject to one eternal law and government. Diversities and pluralities were held to exist in the world of fact, but their reason for existence was related to a higher Whole possessing a unity to which they were subordinate.

The duality of man's body and soul was reflected in the two orders of the spiritual and mundane powers, church and empire, each claiming, in theory at least, universal jurisdiction. Both the papalist and imperialist parties were reluctant, in typical medieval fashion, to accept the dualism of church and empire as final. They agreed that there had to be a unifying principle within which the diversity of ecclesiastical and secular powers could be harmonized. The disagreement between papalists and imperialists arose over the nature of the unifying principle and the method of incorporating it into the solution of practical issues. Partisans of the church as well as of the empire also agreed on another major premise: that the *monarchical form of government in church and empire* was the necessary result of the unitary principle, which finds its highest embodiment in God's rule of the universe.

In the realm of thought, the medieval mind drew its nourishment and vitality from two sources: the religious inspiration of Christianity and the intellectual heritage of antiquity. The task of reconciling these two sources, Christian faith and pre-Christian philosophy, was relatively easy in the early medieval period: first, the classical heritage of thought was mainly kept alive in isolated islands of learning in churches and monasteries, and the *major ideological conflicts* in the *early Middle Ages* were *between church and heresy,* and not between theology and philosophy. Second, the relative quietude in this earlier period lay in the fact that, of the great classical philosophers, *Plato* was the *dominant influence,* whereas Aristotle, known only by a few writings on logic, played a minor part.

Plato's doctrine of vision as the ultimate form of knowing the Good, his concept of God, his tendency toward mysticism, his contempt of matter and idealization of spirit, his conception of Ideas as the essence of reality, his scheme of an ideal society in which the spiritual element would rule—all these Platonic strands could be easily woven into the texture of early Christian life and thought. As long as Christianity was still primarily faith and revelation, idea rather than institution, a fraternal community of love rather than an hierarchical organization endowed with the sword of law, Plato seemed to fit the mood and temper of Christian speculation. Of the two giants of the Christian tradition, St. Augustine and St. Thomas Aquinas, the first, St. Augustine, was thoroughly imbued with Platonic ideas; he was a Platonist not only on intellectual grounds, but also in personality, character, and style. And that he was clearly aware of his affinity is evidenced in *The City of God,* where he says that Plato was "justly preferred to all the other philosophers" of paganism, and that "it is evident that none come nearer to us than the Platonists."

But as the church became more and more a political organization struggling for world hegemony, possessing the best-trained bureaucracy of the Great Powers and utilizing diplomacy in peace and armies in war, its entire outlook changed. The original Augustinian conception of the Christian community as a community of the Elect and the conception of the direct participation of the Christian individual in divine grace and salvation were relegated to the background. When papal power reached its peak in the thirteenth century, the intellectual need of the institutionalized church was not so much mystic visions of a highly individual and personal kind but systematic and realistic elaboration of all thought in the light of collective traditions and newly emerging forces pointing to the future.

Particularly as humanistic studies spread in the eleventh and twelfth centuries in Bologna, Paris, Chartres, and Oxford, and classical knowledge became more easily accessible, the labors of publicists, philosophers, and theologians were increasingly devoted to the construction of a unified system of thought in which faith and reason, theology and philosophy, Christianity and pagan antiquity would be reconciled in harmony and lasting accord. The rising universities in Italy, France, England, and Germany—perhaps the most important single contribution of the Middle Ages to western civilization—provided an opportunity for general study and analysis. Originally intended for the training of the young in a single craft (medicine, law, theology), and therein resembling the medieval trade guilds, the universities soon followed the example set by the University of Paris, which was the first to include, early in the thirteenth century, the four faculties of theology, arts, law, and medicine. Henceforth the ideal of unity of knowledge remained the driving force of European universities; the application of the ideal changed with the outlook of the times.

Medieval scholasticism was the first great attempt, after the fall of the Roman empire, to unite in one body knowledge and revelation, philosophy and theology. The principle of unity was the *primacy of religion over philosophy,* of revelation over empirical verification, of faith over knowledge, of dogma over science. The scholastic philosophers did not invent the doctrine of the primacy of religion over philosophy but refined it in accordance with the needs of the time.

Tertullian (A.D. 160–220), one of the early church Fathers and like St. Augustine, a North African, had stated an extreme position by declaring that Christianity and philosophy were utterly irreconcilable, that heresies are the result of philosophy, and that there was the danger of a "mottled Christianity" of Platonic, Aristotelian, and Stoic elements. Sensing acutely that attempts to buttress religion by philosophy would eventually lead to the decline of faith, Tertullian sought to return to the primitive

doctrine that religious belief should be based on simplicity of heart and not on subtlety of intellect.

St. Augustine was less extreme than Tertullian; he was not opposed to philosophy as
such. According to St. Augustine, the possibility of reasoning originates in the act of
faith. The road to truth begins with faith and revelation: "Seek not to understand that
you may believe, but believe that you may understand." The Augustinian doctrine is
thus an advance over the earlier church fathers because it is not hostile to understanding, provided that the basis and starting point of understanding are the acceptance of
nonrational premises: faith and dogma. Yet in effect St. Augustine's method resulted in
the enthronement of theology, and both his philosophy and his political thought are essentially theological speculation in content, expression, and symbolism.

From the fifth to the eighth century the main issue confronting western thought was
not the struggle of one school against another but the very survival of traditional values
and ideas in the aftermath of material and spiritual devastation on an unprecedented
scale. Only in monasteries and churches was the connection between the tradition of
civilization and the newly emerging medieval world always continued, and the link may
have appeared at times to be tenuous indeed. But by the ninth century, physical recovery
and consolidation had been attained to a considerable extent, and a more independent
and typically medieval intellectual trend began to emerge: *scholasticism*. It was, in fact,
as typical of the intellectual character of the Middle Ages as was feudalism of their social and economic system. From the ninth to the thirteenth century, scholasticism was
the predominant pattern of thought.

The ecclesiastical domination of scholastic philosophy was assured in more than one
way. Most philosophical writers and teachers were clerics, nurtured on church doctrine
and subject to church discipline, and the one principle underlying their speculations was
that reason should never contradict faith. Thus before the argument starts, the writer
knows the answer. It is to be found in faith and belief, as stated by authoritative ecclesiastical sources.

In this respect, in scholastic philosophy the search for truth loses the dynamic and
evolutionary quality of Greek philosophy, for among the exciting traits of Greek philosophy is that one never knows at the outset where the argument will lead, what the results
of reasoning will be. Less influenced by experimental science than is modern thought,
Greek philosophy, unhampered by ecclesiastical discipline, developed into greatness
because it refused to take anything for granted. Whatever one may think of the conclusions arrived at by the various schools of Greek philosophy, one is always astounded
anew by its exhilarating and bold spirit that challenges everything, that allows no argument to hide behind the protective cloak of authority, whatever its source may be.

The authoritative sources of the scholastic philosophers were the Bible, on which
they relied heavily, the church fathers, and the relatively few known works of Greek
and Roman antiquity. Aristotle, for example, was not adopted by the church until the
thirteenth century; thereafter it became impious to attack him, although he had not
been a Christian, and he was generally referred to as "the philosopher." Writers in ancient times relied far less on authority, and the literary technique of copious references
and quotations in support of one's argument is largely an invention of these scholastic
philosophers of the Middle Ages.

Another link between theology and philosophy in scholasticism was forged in the
choice of issues. For example, the problem of free will was discussed in relation to the
activities of God and the angels, from the spiritual nature of which deductions were
made about analogous human problems. Revealed doctrine was the main source of
chosen topics, and dogma was the method of regulation and control of philosophical

writing. Finally, the influence of the Inquisition was also a limitation of untrammeled research and inquiry; the prospect of being burned alive probably tended to discourage unorthodox thinkers from going too far in the exploration of new ideas.

Scholastic philosophy reached its "golden age" in the thirteenth century, which was also the peak of papal power. The evolution of the church as an institution of universal aspirations demanded a universal, comprehensive, and systematic philosophy. The synthesis of theological doctrine, as elaborated and refined over a thousand years, provided one cornerstone of the new edifice. The rediscovery of Aristotle provided the other.

In the East the tradition of Aristotelian learning had never been abandoned; Constantinople in particular had long been a center of Greek scholarship. From Constantinople Greek studies spread to the Near East and were then carried by Arab and Jewish scholars to Spain. In the West, however, only a few of Aristotle's writings on logic were known before the middle of the twelfth century. From then on, and especially in the thirteenth century, the spread of Aristotelian studies was the outstanding intellectual event of the age. It began in Spain with translations of Arab and Hebrew versions of Aristotle into Latin. Toledo was one of the first centers of the Aristotelian revival, and it spread from there to Paris and Oxford, the two liveliest clearinghouses of new philosophical ideas in the thirteenth century. Gradually most of Aristotle's works were translated directly from Greek into Latin, and his metaphysics, physics, biology, psychology, politics, and ethics, in addition to his writings on logic already known, became the common property of the western world. At first the church was concerned about the spread of the new doctrines and sought to stem the tide of Aristotelianism by prohibition. But gradually the attitude of the church changed, and Aristotle moved from toleration into official acceptance.

The triumph of Aristotle in the thirteenth century was the work of many men, schools, and universities, but above all it was due to the influence of St. Thomas Aquinas (c. 1225–1274). He was born at the family castle at Roccasecca, halfway between Rome and Naples, of a landed family with an old military and political reputation. From an early age he was brought up by the Benedictines at the nearby monastery of Montecassino. At the age of barely eighteen, he joined the mendicant order of the Dominicans, against the vehement opposition of his family. He studied in Naples, Cologne, and Paris; in Paris he became well known, first as an outstanding student, and then as a teacher of theology and philosophy.

Although St. Thomas Aquinas died before he was fifty, his literary output, about seventy works of all kinds and sizes, was truly encyclopedic. It marks the crowning achievement and summation of scholastic philosophy, his lasting accomplishment being the incorporation of Aristotelianism into Christian thought. With St. Augustine, St. Thomas Aquinas is one of the two leaders in the development of church doctrine. *Augustinianism* is the fusion of *Plato* and Christianity. *Thomism* is the synthesis of *Aristotle* and Christianity.

In the first few centuries of its existence, the strong mystical and idealistic tendency in Christianity found philosophical kinship and affinity in Plato; as St. Augustine himself said, Plato came near to Christian knowledge and revelation, and in a sense Christianity was Platonic from the beginning. By the thirteenth century, the nature of the Christian idea and church had changed considerably, and Platonism could no longer serve as the philosophical and metaphysical foundation of an institution in which the accent had changed from individual inspiration and illumination to institutional stability and sobriety. By accepting Thomism over Augustianism as its official doctrinal system, the church signified its preference of Aristotle to Plato. St. Augustine, the North African in whom the fires of faith burned with the intensity of his native sun, sought to reaffirm the spirit of the first Christians, for whom Christianity was faith and love, devoid of philosophy, argument, and law. The victory of Thomism over Augustinianism was the final commitment of the church to the long-term institutional, rational, legal viewpoint.

This victory is remarkable for two reasons. In the first place, it shows that the most decisive issue in the philosophical evolution of the church was in effect a repetition of the dialogue between Plato and Aristotle, adapted to the Christian world and its theology. Until the seventeenth century at least, it seemed that Plato and Aristotle had laid down for all time the two possible basic philosophical systems; with all its hostility to pre-Christian pagan philosophy, medieval scholasticism nevertheless was completely under the spell of Plato and Aristotle.

The second remarkable aspect of the victory of Thomism is the light it throws on the adaptability and high survival capacity of the church. As time went by, particularly from the eleventh century on, it became evident that theology was not enough, and that the challenge of budding humanism and secularism had to be met on its own ground. The adoption of Aristotle by the church, through St. Thomas, indicated its tremendous intellectual vitality and flexibility. In Aristotle the church found a systematic and encyclopedic body of thought, encompassing many disciplines and forming a coherent whole; it was moderate in temper and outlook, adaptable to changing circumstances, full of common sense, and therefore altogether human, supranational, and timeless. Though it lacked the spark and brilliance of Plato's philosophy, it was rich in solidity and endurance, characteristics that are prosaic but that wear well under all conditions. To be born, the church needed Plato. To last, it needed Aristotle.

Aristotle himself, as is true of any great disciple of any great teacher, never ceased to be a Platonist in a profound sense; the victory of Thomism over Augustinianism did not mean the elimination of the latter, or of Platonism, from the intellectual heritage of the church, but the relative stress of the Aristotelian over the Platonic system. Augustinian mysticism and emphasis on faith and individual illumination and grace, when politely relegated to a subordinate position in the official church theology, fled into the developing sects and creeds that sought to revive the original character of Christianity in the late Middle Ages. Their Augustinianism was later championed by the Protestant reformers, who were generally opposed to Thomism, in which they saw too much cold logic and too little personal inspiration. Martin Luther, himself an Augustinian monk, declared that he had not found any book that taught him as much of the meaning of God, Christ, man, and the world as he had learned from the Bible and St. Augustine, and that Aristotle is to theology what darkness is to light: "Only without Aristotle can we become theologians." Protestantism was thus a return to the beginnings of Christianity not only because of its stress on the earlier religious sources over the later, but because of its preference of St. Augustine to St. Thomas Aquinas, of Plato to Aristotle.

St. Thomas Aquinas' approach to the problem of faith and reason denoted as great a concession to rationalism in relation to the Augustinian solution, as the Augustinian solution had been an advance in relation to the antirationalism of Tertullian. St. Thomas conceived of faith and knowledge as divine in origin; therefore conflict between them could never be real, only apparent. He thought that the previous trouble had been due largely to the fact that theologians introduced theological criteria into philosophy, and philosophers attempted to philosophize in theology. However, once it is assumed that knowledge and faith are not opposing but supplementary modes of understanding God and the world, there is no need to reconcile conflict where there is no conflict.

Faith is not contrary to reason but *above reason,* and the results of faith are no less certain than those of reason; they are, in fact, more certain because faith is based on direct revelation of God and therefore closer to the source of all truth than is philosophy, which is based on human insight. If articles of faith could be rationally proved, they would become philosophy, and theology as a separate branch of thought would become unnecessary and disappear: the articles of faith, because of their very nature, however, cannot be intellectually proved; they have to be accepted by an act of *will*. Rational evidence can only support further rational propositions; it can never lead to the foundations of faith, which have to be accepted, not because they correspond to rational evidence, but because they are revealed by God as true. What man can therefore believe, he cannot know, and what he can know, he cannot believe.

If theological truth cannot be proved true by philosophy, neither can it be disproved. Conflict is thus impossible. Where it seems to arise, St. Thomas categorically states that faith is higher than knowledge in the hierarchy of truth, and that something must be wrong with philosophy if it seems to contradict revelation: philosophy is only relatively certain, whereas theology is absolutely certain, inasmuch as it is based on divine authority. St. Thomas thus conceives of faith and knowledge as autonomous in their respective spheres, yet does not separate them in tight compartments. Although faith does not interfere with the ordinary operations of reason, it keeps an overall watch over it, and gives it guidance and purpose.

No one in the history of the church has equaled St. Thomas Aquinas in blending the religious and rational motifs in one vast and rich pattern of thought in which there seems to be room, as in the work of Aristotle, for almost all forms of knowledge and insight. St. Thomas represents the high point of equilibrium that was compatible with the long-term interests of the church, and his position is an enormous concession to rationalism, compared with Tertullian's and St. Augustine's. After St. Thomas, and as early as the fourteenth century, the balance begins to move in the direction of rationalism; the fifteenth century, the cradle of the Renaissance, sees the rebirth of classical humanism, in which knowledge breaks with faith and claims supremacy over it.

The method of argument in St. Thomas' main treatise, the *Summa Theologica,* is characteristic of scholasticism. The entire work (three parts in twenty volumes) is arranged uniformly. Each major subject begins with a question and is subdivided into articles. Each article's heading is again a question, for example, "Whether the Angels Exist in Any Great Number?" The text of the article starts out with a series of "objections" presenting the incorrect doctrinal view (in this particular case, that the number of angels is not great). Immediately following the incorrect arguments presented in the objections, the correct doctrine is given, almost invariably in the form of a direct quotation from an authoritative source. Concerning the problem of the number of angels, St. Thomas quotes (Dan. 7:10): "Thousands of thousands ministered to Him, and ten thousand times a hundred thousand stood before Him." After thus establishing the large number of angels as incontrovertible, St. Thomas then adduces a number of reasons in support of the true doctrine stated in the quotation. Finally he replies specifically to each objection, demolishing them one by one.

A sense of complete certainty pervades the work. There is no slow and groping search toward the discovery of truth, and there are no questions (among the many thousand discussed) that must be kept open for further thought and inquiry. An element of dialectical reasoning in the method gives it its strength: the erroneous views are given a fair and full hearing. However, the end of the dialectical process, the truth, is not derived from the process of reasoning itself but from an authoritative source that reveals the true doctrine. After the true position is made known, reason then finds the supporting arguments. The medieval conception of *philosophy* as the *handmaiden of theology* is thus exemplified in the substance of scholasticism as well as in its method of argument.

St. Thomas Aquinas did not think of himself principally as a philosopher, and much less as a political philosopher, but as a theologian, a "catholic doctor" fervently devoted to Holy Doctrine. His political views may be best culled from two of his works, the short fragment, *On Kingship (De regno),* and *The Sum of Theology (Summa Theologica),* his chief work.

The pre-Thomistic medieval theory of the state, unfamiliar with Aristotle's *Politics* and *Ethics,* viewed the origin of political association, of government, as the result of sin and evil, of the distortion of man's natural and original impulses. St. Augustine had been a typical exponent of this Christian-Stoic conception of the state: God did not intend that man, "His rational creature, who was made in His image, should have dominion over anything but the irrational creation—not man over man, but man over the beasts." St. Thomas meets the Augustinian argument by interpreting the concept of "dominion" in two ways: if dominion refers to slavery, St. Thomas is willing to concede (with the Stoics and Roman lawyers) that there is no slavery in the state of nature. But if dominion refers to the "office of governing and directing free men," it is not incompatible with the state of innocence.

St. Thomas suggests two reasons for the necessity of government even in the state of innocence, before the occurrence of sin and evil: first, "Man is naturally a social being and so in the state of innocence he would have led a social life." Because there must be some organization of social life, government emerges as the specific organ of looking after the common good. Second, if one man surpasses others in knowledge and justice, it would be wrong to disregard such superiority for the benefit of all. St. Thomas thus bases the *need for government* on *man's social nature,* and the *organization of government* on the *superior wisdom and morality of the ruler for the benefit of the ruled.* In both views, his kinship to Aristotle is evident, and it constitutes a sharp break with the typical conceptions of state that had been prevalent until Aristotle's *Politics* became known again in the thirteenth century.

St. Thomas agrees with Aristotle that man's social impulse is the origin of the state, and the good life its purpose. But from here on, St. Thomas, the Christian theologian, goes beyond Aristotle. For the Greek, bound to this world, the good life of the community—though nowhere clearly defined—included practical and spiritual ends that could be attained by joint communal effort *here and now.* St. Thomas cannot be satisfied with the community as the ultimate point of reference and the creative source of spiritual values. His Christian, *other-worldy* concern leads him to the view that the Aristotelian doctrine of the good life is still one step short of the ultimate purpose of existence, because "through virtuous living man is further ordained to a higher end, which consists in the enjoyment of God." Whereas Aristotle, whose philosophy and ethics were humanistic and this-worldly, saw the end of man in values that exist within himself, St. Thomas sees, in addition to such man-centered values, an "extrinsic" good that does not exist in man himself and that is yet the supreme value, namely, "final beatitude which is looked for after death in the enjoyment of God."

Because society has the same end as the individual, the ultimate purpose of social life is not merely virtuous living, "but through virtuous living to attain to the possession of God." If man and society could attain this supreme end by human power, the king (as the supreme representative of human power) could guide them in the right direction. However, St. Thomas argues, the possession of God can be attained only by divine power, and human government is unable to guide men toward this end. The ministry of the kingdom of God is not in the hands of earthly kings, but of priests, and—above all—"the chief priest, the successor of St. Peter, the Vicar of Christ, the Roman Pontiff," to whom all kings are to be subject as to Christ himself.

St. Thomas always looks on the world in hierarchical terms, and his system of values is hierarchical, too. From the viewpoint of human and practical needs, the purposes of secular government are legitimate ends. But those ends are themselves means if viewed in relation to a still higher end, the highest of all: the possession of God. Applying the Aristotelian principle that "the one to whom it pertains to achieve the final end commands those who execute the things that are ordained to that end," St. Thomas arrives at the conclusion that *secular government* is *subject to the church* because the former is concerned with intermediate ends, whereas the latter is concerned with the ultimate end, the salvation of souls.

The question of toleration of heretics illustrates St. Thomas Aquinas' conception of the relation of state and church and also shows how seriously he took his religion. St. Thomas defines heretics as persons who profess the Christian faith "but corrupt its dogmas." The church treats heretics patiently, because it admonishes them twice before it takes drastic action. If the heretic remains stubborn, his crime is graver than other offenses; if forgers of money and other evildoers are put to death, "much more reason is there for heretics, as soon as they are convicted of heresy, to be not only excommunicated but even put to death." Excommunication separates the heretic from the church. In its mercy, the church, because it abhors the shedding of blood by its own organs, "delivers him to the secular tribunal to be exterminated thereby from the world by death." The church thus uses only spiritual weapons, whereas the state, as a temporal power, uses temporal weapons. Yet this separate of ecclesiastical and secular authorities is not final, because church and state cooperate in the highest task of all—the salvation of souls. The church possesses indirect power over secular authorities, employing them for its purposes whenever the defense of the faith so requires.

The death penalty in this world is mild compared with the punishment that awaits the sinner in hell. Of all crimes, the offenses against God are the most serious, and heresy ranks among them. The punishment for such crimes is eternal: first, the souls are punished by the real fire of hell; after the resurrection of the bodies, they, too, are burned in the fire of hell, but miraculously the bodies are never consumed by the fire. The degree of fire depends on the gravity of the sin committed, and heretics will be assigned to the hottest mansions in hell. Another miraculous provision prevents the dulling of the senses or loss of consciousness of the damned who are exposed to eternal hell-fire. The eternity of the penalty ensures that the degree of suffering is constant throughout and that there is no lessening of the pain through habit. The blessed in heaven will watch the sufferings of the damned in hell, in order that "the happiness of the saints may be more delightful to them"; they will rejoice not out of cruelty and hatred, but because they will recognize in these sufferings "the order of divine justice and their own deliverance which will fill them with joy."

St. Thomas was a man of kindness, charity, humility, moderation, and saintliness. His views on heresy, the treatment to be meted out to heretics in this world, and the eternal damnation awaiting them in the hottest chambers of hell are in stark contrast to St. Thomas the man; they reflect the nature of scholasticism at its peak. That dogmatic certainty is likely to lead to persecution of dissenters and eventually to death has been proved time and again in history, regardless of whether the dogmas are religious or political. Scholasticism must have been particularly certain of its premises and conclusions if a saintly and kindly man like St. Thomas Aquinas could hold such extreme views, however inextricably they were bound up with the theological and philosophical system he accepted as valid. Yet he could not go the whole way. He conceded that under certain circumstances heresy be tolerated: when heretics and unbelievers are numerous, the church may tolerate them in order to avoid disturbances of the peace.

As to the nature and form of political authority, St. Thomas Aquinas starts with the premise that government is related to the divine order. Therefore, because the commandments of God include the duty of obedience to superiors, "disobedience to the commands of a superior is a mortal sin." St. Thomas follows Aristotle in classifying the forms of government into good types, in which the interest of the governed is served, and bad types, in which the interest of the ruler or rulers prevails. But, whereas Aristotle, with some hesitation and only under qualified circumstances, preferred monarchy as the best form of government, St. Thomas is much more unequivocal in his choice of *monarchy*.

Aristotle preferred monarchy because he believed that it was not likely that superior moral and intellectual qualities could be found in more than one man; his hesitation in committing himself absolutely can be attributed to his doubt that the right man can be found. St. Thomas, on the other hand, derives his preference for the monarchial form of government from his religious view of the world. He notices that "in the whole universe there is one God, Maker and Ruler of all things." In the multitude of bodily members, the heart rules all the others; among the bees, there is "one king bee," and generally "every natural government is government by one." The governing element represents, in a multiplicity of things, their purpose and guiding principle. In political society, the main practical task and purpose is the unity of peace. St. Thomas identifies unity with peace; he is therefore led to the conclusion that one ruler is most likely to maintain the peace that goes with complete unity, whereas a government made up of several persons might endanger social peace and stability through disagreement.

But St. Thomas seeks to delimit monarchy so that it will not degenerate into tyranny. First, he prefers elective to hereditary kingship: both papacy and empire were ruled by elective heads, as contrasted with the national dynasties in England and France that tended to become hereditary. Second, he suggests that the king's power "be so tempered that he cannot easily fall into tyranny." Without indicating in detail how this tempering is to be accomplished, St. Thomas in one passage stresses the important concept that "all should take some share in the government," and he also views sympathetically the idea of the *mixed constitution* in which monarchy is supplemented by aristocratic and popular elements of participation in government.

St. Thomas is aware that even a limited, or constitutional, monarchy, is no cure-all in itself and that it, too, may degenerate into tyranny. But he distinguishes minor tyranny from excessive tyranny. Regarding the first, he warns that hasty action against the tyrant may unleash unforeseen consequences worse than the evil to be remedied. He also says that *revolutionary resistance to minor tyranny,* if successful, is likely to lead to *even worse tyranny,* because the leader of the victorious revolution, "fearing to suffer from another what he did to his predecessor, oppresses the subjects with an even more grievous slavery." St. Thomas is perhaps the first writer on the problem of revolution who understands its inner dynamic, which cannot be halted at will once it is set in motion. He feared that revolution is nearly always a higher price than the evil it seeks to remedy; Edmund Burke was later to apply this Thomistic doctrine to the analysis and condemnation of the French Revolution.

Regarding *excessive tyranny* that becomes unbearable, St. Thomas does not endorse John of Salisbury's justification of *tyrannicide;* it is not up to private persons to decide that the king is a tyrant and then slay him. Such assumption of authority by subjects would be dangerous to the rulers as well as to the people, particularly because wicked men find the rule of a good king no less burdensome than that of a tyrant. If any action is to be taken against tyrants, it can be done only through public authority. Thus, if the people have the right to elect their king, they may lawfully depose him or restrict his power should he abuse it. But if the prince has been appointed by a higher sovereign, only that sovereign may depose him. In the event there is no human remedy, God alone can bring relief, for "it lies in his power to turn the cruel heart of the tyrant to mild-ness." St. Thomas relates the tyranny of the ruler to the sins of the ruled; tyrants rule by divine permission, as a punishment for the sins of the subjects. If God is to help them against the tyrant, the people must desist from sin.

The part of St. Thomas' political theory that is not primarily Aristotelian is his philosophy of law as developed in the *Summa Theologica*. The great contribution of the Middle Ages to the store of civilization is the conception of the *supremacy of law* based on the *custom of the community*. The origins of this conception are partly to be found in the Jewish-Christian doctrine of a divine law above the human law, and partly in the Stoic-Roman consciousness of the rational ordering of the world and its reflection in human society. The feudal system itself was largely a product of custom, and the relations between feudal lord and vassal were determined by custom, or law based on custom. The concept of sovereignty was not alien to the Middle Ages; but it was a sovereignty of the *law,* whereas in antiquity and in modern times the idea of sovereignty is attached to the *lawgiver*—a monarch or an aristocracy in the nondemocratic form of sovereignty, and the people in the democratic application of sovereignty. The medieval preference of communal custom to deliberate decision as the basis of the law was not mere philosophical predilection but the ideological reflection of a social reality in which status rather than contract was predominant, in which mobility was relatively low, and political authority greatly decentralized.

In his analysis of law, St. Thomas distinguishes four forms: eternal law, natural law, divine law, and human law. *Eternal law* is identical with the divine reason that governs the universe, and St. Thomas calls it eternal, because God's reason, God's rule of the world, "is not subject to time but is eternal."

As to *natural law,* St. Thomas says that all things, irrational animals and rational man, are subject to divine reason, to eternal law. But only man, as a rational creature, participates in divine providence and reason in a special way, for he provides for himself and for others, whereas all other creations of God, irrational animals and inanimate things, reflect divine reason only by receiving from it the inclinations to their proper acts and ends. Natural law is therefore man's active and transpersonal rationality, his "participation of the eternal law."

More specifically, St. Thomas divides natural law into three species: first, there is the good that man pursues in accordance with the nature he has in common with all substances, such as self-preservation. Next, there is the inclination he has toward certain forms of conduct that he shares with animals, such as "sexual intercourse, education of offspring and so forth." Third, there is the inclination in him that is specifically human, such as the desire to know God, live in society, and avoid offending those with whom one lives.

Divine law is related by St. Thomas to the fact that man's reason is neither the sole nor the most reliable guide to his apprehension of truth and justice. Divine law is communicated to man through revelation in the Old and New Testaments, and it is in no way contradictory to natural law apprehended by reason. St. Thomas' general doctrine that "grace does not abolish nature but perfects it" also applies to divine law, which is revealed by God as an act of grace.

The fourth, and lowest, form of law is *human law;* it is defined by St. Thomas as an "ordinance of reason for the common good, made by him who has care of the community, and promulgated." The need for human law arises out of two difficulties: first, the impossibility of perfectly apprehending, through the human mind, the dictates of divine reason; second, the difficulty of properly applying general principles of natural law to specific situations and circumstances.

There is little room for arbitrariness in St. Thomas' conception of human law, because it must meet several critical tests. First, for a command to have the nature of law, "it needs to be in accord with some rule of reason." Imperfect as the connection between a specific rule of law and first principles of reason may be, some link between the two must exist. The second major characteristic of law is, according to St. Thomas, that it be just and in harmony with the common good; otherwise it is "devoid of the nature of law." The third essential characteristic of the law is legitimacy: it must derive either from the people or from someone who has been entrusted by the people with the office of governing them. Though St. Thomas preferred monarchy to other forms of state, he sharply distinguished it from tyranny, which is illegitimate government. Finally, St. Thomas held that law, to be valid, must be duly promulgated. Unlike the precepts of reason and natural law, which can be grasped by logical deduction, human laws are not endowed with unerring finality; they apply to specific circumstances and therefore must be clearly and publicly promulgated. St. Thomas' insistence on publicity in the legal system is an important contribution to a principle that is one of the primary services the law renders to social life: security.

Forty-nine years after his death, St. Thomas Aquinas was canonized. It was officially held by the church that his doctrine could, not have come into existence without a miracle of God, and that his doctrine had done more to illuminate the church then the teachings of all other writers, teachers, and doctors together. From then on, the acceptance of Thomism as the official doctrine of the church has been steady. A large number of popes in the Middle Ages and in the modern period have declared Thomism to be the authoritative guide to doctrine and faith. Leo XIII issued the Encyclical *Aeterni Patris* on August 4, 1879, in which he ordered that the doctrines of St. Thomas, "the preeminent guardian and glory of the Catholic Church," be henceforth taught in its academies and schools. In later official pronouncements, Pope Leo XIII decreed that if other writers and theologians disagree with St. Thomas, the "former must be sacrificed to the latter."

The *Summa Theologica* was prescribed as the text of theology in Catholic universities and academies authorized to grant academic degrees and doctorates in philosophy, and all Catholic universities, colleges, and schools were put under the patronage of St. Thomas Aquinas. Pope Pius X declared in his pronouncement of June 29, 1914, that the "capital theses in the philosophy of St. Thomas are not to be placed in the category of opinions capable of being debated one way or another," and he warned all teachers of philosophy and theology that "if they deviated so much as a step, in metaphysics especially, from Aquinas, they exposed themselves to grave risk." The Code of Canon Law, promulgated on May 27, 1917, ordered teachers in Catholic schools to "deal in every particular with the studies of mental philosophy and theology and the education of pupils in such sciences according to the method, doctrine and principles of the Angelic Doctor and religiously to adhere thereto."

Since that time Thomism has been reaffirmed as the official doctrine of the Roman Catholic Church; in addition to conservative Catholic philosophers who are completely committed to the Thomistic line of thought, outstanding liberal Catholic thinkers like Jacques Maritain have also enthusiastically contributed to the renaissance of Thomism. This fact in itself demonstrates the vitality and flexibility of St. Thomas Aquinas' ideas.

How St. Thomas himself would react to the movement of setting him up as the authoritative source of doctrine is difficult to envision. He lived in a turbulent intellectual age that experimented with new sources and materials, and he refashioned the traditional approaches to basic philosophical problems. A profound believer, he nevertheless did not hesitate to reconstruct belief on new foundations. He might have felt that he was not a "Thomist" but a student and teacher seeking to reconcile faith and reason, and he might have doubted, in his modesty and humility, that his views commanded timeless authority.

ST. THOMAS AQUINAS

On Kingship*

DEFINITION OF KINGSHIP

The first step in our undertaking must be to set forth what is to be understood by the term *king*.

In all things which are ordered towards an end, wherein this or that course may be adopted, some directive principle is needed through which the due end may be reached by the most direct route. A ship, for example, which moves in different directions according to the impulse of the changing winds, would never reach its destination were it not brought to port by the skill of the pilot. Now, man has an end to which his whole life and all his actions are ordered; for man is an intelligent agent, and it is clearly the part of an intelligent agent to act in view of an end. Men also adopt different methods in proceeding towards their proposed end, as the diversity of men's pursuits and actions clearly indicates. Consequently man needs some directive principle to guide him towards his end.

To be sure, the light of reason is placed by nature in every man, to guide him in his acts towards his end. Wherefore, if man were intended to live alone, as many animals do, he would require no other guide to his end. Each man would be a king unto himself, under God, the highest King, inasmuch as he would direct himself in his acts by the light of reason given him from on high. Yet it is natural for man, more than for any other animal, to be a social and political animal, to live in a group.

This is clearly a necessity of man's nature. For all other animals, nature has prepared food, hair as a covering, teeth, horns, claws as means of defence or at least speed in flight, while man alone was made without any natural provisions for these things. Instead of all these, man was endowed with reason, by the use of which he could procure all these things for himself by the work of his hands. Now, one man alone is not able to procure them all for himself, for one man could not sufficiently provide for life, unassisted. It is therefore natural that man should live in the society of many.

Moreover, all other animals are able to discern, by inborn skill, what is useful and what is injurious, even as the sheep naturally regards the wolf as his enemy. Some animals also recognize by natural skill certain medicinal herbs and other things necessary for their life. Man, on the contrary, has a natural knowledge of the things which are essential for his life only in a general fashion, inasmuch as he is able to attain knowledge of the particular things necessary for human life by reasoning from natural principles. But it is not possible for one man to arrive at a knowledge of all these things by his own individual reason. It is therefore necessary for man to live in a multitude so that each one may assist his fellows, and different men may be occupied in seeking, by their reason, to make different discoveries—one, for example, in medicine, one in this and another in that.

This point is further and most plainly evidenced by the fact that the use of speech is a prerogative proper to man. By this means, one man is able fully to express his conceptions to others. Other animals, it is true, express their feelings to one another in a

---

*From St. Thomas Aquinas, *On Kingship* (trans. Gerald B. Phelan, rev., with introduction and notes, by I. T. Eschmann; copyright, 1949, by The Pontifical Institute of Medieval Studies, Toronto). By permission.

general way, as a dog may express anger by barking and other animals give vent to other feelings in various fashions. But man communicates with his kind more completely than any other animal known to be gregarious, such as the crane, the ant or the bee.— With this in mind, Solomon says: "It is better that there be two than one; for they have the advantage of their company."

If, then, it is natural for man to live in the society of many, it is necessary that there exist among men some means by which the group may be governed. For where there are many men together and each one is looking after his own interest, the multitude would be broken up and scattered unless there were also an agency to take care of what appertains to the commonweal. In like manner, the body of a man or any other animal would disintegrate unless there were a general ruling force within the body which watches over the common good of all members.—With this in mind, Solomon says: "Where there is no governor, the people shall fall."

Indeed it is reasonable that this should happen, for what is proper and what is common are not identical. Things differ by what is proper to each: they are united by what they have in common. But diversity of effects is due to diversity of causes. Consequently, there must exist something which impels towards the common good of the many, over and above that which impels towards the particular good of each individual. Wherefore also in all things that are ordained towards one end, one thing is found to rule the rest. Thus in the corporeal universe, by the first body, *i.e.* the celestial body, the other bodies are regulated according to the order of Divine Providence; and all bodies are ruled by a rational creature. So, too, in the individual man, the soul rules the body; and among the parts of the soul, the irascible and the concupiscible parts are ruled by reason. Likewise, among the members of a body, one, such as the heart or the head, is the principal and moves all the others. Therefore in every multitude there must be some governing power.

Now it happens in certain things which are ordained towards an end that one may proceed in a right way and also in a wrong way. So, too, in the government of a multitude there is a distinction between right and wrong. A thing is rightly directed when it is led towards a befitting end; wrongly when it is led towards an unbefitting end. Now the end which befits a multitude of free men is different from that which befits a multitude of slaves, for the free man is one who exists for his own sake, while the slave, as such, exists for the sake of another. If, therefore, a multitude of free men is ordered by the ruler towards the common good of the multitude, that rulership will be right and just, as is suitable to free men. If, on the other hand, a rulership aims, not at the common good of the multitude, but at the private good of the ruler, it will be an unjust and perverted rulership. The Lord, therefore, threatens such rulers, saying by the mouth of Ezechiel: "Woe to the shepherds that feed themselves (seeking, that is, their own interest): should not the flocks be fed by the shepherd?" Shepherds indeed should seek the good of their flocks, and every ruler, the good of the multitude subject to him.

If an unjust government is carried on by one man alone, who seeks his own benefit from his rule and not the good of the multitude subject to him, such a ruler is called a *tyrant*—a word derived from *strength*—because he oppresses by might instead of ruling by justice. Thus among the ancients all powerful men were called tyrants. If an unjust government is carried on, not by one but by several, and if they be few, it is called an *oligarchy,* that is, the rule of a few. This occurs when a few, who differ from the tyrant only by the fact that they are more than one, oppress the people by means of their wealth. If, finally, the bad government is carried on by the multitude, it is called a *democracy,* *i.e.* control by the populace, which comes about when the plebeian people by force of numbers oppress the rich. In this way the whole people will be as one tyrant.

In like manner we must divide just governments. If the government is administered by many, it is given the name common to all forms of government, *viz. polity,* as for instance when a group of warriors exercise dominion over a city or province. If it is administered by a few men of virtue, this kind of government is called an *aristocracy, i.e.* noble governance, or governance by noble men, who for this reason are called the *Optimates.* And if a just government is in the hands of one man alone, he is properly called a *king.* Wherefore the Lord says by the mouth of Ezechiel: "My servant, David, shall be king over them and all of them shall have one shepherd."

From this it is clearly shown that the idea of king implies that he be one man who is chief and that he be a shepherd seeking the common good of the multitude and not his own.

Now since man must live in a group, because he is not sufficient unto himself to procure the necessities of life were he to remain solitary, it follows that a society will be the more perfect the more it is sufficient unto itself to procure the necessities of life. There is, to some extent, sufficiency for life in one *family of one household,* namely, insofar as pertains to the natural acts of nourishment and the begetting of offspring and other things of this kind. Self-sufficiency exists, furthermore, in one *street* with regard to those things which belong to the trade of one guild. In a *city,* which is the perfect community, it exists with regard to all the necessities of life. Still more self-sufficiency is found in a *province* because of the need of fighting together and of mutual help against enemies. Hence the man ruling a perfect community, *i.e.* a city or a province, is antonomastically called *the* king. The ruler of a household is called father, not king, although he bears a certain resemblance to the king, for which reason kings are sometimes called the fathers of their peoples.

It is plain, therefore, from what has been said, that a king is one who rules the people of one city or province, and rules them for the common good. Wherefore Solomon says: "The king ruleth over all the land subject to him."

RULE BY ONE OR BY MANY?

Having set forth these preliminary points we must now inquire what is better for a province or a city: whether to be ruled by one man or by many.

This question may be considered first from the viewpoint of the purpose of government. The aim of any ruler should be directed towards securing the welfare of that which he undertakes to rule. The duty of the pilot, for instance, is to preserve his ship amidst the perils of the sea and to bring it unharmed to the port of safety. Now the welfare and safety of a multitude formed into a society lies in the preservation of its unity, which is called peace. If this is removed, the benefit of social life is lost and, moreover, the multitude in its disagreement becomes a burden to itself. The chief concern of the ruler of a multitude, therefore, is to procure the unity of peace. It is not even legitimate for him to deliberate whether he shall establish peace in the multitude subject to him, just as a physician does not deliberate whether he shall heal the sick man encharged to him, for no one should deliberate about an end which he is obliged to seek, but only about the means to attain that end. Wherefore the Apostle, having commended the unity of the faithful people, says: "Be ye careful to keep the unity of the spirit in the bond of peace." Thus, the more efficacious a government is in keeping the unity of peace, the more useful it will be. For we call that more useful which leads more directly to the end. Now it is manifest that what is itself one can more efficaciously bring about unity than several—just as the most efficacious cause of heat is that which is by its nature hot. Therefore the rule of one man is more useful than the rule of many.

Furthermore, it is evident that several persons could by no means preserve the stability of the community if they totally disagreed. For union is necessary among them if they are to rule at all: several men, for instance, could not pull a ship in one direction unless joined together in some fashion. Now several are said to be united according as they come closer to being one. So one man rules better than several who come near being one.

Again, whatever is in accord with nature is best, for in all things nature does what is best. Now, every natural governance is governance by one. In the multitude of bodily members there is one which is the principal mover, namely, the heart; and among the powers of the soul one power presides as chief, namely, the reason. Among bees there is one king bee and in the whole universe there is One God, Maker and Ruler of all things. And there is a reason for this. Every multitude is derived from unity. Wherefore, if artificial things are an imitation of natural things and a work of art is better according as it attains a closer likeness to what is in nature, it follows that it is best for a human multitude to be ruled by one person.

This is also evident from experience. For provinces or cities which are not ruled by one person are torn with dissensions and tossed about without peace, so that the complaint seems to be fulfilled which the Lord uttered through the Prophet: "Many pastors have destroyed my vineyard." On the other hand, provinces and cities which are ruled under one king enjoy peace, flourish in justice, and delight in prosperity. Hence, the Lord by His prophets promises to His people as a great reward that He will give them one head and that "one Prince will be in the midst of them."

RESISTANCE TO TYRANTS

Therefore, since the rule of one man, which is the best, is to be preferred, and since it may happen that it be changed into a tyranny, which is the worst (all this is clear from what has been said), a scheme should be carefully worked out which would prevent the multitude ruled by a king from falling into the hands of a tyrant.

First, it is necessary that the man who is raised up to be king by those whom it concerns should be of such condition that it is improbable that he should become a tyrant. Wherefore Daniel, commending the providence of God with respect to the institution of the king says: "The Lord hath sought him a man according to his own heart, and the Lord hath appointed him to be prince over his people." Then, once the king is established, the government of the kingdom must be so arranged that opportunity to tyrannize is removed. At the same time his power should be so tempered that he cannot easily fall into tyranny. How these things may be done we must consider in what follows.

Finally, provision must be made for facing the situation should the king stray into tyranny.

Indeed, if there be not an excess of tyranny it is more expedient to tolerate the milder tyranny for a while than, by acting against the tyrant, to become involved in many perils more grievous than the tyranny itself. For it may happen that those who act against the tyrant are unable to prevail and the tyrant then will rage the more. But should one be able to prevail against the tyrant, from this fact itself very grave dissensions among the people frequently ensue: the multitude may be broken up into factions either during their revolt against the tyrant, or in process of the organization of the government, after the tyrant has been overthrown. Moreover, it sometimes happens that while the multitude is driving out the tyrant by the help of some man, the latter, having received the power, thereupon seizes the tyranny. Then, fearing to suffer from another what he did to his predecessor, he oppresses his subjects with an even more grievous slavery. This is wont to happen in tyranny, namely, that the second becomes more grievous than the one preceding, inasmuch as, without abandoning the previous oppressions, he himself thinks up fresh ones from the malice of his heart. Whence in Syracuse, at a time when everyone desired the death of Dionysius, a certain old woman kept constantly praying that he might be unharmed and that he might survive her. When the tyrant learned this he asked why she did it. Then she said: "When I was a girl we had a harsh tyrant and I wished for his death; when he was killed, there succeeded him one who was a little harsher. I was very eager to see the end of his dominion also, and we began to have a third ruler still more harsh—that was you. So if you should be taken away, a worse would succeed in your place."

If the excess of tyranny is unbearable, some have been of the opinion that it would be an act of virtue for strong men to slay the tyrant and to expose themselves to the danger of death in order to set the multitude free. An example of this occurs even in the Old Testament, for a certain Aioth slew Eglon, King of Moab, who was oppressing the people of God under harsh slavery, thrusting a dagger into his thigh; and he was made a judge of the people.

But this opinion is not in accord with apostolic teaching. For Peter admonishes us to be reverently subject to our masters, not only to the good and gentle but also the froward: "For if one who suffers unjustly bear his trouble for conscience's sake, this is grace." Wherefore, when many emperors of the Romans tyrannically persecuted the faith of Christ, a great number both of the nobility and the common people were converted to the faith and were praised for patiently bearing death for Christ. They did not resist although they were armed, and this is plainly manifested in the case of the holy Theban legion. Aioth, then, must be considered rather as having slain a foe than assassinated a ruler, however tyrannical, of the people. Hence in the Old Testament we also read that they who killed Joas, the king of Juda, who had fallen away from the worship of God, were slain and their children spared according to the precept of the law.

Should private persons attempt on their own private presumption to kill the rulers, even though tyrants, this would be dangerous for the multitude as well as for their rulers. This is because the wicked usually expose themselves to dangers of this kind more than the good, for the rule of a king, no less than that of a tyrant, is burdensome to them since, according to the words of Solomon: "A wise king scattereth the wicked." Consequently, by presumption of this kind, danger to the people from the loss of a good king would be more probable than relief through the removal of a tyrant.

Furthermore, it seems that to proceed against the cruelty of tyrants is an action to be undertaken, not through the private presumption of a few, but rather by public authority.

If to provide itself with a king belongs to the right of a given multitude, it is not unjust that the king be deposed or have his power restricted by that same multitude if, becoming a tyrant, he abuses the royal power. It must not be thought that such a multitude is acting unfaithfully in deposing the tyrant, even though it had previously subjected itself to him in perpetuity, because he himself has deserved that the covenant with his subjects should not be kept, since, in ruling the multitude, he did not act faithfully as the office of a king demands. Thus did the Romans, who had accepted Tarquin the Proud as their king, cast him out from the kingship on account of his tyranny and the tyranny of his sons; and they set up in their place a lesser power, namely, the consular power. Similarly Domitian, who had succeeded those most moderate emperors, Vespasian, his father, and Titus, his brother, was slain by the Roman senate when he exercised tyranny, and all his wicked deeds were justly and profitably declared null and void by a decree of the senate. Thus it came about that Blessed

John the Evangelist, the beloved disciple of God, who had been exiled to the island of Patmos by that very Domitian, was sent back to Ephesus by a decree of the senate.

If, on the other hand, it pertains to the right of a higher authority to provide a king for a certain multitude, a remedy against the wickedness of a tyrant is to be looked for from him. Thus when Archelaus, who had already begun to reign in Judaea in the place of Herod his father, was imitating his father's wickedness, a complaint against him having been laid before Caesar Augustus by the Jews, his power was at first diminished by depriving him of his title of king and by dividing one-half of his kingdom between his two brothers. Later, since he was not restrained from tyranny even by this means, Tiberius Caesar sent him into exile to Lugdunum, a city in Gaul.

Should no human aid whatsoever against a tyrant be forthcoming, recourse must be had to God, the King of all, Who is a helper in due time in tribulation. For it lies in His power to turn the cruel heart of the tyrant to mildness. According to Solomon: "The heart of the king is in the hand of the Lord, whithersoever He will He shall turn it." He it was who turned into mildness the cruelty of King Assuerus, who was preparing death for the Jews. He it was who so filled the cruel king Nabuchodonosor with piety that he became a proclaimer of the divine power. "Therefore," he said, "I, Nabuchodonosor do now praise and magnify and glorify the King of Heaven; because all His works are true and His ways judgments, and they that walk in pride He is able to abase." Those tyrants, however, whom he deems unworthy of conversion, he is able to put out of the way or to degrade, according to the words of the Wise Man: "God hath overturned the thrones of proud princes and hath set up the meek in their stead." He it was who, seeing the affliction of his people in Egypt and hearing their cry, hurled Pharaoh, a tyrant over God's people, with all his army into the sea. He it was who not only banished from his kingly throne the above-mentioned Nabuchodonosor because of his former pride, but also cast him from the fellowship of men and changed him into the likeness of a beast. Indeed, his hand is not shortened that He cannot free His people from tyrants. For by Isaias He promised to give his people rest from their labours and lashings and harsh slavery in which they had formerly served; and by Ezechiel He says: "I will deliver my flock from their mouth," *i.e.* from the mouth of shepherds who feed themselves.

But to deserve to secure this benefit from God, the people must desist from sin, for it is by divine permission that wicked men receive power to rule as a punishment for sin, as the Lord says by the Prophet Osee: "I will give thee a king in my wrath" and it is said in *Job* that he "maketh a man that is a hypocrite to reign for the sins of the people." Sin must therefore be done away with in order that the scourge of tyrants may cease.

KINGS ARE SUBJECT TO PRIESTS

Just as the founding of a city or kingdom may suitably be learned from the way in which the world was created, so too the way to govern may be learned from the divine government of the world.

Before going into that, however, we should consider that to govern is to lead the thing governed in a suitable way towards its proper end. Thus a ship is said to be governed when, through the skill of the pilot, it is brought unharmed and by a direct route to harbour. Consequently, if a thing be directed to an end outside itself (as a ship to the harbour), it is the governor's duty, not only to preserve the thing unharmed, but further to guide it towards this end. If, on the contrary, there be a thing whose end is not outside itself, then the governor's endeavours will merely tend to preserve the thing undamaged in its proper perfection.

Nothing of this kind is to be found in reality, except God Himself, Who is the end of all. However, as concerns the thing which is directed to an end outside itself, care is exercised by different providers in different ways. One might have the task of preserving a thing in its being, another of bringing it to a further perfection. Such is clearly the case in the example of the ship; (the first meaning of the word *gubernator* [governor] is *pilot*). It is the carpenter's business to repair anything which might be broken, while the pilot bears the responsibility of bringing the ship to port. It is the same with man. The doctor sees to it that a man's life is pre-

served; the tradesman supplies the necessities of life; the teacher takes care that man may learn the truth; and the tutor sees that he lives according to reason.

Now if man were not ordained to another end outside himself, the above-mentioned cares would be sufficient for him. But as long as man's mortal life endures there is an extrinsic good for him, namely, final beatitude which is looked for after death in the enjoyment of God, for as the Apostle says: "As long as we are in the body we are far from the Lord." Consequently the Christian man, for whom that beatitude has been purchased by the blood of Christ, and who, in order to attain it, has received the earnest of the Holy Ghost, needs another and spiritual care to direct him to the harbour of eternal salvation, and this care is provided for the faithful by the ministers of the church of Christ.

Now the same judgment is to be formed about the end of society as a whole as about the end of one man. If, therefore, the ultimate end of man were some good that existed in himself, then the ultimate end of the multitude to be governed would likewise be for the multitude to acquire such good, and persevere in its possession. If such an ultimate end either of an individual man or a multitude were a corporeal one, namely, life and health of body, to govern would then be a physician's charge. If that ultimate end were an abundance of wealth, then knowledge of economics would have the last word in the community's government. If the good of the knowledge of truth were of such a kind that the multitude might attain to it, the king would have to be a teacher. It is, however, clear that the end of a multitude gathered together is to live virtuously. For men form a group for the purpose of *living well* together, a thing which the individual man living alone could not attain, and *good life* is virtuous life. Therefore, virtuous life is the end for which men gather together. The evidence for this lies in the fact that only those who render mutual assistance to one another in living well form a genuine part of an assembled multitude. If men assembled merely to live, then animals and slaves would form a part of the civil community. Or, if men assembled only to accrue wealth, then all those who traded together would belong to one city. Yet we see that only such are regarded as forming one multitude as are directed by the same laws and the same government to live well.

Yet through virtuous living man is further ordained to a higher end, which consists in the enjoyment of God, as we have said above. Consequently, since society must have the same end as the individual man, it is not the ultimate end of an assembled multitude to live virtuously, but through virtuous living to attain to the possession of God.

If this end could be attained by the power of human nature, then the duty of a king would have to include the direction of men to it. We are supposing, of course, that he is called king to whom the supreme power of governing in human affairs is entrusted. Now the higher the end to which a government is ordained, the loftier that government is. Indeed, we always find that the one to whom it pertains to achieve the final end commands those who execute the things that are ordained to that end. For example, the captain, whose business it is to regulate navigation, tells the shipbuilder what kind of ship he must construct to be suitable for navigation; and the ruler of a city, who makes use of arms, tells the blacksmith what kind of arms to make. But because a man does not attain his end, which is the possession of God, by human power but by divine—according to the words of the Apostle: "By the grace of God life everlasting"—, therefore the task of leading him to that last end does not pertain to human but to divine government.

Consequently, government of this kind pertains to that king who is not only a man, but also God, namely, our Lord Jesus Christ, Who by making men sons of God brought them to the glory of Heaven. This then is the government which has been delivered to Him and which "shall not be destroyed," on account of which He is called, in Holy Writ, not Priest only, but King. As Jeremias says: "The king shall reign and he shall be wise." Hence a royal priesthood is derived from Him, and what is more, all those who believe in Christ, insofar as they are His members, are called kings and priests.

Thus, in order that spiritual things might be distinguished from earthly things, the ministry of this kingdom has been entrusted not to earthly kings but to priests, and most of all to the chief priest, the successor of St. Peter, the Vicar of Christ, the Roman Pontiff. To him all the kings of the Christian People are to be subject as to our Lord Jesus Christ Himself. For those to whom pertains the care of intermediate ends should be subject to him to whom pertains the care of the ultimate end, and be directed by his rule.

Because the priesthood of the gentiles and the whole worship of their gods existed merely for the acquisition of temporal goods (which were all ordained to the common good of the multitude, whose care devolved upon the king), the priests of the gentiles were very properly subject to the kings. Similarly, since in the old law earthly goods were promised to the religious people (not indeed by demons but by the true God), the priests of the old law, we read, were also subject to the kings. But in the new law there is a higher priesthood by which men are guided to heavenly goods. Consequently, in the law of Christ, kings must be subject to priests.

It was therefore also a marvellous disposition of Divine Providence that, in the city of Rome, which God had foreseen would be the principal seat of the Christian priesthood, the custom was gradually established that the rulers of the city should be subject to the priests, for as Valerius Maximus relates: "Our city has always considered that everything should yield precedence to religion, even those things in which it aimed to display the splendour of supreme majesty. We therefore unhesitatingly made the imperial dignity minister to religion, considering that the empire would thus hold control of human affairs if faithfully and constantly it were submissive to the divine power."

And because it was to come to pass that the religion of the Christian priesthood should especially thrive in France, God provided that among the Gauls too their tribal priests, called Druids, should lay down the law of all Gaul, as Julius Caesar relates in the book which he wrote about the Gallic war.

Summa Theologica*

WHETHER LAW IS SOMETHING PERTAINING TO REASON?

Objection 1 It seems that law is not something pertaining to reason. For the Apostle says (Rom, vii. 23): *I see another law in my members,* etc. But nothing pertaining to reason is in the members; since the reason does not make use of a bodily organ. Therefore law is not something pertaining to reason.

Obj. 2 Further, in the reason there is nothing else but power, habit, and act. But law is not the power itself of reason. In like manner, neither is it a habit of reason: because the habits of reason are the intellectual virtues of which we have spoken. Nor again is it an act of reason: because then law would cease, when the act of reason ceases, for instance, while we are asleep. Therefore law is nothing pertaining to reason.

Obj. 3 Further, the law moves those who are subject to it to act aright. But it belongs properly to the will to move to act, as is evident from what has been said. Therefore law pertains, not to the reason, but to the will; according to the words of the Jurist *(Lib. i. ff., De Const. Prin.): Whatsoever pleaseth the sovereign, has force of law.*

On the contrary, it belongs to the law to command and to forbid. But it belongs to reason to command. Therefore law is something pertaining to reason.

I answer that, law is a rule and measure of acts, whereby man is induced to act or is restrained from acting: for *lex* (law) is derived from *ligare* (to bind), because it binds one to act. Now the rule and measure of human acts is the reason, which is the first principle of human acts, as is evident from what has been stated above; since it belongs to the reason to direct to the end, which is the first principle in all matters of action, according to the Philosopher *(Phys. ii.).* Now that which is the principle in any genus, is the rule and measure of that genus: for instance, unity in the genus of numbers, and the first movement in the genus of movements. Consequently it follows that law is something pertaining to reason.

Reply Obj. 1 Since law is a kind of rule and measure, it may be in something in two ways. First, as in that which measures and rules: and since this is proper to reason, it follows that, in this way, law is in the reason alone.—Secondly, as in that which is measured and ruled. In this way, law is in all those things that are inclined to something by reason of some law: so that any inclination arising from a law, may be called a law, not essentially but by participation as it were. And thus the inclination of the members to concupiscence is called *the law of the members.*

Reply Obj. 2 Just as, in external action, we may consider the work and the work done, for instance the work of building and the house built; so in the acts of reason, we may consider the act itself of reason, *i.e.,* to understand and to reason, and something produced by this act. With regard to the speculative reason, this is first of all the definition; secondly, the proposition; thirdly, the syllogism or argument. And since also the practical reason makes use of a syllogism in respect of the work to be done, as stated above and as the Philosopher teaches *(Ethic.* vii.); hence we find in the practical reason something that holds the same position in regard to conclusions. Suchlike universal propositions of the practical intellect

*From St. Thomas Aquinas, *Summa Theologica* (trans. the Fathers of the English Dominican Province. Copyright by Benziger Bros., Inc., New York, 1947). By permission.

that are directed to actions have the nature of law. And these propositions are sometimes under our actual consideration, while sometimes they are retained in the reason by means of a habit.

Reply Obj. 3 Reason has its power of moving from the will: for it is due to the fact that one wills the end, that the reason issues its commands as regards things ordained to the end. But in order that the volition of what is commanded may have the nature of law, it needs to be in accord with some rule of reason. And in this sense is to be understood the saying that the will of the sovereign has the force of law; otherwise the sovereign's will would savour of lawlessness rather than of law.

WHETHER THE LAW IS ALWAYS DIRECTED TO THE COMMON GOOD?

Objection 1 It seems that the law is not always directed to the common good as to its end. For it belongs to law to command and to forbid. But commands are directed to certain individual goods. Therefore the end of the law is not always the common good.

Obj. 2 Further, the law directs man in his actions. But human actions are concerned with particular matters. Therefore the law is directed to some particular good.

Obj. 3 Further, Isidore says (*Etym.* ii.): *If the law is based on reason, whatever is based on reason will be a law.* But reason is the foundation not only of what is ordained to the common good, but also of that which is directed to private good. Therefore the law is not only directed to the good of all, but also to the private good of an individual.

On the contrary, Isidore says (*Etym.* v.) that *laws are enacted for no private profit, but for the common benefit of the citizens.*

I answer that the law belongs to that which is a principle of human acts, because it is their rule and measure. Now as reason is a principle of human acts, so in reason itself there is something which is the principle in respect of all the rest: wherefore to this principle chiefly and mainly law must needs be referred.—Now the first principle in practical matters, which are the object of

the practical reason, is the last end: and the last end of human life is bliss or happiness. Consequently the law must needs regard principally the relationship to happiness. Moreover, since every part is ordained to the whole, as imperfect to perfect; and since one man is a part of the perfect community, the law must needs regard properly the relationship to universal happiness. Wherefore the Philosopher, in the above definition of legal matters mentions both happiness and the body politic: for he says (*Ethic.* v.) that we call those legal matters *just, which are adapted to produce and preserve happiness and its parts for the body politic:* since the state is a perfect community, as he says in *Polit.* i.

Now in every genus, that which belongs to it chiefly is the principle of the others, and the others belong to that genus in subordination to that thing: thus fire, which is chief among hot things, is the cause of heat in mixed bodies, and these are said to be hot in so far as they have a share of fire. Consequently, since the law is chiefly ordained to the common good, any other precept in regard to some individual work, must needs be devoid of the nature of a law, save in so far as it regards the common good. Therefore every law is ordained to the common good.

Reply Obj. 1 A command denotes an application of a law to matters regulated by the law. Now the order to the common good, at which the law aims, is applicable to particular ends. And in this way commands are given even concerning particular matters.

Reply Obj. 2 Actions are indeed concerned with particular matters: but those particular matters are referable to the common good, not as to a common genus or species, but as to a common final cause, according as the common good is said to be the common end.

Reply Obj. 3 Just as nothing stands firm with regard to the speculative reason except that which is traced back to the first indemonstrable principles, so nothing stands firm with regard to the practical reason, unless it be directed to the last end which is the common good: and whatever stands to reason in this sense, has the nature of a law.

WHETHER THE REASON OF ANY MAN IS COMPETENT TO MAKE LAWS?

Objection 1 It seems that the reason of any man is competent to make laws. For the Apostle says: (Rom. ii. 14) that *when the Gentiles, who have not the law, do by nature those things that are of the law, . . . they are a law to themselves.* Now he says this of all in general. Therefore anyone can make a law for himself.

Obj. 2 Further, as the Philosopher says (*Ethic.* ii), *the intention of the lawgiver is to lead men to virtue.* But every man can lead another to virtue. Therefore the reason of any man is competent to make laws.

Obj. 3 Further, just as the sovereign of a state governs the state, so every father of a family governs his household. But the sovereign of a state can make laws for the state. Therefore every father of a family can make laws for his household.

On the contrary, Isidore says (*Etym.* v.; and the passage is quoted in *Decretals, Dist.* ii): *A law is an ordinance of the people, whereby something is sanctioned by the Elders together with the Commonalty.*

I answer that, a law, properly speaking, regards first and foremost the order to the common good. Now to order anything to the common good, belongs either to the whole people, or to someone who is the vice-gerent of the whole people. And therefore the making of a law belongs either to the whole people or to a public personage who has care of the whole people: since in all other matters the directing of anything to the end concerns him to whom the end belongs.

Reply Obj. 1 As stated above, a law is in a person not only as in one that rules, but also by participation as in one that is ruled. In the latter way each one is a law to himself, in so far as he shares the direction that he receives from one who rules him. Hence the same text goes on: *Who show the work of the law written in their hearts.*

Reply Obj. 2 A private person cannot lead another to virtue efficaciously: for he can only advise, and if his advice be not taken, it has no coercive power, such as the law

should have, in order to prove an efficacious inducement to virtue, as the Philosopher says (*Ethic.* x.). But this coercive power is vested in the whole people or in some public personage, to whom it belongs to inflict penalties. Wherefore the framing of laws belongs to him alone.

Reply Obj. 3 As one man is a part of the household, so a household is a part of the state: and the state is a perfect community, according to *Polit.* i. And therefore, as the good of one man is not the last end, but is ordained to the common good, so too the good of one household is ordained to the good of a single state, which is a perfect community. Consequently he that governs a family, can indeed make certain commands or ordinances, but not such as to have properly the force of law.

WHETHER PROMULGATION IS ESSENTIAL TO THE LAW?

Objection 1 It seems that promulgation is not essential to a law. For the natural law above all has the character of law. But the natural law needs no promulgation. Therefore it is not essential to a law that it be promulgated.

Obj. 2 Further, it belongs properly to a law to bind one to do or not to do something. But the obligation of fulfilling a law touches not only those in whose presence it is promulgated, but also others. Therefore promulgation is not essential to a law.

Obj. 3 Further, the binding force of a law extends even to the future, since *laws are binding in matters of the future,* as the jurists say (*Cod.* i., tit. *De lege et constit.*). But promulgation concerns those who are present. Therefore it is not essential to a law.

On the contrary, it is laid down in the *Decretals* (*Append. Grat.*) that *laws are established when they are promulgated.*

I answer that a law is imposed on others by way of a rule and measure. Now a rule or measure is imposed by being applied to those who are to be ruled and measured by it. Wherefore, in order that a law obtain the binding force which is proper to a law, it must needs be applied to the men who have to be ruled by it. Such application is made by its being notified to them by promulgation. Wherefore promulgation is necessary for the law to obtain its force.

Thus from the four preceding articles, the definition of law may be gathered; and it is nothing else than an ordinance of reason for the common good, made by him who has care of the community, and promulgated.

Reply Obj. 1 The natural law is promulgated by the very fact that God instilled it into man's mind so as to be known by him naturally.

Reply Obj. 2 Those who are not present when a law is promulgated, are bound to observe the law, in so far as it is notified or can be notified to them by others, after it has been promulgated.

Reply Obj. 3 The promulgation that takes place now, extends to future time by reason of the durability of written characters, by which means it is continually promulgated. Hence Isidore says (*Etym.* ii) that *lex* (law) *is derived from legere* (to read) *because it is written.*

WHETHER THE NATURAL LAW IS THE SAME IN ALL MEN?

Objection 1 It seems that the natural law is not the same in all. For it is stated in the *Decretals (Dist.* i.) that *the natural law is that which is contained in the Law and the Gospel.* But this is not common to all men; because, as it is written (Rom. x. 16), *all do not obey the Gospel.* Therefore the natural law is not the same in all men.

Obj. 2 Further, *things which are according to the law are said to be just,* as stated in *Ethic.* v. But it is stated in the same book that nothing is so universally just as not to be subject to change in regard to some men. Therefore even the natural law is not the same in all men.

Obj. 3 Further, to the natural law belongs everything to which a man is inclined according to his nature. Now different men are naturally inclined to different things; some to the desire of pleasures, others to the desire of honours, and other men to other

things. Therefore there is not one natural law for all.

On the contrary, Isidore says (*Etym.* v.): *The natural law is common to all nations.*

I answer that to the natural law belong those things to which a man is inclined naturally: and among these it is proper to man to be inclined to act according to reason. Now the process of reason is from the common to the proper, as stated in *Phys.* i. The speculative reason, however, is differently situated in this matter, from the practical reason. For, since the speculative reason is busied chiefly with necessary things, which cannot be otherwise than they are, its proper conclusions, like the universal principles, contain the truth without fail. The practical reason, on the other hand, is busied with contingent matters, about which human actions are concerned: and consequently, although there is necessity in the general principles, the more we descend to matters of detail, the more frequently we encounter defects. Accordingly then in speculative matters truth is the same in all men, both as to principles and as to conclusions: although the truth is not known to all as regards the conclusions, but only as regards the principles which are called common notions. But in matters of action, truth or practical rectitude is not the same for all, as to matters of detail, but only as to the general principles: and where there is the same rectitude in matters of detail, it is not equally known to all.

It is therefore evident that, as regards the general principles whether of speculative or of practical reason, truth or rectitude is the same for all, and is equally known by all. As to the proper conclusions of the speculative reason, the truth is the same for all, but is not equally known to all: thus it is true for all that the three angles of a triangle are together equal to two right angles, although it is not known to all. But as to the proper conclusions of the practical reason, neither is the truth or rectitude the same for all, nor, where it is the same, is it equally known by all. Thus it is right and true for all to act according to reason: and from this principle it follows as a proper conclusion, that goods entrusted to another should be restored to their owner. Now this is true for the majority of cases: but it may happen in a particular case that it would be injurious, and therefore unreasonable, to restore goods held in trust; for instance if they are claimed for the purpose of fighting against one's country. And this principle will be found to fail the more, according as we descend further into detail, *e.g.*, if one were to say that goods held in trust should be restored with such and such a guarantee, or in such and such a way; because the greater the number of conditions added, the greater the number of ways in which the principle may fail, so that it be not right to restore or not to restore.

Consequently we must say that the natural law, as to general principles, is the same for all, both as to rectitude and as to knowledge. But as to certain matters of detail, which are conclusions, as it were, of those general principles, it is the same for all in the majority of cases, both as to rectitude and as to knowledge; and yet in some few cases it may fail, both as to rectitude, by reason of certain obstacles (just as natures subject to generation and corruption fail in some few cases on account of some obstacle), and as to knowledge, since in some the reason is perverted by passion, or evil habit, or an evil disposition of nature; thus formerly, theft, although it is expressly contrary to the natural law, was not considered wrong among the Germans, as Julius Caesar relates (*De Bello Gall,* vi.).

Reply Obj. 1   The meaning of the sentence quoted is not that whatever is contained in the Law and the Gospel belongs to the natural law, since they contain many things that are above nature; but that whatever belongs to the natural law is fully contained in them. Wherefore Gratian, after saying that *the natural law is what is contained in the Law and the Gospel,* adds at once, by way of example, *by which everyone is commanded to do to others as he would be done by.*

Reply Obj. 2   The saying of the Philosopher is to be understood of things that are naturally just, not as general principles, but as conclusions drawn from them, having rectitude in the majority of cases, but failing in a few.

Reply Obj. 3   As, in man, reason rules and commands the other powers, so all the natural inclinations belonging to the other powers must needs be directed according to reason. Wherefore it is universally right for all men, that all their inclinations should be directed according to reason.

WHETHER EVERY HUMAN LAW IS DERIVED FROM THE NATURAL LAW?

Objection 1   It seems that not every human law is derived from the natural law. For the Philosopher says (*Ethic.* v.) that *the legal just is that which originally was a matter of indifference.* But those things which arise from the natural law are not matters of indifference. Therefore the enactments of human laws are not all derived from the natural law.

Obj. 2   Further, positive law is contrasted with natural law, as stated by Isidore (*Etym.* v.) and the Philosopher (*Ethic.* v.). But those things which flow as conclusions from the general principles of the natural law belong to the natural law. Therefore that which is established by human law does not belong to the natural law.

Obj. 3   Further, the law of nature is the same for all; since the Philosopher says (*Ethic.* v.) that *the natural just is that which is equally valid everywhere.* If therefore human laws were derived from the natural law, it would follow that they too are the same for all: which is clearly false.

Obj. 4   Further, it is possible to give a reason for things which are derived from the natural law. But *it is not possible to give the reason for all the legal enactments of the lawgivers* (*Pandect. Justin.* Lib. I, Tit. III, Art. V, *De legibus,* etc.) Therefore not all human laws are derived from the natural law.

On the contrary, Tully says (*Rhetor.* ii.): *Things which emanated from nature and were approved by custom, were sanctioned by fear and reverence for the laws.*

I answer that, as Augustine says (*De Lib. Arb.* i.), *that which is not just seems to be no law at all:* wherefore the force of law depends on the extent of its justice. Now in human affairs a thing is said to be just, from being right, according to the rule of reason. But the first rule of reason is the law of nature, as is clear from what has been stated. Consequently every human law has just so much of the nature of law, as it is derived from the law of nature. But if in any point it deflects from the law of nature, it is no longer a law but a perversion of law.

But it must be noted that something may be derived from the natural law in two ways: first, as a conclusion from premises, secondly, by way of determination of certain generalities. The first way is like to that by which, in sciences, demonstrated conclusions are drawn from the principles: while the second mode is likened to that whereby, in the arts, general forms are particularized as to details: thus the craftsman needs to determine the general form of a house to some particular shape. Some things are therefore derived from the general principles of the natural law, by way of conclusions: *e.g.,* that *one must not kill* may be derived as a conclusion from the principle that *one should do harm to no man:* while some are derived therefrom by way of determination; *e.g.,* the law of nature has it that the evil-doer should be punished: but that he be punished in this or that way, is a determination of the law of nature.

Accordingly both modes of derivation are found in the human law. But those things which are derived in the first way, are contained in human law not as emanating therefrom exclusively, but have some force from the natural law also. But those things which are derived in the second way, have no other force than that of human law.

Reply Obj. 1 The Philosopher is speaking of those enactments which are by way of determination or specification of the precepts of the natural law.

Reply Obj. 2 This argument avails for those things that are derived from the natural law, by way of conclusions.

Reply Obj. 3 The general principles of the natural law cannot be applied to all men in the same way on account of the great variety of human affairs: and hence arises the diversity of positive laws among various people.

Reply Obj. 4 These words of the Jurist are to be understood as referring to decisions of rulers in determining particular points of the natural law: on which determinations the judgment of expert and prudent men is based as on its principles; in so far, to wit, as they see at once what is the best thing to decide.

Hence the Philosopher says (*Ethic.* vi.) that in such matters, *we ought to pay as much attention to the undemonstrated sayings and opinions of persons who surpass us in experience, age and prudence, as to their demonstrations.*

WHETHER HUMAN LAW BINDS A MAN IN CONSCIENCE?

Objection 1 It seems that human law does not bind a man in conscience. For an inferior power has no jurisdiction in a court of higher power. But the power of man, which frames human law, is beneath the Divine power. Therefore human law cannot impose its precept in a Divine court, such as is the court of conscience.

Obj. 2 Further, the judgment of conscience depends chiefly on the commandments of God. But sometimes God's commandments are made void by human laws, according to Matth. xv. 6: *You have made void the commandment of God for your tradition.* Therefore human law does not bind a man in conscience.

Obj. 3 Further, human laws often bring loss of character and injury on man, according to Isa. x. 1 *et seq.: Woe to them that make wicked laws, and when they write, write injustice; to oppress the poor in judgment, and do violence to the cause of the humble of My people.* But it is lawful for anyone to avoid oppression and violence. Therefore human laws do not bind man in conscience.

On the contrary, it is written (I Pet. ii. 19.): *This is thanksworthy, if for conscience . . . a man endure sorrow, suffering wrongfully.*

I answer that, laws framed by man are either just or unjust. If they be just, they have the power of binding in conscience, from the eternal law whence they are derived, according to Prov. viii. 15: *By Me kings reign, and lawgivers decree just things.* Now laws are said to be just, both from the end, when, to wit, they are ordained to the common good,—and from their author, that is to say, when the law that is made does not exceed the power of the law-giver,—and from their form, when, to wit, burdens are laid on the subjects, according to an equality of proportion and with a view to the common good. For, since one man is a part of the community, each man, in all that he is and has, belongs to the community; just as a part, in all that it is, belongs to the whole; wherefore nature inflicts a loss on the part, in order to save the whole: so that on this account, such laws as these, which impose proportionate burdens, are just and binding in conscience, and are legal laws.

On the other hand laws may be unjust in two ways: first, by being contrary to human good, through being opposed to the things mentioned above:—either in respect of the end, as when an authority imposes on his subjects burdensome laws, conducive, not to the common good, but rather to his own cupidity or vainglory;—or in respect of the author, as when a man makes a law that goes beyond the power committed to him;—or in respect of the form, as when burdens are imposed unequally on the community, although with a view to the common good. The like are acts of violence rather than laws; because, as Augustine says (*De Lib. A rb.i.*), *a law that is not just, seems to be no law at all.* Wherefore such laws do not bind in conscience, except perhaps in order to avoid scandal or disturbance, for which cause a man should even yield his right, ccording to Matth. v. 40, 41: *If a man . . . take away thy coat, let go thy cloak also unto him; and whosoever will force thee one mile, go with him two.*

Secondly, laws may be unjust through being opposed to the Divine good: such are the laws of tyrants inducing to idolatry, or to anything else contrary to the Divine law: and laws of this kind must nowise be observed, because, as stated in Acts v. 29, *we ought to obey God rather than men.*

Reply Obj. 1 As the Apostle says (Rom. xiii. 1, 2), all human power is from God . . . *therefore he that resisteth the power,* in matters that are within its scope, *resisteth the ordinance of God:* so that he becomes guilty according to his conscience.

Reply Obj. 2 This argument is true of laws that are contrary to the commandments of God, and which go beyond the scope of (human) power. Wherefore in such matters human law should not be obeyed.

Reply Obj. 3 This argument is true of a law that inflicts unjust hurt on its subjects. The power that man holds from God does not extend to this: wherefore neither in such matters is man bound to obey the law, provided he avoid giving scandal or inflicting a more grievous hurt.

WHETHER HUMAN LAW SHOULD ALWAYS BE CHANGED, WHENEVER SOMETHING BETTER OCCURS?

Objection 1 It seems that human law should be changed, whenever something better occurs. Because human laws are devised by human reason, like other arts. But in the other arts, the tenets of former times give place to others, if something better occurs. Therefore the same should apply to human laws.

Obj. 2 Further, by taking note of the past we can provide for the future. Now unless human laws had been changed when it was found possible to improve them, considerable inconvenience would have ensued; because the laws of old were crude in many points. Therefore it seems that laws should be changed, whenever anything better occurs to be enacted.

Obj. 3 Further, human laws are enacted about single acts of man. But we cannot acquire perfect knowledge in singular matters, except by experience, which *requires time,* as stated in *Ethic.* ii. Therefore it seems that as time goes on it is possible for something better to occur for legislation.

On the contrary, it is stated in the *Decretals* (*Dist.* xii.): *It is absurd, and a detestable shame, that we should suffer those traditions to be changed which we have received from the fathers of old.*

I answer that human law is rightly changed, in so far as such change is conducive to the common weal. But, to a certain extent, the mere change of law is of itself prejudicial to the common good: because custom avails much for the observance of laws, seeing that what is done contrary to general custom, even in slight matters, is looked upon as grave. Consequently, when a law is changed, the binding power of the law is diminished, in so far as custom is abolished. Wherefore human law should never be changed, unless, in some way or other, the common weal be compensated according to the extent of the harm done in this respect. Such compensation may arise either from some very great and very evident benefit conferred by the new enactment; or from the extreme urgency of the case, due to the fact that either the existing law is clearly unjust, or its observance extremely harmful. Wherefore the Jurist says (*Pandect. Justin.* i.) *that in establishing new laws, there should be evidence of the benefit to be derived, before departing from a law which has long been considered just.*

Reply Obj. 1   Rules of art derive their force from reason alone: and therefore whenever something better occurs, the rule followed hitherto should be changed. But *laws derive very great force from custom,* as the Philosopher states (*Polit.* ii.): consequently they should not be quickly changed.

Reply Obj. 2   This argument proves that laws ought to be changed: not in view of any improvement, but for the sake of a great benefit or in a case of great urgency. This answer applies also to the Third Objection.

CHAPTER TWELVE

DANTE

Roman civilization reached its fullest flowering in the great urban centers; in fact, "city" and "civilization" come from the same Latin word, *civis*. The countryside, according to the Romans, was good enough as a source of agricultural supplies and a place of occasional refuge and retreat from the cares of the world, but the amenities of civilized living were to be found only in the cities. Unfortunately, many of these amenities were soon to be denied the Romans, for one of the main effects of the invasions that swept over Europe in the early Middle Ages, first of the Germanic tribes, and then of the Arabs and Magyars, was the progressive relapse of Europe into a primitive agrarian way of life. Cities shrank in physical size and, more important, declined as centers of political, economic, and intellectual activity. The city of Rome, which had about a million inhabitants in the first century A.D., dropped to less than half a million in the fourth century and shrank to a small town of seventeen thousand in the census of 1377.

The appearance of feudalism was the outward expression of the disintegration of urban civilization in western Europe. The complex international economy based on trade and transport was replaced, to a considerable extent, by the self-sufficient estate. Actually, the large estates had existed before the coming of medieval feudalism; what was new in the feudal estate was that it no longer produced for an exchange economy but for its own needs. With the decline of the towns and the virtual disappearance of professional merchants, land increasingly defined, from the highest prince and potentate to the lowest serf and slave, a person's wealth, social status, and political position. In politics, too, feudalism connoted a shrinkage of effective range of operation. The prefeudal concept of state and empire, of administration on a large scale, was replaced (in practice at least, though not in theory) by the conception that authority was in the hands of those who possessed land.

The church had a favored position in the feudal system both economically and culturally. As a large owner of land, in some countries the single largest landlord, it directly benefited from a way of life in which land was the measure of all social power and prestige. Culturally, the destruction of urban civilization in the barbarian invasions gave the churches and monasteries a unique position of influence: for centuries they were the only centers of intellectual activity and continuity, saving for posterity the tradition and heritage of art and philosophy that the martial conquerors little understood. Moreover, the general ignorance and illiteracy of laymen compelled emperors and kings to employ clerics in all levels of government, because literacy—not to speak of more advanced accomplishments—was for several centuries confined to priests and ecclesiastics.

The growth of cities from the eleventh century on produced new centers of economic and intellectual life that the church viewed with anxiety and hostility. As a powerful landowner, the church shared the prejudices and fears of all landowners in the face of a new commercial, capitalist economy whose dynamic vitality and immense productivity threatened to overshadow the static, agrarian economy of feudalism. In addition, the church saw in the rise of towns and cities a serious menace to its intellectual predominance. The restless spirit of the urban populations challenged the existing order in which church and aristocracy divided all power between themselves: the existing order recommended itself to church and aristocracy, they argued, not because they were its main beneficiaries, but because it seemed to be in harmony with religion, morals, and custom.

By contrast, the rising bourgeoisie saw in the existing social system unjustifiable privilege and ecclesiastical domination. The legal status of city inhabitants implied freedom and mobility, whereas those who lived and worked on the manorial estates were in complete or partial serfdom. Immigrants from estates into towns shook off the bonds of servitude by mere residence of a year or so, and the medieval saying, "City air makes free," expressed a fact of revolutionary impact in the growth of cities.

The church soon lost its monopoly of learning and technical knowledge in the arts and crafts, and the newly developing cities increasingly assumed the role of intellectual leadership, first apart from the churches and monasteries, and later in direct opposition to them. The accumulation of wealth permitted the growth of a new class of artists, writers, and teachers who were laymen. In nearly every respect the traditional civilization based on church dogma and landed power was challenged, altered, and replaced by a new way of life that was more productive in economics, more equalitarian in government, and more secular in general outlook.

A new elite was thus added to the existing two ruling groups of the clergy and aristocracy: men of wealth, whose claim to greatness ("magnates") and influence was based on financial power. In the beginning this class was primarily concerned about its own privileges in the struggle against the old landed aristocracy and the church, but as time went on, the shared experiences, sorrows, and joys of all townfolk created a new sense of urban solidarity.

The revival of urban life was particularly vigorous in Italy from the twelfth to the fourteenth centuries, and Italian leadership in this rebirth was followed by pre-eminence in the revival of ancient Greek and Roman thought that culminated in the Renaissance. Among Italian cities, Florence, Genoa, and Venice were the most important centers of international trade and finance, not only in Italy but in all Europe. Italians discovered the methods and techniques of banking and credit on domestic and international lines, and Italian terms in banking and finance service to this day.

The capitalist system did not start with the Industrial Revolution in eighteenth-century England but with these bold commercial and financial enterprises in thirteenth-century Italy; in outlook and impact this early phase of capitalism, which lasted until the middle of the eighteenth century, was perhaps as revolutionary as the later phase of industrial capitalism. The early Italian international traders and financiers clearly exhibited the main impulses and methods of capitalism: pursuit of profit for the sake of accumulating wealth, long-distance operations, and long-term planning. *Contract* and *exchange* became the basic economic patterns in lieu of precapitalist *status* and *servitude,* and competition was condoned as the inevitable result of acquisitiveness. Faith in an all-pervading rationality permeated all activities of life, translated them into market transactions, and infused them with utilitarian standards of business ethics.

The hold of the church was weaker over the towns than over the countryside from the beginning, and the secular, or lay, outlook of the later Middle Ages is the product of the new urban, commercial civilization. The most important antipapalist, imperialist tract of the Middle Ages, *De monarchia* (*On Monarchy,* about 1310), is the work of a Florentine, Dante Alighieri (1265–1321), one of the first learned medieval laymen and the greatest poet of the medieval period. By his use of the vernacular in *The Divine Comedy* and other works he helped to create a national Italian language and at the same time to break the monopoly of Latin as the only means of literary communication. Until very recent years, the Roman Catholic Church did not permit the printing of the Bible, without authorization, in any language except Latin, and the use of the vernacular by Dante was, in more than a literary way, an act of revolt against traditional thought and expression.

As an artist, Dante clearly announces the dawn of the Renaissance; he is "modern"— from the twentieth-century viewpoint, at least. His versatility is also of the classical Renaissance style. As a poet, he belongs to the half-dozen immortals, for he moves away from the stereotypes of feeling and expression of the Middle Ages and discovers the intensely personal and individual qualities of man that transcend nationality, religion, class, and caste. But Dante was also, with varying success, a diplomat, soldier, politician, pamphleteer, philologist, theologian, and philosopher. Although he was forced to spend the last third of his life in exile, forbidden to return to Florence under the threat of being burned alive, he made use of his wanderings to enrich his experience and enlarge his horizon.

As a member of the lower nobility, Dante personally abhorred the new business classes, the *nouveaux riches* and their manner of living, and he felt bitter about what seemed to him the vulgarity and coarseness of the new society. Yet such was the force of his environment that his political philosophy, a curious mixture of backward- and forward-looking ideas, of theological scholasticism and pungent antipapalism, was nevertheless a typical product of his age.

In his chief political work, *De monarchia,* Dante raises three questions. The first is whether a *world government, ruled by a monarch,* is necessary for the welfare of the human race. In actuality, two issues are involved in this question: first, the issue of universal government, and, second, the monarchical form of such a world state. Dante derives the need for world government from a philosophical a priori as well as from his conception of man's nature and goals. Philosophically, Dante relates essence and reality to unity, and holds that true being is expressed in the greatest unity, and "where Unity is greatest, there Good is also greatest; and in proportion as anything is far from Being in its highest form, it is far from Unity, and therefore from the Good." Because the distinguishing quality of man is faculty of reasoning and understanding, he cannot develop what is most specifically human in isolation, particularly if his speculative faculties are to be extended into action. Just as the individual can become perfect in wisdom and prudence only by rest and quiet, so the entire human race develops most freely and applies itself best to its proper work, which is "almost divine," if it can do so in the calm and tranquillity of peace. Of all things designed to secure blessings to man, individually and collectively, "peace is the best."

Dante also stresses an argument in support of world government that has a distinctly practical and modern flavor: the need for *settlement of disputes between states without war:* "Wherever there is controversy, there ought to be judgment," and there can be judgment only if the decision of some authority is recognized as final. In the most recent and contemporary thinking about the possibilities of world order it is generally recognized, as was realized by Dante over six centuries ago, that the first institutional development toward world government is likely to occur in the field of judicial settlement of specific disputes rather than in the legislative enactment and executive enforcement of universal laws. Judicial decisions deal with *individual* issues of the *past,* legislative acts with *general* issues of the *future.* The acceptance of universal arbitration and adjudication on the part of states therefore involves a lesser commitment than the submission to universal legislation.

Concerning the necessity of *monarchical* world government, Dante starts again with a philosophical a priori: that "when a number of things are arranged to attain an end, it behooves one of them to regulate or govern the others, and the others to submit." Within the individual, reason governs all other faculties in pursuing happiness. Within associations—from the household, the village, the city, to the kingdom—one individual must rule if unity and peace are to be preserved for the benefit of all. The end of the human race is the fullest development of its potential capacities: "There must, therefore, be one to guide and govern, and the proper title for this office is Monarch or Emperor. And so it is plain that Monarchy or the Empire is necessary for the welfare of the world."

Dante also refers, in Thomistic fashion, to the example of God as the monarchical ruler of the universe. Mankind is a part of the universe, and all created things should represent God as much as possible. The human race is most like God when it is one and united, and it is most one "when it is united wholly in one body, and it is evident that this cannot be, except when it is subject to one prince."

Dante is far from advocating universal tyranny, however, and he stresses the values of *justice* and freedom. The greatest enemy of justice, he says, is greed and avarice, the inability to be *disinterested* and content. He therefore holds that justice would be strongest in a world government headed by a monarch; there is nothing left for him to desire, "for the passions cannot exist if their objects are destroyed." Even kings are corrupted by the springs of injustice—cupidity and ambition—inasmuch as they seek to enlarge their territory and wealth. Dante stresses the Aristotelian idea that the *rule of law* is to be preferred to the personal judgment of men, because such judgment is likely to be perverted by personal interests, whereas the monarchical head of a world state would be in the best position to dispense justice in accordance with general rules of law, because, having no personal interests at stake, he would care for all men in the world. Lacking avarice and cupidity, the monarch would even go beyond justice and dispense charity, in order to strengthen the bonds of solidarity and peace among men.

Freedom, too, is best realized, according to Dante, in a world monarchy. Dante calls freedom "the greatest gift bestowed by God on mankind," but the attainment of liberty is difficult in perverted forms of government in which the ruled exist for the sake of the rulers, rather than the rulers for the ruled. By contrast, good states "aim at liberty, that in them men may live for themselves." Because the monarch of the world state is "the servant of all," mankind will be freer under such a government than under any regime of local or national monarchies in which the ruler can at best identify himself with only a part of humanity.

With all his enthusiasm for a universal state under a monarchical ruler, Dante does not believe in uniformity for its own sake. He recognizes that although a world state would unify mankind with respect to law and government, many ethnic, cultural, and linguistic groups and nations would continue to exist, each with its own traditions and needs dictated by history and external circumstances, such as climate. Trifling matters would therefore not be brought to the attention of the monarch of the world state but would be regulated by municipal and national laws and authorities. Only *matters that affect all mankind* require a *common rule of law* and a *common authority.* Dante is thus one of the first writers on the problem of world government to separate the issue of *political sovereignty,* which must be vested in the central organ of world government, from the issue of *cultural autonomy,* which the individual nations and nationalities will fully preserve in a political world community, "for nations and kingdoms and states have, each of them, certain peculiarities which must be regulated by different laws."

The second main question Dante proposes to answer in *De monarchia* is whether the *Roman people* acquired *world domination* by right. One of Dante's chief authorities in this argument is Virgil, "our divine poet"; his completely natural and uninhibited acceptance of pagans as highest authorities marks Dante off and draws him closer to the Renaissance. Dante betrays Italian national pride in his belief that the Roman people were the noblest and therefore the most fitting to be preferred by God for the government of the world. He notices that the record of the Roman achievement is full of miracles, and that the Roman empire was helped "to its perfection by miracles; therefore it was willed by God and consequently was and is by right."

Although Dante was orthodox in his religious faith, it is apparent from the above statements that he has none of the hostility toward pagan Rome that was so typical of the earlier Middle Ages, as expressed by St. Augustine. Dante says that in bringing the whole world into subjection the Romans aimed at the universal good, renouncing all selfishness, and "that sacred, pious, and glorious people are seen to have neglected their own private interests that they might follow public objects for the good of all mankind." Dante also bases his case on the record of history: Babylonians, Assyrians, Persians, and Egyptians had unsuccessfully tried to subject the whole world, and Alexander the Great came nearest to the prize of world dominion. Only the Romans succeeded in setting up a world empire, and therefore "it was by the judgment of God that it prevailed." In medieval fashion Dante compares the victory of Rome to victory in a duel: according to medieval legal principles what is acquired by duel is "gained by right." Dante anticipates Hegel's famous dictum that "world history is the world court."

Dante never discusses specifically the problem of who the Roman people in the thirteenth century were, because he takes for granted the continuity of the Roman empire and the Holy Roman empire of the German monarchs. Dante was free from political nationalism in the modern sense, and therefore he did not advocate an Italian kingdom on the French or English models. His conception of world monarchy was entirely medieval, though—as an Italian—he thought of Rome as the natural capital of a world monarchy, and of Italy as the preferred "province," which would include the Italian-speaking communes and regions. In this way he hoped that universal monarchy would also bring peace to an Italy whose city-states were rent by civil and foreign wars. But his political thought was focused on world, not nationality, problems, although he was keenly aware of Italy as a cultural and linguistic nation: "To me the world is my country, as the sea is to the fish."

The third main question of *De monarchia* is whether the *authority of the emperor* derives *directly from God* or from some minister or vicar of God, that is, the pope. Dante conceives man as dual in nature, his two essential parts being his body and soul. Following the Aristotelian idea that "every nature is ordained to gain some final end," Dante deduces from man's dual nature two ends: the first is the blessedness of *earthy life,* and the second is the blessedness of *heavenly paradise.* The two ends of man being different, the means to their attainment must be different, too. The blessings of earthly life can be ascertained, Dante says, through the lessons of *reason and philosophy,* whereas we can arrive at the blessings of heavenly paradise by the spiritual lessons, transcending human reason, of *theology, faith, hope,* and *charity.* The truths of philosophy are made manifest by reason and the writings of philosophers, and the supernatural truths of theology are made known in the revelations of the Scriptures. All these considerations lead Dante to this decisive conclusion: "Therefore man had need of two guides for his life, as he had a twofold end in life; whereof one is the Supreme Pontiff, to lead mankind to eternal life, according to the things revealed to us; and the other is the Emperor, to guide mankind to happiness in this world, in accordance with the teaching of philosophy."

Dante's second main argument in support of his antipapalist position is that the Roman empire possessed power and authority before the church even existed. Therefore, Dante holds, the church cannot possibly be the cause of the power or authority of the empire. The authority of the emperor "comes down, with no intermediate will, from the fountain of universal authority; and this fountain, one in its unity, flows through many channels out of the abundance of the goodness of God."

The medieval man in Dante, however, could not be satisfied with a solution under which both church and empire are supreme in their respective spheres of activity. The yearning for ultimate unity, in which the *coordinate powers of pope and emperor* can be brought together again, finds expression in the thought that above the relative superiorities of pope and emperor there is the one absolute superiority in which all others are united: the *unity and supremacy of God.*

Behind Dante's scholastic method of argument, his strictly orthodox religious belief, his use of characteristically medieval symbols, allegories, and quotations, lies considerable originality of thought. The Christian conception of the state appeared in two versions in the Middle Ages: according to the earlier view of St. Augustine and the church fathers the origin of government lies in human frailty and sinfulness, and the state is set up by divine providence as the penalty and remedy of sin. The later Thomistic view, developed under the influence of Aristotle, holds, by contrast, that the state is the natural expression of man's social impulses. Dante is the first writer in the Middle Ages who ingeniously combines Augustinian and Thomistic elements in a new synthesis that surpasses, and is contradictory to, the political theories of both St. Augustine and St. Thomas Aquinas. In approaching the general problem of political life, Dante follows the Aristotelian-Thomistic tradition that man needs collective associations, governmental institutions, the state, for the full development of his natural capacities and the satisfaction of his physical and intellectual wants. However, the natural forms of political organization—communes, city-states, principalities, kingdoms—are particularistic and inadequate because the sins of greed and avarice pervert their natures and purposes. The remedy for these sins—and here Dante skillfully utilizes Augustinian elements for his own theory—is the institution of *universal government* by divine providence, so that man may partake of the blessings of earthly peace, justice, and freedom, just as he may partake of the universal church that God has provided for the attainment of the blessings in heaven.

St. Augustine himself thought of the *church* as the *only universal community* of mankind; not identical with the City of God, the church nevertheless approximates and "mystically" reflects it on earth. As for the earthly city, St. Augustine says that as a way of life, in which the love of self rather than of God prevails, it is a universal phenomenon, but he speaks nowhere of a symbolical or "mystical" reflection of the earthly city in a universal temporal organization, but only of *states.* Even the Roman empire could hardly appear to St. Augustine as a universal temporal community of mankind, first, because of its predominantly pagan background, and, secondly, because of its ruin and disintegration before his own eyes.

Similarly, St. Thomas Aquinas reserves the concept of a universal community for the church, headed by the *pope,* but speaks of *princes,* and not of the emperor, when discussing the issue of government in its most general aspects. According to its own view, the church was the only universal community, exercising universal spiritual authority directly, and universal temporal authority indirectly through a variety of kings and princes. The church therefore discouraged the concept of "emperor," and encouraged instead the local rulers who defended their independence against the encroachments of the Holy Roman Empire. The latter became in effect a German-Italian empire and lost all claim to universality because of its internal decay and its humiliation by the papacy in the twelfth and thirteenth centuries. The more independent the small states and local kingdoms were, the easier it was for the church to exercise control over them, and St. Thomas therefore expressed the customary views of the canonists and papalist advocates when he juxtaposed to the church, princes, and not an emperor claiming universal jurisdiction. Dante's concept of a universal temporal community, a world government headed by a monarch with world-wide authority, contradicts and transcends both the Augustinian and Thomistic roots of medieval philosophy.

What makes Dante's secularization of the religious idea of universal community even more revolutionary is his claim that the authority of the monarchical ruler of the world derives directly from God, without any intermediary, minister, vicar, or pope. The concept of man's two "beatitudes," the blessings of earthly life and the blessings of heavenly paradise, was taken over by Dante from traditional Christian doctrines. St. Thomas Aquinas represented the orthodox view in stating that the attainment of earthly blessings, such as peace, was no more than a means to the final end, the blessing of enjoying God after death. Dante's revolutionary break with this medieval conception consists in his refusal to assign a subordinate role to political life, and his insistence that it, too, was a final goal, and that of the two universal orders, church and world-state, each was supreme in its own sphere, equal in relation to the other, and neither subordinate to the other.

Instead of the traditional medieval hierarchy, in which earthly ends are subordinated to heavenly ends, and consequently temporal authority to the church, Dante construes two coordinate authorities, church and universal empire, each reflecting and realizing a different goal of man. Instead of the previous hierarchy, there is a double supremacy, in this world at least. The pope has no superior—as pope; the universal monarch has no superior—as monarch. Both have a point of hierarchical reference, but it is not of this world: God. To him both pope and emperor are subordinate and responsible.

By strictly separating church and empire, and setting them up as virtually "closed systems," Dante does much more than diminish the temporal authority of the church. He notes that the different ends of church and universal government imply different means: reason and philosophy guide the temporal ruler in the attainment of earthly happiness for mankind, whereas theology, faith, and revelation are the means by which the church seeks to secure for its members the blessings of heavenly paradise. By severing the temporal authority of government from the ecclesiastical authority of the church, Dante thus declares the *independence of philosophy from theology:* if their masters are independent of each other, so are they, as the means of the masters.

Dante's separation of philosophy from theology is more important, from the long-term viewpoint, than his separation of church and empire. St. Thomas Aquinas marks the culmination of the scholastic doctrine that philosophy was the "handmaiden" *(ancilla)* of theology. Dante affirms the revolutionary tenet of separation of philosophy and theology on a basis of equality and independence. His challenge is the transition to the next revolutionary transformation, the growing subordination of theology to philosophy in Humanism and Renaissance.

The church was fully aware of the dangerous ideas contained in *De monarchia.* It was burned as heretical by order of Pope John XXII in 1329 and put on the *Index of Forbidden Books* in 1554, before it was printed (it was first printed in Basle in 1559). *De monarchia* stayed on the *Index* for about three-hundred fifty years, until it was finally removed as being no longer dangerous.

DANTE

De Monarchia*

THE END OF
POLITICAL ORGANIZATION:
UNIVERSAL PEACE

The proper work of the human race, taken as
a whole, is to set in action the whole capacity of that understanding which is capable of
development: first in the way of speculation,
and then, by its extension, in the way of action. And seeing that what is true of a part is
true also of the whole, and that it is by rest
and quiet that the individual man becomes
perfect in wisdom and prudence; so the
human race, by living in the calm and tranquillity of peace, applies itself most freely
and easily to its proper work; a work which,
according to the saying, "Thou has made
him a little lower than the angels," is almost
divine. Whence it is manifest that of all
things that are ordered to secure blessings to
men, peace is the best. And hence the word
which sounded to the shepherds from above
was not riches, nor pleasure, nor honour, nor
length of life, nor health, nor strength, nor
beauty; but peace. For the heavenly host
said: "Glory to God in the highest, and on
earth, peace to men of good will." Therefore
also, "Peace be with you," was the salutation
of the Saviour of mankind. For it behoved
Him, who was the greatest of saviours, to
utter in His greeting the greatest of saving
blessings. And this custom His disciples too
chose to preserve; and Paul also did the same
in his greetings, as may appear manifest
to all.

Now that we have declared these matters,
it is plain what is the better, nay the best,

---

*From Dante, *De Monarchia* (trans. F. C.
Church, in R. W. Church, *Dante: An Essay,* London, 1878).

way in which mankind may attain to do its
proper work. And consequently we have
seen the readiest means by which to arrive
at the point, for which all our works are ordered, as their ultimate end; namely, the
universal peace, which is to be assumed as
the first principle for our deductions. As we
said, this assumption was necessary, for it is
as a sign-post to us, that into it we may resolve all that has to be proved, as into a most
manifest truth.

WORLD PEACE THROUGH
WORLD EMPIRE

As therefore we have already said, there are
three doubts, and these doubts suggest three
questions, concerning temporal Monarchy,
which in more common speech is called the
Empire; and our purpose is, as we explained, to inquire concerning these questions in their given order, and starting from
the first principle which we have just laid
down. The first question, then, is whether
temporal Monarchy is necessary for the
welfare of the world; and that it is necessary can, I think, be shown by the
strongest and most manifest arguments;
for nothing, either of reason or of authority, opposes me. Let us first take the authority of the Philosopher in his *Politics.*
There, on his venerable authority, it is said
that where a number of things are arranged
to attain an end, it behoves one of them to
regulate or govern the others, and the others to submit. And it is not only the authority of his illustrious name which makes
this worthy of belief, but also reason, in-
stancing particulars.

If we take the case of a single man, we
shall see the same rule manifested in him:

all his powers are ordered to gain happiness; but his understanding is what regulates and governs all the others; and otherwise he would never attain to happiness. Again, take a single household: its end is to fit the members thereof to live well; but there must be one to regulate and rule it, who is called the father of the family, or, it may be, one who holds his office. As the Philosopher says: "Every house is ruled by the oldest." And, as Homer says, it is his duty to make rules and laws for the rest. Hence the proverbial curse: "Mayst thou have an equal at home." Take a single village: its end is suitable assistance as regards persons and goods, but one in it must be the ruler of the rest, either set over them by another, or with their consent, the head man amongst them. If it be not so, not only do its inhabitants fail of this mutual assistance, but the whole neighbourhood is sometimes wholly ruined by the ambition of many, who each of them wish to rule. If, again, we take a single city: its end is to secure a good and sufficient life to the citizens; but one man must be ruler in imperfect as well as in good forms of the state. If it is otherwise, not only is the end of civil life lost, but the city too ceases to be what it was. Lastly, if we take any one kingdom, of which the end is the same as that of a city, only with greater security for its tranquillity, there must be one king to rule and govern. For if this is not so, not only do his subjects miss their end, but the kingdom itself falls to destruction, according to that word of the infallible truth: "Every kingdom divided against itself shall be brought to desolation." If then this holds good in these cases, and in each individual thing which is ordered to one certain end, what we have laid down is true.

Now it is plain that the whole human race is ordered to gain some end, as has been before shown. There must, therefore, be one to guide and govern, and the proper title for this office is Monarch or Emperor. And so it is plain that Monarchy or the Empire is necessary for the welfare of the world.

MONARCHY AS THE FORM OF WORLD GOVERNMENT

Further, the whole human race is a whole with reference to certain parts, and, with reference to another whole, it is a part. For it is a whole with reference to particular kingdoms and nations, as we have shown; and it is a part with reference to the whole universe, as is manifest without argument. Therefore, as the lower portions of the whole system of humanity are well adapted to that whole, so that whole is said to be well adapted to the whole which is above it. It is only under the rule of one prince that the parts of humanity are well adapted to their whole, as may easily be collected from what we have said; therefore it is only by being under one Princedom, or the rule of a single Prince, that humanity as a whole is well adapted to the Universe, or its Prince, who is the One God. And it therefore follows that Monarchy is necessary for the welfare of the world.

THE ONENESS OF MANKIND AND THE ONENESS OF GOD

And all is well and at its best which exists according to the will of the first agent, who is God. This is self-evident, except to those who deny that the divine goodness attains to absolute perfection. Now, it is the intention of God that all created things should represent the likeness of God, so far as their proper nature will admit. Therefore was it said: "Let us make man in our image, after our likeness." And though it could not be said that the lower part of creation was made in the image of God, yet all things may be said to be after His likeness, for what is the whole universe but the footprint of the divine goodness? The human race, therefore, is well, nay at its best state, when, so far as can be, it is made like unto God. But the human race is then most made like unto God when most it is one; for the true principle of oneness is in Him alone. Wherefore it is written: "Hear, O Israel; the Lord thy God is one God." But the race of man is most one when it is united wholly in one body, and it is evident that this cannot be, except when it is subject to one prince. Therefore in this subjection mankind is most made like unto God, and, in consequence, such a subjection is in accordance with the divine intention, and it is indeed well and best for man when this is so, as we showed at the beginning of this chapter.

THE NEED FOR AUTHORITATIVE SETTLEMENT OF DISPUTES BETWEEN STATES

Wherever there is controversy, there ought to be judgment, otherwise there would be imperfection without its proper remedy, which is impossible; for God and Nature, in things necessary, do not fill in their provisions. But it is manifest that there may be controversy between any two princes, where the one is not subject to the other, either from the fault of themselves, or even of their subjects. Therefore between them there should be means of judgment. And since, when one is not subject to the other, he cannot be judged by the other (for there is no rule of equals over equals), there must be a third prince of wider jurisdiction, within the circle of whose laws both may come. Either he will or he will not be a Monarch. If he is, we have what we sought; if not, then this one again will have an equal, who is not subject to his jurisdiction, and then again we have need of a third. And so we must either go on to infinity, which is impossible, or we must come to that judge who is first and highest; by whose judgment all controversies shall be either directly or indirectly decided; and he will be Monarch or Emperor. Monarchy is therefore necessary to the world, and this the Philosopher saw when he said: "The world is not intended to be disposed in evil order; 'in a multitude of rulers there is evil, therefore let there be one prince.'"

FREEDOM UNDER MONARCHY

Again, the human race is ordered best when it is most free. This will be manifest if we see what is the principle of freedom. It must be understood that the first principle of our freedom is freedom of will, which many have in their mouth, but few indeed understand. For they come so far as to say that the freedom of the will means a free judgment concerning will. And this is true. But what is meant by the words is far from them: and they do just as our logicians do all day long with certain propositions which are set as examples in the books of logic, as that, "the three angles of a triangle are equal to two right angles."

Therefore I say that Judgment is between Apprehension and Appetite. First, a man apprehends a thing; then he judges it to be good or bad; then he pursues or avoids it accordingly. If therefore the Judgment guides the Appetite wholly, and in no way is forestalled by the Appetite, then is the Judgment free. But if the Appetite in any way at all forestalls the Judgment and guides it, then the Judgment cannot be free: it is not its own: it is captive to another power. Therefore the brute beasts cannot have freedom of Judgment; for in them the Appetite always forestalls the Judgment. Therefore, too, it is that intellectual beings whose wills are unchangeable, and souls which are separate from the body, which have gone hence in peace, do not lose the freedom of their wills, because their wishes cannot change; nay, it is in full strength and completeness that their wills are free.

It is therefore again manifest that this liberty, or this principle of all our liberty, is the greatest gift bestowed by God on mankind: by it alone we gain happiness as men: by it alone we gain happiness elsewhere as gods. But if this is so, who will say that human kind is not in its best state, when it can most use this principle? But he who lives under a Monarchy is most free. Therefore let it be understood that he is free who exists not for another's sake but for his own, as the Philosopher, in his Treatise of simple Being, thought. For everything which exists for the sake of some other thing, is necessitated by that other thing, as a road has to run to its ordained end. Men exist for themselves, and not at the pleasure of others, only if a Monarch rules; for then only are the perverted forms of government set right, while democracies, oligarchies, and tyrannies drive mankind into slavery, as is obvious to any who goes about among them all; and public power is in the hands of kings and aristocracies, which they call the rule of the best, and champions of popular liberty. And because the Monarch loves his subjects much, as we have seen, he wishes all men to be good, which cannot be the case in perverted forms of government: therefore the Philosopher says, in his *Politics:* "In the bad state the good man is a bad citizen, but in a good state the two coincide." Good states in this way aim at liberty, that in them men may live for themselves. The citizens exist not for the good of consuls, nor the nation for the good of its king; but the consuls for the good of the citizens, and the king for the good of his nation. For as the laws are made to suit the state, and not the state to suit the laws, so those who live under the laws are not ordered for the legislator, but he for them; as also the Philosopher holds, in what he has left us on the present subject. Hence, too, it is clear that although the king or the consul rule over the other citizens in respect of the means of government, yet in respect of the end of government they are the servants of the citizens, and especially the Monarch, who, without doubt, must be held the servant of all. Thus it becomes clear that the Monarch is bound by the end appointed to himself in making his laws. Therefore mankind is best off under a Monarchy, and hence it follows that Monarchy is necessary for the welfare of the world.

THE *PAX ROMANA*

To all these reasons alleged above, a memorable experience adds its confirmation. I mean that condition of mankind which the Son of God, when, for the salvation of man, He was about to put on man, either waited for, or, at the moment when He willed, Himself so ordered. For it, from the fall of our first parents, which was the turning point at which all our going astray began, we carry our thoughts over the distribution of the human race and the order of its times, we shall find that never but under the divine Augustus, who was sole ruler, and under whom a perfect Monarchy existed, was the world everywhere quiet. And that then the human race was happy in the tranquillity of universal peace, this is the witness of all writers of history; this is the witness of famous poets; this, too, he who wrote the story of the "meekness and gentleness of Christ" has thought fit to attest. And last of all, Paul has called that most blessed condition "the fullness of the times." For then, indeed, time was full, and all of the things of time; because no office belonging to our felicity wanted its minister. But how the world has fared since that "seamless robe" has suffered rending by the talons of ambition, we may read in books; would that we

might not see it with our eyes. Oh, race of mankind! what storms must toss thee, what losses must thou endure, what shipwrecks must buffet thee, as long as thou, a beast of many heads, strivest after contrary things. Thou art sick in both thy faculties of understanding; thou art sick in thine affections. Unanswerable reasons fail to heal thy higher understanding; the very sight of experience convinces not thy lower understanding; not even the sweetness of divine persuasion charms thy affections, when it breathes into thee through the music of the Holy Ghost: "Behold, how good and how pleasant a thing it is, brethren, to dwell together in unity."

THE VOCATION OF THE ROMANS FOR WORLD RULE

What nature has ordained is maintained of right. For nature in its providence does not come short of men's providence; for if it were to come short, the effect would excel the cause in goodness, which is impossible. But we see that when public bodies are founded, not only are the relations of the members to each other considered, but also their capacities for exercising offices; and this is to consider the end of right in the society or order which is founded, for right is not extended beyond what is possible. Nature then, in her ordinances, does not come short in this foresight. Therefore it is clear that nature, in ordaining a thing, has regard to its capacities; and this regard is the fundamental principle of right which nature lays down. From this it follows that the natural order of things cannot be maintained without right; for this fundamental principle of right is inseparably joined to the natural order of things. It is necessary, therefore, that it is of right that this order is preserved.

The Roman people was ordained for empire, by nature, and this may be shown as follows: The man would come short of perfection in his art, who aimed only to produce his ultimate form, and neglected the means of reaching it; in the same way, if nature only aimed at reproducing in the world the universal form of the divine likeness, and neglected the means of doing so, she would be imperfect. But nature, which is the work of the divine intelligence, is wholly perfect; she therefore aims at all the means by which her final end is arrived at.

Since then mankind has a certain end, and since there is a certain means necessary for the universal end of nature, it necessarily follows that nature aims at obtaining that means. And therefore the Philosopher, in the second book of *Natural Learning,* well shows that nature always acts for the end. And since nature cannot reach this end through one man, because that there are many actions necessary to it, which need many to act, therefore nature must produce many men and set them to act. And besides the higher influence, the powers and properties of inferior spheres contribute much to this. And therefore we see not only that individual men, but also that certain races are born to govern, and certain others to be governed and to serve, as the Philosopher argues in the *Politics;* and for the latter, as he himself says, subjection is not only expedient, but just, even though they be forced into subjection.

And if this is so, it cannot be doubted that nature ordained in the world a country and a nation for universal sovereignty; if this were not so, she would have been untrue to herself, which is impossible. But as to where that country is, and which is that nation, it is sufficiently manifest, both from what we have said and from we shall say, that it was Rome and her citizens or people; and this our poet very skilfully touches on in the sixth *Aeneid,* where he introduces Anchises prophesying to Aeneas, the ancestor of the Romans: "Others may mould the breathing bronze more delicately—I doubt it not; they may chisel from marble the living countenance; they may surpass thee in pleading causes; they may track the course of the heavens with the rod, and tell when the stars will rise; but thou, Roman, remember to rule the nations with thy sway. These shall be thy endowments—to make peace to be the custom of the world; to spare thy foes when they submit, and to crush the proud." And again, Virgil skilfully notes the appointment of the *place,* in the fourth *Aeneid,* when he brings in Jupiter speaking to Mercury concerning Aeneas: "His fair mother did not promise him to us to be such as this: it was not for this that twice she rescues him from Grecian arms; but that there should be one to rule over Italy, teeming with empires,

tempestuous with wars." It has, therefore, sufficiently been shown that the Roman people was by nature ordained to empire. Therefore it was of right that they gained empire, by subduing to themselves the world.

THE SOURCE OF
TEMPORAL POWER

"He hath shut the lions' mouths and they have not hurt me, forasmuch as before Him justice was found in me." At the beginning of this work I proposed to examine into three questions, according as the subject-matter would permit me. Concerning the two first questions our inquiry, as I think, has been sufficiently accomplished in the preceding books. It remains to treat of the third question; and, perchance, it may arouse a certain amount of indignation against me, for the truth of it cannot appear without causing shame to certain men. But seeing that truth from its changeless throne appeals to me—that Solomon too, entering on the forest of his proverbs, teaches me in his own person "to meditate on truth, to hate the wicked"; seeing that the Philosopher, my instructor in morals, bids me, for the sake of truth, to put aside what is dearest; I will, therefore, take confidence from the words of Daniel in which the power of God, the shield of the defenders of truth, is set forth, and, according to the exhortation of St. Paul, "putting on the breastplate of faith," and in the heat of that coal which one of seraphim had taken from off the altar, and laid on the lips of Isaiah, I will enter on the present contest, and, by the arm of Him who delivered us by His blood from the powers of darkness, drive out from the lists the wicked and the liar, in the sight of all the world. Why should I fear, when the Spirit, which is co-eternal with the Father and the Son, saith by the mouth of David: "The righteous shall be had in everlasting remembrance, he shall not be afraid of evil tidings"?

The present question, then, concerning which we have to inquire, is between two great luminaries, the Roman Pontiff and the Roman Prince: and the question is, does the authority of the Roman Monarch, who, as we have proved, is the monarch of the world, depend immediately on God, or on some minister or vicar of God; by whom I understand the successor of Peter, who truly has the keys of the kingdom of heaven?

THE FOUNDATIONS OF CHURCH AUTHORITY

At the outset we must note in reference to this third question, that the truth of the first question had to be made manifest rather to remove ignorance than to end a dispute. In the second question we sought equally to remove ignorance and to end a dispute. For there are many things of which we are ignorant, but concerning which we do not quarrel. In geometry we know not how to square the circle, but we do not quarrel on that point. The theologian does not know the number of the angels, but he does not quarrel about the number. The Egyptian is ignorant of the political system of the Scythians, but he does not therefore quarrel concerning it. But the truth in this third question provokes so much quarrelling that, whereas in other matters ignorance is commonly the cause of quarrelling, here quarrelling is the cause of ignorance. For this always happens where men are hurried by their wishes past what they see by their reason; in this evil bias they lay aside the light of reason, and being dragged on blindly by their desires, they obstinately deny that they are blind. And, therefore, it often follows not only that falsehood has its own inheritance, but that many men issue forth from their own bounds and stray through the foreign camp, where they understand nothing, and no man understands them; and so they provoke some to anger, and some to scorn, and not a few to laughter.

Now three classes of men chiefly strive against the truth which we are trying to prove.

First, the Chief Pontiff, Vicar of our Lord Jesus Christ and the successor of Peter, to whom we owe, not indeed all that we owe to Christ, but all that we owe to Peter, contradicts this truth, urged it may be by zeal for the keys; and also other pastors of the Christian sheepfolds, and others whom I believe to be only led by zeal for our mother, the Church. These all, perchance from zeal and not from pride, withstand the truth which I am about to prove.

But there are certain others in whom obstinate greed has extinguished the light of reason, who are of their father the devil, and yet pretend to be sons of the Church. They not only stir up quarrels in this question, but they hate the name of the most sacred office of Prince, and would shamelessly deny the principles which we have laid down for this and the previous questions.

There is also a third class called Decretalists, utterly without knowledge or skill in philosophy or theology, who, relying entirely on their Decretals (which doubtless, I think, should be venerated), and hoping, I believe, that these Decretals will prevail, disparage the power of the Empire. And no wonder, for I have heard one of them, speaking of these Decretals, assert shamelessly that the traditions of the Church are the foundation of the faith. May this wickedness be taken away from the thoughts of men by those who, antecedently to the traditions of the Church, have believed in Christ the Son of God, whether to come, or present, or as having already suffered; and who from their faith have hoped, and from their hope have kindled into love, and who, burning with love, will, the world doubts not, be made co-heirs with Him.

And that such arguers may be excluded once for all from the present debate, it must be noted that part of Scripture was *before* the Church, that part of it came *with* the Church, and part *after* the Church.

Before the Church were the Old and the New Testament—the covenant which the Psalmist says was "commanded for ever," of which the Church speaks to her Bridegroom, saying: "Draw me after thee."

With the Church came those venerable chief Councils, with which no faithful Christian doubts but that Christ was present. For we have His own words to His disciples when He was about to ascend into heaven: "Lo, I am with you always, even unto the end of the world," to which Matthew testifies. There are also the writings of the doctors, Augustine and others, of whom, if any doubt that they were aided by the Holy Spirit, either he has never beheld their fruit, or if he has beheld, he has never tasted thereof.

After the Church are the traditions which they call Decretals, which, although they are to be venerated for their apostolical authority, yet we must not doubt that they are to be held inferior to fundamental Scripture, seeing that Christ rebuked the Pharisees for this very thing; for when they asked: "Why do thy disciples transgress the tradition of the elders?" (for they neglected the washing of hands), He answered them, as Matthew testifies: "Why do ye also transgress the commandment of God by your tradition?" Thus he intimates plainly that tradition was to have a lower place.

But if the traditions of the Church are *after* the Church, it follows that the Church had not its authority from traditions, but rather traditions from the Church; and, therefore, the men of whom we speak, seeing that they have nought but traditions, must be excluded from the debate. For those who seek after this truth must proceed in their inquiry from those things from which flows the authority of the Church.

Further, we must exclude others who boast themselves to be white sheep in the flock of the Lord, when they have the plumage of crows. These are the children of wickedness, who, that they may be able to follow their evil ways, put shame on their mother, drive out their brethren, and when they have done all will allow none to judge them. Why should we seek to reason with these, when they are led astray by their evil desires, and so cannot see even our first principle?

Therefore there remains the controversy only with the other sort of men who are influenced by a certain kind of zeal for their mother the Church, and yet know not the truth which is sought for. With these men, therefore—strong in the reverence which a dutiful son owes to his father, which a dutiful son owes to his mother, dutiful to Christ, dutiful to the Church, dutiful to the Chief Shepherd, dutiful to all who profess the religion of Christ—I begin in this book the contest for the maintenance of the truth.

CHURCH AND EMPIRE

Certain persons say further that the Emperor Constantine, having been cleansed from leprosy by the intercession of Sylvester, then the Supreme Pontiff, gave unto the Church the seat of Empire which was Rome, together with many other dignities belonging to the Empire. Hence they argue that no man can take unto himself these dignities unless he receive them from the Church, whose they are said to be. From this it would rightly follow, that one authority depends on the other, as they maintain.

The arguments which seemed to have their roots in the Divine words, have been stated and disproved. It remains to state and disprove those which are grounded on Roman history and in the reason of mankind. The first of these is the one which we have mentioned, in which the syllogism runs as follows: No one has a right to those things which belong to the Church, unless he has them from the Church; and this we grant. The government of Rome belongs to the Church; therefore no one has a right to it unless it be given him by the Church. The minor premiss is proved by the facts concerning Constantine, which we have touched on.

This minor premiss then will I destroy; and as for their proof, I say that it proves nothing. For the dignity of the Empire was what Constantine could not alienate, nor the Church receive. And when they insist, I prove my words as follows: No man on the strength of the office which is committed to him, may do aught that is contrary to that office; for so one and the same man, viewed as one man, would be contrary to himself, which is impossible. But to divide the Empire is contrary to the office committed to the Emperor; for his office is to hold mankind in all things subject to one will. Therefore it is not permitted to the Emperor to divide the Empire. If, therefore, as they say, any dignities had been alienated by Constantine, and had passed to the Church, the "coat without seam"—which even they, who pierced Christ, the true God, with a spear, dared not rend—would have been rent.

Further, just as the Church has its foundation, so has the Empire its foundation. The foundation of the Church is Christ, as Paul says in his first Epistle to the Corinthians: "For other foundation can no man lay than that which is laid, which is Jesus Christ." He is the rock on which the Church is built; but the foundation of the Empire is human right. Now I say that, as the Church may not go contrary to its foundation—but must always rest on its foundation, as the words of the Canticles say: "Who is she that cometh up from the desert, abounding in delights, leaning on her beloved?"—in the same way I say that the Empire may not do aught that transgresses human right. But were the Empire to destroy itself, it would so transgress human right. Therefore the Empire may not destroy itself. Since then to divide the Empire would be to destroy it, because the Empire consists in one single universal Monarchy, it is manifest that he who exercises the authority of the Empire may not destroy it, and from what we have said before, it is manifest that to destroy the Empire is contrary to human right.

Moreover, all jurisdiction is prior in time to the judge who has it; for it is the judge who is ordained for the jurisdiction, not the jurisdiction for the judge. But the Empire is a jurisdiction, comprehending within itself all temporal jurisdiction: therefore it is prior to the judge who has it, who is the Emperor. For it is the Emperor who is ordained for the Empire, and not contrariwise. Therefore it is clear that the Emperor, in so far as he is Emperor, cannot alter the Empire; for it is to the Empire that he owes his being. I say then that he who is said to have conferred on the Church the authority in question either was Emperor, or he was not. If he was not, it is plain that he had no power to give away any part of the Empire. Nor could he, if he was Emperor, in so far as he was Emperor, for such a gift would be a diminishing of his jurisdiction.

Further, if one Emperor were able to cut off a certain portion of the jurisdiction of the Empire, so could another; and since temporal jurisdiction is finite, and since all that is finite is taken away by finite diminutions, it would follow that it is possible for the first of all jurisdictions to be annihilated, which is absurd.

Further, since he that gives is in the position of an agent, and he to whom a thing is given in that of a patient, as the Philosopher holds in the fourth book to Nicomachus, therefore, that a gift may be given, we require not only the fit qualification of the giver, but also of the receiver; for the acts of the agent are completed in a patient who is qualified. But the Church was altogether unqualified to receive temporal things; for there is an express command, forbidding her so to do, which Matthew gives thus: "Provide neither gold, nor silver, nor brass in your purses." For though we find in Luke a relaxation of the command in regard to

certain matters, yet I have not anywhere been able to find that the Church after that prohibition had license given her to possess gold and silver. If therefore the Church was unable to receive temporal power, even granting that Constantine was able to give it, yet the gift was impossible; for the receiver was disqualified. It is therefore plain that neither could the Church receive in the way of possession, nor could Constantine give in the way of alienation; though it is true that the Emperor, as protector of the Church, could allot to the Church a patrimony and other things, if he did not impair his supreme lordship, the unity of which does not allow division. And the Vicar of God could receive such things, not to possess them, but as a steward to dispense the fruits of them to the poor of Christ, on behalf of the Church, as we know the Apostles did.

THE TRUE RELATIONS BETWEEN TEMPORAL AND ECCLESIASTICAL AUTHORITY

Although it has been proved that the authority of the Empire has not its cause in the authority of the Supreme Pontiff; for we have shown that this argument led to absurd results; yet it has not been entirely shown that the authority of the Empire depends directly upon God, except as a result from our argument. For it is a consequence that, if the authority comes not from the vicar of God, it must come from God Himself. And therefore, for the complete determination of the question proposed, we have to prove directly that the emperor or monarch of the world stands in an immediate relation to the King of the universe, who is God.

For the better comprehending of this, it must be recognized that man alone, of all created things, holds a position midway between things corruptible and things incorruptible; and therefore philosophers rightly liken him to a dividing line between two hemispheres. For man consists of two essential parts, namely, the soul and the body. If he be considered in relation to his body only, he is corruptible; but if he be considered in relation to his soul only, he is incorruptible. And therefore the Philosopher spoke well concerning the incorruptible soul when he said in the second book "of the Soul:" "It is this alone which may be separated, as being eternal, from the corruptible."

If, therefore, man holds this position midway between the corruptible and the incorruptible, since every middle nature partakes of both extremes, man must share something of each nature. And since every nature is ordained to gain some final end, it follows that for man there is a double end. For as he alone of all beings participates both in the corruptible and the incorruptible, so he alone of all beings is ordained to gain two ends, whereby one is his end in so far as he is corruptible, and the other in so far as he is incorruptible.

Two ends, therefore, have been laid down by the ineffable providence of God for man to aim at: the blessedness of this life, which consists in the exercise of his natural powers, and which is prefigured in the earthly Paradise; and next, the blessedness of the life eternal, which consists in the fruition of the sight of God's countenance, and to which man by his own natural powers cannot rise, if he be not aided by the divine light; and this blessedness is understood by the heavenly Paradise.

But to these different kinds of blessedness, as to different conclusions, we must come by different means. For at the first we may arrive by the lessons of philosophy, if only we will follow them, by acting in accordance with the moral and intellectual virtues. But at the second we can only arrive by spiritual lessons, transcending human reason, so that we follow them in accordance with the theological virtues, faith, hope, and charity. The truth of the first of these conclusions and of these means is made manifest by human reason, which by the philosophers has been all laid open to us. The other conclusions and means are made manifest by the Holy Spirit, who by the mouth of the Prophets and holy writers, and by Jesus Christ, the co-eternal Son of God, and His disciples, has revealed to us supernatural truth of which we have great need. Nevertheless human passion would cast them all behind its back, unless that men, going astray like the beasts that perish, were restrained in their course by bit and bridle, like horses and mules.

Therefore man had need of two guides for his life, as he had a twofold end in life; whereof one is the Supreme Pontiff, to lead mankind to eternal life, according to the things revealed to us; and the other is the Emperor, to guide mankind to happiness in this world, in accordance with the teaching of philosophy. And since none, or but a few only, and even they with sore difficulty, could arrive at this harbour of happiness, unless the waves and blandishments of human desires were set at rest, and the human race were free to live in peace and quiet, this therefore is the mark at which he who is to care for the world, and whom we call the Roman Prince, must most chiefly aim at: I mean, that in this little plot of earth belonging to mortal men, life may pass in freedom and with peace. And since the order of this world follows the order of the heavens, as they run their course, it is necessary, to the end that the learning which brings liberty and peace may be duly applied by this guardian of the world in fitting season and place, that this power should be dispensed by Him who is ever present to behold the whole order of the heavens. And this is He who alone has preordained this, that by it in His providence He might bind all things together, each in their own order.

But if this is so, God alone elects, God alone confirms: for there is none higher than God. And hence there is the further conclusion, that neither those who now are, nor any other who may, in whatsoever way, have been called, "Electors," ought to have that name; rather they are to be held as declarers and announcers of the providence of God. And, therefore, it is that they to whom is granted the privilege of announcing God's will sometimes fall into disagreement; because that, all of them or some of them have been blinded by their evil desires, and have not discerned the face of God's appointment.

It is therefore clear that the authority of temporal Monarchy comes down, with no intermediate will, from the fountain of universal authority; and this fountain, one in its unity, flows through many channels out of the abundance of the goodness of God.

And now, methinks, I have reached the goal which I set before me. I have unravelled the truth of the questions which I asked: whether the office of Monarchy was necessary to the welfare of the world; whether it was by right that the Roman people assumed to themselves the office of Monarchy; and, further, that last question, whether the authority of the Monarch springs immediately from God, or from some other. Yet the truth of this latter question must not be received so narrowly as to deny that in certain matters the Roman Prince is subject to the Roman Pontiff. For that happiness, which is subject to mortality, in a sense is ordered with a view to the happiness which shall not taste of death. Let, therefore, Caesar be reverent to Peter, as the first-born son should be reverent to his father, that he may be illuminated with the light of his father's grace, and so may be stronger to lighten the world over which he has been placed by Him alone, who is the ruler of all things spiritual as well as temporal.

CHAPTER THIRTEEN

MARSILIO
OF PADUA

The struggle between the papacy and the German emperors seemed to be settled with the victory of the church in the middle of the thirteenth century. The German imperial dynasty, the Hohenstaufen, was destroyed, never to rise again. The authority of the popes was supreme; they made and unmade kings and emperors, their wealth was second to none, and the papalist doctrine of the supremacy of ecclesiastical over temporal power (in contradiction to the older Gelasian doctrine of equilibrium) seemed to have been successfully translated into the reality of a new world order. Yet, as so often happens, absolute and limitless power is its own worst enemy, and less than fifty years after the papacy attained its peak, it was humiliated as never before, and perhaps never since.

Pope Boniface VIII (1294–1303) marks the turning point in the history of church-state relations: he is the last pope to make claims of world rule and the first to descend from the summit of glory to humiliation, even degradation. In defeating the German emperors, the popes had learned to rely heavily on the French monarchs; yet France was the country destined to explode, forever, the papal claim of world hegemony.

The conflict arose over money. The church, like every ambitious Great Power, needed more and more money, and its financial needs came into conflict with those of the new national monarchies, particularly France and England, which were gradually building up an efficient but costly central administrative machine to replace the old feudal system of extreme decentralization. In 1296, Boniface declared (in the bull *Clericis Laicos*) that laymen have no jurisdiction over the clergy, "over both the persons and goods of ecclesiastics," without prior papal permission, and that no mundane authority was permitted to levy taxes on church property, nor the clergy permitted to pay them; the imposition or paying of such taxes without papal approval was put under the sanction of excommunication from the church.

Both England and France, for whom the papal bull was especially meant, refused to recognize a financial state within the state; first, because political sovereignty without tax sovereignty was meaningless, and second, because church property was so vast that neither monarchy could afford to exempt it from taxation. In England, King Edward I threatened that the king's peace could not be had for nothing and that if the clergy were to refuse taxes he would consider them outcasts and treat them as such. Boniface had to give in, and the basic principle was never raised again. In France, King Philip IV firmly rejected Boniface's interference in French finances, and the pope was powerless to enforce his doctrine.

The year 1300 was celebrated in Rome as the first Christian Jubilee. Hundreds of thousands of visitors journeyed from all over Europe to the Eternal City, where a complete indulgence of their sins, hitherto available only to crusaders, awaited them, as well as magnificent spectacles and public ceremonials. Pope Boniface himself, at the height of his power and prestige, appeared in public in the garb of pope and emperor, wearing the imperial scepter and crown, displaying two swords, and proclaiming himself Pontiff, Caesar, and Emperor. Though the Jubilee added large sums of money to the coffers of the Holy See, it did not allay the conflict between Rome and the new national states.

In 1302 Boniface issued the bull *Unam Sanctam,* one of the two or three most important church documents in history. It affirmed no new doctrine but merely expressed, more clearly and irreconcilably than ever before, the extreme and intransigent papalist viewpoint: there is "neither salvation nor remission of sins" outside the "holy catholic and apostolic church"; this "one and only church" had one body and one head, "not two heads as if it were a monster"; there are two swords, a spiritual and a temporal, and "both swords are in the power of the church, the one by the hand of the priest, the other by the hand of kings and knights, but at the will and sufferance of the priest." The key idea in *Unam Sanctam* is contained in the following sentence: "One sword, moreover, ought to be under the other, and the temporal authority to be subjected to the spiritual." *Unam Sanctam* also decreed that each power be judged by its superior authority; if the highest earthly power, the emperor or king, err, he will be judged by the spiritual authority, the priests. But if the highest priest, the pope, err, he can be judged by God alone, not by man: "A spiritual man judges all things, but he himself is judged by no one," because his authority is divine. The last sentence of the bull runs as follows: "We therefore declare, say, define, and pronounce that it is altogether a necessity of salvation for every human creature to be subject to the Roman Pontiff."

Philip IV accepted the challenge thrust at him by papal diplomacy and decree. Although Boniface excommunicated Philip and freed his subjects from allegiance, Philip planned to bring Boniface before a General Council of the church to be held in France, and to have him deposed for heresy, murder, sexual immorality, trafficking in church offices (simony), magic, idol worship—to mention but a few of the twenty-nine charges of his indictment. Significantly, the royal council that approved of such grave charges against the pope included the higher clergy in France; the national support for Philip was overwhelming, because the attitude of the universities, intellectuals, urban middle classes, royal bureaucracy, and nobility was hardly in doubt from the beginning.

While the fulminations were being hurled from pope to monarch and back, Philip proceeded to solve the issue by a *coup.* One of his closest advisers, Nogaret (a man of heretical and bourgeois background), went to Italy, where he organized a small force with the intention of capturing the pope and taking him to France before a General Council of the church that would try, condemn, and depose him. Nogaret's men (about sixteen hundred on horse and foot) broke into Anagni, the papal court southeast of Rome, early in September, 1303, overpowered the small papal guard, and seized Boniface. Before the French could bring Boniface to France, however, he was saved by a local revulsion of feeling against the plot and brought back to Rome. There he died within a few weeks as a result of the shock and strain that the outrage at Anagni had caused him.

Scarcely less remarkable than the *coup* of Anagni was the scant attention it attracted. The victory of Philip over Boniface, of France over Roman ecclesiastical imperialism, was not the outcome of a mere daring act of violence. The French were in a better position than the papacy in at least two major respects: first, the feud had manifestly originated in a quarrel over money—hardly an inspiring issue for the side that claims to represent the highest spiritual values on earth; second, the French monarch was in a morally strong position because he asked for supreme jurisdiction only in his own house, France, whereas Boniface asked for authority, spiritual and temporal, over the entire world.

In 1076, Pope Gregory VII and (the German) Emperor Henry IV had been engaged in as dramatic a conflict as Boniface's and Philip's in 1303. The emperor deposed the pope, on which the pope excommunicated and deposed the emperor. In the ensuing struggle the emperor had to surrender unconditionally to the pope in the famous scene at the mountain fortress of Canossa, in northern Italy. Clothed in penitential garb, the emperor stood barefoot at the gate of the snow-bound fortress, to which the pope had come. For three days the emperor had to wait until the pope was willing to see him. The emperor repented, pledged complete submission for the future, and was pardoned. The Holy Roman Empire of the German Nation still lingered on for centuries, but the idea of a universal empire was dead henceforth.

Paradoxically, when the temporal authority (of the German emperors) claimed like the papacy, universal jurisdiction, it failed; when it sought, with strong domestic support, limited jurisdiction in a national state (as in France) against the papal claims of universal authority, it won. In fighting with the German emperors for supremacy, the popes were colliding with the past; in the struggle with the French monarchy, they were up against the strongest single political institution of the next six centuries: the *sovereign national state*. By destroying the prestige and power of the Holy Roman Empire and its German rulers, the papacy had unknowingly undermined the belief in universal authority as such, and thus had aided in the growth of separatist nationalism. In particular, the papacy had strongly drawn on French support in its conflict with the German) empire and thereby had contributed to making France the first European power. Having helped the papacy to eliminate the temporal claimant to universal authority, the French monarchy completed the job by eliminating the papacy itself as a pretender to world hegemony in spiritual and secular affairs.

Boniface was succeeded by Pope Benedict XI, also an Italian. Benedict reestablished concord between the Holy See and the Kingdom of France by annulling all excommunications, bulls, and decrees of his predecessor against Philip and his counselors, except Nogaret, the author of the "outrage of Anagni." Before having further opportunities to serve the French monarchy, Benedict XI died—after only eight months in office (1304).

In the following year, a French subject, the archbishop of Bordeaux, was elected pope, and he assumed the name of Clement V. Nogaret and other antipapalists who were not satisfied with the death of Boniface sought to assassinate his memory, too, by having him tried, *post mortem,* for various crimes, particularly heresy. Clement, who was anxious to avoid the scandal of having one of his predecessors condemned as an heretic, promised to have the issue examined by a commission of cardinals. In the end the pope annulled again all pronouncements of Boniface against Philip and his advisers, and this time he included Nogaret in the general absolution. Moreover, Philip was now praised by Clement for his zeal in defending the faith against Boniface, and Clement also gave orders to erase from Boniface's register the bulls and offensive pronouncements against Philip.

Clement did not go to Rome but set up his court in Avignon, in southern France, where he and his six successors, all French, resided more or less continuously in what has been called the "Babylonian captivity" of the papacy (1305–1378). The French era of the Avignon papacy was followed by the Great Schism (1378–1417), during which there were usually two popes, one at Avignon, one at Rome, and at times a third pretender. After the Great Schism, the Protestant Reformation drastically diminished the range of papal jurisdiction by reducing the Roman Catholic Church to one among many.

In the East, the rivalry between Constantinople and Rome went back to the fifth century. After the fall of Constantinople in 1453, Russia predominated in the eastern church; in 1589 a new patriarch was created with a claim of universal leadership, and Moscow was hailed as the "Third Rome."

The principal revolutionary changes in the late Middle Ages were the growing vehemence of anticlerical feeling and the decisive defeat of the papacy, the secularization of life, the rise of the bourgeoisie, and the formation of national states. These new developments are most systematically reflected in Marsilio of Padua's *Defensor Pacis,* or *The Defender of Peace* (1324). Marsilio (1275–1343) was a physician by occupation, and a student of philosophy, law, and theology. During his lifetime the Italian republican city-states were a unique phenomenon, and Padua was particularly known for its spirit of liberty and independence in defending itself against the local clergy and the Roman Curia.

Marsilio was of middle-class origin, and his mold of thought, skeptical, realistic, and empirical, is characteristic of the inhabitant of a free Italian city-republic with ancient secular traditions. His practice of medicine during many years added to his outlook a more critical and scientific cast. Marsilio quotes Aristotle's *Politics* more than all other classical authors put together, and in this respect he is typically medieval. But to most other medieval writers Aristotle was little more than a source of authority and verbal incantation; the two main assumptions of medieval political speculation—the supremacy of theology over philosophy, and the universality of theological-political rule in papacy and empire—were the exact opposite of Aristotle's two main ideals—empirical observation in philosophy, and the city-state in politics. Marsilio's use of Aristotle is more than verbal: he, too, has the background of an urban, secular civilization, and like Aristotle (who also practiced medicine for some time) he tries to use common sense and empirical verification rather than abstract speculation and authoritative dogma.

Next in importance in Marsilio's background is his intellectual experience in France. He spent a considerable portion of his formative years as a student and teacher at the University of Paris, of which he was Rector for a short period in 1312. Paris was then the world's leading university, particularly in philosophy, art, and letters, and the defeat of the papacy by France made Paris the center of secularist groups and ideas. In this lively political and intellectual atmosphere Marsilio received his formal education, and part of the authorship of *The Defender of Peace* is attributed by some to John of Jandun, a leading French scholar and Marsilio's close friend and collaborator during many years.

Taken individually, most of Marsilio's ideas can be traced to the flourishing and fertile school of publicists, pamphleteers, and politicians who congregated in Paris and established there a new kind of political literature and journalism soon to be copied all over Europe. Yet Marsilio was the first to develop a full-fledged doctrine from current isolated arguments and to discern in contemporary events the shape of a future world.

Like Dante, Marsilio is a link in the transition from the medieval to the modern age. But, whereas Dante was still essentially medieval in the formulation and solution of his main problems, Marsilio is essentially modern, though still encumbered by medieval forms of thought and argument. In fact, he is regarded by some as the most original medieval political writer, precisely because he seeks so consciously to break the fetters of his age and because he rejects vigorously and unequivocally any clerical control of thought or government.

Marsilio's irony and skepticism contrast with the deadly seriousness and dogmatic certainty of most medieval political writing. He occasionally admits that he is not sure, that a position he defends may be wrong—concessions that are more modern than medieval in spirit. Where there is complete certainty based on divine knowledge and revelation, there is no room for probabilities and possibilities, attributes of human, not divine, knowledge.

In his discussion of the forms of state, Marsilio merely repeats the Aristotelian division of the three good types (monarchy, aristocracy, constitutionalism) and the three diseased kinds (tyranny, oligarchy, mob dictatorship). He also says that the criterion of distinction is, following Aristotle, whether a government serves the rulers or the ruled. So far, Marsilio offers few surprises. But he differs radically from Aristotle (without, perhaps, being fully aware of it) by adding that in the good forms of government the ruler governs for the common benefit *in accordance with the will of the people*. Conversely, the diseased forms of government are for the benefit of the rulers *without the consent of the people*. This is not a minor addition to Aristotle but a fundamental revision and transformation. It could be argued, logically, that the postulate of government for the benefit of the ruled implies some measure of consent, but Aristotle himself did not see this logic in its full implication, perhaps because of his belief that some men are born to rule and others to obey.

In one passage Marsilio departs from Aristotle even more drastically by abandoning entirely the criterion of the *object of government* (the common benefit), and by replacing it with that of the *method of government,* according to which political rule is "over either voluntary or involuntary subjects." Similarly, recent and contemporary political theory emphasizes that democracy in government is primarily a question of method, the results and consequences of which can be good or bad. It is an assumption of modern democratic thought, as of Marsilio, that the proper method of government, that is, consent, is more likely (though by no means certain) to produce goods ends than are undemocratic methods, though the latter, too, may be employed for the pursuit of the common benefit. The consciousness of the *dynamic relations between means and ends* is one of the main contributions of modern philosophy, and Marsilio points in this direction by stressing that the problem of government is one of means as much as of ends.

Marsilio's break with Aristotle and the Middle Ages becomes especially clear in his conception of law as the manifestation of political authority. The general tendency of medieval writers was to assume that law is intimately related to reason and the common good; because they sincerely believed that such a relation is essential, they often stated, in the words of St. Thomas Aquinas, that law is "an ordinance of reason for the common good." Marsilio defines *law* in a less substantive and more formal way as a *coercive command* of the legislator *enforceable in the courts.* Marsilio hopes that human law will ordinarily be in harmony with divine and natural law, but he concedes the possibility that "sometimes false conceptions of the just and the beneficial become laws, when there is given a command to observe them."

This *positivist conception of law* is a significant deviation from the medieval tradition of natural law, and it reminds one of modern antimetaphysical views. Thus Holmes, perhaps the greatest of many great American jurists, defined the law as "the prophecies of what the courts will do in fact, and nothing more pretentious"; another leading jurist, Hans Kelsen, saw in the threat of coercion an essential element of the law.

Marsilio is aware that human law is, in dignity, below divine and natural law. However, he denudes this concession to his medieval environment of any practical effect by stating that the divine law is binding on the conscience, but that punishment for transgressing it is reserved for the next world. It is also important that Marsilio restricts the divine law to its revelation in the Bible but will have nothing to do with canon law, which to him is a set of statutes and rules of a human organization, the church, and no more. Because of his refusal to identify human law with divine authority or reason, Marsilio is driven to look for another source of validating human law. This source he finds in human society itself. Marsilio did not know the concept of *sovereignty,* although he was groping toward it and clearly described its substance. He says that "the legislator, or the primary and proper efficient cause of the law, is the people or the whole body of citizens, or the weightier part thereof," and that the "weightier part" of the citizens is to be understood in terms of quantity and quality.

Marsilio's use of the Latin word *legislator* is a source of confusion if the translation is simply rendered as "legislator" in English. Marsilio's legislator (whether it be understood as the whole body of citizens, the numerical majority, or the qualitatively weightier part) may mean two different things. The first is the *political sovereign,* the *constituent power* in the state, which alone has the authority to make the constitution; Marsilio comes somewhat closer to the concept of the sovereign, or constituent power, by calling it, in this context, a "primary" or "absolute" legislator.

The second meaning of legislator as used by Marsilio approximates more closely the modern *legislative function,* and here Marsilio distinguishes again two possibilities: either the people in assembly make the laws, are the legislator (as would be possible in small communities), or the people entrust the legislative function to "some person or persons, who are not and cannot be the legislator in the absolute sense, but only in a relative sense and for a particular time and in accordance with the authority of the primary legislator." Even if the political sovereign is made up of the whole people, the concept of citizenship is still not all-inclusive, for children, slaves, women, and foreigners are excluded from active participation in public life.

The people as the source of political authority was a basic conception in Roman jurisprudence and in its revived form during the Middle Ages, and medieval society itself evolved the idea that the community is the source of the law. Marsilio's originality consists, not so much in having discovered the idea of the people as the source of law, but in having shorn the conception of all its encumbrances and ornamentations so that it could evolve from a juridical fiction into a call for action.

As to his complex conception of the "weightier part" of the citizens, which in some instances may take the place of the entire body of citizens as the political sovereign, it should first be noted that Marsilio says that both the quantity *and* quality should be taken into account. He nowhere holds a brief for the idea of an elite; he merely says that the quantitative element alone is not sufficient, and that the qualitative factor should also be considered. He is undogmatic enough to know that qualitative standards cannot be described in detail in advance; they are the result of varying "honorable customs" in different political communities. In his own day Marsilio undoubtedly saw that even in the free city-republics of northern Italy there was no equality of groups and individuals, and yet there was a strong sense that the assembly of the people, the *arengo* or *parlamento,* was the ultimate source of sovereignty.

Marsilio's concept of a "weightier part" of the citizenry may be seen in a broader perspective with the aid of the British experience. The Glorious Revolution of 1688 and the Settlement of 1689 established in England the principle of *parliamentary supremacy,* rather than *popular sovereignty* in the sense of universal and equal suffrage. The recognition of parliamentary supremacy—under which only the "weightier part" of the citizenry (and a small part in numbers) governed the country—made, however, full democratic sovereignty as developed in the nineteenth and twentieth centuries a practical possibility. It was not until 1948 that the principle of "one man, one vote" was finally attained completely, when the Representation of the People Act abolished extra business and university votes, the last remnants of plural voting.

Similarly, Marsilio's concept of the *legislator* certainly implied *constitutional supremacy* and, to a considerable extent, legislative parliamentary supremacy, although hardly popular sovereignty in the strictly democratic sense that each man counts for one vote. In the United States, too, the element of quantity in politics is modified, first, by the deliberate overrepresentation of less populous states in the senate; this deviation from arithmetic implies the value judgment that in some instances historical or geographical considerations override the democratic argument of pure numbers. In addition, social power, prestige, and influence count, in the United Sates as in other democracies, when it comes to the making of crucial political decisions.

In effect, therefore, the political impact of the individual citizen depends on whether he belongs to the "weightier part" of society, or whether he is a mere quantitative unit whose political influence is confined to the periodic act of voting. Moreover, it should be remembered that Marsilio wrote in the fourteenth century, in which social and economic inequality was taken for granted, and that he cannot be fairly measured by twentieth-century standards.

Whereas Marsilio does not describe in detail how the qualitatively weightier part of the body politic is to be ascertained in practice, he enthusiastically defends the basically democratic doctrine of the *common sense of the people* against the theory that a superior elite alone is possessed of political wisdom. Marsilio argues that a defect in a proposed law can be better detected by a large number than by a small fraction of the community, because every whole "is greater in mass and virtue than any part of it taken separately." From the viewpoint of expediency, too, Marsilio says, the utility of a proposed law will be better judged by the whole people, "because no one knowingly harms himself." By contrast, Marsilio thinks that if the law were made by only one or a few, they would be more likely to consider their own private profit than that of society as a whole.

From a psychological viewpoint, too, popular consent is an advantage: the law has a better chance of being observed by all if everybody has an opportunity to comment freely on its merits. Marsilio introduces again a formal, procedural criterion in discussing freedom and despotism, as he has done in defining the law. Abandoning the substantive definitions of representative medieval writers, Marsilio sees *freedom* primarily as the procedure and method of *self-government,* whereas despotism is the lack of self-government, regardless how good the law of the despot is. Conversely, even if the law is bad, citizens will feel a moral obligation to observe it if they have given their consent to it. Marsilio states the heart of the democratic creed as follows: "Those matters, therefore, which can affect the benefit and harm of all ought to be known and heard by all, who thus may attain the beneficial and repel the opposite."

Marsilio is aware of the argument, made then as now, that the majority of men are vicious, undiscerning, and stupid, and that the few who are wise, learned, and virtuous should therefore rule. Marsilio agrees that the vicious and undiscerning should not make the law, but he denies that most citizens are vicious and undiscerning most of the time: "All or most of them are of sound reason and have a right desire for the polity and for the things necessary for it to endure." A minimum of optimism about human nature is a basic condition, in Marsilio as in other political thinkers, for any faith in democracy, modest and limited as it may be. Marsilio concedes that only few have the ability to make wise laws, yet *every citizen can be a proper judge of the law* because "by induction we can see that many men judge rightly about the quality of a picture, a house, a ship, and other works of art, even though they would have been unable to discover or produce them." Marsilio quotes Aristotle's statement that man is not always the best judge of something he makes himself, and he might have quoted the further Aristotelian dictum that "the guest will judge better of a feast then the cook."

Since the active citizens who from the political sovereign (or *legislator*) cannot themselves carry on the work of legislation, government, and administration, there must be a group of persons who act in the name of the citizenry. Marsilio distinguishes clearly, perhaps more than any writer before him, the *state* as the *source of sovereignty* from the *personnel and process of government* as the *instrumentality of sovereignty*. Marsilio calls the instrumentality of sovereignty the ruling part *(pars principans)* of the state, a decidedly different concept from that of the modern executive, and much broader than the latter. The function of the ruling part, Marsilio says, is "to regulate, in accordance with the law, the political or civil acts of men." He stresses that "the elected kind of government is superior to the non-elected," and in monarchy, too, he strongly prefers the elective ruler. Governments established by force or fraud are, by contrast, "diseased."

According to the traditional medieval view, the ruler holds his office by divine sanction, and he is supposed to be superior in virtue and wisdom. Marsilio deals with this question in a more empirical and democratic, and less metaphysical, manner. The authority of the ruler derives its validity and existence from the observable fact of election, and a person becomes a ruler because he is elected, "and not by his knowledge of the laws, his prudence, or moral virtue, although these are qualities of the perfect ruler." Marsilio also mentions that many men may possess these qualities of ruling, yet, lacking the formal and empirical authority by election, they are not rulers.

Just as Marsilio derives the law from an empirical source, the will of the community, rather than from divine providence or natural reason, so he bases the *authority of the rulers* on the *will of the community* as expressed in *election*. He therefore also stresses the nature of political office as an instrumentality of the *legislator*. The rulers must be guided and controlled by respect for the law, and the armed forces at their disposal should be kept at a level that is at once high enough to maintain order and yet not so high that it will give the rulers despotic power.

If the ruler or rulers violate the trust of office, the *legislator*—which sets them up— has the right to correct and punish them. If their offense is serious, they may even be removed from office. The *legislator* suspends the offending ruler while the proceedings against him are on, because there must never be two competing authorities and also "because he is corrected not as a ruler but as a subject who has transgressed the law." Marsilio's conception of the accountability of the ruler to the people is not new and is typical of the Middle Ages; but, whereas most medieval writers looked for divine punishment or, in more extreme instances, for tyrannicide as a remedy, Marsilio gropes toward an institutionalized method of keeping the ruler responsible to the entire community, should he exceed his authority.

Marsilio's conception of law and government as social regulation owing its coercive authority to the will of the politically organized community (*legislator* or *legislator humanus*) was pointed at lay and clerical despotism. Whereas in the past two hundred years interest in Marsilio's political theory has been steadily growing, in his own time and in the subsequent three centuries his views on the church were more influential. His most revolutionary doctrine in his analysis of the church, and one that was to leave its mark on Protestantism, is the idea of *congregational authority in the church*. The church is a community of believers *(universitas fidelium)*, and, as in the political community *(universitas civium)*, the only source of authority is the body of its members.

Marsilio does not attack the institution of the papacy as such, but he insists that if the Roman bishop (that is, the pope) has any special authority "it belongs to him through human appointment or election." The papacy started out as a simple headship of prestige and honor in view of the strategic position of Rome, but by a gradual and consistent process of usurpation it finally claimed full and universal jurisdiction over clergy and civil government. Selecting Boniface as one of the chief culprits, Marsilio says that the doctrine of papal plenitude of power was expressed by Boniface "in language as insolent as it is harmful and contrary to the meaning of Scripture, and based upon metaphysical demonstrations."

With regard to the right of appointing bishops and priests, Marsilio holds that it belongs to neither Caesar nor pope, "but rather to the whole body of believers," or to an agency set up by this body for the purpose. As to the rank and status of priests, "all bishops are of equal authority immediately through Christ, nor can it be proved by divine law that there is any superiority or subjection among them in spiritual or temporal affairs." The functions of the priesthood in the church, and it has none outside the church, are administration, teaching, and worship; but—and this is one of the main principles of Marsilio's political theory—the priests, the *church,* have *no coercive authority,* spiritual or temporal, over either clergy or laymen.

Marsilio adds the bold thought that the church has even no coercive authority over heretics. If heresy be a sin, it can—like all violations of divine law—be judged and punished on the day of judgment in the next world; if heresy be a civil offense, it must first be so declared by the secular government, and in this event the purpose is not to save souls but to protect secular interests, such as the unity of the state. If there are to be any penalties for heresy, they are to be fixed by secular authorities and meted out by them. However, Marsilio is not certain that heresy is really a moral offense, but he does not examine the matter in any great detail. He is primarily concerned with destroying the claim of the church to coercive authority, and he deliberately picks an extreme instance to illustrate his argument.

For practical purposes the church becomes, according to Marsilio, a department of the state, and he goes so far as to say that only the civil government has the authority to regulate the number of churches and temples, priests, and ministers. Because teaching has always been claimed by the church as its own domain, Marsilio specifically emphasizes that no license for the public teaching or practice of any art or discipline can be granted by bishops collectively or individually; only the civil government has this authority. Marsilio also recalls that Christ himself had no ambition for secular rule or property, and he therefore admonishes the church, in the Franciscan and Dantean tradition, to return to the original ways of Christianity. Existent church property should be used only for the maintenance of priests and "other gospel ministers," for divine worship, and for the aid of the needy and helpless poor. Whatever church property remains over and above such uses may be appropriated by the state "for the common or public welfare and protection."

Marsilio calls his treatise *The Defender of Peace* because he sees the task of civil government primarily as one of peace. In addition to the older causes of social unrest and discord known to Aristotle and other masters of political thought there is a new element, not known to Aristotle, that produces civil discord and intranquillity, and this new cause "is the belief, desire, and undertaking whereby the Roman bishop and his clerical coterie, in particular, are aiming to seize secular rulerships and to possess excessive temporal wealth." The indictment of the church on these two major grounds was to become one of the driving forces that led, first, to reform movements within the church and, later, to schism and separation in the Protestant Reformation.

In matters of religious faith and doctrine generally, Marsilio believes only in the truth of divine Scriptures, not in the additions and accretions of papal decrees and pronouncements. If the divine law is open to different interpretations, such interpretations may be made only by the general council of the believers, and "no partial group or particular individual, whatever his status, has the authority to make such definitions." Marsilio's insistence on the return to the Scriptures as the sole source of religious faith and divine law, his ruthless demolition of the edifice of dogma and power built up by the church over centuries of institutional growth, is one of the early winds that finally gathered in the hurricane of the Protestant Reformation.

Despite his intense concern with church problems, Marsilio is essentially skeptical in matters of faith and religion. His doctrine leads, not to the Protestant state of Luther or Calvin, but to the secular, national, lay state of Machiavelli. Unlike Dante, whose political conceptions centered on the typically medieval image of universal empire, Marsilio shows no great interest in the issue of world government. He briefly notes that mankind is divided into different societies with diverse languages, religions, manners, and customs, and that—in the light of the needs of his time—separate governments suffice for the quiet living together of men in this world. When the conception of the secular national state as the largest sovereign unit displaced the idea of universal papal and imperial authority, the Middle Ages came to a close.

MARSILIO OF PADUA

The Defender of Peace*

FORMS OF GOVERNMENT

There are two genera of ruling parts or governments, one well-tempered, the other diseased. With Aristotle in the *Politics,* Book III, Chapter 5, I call that genus *well-tempered* in which the ruler governs for the common benefit, in accordance with the will of the subjects; while the *diseased* genus is that which is deficient in this respect. Each of these genera, again, is divided into three species: the temperate into kingly monarchy, aristocracy, and polity; the diseased into the three opposite species of tyrannical monarchy, oligarchy, and democracy. And each of these again has subspecies, the detailed discussion of which is not part of our present task.

To obtain a fuller conception of these species of government, which is necessary for the clear understanding of what follows, let us define each species in accordance with the view of Aristotle. A *kingly monarchy* then, is a temperate government wherein there is a single ruler who aims at the common benefit, and in accordance with the will or consent of the subjects. *Tyranny,* its opposite, is a diseased government wherein there is a single ruler who aims at his own benefit apart from the will of his subjects. *Aristocracy* is a temperate government in which the honorable class [*honorabilitas*] alone rules in accordance with the will or consent of the subjects and for the common benefit. *Oligarchy,* its opposite, is a diseased government in which some of the wealthier or more powerful rule for their own benefit apart from the will of the subjects. A *polity,* although in

one sense it is something common to every genus or species of regime or government, means in another sense a certain species of temperate government, in which every citizen participates in some way in the government or in the deliberative function in turn according to his rank and ability or condition, for the common benefit and with the will or consent of the citizens. *Democracy,* its opposite, is a government in which the masses [*vulgus*] or the multitude of the needy establish the government and rule alone, apart from the will or consent of the other citizens and not entirely for the common benefit according to proper proportion.

As to which of the temperate governments is best or which of the diseased governments is worst, and the relative goodness or badness of the other species, the discussion of these points is not part of our present concern. Let it suffice to have said this much about the division of governments into their species and the definition of each.

To make clearer these concepts of Aristotle, and to summarize all the methods of establishing the other kinds of government, we shall say that every government is over either voluntary or involuntary subjects. The first is the genus of well-tempered governments, the second of diseased governments. Each of these genera is divided into three species or kinds. And since one of the species of well-tempered government, and perhaps the more perfect, is kingly monarchy, let us resume our previous statements about its various kinds or methods, by saying that the king or monarch either is named by the election of the inhabitants or citizens, or duly obtains the rulership without their election. If without the election of the

* From Marsilio of Padua, *The Defender of Peace* (1324; trans. Alan Gewirth, Columbia University Press, 1952). By permission.

citizens, this is either because he or his ancestors first inhabited the region, or because he bought the land and jurisdiction, or
acquired it by a just war, or by some other
lawful method, such as by gift made to him
for some great service. Each of these kinds
of monarchy participates so much the more
in true kingship, the more it is over voluntary subjects and according to law made for
the common benefit of the subjects; and it
savors so much the more of tyranny the
more it departs from these features, i.e., the
consent of the subjects and law established
for their common benefit. Hence it is written in the *Politics*, Book IV, Chapter 8:
"These monarchies were kingly because
they were according to law, and ruled voluntary subjects; but they were tyrannical because they ruled despotically and in
accordance with their [i.e., the monarchs']
own judgment." These two features, then,
distinguish temperate from diseased government, as is apparent from the clear statement of Aristotle, but absolutely or in
greater degree it is the consent of the subjects which is the distinguishing criterion.
Now if the ruling monarch is elected by the
inhabitants, it is either with all his posterity
succeeding him or not. If the latter, this may
be in several ways, as be named either for
his own lifetime alone, or for his own lifetime and that of one or more of his successors, or not for the whole lifetime either of
himself or of any of his successors but only
for some determinate period, such as one or
two years, more or less. Again, he is named
to exercise either every judicial office, or
only one office such as leading the army.

The elected and the non-elected kingly
monarchs agree in that each rules voluntary
subjects. They differ, however, in that the
non-elected kings rule less voluntary subjects, and by laws which are less politic for
the common benefit, as we said before in the
case of the barbarians. The elected kings,
on the other hand, rule more willing subjects, and by laws which are more politic, in
that they are made for the common benefit.

From these considerations it is clear, and
will be even more apparent in the sequel,
that the elected kind of government is superior to the non-elected. This is also the view
of Aristotle in that passage of the *Politics*,
Book III, Chapter 8, which we cited above
with reference to those who were made

rulers in the heroic days. Again, this method
of establishing governments is more permanent in perfect communities. For at some
time or other it becomes necessary to have
recourse to this from among all the other
methods of establishing governments, but
not conversely. For example, if hereditary
succession fails, or if for some reason the
multitude cannot bear the excessive malice
of that family's rule, they must then turn to
the method of election, which can never fail
so long as the generation of men does not
fail. Moreover, by the method of election
alone is the best ruler obtained. For it is expedient that the ruler be the best man in the
polity, since he must regulate the civil acts
of all the rest.

The method of establishing the other
species of temperate government is usually
election; in some cases the ruler is chosen
by lot, without subsequent hereditary succession. Diseased governments, on the other
hand, are usually established by fraud or
force or both.

AUTHORITY BASED
ON ELECTION

We must next discuss that efficient cause of
the laws which is capable of being demonstrated. For I do not intend to deal here with
that method of establishing laws which can
be effected by the immediate act or oracle
of God apart from the human will, or which
has been so effected in the past. It was by
this method, as we have said, that the Mo-
saic law was established; but I shall not deal
with it here even insofar as it contains commands with regard to civil acts for the status of the present world. I shall discuss the
establishment of only those laws and governments which emerge immediately from
the decision of the human mind.

Let us say, to begin with, that it can pertain to any citizen to discover the law taken
materially and in its third sense, as the
science of civil justice and benefit. Such inquiry, however, can be carried on more
appropriately and be completed better by
those men who are able to have leisure, who
are older and experienced in practical affairs, and who are called "prudent men,"
than by the mechanics who must bend all
their efforts to acquiring the necessities of
life. But it must be remembered that the true

knowledge or discovery of the just and the beneficial, and of their opposites, is not law taken in its last and most proper sense, whereby it is the measure of human civil acts, unless there is given a coercive command as to its observance, or it is made by way of such a command, by someone through whose authority its transgressors must and can be punished. Hence, we must now say who has the authority to make such a command and to punish its transgressors. This, indeed, is to inquire into the legislator or the maker of the law.

Let us say, then, in accordance with the truth and the counsel of Aristotle in the *Politics,* Book III, Chapter 6, that the legislator, or the primary and proper efficient cause of the law, is the people or the whole body of citizens, or the weightier part thereof, through its election or will expressed by words in the general assembly of the citizens, commanding or determining that something be done or omitted with regard to civil human acts under threat of temporal punishment. By the *weightier part* I mean to take into consideration the quantity and the quality of the persons in that community over which the law is made. The aforesaid whole body of citizens or the weightier part thereof is the legislator regardless of whether it makes the law directly by itself or entrusts the making of it to some person or persons, who are not and cannot be the legislator in the absolute sense, but only in a relative sense and for a particular time and in accordance with the authority of the primary legislator. And I say further that the laws and anything else established through election must receive their necessary approval by that same primary authority and no other, whatever be the case with regard to certain ceremonies or solemnities, which are required not for the being of the matters elected but for their well-being, since the election would be no less valid even if these ceremonies were not performed. Moreover, by the same authority must the laws and other things established through election undergo addition, subtraction, complete change, interpretation, or suspension, insofar as the exigencies of time or place or other circumstances make any such action opportune for the common benefit. And by the same authority, also, must the laws be promulgated or proclaimed after their enactment, so that no citizen or foreigner who is delinquent in observing them may be excused because of ignorance.

A citizen I define in accordance with Aristotle in the *Politics,* Book III, Chapters 1, 3, and 7, as one who participates in the civil community in the government or the deliberative or judicial function according to his rank. By this definition, children, slaves, foreigners, and women are distinguished from citizens, although in different ways. For the sons of citizens are citizens in proximate potentiality, lacking only in years. The weightier part of the citizens should be viewed in accordance with the honorable custom of politics or else should be determined in accordance with the doctrine of Aristotle in the *Politics,* Book VI, Chapter 2.

Having thus defined the citizen and the weightier part of the citizens, let us return to our proposed objective, namely, to demonstrate that the human authority to make laws belongs only to the whole body of the citizens or to the weightier part thereof. Our first proof is as follows. The absolutely primary human authority to make or establish human laws belongs only to those men from whom alone the best laws can emerge. But these are the whole body of the citizens, or the weightier part thereof, which represents that whole body; since it is difficult or impossible for all persons to agree upon one decision, because some men have a deformed nature, disagreeing with the common decision through singular malice or ignorance. The common benefit should not, however, be impeded or neglected because of the unreasonable protest or opposition of these men. The authority to make or establish laws, therefore, belongs only to the whole body of the citizens or to the weightier part thereof.

The first proposition of this demonstration is very nearly self-evident, although its force and its ultimate certainty can be grasped from what has been said earlier. The second proposition, that is, that the best law is made only through the hearing and command of the entire multitude, I prove by assuming with Aristotle in the *Politics,* Book III, Chapter 7, that the best law is that which is made for the common benefit of the citizens. As Aristotle said: "That is presumably right [i.e., in the laws] which is for the common benefit of the state and the citizens."

But that this is best achieved only by the whole body of the citizens or by the weightier part thereof, which is assumed to be the same thing, I show as follows: that at which the entire body of the citizens aims intellectually and emotionally is more certainly judged as to its truth and more diligently considered as to its common utility. For a defect in some proposed law can be better noted by the greater number than by any part thereof, since every whole, or at least every corporeal whole, is greater in mass and in virtue than any part of it taken separately. Moreover, the common utility of a law is better considered by the entire multitude, because no one knowingly harms himself. Anyone can look to see whether a proposed law leans toward the benefit of one or a few persons more than of the others or of the community, and can protest against it. Such, however, would not be the case were the law made by one or a few persons, considering their own private benefit rather than that of the community.

Another argument to the principal conclusion is as follows. The authority to make the law belongs only to those men whose making of it will cause the law to be better observed or observed at all. Only the whole body of the citizens are such men. To them, therefore, belongs the authority to make the law. The first proposition of this demonstration is very nearly self-evident, for a law would be useless unless it were observed. Hence Aristotle said in the *Politics,* Book IV, Chapter 6: "Laws are not well ordered when they are well made but not obeyed." He also said in Book VI, Chapter 5: "Nothing is accomplished by forming opinions about justice and not carrying them into effect." The second proposition I prove as follows. That law is better observed by every citizen which each one seems to have imposed upon himself. But such is the law which is made through the hearing and command of the entire multitude of the citizens. The first proposition of this prosyllogism is almost self-evident: "for since the state is a community of free men," as is written in the *Politics,* Book III, Chapter 4, every citizen must be free, and not undergo someone else's despotism, i.e., slavish dominion. But this would not be the case if one or a few of the citizens by their own authority made the law over the whole body of citizens. For

those who thus made the law would be despots over the others, and hence such a law, however good it was, would be endured only with reluctance, or not at all, by the rest of the citizens, the more ample part. Having suffered contempt, they would protest against it, and not having been called upon to make it, they would not observe it. On the other hand, a law made by the hearing or consent of the whole multitude, even though it were less useful, would be willingly observed and endured by every one of the citizens, because then each would seem to have set the law upon himself, and hence would have no protest against it, but would rather tolerate it with equanimity. The second proposition of the first syllogism I also prove in this way: the power to cause the law to be observed belongs only to those men to whom belongs coercive force over the transgressors of the law. But these men are the whole body of citizens, or the weightier part thereof. Therefore, to them alone belongs the authority to make the law.

The principal conclusion is also proved in this way. That practical matter whose proper establishment is of greatest importance for the common sufficiency of the citizens in this life, and whose poor establishment threatens harm for the community, must be established by the whole body of the citizens. But such a matter is the law. Therefore, the establishment of the law pertains to the whole body of the citizens. The major proposition of this demonstration is almost self-evident. For men came together to the civil community in order to attain what was beneficial for sufficiency of life, and to avoid the opposite. Those matters, therefore, which can affect the benefit and harm of all ought to be known and heard by all, in order that they may attain the beneficial and repel the opposite. Such matters are the laws, as was assumed in the minor proposition. For in the laws being rightly made consists a large part of the whole common sufficiency of men, whereas under bad laws there arise unbearable slavery, oppression, and misery of the citizens, the final result of which is that the state is destroyed.

Again, and this is an abbreviation and summary of the previous demonstrations: the authority to make laws belongs only to the whole body of the citizens, as we have said, or else it belongs to one or a few men. But it cannot belong to one man alone, for through ignorance or malice or both, this one man could make a bad law, looking more to his own private benefit than to that of the community, so that the law would be tyrannical. For the same reason, the authority to make laws cannot belong to a few; for they too could sin, as before, in making the law for the benefit of a certain few and not for the common benefit, as can be seen in oligarchies. The authority to make the laws belongs, therefore, to the whole body of citizens or to the weightier part thereof, for precisely the opposite reason. For since all the citizens must be measured by the law in due proportion, and no one knowingly harms or wishes injustice to himself, it follows that all or most wish a law conducing to the common benefit of the citizens.

From these same demonstrations it can also be proved, merely by changing the minor term, that the approval, interpretation, and suspension of the laws pertain to the authority of the legislator alone. And the same must be thought of everything else which is established by election. For the authority to approve or disapprove rests with those who have the primary authority to elect, or with those to whom they have granted this authority of election. For otherwise, if the part could dissolve, by its own authority, what had been established by the whole, the part would be greater than the whole, or at least equal to it.

IS THE MULTITUDE
FIT TO RULE?

Objections will be made to our above statements, to the effect that the authority to make or establish laws does not belong to the whole body of the citizens. The first objection is that those who are vicious and undiscerning in most cases should not make the law. For these two sins, malice and ignorance, must be excluded from the legislator, and it was to avoid them in civil judgments that we upheld the necessity of law. But the people or the whole body of citizens have these sins; for men in most cases seem to be vicious and stupid: "The number of the stupid is infinite," as is said in the first chapter of *Ecclesiastes.* Another objection is that it is very difficult, or impossible, to harmonize

the views of many vicious and unintelligent persons; but such is not the case with the few and virtuous. It is more useful, therefore, that the law be made by the few than by the whole body of the citizens or the overwhelming majority of them. Again, in every civil community the wise and learned are few in comparison with the multitude of the unlearned. Since, therefore, the law is more usefully made by the wise and learned than by the unlearned and uncultivated, it seems that the authority to make laws belongs to the few, not to the many or to all. Furthermore, that which can be done by fewer persons is needlessly done by more. Since, therefore, the law can be made by the wise, who are few, as has been said, the entire multitude or the greater part of it would needlessly be occupied therein. The authority to make laws does not belong, therefore, to the whole body of the citizens or the weightier part thereof.

As for the first objection, that the authority to make laws does not belong to those who in most cases are vicious and undiscerning, this we grant. But when it is added that the whole body of citizens is such, this must be denied. For most of the citizens are neither vicious nor undiscerning most of the time; all or most of them are of sound mind and reason and have a right desire for the polity and for the things necessary for it to endure, like laws and other statutes or customs. For although not every citizen nor the greater number of the citizens be discoverers of the laws, yet every citizen can judge of what has been discovered and proposed to him by someone else, and can discern what must be added, subtracted, or changed. Hence in the major premiss' reference to the *undiscerning,* if what is meant is that those who cannot, in most of their parts or members, discover the law by themselves, ought not to establish the law, this must be denied as manifestly false, as is borne out by sense induction and by Aristotle in the *Politics,* Book III, Chapter 6. By induction we can see that many men judge rightly about the quality of a picture, a house, a ship, and other works of art, even though they would have been unable to discover or produce them. Aristotle also attests to this in the place just cited, answering the proposed objection with these words: "About some things the man who made them is not the only or the best judge." He proves this in many species of arts, and indicates that the same is true for all the others.

Nor is this position invalidated by those who say that *the wise who are few can discern what should be enacted with regard to practical matters better than can the rest of the multitude.* For even if this be true, it still does not follow that the wise can discern what should be enacted better than can the whole multitude, in which the wise are included together with the less learned. For *every whole is greater than its part* both in acting and in discerning.

The second objection carries little weight, for even though it be easier to harmonize the views of fewer persons than of many, it does not follow that the views of the few, or of the part, are superior to those of the whole multitude, of which the few are a part. For the few would not discern or wish the common benefit equally as well as would the entire multitude of the citizens. Indeed, it would be insecure, as we have already shown, to entrust lawmaking to the will of the few. For they would consult therein their own private benefit, as individuals or as a group, rather than the common benefit.

The third objection can be easily refuted from what we have already said: for although the laws can be better made by the wise than by the less learned, it is not therefore to be concluded that they are better made by the wise alone than by the entire multitude of citizens, in which the wise are included. For the assembled multitude of all of these can better discern and desire the common justice and benefit than any part of it taken separately, however prudent that part may be.

Hence those do not speak the truth who hold that the less learned multitude hinders the election and approval of the true or common good; rather, the multitude is of help in this function when it is joined to those who are more learned and more experienced. For although the multitude cannot by itself discover true and useful measures, it can nevertheless discern and judge the measures discovered and proposed to it by others, as to whether they should be added to, or subtracted from, or completely changed, or re-jected. For many things which a man would have been unable to initiate or discover by himself, he can comprehend and bring to completion after they have been explained to him by someone else.

It is hence appropriate and highly useful that the whole body of citizens entrust to those who are prudent and experienced the investigation, discovery, and examination of the standards, the future laws or statutes, bearing upon civil justice and benefit, common difficulties or burdens, and other similar matters. Either some of these prudent and experienced men may be elected by each of the primary parts of the state, according to the proportion of each part; or else all these men may be elected by all the citizens assembled together. And this will be an appropriate and useful method whereby to come together to discover the laws without detriment to the rest of the multitude, i.e., the less learned, who would be of little help in the investigation of such standards, and would be disturbed in their performance of the other functions necessary both to themselves and to others, which would be troublesome both to each individual and to the community.

After such standards, the future laws, have been discovered and diligently examined, they must be laid before the assembled whole body of citizens for their approval or disapproval, so that if any citizen thinks that something should be added, subtracted, changed, or completely rejected, he can say so, since in this way the law will be more usefully ordained. For as we have said, the less learned citizens can sometimes perceive something which must be corrected in a proposed law even though they could not have discovered the law itself. Also, the laws thus made by the hearing and consent of the entire multitude will be better observed, nor will anyone have any protest to make against them.

These standards, the future laws, will thus have been made public, and in the general assembly of the citizens those citizens will have been heard who have wanted to make some reasonable statements with regard to them. Then there must again be elected men of the qualities and by the method indicated above, or else the aforesaid men must be confirmed; and they, representing the position and authority of the whole body of the citizens, will approve or disapprove in whole or in part the aforementioned standards which had been investigated and proposed, or else, if it so wishes, the whole body of the citizens or the weightier part thereof will do this same thing. After this approval, the aforesaid standards are laws and deserve to be so called, not before; and after their publication or proclamation, they alone among human commands make transgressors liable to civil guilt and punishment.

We think we have adequately shown, then, that the authority to make or establish laws, and to give a command with regard to their observance, belongs only to the whole body of the citizens or to the weightier part thereof as efficient cause, or else to the person or persons to whom the aforesaid whole body has granted this authority.

THE ACCOUNTABILITY OF RULERS

We have previously stated that it pertains to the legislator to correct governments or to change them completely, just as to establish them. In this connection, someone may well wonder whether it is expedient that rulers be corrected by coercive judgment and force; and if it is exepdient, whether they should be corrected for every kind of excess, or only for some and not for others; also who should make such judgments against the rulers, and execute them by coercive force—for it was said above that it pertains to the rulers alone to issue civil sentences and to punish transgressors of the laws by coercive force.

Let us say that the ruler through his action in accordance with the law and the authority given to him is the standard and measure of every civil act, like the heart in an animal. Now if the ruler received no other form beside the law, and the authority and the desire to act in accordance with it, he would never perform any action which was wrong or corrigible or measurable by someone else. And therefore he and his action would be the measure of every civil act of men other than himself, in such manner that he would never be measured by others, like the well-formed heart in an animal. For since the heart receives no form that inclines it to an action contrary to the action

which has to emerge from its natural virtue and heat, it always does naturally the appropriate action and never the contrary. Hence it regulates and measures, through its influence or action, the other parts of the animal, in such manner that it is not regulated by them nor does it receive any influence from them.

But since the ruler is a human being, he has understanding and desire, which may receive other forms, like false opinion or perverted desire or both, as a result of which he comes to do the contraries of the things determined by the law. Because of these actions, the ruler is rendered measurable by someone else who has the authority to measure or regulate him, or his unlawful actions, in accordance with the law. For otherwise every government would become despotic, and the life of the citizens servile and insufficient. This is an evil to be avoided.

Now the judgment, command, and execution of any correction of the ruler, in accordance with his demerit or transgression, must be done by the legislator, or by a person or persons appointed for this purpose by the authority of the legislator. And it is well to suspend for some time the office of the ruler who is to be corrected, especially in relation to the person or persons who must judge of his transgression, because otherwise there would then be a plurality of governments in the community, from which would result schism, agitation, and fighting; and also because he is corrected not as a ruler but as a subject who has transgressed the law.

Coming now to the questions which were raised above, let us say that the ruler's excess is either grave or slight; it may occur frequently or only rarely; and, it is among the things determined by law or it is not. If the ruler's excess be grave, such as against the commonwealth or against a notable or any other person, from failure to correct which there could likely arise scandal or agitation among the people, then whether the excess be one which occurs frequently or rarely, the ruler must be corrected for it. For if the excess is not avenged, agitation might arise among the people, and upheaval and destruction of the polity. If the excess is determined by law, it must be corrected according to the law; but if not, then it must be corrected according to the sentence of the legislator; and it must be determined by law as much as possible.

If the ruler's excess be small, then its occurrence and its commission by the ruler may be either rare or frequent. If it is rarely committed or rarely capable of being committed by the ruler, then it must be allowed to pass and be glossed over rather than having the ruler corrected for it. For if the ruler is corrected for every small and infrequent excess, he will be made an object of contempt; which will result in no slight harm to the community, since the citizens then exhibit less respect and obedience for the law and the ruler. Again, since the ruler is unwilling to undergo correction for every slight offense, because he will regard this as bringing him into low repute, there will be a possibility of grave scandal. But such a condition must not be stirred up in communities when no evident utility can emerge therefrom, but rather harm.

Such was clearly the view of Aristotle on this question, in the *Politics,* Book II, Chapter 4, where he said: "It is manifest that some errors of both legislators and rulers should be allowed to pass. For he will do less good by making changes than he will do harm by becoming accustomed to rebelling against the rulers." By *legislator* Aristotle meant an established law; and he says that if men have become accustomed to observing it, then it must not be changed in order to make a slight correction in it, but must rather be allowed to pass. For frequent changing of the laws saps their strength, which is the custom of obeying and observing what the laws command. As Aristotle said in the same book and chapter: "The law has no power for persuasion except that of custom," *i.e.,* for the law to be observed by the subjects, the most important factor is custom. And the case is very similar with regard to respecting and obeying the ruler.

But if the ruler's excess, while slight in extent, be capable of frequent occurrence, then it must be determined by law, and the ruler who frequently commits the offense must be given the appropriate punishment. For an offense, however slight, would be of notable harm to the polity if it were frequently committed, just as small expenses frequently incurred consume a fortune, *i.e.,* in riches. "For the whole sum is not small,

although it is made up of small sums" as is written in the *Politics,* Book V, Chapter 4.

Such then are our conclusions concerning the correction of rulers, by whom it should be done, and for what reasons.

THE CHURCH AND COERCIVE AUTHORITY

In this way, then, have the Roman bishops entered upon these affairs: First, under the guise of seeking peace among the Christian believers, they have excommunicated certain men who are unwilling to obey their decree. Then they impose on them penalties both real and personal, more harshly against those who are less able to resist their power, such as communities and individuals among the Italians, whose state, divided and wounded in almost all its parts, can more easily be oppressed, but more mildly against those, like kings and rulers, whose resistance and coercive power they fear. On these latter, however, they are gradually creeping up in the attempt to usurp their jurisdictions, not daring to invade them all at once. Hence their stealthy double-dealing has hitherto been concealed even from the Roman rulers and the peoples subject to them. For the Roman bishops have gradually seized one jurisdiction after another, especially when the imperial seat was vacant; so that now they finally say that they have total coercive temporal jurisdiction over the Roman ruler. Most recently and most obviously, the present bishop has written that he has supreme jurisdiction over the ruler of the Romans, both in the Italian and the German provinces, and also over all the lesser rulers, communities, groups, and individuals of the aforesaid provinces, of whatever dignity and condition they may be, and over all their fiefs and other temporalities. This bishop openly ascribes to himself the power to give and transfer their governments, as all can clearly see from certain writings of this bishop, which he calls *edicts* or *sentences.*

This wrong opinion of certain Roman bishops, and also perhaps their perverted desire for rulership, which they assert is owed to them because of the plenitude of power given to them, as they say, by Christ—this is that singular cause which we have said produces the intranquillity or discord of the city or state. For it is prone to creep up on all

states, as was said in our introductory remarks, and by its hateful action it has for a
long time distressed the Italian state, and has
kept and still keeps it from tranquillity or
peace, by preventing with all its force the appointment or institution of the ruler, the
Roman emperor, and his functioning in the
said empire. From lack of this function,
which is the just regulation of civil acts,
there readily emerge injuries and contentions, and these, if not measured by the standard of justice or law because of the absence
of the measurer, cause battles, whence there
have resulted the separation of the citizens
and finally the destruction of the Italian
polities or cities, as we have said. With this
opinion, therefore, and perhaps also with
what we have called a desire for ruling, the
Roman bishop strives to make the Roman
ruler subject to him in coercive or temporal
jurisdiction, whereas that ruler neither
rightly ought to be, nor wishes to be subject
to him in such judgment. From this there has
arisen so much strife and discord that it cannot be extinguished without great effort of
souls and bodies and expenditure of wealth.
For the office of coercive rulership over any
individual, of whatever condition he may be,
or over any community or group, does not
belong to the Roman or any other bishop,
priest, or spiritual minister, as such.

PART II

Sixteenth through Eighteenth Centuries

CHAPTER FOURTEEN

MACHIAVELLI

Only in fifth-century Athens has the world seen the dazzling artistic brilliance and intellectual vitality that characterized the Renaissance. The rebirth and rediscovery of antiquity were both cause and effect: on the one hand, the Renaissance helped to revive the rational, this-worldly, secular, scientific spirit that had lain dormant through many centuries of medieval encasement; on the other hand, the Renaissance was itself the effect of man's growing restlessness as well as of changing social and technological conditions. In particular, printing destroyed the monopoly of knowledge that the clergy had enjoyed for a thousand years, and gunpowder destroyed the military monopoly of the nobility. Like travelers who return from their journey with their prejudices confirmed and strengthened, the men of the Renaissance, in traveling to the remote centuries of classical Greece and Rome, found what they looked for—an exciting world, the image of which had guided them on their voyage.

The most important discovery of the Renaissance—more significant than any single work of art or any one genius—was the *discovery of man*. In antiquity the sense of tribal kinship had not favored the growth of individualism, of isolation from the community. Stoicism and Christianity had been the first to contribute new and lasting elements to a conception of individuality: Stoicism, by stressing the idea of moral selfhood and responsibility, and Christianity, by insisting that man's innermost reality, his soul, was outside the sphere and jurisdiction of mundane authority, and that his salvation depended ultimately on his own decisions, his own works. But the social system of the Middle Ages, built on status and custom, discouraged the mobility and change that favor individualistic attitudes; it emphasized instead the class or group to which a person belonged. The Renaissance goes beyond the moral selfhood of Stoicism, the spiritual uniqueness of Christianity, the aesthetic individuality of the ancient Greeks, and views man in his totality, in his flesh and blood as well as in his mind and spirit—man in relation to himself, to society, to the world. Displacing God, *man* becomes the *center of the universe;* the values of this new solar system are inevitably different from those of the God-centered universe.

The Renaissance was the confluence of many streams and tributaries, yet the Italian share was predominant from beginning to end. Italy had never lost living contacts with its ancient past: The country was full of splendid cities founded in antiquity, it abounded in relics and monuments of past glories, and the language was still the language (with some minor changes) of Caesar and Cicero. The dead hand of uniformity had never lain as heavily on Italy as on other European countries in the Middle Ages, and the feudal system never permeated it as it did, for example, France, England, and Germany. Italy remained the only major area in which a vigorous communal life had weathered the storms of wars and invasions, and its city-states were for a long time islands of individualistic republicanism in a sea of European monarchical loyalties. The virtual destruction of the German empire as a world power by the papacy in the thirteenth century, and the later enslavement of the papacy to the French monarchy in the fourteenth century, gave the independent Italian city-states new opportunities for self-affirmation and increased self-confidence. Leadership in international trade, business, and finance made numerous Italian cities wealthy and prosperous, and provided the economic means for the literary, artistic, and scholarly activities of a new elite.

Among the centers of the Renaissance, Florence was always first, reaching its climax in Leonardo da Vinci (1452–1519), who most perfectly represented, and lived, the Renaissance ideal of *universal man,* creative in painting and the arts, inventive in science and engineering, and accomplished in philosophy and letters. In the study of politics, the New Learning finds its clearest expression in Niccolò Machiavelli (1469–1527).

At the age of twenty-nine Machiavelli entered the public service of his city, and there he remained for fourteen years. Although not employed on the highest levels of policy making, he was close enough to the inner circles of the administration to acquire first-hand knowledge of the mechanics of politics. Florence was at that time an independent republic, and Machiavelli was frequently sent on diplomatic missions to other Italian states and to great foreign powers like France and Germany. In 1512 he lost his job when the republican government, based on French support, was replaced by the absolutist regime of the Medici, who had been restored to power with papal help. Machiavelli was accused of serious crimes and tortured, but he was found innocent and banished to his small farm near Florence.

It was in such enforced leisure that he wrote *The Prince* (1513). The book was dedicated to Lorenzo di Medici, and Machiavelli fulsomely praised the dynasty that stood for the exact opposite of his erstwhile republican sentiments. He even hoped to have his political conversion rewarded by an opportunity to serve the new antirepublican regime, but in this expectation he failed. The further imposed idleness gave him enough time to work on his most elaborate political book, *The Discourses on the First Ten Books of Titus Livius* (1521). Taking Roman history as a starting point, *The Discourses* attempts to dissect the anatomy of the body politic, and on a much more philosophical and historical foundation than that of *The Prince. The Discourses* is interesting because Machiavelli affirms in it his republican sentiment; yet this personal preference does not alter his basic views on the process of politics, regardless of the form of its constitution, republican or despotic.

For all its breadth and elaborateness, and frequent depth and penetration, *The Discourses* is of interest primarily to students of political philosophy, whereas *The Prince,* pithy, shocking, persuasive, provocative, hard-hitting, is destined to remain one of the half-dozen political writings that have entered the general body of world literature. It is a reflection not only of man's political ambitions and passions but of man himself. If Machiavelli had painted, in medieval fashion, the devils who inhabit hell, his impact would have been much less intense on his contemporaries and on posterity. What Machiavelli did, however, was to portray something worse, real human beings; the shock of recognition has created around his work an aura of mixed horror and fascination, and it is hard to tell what is the stronger.

The most revolutionary aspect of *The Prince* is not so much what it says as what it ignores. Before Machiavelli, all political writing—from Plato and Aristotle through the Middle Ages to the Renaissance—had one central question: the *end of the state.*

Political power was assumed to be a means only—a means in the service of higher ends, such as justice, the good life, freedom, or God. Machiavelli ignores the issue of the end of the state in extrapolitical (ethical, religious, cultural) terms. He assumes that *power* is *an end in itself,* and he confines his inquiries into the *means* that are best suited to *acquire, retain,* and *expand power.* Machiavelli thus separates power from morality, ethics, religion, and metaphysics, and sets up the *state* as an *autonomous system of values* independent of any other source.

If he follows the value system of the state, the statesman may violate other value systems, such as religion, ethics, or morality. Machiavelli thus develops the idea of the *reason of state,* under which many acts are permissive, even obligatory, that would be considered heinous crimes if judged in the court of religion or morality. Machiavelli does not assert that ethics and morality as such are inferior to the precepts of power, the reason of state; from a general, theoretical viewpoint, the canons of power and the tenets of morality are independent of each other. When it comes to practical collisions, it depends on who faces the alternatives. The moralist will recognize the supremacy of his moral code over competing systems of values. The ecclesiastic will not admit a rival to his religious code. Similarly, the statesman will be guided solely by the precepts of his code, whose end—the acquisition, retention, and expansion of power—is different from other codes, and whose means are therefore different, too.

In the actions of rulers "the end justifies the means. Let a prince therefore aim at conquering and maintaining the state, and the means will always be judged honourable and praised by every one." In *The Discourses,* Machiavelli defines the reason of state even more clearly: "For where the very safety of the country depends upon the resolution to be taken, no consideration of justice or injustice, humanity or cruelty, nor of glory or of shame, should be allowed to prevail. But putting all other considerations aside, the only question should be: What course will save the life and liberty of the country?"

Machiavelli never praises immorality for its own sake; his basic attitude is not one of nihilism: he neither assumes that there are no values in this world, nor wishes to create a world in which all values would be destroyed. Machiavelli is aware that civilization implies some sort of values. His *amorality* implies therefore, not the denial of moral values in all situations, but the affirmation that, in the specific situation of the statesman, the rules of power have priority over those of ethics and morality.

Machiavelli did not invent political murder, treachery, and fraud. But before his time such crimes were committed *de facto,* and no attempt was made to integrate them into a moral world of their own. The traditional reaction to political immorality had been either one of polite neglect, half-hearted excuse, or, at best, severe censure of individual violations of ethics and morality. The sanctity and inviolability of the moral code seemed, before Machiavelli, in no way impaired by the regrettable exceptions to the rule, regardless of how frequent they were. In Machiavelli, the traditional attitude of polite neglect and hypocritical, or sincere, regret is replaced by the positive affirmation that the reason of state is for the statesman the determining code of conduct, and that statecraft constitutes a value system of its own which is different from that of ethics and religion. What is evil from the viewpoint of morality and religion may therefore be good from the viewpoint of the reason of state, if it serves to acquire, retain, or expand power.

Good and *evil* are thus reduced from absolute to *relative* categories, and it depends on the basic assumption of a system of values whether a particular action is good or bad. If the basic assumption and objective of conduct is friendship, service, fellowship, justice, or God, the individual action will be judged good or bad to the extent that it agrees with, or deviates from, such assumptions and goals. If, as for the ruler, the basic assumption is power, the decision about whether a particular action is good or bad will depend on the extent to which it furthers the gain, retention, and growth of power. In this sense the use of poison may be called "good" if it does a good job in eliminating a political opponent, perhaps by acting slowly and imperceptibly so that the author of the crime cannot be easily detected. The attribution of "goodness" to poison in a specific case of political necessity does not imply a general justification for the use of poison. Assuming *power* as the *end of politics, goodness* thus *coincides with efficiency:* an efficient means of acquiring, consolidating, and expanding power is good; an inefficient means, bad.

Efficiency in politics is thus analogous to virtue in morals or religion, and inefficiency replaces the concept of sin. Machiavelli still uses the term "virtue" *(virtù),* but its meaning is different from, and even antithetical to, the Christian concept of virtue. As in so many other cases, Machiavelli—in typical Renaissance fashion—uses the term *virtù* in its original Roman meaning, and even adds some shades of meaning of his own. In classical, pre-Christian, Rome *virtus* (deriving from *vir,* man) meant "manliness," that is, military courage and intelligence combined with civic responsibility and personal integrity. In later Christian usage, "virtue" entirely lost its military connotation, and Christian virtue stood for humility and cheerful acceptance of suffering, and even female chastity, rather than for manly self-assertion. But even the classical Roman element of civic integrity in the concept of virtue was transformed by Christianity into religious and moral integrity, concerned above all with limitless faith in God and his commands rather than with the practice of political participation. Machiavelli goes back to the original pagan meaning of Roman virtue, but expands and adapts it to his thought and to the restless and violent world he lives in. Virtue for Machiavelli means *military valor,* and appropriately, therefore, the most comprehensive analysis of *virtù* is to be found in his *Art of War* (1521), although he frequently uses the concept in many of his other works, including *The Prince* and *The Discourses.*

Yet, as Machiavelli sees it, the quality of military valor is required in actual warfare as well as in extreme political crisis situations of acquiring, consolidating, and expanding of power, for in such conditions the boundary between conflict and peace, between chaos and stability is largely blurred. In such crisis situations, whether of actual warfare or of decisive political conflict, the concept of virtue implies the ability to understand reality and to adapt action to reality in a flexible and non-ideological, nondogmatic manner. This is the element of *prudence* in Machiavelli's concept of virtue, replacing the Roman quality of civic integrity and the Christian element of religious and moral loyalty in the pre-Renaissance and pre-Machiavellian meaning of virtue.

As in so many other areas of his thought, Machiavelli is more interested in means than in ends; in politics, for example, the end—the acquiring, consolidating, and expanding of power—is presumed to be naturally inherent in the ruler or would-be ruler, and need not be further argued. What captures Machiavelli's intellectual curiosity and literary imagination is the problem of technical skill of ruling, the ability of the leader to fight his way into political power by forcible or other means, coupled with the ability to "stay in business" and to expand his power. Consequently, when Machiavelli applies the term "virtue" *(virtù)* to the successful ruler, he means the ambitious, ruthless, crafty, successful ruler, and not the ruler who is a regular churchgoer, mindful of other men's wives, and generally a practicing moralist. In typical Renaissance style, Machiavelli even sees "grandeur" in elegant and magnificent crimes; this concept of an elegant or beautiful crime would have been unthinkable before a collapse of traditional standards of ethics.

Machiavelli's attitude to the Borgias is a revealing illustration of his more abstract concepts. Cardinal Rodrigo Borgia had four living children, three sons and one daughter, when he became pope in 1492 and assumed the name of Alexander VI. He appointed two of his sons as cardinals, and when he was away from Rome in 1501, he left his daughter, Lucrezia, in charge of the Vatican. Alexander VI had his personal hangman and poisoner. The latter, in particular, was constantly busy, and his victims included several cardinals. Alexander VI was one of the men whom Machiavelli most admired, and he writes of him as follows: "Alexander VI did nothing else but deceive men, he thought of nothing else, and found the occasion for it; no man was ever more able to give assurances, or affirmed things with stronger oaths, and no man observed them less; however, he always succeeded in his deceptions, as he well knew this aspect of things."

If Machiavelli admired Alexander VI, then he idolized his son, Caesar Borgia, Caesar assassinated his older brother and murdered the husband of his sister Lucrezia—hardly a typical family idyll of the Renaissance. The number of his other assassinations is legion, and his cruelty was matched only by his treachery and debauchery. Machiavelli knew Caesar Borgia personally and was fully aware of his criminal record. Yet it is generally believed that Caesar Borgia was Machiavelli's model in writing *The Prince;* certainly he is held up "as an example to be imitated by all who by fortune and with the arms of others have risen to power," and "one can find no better example than the actions of this man." Machiavelli had only one fault to find with Caesar Borgia: that he allowed, after the death of his father, Alexander VI, the election of Julian II as pope, because Julian was an enemy of the Borgias. What Machiavelli criticized in the career of his most admired hero was his one failure and not his life of crime.

Machiavelli's views on morals and religion illustrate his belief in the supremacy of power over other social values. He has no sense of religion as a deep personal experience, and the mystical element in religion—its supranatural and suprarational character—is alien to his outlook. Yet he has a positive attitude toward religion; albeit his *religion* becomes a *tool of influence and control* in the hands of the ruler over the ruled. Machiavelli sees in religion the poor man's reason, ethics, and morality put together, and "where religion exists it is easy to introduce armies and discipline." From his reading of history, however, Machiavelli is led to the generalization that "as the observance of divine institutions is the cause of the greatness of republics, so the disregard of them produces their ruin." The fear of the prince, Machiavelli adds, may temporarily supplant the fear of God, but the life of even an efficient ruler is short.

The role of religion as a mere instrument of political domination, cohesion, and unity becomes even clearer in Machiavelli's advice that the ruler support and spread religious doctrines and beliefs in miracles *that he knows to be false.* The main value of religion to the ruler lies in the fact that it helps him to keep the people "well conducted and united," and from this viewpoint of utility it makes no difference whether he spreads among them true or false religious ideas and beliefs.

Machiavelli's interest in Christianity is not philosophical or theological, but purely pragmatic and political. He is critical of Christianity because "it glorifies more the humble and contemplative men than the men of action," whereas the Roman pagan religion "deified only men who had achieved great glory, such as commanders of republics and chiefs of republics." Christianity idealizes, Machiavelli charges, "humility, lowliness, and a contempt for worldly objects," as contrasted with the pagan qualities of grandeur of soul, strength of body, and other qualities that "render men formidable." The only kind of strength that Christianity teaches is fortitude of soul in suffering; it does not teach the strength that goes into the achievement of great deeds.

Concerning the church, Machiavelli preferred two main charges. First, he states that the Italians have become "irreligious and bad" because of the "evil example of the court of Rome." The second and more serious accusation is that the church "has kept and still keeps our country divided." He goes on to say that the sole cause of Italian political disunity is the church. Having acquired jurisdiction over a considerable portion of Italy, "she has never had sufficient power or courage to enable her to make herself sole sovereign of all Italy." Though Machiavelli hated the papacy, he nevertheless would have been happy to see the papacy govern all Italy if her unity could not be attained by any other means. What Machiavelli primarily reproaches the papacy for is not its record of crime and iniquity but its political failure to rule the whole country.

The clue to Machiavelli is his *pessimism*. The pessimist sees mankind as essentially unchangeable, incapable of progressive improvability, and he denies that reason can cope with the hard and limiting facts of nature and history. By contrast, the optimist believes that man is improvable, that progress is possible, and that the chains of nature and history can be relaxed by the liberating and uplifting force of reason. Whereas the pessimist tends to look into the *past* and is primarily conscious of what *has* happened, the optimist looks into the *future* and wonders what *might* happen.

Machiavelli's pessimism is reflected in his conviction that moral considerations may be laudable in themselves (and in this he is less of a nihilist than the later nihilists and Machiavellians), but that the statesman cannot afford the luxury of practicing morality: "For how we live is so far removed from how we ought to live, that he who abandons what is done for what ought to be done, will rather learn to bring about his own ruin than his preservation." In the struggle between rulers, Machiavelli says, "There are two methods of fighting, the one by law, the other by force: the first method is that of men, the second of beasts; but as the first method is often insufficient, one must have recourse to the second. It is therefore necessary for a prince to know well how to use both the beast and the man."

Specifically, the *ruler must imitate the fox and the lion,* "for the lion cannot protect himself from the traps, and the fox cannot defend himself from wolves."

Should a ruler keep faith? This is Machiavelli's most famous question, and his answer to it is the best-known passage in *The Prince.* He admits that everybody knows how "laudable" it is for a ruler to keep faith. However, in the world of actual politics such laudable intentions may be irreconcilable with expediency and interest: "Therefore, a prudent ruler ought not to keep faith when by doing so it would be against his interest, and when the reasons which made him bind himself no longer exist. If men were all good, this precept would not be a good one; but as they are bad, and would not observe their faith with you, so you are not bound to keep faith with them."

Machiavelli thus takes a radically pessimistic view of human nature, and his psychological outlook is intimately related to his political philosophy. The theological conception of man's depravity, one of the central doctrines of the Reformation, must also have influenced Machiavelli and his contemporaries. Indeed, the political methods of the Renaissance were not known for their humanitarian mellowness. Death by poison and the silent dagger was a mere technical detail in the efficient execution of a political program, and there was little difference between kings and popes, princes and bishops. As a result, it was perhaps not unnatural for Machiavelli, as for many of his contemporaries, to take a dim view of human nature in general, and of human nature in the struggle for power in particular. Such skepticism easily developed into pessimism and outright cynicism.

Unlike later Machiavellians, Machiavelli himself was saved from extremism by prudence and moderation. In both *The Prince* and *The Discourses* there are numerous passages in which Machiavelli counsels rulers to be temperate, not to be uselessly cruel or arrogant, "for to incur hatred without any advantage is the greatest temerity and imprudence." The ruler should not use threats or insults, because neither diminishes the strength of the enemy but makes him only more cautious and disposed to hate. Machiavelli's rational skepticism, his horror of panaceas and cure-alls, his moderation and relativism, are apparent in his warning that no state should believe "that it can always follow a safe policy; rather let it think that all are doubtful. This is found in the nature of things, that one never tries to avoid one difficulty without running into another, but prudence consists in being able to know the nature of the difficulties, and taking the least harmful as good."

Machiavelli's sense of the complexity of human affairs, his realization that no policy can ever assure absolute safety, and his understanding that in practical politics the choice is often between a larger and a lesser evil rather than between evil and good—all these insights are intimately linked to the absence of ideological passion and fanaticism in his thought and feeling. What in some respects is the least satisfactory element in Machiavelli's thought—his scant concern for ends—is in other respects a source of strength which saves him from the excesses of ideological passion, in which hypocrisy easily mixes with cruelty. *Ideology* is essentially an *idea* (or ideas) *in the service of interest,* and to cover up this simple relation, ideologists rationalize, justify, obfuscate, and in extreme cases prevaricate and lie. Machiavelli's lack of commitment to ideological simplification and passionate abstraction is a built-in stabilizing and moderating force in his outlook. By contrast, this stabilizing element was lacking in some later self-styled Machiavellians who combined Machiavellian means with un-Machiavellian ends.

Machiavelli's fine *sense of the possible* makes his thought utilitarian, experimental, and relativistic. This basic quality—if not scientific in a strict sense—nevertheless partakes of one important aspect of science: empiricism, or the refusal to accept any solution as final.

Where Machiavelli is least scientific is where he thinks himself most scientific: in his belief that his analysis of power is based on solid facts of historical experience, that the record of man's behavior proves him a depraved and wily creature, and that a realistic theory of power must be based on such a pessimistic view of man. If Machiavelli's pessimism is the clue to his political philosophy, the weakness of his theory must be sought in his psychological conceptions. In detail a moderate, Machiavelli is an extremist when it comes to the whole. His doctrine of the badness of man is just as much an unscientific oversimplification as is the opposite extreme of the goodness of man. Man is somewhere between *angel and beast;* but Machiavelli says that the ruler is somewhere between *man and beast,* and that he "must know how to use both natures, and that the one without the other is not durable."

It would not be difficult to prove that human history has as much evidence of human goodness as of wickedness. It is a matter of ultimate—unprovable—personal philosophy of history whether one is more impressed by man's goodness than by his badness. But it is not sound philosophy of history, and still less is it sound science of politics, to reduce all history to one common denominator, be it goodness or badness.

Like other "realists" after him, Machiavelli identifies all too readily naked power politics with the whole of political reality, and he thus fails to grasp that ideas and ideals, if properly mobilized, can become potent facts, even decisive weapons, in the struggle for political survival. History is a vast graveyard filled with self-styled "realists" like Napoleon, Hitler, and Mussolini. They all underestimated the important imponderables in the equation of power and missed, in particular, the one component that in the end proved decisive: the will of man to be free, to put freedom above all other goods, even above life itself.

Machiavellian "realists" are usually realistic and rational in the choice of means with which they carry out their schemes of aggrandizement and expansion. But of what use is realism of means, if the ends themselves are utterly megalomaniac and unrealistic? Because Machiavelli was interested only in the means of acquiring, retaining, and expanding power, and not in the end of the state, he remained unaware of the *relations between means and ends*. Ends lead no existence apart from means but are continuously shaped by them. In the short run this inner connection may be concealed, but in the long run no great end can be accomplished by small means. The question, therefore, whether the political techniques and methods in *The Prince* are realistic even from the viewpoint of power cannot be separated from the still more basic issue of the end of power, inasmuch as the nature of the end determines the means most suited to it.

As one examines the references to rulers in *The Prince* more closely, one finds that Machiavelli was not interested in all forms of state, nor in all forms of power. What fascinated him above all was the *dynamics of illegitimate power;* he was little interested in states whose authority was legitimate, as in hereditary monarchies, but was primarily concerned with "new dominions both as to prince and state." He realized that "there is nothing more difficult to carry out, nor more doubtful of success, nor more dangerous to handle, than to initiate a new order of things." His primary concern with founders of new governments and states illuminates his attitude on the use of unethical means in politics. The "founders" of new states are, in effect, revolutionaries, and it is inevitable that in *reducing politics to war and revolution,* one arrives at an outlook in which the extraordinary becomes the ordinary, the abnormal the normal.

Because of his admiration for the outstanding man (and only outstanding men can successfully found "new dominions"), Machiavelli was little interested in the *institutional* framework of politics. He realized that in a period of institutional stability there is less need for the adventurer. In fact, as Machiavelli clearly sees, democrats hate war and revolution: The normal restraints and decencies are then imperiled by the necessity for sheer physical survival, and the habits of institutional stability are more easily subverted than in normal peacetime. The democratic theory of politics therefore tends to stress more the institutional framework of power than unique leader personalities, peace rather than war and revolution. Democrats have learned from long and painful experience that kindliness and decency flourish best in peaceful societies in which stable and just institutions make it difficult for lawless adventurers to thrive.

To the extent that democracies succeed in creating such societies, Machiavelli is wrong. To the extent that they fail, he is right. The ultimate commentary on *The Prince* is not in logic or morality, but in experience and history. Machiavelli laid bare the springs of human motivation with consummate and ruthless insight. It is hard to tell, in reading him, whether we shudder more when he tells the truth about human conduct, or more when he distorts the truth. He has, perhaps, rendered a service to humanity by pointing out the abysmal depth of demoralization and bestiality into which humans will sink for the sake of power. The twentieth century, in particular, has witnessed crimes of mass murder and genocide on a scale of which even Machiavelli, with all his interest in necessary, skillful, even elegant crimes, could never have dreamed. Our age is not one of facile optimism, and a balance will have to be struck between Machiavelli's pessimism about human nature and overconfident optimism, if an adequate approach to the theory and practice of politics is to be discovered.

MACHIAVELLI

*The Prince**

CONSTANT READINESS
FOR WAR

A prince should therefore have no other aim or thought, nor take up any other thing for his study, but war and its organisation and discipline, for that is the only art that is necessary to one who commands, and it is of such virtue that it not only maintains those who are born princes, but often enables men of private fortune to attain to that rank. And one sees, on the other hand, that when princes think more of luxury than of arms, they lose their state. The chief cause of the loss of states, is the contempt of this art, and the way to acquire them is to be well versed in the same.

Francesco Sforza, through being well armed, became, from private status, Duke of Milan; his sons, through wishing to avoid the fatigue and hardship of war, from dukes became private persons. For among other evils caused by being disarmed, it renders you contemptible; which is one of those disgraceful things which a prince must guard against, as will be explained later. Because there is no comparison whatever between an armed and a disarmed man, it is not reasonable to suppose that one who is armed will obey willingly one who is unarmed; or that any unarmed man will remain safe among armed servants. For one being disdainful and the other suspicious, it is not possible for them to act well together. And therefore a prince who is ignorant of military matters, besides the other misfortunes already mentioned, cannot be esteemed by his soldiers, nor have confidence in them.

He ought, therefore, never to let his thoughts stray from the exercise of war; and in peace he ought to practise it more than in war, which he can do in two ways: by action and by study. As to action, he must, besides keeping his men well disciplined and exercised, engage continually in hunting, and thus accustom his body to hardships; and meanwhile learn the nature of the land, how steep the mountains are, how the valleys debouch, where the plains lie, and understand the nature of rivers and swamps. To all this he should devote great attention. This knowledge is useful in two ways. In the first place, one learns to know one's country, and can the better see how to defend it. Then by means of the knowledge and experience gained in one locality, one can easily understand any other that it may be necessary to observe; for the hills and valleys, plains and rivers of Tuscany, for instance, have a certain resemblance to those of other provinces, so that from a knowledge of the country in one province one can easily arrive at a knowledge of others. And that prince who is lacking in this skill is wanting in the first essentials of a leader; for it is this which teaches how to find the enemy, take up quarters, lead armies, plan battles and lay siege to towns with advantage.

Philopœmen, prince of the Achaei, among other praises bestowed on him by writers, is lauded because in times of peace he thought of nothing but the methods of warfare, and when he was in the country with his friends, he often stopped and asked them: If the enemy were on that hill and we found ourselves here with our army, which of us would have the advantage? How could we safely approach him maintaining our order? If we wished to retire, what ought we to do?

---

*From Niccolò Machiavelli, *The Prince* (1513). Modern Library Edition. By permission of Random House, Inc.

If they retired, how should we follow them?
And he put before them as they went along
all the contingencies that might happen to an
army, heard their opinion, gave his own, fortifying it by argument; so that thanks to
these constant reflections there could never
happen any incident when actually leading
his armies for which he was not prepared.

But as to exercise for the mind, the prince
ought to read history and study the actions
of eminent men, see how they acted in warfare, examine the causes of their victories
and defeats in order to imitate the former
and avoid the latter, and above all, do as
some men have done in the past, who have
imitated some one, who has been much
praised and glorified, and have always kept
his deeds and actions before them, as they
say Alexander the Great imitated Achilles,
Cæsar Alexander, and Scipio Cyrus. And
whoever reads the life of Cyrus written by
Xenophon, will perceive in the life of Scipio
how gloriously he imitated the former, and
how, in chastity, affability, humanity, and
liberality Scipio conformed to those qualities of Cyrus as described by Xenophon.

A wise prince should follow similar
methods and never remain idle in peaceful
times, but industriously make good use of
them, so that when fortune changes she may
find him prepared to resist her blows, and to
prevail in adversity.

WHY PRINCES ARE PRAISED
OR BLAMED

It now remains to be seen what are the
methods and rules for a prince as regards
his subjects and friends. And as I know
that many have written of this, I fear that
my writing about it may be deemed presumptuous, differing as I do, especially in
this matter, from the opinions of others.
But my intention being to write something
of use to those who understand, it appears
to me more proper to go to the real truth of
the matter than to its imagination; and
many have imagined republics and principalities which have never been seen or
known to exist in reality; for how we live is
so far removed from bow we ought to live,
that he who abandons what is done for what
ought to be done, will rather learn to bring
about his own ruin than his preservation. A
man who wishes to make a profession of
goodness in everything must necessarily
come to grief among so many who are not
good. Therefore it is necessary for a prince,
who wishes to maintain himself, to learn
how not to be good, and to use this knowledge and not use it, according to the necessity of the case.

Leaving on one side, then, those things
which concern only an imaginary prince,
and speaking of those that are real, I state
that all men, and especially princes, who
are placed at a greater height, are reputed
for certain qualities which bring them
either praise or blame. Thus one is considered liberal, another *misero* or miserly
(using a Tuscan term, seeing that *avaro* with
us still means one who is rapaciously acquisitive and *misero* one who makes grudg-
ing use of his own); one a free giver, another
rapacious; one cruel, another merciful; one
a breaker of his word, another trustworthy;
one effeminate and pusillanimous, another
fierce and high-spirited; one humane, another haughty; one lascivious, another
chaste; one frank, another astute; one hard,
another easy; one serious, another frivolous;
one religious, another an unbeliever, and so
on. I know that every one will admit that it
would be highly praiseworthy in a prince to
possess all the above-named qualities that
are reputed good, but as they cannot all be
possessed or observed, human conditions
not permitting of it, it is necessary that he
should be prudent enough to avoid scandal
of those vices which would lose him the
state, and guard himself if possible against
those which will not lose it him, but if not
able to, he can indulge them with less scruple. And yet he must not mind incurring
the scandal of those vices, without which it
would be difficult to save the state, for if
one considers well, it will be found that
some things which seem virtues would, if
followed, lead to one's ruin, and some others which appear vices result in one's
greater security and well-being.

LIBERALITY
AND NIGGARDLINESS

Beginning now with the first qualities above
named, say that it would be well to be considered liberal; nevertheless liberality such
as the world understands it will injure you,
because if used virtuously and in the proper

way, it will not be known, and you will incur the disgrace of the contrary vice. But one who wishes to obtain the reputation of liberality among men, must not omit every kind of sumptuous display, and to such an extent that a prince of this character will consume by such means all his resources, and will be compelled, if he wishes to maintain his name for liberality, to impose heavy taxes on his people, become extortionate, and do everything possible to obtain money. This will make his subjects begin to hate him, and he will be little esteemed being poor, so that having by this liberality injured many and benefited but few, he will feel the first little disturbance and be endangered by every peril. If he recognises this and wishes to change his system, he incurs at once the charge of niggardliness.

A prince, therefore, not being able to exercise this virtue of liberality without risk if it be known, must not, if he be prudent, object to be called miserly. In course of time he will be thought more liberal, when it is seen that by his parsimony his revenue is sufficient, that he can defend himself against those who make war on him, and undertake enterprises without burdening his people, so that he is really liberal to all those from whom he does not take, who are infinite in number, and niggardly to all to whom he does not give, who are few. In our times we have seen nothing great done except by those who have been esteemed niggardly; the others have all been ruined. Pope Julius II, although he had made use of a reputation for liberality in order to attain the papacy, did not seek to retain it afterwards, so that he might be able to wage war. The present King of France has carried on so many wars without imposing an extraordinary tax, because his extra expenses were covered by the parsimony he had so long practised. The present King of Spain, if he had been thought liberal, would not have engaged in and been successful in so many enterprises.

For these reasons a prince must care little for the reputation of being a miser, if he wishes to avoid robbing his subjects, if he wishes to be able to defend himself, to avoid becoming poor and contemptible, and not to be forced to become rapacious; this niggardliness is one of those vices which enable him to reign. If it is said that Cæsar attained the empire through liberality, and that many others have reached the highest positions through being liberal or being thought so, I would reply that you are either a prince already or else on the way to become one. In the first case, this liberality is harmful; in the second, it is certainly necessary to be considered liberal. Cæsar was one of those who wished to attain the mastery over Rome, but if after attaining it he had lived and had not moderated his expenses, he would have destroyed that empire. And should any one reply that there have been many princes, who have done great things with their armies, who have been thought extremely liberal, I would answer by saying that the prince may either spend his own wealth and that of his subjects or the wealth of others. In the first case he must be sparing, but for the rest he must not neglect to be very liberal. The liberality is very necessary to a prince who marches with his armies, and lives by plunder, sack and ransom, and is dealing with the wealth of others, for without it he would not be followed by his soldiers. And you may be very generous indeed with what is not the property of yourself or your subjects, as were Cyrus, Cæsar, and Alexander, for spending the wealth of others will not diminish your reputation, but increase it, only spending your own resources will injure you. There is nothing which destroys itself so much as liberality, for by using it you lose the power of using it, and become either poor and despicable, or, to escape poverty, rapacious and hated. And of all things that a prince must guard against, the most important are being despicable or hated, and liberality will lead you to one or other of these conditions. It is, therefore, wiser to have the name of a miser, which produces disgrace without hatred, than to incur of necessity the name of being rapacious, which produces both disgrace and hatred.

CRUELTY AND CLEMENCY: IS IT BETTER TO BE LOVED OR FEARED?

Proceeding to the other qualities before named, I say that every prince must desire to be considered merciful and not cruel. He must, however, take care not to misuse this mercifulness. Cesare Borgia was considered cruel, but his cruelty had brought order to the Romagna, united it, and reduced it to peace and fealty. If this is considered well, it will be seen that he was really much more merciful than the Florentine people, who, to avoid the name of cruelty, allowed Pistoia to be destroyed. A prince, therefore, must not mind incurring the charge of cruelty for the purpose of keeping his subjects united and faithful; for, with a very few examples, he will be more merciful than those who, from excess of tenderness, allow disorders to arise, from whence spring bloodshed and rapine; for these as a rule injure the whole community, while the executions carried out by the prince injure only individuals. And of all princes, it is impossible for a new prince to escape the reputation of cruelty, new states being always full of dangers. Wherefore Virgil through the mouth of Dido says:

Res dura, et regni novitas me talia cogunt
Moliri, et late fines custode tueri.

Nevertheless, he must be cautious in believing and acting, and must not be afraid of his own shadow, and must proceed in a temperate manner with prudence and humanity, so that too much confidence does not render him incautious, and too much diffidence does not render him intolerant.

From this arises the question whether it is better to be loved more than feared, or feared more than loved. The reply is, that one ought to be both feared and loved, but as it is difficult for the two to go together, it is much safer to be feared than loved if one of the two has to be wanting. For it may be said of men in general that they are ungrateful, voluble, dissemblers, anxious to avoid danger, and covetous of gain; as long as you benefit them, they are entirely yours; they offer you their blood, their goods, their life, and their children, as I have before said, when the necessity is remote; but when it approaches, they revolt. And the prince who has relied solely on their words, without making other preparations, is ruined; for the friendship which is gained by, purchase and not through grandeur and nobility of spirit is bought but not secured, and in a pinch is not to be expended in your service. And men have less scruple in offending one who makes himself loved than one who makes

himself feared; for love is held by a chain of obligation which, men being selfish, is broken whenever it serves their purpose; but fear is maintained by a dread of punishment which never fails.

Still, a prince should make himself feared in such a way that if he does not gain love, he at any rate avoids hatred; for fear and the absence of hatred may well go together, and will be always attained by one who abstains from interfering with the property of his citizens and subjects or with their women. And when he is obliged to take the life of any one, let him do so when there is a proper justification and manifest reason for it; but above all he must abstain from taking the property of others, for men forget more easily the death of their father than the loss of their patrimony. Then also pretexts for seizing property are never wanting, and one who begins to live by rapine will always find some reason for taking the goods of others, whereas causes for taking life are rarer and more fleeting.

But when the prince is with his army and has a large number of soldiers under his control, then it is extremely necessary that he should not mind being thought cruel; for without this reputation he could not keep an army united or disposed to any duty. Among the noteworthy actions of Hannibal is numbered this, that although he had an enormous army, composed of men of all nations and fighting in foreign countries, there never arose any dissension either among them or against the prince, either in good fortune or in bad. This could not be due to anything but his inhuman cruelty, which together with his infinite other virtues, made him always venerated and terrible in the sight of his soldiers, and without it his other virtues would not have sufficed to produce that effect. Thoughtless writers admire on the one hand his actions, and on the other blame the principal cause of them.

And that it is true that his other virtues would not have sufficed may be seen from the case of Scipio (famous not only in regard to his own times, but all times of which memory remains), whose armies rebelled against him in Spain, which arose from nothing but his excessive kindness, which allowed more licence to the soldiers than was consonant with military discipline. He was reproached with this in the senate by Fabius Maximus, who called him a corrupter of the Roman militia. Locri having been destroyed by one of Scipio's officers was not revenged by him, nor was the insolence of that officer punished, simply by reason of his easy nature; so much so, that some one wishing to excuse him in the senate, said that there were many men who knew rather how not to err, than how to correct the errors of others. This disposition would in time have tarnished the fame and glory of Scipio had he persevered in it under the empire, but living under the rule of the senate this harmful quality was not only concealed but became a glory to him.

I conclude, therefore, with regard to being feared and loved, that men love at their own free will, but fear at the will of the prince, and that a wise prince must rely on what is in his power and not on what is in the power of others, and he must only contrive to avoid incurring hatred, as has been explained.

IN WHAT WAY PRINCES MUST KEEP FAITH

How laudable is it for a prince to keep good faith and live with integrity, and not with astuteness, every one knows. Still the experience of our times shows those princes to have done great things who have had little regard for good faith, and have been able by astuteness to confuse men's brains, and who have ultimately overcome those who have made loyalty their foundation.

You must know, then, that there are two methods of fighting, the one by law, the other by force: the first method is that of men, the second of beasts; but as the first method is often insufficient, one must have recourse to the second. It is therefore necessary for a prince to know well how to use both the beast and the man. This was covertly taught to rulers by ancient writers, who relate how Achilles and many others of those ancient princes were given to Chiron the centaur to be brought up and educated under his discipline. The parable of this semi-animal, semi-human teacher is meant to indicate that a prince must know how to use both natures, and that the one without the other is not durable.

A prince being thus obliged to know well how to act as a beast must imitate the fox and the lion, for the lion cannot protect himself from traps, and the fox cannot defend himself from wolves. One must therefore be a fox to recognise traps, and a lion to frighten wolves. Those that wish to be only lions do not understand this. Therefore, a prudent ruler ought not to keep faith when by so doing it would be against his interest, and when the reasons which made him bind himself no longer exist. If men were all good, this precept would not be a good one; but as they are bad, and would not observe their faith with you, so you are not bound to keep faith with them. Nor have legitimate grounds ever failed a prince who wished to show colourable excuse for the nonfulfilment of his promise. Of this one could furnish an infinite number of modern examples, and show how many times peace has been broken, and how many promises rendered worthless, by the faithlessness of princes, and those that have been best able to imitate the fox have succeeded best. But it is necessary to be able to disguise this character well, and to be a great feigner and dissembler; and men are so simple and so ready to obey present necessities, that one who deceives will always find those who allow themselves to be deceived.

I will only mention one modern instance. Alexander VI did nothing else but deceive men, he thought of nothing else, and found the occasion for it; no man was ever more able to give assurances, or affirmed things with stronger oaths, and no man observed them less; however, he always succeeded in his deceptions, as he well knew this aspect of things.

It is not, therefore, necessary for a prince to have all the above-named qualities, but it is very necessary to seem to have them. I would even be bold to say that to possess them and always to observe them is dangerous, but to appear to possess them is useful. Thus it is well to seem merciful, faithful, humane, sincere, religious, and also to be so; but you must have the mind so disposed that when it is needful to be otherwise you may be able to change to the opposite qualities. And it must be understood that a prince, and especially a new prince, cannot observe all those things which are considered good in men, being often obliged, in order to maintain the state, to act against faith, against charity, against humanity, and against religion. And, therefore, he must have a mind disposed to adapt itself according to the wind, and as the variations of fortune dictate, and, as I said before, not deviate from what is good, if possible, but be able to do evil if constrained.

A prince must take great care that nothing goes out of his mouth which is not full of the above-named five qualities, and, to see and hear him, he should seem to be all mercy, faith, integrity, humanity, and religion. And nothing is more necessary than to seem to have this last quality, for men in general judge more by the eyes than by the hands, for every one can see, but very few have to feel. Everybody sees what you appear to be, few feel what you are, and those few will not dare to oppose themselves to the many, who have the majesty of the state to defend them; and in the actions of men, and especially of princes, from which there is no appeal, the end justifies the means. Let a prince therefore aim at conquering and maintaining the state, and the means will always be judged honourable and praised by every one, for the vulgar is always taken by appearances and the issue of the event; and the world consists only of the vulgar, and the few who are not vulgar are isolated when the many have a rallying point in the prince. A certain prince of the present time, whom it is well not to name, never does anything but preach peace and good faith, but he is really a great enemy to both, and either of them, had he observed them, would have lost him state or reputation on many occasions.

PRINCES MUST AVOID BEING DESPISED OR HATED

But as I have now spoken of the most important of the qualities in question, I will now deal briefly and generally with the rest. The prince must, as already stated, avoid those things which will make him hated or despised; and whenever he succeeds in this, he will have done his part, and will find no danger in other vices. He will chiefly become hated, as I said, by being rapacious, and usurping the property and women of his subjects, which he must abstain from doing, and whenever one does not attack the property or honour of the generality of men, they will five contented; and one will only have

to combat the ambition of a few, who can be easily held in check in many ways. He is rendered despicable by being thought changeable, frivolous, effeminate, timid, and irresolute; which a prince must guard against as a rock of danger, and so contrive that his actions show grandeur, spirit, gravity, and fortitude; and as to the government of his subjects, let his sentence be irrevocable, and let him adhere to his decisions so that no one may think of deceiving or cozening him.

The prince who creates such an opinion of himself gets a great reputation, and it is very difficult to conspire against one who has a great reputation, and he will not easily be attacked, so long as it is known that he is capable and reverenced by his subjects. For a prince must have two kinds of fear: one internal as regards his subjects, one external as regards foreign powers. From the latter he can defend himself with good arms and good friends, and he will always have good friends if he has good arms; and internal matters will always remain quiet, if they are not perturbed by conspiracy and there is no disturbance from without; and even if external powers sought to attack him, if he has ruled and lived as I have described, he will always if he stands firm, be able to sustain every shock, as I have shown that Nabis the Spartan did. But with regard to the subjects, if not acted on from outside, it is still to be feared lest they conspire in secret, from which the prince may guard himself well by avoiding hatred and contempt, and keeping the people satisfied with him, which it is necessary to accomplish, as has been related at length. And one of the most potent remedies that a prince has against conspiracies, is that of not being hated by the mass of the people; for whoever conspires always believes that he will satisfy the people by the death of their prince; but if he thought to offend them by doing this, he would fear to engage in such an undertaking, for the difficulties that conspirators have to meet are infinite. Experience shows that there have been very many conspiracies, but few have turned out well, for whoever conspires cannot act alone, and cannot find companions except among those who are discontented; and as soon as you have disclosed your intention to a malcontent, you give him the means of satisfying himself, for by revealing it he can hope to secure everything he wants; to such an extent that seeing a certain gain by doing this, and seeing on the other hand only a doubtful one and full of danger, he must either be a rare friend to you or else a very bitter enemy to the prince if he keeps faith with you. And to express the matter in a few words, I say, that on the side of the conspirator there is nothing but fear, jealousy, suspicion, and dread of punishment which frightens him; and on the side of the prince there is the majesty of government, the laws, the protection of friends and of the state which guard him. When to these things is added the goodwill of the people, it is impossible that any one should have the temerity to conspire. For whereas generally a conspirator has to fear before the execution of his plot, in this case, having the people for an enemy, he must also fear after his crime is accomplished, and thus he is not able to hope for any refuge.

Numberless instances might be given of this, but I will content myself with one which took place within the memory of our fathers. Messer Annibale Bentivogli, Prince of Bologna, ancestor of the present Messer Annibale, was killed by the Canneschi, who conspired against him. He left no relations but Messer Giovanni, who was then an infant, but after the murder the people rose up and killed all the Canneschi. This arose from the popular goodwill that the house of Bentivogli enjoyed at that time, which was so great that, as there was nobody left after the death of Annibale who could govern the state, the Bolognese hearing that there was one of the Bentivogli family in Florence, who had till then been thought the son of a blacksmith, came to fetch him and gave him the government of the city, and it was governed by him until Messer Giovanni was old enough to assume the government.

I conclude, therefore, that a prince need trouble little about conspiracies when the people are well disposed, but when they are hostile and hold him in hatred, then he must fear everything and everybody. Well-ordered states and wise princes have studied diligently not to drive the nobles to desperation, and to satisfy the populace and keep it contented, for this is one of the most important matters that a prince has to deal with.

Among the kingdoms that are well ordered and governed in our time is France, and there we find numberless good institutions on which depend the liberty and security of the king; of these the chief is the parliament and its authority, because he who established that kingdom, knowing the ambition and insolence of the great nobles, deemed it necessary to have a bit in their mouths to check them. And knowing on the other hand the hatred of the mass of the people against the great, based on fear, and wishing to secure them, he did not wish to make this the special care of the king, to relieve him of the dissatisfaction that he might incur among the nobles by favouring the people, and among the people by favouring the nobles, He therefore established a third judge that, without direct charge of the king, kept in check the great and favoured the lesser people. Nor could any better or more prudent measure have been adopted, nor better precaution for the safety of the king and the kingdom. From which another notable rule can be drawn, that princes should let the carrying out of unpopular duties devolve on others, and bestow favours themselves. I conclude again by saying that a prince must esteem his nobles, but not make himself hated by the populace.

THE USEFULNESS OF FORTRESSES

Some princes, in order to hold their possessions securely, have disarmed their citizens, some others have kept their subject lands divided into parts, others have fomented enmities against themselves, others have endeavoured to win over those whom they suspected at the commencement of their rule: some have constructed fortresses, others have cast them down and destroyed them. And although one cannot pronounce a definite judgment as to these things without going into the particulars of the state to which such a deliberation is to be applied, still I will speak in such a general way as the matter will permit.

A new prince has never been known to disarm his subjects, on the contrary, when he has found them disarmed he has always armed them, for by arming them these arms become your own, those that you suspected become faithful and those that were faithful remain so, and from being merely subjects become your partisans. And since all the subjects cannot be armed, when you give the privilege of arms to some, you can deal more safely with the others; and this different treatment that they recognise renders your men more obliged to you. The others will excuse you, judging that those have necessarily greater merit who have greater danger and heavier duties. But when you disarm them, you commence to offend them and show that you distrust them either through cowardice or lack of confidence, and both of these opinions generate hatred against you. And as you cannot remain unarmed, you are obliged to resort to a mercenary militia, of which we have already stated the value; and even if it were good it cannot be sufficient in number to defend you against powerful enemies and suspected subjects. Therefore, as I have said, a new prince in a new dominion always has his subjects armed. History is full of such examples.

But when a prince acquires a new state as an addition to his old one, then it is necessary to disarm that state, except those who in acquiring it have sided with you; and even these one must, when time and opportunity serve, render weak and effeminate, and arrange things so that all the arms of the new state are in the hands of your soldiers who live near you in your old state.

Our forefathers and those who were esteemed wise used to say that it was necessary to hold Pistoia by means of factions and Pisa with fortresses, and for this purpose they fomented differences in some of their subject towns in order to possess them more easily. In those days when there was a balance of power in Italy, this was doubtless well done, but does not seem to me to be a good precept for the present time, for I do not believe that the divisions thus created ever do any good; on the contrary it is certain that when the enemy approaches, the cities thus divided will be at once lost, for the weaker faction will always side with the enemy and the other will not be able to stand.

The Venetians, actuated, I believe, by the aforesaid motives, fomented the Guelf and Ghibelline factions in the cities subject to them, and although they never allowed them to come to bloodshed, they yet encouraged these differences among them, so that the citizens, being occupied in their own quarrels, might not act against them. This, however, did not avail them anything, as was seen when, after the defeat of Vailà, a part of those subjects immediately took courage and seized the whole state. Such methods, besides, argue weakness in a prince, for in a strong government such dissensions will never be permitted. They are profitable only in time of peace, as by such means it is easy to manage one's subjects, but when it comes to war, the fallacy of such a policy is at once shown.

Without doubt princes become great when they overcome difficulties and opposition, and therefore fortune, especially when it wants to render a new prince great, who has greater need of gaining a great reputation than a hereditary prince, raises up enemies and compels him to undertake wars against them, so that he may have cause to overcome them, and thus climb up higher by means of that ladder which his enemies have brought him. There are many who think therefore that a wise prince ought, when he has the chance, to foment astutely some enmity, so that by suppressing it he will augment his greatness.

Princes, and especially new ones, have found more faith and more usefulness in those men, whom at the beginning of their power they regarded with suspicion, than in those they at first confided in. Pandolfo Petrucci, Prince of Siena, governed his state more by those whom he suspected than by others. But of this we cannot speak at large, as it strays from the subject; I will merely say that these men who at the beginning of a new government were enemies, if they are of a kind to need support to maintain their position, can be very easily gained by the prince, and they are the more compelled to serve him faithfully as they know they must by their deeds cancel the bad opinion previously held of them, and thus the prince will always derive greater help from them than from those who, serving him with greater security, neglect his interests.

And as the matter requires it, I will not omit to remind a prince who has newly taken a state with the secret help of its inhabitants, that he must consider well the motives that have induced those who have favoured him to do so, and if it is not natural affection for him, but only because they were not contented with the state as it was, he will have great trouble and difficulty in maintaining their friendship, because it will be impossible for him to content them. And on well examining the cause of this in the examples drawn from ancient and modern times it will be seen that it is much easier to gain the friendship of those men who were contented with the previous condition and were therefore at first enemies, than that those who not being contented, became his friends and helped him to occupy it.

It has been the custom of princes in order to be able to hold their state securly, to erect fortresses, as a bridle and bit to those who have designs against them, and in order to have a secure refuge against a sudden assault. I approve this method, because it was anciently used. Nevertheless, Messer Niccolò Vitelli has been seen in our own time to destroy two fortresses in Città di Castello in order to keep that state. Guid'Ubaldo, Duke of Urbino, on returning to his dominions from which he had been driven by Cesare Borgia, razed to their foundations all the fortresses of that province, and considered that without them it would be more difficult for him to lose the state again. The Bentivogli, on returning to Bologna, took similar measures. Therefore fortresses may or may not be useful according to the times; if they do good in one way, they do harm in another. The question may be discussed thus: a prince who fears his own people more than foreigners ought to build fortresses, but he who has greater fear of foreigners than of his own people ought to do without them. The castle of Milan built by Francesco Sforza has given and will give more trouble to the house of Sforza than any other disorder in that state. Therefore the best fortress is to be found in the love of the people, for although you may have fortresses they will not save you if you are hated by the people. When once the people have taken arms against you, there will never be lacking foreigners to assist them. In our times we do not see that they have profited any ruler, except the Countess of Forli on the death of her consort Count Girolamo, for she was thus enabled to escape the popular rising and await help from Milan and recover the state; the circumstances being then such that no foreigner could assist the people. But afterwards they were of little use to her when Cesare Borgia attacked her and the people being hostile to her allied themselves with the foreigner. So that then and before it would have been safer for her not to have been hated by the people than to have had the fortresses. Having considered these things I would therefore praise the one who erects fortresses and the one who does not, and would blame any one who, trusting in them, recks little of being hated by his people.

HOW PRINCES
GAIN REPUTATION

Nothing causes a prince to be so much esteemed as great enterprises and giving proof of prowess. We have in our own day Ferdinand, King of Aragon, the present King of Spain. He may almost be termed a new prince, because from a weak king he has become for fame and glory the first king in Christendom, and if you regard his actions you will find them all very great and some of them extraordinary. At the beginning of his reign he assailed Granada, and that enterprise was the foundation of his state. At first he did it at his leisure and with out fear of being interfered with; he kept the minds of the barons of Castile occupied in this enterprise, so that thinking only of that war they did not think of making innovations, and be thus acquired reputation and power over them without their being aware of it. He was able with the money of the Church and the people to maintain his armies, and by that long war to lay the foundations of his military power, which afterwards has made him famous. Besides this, to be able to undertake greater enterprises, and always under the pretext of religion, he had recourse to a pious cruelty, driving out the Moors from his kingdom and despoiling them. No more miserable or unusual example can be found. He also attacked Africa under the same pretext, undertook his Italian enterprise, and has lately attacked France; so that he has continually contrived great things, which have kept his subjects' minds uncertain and astonished, and occupied in watching their result. And these actions have arisen one out of the other, so that they have left no time for men to settle down and act against him.

It is also very profitable for a prince to give some outstanding example of his greatness in the internal administration, like those related of Messer Bernabò of Milan. When it happens that some one does something extraordinary, either good or evil, in civil life, he must find such means of rewarding or punishing him which will be much talked about. And above all a prince must endeavour in every action to obtain fame for being great and excellent.

A prince is further esteemed when he is a true friend or a true enemy, when, that is, he declares himself without reserve in favour of some one or against another. This policy is always more useful than remaining neutral. For if two neighbouring powers come to blows, they are either such that if one wins, you will have to fear the victor, or else not. In either of these two cases it will be better for you to declare yourself openly and make war, because in the first case if you do not declare yourself, you will fall a prey to the victor, to the pleasure and satisfaction of the one who has been defeated, and you will have no reason nor anything to defend you and nobody to receive you. For, whoever wins will not desire friends whom he suspects and who do not help him when in trouble, and whoever loses will not receive you as you did not take up arms to venture yourself in his cause.

Antiochus went to Greece, being sent by the Ætolians to expel the Romans. He sent orators to the Achaeans who were friends of the Romans to encourage them to remain neutral; on the other hand the Romans persuaded them to take up arms on their side. The matter was brought before the council of the Achaeans for deliberation, where the ambassador of Antiochus sought to persuade them to remain neutral, to which the Roman ambassador replied: "As to what is said that it is best and most useful for your state not to meddle in our war, nothing is further from the truth; for if you do not meddle in it you will become, without any favour or any reputation, the prize of the victor."

And it will always happen that the one who is not your friend will want you to remain neutral, and the one who is your friend will require you to declare yourself by taking arms. Irresolute princes, to avoid present dangers, usually follow the way of neutrality and are mostly ruined by it. But when the prince declares himself frankly in favour of one side, if the one to whom you adhere conquers, even if he is powerful and you remain at his discretion, he is under an obligation to you and friendship has been established, and men are never so dishonest as to oppress you with such a patent ingratitude. Moreover, victories are never so prosperous that the victor does not need to have some scruples, especially as to justice. But if your ally loses, you are sheltered by him, and so long as he can, he will assist you; you become the companion of a fortune which may rise again. In the second case, when those who fight are such that you have nothing to fear from the victor, it is still more prudent on your part to adhere to one; for you go to the ruin of one with the help of him who ought to save him if he were wise, and if he conquers he rests at your discretion, and it is impossible that he should not conquer with your help.

And here it should be noted that a prince ought never to make common cause with one more powerful than himself to injure another, unless necessity forces him to it, as before said; for if he wins you rest in his power, and princes must avoid as much as possible being under the will and pleasure of others. The Venetians united with France against the Duke of Milan, although they could have avoided that alliance, and from it resulted their own ruin. But when one cannot avoid it, as happened in the case of the Florentines when the Pope and Spain went with their armies to attack Lombardy, then the prince ought to join for the above reasons. Let no state believe that it can always follow a safe policy, rather let it think that all are doubtful. This is found in the nature of things, that one never tries to avoid one difficulty without running into another, but prudence consists in being able to know the nature of the difficulties, and taking the least harmful as good.

A prince must also show himself a lover of merit, give preferment to the able, and honour those who excel in every art. Moreover he must encourage his citizens to follow their callings quietly, whether in commerce, or agriculture, or any other trade that men follow, so that this one shall not refrain from improving his possessions through fear that they may be taken from him, and that one from starting a trade for fear of taxes; but he should offer rewards to whoever does these things, and to whoever seeks in any way to improve his city or state. Besides this, he ought, at convenient seasons of the year, to keep the people occupied with festivals and shows; and as every city is divided either into guilds or into classes, he ought to pay attention to all these groups, mingle with them from time to time, and give them an example of his humanity and munificence, always upholding, however, the majesty of his dignity, which must never be allowed to fail in anything whatever.

CHAPTER FIFTEEN

THE PROTESTANT REFORMATION

Renaissance and Reformation are inextricably interwoven with the birth and growth of the modern national state. In the field of secular thought and experience, the Renaissance brought about the rediscovery of the ancient world and witnessed the immense broadening of man's horizon through the discovery of the New World of the Americas. In the field of religious thought and experience, the Renaissance opened the gates to a new religious world through the Protestant Reformation.

The first leaders of the Reformation denied any revolutionary intentions and merely claimed to return to the early sources of Christianity, faith and the Scriptures. In this sense, Protestantism was a part of the general process of rebirth, the religious aspect of the Renaissance. In the fifteenth century, the conciliar movement had attempted to reform the church from within by transferring supreme power from the pope to general councils meeting periodically for the specific purpose of reforming the church and invigorating its administration by making its authority more representative of the whole Christian community. Two councils were convened (Constance, 1414–1418, and Basel, 1431–1439), but both failed. Yet, despite its failure the conciliar movement had revived the important conception of the congregational character of church authority, with its corollary that office was in the nature of a trusteeship rather than an inalienable power. When reform from within failed, revolution from without took its place.

Prior to the thirteenth century, as long as the church had to withstand the attacks of critics who did not take any religion seriously, it was able to win easily, either by disregarding its critics, by trying to persuade them, or by burning them alive on the stake. The strength of reform movements from the thirteenth century on lay in the fact that the critics of Rome were passionately religious. They assailed the papacy for having lost the original ideals of the Christian faith and for having become corrupted by the worldly ambitions of lust, wealth, and power. Some of these reformers believed that the hope lay in reforming Christians as individuals rather than in attempting basic institutional change of the church as an organization. The best known example is that of Savonarola, a Dominican friar and preacher in Florence, who managed to exercise complete control over Florence for four years (1494–1498). Yet, in the end, Pope Alexander VI excommunicated him, and he was tried and burned. Finally, there were men who hoped that the church could be reformed through an enlightened fusion of the ethics of early Christianity with the humanism of classical culture. The "Christian Humanists" included some of the leading scholars in Europe, such as Luis Vives in Spain, Pico della Mirandola in Italy, Sir Thomas More in England, and, greatest of them all, Erasmus of Rotterdam. While undoubtedly contributing to a significant change in the moral and intellectual climate of Europe, the Christian Humanists failed in the immediate goal of reforming the church from within through peaceful appeals to reason and faith.

In the sixteenth century, however, the reformist tendencies—now driven into revolution by the obstinacy of the church—were more successful because they were allied with other social forces of the time. In particular, wherever Protestant Reform, as in Northern Germany, England, Scandinavia, was associated with monarchy, the strongest power of the age, its victory was never in question. Where, on the other hand, Protestantism was not favored by royal encouragement, as in France, it did not succeed. Nowhere was the issue purely religious; in all countries it was mixed with political, dynastic, economic, and diplomatic considerations. Although the age of the Reformation itself was truly religious, religion was readily used to cloak less lofty aspirations.

From the viewpoint of the expansion of political liberty, the first Protestant church, Lutheranism, had little effect, either in Germany or elsewhere. Martin Luther (1483–1546) stressed the inner aspects of religious experience, faith rather than good works: "Faith alone is the righteousness of a Christian and the fulfilling of all the commandments" (*Treatise on Christian Liberty,* 1520). Luther argued that liberty is in the conscience and spirit of man and has no relation to his political or social condition, for "that is making Christian liberty an utterly carnal thing." His ideas on government and the relations of rulers and ruled were most clearly and systematically expressed in his *Secular Authority: To What Extent It Should Be Obeyed* (1523). Luther emphasized that government is ordained by God, and that the subjects must obey their rulers, even though their rule be unjust or cruel. His profound pessimism about men in all stations—rulers or ruled—was reflected in his statement that "the world is too wicked, and does not deserve to have many wise and pious princes. Frogs need storks."

In his assertion of the equality of all Christians as Christians he was of revolutionary import, and his doctrine of the priesthood of all Christians contained possibilities that were more fully exploited later on in England, Scotland, and North America. Though he defended the highly unorthodox view that belief or unbelief is a matter of one's conscience, that faith is an act and expression of freedom, and that it cannot be imposed by force, the bold break with Rome was not accompanied in Luther or Lutheranism by any parallel social or political philosophy. On the contrary, Luther's religious radicalism was matched by extreme conservatism in social and political affairs. Supported by the absolutist princes of Northern Germany, Luther stressed the duty of the subject to obey the commands of his king.

Shortly after Luther published his revolutionary religious theses, German peasants—driven by social and political oppression, and translating too quickly the Lutheran ideals of Christian equality from theological into practical terms—began to rebel. This rebellion of 1525 was the only genuine popular revolution in German history, and the subsequent history of the German people might have been different if the rebellion had succeeded at least in part. Luther instigated the princes to take the sternest measures, including wholesale bloodshed, against the "mad dogs," "scoundrels," and "swine"—as he called the rebelling peasants.

Thus for practical purposes Lutheranism evolved into a faithful ally of political absolutism. Its most serious effect on the German people was to strengthen their fatal habit of nourishing ideals of freedom in the realm of the spirit but of submitting without question to the authority of the state in practical affairs. Luther himself was fully aware that princes are "usually the greatest fools or scoundrels on earth"; yet he insisted on the duty of subjects to obey such impious princes, because, he said, the rest of the world is wicked, too, and does not deserve virtuous rulers. Luther added to his strong respect for the state an equally passionate feeling of German nationalism and even racialism; thus he became—the only Protestant leader to have such progeny—one of the spiritual ancestors of Prussian statism and German Nazism.

After Luther's death, the Religious Peace of Augsburg (1555) settled the problem of religious division in the German states by the principle of *cuius regio eius religio,* according to which the ruler of the country determined the religion of its inhabitants. This principle was more liberal than the medieval method of imposing uniformity of belief from which there was no escape, because under the policy of the Peace of Augsburg, religious dissidents were free to adhere to their religion, provided they emigrated.

No doubt emigration was less harsh than the stake; yet by accepting such a principle Germany lost a vital opportunity of learning toleration. In Holland, England, and North America toleration of religious minorities preceded that of political opposition, and the tradition of liberalism in the English-speaking countries in particular cannot be understood apart from the tradition of religious nonconformity. Frederick the Great referred to himself in his *Political Testament* as the "Pope of the Lutherans," and until 1918 the rulers of Protestant states in Germany were simultaneously the supreme bishops of their state churches. Thus, instead of one religious authoritarianism, Germany had two after the Reformation. Yet by the fact of establishing itself as the first Reform church independent of Rome, Lutheranism encouraged the formation of independent churches elsewhere. As more churches came into existence, increased mutual toleration was inevitable; the relative power of each religion or sect declined in proportion to the growing number of all.

As long as Protestantism was mainly Lutheran, it made little headway in France. But there was a vigorous tradition of anticlericalism and antipapalism in France from the Middle Ages on, and the sense of urgent change grew stronger in the sixteenth century. Protestantism became a national force in France, with an intellectual character of its own, after the appearance of a French leader, John Calvin (1509–1564). In 1534 Calvin, forced to leave France for religious reasons, went to Switzerland, where Protestantism had spread rapidly. In 1536 he wrote the *Institutes of the Christian Religion,* his principal work and still the chief source of Calvinist doctrine. With only a few short interruptions, he stayed in Switzerland for the rest of his life; he governed Geneva from 1536 to 1538, and again from 1541 to 1564, the year of his death. His regime was one of ruthless terror. Though Calvin's theological doctrines did not differ substantially from those of Luther, his impact on history did. Calvinism spread to France, Holland, Scotland, and the English colonies in North America.

Unlike Luther, Calvin admitted—in exceptional cases only, to be sure—the right of resistance to tyrannical rulers, provided that resistance was in the hands of magistrates and organized estates, rather than lawless mobs, or in the hands of a secular savior selected by God to deliver the people from tyranny. In the total doctrine of Calvin, the stress was more on obedience than on resistance. Yet the circumstances of persecution in France and Holland in particular drove Calvinists into active resistance. In Holland, Calvinism was allied with the national movement of liberation from Spain, and in the end it won over the majority of the nation. In France, the monarchy needed the friendship of the papacy against the Habsburgs in the struggle for Italy, and, domestically, the strongly centralizing tendencies of the newly developing national state were opposed to the Calvinist demands for local autonomy. Calvinism was thus put in a position in which it could be easily attacked by its opponents as antinational. A considerable proportion of the French aristocracy, perhaps one-third, sympathized with the Protestant cause, and regional, provincial issues were also dragged into the religious controversy.

Passion ran high on both sides. Shortly after the "War of Religion" had broken out in France (it lasted, with interruptions, from 1562 to 1593), the Huguenots invited German and English troops to aid them in the civil war. Foreign intervention in civil war is particularly odious if unsuccessful—and the Huguenots lost. On its side, the royalist, nationalist, Catholic party acted with more ruthlessness against its opponents than was customary in French life, and it is doubtful whether the Revolution of 1789, another "war of religion," witnessed as much brutality as the War of Religion in the sixteenth century.

The anti-Protestant frenzy, carefully nursed, with the blessing of Rome, by the royalist-Catholic party, came to a climax in the Massacre of St. Bartholomew (August 24, 1572), in which thirty thousand Huguenots lost their lives. The head of Admiral Coligny, the military and political leader of the Huguenots, was sent to Pope Gregory XIII in Rome, who had also received Coligny's assassin. The happy outcome of the massacre was celebrated by the pope in a public procession and solemn mass of thanksgiving, attended by thirty-three cardinals and many other high ecclesiastic dignitaries. On September 11, 1572, Gregory praised the French king for his punishment of heretics and expressed the hope that the enterprise of suppressing Protestantism, so auspiciously begun on St. Bartholomew's day, would be carried on to the end.

Deprived of their leaders, hacked into a small minority, the Huguenots produced, in the decade following the massacre, a mass of tracts that belong to the most provocative political literature inspired by the Reformation. The best known of these Huguenot pamphlets and books is *A Defense of Liberty against Tyrants (Vindiciae contra tyrannos),* published in Latin under the pseudonym Stephen Junius Brutus in 1579 and translated into French in 1581. Both editions were printed in Switzerland, then— as earlier and later—an island of freedom in Europe. Many of the Huguenot pamphlets were published anonymously, for obvious reasons, and their authors were generally exiles; Switzerland, Holland, England, and Germany were among the favorite places of refuge.

The authorship of the *Vindiciae* is not completely certain; according to the longest tradition and best modern judgment, the author was Hubert Languet (1519–1581), a French scholar, lawyer, traveler, and diplomat, who spent many years in Germany. Those who dispute Languet's authorship attribute the book partly or wholly to Philippe Duplessis-Mornay (1549–1623), a young friend of Languet who probably had some connection with the *Vindiciae,* either in aiding Languet in the preparation of the original Latin manuscript or in translating the Latin text into French.

The *Vindiciae* proposes to deal with four main questions: first, whether subjects are bound to obey princes if they command what is against the law of God; second, whether it is lawful to resist a prince who infringes the law of God or ruins the church, and by whom resistance is to be offered, how, and to what extent; third, whether it is lawful to resist a prince who oppresses or ruins the commonwealth, by whom and how far such resistance is to be offered, and by what right it is permitted; fourth, whether neighboring princes or states may lawfully help, or are bound to help, the subjects of other princes who are afflicted for the cause of true religion or oppressed by manifest tyranny. As can be seen from these four questions, the purpose of the *Vindiciae* is not to give a general theory of the state but to inquire into one of its pivotal issues: the problem of *obedience.*

The substance of the answers to the four chief questions raised in the *Vindiciae* lies in the notion of contract. In fact, the argument is based on the theory of *two contracts:* The first is made between God on the one side, and the king and people jointly on the other, "that the people might be the people of God." The second contract is between the king and the people, in which the people promise to obey the king faithfully, provided that he rule justly. Both covenants in the *Vindiciae* are derived from the Old Testament; the Calvinists, like the Puritans a century later, lean heavily on the Old Testament for the idea of the covenant as the foundation of all authority.

The importance of the first convenant, that between God on one side, and king and people on the other, lies in the fact that the king's responsibility does not come to an end if he violates his promises, because the people are bound to see that the covenant, which they, too, have entered into, is fulfilled. If the king violates his share of the joint obligation, the people are entitled, nay, bound, to resist or depose him for the sake of the obligation to God. Similarly, from the second covenant between king and people follows the right of the people to resist or depose the king if he violates his obligations.

The second key idea in the *Vindiciae* is that of *trusteeship.* Speaking in terms of the Bible and Roman law, the *Vindiciae* refers to the king as a "guardian" or "tutor." The nature of trusteeship lies in the fact that whatever authority is given to the trustee, he holds, not for his own benefit, but for that of the person or persons in whose behalf he acts. Kings are made by the people, and they "hold their power and sovereignty from the people." Although God elects the king, the people establish him. No one is ever born with a crown on his head and a scepter in his hand, and no man can be a king without people, whereas people can get along without a king; kings are therefore the creations of the people, even in hereditary monarchies. The right of free election "seems in a sort buried" in hereditary monarchies, but actually it is not dead in them, because new kings receive afresh the symbols of their authority from the hands of the peers and officers of the crown, who represent the people.

The author of the *Vindiciae* anticipates one of the chief ideas of Locke by emphasizing that the purpose of setting up government is to decide civil disputes by *third-party judgments,* particularly disputes about *property.* The king is conceived as a judge rather than a legislator, and the superiority of the law over the king is asserted throughout the *Vindiciae.* The king is but an organ of the law, and it is "more profitable and convenient to obey the law, than the king who is but one man." Taking over the Calvinistic concept of the "priesthood" of all believers, the *Vindiciae* denies that the king's subjects are his "slaves or bondmen," because, considered in one body, "they are lords," and the king should therefore govern his subjects as brethren.

The third key idea of the *Vindiciae* is *resistance to tyranny.* Two kinds of tyranny are distinguished: first, that of the ruler who gains a kingdom by violence; and second, that of the ruler who, lawfully invested with his office, violates his promises and duties by the practice of tyranny. The usurper who rules justly is preferable to the legitimate monarch who rules unjustly: "Certainly I had rather that a thief should feed me, than a shepherd devour me: I had rather receive justice from a robber, than outrage from a judge: I had better be healed by an empiric, than poisoned by a doctor in physic." As to the ruler who is doubly a tyrant, because he had illegally usurped power and because he exercises it unjustly, "the meanest private man may resist and lawfully oppose such an intruding tyrant." Even tyrannicide is lawful when the ruler is a "double" tyrant. When tyrants hold office by law but exercise it unjustly, it is the right and duty of the magistrates and Estates to resist the king and, if necessary, depose and kill him.

Because the tyrant with a legitimate title to rule has been established in his office by the community as a whole, private individuals "may not unsheathe the sword against tyrants by practice." The *Vindiciae* makes it clear in numerous passages that the term "the people" is not to be taken too literally; it means the magistrates and assembly of the Estates. The presbyterian character of early Calvinist church government was aristocratic rather than democratic, and though the position of the *Vindiciae* on the right of resistance is antiauthoritarian and liberal, the liberalism is of the predemocratic age, as it existed from the sixteenth to the eighteenth centuries. The main purpose of the *Vindiciae* was to vindicate the right of conscience in religious matters, yet the general principle involved holds good for any issue of conscience.

The *Vindiciae* quickly established itself as a widely read book and inspired religious, political, and national movements of liberation. Although it was considered dangerous enough to be publicly burned by Cambridge University in 1620 (and by Oxford University, too, but much later, in 1683), an English translation appeared in 1648 under the Cromwellian regime, shortly before Charles I was executed; it was reprinted in 1689, another eventful date in the history of English liberty, when parliamentary supremacy and the right to religious nonconformity became firmly established. The main concepts of the *Vindiciae,* the contractual nature of government, popular sovereignty, political rule as trusteeship, protection of property, and, finally, the right of resistance against unjust rulers, dominated political thought until the appearance of Rousseau in the eighteenth century.

The most powerful impact of the *Vindiciae* has been on Dutch and English thought. Locke's *Two Treatises of Government* was begun in Holland, where Locke, like the author of the *Vindiciae,* lived as a refugee; it was published in 1690 in England, one year after the reprinting of the English translation of the *Vindiciae.* Locke's work had more prestige and influence not only because it was a more systematic treatment of the general theory of the state but also because the *Two Treatises of Government* was published with the self-confidence that is born of victory, whereas the *Vindiciae* showed the marks of bitterness born of defeat. What the Huguenots wanted for France, the Bloodless Revolution achieved for England in 1688.

Democracy is more than a system of government, and the democratic conception of man is based on the hypothesis that there is some area in man's conscience that cannot be subdued from the outside but must be won from within by free assent. The *Vindiciae* belongs to the family of books—not too numerous in the history of thought—that stress freedom rather than authority, consent rather than compulsion, and obedience to the inner voice of conscience rather than to the external force of the state.

I LUTHER

Secular Authority:
*To What Extent It Should Be Obeyed**

SECULAR AUTHORITY
DERIVES FROM GOD

We must firmly establish secular law and the sword, that no one may doubt that it is in the world by God's will and ordinance. The passages which establish this are the following: Romans xiii, "Let every soul be subject to power and authority, for there is no power but from God. The power that is everywhere is ordained of God. He then who resists the power resists God's ordinance. But he who resists God's ordinance shall bring himself under condemnation." Likewise, I Peter ii, "Be subject to every kind of human ordinance, whether to the king as supreme, or to the governors, as to those sent of Him for the punishing of the evil and for the reward of the good."

This penal law existed from the beginning of the world. For when Cain slew his brother he was in such great terror of being in turn killed that God specially forbade it and suspended the sword for his sake,—and no one was to slay him. He would not have had this fear if he had not seen and heard from Adam that murderers should be slain. Moreover God re-established and confirmed it after the Flood in unmistakable terms when He said, "Whoso sheds man's blood, his blood shall be shed again by man." This cannot be understood as a plague and punishment of God upon murderers; for many murderers who repent or are pardoned continue to live, and die by other means than the sword. But it is said of the right of the sword, that a murderer is guilty of death and should in justice be slain by the sword. Though justice be hindered or the sword be tardy, so that the murderer dies a natural death, the Scripture is not on that account false when it says, "Whoso sheddeth man's blood, by man shall his blood be shed." For it is men's fault or merit that this law commanded of God is not carried out; even as other commandments of God are broken.

Afterward it was also confirmed by the law of Moses, Exodus xxi, "If a man presumptuously kill thou shalt take him from My altar that he may die." And again, in the same place, "A life for a life, an eye for an eye, a tooth for a tooth, a foot for a foot, a hand for a hand, a wound for a wound, a bruise for a bruise." Christ also confirms it when He says to Peter in the garden, "He that taketh the sword shall perish by the sword," which is to be interpreted like Genesis ix, "Whoso sheddeth man's blood," etc. Doubtless Christ refers in these words to that passage and incorporates and confirms it in them. John the Baptist teaches the same. When the soldiers asked him what they should do, he answered, "Do injustice or violence to no one, and be content with your wages." If the sword were not divinely appointed he should have commanded them to cease being soldiers, since he was to perfect the people and direct them in a proper Christian way. Hence it is sufficiently clear and certain that it is God's will that the sword and secular law be used for the punishment of the wicked and the protection of the upright.

---

*From Martin Luther, *Secular Authority: To What Extent It Should Be Obeyed* (1523, trans. J. J. Schindel), from *Works*, Vol. 45, 1930. By permission of Fortress Press.

NON-RESISTANCE

There seems to be a powerful argument on the other side. Christ says, Matthew v, "Ye have heard that it was said to them of old: An eye for an eye, a tooth for a tooth. But I say unto you, That a man shall not resist evil, but if any one strikes thee upon the right cheek, turn to him the other also; and whoever will go to law with thee to take thy coat, let him have the cloak also, and whoever forces thee a mile, with him go two miles." Likewise Paul, Romans xii, "Dearly beloved, defend not yourselves, but give place to God's wrath, for it is written, Vengeance is mine, I will repay saith the Lord." Likewise Matthew v, "Love your enemies, do good to them that hate you." And I Peter iii, "Let no one repay evil with evil, nor railing with railing," etc. These and the like passages truly would make it appear as though in the New Testament there should be no secular sword among Christians.

Hence the sophists also say that Christ has abolished Moses' law; of such commandments they make counsels for the perfect, and divide Christian teaching and Christians into two classes. One part they call the perfect, and assign to it such counsels. To the other, the imperfect, they assign the commandments. This they do out of sheer perversity and caprice, without any scriptural basis, They do not see that in the same passage Christ lays such stress on His teaching that He is unwilling to have the least word of it set aside, and condemns to hell those who do not love their enemies. Therefore we must interpret these passages differently, so that Christ's words may apply to all alike whether they be "perfect" or "imperfect." For perfection and imperfection consist not in works and do not establish a distinct external order among Christians; but they exist in the heart, in faith and love, so that they who believe and love the most are the perfect ones, whether outwardly they be male or female, prince or peasant, monk or layman. For love and faith produce no sects or outward differences.

THE TWO KINGDOMS

We must divide all the children of Adam into two classes; the first belong to the kingdom of God, the second to the kingdom of the world. Those belonging to the kingdom of God are all true believers in Christ and are subject to Christ. For Christ is the King and Lord in the kingdom of God, as the second Psalm and all the Scriptures say. For this reason He came into the world, that He might begin God's kingdom and establish it in the world. Therefore He says before Pilate, "My kingdom is not of the world, but whoever is of the truth hears My voice"; and continually in the Gospel He refers to the kingdom of God and says, "Amend your ways, the kingdom of God is at hand." Likewise, "Seek first the kingdom of God and His righteousness." He also calls the Gospel, a Gospel of the kingdom, for the reason that it teaches, governs, and contains God's kingdom.

Now observe, these people need no secular sword or law. And if all the world were composed of real Christians, that is, true believers, no prince, king, lord, sword, or law would be needed. For what were the use of them, since Christians have in their hearts the Holy Spirit, who instructs them and causes them to wrong no one, to love every one, willingly and cheerfully to suffer injustice and even death from every one. Where every wrong is suffered and every right is done, no quarrel, strife, trial, judge, penalty, law or sword is needed. Therefore, it is not possible for the secular sword and law to find any work to do among Christians, since of themselves they do much more than its laws and doctrines can demand. Just as Paul says in I Timothy i, "The law is not given for the righteous, but for the unrighteous."

Why is this? Because the righteous does of himself all and more than all that all the laws demand. But the unrighteous do nothing that the law demands, therefore they need the law to instruct, constrain, and compel them to do what is good. A good tree does not need any teaching or law to bear good fruit, its nature causes it to bear according to its kind without any law and teaching. A man would be a fool to make a book of laws and statutes telling an apple tree how to bear apples and not thorns, when it is able by its own nature to do this better than man with all his books can define and direct. Just so, by the Spirit and by faith all Christians are throughout inclined to do well and keep the law, much more than any one can teach them with all the laws, and need so far as they are concerned no commandments nor law.

You ask, Why then did God give to all men so many commandments, and why did Christ teach in the Gospel so many things to be done? To put it as briefly as possible here, Paul says that the law is given for the sake of the unrighteous, that is, that those who are not Christians may through the law be externally restrained from evil deeds, as we shall hear later. Since, however, no one is by nature Christian or pious, but every one sinful and evil, God places the restraints of the law upon them all, so that they may not dare give rein to their desires and commit outward, wicked deeds. In addition, St. Paul gives the law another function in Romans vii and Galatians iii. It is to teach men to recognize sin, that they may be made humble unto grace and unto faith in Christ. Christ also does this here, when He teaches in Matthew v that we should not resist evil, and thereby glorifies the law and teaches how a real Christian ought to be and must be disposed, as we shall hear further on.

All who are not Christians belong to the kingdom of the world and are under the law. Since few believe and still fewer live a Christian life, do not resist the evil, and themselves do no evil, God has provided for non-Christians a different government outside the Christian estate and God's kingdom, and has subjected them to the sword, so that, even though they would do so, they cannot practice their wickedness, and that, if they do, they may not do it without fear nor in peace and prosperity. Even so a wild, savage beast is fastened with chains and bands, so that it cannot bite and tear as is its wont, although it gladly would do so; whereas a tame and gentle beast does not require this, but without any chains and bands is nevertheless harmless. If it were not so, seeing that the whole world is evil and that among thousands there is scarcely one true Christian, men would devour one another, and no one could preserve wife and child, support himself and serve God; and thus the world would be reduced to chaos. For this reason God has ordained the two governments; the spiritual, which by the Holy Spirit under Christ makes Christians and pious people, and the secular, which restrains the unchristian and wicked so that

they must needs keep the peace outwardly, even against their will. So Paul interprets the secular sword, Romans xiii, and says it is not a terror to good works, but to the evil. And Peter says it is for the punishment of evil doers.

If any one attempted to rule the world by the Gospel, and put aside all secular law and the secular sword, on the plea that all are baptised and Christian, and that according to the Gospel, there is to be among them neither law nor sword, nor necessity for either, pray, what would happen? He would loose the bands and chains of the wild and savage beasts, and let them tear and mangle every one, and at the same time say they were quite tame and gentle creatures; but I would have the proof in my wounds. Just so would the wicked under the name of Christian abuse this freedom of the Gospel, carry on their knavery, and say that they were Christians subject neither to law nor sword, as some are already raving and ranting.

To such a one we must say, It is indeed true that Christians, so far as they themselves are concerned, are subject to neither law nor sword and need neither; but first take heed and fill the world with real Christians before ruling it in a Christian and evangelical manner. This you will never accomplish; for the world and the masses are and always will be "unchristian, although they are all baptised and are nominally Christian. Christians, however, are few and far between, as the saying is. Therefore it is out of the question that there should be a common Christian government over the whole world, nay even over one land or company of people, since the wicked always outnumber the good. Hence a man who would venture to govern an entire country or the world with the Gospel would be like a shepherd who should place in one fold wolves, lions, eagles, and sheep together and let them freely mingle with one another and say, Help yourselves, and be good and peaceful among yourselves; the fold is open, there is plenty of food; have no fear of dogs and clubs. The sheep, forsooth, would keep the peace and would allow themselves to be fed and governed in peace, but they would not live long; nor would any beast keep from molesting another.

For this reason these two kingdoms must be sharply distinguished, and both be permitted to remain; the one to produce piety, the other to bring about external peace and prevent evil deeds; neither is sufficient in the world without the other. For no one can become pious before God by means of the secular government, without Christ's spiritual rule. Hence Christ's rule does not extend over all, but Christians are always in the minority and are in the midst of non-Christians. Where there is only secular rule or law, there, of necessity, is sheer hypocrisy, though the commandments be God's very own. Without the Holy Spirit in the heart no one becomes really pious, he may do as fine works as he will. Where, on the other hand, the spiritual government rules alone over land and people, there evil is given free rein and the door is opened for every kind of knavery; for the natural world cannot receive or comprehend spiritual things.

You see the purpose of Christ's words which we quoted above from Matthew v. They mean that Christians shall not go to law nor use the secular sword among themselves. In reality He says it only to His dear Christians. They alone also accept it and act accordingly, nor do they make counsels of it, as the sophists do, but are so inclined in their heart, through the Spirit, that they do evil to no one and willingly endure evil at every one's hands. If the whole world were Christian, all these words would apply to it and it would keep them. Since, however, it is unchristian the words do not apply to it, nor does it keep them, but is under another rule in which those who are not Christians are under external constraint and are forced to keep the peace and do what is good.

For this reason Christ did not wield the sword nor give it a place in His kingdom; for He is a King over Christians and rules by His Holy Spirit alone, without law. And although He acknowledged the sword, He nevertheless did not use it; for it is of no use in His kingdom, in which are none but the pious. Hence David of old dared not build the temple, because he had shed much blood and had borne the sword; not that he had done wrong thereby, but because he could not be a type of Christ, who without the sword was to have a kingdom of peace. It must be built by Solomon, whose name means "Frederick" or "peaceful," who had a peaceful kingdom, by which the truly peaceful kingdom of Christ, the real Frederick

and Solomon, could be represented. In like manner, during the entire building of the temple not the sound of a tool was heard, as the text says; all for this reason, that Christ, without constraint and force, without law and the sword, was to have a people who serve Him freely.

This is what the prophets mean in Psalm cx, "Thy people shall be willing"; and in Isaiah xi, "They shall not hurt nor destroy in all my holy mountain"; and in Isaiah ii, "They shall beat their swords into plowshares and their spears into pruning hooks, and no one shall lift up the sword against another, neither shall they busy themselves in war anymore," etc. Whoever would apply these and similar passages wherever Christ's name is professed, would entirely pervert the Scriptures; for they are spoken only of true Christians, who really do this among themselves.

OBEDIENCE TO SECULAR AUTHORITY

But perhaps you will say, Since Christians do not need the secular sword and the law, why does Paul say to all Christians, in Romans xiii, "Let all souls be subject to power and authority"? And St. Peter says, "Be subject to every human ordinance," etc., as quoted above. I answer, as I have said, that Christians, among themselves and by and for themselves, need no law or sword, since it is neither necessary nor profitable for them. Since, however, a true Christian lives and labors on earth not for himself, but for his neighbor, therefore the whole spirit of his life impels him to do even that which he need not do, but which is profitable and necessary for his neighbor. Because the sword is a very great benefit and necessary to the whole world, to preserve peace, to punish sin and to prevent evil, he submits most willingly to the rule of the sword, pays tax, honors those in authority, serves, helps, and does all he can to further the government, that it may be sustained and held in honor and fear. Although he needs none of these things for himself and it is not necessary for him to do them, yet he considers what is for the good and profit of others, as Paul teaches in Ephesians v.

He serves the State as be performs all other works of love, which he himself does not need. He visits the sick, not that he may be made well; feeds no one because he himself needs food: so he also serves the State not because be needs it, but because others need it,—that they may be protected and that the wicked may not become worse. He loses nothing by this, and such service in no way harms him, and yet it is of great profit to the world. If he did not do it, he would be acting not as a Christian but contrary even to love, and would also be setting a bad example to others, who like him would not submit to authority, though they were no Christians. In this way the Gospel would be brought into disrepute, as though it taught rebellion and made self-willed people, unwilling to benefit or serve any one, when in reality it makes a Christian the servant of every one. Thus in Matthew xviii, Christ gave the tribute money that He might not offend them, although He did not need to do it.

Thus you observe in the words of Christ quoted above from Matthew v that He indeed teaches that Christians among themselves should have no secular sword nor law. He does not, however, forbid one to serve and obey those who have the secular sword and the law; much rather, since you have no need of them and are not to have them, are you to serve those who have not progressed so far as you and still need them. Allthough you do not need to have your enemy punished, your weak neighbor does. You should help him, that he may have peace and that his enemy may be curbed; which is not possible unless power and authority are honored and feared. Christ does not say, "Thou shalt not serve the State or be subject to it," but "Thou shalt not resist evil." As though He said, "Take heed that you bear everything, so that you may not need the State to help and serve you and be of profit to you, but that you may, on the other hand, help, serve, and be of profit and use to it. I would have you to be far too exalted and noble to have any need of it, but it should have need of you."

CHRISTIANS MAY BEAR THE SWORD

You ask whether a Christian, also, may bear the secular sword and punish the wicked, since Christ's words, "Thou shalt not resist the evil," are so clear and definite that the sophists have had to make a counsel of them. I answer, You have now heard two propositions. The one is, that the sword can have no place among Christians, therefore you cannot bear it among and against Christians, who do not need it. The question, therefore, must be directed to the other side, to the non-Christians, whether as a Christian you may there bear it. Here the other proposition applies, that you are under obligation to serve and further the sword by whatever means you can, with body, soul, honor or goods. For it is nothing that you need, but something quite useful and profitable for the whole world and for your neighbor. Therefore, should you see that there is a lack of hangmen, beadles, judges, lords, or princes, and find that you are qualified, you should offer your services and seek the place, that necessary government may by no means be despised and become inefficient or perish. For the world cannot and dare not dispense with it.

You ask, Why did not Christ and the apostles bear the sword? Tell me, Why did He not also take a wife, or become a cobbler or a tailor? If an occupation or office is not good because Christ Himself did not occupy it, what would become of all occupations and offices, with the exception of the ministry which alone He exercised? Christ fulfilled His own office and vocation, but thereby did not reject any other. It was not meet that He should bear the sword, for He was to bear only that office by which His kingdom is governed and which properly serves His kingdom. Now it does not concern His kingdom that He should be a married man, a cobbler, a tailor, a farmer, a prince, a hangman or a beadle, neither is the sword or secular law of any concern, but only God's Word and Spirit, by which His people are inwardly governed. This office which He exercised then, and still exercises, always bestows God's Word and Spirit; and in this office the apostles and all spiritual rulers must needs follow Him. For they are kept so busily employed with the spiritual sword, the Word of God, in fulfilling this their calling, that they must indeed neglect the worldly sword, and leave it to those who do not have to preach; although it is not contrary to their calling to use it, as I have said. For every one must attend to his own calling and work.

Therefore, even though Christ did not bear the sword nor prescribe it, it is sufficient that He did not forbid or abolish it, but rather endorsed it; just as it is sufficient that He did not abolish the state of matrimony, but endorsed it, though He Himself took no wife and gave no commandment concerning it. He had to identify Himself throughout with the occupation and work which properly and entirely served the furtherance of His kingdom, so that no occasion and binding example might be made of it, to teach and believe that the kingdom of God cannot exist without matrimony and the sword and such externals (since Christ's examples are binding), when it is only by God's Word and Spirit that it does exist. This was and had to be Christ's peculiar work as the supreme King in this kingdom. Since, however, not all Christians have this same office, though innately it belongs to them, it is meet that they should have some other, external one, by which God may also be served.

From all this we see what is the true meaning of Christ's words in Matthew v, "Resist not evil," etc. It is this, that a Christian should be so disposed that he will suffer every evil and injustice, not avenge himself nor bring suit in court, and in nothing make use of secular power and law for himself. For others, however, he may and should seek vengeance, justice, protection and help, and do what he can toward this. Likewise, the State should, either of itself or through the instigation of others, help and protect him without complaint, application or instigation on his part. When the State does not do this, he ought to permit himself to be robbed and despoiled, and not resist the evil, as Christ's words say.

THE EXTENT OF SECULAR AUTHORITY

We come now to the main part of this treatise. For as we have learned that there must be temporal authority on earth, and how it is to be employed in a Christian and salutary way, we must now learn how far its arm extends and how far its hand reaches, lest it extend too far and encroach upon God's kingdom and rule. And it is very necessary to know this, since where it is given too wide a scope, intolerable and terrible injury follows; and, on the other hand, it cannot be too much restricted without working injury. In the latter case the punishment is too light; in the former, too severe. It is more tolerable, however, to err on the latter side and punish too little; since it always is better to let a knave live than to kill a good man, for the world will still have knaves, and must have them, but of good men there are few.

In the first place, it must be noted that the two classes of Adam's children, the one in God's kingdom under Christ, the other in the kingdom of the world under the State, have two kinds of laws, as was said above. Every kingdom must have its own laws and regulations, and without law no kingdom or government can exist, as daily experience sufficiently proves. Worldly government has laws which extend no farther than to life and property and what is external upon earth. For over the soul God can and will let no one rule but Himself. Therefore, where temporal power presumes to prescribe laws for the soul, it encroaches upon God's government and only misleads and destroys the soul. We desire to make this so clear that every one shall grasp it, and that our junkers, the princes and bishops, may see what fools they are when they seek to coerce the people with their laws and commandments into believing one thing or another.

When a man-made law is imposed upon the soul, in order to make it believe this or that, as that man prescribes, there is certainly no word of God for it. If there is no word of God for it, it is uncertain whether God will have it so, for we cannot be certain that what He does not command pleases Him. Nay, we are sure that it does not please Him, for He desires that our faith be grounded simply and entirely on His divine Word, as He says in Matthew xvi, "On this rock will I build my church"; and in John x, "My sheep hear my voice and know me; but the voice of strangers they hear not, but flee from them." It follows from this that the secular power forces souls to eternal death with such an outrageous law, for it compels them to believe as right and certainly pleasing to God what is nevertheless uncertain, nay, what is certainly displeasing to Him, since there is no clear word of God for it. For whoever believes that to be right which is wrong or uncertain denies the truth, which is God Himself, and believes in lies and errors and counts that right which is wrong.

Hence it is the height of folly when they command that one shall believe the Church, the fathers, the councils, though there be no word of God for it. The devil's apostles command such things, not the Church; for the Church commands nothing unless it is sure it is God's Word, as St. Peter says, "If any man speak let him speak as the oracles of God." It will be a very long time, however, before they prove that the statements of the councils are God's Word. Still more foolish is it when they assert that kings and princes and the mass of men believe thus and so. If you please, we are not baptised unto kings, princes, or even unto the mass of men, but unto Christ and unto God Himself; neither are we called kings, princes or common folk, but Christians. No one shall and can command the soul, unless he can show it the way to heaven; but this no man can do, only God. Therefore in matters which concern the salvation of souls nothing but God's Word shall be taught and accepted.

Again, consummate fools though they are, they must confess that they have no power over souls. For no human being can kill a soul or make it alive, conduct it to heaven or hell. And if they will not believe us in this, Christ indeed will certify strongly enough to it, since He says in Matthew x, "Fear not them which kill the body and after that have power to do naught; but rather fear Him Who after He has killed the body has power to condemn to hell." I consider that here it is sufficiently clear that the soul is taken out of human hands and is placed under the power of God alone. Now tell me, how much wit is there in the head of him who imposes commandments where he has no power at all? Who would not regard one as insane if he commanded the moon to shine when he desired it? How fitting it would be if the Leipzigers would impose laws on us Wittenbergers, or again, if we in Wittenberg would lay laws on those in Leipzig. They would certainly send the law-makers a thank-offering of hellebore to clear the brain and cure the snuffles. Nevertheless, our emperors and wise princes continue to permit pope, bishops and sophists to lead them on, one blind man leading the other, to command their subjects to believe, without God's Word, whatever they please,

and still would be known as Christian princes. God help us!

Besides, we can understand how any authority shall and may act only where it can see, know, judge, change and convert. For what kind of judge would he be who should blindly judge matters which he neither heard nor saw? Tell me, how can a man see, know, judge, condemn and change hearts? This is reserved for God alone, as Psalm vii says, "God trieth the heart and reins"; likewise, "The Lord shall judge the people"; and Acts xv, "God knoweth the hearts"; and, Jeremiah xvii, "Wicked and unsearchable is the human heart; who can know it? I the Lord, who search the heart and reins." A court ought and must be quite certain and clear about everything, if it is to pass sentence. But the thoughts and intents of the heart can be known to no one but God; therefore it is useless and impossible to command or compel any one by force to believe one thing or another. It must be taken hold of in a different way; force cannot accomplish it. And I am surprised at the great fools, since they themselves all say, *De occultis non judicat ecclesia,*—the Church does not judge secret things. If the spiritual rule of the Church governs only public matters, how dare the senseless secular power judge and control such a secret, spiritual, hidden matter as faith?

Furthermore, every man is responsible for his own faith, and he must see to it for himself that he believes rightly. As little as another can go to hell or heaven for me, so little can he believe or disbelieve for me; and as little as he can open or shut heaven or hell for me, so little can he drive me to faith or unbelief. Since, then, belief or unbelief is a matter of every one's conscience, and since this is no lessening of the secular power, the latter should be content and attend to its own affairs and permit men to believe one thing or another, as they are able and willing, and constrain no one by force. For faith is a free work, to which no one can be forced. Nay, it is a divine work, done in the Spirit, certainly not a matter which outward authority should compel or create. Hence arises the well-known saying, found also in Augustine, "No one can or ought be constrained to believe."

Besides, the blind, wretched folk do not see how utterly hopeless and impossible a thing they are attempting. For no matter how much they fret and fume, they cannot do more than make the people obey them by word and deed; the heart they cannot constrain, though they wear themselves out trying. For the proverb is true, "Thoughts are free." Why then would they constrain people to believe from the heart, when they see that it is impossible? In this way they compel weak consciences to lie, to deny, and to say what they do not believe in their hearts, and they load themselves down with dreadful alien sins. For all the lies and false confessions which such weak consciences utter fall back upon him who compels them. It were far better, if their subjects erred, simply to let them err, than that they should constrain them to lie and to say what is not in their hearts; neither is it right to defend evil with what is worse.

Would you like to know why God ordains that the temporal princes must offend so frightfully? I will tell you. God has given them over to a perverse mind and will make an end of them, as well as of the spiritual nobles. For my ungracious lords, the pope and the bishops, should be bishops and preach God's Word; this they leave undone and are become temporal princes, and govern with laws which concern only life and property. How thoroughly they have turned things upside down! Inwardly they ought to be ruling souls by God's Word; hence outwardly they rule castles, cities, land and people and torture souls with unspeakable outrages. Similarly, the temporal lords should rule land and people outwardly; this they do not do. All they can do is to flay and scrape, put tax on tax, tribute on tribute, let loose now a bear, now a wolf. Besides this, there is no justice, fidelity or truth to be found among them; what they do would be beneath robbers and knaves, and their temporal rule has sunk quite as low as that of the spiritual tyrants. Hence God also perverts their minds, that they rush on in their senselessness and would establish a spiritual rule over souls, as the others would establish a temporal rule, in order that they may contentedly burden themselves with alien sins, and with God's and all men's hate, until they go under with bishops, priests and monks, one knave with the other. Then they lay all the blame on the Gospel, and instead of doing penance, blaspheme God and say that our preaching has

brought about what their perverse wickedness has merited and still unceasingly merits, as the Romans did when they were destroyed. Here then you have God's decree regarding the high and mighty. But they are not to believe it, lest this severe decree of God be hindered by their repentance.

You reply, But Paul said in Romans xiii, "Every soul shall be subject to power and authority," and Peter says, "We should be subject to every ordinance of man." I answer, That is just what I want! These sayings are in my favor. St. Paul speaks of authority and power. Now, you have just heard that no one but God can have authority over souls. Hence Paul cannot be speaking of any obedience except where there can be corresponding authority. From this it follows that he does not speak of faith, and does not say that secular authority should have the right to command faith, but he is speaking of external goods, and that these are to be set in order and controlled on earth. This his words also clearly indicate, when be prescribes the limits to both authority and obedience, and says, "Render to every one his dues, tribute to whom tribute is due, custom to whom custom; honor to whom honor; fear to whom fear." You see, temporal obedience and power apply only externally to tribute, custom, honor and fear. Likewise when he says, "The power is not a terror to good, but to evil works," he again limits the power, so that it is to have the mastery not over faith or the Word of God, but over evil works.

This is what St. Peter also desires, when he says, "Ordinance of man." Human ordinance cannot possibly extend its authority to heaven and over souls, but belongs only to earth, to the external intercourse of men with each other, where men can see, know, judge, sentence punish and acquit. Christ Himself made this nice distinction and summed it all up briefly when He said, "Give unto Cæsar the things that are Cæsar's, and unto God the things that are God's." If, then, imperial power extended to God's kingdom and power, and were not something by itself, He would not thus have made it a separate thing. For, as was said, the soul is not under Cæsar's power; he can neither teach nor guide it, neither kill it nor make it alive, neither bind it nor loose it, neither judge it nor condemn it, neither hold it nor release it, which he must do had he power to command it and impose laws upon it; but over life, goods and honor he indeed has this right, for such things are under his authority.

David, too, stated this long ago in one of his short sayings when he says in Psalm cxv, "The heavens hath he given to the Lord of heaven; but the earth hath he given to the children of men." That is, over what is on earth and belongs to the temporal, earthly kingdom, man has authority from God, but that which belongs to the heavenly eternal kingdom is entirely under the heavenly Lord. Nor does Moses forget this when he says in Genesis i, "God said, Let us make man to rule over the beasts of the earth, over the fish in the waters, over the birds in the air." There only external rule is ascribed to men. And, in short, this is the meaning, as St. Peter says, Acts v, "We must obey God rather than men." Thereby he clearly sets a limit to worldly government, for if we had to do all that worldly government demands it would be to no purpose to say, "We must obey God rather than men."

If then your prince or temporal lord commands you to hold with the pope, to believe this or that, or commands you to give up certain books, you should say, It does not befit Lucifer to sit by the side of God. Dear Lord, I owe you obedience with life and goods; command me within the limits of your power on earth, and I will obey. But if you command me to believe, and to put away books, I will not obey; for in this case you are a tyrant and overreach yourself, and command where you have neither right nor power, etc. Should he take your property for this, and punish such disobedience, blessed are you. Thank God that you are worthy to suffer for the sake of the divine Word, and let him rave, fool that he is. He will meet his judge. For I tell you, if you do not resist him but give him his way, and let him take your faith or your books, you have really denied God.

Let me illustrate. In Meissen, Bavaria, in the Mark, and other places, the tyrants have issued an order that the New Testament be delivered to the courts everywhere. In this case their subjects ought not deliver a page or a letter, at risk of their salvation. For whoever does so, delivers Christ into Herod's hands, since they act as murderers of Christ, like Herod. But if their houses are ordered searched and books or goods taken by force, they should suffer it to be done. Outrage is not to be resisted, but endured, yet they should not sanction it, nor serve or obey or follow by moving foot or finger. For such tyrants act as wordly princes should act,—"wordly" princes they are; but the world is God's enemy. Therefore they must also do what is opposed to God, and in accord with the world, that they may by no means lose all honor, but remain worldly princes. Hence do not wonder that they rage and mock at the Gospel; they must live up to their name and title.

You must know that from the beginning of the world a wise prince is a rare bird indeed; still more so a pious prince. They are usually the greatest fools or the worst knaves on earth; therefore one must constantly expect the worst from them and look for little good from them, especially in divine matters, which concern the salvation of souls. They are God's jailers and hangmen, and His divine wrath needs them to punish the wicked and preserve outward peace. Our God is a great Lord, and therefore must have such noble, honorable and rich hangmen and beadles, and desires that they shall have riches, honor and fear, in full and plenty, from every one. It pleases His divine will that we call His hangmen gracious lords, fall at their feet and be subject to them in all humility, so long as they do not ply their trade too far and desire to become shepherds instead of hangmen. If a prince becomes wise, pious or a Christian, it is one of the great wonders, and one of the most precious tokens of divine grace upon that land. For the usual course is according to the saying in Isaiah iii, "I will give children to be their princes and babes shall rule over them," and in Hosea xiii, "I will give thee a king in my anger and take him away in my wrath." The world is too wicked, and does not deserve to have many wise and pious princes. Frogs need storks.

Again you say, Temporal power does not force men to believe, but simply prevents them from being misled by false doctrine; otherwise how could heretics be prevented from preaching? I answer, This the bishops should do, to whom, and not to the princes, such duty is entrusted. Heresy can never be prevented by force. That must be taken hold of in a different way, and must be opposed and dealt with otherwise than with the sword. Here God's Word must strive; if that does not accomplish the end it will remain unaccomplished through secular power, though it fill the world with blood. Heresy is a spiritual matter, which no iron can strike, no fire burn, no water drown. God's Word alone avails here, as Paul says, II Corinthians x, "Our weapons are not carnal, but mighty through God to destroy every counsel and high thing that exalteth itself against the knowledge of God, and to bring into captivity every thought to the obedience of Christ."

Moreover, faith and heresy are never so strong as when men oppose them by sheer force, without God's Word. For men count it certain that such force is for a wrong cause and is directed against the right, since it proceeds without God's Word, and does not know how to further its cause except by force, just as the brute beasts do. For even in secular affairs force can be used only after the wrong has been legally condemned. How much less possible is it to act with force, without justice and God's Word, in these high, spiritual matters! See, therefore what fine, shrewd nobles they are. They would drive out heresy, and set about it in such a way that they only strengthen the opposition, make themselves suspected, and justify the heretics. Friend, would you drive out heresy, then you must find a plan to tear it first of all from the heart and altogether to turn men's wills away from it; force will not accomplish this, but only strengthen the heresy. What avails it to strengthen heresy in the heart and to weaken only its outward expression, and to force the tongue to lie? God's Word, however, enlightens the heart; and so all heresies and errors perish of themselves from the heart.

Such overpowering of heresy the prophet Isaiah proclaimed in his eleventh chapter when he said, "He shall smite the earth with the rod of His mouth, and slay the wicked with the breath of His lips." You see, if the wicked is to be smitten and converted, it is accomplished by the mouth. In short, such princes and tyrants do not know that to fight against heresy is to fight against the devil, who fills men's hearts with error, as Paul says in Ephesians vi, "We fight not with flesh and blood, but with spiritual wickedness, with the rulers of the darkness of this world." Therefore, as long as the devil is not repelled and

driven from the heart, it matters as little to him that I destroy his vessels with fire or sword, as it would if I fought lightning with a straw. Job bore abundant witness to this, when in his forty-first chapter he said that the devil esteemeth iron as straw and fears no power on earth. We learn it also from experience, for although all the Jews and heretics were burned, yet no one has been or will be convinced and converted thereby.

Nevertheless such a world as this deserves such princes, none of whom do their duty. The bishops are to leave the Word of God alone and not rule souls by it, but command the worldly princes to rule them with the sword. The worldly princes, in their turn, are to permit usury, theft, adultery, murder, and other evil works, and themselves do them; and then allow the bishops to punish with the ban. Thus they turn things topsy-turvy, and rule souls with iron and the body with bans, so that worldly princes rule in a spiritual, and spiritual princes in a wordly way. What else does the devil have to do on earth than thus to play the fool and hold carnival with his folk? These are our Christian princes, who defend the faith and devour the Turk. Fine fellows, to be sure, whom we may well trust to accomplish something by such refined wisdom, namely, break their necks and plunge land and people into suffering and want.

I would, however, in all fidelity advise the blinded folk to take heed to the short saying is Psalm cvii, *"Effundit contemptum super principes"* ("He poureth contempt upon princes"). I swear unto you by God that, if through your fault this little text becomes effective against you, you are lost, though every one of you be as mighty as the Turk; and your snorting and raving will help you nothing. A large part has already come true. For there are very few princes that are not reckoned fools or knaves. That is because they show themselves to be such; the common man is learning to think, and the prince's scourge, which God calls *contemptum,* is gathering force among the mob and with the common man. I fear there is no way to stop it, unless the princes conduct themselves in a princely manner and begin again to rule reasonably and thoroughly. Men ought not, men cannot, men will not suffer your tyranny and presumption much longer. Dear princes and lords, be wise and guide yourselves accordingly. God will no longer tolerate it. The world is no longer what it was when you hunted and drove the people like so much game. Therefore drop your outrage and force, and remember to deal justly and let God's Word have its course, as it will and must and shall, nor will you prevent it. If there is heresy abroad, let it be overcome, as is proper, with God's Word. But if you will keep on brandishing the sword, take heed lest there come one who shall bid you sheath it, and that not in God's name.

But should you ask, Since there is to be no secular sword among Christians, how are they to be ruled outwardly? There certainly must be authority also among Christians. I answer, Among Christians there shall and can be no authority; but all are alike subject to one another, as Paul says in Romans xii, "Each shall count the other his superior," and Peter in I Peter v, "All of you be subject one to another." This is also what Christ means in Luke xiv, "When you are bidden to a wedding sit down in the lowest room." There is no superior among Christians, but Christ Himself and Christ alone. And what kind of authority can there be where all are equal and have the same right, power, possession, and honor, and no one desires to be the other's superior, but each the other's inferior? One could not establish authority where there are such people, even if one would, since their character and nature will not permit them to have superiors, for no one is willing or able to be the superior. But when there are no such people, there are no real Christians.

What, then, are the priests and bishops? I answer, Their government is not one of authority or power, but a service and an office; for they are neither higher nor better than other Christians. Therefore they should not impose any law or decree on others without their will and consent; their rule consists in nothing else than in dealing with God's Word, leading Christians by it and overcoming heresy by its means. For, as was said, Christians can be ruled by nothing but by God's Word. For Christians must be ruled in faith, not by outward works. Faith, however, can come through no word of man, but only through the Word of God, as Paul says in Romans x, "Faith cometh by hearing, and hearing by the Word of God." Those who do not believe are not Christians, do not belong to Christ's kingdom, but to the worldly kingdom, and are constrained and ruled by the sword and by outward rule. Christians do of themselves, without constraint, every good thing, and find God's Word alone sufficient for them.

II CALVIN

*Institutes of the Christian Religion**

SPIRITUAL AND POLITICAL GOVERNMENT

Man is under two kinds of government: one spiritual, by which the conscience is formed to piety and the service of God; the other political, by which a man is instructed in the duties of humanity and civility, which are to be observed in an intercourse with mankind. They are generally, and not improperly, denominated the spiritual and the temporal jurisdiction, indicating that the former species of government pertains to the life of the soul, and that the latter relates to the concerns of the present state, not only to the provision of food and clothing, but to the enactment of laws to regulate a man's life among his neighbors by the rules of holiness, integrity, and sobriety. For the former has its seat in the interior of the mind, whilst the latter only directs the external conduct: one may be termed a spiritual kingdom, and the other a political one. But these two, as we have distinguished them, always require to be considered separately; and while the one is under discussion, the mind must be abstracted from all consideration of the other. For man contains, as it were, two worlds, capable of being governed by various rulers and various laws. This distinction will prevent what the Gospel inculcates concerning spiritual liberty from being misapplied to political regulations, as though Christians were less subject to the external government of human laws because their consciences have been set at liberty before God, as though their freedom of spirit necessarily exempted them from all carnal servitude. Again, because even in those constitutions which seem to pertain to the spiritual kingdom, there may possibly be some deception, it is necessary to discriminate between these also—which are to be accounted legitimate, as according with the Divine word, and which, on the contrary, ought not to be received among believers.

The question which, as I have observed, is in itself not very obscure or intricate, greatly perplexes many because they do not distinguish with sufficient precision between the external jurisdiction and the court of conscience. The difficulty is increased by Paul's injunction to obey magistrates "not only for wrath, but also for conscience's sake,"[1] from which should follow that the conscience also is bound by political laws. But if this were true, it would supersede all that we have already said, or are now about to say, respecting spiritual government. For the solution of this difficulty it will be of use, first, to know what conscience is. And the definition of it must be derived from the etymology of the word. For as, when men apprehend the knowledge of things in the mind and understanding, they are thence said *scire,* "to know," whence is derived the word *scientia,* "science" or "knowledge," so when they have a sense of Divine justice, as an additional witness, which permits them not to conceal their sins or to elude accusation at the tribunal of the supreme Judge, this sense is termed *conscientia,* "conscience." For it is a kind of medium between God and man, because it does not suffer a man to suppress what he knows within himself, but pursues him till it brings him to conviction. This is

---

*From Jean Calvin, *Institutes of the Christian Religion* (1536, trans. John Allen, 1813).

[1] Rom. 8:1, 5.

what Paul means by "their conscience also bearing witness, and their thoughts accusing, or else excusing, one another."[2] Simple knowledge might remain, as it were, confined within a man. This sentiment, therefore, which places man before the Divine tribunal is appointed, as it were, to watch over man, to observe and examine all his secrets, that nothing may remain enveloped in darkness. Hence the old proverb, "Conscience is as a thousand witnesses." For the same reason Peter speaks of "the answer of a good conscience toward God,"[3] to express our tranquillity of mind when, persuaded of the favor of Christ, we present ourselves with boldness in the presence of God. And the author of the Epistle to the Hebrews expresses absolution or freedom from every future charge of sin, by "having no more conscience of sin."[4]

THE DISCIPLINE OF THE CHURCH: NO ONE EXEMPTED

The discipline of the Church depends chiefly on the power of the keys and the spiritual jurisdiction. To make this more easily understood, let us divide the Church into two principal orders—the clergy and the people. I use the word *clergy* as the common, though improper appelation of those who execute the public ministry in the Church. We shall, first, speak of the common discipline to which all ought to be subject; and then we shall proceed to the clergy, who, besides this common discipline, have a discipline peculiar to themselves. But as some have such a hatred of discipline, as to abhor the very name, they should consider the following: that if no society, and even no house, though containing only a small family, can be preserved in a proper state without discipline, this is far more necessary in the Church, the state of which ought to be the most orderly of all. As the saving doctrine of Christ is the soul of the Church, so discipline forms the ligaments which connect the members together, and keep each other in its proper place. Whoever, therefore, either desire the abolition of all discipline, or obstruct its restoration, whether they act from design or

inadvertency, they certainly promote the entire dissolution of the Church. For what will be the consequence if every man be at liberty to follow his own inclinations? But such would be the case, unless the preaching of the doctrine were accompanied with private admonitions, reproofs, and other means to enforce the doctrine, and prevent it from being altogether ineffectual. Discipline, therefore, serves as a bridle to curb and restrain the refractory who resist the doctrine of Christ; or as a spur to stimulate the inactive; and sometimes as a father's rod, with which those who have grievously fallen may be chastised in mercy, and with the gentleness of the Spirit of Christ. When we see the approach of certain beginnings of a dreadful desolation in the Church, since there is no solicitude or means to keep the people in obedience to our Lord, necessity itself proclaims the want of a remedy; and this is the only remedy which has been commanded by Christ, or which has ever been adopted among believers.

From this discipline none were exempted; so that princes and plebeians yielded the same submission to it; and that with the greatest propriety, since it is evidently the discipline of Christ, to whom it is reasonable that all the sceptres and diadems of kings should be subject. Thus Theodosius, when Ambrose excluded him from the privilege of communion on account of a massacre perpetrated at Thessalonica, laid aside the ensigns of royalty with which he was invested, publicly in the Church bewailed his sin, which the deceitful suggestions of others had tempted him to commit, and implored pardon with groans and tears. For great kings ought not to think it any dishonor to prostrate themselves as suppliants before Christ the King of kings, nor ought they be displeased at being judged by the Church. As they hear scarcely anything in their courts but mere flatteries, it is the more highly necessary for them to receive correction from the Lord by the mouth of his *ministers;* they ought even to wish not to be spared by the *pastors,* that they may be spared by the Lord. The legitimate process in excommunicating an offender, as is pointed out by Paul, requires it to be done, not by the elders alone, but with the knowledge and approbation of the Church: in such a manner, however, that the multitude of

---

[2] Rom. 2:15.
[3] I Pet. 3:21.
[4] Heb. 10:2.

the people may not direct the proceeding, but may watch over it as witnesses and guardians, that nothing may be done by a few persons from any improper motive. Beside the invocation of the name of God, the whole of the proceeding ought to be conducted with a gravity declarative of the presence of Christ, so that there be no doubt of his presiding over the sentence.

ON CIVIL GOVERNMENT

Having already stated that man is the subject of two kinds of government, and having sufficiently discussed that which is situated in the soul, or the inner man, and relates to eternal life, we shall now say something of the other kind which relates to civil justice and the regulation of the external conduct. For, though the nature of this argument seems to have no connection with the spiritual doctrine of faith which I have undertaken to discuss, the sequel will show that I have sufficient reason for connecting them together, and, indeed, that necessity obliges me to it, especially since, on the one hand, infatuated and barbarous men madly endeavor to subvert this ordinance established by God, and, on the other hand, the flatterers of princes, extolling their power beyond all just bounds, hesitate not to oppose it to the authority of God himself. Unless both these errors be resisted, the purity of the faith will be destroyed. Besides, it is of no small importance for us to know what benevolent provision God has made for mankind in this instance, that we may be stimulated by a greater degree of pious zeal to testify our gratitude. In the first place, before we enter on the subject itself, it is necessary for us to recur to the distinction which we have already established, lest we fall into an error very common in the world, and injudiciously confound together these two things the nature of which is altogether different.

For some men, when they hear that the Gospel promises a liberty which acknowledges no king or magistrate among them, but submits to Christ alone, think they can enjoy no advantage of their liberty while they see any power exalted above them. They imagine, therefore, that nothing will prosper unless the whole world be modeled in a new form, without any tribunals or laws, or magistrates, or anything of a similar kind which they consider injurious to their liberty. But he who knows how to distinguish between the body and the soul, between this present transitory life and the future eternal one, will find no difficulty in understanding that the spiritual kingdom of Christ and civil government are things very different and remote from each other. Since it is a Jewish folly, therefore, to seek and include the kingdom of Christ under the elements of this world, let us, on the contrary, considering what the Scripture clearly inculcates, that the benefit which is received from the grace of Christ is spiritual—let us, I say, remember to confine within its proper limits all this liberty which is promised and offered to us in him. For why is it that the same apostle who, in one place, exhorts to "stand fast in the liberty wherewith Christ hath made us free and be not entangled again with the yoke of bondage,"[5] in another enjoins servants to "care not for" their servile condition,[6] except that spiritual liberty may very well consist with civil servitude? In this sense we are likewise to understand him in these passages: "There is neither Jew nor Greek, there is neither bond nor free, there is neither male nor female."[7] Again: "There is neither Greek nor Jew, circumcision nor uncircumcision, Barbarian, Scythian, bond nor free: but Christ is all, and in all,"[8] in which he signifies that it is of no importance what is our condition among men or under the laws of what nation we live, as the kingdom of Christ consists not in these things.

Yet this distinction does not lead us to consider the whole system of civil government as a polluted thing which has nothing to do with Christian men. Some fanatics who are pleased with nothing but liberty, or rather licentiousness without any restraint, do indeed boast and vociferate, That since we are dead with Christ to the elements of this world and, being translated into the kingdom of God, sit among the celestials, it is a degradation to us and far beneath our dignity to be occupied with those secular and impure cares which relate to

[5] Gal. 5:1.
[6] I Cor. 7:21.
[7] Gal. 3:28.
[8] Col. 3:11.

things altogether uninteresting to a Christian man. Of what use, they ask, are laws without judgments and tribunals? But what have judgments to do with a Christian man? And if it be unlawful to kill, of what use are laws and judgments to us? But as we have just suggested that this kind of government is distinct from that spiritual and internal reign of Christ, so it ought to be known that they are in no respect at variance with each other. For that spiritual reign, even now upon earth, commences within us some preludes of the heavenly kingdom, and in this mortal and transitory life affords us some prelibations of immortal and incorruptible blessedness; but this civil government is designed, as long as we live in this world, to cherish and support the external worship of God, to preserve the pure doctrine of religion, to defend the constitution of the Church, to regulate our lives in a manner requisite for the society of men, to form our manners to civil justice, to promote our concord with each other, and to establish general peace and tranquillity—all of which I confess to be superfluous if the kingdom of God, as it now exists in us, extinguishes the present life. But if it is the will of God that while we are aspiring toward our true country, we be pilgrims on the earth, and if such aids are necessary to our pilgrimage, they who take them from man deprive him of his human nature. They plead that there should be so much perfection in the Church of God that its order would suffice to supply the place of all laws; but they foolishly imagine a perfection which can never be found in any community of men. For since the insolence of the wicked is so great, and their iniquity so obstinate, that it can scarcely be restrained by all the severity of the laws, what may we expect they would do if they found themselves at liberty to perpetuate crimes with impunity whose outrages even the arm of power cannot altogether prevent?

But for speaking of the exercise of civil polity, there will be another place more suitable. At present we only wish it to be understood that to entertain a thought of its extermination is inhuman barbarism; it is equally as necessary to mankind as bread and water, light and air, and far more excellent. For it not only tends to secure the accommodations arising from all these things, that men may breathe, eat, drink, and be sustained in life, though it comprehends all these things while it causes them to live together, yet I say this is not its only tendency; its objects also are that idolatry, sacrileges against the name of God, blasphemies against his truth, and other offenses against religion may not openly appear and be disseminated among the people; that the public tranquillity may not be disturbed; that every person may enjoy his property without molestation; that men may transact their business together without fraud or injustice; that integrity and modesty may be cultivated among them; in short, that there may be a public form of religion among Christians, and that humanity may be maintained among men. Nor let anyone think it strange that I now refer to human polity the charge of the due maintenance of religion, which I may appear to have placed beyond the jurisdiction of men. For I do not allow men to make laws respecting religion and the worship of God now any more than I did before, though I approve of civil government which provides that the true religion contained in the law of God be not violated and polluted by public blasphemies with impunity. But the perspicuity of order will assist the readers to attain a clearer understanding of what sentiments ought to be entertained respecting the whole system of civil administration, if we enter on a discussion of each branch of it. These are three: The magistrate, who is the guardian and conservator of the laws; the laws according to which he governs; the people, who are governed by the laws and obey the magistrate. Let us, therefore, examine, first, the function of a magistrate, whether it be a legitimate calling and approved by God, the nature of the duty, and the extent of the power; secondly, by what laws Christian government ought to be regulated; and lastly, what advantage the people derive from the laws, and what obedience they owe to the magistrate.

THE DUTY OF
POLITICAL RULERS

Here it is necessary to state in a brief manner the nature of the office of magistracy, as described in the word of God, and wherein it consists. If the Scripture did not teach that this office extends to both tables of the law, we might learn it from heathen writers; for not one of them has treated of the office of magistrates, of legislation, and civil government, without beginning with religion and Divine worship. And thus they have all confessed that no government can be happily constituted unless its first object be the promotion of piety, and that all laws are preposterous which neglect the claims of God and merely provide for the interests of men. Therefore, as religion holds the first place among all the philosophers, and as this has always been regarded by the universal consent of all nations, Christian princes and magistrates ought to be ashamed of their indolence if they do not make it the object of their most serious care. We have already shown that this duty is particularly enjoined upon them by God; for it is reasonable that they should employ their utmost efforts in asserting and defending the honor of Him whose vicegerents they are and by whose favor they govern. And the principal commendations given in the Scripture to the good kings are for having restored the worship of God when it had been corrupted or abolished, or for having devoted their attention to religion, that it might flourish in purity and safety under their reigns. On the contrary, the sacred history represents it as one of the evils arising from anarchy, or a want of good government, that when "there was no king in Israel, every man did that which was right in his own eyes."[9] These things evince the folly of those who would wish magistrates to neglect all thoughts of God, and to confine themselves entirely to the administration of justice among men, as though God appointed governors in his name to decide secular controversies, and disregarded that which is of far greater importance—the pure worship of himself according to the rule of his law. But a rage for universal innovation, and a desire to escape with impunity, instigate men of turbulent spirits to wish that all the avengers of violated piety were removed out of the world. With respect to the second table, Jeremiah admonishes kings in the following manner: "Execute ye judgment and righteousness, and deliver the spoiled out of the hand of the oppressor; and do no wrong, do no violence to the stranger, the fatherless, nor the widow, neither shed innocent blood."[10] To the same purpose is the exhortation in the eighty-second psalm: "Defend the poor and fatherless: do justice to the afflicted and needy: deliver the poor and needy: rid them out of the hand of the wicked."[11] And Moses "charged the judges" whom he appointed to supply his place, saying—

Hear the causes between your brethren, and judge righteously between every man and his brother, and the stranger that is with him: ye shall not respect persons in judgment; but ye shall hear the small as well as the great; ye shall not be afraid of the face of man; for the judgment is God's.[12]

I forbear to remark the directions given by him in another place respecting their future kings: "He shall not multiply horses to himself; neither shall he greatly multiply to himself silver and gold; his heart shall not be lifted up above his brethren; he shall read in the law all the days of his life";[13] also that judges show no partiality nor take bribes, with similar injunctions, which abound in the Scriptures; because, in describing the office of magistrates in this treatise, my design is not so much to instruct magistrates themselves, as to show to others what magistrates are and for what end God has appointed them. We see, therefore, that they are constituted the protectors and vindicators of the public innocence, modesty, probity, and tranquillity, whose sole object it ought to be to promote the common peace and security of all. Of these virtues, David declares that he will be an example when he shall be exalted to the royal throne.

I will set no wicked thing before mine eyes. I will not know a wicked person. Whoso privily slandereth his neighbour, him will I cut off: him that hath a high look and a proud heart will I not suffer. Mine eyes shall be upon the faithful of the land, that they may dwell with me: he that walketh in a perfect way, he shall serve me.[14]

---

[9] Judg. 21:25.
[10] Jer. 22:3.
[11] Ps. 82:3–4.
[12] Deut. 1:16–17.
[13] Deut. 17:16–17, 19–20.
[14] Ps. 101:3–6.

But as they cannot do this unless they defend good men from the injuries of the wicked and aid the oppressed by their relief and protection, they are likewise armed with power for the suppression of crimes, and the severe punishment of malefactors whose wickedness disturbs the public peace. For experience fully verifies the observation of Solon: "That all states are supported by reward and punishment; and that when these two things are removed, all the discipline of human societies is broken and destroyed." For the minds of many lose their regard for equity and justice unless virtue be rewarded with due honor; nor can the violence of the wicked be restrained unless crimes are followed by severe punishments. And these two parts are included in the injunction of the prophet to kings and other governors to "execute judgment and righteousness."[15] "Righteousness" means the care, patronage, defense, vindication, and liberation of the innocent; "judgment" imports the repression of the audacity, the coercion of the violence, and the punishment of the crime of the impious.

THE DUTY OF SUBJECTS

The first duty of subjects toward their magistrates is to entertain the most honorable sentiments of their function, which they know to be a jurisdiction delegated to them from God, and on that account to esteem and reverence them as God's ministers and vicegerents. For there are some persons to be found who show themselves very obedient to their magistrates and have not the least wish that there were no magistrates for them to obey, because they know them to be so necessary to the public good, but who, nevertheless, consider the magistrates themselves as no other than necessary evils. But something more than this is required of us by Peter when he commands us to "honor the king";[16] and by Solomon, when he says, "Fear thou the Lord and the king";[17] for Peter, under the term "honor," comprehends a sincere and candid esteem; and Solomon, by connecting the king with the Lord, attributes to him a kind of sacred veneration and

dignity. It is also a remarkable commendation of magistrates which is given by Paul, when he says that we "must needs be subject, not only for wrath, but also for conscience's sake";[18] by which he means that subjects ought to be induced to submit to princes and governors, not merely from a dread of their power, as persons are accustomed to yield to an armed enemy, who they know will immediately take vengeance upon them if they resist; but because the obedience which is rendered to princes and magistrates is rendered to God, from whom they have received their authority. I am not speaking of the persons as if the mask of dignity ought to palliate or excuse folly, ignorance, or cruelty, and conduct the most nefarious and flagitious, and so to acquire for vices the praise due to virtues; but I affirm that the station itself is worthy of honor and reverence, so that, whoever our governors are, they ought to possess our esteem and veneration on account of the office which they fill.

Now, as we have hitherto described a magistrate who truly answers to his title—who is the father of his country and, as the poet calls him, the pastor of his people, the guardian of peace, the protector of justice, the avenger of innocence; he would justly be deemed insane who disapproved of such a government. But, as it has happened, in almost all ages, that some princes, regardless of everything to which they ought to have directed their attention and provision, give themselves up to their pleasures in indolent exemption from every care; others, absorbed in their own interest, expose to sale all laws, privileges, rights, and judgments; others plunder the public wealth which they afterwards lavish in mad prodigality; others commit flagrant outrages, pillaging houses, violating virgins and matrons, and murdering infants; many persons cannot be persuaded that such ought to be acknowledged as princes whom, as far as possible, they ought to obey. For in such enormities and actions so completely incompatible, not only with the office of a magistrate, but with the duty of every man, they discover no appearance of the image of God, which ought to be conspicuous in a magistrate;

---

[15] Jer. 22:3.
[16] I Pet. 2:17.
[17] Prov. 24:21.

[18] Rom. 13:5.

while they perceive no vestige of that minister of God who is "not a terror to good works, but to the evil," who is sent "for the punishment of evildoers, and for the praise of them that do well"; nor recognize that governor whose dignity and authority the Scripture recommends to us. And certainly the minds of men have always been naturally disposed to hate and execrate tyrants as much as to love and reverence legitimate kings.

But, if we direct our attention to the word of God, it will carry us much farther: even to submit to the government, not only of those princes who discharge their duty to us with becoming integrity and fidelity, but of all who possess the sovereignty, even though they perform none of the duties of their function. For, though the Lord testifies that the magistrate is an eminent gift of his liberality to preserve the safety of men, and prescribes to magistrates themselves the extent of their duty, yet he at the same time declares that whatever be their characters, they have their government only from him; that those who govern for the public good are true specimens and mirrors of his beneficence; and that those who rule in an unjust and tyrannical manner are raised up by him to punish the iniquity of the people; that all equally possess that sacred majesty with which he has invested legitimate authority. I will not proceed any further till I have subjoined a few testimonies in proof of this point. It is unnecessary, however, to labor much to evince an impious king to be a judgment of God's wrath upon the world, as I have no expectation that anyone will deny it; and in this we say no more of a king than of any other robber who plunders our property, or adulterer who violates our bed, or assassin who attempts to murder us; since the Scripture enumerates all these calamities among the curses inflicted by God. But let us rather insist on the proof of that which the minds of men do not so easily admit— that a man of the worst character, and most undeserving of all honor, who holds the sovereign power, really possesses that eminent and Divine authority which the Lord has given by his word to the ministers of his justice and judgment; and, therefore, that he ought to be regarded by his subjects, as far as pertains to public obedience, with the same reverence and esteem which they would show to the best of kings, if such a one were granted to them.

I request my readers to observe and consider with attention what is so frequently and justly mentioned in the Scriptures—the providence and peculiar dispensation of God in distributing kingdoms and appointing whom he pleases to be kings. Daniel says, "God changes the times and the seasons: he removes kings and sets up kings." Again: "That the living may know that the Most High rules in the kingdom of men, and gives it to whomsoever he will." Passages of this kind abound in the Scriptures, but particularly in this prophecy. Now, the character of Nebuchadnezzar, who conquered Jerusalem, is sufficiently known, that he was an invader and depopulator of the territories of others. Yet by the mouth of Ezekiel the Lord declares that he had given him the land of Egypt as a reward for the service which he had performed in devastating Tyre. And Daniel said to him: "Thou, O king, art a king of kings; for the God of heaven has given thee a kingdom, power, strength, and glory; and wheresoever the children of men dwell, the beasts of the field, and the fowls of the heaven, has he given into thine hand, and has made thee ruler over all."

In vain will any one object that this was a special command to the Israelites. For we must observe the reason upon which the Lord founds it. He says: "I have given these lands to Nebuchadnezzar; therefore serve him and live." To whomsoever, therefore, a kingdom shall evidently be given, we have no room to doubt that subjection is due to him. And as soon as he exalts any person to royal dignity, he gives us a declaration of his pleasure that he shall reign. The Scripture contains general testimonies on this subject. Solomon says: "For the transgression of a land, many are the princes thereof." Job says, "He looses the bonds of kings," or divests them of their power, "and girds their loin with a girdle," or restores them to their former dignity. This being admitted, nothing remains for us but to serve and live.

We owe these sentiments of affection and reverence to all our rulers, whatever their characters may be; which I the more frequently repeat that we may learn not to scrutinize the persons themselves, but may be satisfied with knowing that they are invested by the will of the Lord with that function, upon which he has impressed an inviolable majesty. But it will be said that rulers owe mutual duties to their subjects. That I have already admitted. But he who infers from this that obedience ought to be rendered to none but just rulers, is a very bad reasoner. For husbands owe mutual duties to their wives, and parents to their children. Now, if husbands and parents violate their obligations; if parents conduct themselves with discouraging severity and fastidious moroseness towards their children, whom they are forbidden to provoke to wrath; if husbands despise and vex their wives, whom they are commanded to love and to spare as the weaker vessels; does it follow that children should be less obedient to their parents, or wives to their husbands? They are still subject, even to those who are wicked and unkind. As it is incumbent on all not to inquire into the duties of one another, but to confine their attention respectively to their own, this consideration ought particularly to be regarded by those who are subject to the authority of others. Wherefore, if we are inhumanly harassed by a cruel prince; if we are rapaciously plundered by an avaricious or luxurious one; if we are neglected by an indolent one; or if we are persecuted, on account of piety, by an impious and sacrilegious one—let us first call to mind our transgressions against God, which he undoubtedly chastises by these scourges. Thus our impatience will be restrained by humility. Let us, in the next place, consider that it is not in our province to remedy these evils, and that nothing remains for us but to implore the aid of the Lord, in whose hands are the hearts of kings and the revolutions of kingdoms.

RESISTANCE TO TYRANNY

And here is displayed God's wonderful goodness and power and providence; for sometimes he raises up some of his servants as public avengers and arms them with his commission to punish unrighteous domination, and to deliver from their distressing calamities a people who have been unjustly oppressed; sometimes he accomplishes this end by the fury of men who meditate and attempt something altogether different. Thus he liberated the people of Israel from the tyranny of Pharaoh by Moses; from the oppression of Chusan by Othniel; and from other yokes by other kings and judges. Thus he subdued the pride of Tyre by the Egyptians; the insolence of the Egyptians by the Assyrians; the haughtiness of the Assyrians by the Chaldeans; the confidence of Babylon by the Medes and Persians, after Cyrus had subjugated the Medes. The ingratitude of the kings of Israel and Judah and their impious rebellion, notwithstanding his numerous favors, he repressed and punished sometimes by the Assyrians, sometimes by the Babylonians. These were all the executioners of his vengeance, but not all in the same manner. The former, when they were called forth to the performance of such acts by a legitimate commission from God, in taking arms against kings, were not chargeable with the least violation of that majesty with which kings are invested by the ordination of God; but, being armed with authority from Heaven, they punished an inferior power by a superior one, as it is lawful for kings to punish their inferior officers. The latter, though they were guided by the hand of God in such directions as he pleased, and performed his work without being conscious of it, nevertheless contemplated in their hearts nothing but evil.

But whatever opinion be formed of the acts of men, yet the Lord equally executed his work by them when he broke the sanguinary scepters of insolent kings and overturned tyrannical governments. Let princes hear and fear. But, in the meanwhile, it behooves us to use the greatest caution, that we do not despise or violate that authority of magistrates which is entitled to the greatest veneration, which God has established by the most solemn commands, even though it reside in those who are most unworthy of it, and who, as far as in them lies, pollute it by their iniquity. For though the correction of tyrannical domination is the vengeance of God, we are not, therefore, to conclude that it is committed to us who have received no other command than to obey and suffer. This observation I always apply to private persons. For if there be, in the present day, any magistrates appointed for the protection of the people and the moderation of the power of kings, such as were, in ancient times, the Ephori, who were a check upon the kings among the Lacedaemonians, or the popular tribunes upon the consuls among the Romans, or the Demarchi upon the senate among the Athenians; or with power such as perhaps is now possessed by the three estates in every kingdom when they are assembled; I am so far from prohibiting them, in the discharge of their duty, to oppose the violence or cruelty of kings that I affirm that if they connive at kings in their oppression of their people, such forbearance involves the most nefarious perfidy because they fraudulently betray the liberty of the people, of which they know that they have been appointed protectors by the ordination of God.

But in the obedience which we have shown to be due to the authority of governors, it is always necessary to make one exception, and that is entitled to our first attention—that it do not seduce us from obedience to him to whose will the desires of all kings ought to be subject, to whose decrees all their commands ought to yield, to whose majesty all their scepters ought to submit. And, indeed, how preposterous it would be for us, with a view to satisfy men, to incur the displeasure of him on whose account we yield obedience to men! The Lord, therefore, is the King of kings; who, when he has opened his sacred mouth, is to be heard alone, above all, for all, and before all; in the next place, we are subject to those men who preside over us, but no otherwise than in him. If they command anything against him, it ought not to have the least attention, nor, in this case, ought we to pay any regard to all that dignity attached to magistrates, to which no injury is done when it is subjected to the unrivaled and supreme power of God. On this principle Daniel denied that he had committed any crime against the king in disobeying his impious decree;[19] because the king had ex-

ceeded the limits of his office, and had not only done an injury to men, but, by raising his arm against God, had degraded his own authority. On the other hand, the Israelites are condemned for having been too submissive to the impious edict of their king. For when Jeroboam had made his golden calves, in compliance with his will, they deserted the temple of God and revolted to new superstitions. Their posterity conformed to the decrees of their idolatrous kings with the same facility. The prophet severely condemns them for having "willingly walked after the commandment";[20] so far is any praise from being due to the pretext of humility with which courtly flatterers excuse themselves and deceive the unwary, when they deny that it is lawful for them to refuse compliance with any command of their kings, as if God had resigned his right to mortal men when he made them rulers of mankind, or as if earthly power were diminished by being subordinated to its author before whom even the principalities of heaven tremble with awe. I know what great and present danger awaits this constancy, for kings cannot bear to be disregarded without the greatest indignation; and "the wrath of a king," says Solomon, "is as messengers of death."[21] But since this edict has been proclaimed by that celestial herald, Peter, "We ought to obey God rather than men,"[22]—let us console ourselves with this thought, that we truly perform the obedience which God requires of us when we suffer anything rather than deviate from piety. And that our hearts may not fail us, Paul stimulates us with another consideration—that Christ has redeemed us at the immense price which our redemption cost him, that we may not be submissive to the corrupt desires of men, much less be slaves to their impiety.[23]

---

[19] Dan. 6:22.

[20] Hos. 5:11.
[21] Prov. 16:14.
[22] Acts 5:29.
[23] I Cor. 7:23.

III STEPHEN JUNIUS BRUTUS

*A Defense of Liberty against Tyrants**

OBEDIENCE TO PRINCES
OR TO GOD?

This question happily may seem at the first view to be altogether superfluous and unprofitable, for that it seems to make a doubt of an axiom always held infallible among Christians, confirmed by many testimonies in Holy Scripture, divers examples of the histories of all ages, and by the death of all the holy martyrs. For it may be well demanded wherefore Christians have endured so many afflictions, but that they were always persuaded that God must be obeyed simply and absolutely, and kings with this exception, that they command not that which is repugnant to the law of God. Otherways wherefore should the apostles have answered, that God must rather be obeyed than men, and also seeing that the only will of God is always just, and that of men may be, and is, oftentimes unjust, who can doubt but that we must always obey God's commandments without any exception, and men's ever with limitation?

There are no estates which ought to be esteemed firm and stable, but those in whom the temple of God is built, and which are indeed the temple itself, and these we may truly call kings, which reign with God, seeing that it is by him only that kings reign: On the contrary, what beastly foolishness it is to think that the state and kingdom cannot subsist if God Almighty be not excluded,

and his temple demolished. From hence proceed so many tyrannous enterprises, unhappy and tragic death of kings, and ruins of people. If these sycophants knew what difference there is between God and Caesar, between the King of Kings and a simple king, between the lord and the vassal, and what tributes this lord requires of his subjects, and what authority he gives to kings over those his subjects, certainly so many princes would not strive to trouble the kingdom of God, and we should not see some of them precipitated from their thrones by the just instigation of the Almighty, revenging himself of them, in the midst of their greatest strength, and the people should not be sacked and pillaged and trodden down.

It then belongs to princes to know how far they may extend their authority, and to subjects in what they may obey them, lest the one encroaching on that jurisdiction, which no way belongs to them, and the others obeying him which commands further than he ought, they be both chastised, when they shall give an account thereof before another judge. Now the end and scope of the question propounded, whereof the Holy Scripture shall principally give the resolution, is that which follows. The question is, if subjects be bound to obey kings, in case they command that which is against the law of God: that is to say, to which of the two (God or king) must we rather obey, when the question shall be resolved concerning the king, to whom is attributed absolute power, that concerning other magistrates shall be also determined.

---

*From Stephen Junius Brutus, *A Defense of Liberty against Tyrants* (1579; trans. anon., 1648). Spelling and punctuation have been modernized for this selection.

First, the Holy Scripture does teach that God reigns by his own proper authority, and kings by derivation. God from himself, kings from God, that God has a jurisdiction proper, kings are his delegates. It follows then, that the jurisdiction of God has no limits, that of kings bounded, that the power of God is infinite, that of kings confined, that the kingdom of God extends itself to all places, that of kings is restrained within the confines of certain countries. In like manner God had created of nothing both heaven and earth; wherefore by good right He is lord, and true proprietor, both of the one and the other. All the inhabitants of the earth hold of Him that which they have, and are but His tenants and farmers; all the princes and governors of the world are His stipendiaries and vassals, and are bound to take and acknowledge their investitures from Him. Briefly, God alone is the owner and lord, and all men of what degree or quality soever they be, are His servants, farmers, officers and vassals, and owe account and acknowledgement to Him, according to that which He has committed to their dispensation; the higher their place is, the greater their account must be, and according to the ranks whereunto God has raised them, must they make their reckoning before His divine majesty, which the Holy Scriptures teach in infinite places, and all the faithful, yea, and the wisest among the heathen have ever acknowledged.

Now if we consider what is the duty of vassals, we shall find that what may be said of them, agrees properly to kings. The vassal receives his fee of his lord with right of justice, and charge to serve him in his wars. The king is established by the Lord God, the King of Kings, to the end he should administer justice to his people and defend them against all their enemies. The vassal receives laws and conditions from his sovereign. God commands the king to observe his laws and to have them always before his eyes, promising that he and his successors shall possess long the kingdom, if they be obedient, and on the contrary, that their reign shall be of small continuance, if they prove rebellious to their sovereign king. The vassal obliges himself by oath unto his lord, and swears that he will be faithful and obedient. In like manner the king promises

solemnly to command, according to the express law of God. Briefly, the vassal loses his fee, if he commit a felony, and by law forfeits all his privileges. In the like case the king loses his right, and many times his realm also, if he despise God, if he complot with his enemies, and if he commit felony against that royal majesty. This will appear more clearly by the consideration of the covenant which is contracted between God and the king, for God does that honor to His servants to call them His confederates. Now we read of two sorts of covenants at the inaugurating of kings, the first between God, the king, and the people, that the people might be the people of God. The second, between the king and the people, that the people shall obey faithfully, and the king command justly.

Briefly, even as those rebellious vassals who endeavor to possess themselves of the kingdom, do commit felony by the testimony of all laws, and deserve to be extirpated; in like manner those are as really guilty which will not observe the divine law, whereunto all men without exception owe their obedience, or who persecute those who desire to conform themselves thereunto, without hearing them in their just defenses: now for that we see that God invests kings into their kingdoms, almost in the same manner that vassals are invested into their fees by their sovereign, we must needs conclude that kings are the vassals of God, and deserve to be deprived of the benefit they receive from their lord if they commit felony, in the same fashion as rebellious vassals are of their estates. These premises being allowed, this question may be easily resolved; for if God hold the place of sovereign Lord, and the king as vassal, who dare deny but that we must rather obey the sovereign than the vassal? If God commands one thing, and the king commands the contrary, what is that proud man that would term him a rebel who refuses to obey the king, when else he must disobey God? But, on the contrary, he should rather be condemned, and held for truly rebellious, who omits to obey God, or who will obey the king, when he forbids him to yield obedience to God.

Briefly, if God calls us on the one side to enrol us in His service, and the king on the other, is any man so void of reason that he will not say we must leave the king, and apply ourselves to God's service: so far be it from us to believe, that we are bound to obey a king, commanding anything contrary to the law of God, that, contrarily, in obeying him we become rebels to God; no more nor less than we would esteem a countryman a rebel who, for the love he bears to some rich and ancient inferior lord, would bear arms against the sovereign prince, or who had rather obey the writs of an inferior judge than of a superior, the commandments of a lieutenant of a province, than of a prince; to be brief, the directions of an officer rather than the express ordinances of the king himself. In doing this we justly incur the malediction of the prophet Micah, who does detest and curse, in the name of God, all those who obey the wicked and perverse ordinances of kings. By the law of God we understand the two tables given to Moses, in the which, as in unremovable bounds, the authority of all princes ought to be fixed. The first comprehends that which we owe to God, the second that which we must do to our neighbors; briefly, they contain piety and justice conjoined with charity, from which the preaching of the gospel does not derogate, but rather authorize and confirm. The first table is esteemed the principal, as well in order as in dignity. If the prince commands to cut the throat of an innocent, to pillage and commit extortion, there is no man (provided he has some feeling of conscience) who would execute such a commandment.

LAWFUL RESISTANCE
TO PRINCES IN DEFENSE
OF DIVINE LAW

This question seems at the first view to be of a high and difficult nature, for so much as there being small occasion to speak to princes that fear God. On the contrary, there will be much danger to trouble the ears of those who acknowledge no other sovereign but themselves, for which reason few or none have meddled with it, and if any have at all touched it, it has been but as it were in passing by. The question is, if it be lawful to resist a prince violating the law of God, or ruining the church, or hindering the restoring of it? If we hold ourselves to the tenure of the Holy Scripture it will resolve us. For,

if in this case it had been lawful to the Jewish people (which may be easily gathered from the books of the Old Testament), yea, if it had been enjoined them, I believe it will not be denied, that the same must be allowed to the whole people of any Christian kingdom or country whatsoever.

But who may punish the king (for here is question of corporal and temporal punishment) if it be not the whole body of the people to whom the king swears and obliges himself, no more nor less, than the people do to the king? We read also that king Josias, being of the age of twenty-and-five years, together with the whole people, makes a covenant with the Lord, the king and the people promising to keep the laws and ordinances of God; and even then for the better accomplishing of the tenure of this agreement, the idolatry of Baal was presently destroyed. If any will more exactly turn over the Holy Bible, he may well find other testimonies to this purpose.

But I see well, here will be an objection made. What will you say? That a whole people, that beast of many heads, must they run in a mutinous disorder, to order the business of the commonwealth? What address or direction is there in an unruly and unbridled multitude? What counsel or wisdom, to manage the affairs of state?

When we speak of all the people, we understand by that, only those who hold their authority from the people, to wit, the magistrates, who are inferior to the king, and whom the people have substituted, or established, as it were, consorts in the empire, and with a kind of tribunitial authority, to restrain the encroachments of sovereignty, and to represent the whole body of the people. We understand also, the assembly of the estates, which is nothing else but an epitome, or brief collection of the kingdom, to whom all public affairs have special and absolute reference; such were the seventy ancients in the kingdom of Israel, amongst whom the high priest was as it were president, and they judged all matters of greatest importance, those seventy being first chosen by six out of each tribe, which came out of the land of Egypt, then the heads or governors of provinces. In like manner the judges and provosts of towns, the captains of thousands, the centurions and others who commanded over families, the most valiant, noble, and otherwise notable personages, of whom was composed the body of the states, assembled divers times as it plainly appears by the word of the holy scripture. At the election of the first king, who was Saul, all the ancients of Israel assembled together at Kama. In like manner all Israel was assembled, or all Judah and Benjamin, etc. Now, it is no way probable, that all the people, one by one, met together there. Of this rank there are in every well governed kingdom, the princes, the officers of the crown, the peers, the greatest and most notable lords, the deputies of provinces, of whom the ordinary body of the estate is composed, or the parliament or the diet, or other assembly, according to the different names used in divers countries of the world; in which assemblies, the principal care is had both for the preventing and reforming either of disorder or detriment in church or commonwealth.

For as the councils of Basle and Constance have decreed (and well decreed) that the universal council is in authority above the bishop of Rome, so in like manner, the whole chapter may overrule the bishop, the University the rector, the court the president. Briefly, he, whosoever he is, who has received authority from a company, is inferior to that whole company, although he be superior to any of the particular members of it.

A combination or conjuration is good or ill, according as the end whereunto it is addressed is good or ill; and perhaps also according as they are affected who are the managers of it. We say then, that the princes of Judah have done well, and that in following any other course they had failed of the right way. For even as the guardian ought to take charge and care that the goods of his pupil fall not into loss and detriment, and if he omits his duty therein, he may be compelled to give an account thereof, in like manner, those to whose custody and tuition the people have committed themselves, and whom they have constituted their tutors and defenders ought to maintain them safe and entire in all their rights and privileges. To be short, as it is lawful for a whole people to resist and oppose tyranny, so likewise the principal persons of the kingdom may as heads, and for the good of the whole body, confederate and associate themselves together; and as in a public state, that which is done by the greatest part is esteemed and taken as the act of all, so in like manner must it be said to be done, which the better part of the most principal have acted, briefly, that all the people had their hand in it.

KINGS MADE
BY THE PEOPLE

We have shown before that it is God that does appoint kings, who chooses them, who gives the kingdom to them: now we say that the people establish kings, put the scepter into their hands, and who with their suffrages, approve the election. God would have it done in this manner, to the end that the kings should acknowledge, that after God they hold their power and sovereignty from the people, and that it might the rather induce them to apply and address the utmost of their care and thoughts for the profit of the people, without being puffed with any vain imagination, that they were formed of any matter more excellent than other men, for which they were raised so high above others; as if they were to command our flocks of sheep, or herds of cattle. But let them remember and know, that they are of the same mold and condition as others, raised from the earth by the voice and acclamations, now as it were upon the shoulders of the people unto their thrones, that they might afterward bear on their own shoulders the greatest burdens of the commonwealth. Divers ages before that, the people of Israel demanded a king. God gave and appointed the law of royal government contained in the seventeenth chapter, verse fourteen of Deuteronomy, when says Moses, "thou art come unto the land which the Lord thy God giveth thee, and shall possess it, and shalt dwell therein, and shalt say, I will set a king over me like as all the nations that are about me, thou shalt in any wise set him whom the Lord thy God shall choose from amongst thy brethren, etc." You see here, that the election of the king is attributed to God, the establishment to the people; now when the practice of this law came in use, see in what manner they proceeded.

The elders of Israel, who presented the whole body of the people (under this name of elders are comprehended the captains, the centurions, commanders over fifties and tens, judges, provosts, but principally the chiefs of tribes) came to meet Samuel in Ramah, and not being willing longer to endure the government of the sons of Samuel, whose ill carriage had justly drawn on them the people's dislike, and withal persuading themselves that they had found the means to make their wars hereafter with more advantage, they demanded a king of Samuel, who asking counsel of the Lord, he made known that He had chosen Saul for the governor of His people. Then Samuel anointed Saul, and performed all those rights which belong to the election of a king required by the people. Now this might, perhaps, have seemed sufficient, if Samuel had presented to the people the king who was chosen by God, and had admonished them all to become good and obedient subjects. Notwithstanding, to the end that the king might know that he was established by the people, Samuel appointed the estates to meet at Mizpah, where being assembled as if the business were but then to begin, and nothing bad already been done, to be brief, as if the election of Saul were then only to be treated of, the lot is cast and falls on the tribe of Benjamin, after on the family of Matri, and lastly on Saul, born of that family, who was the same whom God had chosen. Then by the consent of all the people Saul was declared king. Finally, that Saul nor any other might attribute the aforesaid business to chance or lot, after that Saul had made some proof of his valor in raising the siege of the Ammonites in Jabish Gilead, some of the people pressing the business, he was again confirmed king in a full assembly at Gilgal. You see that he whom God had chosen, and the lot had separated from all the rest, is established king by the suffrages of the people.

Briefly, for so much as none were ever born with crowns on their heads, and scepters in their hands, and that no man can be a king by himself, nor reign without people, whereas on the contrary, the people may subsist of themselves, and were, long before they had any kings, it must of necessity follow that kings were at the first constituted by the people; and although the sons and dependents of such kings, inheriting their fathers' virtues, may in a sort seem to have rendered their kingdoms hereditary to their offsprings, and that in some kingdoms and countries the right of free election seems in a sort buried; yet, notwithstanding, in all well-ordered kingdoms, this custom is yet remaining. The sons do not succeed the fathers, before the people have first, as it were, anew established them by their new approbation: neither were they acknowledged in quality, as inheriting it from the dead; but approved and accounted kings then only, when they were invested with the kingdom, by receiving the scepter and diadem from the hands of those who represent the majesty of the people. One may see most evident marks of this in Christian kingdoms, which are at this day esteemed hereditary; for the French king, he of Spain and England, and others, are commonly sacred, and, as it were, put into possession of their authority by the peers, lords of the kingdom, and officers of the crown, who represent the body of the people.

THE PEOPLE
ABOVE THE KING

Now, seeing that the people choose and establish their kings, it follows that the whole body of the people is above the king; for it is a thing most evident, that he who is established by another, is accounted under him who has established him, and he who receives his authority from another, is less than he from whom he derives his power. Potiphar the Egyptian sets Joseph over all his house; Nebuchadnezzar, Daniel over the province of Babylon; Darius, the six score governors over the kingdom. It is commonly said that masters establish their servants, kings their officers. In like manner, also, the people establish the king as administrator of the commonwealth. Good kings have not disdained this title; yea, the bad ones themselves have affected it; insomuch, as for the space of divers ages, no Roman emperor (if it were not some absolute tyrant, as Nero, Domitian, Caligula) would suffer himself to be called lord. Furthermore, it must necessarily be that kings were instituted for the people's sake, neither can it be that for the pleasure of some hundreds of men, and without doubt more foolish and worse than many of the other, all the rest were made, but much rather that these hundred were made for the use and service of all the other, and reason requires that he be preferred above the other, who was made only to and for his occasion: so it is, that for the ship's sail, the owner appoints a pilot over her, who sits at the helm, and looks that she keep her course, nor run not upon any dangerous shelf; the pilot doing his duty, is obeyed by the mariners; yea, and of himself who is owner of the vessel, notwithstanding, the pilot is a servant as well as the least in the ship, from whom he only differs in this, that he serves in a better place than they do.

In a commonwealth, commonly compared to a ship, the king holds the place of pilot, the people in general are owners of the vessel, obeying the pilot, while he is careful of the public good; as though this pilot neither is nor ought to be esteemed other than servant to the public; as a judge or general in war differs little from other officers, but that he is bound to bear greater burdens, and expose himself to more dangers. By the same reason also which the king gains by acquist of arms, be it that he possesses himself of frontier places in warring on the enemy, or that which he gets by escheats or confiscations, he gets it to the kingdom, and not to himself, to wit, to the people, of whom the kingdom is composed, no more nor less than the servant does for his master; neither may one contract or oblige themselves to him, but by and with reference to the authority derived from the people. Furthermore, there is an infinite sort of people who live without a king, but we cannot imagine a king without people. And those who have been raised to the royal dignity were not advanced because they excelled other men in beauty and comeliness, nor in some excellency of nature to govern them as shepherds do their flocks, but rather being made out of the same mass with the rest of the people, they would acknowledge that for them, they, as it were, borrow their power and authority.

The ancient custom of the French represents that exceeding well, for they used to lift up on a buckler, and salute him king whom they had chosen. And wherefore is it said, "I pray you, that kings have an infinite number of eyes, a million of ears, with extreme long hands and feet exceeding swift"? Is it because they are like to Argos, Gerien, Midas, and divers others so celebrated by the poets? No, truly, but it is said in regard to all the people, whom the business principally concerns, who lend to the king for the good of the commonwealth, their eyes, their ears, their means, their faculties. Let the people forsake the king, he presently falls to the ground, although before, his hearing and sight seemed most excellent, and that he was strong and in the best disposition that might be; yea, that he seemed to triumph in all magnificence, yet in an instant he will become most vile and contemptible: to be brief, instead of those divine honours wherewith all men adore him, he shall be compelled to become a pendant, and whip children in the school at Corinth. Take away but the basis to this giant, and like the Rhodian Colossus he presently tumbles on the ground and falls into pieces. Seeing then that the king is established in this degree by the people, and for their sake, and that he cannot subsist without them, who can think it strange, then, for us to conclude that the people are above the king?

Now that which we speak of all the people universally, ought also to be understood of those who in every kingdom or town do lawfully represent the body of the people, and who ordinarily are (or at least should be) called the officers of the kingdom, or crown, and not of the king; for the officers of the king, it is he who places and displaces them at his pleasure, yea, after his death they have no more power, and are accounted as dead. On the contrary, the officers of the kingdom receive their authority from the people in the general assembly of the states (or, at the least were accustomed so anciently to have done) and cannot be disauthorized but by them, so then the one depends of the king, the other of the kingdom, those of the sovereign officer of the kingdom, who is the king himself, those of the sovereignty itself, that is of the people, of which sovereignty both the king and all his officers of the kingdom ought to depend, the charge of the one has proper relation to the care of the king's person; that of the other, to look that the commonwealth receive no damage; the first ought to serve and assist the king, as all domestic servants are bound to do to their masters; the other to preserve the rights and privileges of the people, and to carefully hinder the prince, that he neither omit the things that may advantage the state, nor commit anything that may damage the public.

Briefly, the one are servants and domestics of the king, and received into their places to obey his person; the other, on the contrary, are as associates to the king, in the administration of justice, participating of the royal power and authority, being bound to the utmost of their power to be assisting in the managing of the affairs of state, as well as the king, who is, as it were, president amongst them, and principal only in order and degree.

WHY KINGS WERE CREATED

Now, seeing that kings have been ever established by the people, and that they have had associates joined with them, to contain them within the limits of their duties, the which associates considered in particular one by one, are under the king, and altogether in one entire body are above him: We must consequently see wherefore first kings were established, and what is principally their duty. We usually esteem a thing just and good when it attains to the proper end for which it is ordained.

In the first place every one consents, that men by nature loving liberty, and hating servitude, born rather to command, than obey, have not willingly admitted to be governed by another, and renounced as it were the privilege of nature, by submitting themselves to the commands of others, but for some special and great profit that they expected from it. For as Aesop says, "That the horse being before accustomed to wander at his pleasure, would never have received the bit into his mouth, nor the rider on his back, but that he hoped by that means to overmatch the bull." Neither let us imagine, that kings were chosen to apply to their own proper use the goods that are gotten by the sweat of their subjects; for every man loves and cherishes his own. They have not received the power and authority of the people to make it serve as a pander to their pleasures: for ordinarily the inferiors hate, or at least envy, their superiors.

Let us then conclude, that they are established in this place to maintain by justice, and to defend by force of arms, both the public state, and particular persons from all damages and outrages, wherefore Saint Augustine said, "Those are properly called lords and masters who provide for the good and profit of others, as the husband for the wife, fathers for their children." They must therefore obey them who provide for them; although, indeed, to speak truly, those who govern in this manner may in a sort be said to serve those whom they command over.

For, as says the same doctor, they command not for the desire of dominion, but for the duty they owe to provide for the good of those who are subjected to them: not affecting any lordlike domineering, but with charity and singular affection, desiring the welfare of those who are committed to them.

Seneca in the eighty-first epistle says, "That in the golden age, wise men only governed kingdoms; they kept themselves within the bounds of moderation, and preserved the meanest from the oppression of the greatest. They persuaded and dissuaded, according as it advantaged or disadvantaged the public profit; by their wisdom, they furnished the public with plenty of all necessaries, and by their discretion prevented scarcity, by their valor and courage they expelled dangers, by their many benefits they increased and enriched their subjects; they pleaded not their duty in making pompous shows, but in well governing their people. No man made trial what he was able to do against them, because every one received what he was capable of from them," etc.

Therefore then, to govern is nothing else but to provide for. These proper ends of commanding, being for the people's commodity, the only duty of kings and emperors is to provide for the people's good. The kingly dignity to speak properly, is not a title of honor, but a weighty and burdensome office. It is not a discharge or vacation from affairs to run a licentious course of liberty, but a charge and vocation to all industrious employments, for the service of the commonwealth; the which has some glimpse of honor with it, because in those first and golden ages, no man would have tasted of such continual troubles, if they had not been sweetened with some relish of honor; insomuch as there was nothing more true than that which was commonly said in those times, "If every man knew with what turmoils and troubles the royal wreath was wrapt withal, no man would take it up, although it lay at his feet."

When, therefore, that these words of "mine" and "thine" entered into the world, and that differences fell amongst fellow citizens, touching the propriety of goods, and wars amongst neighboring people about the right of their confines, the people bethought themselves to have recourse to some one who both could and should take order that the poor were not oppressed by the rich, nor the patriots wronged by strangers.

Nor as wars and suits increased, they chose someone, in whose wisdom and valor they reposed most confidence. See, then, wherefore kings were created in the first ages; to wit, to administer justice at home, and to be leaders in the wars abroad, and not only to repulse the incursions of the enemy, but also to repress and hinder the devastation and spoiling of the subjects and their goods at home; but above all, to expel and drive away all devices and debauchments ar from their dominions.

ARE KINGS ABOVE THE LAW?

We must here yet proceed a little further: for it is demanded whether the king who presides in the administration of justice has power to resolve and determine business according to his own will and pleasure. Must the kings be subject to the law, or does the law depend upon the king? The law (says an ancient) is respected by those who otherways condemn virtue, for it enforces obedience, and ministers' conduct in warfaring, and gives vigor and luster to justice and equity. Pausanias the Spartan will answer in a word, that it becomes laws to direct, and men to yield obedience to their authority. Agesilaus, king of Sparta, says that all commanders must obey the commandments of the laws. But it shall not be amiss to carry this matter a little higher. When people began to seek for justice to determine their differences, if they met with any private man that did justly appoint them, they were satisfied with it. Now for so much as such

men were rarely and with much difficulty met withal, and for that the judgments of kings received as laws were oftentimes found contrary and difficult, then the magistrates and others of great wisdom invented laws, which might speak to all men in one and the same voice.

This being done, it was expressly enjoined to kings that they should be the guardians and administrators, and sometimes also, for so much as the laws could not foresee the particularities of actions to resolve exactly, it was permitted the king to supply this defect by the same natural equity by which the laws were drawn; and for fear lest they should go against law, the people appointed them from time to time associates, counselors, of whom we have formerly made mention, wherefore there is nothing which exempts the king from obedience which he owes to the law, which he ought to acknowledge as his lady and mistress, esteeming nothing can become him worse than that feminine of which Juvenal speaks: *Sic volo, sic jubeo, sic pro ratione voluntas.* I will, I command, my will shall serve instead of reason. Neither should they think their authority the less because they are confined to laws, for seeing the law is a divine gift coming from above, which human societies are happily governed and addressed to their best and blessedest end; those kings are as ridiculous and worthy of contempt, who repute it a dishonor to conform themselves to law, as those surveyors who think themselves disgraced by using of a rule, a compass, a chain or other instruments, which men understanding the art of surveying are accustomed to do, or a pilot who had rather fail, according to his fantasy and imagination, than steer his course by his needle and sea-card. Who can doubt, but that it is a thing more profitable and convenient to obey the law, than the king who is but one man? The law is the soul of a good king, it gives him motion, sense and life. The king is the organ and as it were the body by which the law displays her forces, exercises her function, and expresses her conceptions. Now it is a thing much more reasonable to obey the soul, than the body; the law is the wisdom of diverse sages, recollected in few words, but many see more clear and further than one alone. It is much better to follow the law than any one man's opinion, be he never so acute. The law is reason and wisdom itself, free from all perturbation, not subject to be moved with choler, ambition, hate, or acceptances of persons.

For, if the welfare of the kingdom depends on the observation of the laws, and the laws are enthralled to the pleasure of one man, is it not most certain, that there can be no permanent stability in that government? Must it not then necessarily come to pass, that if the king (as some have been) be infected with lunacy, either continually, or by intervals, that the whole state fall inevitably to ruin? But if the laws be superior to the king, as we have already proved, and that the king be tied in the same respect of obedience to the laws as the servant is to his master, who will be so senseless, who will not rather obey the law than the king or will not readily yield his best assistance against those who seek to violate or infringe them?

SUBJECTS NOT
THE KING'S SLAVES

For truly neither are the subjects, as it is commonly said, the king's slaves, or bondmen: being neither prisoners taken in the wars, nor bought for money. But as considered in one entire body they are lords, as we have formerly proved; so each of them in particular ought to be held as the king's brothers and kinsmen. And to the end that we think not this strange, let us hear what God Himself says when He prescribes a law to kings: That they lift not their heart above their brethren from amongst whom they were chosen. Whereupon Bartolus, a famous lawyer, who lived in an age that bred many tyrants, did yet draw this conclusion from that law, that subjects were to be held and used in the quality and condition of the king's brethren, and not of his slaves. Also king David was not ashamed to call his subjects his brethren. The ancient kings were called Abimelech, an Hebrew word which signifies, my father the king. The almighty and all good God, of whose great gentleness and mercy we are daily partakers, and very seldom feel His severity, although we justly deserve it, yet is it always mercifully mixed with compassion; whereby He teaches princes, His lieutenants, that subjects ought

rather to be held in obedience by love, than by fear.

But, lest they should except against me, as if I sought to entrench too much upon the royal authority, I verily believe it is so much the greater, by how much it is likely to be of longer continuance. For, says one, servile fear is a bad guardian, for that authority we desire should continue; for those in subjection hate them they fear, and whom we hate, we naturally wish their destruction. On the contrary, there is nothing more proper to maintain their authority than the affection of their subjects, on whose love they may safely and with most security lay the foundation of their greatness. And therefore that prince who governs his subjects as brethren, may confidently assure himself to live securely in the midst of dangers: whereas he who uses them like slaves, must needs live in much anxiety and fear, and may well be resembled to the condition of that master who remains alone in some desert in the midst of a great troop of slaves; for look how many slaves any has, he must make account of so many enemies, which almost all tyrants who have been killed by their subjects have experienced. Whereas, on the contrary, the subjects of good kings are ever as solicitously careful of their safety, as of their own welfare.

AUTHORITY BASED
ON CONTRACT

We have shown already that in the establishing of the king there were two alliances or covenants contracted: the first between God, the king, and the people, of which we have formerly treated; the second, between the king and the people, of which we must now say somewhat. After that Saul was established king, the royal law was given him, according to which he ought to govern. David made a covenant in Hebron before the Lord, that is to say, taking God for witness, with all the ancients of Israel, who represented the whole body of the people, and even then he was made king. Joas also by the mouth of Johoiada the high priest, entered into covenant with the whole people of the land in the house of the Lord. And when the crown was set on his head, together with it was the law of the testimony put into his hand, which most expounds to be the law of God; likewise Josias promises to observe and keep the commandments, testimonies, and statutes comprised in the book of the covenant: under which words are contained all which belongs to the duties both of the first and second table of the law of God. In all the before-remembered places of the holy story, it is ever said, "that a covenant was made with all the people, with all the multitude, with all the elders, with all the men of Judah": to the end that we might know, as it is also fully expressed, that not only the principals of the tribes, but also all the milleniers, centurions, and subaltern magistrates should meet together, each of them in the name, and for their towns and communalties, to covenant and contract with the king. In this assembly was the creating of the king determined of, for it was the people who made the king, and not the king the people.

It is certain, then, that the people by way or stipulation require a performance of covenants. The king promises it. Now the condition of a stipulator is in terms of law more worthy than of a promiser. The people ask the king, whether he will govern justly and according to the laws? He promises he will. Then the people answer, and not before, that while he governs uprightly, they will obey faithfully. The king therefore promises simply and absolutely, the people upon condition: the which failing to be accomplished, the people rest according to equity and reason quit from their promise.

In the first covenant or contract there is only an obligation to piety: in the second, to justice. In that, the king promises to serve God religiously: in this, to rule the people justly. By the one he is obliged with the utmost of his endeavors to procure the glory of God: by the other, the profit of the people. In the first, there is a condition expressed "if thou keep my commandments": in the second, "if thou distribute justice equally to every man." God is the proper revenger of deficiency in the former, and the whole people the lawful punisher of delinquency in the latter, or the estates, the representative body thereof who have assumed to themselves the protection of the people. This has been always practiced in all well-governed estates.

I would ask here, wherefore a man does swear, if it be not to declare that what he delivers he sincerely intends from his heart? Can anything be judged more near to the law of nature, than to observe that which we approve? Furthermore, what is the reason the king swears first, and at the instance, and required by the people, but to accept a condition either tacit or expressed? Wherefore is there a condition opposed to the contract, if it be not that in failing to perform the condition, the contract, according to law, remains void? And if for want of satisfying the condition by right, the contract is of no force, who shall dare to call that people perjured, which refuses to obey a king who makes no account of his promise, which he might and ought to have kept, and willfully breaks those laws which he did swear to observe? On the contrary, may we not rather esteem such a king perfidious, perjured, and unworthy of his place? For if the law free the vassal from his lord, who dealt feloniously with him, although that to speak properly, the lord swears not fealty to his vassal, but he to him: if the law of the twelve tables does detest and hold in execration the protector who defrauds him that is under his tuition: if the civil law permit an enfranchised servant to bring his action against his patron, for any grievous usage: if in such cases the same law delivers the slave from the power of his master, although the obligation be natural only, and not civil: is it not much more reasonable that the people be loosed from that oath of allegiance which they have taken, if the king (who may be not unfitly resembled by an attorney, sworn to look to his client's cause) first break his oath solemnly taken? And what if all these ceremonies, solemn oaths, nay, sacramental promises, had never been taken? Does not nature herself sufficiently teach that kings were on this condition ordained by the people, that they should govern well: judges, that they should distribute justice uprightly; captains in the war, that they should lead their armies against their enemies? If, on the contrary, they themselves forage and spoil their subjects, and instead of governors become enemies, as they leave indeed the true and essential qualities of a king, so neither ought the people to acknowledge them for lawful princes. But what if a people (you will reply) subdued by force, be compelled by the king to take an oath of servitude? And what if a robber, pirate, or tyrant (I will answer) with whom no bond of human society can be effectual, holding his dagger to your throat, constrain you presently to become bound in a great sum of money? Is it not an unquestionable maxim in law, that a promise exacted by violence cannot bind, especially if anything be promised against common reason, or the law of nature? Is there anything more repugnant to nature and reason, than that a people should manacle and fetter themselves; and to be obliged by promise to the prince, with their own hands and weapons to be their own executioners? There is, therefore, a mutual obligation between the king and the people, which, whether it be civil or natural only, whether tacit or expressed in words, it cannot by any means be annihilated, or by any law be abrogated, much less by force made void. And this obligation is of such power that the prince who willfully violates it, is a tyrant. And the people who purposely break it, may be justly termed seditious.

RESISTANCE TO TYRANTS

Hitherto we have treated of a king. It now rests we do somewhat more fully describe a tyrant. We have shown that he is a king, who lawfully governs a kingdom, either derived to him by succession, or committed to him by election. It follows, therefore, that he is reputed a tyrant, which, as opposite to a king, either gains a kingdom by violence or indirect means, or being invested therewith by lawful election, or succession, governs it not according to law and equity, or neglects those contracts and agreements, to the observation whereof he was strictly obliged at his reception. All which may very well occur in one and the same person. The first is commonly called a tyrant without title: the second a tyrant by practice. Now, it may well so come to pass, that he who possesses himself of a kingdom by force, to govern justly, and he on whom it descends by a lawful title, to rule unjustly. But for so much as a kingdom is rather a right than an inheritance, and an office than a possession, he seems rather worthy of the name of a tyrant, who unworthily acquits himself of his

charge, than he who entered into his place by a wrong door. In the same sense is the pope called an intruder who entered by indirect means into the papacy: and he an abuser who governs ill in it.

Pythagoras says "that a worthy stranger is to be preferred before an unworthy citizen, yea, though he be a kinsman." Let it be lawful also for us to say, that a prince who gained his principality by indirect courses, provided he govern according to law, and administer justice equally, is much to be preferred before him, who carries himself tyrannously, although he were legally invested into his government with all the ceremonies and rites thereunto appertaining.

For seeing that kings were instituted to feed, to judge, to cure the diseases of the people: Certainly I had rather that a thief should feed me, than a shepherd devour me: I had rather receive justice from a robber, than outrage from a judge: I had better be healed by an empiric, than poisoned by a doctor in physic. It were much more profitable for me to have my estate carefully managed by an intruding guardian, than to have it wasted and dissipated by one legally appointed.

Now, at the last we are come as it were by degrees to the chief and principal point of the question. We have seen how that kings have been chosen by God, either with relation to their families or their persons only, and after installed by the people. In like manner what is the duty of the king, and of the officers of the kingdom, how far the authority, power, and duty both of the one and the other extends, and what and how sacred are the covenants and contracts which are made at the inauguration of kings, and what conditions are intermixed, both tacit and expressed; finally, who is a tyrant without title, and who by practice, seeing it is a thing unquestionable that we are bound to obey a lawful king, which both to God and people carries himself according to those covenants whereunto he stands obliged, as it were to God Himself, seeing in a sort he represents his divine Majesty? It now follows that we treat, how, and by whom a tyrant may be lawfully resisted, and who are the persons who ought to be chiefly actors therein, and what course is to be held, that the action may be managed according to right and reason. We must first speak of him who is commonly called a tyrant without title. Let us suppose then that some Ninus, having neither received outrage nor offense, invades a people over whom he has no color of pretension: that Caesar seeks to oppress his country, and the Roman commonwealth: that Popiclus endeavors by murders and treasons to make the elective kingdom of Polonia to become hereditary to him and his posterity: or some Bruniehilde draws to herself and her Protadius the absolute government of France, or Ebronius, taking advantage of Theoderick's weakness and idleness, gains the entire administration of the state, and oppresses the people, what shall be our lawful refuge herein?

First, the law of nature teaches and commands us to maintain and defend our lives and liberties, without which life is scant worth the enjoying, against all injury and violence. Nature has imprinted this by instinct in dogs against wolves, in bulls against lions, betwixt pigeons and sparrow hawks, betwixt pullen and kites, and yet much more in man against man himself, if man become a beast, and therefore he who questions the lawfulness of defending oneself, does, as much as in him lies, question the law of nature. To this must be added the law of nations, which distinguishes possessions and dominions, fixes limits, and makes out confines, which every man is bound to defend against all invaders. And, therefore, it is no less lawful to resist Alexander the Great, if without any right or being justly provoked, he invades a country with a mighty navy, as well as Diomedes the pirate who scours the seas in a small vessel. For in this case Alexander's right is no more than Diomedes' but only he has more power to do wrong, and not so easily to be compelled to reason as the other. Briefly, one may as well oppose Alexander in pillaging a country, as a thief in purloining a cloak; as well him when he seeks to batter down the walls of a city, as a robber who offers to break into a private house.

There is, besides this, the civil law, or municipal laws of several countries which govern the societies of men, by certain rules, some in one manner, some in another; some submit themselves to the government of one man, some to more; others are ruled by a whole commonalty, some absolutely exclude women from the royal throne, others

admit them; these here choose their king descended of such a family, those there make election of whom they please, besides other customs practiced among several nations. If, therefore, any offer either by fraud or force to violate this law, we are all bound to resist him, because he wrongs that society to which we owe all that we have, and would ruin our country, to the preservation whereof all men by nature, by law and by solemn oath, are strickly obliged: insomuch that fear or negligence, or bad purposes, make us omit this duty, we may justly be accounted breakers of the laws, betrayers of our country, and contemners of religion. Now as the laws of nature, of nations, and the Civil commands us to take arms against such tyrants; so, is there not any manner of reason that should persuade us to the contrary; neither is there any oath, covenant, or obligation, public or private, of power justly to restrain us; therefore the meanest private man may resist and lawfully oppose such an intruding tyrant. The law Julia, which condemns to death those who raise rebellion against their country or prince, has here no place; for he is no prince, who, without any lawful title invades the commonwealth or confines of another; nor he a rebel, who by arms defends his country; but rather to this had relation the oath which all the youth of Athens were accustomed to take in the temple of Aglaura, "I will fight for religion, for the laws, for the altars, and for our possessions, either alone, or with others; and will do the utmost of my endeavor to leave to posterity our country, at the least, in as good estate as I found it." To as little purpose can the laws made against seditious persons be alleged here; for he is seditious who undertakes to defend the people, in opposition of order and public discipline; but he is no raiser, but a suppressor of sedition, who restrains within the limits of reason the subverter of his country's welfare, and public discipline.

On the contrary, to this has proper relation the law of tyrannicide, which honors the living with great and memorable recompenses, and the dead with worthy epitaphs, and glorious statues, that have been their country's liberators from tyrants; as Harmodius and Aristogiton at Athens, Brutus and Cassius in Rome, and Aratus of Sycione.

We must remember that all princes are born men, and therefore reason and passion are as hardly to be separated in them, as the soul is from the body while the man lives. We must not then expect princes absolute in perfection, but rather repute ourselves happy if those who govern us be indifferently good. And therefore, although the prince observe not exact mediocrity in state affairs; if sometimes passion overrule his reason, if some careless omission make him neglect the public utility, or if he do not always carefully execute justice with equality, or repulse not with ready valor an invading enemy; he must not therefore be presently declared a tyrant. And certainly, seeing he rules not as a god over men, nor as men over beasts, but is a man composed of the same matter, and of the same nature with the rest: as we would questionless judge that prince unreasonably insolent, who should insult over and abuse his subjects, as if they were brute beasts; so those people are doubtless as much void of reason, who imagine a prince should be complete in perfection, or expect divine abilities in a nature so frail and subject to imperfections. But if a prince purposely ruin the commonwealth, if he presumptuously pervert and resist legal proceedings or lawful rights, if he make no reckoning of faith, covenants, justice nor piety, if he prosecute his subject as enemies; briefly, if he express all or the chiefest of those wicked practices we have formerly spoken of; then we may certainly declare him a tyrant, who is as much an enemy both to God and men. We do not therefore speak of a prince less good, but of one absolutely bad; not of one less wise, but of one malicious and, treacherous; not of one less able, judiciously to discuss legal differences, but of one perversely bent to pervert justice and equity; not of an unwarlike, but of one furiously disposed to ruin the people, and ransack the state.

For the wisdom of a senate, the integrity of a judge, the valor of a captain, may peradventure enable a weak prince to govern well. But a tyrant could be content that all the nobility, the counselors of state, the commanders for the wars, had but one head that he might take it off at one blow: those being the proper objects of his distrust and fear, and by consequence the principal sub-jects on whom he desires to execute his malice and cruelty. A foolish prince, although (to speak according to right and equity) he ought to be deposed, yet may he perhaps in some sort be borne withal. But a tyrant, the more he is tolerated, the more he becomes intolerable.

Furthermore, as the princes' pleasure is not always law, so many times it is not expedient that the people do all that which may lawfully be done; for it may oftentimes chance that the medicine proves more dangerous than the disease. Therefore it becomes wise men to try all ways before they come to blows, to use all other remedies before they suffer the sword to decide the controversy. If then those who represent the body of the people foresee any innovation or machination against the state, or that it be already embarked into a course of perdition; their duty is, first to admonish the prince, and not to attend that the disease by accession of time and accidents becomes unrecoverable. For tyranny may be properly resembled unto a fever hectic, the which at the first is easy to be cured, but with much difficulty to be known; but after it is sufficiently known, it becomes incurable. Therefore small beginnings are to be carefully observed, and by those whom it concerns diligently prevented.

If the prince therefore persist in his violent courses, and contemn frequent admonitions, addressing his designs only to that end, that he may oppress at his pleasure, and effect his own desires without fear or restraint; he then doubtless makes himself liable to that detested crime of tyranny: and whatsoever either the law, or lawful authority permits against a tyrant, may be lawfully practiced against him. Tyranny is not only a will, but the chief, and as it were the complement and abstract of vices. A tyrant subverts the state, pillages the people, lays stratagems to entrap their lives, breaks promise with all, scoffs at the sacred obligations of a solemn oath, and therefore is he so much more vile than the vilest of usual malefactors. By how much offences committed against a generality, are worthy of greater punishment than those which concern only particular and private persons. If thieves and those who commit sacrilege be declared infamous; nay, if they justly suffer corporal punishment by death, can we invent any that may be worthily equivalent for so outrageous a crime.

Furthermore, we have already proved that all kings receive their royal authority from the people, that the whole people considered in one body is above and greater than the king; and that the king and emperor are only the prime and supreme governors and ministers of the kingdom and empire; but the people the absolute lord and owner thereof. It therefore necessarily follows that a tyrant is in the same manner guilty of rebellion against the majesty of the people as the lord of a fee, who feloniously transgresses the conditions of his investitures, and is liable to the same punishment, yea, and certainly deserves a much greater one than the equity of those laws inflicts on the delinquents. Therefore as Bartolus says, "He may either be deposed by those who are lords in sovereignty over him, or else justly punished according to the law Julia, which condemns those who offer violence to the public." The body of the people must needs be the sovereign of those who represent it, which in some places are the electors, palatines, peers; in other, the assembly of the general estates. And, if the tyranny have gotten such sure footing, as there is no other means but force to remove him, then it is lawful for them to call the people to arms, to enroll and raise forces, and to employ the utmost of their power, and use against him all advantages and stratagems of war, as against the enemy of the commonwealth, and the disturber of the public peace. Briefly, the same sentence may be justly pronounced against him, as was against Manlius Capitolinus at Rome. "Thou wast to me, Manlius, when thou didst tumble down the Gaules that scaled the capital: but since thou art now become an enemy, like one of them, thou shalt be precipitated down from the same place from whence thou formerly tumbled those enemies."

The officers of the kingdom cannot for this be rightly taxed of sedition; for in a sedition there must necessarily concur but two parts, or sides, the which preemptorily contest together, so that it is necessary that the one be in the right, and the other in the wrong. That part undoubtedly has the right on their side, which defends the laws, and strives to advance the public profit of the kingdom. And those, on the contrary, are questionless in the wrong, who break the laws, and protect those who violate justice, and oppress the commonwealth. Those are certainly in the right way, as said Bartolus, "who endeavor to suppress tyrannical government, and those in the wrong, who oppose lawful authority." And that must ever be accounted just, which is intended only for the public benefit, and that unjust, which aims chiefly at private commodity. Wherefore Thomas Aquinas says, "That a tyrannical rule, having no proper address for the public welfare, but only to satisfy a private will, with increase of particular profit to the ruler, cannot in any reasonable construction be accounted lawful, and therefore the disturbance of such a government cannot be esteemed seditious, much less traitorous"; for that offense has proper relation only to a lawful prince, who indeed is an inanimated or speaking law; therefore, seeing that he who employs the utmost of his means and power to annihilate the laws, and quell their virtue and vigor, can no ways be justly intituled therewith. So neither, likewise, can those who oppose and take arms against him, be branded with so notorious a crime. Also this offense is committed against the commonwealth; but for so much as the commonwealth is there only where the laws are in force, and not where a tyrant devours the state at his own pleasure and liking, he certainly is quit of that crime which ruins the majesty of the public state, and those questionless are worthily protectors and preservers of the commonwealth, who, confident in the lawfulness of their authority, and summoned thereunto by their duty, do courageously resist the unjust proceedings of the tyrant.

And in this their action, we must not esteem them as private men and subjects, but as the representative body of the people, yea, and as the sovereignty itself, which demands of his minister an account of his administration. Neither can we in any good reason account the officers of the kingdom disloyal, who in this manner acquit themselves of their charge.

There is ever, and in all places, a mutual and reciprocal obligation between the people and the prince; the one promises to be a good and wise prince, the other to obey faithfully, provided he govern justly. The people therefore are obliged to the prince under condition, the prince to the people simply and purely. Therefore, if the prince fail in his promise, the people are exempt from obedience, the contract is made void, the right of obligation of no force. Then the king if he govern unjustly is perjured, and the people likewise forsworn if they obey not his lawful commands. But that people are truly acquit from all perfidiousness, who publicly renounce the unjust dominion of a tyrant, or he, striving unjustly by strong hand to continue the possession, do constantly endeavor to expulse him by force of arms.

It is therefore permitted the officers of a kingdom, either all, or some good number of them, to suppress a tyrant; and it is not only lawful for them to do it, but their duty expressly requires it; and, if they do it not, they can by no excuse color their baseness. For the electors, palatines, peers, and other officers of state, must not think they were established only to make pompous paradoes and shows, when they are at the coronation of the king, habited in their robes of state, as if there were some masque or interlude to be represented; or as if they were that day to act the parts of Roland, Oliver, or Renaldo, and such other personages on a stage, or to counterfeit and revive the memory of the knights of the round table; and after the dismissing of that day's assembly, to suppose they have sufficiently acquitted themselves of their duty, until a recess of the like solemnity. Those solemn rites and ceremonies were not instituted for vain ostentation, nor to pass, as in a dumb show, to please the spectators, nor in children's sports, as it is with Horace, to create a king in jest; but those grandees must know that as well for office and duty, as for honor, they are called to the performance of those rites, and that in them, the commonwealth is committed and recommended to the king, as to her supreme and principal tutor and protector, and to them as coadjutors and assistants to him: and therefore, as the tutors or guardians (yea, even those who are appointed by way of honor) are chosen to have care of and observe the actions and importments of him who holds the principal rank in the tutorship, and to look how he carries himself in the administration of the goods of his pupil. So likewise are the former ordained to have an eye to the courses of the king, for, with an equivalent authority, as the others for the pupil, so are they to hinder and prevent the damage and detriment of the people, the king being properly reputed as the prime guardian, and they his coadjutors.

In like manner, as the faults of the principal tutor who manages the affairs are justly imputed to the coadjoints in the tutorship, if when they ought and might, they did not discover his errors, and cause him to be despoiled, especially failing in the main points of his charge, to wit, in not communicating unto them the affairs of his administration, in dealing unfaithfully in his place, in doing anything to the dishonor or detriment of his pupil, in embezzling of his goods or estate, or if he be an enemy to his pupil: briefly, if either in regard of the worthlessness of his person, or weakness of his judgment, he be unable well to discharge so weighty a charge, so also, are the peers and principal officers of the kingdom accountable for the government thereof, and must both prevent, and if occasion require, suppress the tyranny of the prince, as also supply with their care and diligence, his inability and weakness.

Princes are chosen by God, and established by the people. As all particulars considered one by one, are inferior to the prince; so the whole body of the people and officers of state, who represent that body, are the princes' superiors. In the receiving and inauguration of a prince, there are covenants and contracts passed between him and the people, which are tacit and expressed, natural or civil; to wit, to obey him faithfully while he commands justly, that he serving the commonwealth, all men shall serve him, that while he governs according to law, all shall be submitted to his government, etc. The officers of the kingdom are the guardians and protectors of these covenants and contracts. He who maliciously or willfully violates these conditions, is questionless a tyrant by practice. And therefore the officers of state may judge him according to the laws. And if he support his tyranny by strong hands, their duty binds them, when by no other means it can be effected by force of arms to suppress him.

Of these officers there be two kinds, those who have generally undertaken the protection of the kingdom; as a constable, marshals, peers, palatines, and the rest, every one of whom, although all the rest do either connive or consort with the tyranny, are bound to oppose and repress the tyrant; and those who have undertaken the government of any province, city, or part of the kingdom, as dukes, marquesses, earls, consuls, mayors, sheriffs, etc., they may according to right expel and drive tyranny and tyrants from their cities, confines, and governments.

But particular and private persons may not unsheathe the sword against tyrants by practice, because they were not established by particulars, but by the whole body of the people. But for tyrants who without title intrude themselves, for so much as there is no contract or agreement between them and the people, it is indifferently permitted all to oppose and depose them; and in this rank of tyrants may those be ranged, who, abusing the weakness and sloth of a lawful prince, tyrannously insult over his subjects.

Finally, as there have ever been tyrants distressed here and there, so also all histories testify that there have been neighboring princes to oppose tyranny, and maintain the people in their right. The princes of these times by imitating so worthy examples, should suppress the tyrants both of bodies and souls, and restrain the oppressors both of the commonwealth, and of the church of Christ: otherwise, they themselves, may most deservedly be branded with that infamous title of tyrant.

And to conclude this discourse in a word, piety commands that the law and church of God be maintained. Justice requires that tyrants and destroyers of the commonwealth be compelled to reason. Charity challenges the right of relieving and restoring the oppressed. Those who make no account of these things, do as much as in them lies to drive piety, justice, and charity out of this world, that they may never more be heard of.

CHAPTER SIXTEEN

BODIN

The national state is the central concept of modern political thought, its tacit assumption, just as the city-state was that of antiquity, and universal empire that of the Middle Ages. Machiavelli came close to the idea of the state; he was the first to coin the term "state" *(lo stato)*. However, as he was primarily interested in power and the rulers who struggled for it, but not in institutions, his use of the word "state" is strongly permeated with the meaning of "government," the state being essentially the ruler and his political, military, and administrative machine—all still viewed from a personal angle.

A clear formulation of the concepts of state and state sovereignty could occur only in a nation that was actually developing the appropriate judicial, administrative, and legislative institutions. Such institutions had been evolving in France since the late Middle Ages, and a strong sentiment of nationalism and sense of national sovereignty could be seen in the struggle between King Philip IV and Pope Boniface VIII at the end of the thirteenth century. But the appreciation of these changes was slow, and it was not until the sixteenth century that the first systematic and clear conception of *sovereignty* was worked out in *The Six Books on the State (Les six livres de la République,* 1576), by Jean Bodin (1530–1596).

Bodin was a native of Angers, and studied law at Toulouse, where he also taught for some time. Toulouse was an important formative phase in Bodin's life, because its university was outstanding in jurisprudence and also because its population included a considerable number of Protestants. Bodin was of middle-class origin and represented the Third Estate in the Estates-General in 1576. He became closely attached to the brother of King Henry III and served in the legal branch of the royal administration. His vast erudition (of which he put too much into his *Six Books on the State,* thus depriving it of many readers, who find its length forbidding) was aptly supplemented by public experience in both the legislative and administrative parts of government.

Bodin lived at a time when the unity of France, though finally accomplished territorially, was seriously threatened by religious conflict. Calvinist Protestantism made incessant progress in France during the sixteenth century, and the attempt to eradicate it by force was met by resistance. The "War of Religion" started in 1562 and went on intermittently for over a generation. In the Massacre of St. Bartholomew (August 24, 1572) religious conflict degenerated into murder, and the spirit of intransigence grew on both sides. The religious divisions engendered by the Reformation were intertwined with deep-seated social and economic issues, which made reconciliation even more difficult. What France needed for its preservation was more moderation and compromise, and less fanaticism and radicalism; it needed citizens who preferred the prosaic stability of France in the present to the poetic bliss of heaven in the future.

From the 1560s on, a group of administrators, lawyers, and publicists sought to stem the tide of fanaticism that was ruining the nation. They were called *Politiques*. At first the name was meant to be opprobrious, inasmuch as the *Politiques* were charged with putting practical politics above pure principles, and the charge was true as far as it went. The *Politiques* were Catholic, but they were unwilling to sacrifice the interests of the French state and nation to those of the Roman Catholic Church. Their attitude of toleration was generally not based on philosophy but on expediency. Michel de l'Hôpital, Chancellor of France, and an outstanding leader of the *Politiques,* had urged as early as 1560 to get rid "of these devilish words, these names of party, of faction, of sedition—Lutheran, Huguenot, Papist," and had asserted that "a man does not cease to be a citizen for being excommunicated."

If possible, the *Politiques* preferred religious unity because they felt that political unity would thereby be furthered. Hence they were not opposed to a little persecution at the beginning of a new religious creed, provided that such dissent could be eliminated quickly and without much violence or bloodshed. But when a new faith has been embraced by a substantial portion of the community, as was true of the Huguenots, the *Politiques* were willing to accept the fact of Protestantism, because they believed that the unity of France could not stand the strain of wholesale massacre and permanent civil war.

Bodin is the best-known theorist of the *Politiques,* and his *Six Books on the State* expresses the desire for strong government that makes contented and secure citizenship possible. Bodin defines sovereignty—he was the first to use this word—as "the absolute and perpetual power of the state, that is, the greatest power to command." Bodin distinguishes the government from the state, in other words, the exercise of sovereign functions, which may be for a limited time, from sovereignty itself, which is unlimited in time—*perpetual.* Sovereignty exists as long as the state, regardless of its changing forms of government. The *absolute* quality of sovereignty consists in the fact that the sovereign state tolerates no rival legal authority above it: "Only he is absolutely sovereign who, after God, acknowledges no one greater than himself."

Sovereignty is here markedly pointed at two sources that threatened it: universal church and empire. Both were henceforth denied any interference in the ecclesiastical and temporal affairs of the developing national states. Politically the kings looked on themselves as "emperors" in their realms, and ecclesiastically they either became the official heads of their national churches, as in Protestant states, or controlled, according to the theory of "Gallicanism," the clergy in predominantly Catholic states.

The doctrine of sovereignty, however, is directed above all against forces threatening the state from within. Bodin saw more clearly than anyone before him that the essence of sovereignty consists in the *making of general laws.* During the Middle Ages the law was something that was found by judges, not made by legislators; the process of the creation of law was thought of as a slow and imperceptible synthesis of the immemorial custom of the land, the law of nature, and the will of God. The concept of making the law marks a revolutionary break with the medieval tradition, and Bodin specifically refers to local customs and local parliaments; the feudal system of diffusion and decentralization of authority gave way to an authority that was one and indivisible. The nobility, in particular, was the target of the new doctrine of sovereignty. Bodin, like most writers of the *Politiques,* belonged to the Third Estate, and the bourgeoisie also provided the new class of administrators and judges for the constantly expanding activities of the state.

Bodin's attribution of absoluteness to the sovereign is to be understood only in relation to human laws. Still close to the medieval sentiment that the ruler is under a moral obligation to the community and God, Bodin says that the sovereign prince has no authority to violate the laws of God and nature: "In doing so a prince would become guilty of high treason against God." By defining sovereignty at the outset of his treatise as "lawful government," Bodin seeks to distinguish it from the order that bands of robbers and pirates maintain among themselves. Bodin also distinguishes between the sovereign's right to break his laws and his right to break his contracts. The sovereign ruler is not bound by his predecessors' laws or his own, because the authority of lawmaking is unilateral, deriving from the sole authority of the sovereign. But when a contract is made by the prince with his subjects or other rulers, the obligation is mutual and cannot be broken by him at will. Natural law prescribes that agreements be kept *(pacta sunt servanda),* and the prince may not free himself from this obligation by unilateral action any more than the subject may.

Bodin does not discuss in detail how the precepts of divine and natural law limit sovereignty, and in what manner a ruler's violation of divine and natural law is to be ascertained and punished. He cites murder as a case in point. If the sovereign forbids to kill, he is even more bound by it than his subjects, because "such a law is not his, but the law of God and nature."

In addition to divine and natural law, Bodin mentions limitations of sovereignty that derive from human law. First, the sovereign ruler does not have the legal authority to alter the rules of succession to the French crown; second, he has no right to alienate the public domain; third, he may not levy taxes without the consent of the Estates or deprive a subject of his property without "just cause." In the first two instances, Bodin implies that the monarch, though not bound by ordinary statutory law, is bound by the fundamental laws of the realm *(leges imperii)* governing succession and the public domain, because such fundamental laws are the legal basis of the very authority of the sovereign. As for property, Bodin felt that in violating the rights of property without due process the sovereign destroys one of the main purposes of the state, which is the protection of property and the family.

Unlike later protagonists of the doctrine of sovereignty, Bodin was unwilling to deduce limitless *power* of the monarch from his *supreme legal authority.* Parliament is legally supreme as the lawmaking body in Great Britain, yet this fact does not mean that it is able, in actuality, to pass any law whatsoever. Although there are no legal curbs on Parliament as the highest legal authority, there are extralegal and nonlegal forces, such as the electorate, parties, public opinion, trade-unions, churches, and business organizations, that effectively limit and direct its power. The British monarch is even more illustrative of the difference between sovereign authority and political power. Though he has the legal authority to refuse his assent to bills passed by both Houses of Parliament, he has not done so since 1707.

In the field of external relations, too, Bodin felt that sovereignty must be understood as a concept of legal status, and not of political power. A state is sovereign if it is not legally subject to the authority of another state and if its relations with other states are carried on in accordance with international, rather than municipal, law. This definition does not necessarily imply *factual* independence. Small states are often dependent on large states militarily, economically, and politically, but as long as their dependence is one of fact rather than of law, they are sovereign. Bodin himself occasionally blurred the distinction between the highest legal authority of the sovereign and political omnipotence. Yet his line of thought is, in general, unmistakable, and he is saved from confusing legal sovereignty with political despotism by his acute legal learning as well as by his strong sense of the rule of law, which he conceives as the confluence of constitutional, natural, and divine law.

Bodin prefers monarchy to aristocracy and democracy because the unity and indivisibility of authority seem best safeguarded in one man. But in his account of monarchical government he sharply distinguishes between *legitimate* and *illegitimate* monarchy. Royal descent or conquest in lawful war supplies the title of legitimate monarchy, whereas the tyrant, the illegitimate monarch, sets himself up as sovereign prince without rightful claim of election, descent, or lawful war. If the monarch is legitimate, the subjects have no right to encroach, acting individually or jointly, on "the honor or life of the monarch by judicial or other means, though he may have committed all the wicked, impious and cruel misdeeds one can think of." Even less have subjects the right to proceed against the prince by force. As for the tyrant, it is lawful to kill him without formal proceedings because he has put himself outside the law by seizing power illegally; if the tyrant surrenders himself into the hands of the people, thereby recognizing their sovereignty, he may be tried in court. Bodin adds the important observation that it makes no difference whether the tyrant is virtuous or villainous; he may be put to death, regardless of his personal goodness, because he has invaded sovereignty.

Whereas most of the *Politiques* tolerated religious dissent primarily on grounds of expediency, Bodin accepts religious diversity on philosophical grounds. He advises the ruler of a country divided into various churches and religions not to impose forcibly his own religion, because "the more the will of men is forced, the more it becomes obstinate." In a later book, *Colloquium heptaplomeres* (written in 1588, but not printed before 1841), Bodin, presenting seven spokesmen (therefore the title) of various Christian and non-Christian creeds in the world, arrives at a theistic position of rational belief in God, above any particular church or organized religion. Bodin's view on slavery is in harmony with his liberal outlook. Despite his admiration for Aristotle, he felt that slavery was unjust, and that it was not supported by facts, as Aristotle had said, inasmuch as good men may be kept as slaves by masters who are wicked.

Bodin's bourgeois outlook is clearly expressed in his views on property and war. He held that the prince cannot impose taxation without the consent of the Estates, and that he cannot deprive a subject of his property "without just cause." Although recognizing that no cause of revolution is more important than "excessive wealth of the few and extreme poverty of the many," he is strongly opposed to equality of property; the foundation of the state is good faith, and the equalization of property subverts the state by destroying legitimate expectations and conventions. Bodin's views on war are as different from those of Machiavelli as a sixteenth-century French bourgeois from an Italian *condottiere* of the Renaissance. Bodin abhors war because it is destructive of the very purpose of human associations, be it material ease or spiritual elevation. He justifies war only to repel aggression.

Bodin's state is strong but not aggressive; monarchical but not tyrannical. It became the model for the new national state in which the interests of the monarchy were allied with those of the rising merchant and middle classes against church and aristocracy. In this new state the bourgeoisie was willing to accept a strong government under kingly command, provided that it was allowed to make money and enjoy reasonable legal and political security. This alliance was to last over two hundred years, until the French Revolution raised the fundamental issue whether sovereignty should be vested in the king or in the people.

BODIN

*Six Books on the State**

THE STATE

The state is a lawful government, with sovereign power, of different households and their common affairs. We put this definition at the outset because in all things, it is necessary to look first for the chief end, and then for the means of attaining it. A definition is nothing else than the end of a problem that is being considered, and unless it is well founded, whatever is based upon it will soon collapse.

Let us now examine each part of the definition of the state. In the first place, we speak of the state as "lawful government" in order to distinguish it from bands of robbers and pirates, with whom it can have no part, commerce, or alliance. In all well-ordered states, therefore, robbers and pirates have always been excluded from recognition, whether it be a question of making a pledge in negotiating peace, calling off war, setting up offensive or defensive alliances, defining boundaries, or settling disputes between kings and territorial rulers. The law of mankind sharply differentiates between wartime enemies who maintain lawful government in their states, and brigands and pirates who seek to subvert and destroy them.

SOVEREIGNTY

Sovereignty is the absolute and perpetual power of the state, that is, the greatest power to command. It is necessary to arrive at a definition of sovereignty because neither jurists nor political philosophers have so far defined it, although it is the principal and most urgent point for an understanding

of the nature of the state. Having said before that the state is a lawful government, with sovereign power, of many households and their common affairs, the meaning of sovereign power must now be explained. I have said that this power is perpetual, for absolute power may be given to one or several for a certain time only, at the end of which they are subjects again. While they are in authority they still cannot call themselves sovereign rulers, inasmuch as they are only custodians and keepers of sovereign power until it shall please the people or the prince to recall it, just as those who have lent or pawned their goods to others remain the true owners and possessors. Likewise, those who give to others the power and authority to judge and command for a defined period of time, or to be recalled at pleasure, retain power and authority that the others exercise but in the nature of a temporary lease or loan. The governor of a country or the lieutenant of a prince surrenders his power at the expiration of his term, being but the depository and keeper for someone else. It makes no difference whether the official is of high or low rank. If the absolute power granted to the lieutenant of the prince were sovereign, it could be used against the prince himself, who would be left with nothing but an empty title, and the subject would command his lord, the servant his master—which would be absurd. Whatever power and authority the sovereign prince confers upon others, his own person remains excepted. He always retains more authority than he gives away, and he is never divested of his right to command and examine his officials by way of prevention, concurrence, or challenge, to withdraw their authority altogether, or to permit it to go on to the extent, and as long as, it shall please him.

---

*From Jean Bodin, *Six Books on the State* (1576; trans. William Ebenstein).

If the people grant annually absolute power to one or several citizens, without control or appeal, shall we say that they possess sovereignty? Only he is absolutely sovereign who, after God, acknowledges no one greater than himself. These citizens elected to highest office therefore do not possess sovereignty, as they are but trustees of the power lent to them for a given time. The people do not deprive themselves of sovereignty when they entrust absolute authority to one or several rulers, either for a limited time set in advance or to be revoked at their pleasure. In both instances the holders of power remain accountable to those from whom they have received the power to command. This is not true of the sovereign prince, who is accountable to God alone.

But suppose such absolute power be given to a king's lieutenant for life. Is that not sovereign and perpetural power? Otherwise, if we should call perpetual power only that which never came to an end, sovereignty could exist only in aristocratic and popular governments that do not die. Or if the word "perpetual" would apply to a monarch and his heirs, there would be few sovereign monarchs, in view of the fact that only very few monarchies are hereditary, and in view of the fact those who arrive on the throne by the right of election would not be sovereign. "Perpetual" therefore means the lifetime of him who has the power. If the sovereign magistrate, elected for a year or for a defined time limit, continues to exercise the power that has been entrusted to him, he must do so either with the acquiescence of the governed or by force. If by force, the tyrant is sovereign, just as the violent possession of the thief is genuine possession in nature, although contrary to law, and they who had possession before, no longer have it. But if the magistrate continues his sovereign power with the acquiescence of the people, he is not a sovereign prince, as he exercises it only on sufferance; he is even less sovereign if his term is not defined in advance, as he then holds whatever authority is his as a temporary trust and loan to be revoked at pleasure by the people.

Let us now examine the second part of our definition, and ascertain what the words "absolute power" mean. The people or the aristocracy in a commonwealth may purely and simply give someone the sovereign and perpetual power to dispose of their property and persons, and of all the state, as it may please him, and afterward leave all to whomever he may choose; just as an owner may give away his goods purely and simply, without any cause other than his liberality. Such a gift is a true one, with no conditions asked or received, once the donation is transacted and accomplished, whereas gifts that are granted under charges and conditions are not true gifts. Likewise, the transfer of sovereignty to a prince with charges and conditions does not result in true sovereign authority or absolute power, except when the conditions thus attached to the creation of the sovereign are of divine or natural law.

A prince is not bound by the laws of his predecessors, and much less by his own laws and ordinances. It is possible to receive a law from someone else, but it is impossible, in the nature of things, to give to oneself a law that depends on one's own will, as is stated in the legal maxim: *Nulla obligatio consistere potest, quae a voluntate promittentis statum capit* ("There can be no obligation that derives its validity from the will of him who makes the promise"). This necessary reason evidently proves that the prince cannot be subject to his own laws. As the Pope never ties his hands, according to the canonists, so the sovereign prince cannot tie his hands, even if he desires to do so. Therefore we see at the end of laws and ordinances the words "Because it has so pleased Us," in order to indicate that the laws of the sovereign prince, though they may be based on good and valid reasons, depend nevertheless on nothing but his pure and free will.

As for the laws of God and nature, all princes in the world are bound by them, and they have no authority to violate them. In so doing, a prince would become guilty of high treason against God and of making war on him, under whose greatness all the rulers on earth must bear their yoke and bow their heads in fear and reverence. The absolute power of princes and lords in no way extends, therefore, to the laws of God and nature, and the Pope who has best understood the nature of absolute power and who has brought kings and emperors under his control said that a sovereign can abrogate ordinary law but not divine or natural law.

But is a prince not subject to the laws of his country, which he has sworn to keep? A distinction has to be made here between two possible situations: if the prince has sworn to himself that he will abide by his laws, he is no more bound by them than by any oath made to himself, just as private citizens are not bound by oaths and agreements that the law does not consider binding, however honorable and reasonable they be. If the sovereign prince promises, however, to another ruler to keep the laws that he or his predecessors have made, he is obliged to abide by them, if the other prince has an interest therein, although no oath was included in the promise. But when the ruler, to whom the promise has been made, has no interest in the matter, neither the promise nor the oath is binding.

The same holds true if the promise has been made by the prince to his subjects, either before or after ascending the throne. Not that the prince is bound by his own laws or those of his predecessors, but anyone, ruler or subject, is obliged to keep his just covenants and promises, whether made under oath or not. Similarly, as a private citizen may be relieved of an unjust and unreasonable promise that grieves him too much and into which he has been beguiled by trickery, fraud, error, force, or fear, so as to cause him major damage, the prince too, may be released from promises that affect the diminution of his majesty, if he is a sovereign prince. Our general rule thus remains, that the prince is not bound by his own laws or those of his predecessors but is obliged to keep his just and reasonable agreements, in the observance of which his subjects in general, or a particular private person, may have an interest.

Law and contracts must not be confused. Law depends on him who possesses sovereignty, and who can bind all his subjects but cannot bind himself. By contrast, a contract is a mutual obligation between prince and subjects that binds them reciprocally, and it cannot be altered except by mutual consent. In this situation, the prince is in no way above the subject, except that, when the justice of the law he has sworn to maintain has ceased to exist, he is no longer bound by his word; this the subjects cannot do, in their private agreements, unless they be relieved by the prince.

The sovereignty of the monarch is in no way altered or diminished by the calling together and deliberations of the estates. On the contrary, seeing all his people recognize him as their sovereign, he finds his majesty thereby enhanced and more illustrious. In such representative assemblies the princes are not unwilling to grant their subjects concessions and favors that they would not otherwise yield, as they are overcome by the requests, petitions, and just grievances of the people, suffering most often without the knowledge of the prince, who sees and hears but through the eyes, ears, and reports of others. We thus conclude that the principal aspect of sovereign rule and absolute power consists in making general laws for the subjects without their consent. Without looking at other countries, we have often seen in our own realm that general customs have been abolished by the edicts of our kings, without hearing the estates, when the injustice of common law and custom was clearly to be seen.

But what if the prince forbids to kill, under the sanction of the death penalty, is he then bound by his own law? I say that such a law is not his, but the law of God and nature. In fact, he is more strictly bound by it than are his subjects, and cannot be freed from its obligation by the people or the senate, being held responsible by the judgment of God, as King Solomon said. Marcus Aurelius said that the magistrates are the judges of private individuals, the princes of magistrates, and God of the princes. Such were the views of two rulers who have been held among the wisest. I shall conclude with that of Antigon, king of Asia, who, on being told by a flatterer that all things were lawful to kings, said: "Yes, to barbarian and tyrannical kings."

The first characteristic of the sovereign prince is the power to make general and special laws, but—and this qualification is important—without the consent of superiors, equals, or inferiors. If the prince requires the consent of superiors, then he is a subject himself; if that of equals, he shares his authority with others; if that of his subjects, senate or people, he is not sovereign. The names of notables that one sees affixed to laws are not put there to endow them with authority but to serve as testimony and additional weight.

LEGITIMATE AND DESPOTIC MONARCHIES

Monarchy is based on conquest, legitimate descent, or tyranny. This diversity of government does not signify a similar diversity of state, because state and government are different things. Government is actual policy and administration, as distinguished from the framework of the state. The state may be a monarchy, and yet popularly governed, if the representative assemblies, magistrates, offices, and grants are open to all, without distinctions of birth, wealth, or virtue. A monarchy is aristocratically governed if political representation and public offices are reserved by the king to the noble, the virtuous, or the rich. The aristocratic state may also be governed popularly, when honors and offices are distributed equally among all subjects, or aristocratically, if reserved exclusively for the noble and the rich. This variety of government has confused those who have deduced therefrom a like variety of states, overlooking the fact that the basic constitution of a state is different from its government and administration.

The royal, or legitimate, monarchy is that in which the subjects obey the laws of the monarch, and the monarch the laws of nature, the subjects retaining their natural liberty and property. The monarchy based on conquest is that in which the prince has made himself lord over persons and property by the force of arms in lawful war, ruling over his subjects as the head of the family over his slaves. The tyrannical monarchy is that in which the monarch, in contempt of the laws of nature, abuses free citizens as slaves and treats their property as his own. The same difference between legitimate rule and tyranny is also to be found in 'aristocracies and democracies; specifically, tyranny may also appear in the democratic state of a frenzied people, as Cicero has so well pointed out.

I have said in the definition of monarchy that the subjects owe obedience to the legitimate king, the sole source of sovereign majesty, and that the king must obey the law of nature, that is to say, govern his subjects and guide his actions by natural justice, which can be seen and perceived as clearly and brightly as the splendor of the sun. It is the true sign of legitimate monarchy when the king obeys and follows the laws of nature as he would like his subjects to do with respect to his own laws. He will accomplish this by fearing God and being merciful toward the afflicted, prudent in his enterprises, bold in his deeds, modest in prosperity, steadfast in adversity, loyal to his given word, wise in counsel, helpful to friends, mindful of his subjects, terrible to enemies, courteous to the good, awe-inspiring to the evil, and just toward all. If the subjects obey the laws of the king, and the king the laws of nature, justice will be mistress or, as Pindar said, queen. Mutual friendship between ruler and people will ensue, as well as harmony of subjects among one another, and of all with the king.

The greatest difference between a king and a tyrant is that the former conducts himself according to the laws of nature, whereas the latter treads them under his feet. The one adheres to piety, justice and faith; the other has no God, no faith, no law. The one does all to serve the public good and the protection of his subjects; the other acts only for his personal profit, vengeance, or pleasure. The one endeavors to enrich his subjects by all means he can think of; the other builds his castle on the ruin of his subjects. The one revenges the injuries inflicted on the people and easily pardons those done to him; the other revenges cruelly the injuries done to him and pardons those of others. The one spares the honor of virtuous women; the other rejoices in their shame. The one takes pleasure in receiving warnings freely expressed and reproof wisely broached; the other hates nothing more than the man who is serious, free, and virtuous. The one endeavors to keep his subjects in peace and unity; the other sows division among them so that they ruin one another, and then enriches himself by confiscating their property. The one takes pleasure in being seen and heard by his subjects; the other hides from them as from his enemies. The one puts his faith in the love of his people; the other, in their fear. The one fears for nothing more than for his subjects; the other fears nothing more than his subjects. The one imposes upon his subjects as light financial charges as possible, and only for the public good; the other drinks his subjects' blood, gnaws their bones, and sucks the very marrow out of them, in order to weaken them. The one appoints to public office men of integrity; the other employs only thieves and the worst rascals.

JUST TYRANNICIDE AND UNJUST REGICIDE

We have said that he is a tyrant who by his own authority sets himself up as sovereign prince, without election, right to succession, lot, just war, or by special divine summons. Both the ancient writings and laws agree that the tyrant may be put to death and that his assassins even receive rich awards: titles of nobility, prowess, chivalry, statues and crowns, and the property of the tyrant, as is due to real liberators of home and country. The ancients made no distinction between the tyrannical ruler who is good and virtuous or wicked and villainous, because no man has the right to invade sovereignty and set himself up as master over his fellow citizens under the guise of justice and virtue. In law, he is guilty of death who assumes the marks reserved for sovereignty. If therefore the subject attempts, by whatever means, to steal from the king his rank and status, or—in the popular or aristocratic state—seeks to make himself from an equal into a lord, he deserves death.

One may ask the question whether the tyrant may be slain who, having seized sovereignty by force or fraud, has himself elected by the representatives of the people, for it seems that the solemn act of election is a genuine ratification of his tyranny, agreed to by the people. I say nevertheless that it is lawful to kill him without any trial or formal proceedings, unless the tyrant has surrendered his authority into the hands of the people in order to be judged in court.

Where the prince is a legitimate absolute sovereign, as are the true monarchs of France, Spain, England, Scotland, Ethiopia, Turkey, Persia, Muscovy, his authority is neither shared nor challenged by anyone. In this case, subjects may not, acting individually or jointly, encroach upon the honor or life of the monarch by judicial or other means, though he may have committed all the wicked, impious, and cruel misdeeds one can think of. As to proceeding against the monarch by judicial means, the subjects have no jurisdiction over their prince, upon whom all power and authority to command depend, and who may not only revoke all the power of his magistrates but in whose very presence the power and jurisdiction of magistrates, corporations, colleges, estates, and communities cease to exist. It is not lawful for the subject to bring his prince to trial, for the vassal his lord, nor for the servant his master. In short, if it is not lawful to proceed against the king by judicial means, how could it be lawful to do so by force? The question at issue here is not who is the strongest, but whether the subject has the lawful authority to condemn his sovereign prince.

RELIGION AND SOCIAL PEACE

I do not wish to go into the question of which religion is the best (though there is only one religion, one truth, one divine law revealed by the mouth of God). But the prince who has complete certainty of the true religion and desires to attract to it his subjects divided into sects and factions should not be driven into the use of force, because the more the will of men is forced, the more it becomes obstinate. On the other hand, if the prince follows the true religion without sham or make-believe, be will be able to turn the hearts of his subjects to his religion, without using violence or punishments. In so doing he will avoid hard feelings, troubles and civil war, while leading the subjects who had gone astray into the haven of salvation.

THE SOCIAL CAUSES OF REVOLUTION

Among all the causes of sedition and basic changes of the state, none is more important than excessive wealth of the few and extreme poverty of the many. The record of history is full of examples. Those who have advanced several causes of discontent against the state have taken advantage of the first opportunity that presented itself to them to despoil the rich of their fortunes. These revolutionary changes were more frequent in ancient times than at present because of the infinite number of slaves, who were thirty or forty times more numerous than those who were free. The greatest reward for their services was to be freed, even though they would obtain no other benefit. Many were able to buy liberty only by sacrificing their life-long savings or by borrowing, apart from the servitudes that they owed to their former masters. Despite these wretched conditions, they had an infinite number of children, as usually happens to those who labor most and live most frugally; being free, but oppressed by poverty, they were forced, in order to subsist, to borrow and pay their creditors in cash, crops, or services. The longer they lived, the more heavily they became indebted and the less able to meet their obligations; the Hebrews called usury a biting, because it gnaws the debtor to the very bone and sucks his blood and the marrow of his bones. Swollen in numbers and starved, the poor finally arose against the rich, drove them out of their houses and mansions, or had to be fed at their expense.

This is why Plato called wealth and poverty the ancient pests of states, not only on the ground of the material want that oppresses the starving, but also because of their abjection, which is a very evil and dangerous pestilence. To prevent it, men have searched for equality, which has been praised by many as the nourishing source of peace and friendship among citizens, as contrasted with the effects of inequality, namely, enmities, factions, hatreds, and prejudices. For he who possesses more than another and sees himself richer in property also desires more honors, delights, pleasures, food, and clothes. He wishes to be revered by the poor, whom he despises and tramples under his feet. On their part, the poor feel extreme envy and jealousy; though considering themselves as worthy as the rich, or even more so, they find themselves oppressed by poverty, hunger, misery, and disgrace.

For this reason, several ancient legislators divided the goods equally among a subjects; within recent memory, Thomas More, Chancellor of England, said in his book on the state that the public welfare can be attained only if men live in a community of goods, and that public welfare is impossible where private property exists. When Plato had the power, by the consent of the citizens who sent their ambassadors to him, to set up a new commonwealth, the colony of the Thebans and Phocians, he left without accomplishing anything because the rich were unwilling to share any of their wealth with the poor. Lycurgus endangered his life when, having banned the use of gold and silver, he also equally divided all estates. If Solon was unable to do the same, it was not because of lack of will, for he granted an annulment of bonds and a general abolition of debts.

On the other hand, it may be affirmed that equality of property is very harmful to the state, which has no safer support and foundation than good faith, without which neither justice nor any form of society can endure. Faith inheres in promises of legitimate conventions; if obligations are broken, contracts annulled, debt abolished, what can one then expect but the complete subversion of the state? There will be no trust whatsoever in one another. Moreover, such general abolitions of debts often harm and even ruin the poor, because poor widows, orphans, and little people who have nothing but a small annuity are lost when debts are generally abolished. By contrast, the usurers take their precaution in time and profit from such abolitions of debts, as happened under Solon and Agis: the usurers, having had advance information about the cancellation of all debts, borrowed money from all sides to defraud their creditors. In addition, the hope of such general abolition of debts encourages the spendthrifts to borrow at any rate of interest; later they join the ranks of the malcontent and desperate poor, and stir up sedition among them, whereas, had there been no expectation of the cancellation of debts at the time of contracting them, everybody would seek to husband his property wisely and live in peace.

If the evil effects of such abolitions are great, they are still worse in the case of the equal division of land and other goods that had been lawfully acquired and held in possession. With regard to debts, there is the pretense of usury and the sterility of money, arguments that cannot be used with respect to lawful estates, so that one is led to conclude that such division of the property of others is nothing but theft under the cloak of equality. And to say that equality nourishes friendship is to abuse the ignorant; for it is certain that there is no greater hatred, nor fiercer enmity than among equals, and the jealousy among equals is the source of turmoil, sedition, and civil war. By contrast, the poor, small, and weak willingly submit to, and obey, the great, rich, and powerful for the aid and profit that they hope to receive from them.

WAR

Should citizens be prepared and trained in the military arts? Should the state seek war rather than peace? There is no doubt on these issues. We firmly hold that commonwealth to be happy in which the king obeys the laws of God and nature, in which the magistrates obey the king, the subjects the magistrates, the children their parents, servants their masters, and whose subjects are bound by friendship to one other, and all with the prince, so as to enjoy the sweetness of peace and the true calmness of spirit. War is contrary to all this, and warlike men are the sworn enemies of this kind of life. Also, it is impossible to see a commonwealth flourish in religion, justice, charity, integrity, and, in short, in all the liberal sciences and mechanical arts unless the citizens enjoy a firm and assured peace— which is the ruin of warriors, who, like their equipment, are useless in time of good peace. And who is more hostile to a peaceable man than the furious soldier; to the mild farmer, than the bloodthirsty warrior; to the philosopher, than the captain; to the wise, than fools? For the greatest pleasure of warriors is to forage the open country, rob the peasants, burn the villages, besiege, batter, force, and pillage the towns, massacre the good and bad, the young and old, all ages and sexes, rape the virgins, wash in the blood of their victims, desecrate holy objects, raze temples, blaspheme the name of God, and trample under their feet all divine and human laws. Such are the fruits of war, pleasant and agreeable to warriors, abominable to good men, and detestable to God.

It is unnecessary to amplify in words what one sees happen in so many places, for the memory of these happenings alone fills one with horror. One must therefore beware of raising a warlike spirit among the subjects, guiding them toward such an execrable life, nor seek war under any circumstances, except when it is a matter of repelling violence in an extreme emergency. For those who make use of the slightest occasion to make war, resemble the flies who cannot stay on a well polished mirror, but prefer rough places. They who seek war to aggrandize themselves out of the ruin of others will be in perpetual torment, leading a life of misery, because greed has no limits, though in appearances one may promise oneself to have enough after the conquest of a kingdom. They resemble a slave who first only demands to be unchained; free of his shackles, he desires freedom; emancipated, he wishes to have the status of a citizen; given citizenship rights, he would like to be a public official; having reached the highest ranks of office, he aspires to be king; being king, he seeks to be the sole monarch; and, finally, he wants to be God.

How much happier then is a small prince or a small commonwealth (though there is nothing small in contentment), enjoying the assurance of tranquillity and peace without enemies, without war or envy? The boundary of a well ordered commonwealth is justice, as Pompey said to the king of the Parthians, and not the point of the sword, as King Agesilaus said.

CHAPTER SEVENTEEN

HOBBES

The modern age, conceived in the Renaissance and Reformation, was born in the crucible of civil and international war in the seventeenth century. A host of old and new issues—social, economic, constitutional—produced intense passions transformed by religion into irreconcilable hatreds. The Thirty Years' War (1618–1648) started with a Protestant revolt in Bohemia. The conflict soon broadened into a major conflagration, until most European states were finally involved; civil wars and revolutions sprang up in half a dozen countries, from Italy to England. Germany, the principal theater of military operations, was depopulated, impoverished, and ruined by the war. Neither Protestantism nor Catholicism won a conclusive victory, and men began to ask themselves whether moral and physical devastation could be justified by theological differences.

Until the age of discovery, that is, as long as the Mediterranean held the pivotal position in commerce and civilization, England lived on the rim of the world's center. But when geographical discovery and overseas expansion shifted the world's focal area from the Mediterranean basin—the "middle of the earth"—to the Atlantic shores of western Europe, England became the center of a new oceanic world largely of her own making, and her rising commercial and industrial wealth quickly put her in the front rank of European nations. Moreover, in the seventeenth century the foundations were laid for the future greatness of England in science, medicine, navigation, philosophy, economics, and politics. The nineteenth century is often called the "English century" because England then attained the peak of her visible power and world-wide influence. Yet the seventeenth is probably the most creative century in English history, and the success of the nineteenth century was built on the greatness of the seventeenth.

The turning point was marked by the Puritan Revolution and two civil wars 1642–1649), fought over fundamental issues that could not be resolved peaceably. First, there was the issue of *religious* liberty: the Church of England was criticized for being a state church, and its episcopal organization as well as its liturgy was rejected by many as being too close to Roman Catholicism. A sizable body of respectable Protestants favored presbyterianism as an alternative, and—on the theological left—the independent congregationalist sects began to press their demands. The slogan of King James I, "No Bishop, no King," made compromise with the Puritans difficult, and with the congregationalist sectarians impossible. The second main issue of the civil war was *constitutional:* who was sovereign, Parliament or the King? The third issue, cutting across religion and politics, was *social* and *economic:* to what extent should the merchants, financiers, lawyers, and tradesmen be included in the governing classes of the nation?

The class lines were by no means neatly drawn. The most prominent generals on the parliamentary side came from distinguished aristocratic or landowning families. Conversely, many urban elements, particularly in the North and West, supported the royalist side in the war. Yet on the whole the middle classes, tradesmen and yeoman farmers, supported the parliamentary party; and, though they were not agreed on the form of church government they wanted, they all abhorred the High Anglicanism and episcopalianism of the royalists, which seemed little different from Roman Catholicism—and Romanism meant Spain and France, the two national enemies of England. The parliamentary party was the more nationalistic; nationalism was of less import to those who upheld the doctrine of the divine right of kings.

The parliamentary party won because it commanded superior economic and financial resources, because the fleet was on its side, and because the New Model Army fought with invincible faith in its cause. King Charles I was publicly beheaded in London on January 30, 1649. The first middle-class revolution in history thus asserted itself successfully with decisive and unheard-of audacity. With the head of Charles I, the doctrine of the divine rights of kings rolled to the ground. His fate warned all rulers that political authority is closer to the earth and the people than to God and heaven.

The turbulent first half of the seventeenth century in England provides the background for the political philosophy of a lonely and complex figure, Thomas Hobbes (1588–1679). Hobbes' father was an impecunious vicar and something of a "character." Once, after a Saturday night of playing cards, he dozed in the pulpit and surprised the congregation by awakening with the cry of "Clubs is trumps." He got into a brawl with another parson and was forced to get away, abandoning his wife and three children. His brother, a well-to-do glover, who took charge of the deserted children, became particularly interested in young Thomas, who read and wrote at four, learned Greek and Latin at six, and went to Oxford at fifteen. Hobbes stayed at Oxford for five years but was not too happy about the course of studies, which seemed to him arid and old-fashioned.

On receiving his degree, Hobbes was recommended to Lord Cavendish (afterward the first Earl of Devonshire) for the post of companion and tutor of his eldest son, who was about the same age as Hobbes. The association with the Cavendish family lasted, with some interruptions, until Hobbes' death. Through his close connection with this family, one of the most aristocratic in England, he met men of affairs as well as outstanding scientists of the day, such as Bacon, Harvey, Descartes, and Galileo. Hobbes also traveled widely, and spent—in company with his Cavendish charges or on his own—about twenty years on the Continent, mostly in Paris; there he came in touch with the new philosophical and scientific developments of the time.

In 1640, when Parliament began to assert its authority, Hobbes fled to France, "the first of all that fled," as he later said of himself. He feared that his intimate associations with royalist circles might endanger his safety; in addition, his writings up to his flight to France had been clearly antiparliamentarian and antidemocratic. During his stay in Paris he instructed, from 1646 to 1648, Charles II, the son of the executed monarch, in mathematics. In 1651, Hobbes went back to England, because he "would not trust his safety with the French clergy," as he later explained. He declared his submission to the new republican regime and stayed in England until his death in 1679.

Hobbes' greatest work, the *Leviathan,* appeared in 1651, shortly before his return to England. The civil war provided some of the atmosphere of the book but little more. Hobbes' main views were formed long before the actual conflict broke out, although there had been no real peace in England since the ascension to the throne of James I in 1603. The *Leviathan* is not an apology for the Stuart monarchy, nor a grammar of despotic government, but the first general theory of politics in the English language.

Unlike most defenders of absolute government, who start out with the gospel of inequality, Hobbes argues that men are naturally equal in mind and body. As to strength of body, the weakest has enough strength to kill the strongest, either by slaying him secretly or by allying himself with others for the purpose. With regard to mental faculties, Hobbes finds an even greater natural equality. Prudence is a matter of time and experience that can be acquired by everybody. Most persons think that they have more wisdom than their fellow men, but this in itself, Hobbes remarks sardonically, is proof that men are equal rather than unequal.

This *basic equality of men* is a principal source of trouble and misery. Men have, in general, equal faculties; they also cherish like hopes and desires. If two men desire the same thing, which they cannot both obtain, they become enemies and seek to destroy each other. In the *state of nature,* therefore, men are in a *condition of war,* of "every man against every man," and Hobbes adds that the nature of the war consists, not in actual fighting, "but in the known disposition thereto." Force and fraud, the two cardinal virtues of war, flourish in this atmosphere of perpetual fear and strife, fed by three psychological causes: competition, diffidence, and glory. In such a condition, there is no place for industry, agriculture, navigation, trade; there are no arts or letters; no society; no amenities of civilized living, and, worst of all, there is "continual fear and danger of violent death; and the life of man, solitary, poor, nasty, brutish, and short."

Hobbes does not extensively discuss the question whether men have actually ever lived in such a state of nature. He notes that the "savage people in many places of America" have no government and live in the brutish manner described. Yet, even if the state of nature has never existed generally all over the world, one could envisage the kind of life men would lead if there were no government. His argument of the *state of nature* is, in other words, *philosophical* and *not historical.* On the basis of the anthropological data that we possess today but that were not accessible to Hobbes, we know that life is actually more regulated in the so-called primitive group than in the community of the more advanced stage. As a thoroughgoing individualist and rationalist, Hobbes was unaware that the family or clan, and not the individual, is the basic social unit in primitive society, and custom or social pressure, and not law, its mechanism of enforcing conformity.

Pessimistic as Hobbes may seem, he is not despondent about man's ability to overcome the predicament in which he finds himself in the state of nature. The *fear of death* is the passion that inclines men to peace: the attractions of power and glory give way to the desire for securing, as a minimum, life, and—if possible—the means of a commodious existence. Hobbes is a strong rationalist, but reason is for him not a *deus ex machina* that appears from nowhere to work miracles, but an integral part of man, his essential faculty that distinguishes him from animals. Once man realizes that his fear of death is primarily due to brutal competition, resulting in perpetual war of all against all, reason shows the way out: to accept the principle of not doing that to another "which thou thinkest unreasonable to be done by another to yourself."

However, on the basis of Hobbes' analysis of the nature of man, a contract among men not to do to one another what they would not wish to have done to themselves would not be sufficient. Though man has the capacity to learn prudence and moderation from his fear of death, his desire for power and glory may tempt him to break his pledge unless there is a restraining power strong enough to keep him to his promise, because "covenants, without the sword, are but words, and of no strength to secure a man at all." If men were peaceable enough, Hobbes notes, to observe covenants without a superior authority for their enforcement, there would be no need for government in the first place, because there would be peace without compulsion. To make the counsel of prudence, born of the fear of death, issue in effective peace, a sovereign authority—one man or an assembly of men—must be created to whom all power is transferred.

The *social contract* of Hobbes is made *between subjects and subjects, not between subjects and sovereign.* The sovereign is not a party to the contract, but its creation. In this conception of the social contract, the sovereign cannot commit any breach of covenant, because he is not a party to it. By participating in the creation of the sovereign, the subject is the author of all that the ruler does and must therefore not complain of any of the ruler's actions, because he would then be deliberately doing injury to himself. Hobbes concedes that the sovereign may commit iniquity but not "injustice or injury in the proper signification," because he cannot, by definition, act illegally: he determines what is just and unjust, and his action is law.

The question of the best form of state is not one of logic, according to Hobbes, but of convenience, that is, of the aptitude of the state to produce the security and peace of the people for which a government is instituted. However, on purely practical grounds Hobbes considers monarchy the best form of state because it suffers less from competition for office and power than do aristocracies and democracies; also, it is easier for one than for many to act resolutely and consistently.

Sovereign power is "incommunicable and inseparable," and Hobbes attacks any institution, town or private corporation, that may weaken the omnipotence of the state. He is vehemently opposed to division of powers or mixed government, and he goes so far as to say that there would have been no civil war in England if it had not been for the widespread opinion that sovereignty was divided between King, Lords, and Commons. There is particular danger in the liberty of the subject to challenge the wisdom of legality of the sovereign's actions, the "poisonous doctrine" that "every private man is judge of good and evil actions," and that "whatsoever a man does against his conscience is sin." Against such "seditious doctrines" Hobbes demands the unqualified obedience of the subject.

To keep the authority of the state strong, Hobbes advises the sovereign not to allow the growth of groups and institutions that intervene between state and individual. Hobbes is particularly anxious to prevent churches from interfering in any way with the activities of the state, and in his doctrine the church becomes, in effect, a department of the state. He reminds the clergy that it is not essential to the commonwealth, and that the safety of the church depends on the state rather than the state on the safety of the church.

Hobbes had no religion. He defines religion in general, together with true religion and superstition, as follows: *"Fear* of power invisible, feigned by the mind, or imagined from tales publicly allowed, *religion;* not allowed, *superstition.* And when the power imagined is truly such as we imagine, *true religion."* These definitions are included, not in a discussion of theology or metaphysics, but in a catalogue of human passions and their forms of expression. His approach to religion is by way of psychology and public policy, and not by way of theology or philosophy. His definitions of religion, superstition, and true religion are placed between "curiosity" and "panic terror," which placement suggests itself Hobbes' approach to religion.

From a strictly political viewpoint Hobbes saw in religions and churches the most serious danger of civil disobedience and disunity, and in the conflict of secular and divine commandments the most frequent pretext of sedition and civil war. He is skeptical about the origin of many commands that claim divine provenance, because it is difficult to know whether a command comes from God or from someone who abuses His name for private ends. But if there is a bona fide conflict between secular and divine laws, the subject should obey the civil sovereign, if compliance does not involve forfeiture of life eternal; if it does, the subject may prefer death of the body to eternal damnation of the soul.

Hobbes' advice to subjects to become martyrs for their consciences' sake, or obey the sovereign, is tantamount to establishing—for most people—the duty of unlimited obedience. Not feeling any deep sympathy for religion, Hobbes invites believers to prove their faith by their willingness to die for it. In his personal attitude, Hobbes preferred the "episcopacy" of the Anglican state church because it was the official church, and "the most commodious that a Christian King can use for the governing of Christ's flock." By contrast, Presbyterians and Puritans encroach on civil authority and encourage men to set themselves up as their own judges—a bad habit easily carried over into secular affairs.

Hobbes' heaviest assaults are directed against the Roman Catholic Church. Hobbes remembered—and the memory is maintained in England to this day by annual public ceremonies—the Catholic conspiracy of the Gunpowder Plot in 1605. The conspirators managed to introduce barrels of gunpowder into the cellars of Parliament just before it was to be opened by King James I, with the aim of blowing up King, Lords, and Commons in one big explosion. The plot failed, and the conspirators were executed, including the Provincial of the Jesuits in England. In 1610, while Hobbes was in Paris with young Cavendish on their first grand tour, King Henry IV of France, at first a Huguenot and later a convert to Catholicism, a conciliatory and temperate ruler, was stabbed to death by François Ravaillac, a Catholic fanatic. The murder made a lifelong impression on Hobbes, and he saw in the Roman Catholic Church the true exemplification of the kingdom of darkness: "For from the time that the Bishop of Rome had gotten to be acknowledged for bishop universal, by pretense of succession to St. Peter, their whole hierarchy, or kingdom of darkness, may be compared not unfitly to the *kingdom of fairies;* that is, to the old wives' *fables* in England concerning *ghosts* and *spirits,* and the feats they play in the night. And if a man consider the original of this ecclesiastical dominion, he will easily perceive that the Papacy is no other than the *ghost* of the deceased *Roman empire,* sitting crowned upon the grave thereof."

Called "father of atheists" even in the entourage of Charles II, Hobbes had to leave France in 1651 because he was afraid of the French clergy, not of politicians. After Charles II returned to England in 1660, Hobbes got into difficulties because of his alleged atheism, and the *Leviathan* could not be reprinted for several years, owing to the opposition of the bishops. In 1666 Hobbes—fearful of official proceedings against him—wrote an essay on heresy to prove why he could not be legally burned for his opinions. The first collected edition of his works in 1688 was published not in England, but in Holland.

In his treatment of the problem of *natural law* Hobbes reveals his novel doctrine. Since the Stoics, the conception has never died out in the West that civil (or positive) law is derived from, and inferior to, a higher law, a "law behind the law"—the law of nature. In the Bible, too, the law of kings and princes is held to be subordinate to the law of God. This Stoic-Jewish-Christian tradition has had a civilizing effect on the western world because it has always reminded rulers that above their edicts and commands there is a higher law, founded on natural reason or divine revelation. Hobbes rejects this approach to the problem of the validity of law on the ground that it places validity beyond the formal source of the legal sovereign. According to Hobbes, there can be no unjust law—the cardinal issue of legal philosophy—because laws are the "rules of just and unjust." As to the relations between civil law and natural law, Hobbes maintains that they "contain each other." In fact, the law of nature is not law at all, but only "qualities that dispose men to peace and obedience."

Hobbes lists equity, justice, gratitude, and "other moral virtues" as the laws of nature. These qualities are not true laws, because, before the state is established, there is no authority to decide finally which idea of the law is binding. In practice, therefore, the law of nature is nothing but a set of general principles of the civil law; the main formal difference lies in the fact that the civil law is written, whereas the natural law is unwritten. Thus Hobbes sought to sweep away the doctrine of natural law from the theory of the state. With penetrating insight he foresaw the revolutionary implications of natural law ideas as they became manifest only a century later in the American and French revolutions. Locke, too, admitted the revolutionary possibilities of the doctrine of natural law, but, unlike Hobbes, he was not overly frightened by the prospect.

Hobbes' hostility to natural law, whether based on reason or religious faith, is not only linked to his conception of sovereignty and government, but is closely related to his total rejection of values and universally valid ethical ideas. According to Hobbes, "good" and "evil" are not ethical qualities of an object or action, but merely expressions of an individual's feelings about them: "But whatsoever is the object of any man's appetite or desire, that is it which he for his part calls *good:* and the object of his hate and aversion, *evil;* and of his contempt, *vile* and *inconsiderable.* For these words of good, evil, and contemptible are ever used with relation to the person that uses them: there being nothing simply and absolutely so; nor any common rule of good and evil, to be taken from the nature of the objects themselves." This *emotive theory of value,* as the modern philosophical school of logical positivism calls it, thus denies to statements of value any objective validity or even meaning, since such statements—in the eyes of both Hobbes and the logical positivists—merely tell us something about the feelings of a person with respect to some actions, but say nothing meaningful or valid about the actions themselves.

This general rejection by Hobbes of any concept of universal values can also be seen in his treatment of the problem of the *forms of government* Aristotle divided all forms of government into two broad groups, and the basic criterion of his distinction was entirely ethical: whether a government operates in the interests of the people (monarchy, aristocracy, constitutional government) or of the rulers (tyranny, oligarchy, dictatorship of the poor). Hobbes rejects this ethical distinction completely, and holds that governments can only differ as to their numerical composition, that is, government by one (monarchy), by a few (aristocracy), or by the people (democracy). Terms like "tyranny," "oligarchy," and "anarchy" are not, according to Hobbes, names for ethically deficient forms of government, but simply indicate that a particular person "mislikes" a monarchical, aristocratic, or democratic form of government. Hobbes rejects here again, as in his analysis of natural law and the more general problem of values, the possibility of rational argument and valid ethical conclusions: if he comes out in favor of monarchy against aristocracy and democracy, his preference is not based on any moral position, but solely on his assertion that monarchy is more "convenient," in the sense that it is likely to be more effective than its rivals, and will result in more peace and security for the people.

On the whole, the practical effect of Hobbes has been to strengthen the *doctrine of the absolute state.* Yet the complex character of his ideas has puzzled his political friends and opponents. Conservatives who believe in legitimate monarchy criticize Hobbes first for being little interested in the divine right of monarchs and in monarchy as a moral institution. Hobbes was solely concerned with the pragmatic question of *effective* government, and legitimacy did not interest him at all. Thus, when he returned to England in 1651, he sent his submission to the Council of State. Though he was a lifelong supporter of the royalist cause, he was willing to submit to Cromwell's regime, because at the time it was the effective government that maintained law and order in

England. In 1656, Hobbes boasted of the influence of the *Leviathan* on "the minds of a thousand gentlemen to a conscientious obedience to the present government [of Cromwell], which otherwise would have wavered in that point." After King Charles II returned to England in 1660, and the monarchy was restored, Hobbes explained that the "gentlemen" had appeased Cromwell in order to protect their property and influence for serving the king better later on. This may be realism, but it cannot appeal to a conservative who bases loyalty on moral sentiment.

Moreover, monarchists could never be satisfied with Hobbes' preference for monarchy as the best form of government. No theory of monarchy can be construed without some element of mysticism to make its authority acceptable. Hobbes' preference was entirely devoid of mysticism; his approach was utilitarian and pragmatic. The Hobbesian monarch cannot hide his ineffectiveness behind the cloak of divine or traditional authority. He must "deliver the goods," if he is to retain his regal office. Religious conservatives have charged Hobbes with atheism because he treats the church as he treats other associations, that is, subordinates it to the state, as he subordinates theology to philosophy. For a long time, atheism and agnosticism were branded as Hobbism.

Hobbes' main opponents have been the adherents of parliamentary government and limited powers; because this doctrine has become the dominant tradition in the English-speaking countries, there has been no Hobbesian school in British and American political thought. By contrast, Hobbes has markedly influenced various countries with traditions of absolute, despotic government.

Yet to call Hobbes a spiritual father of modern totalitarianism is more untenable than would appear from a cursory glance at several key phrases in the *Leviathan*. First, government is set up, according to Hobbes, by a covenant that transfers all power and authority to the sovereign. This *contractual foundation of government* is anathema to modern totalitarians who attacked the contractual theory of the state because contract implies mutuality of some sort, and, still more important because there can be no contract without consent. Democracy is government by consent.

Second, Hobbes assigns to the state a prosaic business: to maintain *order and security for the benefit of the citizens*. By contrast, the aim of the modern totalitarian state was anti-individualistic and antihedonistic: the goal of public policy was dictated, not by the longing of citizens for happiness, but by a collective purpose, such as the glory of the master race in Nazi Germany, the revival of the Roman empire in Fascist Italy, and the triumph of the proletariat in Soviet Russia. Race, Empire, and Class are modern totalitarian substitutes for Hobbes' bourgeois ideals of Thrift, Industry, and "Commodious Living."

Third, the Hobbesian state is *authoritarian*, not totalitarian. Above all, Hobbes pleads for equality before the law, so that the "rich and mighty" have no legal advantage over "poor and obscure persons." Hobbes' authoritarianism thus lacks one of the most characteristic features of the modern totalitarian state: inequality before the law, and the resulting sense of personal insecurity. Authority in the Hobbesian state is concentrated in the political sphere, and in it alone. The sovereign will normally permit his subjects "the liberty to buy and sell and otherwise to contract with one another, to choose their own abode, their own diet, their own trade of life, and institute their children as they themselves see fit; and the like." The Hobbesian belief in economic *laissez faire* is the exact opposite of rigid economic planning. Similarly, the Hobbesian freedom of bringing up one's children is antithetical to the regimenting and drilling of children in modern totalitarian regimes.

Fourth, Hobbes holds that the sovereign may be one man or an assembly of men, whereas modern totalitarianism—in fact, if not always in theory—was addicted to the leadership principle. Hobbes preferred monarchy for practical reasons, but he was free from the mysticism that has endowed totalitarian leaders with alleged charismatic and prophetic gifts. The Hobbesian sovereign is a *supreme administrator and lawgiver* but not a top spellbinder, propagandist, or showman.

Fifth, Hobbes recognizes that war is one of the two main forces (the other being the danger of internal disorder) that drive men to set up a state. But whenever he speaks of war, it is *defensive war,* and there is no glorification of war, let alone of aggressive war, in the *Leviathan.* By contrast, totalitarian fascists looked on war as something highly *desirable,* and on imperialist war as the highest form of national life; communists— while rejecting, in theory, war between nations—accepted the inevitability of war be- tween classes, and the liquidation of the bourgeoisie by violent means.

Sixth, the totalitarian state insisted on outer as well as inner conformity; in fact, it considered ideas more dangerous than actions. By contrast, the Hobbesian sovereign de- sires merely—for purposes of maintaining the peace—*outer conformity* of the subjects to the law. The subject is bound to obey the law, but "not bound to believe it," and human governors can take no notice of his "belief and interior cogitations." What Hobbes is concerned about is social peace, not Truth, whereas totalitarians of all times are willing to destroy man for the sake of preserving Truth, if a choice has to be made.

Seventh, and finally, the Hobbesian state does not completely swallow the individual: "A man cannot lay down the right of resisting them that assault him by force to take away his life." Since the purpose of civil society is the preservation and protection of man's life, Hobbes recognizes the inalienable *right of the individual to resist* when his life is at stake, because "man by nature chooses the lesser evil, which is danger of death in resisting, rather than the greater, which is certain and present death in not resisting." For a long time this cautionary qualification seemed unimportant, because the sanctity of human life, as a principle at least, was universally accepted. But when, in World War II, millions of people were murdered in gas chambers and concentration camps in pur- suance of deliberate state policy, the Hobbesian stress on the inalienability of human life as the irreducible minimum of the state's purpose acquired new meaning.

The fact that Hobbes was not—intellectually or emotionally—of the totalitarian cast should not create the impression that he was a democrat in disguise. He was not. The Hobbesian state finds its realization in neither the modern democratic state nor the to- talitarian dictatorship of the fascist or communist brand. In modern times, political Hobbism is to be found in countries that possess social and economic conditions similar to those of seventeenth century England—some nations in Latin America and Asia. Dictatorships in Latin America in the nineteenth and twentieth centuries closely ap- proximated the Hobbesian state: society was still in a precapitalist or, at best, early capitalist stage. Economic *laisez faire* was mingled, in such countries, with strong polit- ical authority, usually in the form of an open or concealed dictatorship. But the dicta- torship was authoritarian, not totalitarian. In cultural, religious, educational, social, and economic affairs it was often very lenient. Compared with an advanced democracy, the Hobbesian state may appear dismal enough. Compared with twentieth-century to- talitarianism, it is a vision of refined political civilization.

The Hobbesian theory of politics rests largely on a hypothesis—the solitary, com- bative, competitive character of man—that is only a half-truth. It is difficult to see how the brutes who lead a life of nasty savagery in the Hobbesian state of nature should suddenly display the prudent reasoning and cooperative effort that go into the making of the social contract creating the sovereign. A group that knows the institu- tion of the contract is well beyond the state of nature, and it would perhaps be truer to say that contact is the product of society rather than society the product of contract.

Yet these difficulties rest, not on varying sets of historical facts, but on different interpretations of human nature. If one rejects Hobbes' psychological assumptions as too pessimistic and mechanistic, one will be unable to accept, to that extent, the political ideas derived from them.

The truth of Hobbes' psychological tenets will ultimately be tested by the facts of social life rather than by philosophical arguments. In the area of domestic political organization, the state of nature with its horrors and barbarisms has disappeared. In the area of international relations, Hobbes noted in 1651, independent sovereign states live in the state of nature, "are in continual jealousies, and in the state and posture of gladiators; having their weapons pointing, and their eyes fixed, on one another; that is, their forts, garrisons, and guns upon the frontiers of their kingdoms, and continual spies upon their neighbors; which is a posture of war. But because they uphold thereby the industry of their subjects, there does not follow from it that misery which accompanies the liberty of particular men." As long as the sovereign states of the world continue to exist in the state of nature, a condition of brutish savagery, the Hobbesian view of man will continue to be true of the behavior of states toward one another.

Hobbes' observation that the fear of death is an important motive in creating a social order is profound. In the forty-five years after World War II, relative peace between the Soviet Union and the United States was maintained as the result of this fear, which took on new meaning in the atomic age. If humanity cannot find its purpose in the pursuit of more positive goals, then perhaps its best chance of survival may be in the more modest Hobbesian motive.

HOBBES

*Leviathan**

THE STATE OF NATURE

Nature has made men so equal in the faculties of the body and mind, as that though there be found one man sometimes manifestly stronger in body, or of quicker mind than another, yet when all is reckoned together, the difference between man and man is not so considerable, as that one man can thereupon claim to himself any benefit to which another man may not pretend as well as he. For as to the strength of body, the weakest has strength enough to kill the strongest, either by secret machinations, or by confederacy with others that are in the same danger with himself.

And as to the faculties of the mind, setting aside the arts grounded upon words, and especially that skill of proceeding upon general and infallible rules, called science, which very few have, and but in few things, as being not a native faculty, born with us, nor attained, as prudence, while we look after somewhat else, I find yet a greater equality among men than that of strength. For prudence is but experience, which equal time equally bestows on all men in those things they equally apply themselves unto. That which may perhaps make such equality incredible is but a vain conceit of one's own wisdom, which almost all men think they have in a greater degree than the vulgar; that is, than all men but themselves, and a few others, whom by fame, or for concurring with themselves, they approve. For such is the nature of men, that howsoever they may acknowledge many others to be more witty, or more eloquent, or more learned,

yet they will hardly believe there be many so wise as themselves; for they see their own wit at hand, and other men's at a distance. But this proves rather that men are in that point equal, than unequal. For there is not ordinarily a greater sign of the equal distribution of anything than that every man is contented with his share.

From this equality or ability arises equality of hope in the attaining of our ends. And therefore if any two men desire the same thing, which nevertheless they cannot both enjoy, they become enemies; and in the way to their end, which is principally their own conservation, and sometimes their delectation only, endeavour to destroy or subdue one another. And from hence it comes to pass that where an invader has no more to fear than another man's single power, if one plant, sow, build, or possess a convenient seat, others may probably be expected to come prepared with forces united, to dispossess and deprive him, not only of the fruit of his labour, but also of his life or liberty. And the invader again is in the like danger of another.

And from this diffidence of one another, there is no way for any man to secure himself, so reasonable, as anticipation; that is, by force, or wiles, to master the persons of all men he can, so long till he see no other power great enough to endanger him; and this is no more than his own conservation requires, and is generally allowed. Also because there be some that, taking pleasure in contemplating their own power in the acts of conquest, which they pursue farther than their security requires, if others, that otherwise would be glad to be at case within modest bounds, should not by invasion increase their power, they would not be able,

---

*From Thomas Hobbes, *Leviathan* (1651). Spelling and punctuation have been modernized for this selection.

long time, by standing only on their defence, to subsist. And by consequence, such augmentation of dominion over men being necessary to a man's conservation, it ought to be allowed him.

Again, men have no pleasure, but on the contrary a great deal of grief, in keeping company where there is no power able to over-awe them all. For every man looks that his companion should value him at the same rate he sets upon himself; and upon all signs of contempt, or undervaluing, naturally endeavours, as far as he dares (which, among them that have no common power to keep them in quiet, is far enough to make them destroy each other), to extort a greater value from his contemners, by damage; and from others, by the example.

So that in the nature of man, we find three principal causes of quarrel. First, competition; secondly, diffidence; thirdly, glory.

The first makes men invade for gain; the second, for safety; and the third, for reputation. The first use violence, to make themselves masters of other men's persons, wives, children, and cattle; the second, to defend them; the third, for trifles, as a word, a smile, a different opinion, and any other sign of undervalue, either direct in their persons, or by reflection in their kindred, their friends, their nation, their profession, or other name.

Hereby it is manifest that, during the time men live without a common power to keep them all in awe, they are in that condition which is called war; and such a war as is of every man against every man. For *war* consists not in battle only, or the act of fighting, but in a tract of time, wherein the will to contend by battle is sufficiently known; and therefore the notion of *time* is to be considered in the nature of war, as it is in the nature of weather. For as the nature of foul weather lies not in a shower or two or rain, but in an inclination thereto of many days together, so the nature of war consists not in actual fighting, but in the known disposition thereto, during all the time there is no assurance to the contrary. All other time is *peace*.

Whatsoever therefore is consequent to a time of war, where every man is enemy to every man, the same is consequent to the time wherein men live without other security than what their own strength, and their own invention, shall furnish them withal. In such condition, there is no place for industry, because the fruit thereof is uncertain; and consequently no culture of the earth; no navigation nor use of the commodities that may be imported by sea; no commodious building; no instruments of moving, and removing, such things as require much force; no knowledge of the face of the earth; no account of time; no arts; no letters; no society and, which is the worst of all, continual fear, and danger of violent death; and the life of man, solitary, poor, nasty, brutish, and short.

It may seem strange to some man that has not well weighted these things that nature should thus dissociate, and render men apt to invade and destroy one another; and he may therefore, not trusting to this inference, made from the passions, desire perhaps to have the same confirmed by experience. Let him therefore consider with himself: when taking a journey, he arms himself, and seeks to go well accompanied; when going to sleep, he locks his doors; when even in his house he locks his chests; and this when he knows there be laws, and public officers, armed, to revenge all injuries shall be done him; what opinion he has of his fellow-subjects, when he rides armed; of his fellow citizens, when he locks his doors; and of his children and servants, when he locks his chests. Does he not there as much accuse mankind by his actions as I do by my words? But neither of us accuse man's nature in it. The desire, and other passions of man, are in themselves no sin. No more are the actions that proceed from those passions, till they know a law that forbids them, which till laws be made they cannot know, nor can any law be made till they have agreed upon the person that shall make it.

It may peradventure be thought there was never such a time, nor condition of war, as this; and I believe it was never generally so over all the world; but there are many places where they live so now. For the savage people in many places of America, except the government of small families, the concord whereof depends on natural lust, have no government at all, and live at this day in that brutish manner, as I said before. Howsoever, it may be perceived what manner of life there would be, where there were no common power to fear, by the manner of life which men that have formerly lived under a peaceful government used to degenerate into in civil war.

But though there had never been any time wherein particular men were in a condition of war one against another, yet in all times kings and persons of sovereign authority, because of their independency, are in continual jealousies and in the state and posture of gladiators, having their weapons pointing and their eyes fixed on one another; that is, their forts, garrisons and guns upon the frontiers of their kingdoms, and continual spies upon their neighbours, which is a posture of war. But because they uphold thereby the industry of their subjects, there does not follow from it that misery which accompanies the liberty of particular men.

To this war of every man against every man this also is consequent: that nothing can be unjust. The notions of right and wrong, justice and injustice, have there no place. Where there is no common power, there is no law: where no law, no injustice. Force and fraud are in war the two cardinal virtues. Justice and injustice are none of the faculties neither of the body nor mind. If they were, they might be in a man that were alone in the world, as well as his senses and passions. They are qualities that relate to men in society, not in solitude. It is consequent also to the same condition that there be no propriety, no dominion, no *mine* and *thine* distinct, but only that to be every man's that he can get, and for so long as he can keep it. And thus much for the ill condition which man by mere nature is actually placed in, though with a possibility to come out of it, consisting partly in the passions, partly in his reason.

The passions that incline men to peace are fear of death, desire of such things as are necessary to commodious living, and a hope by their industry to obtain them. And reason suggests convenient articles of peace, upon which men may be drawn to agreement. These articles are they which otherwise are called the laws of nature.

THE SOCIAL CONTRACT

The *right of nature,* which writers commonly call *jus naturale,* is the liberty each man has to use his own power, as he will himself, for the preservation of his own nature, that is to say, of his own life, and consequently of doing anything which in his own judgment and reason he shall conceive to be the aptest means thereunto.

By *liberty* is understood, according to the proper signification of the word, the absence of external impediments, which impediments may oft take away part of a man's power to do what he would, but cannot hinder him from using the power left him, according as his judgment and reason shall dictate to him.

A law of nature, *lex naturalis,* is a precept or general rule, found out by reason, by which a man is forbidden to do that which is destructive of his life or takes away the means of preserving the same, and to omit that by which he thinks it may be best preserved. For though they that speak of this subject use to confound *jus* and *lex, right* and *law,* yet they ought to be distinguished, because right consists in liberty to do or to forbear, whereas law determines and binds to one of them, so that law and right differ as much as obligation and liberty, which in one and the same matter are inconsistent.

And because the condition of man, as has been declared in the precedent chapter, is a condition of war of every one against every one, in which case every one is governed by his own reason, and there is nothing he can make use of that may not be a help unto him in preserving his life against his enemies; it follows that in such a condition every man has a right to every thing, even to one another's body. And therefore, as long as this natural right of every man to every thing endures, there can be no security to any man, how strong or wise soever he be, of living out the time which nature ordinarily allows men to live. And consequently it is a precept, or general rule of reason, *that every man ought to endeavour peace as far as he has hope of obtaining it, and when he cannot obtain it, that he may seek, and use, all helps and advantages of war.* The first branch of which rule contains the first, and fundamental, law of nature: which is, *to seek peace and follow it.* The second, the sum of the right of nature: which is, *by all means we can to defend ourselves.*

From this fundamental law of nature, by which men are commanded to endeavour peace, is derived this second law: *that a man be willing, when others are so too, as far-forth as for peace and defence of himself he shall think it necessary, to lay down this right to all things, and be contented with so much liberty against other men as he would allow other men against himself.* For as long as every man holds this right of doing any thing he likes, so long are all men in the condition of war. But if other men will not lay down their right as well as he, then there is no reason for any one to divest himself of his, for that were to expose himself to prey, which no man is bound to, rather than to dispose himself to peace. This is that law of the Gospel: *whatsoever you require that others should do to you, that do ye to them.* And that law of all men: *quod tibi fieri non vis, alteri ne feceris.*

To *lay down* a man's *right* to any thing is to *divest* himself of the *liberty* of hindering another of the benefit of his own right to the same. For he that renounces or passes away his right, gives not to any other man a right which he had not before, because there is nothing to which every man had not right by nature, but only stands out of his way that he may enjoy his own original right without hindrance from him, not without hindrance from another. So that the effect which redounds to one man by another man's defect of right, is but so much diminution of impediments to the use of his own right original. Right is laid aside either by simply renouncing it or by transferring it to another. By *simply* renouncing: when he cares not to whom the benefit thereof redounds. By transferring: when he intends the benefit thereof to some certain person or persons. And when a man has in either manner abandoned or granted away his right, then he is said to be obliged, or bound, not to hinder those to whom such right is granted or abandoned from the benefit of it, and that he *ought,* and it is his duty, not to make void that voluntary act of his own, and that such hindrance is injustice and injury, as being *sine jure,* the right being before being renounced or transferred. So that *injury,* or *injustice,* in the controversies of the world is somewhat like to that which in the disputations of scholars is called *absurdity.* For as it is there called an absurdity to contradict what one maintained in the beginning, so in the world it is called injustice and injury voluntarily to undo that which from the beginning he had voluntarily done. The way by which a man either simply renounces or

transfers his right, is a declaration, or signification, by some voluntary and sufficient sign, or signs, that he does so renounce or transfer, or has so renounced or transferred the same to him that accepts it. And these signs are either words only, or actions only, or—as it happens most often—both words and actions. And the same are the bonds by which men are bound and obliged: bonds that have their strength, not from their own nature, for nothing is more easily broken than a man's word, but from fear of some evil consequence upon the rupture.

Whensoever a man transfers his right or renounces it, it is either in consideration of some right reciprocally transferred to himself, or for some other good he hopes for thereby. For it is a voluntary act: and of the voluntary acts of every man the object is some *good to himself.* And therefore there be some rights which no man can be understood by any words, or other signs, to have abandoned or transferred. As first a man cannot lay down the right of resisting them that assault him by force to take away his life, because he cannot be understood to aim thereby at any good to himself. The same may be said of wounds, and chains, and imprisonment: both because there is no benefit consequent to such patience, as there is to the patience of suffering another to be wounded or imprisoned, as also because a man cannot tell, when he sees men proceed against him by violence, whether they intend his death or not. And lastly, the motive and end for which this renouncing and transferring of right is introduced, is nothing else but the security of a man's person in his life and in the means of so preserving life as not to be weary of it. And therefore if a man by words, or other signs, seems to despoil himself of the end for which those signs were intended, he is not to be understood as if he meant it or that it was his will, but that he was ignorant of how such words and actions were to be interpreted. The mutual transferring of right is that which men call *contract.*

A covenant not to defend myself from force, by force, is always void. For, as I have showed before, no man can transfer, or lay down, his right to save himself from death, wounds, and imprisonment, the avoiding whereof is the only end of laying down any right; and therefore the promise of not resisting force in no covenant transfers any right nor is obliging. For though a man may covenant thus, *unless I do so or so, kill me,* he cannot covenant thus, *unless I do so or so, I will not resist you when you come to kill me.* For man by nature chooses the lesser evil, which is danger of death in resisting, rather than the greater, which is certain and present death in not resisting. And this is granted to be true by all men, in that they lead criminals to execution and prison with armed men, notwithstanding that such criminals have consented to the law by which they are condemned.

A covenant to accuse oneself, without assurance of pardon, is likewise invalid. For in the condition of nature, where every man is judge, there is no place for accusation, and in the civil state the accusation is followed with punishment which, being force, a man is not obliged not to resist. The same is also true of the accusation of those, by whose condemnation a man falls into misery, as of a father, wife, or benefactor. For the testimony of such an accuser, if it be not willingly given, is presumed to be corrupted by nature, and therefore not to be received: and where a man's testimony is not to be credited, he is not bound to give it. Also accusations upon torture are not to be reputed as testimonies. For torture is to be used but as means of conjecture and light in the further examination and search of truth; and what is in that case confessed, tends to the ease of him that is tortured, not to the informing of the torturers, and therefore ought not to have the credit of a sufficient testimony: for whether he deliver himself by true or false accusation, he does it by the right of preserving his own life.

THE COMMONWEALTH

The final cause, end, or design of men who naturally love liberty and dominion over others, in the introduction of that restraint upon themselves in which we see them live in commonwealths, is the foresight of their own preservation and of a more contented life thereby; that is to say, of getting themselves out from that miserable condition of war which is necessarily consequent, as has been shown, to the natural passions of men, when there is no visible power to keep them in awe, and tie them by fear of punishment to the performance of their covenants and observation of the laws of nature.

For the laws of nature, as *justice, equity, modesty, mercy,* and, in sum, *doing to others, as we would be done to,* of themselves, without the terror of some power to cause them to be observed, are contrary to our natural passions that carry us to partiality, pride, revenge, and the like. And covenants, without the sword, are but words, and of no strength to secure a man at all. Therefore notwithstanding the laws of nature (which everyone has then kept, when he has the will to keep them, when he can do it safely), if there be no power erected, or not great enough for our security, every man will, and may, lawfully rely on his own strength and art for caution against all other men. And in all places where men have lived by small families, to rob and spoil one another has been a trade, and so far from being reputed against the law of nature, that the greater spoils they gained, the greater was their honour; and men observed no other laws therein, but the laws of honour, that is, to abstain from cruelty, leaving to men their lives and instruments of husbandry.

The only way to erect such a common power, as may be able to defend them from the invasion of foreigners and the injuries of one another, and thereby to secure them in such sort as that by their own industry and by the fruits of the earth they may nourish themselves and live contentedly, is to confer all their power and strength upon one man, or upon one assembly of men, that may reduce all their wills, by plurality of voices, unto one will: which is as much as to say, to appoint one man, or assembly of men, to bear their persons, and every one to own and acknowledge himself to be author of whatsoever he that so bears their person shall act, or cause to be acted, in those things which concern the common peace and safety, and therein to submit their wills, every one to his will, and their judgments to his judgment. This is more than consent, or concord; it is a real unity of them all, in one and the same person, made by covenant of every man with every man, in such manner as if every man should say to every man, *I authorize and give up my right of governing myself, to this man, or to this assembly of men, on this condition, that thou give up thy right to him, and authorize all his actions in like manner.* This done, the multitude so united in one person is called a Commonwealth, in Latin, *civitas.* This is the generation of that great *Leviathan,* or rather, to speak more reverently, of that *mortal god* to which we owe, under the *immortal God,* our peace and defence. For by this authority, given him by every particular man in the commonwealth, he has the use of so much power and strength conferred on him that by terror thereof he is enabled to form the wills of them all, to peace at home, and mutual aid against their enemies abroad. And in him consists the essence of the commonwealth; which, to define it, is *one person, of whose acts a great multitude, by mutual covenants one with another, have made themselves every one the author, to the end he may use the strength and means of them all, as he shall think expedient, for their peace and common defence.*

And he that carries this person is called Sovereign, and said to have *sovereign power;* and every one besides, his subject.

The attaining to this sovereign power is by two ways. One, by natural force, as when a man makes his children to submit themselves and their children to his government, as being able to destroy them if they refuse, or by war subdues his enemies to his will, giving them their lives on that condition. The other is when men agree among themselves to submit to some man, or assembly of men, voluntarily, on confidence to be protected by him against all others. This latter may be called a political commonwealth, or commonwealth by *institution;* and the former, a commonwealth by *acquistion.*

RIGHTS OF THE SOVEREIGN

A *commonwealth* is said to be *instituted* when a *multitude* of men do agree and *covenant, every one with every one,* that to whatsoever *man,* or *assembly of men,* shall be given by the major part the *right to present* the person of them all, that is to say, to be their *representative,* every one—as well he that *voted for it,* as he that *voted against it,* shall *authorize* all the actions and judgments of that man, or assembly of men, in the same manner as if they were his own, to the end, to live peaceably amongst themselves, and be protected against other men.

From this institution of a commonwealth are derived all the *rights* and *faculties* of him, or them, on whom the sovereign power is conferred by the consent of the people assembled.

First, because they covenant, it is to be understood, they are not obliged by former covenant to any thing repugnant hereunto. And consequently they that have already instituted a commonwealth, being thereby bound by covenant to own the actions and judgments of one, cannot lawfully make a new covenant, among themselves, to be obedient to any other, in any thing whatsoever, without his permission. And therefore, they that are subjects to a monarch cannot without his leave cast off monarchy, and return to the confusion of a disunited multitude, nor transfer their person from him that bears it to another man, or other assembly of men: for they are bound, every man to every man, to own and be reputed author of all that he that already is their sovereign, shall do and judge fit to be done; so that any one man dissenting, all the rest should break their covenant made to that man, which is injustice, and they have also every man given the sovereignty to him that bears their person, and therefore if they depose him, they take from him that which is his own, and so again it is injustice. Besides, if he that attempts to depose his sovereign be killed, or punished by him for such attempt, he is author of his own punishment, as being by the institution author of all his sovereign shall do; and because it is injustice for a man to do any thing for which he may be punished by his own authorty, he is also, upon that title, unjust. And whereas some men have pretended for their disobedience to their sovereign a new covenant made, not with men, but with God, this also is unjust, for there is no covenant with God but by mediation of somebody that represents God's person, which none does but God's lieutenant, who has the sovereignty under God. But this pretence of covenant with God is so evident a lie, even in the pretenders' own consciences, that it is not only an act of an unjust, but also of a vile and unmanly disposition.

Secondly, because the right of bearing the person of them all is given to him they make sovereign, by covenant only of one to another, and not of him to any of them, there can happen no breach of covenant on the part of the sovereign, and consequently none of his subjects, by any pretence of forfeiture, can be freed from his subjection. That he which is made sovereign makes no covenant with his subjects beforehand, is manifest, because either he must make it with the whole multitude, as one party to the covenant, or he must make a several covenant with every man. With the whole, as one party, it is impossible, because as yet they are not one person; and if he make so many covenants as there be men, those covenants after he has the sovereignty are void, because what act soever can be pretended by any one of them for breach thereof, is the act both of himself and of all the rest, because done in the person and by the right of every one of them in particular. Besides, if any one, or more of them, pretend a breach of the covenant made by the sovereign at his institution, and others, or one other of his subjects, or himself alone, pretend there was no such breach, there is in this case no judge to decide the controversy. It returns therefore to the sword again, and every man recovers the right of protecting himself by his own strength, contrary to the design they had in the institution. It is therefore in vain to grant sovereignty by way of precedent covenant. The opinion that any monarch receives his power by covenant, that is to say, on condition, proceeds from want of understanding this easy truth: that covenants, being but words and breath, have no force to oblige, contain, constrain, or protect any man, but what it has from the public sword, that is, from the united hands of that man, or assembly of men, that has the sovereignty, and whose actions are avouched by them all and performed by the strength of them all, in him united. But when an assembly of men is made sovereign, then no man imagines any such covenant to have passed in the institution, for no man is so dull as to say for example, the people of Rome made a covenant with the Romans to hold the sovereignty on such or such conditions which, not performed, the Romans might lawfully depose the Roman people. That men see not the reason to be alike in a monarchy and in a popular government, proceeds from the ambition of some that are kinder to the government of an assembly, whereof they may hope to participate, than of monarchy, which they despair to enjoy.

Thirdly, because the major part has by consenting voices declared a sovereign, he that dissented must now consent with the rest, that is, be contented to avow all the actions he shall do, or else justly be destroyed by the rest. For if he voluntarily entered into the congregation of them that were assembled, he sufficiently declared thereby his will, and therefore tacitly covenanted, to stand to what the major part should ordain; and therefore if he refuse to stand thereto, or make protestation against any of their decrees, he does contrary to his covenant, and therefore unjustly. And whether he be of the congregation or not, and whether his consent be asked or not, he must either submit to their decrees, or be left in the condition of war he was in before; wherein he might without injustice be destroyed by any man whatsoever.

Fourthly, because every subject is by this institution author of all the actions and judgments of the sovereign instituted, it follows that whatsoever he does, it can be no injury to any of his subjects, nor ought he to be by any of them accused of injustice. For he that does anything by authority from another, does therein no injury to him by whose authority he acts, but by this institution of a commonwealth every particular man is author of all the sovereign does, and consequently he that complains of injury from his sovereign, complains of that whereof he himself is author, and therefore ought not to accuse any man but himself; no, nor himself of injury, because to do injury to one's self is impossible. It is true that they that have sovereign power may commit iniquity, but not injustice, or injury, in the proper signification.

Fifthly, and consequently to that which was said last, no man that has sovereign power can justly be put to death, or otherwise in any manner by his subjects punished. For seeing every subject is author of the actions of his sovereign, he punishes another for the actions committed by himself.

And because the end of this institution is the peace and defence of them all, and whosoever has right to the end has right to the means, it belongs of right to whatsoever man or assembly that has the sovereignty, to be judge both of the means of peace and defence and also of the hindrances and disturbances of the same, and to do whatsoever he shall think necessary to be done, both beforehand for the preserving of peace and security, by prevention of discord at home and hostility from abroad, and, when peace and security are lost, for the recovery of the same. And therefore:

Sixthly, it is annexed to the sovereignty to be judge of what opinions and doctrines are averse, and what conducing to peace, and consequently on what occasions, how far, and what men are to be trusted withal, in speaking to multitudes of people, and who shall examine the doctrines of all books before they be published. For the actions of men proceed from their opinions, and in the well-governing of opinions consists the well-governing of men's actions, in order to their peace and concord. And though in matter of doctrine nothing ought to be regarded but the truth, yet this is not repugnant to regulating the same by peace. For doctrine repugnant to peace can no more be true than peace and concord can be against the law of nature. It is true that in a commonwealth where by the negligence or unskilfulness of governors and teachers false doctrines are by time generally received, the contrary truths may be generally offensive. Yet the most sudden and rough bustling in of a new truth that can be, does never break the peace, but only sometimes awake the war. For those men that are so remissly governed that they dare take up arms to defend or introduce an opinion, are still in war, and their condition not peace, but only a cessation of arms for fear of one another; and they live, as it were, in the precincts of battle continually. It belongs therefore to him that has the sovereign power to be judge, or constitute all judges of opinions and doctrines as a thing necessary to peace, thereby to prevent discord and civil war.

Seventhly, is annexed to the sovereignty the whole power of prescribing the rules whereby every man may know what goods he may enjoy, and what actions he may do, without being molested by any of his fellow-subjects; and this is it men call *propriety.* For before constitution of sovereign power, as has already been shown, all men had right to all things, which necessarily causes war: and therefore this propriety, being necessary to peace and depending on sovereign power, is the act of that power, in order to the public peace. These rules of propriety,

or *meum* and *tuum,* and of *good, evil, lawful* and *unlawful* in the actions of subjects, are the civil laws, that is to say, the laws of each commonwealth in particular, though the name of civil law be now restrained to the ancient civil laws of the city of Rome which being the head of a great part of the world, her laws at that time were in these parts the civil law.

Eighthly, is annexed to the sovereignty the right of judicature, that is to say, of hearing and deciding all controversies which may arise concerning law, either civil or natural, or concerning fact. For without the decision of controversies, there is no protection of one subject against the injuries of another; the laws concerning *meum* and *tuum* are in vain; and to every man remains, from the natural and necessary appetite of his own conservation, the right of protecting himself by his private strength, which is the condition of war and contrary to the end for which every commonwealth is instituted.

These are the rights which make the essence of sovereignty, and which are the marks whereby a man may discern in what man, or assembly of men, the sovereign power is placed and resides. For these are incommunicable and inseparable. The power to coin money, to dispose of the estate and persons of infant heirs, to have preemption in markets, and all other statute prerogatives may be transferred by the sovereign, and yet the power to protect his subjects be retained. But if he transfer the *militia,* he retains the judicature in vain, for want of execution of the laws; or if he grant away the power of raising money, the *militia* is in vain; or if he give away the government of doctrines, men will be frightened into rebellion with the fear of spirits. And so if we consider any one of the said rights, we shall presently see that the holding of all the rest will produce no effect in the conservation of peace and justice, the end for which all commonwealths are instituted. And this division is it, whereof it is said, *a kingdom divided in itself cannot stand:* for unless this division precede, division into opposite armies can never happen. If there had not first been an opinion received of the greatest part of England that these powers were divided between the King and the Lords and the House of Commons, the people had never been divided and fallen into this civil war; first between those that disagreed in politics; and after between the dissenters about the liberty of religion; which have so instructed men in this point of sovereign right that there be few now in England that do not see that these rights are inseparable, and will be so generally acknowledged at the next return of peace, and so continue till their miseries are forgotten, and no longer, except the vulgar be better taught than they have hitherto been.

But a man may here object that the condition of subjects is very miserable, as being obnoxious to the lusts and other irregular passions of him or them that have so unlimited a power in their hands. And commonly they that live under a monarch, think it the fault of monarchy; and they that live under the government of democracy or other sovereign assembly, attribute all the inconvenience to that form of commonwealth; whereas the power in all forms, if they be perfect enough to protect them, is the same: not considering that the state of man can never be without some incommodity or other, and that the greatest that in any form of government can possibly happen to the people in general is scarce sensible in respect of the miseries and horrible calamities that accompany a civil war or that dissolute condition of masterless men, without subjection to laws and a coercive power to tie their hands from rapine and revenge: nor considering that the greatest pressure of sovereign governors proceeds not from any delight or profit they can expect in the damage or weakening of their subjects, in whose vigour consists their own strength and glory, but in the restiveness of themselves that, unwillingly contributing to their own defence, make it necessary for their governors to draw from them what they can in time of peace, that they may have means on any emergent occasion, or sudden need, to resist, or take advantage on their enemies. For all men are by nature provided of notable multiplying glasses, that is their passions and self-love, through which every little payment appears a great grievance, but are destitute of those prospective glasses, namely moral and civil science, to see afar off the miseries that hang over them, and cannot without such payments be avoided.

LIBERTY OF THE SUBJECT

But as men, for the attaining of peace and conservation of themselves thereby, have made an artificial man, which we call a commonwealth, so also have they made artificial chains, called *civil laws,* which they themselves, by mutual covenants, have fastened at one end to the lips of that man, or assembly, to whom they have given the sovereign power, and at the other end to their own cars. These bonds, in their own nature but weak, may nevertheless be made to hold by the danger, though not by the difficulty, of breaking them.

In relation to these bonds only it is that I am to speak now of the *liberty* of *subjects.* For seeing there is no commonwealth in the world, wherein there be rules enough set down for the regulating of all the actions and words of men, as being a thing impossible, it follows necessarily that in all kinds of actions by the laws praetermitted, men have the liberty of doing what their own reasons shall suggest, for the most profitable to themselves. For if we take liberty in the proper sense for corporal liberty, that is to say, freedom from chains and prison, it were very absurd for men to clamour, as they do, for the liberty they so manifestly enjoy. Again, if we take liberty for an exemption from laws, it is no less absurd for men to demand, as they do, that liberty by which all other men may be masters of their lives. And yet, as absurd as it is, this is it they demand, not knowing that the laws are of no power to protect them without a sword in the hands of a man, or men, to cause those laws to be put in execution. The liberty of a subject lies therefore only in those things which, in regulating their actions, the sovereign has praetermitted: such as is the liberty to buy, and sell, and otherwise contract with one another; to choose their own abode, their own diet, their own trade of life, and institute their children as they themselves think fit; and the like.

Nevertheless we are not to understand that by such liberty the sovereign power of life and death is either abolished or limited. For it has been already shown that nothing the sovereign representative can do to a subject, on what pretence soever, can properly be called injustice or injury, because every subject is author of every act the sovereign does, so that he never wants right to any thing, otherwise than as he is himself the subject of God, and bound thereby to observe the laws of nature. And therefore it may, and does often, happen in commonwealths that a subject may be put to death by the command of the sovereign power, and yet neither do the other wrong: as when Jephtha caused his daughter to be sacrificed, in which—and the like cases—he that so dies, had liberty to do the action for which he is nevertheless without injury put to death. And the same holds also in a sovereign prince that puts to death an innocent subject. For though the action be against the law of nature as being contrary to equity, as was the killing of Uriah by David, yet it was not an injury to Uriah, but to God. Not to Uriah, because the right to do what he pleased was given him by Uriah himself: and yet to God, because David was God's subject and prohibited all iniquity by the law of nature, which distinction David himself, when he repented the fact, evidently confirmed saying, *To thee only have I sinned.* In the same manner, the people of Athens, when they banished the most potent of their commonwealth for ten years, thought they committed no injustice; and yet they never questioned what crime he had done, but what hurt he would do: nay, they commanded the banishment of they knew not whom; and every citizen bringing his oystershell into the market place, written with the name of him he desired should be banished, without actually accusing him, sometimes banished an Aristides for his reputation of justice, and sometimes a scurrilous jester, as Hyperbolus, to make a jest of it. And yet a man cannot say the sovereign people of Athens wanted right to banish them, or an Athenian the liberty to jest, or to be just.

The liberty whereof there is so frequent and honourable mention in the histories and philosophy of the ancient Greeks and Romans, and in the writings and discourse of those that from them have received all their learning in the politics, is not the liberty of particular men, but the liberty of the commonwealth: which is the same with that which every man then should have if there were no civil laws, nor commonwealth at all. And the effects of it also be the same. For as among masterless men there is per-

petual war of every man against his neighbour; no inheritance to transmit to the son, nor to expect from the father; no propriety of goods or lands; no security; but a full and absolute liberty in every particular man: so in states and commonwealths not dependent on one another, every commonwealth, not every man, has an absolute liberty to do what it shall judge, that is to say, what that man, or assembly that represents it, shall judge most conducing to their benefit. But withal, they live in the condition of a perpetual war and upon the confines of battle, with their frontiers armed and cannons planted against their neighbours round about. The Athenians and Romans were free, that is, free commonwealths: not that any particular men had the liberty to resist their own representative, but that their representative had the liberty to resist or invade other people. There is written on the turrets of the city of Lucca in great characters at this day the word "Libertas"; yet no man can thence infer that a particular man has more liberty or immunity from the service of the commonwealth there than in Constantinople. Whether a commonwealth be monarchical, or popular, the freedom is still the same.

But it is an easy thing for men to be deceived by the specious name of liberty, and for want of judgment to distinguish, mistake that for their private inheritance and birthright which is the right of the public only. And when the same error is confirmed by the authority of men in reputation for their writings on this subject, it is no wonder if it produce sedition and change of government. In these western parts of the world, we are made to receive our opinions concerning the institution and rights of commonwealths from Aristotle, Cicero, and other men, Greeks and Romans, that, living under popular states, derived those rights, not from the principles of nature, but transcribed them into their books out of the practice of their own commonwealths which were popular; as the grammarians describe the rules of language out of the practice of the time, or the rules of poetry out of the poems of Homer and Virgil. And because the Athenians were taught, to keep them from desire of changing their government, that they were freemen, and all that lived under monarchy were slaves, therefore Aristotle puts it down in his *Politics* (*lib.* 6, *cap.* ii): "In democracy, liberty is to be supposed: for it is commonly held that no man is free in any other government." And as Aristotle, so Cicero and other writers have grounded their civil doctrine on the opinions of the Romans, who were taught to hate monarchy, at first, by them that, having deposed their sovereign, shared among them the sovereignty of Rome, and afterwards by their successors. And by reading of these Greek and Latin authors, men from their childhood have gotten a habit, under a false show of liberty, of favouring tumults and of licentious controlling the actions of their sovereigns, and again of controlling those controllers; with the effusion of so much blood, as I think I may truly say, there was never any thing so dearly bought as these western parts have bought the learning of the Greek and Latin tongues.

To come now to the particulars of the true liberty of a subject; that is to say, what are the things which, though commanded by the sovereign, be may nevertheless, without injustice, refuse to do; we are to consider what rights we pass away when we make a commonwealth, or, which is all one, what liberty we deny ourselves by owning all the actions, without exception, of the man, or assembly, we make our sovereign. For in the act of our *submission* consists both our *obligation* and our *liberty,* which must therefore be inferred by arguments taken from thence, there being no obligation on any man which arises not from some act of his own, for all men equally are by nature free. And because such arguments must either be drawn from the express words, *I authorize all his actions,* or from the intention of him that submits himself to his power, which intention is to be understood by the end for which he so submits, the obligation and liberty of the subject is to be derived either from those words or others equivalent, or else from the end of the institution of sovereignty, namely, the peace of the subjects within themselves, and their defence against a common enemy.

First therefore, seeing sovereignty by institution is by covenant of every one to every one, and sovereignty by acquisition, by covenants of the vanquished to the victor, or the child to the parent, it is manifest that every subject has liberty in all those things,

the right whereof cannot by covenant be transferred. I have shown before that covenants not to defend a man's own body are void. Therefore, if the sovereign command a man, though justly condemned, to kill, wound, or maim himself, or not to resist those that assault him, or to abstain from the use of food, air, medicine, or any other thing without which he cannot live, yet has that man the liberty to disobey.

If a man be interrogated by the sovereign, or his authority, concerning a crime done by himself, he is not bound, without assurance of pardon, to confess it, because no man can be obliged by covenant to accuse himself.

Again, the consent of a subject to sovereign power is contained in these words, *I authorize, or take upon me, all his actions,* in which there is no restriction at all of his former natural liberty: for by allowing him to *kill* me, I am not bound to kill myself when he commands me. It is one thing to say, *kill me, or my fellow, if you please;* another thing to say, *I will kill myself, or my fellow.* It follows therefore that no man is bound by the words themselves either to kill himself, or any other man, and consequently, that the obligation a man may sometimes have, upon the command of the sovereign to execute any dangerous or dishonourable office, depends not on the words of our submission, but on the intention, which is to be understood by the end thereof. When therefore our refusal to obey frustrates the end for which the sovereignty was ordained, then there is no liberty to refuse: otherwise there is.

The obligation of subjects to the sovereign is understood to last as long, and no longer, than the power lasts by which he is able to protect them. For the right men have by nature to protect themselves when none else can protect them, can by no covenant be relinquished. The sovereignty is the soul of the commonwealth which, once departed from the body, the members do no more receive their motion from it. The end of obedience is protection which, wheresoever a man sees it either in his own or in another's sword, nature applies his obedience to it, and his endeavour to maintain it. And though sovereignty, in the intention of them that make it, be immortal, yet is it in its own nature, not only subject to violent death by foreign war, but also through the ignorance and passions of men, it has in it—from the very institution—many seeds of a natural mortality by intestine discord.

CIVIL LAW AND NATURAL LAW

By civil laws I understand the laws that men are therefore bound to observe because they are members, not of this or that commonwealth in particular, but of a commonwealth. For the knowledge of particular laws belongs to them that profess the study of the laws of their several countries; but the knowledge of civil law in general, to any man. The ancient law of Rome was called their *civil law,* from the word *civitas,* which signifies a commonwealth: and those countries which, having been under the Roman empire and governed by that law, retain still such part thereof as they think fit, call that part the civil law, to distinguish it from the rest of their own civil laws. But that is not it I intend to speak of here; my design being not to show what is law here and there, but what is law, as Plato. Aristotle, Cicero and divers others have done, without taking upon them the profession of the study of the law.

And first it is manifest that law in general is not counsel, but command; nor a command of any man to any man, but only of him whose command is addressed to one formerly obliged to obey him. And as for civil law, it adds only the name of the, person commanding, which is *persona civitatis,* the person of the commonwealth.

Which considered, I define civil law in this manner. Civil law *is to every subject those rules which the commonwealth has commanded him, by word, writing, or other sufficient sign of the will, to make use of, for the distinction of right and wrong; that is to say, of what is contrary, and what is not contrary to the rule.*

In which definition, there is nothing that is not at first sight evident. For every man sees that some laws are addressed to all the subjects in general, some to particular provinces; some to particular vocations; and some to particular men; and are therefore laws to every of those to whom the command is directed, and to none else. As also, that laws are the rules of just and unjust; nothing being reputed unjust that is not contrary to some law. Likewise, that none can make laws but the commonwealth, because our subjection is to the commonwealth only, and that commands are to be signified by sufficient signs, because a man knows not otherwise bow to obey them. And therefore, whatsoever can from this definition by necessary consequence be deduced, ought to be acknowledged for truth. Now I deduce from it this that follows.

The legislator in all commonwealths is only the sovereign, be he one man, as in a monarchy, or one assembly of men, as in a democracy or aristocracy. For the legislator is he that makes the law. And the commonwealth only prescribes and commands the observation of those rules which we call law: therefore the commonwealth is the legislator. But the commonwealth is no person, nor has capacity to do any thing, but by the representative, that is, the sovereign; and therefore the sovereign is the sole legislator. For the same reason, none can abrogate a law made, but the sovereign; because a law is not abrogated, but by another law that forbids it to be put in execution.

The sovereign of a commonwealth, be it an assembly, or one man, is not subject to the civil laws. For having power to make and repeal laws, he may, when he pleases, free himself from that subjection by repealing those laws that trouble him, and making of new; and consequently he was free before. For he is free that can be free when he will: nor is it possible for any person to be bound to himself, because he that can bind can release; and therefore he that is bound to himself only, is not bound.

When long use obtains the authority of a law, it is not the length of time that makes the authority, but the will of the sovereign signified by his silence, for silence is sometimes an argument of consent; and it is no longer law than the sovereign shall be silent therein. And therefore if the sovereign shall have a question of right grounded, not upon his present will, but upon the laws formerly made, the length of time shall bring no prejudice to his right, but the question shall be judged by equity. For many unjust actions and unjust sentences go uncontrolled a longer time than any man can remember. And our lawyers account no customs law, but such as are reasonable, and that evil customs are to be abolished. But the judgment of what is reasonable, and of what is to be abolished, belongs to him that makes the law, which is the sovereign assembly, or monarch.

The law of nature and the civil law contain each other, and are of equal extent. For the laws of nature, which consist in equity, justice, gratitude and other moral virtues on these depending in the condition of mere nature, as I have said before, are not properly laws, but qualities that dispose men to peace and obedience. When a commonwealth is once settled, then are they actually laws, and not before, as being then the commands of the commonwealth, and therefore also civil laws: for it is the sovereign power that obliges men to obey them. For in the differences of private men to declare what is equity, what is justice, and what is moral virtue, and to make them binding, there is need of the ordinances of sovereign power, and punishments to be ordained for such as shall break them, which ordinances are therefore part of the civil law. The law of nature therefore is a part of the civil law in all commonwealths of the world. Reciprocally also, the civil law is a part of the dictates of nature. For justice, that is to say, performance of covenant, and giving to every man his own, is a dictate of the law of nature. But every subject in a commonwealth has covenanted to obey the civil law, either one with another, as when they assemble to make a common representative, or with the representative itself one by one, when subdued by the sword they promise obedience that they may receive life; and therefore obedience to the civil law is part also of the law of nature. Civil and natural law are not different kinds, but different parts of law, whereof one part, being written, is called civil, the other, unwritten, natural. But the right of nature, that is, the natural liberty of man, may by the civil law be abridged and restrained: nay, the end of making laws is no other but such restraint, without the which there cannot possibly be any peace. And law was brought into the world for nothing else but to limit the natural liberty of particular men in such manner, as they might not hurt, but assist one another and join together against a common enemy.

That law can never be against reason, our lawyers are agreed; and that not the letter, that is, every construction of it, but that which is according to the intention of the legislator, is the law. And it is true: but the doubt is of whose reason it is that shall be received for law. It is not meant of any private reason; for then there would be as much contradiction in the laws, as there is in the Schools, nor yet, as Sir Edward Coke makes it, *an artificial perfection of reason, gotten by long study, observation, and experience,* as his was. For it is possible long study may increase and confirm erroneous sentences: and when men build on false grounds, the more they build, the greater is the ruin: and of those that study and observe with equal time and diligence, the reasons and resolutions are, and must remain, discordant: and therefore it is not that *juris prudentia,* or wisdom of subordinate judges, but the reason of this our artificial man the commonwealth, and his command, that makes law: and the commonwealth being in their representative but one person, there cannot easily arise any contradiction in the laws; and when there does, the same reason is able, by interpretation, or alteration, to take it away. In all courts of justice, the sovereign, which is the person of the commonwealth, is he that judges: the subordinate judge ought to have regard to the reason which moved his sovereign to make such law, that his sentence may be according thereunto; which then is his sovereign's sentence; otherwise it is his own, and an unjust one.

The interpretation of the laws of nature, in a commonwealth, depends not on the books of moral philosophy. The authority of writers, without the authority of the commonwealth, makes not their opinions law, be they never so true. That which I have written in this treatise concerning the moral virtues, and of their necessity for the procuring and maintaining peace, though it be evident truth, is not therefore presently law; but because in all commonwealths in the world it is part of the civil law. For though it be naturally reasonable, yet it is by the sovereign power that it is law: otherwise it were a great error to call the laws of nature unwritten laws; whereof we see so many volumes published, and in them so many contradictions of one another, and of themselves.

The interpretation of the law of nature is the sentence of the judge constituted by the sovereign authority, to hear and determine such controversies, as depend thereon, and consists in the application of the law to the present case. For in the act of judicature, the judge does no more but consider whether the demand of the party be consonant to natural reason and equity, and the sentence he gives is therefore the interpretation of the law of nature; which interpretation is authentic, not because it is his private sentence, but because he gives it by authority of the sovereign, whereby it becomes the sovereign's sentence; which is law for that time, to the parties pleading.

SUBVERSIVE POLITICAL DOCTRINES

Though nothing can be immortal which mortals make, yet, if men had the use of reason they pretend to, their commonwealths might be secured at least from perishing by internal diseases. For by the nature of their institution they are designed to live as long as mankind, or as the laws of nature, or as justice itself which gives them life. Therefore when they come to be dissolved, not by external violence, but intestine disorder, the fault is not in men as they are the *matter,* but as they are the *makers* and orderers of them. For men, as they become at least weary of irregular jostling and hewing one another, and desire with all their hearts to conform themselves into one firm and lasting edifice, so for want both of the art of making fit laws to square their actions by, and also of humility and patience to suffer the rude and cumbersome points of their present greatness to be taken off, they cannot without the help of a very able architect be compiled into any other than a crazy building, such as hardly lasting out their own time, must assuredly fall upon the heads of their posterity.

Among the *infirmities* therefore of a commonwealth, I will reckon in the first place those that arise from an imperfect institution, and resemble the diseases of a natural body which proceed from a defectuous procreation.

Of which this is one, *that a man, to obtain a kingdom, is sometimes content with less power than to the peace and defence of the commonwealth is necessarily required.* From whence it comes to pass that when the exercise of the power laid by is for the public safety to be resumed, it has the resemblance of an unjust act, which disposes great numbers of men, when occasion is presented, to rebel, in the same manner as the bodies of children, gotten by diseased parents, are subject either to untimely death or, to purge the ill quality derived from their vicious conception, by breaking out into biles and scabs. And when kings deny themselves some such necessary power, it is not always, though sometimes, out of ignorance of what is necessary to the office they undertake, but many times out of a hope to recover the same again at their pleasure. Wherein they reason not well, because such as will hold them to their promises shall be maintained against them by foreign commonwealths, who in order to the good of their own subjects let slip few occasions to *weaken* the estate of their neighbours. So was Thomas Becket, archbishop of Canterbury, supported against Henry the Second by the Pope, the subjection of ecclesiastics to the commonwealth having been dispensed with by William the Conqueror at his reception, when he took an oath not to infringe the liberty of the church. And so were the barons, whose power was by William Rufus, to have their help in transferring the succession from his elder brother to himself, increased to a degree inconsistent with the sovereign power, maintained in their rebellion against King John, by the French.

Nor does this happen in monarchy only. For whereas the style of the ancient Roman commonwealth was *The Senate and People of Rome,* neither senate nor people pretended to the whole power, which first caused the seditions of Tiberius Gracchus, Caius Gracchus, Lucius Saturninus, and others, and afterwards the wars between the senate and the people, under Marius and Sulla; and again under Pompey and Caesar, to the extinction of their democracy, and the setting up of monarchy.

The people of Athens bound themselves but from one only action, which was that no man on pain of death should propound the renewing of the war for the island of Salamis; and yet thereby, if Solon had not caused to be given out he was mad, and afterwards in gesture and habit of a madman, and in verse, propounded it to the people that flocked about him, they had had an enemy perpetually in readiness, even at the gates of their city; such damage, or shifts, are all commonwealths forced to that have their power never so little limited.

In the second place, *diseases* of a commonwealth that proceed from the poison of seditious doctrines, whereof one is *that every private man is judge of good and evil actions.* This is true in the condition of mere nature, where there are no civil laws, and also under civil government in such cases as are not determined by the law. But otherwise, it is manifest that the measure of good and evil actions is the civil law, and the judge the legislator who is always representative of the commonwealth. From this false doctrine, men are disposed to debate with themselves and dispute the commands of the commonwealth, and afterwards to obey or disobey them, as in their private judgments they shall think fit; whereby the commonwealth is distracted and *weakened.*

Another doctrine repugnant to civil society is that *whatsoever a man does against his conscience is sin,* and it depends on the presumption of making himself judge of good and evil. For a man's conscience and his judgment is the same thing, and as the judgment, so also the conscience may be erroneous. Therefore, though he that is subject to no civil law sins in all he does against his conscience, because he has no other rule to follow but his own reason, yet it is not so with him that lives in a commonwealth, because the law is the public conscience, by which he has already undertaken to be guided. Otherwise in such diversity as there is of private consciences, which are but private opinions, the commonwealth must needs be distracted, and no man dare to obey the sovereign power further than it shall seem good in his own eyes.

It has been also commonly taught *that faith and sanctity are not to be attained by study and reason, but by supernatural inspiration or infusion.* Which granted, I see not why any man should render a reason of his faith; or why every Christian should not be also a prophet; or why any man should take the law of his country, rather than his own inspiration, for the rule of his action. And thus we fall again in the fault of taking upon us to judge of good and evil, or to make

judges of it such private men as pretend to be supernaturally inspired, to the dissolution of all civil government. Faith comes by hearing, and hearing by those accidents which guide us into the presence of them that speak to us; which accidents are all contrived by God Almighty, and yet are not supernatural, but only, for the great number of them that concur to every effect, unobservable. Faith and sanctity are indeed not very frequent; but yet they are not miracles, but brought to pass by education, discipline, correction, and other natural ways by which God works them in his elect, at such times as he thinks fit. And these three opinions, pernicious to peace and government, have in this part of the world proceeded chiefly from the tongues and pens of unlearned divines who, joining the words of Holy Scripture together otherwise than is agreeable to reason, do what they can to make men think that sanctity and natural reason cannot stand together.

A fourth opinion, repugnant to the nature of commonwealth, is this, *that he that has the sovereign power is subject to the civil laws.* It is true that sovereigns are all subject to the laws of nature, because such laws be divine and cannot by any man or commonwealth be abrogated. But to those laws which the sovereign himself, that is, which the commonwealth makes, he is not subject. For to be subject to laws is to be subject to the commonwealth, that is, to the sovereign representative, that is to himself; which is not subjection, but freedom from the laws. Which error, because it sets the laws above the sovereign, sets also a judge above him, and a power to punish him; which is to make a new sovereign; and again for the same reason a third, to punish the second; and so continually without end, to the confusion and dissolution of the commonwealth.

A fifth doctrine, that tends to the dissolution of the commonwealth, is *that every private man has an absolute propriety in his goods, such as excludes the right of the sovereign.* Every man has indeed a propriety that excludes the right of every other subject; and he has it only from the sovereign power, without the protection whereof every other man should have equal right to the same. But if the right of the sovereign also be excluded, he cannot perform the office they have put him into, which is to defend them both from foreign enemies and from the injuries of one another; and consequently there is no longer a commonwealth.

And if the propriety of subjects exclude not the right of the sovereign representative to their goods, much less to their offices of judicature, or execution, in which they represent the sovereign himself.

There is a sixth doctrine, plainly and directly against the essence of a commonwealth; and it is this, *that the sovereign power may be divided.* For what is it to divide the power of a commonwealth, but to dissolve it; for powers divided mutually destroy each other. And for these doctrines men are chiefly beholding to some of those that, making profession of the laws, endeavour to make them depend upon their own learning and not upon the legislative power.

CHAPTER EIGHTEEN

LOCKE

Revolutionary Puritanism ruled England until 1660 but was unable to establish itself permanently. Cromwell died in 1658, and in less than two years Charles II was restored to the throne. After civil war and dictatorship the return to monarchy seemed the best prospect of peace. In bringing Charles II back to a throne, no clear delimitation between royal and parliamentary authority was made. It was hoped that a practical equilibrium could be obtained without formal constitutional charters, if the King would avoid the arbitrary government of his executed father, and if Parliament would be satisfied with less than absolute supremacy, such as it had exercised in the years 1642–1649, the period of civil war. Yet Charles II lacked the wisdom, or even desire, to contribute his share to the growth of a balanced constitution. His reign lasted from 1660–1685, during which years he increasingly antagonized his subjects on the two key issues of religion and Parliament. A crypto-Catholic, he sought to strengthen the influence of Catholics and fatally returned to the ways of his father by ruling without summoning Parliament for several years.

Charles II was succeeded by his brother, James II, who was an open Catholic and more authoritarian than Charles. James II sought to convert England to Catholicism by prerogative and force, and he methodically subverted the authority of Parliament either by exempting individuals from the law or by suspending laws altogether. He appointed and dismissed judges arbitrarily and built up a standing army to buttress his autocracy. By identifying despotism with Roman Catholicism he outraged not only his subjects' religion and liberty but their very patriotism.

France and Spain were England's chief opponents in the struggle for hegemony, and James II sealed his position as a traitor to the nation when it became known that he, like Charles II and many politicians, was secretly receiving money from Louis XIV of France. In 1688, Whig and Tory leaders invited Prince William of Orange to come to England and deliver it from Romanism and absolutism. William arrived in England in November, and there was great jubilation and almost no resistance. James II saw himself abandoned by Parliament, church, and army, and on December 22, 1688, stealthily sailed for France, never to return. Royal absolutism in England was dead.

Prince William summoned a "Convention Parliament" that met in January of 1689. The first business was to fill the vacant throne. James II was declared to have subverted the Constitution of the Kingdom by breaking the "original contract" between King and people and to have violated the fundamental laws "by the advice of Jesuits and other wicked persons," and to have, by his flight and misdeeds, abdicated the throne. Parliament then invited Prince William and his wife Mary to become King and Queen of England. But the Crown was not given to them without condition. The "Declaration of Right" (passed later in the year as the Bill of Rights) was the instrument that conferred the Crown on William and Mary.

The Bill of Rights begins with a recital of the iniquities and illegalities of James II. The first of the twelve charges accuses him of having assumed and exercised the power to dispense with and suspend laws, and to execute laws, without consent of Parliament. This was the crux of the "Glorious" or "Bloodless" Revolution of 1688: who is to be supreme, king or Parliament? The clear and unmistakable words of the Bill of Rights settled the question once and for all. By denying the king the right to levy money without grant of Parliament, and by prohibiting the raising or keeping of a standing army in time of peace without the consent of Parliament, the Bill of Rights deprived the king of the fiscal and military means of governing without the active consent of Parliament.

Another important condition was attached by Parliament to the British monarchy: no person who professes the Roman Catholic religion or is married to a Roman Catholic may inherit or hold the throne. The work of the Glorious Revolution went further. Judges were made irremovable during good behavior; they could no longer be removed by the arbitrary will of the king, as James II had removed judges who interpreted the law contrary to his wishes. To make the change of the times even more marked, judges were henceforth to be removable only on the address of both Houses of Parliament. The abolition of censorship made for free expression of thought in religious and political matters, and toleration was legally granted to Protestant dissenters; thus the road was opened for the general principle of separating religious faith from political loyalty.

The Glorious Revolution established the first constitutional monarchy in a major European country, and its general character remained unchanged until the reform of parliamentary representation in 1832. The bloodless revolution of 1832, transferring political power from the gentry to the middle class, would have been impossible without the Bloodless Revolution of 1688. At that time the liberal foundations of British government were judiciously laid, and the British system of today is the direct descendant of the Revolution of 1688. The peaceful revolution of 1945, by which the British working class became one of the principal political elements in the state through the election of a Labour Party majority in Parliament, is the twentieth-century version of the Reform Act of 1832, and both go back to 1688–1689. *Revolution by consent* sounds like a contradiction in itself, yet the examples of 1688, 1832, and 1945 prove that it is possible to effect fundamental political and social change without bloodshed.

The spirit of this rational liberalism is best reflected in the work of John Locke (1632–1704), specifically, in his *Two Treatises of Government* (1690). Locke was born of a middle-class Puritan family; his father had fought in the civil war on the side of the Parliamentary party. He went to Oxford in 1652, and stayed on after graduation as a senior student and tutor. His connection with the university lasted until 1684, when he was deprived of his appointment for political reasons. His interests were at first concentrated on philosophy, then on science, and he became a fellow of the Royal Society, England's first scientific society, shortly after its incorporation. Locke also studied and, on many occasions, practiced medicine. In 1667, he met Thomas Sydenham, the leading English medical figure in both clinical work and research. The two men became life-long close friends, and Locke worked with Sydenham both in his clinical practice and in his research. Sydenham believed that medical experience was the only "true teacher" and there is no doubt that Sydenham's medical views, then strongly rejected by the more conservative "establishment" of the medical profession, influenced and reinforced Locke's general sympathies toward experience as the source of knowledge.

Locke's knowledge of medicine led to a chance meeting with Lord Ashley in 1666. Lord Ashley was the leader of the Whig party and one of the central figures in public life. Locke, who saved the statesman's life by a skillful operation, became attached to his career and household for the next fifteen years. He assisted him in political and commercial affairs, and helped him draw up the *Fundamental Constitutions of Carolina* (1669), of which colony Lord Ashley was one of the founders and chief owners. The Carolina constitution guaranteed religious toleration but accepted Negro slavery as a form of rightful property. In 1672 Lord Ashley was raised to the peerage as Earl of Shaftesbury, and shortly thereafter he was appointed Lord High Chancellor of England. Locke followed Shaftesbury into the government and retained his position until 1675, when Shaftesbury fell in disgrace.

Locke then went to France, where he spent four years, mostly in Montpellier and Paris. On his return to England in 1679 he found political unrest growing. Shaftesbury became the principal leader of the opposition against the court, and he was finally forced to flee to Holland, where he died in 1683. Later in the same year Locke himself, fearful for his safety in England, fled to Holland, where he stayed until early in 1689. He left Holland on the same boat that carried Princess Mary of Orange to England.

Locke's exile in Holland was not free from harassment and uncertainty; yet he always looked back on it with nostalgia. He was captivated by the spirit of freedom and manliness he saw in Holland, and he envied the country that had become the center of political and religious refugees from all Europe, including the British Isles. Locke's liberalism was formed in its fundamentals before he set foot on Dutch soil, but his experience there showed him that liberalism in religion and politics could work, and it reinforced his determination to help rid England of the illiberal government of Charles II, and—later—the despotic obscurantism of James II. The first of Locke's four *Letters Concerning Toleration* was composed and first published in Holland, and an abstract of Locke's chief philosophical work, the *Essay Concerning Human Understanding*, the foundation of modern empiricism, was also first published there.

On his arrival in England the new government offered Locke an ambassadorship in Vienna or Berlin, but, as he preferred to remain in England, he accepted instead an appointment as Commissioner of Appeals, which enabled him to stay away from London much of the time, his health having begun to fail him. In 1696 he was made Commissioner of Trade and Plantations, the forerunner of the later Board of Trade and Colonial Office. Whereas Hobbes had little or no practical acquaintance with government, Locke had wide administrative and political experience both before and after his exile. Hobbes had spent his years of exile in absolutist France, Locke in liberal Holland.

Locke's *Two Treatises of Government* is often dismissed as a mere apology for the victorious Whigs in the Revolution of 1688–1689. Such dismissal is clearly not borne out by the facts relating to the history and publication of the book. The *Two Treatises* was begun in 1679 and substantially finished in 1681. Its purpose was to provide the intellectual armory for the planned revolutionary overthrow of Charles II by the Earl of Shaftesbury and his Whig friends. After Locke returned to England in February, 1689, he revised the *Two Treatises* to take into account the fact that the revolution had already occurred. Although the first edition of the *Two Treatises* carries the year 1690 as the date of publication, the book was actually on sale in October of 1689, since publishers then—as now—had the habit of putting a later date on publications than the actual date on which they appeared. In the Preface to the *Two Treatises* Locke implies that the text presented to the public is only part of a larger work, written at an earlier date.

Yet Locke seems to lend some weight to the idea of looking at the *Two Treatises* as an apology for the victorious Whigs in the Revolution of 1688–1689, for in the Preface to the *Two Treatises,* obviously written after his return in 1689, he expresses the hope that the pages of the *Two Treatises* as published "are sufficient to establish the throne of our great restorer, our present King William," and "to justify to the world the people of England whose love of their just and natural rights, with their resolution to preserve them, saved the nation when it was on the very brink of slavery and ruin." Locke nowhere says or implies that he wrote the *Two Treatises* for the purpose of justifying the Revolution of 1688–1689. He was confident that the book which he composed in 1679–1681 and in which he, in principle, both attacked despotism and justified its overthrow by revolution would also hold good in 1689, although the specific circumstances of English politics had changed in the meantime. The specific issue was no longer a revolution to be carried out by the Liberal political leaders, but a Liberal revolution which had actually taken place.

Every piece of significant political writing is a fragment of the autobiography of its age; yet it becomes great only if, in addition to its vital connection with the period from which it springs, it possesses a universal appeal because of its general human interest. A political treatise that is wholly submerged in the issues of its own age can never rise above the level of a partisan pamphlet. On the other hand, a political work that is isolated from its own age is bound to be and and abstract. The *Two Treatises* could not have been written by someone without the practical experience and interest of Locke; yet without Locke's philosophical rationalism, luminous common sense, and liberality of spirit it could never have become the Bible of modern liberalism.

Like Hobbes, Locke starts out with the concept of the *state of nature.* Yet from this starting point on, Locke travels a different road and arrives at a different destination. Unlike Hobbes, whose state of nature is little different from the jungle in which force and fraud reign supreme, Locke takes an optimistic view. In Hobbes' state of nature there is no natural law, only natural right, each individual doing as he sees fit for his preservation and enhancement of power. By contrast, Locke's conception of man in the state of nature is not noticeably different from man in organized society. Locke cannot conceive of human beings living together without some sort of law and order, and in the state of nature it is the *law of nature* that rules: "The state of nature has a law of nature to govern it, which obliges every one; and reason, which is that law, teaches all mankind who will but consult it, that, being all equal and independent, no one ought to harm another in his life, health, liberty, or possessions."

The law of nature, through the instrument of reason, defines what is right and wrong; if a violation of the law occurs, the execution of the penalty is, in the state of nature, "put into every man's hands, whereby every one has a right to punish the transgressors of that law to such a degree, as may hinder its violation." Locke penetratingly notes that without some agency of enforcement there can be no law, and that in the law of nature the injured party is authorized to be judge in his own case and to execute the judgment against the culprit.

In actuality, the legal situation that Locke describes as the state of nature still exists (as it did in Locke's time) in two areas. First, within the so-called primitive community there is a body of law that is generally known to its members. In the event of transgression, the injured party (or his family) pursues the malefactor, punishes him, or takes reparation from him. The kin of the murdered victim, who slays the assassin, does not commit murder in the eyes of the primitive community, but reestablishes thereby the sanctity of the law: he is the authorized agent of the law to defend it against the assassin, because as yet there are no third-party judges and specialized law-enforcement agencies. Second, the state of nature still exists between so-called advanced nations. To be sure, there is a body of law, international law, that is binding and recognized as such;

yet, when a violation of international law occurs and there is no international judicature and enforcement agency, the injured state is authorized to punish the transgressor. Such penalties or reprisals are not considered contrary to international law but are viewed as acts in behalf of its defense and reestablishment.

The law of the state of nature is thus deficient in three important points. First, it is not sufficiently clear. If all men were guided by pure reason, they would all see the same law. But men are biased by their interests and mistake their interest for general rules of law. Second, there is no third-party judge who has no personal stake in disputes. Men who judge their own conflicts are apt to be carried away by passion and revenge. Third, in the state of nature the injured party is not always strong enough to execute the just sentence of the law: "Thus mankind, notwithstanding all the privileges of the state of nature, but being in an ill condition while they remain in it, are quickly driven into society." The purpose of the social contract is to establish organized law and order so that the uncertainties of the state of nature will be replaced by the predictability of known laws and impartial institutions.

Within a group, men quickly form society, because the advantages of the state of nature seem to them to be outweighed by its disadvantages. After society is set up by contract, government is established, not by a contract, but by a *fiduciary trust*. The legislature is "the supreme power" to which all other powers, particularly the executive, "must be subordinate." Yet the legislature is only relatively supreme among organs of government. Above the legislature there is still something higher: the people. Locke conceives of the institution of the legislature as a "fiduciary power." Ordinarily there are three parties to a trust: the trustor, who creates the trust; the trustee, who is charged with the administration of the trust; and the beneficiary, in whose interest the trust is created. According to Locke's view of government, there are only two parties to the trust: the people, who are both trustor and beneficiary, and the legislature, who is trustee.

The principal characteristic of a trust is the fact that the trustee assumes primarily obligations rather than rights. The purpose of the trust is determined by the interest of the beneficiary and not by the will of the trustee. The trustee is little more than a servant of both trustor and beneficiary, and he may be recalled by the trustor in the event of neglect of duty. Because the legislature is no more than a trustee, "there remains still in the people a supreme power to remove or alter the legislative when they find the legislative act contrary to the trust reposed in them; for all power given with trust for the attaining an end, being limited by that end, whenever that end is manifestly neglected or opposed, the trust must necessarily be forfeited, and the power devolve to the hands of those that gave it, who may place it anew where they shall think best for their safety and security."

Locke thus goes further than the makers of the Glorious Revolution who accused James II of having violated the "original contract between King and people." The contractual conception of kingship was a tremendous attack on the theory of kingship by divine right, according to which the king—and the king only—received his right to govern from God. In the doctrine of contract, people and king were put on the same plane as equals. Locke completes this progression by his conception of government as trust: only the people as trustor (and beneficiary) have rights; the government as trustee has only duties, which are defined by the interests of the trustor and beneficiary, and not by those of the trustee. In the theory of divine right, only the ruler has rights; in the theory of contract, both people and government have rights; in Locke's conception of *government as trust, only the people have rights.*

When Hobbes described the establishment of society and government, he carefully confined the act of covenant to the subjects; they set up the sovereign, transferring to him all power. There was no contract between subjects and sovereign, only between subjects and subjects, because Hobbes was anxious to avoid a conception of government that had duties, under a contract, toward the governed. Similarly, Locke confines the act of covenant to the setting up of society but not of government; yet his aim is exactly the opposite of Hobbes'. Locke's government is not a party to any contract with the people, because he does not wish to give the state any rights against the people. Locke's state never becomes the Hobbesian sovereign but always remains an instrument of the purposes that society sets for it. As a strong believer in natural law, Locke assigned to government the task of *finding the law* rather than of making it in the Hobbesian manner. *Law precedes the state* in Locke, but follows it in Hobbes.

Among the rights which precede government Locke stresses that of *property*. The principal purpose of government, the reason why men give up the state of nature for civil society, is "for the mutual preservation of their lives, liberties, and estates, which I call by the general name, property." This broad Lockean concept of property exceeds man's purely economic needs and interests and encompasses almost the whole orbit of his "life, liberty, and pursuit of happiness." When Locke speaks of property, he thinks of a wider range of action and opportunity that is implied in ordinary language. By linking property with life and liberty, Locke undoubtedly showed how important it seemed to him. Yet by the same token, the link of property with life and liberty also shows that Locke thought of property as liberating its owner rather than as enslaving others. To Locke, property meant, not the exercise of power over others, but the protection against power of others—particularly the power of government or of custom or privilege.

Locke's theory of property starts with the inquiry of how private property can be justified at all. Because every man has a property in his own person, the "labor of his body and the work of his hands we may say are properly his." *Labor creates property;* the human effort that is "mixed" with natural resources is the determining criterion which alone justifies private property. Thus Locke avoids justifying property on the ground that "the law" protects it, and instead goes back to the law behind the law, the law of nature, according to which man's property in his own body also extends to its labor.

But labor does more than create property. It also *determines the value of property.* "It is labor indeed," Locke says, "that puts the difference of value on everything." In fact, he stresses the proportion of labor in value highly enough to say that "of the products of the earth useful to the life of man nine-tenths are the effects of labor."

The Lockean theory of property was later used in defense of capitalism; but in the hands of pre-Marxian socialists it became a powerful weapon of attacking capitalism. When Locke defended property on the ground of individual effort and initiative, he protected the productive capacities of a new system of commercial and industrial capitalism against the restrictive traditions of a repressive state. By making labor the title to property and the source of value, Locke translated the rise of a new class to power into terms of a new political economy. Although himself a mercantilist, Locke's economic philosophy helped to liberate the ingenious and industrious entrepreneur from paralyzing force and custom. The socialists used—a century and a half after Locke—his labor theory of property to demand communal control or ownership of the basic means of production; they did not thereby prove that they were more progressive than Locke, but that economic facts had changed since 1690, resulting in the concentration of property and control in industry and finance.

Locke did not work out a consistently clear theory as to *how much property* a person may fairly claim for himself. In general, he acknowledges that the right to property is limited: "As much as anyone can make use of to any advantage of life before it spoils, so much he may by his labor fix a property in; whatever is beyond this, is more than his share, and belongs to others. Nothing was made by God for man to spoil or destroy." This relative equality of property, based on man's limited capacity to consume, would have lasted forever, "had not the invention of money, and by tacit agreement of men to put a value on it, introduced (by consent) larger possessions and a right to them."

The criterion which Locke here applies is that of waste. Before money was invented, man had no moral right to hoard the products of the earth and allow them to rot and spoil. His ability to use perishable goods determined the amount of property he could rightfully own. In a later phase, man would exchange perishable fruit (like plums) for durable ones (like nuts). By disposing of the plums he had done his duty toward society, for he had prevented them from wasting in his possession. From durable nuts to even more durable gold, or "a sparkling pebble or diamond," was only a small and logical step. And if he kept on hoarding these durable goods (like gold and diamonds and money) "all his life, he invaded not the right of others."

Thus Locke arrives at defining money "as some lasting thing that men might keep without spoiling, and that, by mutual consent, men would take in exchange for the truly useful but perishable supports of life." In his doctrine of property Locke makes no serious attempt to reconcile the teaching of natural law, which postulates a reasonable equality of property, with the inequality of property that stems, by consent among men, from the use of money.

Property precedes government and is the "great and chief end" for which men unite into political society. It follows that the state "cannot take from any man any part of his property without his own consent." Even if a commonwealth is based on freely elected representative institutions, it cannot "dispose of the estates of the subjects arbitrarily." The Fourteenth Amendment to the Constitution of the United States embodies this Lockean idea, that no State shall "deprive any person of life, liberty, or property, without due process of law."

Locke felt—understandably enough in the light of Stuart despotism—a profound distrust of executive power; he had more confidence in the legislature, as representing the will of the people or at least the majority of the electorate. The executive power "is visibly subordinate and accountable" to the legislature, "and may be at pleasure changed and displaced." The legislature is supreme, but not absolutely; it is supreme only in relation to other organs of government, and the limitations of the legislature are the end of government, that is, the protection of life, liberty and property of men.

Specifically, Locke lists four major limitations on the powers of the legislature: first, the law must apply equally to all, rich and poor, favorite at court and countryman at plough; second, the law must not be arbitrary and oppressive, but must be designed for the good of the people; third, the legislature must not raise taxes without the consent of the people or their representatives; fourth, the legislature must not transfer its lawmaking power to anybody else. In this fourth limitation Locke expresses his opposition to government by administrative decree instead of by legislative assembly. Executive power always harbors the peril of uncertainty and arbitrariness, whereas government by legislature means certainty and the Rule of Law.

This part of Locke's political philosophy has retained more vitality in the United States than in England. There the development of cabinet government since the eighteenth century has controverted some of Locke's misgivings about the inherent evil of a strong and effective executive. Despite Locke's fears, England has not become a despotism, although her legislature has been overshadowed by the executive (itself, however, a committee of the legislature). In the United States, on the other hand, the Lockean sanctification of the legislature as contrasted with the devil theory of the executive has not lost its vote-getting magic.

Hobbes was so strongly impressed with the need for compulsion to maintain social cohesion that he could not envisage society without government. The dissolution of government meant for him the end of all order and restraint, the cessation of civilized living, and the return to the barbarous state of nature. Locke enunciates one of the principal doctrines of classical liberalism by drawing a *sharp distinction between state and society.* Of the two, society is by far the more important and enduring. The dissolution of government does not entail that of society, whereas if society "is dissolved, it is certain that the government of that society cannot remain." Locke mentions that the destruction of society usually occurs by external force, by conquerors' swords that "mangle society to pieces." But when government is dissolved from within, Locke does not anticipate chaos—as did Hobbes—but trusts that society will set up a new government to serve its ends and purposes. In general, government dissolves from within if it violates the trust given to it by the people, who then set up a new government.

Absolute monarchy is, according to Locke, *no form of civil government* at all, and, in fact, worse than the state of nature. In the latter, everybody is judge in his own case, whereas in absolute monarchy there is only one person who has that liberty: the king. In civil society, government approaches dissolution whenever the legislators "endeavor to take away and destroy the property of the people, or to reduce them to slavery under arbitrary power." Similarly, government may be destroyed from within by the chief executive if he overrides the laws of the legislature by his own arbitrary will, hinders the legislative assembly from meeting or acting freely, prevents free elections, or delivers the people into the subjection of a foreign power: "In these, and the like cases, when the government is dissolved, the people are at liberty to provide for themselves by erecting a new legislature differing from the other by the change of persons, or form, or both, as they shall find it most for their safety and good."

Before Locke, theories of disobedience usually contained an element of apology when it came to justifying resistance to authority. Locke reversed the position by declaring the arbitrary ruler an outcast and rebel against the law, whereas the people defined the law by revolting against such despots: "In all states and conditions the true remedy of force without authority is to oppose force to it," and the ruler who uses force without authority should be treated like an aggressor in war. Locke qualifies his theory of resistance in two ways; first, force is to be used by the people only against unjust and unlawful force; second, the right of disobedience may not be exercised by one man or a small group of citizens who feel themselves oppressed, but only by the majority of the people when they have suffered from mischief and oppression.

Locke's insistence that there is a higher law above the law of the state has led to the conception, so deeply ingrained in the traditions of democratic nations, that obedience to the law is a high, but not the highest, civic virtue. Opponents of democratic government have charged that making political rule dependent on consent of the ruled "lays a ferment for frequent rebellion," as Locke puts it. Locke does not deny the charge, but asserts that his hypothesis invites *anarchy and rebellion* no more than any other. First, when the people are made miserable, they will rebel under any form of government, let the governors be "sacred and divine, descended or authorized from heaven, give them out for whom or what you please, the same will happen." Second, Locke emphasizes that men do not revolt "upon every little mismanagement in public affairs" (or "for light and transient causes," as the Declaration of Independence puts it). Third, and here Locke moves from the defensive to the offensive, government by consent coupled with the right of the people to rebel is "the best fence against rebellion." The more the channels of free communication and consent are maintained in a society, the less the need for revolution.

What was an argument in 1690 has since become a matter of experience. The most effective reply to the charge that democracy contains within itself the seeds of anarchy and rebellion is to be found in the political history of the last three centuries. The British and American systems of government, based on the Lockean recognition of the right to rebel, have proved themselves the strongest and most enduring political societies the world has seen, and the same could be said of smaller countries like Holland, Switzerland, and the Scandinavian nations. By contrast, where the right to revolution has been rejected in the name of order and stability, the political results have been *coups d'état,* blood purges, plots and counterplots, conspiracies, and violent swings from one extreme to another—the political record, specifically, of militaristic dictatorships and totalitarian regimes.

By committing themselves to Locke's theories of government, the British supplied the case for the American Revolution and the later peaceful attainment of independence by other colonies, culminating in the virtually complete liquidation of the British Empire in the two decades following World War II. The text of the Declaration is pure Locke, and the main elements of the American constitutional system—limited government, inalienable individual rights, inviolability of property—are all directly traceable to Locke. Writing in the expanding commercial society of his own, his ideas fitted even more the needs of a dynamic pioneering society on the American continent.

Above all, Locke's defense of the right to rebel seemed to the makers of the American Revolution eminently reasonable. Thomas Jefferson, in many respects a Lockean rationalist and lover of freedom and toleration, expressed the American version of Locke's theory of rebellion in the classical phrase that the "tree of liberty must be refreshed from time to time with the blood of patriots and tyrants." Whatever the social or economic system that may exist at a particular time, the right to rebel remains the great, perhaps the greatest, tradition of British and American politics. Rebelliousness too, can, paradoxically, grow into tradition: the tradition of the dignity of man and of his unbreakable spirit.

LOCKE

*Two Treatises of Government**

THE STATE OF NATURE

To understand political power aright, and derive it from its original, we must consider, what state all men are naturally in, and that is, a state of perfect freedom to order their actions, and dispose of their possessions and persons, as they think fit, within the bounds of the law of nature, without asking leave, or depending upon the will of any other man.

A state also of equality, wherein all the power and jurisdiction is reciprocal, no one having more than another; there being nothing more evident, than that creatures of the same species and rank, promiscuously born to all the same advantages of nature, and the use of the same faculties, should also be equal one amongst another without subordination or subjection, unless the lord and master of them all should, by any manifest declaration of his will, set one above another, and confer on him, by an evident and clear appointment, an undoubted right to dominion and sovereignty.

This equality of men by nature, the judicious Hooker looks upon as so evident in itself, and beyond all question, that he makes it the foundation of that obligation to mutual love amongst men, on which he builds the duties they owe one another, and from whence he derives the great maxims of justice and charity. His words are:

The like natural inducement hath brought men to know that it is no less their duty, to love others than themselves; for seeing those things which are equal, must needs all have one measure; if I cannot but wish to receive

good, even as much at every man's hands, as any man can wish unto his own soul, how should I look to have any part of my desire herein satisfied, unless myself be careful to satisfy the like desire, which is undoubtedly in other men. We all being of one and the same nature; to have any thing offered them repugnant to this desire, must needs in all respects grieve them as much as me; so that if I do harm, I must look to suffer, there being no reason that others should shew greater measure of love to me, than they have by me shewed unto them; my desire therefore to be loved of my equals in nature, as much as possible may be, imposeth upon me a natural duty of bearing to themward fully the like affection; from which relation of equality between ourselves and them that are as ourselves, what several rules and canons natural reason hath drawn, for direction of life, no man is ignorant.

—*Eccl. Pol.*, lib.i.

But though this be a state of liberty, yet it is not a state of licence: though man in that state have an uncontrollable liberty to dispose of his person or possessions, yet he has not liberty to destroy himself, or so much as any creature in his possession, but where some nobler use than its bare preservation calls for it. The state of nature has a law of nature to govern it, which obliges every one, and reason, which is that law, teaches all mankind, who will but consult it, that being all equal and independent, no one ought to harm another in his life, health, liberty, or possessions: for men being all the workmanship of one omnipotent, and infinitely wise maker; all the servants of one sovereign master, sent into the world by his order, and about his business; they are his property,

*From John Locke, *Two Treatises of Government* (1690).

whose workmanship they are, made to last during his, not one another's pleasure: and being furnished with like faculties, sharing all in one community of nature, there cannot be supposed any such subordination among us, that may authorize us to destroy one another, as if we were made for one another's uses, as the inferior ranks of creatures are for ours. Every one, as he is bound to preserve himself, and not to quit his station wilfully, so by the like reason, when his own preservation comes not in competition, ought he as much as he can to preserve the rest of mankind, and not unless it be to do justice on an offender, take away, or impair the life, or what tends to the preservation of the life, the liberty, health, limb or goods of another.

And that all men may be restrained from invading others rights, and from doing hurt to one another, and the law of nature be observed, which willeth the peace and preservation of all mankind, the execution of the law of nature is, in that state, put into every man's hands, whereby every one has a right to punish the transgressors of that law to such a degree, as may hinder its violation. For the law of nature would, as all other laws that concern men in this world, be in vain, if there were nobody that in the state of nature had a power to execute that law, and thereby preserve the innocent and restrain offenders. And if any one in the state of nature may punish another for any evil he has done, every one may do so: for in that state of perfect equality where naturally there is no superiority or jurisdiction of one over another, what any may do in prosecution of that law, every one must needs have a right to do.

And thus, in the state of nature, one man comes by a power over another; but yet no absolute or arbitrary power, to use a criminal, when he has got him in his hands, according to the passionate heats, or boundless extravagancy of his own will; but only to retribute to him, so far as calm reason and conscience dictates, what is proportionate to his transgression, which is so much as may serve for reparation and restraint: for these two are the only reasons why one man may lawfully do harm to another, which is that we call punishment. In transgressing the law of nature, the offender declares himself to live by another rule than that of reason and

common equity, which is that measure God has set to the actions of men for their mutual security, and so he becomes dangerous to mankind, the tie, which is to secure them from injury and violence, being slighted and broken by him, which being a trespass against the whole species, and the peace and safety of it, provided for by the law of nature, every man upon this score, by the right he hath to preserve mankind in general, may restrain, or where it is necessary, destroy things noxious to them, and so may bring such evil on any one, who hath transgressed that law, as may make him repent the doing of it, and thereby deter him, and, by his example others, from doing the like mischief. And in this case, and upon this ground, every man hath a right to punish the offender, and be executioner of the law of nature.

I doubt not but this will seem a very strange doctrine to some men; but before they condemn it, I desire them to resolve me, by what right any prince or state can put to death, or punish an alien, for any crime he commits in their country. 'Tis certain their laws, by virtue of any sanction they receive from the promulgated will of the legislative, reach not a stranger: they speak not to him, nor, if they did, is he bound to hearken to them. The legislative authority, by which they are in force over the subjects of that commonwealth, hath no power over him. Those who have the supreme power of making laws in England, France or Holland, are to an Indian, but like the rest of the world, men without authority: and therefore, if by the law of nature every man hath not a power to punish offences against it, as he soberly judges the case to require, I see not how the magistrates of any community can punish an alien of another country; since, in reference to him, they can have no more power than what every man naturally may have over another.

Besides the crime which consists in violating the law, and varying from the right rule of reason, whereby a man so far becomes degenerate, and declares himself to quit the principles of human nature and to be a noxious creature, there is commonly injury done, and some person or other, some other man receives damage by his transgression; in which case he who hath received any damage, has, besides the right of punishment common to him with other men, a particular right to seek reparation from him that has done it: and any other person, who finds it just, may also join with him that is injured, and assist him in recovering from the offender so much as may make satisfaction for the harm he has suffered.

From these two distinct rights, the one of punishing the crime for restraint, and preventing the like offence, which right of punishing is in everybody; the other of taking reparation, which belongs only to the injured party, comes it to pass that the magistrate, who by being magistrate hath the common right of punishing put into his hands, can often, where the public good demands not the execution of the law, remit the punishment of criminal offences by his own authority, but yet cannot remit the satisfaction due to any private man for the damage he has received. That, he who has suffered the damage has a right to demand in his own name, and he alone can remit: the damnified person has this power of appropriating to himself the goods or service of the offender, by right of self-preservation, as every man has a power to punish the crime, to prevent its being committed again, by the right he has of preserving all mankind, and doing all reasonable things he can in order to that end: and thus it is, that every man, in the state of nature, has a power to kill a murderer, both to deter others from doing the like injury, which no reparation can compensate, by the example of the punishment that attends it from every body, and also to secure men from the attempts of a criminal, who having renounced reason, the common rule and measure God hath given to mankind, hath, by the unjust violence and slaughter he hath committed upon one, declared war against all mankind, and therefore may be destroyed as a lion or a tiger, one of those wild savage beasts, with whom men can have no society nor security: and upon this is grounded that great law of nature, *Whoso sheddeth man's blood, by man shall his blood be shed.* And Cain was so fully convinced, that every one had a right to destroy such a criminal, that after the murder of his brother, he cries out, *Every one that findeth me shall slay me;* so plain was it writ in the hearts of all mankind.

By the same reason may a man in the state of nature punish the lesser breaches of that law. It will perhaps be demanded, with

death? I answer, each transgression may be punished to that degree, and with so much severity, as will suffice to make it an ill bargain to the offender, give him cause to repent, and terrify others from doing the like. Every offence, that can be committed in the state of nature, may in the state of nature be also punished equally, and as far forth as it may, in a commonwealth: for though it would be besides my present purpose, to enter here into the particulars of the law of nature, or its measures of punishment; yet, it is certain there is such a law, and that too as intelligible and plain to a rational creature, and a studier of that law, as the positive laws of commonwealths: nay, possibly plainer; as much as reason is easier to be understood, than the fancies and intricate contrivances of men, following contrary and hidden interests put into words; for so truly are a great part of the municipal laws of countries, which are only so far right, as they are founded on the law of nature, by which they are to be regulated and interpreted.

To this strange doctrine, *viz.,* that in the state of nature every one has the executive power of the law of nature, I doubt not but it will be objected, that it is unreasonable for men to be judges in their own cases, that self-love will make men partial to themselves and their friends: and on the other side, ill-nature, passion and revenge will carry them too far in punishing others; and hence nothing but confusion and disorder will follow; and that therefore God hath certainly appointed government to restrain the partiality and violence of men. I easily grant that civil government is the proper remedy for the inconveniences of the state of nature, which must certainly be great where men may be judges in their own case, since 'tis easy to be imagined, that he who was so unjust as to do his brother an injury, will scarce be so just as to condemn himself for it; but I shall desire those who make this objection, to remember, that absolute monarchs are but men; and if government is to be the remedy of those evils, which necessarily follow from men's being judges in their own cases, and the state of nature is therefore not to be endured, I desire to know what kind of government that is, and bow much better it is than the state of nature, where one man commanding a multitude, has the liberty to be judge in his own case, and may do to all his subjects whatever he pleases, without the least question or control of those who execute his pleasure? and in whatsoever he doth, whether led by reason, mistake or passion, must be submitted to? which men in the state of nature are not bound to do one to another. And if he that judges, judges amiss in his own, or any other case, he is answerable for it to the rest of mankind.

'Tis often asked as a mighty objection, where are, or ever were there any men in such a state of nature? To which it may suffice as an answer at present, that since all princes and rulers of *independent* governments all through the world, are in a state of nature, 'tis plain the world never was, nor never will be, without numbers of men in that state. I have named all governors of *independent* communities, whether they are, or are not, in league with others: for 'tis not every compact that puts an end to the state of nature between men, but only this one of agreeing together mutually to enter into one community, and make one body politic; other promises, and compacts, men may make one with another, and yet still be in the state of nature. The promises and bargains for truck, etc. between the two men in the desert island, mentioned by Garcilasso de la Vega, in his history of Peru; or between a Swiss and an Indian, in the woods of America, are binding to them, though they are perfectly in a state of nature, in reference to one another: for truth and keeping of faith belongs to men as men, and not as members of society.

To those that say, there were never any men in the state of nature, I will not only oppose the authority of the judicious Hooker, *Eccl. Pol.* lib. i. *sect.* 10, where he says,

> the laws which have been hitherto mentioned, *i.e.,* the laws of nature, do bind men absolutely, even as they are men, although they have never any settled fellowship, never any solemn agreement amongst themselves what to do, or not to do: but forasmuch as we are not by ourselves sufficient to furnish ourselves with competent store of things, needful for such a life as our nature doth desire, a life fit for the dignity of man; therefore to supply those defects and imperfections which are in us, as living singly

and solely by ourselves, we are naturally induced to seek communion and fellowship with others: this was the cause of men uniting themselves at first in politic societies.

But I moreover affirm, that all men are naturally in that state, and remain so, till by their own consents they make themselves members of some politic society; and I doubt not in the sequel of this discourse, to make it very clear.

THE STATE OF WAR

The state of war is a state of enmity and destruction; and therefore declaring by word or action, not a passionate and hasty, but sedate, settled design upon another man's life, puts him in a state of war with him against whom he has declared such an intention, and so has exposed his life to the other's power to be taken away by him, or any one that joins with him in his defence, and espouses his quarrel, it being reasonable and just I should have a right to destroy that which threatens me with destruction; for by the fundamental law of nature, man being to be preserved, as much as possible, when all cannot be preserved, the safety of the innocent is to be preferred; and one may destroy a man who makes war upon him, or has discovered an enmity to his being, for the same reason that he may kill a wolf or a lion, because such men are not under the ties of the common law of reason, have no other rule but that of force and violence, and so may be treated as beasts of prey, those dangerous and noxious creatures that will be sure to destroy him whenever he falls into their power.

And hence it is that he who attempts to get another man into his absolute power does thereby put himself into a state of war with him; it being to be understood as a declaration of a design upon his life. For I have reason to conclude that he who would get me into his power without my consent would use me as he pleased when he had got me there, and destroy me too when he had a fancy to it, for nobody can desire to have me in his absolute power unless it be to compel me by force to that which is against the right of my freedom—*i.e.,* make me a slave. To be free from such force is the only security of my preservation, and reason bids me look on him as an enemy to my preservation who would take away that freedom which is the fence to it; so that he who makes an attempt to enslave me thereby puts himself into a state of war with me. He that in the state of nature would take away the freedom that belongs to any one in that state must necessarily be supposed to have a design to take away everything else, that freedom being the foundation of all the rest; as he that in the state of society would take away the freedom belonging to those of that society or commonwealth must be supposed to design to take away from them everything else, and so be looked on as in a state of war.

This makes it lawful for a man to kill a thief who has not in the least hurt him, nor declared any design upon his life, any farther than by the use of force, so to get him in his power as to take away his money, or what he pleases, from him; because using force, where he has no right to get me into his power, let his pretence be what it will, I have no reason to suppose that he who would take away my liberty would not, when he had me in his power, take away everything else. And therefore it is lawful for me to treat him as one who has put himself into a state of war with me—*i.e.,* kill him if I can; for to that hazard does he justly expose himself whoever introduces a state of war, and is aggressor in it.

And here we have the plain difference between the state of nature and the state of war, which however some men have confounded, are as far distant as a state of peace, goodwill, mutual assistance, and preservation; and a state of enmity, malice, violence and mutual destruction are one from another. Men living together according to reason without a common superior on earth, with authority to judge between them, are properly in the state of nature. But force, or a declared design of force upon the person of another, where there is no common superior on earth to appeal to for relief, is the state of war; and 'tis the want of such an appeal gives a man the right of war even against an aggressor, though he be in society and a fellow-subject. Thus, a thief whom I cannot harm, but by appeal to the law, for having stolen all that I am worth, I

may kill when he sets on me to rob me but of my horse or coat, because the law, which was made for my preservation, where it cannot interpose to secure my life from present force, which if lost is capable of no reparation, permits me my own defence and the right of war, a liberty to kill the aggressor, because the aggressor allows not time to appeal to our common judge, nor the decision of the law, for remedy in a case where the mischief may be irreparable. Want of a common judge with authority puts all men in a state of nature; force without right upon a man's person makes a state of war both where there is, and is not, a common judge.

But when the actual force is over, the state of war ceases between those that are in society and are equally on both sides subjected to the fair determination of the law; because then there lies open the remedy of appeal for the past injury, and to prevent future harm; but where no such appeal is, as in the state of nature, for want of positive laws, and judges with authority to appeal to, the state of war, once begun, continues with a right to the innocent party to destroy the other whenever he can, until the aggressor offers peace, and desires reconciliation on such terms as may repair any wrongs he has already done, and secure the innocent for the future; nay, where an appeal to the law and constituted judges lies open, but the remedy is denied by a manifest perverting of justice, and a barefaced wresting of the laws to protect or indemnify the violence or injuries of some men or party of men, there it is hard to imagine any thing but a state of war: for wherever violence is used, and injury done, though by hands appointed to administer justice, it is still violence and injury, however coloured with the name, pretences, or forms of law, the end whereof being to protect and redress the innocent, by an unbiased application of it, to all who are under it; wherever that is not *bona fide* done, war is made upon the sufferers, who having no appeal on earth to right them, they are left to the only remedy in such cases, an appeal to heaven.

To avoid this state of war (wherein there is no appeal but to heaven, and wherein every the least difference is apt to end, where there is no authority to decide between the contenders) is one great reason of men's putting themselves into society, and quitting the state of nature. For where there is an authority, a power on earth from which relief can be had by appeal, there the continuance of the state of war is excluded, and the controversy is decided by that power.

SLAVERY

The natural liberty of man is to be free from any superior power on earth, and not to be under the will or legislative authority of man, but to have only the law of nature for his rule. The liberty of man in society is to be under no other legislative power but that established by consent in the commonwealth, nor under the dominion of any will, or restraint of any law, but what the legislative shall enact according to the trust put in it. Freedom, then, is not what Sir Robert Filmer tells us, *O.A. 55. A liberty for every one to do what he lists, to live as he pleases, and not to be tied by any laws,* but freedom of men under government is to have a standing rule to live by, common to every one of that society, and made by the legislative power erected in it. A liberty to follow my own will in all things where the rule prescribes not, not to be subject to the inconstant, uncertain, unknown, arbitrary will of another man, as freedom of nature is to be under no other restraint but the law of nature.

This freedom from absolute, arbitrary power is so necessary to, and closely joined with, a man's preservation, that he cannot part with it but by what forfeits his preservation and life together. For a man, not having the power of his own life, cannot, by compact or his own consent, enslave himself to any one, nor put himself under the absolute, arbitrary power of another to take away his life when he pleases. Nobody can give more power than he has himself, and he that cannot take away his own life cannot give another power over it. Indeed, having by his fault forfeited his own life by some act that deserves death, he to whom he has forfeited it may, when he has him in his power, delay to take it, and make use of him to his own service; and he does him no injury by it. For, whenever he finds the hardship of his slavery outweigh the value of his life, 'tis in his power, by resisting the will of his master, to draw on himself the death he desires.

PROPERTY

God, who hath given the world to men in common, hath also given them reason to make use of it to the best advantage of life and convenience. The earth and all that is therein is given to men for the support and comfort of their being. And though all the fruits it naturally produces, and beasts it feeds, belong to mankind in common, as they are produced by the spontaneous hand of nature, and no body has originally a private dominion exclusive of the rest of mankind in any of them, as they are thus in their natural state, yet being given for the use of men, there must of necessity be a means to appropriate them some way or other before they can be of any use, or at all beneficial, to any particular man. The fruit or venison which nourishes the wild Indian, who knows no enclosure, and is still a tenant in common, must be his, and so his—*i.e.,* a part of him, that another can no longer have any right to it before it can do him any good for the support of his life.

Though the earth and all inferior creatures be common to all men, yet every man has a *property* in his own *person.* This nobody has any right to but himself. The *labour* of his body and the *work* of his hands, we may say, are properly his. Whatsoever, then, he removes out of the state that nature hath provided and left it in, he hath mixed his labour with it, and joined to it something that is his own, and thereby makes it his property. It being by him removed from the common state nature placed it in, it hath by this labour something annexed to it that excludes the common right of other men. For this labour being the unquestionable property of the labourer, no man but he can have a right to what that is once joined to, at least where there is enough, and as good left in common for others.

He that is nourished by the acorns he picked up under an oak, or the apples he gathered from the trees in the wood, has certainly appropriated them to himself. Nobody can deny but the nourishment is his. I ask, then, when did they begin to be his? when he digested? or when he ate? or when he boiled? or when he brought them home?

or when he picked them up? And 'tis plain, if the first gathering made them not his, nothing else could. That labour put a distinction between them and common. That added something to them more than Nature, the common mother of all, had done, and so they became his private right. And will any one say he had no right to those acorns or apples he thus appropriated because he had not the consent of all mankind to make them his? Was it a robbery thus to assume to himself what belonged to all in common? If such a consent as that was necessary, man had starved, notwithstanding the plenty God had given him. We see in commons, which remain so by compact, that 'tis the taking any part of what is common, and removing it out of the state Nature leaves it in, which begins the property, without which the common is of no use. And the taking of this or that part does not depend on the express consent of all the commoners. Thus, the grass my horse has bit, the turfs my servant has cut, and the ore I have digged in any place, where I have a right to them in common with others, become my property without the assignation or consent of any body. The labour that was mine, removing them out of that common state they were in, hath fixed my property in them.

It will perhaps be objected to this, that if gathering the acorns or other fruits of the earth, etc., makes a right to them, then any one may engross as much as he will. To which I answer, Not so. The same law of nature that does by this means give us property, does also bound that property too. *God has given us all things richly,* I *Tim.* vi. 12. Is the voice of reason confirmed by inspiration? But how far has he given it us, *to enjoy?* As much as any one can make use of to any advantage of life before it spoils, so much he may by his labour fix a property in. Whatever is beyond this is more than his share, and belongs to others. Nothing was made by God for man to spoil or destroy. And thus considering the plenty of natural provisions there was a long time in the world, and the few spenders, and to how small a part of that provision the industry of one man could extend itself and engross it to the prejudice of others, especially keeping within the bonds set by reason of what might serve for his use, there could be

then little room for quarrels or contentions about property so established.

But the chief matter of property being now not the fruits of the earth and the beasts that subsist on it, but the earth itself, as that which takes in and carries with it all the rest, I think it is plain that property in that too is acquired as the former. As much land as a man tills, plants, improves, cultivates, and can use the product of, so much is his property. He by his labour does, as it were, enclose it from the common. Nor will it invalidate his right to say, Every body else has an equal title to it, and therefore he cannot appropriate, he cannot enclose, without the consent of all his fellowcommoners, all mankind. God, when he gave the world in common to all mankind, commanded man also to labour, and the penury of his condition required it of him. God and his reason commanded him to subdue the earth—*i.e.,* improve it for the benefit of life and therein lay out something upon it that was his own, his labour. He that, in obedience to this command of God, subdued, tilled, and sowed any part of it, thereby annexed to it something that was his property, which another had no title to, nor could without injury take from him.

Nor was this appropriation of any parcel of land, by improving it, any prejudice to any other man, since there was still enough and as good left, and more than the yet unprovided could use. So that, in effect, there was never the less left for others because of his enclosure for himself. For he that leaves as much as another can make use of does as good as take nothing at all. No body could think himself injured by the drinking of another man, though he took a good draught, who had a whole river of the same water left him to quench his thirst. And the case of land and water, where there is enough of both, is perfectly the same.

God gave the world to men in common, but since he gave it them for their benefit and the greatest conveniences of life they were capable to draw from it, it cannot be supposed he meant it should always remain common and uncultivated. He gave it to the use of the industrious and rational (and labour was to be his title to it); not to the fancy or covetousness of the quarrelsome and contentious. He that had as good left for his improvement as was already taken up needed not complain, ought not to meddle with what was already improved by another's labour; if he did 'tis plain he desired the benefit of another's pains, which he had no right to, and not the ground which God had given him, in common with others, to labour on, and whereof there was as good left as that already possessed, and more than he knew what to do with, or his industry could reach to.

Nor is it so strange as perhaps before consideration, it may appear, that the property of labour should be able to overbalance the community of land, for 'tis labour indeed that puts the difference of value on every thing; and let any one consider what the difference is between an acre of land planted with tobacco or sugar, sown with wheat or barley, and an acre of the same land lying in common without any husbandry upon it, and he will find that the improvement of labour makes the far greater part of the value. I think it will be but a very modest computation to say, that of the products of the earth useful to the life of man, nine-tenths are the effects of labour: nay, if we will rightly estimate things as they come to our use, and cast up the several expenses about them, what in them is purely owing to nature and what to labour, we shall find that in most of them ninety-nine hundredths are wholly to be put on the account of labour.

There cannot be a clearer demonstration of any thing than several nations of the Americans are of this, who are rich in land and poor in all the comforts of life; whom nature, having furnished as liberally as any other people with the materials of plenty, *i.e.,* a fruitful soil, apt to produce in abundance what might serve for food, raiment, and delight; yet, for want of improving it by labour, have not one hundredth part of the conveniences we enjoy. And a king of a large and fruitful territory there feeds, lodges, and is clad worse than a day labourer in England.

From all which it is evident, that though the things of nature are given in common, man (by being master of himself, and proprietor of his own person, and the actions or labour of it) had still in himself the great foundation of property; and that which made up the great part of what he applied to the support or comfort of his being, when invention and arts had improved the conveniences of life, was perfectly his own, and did not belong in common to others.

Thus labour, in the beginning, gave a right of property, wherever any one was pleased to employ it, upon what was common, which remained a long while, the far greater part, and is yet more than mankind makes use of. Men at first, for the most part, contented themselves with what unassisted nature offered to their necessities, and though afterwards, in some parts of the world, where the increase of people and stock, with the use of money, had made land scarce, and so of some value, the several communities settled the bounds of their distinct territories, and, by laws, within themselves, regulated the properties of the private men of their society, and so, by compact and agreement, settled the property which labour and industry began; and the leagues that have been made between several states and kingdoms, either expressly or tacitly disowning all claim and right to the land in the other's possession, have, by common consent, given up their pretences to their natural common right, which originally they had to those countries; and so have, by positive agreement, settled a property amongst themselves, in distinct parts of the world; yet there are still great tracts of ground to be found, which the inhabitants thereof, not having joined with the rest of mankind in the consent of the use of their common money, lie waste, and are more than the people who dwell on it do, or can make use of, and so still lie in common; though this can scarce happen amongst that part of mankind that have consented to the use of money.

The greatest part of things really useful to the life of man, and such as the necessity of subsisting made the first commoners of the world look after, as it doth the Americans now, are generally things of short duration, such as, if they are not consumed by use, will decay and perish of themselves. Gold, silver, and diamonds are things that fancy or agreement hath put the value on, more than real use and the necessary support of life. Now of those good things which nature hath provided in common, every one had a right (as hath been said) to as much as he could use, and had a property in all that he could effect with his labour; all that his industry could extend to, to alter from the state nature had put it in, was his. He that gathered a hundred bushels of acorns or apples had thereby a property in them, they were his goods as soon as gathered. He was only to look that he used them before they spoiled, else he took more than his share, and robbed others. And, indeed, it was a foolish thing, as well as dishonest, to hoard up more than he could make use of. If he gave away a part to any body else, so that it perished not uselessly in his possession, these he also made use of. And if he also bartered away plums that would have rotted in a week, for nuts that would last good for his eating a whole year, he did no injury; he wasted not the common stock; destroyed no part of the portion of goods that belonged to others, so long as nothing perished uselessly in his hands. Again, if he would give his nuts for a piece of metal, pleased with its colour, or exchange his sheep for shells, or wool for a sparkling pebble or a diamond, and keep those by him all his life, he invaded not the right of others; he might heap up as much of these durable things as he pleased; the exceeding of the bounds of his just property not lying in the largeness of his possession, but the perishing of anything uselessly in it.

And thus came in the use of money, some lasting thing that men might keep without spoiling, and that, by mutual consent, men would take in exchange for the truly useful but perishable supports of life.

And as different degrees of industry were apt to give men possessions in different proportions, so this invention of money gave them the opportunity to continue and enlarge them. For supposing an island, separate from all possible commerce with the rest of the world, wherein there were but a hundred families, but there were sheep, horses, and cows, with other useful animals, wholesome fruits, and land enough for corn for a hundred thousand times as many, but nothing in the island, either because of its commonness or perishableness, fit to supply the place of money. What reason could any one have there to enlarge his possessions beyond the use of his family, and a plentiful supply to its consumption, either in what their own industry produced, or they could barter for like perishable, useful commodities with others? Where there is not something both lasting

and scarce, and so valuable to be hoarded up, there men will not be apt to enlarge their possessions of land, were it never so rich, never so free for them to take. For I ask, what would a man value ten thousand or an hundred thousand acres of excellent land, ready cultivated and well stocked, too, with cattle, in the middle of the inland parts of America, where he had no hopes of commerce with other parts of the world, to draw money to him by the sale of the product? It would not be worth the enclosing, and we should see him give up again to the wild common of nature whatever was more than would supply the conveniences of life, to be had there for him and his family.

Thus, in the beginning, all the world was America, and more so than that is now; for no such thing as money was any where known. Find out something that hath the use and value of money amongst his neighbours, you shall see the same man will begin presently to enlarge his possessions.

But since gold and silver, being little useful to the life of man, in proportion to food, raiment, and carriage, has its value only from the consent of men, whereof labour yet makes in great part the measure, it is plain that the consent of men have agreed to a disproportionate and unequal possession of the earth, I mean out of the bounds of society and compact; for in governments the laws regulate it., they having, by consent, found out and agreed in a way how a man may rightfully, and without injury, possess more than he himself can make use of by receiving gold and silver, which may continue long in a man's possession without decaying for the overplus, and agreeing those metals should have a value.

POLITICAL SOCIETY

Man being born, as has been proved, with a title to perfect freedom and an uncontrolled enjoyment of all the rights and privileges of the law of nature, equally with any other man, or number of men in the world, hath by nature a power not only to preserve his property, that is, his life, liberty, and estate, against the injuries and attempts of other men, but to judge of and punish the breaches of that law in others, as he is persuaded the offence deserves, even with death itself, in crimes where the heinousness of the fact, in his opinion, requires it. But because no political society can be, nor subsist, without having in itself the power to preserve the property, and in order thereunto punish the offences of all those of that society: there, and there only, is political society, where every one of the members hath quitted this natural power, resigned it up into the hands of the community in all cases that exclude him not from appealing for protection to the law established by it. And thus all private judgement of every particular member being excluded, the community comes to be umpire, by settled standing rules; indifferent, and the same to all parties: And by men having authority from the community for the execution of those rules, decides all the differences that may happen between any members of that society concerning any matter of right, and punishes those offences which any member hath committed against the society with such penalties as the law has established; whereby it is easy to discern who are, and who are not, in political society together. Those who are united into one body, and have a common established law and judicature to appeal to, with authority to decide controversies between them and punish offenders, are in civil society one with, another; but those who have no such common appeal, I mean on earth, are still in the state of nature, each being, where there is no other, judge for himself and executioner; which is, as I have before showed it, the perfect state of nature.

And thus the commonwealth comes by a power to set down what punishment shall belong to the several transgressions they think worthy of it, committed amongst the members of that society (which is the power of making laws) as well as it has the power to punish any injury done unto any of its members by anyone that is not of it (which is the power of war and peace); and all this for the preservation of the property of all the members of that society, as far as is possible. But though every man entered into society has quitted his power to punish offences against the law of nature in prosecution of his own private judgement, yet with the judgement of offences which he has given up to the legislative in all cases where he can appeal to the magistrate, he has given up a right to the commonwealth to employ his force for the execution of the judgements of the commonwealth whenever he shall be called to it, which, indeed, are his own judgements, they being made by himself or his representative. And herein we have the original of the legislative and executive power of civil society, which is to judge by standing laws how far offences are to be punished when committed within the commonwealth; and also by occasional judgements founded on the present circumstances of the fact, how far injuries from without are to be vindicated, and in both these to employ all the force of all the members when there shall be need.

Wherever therefore any number of men are so united into one society as to quit every one his executive power of the law of nature, and to resign it to the public, there and there only is a political or civil society. And this is done wherever any number of men, in the state of nature, enter into society to make one people, one body politic under one supreme government: or else when anyone joins himself to and incorporates with any government already made. For hereby he authorizes the society, or which is all one, the legislative thereof, to make laws for him as the public good of he society shall require, to the execution whereof his own assistance (as to his own decrees) is due. And this puts men out of a state of nature into that of a commonwealth, by setting up a judge on earth with authority to determine all the controversies and redress the injuries that may happen to any member of the commonwealth; which judge is the legislative or magistrates appointed by it. And wherever there are any number of men, however associated, that have no such decisive power to appeal to, there they are still in the state of nature.

And hence it is evident that absolute monarchy, which by some men is counted for the only government in the world, is indeed inconsistent with civil society, and so can be no form of civil government at all. For the end of civil society being to avoid and remedy those inconveniences of the state of nature which necessarily follow from every man's being judge in his own case, by setting up a known authority, to which everyone of that society may appeal upon any injury received, or controversy that may arise, and which everyone of the society ought to obey, wherever any persons are who have not such an authority to appeal to, for the decision of any difference between them there, those persons are still in the state of nature. And so is every absolute prince in respect of those who are under his *dominion.*

For he being supposed to have all, both legislative and executive, power in himself alone, there is no judge to be found, no appeal lies open to anyone, who may fairly and indifferently, and with authority decide, and from whence relief and redress may by expected of any injury or inconveniency that may be suffered from him, or by his order. So that such a man, however entitled, Czar, or Grand Signior, or how you please, is as much in the state of nature, with all under his dominion, as he is with the rest of mankind. For wherever any two men are, who have no standing rule and common judge to appeal to on earth, for the determination of controversies of right betwixt them, there they are still in the state of nature, and under all the inconveniences of it, with only this woeful difference to the subject, or rather slave of an absolute prince. That whereas, in the ordinary state of nature, he has a liberty to judge of his right, and according to the best of his power, to maintain it; but whenever his property is invaded by the will and order of his monarch, he has not only no appeal, as those in society ought to have, but, as if he were degraded from the common state of rational creatures, is denied a liberty to judge of, or defend his right, and so is exposed to all the misery and inconveniences that a man can fear from one, who being in the unrestrained state of nature, is yet corrupted with flattery and armed with power.

THE END OF GOVERNMENT

If man in the state of nature be so free as has been said; if he be absolute lord of his own person and possessions; equal to the greatest and subject to no body, why will he part with his freedom? Why will he give up this empire, and subject himself to the dominion and control of any other power? To which 'tis obvious to answer, that though in the state of nature he hath such a right, yet the enjoyment of it is very uncertain and constantly exposed to the invasion of others; for all being kings as much as he, every man

his equal, and the greater part no strict observers of equity and justice, the enjoyment of the property he has in this state is very unsafe, very unsecure. This makes him willing to quit this condition which, however free, is full of fears and continual dangers; and 'tis not without reason that he seeks out and is willing to join in society with others who are already united, or have a mind to unite for the mutual preservation of their lives, liberties, and estates, which I call by the general name, property.

The great and chief end therefore, of men's uniting into commonwealths, and putting themselves under government, is the preservation of their property; to which in the state of nature there are many things wanting.

First, There wants an established, settled, known law, received and allowed by common consent to be the standard of right and wrong, and the common measure to decide all controversies between them. For though the law of nature be plain and intelligible to all rational creatures, yet men, being biased by their interest, as well as ignorant for want of study of it, are not apt to allow of it as a law binding to them in the application of it to their particular cases.

Secondly, In the state of nature there wants a known and indifferent judge, with authority to determine all differences according to the established law. For everyone in that state being both judge and executioner of the law of nature, men being partial to themselves, passion and revenge is very apt to carry them too far, and with too much heat in their own cases, as well as negligence and unconcernedness, make them too remiss in other men's.

Thirdly, In the state of nature there often wants power to back and support the sentence when right, and to give it due execution. They who by any injustice offended, will seldom fail where they are able by force to make good their injustice. Such resistance many times makes the punishment dangerous, and frequently destructive to those who attempt it.

Thus mankind, notwithstanding all the privileges of the state of nature, being but in an ill condition while they remain in it, are quickly driven into society. Hence it comes to pass, that we seldom find any number of men live any time together in this state. The inconveniences that they are therein exposed to by the irregular and uncertain exercise of the power every man has of punishing the transgressions of others, make them take sanctuary under the established laws of government, and therein seek the preservation of their property. 'Tis this makes them so willingly give up every one his single power of punishing to be exercised by such alone as shall be appointed to it amongst them, and by such rules as the community, or those authorized by them to that purpose, shall agree on. And in this we have the original right and rise of both the legislative and executive power as well as of the governments and societies themselves.

THE LIMITS OF GOVERNMENT

The great end of men's entering into society being the enjoyment of their properties in peace and safety, and the great instrument and means of that being the laws established in that society, the first and fundamental positive law of all commonwealths is the establishing of the legislative power; as the first and fundamental natural law, which is to govern even the legislative itself, is the preservation of the society, and (as far as will consist with the public good) of every person in it. This legislative is not only the supreme power of the commonwealth, but sacred and unalterable in the hands where the community have once placed it; nor can any edict of anybody else, in what form soever conceived, or by what power soever backed, have the force and obligation of a law which has not its sanction from that legislative which the public has chosen and appointed; for without this the law could not have that which is absolutely necessary to its being a law, the consent of the society, over whom nobody can have a power to make laws but by their own consent and by authority received from them; and therefore all the obedience, which by the most solemn ties anyone can be obliged to pay, ultimately terminates in this supreme power, and is directed by those laws which it enacts. Nor can any oaths to any foreign power whatsoever, or any domestic subordinate power, discharge any member of the society from his obedience to the legislative, acting pursuant to their trust, nor oblige him to any obedience contrary to the laws so enacted or

farther than they do allow, it being ridiculous to imagine one can be tied ultimately to obey any power in the society which is not the supreme.

Though the legislative, whether placed in one or more, whether it be always in being or only by intervals, though it be the supreme power in every commonwealth, yet.

First, It is not, nor can possibly be, absolutely arbitrary over the lives and fortunes of the people. For it being but the joint power of every member of the society given up to that person or assembly which is legislator, it can be no more than those persons had in a state of nature before they entered into society, and gave it up to the community. For nobody can transfer to another more power than he has in himself, and nobody has an absolute arbitrary power over himself, or over any other, to destroy his own life, or take away the life or property of another. A man, as has been proved, cannot subject himself to the arbitrary power of another; and having, in the state of nature, no arbitrary power over the life, liberty, or possession of another, but only so much as the law of nature gave him for the preservation of himself and the rest of mankind, this is all he doth, or can give up to the commonwealth, and by it to the legislative power, so that the legislative can have no more than this. Their power in the utmost bounds of it is limited to the public good of the society. It is a power that hath no other end but preservation, and therefore can never have a right to destroy, enslave, or designedly to impoverish the subjects; the obligations of the law of nature cease not in society, but only in many cases are drawn closer, and have, by human laws, known penalties annexed to them to enforce their observation. Thus the law of nature stands as an eternal rule to all men, legislators as well as others. The rules that they make for other men's actions must, as well as their own and other men's actions, be conformable to the law of nature, *i.e.* to the will of God, of which that is a declaration, and the fundamental law of nature being the preservation of mankind, no human sanction can be good or valid against it.

Secondly, The legislative or supreme authority cannot assume to itself a power to rule by extemporary arbitrary decrees, but is bound to dispense justice and decide the rights of the subject by promulgated standing laws, and known authorized judges. For the law of nature being unwritten, and so nowhere to be found but in the minds of men, they who, through passion or interest, shall miscite or misapply it, cannot so easily be convinced of their mistake where there is no established judge; and so it serves not as it ought, to determine the rights and fence the properties of those that live under it, especially where everyone is judge, interpreter, and executioner of it too, and that in his own case; and he that has right on his side, having ordinarily but his own single strength, hath not force enough to defend himself from injuries or to punish delinquents. To avoid these inconveniencies which disorder men's properties in the state of nature, men unite into societies that they may have the united strength of the whole society to secure and defend their properties, and may have standing rules to bound it by which everyone may know what is his. To this end it is that men give up all their natural power to the society they enter into, and the community put the legislative power into such hands as they think fit, with this trust, that they shall be governed by declared laws, or else their peace, quiet, and property will still be at the same uncertainty as it was in the state of nature.

Absolute arbitrary power, or governing without settled standing laws, can neither of them consist with the ends of society and government, which men would not quit the freedom of the state of nature for, and tie themselves up under, were it not to preserve their lives, liberties, and fortunes, and by stated rules of right and property to secure their peace and quiet. It cannot be supposed that they should intend, had they a power so to do, to give to any one or more an absolute arbitrary power over their persons and estates, and put a force into the magistrate's hand to execute his unlimited will arbitrarily upon them; this were to put themselves into a worse condition than the state of nature, wherein they had a liberty to defend their right against the injuries of others, and were upon equal terms of force to maintain it, whether invaded by a single man or many in combination. Whereas by supposing they have given up themselves to the absolute arbitrary power and will of a legislator, they have disarmed themselves, and armed him

to make a prey of them when he pleases; he being in a much worse condition that is exposed to the arbitrary power of one man who has the command of a hundred thousand than he that is exposed to the arbitrary power of a hundred thousand single men, nobody being secure, that his will who has such a command is better than that of other men, though his force be a hundred thousand times stronger. And, therefore, whatever form the commonwealth is under, the ruling power ought to govern by declared and received laws, and not by extemporary dictates and undetermined resolutions, for then mankind will be in a far worse condition than in the state of nature if they shall have armed one or a few men with the joint power of a multitude, to force them to obey at pleasure the exorbitant and unlimited decrees of their sudden thoughts, or unrestrained, and till that moment, unknown wills, without having any measures set down which may guide and justify their actions. For all the power the government has, being only for the good of the society, as it ought not to be arbitrary and at pleasure, so it ought to be exercised by established and promulgated laws, that both the people may know their duty, and be safe and secure within the limits of the law, and the rulers, too, kept within their due bounds, and not to be tempted by the power they have in their hands to employ it to purposes, and by such measures as they would not have known, and own not willingly.

Thirdly, The supreme power cannot take from any man any part of his property without his own consent. For the preservation of property being the end of government, and that for which men enter into society, it necessarily supposes and requires that the people should have property, without which they must be supposed to lose that by entering into society which was the end for which they entered into it; too gross an absurdity for any man to own. Men therefore in society having property, they have such a right to the goods, which by the law of the community are theirs, that nobody hath a right to their substance, or any part of it, from them without their own consent; without this they have no property at all. For I have truly no property in that which another can by right take from me when he pleases against my consent. Hence it is a mistake to think that the supreme or legislative power of any commonwealth can do what it will, and dispose of the estates of the subject arbitrarily, or take any part of them at pleasure. This is not much to be feared in governments where the legislative consists wholly or in part in assemblies which are variable, whose members upon the dissolution of the assembly are subjects under the common laws of their country, equally with the rest. But in governments where the legislative is in one lasting assembly, always in being, or in one man as in absolute monarchies, there is danger still, that they will think themselves to have a distinct interest from the rest of the community, and so will be apt to increase their own riches and power by taking what they think fit from the people. For a man's property is not at all secure, though there be good and equitable laws to set the bounds of it between him and his fellow-subjects, if he who commands those subjects have power to take from any private man what part he pleases of his property, and use and dispose of it as he thinks good.

But government, into whatsoever hands it is put, being as I have before showed, entrusted with this condition, and for this end, that men might have and secure their properties, the prince or senate, however it may have power to make laws for the regulating of property between the subjects one amongst another, yet can never have a power to take to themselves the whole, or any part of the subjects' property, without their own consent; for this would be in effect to leave them no property at all. And to let us see that even absolute power, where it is necessary, is not arbitrary by being absolute, but is still limited by that reason, and confined to those ends which required it in some cases to be absolute, we need look no farther than the common practice of martial discipline. For the preservation of the army, and in it of the whole commonwealth, requires an absolute obedience to the command of every superior officer, and it is justly death to disobey or dispute the most dangerous or unreasonable of them; but yet we see that neither the sergeant that could command a soldier to march up to the mouth of a cannon, or stand in a breach where he is almost sure to perish, can command that soldier to give him one penny of his money; nor the general that can condemn him to death for

deserting his post, or not obeying the most desperate orders, cannot yet with all his absolute power of life and death dispose of one farthing of that soldier's estate, or seize one jot of his goods; whom yet be can command anything, and hang for the least disobedience. Because such a blind obedience is necessary to that end for which the commander has his power, *viz.* the preservation of the rest, but the disposing of his goods has nothing to do with it.

'Tis true, governments cannot be supported without great charge, and 'tis fit everyone who enjoys his share of the protection should pay out of his estate his proportion for the maintenance of it. But still it must be with his own consent, *i.e.* the consent of the majority, giving it either by themselves or their representatives chosen by them; for if anyone shall claim a power to lay and levy taxes on the people by his own authority, and without such consent of the people, he thereby invades the fundamental law of property, and subverts the end of government. For what property have I in that which another may by right take when he pleases himself?

Fourthly, The legislative cannot transfer the power of making laws to any other hands, for it being but a delegated power from the people, they who have it cannot pass it over to others. The people alone can appoint the form of the commonwealth, which is by constituting the legislative, and appointing in whose hands that shall be. And when the people have said, We will submit, and be governed by laws made by such men, and in such forms, nobody else can say other men shall make laws for them; nor can they be bound by any laws but such as are enacted by those whom they have chosen and authorized to make laws for them. The power of the legislative being derived from the people by a positive voluntary grant and institution, can be no other than what that positive grant conveyed, which being only to make laws, and not to make legislators, the legislative can have no power to transfer their authority of making laws, and place it in other hands.

These are the bounds which the trust that is put in them by the society and the law of God and nature have set to the legislative power of every commonwealth, in all forms of government.

First, They are to govern by promulgated established laws, not to be varied in particular cases, but to have one rule for rich and poor, for the favourite at Court, and the countryman at plough.

Secondly, These laws also ought to be designed for no other end ultimately but the good of the people.

Thirdly, They must not raise taxes on the property of the people without the consent of the people given by themselves or their deputies. And this properly concerns only such governments where the legislative is always in being, or at least where the people have not reserved any part of the legislative to deputies, to be from time to time chosen by themselves.

Fourthly, The legislative neither must nor can transfer the power of making laws to anybody else, or place it anywhere but where the people have.

THE RIGHT TO REBEL

The reason why men enter into society is the preservation of their property; and the end why they choose and authorize a legislative is that there may be laws made, and rules set, as guards and fences to the properties of all the members of the society, to limit the power and moderate the dominion of every part and member of the society. For since it can never be supposed to be the will of the society that the legislative should have a power to destroy that which every one designs to, secure by entering into society, and for which the people submitted themselves to legislators of their own making: whenever the legislators endeavour to take away and destroy the property of the people, or to reduce them to slavery under arbitrary power, they put themselves into a state of war with the people, who are thereupon absolved from any farther obedience, and are left to the common refuge which God hath provided for all men against force and violence. Whensoever therefore the legislative shall transgress this fundamental rule of society, and either by ambition, fear, folly, or corruption, endeavour to grasp themselves, or put into the hands of any other, an absolute power over the lives, liberties, and estates of the people, by this breach of trust they forfeit the power the people had put into their hands for quite

contrary ends, and it devolves to the people; who have a right to resume their original liberty, and by the establishment of a new legislative (such as they shall think fit), provide for their own safety and security, which is the end for which they are in society. What I have said here concerning the legislative in general holds true also concerning the supreme executor, who having a double trust put in him, both to have a part in the legislative and the supreme execution of the law, acts against both, when he goes about to set up his own arbitrary will as the law of the society. He acts also contrary to his trust when he employs the force, treasure, and offices of the society to corrupt the representatives and gain them to his purposes, when he openly pre-engages the electors, and prescribes, to their choice, such whom he has, by solicitations, threats, promises, or otherwise, won to his designs, and employs them to bring in such who have promised beforehand what to vote and what to enact. Thus to regulate candidates and electors, and new model the ways of election, what is it but to cut up the government by the roots, and poison the very fountain of public security? For the people having reserved to themselves the choice of their representatives as the fence to their properties, could do it for no other end but that they might always be freely chosen, and so chosen, freely act and advise as the necessity of the commonwealth and the public good should, upon examination and mature debate, be judged to require. This, those who give their votes before they hear the debate, and have weighed the reasons on all sides, are not capable of doing. To prepare such an assembly as this, and endeavour to set up the declared abettors of his own will, for the true representatives of the people, and the law-makers of the society, is certainly as great a breach of trust, and as perfect a declaration of a design to subvert the government, as is possible to be met with. To which, if one shall add rewards and punishments visibly employed to the same end, and all the arts of perverted law made use of to take off and destroy all that stand in the way of such a design, and will not comply and consent to betray the liberties of their country, 'twill be past doubt what is doing. What power they ought to have in the society who thus employ it contrary to the trust went along with it in its first institution, is easy to determine; and one cannot but see that he who has once attempted any such thing as this cannot any longer be trusted.

To this, perhaps, it will be said, that the people being ignorant and always discontented, to lay the foundation of government in the unsteady opinion and uncertain humour of the people, is to expose it to certain ruin; and no government will be able long to subsist if the people may set up a new legislative whenever they take offence at the old one. To this I answer, quite the contrary. People are not so easily got out of their old forms as some are apt to suggest. They are hardly to be prevailed with to amend the acknowledged faults in the frame they have been accustomed to. And if there be any original defects, or adventitious ones introduced by time or corruption, 'tis not an easy thing to get them changed, even when all the world sees there is an opportunity for it. This slowness and aversion in the people to quit their old constitutions has in the many revolutions [that] have been seen in this kingdom, in this and former ages, still kept us to, or after some interval of fruitless attempts, still brought us back again to our old legislative king, lords and commons; and whatever provocations have made the crown be taken from some of our princes' heads, they never carried the people so far as to place it in another line.

But 'twill be said, this hypothesis lays a ferment for frequent rebellion. To which I answer:

First, No more than any other hypothesis. For when the people are made miserable, and find themselves exposed to the ill usage of arbitrary power; cry up their governors as much as you will for sons of *Jupiter,* let them be sacred and divine, descended or authorized from Heaven; give them out for whom or what you please, the same will happen. The people generally ill treated, and contrary to right, will be ready upon any occasion to ease themselves of a burden that sits heavy upon them. They will wish and seek for the opportunity, which in the change, weakness, and accidents of human affairs, seldom delays long to offer itself. He must have lived but a little while in the world, who has not seen examples of this in his time; and he must have read very little

who cannot produce examples of it in all sorts of governments in the world.

Secondly, I answer, such revolutions happen not upon every little mismanagement in public affairs. Great mistakes in the ruling part, many wrong and inconvenient laws, and all the slips of human frailty will be borne by the people without mutiny or murmur. But if a long train of abuses, prevarications, and artifices, all tending the same way, make the design visible to the people, and they cannot but feel what they lie under, and see whither they are going, 'tis not to be wondered that they should then rouse themselves, and endeavour to put the rule into such hands which may secure to them the ends for which government was at first erected, and without which, ancient names and specious forms are so far from being better, that they are much worse than the state of nature or pure anarchy; the inconveniencies being all as great and as near, but the remedy farther off and more difficult.

Thirdly, I answer, That this power in the people of providing for their safety anew by a new legislative when their legislators have acted contrary to their trust by invading their property, is the best fence against rebellion, and the probablest means to hinder it. For rebellion being an opposition, not to persons, but authority, which is founded only in the constitutions and laws of the government; those, whoever they be, who by force break through, and by force justify their violation of them, are truly and properly rebels. For when men, by entering into society and civil government, have excluded force, and introduced laws for the preservation of property, peace, and unity amongst themselves; those who set up force again in opposition to the laws, do *rebellare*—that is, bring back again the state of war, and are properly rebels, which they who are in power, by the pretence they have to authority, the temptation of force they have in their hands, and the flattery of those about them being likeliest to do, the properest way to prevent the evil is to shew them the danger and injustice of it who are under the greatest temptation to run into it.

In both the forementioned cases, when either the legislative is changed, or the legislators act contrary to the end for which they were constituted, those who are guilty are guilty of rebellion. For if any one by force takes away the established legislative of any society, and the laws by them made, pursuant to their trust, he thereby takes away the umpirage which every one had consented to for a peaceable decision of all their controversies, and a bar to the state of war amongst them. They who remove or change the legislative take away this decisive power, which no body can have but by the appointment and consent of the people; and so destroying the authority which the people did, and no body else can set up, and introducing a power which the people hath not authorized, actually introduce a state of war, which is that of force without authority; and thus by removing the legislative established by the society, in whose decisions the people acquiesced and united as to that of their own will, they untie the knot, and expose the people anew to the state of war. And if those, who by force take away the legislative, are rebels, the legislators themselves, as has been shown, can be no less esteemed so, when they who were set up for the protection and preservation of the people, their liberties and properties shall by force invade and endeavour to take them away; and so they putting themselves into a state of war with those who made them the protectors and guardians of their peace, are properly, and with the greatest aggravation, *rebellantes,* rebels.

But if they who say it lays a foundation for rebellion mean that it may occasion civil wars or intestine broils to tell the people they are absolved from obedience when illegal attempts are made upon their liberties or properties, and may oppose the unlawful violence of those who were their magistrates when they invade their properties, contrary to the trust put in them; and that, therefore, this doctrine is not to be allowed, being so destructive to the peace of the world; they may as well say, upon the same ground, that honest men may not oppose robbers or pirates, because this may occasion disorder or bloodshed. If any mischief come in such cases, it is not to be charged upon him who defends his own right, but on him that invades his neighbour's. If the innocent honest man must quietly quit all he has for peace sake to him who will lay violent hands upon it, I desire it may be considered what a kind of peace

there will be in the world which consists only in violence and rapine, and which is to be maintained only for the benefit of robbers and oppressors. Who would not think it an admirable peace betwixt the mighty and the mean, when the lamb, without resistance, yielded his throat to be torn by the imperious wolf? *Polyphemus's* den gives us a perfect pattern of such a peace. Such a government wherein *Ulysses* and his companions had nothing to do but quietly to suffer themselves to be devoured. And no doubt, *Ulysses,* who was a prudent man, preached up passive obedience, and exhorted them to a quiet submission by representing to them of what concernment peace was to mankind, and by showing the inconveniences might happen if they should offer to resist *Polyphemus,* who had now the power over them.

The end of government is the good of mankind; and which is best for mankind, that the people should be always exposed to the boundless will of tyranny, or that the rulers should be sometimes liable to be opposed when they grow exorbitant in the use of their power, and employ it for the destruction, and not the preservation, of the properties of their people?

Nor let any one say that mischief can arise from hence as often as it shall please a busy head or turbulent spirit to desire the alteration of the government. 'Tis true such men may stir whenever they please, but it will be only to their own just ruin and perdition. For till the mischief be grown general, and the ill designs of the rulers become visible, or their attempts sensible to the greater part, the people, who are more disposed to suffer than right themselves by resistance, are not apt to stir. The examples of particular injustice or oppression of here and there an unfortunate man moves them not. But if they universally have a persuasion grounded upon manifest evidence that designs are carrying on against their liberties, and the general course and tendency of things cannot but give them strong suspicions of the evil intention of their governors, who is to be blamed for it? Who can help it if they, who might avoid it, bring themselves into this suspicion? Are the people to be blamed if they have the sense of rational creatures, and can think of things no otherwise than as they find and feel them? And is it not rather their fault who put things in such a posture that they would not have them thought as they are? I grant that the pride, ambition, and turbulency of private men have sometimes caused great disorders in commonwealths, and factions have been fatal to states and kingdoms. But whether the mischief has oftener begun in the people's wantonness, and a desire to cast off the lawful authority of their rulers, or in the rulers' insolence and endeavours to get and exercise an arbitrary power over their people, whether oppression or disobedience gave the first rise to the disorder, I leave it to impartial history to determine. This I am sure, whoever, either ruler or subject, by force goes about to invade the rights of either prince 'or people, and lays the foundation for overturning the constitution and frame of any just government, he is guilty of the greatest crime I think a man is capable of, being to answer for all those mischiefs of blood, rapine, and desolation, which the breaking to pieces of governments bring on a country; and he who does it is justly to be esteemed the common enemy and pest of mankind, and is to be treated accordingly.

That subjects or foreigners attempting by force on the properties of any people may be resisted with force is agreed on all hands; but that magistrates doing the same thing may be resisted, has of late been denied; as if those who had the greatest privileges and advantages by the law had thereby a power to break those laws by which alone they were set in a better place than their brethren; whereas their offence is thereby the greater, both as being ungrateful for the greater share hey have by the law, and breaking also that trust which is put into their hands by their brethren.

Whosoever uses force without right, as every one does in society who does it without law, puts himself into a state of war with those against whom he so uses it, and in that state all former ties are cancelled, all other rights cease, and every one has a right to defend himself, and to resist the aggressor.

Here 'tis like the common question will be made, Who shall be judge whether the prince or legislative act contrary to their trust? This, perhaps, ill-affected and factious men may spread amongst the people, when the prince only makes use of his due prerogative. To this I reply, The people shall be judge; for who shall be judge whether his trustee or deputy acts well and according to the trust reposed in him, but he who deputes him and must, by having deputed him, have still a power to discard him when he fails in his trust? If this be reasonable in particular cases of private men, why should it be otherwise in that of the greatest moment, where the welfare of millions is concerned and also where the evil, if not prevented, is greater, and the redress very difficult, dear, and dangerous?

But, farther, this question, (Who shall be judge?) cannot mean that there is no judge at all. For where there is no judicature on earth to decide controversies amongst men, God in Heaven is judge. He alone, 'tis true, is judge of the right. But every man is judge for himself, as in all other cases so in this, whether another hath put himself into a state of war with him, and whether he should appeal to the supreme Judge, as *Jephtha* did.

If a controversy arise betwixt a prince and some of the people in a matter where the law is silent or doubtful, and the thing be of great consequence, I should think the proper umpire, in such a case, should be the body of the people. For in such cases where the prince hath a trust reposed in him, and is dispensed from the common, ordinary rules of the law; there, if any men find themselves aggrieved, and think the prince acts contrary to, or beyond that trust, who so proper to judge as the body of the people (who at first lodged that trust in him) how far they meant it should extend? But if the prince, or whoever they be in the administration, decline that way of determination, the appeal then lies nowhere but to Heaven. Force between either persons, who have no known superior on earth, or which permits no appeal to a judge on earth, being properly a state of war, wherein the appeal lies only to Heaven; and in that state the injured party must judge for himself when he will think fit to make use of that appeal and put himself upon it.

To conclude, The power that every individual gave the society when he entered into it, can never revert to the individuals again, as long as the society lasts, but will always remain in the community; because without this there can be no community, no commonwealth, which is contrary to the original agreement; so also when the society hath placed the legislative in any assembly of men, to continue in them and their successors, with direction and authority for providing such successors, the legislative can never revert to the people whilst that government lasts; because, having provided a legislative with power to continue for ever, they have given up their political power to the legislative, and cannot resume it. But if they have set limits to the duration of their legislative, and made this supreme power in any person or assembly only temporary; or else when, by the miscarriages of those in authority, it is forfeited; upon the forfeiture of their rulers or at the determination of the time set, it reverts to the society, and the people have a right to act as supreme, and continue the legislative in themselves or place it in a new form, or new hands, as they think good.

CHAPTER NINETEEN

MONTESQUIEU

The seventeenth century was dominated by the struggle for sovereignty between monarchy and parliament. In England, parliamentary supremacy was decisively asserted in the Revolution of 1688. In France, the monarchy was able to overcome all resistance to its power, and after 1614 the Estates General did not meet until 1789—and in 1789 it was too late. The fifty-four years of Louis XIV's personal government (1661–1715) set a standard for royal absolutism in Europe; France was the acknowledged mistress in the arts and letters as well as the first power in population and wealth.

Yet the cost of the glorious rule of *le grand monarque* was immense. In 1685 he revoked the Edict of Nantes, which had granted religious toleration to Protestants a century earlier (1598). Many Protestants were thus forced to leave France. As the Huguenots had been a vigorous element in French trade and industry, their emigration contributed to the growing economic malaise and bankruptcy that threatened France during the latter part of Louis XIV's regime.

Politically, the revocation of the Edict of Nantes was no less disastrous to French clericalism and absolutism, because it was largely through the writings of the Huguenot refugees in England that France—and through the French language the educated classes all over Europe—acquired a direct knowledge of the English Revolution of 1688 and its underlying liberal philosophy. In science, the English influence was left most directly through the work of Newton; in philosophy and political thought, Locke's name dominated eighteenth-century France. Locke's *Essay Concerning Human Understanding* stressed experience as the sole source of knowledge and thus indirectly opposed a scheme of life that emphasized authority rather than reason and observation. More directly, Locke's *Two Treatises of Government and Letters Concerning Toleration* showed the outlines of a new social order in which despotic kingship by divine right and clerical control of thought and education were replaced by political liberalism and intellectual individualism.

Voltaire (1694–1778) spent three years in England, from 1726 to 1729, and his *Letters on the English* (1734) showed the French—and European—reading public a land of freedom and common sense, secular in outlook, tolerant in religion, and respectful of the rule of law. Voltaire was favorably impressed with the rising social prestige of the middle classes in England and with the individual freedom that resulted from wealth earned in trade and commerce. Like most of the French eighteenth-century *philosophes,* Voltaire was satisfied with a political order that secured stability of property and freedom of individual thought and opinion; democratic rule by the people was still an ideal that was not seriously discussed before the latter part of the century.

During the year of Voltaire's return to France, another distinguished French writer, Montesquieu, went to England to see things for himself. Charles-Louis de Secondat, Baron de la Brède et de Montesquieu (1689–1755), came from a noble family of good standing. At one time his family had accepted Protestantism but later abandoned it. Montesquieu received, as was customary at the time, a classical education, and from his Latin studies he derived a deep affection for Stoicism that he retained for the rest of his life. Imbued with the religious tolerance of the Stoics, he wrote, at the age of twenty-two, an essay in which he maintained that the pagan philosophers of antiquity did not deserve eternal damnation. Montesquieu was trained in law and early became associated with the administration of justice in Bordeaux, his parental castle and birthplace being only a few miles from this flourishing city. In 1716 his uncle died and bequeathed to him the office of chief justice. He held that office for only ten years, and then resigned, in order to devote himself entirely to his favorite activity of writing.

By this time Montesquieu had become a European celebrity. In 1721, when he was thirty-two, he had published (anonymously in Geneva) the *Persian Letters,* which had the effect of a literary bombshell in the Parisian *salons.* Through the letters of two imaginary Persian visitors to Paris, Montesquieu showed the reactions of unprejudiced observers to the irrationalities and imperfections of the western world, and the device of two fictional Persians enabled him to comment on taboos that would otherwise be too delicate to handle. The success of the book was increased by the detailed observations of the foreign visitors on the love life of Paris, and the detailed reports that they in turn received from their eunuchs about their harems in Persia. Also, Montesquieu satirized the Roman Catholic Church in a manner that would have been well-nigh impossible without the disguise of the Persians. The pope is described as a magician who makes believe "that three are but one, that the bread one eats is not bread, that the wine one drinks is not wine, and a thousand similar things," and the clergy is characterized as a "society of persons who always take, and never give." In a more serious vein, the statement is made that the "Protestants will become every day richer and stronger, and the Catholics weaker."

The political satire of the *Persian Letters* was thus well couched in the anonymity of the two Persians, the ironical anticlericalism, and the comparative study of erotics in East and West. In 1726 Montesquieu was proposed—at an unusually early age—for membership in the French Academy, but King Louis XV objected. In 1728 he was able to win entry into the ranks of the "immortals" in French letters.

During the same year he set out on his travels, which took him to Austria, Hungary, Italy, Switzerland, Germany, and Holland; from Holland, in the fall of 1729, he went to England, where he stayed until the spring of 1731. As he traveled to England with the Earl of Chesterfield, British Ambassador at the Hague, he was quickly introduced to the most fashionable society in London. He was also presented at court, where he became a favorite of Queen Caroline, who was charmed by his wit and gallantry. Because of his scientific interests (in his younger years Montesquieu had composed papers on natural history, anatomy, and botany) he was elected a member of the Royal Society, then the world's leading scientific society; the close friendships he formed with some of England's foremost scientists he continued throughout the remainder of his life.

Montesquieu made a serious effort to understand English government. He attended both Houses of Parliament, took notes on debates, and met numerous politicians. He also studied the theory of British government and was a great admirer of Locke, whom he called the great instructor of mankind. Montesquieu was fully aware of the corruption of British politics at that time, and he saw other serious shortcomings. Yet his over-all impression was favorable when he compared the social and political conditions of England with those in France.

Like Voltaire, Montesquieu admired the sound common sense of the English aristocracy and middle classes. Political journalism was free and vigorous, and after the cynicism, corruption, and censorship of France the seriousness of English public life captivated him. There was more color and verve in French life, but he believed that the solidity—and often mediocrity—of England was politically more desirable than the dazzling brilliance of the Paris *salons,* in which there was no subject serious enough not to be corroded by cynicism. During his stay in England, Montesquieu made no effort to study the condition of the "lower" classes but confined himself to contacts with the upper classes and distinguished scientists. His picture of England had little relation to her poverty and rotten boroughs, because Montesquieu, like Voltaire, was more interested in political than in social or economic problems.

Montesquieu returned to France in 1731, full of ideas and projects for future books. In 1734 he published his *Considerations on the Greatness and Decline of Rome.* Roman history was a convenient starting point for his favorite theories, soon to be developed more fully. Speaking of the capacity of a state to correct its own mistakes and abuses, Montesquieu mentions Rome, Carthage, Athens, and the Italian city-republics; lamenting their shortcomings in self-analysis and self-correction, he says: "The government of England is wiser, because there is a body which examines it continuously and continuously examines itself; its errors never last long, and are often useful because of the spirit of attention they give to the people. In a word, a free government, that is, one that is always agitated, cannot be maintained if it is not capable of correction through its own laws."

Montesquieu's chief work, on which his reputation is founded, is his *Spirit of the Laws (De l'esprit des lois,* 1748). He had been working on it, he said, all his life; in fact, his earlier writings anticipate the main ideas of *The Spirit of the Laws.* The impact of the work was powerful both intellectually and politically. Montesquieu shared with the eighteenth-century French *philosophes*—rational, cosmopolitan humanists—their optimism and faith in human progress through reason; yet the title of the book suggests that Montesquieu, though completely of the Age of Reason, goes beyond it. He is interested in the spirit of the *laws,* not the law.

From the traditional viewpoint, the basic principles of law could be rationally ascertained, and law was characteristically thought of in universal terms. The tendency of the philosophy of natural law was to minimize actual legal differences, treat them as accidental, and as not pertaining to the essence of law. Montesquieu confines, by contrast, the concept of natural law to the state of nature, "before the establishment of society." Once mankind sets up society and government, there are three kinds of law: first, the law of nations, which applies to their mutual intercourse; second, political law, which applies to the relations between government and the governed (constitutional, public, and administrative law); third, civil law, which regulates the relations of citizens among themselves (private law, such as the law of contracts). Montesquieu makes a bow to the traditional viewpoint by saying that "law in general is the human reason, inasmuch as it governs all the inhabitants of the earth; the political and civil laws of each nation ought to be only the particular cases in which human reason is applied." But it is evident that he is interested in the particular applications of law rather than in general law.

Montesquieu outlines his program of combining rationalism (which emphasizes the universal) with the historical method (which emphasizes the uniquely individual) by describing laws as follows: "They should be relative to the climate of each country, to the quality of its soil, to its situation and extent, to the principal occupation of the natives, whether husbandmen, huntsmen, or shepherds: they should have a relation to the degree of liberty which the constitution will bear; to the religion of the inhabitants, to their inclinations, riches, numbers, commerce, manners, and customs." By indicating how laws *ought* to be made, Montesquieu retains his link with the Age of Enlightenment from which he springs. Yet he places his rationalism on the empirical basis of social institutions, history, and environment, in the light of which one cannot produce laws by following mere fancy and imagination, because "laws, in their most general signification, are the necessary relations arising from the nature of things."

This awareness of the toughness of facts gives Montesquieu's work a massive strength that has stood the test of time. Forms of government are therefore, for Montesquieu, complex combinations of physical and environmental factors, on the one hand, and of psychological motivations—ways of life—on the other. His profound remark that the "beautiful system" of the English constitution "was invented first in the woods" showed an amazing historical awareness at a time when constitutions were discussed in the light of first principles of logic and reason. Montesquieu surmised that the origins of English political life had to be searched for in the remote history of the English people rather than in a constitutional charter. Although Montesquieu was anticipated by Aristotle, Polybius, and Bodin (to mention but a few) in the institutional and environmental study of politics, none of his predecessors surpassed him in breadth of interest, detachment of observation, and balance of spirit that sympathetically comprehended the reality of the past as much as the ideal possibilities of the future.

Montesquieu's second key idea is that of the *balanced constitution,* of which the doctrine of the *separation of powers* has become politically the most influential expression. Both concepts are elaborated and illustrated in *The Spirit of the Laws* by references to English government and politics. He characterizes England as a nation "passionately fond of liberty, because this liberty is real," willing to sacrifice its wealth, ease, and interest in defense of its freedom. Obviously alluding to the military adventurism of Louis XIV and the high respect for military virtues in the *ancien régime,* Montesquieu (though of a family that had given a number of professional officers to France) enviously notes that in England military men are regarded "as belonging to a profession which may be useful, but is often dangerous," and that civilians are more esteemed than the military.

The eighteenth century was full of colonial quarrels, particularly between France and England, and Montesquieu was attracted by the intricacies of colonial questions. He observes that English settlers introduced in the colonies their own form of government, and "raised great nations in the forests they were sent to inhabit." At the same time, Montesquieu prophetically foresaw that England, having granted a large measure of self-government to its colonies, would be the first nation to lose them. Similarly, in studying the impact of domestic institutions on foreign policy, Montesquieu thought that English statesmen, "being frequently obliged to justify their conduct before a popular council," would be forced to be "a little more honest" than statesmen who were not accountable to either parliament or public opinion.

The secret of England's freedom lay, for Montesquieu, in her system of government; as a liberal aristocrat who favored individual liberty, property, and the ancient privileges of the aristocracy, Montesquieu was impressed by the fact that the English system of government combined within itself the best features of monarchy (in the executive), aristocracy (the House of Lords as the supreme court and as part of the legislative), and democracy (in part of the legislative). Although the forms of state—monarchy, aristocracy, and democracy—were united in English government, the powers of government were separated from one another. There can be no liberty where the executive, legislative, and judicial powers are united in one person or body of persons, because such concentration is bound to result in arbitrary despotism. Montesquieu acutely noted that the English system had an additional check on despotism: the legislative itself was divided into two bodies, the House of Lords, representing the privileges of an hereditary aristocracy, and the House of Commons, representing the popular interests.

Montesquieu holds that the executive power should be in the hands of a monarch, independent of the legislative. He predicted that if the executive power "should be committed to a certain number of persons elected from the legislative body, there would be an end then of liberty." The development of cabinet government was beginning to take place in England when Montesquieu was there, but his picture of the English constitution is more the theory of 1689 than the practice of 1730. Montesquieu's fears were shared, however, by the makers of the Constitution of the United States, and the doctrine of separation of powers has resulted in the exclusion of cabinet ministers from Congress. It has therefore been maintained that the American political system of the twentieth century, in which the independence of executive and legislative from each other is still real, resembles the British constitution of the eighteenth century, in which the Crown, Lords, and Commons were balanced against one another, rather than that of the twentieth century, in which the House of Commons has become the final arbiter.

Underlying Montesquieu's doctrine of the separation of powers is the unstated premise of the *negative state,* the state that acts primarily as a night watchman maintaining law and order, and protecting the liberty and property of the individual. As long as liberalism was imbued with the philosophy of *laissez faire,* Montesquieu was one of its apostles. As liberalism—since the early twentieth century—became increasingly oriented toward the positive state, the state of broadened scope and enlarged activity, the doctrine of separation of powers as a philosophy of governmental paralysis and do-nothing lost its erstwhile appeal. In the eighteenth century the purpose of the doctrine of separation of powers was to strengthen the popular element of government at the expense of the king. In the nineteenth century Montesquieu's formula was used by conservatives to keep—in the executive branch at least—the power of the monarch intact against demands for full democratic, popular government.

In the final analysis it is not easy to classify Montesquieu's political philosophy. In his explicit beliefs there is a curious mixture of hatred of clericalism and despotism, profound concern for individual liberty, and a strong sense of aristocratic privilege, property, and class. Similarly, the implicit hypotheses of his political theory are complex: his faith in reason, humanity, and progress mark him out as a typical representative of the Age of Enlightenment. At the same time, Montesquieu was institution-minded to the point of venerating the past, and he therefore became suspect with many *philosophes.*

This element in Montesquieu leads straight to Burke, and—by means of some distortion—to the romantic, nationalist school of thought. Montesquieu's belief that "nothing must be changed by laws which can be changed by custom and morality" differed strongly from the optimistic faith of the Age of Reason in the possibility of wholesale social change through proper legislation. Yet the peculiar mixture of history and reason, of awareness of the past and concern for the future, of objective observation and desire for reform, has made Montesquieu one of the most influential political writers of the modern age.

MONTESQUIEU

*The Spirit of the Laws**

THE SOCIAL AND PHYSICAL FOUNDATIONS OF GOVERNMENT

As soon as mankind enter into a state of society they lose the sense of their weakness; equality ceases, and then commences the state of war.

Each particular society begins to feel its strength, whence arises a state of war betwixt different nations. The individuals likewise of each society become sensible of their force; hence the principal advantages of this society they endeavour to convert to their own emolument, which constitutes a state of war betwixt individuals.

These two different kinds of states give rise to human laws. Considered as inhabitants of so great a planet, which necessarily contains a variety of nations, they have laws relative to their mutual intercourse, which is what we call the *law of nations*. As members of a society that must be properly supported, they have laws relative to the governors and the governed, and this we distinguish by the name of *politic law*. They have also another sort of laws, as they stand in relation to each other; by which is understood the *civil law*.

The law of nations is naturally founded on this principle, that different nations ought in time of peace to do one another all the good they can, and in time of war as little injury as possible, without prejudicing their real interests.

The object of war is victory; that of victory is conquest; and that of conquest,

preservation. From this and the preceding principle all those rules are derived which constitute the *law of nations*.

All countries have a law of nations, not excepting the Iroquois themselves, though they devour their prisoners; for they send and receive ambassadors, and understand the rights of war and peace. The mischief is, that their law of nations is not founded on true principles.

Besides the law of nations relating to all societies, there is a polity or civil constitution for each particularly considered. No society can subsist without a form of government. "The united strength of individuals," as Gravina well observes, "constitutes what we call the body politic."

The general strength may be in the hands of a single person, or of many. Some think that nature having established paternal authority, the most natural government was that of a single person. But the example of paternal authority proves nothing. For if the power of a father be relative to a single government, that of brothers after the death of a father, and that of cousins german after the decease of brother, refer to a government of many. The political power necessarily comprehends the union of several families.

Better is it to say, that the government most conformable to nature, is that which best agrees with the humour and disposition of the people in whose favour it is established.

The strength of individuals cannot be united without a conjunction of all their wills. "The conjunction of those wills," as Gravina again very justly observes, "is what we call the *civil state*."

Law in general is human reason, inasmuch as it governs all the inhabitants of the

---

*From Charles-Louis de Montesquieu, *The Spirit of the Laws* (1748; rev. ed., trans. Thomas Nugent, 1873).

earth; the political and civil laws of each nation ought to be only the particular cases in which human reason is applied.

They should be adapted in such a manner to the people for whom they are framed, that it is a great chance if those of one nation suit another.

They should be relative to the nature and principle of each government; whether they form it, as may be said of politic laws; or whether they support it, as in the case of civil institutions.

They should be relative to the climate of each country, to the quality of its soil, to its situation and extent, to the principal occupation of the natives, whether husbandmen, huntsmen, or shepherds; they should have a relation to the degree of liberty which the constitution will bear; to the religion of the inhabitants, to their inclinations, riches, numbers, commerce, manners, and customs. In fine, they have relations to each other, as also to their origin, to the intent of the legislator, and to the order of things on which they are established; in all which different lights they ought to be considered.

This is what I have undertaken to perform in the following work. These relations I shall examine, since all these together constitute what I call the *Spirit of Laws.*

I have not separated the political from the civil institutions: for as I do not pretend to treat of laws, but of their spirit; and as this spirit consists in the various relations which the laws may have to different objects, it is not so much my business to follow the natural order of laws, as that of these relations and objects.

REPUBLICAN GOVERNMENT AND THE LAWS RELATIVE TO DEMOCRACY

When the body of the people is possessed of the supreme power, this is called a *democracy.* When the supreme power is lodged in the hands of a part of the people, it is then an *aristocracy.*

In a democracy the people are in some respects the sovereign, and in others the subject.

There can be no exercise of sovereignty but by their suffrages, which are their own will; now the sovereign's will is the sovereign himself. The laws therefore which establish the right of suffrage, are fundamental to this government. And indeed it is as important to regulate in a republic, in what manner, by whom, to whom, and concerning what, suffrages are to be given, as it is in a monarchy to know who is the prince, and after what manner he ought to govern.

Libanius says that at "Athens a stranger, who intermeddled in the assemblies of the people, was punished with death." This is because such a man usurped the rights of sovereignty.

It is an essential point to fix the number of citizens who are to form the public assemblies; otherwise it would be uncertain whether the whole, or only a part of the people, had given their votes. At Sparta the number was fixed to ten thousand. But Rome, designed by Providence to rise from the weakest beginnings to the highest pitch of grandeur; Rome, doomed to experience all the vicissitudes of fortune; Rome, who had sometimes all her inhabitants without her walls, and sometimes all Italy and a considerable part of the world within them: Rome, I say, never fixed the number; and this was one of the principal causes of her ruin.

The people, in whom the supreme power resides, ought to have the management of every thing within their reach: what exceeds their abilities, must be conducted by their ministers.

But they can not properly be said to have their ministers, without the power of nominating them: it is, therefore, a fundamental maxim in this government, that the people should choose their ministers, that is, their magistrates.

They have occasion, as well as monarchs, and even more so, to be directed by a council or senate. But to have a proper confidence in these, they should have the choosing of the members; whether the election be made by themselves, as at Athens; or by some magistrate deputed for that purpose, as on certain occasions was customary at Rome.

The people are extremely well qualified for choosing those whom they are to intrust with part of their authority. They have only to be determined by things to which they cannot be strangers, and by facts that are obvious to sense. They can tell when a person has fought many battles, and been crowned with success; they are, therefore, very capable of electing a general. They can tell when a judge is assiduous in his office, gives general satisfaction, and has never been charged with bribery: this is sufficient for choosing a praetor They are struck with the magnificence or riches of a fellow-citizen; no more is requisite for electing an edile. These are facts of which they can have better information in a public forum, than a monarch in his palace. But are they capable of conducting an intricate affair, of seizing and improving the opportunity and critical amount of action? No; this surpasses their abilities.

Should we doubt of the people's natural capacity, in respect to the discernment of merit, we need only cast an eye on the series of surprising elections made by the Athenians and Romans; which no one surely will attribute to hazard.

We know, that though the people of Rome assumed to themselves the right of raising plebeians to public offices, yet they never would exert this power; and though at Athens the magistrates were allowed, by the law of Aristides, to be elected from all the different classes of inhabitants, there never was a case, says Xenophon, that the common people petitioned for employments which could endanger either their security or their glory.

As most citizens have sufficient abilities to choose, though unqualified to be chosen; so the people, though capable of calling others to an account for their administration, are incapable of conducting the administration themselves.

The public business must be carried on with a certain motion, neither too quick nor too slow. But the motion of the people is always either too remiss or too violent. Sometimes with a hundred thousand arms they overturn all before them; and sometimes with a hundred thousand feet they creep like insects.

In a popular state the inhabitants are divided into certain classes. It is in the manner of making this division that great legislators have signalized themselves; and it is on this the duration and prosperity of democracy have ever depended.

Servius Tullius followed the spirit of aristocracy in the distribution of his classes. We find in Livy and in Dionysius Halicarnassus, in what manner he lodged the right of suffrage in the hands of the principal citizens. He had divided the people of Rome into a hundred and ninety-three centuries, which formed six classes; and ranking the rich, who were in smaller numbers, in the first centuries; and those in middling circumstances, who were more numerous, in the next, he flung the indigent multitude into the last; and as each century had but one vote, it was property rather than numbers that decided the elections.

Solon divided the people of Athens into four classes. In this he was directed by the spirit of democracy, his intention not being to fix those who were to choose, but such as were eligible: therefore, leaving to every citizen the right of election, he made the judges eligible from each of those four classes; but the magistrates he ordered to be chosen only out of the first three, consisting of persons of easy fortunes.

As the division of those who have a right of suffrage is a fundamental law in republics, the manner also of giving this suffrage is another fundamental.

The suffrage by *lot* is natural to democracy, as that by *choice* is to aristocracy.

The suffrage by *lot* is a method of electing that offends no one; but animates each citizen with the pleasing hope of serving his country.

Yet as this method is in itself defective, it has been the endeavour of the most eminent legislators to regulate and amend it.

Solon made a law at Athens, that military employments should be conferred by choice; but that senators and judges should be elected by *lot*.

The same legislator ordained that civil magistrates, attended with great expense, should be given by choice; and the others by lot.

In order, however, to amend the suffrage by lot, he made a rule, that none but those who presented themselves should be elected; that the person elected should be examined by judges, and that every one should have a right to accuse him if he were unworthy of the office: this participated at the same time of the suffrage by lot, and of that by choice. When the time of their magistracy was expired, they were obliged to submit to another judgment in regard to their conduct. Persons utterly unqualified, must have been extremely backward in giving in their names to be drawn by lot.

The law which determines the manner of giving suffrage, is likewise fundamental in a democracy. It is a question of some importance, whether the suffrages ought to be public or secret. Cicero observes, that the laws which rendered them secret towards the close of the republic, were the cause of its decline. But as this is differently practised in different republics, I shall offer here my thoughts concerning this subject.

The people's suffrages ought doubtless to be public; and this should be considered as a fundamental law of democracy. The lower class ought to be directed by those of higher rank, and restrained within bounds by the gravity of eminent personages. Hence, by rendering the suffrages secret in the Roman republic, all was lost; it was no longer possible to direct a populace that sought its own destruction. But when the body of the nobles are to vote in an aristocracy; or in a democracy, the senate; as the business is then only to prevent intrigues, the suffrages cannot be too secret.

Intriguing in a senate is dangerous; dangerous it is also in a body of nobles; but not so in the people, whose nature is to act through passion. In countries where they have no share in the government, we often see them as much inflamed on the account of an actor, as ever they could be for the welfare of the state. The misfortune of a republic is, when intrigues are at an end; which happens when the people are gained by bribery and corruption: in this case they grow indifferent to public affairs, and avarice becomes their predominant passion. Unconcerned about the government, and every thing belonging to it, they quietly wait for their hire.

It is likewise a fundamental law in democracies, that the people should have the sole power to enact laws. And yet there are a thousand occasions on which it is necessary the senate should have a power of decreeing; nay, it is frequently proper to make some trial of a law before it is established. The constitutions of Rome and Athens were excellent. The decrees of the senate had the force of laws for the space of a year; but did not become perpetual till they were ratified by the consent of the people.

THE PRINCIPLE
OF DEMOCRACY

There is no great share of probity necessary to support a monarchical or despotic government. The force of laws in one, and the prince's arm in the other, are sufficient to direct and maintain the whole. But in a popular state, one spring more is necessary, namely, *virtue*.

What I have here advanced, is confirmed by the unanimous testimony of historians, and is extremely agreeable to the nature of things. For it is clear that in a monarchy, where he who commands the execution of the laws, generally thinks himself above them, there is less need of virtue than in a popular government, where the person entrusted with the execution of the laws, is sensible of his being subject to their direction.

Clear it is also, that a monarch, who, through bad advice or indolence, ceases to enforce the execution of the laws, may easily repair the evil; he has only to follow other advice; or to shake off this indolence. But when, in a popular government, there is a suspension of the laws, as this can proceed only from the corruption of the republic, the state is certainly undone.

A very droll spectacle it was in the last century to behold the impotent efforts of the English towards the establishment of democracy. As they who had a share in the direction of public affairs were void of virtue; as their ambition was inflamed by the success of the most daring of their members; as the prevailing parties were successively animated by the spirit of faction, the government was continually changing: the people, amazed at so many revolutions, in vain attempted to erect a commonwealth. At length, when the country had undergone the most violent shocks, they were obliged to have recourse to the very government which they had so wantonly proscribed.

When Sulla thought of restoring Rome to her liberty, this unhappy city was incapable of that blessing. She had only the feeble remains of virtue, which were continually diminishing: instead of being roused out of her lethargy, by Caesar, Tiberius, Caius Claudius, Nero, Domitian, she riveted every day her chains; if she struck some blows, her aim was at the tyrant, but not at the usurpation.

The politic Greeks, who lived under a popular government, knew no other support than virtue. The modern inhabitants of that country are entirely taken up with manufacture, commerce, finances, opulence, and luxury.

When virtue is banished, ambition invades the minds of those who are disposed to receive it, and avarice possesses the whole community. The objects of their desires are changed; what they were fond of before, is become indifferent; they were free, while under the restraint of laws, but they would fain now be free to act against law; and as each citizen is like a slave who has run away from his master, what was a maxim of equity, he calls rigour; what was a rule of action, he styles constraint; and to precaution, he gives the name of fear. Frugality, and not the thirst of gain, now passes for avarice. Formerly the wealth of individuals constituted the public treasure; but now this is become the patrimony of private persons. The members of the commonwealth riot on the public spoils, and its strength is only the power of a few, and the licentiousness of many.

Athens was possessed of the same number of forces, when she triumphed so gloriously, and when with so much infarny she was enslaved. She had twenty thousand citizens, when she defended the Greeks against the Persians, when she contended for empire with Sparta, and invaded Sicily. She had twenty thousand when Demetrius Phalereus numbered them, as slaves are told by the head in a market-place. When Philip attempted to lord it over Greece, and appeared at the gates of Athens, she had even then lost nothing but time. We may see in Demosthenes how difficult it was to awake her: she dreaded Philip, not as the enemy of her liberty, but of her pleasures. This famous city, which had withstood so many defeats, and after having been so often destroyed, had as often risen out of her ashes, was overthrown of Chæronea, and at one blow deprived of all hopes of resource. What does it avail her, that Philip sends back her prisoners, if he does not return her men? It was ever after as easy to triumph over the Athenian forces, as it had been difficult to subdue her virtue.

How was it possible for Carthage to maintain her ground? When Hannibal, upon his being made prætor, endeavoured to hinder the magistrates from plundering the republic, did not they complain of him to the Romans? Wretches, who would fain be citizens without a city, and beholden for their riches to their very destroyers! Rome soon insisted upon having three hundred of their principal citizens as hostages; she obliged them next to surrender their arms and ships; and then she declared war. From the desperate efforts of this defenceless city, one may judge of what she might have performed in her full vigour, and assisted by virtue.

THE PRINCIPLE OF DESPOTIC GOVERNMENT

As virtue is necessary in a republic, and in a monarchy honour, so fear is necessary in a despotic government: with regard to virtue, there is no occasion for it, and honour would be extremely dangerous.

Here the immense power of the prince is devolved entirely upon those whom he is pleased to intrust with the administration. Persons capable of setting a value upon themselves, would be likely to create disturbances. Fear must therefore depress their spirits, and extinguish even the least sense of ambition.

A moderate government may, whenever it pleases, and without the least danger, relax its springs. It supports itself by the laws, and by its own internal strength. But when a despotic prince ceases one single moment to lift up his arm, when he cannot instantly demolish those whom he has entrusted with the first employments, all is over: for as fear, the spring of this government, no longer subsists, the people are left without a protector.

It is probably in this sense the Cadis maintained that the Grand Seignior was not obliged to keep his word or oath, when he limited thereby his authority.

It is necessary that the people should be judged by laws, and the great men by the caprice of the prince, that the lives of the lowest subjects should be safe, and the bashaw's head ever in danger. We cannot mention these monstrous governments without horror. The Sophi of Persia, dethroned in our days by Mahomet, the son of Miriveis, saw the constitution subverted before this revolution, because he had been too sparing of blood.

History informs us, that the horrid cruelties of Domitian struck such a terror into the governors, that the people recovered themselves a little under his reign. Thus a torrent overflows one side of a country, and on the other leaves fields untouched, where the eye is refreshed by the prospect of fine meadows.

CORRUPTION OF THE PRINCIPLES OF DEMOCRACY

The principle of democracy is corrupted not only when the spirit of equality is extinct, but likewise when they fall into a spirit of extreme equality, and when each citizen would fain be upon a level with those whom he has chosen to command him. Then the people, incapable of bearing the very power they have delegated, want to manage every thing themselves, to debate for the senate, to execute for the magistrate, and to decide for the judges.

When this is the case, virtue can no longer subsist in the republic. The people are desirous of exercising the functions of the magistrates, who cease to be revered. The deliberations of the senate are slighted; all respect is then laid aside for the senators, and consequently for old age. If there is no more respect for old age, there will be none presently for parents; deference to husbands will be likewise thrown off, and submission to masters. This licentiousness will soon become general; and the trouble of command be as fatiguing as that of obedience. Wives, children, slaves will shake off all subjection. No longer will there be any such things as manners, order or virtue.

We find in Xenophon's banquet a very lively description of a republic in which the people abused their equality. Each guest gives in his turn the reason why he is satisfied. "Content I am," says Chamides, "because of my poverty. When I was rich, I was obliged to pay my court to informers, knowing I were more liable to be hurt by them, than capable of doing them harm. The republic constantly demanded some new tax of me; and I could not decline paying. Since I am grown poor, I have acquired authority; nobody threatens me; I rather threaten others. I can go or stay where I please. The rich already rise from their seats and give me the way. I am a king, I was before a slave; I paid taxes to the republic, now it maintains me: I am no longer afraid of losing, but I hope to acquire."

The people fall into this misfortune, when those in whom they confide, desirous of concealing their own corruption, endeavour to corrupt them. To disguise their own ambition, they speak to them only of the grandeur of the state; to conceal their own avarice, they incessantly flatter theirs.

The corruption will increase among the corrupters, and likewise among those who are already corrupted. The people will divide the public money among themselves, and having added the administration of affairs to their indolence, will be for blending their poverty with the amusements of luxury. But with their indolence and luxury, nothing but the public treasure will be able to satisfy their demands.

We must not be surprised to see their suffrages given for money. It is impossible to make great largesses to the people without great extortion: and to compass this, the state must be subverted. The greater the advantages they seem to derive from their liberty, the nearer they approach towards the critical moment of losing it. Petty tyrants arise, who have all the vices of a single tyrant. The small remains of liberty soon become unsupportable; a single tyrant starts up, and the people are stripped of every thing, even of the profits of their corruption.

Democracy has, therefore, two excesses to avoid; the spirit of inequality, which leads to aristocracy or monarchy; and the spirit of extreme equality, which leads to despotic power, as the latter is completed by conquest.

True it is, that those who corrupted the Greek republics, did not always become tyrants. This was because they had a greater passion for eloquence than for the military art. Besides there reigned an implacable hatred in the breasts of the Greeks against those who subverted a republican government; and for this reason anarchy degenerated into annihilation, instead of being changed into tyranny.

But Syracuse being situated in the midst of a great number of petty states, whose government had been changed from oligarchy to tyranny; and being governed by a senate scarce ever mentioned in history, underwent such miseries as are the consequence of a more than ordinary corruption. This city, ever a prey to licentiousness or oppression, equally labouring under the sudden and alternate succession of liberty and servitude, and notwithstanding her external strength, constantly determined to a revolution by the least foreign power: this city, I say, had in her bosom an immense multitude of people, whose fate it was to have always this cruel alternative, either of choosing a tyrant to govern them, or of acting the tyrant themselves.

THE CONFEDERATE REPUBLIC

If a republic be small, it is destroyed by a foreign force; if it be large, it is ruined by an internal imperfection.

To this twofold inconveniency Democracies and Aristocracies are equally liable, whether they be good or bad. The evil is in the very thing itself, and no form can redress it.

It is, therefore, very probable that mankind would have been, at length, obliged to live constantly under the government of a single person, had they not contrived a kind of constitution that has all the internal advantages of a republican, together with the external force of a monarchical, government. I mean a confederate republic.

This form of government is a convention by which several petty states agree to become members of a larger one, which they intend to establish. It is a kind of assemblage of societies, that constitute a new one, capable of increasing by means of farther associations, till they arrive to such a degree of power, as to be able to provide for the security of the whole body.

It was these associations that so long contributed to the prosperity of Greece. By these the Romans attacked the whole globe, and by these alone the whole globe withstood them; for when Rome was arrived to her highest pitch of grandeur, it was the associations beyond the Danube and the Rhine, associations formed by the terror of her arms, that enabled the Barbarians to resist her.

From hence it proceeds that Holland, Germany, and the Swiss Cantons, are considered in Europe as perpetual republics.

The associations of cities were formerly more necessary than in our times. A weak, defenceless town was exposed to greater danger. By conquest it was deprived not only of the executive and legislative power, as at present, but moreover of all human property.

A republic of this kind, able to withstand an external force, may support itself without any internal corruption; the form of this society prevents all manner of inconveniences.

If a single member should attempt to usurp the supreme power, he could not be supposed to have an equal authority and credit in all the confederate states. Were he to have too great an influence over one, this would alarm the rest; were he to subdue a part, that which would still remain free, might oppose him with forces independent of those which he had usurped, and overpower him before he could be settled in his usurpation.

Should a popular insurrection happen in one of the confederate states, the others are able to quell it. Should abuses creep into one part, they are reformed by those that remain sound. The state may be destroyed on one side, and not on the other; the confederacy may be dissolved, and the confederates preserve their sovereignty.

As this government is composed of petty republics, it enjoys the internal happiness of each, and with regard to its external situation, by means of the association, it possesses all the advantages of large monarchies.

MEANING OF LIBERTY

There is no word that admits of more various significations, and has made more different impressions on the human mind, than that of *Liberty*. Some have taken it for a facility of deposing a person on whom they had conferred a tyrannical authority; others for the power of choosing a superior whom they are obliged to obey; others for the right of bearing arms, and of being thereby enabled to use violence; others, in fine, for the privilege of being governed by a native of their own country, or by their own laws. A certain nation for a long time thought liberty consisted in the privilege of wearing a long beard. Some have annexed this name to one form of government exclusive of others: those who had a republican taste, applied it to this species of policy; those who liked a monarchical state, gave it to monarchy. Thus they have all applied the name of *liberty* to the government most suitable to their own customs and inclinations; and as in republics the people have not so constant and so present a view of the causes of their misery, and as the magistrates seem to act only in conformity to the laws, hence liberty is generally said to reside in republics, and to be banished from monarchies. In fine, as in democracies the people seem to act almost as they please; this sort of government has been deemed the most free; and the power of the people has been confounded with their liberty.

It is true that in democracies the people seem to act as they please; but political liberty does not consist in an unlimited freedom. In governments, that is, in societies directed by laws, liberty can consist only in the power of doing what we ought to will, and in not being constrained to do what we ought not to will.

We must have continually present to our minds the difference between independence and liberty. Liberty is a right of doing whatever the laws permit; and if a citizen could do what they forbid, he would be no longer possessed of liberty, because all his fellow-citizens would have the same power.

Democratic and aristocratic states are not in their own nature free. Political liberty is to be found only in moderate governments; and even in these, it is not always found. It is there only when there is no abuse of power; but constant experience shows us, that every man invested with power is apt to abuse it, and to carry his authority as far as it will go. Is it not strange, though true, to say, that virtue itself has need of limits?

To prevent this abuse, it is necessary from the very nature of things, power should be a check to power. A government may be so constituted as no man shall be compelled to do things to which the law does not oblige him, nor forced to abstain from things which the law permits.

THE CONSTITUTION
OF ENGLAND

In every government there are three sorts of power: the legislative; the executive, in respect to things dependent on the law of nations; and the executive, in regard to matters that depend on the civil law.

By virtue of the first, the prince or magistrate enacts temporary or perpetual laws, and amends or abrogates those that have been already enacted. By the second, he makes peace or war, sends or receives embassies, establishes the public security, and provides against invasions. By the third, he punishes criminals, or determines the disputes that arise between individuals. The latter we shall call the judiciary power, and the other simply the executive power of he state.

The political liberty of the subject is a tranquillity of mind arising from the opinion each person has of his safety. In order to have this liberty, it is requisite the government be so constituted as one man needs not be afraid of another.

When the legislative and executive powers are united in the same person, or in the same body of magistrates, there can be no liberty; because apprehensions may arise, lest the same monarch or senate should enact tyrannical laws, to execute them in a tyrannical manner.

Again there is no liberty, if the judiciary power be not separated from the legislative and executive. Were it joined with the legislative, the life and liberty of the subject would be exposed to arbitrary control; for the judge would be then the legislator. Were it joined to the executive power, the judge might behave with violence and oppression.

There would be an end of everything, were the same man, or the same body, whether of the nobles or of the people, to exercise those three powers, that of enacting laws, that of executing the public resolutions, and of trying the causes of individuals.

Most kingdoms in Europe enjoy a moderate government, because the prince who is invested with the two first powers, leaves the third to his subjects. In Turkey, where these three powers are united in the Sultan's person, the subjects groan under the most dreadful oppression.

THE CRIME OF HIGH TREASON
IN REPUBLICS

As soon as a republic has compassed the destruction of those who wanted to subvert it, there should be an end of terrors, punishments, and even of rewards.

Great punishments, and consequently great changes, cannot take place without investing some citizens with an exorbitant power. It is, therefore, more advisable in this case to exceed in lenity, than in severity; to banish but few, rather than many; and to leave them their estates, instead of making a vast number of confiscations. Under pretence of avenging the republic's cause, the avengers would establish tyranny. The business is not to destroy the rebel but the rebellion. They ought to return as quick as possible into the usual track of government, in which every one is protected by the laws, and no one injured.

The Greeks set no bounds to the vengeance they took of tyrants, or of those they suspected of tyranny; they put their children to death, nay sometimes five of their nearest relations; and they proscribed an infinite number of families. By such means their republics suffered the most violent shocks: exiles, or the return of the exiled, were always epochs that indicated a change of the constitution.

The Romans had more sense. When Cassius was put to death for having aimed at tyranny, the question was proposed whether his children should undergo the same fate: but they were preserved. "They," says Dionysius Halicarnassus, "who wanted to change this law at the end of the Marsian and civil wars, and to exclude from public offices the children of those who had been proscribed by Sulla, are very much to blame."

RELIGION AND FORMS OF STATE

When a religion is introduced and fixed in a state, it is commonly such as is most suitable to the plan of government there established; for those who receive it, and those who are the cause of its being received, have scarcely any other idea of policy, than that of the state in which they were born.

When the Christian religion, two centuries ago, became unhappily divided into Catholic and Protestant, the people of the north embraced the Protestant, and those of the south adhered still to the Catholic.

The reason is plain: the people of the north have, and will for ever have, a spirit of liberty and independence, which the people of the south have not; and therefore, a religion which has no visible head, is more agreeable to the independency of the climate, than that which has one.

In the countries themselves, where the Protestant religion became established, the revolutions were made pursuant to the several plans of political government. Luther having great princes on his side, would never have been able to make them relish an ecclesiastical authority that had no exterior pre-eminence; while Calvin, having to do with people who lived under republican governments, or with obscure citizens in monarchies, might very well avoid establishing dignities and preferments.

Each of these two religions was believed to be the most perfect; the Calvinist judging his most conformable to what Christ had said, and the Lutheran to what the Apostles had practised.

RELIGIOUS TOLERATION

We are here politicians, and not divines; but the divines themselves must allow that there is a great difference between tolerating and approving a religion.

When the legislator has believed it a duty to permit the exercise of many religions, it is necessary that he should enforce also a toleration amongst these religions themselves. It is a principle that every religion which is persecuted, becomes itself persecuting: for as soon as by some accidental turn it arises from persecution, it attacks the religion which persecuted it; not as a religion, but as a tyranny.

It is necessary, then, that the laws require from the several religions, not only that they shall not embroil the state, but that they shall not raise disturbances amongst themselves. A citizen does not fulfil the laws by not disturbing the government; it is requisite that he should not trouble any citizen whomsoever.

CHAPTER TWENTY

HUME

The eighteenth century experienced one of the greatest bursts of nonscientific philosophical speculation since ancient Greece. George Berkeley, Kant, Rousseau, Adam Smith, and David Hume (1711–76) all were roughly contemporaries. Hume has the distinction of having known Smith and Rousseau and having influenced Kant.

Hume was a product of, and a major force within, the European Enlightenment, which particularly was strong in his native Scotland. The influence of Isaac Newton on the Enlightenment was fundamental. By making it possible through primary laws of tremendous potency theoretically to determine the properties and movement of every material particle in the universe, Newton not only instructed mankind in physics, but provided an example for others to attempt to follow in the field of human nature. Indeed, Newton himself stated, "If natural philosophy in all its parts by pursuing the inductive method, shall at length be perfected, the bounds of moral philosophy will also be enlarged." Further, by describing the actions of matter precisely, Newton helped finalize the split between natural philosophy (science) and speculative philosophy, because speculative philosophy gave up the hope of attempting to describe its realm as accurately as Newton described his.

The Scottish Enlightenment had great impact on England and around the world. Three future British prime ministers and Charles Darwin studied at Scottish universities during the eighteenth and early nineteenth centuries, under the likes of Francis Hutcheson, professor of moral philosophy at Glasgow University (whom Smith described as "never to be forgotten"), and Smith himself, who held the same position at Edinburgh University. James Mill—a Scot, the father of John Stuart Mill, and a significant utilitarian in his own right—attended lectures given by Dugald Stewart, a successor of Smith's at Edinburgh. The *Edinburgh Review* was a leading British liberal journal. Scotland united with England in 1707, though it previously shared the crown.

Hume's fame today rests mostly upon his philosophy. Indeed, in purely speculative philosophy, he often is considered the greatest thinker who originally has written in English. Hume pushes the philosophical premises of Locke and Berkeley to their logical conclusion, and in so doing undercuts the basis of what they were attempting to accomplish. Like Locke—to whom Hume looked as a master, though he did not always agree with him—Hume attempts to ground knowledge in experience. But where Locke sees experience as the basis for certainty, Hume sees it as the basis only for uncertainty.

Hume's essential epistemology (theory of knowledge) consists of what he terms "impressions" and "ideas." By impressions, he means primary sensory experience—what humans see, hear, touch, taste, and smell—together with certain emotions. By ideas, Hume means the mind's subsequent (and less forceful and lively) thinking and reasoning about these impressions. The next step in Hume's logical train is to postulate that in no way can one be sure that what he is experiencing is real. Experience could just be, as it were, a figment of one's imagination. Hume is particularly concerned with rebutting the notion of cause and effect as it traditionally is understood; for him, these are simply juxtaposition in time and/or place.

Hume's philosophy is scepticism. As he states in his earliest work, *A Treatise of Human Nature* (1739–40), "the understanding, when it acts alone . . . entirely subverts itself, and leaves not the lowest degree of evidence in any proposition." He notes that when one closes his eyes, one cannot even be certain that the room he was just in still exists. He defines the self as merely "nothing but a bundle or collection of different perceptions." What saves Hume from solipsism (the theory that the self is the only existent thing) is his scepticism itself. Though "we can never pretend to know body otherwise than by those external properties, which discover themselves to the senses . . . I content myself with knowing perfectly the manner in which objects affect my senses."

Hume's scepticism personally caused him problems. He was unable to obtain certain academic positions because his philosophy was considered incompatible with Christianity, and, at one point, the Church of Scotland attempted to excommunicate him. He did not have his *Dialogues Concerning Natural Religion* published during his lifetime for fear of the controversy it would engender.

In the history of political theory, Hume's primary significance stems from his role as a predecessor of Benthamite utilitarianism. Bentham first came across the term *utility* in Hume's section "Why Utility Pleases" from *An Enquiry Concerning the Principles of Morals* (1751). Further, Bentham wrote, "When I came out with the principle of utility . . . in the *[F]ragment [on Government]*, I took it from Hume's Essays," and that, particularly regarding the third book of the *Treatise,* "I felt as if the scales had fallen from my eyes," when originally reading it. In Bentham's "Article on Utilitarianism" (both the long and short versions), he gives the place of honor to Hume as the first in modern times to suggest utility as the cornerstone of a scientific theory of morals, though Bentham also considers that Hume did not work the utilitarian system fully out.

Hume is a sometimes careless—although usually clear—writer. He occasionally uses the same word to denote more than one meaning. Consequently, one must exercise caution in determining his system. There is, additionally, so much in his thought that it is possible to find systems other than proto-utilitarianism in it. Nevertheless, a careful reading of him reveals the extent to which later utilitarians followed him—a debt they were not always willing to acknowledge—due to his unpopularity, which arose in response to his scepticism.

Hume's philosophical beliefs underpin his moral ones, and this congruence between theory and practice holds true as well for other utilitarian writers. Hume's philosophy is radical subjectivism. All that certainly exists is each person's own impressions and the ideas founded upon these (to use Hume's terminology). The relationship between Hume's philosophy and moral system is that philosophical outlooks grounded in subjectivism are much more likely to result in individualist theories of ethics than those that perceive objective facts ineluctably existing in external nature. Plato, by this interpretation, is almost the antithesis of Hume: Plato ultimately sees only objective facts (the "forms"). Moreover, whereas Plato thus finds something moral existing in nature that should be replicated in the ideal city—justice—Hume and other utilitarians are inclined more modestly to place the good in what individuals themselves experience—happiness and unhappiness.

In the *Treatise,* Hume expresses the psychological portion of utilitarianism: "The chief spring or actuating principle of the human mind is pleasure or pain." Pleasure and pain mold the will to pursue certain actions and shun others. Hume is not, however, a believer only in psychological utilitarianism; he also subscribes to ethical utilitarianism. He identifies "Good and evil, or in other words, pain and pleasure." From the subjectivist viewpoint, again, there is little alternative but to ground moral good and evil in what individuals feel.

Quite similarly to J.S. Mill, Hume holds that there are different types of pleasures and pains: "Under the term *pleasure,* we comprehend sensations which are very different from each other." Again like Mill, he believes that individuals feel personal pleasure and pain in performing moral acts: "The distinguishing impressions, by which moral good or evil is known, are nothing but particular pains or pleasures." In this view, Hume is able to postulate a consistent psychological-ethical utilitarianism. Individuals are motivated by pleasure and pain; however, because they find pleasure and pain in the pleasures and pains of others, there is no necessary incongruence between individuals acting according to their own happiness and thereby promoting the happiness of others. Significantly, Hume does not consider that all of an individual's actions are strictly selfish or a convoluted form of self-love, as other philosophers have. Instead, he believes humans are quite directly able to experience social pleasures and pains.

At the same time, Hume recognizes the tendency to self-interest remains strong: "Nothing is more certain than that men are, in a great measure, governed by interest." Hume is unclear on the extent to which people find happiness in others' happiness, or simply are motivated by their own gain more narrowly construed. For example, he also holds that "sympathy is a very powerful principle in human nature" and "it is rare . . . to meet with one, in whom all the kind affections, taken together, do not overbalance all the selfish."

It is from self-interest and social feelings that society and justice emerge and are sustained. The original motivation to form the first society of any sort arises from "that natural appetite between the sexes." Sexual attraction creates a family-society between men and women which comes to fruition through their children. Gradually, groups of families learn that through a system of cooperation they all can have more than if they individually attempt to go it alone: This is the self-interest from which society emerges. Society is sustained, however, by mankind's social feelings. Although self-interest is the original motive to form a social order beyond the family-society, "a sympathy with public interest" is what keeps the second stage of society going. By nature, part of the character of men and women is that the sight of an individual exploiting the societal bond in a way that is disadvantageous to another displeases them—even when they are not directly affected. Thus, society is the product of a mix of self- and other-interested motives.

Hume's utilitarian sentiments are apparent in his justification of society: "Public utility is the *sole* origin of justice"; "the rules of equity or justice . . . owe their origin and existence to that utility, which results to the public from their strict and regular observance." Following Montesquieu, he believes justice in a society will vary depending on such factors as its religion and stage of economic development.

Similarly to Hobbes, Hume posits that justice is artificial—it is the result of human contrivance only. There is no justice by nature except to the extent that the natural development of human society invariably leads to certain rules. First among these rules is the importance of private property. Hume identifies three types of goods: "the internal satisfaction of our mind, the external advantages of our body, and the enjoyment of such possessions as we have acquired by our industry and good fortune." Of these, we are "perfectly secure" in our enjoyment of the first, and it is in no one's interest to take away the second. The third class of goods are, however, "exposed to the violence of others," both because they can be transferred without loss, and there are not enough material goods to meet everyone's desires.

Unlike other political theorists who consider the primary value to men and women of coming together in a community to be social interaction, Hume considers this advantage mostly to be material. We can economically produce more if we cooperate—this is the fundamental justification of society, not human beings' social nature (after the initial family-society stage). Consequently, society must, above all else, protect and promote private property: "As the improvement, therefore, of these goods is the chief advantage of society, so the *instability* of their possession, along with their *scarcity,* is the chief impediment." Although humanity has significant social feelings, self-interest remains strong and should be guarded against. Society provides the reinforcement mechanisms that make people's social feelings also their self-interest.

The need for justice is based on four circumstances: selfishness, limited generosity, scarcity, and the ability to exchange material objects. In circumstances of unlimited material objects, or universal, strong benevolence, justice would be unnecessary. As neither of these conditions holds, however, justice is among the most important of virtues and esteemed as such. Hume takes it as axiomatic that individuals will produce more when they have the exclusive right to what they produce, and this is his reason for private property; in addition, when ownership is unclear, continual societal discord results.

Society arises not through an explicit contract (Hume considers the state of nature to be "a mere philosophical fiction"); rather, in a conception similar to Hayek's, it gradually evolves from what is successful in social organization. Society is founded on private possession, from which spring the notions of justice and injustice, right and obligation, and property. Hume speculates that society beyond the family stage possibly developed following a war between groups of families when a group became accustomed to following one leader and perceived benefits to remaining in a larger society even after the war was over. The relationship between justice and political society is that justice is the set of rules which political society enforces.

Hume is adamant that justice is based on property. In reasoning that influenced James Madison (*The Federalist,* No. 51, "Ambition must be made to check ambition"), Hume holds, "There is no passion . . . capable of controlling the interested affection ['of acquiring goods and possessions'], but the very affection itself, by an alteration of its direction." Individuals' acquisitive desires establish society and justice; society and justice are then maintained by the self-interest each has in having society succeed, together with social inclinations. Like Rawls, Hume notes that humans' sense of justice (artificial though it may be in the latter's conception) gains from the observation that it leads to great good for others: "This sense must certainly acquire new force, when reflecting on itself, it approves of those principles, from whence it is derived, and finds nothing but what is great and good in its rise and origin."

Hume says in his brief autobiography that he composed the *Treatise of Human Nature* before he was 25. It is generally—particularly its first part—considered his greatest work, though he also states in his autobiography that "it fell dead-born from the press" without arousing "a murmur among the zealots." Hume exaggerates in this statement. Particularly for a first work published anonymously, the *Treatise* received a considerable amount of attention. Generally, readers dissented from it as the result of its scepticism.

The *Enquiry Concerning the Principles of Morals* and the *Enquiry Concerning the Human Understanding* (1748), correspond to the first and third parts of the *Treatise;*

Hume rewrote these parts of the *Treatise* to broaden their appeal. "Love of literary fame," as he himself says, was his "ruling passion." While Hume considered the *Enquiry Concerning the Principles of Morals,* "of all my writings . . . . incomparably the best," and stated that any discrepancies between the *Treatise* and the *Enquiries* should be resolved in favor of the latter, posterity has judged otherwise. Fortunately, the differences between the *Treatise* and the *Enquiries* are not significant.

Hume states in the *Treatise:* "Morality is a subject that interests us above all others." While he is interested in postulating a philosophical system, he mostly wants it as a foundation for his moral system. In the *Enquiries,* he explicitly uses the word "utility" to describe his ethical goal more than he does in the *Treatise.* Unlike later utilitarians, however, he does not always identify utility with happiness; his most common synonym for "utility" is "useful." He does, though, often define the useful in terms of what produces happiness. There is, thus, little functional difference between him and later utilitarians here. The extent to which Hume popularized the term "utility," and his general influence, is indicated by Bentham, when, referring to his own first use of the term, he says, "Hume was in all his glory. The phrase [utility] was consequently familiar to everybody."

The *Treatise* contains what perhaps is Hume's most famous phrase: "Reason is, and ought only to be the slave of the passions, and can never pretend to any other office than to serve and obey them." By this, he means that, as in his system, good and bad come down to subjective feelings, it is these subjective feelings that must rule humankind. While Hume does not use this example, consider even the extreme case of murder. How does one know this is wrong? Granting Hume's supposition—that right and wrong do not objectively exist in nature—murder is wrong only because human beings feel it is wrong. Many reasons can be advanced for its wrongness (the harm it does to the victim, to his associates, to society, and so forth), but all of these reasons ultimately also dissolve into feelings. Reason, then, does not—because it cannot—rule our moral actions. Instead, these are determined by our passions. Hume's use of "passions" is broad, to designate almost all of a person's internal feelings.

This conception of reason's place is completely different than that of ancient political philosophers, who saw in reason the purpose of human existence, at least the purpose of those men and women who were able to experience it. Hume's conception of reason's place is also different than some of his philosophical successors, such as Kant, who again see in reason the determinant of humans' passions, not their slave. Hume posits a rigid distinction between facts and values: Values remain subjective, while facts (to the extent they exist in his philosophical system) are strictly limited to empirical experience.

Having exiled reason, Hume recalls it. The place of reason in morals is: "Judgments may often be false and erroneous. A person may be affected with passion, by supposing a pain or pleasure to lie in an object, which has no tendency to produce either of these sensations, or which produces the contrary to what is imagined." Reason, in this case, truly is only the servant of the passions, but a very important one. It informs human beings of how most effectively to produce pleasure and limit pain. Importantly, government serves a similar sort of regulative function in Hume's conception of society. Government and justice arise in considerable part from humanity's inclination to reason improperly. Hume takes it for granted that individuals will often prefer a lesser near good to a greater good farther away, and thus government and justice compensate for short-sightedness as well as for self-interest.

Hume considers the fundamental laws of society to be stability of property, its transfer by consent, and the performance of promises. Even the third of these ultimately dissolves into property of a certain type; if a promise does not concern property explicitly, then at least often it is connected to some sort of remuneration for an individual's time. Like Locke, Hume holds that a person's time is his or her own. Taking a person's time, through breaking a promise, is taking something belonging to that person. As noted earlier, society's three fundamental laws are not actually restraints on people's passions; rather, "they are the real offspring of those passions, and are only a more artful and more refined way of satisfying them." Hume also recognizes government as an instrument for individuals to engage in certain common actions that otherwise would be almost impossible to perform, such as constructing public works and forming armies.

Hume was the first British man of letters to become wealthy through the sale of his works. After the failure, from his perspective, of the *Treatise,* he wrote the *Essays Moral, Political, and Literary* (1742, 1752), which were intended for a wider audience, and which did achieve greater popular success. The *Essays* were revised several times in Hume's life, and though some were described even by Hume as "frivolous," others are important.

In several essays, Hume takes up economic topics, and in doing so anticipates Smith, whose *The Wealth of Nations* was published a few months before Hume's death. Hume wrote to Smith regarding an advance copy of *The Wealth of Nations,* "I am much pleased with your performance." Hume was completely in favor of free trade and subscribed to monetarist theory. In the essay "Of Money," he states: "It seems a maxim almost self-evident, that the prices of everything depend on the proportion between commodities and money." It is a tribute to Hume's perspicacity that Friedman could comment two centuries later on "Of Money" that it can still be read "with pleasure and profit." In another economic essay, "Of Commerce," Hume writes: "The greatness of a state, and the happiness of its subjects . . . are commonly allowed to be inseparable with regard to commerce . . . the public becomes powerful in proportion to the opulence and extensive commerce of private men."

Hume effectively demolished the myth of an original contract in his essay of this name. He demonstrated that, heretofore, societies had almost never been founded on the basis of consent, and that it was chimerical to claim so. This thought helped pave the way for utilitarian theories of society that see the ties of social union in what is to men and women's interest, and not in divine or natural law. In the essay "Of the Origin of Government," he says that government has "no other object or purpose" than to support justice.

An attitude of scepticism permeates Hume's writings on all topics, and not merely those in philosophy. Somewhat paradoxically, Hume was politically conservative—a Tory, not a Whig. Though an individualist in his philosophy and morals, he questions the ability of men to govern themselves. In his essay "Idea of a Perfect Commonwealth," however, he favored a largely representative form of government. His massive *History of England,* though, which was the major project of his lifetime, was considered a Tory document. Thomas Jefferson thought that the *History* helped to undermine the principles of free government in Britain, and spread "universal toryism over the land."

Politically conservative but philosophically liberal, a sceptic, and a Scot, Hume was never able to attract a personal following in England or anywhere else. His influence has been the result not of popularity, but the force of his mind.

HUME

Essays Moral, Political and Literary and *An Enquiry Concerning The Principles of Morals**

OF THE ORIGIN OF GOVERNMENT[†]

Man, born in a family, is compelled to maintain society, from necessity, from natural inclination, and from habit. The same creature, in his farther progress, is engaged to establish political society, in order to administer justice; without which there can be no peace among them, nor safety, nor mutual intercourse. We are, therefore, to look upon all the vast apparatus of our government, as having ultimately no other object or purpose but the distribution of justice, or, in other words, the support of the twelve judges.[1] Kings and parliaments, fleets and armies, officers of the court and revenue, ambassadors, ministers, and privy-counsellors, are all subordinate in their end to this part of administration. Even the clergy, as their duty leads them to inculcate morality, may justly be thought, so far as regards this world, to have no other useful object of their institution.

All men are sensible of the necessity of justice to maintain peace and order; and all men are sensible of the necessity of peace and order for the maintenance of society. Yet, notwithstanding this strong and obvious necessity, such is the frailty or perverseness of our nature! It is impossible to keep men, faithfully and unerringly, in the paths of jus-

tice. Some extraordinary circumstances may happen, in which a man finds his interests to be more promoted by fraud or rapine, than hurt by the breach which his injustice makes in the social union. But much more frequently, he is seduced from his great and important, but distant interests, by the allurement of present, though often very frivolous temptations. This great weakness is incurable in human nature.

Men must, therefore, endeavor to palliate what they cannot cure. They must institute some persons, under the appellation of magistrates, whose peculiar office it is, to point out the decrees of equity, to punish transgressors, to correct fraud and violence, and to oblige men, however reluctant, to consult their own real and permanent interests. In a word, OBEDIENCE is a new duty which must be invented to support that of JUSTICE; and the ties of equity must be corroborated by those of allegiance.

But still, viewing matters in an abstract light, it may be thought, that nothing is gained by this alliance, and that the factitious duty of obedience, from its very nature, lays as feeble a hold of the human mind, as the primitive and natural duty of justice. Peculiar interests and present temptations may overcome the one as well as the other. They are equally exposed to the same inconvenience. And the man, who is inclined to be a bad neighbor, must be led by the same motives, well or ill understood, to be a bad citizen and subject. Not to mention, that the magistrate himself may often be negligent, or partial, or unjust in his administration.

---

* Some spellings and punctuations have been modernized.

[†] From David Hume, *Essays Moral, Political, and Literary* (1758).

[1] i.e., of Israel, who dispensed justice.

Experience, however, proves, that there is a great difference between the cases. Order in society, we find, is much better maintained by means of government; and our duty to the magistrate is more strictly guarded by the principles of human nature, than our duty to our fellow-citizens. The love of dominion is so strong in the breast of man, that many, not only submit to, but court all the dangers, and fatigues, and cares of government; and men, once raised to that station, though often led astray by private passions, find, in ordinary cases, a visible interest in the impartial administration of justice. The persons, who first attain this distinction by the consent, tacit or express, of the people, must be endowed with superior personal qualities of valor, force, integrity, or prudence, which command respect and confidence: and after government is established, a regard to birth, rank, and station has a mighty influence over men, and enforces the decrees of the magistrate. The prince or leader exclaims against every disorder, which disturbs his society. He summons all his partisans and all men of probity to aid him in correcting and redressing it: and he is readily followed by all indifferent persons in the execution of his office. He soon acquires the power of rewarding these services; and in the progress of society, he establishes subordinate ministers and often a military force, who find an immediate and a visible interest, in supporting his authority. Habit soon consolidates what other principles of human nature had imperfectly founded; and men, once accustomed to obedience, never think of departing from that path, in which they and their ancestors have constantly trod, and to which they are confined by so many urgent and visible motives.

But though this progress of human affairs may appear certain and inevitable, and though the support which allegiance brings to justice, be founded on obvious principles of human nature, it cannot be expected that men should beforehand be able to discover them, or foresee their operation. Government commences more casually and more imperfectly. It is probable, that the first ascendant of one man over multitudes began during a state of war; where the superiority of courage and of genius discovers itself most visibly, where unanimity and concert are most requisite, and where the pernicious effects of disorder are most sensibly felt. The long continuance of that state, an incident common among savage tribes, inured the people to submission; and if the chieftain possessed as much equity as prudence and valor, he became, even during peace, the arbiter of all differences, and could gradually, by a mixture of force and consent, establish his authority. The benefit sensibly felt from his influence, made it be cherished by the people, at least by the peaceable and well disposed among them; and if his son enjoyed the same good qualities, government advanced the sooner to maturity and perfection; but was still in a feeble state, till the farther progress of improvement procured the magistrate a revenue, and enabled him to bestow rewards on the several instruments of his administration, and to inflict punishments on the refractory and disobedient. Before that period, each exertion of his influence must have been particular, and founded on the peculiar circumstances of the case. After it, submission was no longer a matter of choice in the bulk of the community, but was rigorously exacted by the authority of the supreme magistrate.

In all governments, there is a perpetual intestine struggle, open or secret, between AUTHORITY and LIBERTY; and neither of them can ever absolutely prevail in the contest. A great sacrifice of liberty must necessarily be made in every government; yet even the authority, which confines liberty, can never, and perhaps ought never, in any constitution, to become quite entire and uncontrollable. The sultan is master of the life and fortune of any individual; but will not be permitted to impose new taxes on his subjects: a French monarch can impose taxes at pleasure; but would find it dangerous to attempt the lives and fortunes of individuals. Religion also, in most countries, is commonly found to be a very intractable principle; and other principles or prejudices frequently resist all the authority of the civil magistrate; whose power, being founded on opinion, can never subvert other opinions, equally rooted with that of his title to dominion. The government, which, in common appellation, receives the appellation of free, is that which admits of a partition of power among several members, whose united authority is no less, or is commonly greater than that of any monarch; but who, in the usual course of administration, must act by general and equal laws, that are previously known to all the members and to all their subjects. In this sense, it must be owned, that liberty is the perfection of civil society; but still authority must be acknowledged essential to its very existence: and in those contests, which so often take place between the one and the other, the latter may, on that account, challenge the preference. Unless perhaps one may say (and it may be said with some reason) that a circumstance, which is essential to the existence of civil society, must always support itself, and needs be guarded with less jealousy, than one that contributes only to its perfection, which the indolence of men is so apt to neglect, or their ignorance to overlook.

OF THE ORIGINAL CONTRACT*

As no party, in the present age, can well support itself, without a philosophical or speculative system of principles, annexed to its political or practical one; we accordingly find, that each of the factions, into which this nation is divided, has reared up a fabric of the former kind, in order to protect and cover that scheme of actions, which it pursues. The people being commonly very rude builders, especially in this speculative way, and more especially still, when actuated by party-zeal; it is natural to imagine, that their workmanship must be a little unshapely, and discover evident marks of that violence and hurry, in which it was raised. The one party, by tracing up government to the DEITY, endeavor to render it so sacred and inviolate, that it must be little less than sacrilege, however tyrannical it may become, to touch or invade it, in the smallest article. The other party, by founding government altogether on the consent of the PEOPLE, suppose that there is a kind of *original contract,* by which the subjects have tacitly reserved the power of resisting their sovereign, whenever they find themselves aggrieved by that authority, with which they have, for certain purposes, voluntarily entrusted him. These are the speculative principles of the two parties; and these too are the practical consequences deduced from them.

I shall venture to affirm, *That both these* systems of *speculative principles are just; though not in the sense, intended by the parties:* And, *That both the* schemes *of practical consequences are prudent; though not in the extremes, to which each party, in opposition to the other, has commonly endeavoured to carry them.*

That the DIETY is the ultimate author of all government, will never be denied by any, who admit a general providence, and allow, that all events in the universe are conducted by an uniform plan, and directed to wise purposes. As it is impossible for the human race to subsist, at least in any comfortable or secure state, without the protection of government; this institution must certainly have been intended by that beneficent Being, who means the good of all his creatures. And as it has universally, in fact, taken place, in all countries, and all ages; we may conclude, with still greater certainty, that it was intended by that omniscient Being, who can never be deceived by any event or operation. But since he gave rise to it, not by any particular or miraculous interposition, but by his concealed and universal efficacy; a sovereign cannot, properly speaking, be called his vice-regent, in any other sense than every power or force, being derived from him, may be said to act by his commission. Whatever actually happens is comprehended in the general plan or intention of providence; nor has the greatest and most lawful prince any more reason, upon that account, to plead a peculiar sacredness or inviolable authority, than an inferior magistrate, or even an usurper, or even a robber and a pirate. The same divine superintendent, who, for wise purposes, invested a TITUS or a TRAJAN with authority, did also, for purposes, no doubt, equally wise, though unknown, bestow power on a BORGIA or an ANGRIA. The same causes, which gave rise to the sovereign power in every state, established likewise every petty jurisdiction in it, and every limited authority. A constable, therefore, no less than a king, acts by a divine commission, and possesses an indefeasible right.

When we consider how nearly equal all men are in their bodily force, and even in their mental powers and faculties, till

---

*From David Hume, *Essays Moral, Political, and Literary* (1758).

cultivated by education; we must necessarily allow, that nothing but their own consent could, at first, associate them together, and subject them to any authority. The people, if we trace government to its first origin in the woods and deserts, are the source of all power and jurisdiction, and voluntarily, for the sake of peace and order, abandoned their native liberty, and received laws from their equal and companion. The conditions, upon which they were willing to submit, were either expressed, or were so clear and obvious, that it might well be esteemed superfluous to express them. If this, then, be meant by the *original contract,* it cannot be denied, that all government is, at first, founded on a contract, and that the most ancient rude combinations of mankind were formed chiefly by that principle. In vain, are we asked in what records this charter of our liberties is registered. It was not written on parchment, nor yet on leaves or barks of trees. It preceded the use of writing and all the other civilized arts of life. But we trace it plainly in the nature of man, and in the equality, or something approaching equality, which we find in all the individuals of that species. The force, which now prevails, and which is founded on fleets and armies, is plainly political, and derived from authority, the effect of established government. A man's natural force consists only in the vigor of his limbs, and the firmness of his courage; which could never subject multitudes to the command of one. Nothing but their own consent, and their sense of the advantages resulting from peace and order, could have had that influence.

Yet even this consent was long very imperfect, and could not be the basis of a regular administration. The chieftain, who had probably acquired his influence during the continuance of war, ruled more by persuasion than command; and till he could employ force to reduce the refractory and disobedient, the society could scarcely be said to have attained a state of civil government. No compact or agreement, it is evident, was expressly formed for general submission; an idea far beyond the comprehension of savages. Each exertion of authority in the chieftain must have been particular, and called forth by the present exigencies of the case. The sensible utility, resulting from his interposition, made these exertions become daily more frequent; and their frequency gradually produced an habitual, and, if you please to call it so, a voluntary, and therefore precarious, acquiescence in the people.

But philosophers, who have embraced a party (if that be not a contradiction in terms) are not contented with these concessions. They assert, not only that government in its earliest infancy arose from consent or rather the voluntary acquiescence of the people; but also, that, even at present, when it has attained full maturity, it rests on no other foundation. They affirm, that all men are still born equal, and owe allegiance to no prince or government, unless bound by the obligation and sanction of a *promise.* And as no man, without some equivalent, would forego the advantages of his native liberty, and subject himself to the will of another, this promise is always understood to be conditional, and imposes on him no obligation, unless he meet with justice and protection from his sovereign. These advantages the sovereign promises him in return; and if he fail in the execution, he has broken, on his part, the articles of engagement, and has thereby freed his subject from all obligations to allegiance. Such, according to these philosophers, is the foundation of authority in every government; and such the right of resistance, possessed by every subject.

But would these reasoners look abroad into the world, they would meet with nothing that, in the least, corresponds to their ideas, or can warrant so refined and philosophical a system. On the contrary, we find, everywhere, princes, who claim their subjects as their property, and assert their independent right of sovereignty, from conquest or succession. We find also, everywhere, subjects, who acknowledge this right in their prince, and suppose themselves born under obligations of obedience to a certain sovereign, as much as under the ties of reverence and duty to certain parents. These connections are always conceived to be equally independent of our consent, in Persia and China; in France and Spain; and even in Holland and England, wherever the doctrines abovementioned have not been carefully inculcated. Obedience or subjection becomes so familiar, that most men never make any inquiry about its origin or cause, more than about the principle of gravity, resistance, or the most universal laws of nature. Or if curiosity ever move them; as soon as they learn, that they themselves and their ancestors have, for several ages, or from time immemorial, been subject to such a form of government or such a family; they immediately acquiesce, and acknowledge their obligation to allegiance. Were you to preach, in most parts of the world, that political connections are founded altogether on voluntary consent or a mutual promise, the magistrate would soon imprison you, as seditious, for loosening the ties of obedience; if your friends did not before shut you up as delirious, for advancing such absurdities. It is strange, that an act of the mind, which every individual is supposed to have formed, and after he came to the use of reason too, otherwise it could have no authority; that this act, I say, should be so much unknown to all of them, that, over the face of the whole earth, there scarcely remain any traces or memory of it.

But the contract, on which government is founded, is said to be the *original contract;* and consequently may be supposed too old to fall under the knowledge of the present generation. If the agreement, by which savage men first associated and conjoined their force, be here meant, this is acknowledged to be real; but being so ancient, and being obliterated by a thousand changes of government and princes, it cannot now be supposed to retain any authority. If we would say anything to the purpose, we must assert, that every particular government, which is lawful, and which imposes any duty of allegiance on the subject, was, at first, founded on consent and a voluntary compact. But besides that this supposes the consent of the fathers to bind the children, even to the most remote generations (which republican writers will never allow), besides this, I say, it is not justified by history or experience, in any age or country of the world.

Almost all the governments, which exist at present, or of which there remains any record in story, have been founded originally, either on usurpation or conquest, or both, without any pretense of a fair consent, or voluntary subjection of the people. When an artful and bold man is placed at the head of an army or faction, it is often easy for him, by employing, sometimes violence, sometimes false pretenses, to establish his dominion over a people a hundred times more numerous than his partisans. He allows no such open communication, that his enemies can know, with certainty, their number or force. He gives them no leisure to assemble together in a body to oppose him. Even all those, who are the instruments of his usurpation, may wish his fall; but their ignorance of each other's intention keeps them in awe, and is the sole cause of his security. By such arts as these, many governments have been established; and this is all the *original contract,* which they have to boast of.

The face of the earth is continually changing, by the increase of small kingdoms into great empires, by the dissolution of great empires into smaller kingdoms, by the planting of colonies, by the migration of tribes. Is there anything discoverable in all these events, but force and violence? Where is the mutual agreement or voluntary association so much talked of?

Even the smoothest way, by which a nation may receive a foreign master, by marriage or a will, is not extremely honorable for the people; but supposes them to be disposed of, like a dowry or a legacy, according to the pleasure or interest of their rulers.

But where no force interposes, and election takes place; what is this election so highly vaunted? It is either the combination of a few great men, who decide for the whole, and will allow of no opposition, or it is the fury of a multitude, that follow a seditious ringleader, who is not known, perhaps, to a dozen among them, and who owes his advancement merely to his own impudence, or to the momentary caprice of his fellows.

Are these disorderly elections, which are rare too, of such mighty authority, as to be the only lawful foundation of all government and allegiance?

In reality, there is not a more terrible event, than a total dissolution of government, which gives liberty to the multitude, and makes the determination or choice of a new establishment depend upon a number, which nearly approaches to that of the body of the people. For it never comes entirely to the whole body of them. Every wise man, then, wishes to see, at the head of a powerful and obedient army, a general, who may speedily seize the prize, and give to the people a master, which they are so unfit to choose for themselves. So little correspondent is fact and reality to those philosophical notions.

Let not the establishment at the *Revolution* deceive us, or make us so much in love with a philosophical origin to government, as to imagine all others monstrous and irregular. Even that event was far from corresponding to these refined ideas. It was only the succession, and that only in the regal part of the government, which was then changed. And it was only the majority of seven hundred, who determined that change for near ten millions.[2] I doubt not, indeed, but the bulk of those ten millions acquiesced willingly in the determination: But was the matter left, in the least, to their choice? Was it not justly supposed to be, from that moment, decided, and every man punished, who refused to submit to the new sovereign? How otherwise could the matter have ever been brought to any issue or conclusion?

The republic of ATHENS was, I believe, the most extensive democracy, that we read of in history. Yet if we make the requisite allowances for the women, the slaves, and the strangers, we shall find, that that establishment was not, at first, made, nor any law ever voted, by a tenth part of those who were bound to pay obedience to it. Not to mention the islands and foreign dominions, which the ATHENIANS claimed as theirs by right of conquest. And as it is well known, that popular assemblies in that city were always full of license and disorder, notwithstanding the institutions and laws by which they were checked. How much more disorderly must they prove, where they form not the established constitution, but meet tumultuously on the dissolution of the ancient government, in order to give rise to a new one? How chimerical must it be to talk of a choice in such circumstances?

The ACHAEANS enjoyed the freest and most perfect democracy of all antiquity; yet they employed force to oblige some cities to enter into their league, as we learn from POLYBIUS.

HARRY the IVth and HARRY the VIIth of ENGLAND, had really no title to the throne but a parliamentary election; yet they never

would acknowledge it, lest they should thereby weaken their authority. Strange, if the only real foundation of all authority be consent and promise!

It is in vain to say, that all governments are or should be, at first, founded on popular consent, as much as the necessity of human affairs will admit. This favors entirely my pretension. I maintain, that human affairs will never admit of this consent; seldom of the appearance of it. But that conquest or usurpation, that is, in plain terms, force, by dissolving the ancient governments, is the origin of almost all the new ones, which were ever established in the world. And that in the few cases, where consent may seem to have taken place, it was commonly so irregular, so confined, or so much intermixed either with fraud or violence, that it cannot have any great authority.

My intention here is not to exclude the consent of the people from being one just foundation of government where it has place. It is surely the best and most sacred of any. I only pretend, that it has very seldom had place in any degree, and never almost in its full extent. And that therefore some other foundation of government must also be admitted.

Were all men possessed of so inflexible a regard to justice, that, of themselves, they would totally abstain from the properties of others; they had forever remained in a state of absolute liberty, without subjection to any magistrate or political society. But this is a state of perfection, of which human nature is justly deemed incapable. Again, were all men possessed of so perfect an understanding, as always to know their own interests, no form of government had ever been submitted to, but what was established on consent, and was fully canvassed by every member of the society. But this state of perfection is likewise much superior to human nature. Reason, history, and experience show us, that all political societies have had an origin much less accurate and regular; and were one to choose a period of time, when the people's consent was the least regarded in public transactions, it would be precisely on the establishment of a new government. In a settled constitution, their inclinations are often consulted; but during the fury of revolutions, conquests, and public convulsions,

---

[2] in England, following the Glorious Revolution.

military force or political craft usually decides the controversy.

When a new government is established, by whatever means, the people are commonly dissatisfied with it, and pay obedience more from fear and necessity, than from any idea of allegiance or of moral obligation. The prince is watchful and jealous, and must carefully guard against every beginning or appearance of insurrection. Time, by degrees, removes all these difficulties, and accustoms the nation to regard, as their lawful or native princes, that family, which, at first, they considered as usurpers or foreign conquerors. In order to found this opinion, they have no recourse to any notion of voluntary consent or promise, which, they know, never was, in this case, either expected or demanded. The original establishment was formed by violence, and submitted to from necessity. The subsequent administration is also supported by power, and acquiesced in by the people not as a matter of choice, but of obligation. They imagine not that their consent gives their prince a title. But they willingly consent, because they think, that, from long possession, he has acquired a title, independent of their choice or inclination.

Should it be said, that, by living under the dominion of a prince, which one might leave, every individual has given a *tacit* consent to his authority, and promised him obedience; it may be answered, that such an implied consent can only have place, where a man imagines, that the matter depends on his choice. But where he thinks (as all mankind do who are born under established governments) that by his birth he owes allegiance to a certain prince or certain form of government; it would be absurd to infer a consent or choice, which he expressly, in this case, renounces and disclaims.

Can we seriously say, that a poor peasant or artisan has a free choice to leave his country, when he knows no foreign language or manners, and lives from day to day, by the small wages which he acquires? We may as well assert, that a man, by remaining in a vessel, freely consents to the dominion of the master; though he was carried on board while asleep, and must leap into the ocean, and perish, the moment he leaves her.

What if the prince forbid his subjects to quit his dominions; as in TIBERIUS's time, it was regarded as a crime in a ROMAN knight that he had attempted to fly to the PARTHIANS, in order to escape the tyranny of that emperor? Or as the ancient MUSCOVITES prohibited all travelling under pain of death? And did a prince observe, that many of his subjects were seized with the frenzy of migrating to foreign countries, he would doubtless, with great reason and justice, restrain them, in order to prevent the depopulation of his own kingdom. Would he forfeit the allegiance of all his subjects, by so wise and reasonable a law? Yet the freedom of their choice is surely, in that case, ravished from them.

A company of men, who should leave their native country, in order to people some uninhabited region, might dream of recovering their native freedom; but they would soon find, that their prince still laid claim to them, and called them his subjects, even in their new settlement. And in this he would but act conformably to the common ideas of mankind.

The truest *tacit* consent of this kind, that is ever observed, is when a foreigner settles in any country, and is beforehand acquainted with the prince, and government, and laws, to which he must submit. Yet is his allegiance, though more voluntary, much less expected or depended on, than that of a natural born subject? On the contrary, his native prince still asserts a claim to him. And if he punish not the renegade, when he seizes him in war with his new prince's commission; this clemency is not founded on the municipal law, which in all countries condemns the prisoner; but on the consent of princes, who have agreed to this indulgence, in order to prevent reprisals.

Did one generation of men go off the stage at once, and another succeed, as is the case with silk-worms and butterflies, the new race, if they had sense enough to choose their government, which surely is never the case with men, might voluntarily, and by general consent, establish their own form of civil polity, without any regard to the laws or precedents, which prevailed among their ancestors. But as human society is in perpetual flux, one man every hour going out of the world, another coming into it, it is necessary, in order to preserve stability in government, that the new brood should conform themselves to the established constitution, and nearly follow the path which their fathers, treading in the footsteps of theirs, had marked out to them. Some innovations must necessarily have place in every human institution, and it is happy where the enlightened genius of the age give these a direction to the side of reason, liberty, and justice: but violent innovations no individual is entitled to make: they are even dangerous to be attempted by the legislature: more ill than good is ever to be expected from them: and if history affords examples to the contrary, they are not to be drawn into precedent, and are only to be regarded as proofs, that the science of politics affords few rules, which will not admit of some exception, and which may not sometimes be controlled by fortune and accident. The violent innovations in the reign of HENRY VIII proceeded from an imperious monarch, seconded by the appearance of legislative authority. Those in the reign of CHARLES I were derived from faction and fanaticism; and both of them have proved happy in the issue. But even the former were long the source of many disorders, and still more dangers; and if the measures of allegiance were to be taken from the latter, a total anarchy must have place in human society, and a final period at once be put to every government.

Suppose, that a usurper, after having banished his lawful prince and royal family, should establish his dominion for ten or a dozen years in any country, and should preserve so exact a discipline in his troops, and so regular a disposition in his garrisons, that no insurrection had ever been raised, or even murmur heard, against his administration. Can it be asserted, that the people, who in their hearts abhor his treason, have tacitly consented to his authority, and promised him allegiance, merely because, from necessity, they live under his dominion? Suppose again their native prince restored, by means of an army, which he levies in foreign countries. They receive him with joy and exultation, and show plainly with what reluctance they had submitted to any other yoke. I may now ask, upon what foundation the prince's title stands? Not on popular consent surely. For though the people willingly acquiesce in his authority, they never imagine, that their consent made him sovereign. They consent; because they apprehend him to be already, by birth, their lawful sovereign. And as to that tacit consent, which may now be inferred from their living under his dominion, this is no more than what they formerly gave to the tyrant and usurper.

When we assert, that all lawful government arises from the consent of the people, we certainly do them a great deal more honor than they deserve, or even expect and desire from us. After the ROMAN dominions became too unwieldy for the republic to govern them, the people, over the whole known world, were extremely grateful to AUGUSTUS for that authority, which, by violence, he had established over them; and they showed an equal disposition to submit to the successor, whom he left them, by his last will and testament. It was afterwards their misfortune, that there never was, in one family, any long regular succession; but that their line of princes was continually broken, either by private assassinations or public rebellions. The *praetorian* bands, on the failure of every family, set up one emperor; the legions in the East a second; those in GERMANY, perhaps, a third: And the sword alone could decide the controversy. The condition of the people, in that mighty monarchy, was to be lamented, not because the choice of the emperor was never left to them; for that was impracticable: But because they never fell under any succession of masters, who might regularly follow each other. As to the violence and wars and bloodshed, occasioned by every new settlement; these were not blameable, because they were inevitable.

The house of LANCASTER ruled in this island about sixty years; yet the partisans of the white rose seemed daily to multiply in ENGLAND. The present establishment has taken place during a still longer period. Have all views of right in another family been utterly extinguished; even though scarce any man now alive had arrived at years of discretion, when it was expelled, or could have consented to its dominion, or have promised it allegiance? A sufficient indication surely of the general sentiment of mankind on this head. For we blame not the partisans of the abdicated family, merely on account of the long time, during which they have preserved their imaginary loyalty. We blame them for adhering to a family, which, we affirm, has been justly expelled, and which, from the moment the new settlement took place, had forfeited all title to authority.

But would we have a more regular, at least a more philosophical, refutation of this principle of an original contract or popular consent; perhaps, the following observations may suffice.

All *moral* duties may be divided into two kinds. The *first* are those, to which men are impelled by a natural instinct or immediate propensity, which operates on them, independent of all ideas of obligation, and of all views, either to public or private utility. Of this nature are, love of children, gratitude to benefactors, pity to the unfortunate, When we reflect on the advantage, which results to society from such humane instincts, we pay them the just tribute of moral approbation and esteem: But the person, actuated by them, feels their power and influence, antecedent to any such reflection.

The *second* kind of moral duties are such as are not supported by any original instinct of nature, but are performed entirely from a sense of obligation, when we consider the necessities of human society, and the impossibility of supporting it, if these duties were neglected. It is thus *justice* or a regard to the property of others, *fidelity* or the observance of promises, become obligatory, and acquire an authority over mankind. For as it is evident, that every man loves himself better than any other person, he is naturally impelled to extend his acquisitions as much as possible; and nothing can restrain him in this propensity, but reflection and experience, by which he learns the pernicious effects of that license, and the total dissolution of society which must ensue from it. His original inclination, therefore, or instinct, is here checked and restrained by a subsequent judgment or observation.

The case is precisely the same with the political or civil duty of *allegiance,* as with the natural duties of justice and fidelity. Our primary instincts lead us either to indulge ourselves in unlimited freedom, or to seek dominion over others. And it is reflection only, which engages us to sacrifice such strong passions to the interests of peace and public order. A small degree of experience and observation suffices to teach us that society cannot possibly be maintained without the authority of magistrates, and that this

authority must soon fall into contempt, where exact obedience is not payed to it. The observation of these general and obvious interests is the source of all allegiance, and of that moral obligation, which we attribute to it.

What necessity, therefore, is there to found the duty of *allegiance* or obedience to magistrates on that of *fidelity* or a regard to promises, and to suppose, that it is the consent of each individual, which subjects him to government; when it appears, that both allegiance and fidelity stand precisely on the same foundation, and are both submitted to by mankind, on account of the apparent interests and necessities of human society? We are bound to obey our sovereign, it is said; because we have given a tacit promise to that purpose. But why are we bound to observe our promise? It must here be asserted, that the commerce and intercourse of mankind, which are of such mighty advantage, can have no security where men pay no regard to their engagements. In like manner, may it be said, that men could not live at all in society, at least in a civilized society, without laws and magistrates and judges, to prevent the encroachments of the strong upon the weak, of the violent upon the just and equitable. The obligation to allegiance being of like force and authority with the obligation to fidelity, we gain nothing by resolving the one into the other. The general interests or necessities of society are sufficient to establish both.

If the reason be asked of that obedience, which we are bound to pay to government, I readily answer, *because society could not otherwise subsist:* And this answer is clear and intelligible to all mankind. Your answer is, *because we should keep our word.* But besides, that no body, till trained in a philosophical system, can either comprehend or relish this answer: Besides this, I say, you find yourself embarrassed, when it is asked, *why we are bound to keep our word?* Nor can you give any answer, but what would, immediately, without any circuit, have accounted for our obligation to allegiance.

But *to whom is allegiance due?* And *who is our lawful sovereign?* This question is often the most difficult of any, and liable to infinite discussions. When people are so happy, that they can answer, *Our present sovereign, who inherits, in a direct line, from ancestors, that have governed us for many ages;* this answer admits of no reply; even though historians, in tracing up to the remotest antiquity, the origin of that royal family, may find, as commonly happens, that its first authority was derived from usurpation and violence. It is confessed, that private justice, or the abstinence from the properties of others, is a most cardinal virtue. Yet reason tells us, that there is no property in durable objects, such as lands or houses, when carefully examined in passing from hand to hand, but must, in some period, have been founded on fraud and injustice. The necessities of human society, neither in private nor public life, will allow of such an accurate enquiry. And there is no virtue or moral duty, but what may, with facility, be refined away, if we indulge a false philosophy, in sifting and scrutinizing it, by every captious rule of logic, in every light or position, in which it may be placed.

The questions with regard to private property have filled infinite volumes of law and philosophy, if in both we add the commentators to the original text; and in the end, we may safely pronounce, that many of the rules, there established, are uncertain, ambiguous, and arbitrary. The like opinion may be formed with regard to the succession and rights of princes and forms of government. Several cases, no doubt, occur, especially in the infancy of any constitution, which admit of no determination from the laws of justice and equity. . . .

Nor can any thing be more unhappy than a despotic government of this kind; where the succession is disjointed and irregular, and must be determined, on every vacancy, by force or election. In a free government, the matter is often unavoidable, and is also much less dangerous. The interests of liberty may there frequently lead the people, in their own defense, to alter the succession of the crown. And the constitution, being compounded of parts, may still maintain a sufficient stability, by resting on the aristocratical or democratical members, though the monarchical be altered, from time to time, in order to accommodate it to the former.

In an absolute government, when there is no legal prince, who has a title to the throne, it may safely be determined to belong to the first occupant. Instances of this kind are but too frequent, especially in the eastern monarchies. When any race of princes expires, the will or destination of the last sovereign will be regarded as a title. Thus the edict of LEWIS the XIVth, who called the bastard princes to the succession in case of the failure of all the legitimate princes, would, in such an event, have some authority. Thus the will of CHARLES the Second disposed of the whole SPANISH monarchy. The cession of the ancient proprietor, especially when joined to conquest, is likewise deemed a good title. The general obligation, which binds us to government, is the interest and necessities of society; and this obligation is very strong. The determination of it to this or that particular prince or form of government is frequently more uncertain and dubious. Present possession has considerable authority in these cases, and greater than in private property; because of the disorders which attend all revolutions and changes of government.

We shall only observe, before we conclude, that, though an appeal to general opinion may justly, in the speculative sciences of metaphysics, natural philosophy, or astronomy, be deemed unfair and inconclusive, yet in all questions with regard to morals, as well as criticism, there is really no other standard, by which any controversy can ever be decided. And nothing is a clearer proof, that a theory of this kind is erroneous, than to find, that it leads to paradoxes, repugnant to the common sentiments of mankind, and to the practice and opinion of all nations and all ages. The doctrine, which founds all lawful government on an *original contract,* or consent of the people, is plainly of this kind; nor has the most noted of its partisans,[3] in prosecution of it, scrupled to affirm, *that absolute monarchy is inconsistent with civil society, and so can be no form of civil government at all; and that the supreme power in a state cannot take from any man, by taxes and impositions, any part of his property, without his own consent or that of his representatives.* What authority any moral reasoning can have, which leads into opinions so wide of the general practice of mankind, in every place but this single kingdom, it is easy to determine.

The only passage I meet with in antiquity, where the obligation of obedience to

---

[3] Locke.

government is ascribed to a promise, is in PLATO'S *Crito:* where SOCRATES refuses to escape from prison, because he had tacitly promised to obey the laws. Thus he builds a *Tory* consequence of passive obedience, on a *Whig* foundation of the original contract.

New discoveries are not to be expected in these matters. If scarce any man, till very lately, ever imagined that government was founded on compact, it is certain, that it cannot, in general, have any such foundation.

OF JUSTICE*

That justice is useful to society, and consequently that *part* of its merit, at least, must arise from that consideration, it would be a superfluous undertaking to prove. That public utility is the *sole* origin of Justice, and that reflections on the beneficial consequences of this virtue are the *sole* foundation of its merit; this proposition, being more curious and important, will better deserve our examination and inquiry.

Let us suppose, that nature has bestowed on the human race such profuse *abundance* of all *external* conveniences, that, without any uncertainty in the event, without any care or industry on our part, every individual finds himself fully provided with whatever his most voracious appetites can want, or luxurious imagination wish or desire. His natural beauty, we shall suppose, surpasses all acquired ornaments. The perpetual clemency of the seasons renders useless all clothes or covering. The raw herbage affords him the most delicious fare; the clear fountain, the richest beverage. No laborious occupation required. No tillage. No navigation. Music, poetry, and contemplation, form his sole business. Conversation, mirth, and friendship, his sole amusement.

It seems evident, that, in such a happy state, every other social virtue would flourish, and receive tenfold increase; but the cautious, jealous virtue of justice, would never once have been dreamed of. For what purpose make a partition of goods, where every one has already more than enough? Why give rise to property, where there cannot possibly be any injury? Why call this object *mine,* when, upon the seizing of it by

*From David Hume, *An Enquiry Concerning the Principles of Morals* (1751).

another, I need but stretch out my hand to possess myself of what is equally valuable? Justice, in that case, being totally USELESS, would be an idle ceremonial, and could never possibly have place in the catalogue of virtues.

We see, even in the present necessitous condition of mankind, that, wherever any benefit is bestowed by nature in an unlimited abundance, we leave it always in common among the whole human race, and make no subdivisions of right and property. Water and air, though the most necessary of all objects, are not challenged as the property of individuals; nor can any man commit injustice by the most lavish use and enjoyment of these blessings. In fertile extensive countries, with few inhabitants, land is regarded on the same footing. And no topic is so much insisted on by those who defend the liberty of the seas, as the unexhausted use of them in navigation. Were the advantages procured by navigation as inexhaustible, these reasoners had never had any adversaries to refute; nor had any claims ever been advanced of a separate, exclusive dominion over the ocean.

It may happen, in some countries, at some periods, that there be established a property in water, none in land; if the latter be in greater abundance than can be used by the inhabitants, and the former be found with difficulty, in very small quantities.

Again: Suppose, that though the necessities of the human race continue the same as at present, yet the mind is so enlarged, and so replete with friendship and generosity, that every man has the utmost tenderness for every man, and feels no more concern for his own interest than for that of his fellows. It seems evident, that the USE of Justice would, in this case, be suspended by such an extensive benevolence, nor would the divisions and barriers of property and obligation have ever been thought of. Why should I bind another, by a deed or promise, to do me any good office, when I know that he is already prompted, by the strongest inclination, to seek my happiness, and would, of himself, perform the desired service; except the hurt he thereby receives be greater than the benefit accruing to me. In which case he knows that, from my innate humanity and friendship, I should be the first to oppose myself to his imprudent generosity.

Why raise landmarks between my neighbor's field and mine, when my heart has made no division between our interests; but shares all his joys and sorrows with the same force and vivacity as if originally my own? Every man, upon this supposition, being a second self to another, would trust all his interests to the discretion of every man; without jealousy, without partition, without distinction. And the whole human race would form only one family; where all would lie in common, and be used freely, without regard to property; but cautiously too, with as entire regard to the necessities of each individual, as if our own interests were most intimately concerned.

In the present disposition of the human heart, it would perhaps be difficult to find complete instances of such enlarged affections; but still we may observe, that the case of families approaches towards it; and the stronger the mutual benevolence is among the individuals, the nearer it approaches; till all distinction of property be, in a great measure, lost and confounded among them. Between married persons, the cement of friendship is by the laws supposed so strong as to abolish all division of possessions, and has often, in reality, the force ascribed to it. And it is observable, that, during the ardor of new enthusiasms, when every principle is inflamed into extravagance, the community of goods has frequently been attempted; and nothing but experience of its inconveniences, from the returning or disguised selfishness of men, could make the imprudent fanatics adopt anew the ideas of justice and of separate property. So true is it that this virtue derives its existence entirely from its necessary *use* to the intercourse and social state of mankind,

To make this truth more evident, let us reverse the foregoing suppositions; and, carrying every thing to the opposite extreme, consider what would be the effect of these new situations. Suppose a society to fall into such want of all common necessaries, that the utmost frugality and industry cannot preserve the greater number from perishing, and the whole from extreme misery. It will readily, I believe, be admitted, that the strict laws of justice are suspended, in such a pressing emergence, and give place to the stronger motives of necessity and self-preservation. Is it any

crime, after a shipwreck, to seize whatever means or instrument of safety one can lay hold of, without regard to former limitations of property? Or if a city besieged were perishing with hunger; can we imagine that men will see any means of preservation before them, and lose their lives, from a scrupulous regard to what, in other situations, would be the rules of equity and justice? The USE and TENDENCY of that virtue is to procure happiness and security, by preserving order in society. But where the society is ready to perish from extreme necessity, no greater evil can be dreaded from violence and injustice, and every man may now provide for himself by all the means which prudence can dictate, or humanity permit. The public, even in less urgent necessities, open granaries without the consent of proprietors; as justly supposing, that the authority of magistracy may, consistent with equity, extend so far. But were any number of men to assemble, without the tie of laws or civil jurisdiction; would an equal partition of bread in a famine, though effected by power and even violence, be regarded as criminal or injurious?

Suppose, likewise, that it should be a virtuous man's fate to fall into the society of ruffians; remote from the protection of laws and government; what conduct must he embrace in that melancholy situation? He sees such a desperate rapaciousness prevail; such a disregard to equity, such contempt of order, such stupid blindness to future consequences, as must immediately have the most tragical conclusion, and must terminate in destruction to the greater number, and in a total dissolution of society to the rest, He meanwhile, can have no other expedient than to arm himself, to whomever the sword he seizes, or the buckler, may belong, to make provision of all means or defence and security. And his particular regard to justice being no longer of USE to his own safety or that of others, he must consult the dictates of self-preservation alone, without concern for those who no longer merit his care and attention.

When any man, even in political society, renders himself by his crimes obnoxious to the public, he is punished by the laws in his goods and person; that is, the ordinary rules of justice are, with regard to him, suspended for a moment; and it becomes equitable to inflict on him, for the *benefit* of society, what otherwise he could not suffer without wrong or injury.

The rage and violence of public war; what is it but a suspension of justice among the warring parties, who perceive that this virtue is now no longer of any *use* or advantage to them? The laws of war, which then succeed to those of equity and justice, are rules calculated for the *advantage* and *utility* of that particular state in which men are now placed. And were a civilized nation engaged with barbarians, who observed no rules even of war; the former must also suspend their observance of them, where they no longer serve to any purpose; and must render every action or rencounter as bloody and pernicious as possible to the first aggressors.

Thus, the rules of equity or justice depend entirely on the particular state and condition in which men are placed, and owe their origin and existence to that UTILITY, which results to the public from their strict and regular observance. Reverse, in any considerable circumstance, the condition of men. Produce extreme abundance or extreme necessity. Implant in the human breast perfect moderation and humanity, or perfect rapaciousness and malice. By rendering justice totally *useless,* you thereby totally destroy its essence, and suspend its obligation upon mankind.

The common situation of society is a medium amidst all these extremes. We are naturally partial to ourselves and to our friends; but are capable of learning the advantage resulting from a more equitable conduct. Few enjoyments are given us from the open and liberal hand of nature; but by art, labor, and industry, we can extract them in great abundance. Hence the ideas of property become necessary in all civil society. Hence justice derives its usefulness to the public. And hence alone arises its merit and moral obligation.

These conclusions are so natural and obvious, that they have not escaped even the poets in their descriptions of the felicity attending the golden age or the reign of Saturn. The seasons, in that first period of nature, were so temperate, if we credit these agreeable fictions, that there was no necessity for men to provide themselves with clothes and houses, as a security against the violence of heat and cold. The rivers flowed with wine and milk. The oaks yielded honey. And Nature spontanaeously produced her greatest delicacies. Nor were these the chief advantages of that happy age. Tempests were not alone removed from nature; but those more furious tempests were unknown to human breasts, which now cause such uproar, and engender such confusion. Avarice, ambition, cruelty, selfishness, were never heard of. Cordial affection, compassion, sympathy, were the only movements with which the mind was yet acquainted. Even the punctilious distinction of *mine* and *thine* was banished from among that happy race of mortals, and carried with it the very notion of property and obligation, justice and injustice.

This *poetical* fiction of the *golden age* is, in some respects, of a piece with the *philosophical* fiction of the *state of nature;* only that the former is represented as the most charming and most peaceable condition which can possibly be imagined; whereas the latter is painted out as a state of mutual war and violence, attended with the most extreme necessity. On the first origin of mankind, we are told, their ignorance and savage nature were so prevalent, that they could give no mutual trust, but must each depend upon himself, and his own force or cunning for protection and security. No law was heard of. No rule of justice known. No distinction of property regarded. Power was the only measure of right; and a perpetual war of all against all was the result of men's untamed selfishness and barbarity.

Whether such a condition of human nature could ever exist, or, if it did, could continue so long as to merit the appellation of a state, may justly be doubted. Men are necessarily born in a family—society at least; and are trained up by their parents to some rule of conduct and behaviour. But this must be admitted, that, if such a state of mutual war and violence was ever real, the suspension of all laws of justice, from their absolute inutility, is a necessary and infallible consequence.

The more we vary our views of human life, and the newer and more unusual the lights are in which we survey it, the more shall we be convinced, that the origin here assigned for the virtue of justice is real and satisfactory.

Were there a species of creatures intermingled with men, which, though rational, were possessed of such inferior strength, both of body and mind, that they were incapable of all resistance, and could never, upon the highest provocation, make us feel the effects of their resentment; the necessary consequence, I think, is, that we should be bound, by the laws of humanity, to give gentle usage to these creatures, but should not, properly speaking, lie under any restraint of justice, with regard to them, nor could they possess any right or property exclusive of such arbitrary lords. Our intercourse with them could not be called society, which supposes a degree of equality; but absolute command on the one side, and servile obedience on the other. Whatever we covet, they must instantly resign. Our permission is the only tenure by which they hold their possessions. Our compassion and kindness the only check by which they curb our lawless will. And as no inconvenience ever results from the exercise of a power so firmly established in nature, the restraints of justice and property, being totally *useless,* would never have place in so unequal a confederacy.

This is plainly the situation of men with regard to animals; and how far these may be said to possess reason, I leave it to others to determine. The great superiority of civilized Europeans above barbarous Indians, tempted us to imagine ourselves on the same footing with regard to them, and made us throw off all restraints of justice, and even of humanity, in our treatment of them. In many nations, the female sex are reduced to like slavery, and are rendered incapable of all property, in opposition to their lordly masters. But though the males, when united, have in all countries bodily force sufficient to maintain this severe tyranny; yet such are the insinuations, address, and charms of their fair companions, that women are commonly able to break the confederacy, and share with the other sex in all the rights and privileges of society.

Were the human species so framed by nature as that each individual possessed within himself every faculty, requisite both for his own preservation, and for the propagation of his kind: Were all society and intercourse cut off between man and man, by the primary intention of the Supreme Creator: It seems evident, that so solitary a being would be as much incapable of justice as of social discourse and conversation. Where mutual regards and forbearance serve to no manner of purpose, they would never direct the conduct of any reasonable man. The headlong course of the passions would be checked by no reflection on future consequences. And as each man is here supposed to love himself alone, and to depend only on himself and his own activity for safety and happiness, he would, on every occasion, to the utmost of his power, challenge the preference above every other being, to none of which he is bound by any ties, either of nature or of interest.

But suppose the conjunction of the sexes to be established in nature, a family immediately arises; and particular rules being found requisite for its subsistence, these are immediately embraced, though without comprehending the rest of mankind within their prescriptions. Suppose that several families unite together into one society, which is totally disjoined from all others, the rules which preserve peace and order enlarge themselves to the utmost extent of that society; but becoming then entirely useless, lose their force when carried one step farther. But again, suppose that several distinct societies maintain a kind of intercourse for mutual convenience and advantage, the boundaries of justice still grow larger, in proportion to the largeness of men's views, and the force of their mutual connection. History, experience, reason, sufficiently instruct us in this natural progress of human sentiments, and in the gradual enlargement of our regards to justice, in proportion as we become acquainted with the extensive utility of that virtue.

CHAPTER TWENTY-ONE

ROUSSEAU

The French Revolution is the dominating event of the eighteenth century, and its impetus is far from being spent even today. Its intellectual preparation ran through three generations, and all significant issues were subjected to critical inquiry and examination. The impact of the debate was intensified by its being carried on in human rather than in national terms, and the universal recognition of France's intellectual leadership in the Age of Reason was a source of her ultimate political leadership, because progressive and democratic forces throughout the world identified themselves with the cause of French freedom.

If the Age of Reason ended, politically, in the Age of Revolution, the fault was not that of philosophers and publicists but of the traditional forces that, by stubbornly resisting mild reform, made radical revolution inevitable. Voltaire and Montesquieu were liberal conservatives of the upper classes, and their purpose was to prevent revolution rather than to promote it; and social revolution was furthest from their thoughts. The England they adored was dominated by a wealthy and vigorous aristocracy. The suffrage was confined to a small number of persons, and Parliament represented primarily the interests of the landowning classes. The political recognition of the English middle classes came in 1832, a century after Voltaire and Montesquieu had visited England, and the acceptance of popular democracy occurred even later.

The whole eighteenth century in France was a race between time and disaster. During the first half of the century, criticism of existing institutions was directed more openly against the church than against the state, although once the principle of ecclesiastical authority was undermined, the issue of political authority was bound to be raised. The social centers of the era were the elegant Parisian *salons,* in which the sparkling wit of the *philosophes* mingled with the charm of beautiful women and the skeptical nonchalance of leisurely aristocrats. The people were still inarticulate; Voltaire spoke of them as *la canaille,* and not a few of the early leaders of the Enlightenment felt the same sentiment toward the masses, whom they met only as untutored servants, workers, or peasants.

Voltaire was little interested in forms of government; a benevolent despot, enlightened enough to protect intellectual liberty and personal property, would have suited his taste best, because he was more interested in the monarch's enlightenment than in his autocratic government. He would rather, he said, "obey a fine lion, much stronger than himself, than two hundred rats of his own species." Though completely unaware of the existence of the social question as a chief driving force of revolution, Voltaire nevertheless opened the way for change by his ruthless and ridiculing attacks on intellectual obscurantism and inequality before the law.

In the second half of the eighteenth century, political criticism and philosophical expression became more daring and outspoken. The monument to that era is the *Encyclopédie* (1751–1772), edited by Diderot and containing contributions from the leading men of the time, d'Alembert, Holbach, Helvétius, Turgot, Haller, Morellet, Quesnay, and, at the beginning, also from Voltaire and Montesquieu. The *Encyclopédie* was originally designed to be mainly a translation of Chambers' *Cyclopaedia,* published in London in 1727, but Diderot desired to produce a work of more original and ambitious scope. The *Encyclopédie* was the first large-scale synthesis of all knowledge, and it represented—more than any other encyclopedia before or after—a whole temper and philosophical outlook.

The *encyclopédistes* belonged to varied schools of thought in science, philosophy, theology, and the arts, yet a collective intellectual denominator soon emerged: naturalism and empiricism in philosophy, deism or agnosticism in theology, utilitarianism in social institutions, constitutionalism in government, and support for industry and commerce in economics. The faith of the *encyclopédistes* was humanitarian, rationalist, and scientific: they believed that nature and society are governed, not by an incomprehensible and arbitrary fate or divine providence, but by an intelligible rational order, and that man's increase of knowledge is the best guide to his happiness and progress.

Despite its novel ideas and emphases, the rational outlook of the Enlightenment was traditional—and the tradition that had sprung from Greece was even older than the rivaling dogmas of church and religion. The historical achievement of the Enlightenment consisted not so much in having discovered the possibilities of reason but in having converted such a large part of the ruling classes of the time to its tenets. There was room for feeling and emotion in this age of rationalism, but they were subordinated to the primacy of reason and stylized in form and expression. The first to attack, not this or that idea or philosophy, but the very foundations of traditional civilization, had to be someone who was not a part of it: Jean Jacques Rousseau (1712–1778).

Before Rousseau appeared on the literary scene in Europe, critics of the existing order had slowly been widening their orbit of interest to include the people in their plans of reform. But "the people" meant primarily the discriminated Third Estate of prosperous and respectable merchants, lawyers, and intellectuals. Rousseau is the first modern writer on politics who was *of* the people: the submerged, inarticulate masses of the *petite bourgeoisie,* the poor artisans and workingmen, the small peasants, the restless and rootless, the *déclassés,* for whom there was no room, and no hope, in the existing order of things.

Rousseau was born of a poor family in Geneva, his French ancestors having migrated there as religious refugees in the sixteenth century. Rousseau's mother died a few days after his birth, and his father, an impecunious watchmaker and more enthusiastic dancing master, was unable to raise Jean Jacques in any coherent fashion. From the age of twelve Rousseau was apprenticed to various masters, but he failed to establish himself in any art or trade. At sixteen he ran away from Geneva, and for the remainder of his life could claim no permanent abode anywhere.

Voltaire and Montesquieu had traveled through Europe in grand style; Rousseau saw much of the Continent through the eyes of a penniless, and at times hunted, vagabond, who did not always know where his next meal would come from and where he would sleep. Poverty made him commit minor thefts and larcenies, change his religion for temporary material advantage, and accept charity from people he detested. He was valet to an Italian aristocrat, secretary to a French diplomat, and a music teacher (with but few pupils); he often survived by dint of his own ingenuity and the charity of others, particularly women, who played a large part in his life from his early youth. He never ceased to attract women and to be attracted by them.

In 1744 Rousseau went to Paris, having visited it first in 1742. He tried his hand at various schemes, the theater, opera, music, poetry, without making much of a success at anything. Yet his personality opened for him the doors of the best *salons* in Paris, where he met leading Encyclopédists as well as influential women, with several of whom he maintained close ties of friendship. But he never became, nor did he wish to become, a part of the fashionable set of Paris. He had love affairs with society women, but of all his associations with women the one that lasted longest was with Thérèse Levasseur, a servant girl who worked in Rousseau's small hotel in Paris. As he said later in his *Confessions:* "At first I sought to give myself amusement, but I saw I had gone further and had given myself a companion."

Though enjoying, out of vanity, the company of the rich and powerful, he resented being admitted to the exalted society as a matter of personal privilege, and he never shed his plebeian, Puritanical background of a low middle-class family in Geneva. His complex feelings of pleasure and resentment regarding his social standing made it difficult for him to establish lasting human relations, except with Thérèse Levasseur, with whom he lived from his early days in Paris to the end of his life.

In 1749 the Academy of Dijon announced a prize for the best essay on the question: "Has the progress of sciences and arts contributed to corrupt or purify morality?" In his *Confessions* Rousseau later describes his immediate reaction: "Instantly I saw another universe, and I become another man." He set to work feverishly on the essay and submitted it to the Academy. In 1750 the Academy rewarded it the first prize, and it was published in 1751 under the title *A Discourse on the Moral Effects of the Arts and Sciences.*

Rousseau's thesis was the exact opposite of what was conventionally thought at that time, and he was bold enough to *extol natural man* at the expense of so-called civilized man, for "our minds have been corrupted in proportion as the arts and sciences have improved." The much vaunted politeness, the glory of civilized refinement, is for Rousseau but a "uniform and perfidious veil" under which he sees "jealousy, suspicion, fear, coolness, reserve, hate, and fraud."

In surveying history in support of his cult of natural simplicity, Rousseau is full of enthusiasm for Sparta, a "republic of demi-gods rather than of men," famous for the happy ignorance of its inhabitants, "eternal proof of the vanity of science." By contrast, he denigrates Athens, the center of vice, doomed to perish because of its elegance, luxury, wealth, art, and science: "From Athens we derive those astonishing performances which will serve as models to every corrupt age."

Rousseau sees a direct causal relation between luxury, constantly expanding needs, and the rise of art and science, after which true courage flags and the virtues disappear. Roman history, Rousseau holds, supports this view: as long as Rome was poor and simple, she was able to command respect and conquer an empire; after having developed luxury and engulfed the riches of the universe, Rome "fell a prey to peoples who knew not even what riches were." Rousseau inveighs against orators and philosophers as guides to superficiality and perversion. Philosophers consecrate themselves to the destruction of "all that men hold sacred," and Rousseau calls them "charlatans" who sow confusion among men and undermine their simple ideas of patriotism and religion.

Anticipating his own later views on education in *Emile* (1762), Rousseau writes in his first *Discourse* that traditional education is too vocational and too highly specialized, that children remain ignorant of their own language while being taught other languages not spoken anywhere, and that the moral virtues are neglected: "But magnanimity, equity, temperance, humanity and courage will be words of which they know not the meaning." Finally, Rousseau makes the charge that is as timely today as in 1749. "We have physicists, geometricians, chemists, astronomers, poets, musicians, and painters in plenty; but we have no longer a citizen among us."

In 1753 Rousseau competed again in a contest of the Academy of Dijon; the subject was "What is the origin of inequality among men, and is it authorized by natural law?" His first *Discourse* had brought him immediate fame and sensational success. In writing his *Discourse on the Origin of Inequality* (1755), Rousseau felt he no longer needed to shock and captivate his audience by paradoxes and one-sided arguments, and he composed a much more systematic essay, one of the most influential in the history of democratic and socialist thought. He did not win this time, but the second *Discourse* is more important than the first, particularly in relation to the development of Rousseau's political ideas.

Rousseau distinguishes two kinds of inequality. The first is *natural* and consists in differences of age, health, bodily strength, and the qualities of mind and soul. The second is moral or *political inequality,* which owes its existence to social institutions and consists in privileges of wealth, honor, and power. Rousseau finds that natural inequalities are not substantial, that the problem of inequality arises with the formation of society. Nature destined man to live a healthy, simple life and to satisfy his essential needs ("food, a female, and sleep"). By contrast, man in society, or civilized man, has developed varied and unhealthful habits of eating and sleeping, and his mental and physical exhaustion is the result of the pains, anxieties, and torments of civilized living. *Civilization* is thus a *hopeless race to discover remedies for the evils it produces.* The man of nature knows less medicine than civilized man, but the latter brings upon himself more diseases than medicine can cure. Reflection is contrary to nature, and a thinking man, Rousseau says, is "a depraved animal."

This motif ran through the first *Discourse on the Arts and Sciences,* and Rousseau now announces the idea—so contrary to the commonplaces of his time—that human understanding is not the sole domain of reason but is "greatly indebted to passions." In the state of nature, man was guided by two sentiments: self-interest and pity, and having no moral obligations with others, he could not be "good or bad, virtuous or vicious." Rousseau specifically rejects Hobbes' view of the state of nature in which man, not knowing goodness, must therefore be wicked, and he asserts that man's sense of compassion is the original sentiment from which all later virtues flow. Reason and thinking come afterward and isolate man from his fellows, whereas compassion unites him with others. Uncivilized man is always "foolishly ready to obey the first promptings of humanity. It is the populace that flocks together at riots and street-brawls, while the wise man prudently makes off. It is the mob and the market-women who part the combatants, and hinder gentle-folks from cutting one another's throats."

Turning to the origin of inequality in society, Rousseau starts out with a passage that has a distinctly socialist and revolutionary flavor: "The first man who, having enclosed a piece of ground, bethought himself of saying *This is mine,* and found people simple enough to believe him, was the real founder of civil society." The natural voice of compassion was stilled by the usurpations of the rich and the robberies of the poor, and the newborn society thus led to a "horrible state of war." The rich then devised a plan by which they would better enjoy their power and possession without the threat of constant war.

The first step was easy, to obtain agreement among the rich themselves to set up a system of law and government for the maintenance of peace. The second step, "the profoundest plan that ever entered the mind of man," was to employ the forces of the poor for the creation of government, under which all would be protected and their possessions safeguarded: "Such was, or may well have been, the origin of society and law, which bound new fetters on the poor, and gave new powers to the rich; which irretrievably destroyed natural liberty, eternally fixed the law of property and inequality, converted clever usurpation into unalterable right, and, for the advantage of a few ambitious individuals, subjected all mankind to perpetual labor, slavery and wretchedness."

In the long run, however, Rousseau foresees that from extreme inequality of fortunes and conditions spring divisions and dissensions that undermine the fabric of society and government. Despotism arises out of these disorders, but despotism is the "last term of inequality." Popular insurrection deposes the despot, or even puts him to death: "As he was maintained by force alone, it is force alone that overthrows him." This was strong language for the middle of the eighteenth century, when revolution was not thought of as yet and when free expression was curbed by both church and state.

The concluding words of the *Discourse on the Origin of Inequality* made it plain that Rousseau was not referring to hypothetical states of nature or society but to the injustices of contemporary France, "since it is plainly contrary to the laws of nature, however defined, that children should command old men, fools wise men, and that the privileged few should gorge themselves with superfluities, while the starving multitude are in want of the bare necessities of life."

At the time of uttering this ringing challenge, Rousseau did not earn enough to rent a house, much less own one, or to provide enough of the bare necessities for himself and the woman who shared his existence. During most of his life Rousseau lived in houses and cottages that his friends gave him rent-free, and Thérèse Levasseur received more gifts (often rather unashamedly soliticiting them from friends) than proud and sensitive Jean Jacques would have cared to know. While he was not of the "starving multitude," he was close enough to its worries, its tragedies, and petty cares, to know how poverty could deprave and degrade men and women who were originally good.

In 1755 Rousseau published the *Discourse on Political Economy* in Diderot's *Encyclopédie*. Rousseau's regular assignments for the *Encyclopédie* covered music, and the *Discourse on Political Economy* is less remarkable for its economic observations than for the fact that it is his first constructive approach to a theory of the state, whereas the first two *Discourses* had been mainly critical. The *Discourse on Political Economy* is important in the development of Rousseau's political ideas, inasmuch as it contains the first statement of the concept of the General Will, his most original contribution to political philosophy. Thus, when Rousseau published his most famous work, *The Social Contract,* in 1762, its chief ideas were not the result of a sudden inspiration; they had matured in him over the years and had been partially expressed in his three *Discourses.*

The main concern of *The Social Contract* is the central issue of all political speculation: *political obligation.* "The problem," Rousseau says, "is to find a form of association which will defend and protect with the whole common force the person and goods of each associate, and in which each, while uniting himself with all, may still obey himself alone, and remain as free as before." In the very beginning of the book, Rousseau puts the same question in a more dramatic form: "Man is born free; and everywhere he is in chains."

Like his predecessors, Rousseau uses the conceptions of the state of nature and the social contract that puts an end to it. Rousseau's conception of man's life in the state of nature is not quite so gloomy as that of Hobbes, nor as optimistic as that of Locke. Each man pursues his self-interest in the state of nature until he discovers that his power to preserve himself individually against the threats and hindrances of others is not strong enough. The purpose of the social contract is thus to combine security, which comes from collective association, with liberty, which the individual had before the making of the contract. But the social contract consists in "the total alienation of each associate, together with all his rights, to the whole community."

The total surrender of the individual to the sovereign community is completely contrary to Locke and recalls Hobbes' view of the social contract, in which the individual also surrenders himself completely to the sovereign. But whereas Hobbes' subject is completely submissive to his sovereign, Rousseau reflects this kind of social peace without liberty: "Tranquillity is also found in dungeons; but is that enough to make them desirable places to live in?" To renounce liberty, Rousseau says, is to renounce being a man, for there can be no obligation that is not, to some extent at least, mutual. In Rousseau's social contract man does not surrender completely to a sovereign ruler, but each man gives himself to all, and therefore gives himself to nobody in particular: "As there is no associate over whom he does not acquire the same right as he yields others over himself, he gains an equivalent for everything he loses, and an increase of force for the preservation of what he has."

Rousseau shows in *The Social Contract* a much greater appreciation of civil society, as compared with the state of nature, than he showed in his earlier writings. In the state of nature, Rousseau now says, man is guided by instinct only, whereas in society he is inspired by justice and morality. Man loses through the social contract his *natural liberty* and an unlimited right to everything he can lay his hands on, but he gains *civil liberty* and property rights in all he possesses. The liberty of the state of nature is no true liberty, because it is merely enslavement to uncontrolled appetites. By contrast, *moral liberty,* which man acquires solely in the civil state, makes him master of himself, because "obedience to a law which we prescribe to ourselves is liberty."

These three forms of liberty progress from the lower to the higher. Natural liberty is devoid of any reflective or rational elements, and its boundary—constantly shifting—is simply the strength of the individual to assert himself. Civil liberty has a firmer and more rational foundation—the laws and rules of the political community which determine what each member may and may not do in relation to other members. However, if the rules and laws of a political community are created by all its members, then civil liberty rises to the level of moral liberty, for in obeying laws we ourselves have made, we remain free. Whereas civil liberty creates individual rights and freedoms in relation to others, moral liberty is the only type of freedom in which the individual is free in relation to himself.

Once men have created society, the alternative is no longer between liberty limited by no rules (or by one's strength only, as in the state of nature) and liberty limited by rules, for the very concept of civil society requires laws. In civil society, the alternative is between obeying laws in the making of which the citizens have not participated, and obeying laws in which we ourselves have participated in making. In the first case, we obey the will of others, which makes us morally unfree. In the second case, we obey the will of ourselves, which condition alone can make us free. If there has to be law—and where there is society, there must be law—self-imposed law is thus the closest approximation to freedom that man can attain in civil society. Rousseau was fully aware of the paradox that law by its very nature limits freedom and that there can be no freedom without law. "By what inconceivable art," he asks, "has a means been found of making men free by making them subject?" and he answers that "these wonders are the work of law. It is to law alone that men owe justice and liberty."

Rousseau's conception of sovereignty differs from both Hobbes' and Locke's. In Hobbes' the people set up a sovereign and transfer all power to him. In Locke's social contract the people set up a limited government for limited purposes, but Locke shuns the conception of sovereignty—popular or monarchical—as a symbol of political absolutism. Rousseau's sovereign is the people, constituted as a political community through the social contract.

Unlike nearly all other major political thinkers, Rousseau considers the *sovereignty of the people inalienable and indivisible.* The people cannot give away, or transfer, to any person or body their ultimate right of self-government, of deciding their own destiny. Whereas Hobbes identified the sovereign with the ruler who exercises sovereignty, Rousseau draws a sharp distinction between sovereignty, which always and wholly resides in the people, and government, which is but a temporary agent (as in Locke's conception) of the sovereign people. Whereas, in Locke, the people transfer the exercise of their supreme authority, legislative, executive, and judicial, to organs of government, Rousseau's concept of inalienable and indivisible sovereignty does not permit the people to transfer their legislative function, the supreme authority in the state. As to the executive and judicial functions, Rousseau realizes that they have to be exercised by special organs of government, but they are completely subordinated to the sovereign people, and there is no hint or suggestion of separation, or balance, of powers.

Rousseau's system of government is unmitigated popular sovereignty, unmodified by competing or balancing powers; this aspect of Rousseau has always strongly appealed to adherents of radical and uncompromising democracy. Rousseau thought that the people of England were mistaken in thinking themselves free; they were actually free only once every few years when electing Members of Parliament. Sovereignty lies in the General Will of the people, and will cannot be represented.

In the *Discourse on Political Economy* Rousseau had already dealt with the problem of the General Will, the key conception in his political philosophy. He sees the body politic "possessed of a will; and this General Will, which tends always to the preservation and welfare of the whole and of every part, and is the source of the laws, constitutes for all the members of the state, in their relation to one another and to it, the rule of what is just or unjust." By introducing the concept of the *General Will,* Rousseau fundamentally alters the mechanistic concept of the state as an instrument (shared by both Hobbes and Locke) and revives the *organic* theory of the state, which goes back to Plato and Aristotle.

Rousseau is keenly aware of the life of groups, which is more than a charter or articles of incorporation. The state is not the only group with a General Will; particular societies and associations, too, have a General Will in relation to their members, though in relation to the state their will is particular, because the General Will of the state is the most comprehensive of all, embracing all members of the community.

Rousseau himself admits, before his critics and commentators made the discovery, that the distinction between the General Will and particular wills is "always very difficult to make." The General Will is not an empirical fact so much as a *moral fact,* and "it is needful only to act justly, to be certain of following the General Will." By establishing the reign of virtue, all particular wills will be brought in conformity with the General Will. The General Will, therefore, is not something that can be legislated against the people from the outside, but is a moral attitude in the heart of the citizens, and "nothing can take the place of morality in the maintenance of government."

The character of the General Will is determined by two elements: first, it *aims at the general good,* and, second, it *must come from all* and *apply to all.* The first refers to the object of the will; the second, to its origin. The Will of All must therefore not be confused with the General Will: "The latter considers only the common interest, while the former takes private interest into account, and is no more than a sum of particular wills."

The generality of the will is not so much a matter of numbers as of intrinsic quality and goodness. The people always will be good, but they do not always understand it, particularly when factions make it difficult for the independent citizen to pursue the common good. Nor can the General Will be represented, because representative assemblies tend to develop particular interests of their own, forgetting those of the community. Obviously referring to the direct democracies of Swiss city-republics, Rousseau glowingly describes how "bands of peasants are seen regulating affairs of state under an oak, and always acting wisely," and he prefers the methods of these "happiest people in the world" to the ingenious methods of party government through representation, as practiced in other nations.

Rousseau recognizes that in direct popular government unanimity is, in practice, impossible, and that the vote of the majority binds the minority. The question of how the minority can be free and yet be bound to obey the majority is rejected by Rousseau as wrongly put: when a citizen objects to a proposed law in the popular assembly and finds himself in a minority, he does not thereby lose his freedom, for his minority vote merely proves that he did not recognize the General Will, rather than that the majority, as such, has a right to rule over him. Rousseau cautiously adds that this conception of freedom of the individual "presupposes, indeed, that all the qualities of the General Will still reside in the majority: when they cease to do so, whatever side a man may take, liberty is no longer possible."

Obeying the General Will is thus the expression of the moral freedom of the individual, and if he refuses to obey, he may be compelled to do so: "This means nothing less than that he will be forced to be free." Here Rousseau revives his basic distinction between the apparent liberty of man in the state of nature, which actually is enslavement to selfish appetites, and his moral liberty in civil society, which consists in obeying laws, general in scope and origin, which he, as a member of the body politic, has helped to make.

Yet it takes more than one brief phrase to interpret a thinker as an authoritarian, particularly a thinker who felt drawn to the lowly, the weak, the oppressed, and who proclaimed liberty, justice, and equality as the ends of law and government. Perhaps this famous phrase—that man can be forced to be free—is an extreme case of Rousseau's love of colorful images and verbal fireworks, as exemplified, for example, by the opening words of the *social contract,* "Man is born free; and everywhere he is in chains," which also cannot be accepted literally and which yet try to say something important.

The phrase "forcing man to be free" is obviously self-contradictory, if one looks at the ordinary meaning of these words. It may be safely presumed that Rousseau was fully aware of this contradiction if one interprets the words force and freedom according to everyday usage in which force and freedom are contradictory. The contradiction becomes, however, less obvious and simple if we recall that Rousseau distinguishes civil liberty from moral liberty, and that moral liberty can be attained only through the General Will creating laws which come from all, apply to all, and aim at the general good. When a civil society is in the process of being set up by the social contract, individuals may stay out of the rights and obligations thereby created by either leaving the civil society, that is, by emigrating, or by remaining "as foreigners among citizens." Once the state is set up, "residence constitutes consent; to dwell in its territory to submit to its sovereignty." In the light of many modern totalitarian practices of preventing people from leaving their country for another, Rousseau adds the interesting comment that residence should be construed as consent to the political institutions of a state only if it is free and voluntary, as is the case in a "free state," for in states which are not free, "lack of a refuge, necessity, or violence may detain a man in a country against his will; and then his residing there no longer by itself implies his consent to the contract or to its violation."

However, the citizen of the free state cannot give his consent selectively to one law but not to another: "The citizen gives his consent to all the laws, including those which are passed in spite of his opposition, and even those which punish him when he dares to break any of them." The concept of the General Will involves the participation of every citizen in the making of laws; by taking part in the process on a free and equal basis with all other citizens, he obliges himself in advance to obey the law even if he has voted against it, since "the vote of the majority always binds the rest." However, Rousseau is no adherent of majoritarian tyranny and caprice, for the obligation of the citizen to obey the law he has opposed or voted against before its being enacted presupposes that "all the qualities of the General Will still reside in the majority," including its quality of aiming at the common good. But if the General Will, as expressed by the majority, meets both its empirical requirement—that it come from all and that it apply to all—and its moral or rational requirement—that it aim at the common good, then liberty—in Rousseau's (and, later, Kant's) sense of *moral liberty*—means no more, *but also no less,* than obeying the laws one has participated in creating. What Rousseau thus tries to convey in the provocative and attention-catching phrase of forcing man to be free if he disobeys the General Will is the notion that one cannot have it both ways, that the very concept of civil society implies the abandonment of natural liberty, in which one's freedom is limited only by his strength. All civilization implies rational self-restraint, and political civilization, too, implies the rational understanding on the part of the citizen in the free state that in the notion of liberty as subjection to self-imposed law the importance of the word "subjection" is equal to that of "self-imposed." In the first draft of the *Social Contract* Rousseau plainly states that the General Will is more than pure will, that, in fact, it is "in each individual a pure act of understanding, which reasons while the passions are silent on what a man may demand of his neighbor and on what his neighbor has a right to demand of him."

Like most democratic theorists of the state, Rousseau was anxious to base political obligation on consent and thus save the idea of individual liberty in the realm of government. Yet he saw beyond the mechanical constructions of liberal political theory, which assumed that the public good would somehow be the final product of all individual private wills and interests. He attributes to the people inalienable sovereignty, but a moral obligation is attached to this precious possession: each citizen must will the general good, because popular sovereignty means the General Will, and self-government is therefore not mere submission to the common good, but its active cultivation: "There can be no patriotism without liberty, no liberty without virtue, no virtue without citizens; create citizens, and you have everything you need; without them, you will have nothing but debased slaves, from the rulers of the state downward."

Some defenders of totalitarian states have sought to claim Rousseau as an intellectual progenitor of unlimited collectivism and oppressive anti-individualism. True, the organic element in Rousseau's doctrine may be abused, and has been abused, for anti-democratic purposes. Yet the master conception of *The Social Contract*—is a community of free men living in a small state in which democracy can be practiced directly by the people, a community of men who see in freedom not only an invitation to personal enjoyment and advantage but also shared responsibility for the welfare of the whole.

Before Rousseau, the classical doctrine of Plato and Aristotle emphasized good government at the expense of self-government. The aim was the good life, not government of the people by the people. The more modern idea of Locke and the liberal school was

concerned principally with self-government; it relegated the problem of good government into the background, or it was assumed that good government would naturally
result from a combination of public *laissez faire* and private pursuit of individual advantage. Rousseau is the first modern writer to attempt, not always successfully, to syn-
thesize *good government with self-government* in the key concept of the General Will:
the realization of what is best for the community is not enough; it must also be *willed* by
the community.

This synthesis explains why Rousseau has been claimed by adherents of the organic
theory of the state as well as by followers of liberal democracy, though their conclusions may be antagonistic to each other. The more one is addicted to an extreme view of
either the organic or the liberal theory in politics, the easier it is to appropriate only one
part of Rousseau. The more one seeks to preserve what is best in the organic theory of
the state and to fuse it with liberal democracy, the more one runs into philosophical difficulties that, in the end, resemble those of Rousseau.

Rousseau also saw more clearly than the conventional liberal doctrinaries that the
end of government is not confined to the protection of individual liberty but also includes *equality,* because "liberty cannot exist without it." Rousseau reverses in *The
Social Contract* the hostility to property that he showed in the first two *Discourses;* here
he accepts property as an essential institution of society. But in *The Social Contract* he
does not abandon the ideal of economic equality, though the concept of equality should
not be taken in a literal sense. No citizen "shall ever be wealthy even to buy another,
and none poor enough to be forced to sell himself." Rousseau realizes that in practice it
is difficult to maintain the ideal of equitable distribution of property, but it "is precisely because the force of circumstances tends continually to destroy equality that the
force of legislation should always tend to its maintenance."

Whereas Locke failed to see property as a relation of domination of man over
man, Rousseau clearly recognized *property* as a form of *private domination* that had to
be kept under control by the General Will, the public interest of the community.
Rousseau's theory of equitable distribution of property was, however, hardly socialist
in the modern sense of the term, because he was not thinking of an industrial society, in
which the problem of socialized property chiefly arises, but of communities of small
peasants and craftsmen (as in Switzerland), in which individual economic independence and an approximation to the ideal of equal property are feasible. Yet indirectly,
this part of Rousseau—the stress on equality—has aided the development of socialist
sentiment by sharpening the awareness that political liberty and crass economic inequality are ultimately incompatible if democracy is to survive and expand.

Since the eighteenth century the record of free government everywhere has proved
that there can be no reliance on contrivances and institutions alone in the eternal struggle for liberty, and that its survival depends, in the last analysis, on those moral qualities that Rousseau calls the General Will, justice, virtue. The General Will, like
individual virtue, cannot be defined in detail; it is an impulse that animates and guides
civic action. It receives its ultimate valid definition in the lives of free men rather than
in philosophical distinctions.

Rousseau was first vindicated historically by the success of the American Revolution,
and the opening words of the Constitution of the United States. "We the people . . . ,"
were of the spirit of Jean Jacques Rousseau. In the French Revolution, only a few years
later, the French nation discovered its communal solidarity in a new birth of individual
freedom and popular government. Since then, the message of Rousseau has been carried
to all corners of the world, and its vitality and persistent timeliness continue to inspire
free men and free women everywhere.

ROUSSEAU

*The Social Contract**

MAN IS BORN FREE

Man is born free; and everywhere he is in chains. One thinks himself the master of others, and still remains a greater slave than they. How did this change come about? I do not know. What can make it legitimate? That question I think I can answer.

If I took into account only force, and the effects derived from it, I should say: "As long as a people is compelled to obey, and obeys, it does well; as soon as it can shake off the yoke, and shakes it off, it does still better; for, regaining its liberty by the same right as took it away, either it is justified in resuming it, or there was no justification for those who took it away." But the social order is a sacred right which is the basis of all other rights. Nevertheless, this right does not come from nature, and must therefore be founded on conventions. Before coming to that, I have to prove what I have just asserted.

THE RIGHT OF
THE STRONGEST

The strongest is never strong enough to be always the master, unless he transforms strength into right, and obedience into duty. Hence the right of the strongest, which, though to all seeming meant ironically, is really laid down as a fundamental principle. But are we never to have an explanation of this phrase? Force is a physical power, and I fail to see what moral effect it can have. To yield to force is an act of necessity, not of will—at the most, an act of prudence. In what sense can it be a duty?

Suppose for a moment that this so-called "right" exists. I maintain that the sole result is a mass of inexplicable nonsense. For, if force creates right, the effect changes with the cause: every force that is greater than the first succeeds to its right. As soon as it is possible to disobey with impunity, disobedience is legitimate; and, the strongest being always in the right, the only thing that matters is to act so as to become the strongest. But what kind of right is that which perishes when force fails? If we must obey perforce, there is no need to obey because we ought; and if we are not forced to obey, we are under no obligation to do so. Clearly, the word "right" adds nothing to force: in this connection, it means absolutely nothing.

Obey the powers that be. If this means yield to force, it is a good precept, but superfluous: I can answer for its never being violated. All power comes from God, I admit; but so does all sickness: does that mean that we are forbidden to call in the doctor? A brigand surprises me at the edge of a wood: must I not merely surrender my purse on compulsion; but, even if I could withhold it, am I in conscience bound to give it up? For certainly the pistol he holds is also a power.

Let us then admit that force does not create right, and that we are obliged to obey only legitimate powers. In that case, my original question recurs.

---

*From Jean Jacques Rousseau, *The Social Contract and Discourses* (1762, trans. G.D.H. Cole, Everyman's Library Edition, 1947). By permission of E.P. Dutton & Co., and J.M. Dent & Sons, Ltd.

SLAVERY

Since no man has a natural authority over his fellow, and force creates no right, we must conclude that conventions form the basis of all legitimate authority among men.

If an individual, says Grotius, can alienate his liberty and make himself the slave of a master, why could not a whole people do the same and make itself subject to a king? There are in this passage plenty of ambiguous words which would need explaining; but let us confine ourselves to the word *alienate*. To alienate is to give or to sell. Now, a man who becomes the slave of another does not give himself; he sells himself, at the least for his subsistence: but for what does a people sell itself? A king is so far from furnishing his subjects with their subsistence that he gets his own only from them; and, according to Rabelais, kings do not live on nothing. Do subjects then give their persons on condition that the king takes their goods also? I fail to see what they have left to preserve.

It will be said that the despot assures his subjects civil tranquillity. Granted; but what do they gain, if the wars his ambition brings down upon them, his insatiable avidity, and the vexatious conduct of his ministers press harder on them than their own dissensions would have done? What do they gain, if the very tranquillity they enjoy is one of their miseries? Tranquillity is found also in dungeons; but is that enough to make them desirable places to live in? The Greeks imprisoned in the cave of the Cyclops lived there very tranquilly, while they were awaiting their turn to be devoured.

To say that a man gives himself gratuitously, is to say what is absurd and inconceivable; such an act is null and illegitimate, from the mere fact that he who does it is out of his mind. To say the same of a whole people is to suppose a people of madmen; and madness creates no right.

Even if each man could alienate himself, he could not alienate his children: they are born men and free; their liberty belongs to them, and no one but they has the right to dispose of it. Before they come to years of discretion, the father can, in their name, lay down conditions for their preservation and well-being, but he cannot give them irrevocably and without conditions: such a gift is contrary to the ends of nature, and exceeds the rights of paternity. It would therefore be necessary, in order to legitimize an arbitrary government, that in every generation the people should be in a position to accept or reject it; but, were this so, the government would be no longer arbitrary.

To renounce liberty is to renounce being a man, to surrender the rights of humanity and even its duties. For him who renounces everything no indemnity is possible. Such a renunciation is incompatible with man's nature; to remove all liberty from his will is to remove all morality from his acts. Finally, it is an empty and contradictory convention that sets up, on the one side, absolute authority, and, on the other, unlimited obedience. Is it not clear that we can be under no obligation to a person from whom we have the right to exact everything? Does not this condition alone, in the absence of equivalence or exchange, in itself involve the nullity of the act? For what right can my slave have against me, when all that he has belongs to me, and, his right being mine, this right of mine against myself is a phrase devoid of meaning?

Grotius and the rest find in war another origin for the so-called right of slavery. The victor having, as they hold, the right of killing the vanquished, the latter can buy back his life at the price of his liberty; and this convention is the more legitimate because it is to the advantage of both parties.

But it is clear that this supposed right to kill the conquered is by no means deducible from the state of war. Men, from the mere fact that, while they are living in their primitive independence, they have no mutual relations stable enough to constitute either the state of peace or the state of war, cannot be naturally enemies. War is constituted by a relation between things, and not between persons; and, as the state of war cannot arise out of simple personal relations, but only out of real relations, private war, or war of man with man, can exist neither in the state of nature, where there is no constant property, nor in the social state, where everything is under the authority of the laws.

Individual combats, duels, and encounters, are acts which cannot constitute a state; while the private wars, authorized by the Establishments of Louis IX, King of France, and suspended by the Peace of God, are abuses of feudalism, in itself an absurd system if ever there was one, and contrary to the principles of natural right and to all good polity.

War then is a relation, not between man and man, but between State and State, and individuals are enemies only accidentally, not as men, nor even as citizens,[1] but as soldiers; not as members of their country, but as its defenders. Finally, each State can have for enemies only other States, and not men; for between things disparate in nature there can be no real relation.

Furthermore, this principle is in conformity with the established rules of all times and the constant practice of all civilized peoples. Declarations of war are intimations less to powers than to their subjects. The foreigner, whether king, individual, or people, who robs, kills, or detains the subjects, without declaring war on the prince, is not an enemy, but a brigand. Even in real war, a just prince, while laying hands, in the enemy's country, on all that belongs to the public, respects the lives and goods of individuals: he respects rights on which his own are founded. The object of the war being the destruction of the hostile State, the other side has a right to kill its defenders, while they are bearing arms; but as soon as they lay them down and surrender, they cease to be enemies or instruments of the enemy, and become once more merely men, whose life no one has any right to take. Sometimes it is possible to kill the State without killing a single one of its members; and war gives no right which is not necessary to the gaining of its object. These principles are not those of Grotius: they are not based on the authority of poets, but derived from the nature of reality and based on reason.

The right of conquest has no foundation other than the right of the strongest. If war does not give the conqueror the right to massacre the conquered peoples, the right to enslave them cannot be based upon a right which does not exist. No one has a right to kill an enemy except when he cannot make him a slave, and the right to enslave him cannot therefore be derived from the right to kill him. It is accordingly an unfair exchange to make him buy at the price of his liberty his life, over which the victor holds no right. Is it not clear that there is a vicious circle in founding the right of life and death on the right of slavery, and the right of slavery on the right of life and death?

Even if we assume this terrible right to kill everybody, I maintain that a slave made in war, or a conquered people, is under no obligation to a master, except to obey him as far as he is compelled to do so. By taking an equivalent for his life, the victor has not done him a favour; instead of killing him without profit, he has killed him usefully. So far then is he from acquiring over him any authority in addition to that of force, that the state of war continues to subsist between them: their mutual relation is the effect of it, and the usage of the right of war does not imply a treaty of peace. A convention has indeed been made; but this convention, so far from destroying the state of war, presupposes its continuance.

So, from whatever aspect we regard the question, the right of slavery is null and void, not only as being illegitimate, but also because it is absurd and meaningless. The words *slave* and *right* contradict each other, and are mutually exclusive. It will always be equally foolish for a man to say to a man or to a people: "I make with you a convention wholly at your expense and wholly to my advantage; I shall keep it as long as I like, and you will keep it as long as I like."

THE FIRST CONVENTION OF SOCIETY

Even if I granted all that I have been refuting, the friends of despotism would be no better off. There will always be a great difference between subduing a multitude and

---

[1] The Romans, who understood and respected the right of war more than any other nation on earth, carried their scruples on this head so far that a citizen was not allowed to serve as a volunteer without engaging himself expressly against the enemy, and against such and such an enemy by name. A legion in which the younger Cato was seeing his first service under Popilius having been reconstructed, the elder Cato wrote to Popilius that, if he wished his son to continue serving under him, he must administer to him a new military oath, because, the first having been annulled, he was no longer able to bear arms against the enemy. The same Cato wrote to his son telling him to take great care not to go into battle before taking this new oath. I know that the siege of Clusium and other isolated events can be quoted against me; but I am citing laws and customs. The Romans are the people that least often transgressed its laws; and no other people has had such good ones.

ruling a society. Even if scattered individuals were successively enslaved by one man, however numerous they might be, I still see no more than a master and his slaves, and certainly not a people and its ruler; I see what may be termed an aggregation, but not an association; there is as yet neither public good nor body politic. The man in question, even if he has enslaved half the world, is still only an individual; his interest, apart from that of others, is still a purely private interest. If this same man comes to die, his empire, after him, remains scattered and without unity, as an oak falls and dissolves into a heap of ashes when the fire has consumed it.

A people, says Grotius, can give itself to a king. Then, according to Grotius, a people is a people before it gives itself. The gift is itself a civil act, and implies public deliberation. It would be better, before examining the act by which a people gives itself to a king, to examine that by which it has become a people; for this act, being necessarily prior to the other, is the true foundation of society.

Indeed, if there were no prior convention, where, unless the election were unanimous, would be the obligation on the minority to submit to the choice of the majority? How have a hundred men who wish for a master the right to vote on behalf of ten who do not? The law of majority voting is itself something established by convention, and presupposes unanimity, on one occasion at least.

THE SOCIAL COMPACT

I suppose men to have reached the point at which the obstacles in the way of their preservation in the state of nature show their power of resistance to be greater than the resources at the disposal of each individual for his maintenance in that state, The primitive condition can then subsist no longer; and the human race would perish unless it changed its manner of existence.

But, as men cannot engender new forces, but only unite and direct existing ones, they have no other means of preserving themselves than the formation, by aggregation, of a sum of forces great enough to overcome the resistance. These they have to bring into play by means of a single motive power, and cause to act in concert.

This sum of forces can arise only where several persons come together: but, as the force and liberty of each man are the chief instruments of his self-preservation, how can he pledge them without harming his own interests, and neglecting the care he owes to himself? This difficulty, in its bearing on my present subject, may be stated in the following terms:

"The problem is to find a form of association which will defend and protect with the whole common force the person and goods of each associate, and in which each, while uniting himself with all, may still obey himself alone, and remain as free as before." This is the fundamental problem of which the *Social Contract* provides the solution.

The clauses of this contract are so determined by the nature of the act that the slightest modification would make them vain and ineffective; so that, although they have perhaps never been formally set forth, they are everywhere the same and everywhere tacitly admitted and recognized, until, on the violation of the social compact, each regains his original rights and resumes his natural liberty, while losing the conventional liberty in favour of which he renounced it.

These clauses, properly understood, may be reduced to one—the total alienation of each associate, together with all his rights, to the whole community; for, in the first place, as each gives himself absolutely, the conditions are the same for all; and, this being so, no one has any interest in making them burdensome to others.

Moreover, the alienation being without reserve, the union is as perfect as it can be, and no associate has anything more to demand: for, if the individuals retained certain rights, as there would be no common superior to decide between them and the public, each, being on one point his own judge, would ask to be so on all; the state of nature would thus continue, and the association would necessarily become inoperative or tyrannical.

Finally, each man, in giving himself to all, gives himself to nobody; and as there is no associate over which he does not acquire the same right as he yields others over himself, he gains an equivalent for everything he loses, and an increase of force for the preservation of what he has.

If then we discard from the social compact what is not of its essence, we shall find that it reduces itself to the following terms:

"Each of us puts his person and all his power in common under the supreme direction of the general will, and, in our corporate capacity, we receive each member as an indivisible part of the whole."

At once, in place of the individual personality of each contracting party, this act of association creates a moral and collective body, composed of as many members as the assembly contains voters, and receiving from this act its unity, its common identity, its life, and its will. This public person, so formed by the union of all other persons, formerly took the name of *city,*[2] and now takes that of *Republic* or *body politic;* it is called by its members *State* when passive, *Sovereign* when active, and *Power* when compared with others like itself. Those who are associated in it take collectively the name of *people,* and severally are called *citizens,* as sharing in the sovereign power, and *subjects,* as being under the laws of the State. But these terms are often confused and taken one for another: it is enough to know how to distinguish them when they are being used with precision.

---

[2] The real meaning of this word has been almost wholly lost in modern times; most people mistake a town for a city, and a townsman for a citizen. They do not know that houses make a town, but citizens a city. The same mistake long ago cost the Carthaginians dear. I have never read of the title of citizens being given to the subjects of any prince, not even the ancient Macedonians or the English of to-day, though they are nearer liberty than any one else. The French alone everywhere familiarly adopt the name of citizens, because, as can be seen from their dictionaries, they have no idea of its meaning, otherwise they would be guilty in usurping it, of the crime of *lèse-majesté:* among them, the name expresses a virtue, and not a right. When Bodin spoke of our citizens and townsmen, he fell into a bad blunder in taking the one class for the other. M. d'Alembert has avoided the error, and, in his article on Geneva, has clearly distinguished the four orders of men (or even five, counting mere foreigners) who dwell in our town, of which two only compose the Republic. No other French writer, to my knowledge, has understood the real meaning of the word citizen.

THE SOVEREIGN

This formula shows us that the act of association comprises a mutual undertaking between the public and the individuals, and that each individual, in making a contract, as we may say, with himself, is bound in a double capacity; as a member of the Sovereign he is bound to the individuals, and as a member of the State to the Sovereign. But the maxim of civil right, that no one is bound by undertakings made to himself, does not apply in this case; for there is a great difference between incurring an obligation to yourself and incurring one to a whole of which you form a part.

Attention must further be called to the fact that public deliberation, while competent to bind all the subjects to the Sovereign, because of the two different capacities in which each of them may be regarded, cannot, for the opposite reason, bind the Sovereign to itself; and that it is consequently against the nature of the body politic for the Sovereign to impose on itself a law which it cannot infringe. Being able to regard itself in only one capacity, it is in the position of an individual who makes a contract with himself; and this makes it clear that there neither is nor can be any kind of fundamental law binding on the body of the people— not even the social contract itself. This does not mean that the body politic cannot enter into undertakings with others, provided the contract is not infringed by them; for in relation to what is external to it, it becomes a simple being, an individual.

But the body politic or the Sovereign, drawing its being wholly from the sanctity of the contract, can never bind itself, even to an outsider, to do anything derogatory to the original act, for instance, to alienate any part of itself, or to submit to another Sovereign. Violation of the act by which it exists would be self-annihilation; and that which is itself nothing can create nothing.

As soon as this multitude is so united in one body, it is impossible to offend against one of the members without attacking the body, and still more to offend against the body without the members resenting it. Duty and interest therefore equally oblige the two contracting parties to give each other help; and the same men should seek to combine, in their double capacity, all the advantages dependent upon that capacity.

Again, the Sovereign, being formed wholly of the individuals who compose it, neither has nor can have any interest contrary to theirs; and consequently the sovereign power need give no guarantee to its subjects, because it is impossible for the body to wish to hurt all its members. We shall also see later on that it cannot hurt any in particular. The Sovereign, merely by virtue of what it is, is always what it should be.

This, however, is not the case with the relation of the subjects to the Sovereign, which, despite the common interest, would have no security that they would fulfil their undertakings, unless it found means to assure itself of their fidelity.

In fact, each individual, as a man, may have a particular will contrary or dissimilar to the general will which he has as a citizen. His particular interest may speak to him quite differently from the common interest: his absolute and naturally independent existence may make him look upon what he owes to the common cause as a gratuitous contribution, the loss of which will do less harm to others than the payment of it is burdensome to himself; and, regarding the moral person which constitutes the State as a *persona ficta*, because not a man, he may wish to enjoy the rights of citizenship without being ready to fulfil the duties of a subject. The continuance of such an injustice could not but prove the undoing of the body politic.

In order then that the social compact may not be an empty formula, it tacitly includes the undertaking, which alone can give force to the rest, that whoever refuses to obey the general will shall be compelled to do so by the whole body. This means nothing less than that he will be forced to be free; for this is the condition which, by giving each citizen to his country, secures him against all personal dependence. In this lies the key to the working of the political machine; this alone legitimizes civil undertakings, which, without it, would be absurd, tyrannical, and liable to the most frightful abuses.

THE CIVIL STATE

The passage from the state of nature to the civil state produces a very remarkable change in man, by substituting justice for instinct in his conduct, and giving his actions the morality they had formerly lacked. Then only, when the voice of duty takes the place of physical impulses and right of appetite, does man, who so far had considered only himself, find that he is forced to act on different principles, and to consult his reason before listening to his inclinations. Although, in this state, he deprives himself of some advantages which he got from nature, he gains in return others so great, his faculties are so stimulated and developed, his ideas so extended, his feelings so ennobled, and his whole soul so uplifted, that, did not the abuses of this new condition often degrade him below that which he left, he would be bound to bless continually the happy moment which took him from it for ever, and, instead of a stupid and unimaginative animal, made him an intelligent being and a man.

Let us draw up the whole account in terms easily commensurable. What man loses by the social contract is his natural liberty and an unlimited right to everything he tries to get and succeeds in getting; what he gains is civil liberty and the proprietorship of all he possesses. If we are to avoid mistakes in weighing one against the other, we must clearly distinguish natural liberty, which is bounded only by the strength of the individual, from civil liberty, which is limited by the general will; and possession, which is merely the effect of force or the right of the first occupier, from property, which can be founded only on a positive title.

We might, over and above all this, add, to what man acquires in the civil state, moral liberty, which alone makes him truly master of himself; for the mere impulse of appetite is slavery, while obedience to a law which we prescribe to ourselves is liberty. But I have already said too much on this head, and the philosophical meaning of the word liberty does not now concern us.

THE INALIENABILITY OF SOVEREIGNTY

The first and most important deduction from the principles we have so far laid down is that the general will alone can direct the State according to the object for which it was instituted, i.e. the common good: for if the clashing of particular interests made the establishment of societies necessary, the agreement of these very interests made it possible. The common element in these different interests is what forms the social tie; and, were there no point of agreement between them all, no society could exist. It is solely on the basis of this common interest that every society should be governed.

I hold then that Sovereignty, being nothing less than the exercise of the general will, can never be alienated, and that the Sovereign, who is no less than a collective being, cannot be represented except by himself: the power indeed may be transmitted, but not the will.

In reality, if it is not impossible for a particular will to agree on some point with the general will, it is at least impossible for the agreement to be lasting and constant; for the particular will tends, by its very nature, to partiality, while the general will tends to equality. It is even more impossible to have any guarantee of this agreement; for even if it should always exist, it would be the effect not of art, but of chance. The Sovereign may indeed say: "I now will actually what this man wills, or at least what he says he wills"; but it cannot say: "What he wills to-morrow, I too shall will" because it is absurd for the will to bind itself for the future, nor is it incumbent on any will to consent to anything that is not for the good of the being who wills. If then the people promises simply to obey, by that very act it dissolves itself and loses what makes it a people; the moment a master exists, there is no longer a Sovereign, and from that moment the body politic has ceased to exist.

This does not mean that the commands of the rulers cannot pass for general wills, so long as the Sovereign, being free to oppose them, offers no opposition. In such a case, universal silence is taken to imply the consent of the people. This will be explained later on.

THE INDIVISIBILITY
OF SOVEREIGNTY

Sovereignty, for the same reason as makes it inalienable, is indivisible; for will either is, or is not, general;[3] it is the will either of the body of the people, or only of a part of it. In the first case, the will, when declared, is an act of Sovereignty and constitutes law: in the second, it is merely a particular will, or act of magistracy—at the most a decree.

But our political theorists, unable to divide Sovereignty in principle, divide it according to its object: into force and will; into legislative power and executive power; into rights of taxation, justice, and war; into internal administration and power of foreign treaty. Sometimes they confuse all these sections, and sometimes they distinguish them; they turn the Sovereign into a fantastic being composed of several connected pieces: it is as if they were making man of several bodies, one with eyes, one with arms, another with feet, and each with nothing besides. We are told that the jugglers of Japan dismember a child before the eyes of the spectators; then they throw all the members into the air one after another, and the child falls down alive and whole. The conjuring tricks of our political theorists are very like that; they first dismember the body politic by an illusion worthy of a fair, and then join it together again we know not how.

This error is due to a lack of exact notions concerning the Sovereign authority, and to taking for parts of it what are only emanations from it. Thus, for example, the acts of declaring war and making peace have been regarded as acts of Sovereignty; but this is not the case, as these acts do not constitute law, but merely the application of a law, a particular act which decides how the law applies, as we shall see clearly when the idea attached to the word "law" has been defined.

If we examined the other divisions in the same manner, we should find, that, whenever Sovereignty seems to be divided, there is an illusion: the rights which are taken as being part of Sovereignty are really all subordinate, and always imply supreme wills of which they only sanction the execution.

It would be impossible to estimate the obscurity this lack of exactness has thrown

---

[3] To be general, a will need not always be unanimous; but every vote must be counted: any exclusion is a breach of generality.

over the decisions of writers who have dealt with political right, when they have used the principles laid down by them to pass judgment on the respective rights of kings and peoples. Every one can see, in Chapters III and IV of the first book of Grotius, how the learned man and his translator, Barbeyrac, entangle and tie themselves up in their own sophistries, for fear of saying too little or too much of what they think, and so offending the interests they have to conciliate. Grotius, a refugee in France, ill content with his own country, and desirous of paying his court to Louis XIII, to whom his book is dedicated, spares no pains to rob the peoples of all their rights and invest kings with them by every conceivable artifice. This would also have been much to the taste of Barbeyrac, who dedicated his translation to George I of England. But unfortunately the expulsion of James II, which he called his "abdication," compelled him to use all reserve, to shuffle and to tergiversate, in order to avoid making William out a usurper. If these two writers had adopted the true principles, all difficulties would have been removed, and they would have been always consistent; but it would have been a sad truth for them to tell, and would have paid court for them to no one save the people. Moreover, truth is no road to fortune, and the people dispenses neither ambassadorships, nor professorships, nor pensions.

INFALLIBILITY OF THE GENERAL WILL

It follows from what has gone before that the general will is always right and tends to the public advantage; but it does not follow that the deliberations of the people are always equally correct. Our will is always for our own good, but we do not always see what that is; the people is never corrupted, but it is often deceived, and on such occasions only does it seem to will what is bad.

There is often a great deal of difference between the will of all and the general will; the latter considers only the common interest, while the former takes private interest into account, and is no more than a sum of particular wills: but take away from these same wills the pluses and minuses that cancel one another,[4] and the general will remains as the sum of the differences.

If, when the people, being furnished with adequate information, held its deliberations, the citizens had no communication one with another, the grand total of the small differences would always give the general will, and the decision would always be good. But when factions arise, and partial associations are formed at the expense of the great association, the will of each of these associations becomes general in relation to its members, while it remains particular in relation to the State: it may then be said that there are no longer as many votes as there are men, but only as many as there are associations. The differences become less numerous and give a less general result. Lastly, when one of these associations is so great as to prevail over all the rest, the result is no longer a sum of small differences, but a single difference; in this case there is no longer a general will, and the opinion which prevails is purely particular.

It is therefore essential, if the general will is to be able to express itself, that there should be no partial society within the State, and that each citizen should think only his own thoughts[5] which was indeed the sublime and unique system established by the great Lycurgus. But if there are partial societies, it is best to have as many as possible and to prevent them from being unequal, as was done by Solon, Numa, and Servius. These precautions are the only

---

[4] "Every interest," says the Marquis d'Argenson, "has different principles. The agreement of two particular interests is formed by opposition to a third." He might have added that the agreement of all interests is formed by opposition to that of each. If there were no different interests, the common interest would be barely felt, as it would encounter no obstacle; all would go on of its own accord, and politics would cease to be an art.

[5] "In fact," says Machiavelli, "there are some divisions that are harmful to a Republic and some that are advantageous. Those which stir up sects and parties are harmful; those attended by neither are advantageous. Since, then, the founder of a Republic cannot help enmities arising, he ought at least to prevent them from growing into sects" (*History of Florence,* Book VII).

ones than can guarantee that the general will shall be always enlightened, and that the people shall in no way deceive itself.

LIMITS OF THE SOVEREIGN POWER

If the State is a moral person whose life is in the union of its members, and if the most important of its cares is the care for its own preservation, it must have a universal and compelling force, in order to move and dispose each part as may be most advantageous to the whole. As nature gives each man absolute power over all his members, the social compact gives the body politic absolute power over all its members also; and it is this power which, under the direction of the general will, bears, as I have said, the name of Sovereignty.

But, besides the public person, we have to consider the private persons composing it, whose life and liberty are naturally independent of it. We are bound then to distinguish clearly between the respective rights of the citizens and the Sovereign,[6] and between the duties the former have to fulfil as subjects, and the natural rights they should enjoy as men.

Each man alienates, I admit, by the social compact, only such part of his powers, goods, and liberty as it is important for the community to control; but it must also be granted that the Sovereign is sole judge of what is important.

Every service a citizen can render the State he ought to render as soon as the Sovereign demands it; but the Sovereign, for its part, cannot impose upon its subjects any fetters that are useless to the community, nor can it even wish to do so; for no more by the law of reason than by the law of nature can anything occur without a cause.

The undertakings which bind us to the social body are obligatory only because they are mutual; and their nature is such that in fulfilling them we cannot work for others without working for ourselves. Why is it that the general will is always in the right,

and that all continually will the happiness of each one, unless it is because there is not a man who does not think of "each" as meaning him, and consider himself in voting for all? This proves that equality of rights and the idea of justice which such equality creates originate in the preference each man gives to himself, and accordingly in the very nature of man. It proves that the general will, to be really such, must be general in its object as well as its essence; that it must both come from all and apply to all; and that it loses its natural rectitude when it is directed to some particular and determinate object, because in such a case we are judging of something foreign to us, and have no true principle of equity to guide us.

Indeed, as soon as a question of particular fact or right arises on a point not previously regulated by a general convention, the matter becomes contentious. It is a case in which the individuals concerned are one party, and the public the other, but in which I can see neither the law that ought to be followed nor the judge who ought to give the decision. In such a case, it would be absurd to propose to refer the question to an express decision of the general will, which can be only the conclusion reached by one of the parties and in consequence will be, for the other party, merely an external and particular will, inclined on this occasion to injustice and subject to error. Thus, just as a particular will cannot stand for the general will, the general will, in turn, changes its nature, when its object is particular, and, as general, cannot pronounce on a man or a fact. When, for instance, the people of Athens nominated or displaced its rulers, decreed honours to one, and imposed penalties on another, and, by a multitude of particular decrees, exercised all the functions of government indiscriminately, it had in such cases no longer a general will in the strict sense; it was acting no longer as Sovereign, but as magistrate. This will seem contrary to current views; but I must be given time to expound my own.

It should be seen from the foregoing that what makes the will general is less the number of votes than the common interest uniting them; for, under this system, each necessarily submits to the conditions he imposes on others: and this admirable agreement between interest and justice gives to

---

[6] Attentive readers, do not, I pray, be in a hurry to charge me with contradicting myself. The terminology made it unavoidable, considering the poverty of the language; but wait and see.

the common deliberations an equitable character which at once vanishes when any particular question is discussed, in the absence of a common interest to unite and identify the ruling of the judge with that of the party.

From whatever side we approach our principle, we reach the same conclusion, that the social compact sets up among the citizens an equality of such a kind, that they all bind themselves to observe the same conditions and should therefore all enjoy the same rights. Thus, from the very nature of the compact, every act of Sovereignty, i.e. every authentic act of the general will, binds or favours all the citizens equally; so that the Sovereign recognizes only the body of the nation, and draws no distinctions between those of whom it is made up. What, then, strictly speaking, is an act of Sovereignty? It is not a convention between a superior and an inferior, but a conviction between the body and each of its members. It is legitimate, because based on the social contract, and equitable, because common to all; useful, because it can have no other object than the general good, and stable, because guaranteed by the public force and the supreme power. So long as the subjects have to submit only to conventions of this sort, they obey no one but their own will; and to ask how far the respective rights of the Sovereign and the citizens extend, is to ask up to what point the latter can enter into undertakings with themselves, each with all, and all with each.

We can see from this that the sovereign power, absolute, sacred, and inviolable as it is, does not and cannot exceed the limits of general conventions, and that every man may dispose at will of such goods and liberty as these conventions leave him; so that the Sovereign never has a right to lay more charges on one subject than on another, because, in that case, the question becomes particular, and ceases to be within its competency.

When these distinctions have once been admitted, it is seen to be so untrue that there is, in the social contract, any real renunciation on the part of the individuals, that the position in which they find themselves as a result of the contract is really preferable to that in which they were before. Instead of a renunciation, they have made an advantageous exchange: instead of an uncertain and

precarious way of living they have got one that is better and more secure; instead of natural independence they have got liberty, instead of the power to harm others security for themselves, and instead of their strength, which others might overcome, a right which social union makes invincible. Their very life, which they have devoted to the State, is by it constantly protected; and when they risk it in the State's defence, what more are they doing than giving back what they have received from it? What are they doing that they would not do more often and with greater danger in the state of nature, in which they would inevitably have to fight battles at the peril of their lives in defence of that which is the means of their preservation? All have indeed to fight when their country needs them; but then no one has ever to fight for himself. Do we not gain something by running, on behalf of what gives us our security, only some of the risks we should have to run for ourselves, as soon as we lost it?

LAW

By the social compact we have given the body politic existence and life; we have now by legislation to give it movement and will. For the original act by which the body is formed and united still in no respect determines what it ought to do for its preservation.

What is well and in conformity with order is so by the nature of things and independently of human conventions. All justice comes from God, who is its sole source; but if we knew how to receive so high an inspiration, we should need neither government nor laws. Doubtless, there is a universal justice emanating from reason alone; but this justice, to be admitted among us, must be mutual. Humanly speaking, in default of natural sanctions, the laws of justice are ineffective among men: they merely make for the good of the wicked and the undoing of the just, when the just man observes them towards everybody and nobody observes them towards him. Conventions and laws are therefore needed to join rights to duties and refer justice to its object. In the state of nature, where everything is common, I owe nothing to him whom I have promised nothing; I recognize as belonging to others only what is of no use to me. In the state of society all rights are fixed by law, and the case becomes different.

But what, after all, is a law? As long as we remain satisfied with attaching purely metaphysical ideas to the word, we shall go on arguing without arriving at an understanding; and when we have defined a law of nature, we shall be no nearer the definition of a law of the State,

I have already said that there can be no general will directed to a particular object. Such an object must be either within or outside the State. If outside, a will which is alien to it cannot be, in relation to it, general; if within, it is part of the State, and in that case there arises a relation between whole and part which makes them two separate beings, of which the part is one, and the whole minus the part the other. But the whole minus a part cannot be the whole; and while this relation persists, there can be no whole, but only two unequal parts; and it follows that the will of one is no longer in any respect general in relation to the other.

But when the whole people decrees for the whole people, it is considering only itself; and if a relation is then formed, it is between two aspects of the entire object, without there being any division of the whole. In that case the matter about which the decree is made is, like the decreeing will, general. This act is what I call a law.

When I say that the object of laws is always general, I mean that law considers subjects *en masse* and actions in the abstract, and never a particular person or action. Thus the law may indeed decree that there shall be privileges, but cannot confer them on anybody by name. It may set up several classes of citizens, and even lay down the qualifications for membership of these classes, but it cannot nominate such and such persons as belonging to them; it may establish a monarchical government and hereditary succession, but it cannot choose a king, or nominate a royal family. In a word, no function which has a particular object belongs to the legislative power.

On this view, we at once see that it can no longer be asked whose business it is to make laws, since they are acts of the general will; nor whether the prince is above the law, since he is a member of the State; nor whether the law can be unjust, since no one is unjust to himself; nor how we can be both free and subject to the laws, since they are but registers of our wills.

We see further that, as the law unites universality of will with universality of object, what a man, whoever he be, commands of his own motion cannot be a law; and even what the Sovereign commands with regard to a particular matter is no nearer being a law, but is a decree, an act, not of sovereignty, but of magistracy.

I therefore give the name "Republic" to every State that is governed by laws, no matter what the form of its administration may be: for only in such a case does the public interest govern, and the *res publica* rank as a *reality*. Every legitimate government is republican;[7] what government is I will explain later on.

Laws are, properly speaking, only the conditions of civil association. The people, being subject to the laws, ought to be their author: the conditions of the society ought to be regulated solely by those who come together to form it. But how are they to regulate them? Is it to be by common agreement, by a sudden inspiration? Has the body politic an organ to declare its will? Who can give it the foresight to formulate and announce its acts in advance? Or how is it to announce them in the hour of need? How can a blind multitude, which often does not know what it wills, because it rarely knows what is good for it, carry out for itself so great and difficult an enterprise as a system of legislation? Of itself the people wills always the good, but of itself it by no means always sees it. The general will is always in the right, but the judgment which guides it is not always enlightened. It must be got to see objects as they are, and sometimes as they ought to appear to it; it must be shown the good road it is in search of, secured from the seductive influences of individual wills, taught to see times and spaces as a series, and made to weigh the attractions of present and sensible advantages against the danger of distant and hidden evils. The individuals

---

[7] I understand by this word, not merely an aristocracy or a democracy, but generally any government directed by the general will, which is the law. To be legitimate, the government must be, not one with the Sovereign, but its minister. In such a case even a monarchy is a Republic.

see the good they reject; the public wills the good it does not see. All stand equally in need of guidance. The former must be compelled to bring their wills into conformity with their reason; the latter must be taught to know what it wills. If that is done, public enlightenment leads to the union of understanding and will in the social body: the parts are made to work exactly together, and the whole is raised to its highest power. This makes a legislator necessary.

THE LEGISLATOR

In order to discover the rules of society best suited to nations, a superior intelligence beholding all the passions of men without experiencing any of them would be needed. This intelligence would have to be wholly unrelated to our nature, while knowing it through and through; its happiness would have to be independent of us, and yet ready to occupy itself with ours; and lastly, it would have, in the march of time, to look forward to a distant glory, and, working in one century, to be able to enjoy in the next.[8] It would take gods to give men laws.

What Caligula argued from the facts, Plato, in the dialogue called the *Politicus,* argued in defining the civil or kingly man, on the basis of right. But if great princes are rare, how much more so are great legislators! The former have only to follow the pattern which the latter have to lay down. The legislator is the engineer who invents the machine, the prince merely the mechanic who sets it up and makes it go. "At the birth of societies," says Montesquieu, "the rulers of Republics establish institutions, and afterwards the institutions mould the rulers."[9]

He who dares to undertake the making of a people's institutions ought to feel himself capable, so to speak, of changing human nature, of transforming each individual, who is by himself a complete and solitary whole, into part of a greater whole from which he in a manner receives his life and being; of altering man's constitution for the purpose of strengthening it; and of substituting a partial and moral existence for the physical and independent existence nature has conferred on us all. He must, in a word, take away from man his own resources and give him instead new ones alien to him, and incapable of being made use of without the help of other men. The more completely these natural resources are annihilated, the greater and more lasting are those which he acquires, and the more stable and perfect the new institutions; so that if each citizen is nothing and can do nothing without the rest, and the resources acquired by the whole are equal or superior to the aggregate of the resources of all the individuals, it may be said that legislation is at the highest possible point of perfection.

The legislator occupies in every respect an extraordinary position in the State. If he should do so by reason of his genius, he does so no less by reason of his office, which is neither magistracy, nor Sovereignty. This office, which sets up the Republic, nowhere enters into its constitution; it is an individual and superior function, which has nothing in common with human empire; for if he who holds command over men ought not to have command over the laws, he who has command over the laws ought not any more to have it over men; or else his laws would be the ministers of his passions and would often merely serve to perpetuate his injustices: his private aims would inevitably mar the sanctity of his work.

When Lycurgus gave laws to his country, he began by resigning the throne. It was the custom of most Greek towns to entrust the establishment of their laws to foreigners. The Republics of modern Italy in many cases followed this examples; Geneva did the same and profited by it.[10] Rome, when it was most prosperous, suffered a revival of

---

[8] A people becomes famous only when its legislation begins to decline. We do not know for how many centuries the system of Lycurgus made the Spartans happy before the rest of Greece took any notice of it.

[9] Montesquieu, *The Greatness and Decadence of the Romans,* chap. i.

[10] Those who know Calvin only as a theologian much underestimate the extent of his genius. The codification of our wise edicts, in which he played a large part, does him no less honour than his *Institutes.* Whatever revolution time may bring in our religion, so long as the spirit of patriotism and liberty still lives among us, the memory of this great man will be for ever blessed.

all the crimes of tyranny, and was brought to the verge of destruction, because it put the legislative authority and the sovereign power into the same hands.

Nevertheless, the decemvirs themselves never claimed the right to pass any law merely on their own authority. "Nothing we propose to you," they said to the people, "can pass into law without your consent. Romans, be yourselves the authors of the laws which are to make you happy."

He, therefore, who draws up the laws has, or should have, no right of legislation, and the people cannot, even if it wishes, deprive itself of this incommunicable right, because, according to the fundamental compact, only the general will can bind the individuals, and there can be no assurance that a particular will is in conformity with the general will, until it has been put to the free vote of the people. This I have said already; but it is worth while to repeat it.

Thus in the task of legislation we find together two things which appear to be incompatible: an enterprise too difficult for human powers, and, for its execution, an authority that is no authority.

There is a further difficulty that deserves attention. Wise men, if they try to speak their language to the common herd instead of its own, cannot possibly make themselves understood. There are a thousand kinds of ideas which it is impossible to translate into popular language. Conceptions that are too general and objects that are too remote are equally out of its range: each individual, having no taste for any other plan of government than that which suits his particular interest, finds it difficult to realize the advantages he might hope to draw from the continual privations good laws impose. For a young people to be able to relish sound principles of political theory and follow the fundamental rules of statecraft, the effect would have to become the cause; the social spirit, which should be created by these institutions, would have to preside over their very foundation; and men would have to be before law what they should become by means of law. The legislator therefore, being unable to appeal to either force or reason, must have recourse to an authority of a different order, capable of constraining without violence and persuading without convincing.

This is what has, in all ages, compelled the fathers of nations to have recourse to divine intervention and credit the gods with their own wisdom, in order that the peoples, submitting to the laws of the State as to those of nature, and recognizing the same power in the formation of the city as in that of man, might obey freely, and bear with docility the yoke of the public happiness.

This sublime reason, far above the range of the common herd, is that whose decisions the legislator puts into the mouth of the immortals, in order to constrain by divine authority those whom human prudence could not move.[11] But it is not anybody who can make the gods speak, or get himself believed when he proclaims himself their interpreter. The great soul of the legislator is the only miracle that can prove his mission. Any man may grave tablets of stone, or buy an oracle, or feign secret intercourse with some divinity, or train a bird to whisper in his ear, or find other vulgar ways of imposing on the people. He whose knowledge goes no further may perhaps gather round him a band of fools; but he will never found an empire, and his extravagances will quickly perish with him. Idle tricks form a passing tie; only wisdom can make it lasting. The Judaic law, which still subsists, and that of the child of Ishmael, which, for ten centuries, has ruled half the world, still proclaim the great men who laid them down; and, while the pride of philosophy or the blind spirit of faction sees in them no more than lucky impostures, the true political theorist admires, in the institutions they set up, the great and powerful genius which presides over things made to endure.

We should not, with Warburton, conclude from this that politics and religion have among us a common object, but that, in the first periods of nations, the one is used as an instrument for the other.

---

[11] "In truth," says Machiavelli, "there has never been, in any country, an extraordinary legislator who has not had recourse to God; for otherwise his laws would not have been accepted: there are, in fact, many useful truths of which a wise man may have knowledge without their having in themselves such clear reasons for their being so as to be able to convince others" (*Discourses on Livy,* Bk. V, chap. xi).

THE PEOPLE

As nature has set bounds to the stature of a well-made man, and, outside those limits, makes nothing but giants or dwarfs, similarly, for the constitution of a State to be at its best, it is possible to fix limits that will make it neither too large for good government, nor too small for self-maintenance. In every body politic there is a maximum strength which it cannot exceed and which it only loses by increasing in size. Every extension of the social tie means its relaxation; and, generally speaking, a small State is stronger in proportion than a great one.

A thousand arguments could be advanced in favour of this principle. First, long distances make administration more difficult, just as a weight becomes heavier at the end of a longer lever. Administration therefore becomes more and more burdensome as the distance grows greater; for, in the first place, each city has its own, which is paid for by the people: each district its own, still paid for by the people: then comes each province, and then the great governments, satrapies, and viceroyalties, always costing more the higher you go, and always at the expense of the unfortunate people. Last of all comes the supreme administration, which eclipses all the rest. All these overcharges are a continual drain upon the subjects; so far from being better governed by all these different orders, they are worse governed than if there were only a single authority over them. In the meantime, there scarce remain resources enough to meet emergencies; and, when recourse must be had to these, the State is always on the eve of destruction.

This is not all; not only has the government less vigour and promptitude for securing the observance of the laws, preventing nuisances, correcting abuses, and guarding against seditious undertakings begun in distant places; the people has less affection for its rulers, whom it never sees, for its country, which, to its eyes, seems like the world, and for its fellow citizens, most of whom are unknown to it. The same laws cannot suit so many diverse provinces with different customs, situated in the most various climates, and incapable of enduring a uniform government. Different laws lead only to trouble and confusion among peoples which, living under the same rulers and in constant communication one with another, intermingle and intermarry, and, coming under the sway of new customs, never know if they can call their very patrimony their own. Talent is buried, virtue unknown, and vice unpunished, among such a multitude of men who do not know one another, gathered together in one place at the seat of the central administration. The leaders, overwhelmed with business, see nothing for themselves; the State is governed by clerks. Finally, the measures which have to be taken to maintain the general authority, which all these distant officials wish to escape or to impose upon, absorb all the energy of the public, so that there is none left for the happiness of the people. There is hardly enough to defend it when need arises, and thus a body which is too big for its constitution gives way and falls crushed under its own weight.

Again, the State must assure itself a safe foundation, if it is to have stability, and to be able to resist the shocks it cannot help experiencing, as well as the efforts it will be forced to make for its maintenance; for all peoples have a kind of centrifugal force that makes them continually act one against another, and tend to aggrandize themselves at their neighbours' expense, like the vortices of Descartes. Thus the weak run the risk of being soon swallowed up; and it is almost impossible for any one to preserve itself except by putting itself in a state of equilibrium with all, so that the pressure is on all sides practically equal.

It may therefore be seen that there are reasons for expansion and reasons for contraction; and it is no small part of the statesman's skill to hit between them the mean that is most favourable to the preservation of the State. It may be said that the reason for expansion, being merely external and relative, ought to be subordinate to the reasons for contraction, which are internal and absolute. A strong and healthy constitution is the first thing to look for; and it is better to count on the vigour which comes of good government than on the resources a great territory furnishes.

It may be added that there have been known States so constituted that the necessity of making conquests entered into their very constitution, and that, in order to maintain themselves, they were forced to expand ceaselessly. It may be that they congratulated themselves greatly on this fortunate necessity, which none the less indicated to them, along with the limits of their greatness, the inevitable moment of their fall.

GOVERNMENT IN GENERAL

I warn the reader that this chapter requires careful reading, and that I am unable to make myself clear to those who refuse to be attentive.

Every free action is produced by the concurrence of two causes; one moral, i.e. the will which determines the act; the other physical, i.e. the power which executes it. When I walk towards an object, it is necessary first that I should will to go there, and, in the second place, that my feet should carry me. If a paralytic wills to run and an active man wills not to, they will both stay where they are. The body politic has the same motive powers; here too force and will are distinguished, will under the name of legislative power and force under that of executive power. Without their concurrence, nothing is, or should be, done.

We have seen that the legislative power belongs to the people, and can belong to it alone. It may, on the other hand, readily be seen, from the principles laid down above, that the executive power cannot belong to the generality as legislature or Sovereign, because it consists wholly of particular acts which fall outside the competency of the law, and consequently of the Sovereign, whose acts must always be laws.

The public force therefore needs an agent of its own to bind it together and set it to work under the direction of the general will, to serve as a means of communication between the State and the Sovereign, and to do for the collective person more or less what the union of soul and body does for man. Here we have what is, in the State, the basis of government, often wrongly confused with the Sovereign, whose minister it is.

What then is government? An intermediate body set up between the subjects and the Sovereign, to secure their mutual correspondence, charged with the execution of the laws and the maintenance of liberty, both civil and political.

The members of this body are called magistrates or *kings,* that is to say *governors,* and the whole body bears the name *prince.*[12] Thus those who hold that the act, by which a people puts itself under a prince, is not a contract, are certainly right. It is simply and solely a commission, an employment, in which the rulers, mere officials of the Sovereign, exercise in their own name the power of which it makes them depositaries. This power it can limit, modify, or recover at pleasure; for the alienation of such a right is incompatible with the nature of the social body, and contrary to the end of association.

I call then *government,* or supreme administration, the legitimate exercise of the executive power, and prince or magistrate the man or the body entrusted with that administration.

In government reside the intermediate forces whose relations make up that of the whole to the whole, or of the Sovereign to the State. This last relation may be represented as that between the extreme terms of the continuous proportion, which has government as its mean proportional. The government gets from the Sovereign the orders it gives the people, and, for the State to be properly balanced, there must, when everything is reckoned in, be equality between the product or power of the government taken in itself, and the product or power of the citizens, who are on the one hand sovereign and on the other subject.

Furthermore, none of these three terms can be altered without the equality being instantly destroyed. If the Sovereign desires to govern, or the magistrate to give laws, or if the subjects refuse to obey, disorder takes the place of regularity, force and will no longer act together, and the State is dissolved and falls into despotism or anarchy. Lastly, as there is only one mean proportional between each relation, there is also only one good government possible for a State. But, as countless events may change the relations of a people, not only may different governments be good for different peoples, but also for the same people at different times.

---

[12] Thus at Venice the College, even in the absence of the Doge, is called "Most Serene Prince."

In attempting to give some idea of the various relations that may hold between these two extreme terms, I shall take as an example the number of a people, which is the most easily expressible.

Suppose the State is composed of ten thousand citizens. The Sovereign can only be considered collectively and as a body; but each member, as being a subject, is regarded as an individual: thus the Sovereign is to the subject as ten thousand to one, i.e. each member of the State has as his share only a ten-thousandth part of the sovereign authority, although he is wholly under its control. If the people numbers a hundred thousand, the condition of the subject undergoes no change, and each equally is under the whole authority of the laws, while his vote, being reduced to one hundred thousandth part, has ten times less influence in drawing them up. The subject therefore remaining always a unit, the relation between him and the Sovereign increases with the number of citizens. From this it follows that, the larger the State, the less the liberty.

When I say the relation increases, I mean that it grows more unequal. Thus the greater it is in the geometrical sense, the less relation there is in the ordinary sense of the word. In the former sense, the relation, considered according to quantity, is expressed by the quotient; in the latter, considered according to identity, it is reckoned by similarity.

Now, the less relation the particular wills have to the general will, that is, morals and manners to laws, the more should the repressive force be increased. The government, then, to be good, should be proportionately stronger as the people is more numerous.

On the other hand, as the growth of the State gives the depositaries of the public authority more temptations and chances of abusing their power, the greater the force with which the government ought to be endowed for keeping the people in hand, the greater too should be the force at the disposal of the Sovereign for keeping the government in hand. I am speaking, not of absolute force, but of the relative force of the different parts of the state.

It follows from this double relation that the continuous proportion between the Sovereign, the prince, and the people, is by no means an arbitrary idea, but a necessary consequence of the nature of the body politic. It follows further that, one of the extreme terms, viz. the people, as subject, being fixed and represented by unity, whenever the duplicate ratio increases or diminishes, the simple ratio does the same, and is changed accordingly. From this we see that there is not a single unique and absolute form of government, but as many governments differing in nature as there are States differing in size.

If, ridiculing this system, any one were to say that, in order to find the mean proportional and give form to the body of the government, it is only necessary, according to me, to find the square root of the number of the people, I should answer that I am here taking this number only as an instance; that the relations of which I am speaking are not measured by the number of men alone, but generally by the amount of action, which is a combination of a multitude of causes; and that, further, if, to save words, I borrow for a moment the terms of geometry, I am none the less well aware that moral quantities do not allow of geometrical accuracy.

The government is on a small scale what the body politic which includes it is on a great one. It is a moral person endowed with certain faculties, active like the Sovereign and passive like the State, and capable of being resolved into other similar relations. This accordingly gives rise to a new proportion, within which there is yet another, according to the arrangement of the magistracies, till an indivisible middle term is reached, i.e. a single ruler or supreme magistrate, who may be represented, in the midst of this progression, as the unity between the fractional and the ordinal series.

Without encumbering ourselves with this multiplication of terms, let us rest content with regarding government as a new body within the State, distinct from the people and the Sovereign, and intermediate between them.

There is between these two bodies this essential difference, that the State exists by itself, and the government only through the Sovereign. Thus the dominant will of the prince is, or should be, nothing but the general will or the law; his force is only the public force concentrated in his hands, and, as soon as he tries to base any absolute and independent act on his own authority, the tie that binds the whole together begins to be loosened. If finally the prince should come to have a particular will more active than the will of the Sovereign, and should employ the public force in his hands in obedience to this particular will, there would be, so to speak, two Sovereigns, one rightful and the other actual, the social union would evaporate instantly, and the body politic would be dissolved.

However, in order that the government may have a true existence and a real life distinguishing it from the body of the State, and in order that all its members may be able to act in concert and fulfil the end for which it was set up, it must have a particular personality, a sensibility common to its members, and a force and will of its own making for its preservation. This particular existence implies assemblies, councils, power of deliberation and decision, rights, titles, and privileges belonging exclusively to the prince and making the office of magistrate more honourable in proportion as it is more troublesome. The difficulties lie in the manner of so ordering this subordinate whole within the whole, that it in no way alters the general constitution by affirmation of its own, and always distinguishes the particular force it possesses, which is destined to aid in its preservation, from the public force, which is destined to the preservation of the State; and, in a word, is always ready to sacrifice the government to the people, and never to sacrifice the people to the government.

Furthermore, although the artificial body of the government is the work of another artificial body, and has, we may say, only a borrowed and subordinate life, this does not prevent it from being able to act with more or less vigour or promptitude, or from being, so to speak, in more or less robust health. Finally, without departing directly from the end for which it was instituted, it may deviate more or less from it, according to the manner of its constitution.

From all these differences arise the various relations which the government ought to bear to the body of the State, according to the accidental and particular relations by which the State itself is modified, for often the government that is best in itself will become the most pernicious, if the relations in which it stands have altered according to the defects of the body politic to which it belongs.

DEMOCRACY

He who makes the law knows better than any one else how it should be executed and interpreted. It seems then impossible to have a better constitution than that in which the executive and legislative powers are united; but this very fact renders the government in certain respects inadequate, because things which should be distinguished are confounded, and the prince and the Sovereign, being the same person, form, so to speak, no more than a government without government.

It is not good for him who makes the laws to execute them, or for the body of the people to turn its attention away from a general standpoint and devote it to particular objects. Nothing is more dangerous than the influence of private interests in public affairs, and the abuse of the laws by the government is a less evil than the corruption of the legislator, which is the inevitable sequel to a particular standpoint. In such a case, the State being altered in substance, all reformation becomes impossible. A people that would never misuse governmental powers would never misuse independence; a people that would always govern well would not need to be governed.

If we take the term in the strict sense, there never has been a real democracy, and there never will be. It is against the natural order for the many to govern and the few to be governed. It is unimaginable that the people should remain continually assembled to devote their time to public affairs, and it is clear that they cannot set up commissions for that purpose without the form of administration being changed.

In fact, I can confidently lay down as a principle that, when the functions of government are shared by several tribunals, the less numerous sooner or later acquire the greatest authority, if only because they are in position to expedite affairs, and power thus naturally comes into their hands.

Besides, how many conditions that are difficult to unite does such a government presuppose! First, a very small State, where the people can readily be got together and where each citizen can with ease know all the rest; secondly, great simplicity of manners, to prevent business from multiplying and raising thorny problems; next, a large measure of equality in rank and fortune, without which equality of rights and authority cannot long subsist; lastly, little or no luxury—for luxury either comes of riches or makes them necessary; it corrupts at once rich and poor, the rich by possession and the poor by covetousness; it sells the country to softness and vanity, and takes away from the State all its citizens, to make them slaves one to another, and one and all to public opinion.

This is why a famous writer has made virtue the fundamental principle of Republics; for all these conditions could not exist without virtue. But, for want of the necessary distinctions, that great thinker was often inexact, and sometimes obscure, and did not see that, the sovereign authority being everywhere the same, the same principle should be found in every well-constituted State, in a greater or less degree, it is true, according to the form of the government.

It may be added that there is no government so subject to civil wars and intestine agitations as democratic or popular government, because there is none which has so strong and continual a tendency to change to another form, or which demands more vigilance and courage for its maintenance as it is. Under such a constitution above all, the citizen should arm himself with strength and constancy, and say, every day of his life, what a virtuous Count Palatine said in the Diet of Poland: "Malo periculosam libertatem quam quieturn servitium."

Were there a people of gods, their government would be democratic. So perfect a government is not for men.

DEPUTIES OR REPRESENTATIVES

As soon as public service ceases to be the chief business of the citizens, and they would rather serve with their money than with their persons, the State is not far from its fall. When it is necessary to march out to war, they pay troops and stay at home: when it is necessary to meet in council, they name deputies and stay at home. By reason of idleness and money, they end by having soldiers to enslave their country and representatives to sell it.

It is through the hustle of commerce and the arts, through the greedy self-interest of profit, and through softness and love of amenities that personal services are replaced by money payments. Men surrender a part of their profits in order to have time to increase them at leisure. Make gifts of money, and you will not be long without chains. The word "finance" is a slavish word, unknown in the city-state. In a country that is truly free, the citizens do everything with their own arms and nothing by means of money; so far from paying to be exempted from their duties, they would even pay for the privilege of fulfilling them themselves. I am far from taking the common view: I hold enforced labour to be less opposed to liberty than taxes.

The better the constitution of a State is, the more do public affairs encroach on private in the minds of the citizens. Private affairs are even of much less importance, because the aggregate of the common happiness furnishes a greater proportion of that of each individual, so that there is less for him to seek in particular cares. In a well-ordered city every man flies to the assemblies: under a bad government no one cares to stir a step to get to them, because no one is interested in what happens there, because it is foreseen that the general will will not prevail, and lastly because domestic cares are all-absorbing. Good laws lead to the making of better ones; bad ones bring about worse. As soon as any man says of the affairs of the State *What does it matter to me?* the State may be given up for lost.

The lukewarmness of patriotism, the activity of private interest, the vastness of States, conquest, and the abuse of government suggested the method of having deputies or representatives of the people in the national assemblies. These are what, in some countries, men have presumed to call the Third Estate. Thus the individual interest of two orders is put first and second; the public interest occupies only the third place.

Sovereignty, for the same reason as makes it inalienable, cannot be represented; it lies essentially in the general will, and will does not admit of representation: it is either the same, or other; there is no intermediate possibility. The deputies of the people, therefore, are not and cannot be its representatives: they are merely its stewards, and can carry through no definitive acts. Every law the people has not ratified in person is null and void—is, in fact, not a law. The people of England regards itself as free; but it is grossly mistaken; it is free only during the election of members of parliament. As soon as they are elected, slavery overtakes it, and it is nothing. The use it makes of the short moments of liberty it enjoys shows indeed that it deserves to lose them.

The idea of representation is modern; it comes to us from feudal government, from that iniquitous and absurd system which degrades humanity and dishonours the name of man. In ancient republics and even in monarchies, the people never had representatives; the word itself was unknown. It is very singular that in Rome, where the tribunes were so sacrosanct, it was never even imagined that they could usurp the functions of the people, and that in the midst of so great a multitude they never attempted to pass on their own authority a single *plebiscitum*. We can, however, form an idea of the difficulties caused sometimes by the people being so numerous, from what happened in the time of the Gracchi, when some of the citizens had to cast their votes from the roofs of buildings.

Where right and liberty are everything, disadvantages count for nothing. Among this wise people everything was given its just value, its lictors were allowed to do what its tribunes would never have dared to attempt; for it had no fear that its lictors would try to represent it.

To explain, however, in what way the tribunes did sometimes represent it, it is enough to conceive how the government represents the Sovereign. Law being purely the declaration of the general will, it is clear that, in the exercise of the legislative power, the people cannot be represented; but in that of the executive power, which is only the force that is applied to give the law effect, it both can and should be represented. We thus see that if we looked closely into the matter we should find that very few nations have any laws. However that may be, it is certain that the tribunes, possessing no executive power,

could never represent the Roman people by right of the powers entrusted to them, but only by usurping those of the senate.

In Greece, all that the people had to do, it did for itself; it was constantly assembled in the public square. The Greeks lived in a mild climate; they had no natural greed; slaves did their work for them; their great concern was with liberty. Lacking the same advantages, how can you preserve the same rights? Your severer climates add to your needs;[13] for half the year your public squares are uninhabitable; the flatness of your languages unfits them for being heard in the open air; you sacrifice more for profit than for liberty, and fear slavery less than poverty.

What then? Is liberty maintained only by the help of slavery? It may be so. Extremes meet. Everything that is not in the course of nature has its disadvantages, civil society most of all. There are some unhappy circumstances in which we can only keep our liberty at others' expense, and where the citizen can be perfectly free only when the slave is most a slave. Such was the case with Sparta. As for you, modern peoples, you have no slaves, but you are slaves yourselves; you pay for their liberty with your own. It is in vain that you boast of this preference; I find in it more cowardice than humanity.

I do not mean by all this that it is necessary to have slaves, or that the right of slavery is legitimate: I am merely giving the reason why modern peoples, believing themselves to be free, have representatives, while ancient peoples had none. In any case, the moment a people allows itself to be represented, it is no longer free: it no longer exists.

All things considered, I do not see that it is possible henceforth for the Sovereign to preserve among us the exercise of its rights, unless the city is very small. But if it is very small, it will be conquered? No. I will show later on how the external strength of a great people may be combined with the convenient polity and good order of a small State.

----

[13] To adopt in cold countries the luxury and effeminacy of the East is to desire to submit to its chains; it is indeed to bow to them far more inevitably in our case than in theirs.

VOTING

It may be seen that the way in which general business is managed may give a clear enough indication of the actual state of morals and the health of the body politic. The more concert reigns in the assemblies, that is, the nearer opinion approaches unanimity, the greater is the dominance of the general will. On the other hand, long debates, dissensions, and tumult proclaim the ascendancy of particular interests and the decline of the State.

This seems less clear when two or more orders enter into the constitution, as patricians and plebeians did at Rome; for quarrels between these two orders often disturbed the comitia, even in the best days of the Republic. But the exception is rather apparent than real; for then, through the defect that is inherent in the body politic, there were, so to speak, two States in one, and what is not true of the two together is true of either separately. Indeed, even in the most stormy times, the *plebiscita* of the people, when the senate did not interfere with them, always went through quietly and by large majorities. The citizens having but one interest, the people had but a single will.

At the other extremity of the circle, unanimity recurs; this is the case when the citizens, having fallen into servitude, have lost both liberty and will. Fear and flattery then change votes into acclamation; deliberation ceases, and only worship or malediction is left. Such was the vile manner in which the senate expressed its views under the emperors. It did so sometimes with absurd precautions. Tacitus observes that, under Otho, the senators, while they heaped curses on Vitellius, contrived at the same time to make a deafening noise, in order that, should he ever become their master, he might not know what each of them had said.

On these various considerations depend the rules by which the methods of counting votes and comparing opinions should be regulated, according as the general will is more or less easy to discover, and the State more or less in its decline.

There is but one law which, from its nature, needs unanimous consent. This is the social compact; for civil association is the most voluntary of all acts. Every man being born free and his own master, no one, under any pretext whatsoever, can make any man subject without his consent. To decide that the son of a slave is born a slave is to decide that he is not born a man.

If then there are opponents when the social compact is made, their opposition does not invalidate the contract, but merely prevents them from being included in it. They are foreigners among citizens. When the State is instituted, residence constitutes consent; to dwell within its territory is to submit to the Sovereign.[14]

Apart from this primitive contract, the vote of the majority always binds all the rest. This follows from the contract itself. But it is asked how a man can be both free and forced to conform to wills that are not his own. How are the opponents at once free and subject to laws they have not agreed to?

I retort that the question is wrongly put. The citizen gives his consent to all the laws, including those which are passed in spite of his opposition, and even those which punish him when he dares to break any of them. The constant will of all the members of the State is the general will; by virtue of it they are citizens and free.[15] When in the poular assembly a law is proposed, what the people is asked is not exactly whether it approves or rejects the proposal, but whether it is in conformity with the general will, which is their will. Each man, in giving his vote, states his opinion on that point; and the general will is found by counting votes. When therefore the opinion that is contrary to my own prevails, this proves neither more nor less than that I was mistaken, and that what I thought to be the general will was not so. If my particular opinion had carried the day I should have achieved the opposite of what

---

[14] This should of course be understood as applying to a free State; for elsewhere family, goods, lack of a refuge, necessity, or violence may detain a man in a country against his will; and then his dwelling there no longer by itself implies his consent to the contract or to its violation.

[15] At Genoa, the word "Liberty" may be read over the front of the prisons and on the chains of the galley-slaves. This application of the device is good and just. It is indeed only malefactors of all estates who prevent the citizen from being free. In the country in which all such men were in the galleys, the most perfect liberty would be enjoyed.

was my will; and it is in that case that I should not have been free.

This presupposes, indeed, that all the qualities of the general will still reside in the majority: when they cease to do so, whatever side a man may take, liberty is no longer possible.

In my earlier demonstration of how particular wills are substituted for the general will in public deliberation, I have adequately pointed out the practicable methods of avoiding this abuse; and I shall have more to say of them later on. I have also given the principles for determining the proportional number of votes for declaring that will. A difference of one vote destroys equality; a single opponent destroys unanimity; but between equality and unanimity, there are several grades of unequal division, at each of which this proportion may be fixed in accordance with the condition and the needs of the body politic.

There are two general rules that may serve to regulate this relation. First, the more grave and important the questions discussed, the nearer should the opinion that is to prevail approach unanimity. Secondly, the more the matter in hand calls for speed, the smaller the prescribed difference in the numbers of votes may be allowed to become: where an instant decision has to be reached, a majority of one vote should be enough. The first of these two rules seems more in harmony with the laws, and the second with practical affairs. In any case, it is the combination of them that gives the best proportions for determining the majority necessary.

CHAPTER TWENTY-TWO

KANT

Most political philosophy produced in Germany before the post-World War II era was different than in Britain, America, and France because of Germany's peculiar national history. Unlike western European nations and the United States, Germany did not attain national unity until late in the nineteenth century and has only recently reachieved this state. Unlike its major neighbors to the west, Germany's boundaries were not clearly demarcated by rivers, mountain ranges, or seas. During the Thirty Years' War (1618–48), stemming from the Reformation, Germany's population was decimated by three-quarters. Following the Treaty of Westphalia, it became divided into 360 sovereign states, "petty principalities." Germany remained disunited until 1871, when, through the effort of the "Iron Chancellor," Otto von Bismarck (and three wars against Denmark, Austria, and France), the German Empire was proclaimed.

Coincident with the rise of Germany was the rise of Prussia. Originally a backward province on the edge of German states, Prussia developed a potent army and began to assert political leadership under Frederick the Great. Ironically, the greatest philosopher Germany has produced, Immanuel Kant (1724–1804), lived his entire life in Prussia. Most of what Kant stood for in his political philosophy was diametrically opposed to the Prussian state, particularly as that state developed. Therefore, Kant is unrepresentative of most German political thought.

Even more so than Hume, Kant was a speculative philosopher rather than political theorist. His three major works—the *Critique(s) of Pure Reason* (1781), *Practical Reason* (1788), and *Judgment* (1790)—barely consider politics explicitly. His fundamental goal was to effect a "Copernican" revolution in philosophy. Copernicus, failing to explain the movements of heavenly bodies based on the assumption that they revolved around the spectator, revised his thesis to assume instead that the spectator revolved around the heavenly bodies. Similarly, Kant attempted a full-scale reconstruction of the premises on which philosophy stood.

Kant states his primary philosophical problem in the *Critique of Pure Reason* as establishing how what he terms "synthetic *a priori*" judgments can exist. By *a priori*, Kant means "before experience." *A priori* knowledge is knowledge that is not based on experience—for example, mathematics. It is distinguished from *a posteriori,* or empirical, knowledge, for which sensory data is necessary. Besides a distinction between *a priori* and *a posteriori* knowledge, Kant also distinguishes between analytic and synthetic judgments. An analytic judgment is one for which the predicate of the judgment lies in the subject (for example, that a short man is a man). A synthetic judgment is, on the other hand, one for which the predicate of the judgment is not contained in the subject, that is, where something new is added to the subject before reaching the predicate.

In the *Critique of Practical Reason,* Kant moves closer to political topics, though he still does not reach them. Having explored theoretical knowledge in the first critique, he discusses practical knowledge in the second. Kant founds his ethical system on the notion that the moral law demands justice. Obviously, this is not the case in this life. Therefore, he postulates that it is necessary that God exists and there is an afterlife in which the wrongs of this life are righted. If this were not the case, then existence would be amoral.

A great dichotomy in Kant's theoretical conception of the world is between what he terms the "phenomenal" and the "noumenal" (things-in-themselves). Following Newton, Kant holds that the phenomenal world and all that is in it—including humanity—is determined and without will. At the same time, Kant is unable to give up individuals' freedom, on which morality is founded. Humanity, therefore, though phenomenally determined are noumenally free. This is a difficult conception to grasp, though it is not entirely dissimilar from Plato's theory of forms; the influence of Gottfried Wilhelm Leibniz is also evident here. The tension which exists between necessity and freedom in Kant's moral and political thought is grounded in the greater tension in his larger conception of the world.

In the same way that he sought principles before experience to understand the physical world, Kant seeks principles before experience to understand the moral world. In the *Critique of Practical Reason,* following his usage in the first critique, he calls these moral principles, "practical synthetic *a priori* judgments." These underlie all moral acts. Kant's essential moral assumption is that humans are beings who can be free—that is, they are noumenal as well as phenomenal. Morality can only exist where there is freedom (in a metaphysical sense); where individuals are not free, they are unable to exercise the choices which make morality possible. Further, as it is in choice that morality is ultimately revealed, all that matters in ethics is the "good will." What is important about an agent is the reason he intends to do something.

As Kant also explained in *Groundwork of the Metaphysics of Morals* (1785), actions are moral only if they are done for the sake of duty. He is completely un-utilitarian in his rejection of satisfaction of desires as a ground for morals. He is thus in a different ethical constellation than many of his contemporary English and French philosophers. Kant bases his moral system on reason. As stated in the *Groundwork of the Metaphysics of Morals,* reason demands the categorical imperative: "act according to a maxim which can be adopted at the same time as a universal law." This is a radically equalitarian premise, implying that an individual must act as all others should in similar circumstances. The categorical imperative is distinguished from the hypothetical imperative (this latter being contingent on what a person wants his action to produce in a specific case)—"act according to a maxim which can be adopted at the same time as a particular law." The categorical imperative holds for entire classes of actions.

Kant does not base his ethics on either self-interest or, again, desires. All moral laws are universal and must also be publicized. The political implications of Kant's ethics are several. First, the emphasis he places on metaphysical freedom clears the way for political freedom. Second, the equality inherent in the categorical imperative leads to political systems that treat humans equally. Third, Kant's admonition to "act always so that you treat humanity whether in your person or in that of another always as an end, but never as a means only" dictates a just social order. Returning to the tension between freedom and necessity, Kant holds that human freedom is living according to self-willed laws. Political freedom, then, is living according to the laws of the community.

In certain respects, Kant represents the end of a line in political thought. Following Hobbes, Locke, and especially Rousseau, he is the last great political thinker in the social contract tradition (with the recent exception of Rawls, who builds on Kantian premises in his theory of justice). From Rousseau, Kant says, he learned respect for the common man, which is evident in the categorical imperative. The social contract theory is based on the notion that the citizens of a state have the collective right to leave the state of nature and form a civil society. Kant is more explicit than some of his predecessors in emphasizing that the departure from the state of nature need not be historical: All that is necessary is that the framework of society would have been agreed to by reasonable men, whether they actually agreed or not (similar to Rawls's contract conception).

Kant recognizes the need for the state in human affairs. He considers a state the "union of a multitude of men under laws." In Kant, one does not yet see the national idea—the state is not a value in itself, though he does think states will form primarily along linguistic and religious lines. The state is only a basis for the development of the morality of its citizens: Politics grows out of ethics in the Kantian framework and is strictly subordinate to it. Again, utilitarian ideas play no role in this. The emphasis is on acting rightly, not maximizing the satisfaction of desires.

Kant's political writings are relatively few and scattered; some care, therefore, must be exercised in defining his political system. Though in terms of pure philosophy he is quite far from British empiricists, his political views are considerably closer to theirs. Kant calls himself a "republican" and favors a worldwide alliance of states to prevent war. His conception of republicanism is somewhat unusual, in that he defines it mainly as a system wherein makers and executors of law are different people. He is generally in favor of the right to vote, although he would restrict voting to economically independent male citizens. He does not see monarchy as incompatible with republicanism; in fact, passages of his writings appear to indicate a preference for monarchical execution of the law. Essentially, he seems to favor a parliamentary democracy with a monarchical executive.

Kant reinforced the idea of the state as subject to the rule of law. His definition of civil liberty is "That condition in which nobody is obliged to obey anything else but that which is decreed by law." He seeks to avoid a situation where individuals may be affected by the particular wills of others; such a situation is not, he thinks, a circumstance of freedom. Following Rousseau, he feels that only a society organized according to the "general will," "collective will," or "united will" is compatible with the members of the society's autonomies, *qua* members of the society (although this does not imply that individuals do not, or should not, retain considerable freedom outside of relationships that are societal). He foresees no all-encompassing or all-powerful state. The purpose of the state is to further the mutual freedom of its citizens through their common obedience to the law.

Surprisingly, Kant denies the right of resistance to government, though he sympathized with the American and French Revolutions, and was made an honorary citizen of France following the latter. He considers the most effective means of ensuring political liberty to be freedom of the press, but does not say what the people should do if this, in addition to political participation rights, were taken away. Notwithstanding the duty to obey a standing government, if a revolt succeeds, then the citizenry has the obligation to obey the new government.

Kant's view of the historical development of governments is well-summarized in a paragraph from the *Critique of Pure Reason* (which is almost the only time in the three *Critiques* that he mentions politics explicitly):

A constitution allowing the *greatest possible human freedom* in accordance with laws which ensure *that the freedom of each can co-exist with the freedom of all the others* . . . , is at all events
a necessary idea which must be made the basis not only of the first outline of a political constitution but of all laws as well. It requires that we should abstract at the outset from present hindrances, which perhaps do not arise inevitably out of human nature, but are rather occasioned
by neglect of genuine ideas in the process of legislation.

Thus politics has an important role to play in humankind's development. Kant develops
this notion further in the *Idea for a Universal History with a Cosmopolitan Purpose*
(1784), wherein he speculates that "the greatest problem for the human species . . . is
that of attaining a *civil society* which can administer justice universally," and that this
problem "is both the most difficult and the last to be solved by the human race."

The *Idea for a Universal History with a Cosmopolitan Purpose* puts forward the thesis
that humanity is essentially distinguished by the ability to reason, and that nature des-
tines that the capacities of a creature are to be fully realized. Because no one individual
can over the course of his lifetime completely develop his reason, such development
must proceed through humanity collectively. Humans obtain reason through civil society, wherein individual and collective freedom are realized through "freedom under
external laws" of a "just civil constitution." Kant sees properly regulated antagonism
among individuals necessary to the development of reason.

Perpetual Peace (1795), Kant's most famous specifically political work, begins
where the *Idea for a Universal History* ends. Freedom for one state demands freedom
for all, because only republican states, wherein the people have some say in their governance, will avoid wars. If some states are unrepublican, they will constantly threaten
the republican states with war, depriving the latter of their freedom. Kant does not foresee a future world-state; rather, his vision is of a federation of free states.

In *Perpetual Peace,* Kant draws an inspiring picture of a world at peace. An international federation of free states, held together by bonds of law rather than separated by
savagery and licentious liberty, will emerge through the full development of reason.
Kant makes the important point that a peace treaty finishes only a particular war,
whereas a pacific alliance would forever terminate all wars. No state may dominate another. States, as individuals once did, must leave the state of nature.

In economics as in politics, Kant largely follows the thinking of his English and French
contemporaries and predecessors. He favors private possession of property and, indeed,
sees it as a way in which the autonomous individual expresses his will. He looks forward
to beneficial consequences of private property in international affairs; as he states in *Perpetual Peace,* "the *spirit of commerce* sooner or later takes hold of every people, and it
cannot exist side by side with war." Kant's emphasis on individual autonomy has been
held by some to be an expression of a bourgeois attitude in which society is an agglomeration of individuals whose chief interest is to live in peace and be left in peace.

Kant was a professional philosopher who taught logic and metaphysics at the University of Konigsberg in East Prussia. He was known as an excellent instructor. In lecture, he
once said to his students: "You will learn from me not philosophy, but how to philosophize." His contribution to philosophy is as much his method as any particular teaching.
In political thought, he was the first German thinker to demand liberty, equality, and security of property as fundamental rights. His philosophical methods, especially the rescue of speculative philosophy from Hume's scepticism, influenced particularly his
German successors, whether they agreed or disagreed with him. Hegel was greatly influenced by Kant's treatment of antinomies (mutually contradictory propositions, each of
which apparently can be proved), and Marx was significantly influenced by Hegel.

KANT

Foundations of the Metaphysics of Morals, Idea for a Universal History with a Cosmopolitan Purpose, and *Perpetual Peace*

FOUNDATIONS OF THE METAPHYSICS OF MORALS*

Nothing in the world—indeed nothing even beyond the world—can possibly be conceived which could be called good without qualification except a *good will.* Intelligence, wit, judgment, and the other talents of the mind, however they may be named, or courage, resoluteness, and perseverance as qualities of temperament, are doubtless in many respects good and desirable. But they can become extremely bad and harmful if the will, which is to make use of these gifts of nature and which in its special constitution is called character, is not good. It is the same with the gifts of fortune. Power, riches, honor, even health, general well-being, and the contentment with one's condition which is called happiness, make for pride and even arrogance if there is not a good will to correct their influence on the mind and on its principles of action so as to make it universally conformable to its end. It need hardly be mentioned that the sight of a being adorned with no feature of a pure and good will, yet enjoying uninterrupted prosperity, can never give pleasure to a rational impartial observer. Thus the good will seems to constitute the indispensable condition even of worthiness to be happy.

---

*From Immanuel Kant, trans. *Foundations of the Metaphysics of Morals* (1785, Lewis White Beck, Indianapolis: Bobbs-Merrill, 1969). By permission.

Some qualities seem to be conducive to this good will and can facilitate its action, but, in spite of that, they have no intrinsic unconditional worth. They rather presuppose a good will, which limits the high esteem which one otherwise rightly has for them and prevents their being held to be absolutely good. Moderation in emotions and passions, self-control, and calm deliberation not only are good in many respects but even seem to constitute a part of the inner worth of the person. But however unconditionally they were esteemed by the ancients, they are far from being good without qualification. For without the principle of a good will they can become extremely bad, and the coolness of a villain makes him not only far more dangerous but also more directly abominable in our eyes than he would have seemed without it.

The good will is not good because of what it effects or accomplishes or because of its adequacy to achieve some proposed end; it is good only because of its willing, i.e., it is good of itself. And, regarded for itself, it is to be esteemed incomparably higher than anything which could be brought about by it in favor of any inclination or even of the sum total of all inclinations. Even if it should happen that, by a particularly unfortunate fate or by the niggardly provision of a step-motherly nature, this will should be wholly lacking in power to accomplish its purpose, and if even the greatest effort should not avail it to achieve anything of its end, and if there remained only the good will (not as a mere wish but as the summoning of all the means in our power), it would sparkle like a jewel in its own right, as something that had its full worth in itself. Usefulness or fruitlessness can neither diminish nor augment this worth. Its usefulness would be only its setting, as it were, so as to enable us to handle it more conveniently in commerce or to attract the attention of those who are not yet connoisseurs, but not to recommend it to those who are experts or to determine its worth.

But there is something so strange in this idea of the absolute worth of the will alone, in which no account is taken of any use, that, notwithstanding the agreement even of common sense, the suspicion must arise that perhaps only high-flown fancy is its hidden basis, and that we may have misunderstood the purpose of nature in its appointment of reason as the ruler of our will. We shall therefore examine this idea from this point of view.

In the natural constitution of an organized being, i.e., one suitably adapted to life, we assume as an axiom that no organ will be found for any purpose which is not the fittest and best adapted to that purpose. Now if its preservation, its welfare—in a word, its happiness—were the real end of nature in a being having reason and will, then nature would have hit upon a very poor arrangement in appointing the reason of the creature to be the executor of this purpose. For all the actions which the creature has to perform with this intention, and the entire rule of its conduct, would be dictated much more exactly by instinct, and that end would be far more certainly attained by instinct than it ever could be by reason. And if, over and above this, reason should have been granted to the favored creature, it would have served only to let it contemplate the happy constitution of its nature, to admire it, to rejoice in it, and to be grateful for it to its beneficent cause. But reason would not have been given in order that the being should subject its faculty of desire to that weak and delusive guidance and to meddle with the purpose of nature. In a word, nature would have taken care that reason did not break forth into practical use nor have the presumption, with its weak insight, to think out for itself the plan of happiness and the means of attaining it. Nature would have taken over not only the choice of ends but also that of the means, and with wise foresight she would have entrusted both to instinct alone.

And, in fact, we find that the more a cultivated reason deliberately devotes itself to the enjoyment of life and happiness, the more the man falls short of true contentment. From this fact there arises in many persons, if only they are candid enough to admit it, a certain degree of misology, hatred of reason. This is particularly the case with those who are most experienced in its use. After counting all the advantages which they draw—I will not say from the invention of the arts of common luxury—from the sciences (which in the end seem to them to be also a luxury of the understanding), they nevertheless find that they have actually brought more trouble on their shoulders instead of gaining in happiness; they finally envy, rather than despise, the common run of men who are better guided by mere natural instinct and who do not permit their reason much influence on their conduct. And we must as least admit that a morose attitude or ingratitude to the goodness with which the world is governed is by no means found always among those who temper or refute the boasting eulogies which are given of the advantages of happiness and contentment with which reason is supposed to supply us. Rather their judgment is based on the idea of another and far more worthy purpose of their existence for which, instead of happiness, their reason is properly intended, this purpose, therefore, being the supreme condition to which the private purposes of men must for the most part defer.

Reason is not, however, competent to guide the will safely with regard to its objects and the satisfaction of all our needs (which it in part multiplies), and to this end an innate instinct would have led with far more certainty. But reason is given to us as a practical faculty, i.e., one which is meant to have an influence on the will. As nature has elsewhere distributed capacities suitable to the functions they are to perform, reason's proper function must be to produce a will good in itself and not only good merely as a means, for to the former reason is absolutely essential. This will must indeed not be the sole and complete good but the highest good and the condition of all others, even of the desire for happiness. In this case it is entirely compatible with the wisdom of nature that the cultivation of reason, which is required for the former unconditional purpose, at least in this life restricts in many ways—indeed can reduce to less than nothing—the achievement of the latter conditional purpose, happiness. For one perceives that nature here does not proceed unsuitably to its purpose, because reason, which recognizes its highest practical vocation in the establishment of a good will, is capable only of a contentment of its own kind, i.e., one that springs from the attainment of a purpose which is determined by reason, even though this injures the ends of inclination.

We have, then, to develop the concept of a will which is to be esteemed as good of itself without regard to anything else. It dwells already in the natural sound understanding and does not need so much to be taught as only to be brought to light. In the estimation of the total worth of our actions it always takes first place and is the condition of everything else. In order to show this, we shall take the concept of duty. It contains that of a good will, though with certain subjective restrictions and hindrances; but these are far from concealing it and making it unrecognizable, for they rather bring it out by contrast and make it shine forth all the brighter. . . .

But what kind of a law can that be, the conception of which must determine the will without reference to the expected result? Under this condition alone the will can be called absolutely good without qualification. Since I have robbed the will of all impulses which could come to it from obedience to any law, nothing remains to serve as a principle of the will except universal conformity of its action to law as such. That is, I should never act in such a way that I could not also will that my maxim should be a universal law. Mere conformity to law as such (without assuming any particular law applicable to certain actions) serves as the principle of the will, and it must serve as such a principle if duty is not to be a vain delusion and chimerical concept. . . .

I do not, therefore, need any penetrating acuteness in order to discern what I have to do in order that my volition may be morally good. Inexperienced in the course of the world, incapable of being prepared for all its

contingencies, I ask myself only: Can I will that my maxim becomes a universal law? If not, it must be rejected, not because of any disadvantage accruing to myself or even to others, but because it cannot enter as a principle into a possible universal legislation, and reason extorts from me an immediate respect for such legislation.

IDEA FOR A UNIVERSAL HISTORY WITH A COSMOPOLITAN PURPOSE*

Whatever conception of the freedom of the will one may form in terms of metaphysics, the will's manifestations in the world of phenomena, i.e. human actions, are determined in accordance with natural laws, as is every other natural event. History is concerned with giving an account of these phenomena, no matter how deeply concealed their causes may be, and it allows us to hope that, if it examines the free exercise of the human will *on a large scale,* it will be able to discover a regular progression among freely willed actions. In the same way, we may hope that what strikes us in the actions of individuals as confused and fortuitous may be recognized, in the history of the entire species, as a steadily advancing but slow development of man's original capacities. Thus marriages, births, and deaths do not seem to be subject to any rule by which their numbers could be calculated in advance, since the free human will has such a great influence upon them; and yet the annual statistics for them in large countries prove that they are just as subject to constant natural laws as are the changes in the weather, which in themselves are so inconsistent that their individual occurrence cannot be determined in advance, but which nevertheless do not fail as a whole to sustain the growth of plants, the flow of rivers, and other natural functions in a uniform and uninterrupted course. Individual men and even entire nations little imagine that, while they are pursuing their own ends, each in his own

---

*From Immanuel Kant, *Idea for a Universal History with a Cosmopolitan Purpose* (1784, in Hans Reiss, ed., and H.B. Nisbet, trans., *Kant's Political Writings,* Cambridge, 1970). By permission of Cambridge University Press. Footnotes deleted.

way and often in opposition to others, they are unwittingly guided in their advance along a course intended by nature. They are unconsciously promoting an end which, even if they knew what it was, would scarcely arouse their interest.

Since men neither pursue their aims purely by instinct, as the animals do, nor act in accordance with any integral, prearranged plan like rational cosmopolitans, it would appear that no law-governed history of mankind is possible (as it would be, for example, with bees or beavers). We can scarcely help feeling a certain distaste on observing their activities as enacted in the great world-drama, for we find that, despite the apparent wisdom of individual actions here and there, everything as a whole is made up of folly and childish vanity, and often of childish malice and destructiveness. The result is that we do not know what sort of opinion we should form of our species, which is so proud of its supposed superiority. The only way out for the philosopher, since he cannot assume that mankind follows any rational *purpose of its own* in its collective actions, is for him to attempt to discover a *purpose in nature* behind this senseless course of human events, and decide whether it is after all possible to formulate in terms of a definite plan of nature a history of creatures who act without a plan of their own.— Let us now see if we can succeed in finding a guiding principle for such a history, and then leave it to nature to produce someone capable of writing it along the lines suggested. Thus nature produced a Kepler who found an unexpected means of reducing the eccentric orbits of the planets to definite laws, and a Newton who explained these laws in terms of a universal natural cause.

FIRST PROPOSITION

All the natural capacities of a creature are destined sooner or later to be developed completely and in conformity with their end. This can be verified in all animals by external and internal or anatomical examination. An organ which is not meant for use or an arrangement which does not fulfill its purpose is a contradiction in the teleological theory of nature. For if we abandon this basic principle, we are faced not with a law-governed nature, but with an aimless,

random process, and the dismal reign of chance replaces the guiding principle of reason.

SECOND PROPOSITION

In man (as the only rational creature on earth), *those natural capacities which are directed towards the use of his reason are such that they could be fully developed only in the species, but not in the individual.* Reason, in a creature, is a faculty which enables that creature to extend far beyond the limits of natural instinct the rules and intentions it follows in using its various powers, and the range of its projects is unbounded. But reason does not itself work instinctively, for it requires trial, practice and instruction to enable it to progress gradually from one stage of insight to the next. Accordingly, every individual man would have to live for a vast length of time if he were to learn how to make complete use of all his natural capacities; or if nature has fixed only a short term for each man's life (as is in fact the case), then it will require a long, perhaps incalculable series of generations, each passing on its enlightenment to the next, before the germs implanted by nature in our species can be developed to that degree which corresponds to nature's original intention. And the point of time at which this degree of development is reached must be the goal of man's aspirations (at least as an idea in his mind), or else his natural capacities would necessarily appear by and large to be purposeless and wasted. In the latter case, all practical principles would have to be abandoned, and nature, whose wisdom we must take as axiomatic in judging all other situations, would incur the suspicion of indulging in childish play in the case of man alone.

THIRD PROPOSITION

Nature has willed that man should produce entirely by his own initiative everything which goes beyond the mechanical ordering of his animal existence, and that he should not partake of any other happiness or perfection than that which he has procured for himself without instinct and by his own reason. For nature does nothing unnecessarily and is not extravagant in the means employed to reach its ends. Nature gave man reason, and freedom of will based upon reason, and this in itself was a clear indication of nature's intention as regards his endowments. For it showed that man was not meant to be guided by instinct or equipped and instructed by innate knowledge; on the contrary, he was meant to produce everything out of himself. Everything had to be entirely of his own making—the discovery of a suitable diet, of clothing, of external security and defense (for which nature gave him neither the bull's horns, the lion's claws, nor the dog's teeth, but only his hands), as well as all the pleasures that can make life agreeable, and even his insight and circumspection and the goodness of his will. Nature seems here to have taken pleasure in exercising the strictest economy and to have measured out the basic animal equipment so sparingly as to be just enough for the most pressing needs of the beginnings of existence. It seems as if nature had intended that man, once he had finally worked his way up from the uttermost barbarism to the highest degree of skill, to inner perfection in his manner of thought and thence (as far as is possible on earth) to happiness, should be able to take for himself the entire credit for doing so and have only himself to thank for it. It seems that nature has worked more with a view to man's rational *self-esteem* than to his mere well-being. For in the actual course of human affairs, a whole host of hardships awaits him. Yet nature does not seem to have been concerned with seeing that man should live agreeably, but with seeing that he should work his way onwards to make himself by his own conduct worthy of life and well-being. What remains disconcerting about all this is firstly, that the earlier generations seem to perform their laborious tasks only for the sake of the later ones, so as to prepare for them a further stage from which they can raise still higher the structure intended by nature; and secondly, that only the later generations will in fact have the good fortune to inhabit the building on which a whole series of their forefathers (admittedly, without any conscious intention) had worked without themselves being able to share in the happiness they were preparing. But no matter how puzzling this may be, it will appear as necessary as it is puzzling if we simply assume

that one animal species was intended to have reason, and that, as a class of rational beings who are mortal as individuals but immortal as a species, it was still meant to develop its capacities completely.

FOURTH PROPOSITION

The means which nature employs to bring about the development of innate capacities is that of antagonism within society, in so far as this antagonism becomes in the long run the cause of a law-governed social order. By antagonism, I mean in this context the *unsocial sociability* of men, that is, their tendency to come together in society, coupled, however, with a continual resistance which constantly threatens to break this society up. This propensity is obviously rooted in human nature. Man has an inclination to *live in society,* since he feels in this state more like a man, that is, he feels able to develop his natural capacities. But he also has a great tendency to *live as an individual,* to isolate himself, since he also encounters in himself the unsocial characteristic of wanting to direct everything in accordance with his own ideas. He therefore expects resistance all around, just as he knows of himself that he is in turn inclined to offer resistance to others. It is this very resistance which awakens all man's powers and induces him to overcome his tendency to laziness. Through the desire for honor, power or property, it drives him to seek status among his fellows, whom he cannot *bear yet cannot bear to leave.* Then the first true steps are taken from barbarism to culture, which in fact consists in the social worthiness of man. All man's talents are now gradually developed, his taste cultivated, and by a continued process of enlightenment, a beginning is made towards establishing a way of thinking which can with time transform the primitive natural capacity for moral discrimination into definite practical principles; and thus a *pathologically* enforced social union is transformed into a *moral* whole. Without these social qualities (far from admirable in themselves) which cause the resistance inevitably encountered by each individual as he furthers his self-seeking pretensions, man would live an Arcadian, pastoral existence of perfect concord, self-sufficiency and mutual love. But all human talents would remain hidden for ever in a dormant state, and men, as good-natured as the sheep they tended, would scarcely render their existence more valuable than that of their animals. The end for which they were created, their rational nature, would be an unfilled void. Nature should thus be thanked for fostering social incompatibility, enviously competitive vanity, and insatiable desires for possession or even power. Without these desires, all man's excellent natural capacities would never be roused to develop. Man wishes concord, but nature, knowing better what is good for his species, wishes discord. Man wishes to live comfortably and pleasantly, but nature intends that he should abandon idleness and inactive self-sufficiency and plunge instead into labor and hardships, so that he may by his own adroitness find means of liberating himself from them in turn. The natural impulses which make this possible, the sources of the very unsociableness and continual resistance which cause so many evils, at the same time encourage man towards new exertions of his powers and thus towards further development of his natural capacities. They would thus seem to indicate the design of a wise creator—not, as it might seem, the hand of a malicious spirit who had meddled in the creator's glorious work or spoiled it out of envy.

FIFTH PROPOSITION

The greatest problem for the human species, the solution of which nature compels him to seek, is that of attaining a civil society which can administer justice universally.

The highest purpose of nature—i.e. the development of all natural capacities—can be fulfilled for mankind only in society, and nature intends that man should accomplish this, and indeed all his appointed ends, by his own efforts. This purpose can be fulfilled only in a society which has not only the greatest freedom, and therefore a continual antagonism among its members, but also the most precise specification and preservation of the limits of this freedom in order that it can co-exist with the freedom of others. The highest task which nature has set for mankind must therefore be that of establishing a society in which *freedom under external laws* would be combined to the greatest

possible extent with irresistible force, in other words of establishing a perfectly *just civil constitution*. For only through the solution and fulfillment of this task can nature accomplish its other intentions with our species. Man, who is otherwise so enamored with unrestrained freedom, is forced to enter this state of restriction by sheer necessity. And this is indeed the most stringent of all forms of necessity, for it is imposed by men upon themselves, in that their inclinations make it impossible for them to exist side by side for long in a state of wild freedom. But once enclosed within a precinct like that of civil union, the same inclinations have the most beneficial effect. In the same way, trees in a forest, by seeking to deprive each other of air and sunlight, compel each other to find these by upward growth, so that they grow beautiful and straight—whereas those which put out branches at will, in freedom and in isolation from others, grow stunted, bent and twisted. All the culture and art which adorn mankind and the finest social order man creates are fruits of his unsociability. For it is compelled by its own nature to discipline itself, and thus, by enforced art, to develop completely the germs which nature implanted.

SIXTH PROPOSITION

This problem is both the most difficult and the last to be solved by the human race. The difficulty (which the very idea of this problem clearly presents) is this: if he lives among others of his own species, man is *an animal who needs a master*. For he certainly abuses his freedom in relation to others of his own kind. And even although, as a rational creature, he desires a law to impose limits on the freedom of all, he is still misled by his self-seeking animal inclinations into exempting himself from the law where he can. He thus requires a *master* to break his self-will and force him to obey a universally valid will under which everyone can be free. But where is he to find such a master? Nowhere else but in the human species. But this master will also be an animal who needs a master. Thus while man may try as he will, it is hard to see how he can obtain for public justice a supreme authority which would itself be just, whether he seeks this authority in a single person or in a group of many persons selected for this purpose. For each one of them will always misuse his freedom if he does not have anyone above him to apply force to him as the laws should require it. Yet, the highest authority has to be just *in itself* and yet also a *man.* This is therefore the most difficult of all tasks, and a perfect solution is impossible. Nothing straight can be constructed from such warped wood as that which man is made of. Nature only requires of us that we should approximate to this idea. A further reason why this task must be the last to be accomplished is that man needs for it a correct conception of the nature of a possible constitution, great experience tested in many affairs of the world, and above all else a good will prepared to accept the findings of this experience. But three factors such as these will not easily be found in conjunction, and if they are, it will happen only at a late stage and after many unsuccessful attempts.

PERPETUAL PEACE: A PHILOSOPHICAL SKETCH*

First Section: Which Contains the Preliminary Articles of a Perpetual Peace Between States

1. 'No conclusion of peace shall be considered valid as such if it was made with a secret reservation of the material for a future war.'

For if this were the case, it would be a mere truce, a suspension of hostilities, not a *peace.* Peace means an end to all hostilities, and to attach the adjective 'perpetual' to it is already suspiciously close to pleonasm [redundancy]. A conclusion of peace nullifies all existing reasons for a future war, even if these are not yet known to the contracting parties, and no matter how acutely and carefully they may later be pieced together out of old documents. It is possible that either party may make a mental reservation with a view to reviving its

old pretensions in the future. Such reservations will not be mentioned explicitly, since both parties may simply be too exhausted to continue the war, although they may nonetheless possess sufficient ill will to seize the first favorable opportunity of attaining their end. But if we consider such reservations in themselves, they soon appear as Jesuitical casuistry; they are beneath the dignity of a ruler, just as it is beneath the dignity of a minister of state to comply with any reasoning of this kind.

• • •

2. 'No independently existing state, whether it be large or small, may be acquired by another state by inheritance, exchange, purchase or gift.'

For a state, unlike the ground on which it is based, is not a possession. It is a society of men, which no one other than itself can command or dispose of. Like a tree, it has its own roots, and to graft it on to another state as if it were a shoot is to terminate its existence as a moral personality and make it into a commodity. This contradicts the idea of the original contract, without which the rights of a people are unthinkable.* Everyone knows what danger the supposed right of acquiring states in this way, even in our own times, has brought upon Europe (for this practice is unknown in other continents). It has been thought that states can marry one another, and this has provided a new kind of industry by which power can be increased through family alliances, without expenditure of energy, while landed property can be extended at the same time. It is the same thing when the troops of one state are hired to another to fight an enemy who is not common to both; for the subjects are thereby used and misused as objects to be manipulated at will.

3. 'Standing armies will gradually be abolished altogether.'

---

* From Immanuel Kant, *Perpetual Peace* (1795, in Hans Reiss, ed., and H.B. Nisbet, trans., *Kant's Political Writings,* Cambridge, 1970). By permission of Cambridge University Press. Most footnotes and Latin translation deleted.

* A hereditary kingdom is not a state which can be inherited by another state. Only the right to rule over it may be bequeathed to another physical person. In this case, the state acquires a ruler, but the ruler as such (i.e. as one who already has another kingdom) does not acquire the state.

For they constantly threaten other states with war by the very fact that they are always prepared for it. They spur on the states to outdo one another in arming unlimited numbers of soldiers, and since the resultant costs eventually make peace more oppressive than a short war, the armies are themselves the cause of wars of aggression which set out to end burdensome military expenditure. Furthermore, the hiring of men to kill or to be killed seems to mean using them as mere machines and instruments in the hands of someone else (the state), which cannot easily be reconciled with the rights of man in one's own person. It is quite a different matter if the citizens undertake voluntary military training from time to time in order to secure themselves and their fatherland against attacks from outside.

· · ·

4. 'No national debt shall be contracted in connection with the external affairs of the state.'

There is no cause for suspicion if help for the national economy is sought inside or outside the state (e.g. for improvements to roads, new settlements, storage of foodstuffs for years of famine, etc.). But a credit system, if used by the powers as an instrument of aggression against one another, shows the power of money in its most dangerous form. For while the debts thereby incurred are always secure against present demands (because not all the creditors will demand payment at the same time), these debts go on growing indefinitely. This ingenious system, invented by a commercial people in the present century, provides a military fund which may exceed the resources of all the other states put together. . . . This ease in making war, coupled with the warlike inclination of those in power (which seems to be an integral feature of human nature), is thus a great obstacle in the way of perpetual peace. . . .

5. 'No state shall forcibly interfere in the constitution and government of another state.'

For what could justify such interference? Surely not any sense of scandal or offense which a state arouses in the subjects of another state. It should rather serve as a warning to others, as an example of the great evils which a people has incurred by its lawlessness. And a bad example which one free person gives to another is not the same as an injury to the latter. But it would be a different matter if a state, through internal discord, were to split into two parts, each of which set itself up as a separate state and claimed authority over the whole. For it could not be reckoned as interference in another state's constitution if an external state were to lend support to one of them, because their condition is one of anarchy. But as long as this internal conflict is not yet decided, the interference of external powers would be a violation of the rights of an independent people which is merely struggling with its internal ills. Such interference would be an active offense and would make the autonomy of all other states insecure.

6. 'No state at war with another shall permit such acts of hostility as would make mutual confidence impossible during a future time of peace. Such acts would include the employment of *assassins or poisoners, breach of agreements, the instigation of treason* within the enemy state, etc.'

These are dishonorable stratagems. For it must still remain possible, even in wartime, to have some sort of trust in the attitude of the enemy, otherwise peace could not be concluded and the hostilities would turn into a war of extermination. After all, war is only a regrettable expedient for asserting one's rights by force within a state of nature, where no court of justice is available to judge with legal authority. In such cases, neither party can be declared an unjust enemy, for this would already presuppose a judge's decision; only the *outcome* of the conflict, as in the case of a so-called 'judgment of God,' can decide who is in the right. A war of punishment between states is inconceivable, since there can be no relationship of superior to inferior among them. It thus follows that a war of extermination, in which both parties and right itself might all be simultaneously annihilated, would allow perpetual peace only on the vast graveyard of the human race. A war of this kind and the employment of all means which might bring it about must thus be absolutely prohibited. But the means listed above would inevitably lead to such a war, because these diabolical arts, besides being intrinsically despicable, would not long be confined to war alone if they were brought into use. This applies, for example, to the employment of spies, for it exploits only the dishonesty of others (which can never be completely eliminated). Such practices will be carried over into peacetime and will thus completely vitiate its purpose.

All of the articles listed above, when regarded objectively or in relation to the intentions of those in power, are *prohibitive laws*. Yet some of them are of the *strictest* sort, being valid irrespective of differing circumstances, and they require that the abuses they prohibit should be abolished *immediately* (Nos. 1, 5, and 6). Others (Nos. 2, 3, and 4), although they are not exceptions to the rule of justice, allow some *subjective* latitude according to the circumstances in which they are applied. The latter need not necessarily be executed at once, so long as their ultimate purpose (e.g. the *restoration* of freedom to certain states in accordance with the second article) is not lost sight of. But their execution may not be *put off* to a non-existent date, for any delay is permitted only as a means of avoiding a premature implementation which might frustrate the whole purpose of the article. For in the case of the second article, the prohibition relates only to the *mode of acquisition,* which is to be forbidden hereforth, but not to the present *state of political possessions.* For although this present state is not backed up by the requisite legal authority, it was considered lawful in the public opinion of every state at the time of the putative acquisition.

Second Section: Which Contains the Definitive Articles of a Perpetual Peace Between States

A state of peace among men living together is not the same as the state of nature, which is rather a state of war. For even if it does not involve active hostilities, it involves a constant threat of their breaking out. Thus the state of peace must be *formally instituted,* for a suspension of hostilities is not in itself a guarantee of peace. And unless one neighbor gives a guarantee to the other at his request (which can happen only in a *lawful* state), the latter may treat him as an enemy.

First Definitive Article of a Perpetual Peace: The Civil Constitution of Every State shall be Republican

A *republican constitution* is founded upon three principles: firstly, the principle of *freedom* for all members of a society (as men);* secondly, the principle of the *dependence* of everyone upon a single common legislation (as subjects); and thirdly, the principle of legal *equality* for everyone (as citizens). It is the only constitution which can be derived from the idea of an original contract, upon which all rightful legislation of a people must be founded. Thus as far as right is concerned, republicanism is in itself the original basis of every kind of civil constitution, and it only remains to ask whether it is the only constitution which can lead to a perpetual peace.

The republican constitution is not only pure in its origin (since it springs from the pure concept of right); it also offers a prospect of attaining the desired result, i.e. a perpetual peace, and the reason for this is as follows.—If, as is inevitably the case under this constitution, the consent of the citizens is required to decide whether or not war is to be declared, it is very natural that they will have great hesitation in embarking on so dangerous an enterprise. For this would mean calling down on themselves all the miseries of war, such as doing the fighting themselves, supplying the costs of the war from their own resources, painfully

---

* My external and rightful *freedom* should be defined as a warrant to obey no external laws except those to which I have been able to give my own consent. Similarly, external and rightful *equality* within a state is that relationship among the citizens whereby no-one can put anyone else under a legal obligation without submitting simultaneously to a law which requires that he can himself be put under the same kind of obligation by the other person. (And we do not need to define the principle of *legal* dependence, since it is always implied in the concept of a political constitution.)

making good the ensuing devastation, and, as the crowning evil, having to take upon themselves a burden of debt which will embitter peace itself and which can never be paid off on account of the constant threat of new wars. But under a constitution where the subject is not a citizen, and which is therefore not republican, it is the simplest thing in the world to go to war. For the head of state is not a fellow citizen, but the owner of the state, and a war will not force him to make the slightest sacrifice so far as his banquets, hunts, pleasure palaces and court festivals are concerned. He can thus decide on war, without any significant reason, as a kind of amusement, and unconcernedly leave it to the diplomatic corps (who are always ready for such purposes) to justify the war for the sake of propriety.

The following remarks are necessary to prevent the republican constitution from being confused with the democratic one, as commonly happens. The various forms of state may be classified either according to the different persons who exercise supreme authority, or according to the way in which the nation is governed by its ruler, whoever he may be. The first classification goes by the form of sovereignty, and only three such forms are possible, depending on whether the ruling power is in the hands of an *individual*, of *several persons* in association, or of *all* those who together constitute civil society (i.e. *autocracy, aristocracy* and *democracy*—the power of a prince, the power of a nobility, and the power of the people). The second classification depends on the form of government, and relates to the way in which the state, setting out from its constitution (i.e. an act of the general will whereby the mass becomes a people), makes use of its plenary power. The form of government, in this case, will be either *republican or despotic. Republicanism* is that political principle whereby the executive power (the government) is separated from the legislative power. Despotism prevails in a state if the laws are made and arbitrarily executed by one and the same power, and it reflects the will of the people only in so far as the ruler treats the will of the people as his own private will. Of the three forms of *sovereignty, democracy,* in the truest sense of the word, is necessarily a *despotism,* because it

establishes an executive power through which all the citizens may make decisions about (and indeed against) the single individual without his consent, so that decisions are made by all the people and yet not by all the people; and this means that the general will is in contradiction with itself, and thus also with freedom.

For any form of government which is not *representative* is essentially an *anomaly,* because one and the same person cannot at the same time be both the legislator and the executor of his own will, just as the general proposition in logical reasoning cannot at the same time be a secondary proposition subsuming the particular within the general. And even if the other two political constitutions (i.e. autocracy and aristocracy) are always defective in as much as they leave room for a despotic form of government, it is at least possible that they will be associated with a form of government which accords with the *spirit* of a representative system. Thus Frederick II at least *said* that he was merely the highest servant of the state, while a democratic constitution makes this attitude impossible, because everyone under it wants to be a ruler. We can therefore say that the smaller the number of ruling persons in a state and the greater their powers of representation, the more the constitution will approximate to its republican potentiality, which it may hope to realize eventually by gradual reforms. For this reason, it is more difficult in an aristocracy than in a monarchy to reach this one and only perfectly lawful kind of constitution, while it is possible in a democracy only by means of violent revolution. But the people are immensely more concerned with the mode of government than with the form of the constitution, although a great deal also depends on the degree to which the constitution fits the purpose of the government. But if the mode of government is to accord with the concept of right, it must be based on the representative system. This system alone makes possible a republican state, and without it, despotism and violence will result, no matter what kind of constitution is in force. None of the so-called 'republics' of antiquity employed such a system, and they thus inevitably ended in despotism, although this is still relatively bearable under the rule of a single individual.

SECOND DEFINITIVE ARTICLE OF A
PERPETUAL PEACE: THE RIGHT OF
NATIONS SHALL BE BASED ON A
FEDERATION OF FREE STATES

Peoples who have grouped themselves into nation states may be judged in the same way as individual men living in a state of nature, independent of external laws; for they are a standing offense to one another by the very fact that they are neighbors. Each nation, for the sake of its own security, can and ought to demand of the others that they should enter along with it into a constitution, similar to the civil one, within which the rights of each could be secured. This would mean establishing a *federation of peoples*. But a federation of this sort would not be the same thing as an international state. For the idea of an international state is contradictory, since every state involves a relationship between a superior (the legislator) and an inferior (the people obeying the laws), whereas a number of nations forming one state would constitute a single nation. And this contradicts our initial assumption, as we are here considering the right of nations in relation to one another in so far as they are a group of separate states which are not to be welded together as a unit.

We look with profound contempt upon the way in which savages cling to their lawless freedom. They would rather engage in incessant strife than submit to a legal constraint which they might impose upon themselves, for they prefer the freedom of folly to the freedom of reason. We regard this as barbarism, coarseness, and brutish debasement of humanity.

We might thus expect that civilized peoples, each united within itself as a state, would hasten to abandon so degrading a condition as soon as possible. But instead of doing so, each *state* sees its own majesty (for it would be absurd to speak of the majesty of a *people*) precisely in not having to submit to any external legal constraint, and the glory of its ruler consists in his power to order thousands of people to immolate themselves for a cause which does not truly concern them, while he need not himself incur any danger whatsoever. And the main difference between the savage nations of Europe and those of America is that

while some American tribes have been entirely eaten up by their enemies, the Europeans know how to make better use of those they have defeated than merely by making a meal of them. They would rather use them to increase the number of their own subjects, thereby augmenting their stock of instruments for conducting even more extensive wars.

Although it is largely concealed by governmental constraints in law-governed civil society, the depravity of human nature is displayed without disguise in the unrestricted relations which obtain between the various nations. It is therefore to be wondered at that the word *right* has not been completely banished from military politics as superfluous pedantry, and that no state has been bold enough to declare itself publicly in favor of doing so. For Hugo Grotius, Pufendorf, Vattel and the rest (sorry comforters as they are) are still dutifully quoted in *justification* of military aggression, although their philosophically or diplomatically formulated codes do not and cannot have the slightest *legal* force, since states as such are not subject to a common external constraint. Yet there is no instance of a state ever having been moved to desist from its purpose by arguments supported by the testimonies of such notable men. This homage which every state pays (in words at least) to the concept of right proves that man possesses a greater moral capacity, still dormant at present, to overcome eventually the evil principle within him (for he cannot deny that it exists), and to hope that others will do likewise. Otherwise the word *right* would never be used by states which intend to make war on one another, unless in a derisory sense, as when a certain Gallic prince declared: 'Nature has given to the strong the prerogative of making the weak obey them.' The way in which states seek their rights can only be by war, since there is no external tribunal to put their claims to trial. But rights cannot be decided by military victory, and a *peace treaty* may put an end to the current war, but not to that general warlike condition within which pretexts can always be found for a new war. And indeed, such a state of affairs cannot be pronounced completely unjust, since it allows each party to act as judge in its own cause. Yet, while natural right allows us to say of men living in a lawless condition that they ought to abandon it, the right of nations does not allow us to say the same of states. For as states, they already have a lawful internal constitution, and have thus outgrown the coercive right of others to subject them to a wider legal constitution in accordance with their conception of right. On the other hand, reason, as the highest legislative moral power, absolutely condemns war as a test of rights and sets up peace as an immediate duty. But peace can neither be inaugurated nor secured without a general agreement between the nations; thus a particular kind of league, which we might call a *pacific federation* is required. It would differ from a *peace treaty* in that the latter terminates *one* war, whereas the former would seek to end *all* wars for good. This federation does not aim to acquire any power like that of a state, but merely to preserve and secure the *freedom* of each state in itself, along with that of the other confederated states, although this does not mean that they need to submit to public laws and to a coercive power which enforces them, as do men in a state of nature. It can be shown that this idea of *federalism,* extending gradually to encompass all states and thus leading to perpetual peace, is practicable and has objective reality. For if by good fortune one powerful and enlightened nation can form a republic (which is by its nature inclined to seek perpetual peace), this will provide a focal point for federal association among other states. These will join up with the first one, thus securing the freedom of each state in accordance with the idea of international right, and the whole will gradually spread further and further by a series of alliances of this kind.

It would be understandable for a people to say: 'There shall be no war among us; for we will form ourselves into a state, appointing for ourselves a supreme legislative, executive and juridical power to resolve our conflicts by peaceful means.' But if this state says: 'There shall be no war between myself and other states, although I do not recognize any supreme legislative power which could secure my rights and whose rights I should in turn secure,' it is impossible to understand what justification I can have for placing any confidence in my rights, unless I can rely on some substitute for the union of civil society, i.e. on a free federation. If the concept of international right is to retain any meaning at all, reason must necessarily couple it with a federation of this kind.

The concept of international right becomes meaningless if interpreted as a right to go to war. For this would make it a right to determine what is lawful not by means of universally valid external laws, but by means of one-sided maxims backed up by physical force. It could be taken to mean that it is perfectly just for men who adopt this attitude to destroy one another, and thus to find perpetual peace in the vast grave where all the horrors of violence and those responsible for them would be buried. There is only one rational way in which states coexisting with other states can emerge from the lawless condition of pure warfare. Just like individual men, they must renounce their savage and lawless freedom, adapt themselves to public coercive laws, and thus form an *international state,* which would necessarily continue to grow until it embraced all the peoples of the earth. But since this is not the will of the nations, according to their present conception of international right (so that they reject *in hypothesi* what is true *in thesi*), the positive idea of a *world republic* cannot be realized. If all is not to be lost, this can at best find a negative substitute in the shape of an enduring and gradually expanding *federation* likely to prevent war. The latter may check the current of man's inclination to defy the law and antagonize his fellows, although there will always be a risk of it bursting forth anew.

THIRD DEFINITIVE ARTICLE
OF A PERPETUAL PEACE:
COSMOPOLITAN RIGHT SHALL BE
LIMITED TO CONDITIONS OF
UNIVERSAL HOSPITALITY

As in the foregoing articles, we are here concerned not with philanthropy, but with *right.* In this context, *hospitality* means the right of a stranger not to be treated with hostility when he arrives on someone else's territory. He can indeed be turned away, if this can be done without causing his death, but he must not be treated with hostility, so long as he behaves in a peaceable manner in the place he happens to be in. The stranger cannot claim the *right of a guest* to be entertained, for this would require a special friendly agreement whereby he might become a member of the native household for a certain time. He may only claim a *right of resort,* for all men are entitled to present themselves in the society of others by virtue of their right to communal possession of the earth's surface. Since the earth is a globe, they cannot disperse over an infinite area, but must necessarily tolerate one another's company. And no one originally has any greater right than anyone else to occupy any particular portion of the earth. The community of man is divided by uninhabitable parts of the earth's surface such as oceans and deserts, but even then, the *ship* or the *camel* (the ship of the desert) make it possible for them to approach their fellows over these ownerless tracts, and to utilize as a means of social intercourse that *right to the earth's surface* which the human race shares in common. The inhospitable behavior of coastal dwellers (as on the Barbary coast) in plundering ships on the adjoining seas or enslaving stranded seafarers, or that of inhabitants of the desert (as with the Arab Bedouins), who regard their proximity to nomadic tribes as a justification for plundering them, is contrary to natural right. But this natural right of hospitality, i.e. the right of strangers, does not extend beyond those conditions which make it possible for them to *attempt* to enter into relations with the native inhabitants. In this way, continents distant from each other can enter into peaceful mutual relations which may eventually be regulated by public laws, thus bringing the human race nearer and nearer to a cosmopolitan constitution.

• • •

The peoples of the earth have entered in varying degrees into a universal community, and it has developed to the point where a violation of rights in *one* part of the world is felt *everywhere*. The idea of a cosmopolitan right is therefore not fantastic and overstrained; it is a necessary complement to the unwritten code of political and international right, transforming it into a universal right of humanity. Only under this condition can we flatter ourselves that we are continually advancing towards a perpetual peace.

First Supplement: On the Guarantee of a Perpetual Peace

Perpetual peace is *guaranteed* by no less an authority than the great artist *Nature* herself. The mechanical process of nature visibly exhibits the purposive plan of producing concord among men, even against their will and indeed by means of their very discord. This design, if we regard it as a compelling cause whose laws of operation are unknown to us, is called *fate*. But if we consider its purposive function within the world's development, whereby it appears as the underlying wisdom of a higher cause, showing the way towards the objective goal of the human race and predetermining the world's evolution, we call it *providence*. We cannot actually observe such an agency in the artifices of nature, nor can we even *infer* its existence from them. But as with all relations between the form of things and their ultimate purposes, we can and must *supply it mentally* in order to conceive of its possibility by analogy with human artifices. Its relationship to and conformity with the end which reason directly prescribes to us (i.e. the end of morality) can only be conceived of as an idea. Yet, while this is indeed far-fetched in *theory,* it does possess dogmatic validity and has a very real foundation in *practice,* as with the concept of *perpetual peace,* which makes it our duty to promote it by using the natural mechanism described above. But in contexts such as this, where we are concerned purely with theory and not with religion, we should also note that it is more in keeping with the limitations of human reason to speak of *nature* and not of *providence,* for reason, in dealing with cause and effect relationships, must keep within the bounds of possible experience. *Modesty* forbids us to speak of providence as something we can recognize, for this would mean donning the wings of Icarus and presuming to approach the mystery of its inscrutable intentions.

• • •

We now come to the essential question regarding the prospect of perpetual peace. What does nature do in relation to the end which man's own reason prescribes to him as a duty, i.e. how does nature help to promote his *moral purpose?* And how does nature guarantee that what man *ought* to do by the laws of his freedom (but does not do) will in fact be done through nature's compulsion, *without* the free agency of man? This question arises, moreover, in all three areas of public right—in *political, international and cosmopolitan right*. For if I say that nature *wills* that this or that should happen, this does not mean that nature imposes on us a *duty* to do it, for duties can only be imposed by practical reason, acting without any external constraint. On the contrary, nature does it herself, whether we are willing or not.

1. Even if people were not compelled by internal dissent to submit to the coercion of public laws, war would produce the same effect from outside. For in accordance with the natural arrangement described above, each people would find itself confronted by another neighboring people pressing in upon it, thus forcing it to form itself internally into a *state* in order to encounter the other as an armed *power*. Now the *republican* constitution is the only one which does complete justice to the rights of man. But it is also the most difficult to establish, and even more so to preserve, so that many maintain that it would only be possible within a state of *angels,* since men, with their self-seeking inclinations, would be incapable of adhering to a constitution of so sublime a nature. But in fact, nature comes to the aid of the universal and rational human will, so admirable in itself but so impotent in practice, and makes use of precisely those self-seeking inclinations in order to do so. It only remains for men to create a good organization for the state, a task which is well within their capability, and to arrange it in such a way that their self-seeking energies are opposed to one another, each thereby neutralizing or eliminating the destructive effects of the rest. And as far as reason is concerned, the result is the same as if man's selfish tendencies were non-existent, so that man, even if he is not morally good in himself, is nevertheless compelled to be a good citizen. As hard as it may sound, the problem of setting up a state can be solved even by a nation of devils (so long as they possess understanding). It may be stated as follows: 'In order to organize a group of rational beings who together require universal laws for their survival, but of whom each separate

individual is secretly inclined to exempt himself from them, the constitution must be so designed that, although the citizens are opposed to one another in their private attitudes, these opposing views may inhibit one another in such a way that the public conduct of the citizens will be the same as if they did not have such evil attitudes.' A problem of this kind must be soluble. For such a task does not involve the moral improvement of man; it only means finding out how the mechanism of nature can be applied to men in such a manner that the antagonism of their hostile attitudes will make them compel one another to submit to coercive laws, thereby producing a condition of peace within which the laws can be enforced. We can even see this principle at work among the actually existing (although as yet very imperfectly organized) states. For in their external relations, they have already approached what the idea of right prescribes, although the reason for this is certainly not their internal moral attitudes. In the same way, we cannot expect their moral attitudes to produce a good political constitution; on the contrary, it is only through the latter that the people can be expected to attain a good level of moral culture. Thus that mechanism of nature by which selfish inclinations are naturally opposed to one another in their external relations can be used by reason to facilitate the attainment of its own end, the reign of established right. Internal and external peace are thereby furthered and assured, so far as it lies within the power of the state itself to do so. We may therefore say that nature *irresistibly wills* that right should eventually gain the upper hand. What men have neglected to do will ultimately happen of its own accord, albeit with much inconvenience.

2. The idea of international right presupposes the separate existence of many independent adjoining states. And such a state of affairs is essentially a state of war, unless there is a federal union to prevent hostilities breaking out. But in the light of the idea of reason, this state is still to be preferred to an amalgamation of the separate nations under a single power which has overruled the rest and created a universal monarchy. For the laws progressively lose their impact as the government increases its range, and a soulless despotism, after crushing the

germs of goodness, will finally lapse into anarchy. It is nonetheless the desire of every state (or its ruler) to achieve lasting peace by thus dominating the whole world, if at all possible. But *nature* wills it otherwise, and uses two means to separate the nations and prevent them from intermingling—*linguistic* and *religious* differences. These may certainly occasion mutual hatred and provide pretexts for wars, but as culture grows and men gradually move towards greater agreement over their principles, they lead to mutual understanding and peace. And unlike that universal despotism which saps all man's energies and ends in the graveyard of freedom, this peace is created and guaranteed by an equilibrium of forces and a most vigorous rivalry.

3. Thus nature wisely separates the nations, although the will of each individual state, even basing its arguments on international right, would gladly unite them under its own sway by force or by cunning. On the other hand, nature also unites nations which the concept of cosmopolitan right would not have protected from violence and war, and does so by means of their mutual self-interest. For the *spirit of commerce* sooner or later takes hold of every people, and it cannot exist side by side with war. And of all the powers (or means) at the disposal of the power of the state, *financial power* can probably be relied on most. Thus states find themselves compelled to promote the noble cause of peace, though not exactly from motives of morality. And wherever in the world there is a threat of war breaking out, they will try to prevent it by mediation, just as if they had entered into a permanent league for this purpose; for by the very nature of things, large military alliances can only rarely be formed, and will even more rarely be successful.

In this way, nature guarantees perpetual peace by the actual mechanism of human inclinations. And while the likelihood of its being attained is not sufficient to enable us to *prophesy* the future theoretically, it is enough for practical purposes. It makes it our duty to work our way towards this goal, which is more than an empty chimera.

SECOND SUPPLEMENT: SECRET ARTICLE OF A PERPETUAL PEACE

In transactions involving public right, a secret article (regarded objectively or in terms of its content) is a contradiction. But in subjective terms, i.e. in relation to the sort of person who dictates it, an article may well contain a secret element, for the person concerned may consider it prejudicial to his own dignity to name himself publicly as its originator.

The only article of this kind is embodied in the following sentence: '*The maxims of the philosophers on the conditions under which public peace is possible shall be consulted by states which are armed for war.*'

Although it may seem humiliating for the legislative authority of a state, to which we must naturally attribute the highest degree of wisdom, to seek instruction from *subjects* (the philosophers) regarding the principles on which it should act in its relations with other states, it is nevertheless extremely advisable that it should do so. The state will therefore invite their help *silently,* making a secret of it. In other words, it will *allow them to speak freely* and publicly on the universal maxims of warfare and peacemaking, and they will indeed do so of their own accord if no one forbids their discussions.

• • •

This does not, however, imply that the state must give the principles of the philosopher precedence over the pronouncements of the jurist (who represents the power of the state), but only that the philosopher should be given a *hearing.*

CHAPTER TWENTY-THREE

SMITH

The *Industrial Revolution* was a part—perhaps the most important part—of the transformations that have shaped the modern age. The discovery of a New World and the rediscovery of antiquity both reflected and furthered the desire to create a more secular European civilization. The Protestant Reformation emphasized individualism and that individuals should be free to play more of a role in controlling their earthly, as well as their eternal, destiny. The times were ripe for change. In politics, change was represented by the English, American, and French Revolutions.

The traditional Christian outlook on economics relatively was to deprecate it. The focus was on the next world, not this one. As late as the 1700s, there were fervent disputes over the "just" prices of commodities and products. Advertising goods was often disallowed. The Protestant work ethic had not yet permeated western culture in proclaiming that earthly material rewards are the best guide to one's likely status in the next life and in exalting the value of earthly work. In a traditional—mostly agricultural—economy, jobs often were passed down from father to son, and relocating to other parts of a country was uncommon. In a general atmosphere of disparagement, the practice of economics became corrupt. Guilds, supposedly established for the benefit of all (along the lines of "just" prices), in fact protected the interests only of their members. A large aristocracy and nobility were able to feed off the land and the people of a country with relative ease; if the people complained, did this not just exemplify sinfulness and excessive desires for the things of this world?

The effect of the discovery of the New World truly should not be minimized. First, the ability to emigrate expanded the opportunities of individuals to leave their traditional societies, helping to free the minds of even the masses who remained, and also facilitating the creation of more open societies in Europe, particularly England. When the people can leave, ruling classes have more of an incentive to form societies that individuals like. Second, the discovery of the New World helped to fuel the rise of the national state, because nations had something worth fighting over—colonies around the globe. While the rise of the national state caused much destructiveness and while the loss of an earlier more porous (though feudal) European society was not without drawbacks, separate national identities established national economies in which the progress of new economic ideas and practices was easier. Third, and perhaps most importantly, the discovery of the New World fired the imagination of Europeans and led to a general attitude of inquisitiveness and questioning of established truths. This general attitude, particularly when combined with questions requiring economic answers (such as, why did prices rise when gold and silver were imported from the New World to Spain and Portugal?) led to new economic outlooks.

The first economic response by Europe to the discovery of the New World was mercantilism. Under this system, the hoarding of gold and silver was the primary national economic goal, colonies were extremely valuable, the import of finished goods (which had to be paid for in gold and silver) was undesirable, and the export of finished goods (for which gold and silver would be received) was highly desirable. To facilitate these policies, nations adopted tariffs and bounties (subsidies to exports).

The period leading up to the Industrial Revolution was thus one of tremendous flux and change. Gradually, through Protestantism, a greater appreciation for the individual and this life had been attained. Freedom began to permeate society. Finally, because slavery (at least of Europeans) was illegal, if economic advances were to be achieved, it would largely have to be through technical advances. There was no industrial revolution in ancient times because of the existence of slavery, which allowed the higher classes to have an affluent life-style without technical innovation. One has only to consider the example of the *ante-bellum* American South to appreciate that the existence of slavery tends to discourage practical science and material innovation. In a very real sense, machines are modern slaves—and machines (unlike slaves) can in time be made available to everyone, not just the rich.

The Industrial Revolution, then, was the product of a number of causes—some social and others technical. It is this revolution, furthermore, more than political ones, which has probably had the most significant impact on those whom it has affected, in terms of molding their day-to-day lives. Modernity came to have a very different culture than that of the Middle Ages. Wealth and its creation were looked upon as great social and personal goals.

Adam Smith (1723–90) is considered the apostle of capitalism. Before his *The Wealth of Nations* (1776), no systemic treatise existed that summed up and explained the economic order that was emerging. In this respect, Smith's primary contribution to political economy was not originality but systematization. While Locke and Smith's good friend Hume (whose literary executor Smith was) had written on economic topics, no great mind had yet propounded a comprehensive and sustained outlook. The newness of the field, indeed, is shown by the fact that the first book in English to carry the words "political economy" in its title appeared just nine years before *The Wealth of Nations:* Sir James Steuart's *Principles of Political Economy,* published in 1767.

Smith was from Scotland, and at the then normal age of 14, he entered the University of Glasgow and met Frances Hutcheson. Three years later, Smith attended Balliol College in Oxford, and six years after this returned to Glasgow. In 1752, he became professor at the University of Glasgow in moral philosophy, encompassing the fields of natural theology, ethics, jurisprudence, and political economy. In 1764, he became tutor to a young duke, and they travelled to France, where Smith met the physiocrats and began *The Wealth of Nations.* He returned to Britain two years later.

Smith was the archetypical absentminded professor. On one occasion, after getting up in the morning and smelling the air in his garden—and then pausing for a moment of reflection—he found himself fifteen miles away, still in his nightclothes. On another occasion, when showing a visitor a tannery and explaining the advantages of the division of labor, he fell into the tanning pit. Obviously, his mind was on more important matters.

The essential element in Smith's philosophy is his concentration on the importance of a free market in ensuring the highest quality goods at the lowest prices. His assumptions about human nature are uncomplicated and representative of the British capitalist-utilitarian era. As he works out comprehensively in *The Theory of Moral Sentiments* (1759), his only other major work besides *The Wealth of Nations,* human beings are at root individualistic. The appropriate reference point is that of the sympathetic, impartial spectator. There is nothing in Smith that suggests an organic view of social life or a historicist approach. According to him, human beings are autonomous, independent entities who may interact either more or less successfully. Human life has no set, predetermined, or inescapable goal or purpose.

Humans will interact most successfully if they live in a society of economic freedom. Individualistic philosophies tend to emphasize what people can do as individuals, not what they can do as groups. Strictly political questions do not much occupy Smith's attention—he does not care so much whether a person may vote as whether he may trade, establish an enterprise, or enter an occupation. In Smith's mind, the latter types of questions are more important than the former. It is important to comment that in his day the major goal of social philosophers was to reduce the extent of government and custom in all areas. Government at that time produced much inefficiency and waste through poor taxation practices, misdirection of resources, and over-regulation of the economy and society generally. It had not yet occurred to political and economic thinkers that government might actually be able to do great positive good for people; it would be enough if government just did no harm. Political liberty and economic *laissez faire* are thus related.

In fact, in an almost Marxian analysis (in that Smith holds the economic structure of society to precede its political one), Smith states, "Commerce and manufactures gradually introduced order and good government." It is when individuals have something worth preserving that they will institute a political system that will protect it.

Individuals, in Smith's conception, are largely, but not completely, motivated by self-interest. But because humans have within themselves a capacity for sympathy, they generally do not pillage at will. Nonetheless, humanity's sympathetic capacities are limited, and are socially more useful in restraining wicked actions than in compelling virtuous ones. For this reason, Smith notes that society is more likely to condemn a malicious character than it is to castigate merely a non-praiseworthy one. The appropriate role for government is to provide a stable social framework within which "the uniform, constant, and uninterrupted effort of every man to better his condition" can be realized.

Smith's famous analogy for the thesis that people, if left alone, will produce not only their own greatest good, but the good of all, is "the invisible hand." He uses this analogy in both *The Theory of Moral Sentiments* and *The Wealth of Nations.* In the latter, he states that—in a free economic system—an individual is "led by an invisible hand to promote an end which was no part of his intention. . . . By pursuing his own interest, he frequently promotes that of the society more effectually than when he really intends to promote it." Because individuals constantly seek to better their condition, they will continually direct resources to higher and better uses, if they are allowed to do so. This will result not only in their personal advantage, but in the advantage of others.

A free market enables individuals' significant self-interest to exercise itself within the limits established by a government that restrains people from performing positively bad actions. Smith states: "Man has almost constant occasion for the help of his brethren, and it is vain for him to expect it from their benevolence only. He will be more likely to prevail if he can interest their self-love in his favor, and show them that it is for their own advantage to do for him what he requires of them. . . . It is not from the benevolence of the butcher, the brewer, or the baker, that we expect our dinner, but from their regard to their own interest. We address ourselves, not to their humanity but to their self-love." Free markets allow all individuals in an economy to improve their conditions; this collective improvement by individuals equals national improvement—the wealth of nations.

In its emphasis on the wealth of a nation being nothing other than the wealth of the members who make up the nation, Smith's philosophy is individualistic. It furthers political theories that emphasize the individual, and proclaims the worth of each individual. Although in a very different way, Smith, like Marx, finds men and women's purpose in work.

The great advantage of free domestic and foreign markets is that they expand individuals' abilities to specialize, and it is through specialization that the wealth of persons and nations really increases. Among Smith's most important concepts, following his emphasis on the importance of free markets, is that as a productive enterprise becomes more complex, it generally can produce far more output. The example Smith uses is a pinmaker. He notes that if one person had to perform all of the functions required by that trade, he "could scarce . . . make one pin in a day, and certainly could not make twenty." But when this enterprise is divided into many branches, with each worker assigned a particular task, "ten persons . . . could make among them forty-eight thousand pins in a day." The *division of labor* is a fundamental component of economic growth to Smith, and it is this division which—more than any other single factor—allows the wealth of nations and persons to develop. In a primitive state of society, an individual's productive capabilities are extremely limited—to what a person can only directly produce.

The division of labor requires, further, a free market in order to be most effective. Where there is a closed market (either at home or abroad), or monopolies or guilds control productive practices, inefficiencies can result, and often do. Individuals' self-love will lead them to use the system for their personal advantage to the detriment of all, if the system allows them to. A free market in labor and capital always directs resources to be used exclusively by those who manage them optimally and provides the rewards necessary to encourage innovation and technical advance. Inefficient practices and producers will lose work. If this means that some producers go out of business or some workers must shift occupations, "the interest of the producer ought to be attended to only so far as it may be necessary for promoting that of the consumer."

Following Locke, Smith sees labor as the ultimate source for all value: "Labor . . . is the real measure of the exchangeable value of all commodities." While there is a partial exception to this in goods that are naturally scarce, such as (in a celebrated example) diamonds, the rule generally holds true. Smith considers the wages of labor to vary based on five components: the agreeableness of the employment, the difficulty in learning it, the constancy of the employment, the amount of trust required by it, and the probability of success in it.

Anything that restricts individuals' abilities to conduct transactions of all sorts is a hindrance to production. If apprenticeship laws and customs restrict the number of producers in an economic endeavor, then this is a restriction on the market. Similarly, if trade between nations is curtailed, then specialization will not occur to the extent that it otherwise would, resulting in inefficiency.

Smith's great target of opposition was mercantilism. This precapitalist phase of economic development saw rivalry between nations—fostered by discovery and colonization of the New World—as inerradicable. Rivalry was both on a territorial and commercial basis. Each nation considered its own interest to be possession of as much gold and silver as possible because these commodities were readily exchangeable in time of war for mercenaries and material. This is why the central concept of mercantilism was balance of trade. It is a measure of the enduring attraction of mercantilist-like ideas that the balance of trade remains topical today. Nations continue to be concerned with exporting more than they import, and, as in Smith's time, engage in various practices to help bring this state of affairs about. Smith's appraisal of mercantilism was that "the interest of the consumer is almost continually sacrificed to that of the producers."

Smith was emphatically opposed to any restraints on foreign trade that were the result of mercantilism. He considered this to result in both a nation—and its competitor—being worse off. Wherever the market is restricted, there is not the same possibility for specialization, and this is what allows maximum economic production. For example, in a simple two-nation economy, if one nation makes cars better and the other is superior in producing food, both will be better off by allowing free trade between them. Otherwise, the one nation will have to devote a disproportionate amount of resources to food production, and the other to car manufactures, and neither will be as well off as it could be. Smith sees a natural harmony of interests that results when freedom is society's governing principle. This implies, broadly speaking, a pacific policy in foreign relations, as well as domestic policies of economic non-interference and political liberty.

Smith opposed restrictions on trade within nations and between them. He was, however, no defender of what would later be called "big business." Along these lines, he wrote, "People of the same trade seldom meet together, even for merriment and diversion, but the conversation ends in a conspiracy against the public, or in some contrivance to raise prices." His solution to monopolies fostered by government was freer exchange through diminished government. He profoundly notes to those who might be tempted to use government for positive ends beyond the maintenance of free markets that, for example, "whenever the legislature attempts to regulate the differences between masters and their workmen, its counsellors are always the masters." In general, people will benefit more from a general principle of non-interference by government than from a principle that allows interference, because there is no telling what the interference will be or whom it will benefit.

Smith was not completely opposed to government, though he saw a limited role for it. The three functions that he allowed government are national defense; administration of an impartial system of justice; and facilitation of certain public works and institutions that are beneficial to society (particularly in furthering commerce), but whose nature does not lend themselves to being performed by individuals. Like Hume, Smith grounds justice in property: "Commerce and manufactures can seldom flourish long in any state which does not enjoy a regular administration of justice, in which the people do not feel themselves secure in the possession of their property, in which the faith of contracts is not supported by law, and in which the authority of the state is not supposed to be regularly employed in enforcing the payment of debts."

Concerning the non-defense and non-judicial functions of government, Smith saw these as essentially two: public works such as bridges, roads, and canals that are (or were) too expensive for individuals to construct; and some support for education. Even in these cases, though, he thought the government role should be as small as possible—the maintenance (if not the construction) of roads could be paid for by tolls; even if government provided the schoolhouse, students could still pay something toward the cost of teachers. Part of Smith's support for education was motivated by his observation that a mode of production, efficient as it might be, that restricted workers to just a "very few simple operations" could produce individuals who would be "as stupid and ignorant as it is possible for any human creature to become." Education would ward off some of the negative side effects of modernization. On taxation, Smith propounds four principles: taxation should be *proportionate* to income, its amount should be *certain* (and not arbitrary), its payment should be at a time when it is *convenient* for the payer, and it should be of a nature that is *uncostly* to administrate. Part of Smith's aversion to much government was that it would run up large debts: "Great nations are never impoverished by private, though they sometimes are by public, prodigality and misconduct."

Wisely, Smith observed that "it is not the actual greatness of national wealth, but its continual increase, which occasions a rise in the wages of labor." If the economic pie is fixed, then those who have the least social power may find their share continually reduced. It is when the national economic pie is growing that individuals have the greatest chance of increasing their standard of living.

Smith's approach to capital is that it is vital to the wealth of nations. Capital, in a very real sense, is stored labor. When capital exists, then people have the opportunity to innovate and experiment, as they are not living, literally, hand to mouth. The more capital that exists in a society, the more a society has the opportunity to enhance its future production. While the accumulation of capital results in a current diminution of standard of living, a higher standard of living in the future is allowed by this. Smith thus praises "private frugality and [the] good conduct of individuals." His economic philosophy was compatible with Victorian morality as well as political liberty.

The Wealth of Nations is for the most part an economic treatise. It provided practical guidance on many pressing issues of the day, including the British corn and poor laws. The former were a remnant of mercantilism; the export of corn was subsidized by the government, thereby also keeping its price high to domestic consumers and inaccessible. The poor laws restricted the movement of the poor to different parishes. Partially under the influence of *The Wealth of Nations,* both of these sets of laws eventually were eliminated, and policies of *laissez faire* generally were practiced in nineteenth-century Britain.

SMITH

The Wealth of Nations

THE DIVISION OF LABOR*

The greatest improvement in the productive powers of labor, and the greater part of the skill, dexterity, and judgment with which it is any where directed, or applied, seem to have been the effects of the division of labor.

The effects of the division of labor, in the general business of society, will be more easily understood, by considering in what manner it operates in some particular manufactures. It is commonly supposed to be carried furthest in some very trifling ones; not perhaps that it really is carried further in them than in others of more importance: but in those trifling manufactures which are destined to supply the small wants of but a small number of people, the whole number of workmen must necessarily be small; and those employed in every different branch of the work can often be collected into the same workhouse, and placed at once under the view of the spectator. In those great manufactures, on the contrary, which are destined to supply the great wants of the great body of the people, every different branch of the work employs so great a number of workmen, that it is impossible to collect them all into the same workhouse. We can seldom see more, at one time, than those employed in one single branch. Though in such manufactures, therefore, the work may really be divided into a much greater number of parts, than in those of a more trifling nature, the division is not near so obvious, and has accordingly been much less observed.

---

*From Adam Smith, *The Wealth of Nations* (1776).

To take an example, therefore, from a very trifling manufacture; but one in which the division of labor has been very often taken notice of, the trade of the pin-maker; a workman not educated to this business (which the division of labor has rendered a distinct trade), nor acquainted with the use of the machinery employed in it (to the invention of which the same division of labor has probably given occasion), could scarce, perhaps, with his utmost industry, make one pin in a day, and certainly could not make twenty. But in the way in which this business is now carried on, not only the whole work is a peculiar trade, but it is divided into a number of branches, of which the greater part are likewise peculiar trades. One man draws out the wire, another straights it, a third cuts it, a fourth points it, a fifth grinds it at the top for receiving the head; to make the head requires two or three distinct operations; to put it on, is a peculiar business, to whiten the pins is another; it is even a trade by itself to put them into the paper, and the important business of making a pin is, in this manner, divided into about eighteen distinct operations, which, in some manufactories, are all performed by distinct hands, though in others the same man will sometimes perform two or three of them. I have seen a small manufactory of this kind where ten men only were employed, and where some of them consequently performed two or three distinct operations. But though they were very poor, and therefore but indifferently accommodated with the necessary machinery, they could, when they exerted themselves, make among them about twelve pounds of pins in a day. There are in a pound upwards of four thousand pins of a middling size. Those ten persons, therefore, could make among them upwards of forty-eight thousand pins in a day. Each person, therefore, making a tenth part of forty-eight thousand pins, might be considered as making four thousand eight hundred pins in a day. But if they had all wrought separately and independently, and without any of them having been educated to this peculiar business, they certainly could not each of them have made twenty, perhaps not one pin in a day; that is, certainly, not the two hundred and fortieth, perhaps not the four thousand eight hundredth part of what they are at present capable of performing, in consequence of a proper division and combination of their different operations.

• • •

It is the great multiplication of the productions of all the different arts, in consequence of the division of labor, which occasions, in a well-governed society, that universal opulence which extends itself to the lowest ranks of the people. Every workman has a great quantity of his own work to dispose of beyond what he himself has occasion for; and every other workman being exactly in the same situation, he is enabled to exchange a great quantity of his own goods for a great quantity, or, what comes to the same thing, for the price of a great quantity of theirs. He supplies them abundantly with what they have occasion for, and they accommodate him as amply with what he has occasion for, and a general plenty diffuses itself through all the different ranks of the society.

Observe the accommodation of the most common artificer or day-laborer in a civilized and thriving country, and you will perceive that the number of people of whose industry a part, though but a small part, has been employed in procuring him this accommodation, exceeds all computation. The woollen coat, for example, which covers the day-laborer, as coarse and rough as it may appear, is the produce of the joint labor of a great multitude of workmen. The shepherd, the sorter of the wool, the wool-comber or carder, the dyer, the scribbler, the spinner, the weaver, the fuller, the dresser, with many others, must all join their different arts in order to complete even this homely production. How many merchants and carriers, besides, must have been employed in transporting the materials from some of those workmen to others who often live in a very distant part of the country! How much commerce and navigation in particular, how many ship-builders, sailors, sailmakers, rope-makers, must have been employed in order to bring together the different drugs made use of by the dyer, which often come from the remotest corners of the world! What a variety of labor too is necessary in order to produce the tools of the meanest of those workmen! To say nothing of such complicated machines as the ship of the sailor, the mill of the fuller, or even the loom of the weaver, let us consider only what a variety of labor is requisite in order to form that very simple machine, the shears with which the shepherd clips the wool. The miner, the builder of the furnace of smelting the ore, the feller of the timber, the burner of the charcoal to be made use of in the smelting-house, the brick-maker, the bricklayer, the work-men who attend the furnace, the mill-wright, the forger, the smith, must all of them join their different arts in order to produce them. Were we to examine, in the same manner, all the different parts of his dress and household furniture, the coarse linen shirt which he wears next his skin, the shoes which cover his feet, the bed which he lies on, and all the different parts which compose it, the kitchen-grate at which he prepares his victuals, the coals which he makes use of for that purpose, dug from the bowels of the earth, and brought to him perhaps by a long sea and a long land carriage, all the other utensils of his kitchen, all the furniture of his table, the knives and forks, the earthen or pewter plates upon which he serves up and divides his victuals, the different hands employed in preparing his bread and his beer, the glass window which lets in the heat and the light, and keeps out the wind and the rain, with all the knowledge and art requisite for preparing that beautiful and happy invention, without which these northern parts of the world could scarce have afforded a very comfortable habitation, together with the tools of all the different workmen employed in producing those different conveniences; if we examine, I say, all these things, and consider what a variety of labour is employed about each of them, we shall be sensible that without the assistance and co-operation of many thousands, the very meanest person in a civilized country could not be provided, even according to, what we very falsely imagine, the easy and simple manner in which he is commonly accommodated. Compared, indeed, with the more extravagant luxury of the great, his accommodation must no doubt appear extremely simple and easy; and yet it may be true, perhaps, that the accommodation of an European prince does not always so much exceed that of an industrious and frugal peasant, as the accommodation of the latter exceeds that of many an African king, the absolute master of the lives and liberties of ten thousand naked savages.

• • •

As it is the power of exchanging that gives occasion to the division of labor, so the extent of this division must always be limited by the extent of that power, or, in other words, by the extent of the market. When the market is very small, no person can have an encouragement to dedicate himself entirely to one employment, for want of the power to exchange all that surplus part of the produce of his own labor, which is over and above his own consumption, for such parts of the produce of other men's labour as he has occasion for.

ECONOMIC VALUE

The word VALUE, it is to be observed, has two different meanings, and sometimes expresses the utility of some particular object, and sometimes the power of purchasing other goods which the possession of that object conveys. The one may be called "value in use"; the other, "value in exchange." The things which have the greatest value in use have frequently little or no value in exchange; and on the contrary, those which have the greatest value in exchange have frequently little or no value in use. Nothing is more useful than water: but it will purchase scarce any thing; scarce any thing can be had in exchange for it. A diamond, on the contrary, has scarce any value in use; but a very great quantity of other goods may frequently be had in exchange for it.

In order to investigate the principles which regulate the exchangeable value of commodities, I shall endeavor to show,

First, what is the real measure of this exchangeable value; or, wherein consists the real price of all commodities.

Secondly, what are the different parts of which this real price is composed or made up.

And, lastly, what are the different circumstances which sometimes raise some or all of these different parts of price above, and sometimes sink them below their natural or ordinary rate; or, what are the causes which sometimes hinder the market price, that is, the actual price of commodities, from coinciding exactly with what may be called their natural price.

• • •

Every man is rich or poor according to the degree in which he can afford to enjoy the necessaries, conveniences, and amusements of human life. But after the division of labor has once thoroughly taken place, it is but a very small part of these with which a man's own labor can supply him. The far greater part of them he must derive from the labor of other people, and he must be rich or poor according to the quantity of that labor which he can command, or which he can afford to purchase. The value of any commodity, therefore, to the person who possesses it, and who means not to use or consume it himself, but to exchange it for other commodities, is equal to the quantity of labor which it enables him to purchase or command. Labor, therefore, is the real measure of the exchangeable value of all commodities.

The real price of every thing, what every thing really costs to the man who wants to acquire it, is the toil and trouble of acquiring it. What everything is really worth to the man who has acquired it and who wants to dispose of it or exchange it for something else, is the toil and trouble which it can save to himself, and which it can impose upon other people. What is bought with money or with goods is purchased by labor, as much as what we acquire by the toil of our own body. That money or those goods indeed save us this toil. They contain the value of a certain quantity of labor which we exchange for what is supposed at the time to contain the value of an equal quantity. Labor was the first price, the original purchase-money that was paid for all things. It was not by gold or by silver, but by labor, that all the wealth of the world was originally purchased; and its value, to those who possess it, and who want to exchange it for some new productions, is precisely equal to the quantity of labor which it can enable them to purchase or command.

But though labor be the real measure of the exchangeable value of all commodities, it is not that by which their value is commonly estimated. It is often difficult to ascertain the proportion between two different quantities of labor. The time spent in two different sorts of work will not always alone determine this proportion. The different degrees of hardship endured, and of ingenuity exercised, must likewise be taken into account. There may be more labor in an hour's hard work than in two hours easy business; or in an hour's application to a trade which it cost ten years labor to learn, than in a month's industry at an ordinary and obvious employment. But it is not easy to find any accurate measure either of hardship or ingenuity. In exchanging indeed the different productions of different sorts of labor for one another, some allowance is commonly made for both. It is adjusted, however, not by any accurate measure, but by the higgling and bargaining of the market, according to that sort of rough equality which, though not exact, is sufficient for carrying on the business of common life.

• • •

In that early and rude state of society which precedes both the accumulation of stock and the appropriation of land, the proportion between the quantities of labor necessary for acquiring different objects seems to be the only circumstance which can afford any rule for exchanging them for one another. If among a nation of hunters, for example, it usually costs twice the labor to kill a beaver which it does to kill a deer, one beaver should naturally exchange for or be worth two deer. It is natural that what is usually the produce of two days or two hours labor, should be worth double of what is usually the produce of one day's or one hour's labor.

If the one species of labor should be more severe than the other, some allowance will naturally be made for this superior hardship; and the produce of one hour's labor in the one way may frequently exchange for that of two hours labor in the other.

Or if the one species of labor requires an uncommon degree of dexterity and ingenuity, the esteem which men have for such talents, will naturally give a value to their produce, superior to what would be due to the time employed about it. Such talents can seldom be acquired but in consequence of long application, and the superior value of their produce may frequently be no more than a reasonable compensation for the time and labor which must be spent in acquiring them. In the advanced state of society, allowances of this kind, for superior hardship and superior skill, are commonly made in the wages of labor, and something of the same kind must probably have taken place in its earliest and rudest period.

As soon as stock has accumulated in the hands of particular persons, some of them will naturally employ it in setting to work industrious people, whom they will supply with materials and subsistence, in order to make a profit by the sale of their work, or by what their labor adds to the value of the materials. In exchanging the complete manufacture either for money, for labor, or for other goods, over and above what may be sufficient to pay the price of the materials, and the wages of the workmen, something must be given for the profits of the undertaker of the work who hazards his stock in this adventure. The value which the workmen add to the materials, therefore, resolves itself in this case into two parts, of which the one pays their wages, the other the profits of their employer upon the whole stock of materials and wages which he advanced. He could have no interest to employ them, unless he expected from the sale of their work something more than what was sufficient to replace his stock to him; and he could have no interest to employ a great stock rather than a small one, unless his profits were to bear some proportion to the extent of his stock.

As soon as the land of any country has all become private property, the landlords, like all other men, love to reap where they never sowed, and demand a rent even for its natural produce. The wood of the forest, the grass of the field, and all the natural fruits of the earth, which, when land was in common, cost the laborer only the trouble of gathering them, come, even to him, to have an additional price fixed upon them. He must give up to the landlord a portion of what his labor either collects or produces. This portion, or, what comes to the same thing, the price of this portion, constitutes the rent of land, and in the price of the greater part of commodities makes a third component part.

As the price or exchangeable value of every particular commodity, taken separately, resolves itself into some one or other, or all of those three parts; so that of all the commodities which compose the whole annual produce of the labor of every country, taken complexly, must resolve itself into the same three parts, and be parcelled out among different inhabitants of the country, either as the wages of their labor, the profits of their stock, or the rent of their land. The whole of what is annually either collected or produced by the labor of every society, or what comes to the same thing, the whole price of it, is in this manner originally distributed among some of its different members. Wages, profit, and rent, are the three original sources of all revenue as well as of all exchangeable value. All other revenue is ultimately derived from some one or other of these.

GOVERNMENT

The first duty of the sovereign is that of protecting the society from the violence and invasion of other independent societies.

• • •

The second duty of the sovereign is that of protecting, as far as possible, every member of the society from the injustice or oppression of every other member of it, or the duty of establishing an exact administration of justice.

• • •

The third and last duty of the sovereign or commonwealth is that of erecting and maintaining those public institutions and those public works, which, though they may be in the highest degree advantageous to a great society, are, however, of such a nature,

that the profit could never repay the expense to any individual or small number of individuals, and which it therefore cannot be expected that any individual or small number of individuals should erect or maintain.

After the public institutions and public works necessary for the defense of the society, and for the administration of justice, the other works and institutions of this kind are chiefly those for facilitating the commerce of the society, and those for promoting the instruction of the people.

It is necessary to premise the four following maxims with regard to taxes in general.

I. The subjects of every state ought to contribute towards the support of the government, as nearly as possible, in proportion to their respective abilities; that is, in proportion to the revenue which they respectively enjoy under the protection of the state. The expense of government to the individuals of a great nation, is like the expense of management to the joint tenants of a great estate, who are all obliged to contribute in proportion to their respective interests in the estate. In the observation or neglect of this maxim consists, what is called the equality or inequality of taxation.

II. The tax which each individual is bound to pay ought to be certain, and not arbitrary. The time of payment, the manner of payment, the quantity to be paid, ought all to be clear and plain to the contributor, and to every other person. Where it is otherwise, every person subject to the tax is put more or less in the power of the tax-gatherer, who can either aggravate the tax upon any obnoxious contributor, or extort, by the terror of such aggravation, some present or perquisite to himself. The uncertainty of taxation encourages the insolence and favors the corruption of an order of men who are naturally unpopular, even where they are neither insolent nor corrupt. The certainty of what each individual ought to pay is, in taxation, a matter of so great importance, that a very considerable degree of inequality, it appears, I believe, from the experience of all nations, is not near so great an evil as a very small degree of uncertainty.

III. Every tax ought to be levied at the time, or in the manner in which it is most likely to be convenient for the contributor to pay it. A tax upon the rent of land or of houses, payable at the same term at which such rents are usually paid, is levied at the time when it is most likely to be convenient for the contributor to pay; or, when he is most likely to have wherewithal to pay. Taxes upon such consumable goods as are articles of luxury, are all finally paid by the consumer, and generally in a manner that is very convenient for him. He pays them by little and little, as he has occasion to buy the goods. As he is at liberty too, either to buy, or not to buy, as he pleases, it must be his own fault if he ever suffers any considerable inconveniency from such taxes.

IV. Every tax ought to be so contrived as both to take out and to keep out of the pockets of the people as little as possible, over and above what it brings into the public treasury of the state. A tax may either take out or keep out of the pockets of the people a great deal more than it brings into the public treasury, in the four following ways. First, the levying of it may require a great number of officers, whose salaries may eat up the greater part of the produce of the tax, and whose perquisites may impose another additional tax upon the people. Secondly, it may obstruct the industry of the people, and discourage them from applying to certain branches of business which might give maintenance and employment to great multitudes. While it obliges the people to pay, it may thus diminish, or perhaps destroy, some of the funds which might enable them more easily to do so. Thirdly, by the forfeitures and other penalties which those unfortunate individuals incur who attempt unsuccessfully to evade the tax, it may frequently ruin them, and thereby put an end to the benefit which the community might have received from the employment of their capitals. An injudicious tax offers a great temptation to smuggling. But the penalties of smuggling must rise in proportion to the temptation. The law, contrary to all the ordinary principles of justice, first creates the temptation, and then punishes those who yield to it; and it commonly enhances the punishment too in proportion to the very circumstance which ought certainly to alleviate it, the temptation to commit the crime. Fourthly, by subjecting the people to the frequent visits and the odious examination of the tax-gatherers, it may expose them to much unnecessary trouble, vexation, and oppression; and though vexation is not, strictly speaking, expense, it is certainly equivalent to the expense at which every man would be willing to redeem himself from it. It is in some one or other of these four different ways that taxes are frequently so much more burdensome to the people than they are beneficial to the sovereign.

CHAPTER TWENTY-FOUR

BURKE

The American Revolution was the second act in the drama of democratic revolution. The colonists derived their political heritage from the English experience of 1640 and 1688, and the Revolution was caused by the attempt of the English—doomed to failure from the beginning—to apply to British subjects in North America doctrines and practices of government that had been repudiated through revolution and civil war at home. Moreover, the American Revolution was not only a war of independence but also a conflict between rivaling social classes. The victory of the American Revolution meant the predominance of the middle classes in the development of the new nation, dedicated to the equalitarian ideals of life, liberty, and the pursuit of happiness for all. As in the English revolutions of the seventeenth century, neither extreme radicalism nor ultraconservatism prevailed in the American Revolution. Internally there was less resistance to the revolutionary achievement in the United States than there was to the Puritan successes of the 1640s in England, because even before the Revolution the absence of an aristocracy and the fuller acceptance of religious diversity in America allowed society to develop more freely than was possible in England before the Reform Act of 1832.

The example of the American Revolution was a standing challenge to the established order of Europe, dominated—from France to the Urals—by absolute monarchy, church, and aristocracy. The significance of the English Revolution of 1688 could not be so quickly discerned, because the monarchy continued as the symbol of traditional authority and the landowning classes still controlled both Houses of Parliament until 1832. As for the American Revolution, the absence of monarchy and aristocracy in the new society unmistakably underlined its belief in equality and opportunity. One of the main arguments of the antidemocratic side in the eighteenth century had been the impracticality of the democratic ideal, the insistence that unpopular government could never work in actuality, that it would quickly degenerate into chaos and anarchy. The sound sense and statesmanship of the American revolutionary leaders quickly turned the revolutionary experiment into a stable order, addressing itself, by its existence and success, to the oppressed everywhere as an invitation to rebellion. In 1824, Prince Metternich, the mouthpiece of European conservatism, said of the United States that "in fostering revolutions wherever they show themselves, in regretting those which have failed, in extending a helping hand to those which seem to prosper, they lend new strength to the apostles of sedition, and reanimate the courage of every conspirator."

The French Revolution, the third act in the drama of modern democratic revolution, began two years after the Constitution of the United States was framed. Peaceful reform would have been possible until the last minute, and the Anglophile, liberal-conservative element was at first in the ascendancy. But the *ancien régime* lacked the most elementary prudence and foresight, and thus made revolution inevitable. The Estates-General met, for the first time since 1614, on May 5, 1789, and on the following day the Third Estate assembled in separate session. The cleavage between the people on the one side, and church and aristocracy on the other, was thereby quickly revealed. Meeting separately, the Third Estate in effect declared itself to be the representative body of the whole nation: the Revolution had started.

No event in modern history so immediately and completely electrified the world as did the French Revolution, particularly after the storming of the Bastille on July 14, 1789. Charles James Fox, the leader of the English Whigs (or Liberals) called it the "greatest event" that had ever happened in the world, and "how much the best!" His remark reveals how, even when politics was mainly the business of a small aristocratic class, attitudes toward foreign countries were largely determined by ideological sympathies. Traditionally, the Tories (or Conservatives) had been the friends of France, although she was England's principal rival for world hegemony, because the *ancien régime* upheld the influence of hierarchy in religion, class in society, and authority in government. Precisely for these reasons the Whigs were anti-French, and also because the Revolution of 1688 was directed against a monarch who was in French pay and in closest sympathy with the French court. But the French Revolution reversed the two traditional attitudes in England. The new anti-French position of the Tories expressed hostility, not to the French people, but to the Jacobin ideals of Liberty, Fraternity, and Equality; similarly, the sudden sympathy of the Whigs, or at least their more radical wing, for France expressed the satisfaction that she had finally done in 1789 what England had accomplished a century before.

In the early stage of the Revolution few understood its long-term impact and significance. Some of the conservative forces in Europe even welcomed the Revolution as a sign of French weakness and decay; they failed to perceive the fresh vitality and vigorous ability of the new democratic leaders, whose aim was to make France not only free but great. The first to raise the issues of the Revolution from the plane of immediate profit and policy to that of principle and philosophy was Edmund Burke (1729–1797), whose *Reflections on the Revolution in France* (1790) was an immediate literary success in England and on the Continent. Moreover, it was a political event of the first order, stemming the flood of sympathy and enthusiasm that until then had been rushing forth from the hearts of the inarticulate masses of Europe, as well as from philosophers and poets who saw in the Revolution the dawn of a new humanity.

Burke's *Reflections* comforted the enemies of the Revolution ("Read it," King George III said to all who came to see him. "It will do you good—do you good! Every gentleman should read it.") as much as it antagonized its friends, and it was at once answered by a mass of prorevolutionary books and pamphlets. The most important of those writings is Tom Paine's *Rights of Man* (1791–1792), a fiery answer to the *Reflections,* and—as a defense of French democracy—a worthy successor to his *Common Sense* (1776), one of the trail blazers of the Declaration of Independence.

Burke was born in Dublin in 1729, the son of a successful Irish-Protestant attorney. His mother was a Catholic who did not change her faith, and Burke's Catholic connection (his sister, too, was brought up as a Catholic) provided him with an early education in practical politics. Although Catholics formed the vast majority of the Irish population, they were cruelly oppressed by the ruling Protestant English aristocracy. A special "penal" code was used to exclude Catholics from property, public service, and the professions, reduce them to the state of second-class citizens in their own country, extirpate the Catholic religion, and destroy the sense, and very existence, of Irish nationality. Though Burke came to identify himself ultimately with England, his Irish background and experience always remained a powerful element in his outlook and sympathies.

In 1750 Burke went to London to prepare himself for the legal profession. But his heart was in literature and politics rather than in law, and he preferred the vagaries and uncertainties of the former to the security of the latter, even though his decision cost him his regular allowance from his father.

In 1756 Burke published his first work, *A Vindication of Natural Society.* A short essay, the *Vindication* contains nevertheless most of the key ideas of Burke, developed more exhaustively in his later, and more elaborate, writings. In the preface to the *Vindication* Burke expresses his lack of faith in the capacity of the ordinary person to think things out for himself, and asks, "What would become of the world if the practice of all moral duties, and the foundations of society, rested upon having their reasons made clear and demonstrative to every individual?" His supernatural approach to problems of politics becomes evident in the proposition that "civil government borrows a strength from ecclesiastical," and that in general the "ideas of religion and government are closely connected."

The chief purpose of the *Vindication* becomes evident—to discourage rational inquiry into political institutions as into religion, because the critical spirit of rationalism is bound to challenge, question, attack, and—finally—undermine the civil and religious foundations of society.

Underlying Burke's philosophy in the *Vindication,* published when he was only twenty-seven, is a deep feeling of *pessimism* that nourishes and colors all his thought: "On considering political societies, their origin, their constitution, and their effects, I have sometimes been in a good deal more than doubt whether the Creator did ever really intend man for a state of happiness. He has mixed in his cup a number of natural evils (in spite of the boasts of stoicism they are evils), and every endeavor which the art and policy of mankind has used from the beginning of the world to this day, in order to alleviate or cure them, has only served to introduce new mischiefs, or to aggravate and inflame the old."

Burke approached problems of society in the knowledge that "we owe an implicit reverence to all the institutions of our ancestors," and that we should consider such institutions "with all that modesty" in which a received opinion should be examined.

Burke was even more eager to get into politics than into literature, and he finally entered Parliament at thirty-seven, a comparatively late age in those days. Although he was one of the most brilliant political speakers and writers of his time, he was never able to attain cabinet office; his sincere and impassioned effort to dedicate his life to the English governing classes did not remove the obstacle of his being a newcomer in English politics. Burke's position was made still more vulnerable by his lifelong financial troubles. He lived above his means, purchased a large estate that he could not pay for, and incurred enormous debts that would have driven him into bankruptcy and disgrace had he not been saved by the generosity of his aristocratic benefactors. Burke's reputation also suffered from speculations, which generally failed, and from his associations with financial adventurers and other persons of doubtful standing. In addition, anti-Catholic bigotry affected his career adversely. His mother was known as a loyal Catholic, he married a Catholic, and he himself was suspected of Catholic sympathies and Jesuit beliefs and practices. In June, 1780, anti-Catholic rioting took place in London for ten days, and Burke's life was openly threatened by the mob.

Burke's *veneration of aristocracy* was not a matter of snobbery but of profound conviction that aristocracy was a part of the divinely ordained scheme of governing society, and he accepted his social inferiority with good cheer. Toward the end of his life he said of himself that he was not "swaddled and rocked and dandled" into a political career: "I possessed not one of the qualities, nor cultivated one of the arts, that recommend men to the favor and protection of the great. I was not made for a minion or a tool. As little did I follow the trade of winning the hearts, by imposing on the understandings of the people. At every step of my progress in life, for in every step was I traversed and opposed, and at every turnpike I met, I was obliged to show my passport, and again and again to prove my sole title to the honor of being useful to my country, by a proof that I was not wholly unacquainted with its laws and the whole system of its interests both abroad and at home; otherwise no rank, no toleration even for me." Although Burke was completely rational in the appraisal of individual members of the aristocracy, especially when they were his political opponents, he never challenged the collective right of the aristocratic class to govern Britain and her empire.

Burke's *Reflections on the Revolution in France* (1790) was the outstanding event in his literary as well as political career. Until the publication of the book, liberal sympathies for the Revolution had been expressed more often and more vigorously than criticisms; the *Reflections* (followed swiftly, in 1791, by *A Letter to a Member of the National Assembly, Thoughts on French Affairs,* and *An Appeal from the Old to the New Whigs*) turned the tables on the liberal sympathizers by enlarging the scope of the debate. What had started out as a discussion of the French Revolution became a searching inquiry into the nature of reform and revolution in general, and out of this inquiry emerged the bible of modern conservatism.

The impact of the *Reflections* was due as much to its subtlety of thought and moral elevation as to its style and language, an arresting mixture of poetry, philosophy, and religious mysticism, all suffused with a penetrating sense of practical wisdom. The French Revolution was, for Burke, not the result of deepseated historical conflicts and forces, but of wrong doctrines of philosophers who were animated by fanatical atheism, and of vile ambitions of politicians who were driven by opportunist lust for power. Burke is particularly vehement in his denunciation of French philosophers and men of letters—"robbers and assassins: Never before, did a den of bravoes and banditti, assume the garb and tone of an academy of philosophers."

Burke was quick enough to realize that the French Revolution was more than an internal French affair, that it was a "revolution of doctrine and theoretic dogma," and he attacked the state that emerged from it as a "college of armed fanatics, for the propagation of the principles of assassination, robbery, fraud, faction, oppression, and impiety." Wisdom is most terrified by fanaticism, its worst enemy, against which it is the least able to furnish any kind of remedy, and Burke therefore called for a European crusade to crush the revolutionary spirit by force of arms. He was convinced that no monarchy would be safe "as long as this strange, nameless, wild, enthusiastic thing is established in the center of Europe." After England, in concert with other European powers, became involved in war with France, Burke emphasized that the war was directed, not against the French people, but against Jacobin democracy, which could not be shut out by fortresses and territorial limits. In the French Revolution Burke saw a tyranny of the multitude, which is but "a multiplied tyranny."

Against the individualist conception of society of Locke and the French philosophers Burke put forward the *organic theory:* "Society is indeed a contract. Subordinate contracts for objects of mere occasional interest may be dissolved at pleasure—but the state ought not to be considered as nothing better than a partnership agreement in a trade of pepper and coffee, calico or tobacco, or some other such low concern, to be taken up for a little temporary interest, and to be dissolved by the fancy of the parties.

It is to be looked on with other reverence; because it is not a partnership in things sub-servient only to the gross animal existence of a temporary and perishable nature. It is a partnership in all science; a partnership in all art; a partnership in every virtue, and in all perfection. As the ends of such a partnership cannot be obtained in many genera-tions, it becomes a partnership not only between those who are living, but between those who are living, those who are dead and those who are to be born." Because soci-ety is the product of a continuous stream of generation cooperating with generation, aiming at the good life in its fullest measure, the burden of proof lies on those "who tear to pieces the whole frame and contexture of their country."

Burke's ideal of statesmanship avoids extremes of tearing down blindly the existing order and of resisting change at all cost: "A disposition to preserve, and an ability to im-prove, taken together, would be my standard of a statesman." This formula may also be seen as the classical definition of the true conservative, as distinct from the stand-pat conservative or the reactionary. The stand-pat conservative is so content with the status quo that he is unwilling to make any changes or reforms. The reactionary wants to change and to move—but to move backward rather than forward. The true conservative possesses a balance between preservation and change, with a slight bias toward preser-vation. As Burke says, the spontaneous, emotional, unreflective "disposition" of the conservative is to preserve, but when the conservative is shown the need for change and improvement, he has the intellectual, reflective "ability" to make necessary changes. By the same token, the liberal could be defined, in Burkean terms, as having "a disposi-tion to improve and an ability to preserve."

Burke sharply distinguishes reform from innovation, which generally derives from a selfish temper and confined views. Whatever innovation, or "hot reformation," can ac-complish is bound to be crude, harsh, indigested, mixed with imprudence and injustice, and contrary to human nature and human institutions. *True reform,* which can be brought about only by disinterested statesmen, must be *early* in the interest of govern-ment, and *temperate* in the interest of the people, because only temperate reforms are permanent and allow room for growth: "Whenever we improve, it is right to leave room for further improvement."

Every revolution contains some evil, Burke says, as it inevitably destroys part of the moral capital, the good will, of the community, and the moral capital of future genera-tions should be considered as a trust that must not be treated lightly. The English Revo-lution of 1688 was "a revolution, not made, but prevented," because the nation was on the defensive, seeking to preserve its institutions rather than to subvert or destroy them. The monarchy was continued, and the nation kept "the same ranks, the same or-ders, the same privileges, the same franchises, the same rules for property, the same subordinations," and, above all, the Revolution was followed by a "happy settlement." Burke contrasts the English Revolution of 1688 with the French Revolution of 1789, in which he sees but destruction, anarchy, and terror.

Burke denies the validity of the central doctrine of democracy: that only the gov-erned have the right to determine who is to govern them, and that all votes count equally. He opposes this democratic method as an "arithmetic" devoid of meaning and thinks of representation in terms of historic interests, such as the Lords, the Commons, the monarchy, the Established Church, rather than in terms of individual citizens. Burke adheres to the medieval idea that man is politically significant, not as an individ-ual citizen, but solely as a member of a group to which he belongs socially or economi-cally. This theory of *corporate representation* was later supported by Hegel and found a distorted expression in the "corporate state" of fascism.

Burke was liberal enough not to desire the oppression of persons of low station, like hairdressers and working tallow chandlers, provided that they stay in their places: "Such descriptions of men ought not to suffer oppression from the state; but the state suffers oppression, if such as they, either individually or collectively, are permitted to rule." Because of his firm conviction that wealth and aristocracy were the repositories of political wisdom and experience, he stubbornly resisted any widening of the suffrage. Under the then existing system of "rotten boroughs," small hamlets were represented in Parliament, whereas large urban communities were not represented at all or grossly under-represented. This system soon brought England to the brink of revolution, but it was adjudged by Burke to be "adequate to all the purposes for which a representation of the people can be desired or devised." In fact, Burke held that the suffrage ought to be further limited, rather than broadened, if any changes were to be made, because of the "prostitute and daring venality, the corruption of manners, the idleness and profligacy of the lower sort of voters."

Whereas Locke attached to *property* the qualification that it was originally equal, Burke frankly states the doctrine that the "characteristic essence of property, formed out of the combined principles of its acquisition and conservation, is to be *unequal*." The inequality of property that Burke defended was closely related to his conception of society in which rank and privilege played such a large part. Similarly, Burke fully perceived and approved of political inequality as the concomitant of economic inequality. "Hereditary property and hereditary distinction" wholly composed the House of Lords, and he was pleased that the House of Commons was also made up (in his time) of large property owners.

As to the unpropertied masses, Burke wanted them to be content with *virtual representation,* under which, as he said in a letter to Sir Hercules Langrishe (January 3, 1792), "There is a communion of interests, and a sympathy in feelings and desires between those who act in the name of any description of people, and the people in whose name they act, though the trustees are not actually chosen by them. This is virtual representation. Such a representation I think to be, in many cases, even better than the actual."

Moreover, apart from the direct and explicit support that Burke gave to the sanctity of property and its privileges in government and society, his indirect and implicit support was even more important. What mattered most was that Burke emphasized the values of prescription, inheritance, rank, and distinction, all of which helped to buttress the cause of inequality of property and political rights.

Burke saw society, not in terms of equal individuals, but of unequal groups and historically recognized interests. Property is such an interest, founded on *prescription,* rather than on natural law or abstract reasoning. Aristocracy and monarchy are also institutions based on prescription. Though property is not the only criterion of the privileged classes and interests that Burke deems worthy to rule the nation, he is keenly conscious of the connections between property and the established order based on privilege and rank. The French Revolution was, for Burke, a direct threat to the traditional connection of property and political rule, and he defines Jacobinism as "the revolt of the enterprising talents of a country against its property." The attempt to level inequality never ends in equality, Burke says. Every society has various descriptions of citizens, and "some description must be uppermost." The levelers therefore merely pervert the natural order of society by their abstract schemes that interfere with its proper constitution.

The only time that Burke seems to relinquish his organic conceptions of man and society, when he talks the cold-blooded language of the profit-seeking entrepreneur, is in his discussion of labor, particularly in his *Thoughts and Details on Scarcity* (1795). There is little in this pamphlet that Herbert Spencer could not have wholeheartedly endorsed. Labor, Burke argues, is "a commodity" and as such an article of trade, subject to the fluctuations of supply and demand on the market: "The impossibility of the subsistence of a man, who carries his labor to a market, is totally beside the question in this way of viewing it. The only question is, what is it worth to the buyer?" The poverty of the laboring people, Burke held, was due to their large numbers: "Numbers in their nature imply poverty." Even if all the throats of the rich were cut, the distribution of their wealth would not yield enough bread and cheese for one night's supper of the laboring classes. But, Burke continues, the throats of the rich ought not to be cut, because the rich are the trustees for those who labor, and their accumulated hoards are the banking houses of the poor. All that the rich receive for their office of trusteeship is a "very trifling commission and discount."

If the worker does not earn enough for his subsistence, the state has no right to interfere by guaranteeing minimum wages, and the worker then passes out of the jurisdiction of economic or political laws and becomes an object of mercy and charity. Burke concedes that the duty to practice charity toward the indigent is "imperfect," that is, it cannot be enforced, but he is unwilling to go beyond such voluntary provision for the helpless poor. Whereas Burke rejects the concept of natural law when discussing the Rights of Man, he thinks differently when it comes to the Rights of Commerce: "We, the people, ought to be made sensible, that it is not in breaking the laws of commerce, which are the laws of nature, and consequently the laws of God, that we are to place our hope of softening the divine displeasure to remove any calamity under which we suffer, or which hangs over us."

Burke never composed a systematic treatise of politics, like Hobbes' *Leviathan* or Locke's *Two Treatises of Government,* partly because he was a busy parliamentarian and partly because he needed a concrete issue around which he could develop his general principles. His political ideas cannot be found in one place but have to be gathered from his books, speeches, essays, and letters, although the *Reflections* will always occupy first place. Yet if Burke does not state anywhere a systematic theory of politics, his thought is always cast in forms which do not vary greatly. Above all, Burke distrusts metaphysics and *a priori* reasoning, and he constantly reiterates the plea that politics is a matter of prudence, expediency, circumstance, utility, experience, history, loyalty, and reverence, and not of abstract speculation: "The science of constructing a commonwealth, or renovating it, or reforming it, is, like every other experimental science, not to be taught *a priori*." Circumstances give to every principle its distinguishing color and discriminating effect: "The circumstances are what render every civil and political scheme beneficial or noxious to mankind." The world of contingency and political combination is always larger than we can imagine in advance, and no lines can be laid down for civil or political wisdom. They are incapable of exact definition.

Politics ought to be adjusted, not to reason, but to human nature, and Burke urges that the practical consequences of any political tenet "go a great way in deciding upon its value. Political problems do not primarily concern truth or falsehood. They relate to good or evil. What in the result is likely to produce evil, is politically false: that which is productive of good, politically true." Burke expresses this purely *utilitarian* and *pragmatic* viewpoint by saying that things that are not practicable are not desirable, and that the consequences of any assumed rights "are of great moment in deciding upon their validity." No universal statement can be made on moral and political subjects, and pure metaphysics does not apply to them. The lines of morality are not like those of mathematics: they admit exceptions and demand modifications, arrived at, not by the process of logic, but by the rules of prudence: "Prudence is not only the first in rank of the virtues political and moral, but she is the director, the regulator, the standard of them all. Metaphysics cannot live without definition; but prudence is cautious how she defines."

In discussing human *liberty* Burke is less interested in the right to freedom than in the aptitude for it. Men are qualified for civil liberty in exact proportion to their self-control, love of justice, sobriety, and soundness of understanding. Society must have a controlling power, and the less of it there is within the minds and hearts of men, the more there must be without: "It is ordained in the eternal constitution of things that men of intemperate minds cannot be free. Their passions forge their fetters." Similarly, Burke refuses to lay down an abstract and general definition of *rights* to which every man is entitled, because they are "a thing to be settled by convention." Government itself is not primarily designed to provide and protect rights but is "a contrivance of human wisdom to provide for human *wants*." The rights of men are their advantages and are in "a sort of *middle*, incapable of definition, but not impossible to be discerned." The balancing of conflicting rights and advantages is a most complex process of compromise, of "adding, subtracting, multiplying, and dividing, morally and not metaphysically or mathematically, true moral denominations."

In appraising the political judgment of Burke it ought to be remembered that he was on the side of the future of three of the principal political issues of his time: Ireland, India, and the American colonies. In all three instances his sympathies were magnanimous, his judgment farsighted, and for these reasons he will always be an abiding inspiration to liberal statesmen. In his attitude toward the French Revolution, Burke (who knew France firsthand from only one visit in 1773) was proved wrong in the light of the future, but he was also wrong from his own viewpoint. France did not degenerate into anarchy, as Burke claimed, and it more than regained its lost military strength and international influence under the impetus of the Revolution. Far from destroying the respect for property, as Burke feared, the French Revolution firmly established a new legal and political order that tenaciously protected the rights of property. Burke profoundly foresaw that the Revolution would end in a military dictatorship; yet it was not the original aims of the Revolution but the military coalition of Europe (including England) against France that paved the way for Napoleon. Moreover, the rule of Napoleon was only an interlude, and the liberating effect of the Revolution proved stronger than the temporary dictatorship.

In comparing the French with the English Revolution, Burke always pointed to the violent and radical character of the first, contrasted with the peaceable and conservative character of the second. Yet the obvious parallel to the French Revolution is not the Bloodless Revolution of 1688, but the very bloody revolution and Civil War of the 1640s, culminating in the execution of Charles I. In cutting off the head of their monarch the French were no more than good disciples of the English, and their Revolution was, at the start, much more peaceful than the Puritan Revolution.

Had there been no military coalition of Europe (for which Burke himself labored with utmost frenzy) against revolutionary France, no invasion of her soil by the Prussians and their allies, it is at least conceivable that France might have worked her passage from royal autocracy to popular government without so much violence and bloodshed. Whereas the English Civil War of the 1640s was wholly the product of irreconcilable domestic forces, the civil strife that developed in France after the outbreak of the Revolution was largely the result of foreign interference, in which the King himself was treacherously implicated.

Above all, Burke failed to see that revolution is not necessarily the result of metaphysical fanaticism but may spring from the soil of experience, the experience of protracted suffering. The breakdown and failure of social and political institutions are just as much a matter of experience as are their growth and development. As Burke himself said, political problems do not primarily concern truth or falsehood, but good or evil, and political principles must be judged by their results. Yet in the matter of the French Revolution, Burke was unwilling to await its consequences because he *knew*, without a shadow of his usual doubt and caution, that the French revolutionaries were no more than a band of robbers and assassins. In the same manner, he also idealized the conditions of prerevolutionary France and its basic institutions, the monarchy, church, and aristocracy. Disregarding the oppressions, humiliations, and frustrations of the French people before the Revolution, Burke was shocked and shaken by the sufferings of Queen Marie Antoinette in a "nation of men of honor, and of cavaliers." Tom Paine's famous reply in the *Rights of Man* to this passage in the *Reflections* is that Burke "pities the plumage, but forgets the dying bird."

Yet, when all is said and done, no reader of Burke, and of his *Reflections* in particular, can escape the impact of a mature, imaginative, and penetrating mind: "The nature of man is intricate; the objects of society are of the greatest possible complexity; and therefore no simple disposition or direction of power can be suitable either to man's nature, or to the quality of his affairs." Bismarck defined politics as the "art of the possible," and this is one of the guiding principles of Burke's approach to politics. Whether or not one accepts the tenets of his political creed, one finds on almost every page of the *Reflections* epigrammatic gems of wisdom and observation that make his thought a permanent inspiration even for those who feel more optimistic about the possibilities of democracy than Burke did.

Burke's conservative political philosophy was, with all its literary charm and persuasive poetry, ineffectual in stemming the course of events. Burke, like other writers and statesmen of his time, failed to see that the French Revolution was a symptom and reflection of something much more profound—the changing class structure in western Europe. The important fact in Burke's lifetime was not, as he thought, the opposition of rationalism to the traditional order of religion and prescription but change of another kind, the implications of which largely escaped him, those of the Industrial Revolution. The conservative reaction to the French Revolution delayed the social forces of the Industrial Revolution, but could not permanently forestall them.

BURKE

*Reflections on the Revolution in France**

THE FRENCH REVOLUTION AND THE BRITISH CONSTITUTION

Our oldest reformation is that of Magna Charta. You will see that Sir Edward Coke, that great oracle of our law, and indeed all the great men who follow him, to Blackstone, are industrious to prove the pedigree of our liberties. They endeavour to prove, that the ancient charter, the Magna Charta of King John, was connected with another positive charter from Henry I, and that both the one and the other were nothing more than a reaffirmance of the still more ancient standing law of the kingdom. In the matter of fact, for the greater part, these authors appear to be in the right; perhaps not always; but if the lawyers mistake in some particulars, it proves my position still the more strongly; because it demonstrates the powerful prepossession towards antiquity, with which the minds of all our lawyers and legislators, and of all the people whom they wish to influence, have been always filled; and the stationary policy of this kingdom in considering their most sacred rights and franchises as an *inheritance.*

In the famous law of the 3rd of Charles I, called the *Petition of Right,* the parliament says to the king, "Your subjects have *inherited* this freedom," claiming their franchises not on abstract principles "as the rights of men," but as the rights of Englishmen, and as a patrimony derived from their forefathers. Selden, and the other profoundly learned men, who drew this Petition of Right, were as well acquainted, at least,

with all the general theories concerning the "rights of men," as any of the discoursers in our pulpits, or on your tribune; full as well as Dr. Price, or as the Abbé Sieyes. But, for reasons worthy of that practical wisdom which superseded their theoretic science, they preferred this positive, recorded, *hereditary* title to all which can be dear to the man and the citizen, to that vague speculative right, which exposed their sure inheritance to be scrambled for and torn to pieces by every wild, litigious spirit.

The same policy pervades all the laws which have since been made for the preservation of our liberties. In the 1st of William and Mary, in the famous statute, called the Declaration of Right, the two Houses utter not a syllable of "a right to frame a government for themselves." You will see, that their whole care was to secure the religion, laws, and liberties, that had been long possessed, and had been lately endangered. "Taking into their most serious consideration the *best* means for making such an establishment, that their religion, laws, and liberties might not be in danger of being again subverted," they auspicate all their proceedings, by stating as some of those *best* means, "in the *first place*" to do "as their *ancestors in like cases have usually* done for vindicating their *ancient* rights and liberties, to *declare*";—and then they pray the king and queen, "that it may be *declared* and enacted, that *all and singular* the rights and liberties *asserted and declared,* are the true *ancient* and indubitable rights and liberties of the people of this kingdom."

You will observe, that from Magna Charta to the Declaration of Right, it has been the uniform policy of our constitution to claim and assert our liberties, as an

---

*From Edmund Burke, *Reflections on the Revolution in France* (1790). In form, it is addressed to a French correspondent of Burke.

entailed inheritance derived to us from our forefathers, and to be transmitted to our posterity; as an estate specially belonging to the people of this kingdom, without any reference whatever to any other more general or prior right. By this means our constitution preserves a unity in so great a diversity of its parts. We have an inheritable crown; an inheritable peerage; and a House of Commons and a people inheriting privileges, franchises, and liberties, from a long line of ancestors.

This policy appears to me to be the result of profound reflection; or rather the happy effect of following nature, which is wisdom without reflection, and above it. A spirit of innovation is generally the result of a selfish temper and confined views. People will not look forward to posterity, who never look backward to their ancestors. Besides, the people of England well know, that the idea of inheritance furnishes a sure principle of conservation and a sure principle of transmission; without at all excluding a principle of improvement. It leaves acquisition free; but it secures what it acquires. Whatever advantages are obtained by a state proceeding on these maxims, are locked fast as in a sort of family settlement; grasped as in a kind of mortmain for ever. By a constitutional policy, working after the pattern of nature, we receive, we hold, we transmit our government and our privileges, in the same manner in which we enjoy and transmit our property and our lives. The institutions of policy, the goods of fortune, the gifts of providence, are handed down to us, and from us, in the same course and order. Our political system is placed in a just correspondence and symmetry with the order of the world, and with the mode of existence decreed to a permanent body composed of transitory parts; wherein, by the disposition of a stupendous wisdom, moulding together the great mysterious incorporation of the human race, the whole, at one time, is never old, or middle-aged, or young, but, in a condition of unchangeable constancy, moves on through the varied tenor of perpetual decay, fall, renovation, and progression. Thus, by preserving the method of nature in the conduct of the state, in what we improve, we are never wholly new; in what we retain, we are never wholly obsolete. By adhering in this manner and on those principles to our forefathers,

we are guided not by the superstition of antiquarians, but by the spirit of philosophic analogy. In this choice of inheritance we have given to our frame of polity the image of a relation in blood; binding up the constitution of our country with our dearest domestic ties; adopting our fundamental laws into the bosom of our family affections; keeping inseparable, and cherishing with the warmth of all their combined and mutually reflected charities, our state, our hearths, our sepulchres, and our altars.

Through the same plan of a conformity to nature in our artificial institutions, and by calling in the aid of her unerring and powerful instincts, to fortify the fallible and feeble contrivances of our reason, we have derived several other, and those no small benefits, from considering our liberties in the light of an inheritance. Always acting as if in the presence of canonized forefathers, the spirit of freedom, leading in itself to misrule and excess, is tempered with an awful gravity. This idea of a liberal descent inspires us with a sense of habitual native dignity, which prevents that upstart insolence almost inevitably adhering to and disgracing those who are the first acquirers of any distinction. By this means our liberty becomes a noble freedom. It carries an imposing and majestic aspect. It has a pedigree and illustrating ancestors. It has its bearings, and its ensigns armorial. It has its gallery of portraits; its monumental inscriptions; its records, evidences, and titles. We procure reverence to our civil institutions on the principle upon which nature teaches us to revere individual men; on account of their age, and on account of those from whom they are descended. All your sophisters cannot produce anything better adapted to preserve a rational and manly freedom than the course that we have pursued, who have chosen our nature rather than our speculations, our breasts rather than our inventions, for the great conservatories and magazines of our rights and privileges.

You might, if you pleased, have profited of our example, and have given to your recovered freedom a correspondent dignity. Your privileges, though discontinued, were not lost to memory. Your constitution, it is true, whilst you were out of possession, suffered waste and dilapidation; but you possessed in some parts the walls, and, in all, the foundations, of a noble and venerable castle. You might have repaired those walls; you might have built on those old foundations. Your constitution was suspended before it was perfected; but you had the elements of a constitution very nearly as good as could be wished. In your old states you possessed that variety of parts corresponding with the various descriptions of which your community was happily composed; you had all that combination, and all that opposition of interests, you had that action and counteraction, which, in the natural and in the political world, from the reciprocal struggle of discordant powers, draws out the harmony of the universe. These opposed and conflicting interests, which you considered as so great a blemish in your old and in our present constitution, interpose a salutary check to all precipitate resolutions. They render deliberation a matter not of choice, but of necessity; they make all change a subject of *compromise,* which naturally begets moderation; they produce *temperaments* preventing the sore evil of harsh, crude, unqualified reformations; and rendering all the headlong exertions of arbitrary power, in the few or in the many, for ever impracticable. Through that diversity of members and interests, general liberty had as many securities as there were separate views in the several orders; whilst by pressing down the whole by the weight of a real monarchy, the separate parts would have been prevented from warping, and starting from their allotted places.

You had all these advantages in your ancient states; but you chose to act as if you had never been moulded into civil society, and had everything to begin anew. You began ill, because you began by despising everything that belonged to you. You set up your trade without a capital. If the last generations of your country appeared without much lustre in your eyes, you might have passed them by, and derived your claims from a more early race of ancestors. Under a pious predilection for those ancestors, your imaginations would have realized in them a standard of virtue and wisdom, beyond the vulgar practice of the hour: and you would have risen with the example to whose imitation you aspired. Respecting your forefathers, you would have been taught to respect yourselves. You would not have chosen to consider the French as a people of yesterday, as a nation of lowborn servile wretches until the emancipating year of 1789. In order to furnish, at the expense of your honour, an excuse to your apologists here for several enormities of yours, you would not have been content to be represented as a gang of Maroon slaves, suddenly broke loose from the house of bondage, and therefore to be pardoned for your abuse of the liberty to which you were not accustomed, and ill fitted. Would it not, my worthy friend, have been wiser to have you thought, what I, for one, always thought you, a generous and gallant nation, long misled to your disadvantage by your high and romantic sentiments of fidelity, honour, and loyalty; that events had been unfavourable to you, but that you were not enslaved through any illiberal or servile disposition; that in your most devoted submission, you were actuated by a principle of public spirit, and that it was your country you worshipped, in the person of your king? Had you made it to be understood, that in the delusion of this amiable error you had gone farther than your wise ancestors; that you were resolved to resume your ancient privileges, whilst you preserved the spirit of your ancient and your recent loyalty and honour; or if, diffident of yourselves, and not clearly discerning the almost obliterated constitution of your ancestors, you had looked to your neighbours in this land, who had kept alive the ancient principles and models of the old common law of Europe meliorated and adapted to its present state—by following wise examples you would have given new examples of wisdom to the world. You would have rendered the cause of liberty venerable in the eyes of every worthy mind in every nation. You would have shamed despotism from the earth, by showing that freedom was not only reconcilable, but, as when well disciplined it is, auxiliary to law. You would have had an unoppressive but a productive revenue. You would have had a flourishing commerce to feed it. You would have had a free constitution; a potent monarchy; a disciplined army; a reformed and venerated clergy; a mitigated but spirited nobility, to lead your virtue, not to overlay it; you would have had a liberal order of commons, to emulate and to recruit that nobility; you would have had a protected, satisfied, laborious, and obedient people, taught to seek and to recognise the happiness that is to be found by virtue in all conditions; in which consists the true moral equality of mankind, and not in that monstrous fiction, which, by inspiring false ideas and vain expectations into men destined to travel in the obscure walk of laborious life, serves only to aggravate and embitter that real inequality, which it never can remove; and which the order of civil life establishes as much for the benefit of those whom it must leave in a humble state, as those whom it is able to exalt to a condition more splendid, but not more happy. You had a smooth and easy career of felicity and glory laid open to you, beyond anything recorded in the history of the world; but you have shown that difficulty is good for man.

Compute your gains: see what is got by those extravagant and presumptuous speculations which have taught your leaders to despise all their predecessors, and all their contemporaries, and even to despise themselves, until the moment in which they became truly despicable. By following those false lights, France has bought undisguised calamities at a higher price than any nation has purchased the most unequivocal blessings! France has bought poverty by crime! France has not sacrificed her virtue to her interest, but she has abandoned her interest, that she might prostitute her virtue. All other nations have begun the fabric of a new government, or the reformation of an old, by establishing originally, or by enforcing with greater exactness, some rites or other of religion. All other people have laid the foundations of civil freedom in severer manners, and a system of a more austere and masculine morality. France, when she let loose the reins of regal authority, doubled the license of a ferocious dissoluteness in manners, and of an insolent irreligion in opinions and practices; and has extended through all ranks of life, as if she were communicating some privilege, or laying open some secluded benefit, all the unhappy corruptions that usually were the disease of wealth and power. This is one of the new principles of equality in France.

In the calling of the states-general of France, the first thing that struck me, was a great departure from the ancient course. I found the representation for the third estate composed of six hundred persons. They were equal in number to the representatives of both the other orders. If the orders were to act separately, the number would not, beyond the consideration of the expense, be of much moment. But when it became apparent that the three orders were to be melted down into one, the policy and necessary effect of this numerous representation became obvious. A very small desertion from either of the other two orders must throw the power of both into the hands of the third. In fact, the whole power of the state was soon resolved into that body. Its due composition became therefore of infinitely the greater importance.

Judge, Sir, of my surprise, when I found that a very great proportion of the Assembly (a majority, I believe, of the members who attended) was composed of practitioners in the laws. It was composed, not of distinguished magistrates, who had given pledges to their country of their science, prudence, and integrity; not of leading advocates, the glory of the bar; not of renowned professors in universities;—but for the far greater part, as it must in such a number, of the inferior, unlearned, mechanical, merely instrumental members of the profession. There were distinguished exceptions; but the general composition was of obscure provincial advocates, of stewards of petty local jurisdictions, country attorneys, notaries, and the whole train of the ministers of municipal litigation, the fomenters and conductors of the petty war of village vexation. From the moment I read the list, I saw distinctly, and very nearly as it has happened, all that was to follow.

The degree of estimation in which any profession is held becomes the standard of the estimation in which the professors hold themselves. Whatever the personal merits of many individual lawyers might have been, and in many it was undoubtedly very considerable, in that military kingdom no part of the profession had been much regarded, except the highest of all, who often united to their professional offices great family splendour, and were invested with great power and authority. These certainly were highly respected, and even with no small degree of awe. The next rank was not much esteemed; the mechanical part was in a very low degree of repute.

Whenever the supreme authority is vested in a body so composed, it must evidently produce the consequences of supreme authority placed in the hands of men not taught habitually to respect themselves; who had no previous fortune in character at stake; who could not be expected to bear with moderation, or to conduct with discretion, a power, which they themselves, more than any others, must be surprised to find in their hands. Who could flatter himself that these men, suddenly, and, as it were, by enchantment, snatched from the humblest rank of subordination, would not be intoxicated with their unprepared greatness? Who could conceive that men, who are habitually meddling, daring, subtle, active, of litigious dispositions and unquiet minds, would easily fall back into their old condition of obscure contention, and laborious, low, and unprofitable chicane? Who could doubt but that, at any expense to the state, of which they understood nothing, they must pursue their private interests which they understood but too well? It was not an event depending on chance, or contingency. It was inevitable; it was necessary; it was planted in the nature of things. They must *join* (if their capacity did not permit them to *lead*) in any project which could procure to them a *litigious constitution;* which could lay open to them those innumerable lucrative jobs, which follow in the train of all great convulsions and revolutions in the state, and particularly in all great and violent permutations of property. Was it to be expected that they would attend to the stability of property, whose existence had always depended upon whatever rendered property questionable, ambiguous, and insecure? Their objects would be enlarged with their elevation, but their disposition and habits, and mode of accomplishing their designs, must remain the same.

Well! but these men were to be tempered and restrained by other descriptions, of more sober and more enlarged understandings. Were they then to be awed by the supereminent authority and awful dignity of a handful of country clowns, who have seats in that Assembly, some of whom are said not to be able to read and write? and by not a greater number of traders, who, though somewhat more instructed, and more conspicuous in the order of society, had never known anything beyond their counting-house. No! both these descriptions were more formed to be overborne and swayed by the intrigues and artifices of lawyers, than to become their counterpoise. With such a dangerous disproportion, the whole must needs be governed by them. To the faculty of law was joined a pretty considerable proportion of the faculty of medicine. This faculty had not, any more than that of the law, possessed in France its just estimation. Its professors, therefore, must have the qualities of men not habituated to sentiments of dignity. But supposing they had ranked as they ought to do, and as with us they do actually, the sides of sick beds are not the academies for forming statesmen and legislators. Then came the dealers in stocks and funds, who must be eager, at any expense, to change their ideal paper wealth for the more solid substance of land. To these were joined men of other descriptions, from whom as little knowledge of, or attention to, the interests of a great state was to be expected, and as little regard to the stability of any institution; men formed to be instruments, not controls. Such in general was the composition of the *Tiers État* in the National Assembly; in which was scarcely to be perceived the slightest traces of what we call the natural landed interest of the country.

We know that the British House of Commons, without shutting its doors to any merit in any class, is, by the sure operation of adequate causes, filled with everything illustrious in rank, in descent, in hereditary and in acquired opulence, in cultivated talents, in military, civil, naval, and politic distinction, that the country can afford. But supposing, what hardly can be supposed as a case, that the House of Commons should be composed in the same manner with the *Tiers État* in France, would this dominion of chicane be borne with patience, or even conceived without horror? God forbid I should insinuate anything derogatory to that profession, which is another priesthood, administrating the rights of sacred justice. But whilst I revere men in the functions which belong to them, and would do as much as one man can do to prevent their exclusion from any, I cannot, to flatter them, give the lie to nature. They are good and useful in the composition; they must be mischievous if they preponderate so as virtually to become the whole. Their very excellence in their peculiar functions may be far from a qualification for others. It cannot escape observation, that when men are too much confined to professional and faculty habits, and as it were inveterate in the recurrent employment of that narrow circle, they are rather disabled than qualified for whatever depends on the knowledge of mankind, on experience in mixed affairs, on a comprehensive, connected view of the various, complicated, external and internal interests, which go to the formation of that multifarious thing called a state.

REPRESENTATION
OF PROPERTY

The Chancellor of France at the opening of the States, said, in a tone of oratorical flourish, that all occupations were honourable. If he meant only, that no honest employment was disgraceful, he would not have gone beyond the truth. But in asserting that anything is honourable, we imply some distinction in its favour. The occupation of a hair-dresser, or of a working tallow-chandler, cannot be a matter of honour to any person—to say nothing of a number of other more servile employments. Such descriptions of men ought not to suffer oppression from the state; but the state suffers oppression, if such as they, either individually or collectively, are permitted to rule. In this you think you are combating prejudice. But you are at war with nature.

I do not, my dear Sir, conceive you to be of that sophistical, captious spirit, or of that uncandid dulness, as to require, for every general observation or sentiment, an explicit detail of the correctives and exceptions, which reason will presume to be included in all the general propositions which come from reasonable men. You do not imagine, that I wish to confine power, authority, and distinction to blood, and names, and titles. No, Sir. There is no qualification for government but virtue and wisdom, actual or presumptive. Wherever they are actually found, they have, in whatever state, condition, profession or trade, the passport of Heaven to human place and honour. Woe to the country which would madly and impiously reject the service of the talents and virtues, civil, military, or religious, that are given to grace and

to serve it; and would condemn to obscurity everything formed to diffuse lustre and glory around a state! Woe to that country too, that, passing into the opposite extreme, considers a low education, a mean contracted view of things, a sordid, mercenary occuption, as a preferable title to command! Everything ought to be open; but not indifferently to every man. No rotation; no appointment by lot; no mode of election operating in the spirit of sortition, or rotation, can be generally good in a government conversant in extensive objects. Because they have no tendency, direct or indirect, to select the man with a view to the duty, or to accommodate the one to the other. I do not hesitate to say, that the road to eminence and power from obscure condition, ought not to be made too easy, nor a thing too much of course. If rare merit be the rarest of all rare things, it ought to pass through some sort of probation. The temple of honour ought to be seated on an eminence. If it be opened through virtue, let it be remembered too, that virtue is never tried but by some difficulty and some struggle.

Nothing is a due and adequate representation of a state, that does not represent its ability, as well as its property. But as ability is a vigorous and active principle, and as property is sluggish, inert, and timid, it never can be safe from the invasions of ability, unless it be, out of all proportion, predominant in the representation. It must be represented too in great masses of accumulation, or it is not rightly protected. The characteristic essence of property, formed out of the combined principles of its acquisition and conservation, is to be *unequal*. The great masses therefore which excite envy, and tempt rapacity, must be put out of the possibility of danger. Then they form a natural rampart about the lesser properties in all their gradations. The same quantity of property, which is by the natural course of things divided among many, has not the same operation. Its defensive power is weakened as it is diffused. In this diffusion each man's portion is less than what, in the eagernes of his desires, he may flatter himself to obtain by dissipating the accumulations of others. The plunder of the few would indeed give but a share inconceivably small in the distribution to the many. But the many are not capable of making this calculation; and those who lead them to rapine never intend this distribution.

The power of perpetuating our property in our families is one of the most valuable and interesting circumstances belonging to it, and that which tends the most to the perpetuation of society itself. It makes our weakness subservient to our virtue; it grafts benevolence even upon avarice. The possessors of family wealth, and of the distinction which attends hereditary possession (as most concerned in it), are the natural securities for this transmission. With us the House of Peers is formed upon this principle. It is wholly composed of hereditary property and hereditary distinction; and made therefore the third of the legislature; and, in the last event, the sole judge of all property in all its subdivisions. The House of Commons too, though not necessarily, yet in fact, is always so composed, in the far greater part. Let those large proprietors be what they will, and they have their chance of being amongst the best, they are, at the very worst, the ballast in the vessel of the commonwealth. For though hereditary wealth, and the rank which goes with it, are too much idolized by creeping sycophants, and the blind, abject admirers of power, they are too rashly slighted in shallow speculations of the petulant, assuming, short-sighted coxcombs of philosophy. Some decent, regulated pre-eminence, some preference (not exclusive appropriation) given to birth, is neither unnatural, nor unjust, nor impolitic.

It is said, that twenty-four millions ought to prevail over two hundred thousand. True; if the constitution of a kingdom be a problem of arithmetic. This sort of discourse does well enough with the lamp-post for its second: to men who *may* reason calmly, it is ridiculous. The will of the many and their interest must very often differ; and great will be the difference when they make an evil choice. A government of five hundred country attorneys and obscure curates is not good for twenty-four millions of men, though it were chosen by eight-and-forty millions; nor is it the better for being guided by a dozen of persons of quality, who have betrayed their trust in order to obtain that power. At present, you seem in everything to have strayed out of the high road of nature. The property of France does not govern it. Of

course property is destroyed, and rational liberty has no existence.

All this violent cry against the nobility I take to be a mere work of art. To be honoured and even privileged by the laws, opinions, and inveterate usages of our country, growing out of the prejudice of ages, has nothing to provoke horror and indignation in any man. Even to be too tenacious of those privileges is not absolutely a crime. The strong struggle in every individual to preserve possession of what he had found to belong to him, and to distinguish him, is one of the securities against injustice and despotism implanted in our nature. It operates as an instinct to secure property, and to preserve communities in a settled state. What is there to shock in this? Nobility is a graceful ornament to the civil order. It is the Corinthian capital of polished society. *Omnes boni nobilitati semper favemus,* was the saying of a wise and good man. It is indeed one sign of a liberal and benevolent mind to incline to it with some sort of partial propensity. He feels no ennobling principle in his own heart, who wishes to level all the artificial institutions which have been adopted for giving a body to opinion, and permanence to fugitive esteem. It is a sour, malignant, envious disposition, without taste for the reality, or for any image or representation of virtue, that sees with joy the unmerited fall of what had long flourished in splendour and in honour. I do not like to see anything destroyed; any void produced in society; any ruin on the face of the land. It was therefore with no disappointment or dissatisfaction that my inquiries and observations did not present to me any incorrigible vices in the noblesse of France, or any abuse which could not be removed by a reform very short of abolition. Your noblesse did not deserve punishment: but to degrade is to punish.

With the National Assembly of France, possession is nothing, law and usage are nothing. I see the National Assembly openly reprobate the doctrine of prescription, which, one of the greatest of their own lawyers tells us, with great truth, is a part of the law of nature. He tells us, that the positive ascertainment of its limits, and its security from invasion, were among the causes for which civil society itself has been instituted. If prescription be once shaken, no species of property is secure, when it once becomes an object large enough to tempt the cupidity of indigent power. I see a practice perfectly correspondent to their contempt of this great fundamental part of natural law. I see the confiscators begin with bishops, and chapters, and monasteries; but I do not see them end there. I see the princes of the blood, who, by the oldest usages of that kingdom, held large landed estates (hardly with the compliment of a debate) deprived of their possessions, and, in lieu of their stable, independent property, reduced to the hope of some precarious, charitable pension, at the pleasure of an assembly, which of course will pay little regard to the rights of pensioners at pleasure, when it despises those of legal proprietors. Flushed with the insolence of their first inglorious victories, and pressed by the distresses caused by their lust of unhallowed lucre, disappointed but not discouraged, they have at length ventured completely to subvert all property of all descriptions throughout the extent of a great kingdom. They have compelled all men, in all transactions of commerce, in the disposal of lands, in civil dealing, and through the whole communion of life, to accept as perfect payment and good and lawful tender, the symbols of their speculations on a projected sale of their plunder. What vestiges of liberty or property have they left? The tenant-right of a cabbage-garden, a year's interest in a hovel, the good-will of an ale-house or a baker's shop, the very shadow of a constructive property, are more ceremoniously treated in our parliament, than with you the oldest and most valuable landed possession, in the hands of the most respectable personages, or than the whole body of the monied and commercial interest of your country. We entertain a high opinion of the legislative authority; but we have never dreamt that parliaments had any right whatever to violate property, to overrule prescription, or to force a currency of their own fiction in the place of that which is real, and recognized by the law of nations. But you, who began with refusing to submit to the most moderate restraints, have ended by establishing an unheard-of despotism. I find the ground upon

which your confiscators go is this; that indeed their proceedings could not be supported in a court of justice; but that the rules of prescription cannot bind a legislative assembly. So that this legislative assembly of a free nation sits, not for the security, but for the destruction, of property, and not of property only, but of every rule and maxim which can give it stability, and of those instruments which can alone give it circulation.

In every prosperous community something more is produced than goes to the immediate support of the producer. This surplus forms the income of the landed capitalist. It will be spent by a proprietor who does not labour. But this idleness is itself the spring of labour; this repose the spur to industry. The only concern of the state is, that the capital taken in rent from the land, should be returned again to the industry from whence it came; and that its expenditure should be with the least possible detriment to the morals of those who expend it, and to those of the people to whom it is returned.

Why should the expenditure of a great landed property, which is a dispersion of the surplus product of the soil, appear intolerable to you or to me, when it takes its course through the accumulation of vast libraries, which are the history of the force and weakness of the human mind; through great collections of ancient records, medals, and coins, which attest and explain laws and customs; through paintings and statues, that, by imitating nature, seem to extend the limits of creation; through grand monuments of the dead, which continue the regards and connexions of life beyond the grave, through collections of the specimens of nature, which become a representative assembly of all the classes and families of the world, that by disposition facilitate, and, by exciting curiosity, open the avenues to science? If by great permanent establishments, all these objects of expense are better secured from the inconstant sport of personal caprice and personal extravagance, are they worse than if the same tastes prevailed in scattered individuals? Does not the sweat of the mason and carpenter, who toil in order to partake the sweat of the peasant, flow as pleasantly and as salubriously, in the construction and repair of the majestic edifices of religion, as in the painted booths and sordid sties of vice and luxury; as honourably and as profitably in repairing those sacred works, which grow hoary with innumerable years, as on the momentary receptacles of transient voluptuousness; in opera-houses, and brothels, and gaming-houses, and club-houses, and obelisks in the Champ de Mars? Is the surplus product of the olive and the vine worse employed in the frugal sustenance of persons, whom the fictions of a pious imagination raise to dignity by construing in the service of God, than in pampering the innumerable multitude of those who are degraded by being made useless domestics, subservient to the pride of man? Are the decorations of temples an expenditure less worthy a wise man, than ribbons, and laces, and national cockades, and petit maisons, and petit soupers, and all the innumerable fopperies and follies, in which opulence sports away the burthen of its superfluity?

We tolerate even these; not from love of them, but for fear of worse. We tolerate them, because property and liberty, to a degree, require that toleration. But why proscribe the other, and surely, in every point of view, the more laudable use of estates? Why, through the violation of all property, through an outrage upon every principle of liberty, forcibly carry them from the better to the worse?

With us the king and the lords are several and joint securities for the equality of each district, each province, each city. When did you hear in Great Britain of any province suffering from the inequality of its representation; what district from having no representation at all? Not only our monarchy and our peerage secure the equality on which our unity depends, but it is the spirit of the House of Commons itself. The very inequality of representation, which is so foolishly complained of, is perhaps the very thing which prevents us from thinking or acting as members for districts. Cornwall elects as many members as all Scotland. But is Cornwall better taken care of than Scotland? Few trouble their heads about any of your bases, out of some giddy clubs.

Good order is the foundation of all good things. To be enabled to acquire, the people, without being servile, must be tractable and obedient. The magistrate must have his reverence, the laws their authority. The body of the people must not find the principles of natural subordination by art rooted out of their minds. They must respect that property of which they cannot partake. They must labour to obtain what by labour can be obtained; and when they find, as they commonly do, the success disproportioned to the endeavour, they must be taught their consolation in the final proportions of eternal justice. Of this consolation whoever deprives them, deadens their industry, and strikes at the root of all acquisition as of all conservation. He that does this is the cruel oppressor, the merciless enemy of the poor and wretched; at the same time that by his wicked speculations he exposes the fruits of successful industry, and the accumulations of fortune, to the plunder of the negligent, the disappointed, and the unprosperous.

Too many of the financiers by profession are apt to see nothing in revenue but banks, and circulations, and annuities on lives, and tontines, and perpetual rents, and all the small wares of the ship. In a settled order of the state, these things are not to be slighted, nor is the skill in them to be held of trivial estimation. They are good, but then only good, when they assume the effects of that settled order, and are built upon it. But when men think that these beggarly contrivances may supply a resource for the evils which result from breaking up the foundations of public order, and from causing or suffering the principles of property to be subverted, they will, in the ruin of their country, leave a melancholy and lasting monument of the effect of preposterous politics, and presumptuous, shortsighted, narrow-minded wisdom.

WHY GOVERNMENT IS COMPLEX

I see that your example is held out to shame us. I know that we are supposed a dull, sluggish race, rendered passive by finding our situation tolerable, and prevented by a mediocrity of freedom from ever attaining to its full perfection. Your leaders in France began by affecting to admire, almost to adore, the British constitution; but as they advanced, they came to look upon it with a sovereign contempt. The friends of your National Assembly amongst us have full as mean an opinion of what was formerly thought the glory of their country. The Revolution Society has discovered that the English nation is not free. They are convinced that the inequality in our representation is a "defect in our constitution *so gross and palpable,* as to make it excellent chiefly in *form* and *theory.*"[1] That a representation in the legislature of a kingdom is not only the basis of all constitutional liberty in it, but of *"all legitimate government; that without it a government* is nothing but an *usurpation";* that *"*when the representation is *partial,* the kingdom possess liberty only *partially;* and if extremely partial, it gives only a *semblance;* and if not only extremely partial, but corruptly chosen, it becomes a *nuisance."* Dr. Price considers this inadequacy of representation as our *fundamental grievance;* and though, as to the corruption of this semblance of representation, he hopes it is not yet arrived to its full perfection of depravity, he fears that "nothing will be done towards gaining for us this *essential blessing,* until some *great abuse of power* again provokes our resentment, or some *great calamity* again alarms our fears, or perhaps till the acquisition of a *pure and equal representation by other countries,* whilst we are *mocked* with the *shadow,* kindles our shame." To this he subjoins a note in these words: "A representation chosen chiefly by the treasury, and a *few* thousand of the *dregs* of the people, who are generally paid for their votes."

You will smile here at the consistency of those democratists, who, when they are not on their guard, treat the humbler part of the community with the greatest contempt, whilst, at the same time, they pretend to make them the depositories of all power. It would require a long discourse to point out to you the many fallacies that lurk in the generality and equivocal nature of the terms "inadequate representation." I shall only say here, in justice to that old-fashioned constitution, under which we have long

prospered, that our representation has been found perfectly adequate to all the purposes for which a representation of the people can be desired or devised. I defy the enemies of our constitution to show the contrary. To detail the particulars in which it is found so well to promote its ends, would demand a treatise on our practical constitution. I state here the doctrine of the Revolutionists, only that you and others may see what an opinion these gentlemen entertain of the constitution of their country, and why they seem to think that some great abuse of power, or some great calamity, as giving a chance for the blessing of a constitution according to their ideas, would be much palliated to their feelings; you see *why they* are so much enamoured of your fair and equal representation, which being once obtained, the same effects might follow. You see they consider our House of Commons as only "a semblance," "a form," "a theory," "a shadow," "a mockery," perhaps "a nuisance."

These gentlemen value themselves on being systematic; and not without reason. They must therefore look on this gross and palpable defect of representation, this fundamental grievance (so they call it), as a thing not only vicious in itself, but as rendering our whole government absolutely *illegitimate,* and not at all better than a downright *usurpation.* Another revolution, to get rid of this illegitimate and usurped government, would of course be perfectly justifiable, if not absolutely necessary. Indeed their principle, if you observe it with any attention, goes much further than to an alteration in the election of the House of Commons; for, if popular representation, or choice, is necessary to the *legitimacy* of all government, the House of Lords is, at one stroke, bastardized and corrupted in blood. That house is no representative of the people at all, even in "semblance or in form." The case of the crown is altogether as bad. In vain the crown may endeavour to screen itself against these gentlemen by the authority of the establishment made on the Revolution. The Revolution which is resorted to for a title, on their system, wants a title itself. The Revolution is built, according to their theory, upon a basis not more solid than our present formalities, as it was made by a House of Lords, not representing any one but themselves; and by a House of Commons

---

[1] *Discourse on the Love of our Country,* 3rd ed., p. 39.

exactly such as the present, that is, as they term it, by a mere "shadow and mockery" of representation.

Something they must destroy, or they seem to themselves to exist for no purpose. One set is for destroying the civil power through the ecclesiastical; another, for demolishing the ecclesiastic through the civil. They are aware that the worst consequences might happen to the public in accomplishing this double ruin of church and state; but they are so heated with their theories, that they give more than hints, that this ruin, with all the mischiefs that must lead to it and attend it, and which to themselves appear quite certain, would not be unacceptable to them, or very remote from their wishes. A man amongst them of great authority, and certainly of great talents, speaking of a supposed alliance between church and state, says, "perhaps *we must wait for the fall of the civil powers* before this most unnatural alliance be broken. Calamitous no doubt will that time be. But what convulsion in the political world ought to be a subject of lamentation, if it be attended with so desirable an effect?" You see with what a steady eye these gentlemen are prepared to view the greatest calamities which can befall their country.

It is no wonder therefore, that with these ideas of everything in their constitution and government at home, either in church or state, as illegitimate and usurped, or at best as a vain mockery, they look abroad with an eager and passionate enthusiasm. Whilst they are possessed by these notions, it is vain to talk to them of the practice of their ancestors, the fundamental laws of their country, the fixed form of a constitution, whose merits are confirmed by the solid test of long experience, and an increasing public strength and national prosperity. They despise experience as the wisdom of unlettered men; and as for the rest, they have wrought under ground a mine that will blow up, at one grand explosion, all examples of antiquity, all precedents, charters, and acts of parliament. They have "the rights of men." Against these there can be no prescription; against these no agreement is binding: these admit no temperament and no compromise: anything withheld from their full demand is so much of fraud and injustice. Against these their rights of men let no

government look for security in the length of its continuance, or in the justice and lenity of its administration. The objections of these speculatists, if its forms do not quadrate with their theories, are as valid against such an old and beneficent government, as against the most violent tyranny, or the greenest usurpation. They are always at issue with governments, not on a question of abuse, but a question of competency, and a question of title. I have nothing to say to the clumsy subtlety of their political metaphysics. Let them be their amusement in the schools.— "*Illa se jactat in aula—Æolus, et clauso ventorurn carcere regnet.*"—But let them not break prison to burst like a *Levanter,* to sweep the earth with their hurricane, and to break up the fountains of the great deep to overwhelm us.

Far am I from denying in theory, full as far is my heart from withholding in practice (if I were of power to give or to withhold), the *real* rights of men. In denying their false claims of right, I do not mean to injure those which are real, and are such as their pretended rights would totally destroy. If civil society be made for the advantage of man, all the advantages for which it is made become his right. It is an institution of beneficence; and law itself is only beneficence acting by a rule. Men have a right to live by that rule; they have a right to do justice, as between their fellows, whether their fellows are in public function or in ordinary occupation. They have a right to the fruits of their industry; and to the means of making their industry fruitful. They have a right to the acquisitions of their parents; to the nourishment and improvement of their offspring; to instruction in life, and to consolation in death. Whatever each man can separately do, without trespassing upon others, he has a right to do for himself; and he has a right to a fair portion of all which society, with all its combinations of skill and force, can do in his favour. In this partnership all men have equal rights; but not to equal things. He that has but five shillings in the partnership, has as good a right to it, as he that has five hundred pounds has to his larger proportion. But he has not a right to an equal dividend in the product of the joint stock; and as to the share of power, authority, and direction which each individual ought to have in the management of the state, that I must deny to be amongst the direct original rights of man in civil society; for I have in my contemplation the civil social man, and no other. It is a thing to be settled by convention.

If civil society be the offspring of convention, that convention must be its law. That convention must limit and modify all the descriptions of constitution which are formed under it. Every sort of legislative, judicial, or executory power are its creatures. They can have no being in any other state of things; and how can any man claim under the conventions of civil society, rights which do not so much as suppose its existence? rights which are absolutely repugnant to it? One of the first motives to civil society, and which becomes one of its fundamental rules, is, *that no man should be judge in his own cause.* By this each person has at once divested himself of the first fundamental right of uncovenanted man, that is, to judge for himself, and to assert his own cause. He abdicates all right to be his own governor. He inclusively, in a great measure, abandons the right of self-defence, the first law of nature. Men cannot enjoy the rights of an uncivil and of a civil state together. That he may obtain justice, he gives up his right of determining what it is in points the most essential to him. That he may secure some liberty, he makes a surrender in trust of the whole of it.

Government is not made in virtue of natural rights, which may and do exist in total independence of it; and exist in much greater clearness, and in a much greater degree of abstract perfection: but their abstract perfection is their practical defect. By having a right to everything they want everything. Government is a contrivance of human wisdom to provide for human *wants.* Men have a right that these wants should be provided for by this wisdom. Among these wants is to be reckoned the want, out of civil society, of a sufficient restraint upon their passions. Society requires not only that the passions of individuals should be subjected, but that even in the mass and body, as well as in the individuals, the inclinations of men should frequently be thwarted, their will controlled, and their passions brought into subjection. This can only be done *by a power out of themselves;* and not, in the exercise of its function, subject to that will and

to those passions which it is its office to bridle and subdue. In this sense the restraints on men, as well as their liberties, are to be reckoned among their rights. But as the liberties and the restrictions vary with times and circumstances, and admit of infinite modifications, they cannot be settled upon any abstract rule; and nothing is so foolish as to discuss them upon that principle.

The moment you abate anything from the full rights of men, each to govern himself, and suffer any artificial, positive limitation upon those rights, from that moment the whole organization of government becomes a consideration of convenience. This it is which makes the constitution of a state, and the due distribution of its powers, a matter of the most delicate and complicated skill. It requires a deep knowledge of human nature and human necessities, and of the things which facilitate or obstruct the various ends, which are to be pursued by the mechanism of civil institutions. The state is to have recruits to its strength, and remedies to its distempers. What is the use of discussing a man's abstract right to food or medicine? The question is upon the method of procuring and administering them. In that deliberation I shall always advise to call in the aid of the farmer and the physician, rather than the professor of metaphysics.

The science of constructing a commonwealth, or renovating it, or reforming it, is, like every other experimental science, not to be taught *a priori.* Nor is it a short experience that can instruct us in that practical science; because the real effects of moral causes are not always immediate; but that which in the first instance is prejudicial may be excellent in its remoter operation; and its excellence may arise even from the ill effects it produces in the beginning. The reverse also happens: and very plausible schemes, with very pleasing commencements, have often shameful and lamentable conclusions. In states there are often some obscure and almost latent causes, things which appear at first view of little moment, on which a very great part of its prosperity or adversity may most essentially depend. The science of government being therefore so practical in itself, and intended for such practical purposes, a matter which requires experience, and even more experience than any person can gain in his whole life, however sagacious and observing he may be, it is with infinite caution that any man ought to venture upon pulling down an edifice, which has answered in any tolerable degree for ages the common purposes of society, or on building it up again, without having models and patterns of approved utility before his eyes.

These metaphysic rights entering into common life, like rays of light which pierce into a dense medium, are, by the laws of nature, refracted from their straight line. Indeed in the gross and complicated mass of human passions and concerns, the primitive rights of men undergo such a variety of refractions and reflections, that it becomes absurd to talk of them as if they continued in the simplicity of their original direction. The nature of man is intricate; the objects of society are of the greatest possible complexity: and therefore no simple disposition or direction of power can be suitable either to man's nature, or to the quality of his affairs. When I hear the simplicity of contrivance aimed at and boasted of in any new political constitutions, I am at no loss to decide that the artificers are grossly ignorant of their trade, or totally negligent of their duty. The simple governments are fundamentally defective, to say no worse of them. If you were to contemplate society in but one point of view, all these simple modes of polity are infinitely captivating. In effect each would answer its single end much more perfectly than the more complex is able to attain all its complex purposes. But it is better that the whole should be imperfectly and anomalously answered, than that, while some parts are provided for with great exactness, others might be totally neglected, or perhaps materially injured, by the over-care of a favourite member.

The pretended rights of these theorists are all extremes: and in proportion as they are metaphysically true, they are morally and politically false. The rights of men are in a sort of *middle,* incapable of definition, but not impossible to be discerned. The rights of men in governments are their advantages; and these are often in balances between differences of good; in compromises sometimes between good and evil, and sometimes between evil and evil. Political reason is a computing principle; adding, subtracting, multiplying, and dividing, morally and not metaphysically, or mathematically, true moral denominations.

By these theorists the right of the people is almost always sophistically confounded with their power. The body of the community, whenever it can come to act, can meet with no effectual resistance; but till power and right are the same, the whole body of them has no right inconsistent with virtue, and the first of all virtues, prudence. Men have no right to what is not reasonable, and to what is not for their benefit, for though a pleasant writer said, *Liceat perire poetis,* when one of them, in cold blood, is said to have leaped into the flames of a volcanic revolution, *Ardentem frigidus Ætnam insiluit,* I consider such a frolic rather as an unjustifiable poetic licence, than as one of the franchises of Parnassus; and whether he were poet, or divine, or politician, that chose to exercise this kind of right, I think that more wise, because more charitable, thoughts would urge me rather to save the man, than to preserve his brazen slippers as the monuments of his folly.

The kind of anniversary sermons to which a great part of what I write refers, if men are not shamed out of their present course, in commemorating the fact, will cheat many out of the principles and deprive them of the benefits, of the revolution they commemorate. I confess to you, Sir, I never liked this continual talk of resistance, and revolution, or the practice of making the extreme medicine of the constitution its daily bread. It renders the habit of society dangerously valetudinary; it is taking periodical doses of mercury sublimate, and swallowing down repeated provocatives of cantharides to our love of liberty.

SENTIMENT AND LOGIC IN POLITICS

We are not the converts of Rousseau; we are not the disciples of Voltaire; Helvetius has made no progress amongst us. Atheists are not our preachers; madmen are not our lawgivers. We know that *we* have made no discoveries, and we think that no discoveries are to be made, in morality; nor many in the great principles of government, nor in the ideas of liberty, which were understood long before we were born, altogether as well as they will be after the grave has heaped its mould upon our presumption, and the silent tomb shall have imposed its law on our pert loquacity. In England we have not yet been completely embowelled of our natural entrails; we still feel within us, and we cherish and cultivate, those inbred sentiments which are the faithful guardians, the active monitors of our duty, the true supporters of all liberal and manly morals. We have not been drawn and trussed, in order that we may be filled, like stuffed birds in a museum, with chaff and rags and paltry blurred shreds of paper about the rights of man. We preserve the whole of our feelings still native and entire, unsophisticated by pedantry and infidelity. We have real hearts of flesh and blood beating in our bosoms. We fear God; we look up with awe to kings; with affection to parliaments; with duty to magistrates; with reverence to priests; and with respect to nobility. Why? Because when such ideas are brought before our minds, it is *natural* to be so affected; because all other feelings are false and spurious, and tend to corrupt our minds, to vitiate our primary morals, to render us unfit for rational liberty; and by teaching us a servile, licentious, and abandoned insolence, to be our low sport for a few holidays, to make us perfectly fit for, and justly deserving of, slavery, through the whole course of our lives.

You see, Sir, that in this enlightened age I am bold enough to confess, that we are generally men of untaught feelings; that instead of casting away all our old prejudices, we cherish them to a very considerable degree, and, to take more shame to ourselves, we cherish them because they are prejudices; and the longer they have lasted, and the more generally they have prevailed, the more we cherish them. We are afraid to put men to live and trade each on his own private stock of reason; because we suspect that this stock in each man is small, and that the individuals would do better to avail themselves of the general bank and capital of nations and of ages. Many of our men of speculation, instead of exploding general prejudices, employ their sagacity to discover the latent wisdom which prevails in them. If they find what they seek, and they seldom fail, they think it more wise to continue the prejudice, with the reason involved, than to cast away the coat of prejudice, and to leave nothing but the naked reason; because prejudice, with its reason, has a motive to give action to that reason, and an affection which will give it permanence. Prejudice is of ready application in the emergency; it previously engages the mind in a steady course of wisdom and virtue, and does not leave the man hesitating in the moment of decision, sceptical, puzzled, and unresolved. Prejudice renders a man's virtue his habit; and not a series of unconnected acts. Through just prejudice, his duty becomes a part of his nature.

Your literary men, and your politicians, and so do the whole clan of the enlightened among us, essentially differ in these points. They have no respect for the wisdom of others; but they pay it off by a very full measure of confidence in their own. With them it is a sufficient motive to destroy an old scheme of things, because it is an old one. As to the new, they are in no sort of fear with regard to the duration of a building run up in haste; because duration is no object to those who think little or nothing has been done before their time, and who place all their hopes in discovery. They conceive, very systematically, that all things which give perpetuity are mischievous, and therefore they are at inexpiable war with all establishments. They think that government may vary like modes of dress, and with as little ill effect: that there needs no principle of attachment, except a sense of present conveniency, to any constitution of the state. They always speak as if they were of opinion that there is a singular species of compact between them and their magistrates, which binds the magistrate, but which has nothing reciprocal in it, but that the majesty of the people has a right to dissolve it without any reason, but its will. Their attachment to their country itself is only so far as it agrees with some of their fleeting projects; it begins and ends with that scheme of polity which falls in with their momentary opinion.

These doctrines, or rather sentiments, seem prevalent with your new statesmen. But they are wholly different from those on which we have always acted in this country.

RELIGION, SOCIETY, POLITICS

We know, and what is better, we feel inwardly, that religion is the basis of civil society, and the source of all good and all comfort. In England we are so convinced of this, that there is no rust of superstition, with which the accumulated absurdity of the human mind might have crusted it over in the course of ages, that ninety-nine in a hundred of the people of England would not prefer to impiety. We shall never be such fools as to call in an enemy to the substance of any system to remove its corruptions, to supply its defects, or to perfect its construction. If our religious tenets should ever want a further elucidation, we shall not call on atheism to explain them. We shall not light up our temple from that unhallowed fire. It will be illuminated with other lights. It will be perfumed with other incense, than the infectious stuff which is imported by the smugglers of adulterated metaphysics. If our ecclesiastical establishment should want a revision, it is not avarice or rapacity, public or private, that we shall employ for the audit, or receipt, or application of its consecrated revenue. Violently condemning neither the Greek nor the Armenian, nor, since heats are subsided, the Roman system of religion, we prefer the Protestant; not because we think it has less of the Christian religion in it, but because, in our judgment, it has more. We are Protestants, not from indifference, but from zeal.

We know, and it is our pride to know, that man is by his constitution a religious animal; that atheism is against, not only our reason, but our instincts; and that it cannot prevail long. But if, in the moment of riot, and in a drunken delirium from the hot spirit drawn out of the alembic of hell, which in France is now so furiously boiling, we should uncover our nakedness, by throwing off that Christian religion which has hitherto been our boast and comfort, and one great source of civilization amongst us and amongst many other nations, we are apprehensive (being well aware that the mind will not endure a void) that some uncouth, pernicious, and degrading superstition might take place of it.

For that reason, before we take from our establishment the natural, human means of estimation, and give it up to contempt, as you have done, and in doing it have incurred the penalties you well deserve to suffer, we desire that some other may be presented to us in the place of it. We shall then form our judgment.

On these ideas, instead of quarrelling with establishments, as some do, who have made a philosophy and a religion of their hostility to such institutions, we cleave closely to them. We are resolved to keep an established church, an established monarchy, an established aristocracy, and an established democracy, each in the degree it exists, and in no greater. I shall show you presently how much of each of these we possess.

It has been the misfortune (not, as these gentlemen think it, the glory) of this age, that everything is to be discussed, as if the constitution of our country were to be always a subject rather of altercation, than enjoyment. For this reason, as well as for the satisfaction of those among you (if any such you have among you) who may wish to profit of examples, I venture to trouble you with a few thoughts upon each of these establishments. I do not think they were unwise in ancient Rome, who, when they wished to new-model their laws, set commissioners to examine the best constituted republics within their reach.

First, I beg leave to speak of our church establishment, which is the first of our prejudices, not a prejudice destitute of reason, but involving in it profound and extensive wisdom. I speak of it first. It is first, and last, and midst in our minds. For, taking ground on that religious system, of which we are now in possession, we continue to act on the early received and uniformly continued sense of mankind. That sense not only, like a wise architect, hath built up the august fabric of states, but like a provident proprietor, to preserve the structure from profanation and ruin, as a sacred temple purged from all the impurities of fraud, and violence, and injustice, and tyranny, hath solemnly and for ever consecrated the commonwealth, and all that officiate in it. This consecration is made, that all who administer in the government of men, in which they stand in the person of God Himself, should have high and worthy notions of their function and destination; that their hope should be full of immortality; that they should not look to the paltry pelf of the moment, nor to the temporary and transient praise of the vulgar, but to a solid, permanent exercise, in the permanent part of their nature, and to a permanent fame and glory, in the example they leave as a rich inheritance to the world.

Such sublime principles ought to be infused into persons of exalted situations; and religious establishments provided, that may continually revive and enforce them. Every sort of moral, every sort of civil, every sort of political institution, aiding the rational and natural ties that connect the human understanding and affections to the divine, are not more than necessary, in order to build up that wonderful structure, Man; whose prerogative it is, to be in a great degree a creature of his own making; and who, when made as he ought to be made, is destined to hold no trivial place in the creation. But whenever man is put over men, as the better nature ought ever to preside, in that case more particularly, he should as nearly as possible be approximated to his perfection.

The consecration of the state, by a state religious establishment, is necessary also to operate with a wholesome awe upon free citizens; because, in order to secure their freedom, they must enjoy some determinate portion of power. To them therefore a religion connected with the state, and with their duty towards it, becomes even more necessary than in such societies, where the people, by the terms of their subjection, are confined to private sentiments, and the management of their own family concerns. All persons possessing any portion of power ought to be strongly and awfully impressed with an idea that they act in trust: and that they are to account for their conduct in that trust to the one great Master, Author, and Founder of society.

To avoid therefore the evils of inconstancy and versatility, ten thousand times worse than those of obstinacy and the blindest prejudice, we have consecrated the state, that no man should approach to look into its defects or corruptions but with due caution; that he should never dream of beginning its reformation by its subversion; that he should approach to the faults of the state

as to the wounds of a father, with pious awe and trembling solicitude. By this wise prejudice we are taught to look with horror on those children of their country, who are prompt rashly to hack that aged parent in pieces, and put him into the kettle of magicians, in hopes that by their poisonous weeds, and wild incantations, they may regenerate the paternal constitution, and renovate their father's life.

Society is indeed a contract. Subordinate contracts for objects of mere occasional interest may be dissolved at pleasure—but the state ought not to be considered as nothing better than a partnership agreement in a trade of pepper and coffee, calico or tobacco, or some other such low concern, to be taken up for a little temporary interest, and to be dissolved by the fancy of the parties. It is to be looked on with other reverence; because it is not a partnership in things subservient only to the gross animal existence of a temporary and perishable nature. It is a partnership in all science; a partnership in all art; a partnership in every virtue, and in all perfection. As the ends of such a partnership cannot be obtained in many generations, it becomes a partnership not only between those who are living, but between those who are living, those who are dead, and those who are to be born. Each contract of each particular state is but a clause in the great primæval contract of eternal society, linking the lower with the higher natures, connecting the visible and invisible world, according to a fixed compact sanctioned by the inviolable oath which holds all physical and all moral natures, each in their appointed place. This law is not subject to the will of those, who by an obligation above them, and infinitely superior, are bound to submit their will to that law. The municipal corporations of that universal kingdom are not morally at liberty at their pleasure, and on their speculations of a contingent improvement, wholly to separate and tear asunder the bands of their subordinate community, and to dissolve it into an unsocial, uncivil, unconnected chaos of elementary principles. It is the first and supreme necessity only, a necessity that is not chosen, but chooses, a necessity paramount to deliberation, that admits no discussion, and demands no evidence, which alone can justify a resort to anarchy. This necessity is no exception to the rule; because this necessity itself is a part too of that moral and physical disposition of things, to which man must be obedient by consent or force: but if that which is only submission to necessity should be made the object of choice, the law is broken, nature is disobeyed, and the rebellious are outlawed, cast forth, and exiled, from this world of reason, and order, and peace, and virtue, and fruitful penitence, into the antagonist world of madness, discord, vice, confusion, and unavailing sorrow.

These, my dear Sir, are, were, and, I think, long will be, the sentiments of not the least learned and reflecting part of this kingdom. They, who are included in this description, form their opinions on such grounds as such persons ought to form them. The less inquiring receive them from an authority, which those whom Providence dooms to live on trust need not be ashamed to rely on. These two sorts of men move in the same direction, though in a different place. They both move with the order of the universe. They all know or feel this great ancient truth: "Quod illi principi et præpotenti Deo qui omnem hunc mundurn regit, nihil eorum quæ quidem fiant in terris acceptius quam concilia et cœtus hominum jute sociati quæ civitates appellantur." They take this tenet of the head and heart, not from the great name which it immediately bears, nor from the greater from whence it is derived; but from that which alone can give true weight and sanction to any learned opinion, the common nature and common relation of men. Persuaded that all things ought to be done with reference, and referring all to the point of reference to which all should be directed, they think themselves bound, not only as individuals in the sanctuary of the heart, or as congregated in that personal capacity, to renew the memory of their high origin and caste; but also in their corporate character to perform their national homage to the institutor, and author, and protector of civil society; without which civil society man could not by any possibility arrive at the perfection of which his nature is capable, nor even make a remote and faint approach to it. They conceive that He who gave our nature to be perfected by our virtue, willed also the necessary means of its perfection.—He willed therefore the state—He willed its connexion with the source and original archetype of all perfection. They who are convinced of this His will, which is the law of laws, and the sovereign of sovereigns, cannot think it reprehensible that this our corporate fealty and homage, that this our recognition of a signiory paramount, I had almost said this oblation of the state itself, as a worthy offering on the high altar of universal praise, should be performed as all public, solemn acts are performed, in buildings, in music, in decoration, in speech, in the dignity of persons, according to the customs of mankind, taught by their nature; this is, with modest splendour and unassuming state, with mild majesty and sober pomp. For those purposes they think some part of the wealth of the country is as usefully employed as it can be in fomenting the luxury of individuals. It is the public ornament. It is the public consolation. It nourishes the public hope. The poorest man finds his own importance and dignity in it, whilst the wealth and pride of individuals at every moment makes the man of humble rank and fortune sensible of his inferiority, and degrades and vilifies his condition. It is for the man in humble life, and to raise his nature, and to put him in mind of a state in which the privileges of opulence will cease, when he will be equal by nature, and may be more than equal by virtue, that this portion of the general wealth of his country is employed and sanctified.

The English people are satisfied, that to the great the consolations of religion are as necessary as its instructions. They too are among the unhappy. They feel personal pain, and domestic sorrow. In these they have no privilege, but are subject to pay their full contingent to the contributions levied on mortality. They want this sovereign balm under their gnawing cares and anxieties, which, being less conversant about the limited wants of animal life, range without limit, and are diversified by infinite combinations, in the wild and unbounded regions of imagination. Some charitable dole is wanting to these, our often very unhappy brethren, to fill the gloomy void that reigns in minds which have nothing on earth to hope or fear; something to relieve in the killing languor and over-laboured lassitude of those who have nothing to do; something to excite an appetite to existence in the palled satiety which attends on all pleasures which may be bought, where nature is not left to her own process, where even desire is anticipated, and therefore fruition defeated by meditated schemes and contrivances of delight; and no interval, no obstacle, is interposed between the wish and the accomplishment.

REFORM AND REVOLUTION

The errors and defects of old establishments are visible and palpable. It calls for little ability to point them out; and where absolute power is given, it requires but a word wholly to abolish the vice and the establishment together. The same lazy but restless disposition, which loves sloth and hates quiet, directs the politicians, when they come to work for supplying the place of what they have destroyed. To make everything the reverse of what they have seen is quite as easy as to destroy. No difficulties occur in what has never been tried. Criticism is almost baffled in discovering the defects of what has not existed; and eager enthusiasm and cheating hope have all the wide field of imagination, in which they may expatiate with little or no opposition.

At once to preserve and to reform is quite another thing. When the useful parts of an old establishment are kept, and what is superadded is to be fitted to what is retained, a vigorous mind, steady, persevering attention, various powers of comparison and combination, and the resources of an understanding fruitful in expedients, are to be exercised; they are to be exercised in a continued conflict with the combined force of opposite vices, with the obstinacy that rejects all improvement, and the levity that is fatigued and disgusted with everything of which it is in possession. But you may object—"A process of this kind is slow. It is not fit for an assembly, which glories in performing in a few months the work of ages. Such a mode of reforming, possibly, might take up many years." Without question it might; and it ought. It is one of the excellencies of a method in which time is amongst the assistants, that its operation is slow, and in some cases almost imperceptible. If circumspection and caution are a part of wisdom, when we work only upon inanimate

matter, surely they become a part of duty too, when the subject of our demolition and construction is not brick and timber, but sentient beings, by the sudden alteration of whose state, condition, and habits, multitudes may be rendered miserable. But it seems as if it were the prevalent opinion in Paris, that an unfeeling heart, and an undoubting confidence, are the sole qualifications for a perfect legislator. Far different are my ideas of that high office. The true lawgiver ought to have a heart full of sensibility. He ought to love and respect his kind, and to fear himself. It may be allowed to his temperament to catch his ultimate object with an intuitive glance; but his movements towards it ought to be deliberate. Political arrangement, as it is a work for social ends, is to be only wrought by social means. There mind must conspire with mind. Time is required to produce that union of minds which alone can produce all the good we aim at. Our patience will achieve more than our force. If I might venture to appeal to what is so much out of fashion in Paris, I mean to experience, I should tell you, that in my course I have known, and, according to my measure, have cooperated with great men; and I have never yet seen any plan which has not been mended by the observations of those who were much inferior in understanding to the person who took the lead in the business. By a slow but well-sustained progress, the effect of each step is watched; the good or ill success of the first gives light to us in the second; and so, from light to light, we are conducted with safety through the whole series. We see that the parts of the system do not clash. The evils latent in the most promising contrivances are provided for as they arise. One advantage is as little as possible sacrificed to another. We compensate, we reconcile, we balance. We are enabled to unite into a consistent whole the various anomalies and contending principles that are found in the minds and affairs of men. From hence arises, not an excellence in simplicity, but one far superior, an excellence in composition. Where the great interests of mankind are concerned through a long succession of generations, that succession ought to be admitted into some share in the councils which are so deeply to affect them. If justice requires this, the work itself requires the aid of more minds than one age can furnish. It is from this view of things that the best legislators have been often satisfied with the establishment of some sure, solid, and ruling principle in government; a power like that which some of the philosophers have called a plastic nature; and having fixed the principle, they have left it afterwards to its own operation.

REVOLUTION AND MILITARY DESPOTISM

It is known, that armies have hitherto yielded a very precarious and uncertain obedience to any senate, or popular authority; and they will least of all yield it to an assembly which is only to have a continuance of two years. The officers must totally lose the characteristic disposition of military men, if they see with perfect submission and due admiration, the dominion of pleaders; especially when they find that they have a new court to pay to an endless succession of those pleaders; whose military policy, and the genius of whose command (if they should have any), must be as uncertain as their duration is transient. In the weakness of one kind of authority, and in the fluctuation of all, the officers of any army will remain for some time mutinous and full of faction, until some popular general, who understands the art of conciliating the soldiery, and who possesses the true spirit of command, shall draw the eyes of all men upon himself. Armies will obey him on his personal account. There is no other way of securing military obedience in this state of things. But the moment in which that event shall happen, the person who really commands the army is your master; the master (that is little) of your king, the master of your assembly, the master of your whole republic.

How came the Assembly by their present power over the army? Chiefly, to be sure, by debauching the soldiers from their officers. They have begun by a most terrible operation. They have touched the central point, about which the particles that compose armies are at repose. They have destroyed the principle of obedience in the great, essential, critical link between the officer and the soldier, just where the chain of military subordination commences and on which the whole of that system depends. The soldier is told he is a citizen, and has the rights of man and citizen. The right of a man, he is told, is to be his own governor, and to be ruled only by those to whom he delegates that self-government. It is very natural he should think that he ought most of all to have his choice where he is to yield the greatest degree of obedience. He will therefore, in all probability, systematically do, what he does at present occasionally; that is, he will exercise at least a negative in the choice of his officers. At present the officers are known at best to be only permissive, and on their good behaviour. In fact, there have been many instances in which they have been cashiered by their corps. Here is a second negative on the choice of the king; a negative as effectual at least as the other of the Assembly. The soldiers know already that it has been a question, not ill received in the National Assembly, whether they ought not to have the direct choice of their officers, or some proportion of them? When such matters are in deliberation it is no extravagant supposition that they will incline to the opinion most favourable to their pretensions. They will not bear to be deemed the army of an imprisoned king, whilst another army in the same country, with whom too they are to feast and confederate, is to be considered as the free army of a free constitution. They will cast their eyes on the other and more permanent army; I mean the municipal. That corps, they will know, does actually elect its own officers. They may not be able to discern the ground of distinction on which they are not to elect a Marquis de la Fayette (or what is his new name?) of their own. If this election of a commander-in-chief be a part of the rights of men, why not of theirs? They see elective justices of peace, elective judges, elective curates, elective bishops, elective municipalities, and elective commanders of the Parisian army. Why should they alone be excluded? Are the brave troops of France the only men in that nation who are not the fit judges of military merit, and of the qualifications necessary for a commander-in-chief? Are they paid by the state, and do they therefore lose the rights of men? They are a part of that nation themselves, and contribute to that pay. And is not the king, is not the

National Assembly, and are not all who elect the National Assembly, likewise paid? Instead of seeing all these forfeit their rights by their receiving a salary, they perceive that in all these cases a salary is given for the exercise of those rights. All your resolutions, all your proceedings, all your debates, all the works of your doctors in religion and politics, have industriously been put into their hands; and you expect that they will apply to their own case just as much of your doctrines and examples as suits your pleasure.

Everything depends upon the army in such a government as yours; for you have industriously destroyed all the opinions, and prejudices, and, as far as in you lay, all the instincts which support government. Therefore the moment any difference arises between your National Assembly and any part of the nation, you must have recourse to force. Nothing else is left to you; or rather you have left nothing else to yourselves.

PART III

NINETEENTH AND TWENTIETH CENTURIES

CHAPTER TWENTY-FIVE

BENTHAM

The nineteenth and twentieth centuries were ones of fantastic and unimagined development within human history. Human control of nature exploded during the two hundred years between 1800 and 2000. Material living conditions in 1800 were more similar to those thousands of years before than those existing merely two centuries later. Humanity entered a new epoch. The change in the human condition between 1800 and 2000 included more than material development. Concomitant with this change came significant alteration in new forms and functions of government. The emerging and new era called forth ideas about government and society.

From the middle of the eighteenth century, England experienced—as the first modern country—a technological and industrial transformation whose impact was revolutionary from the point-of-view of new social ideas and a new material environment. Technologically, the new age was based on coal and iron, later to be supplemented by electricity and steel. Economically, the Industrial Revolution led to the factory as its most characteristic institution, which replaced the farm or landed estate as the principal unit of production and wealth. Socially, the Industrial Revolution was responsible for three complementary developments: first, the growth of new, and the rapid expansion of old, towns and cities; second, an increase in population made possible by higher living standards and improved conditions of health; and third, destruction of the existing social hierarchy headed by the landed aristocracy and its gradual replacement by manufacturers, financiers, merchants, and professional men as the new dominant class.

Prominent among the reformers of government at the start of the Industrial Revolution was the British political and legal philosopher Jeremy Bentham (1748–1832). Though he lived most of his life during the eighteenth century, he achieved most of his influence during the nineteenth, and his thought pointed to the future rather than the past.

Bentham was a child prodigy—he was a true genius. He read at three; he began learning Latin at four; he wrote Latin at five. He learned French at six and took to Voltaire for light reading at eight. What is most amazing about this childhood precocity is that, unlike his successor John Stuart Mill, Bentham's early intellectual accomplishments apparently were not the result of a regimen forced upon him by adults. They were spontaneous manifestations of his great intellect.

When Bentham entered Oxford at the age of twelve, he was forced to sign the Thirty-Nine Articles of the Church of England. Other students readily signed, but not Bentham. He sat down and examined them one-by-one. He believed some had no meaning and others were contrary to reason and Scripture. A few fellow students shared Bentham's apprehensions about signing articles of faith that they did not understand or believe, but Bentham was the one to speak up. He was advised not to substitute his private judgment for the public judgment formed by wise men. Bentham reluctantly signed, and later recalled that "by the view I found myself forced to take of the whole business, such an impression was made, as will never depart from me but with life."

The work for which Bentham most is known is *An Introduction to the Principles of Morals and Legislation* (printed in 1780 and published in 1789). Happiness is the sun around which Bentham's other ideas, like planets, travel. "Happiness," he states in an early, unpublished manuscript, "is the end of every human action, of every human thought. How can it, or why ought it to be otherwise? This is for those to say, who sometime seem to struggle to dispute it."

Continuing along this line, he commenced *An Introduction to the Principles of Morals and Legislation:* "Nature has placed mankind under the governance of two sovereign masters, *pain* and *pleasure.* It is for them alone to point out what we ought to do, as well as to determine what we shall do. On the one hand the standard of right and wrong, on the other the chain of causes and effects, are fastened to their throne. They govern us in all we do, in all we say, in all we think: every effort we can make to throw off our subjection, will serve but to demonstrate and confirm it. In words a man may pretend to abjure their empire: but in reality he will remain subject to it all the while. The *principle of utility* recognizes this subjection, and assumes it for the foundation of that system, the object which is to rear the fabric of felicity by the hands of reason and law. Systems which attempt to question it, deal in sounds instead of senses, in caprice instead of reason, in darkness instead of light."

As an old man, he inscribed the following in the birthday album of the daughter of his editor John Bowring, which reads like the doctrine of Christian love: "Create all the happiness you are able to create; remove all the misery you are able to remove. Everyday will allow you—will invite you to add something to the pleasure of others,—or to diminish something of their pains. And for every grain of enjoyment you sow in the bosom of another, you shall find a harvest in your own bosom,—while every sorrow which you pluck out from the thoughts and feelings of a fellow creature shall be replaced by beautiful flowers of peace and joy in the sanctuary of your soul."

Bentham first enunciated the principle of utility in *A Fragment on Government* (1776): "It is the greatest happiness of the greatest number that is the measure of right and wrong." Neither the phrase nor idea were original to him, of course, but he has the distinction of grounding a theory of ethics and society so extensively upon this principle. There is one moral good for Bentham—the greatest happiness.

In *An Introduction to the Principles of Morals and Legislation,* he humorously contrasts the principle of utility with other supposed moral standards, and finds the others wanting. Whether one otherwise deduces morality from a "moral sense," "common sense," "understanding," a "Rule of Right," the "Fitness of Things," the "Law of Nature," "Law of Reason," "Right Reason," "Natural Justice," Natural Equity," or "Good Order," all of these merely are, in Bentham's opinion, words without meaning unless they refer to happiness.

There must be a criterion of morality in order to give morality meaning. For Bentham, this criterion is happiness. In his *Constitutional Code,* he criticizes the authors of the *Federalist* for saying that justice is the "end of government." "Why not happiness?" Bentham asks. "What happiness is every man knows, because what pleasure is, every man knows, and what pain is, every man knows. But what justice is—this is what on every occasion is the subject-matter of dispute."

When Bentham began writing during the 1770s, English common law largely was under the influence of William Blackstone, whose lectures Bentham attended at Oxford, and whose recently published *Commentaries on the Laws of England* attempted to enshrine existing British legal practice and governmental organization as the *ne plus ultra* of human political thought and development. Bentham had nothing to do with attempts to sanctify the existing as therefore best. He saw great problems in English institutions and laws of his day, and sought to reform them along the lines of the greatest happiness for the greatest number, a phrase he refined late in his career to "the greatest happiness maximized."

Bentham's ethical theory often is confused with egoistic hedonism, which holds that an individual solely should be motivated by his own happiness. This was not Bentham's position, as a later utilitarian, Henry Sidgwick, recognized in his own *The Methods of Ethics:* "The two methods which take happiness as an ultimate end it will be convenient to distinguish as Egoistic and Universalistic Hedonism: and . . . it is the latter of these, as taught by Bentham and his successors, that is more generally understood under the term 'Utilitarianism.'" The principle of utility is not the greatest happiness of an agent, but the greatest happiness of all.

Bentham moved into the top circle of British political life during the 1780s through his friendship with Lord Shelburne, who was prime minister in 1782–83. Shelburne was impressed by *A Fragment on Government,* was Bentham's patron, and introduced him to the elite of British society. Bentham thus had the opportunity to observe British political life from the inside, and was known to and knew leading figures.

Bentham's leading project during the 1780s and '90s was the Panopticon, a scheme for prison reform that entailed a physical lay-out for jails that enables a jailer to observe prisoners at all times. Bentham also published, in 1787, *Defence of Usury,* which argued against Smith that government should not restrict the rate of interest. Bentham was well-known enough by the time of the French Revolution that, together with George Washington, Kant, and others, he was made an honorary citizen of France in 1792.

Bentham's attitude toward the French Revolution never was in line with prevailing fashions. On the one hand, he was opposed to revolution because he believed in progress through peaceful and rational persuasion (such as he thought possible in England through Parliament); on the other hand, he could not be enthusiastic over Burke's and Blackstone's incantations of the glories of history because, in the light of Bentham's Felicific calculus and zeal for reform, history often is little more than a record of folly and crime.

At first, Bentham welcomed the opportunities for fresh legislation unencumbered by tradition and custom that the French Revolution offered to reformers, and he sent several proposals to his French friends and correspondents, but these brought no tangible results. Within a few years, Bentham became disenchanted by the violence and ideological fanatacism of the French Revolution. He became convinced that whatever radical changes had to be made in England, the road to such changes was reform, not revolution.

A vital contact Bentham made through Shelburne was Étienne Dumont, who translated and published, together with other material, an edited version of *An Introduction to the Principles of Morals and Legislation* in French in 1802. Through this French version of his work, *Traités de législation civile et pénale,* Bentham became famous throughout the European world, and it was through Dumont that Bentham had become acquainted with French revolutionary leaders.

Until he was sixty years of age, Bentham never was closely allied with either Tories or Whigs, though he was born a Tory. His philanthropic schemes were above party, and he hoped the force of logic would be sufficient to impel social change. He thought reason universally is human.

Bentham's fundamental jurisprudential point is that law pertains to future action, and deliberately should be structured to produce the greatest happiness. Existing laws and government organization should not be maintained merely because they are the way things are and have been. He once heard that Alexander Wedderburn, a future Chancellor of England, called the principle of utility a "dangerous" principle. "Dangerous it unquestionably is," Bentham later replied, "to every government which has for its *actual* end or object, the greatest happiness of a certain *one*" or few.

An Introduction to the Principles of Morals and Legislation is Bentham's great work. He wrote in the era in which the split between the natural sciences and what has become speculative philosophy was not complete, and in which it was thought by some, including himself, that the same sort of precision that Isaac Newton obtained in the physical world can be obtained in the moral world of ethics and legislation. Four times in the preface of *An Introduction,* Bentham makes reference to the potentially scientific character of morality and law:

an introduction to a work which takes for its subject the totality of any science . . .

the science of law . . .

political and moral science . . .

There is no King's Road, no Stadtholder's Gate, to legislatve any more than to mathematic science.

He thus may have been the first to refer to "political science."

Bentham hoped that *An Introduction to the Principles of Morals and Legislation* would perform the "office which is done, by books of pure mathematics, to books of mixed mathematics and . . . philosophy." That is, *An Introduction* is Bentham's theory. His other writings, by comparison, are practical applications of the principle of utility—they attempt to show how the greatest happiness most feasibly may be realized. As such, his other works are more dated and of less current relevance.

Bentham writes in *An Introduction:*

To a person considered *by himself,* the value of a pleasure or pain considered *by itself,* will be greater or less, according to the four following circumstances:

1. Its *intensity.*
2. Its *duration.*
3. Its *certainty* or *uncertainty.*
4. Its *propinquity* [nearness] or *remoteness.*

Intensity surely is the essence of a pleasure or pain. Intensity is the depth of feeling of joy or sorrow of a particular pleasure or pain. It is its power, vigor, strength, force, or degree. It is the rapture of the most exalted pleasure or sting of the most debilitating pain.

Duration, also, is a property of all pleasures and pains. Does a particular pleasure or pain last for a long or short interval of time? Duration and intensity not only both are properties of all pleasures and pains, they are necessary complements to make sense of each other. A pleasure or pain must last some time (if only a millisecond) to exist. Likewise, duration of an experience, without intensity, would be vapid.

Bentham best states the essentiality of intensity and duration to pleasure and pain in the, in his day, unpublished *Plan of a Penal Code* on which he worked before turning to *An Introduction to the Principles of Morals and Legislation.* He here says:

1. Of whatever nature a pleasure be; a pleasure of the body or a pleasure of the mind; a pleasure of enjoyment, a pleasure of possession, or a pleasure of expectation; a pleasure of the concupiscible appetites or a pleasure of the irascible; what we shall have to say of any pleasure in the present chapter will be found equally to belong to all: and so it is with pains.
2. A pleasure may be more or less intense, hence we come to speak of its intensity: when its intensity is at a high degree, we say (preserving the same expression) that it is intense, when at a low degree, we call it faint or slight.
3. The time it lasts, is either long or short; hence we have to speak of its duration.
4. This is the case with everything called pleasure; to exist it must possess two qualities: it must possess intensity; it must possess duration. They constantly belong to it; they are essential to it: it cannot be conceived without them.

Prospective pleasures and pains do not possess only intensity and duration, however, and this is where the elements of certainty and proximity enter. The certainty or uncertainty of a pleasure or pain is the probability a particular pleasure or pain actually will come to pass. Proximity is "the nearness or remoteness of the time at which, if at all, it is to come into possession." Bentham includes probability and proximity as elements of value in pleasures and pains because his purpose in *An Introduction to the Principles of Morals and Legislation* is to provide an undergirding for laws and ethics. In order to devise effective legislation and ethics, probability and proximity should be considered because they influence individuals' valuations of future prospective pleasures and pains. They affect the present value of future potential pleasures and pains. Neither of these latter two factors affects the pleasure or pain once it actually is experienced. They are relevant only so long as a pleasure or pain is prospective, as long as it has not been experienced. A pleasure or pain, of itself, as it is experienced, remains a function of its intensity and duration.

In introducing the most recent edition of *An Introduction to the Principles of Morals and Legislation,* current Bentham *Collected Works* general editor Fred Rosen remarks that Bentham developed "elaborate classification of different kinds of pleasures and pains." Bentham often is accused of being a philistine with little regard for refined pleasures. While Bentham maintains an ultimate sensory base for pleasure and pain, he does so within a conception that holds mind is capable of developing to experience refined pleasures. In *An Introduction,* he provides one example of a catalog of the pleasures of a particular circumstance, the "pleasures of a country scene":

I. Pleasures of the senses

1. The simple pleasures of sight, excited by the perception of agreeable colours and figures, green fields, waving foliage, glistening water, and the like.
2. The simple pleasures of the ear, excited by the perceptions of the chirping of birds, the murmuring of waters, the rustling of the wind among the trees.
3. The pleasures of the smell, excited by the perceptions of the fragrance of flowers, of the new-mown hay, or other vegetable substances, in the first stages of fermentation.

4. The agreeable inward sensation, produced by a brisk circulation of the blood, and the ventilation of it in the lungs by a pure air, such as that in the country frequently is in comparison of that which is breathed in towns.

II. Pleasures of the imagination produced by association

1. The idea of the plenty, resulting from the possession of the objects that are in view, and of the happiness arising from it.

2. The idea of the innocence and happiness of the birds, sheep, cattle, dogs, and other gentle or domestic animals.

3. The idea of the constant flow of health, supposed to be enjoyed by all these creatures: a notion which is apt to result from the occasional flow of health enjoyed by the supposed spectator.

4. The idea of gratitude, excited by the contemplation of the all-powerful and beneficient Being, who is looked up to as the author of these blessings.

Bentham is no philistine. During the early years of the 1800s, Bentham's fame spread with the *Traités,* far beyond England. In Russia, Greece, Spain, Latin America, Portugal, and elsewhere, he became a well-known figure among government reformers. In England, a group of followers began to form around him who became known as the Philosophical Radicals.

During his latter decades, Bentham became a proponent of democracy. He once naively believed that the good had merely to be pointed out in order for it to be accepted. As he gained more experience with the actual working of government, he realized the form of government affects its outcomes. In order for government to promote the happiness of all, it must be by all. He thus embraced and promoted democracy.

Bentham failed enough to appreciate that in politics, reason only is a party, and that it always has been opposed by parties of irrationalism, custom, and tradition. He also failed to perceive that no one individual is capable of the sort of detailed organization of a society he planned.

Among those who gathered around Bentham was James Mill, father of John Stuart, and a significant thinker and figure in his own right. A number of "Benthamites" were elected to parliament. While Bentham's faction never came close to possessing a majority, they did provide a cutting edge for reform efforts within the Whig Party. In 1824, Bentham founded the *Westminster Review,* which was the chief organ of Philosophical Radicalism and utilitarianism.

Henry Maine wrote in 1875: "I do not know a single law reform effected since Bentham's day which cannot be traced to his influence." In *Constitutional Code,* on which Bentham labored for the last years of his life but remained incomplete, Bentham laid down principles of orderly and rational government that gradually were adopted. A public health service, a system of national education, the collection of social and economic statistics (including the periodic taking of a census, the first of which was in 1801), colonial self-government, proper correlation between central and local government, open competition for entry into the civil service, organization of government departments relating to their functions—these are but a few of the major practical reforms of government and public administrative execution that Bentham and his group suggested and initiated. In the area of workers' combined activity, in part as a result of the Benthamites' influence, labor organizations ceased to be criminal conspiracies in 1824 and thereafter existed on a legal basis.

Bentham's views, like John Stuart Mill's, were ahead of his time in a variety of social areas, not merely in government. In the area of sex, he saw no reason homosexuality should be illegal at a time when its punishment was hanging. In the area of religion, he supported universal tolerance when even Catholics did not possess full civil rights. Regarding race and animals, he wrote in *An Introduction to the Principles of Morals and Legislation:* "The French have already discovered that the blackness of the skin is no reason why a human being should be abandoned without redress to the caprice of a tormentor. It may one day come to be recognized, that the number of the legs, the villosity of the skin, or the termination of the *os sacrum,* are reasons equally insufficient for abandoning a sensitive being to the same fate. . . . [T]he question is not [concerning animals], Can they *reason* . . . but, Can they suffer?"

In criminal law, owing to Bentham's and his follower in Parliament Samuel Romilly's efforts, the worst forms of cruel punishment, such as whipping of women, transportation of criminals from England to the colonies, and the pillory were eliminated. The supreme penalty of death was confined to murder and treason, whereas before Bentham's time there were over two hundred offenses punishable by death.

Bentham emphasized equality. John Stuart Mill in his own *Utilitarianism* quoted "Bentham's dictum" as "everybody to count for one, nobody for more than one." Bentham's view was that the equal happiness of different individuals equally should be considered. In his focus on individualism, Bentham has been criticized, but when he says "the community is a fictitious *body* . . . The interest of the community then is, what?— the sum of the interest of the several members who compose it," he merely means that there is no happiness that is not individually experienced.

Bentham is skeptical with regard to religion because it hinders intellectual progress by supporting belief apart from—in the British philosophical tradition—experience, "its only safe ground." Bentham published one of his books on religion, *Church of Englandism and Its Catechisms Examined,* under his own name, and two others under pseudonyms: *The Analysis of Natural Religion on the Temporal Happiness of Mankind* and *Not Paul, but Jesus.*

One of Bentham's richest legacies was his awareness that good government is more than a matter of tradition, common sense, and intuition, and that it should have a base in empirical investigation and research. Bentham was among the first modern writers to apply the investigative approach to problems of public policy, relating societal facts to legal and administrative practices.

In economics, he was in the Adam Smith tradition, and his criticism of Smith regarding usury was not that Smith's principles were wrong, but that Smith himself did not apply them in this case. Bentham preferred security of property to its equality. But he was not dogmatic and was ready to depart from *laissez-faire* if in a specific instance a case for governmental intervention can be made on grounds of utility. He recognized government is responsible for public health, education, defense, public works, and some form of public charity. He correctly saw that the question of government is not one of pure abstract speculation, but historical and environmental circumstances.

He dismissed natural rights. In *Anarchical Fallacies,* he referred to natural rights as "simple nonsense, . . . rhetorical nonsense, nonsense upon stilts." His argument here was not that people should not have certain things—his argument was, indeed, as seen, that all people, all creatures, should be happy. His position here was definitional—that rights are legally created, not natural: "Reasons for wishing there were such things as rights, are not rights; a reason for wishing that a certain right were established, is not that right; want is not supply; hunger is not bread."

While Bentham's personality and writing style often, not without complete injustice, somewhat are ridiculed, there can be little question that through his emphases on logical, systematic reform of government and law, happiness as the moral good, and democracy, he has had significant influence. John Stuart Mill wrote upon him in 1838: "The changes which have been made, and the greater changes which will be made, in our institutions, are not the work of philosophers, but of the interests and instincts of large portions of society recently grown into strength. . . . Bentham gave voice to those interests and instincts: until he spoke out, those who found our institutions unsuited to them did not dare to say so . . . It was not Bentham by his own writings; it was Bentham through the minds and pens which those writings fed—through the men in more direct contact with the world, into whom his spirit passed. . . . The father of English innovation, both in doctrines and in institutions, is Bentham." Bentham changed the character of British political life during the first half of the nineteenth century as much as any one else.

Bentham's first, and still best, biographer, Leslie Stephen, wrote that "in his later years the United States became his ideal . . ." The great British Reform Bill of 1832 extending the right to vote passed in parliament the day after Bentham died. His final utilitarian act was to leave his body for dissection.

Bentham left his body for posterity as an "auto-icon," and it still may be seen in University College in London, which he played a primary role in founding. In his personal and political support for public educational spending especially at the higher levels, he advanced the causes of governmental and societal reform. The London School of Economics and Political Science emerged from University College.

While Bentham did not, or at least has not yet, achieved his very high ambitions for personal fame, he accomplished his goal of advancing human happiness. Lord Brougham told the House of Commons in 1828: "The age of reform and the age of Jeremy Bentham are one and the same." Mill wrote in his essay on Bentham on "a lesson given to mankind by every age, and always disregarded— . . . that speculative philosophy, which to the superficial appears a thing so remote from the business of life and the outward interests of men, is in reality the thing on earth which most influences them, and in the long run overbears every other influence save those which it must itself obey."

In *Utilitarianism,* Mill introduced "quality" of pleasures and pains to Bentham's "quantity." While this introduction to Bentham's utilitarian system typically is considered a new element, it is not. While Mill never really adequately defined "quality" and "quantity" of pleasures and pains, they may be considered philosophically akin to Bentham's "intensity" and "duration," though Mill emphasizes the mental and sympathetic aspects of pleasure and pain more than Bentham does. Mill here builds upon Bentham's foundation not by grafting something new onto it, but by paring it to its essence. Stephen concludes his biography of Bentham that Bentham's influence demonstrates "the power which belongs to the man of one idea."

BENTHAM

*Principles of Morals and Legislation**

OF THE PRINCIPLE
OF UTILITY

1. Nature has placed mankind under the governance of two sovereign masters, *pain* and *pleasure*. It is for them alone to point out what we ought to do, as well as to determine what we shall do. On the one hand the standard of right and wrong, on the other the chain of causes and effects, are fastened to their throne. They govern us in all we do, in all we say, in all we think: every effort we can make to throw off our subjection will serve but to demonstrate and confirm it. In words a man may pretend to abjure their empire: but in reality he will remain subject to it all the while. The *principle of utility*[1]

recognizes this subjection, and assumes it for the foundation of that system, the object of which is to rear the fabric of felicity by the hands of reason and of law. Systems which attempt to question it, deal in sounds instead of senses, in caprice instead of reason, in darkness instead of light.

But enough of metaphor and declamation: it is not by such means that moral science is to be improved.

2. The principle of utility is the foundation of the present work: it will be proper therefore at the outset to give an explicit and determinate account of what is meant by it. By the principle of utility is meant that principle which approves or disapproves of every action whatsoever, according to the tendency which it appears to have to augment or diminish the happiness of the party whose interest is in question: or, what is the same thing in other words, to promote or to oppose that happiness. I say of every action whatsoever; and therefore not only of every action of a private individual, but of every measure of government.

3. By utility is meant that property in any object, whereby it tends to produce benefit, advantage, pleasure, good, or happiness (all this in the present case comes to the same thing) or (what comes again to the same thing) to prevent the happening of mischief, pain, evil, or unhappiness to the party whose interest is considered: if that party be the community in general, then the happiness of the community: if a particular

---

*From Jeremy Bentham, *An Introduction to the Principles of Morals and Legislation* (1789; rev. ed., 1823).

[1] Note by the Author, July 1822.

To this denomination has of late been added, or substituted, the *greatest happiness* or *greatest felicity* principle: this for shortness, instead of saying at length *that principle* which states the greatest happiness of all those whose interest in question, as being the right and proper, and only right and proper and universally desirable, end of human action: of human action in every situation, and in particular in that of a functionary or set of functionaries exercising the powers of Government. The word *utility* does not so clearly point to the ideas of *pleasure* and *pain* as the words *happiness* and *felicity* do: nor does it lead us to the consideration of the *number,* of the interests affected; to the *number,* as being the circumstance, which contributes, in the largest proportion, to the formation of the standard here in question; the *standard of right and wrong,* by which alone the propriety of human conduct, in every situation, can with propriety be tried. This want of a sufficiently manifest connexion between the ideas of *happiness* and *pleasure* on the

---

one hand, and the idea of *utility* on the other, I have every now and then found operating, and with but too much efficiency, as a bar to the acceptance, that might otherwise have been given, to this principle.

individual, then the happiness of that individual.

4. The interest of the community is one of the most general expressions that can occur in the phraseology of morals: no wonder that the meaning of it is often lost. When it has a meaning, it is this. 'The community is a fictitious *body,* composed of the individual persons who are considered as constituting as it were its *members.* The interest of the community then is, what?—the sum of the interests of the several members who compose it.

5. It is in vain to talk of the interest of the community, without understanding what is the interest of the individual. A thing is said to promote the interest, or to be *for* the interest, of an individual, when it tends to add to the sum total of his pleasures: or, what comes to the same thing, to diminish the sum total of his pains.

6. An action then may be said to be conformable to the principle of utility, or, for shortness sake, to utility (meaning with respect to the community at large) when the tendency it has to augment the happiness of the community is greater than any it has to diminish it.

7. A measure of government (which is but a particular kind of action, performed by a particular person or persons) may be said to be conformable to or dictated by the principle of utility, when in like manner the tendency which it has to augment the happiness of the community is greater than any which it has to diminish it.

8. When an action, or in particular a measure of government, is supposed by a man to be conformable to the principle of utility, it may be convenient, for the purposes of discourse, to imagine a kind of law or dictate, called a law or dictate of utility; and to speak of the action in question, as being conformable to such law or dictate.

9. A man may be said to be a partizan of the principle of utility, when the approbation or disapprobation he annexes to any action, or to any measure, is determined by and proportioned to the tendency which he conceives it to have to augment or to diminish the happiness of the community: or in other words, to its conformity or unconformity to the laws or dictates of utility.

10. Of an action that is conformable to the principle of utility one may always say

either that it is one that ought to be done, or at least that it is not one that ought not to be done. One may say also, that it is right it should be done; at least that it is not wrong it should be done: that it is a right action; at least that it is not a wrong action. When thus interpreted, the words *ought,* and *right* and *wrong,* and others of that stamp, have a meaning: when otherwise, they have none.

11. Has the rectitude of this principle been ever formally contested? It should seem that it had, by those who have not known what they have been meaning. Is it susceptible of any direct proof? It should seem not: for that which is used to prove every thing else, cannot itself be proved: a chain of proofs must have their commencement somewhere. To give such proof is as impossible as it is needless.

12. Not that there is or ever has been that human creature breathing, however stupid or perverse, who has not on many, perhaps on most occasions of his life, deferred to it. By the natural constitution of the human frame, on most occasions of their lives men in general embrace this principle, without thinking of it: if not for the ordering of their own actions, yet for the trying of their own actions, as well as of those of other men. There have been, at the same time, not many, perhaps, even of the most intelligent, who have been disposed to embrace it purely and without reserve. There are even few who have not taken some occasion or other to quarrel with it, either on account of their not understanding always how to apply it, or on account of some prejudice or other which they were afraid to examine into, or could not bear to part with. For such is the stuff that man is made of: in principle and in practice, in a right track and in a wrong one, the rarest of all human qualities is consistency.

13. When a man attempts to combat the principle of utility, it is with reasons drawn, without his being aware of it, from that very principle itself.[2] His arguments, if they

---

[2] "The principle of utility (I have heard it said) is a dangerous principle: it is dangerous on certain occasions to consult it." This is as much as to say, what? that it is not consonant to utility,

prove any thing, prove not that the principle is *wrong,* but that, according to the applications he supposes to be made of it, it is *misapplied.* Is it possible for a man to move the earth? Yes; but he must first find out another earth to stand upon.

14. To disprove the propriety of it by arguments is impossible; but, from the causes that have been mentioned, or from some confused or partial view of it, a man may happen to be disposed not to relish it. Where this is the case, if he thinks the settling of his opinions on such a subject worth the trouble, let him take the following steps and at length, perhaps, he may come to reconcile himself to it.

I. Let him settle with himself, whether he would wish to discard this principle altogether; if so, let him consider what it is that all his reasonings (in matters of politics especially) can amount to?

II. If he would, let him settle with himself, whether he would judge and act without any principle, or whether there is any other he would judge and act by?

III. If there be, let him examine and satisfy himself whether the principle he thinks he has found is really any separate intelligible principle; or whether it be not a mere principle in words, a kind of phrase, which at bottom expresses neither more nor less than the mere averment of his own unfounded sentiments; that is, what in another person he might be apt to call caprice?

IV. If he is inclined to think that his own approbation or disapprobation, annexed to the idea of an act, without any regard to its consequences, is a sufficient foundation for him to judge and act upon, let him ask himself whether his sentiment is to be a standard of right and wrong, with respect to every other man, or whether every man's sentiment has the same privilege of being a standard to itself?

V. In the first case, let him ask himself whether his principle is not despotical, and hostile to all the rest of human race?

---

to consult utility: in short, that it is *not* consulting it, to consult it.

Addition by the Author, July 1822.

Not long after the publication of the *Fragment on Government,* anno 1776, in which, in the character of an all-comprehensive and all-commanding principle, the principle of *utility* was brought to view, one person by whom observation to the above effect was made was *Alexander Wedderburn,* at that time Attorney or Solicitor General, afterwards successively Chief Justice of the Common Pleas, and Chancellor of England, under the successive titles of Lord Loughborough and Earl of Rosslyn. It was made—not indeed in my hearing, but in the hearing of a person by whom it was almost immediately communicated to me. So far from being self-contradictory, it was a shrewd and perfectly true one. By that distinguished functionary, the state of the Government was thoroughly understood: by the obscure individual, at that time not so much as supposed to be so: his disquisitions have not been as yet applied, with any thing like a comprehensive view, to the field of Constitutional Law, nor therefore to those features of the English Government, by which the greatest happiness of the ruling *one* with or without that of a favoured few, are now so plainly seen to be the only ends to which the course of it has at any time been directed. The *principle of utility* was an appellative, at that time employed—employed by me, as it had been by others, to designate that which in a more perspicuous and instructive manner, may, as above, be designated by the name of the *greatest happiness principle.* "This principle (said Wedderburn) is a dangerous one." Saying so, he said that which, to a certain extent, is strictly true: a principle, which lays down, as the only *right* and justifiable end of Government, the greatest happiness of the greatest number—how can it be denied, to be a dangerous one? dangerous it unquestionably is, to every Government which has for its *actual* end or object, the greatest happiness of a certain *one,* with or without the addition of some comparatively small number of others, whom it is a matter of pleasure or accommodation to him to admit, each of them, to a share in the concern, on the footing of so many junior partners. *Dangerous* it therefore really was, to the interest—the sinister interest—of all those functionaries, himself included, whose interest it was, to maximize delay, vexation, and expense, in judicial and other modes of procedure, for the sake of the profit, extractible out of the expense. In a Government which had for its end in view the greatest happiness of the greatest number, Alexander Wedderburn might have been Attorney General and then Chancellor: but he would not have been Attorney General with £15,000 a year, nor Chancellor, with a peerage with a veto upon all justice, with £25,000 a year, and with 500 sinecures at his disposal, under the name of Ecclesiastical Benefices, besides *et coeteras.*

VI. In the second case, whether it is not anarchical, and whether at this rate there are not as many different standards of right and wrong as there are men? and whether even to the sane man, the same thing, which is right to-day, may not (without the least change in its nature) be wrong tomorrow? and whether the same thing is not right and wrong in the same place at the same time? and in either case, whether all argument is not at an end? and whether, when two men have said, "I like this," and "I don't like it," they can (upon such a principle) have any thing more to say?

VII. If he should have said to himself, No: for that the sentiment which he proposes as a standard must be grounded on reflection, let him say on what particulars the reflection is to turn? if on particulars having relation to the utility of the act, then let him say whether this is not deserting his own principle, and borrowing assistance from that very one in opposition to which he sets it up: or if not on those particulars, on what other particulars?

VIII. If he should be for compounding the matter, and adopting his own principle in part, and the principle of utility in part, let him say how far he will adopt it?

IX. When he has settled with himself where he will stop, then let him ask himself how he justifies to himself the adopting it so far? and why he will not adopt it any farther?

X. Admitting any other principle than the principle of utility to be a right principle, a principle that it is right for a man to pursue; admitting (what is not true) that the word *right* can have a meaning without reference to utility, let him say whether there is any such thing as a *motive* that a man can have to pursue the dictates of it: if there is, let him say what that motive is, and how it is to be distinguished from those which enforce the dictates of utility: if not, then lastly let him say what it is this other principle can be good for?

OF PRINCIPLES ADVERSE
TO THAT OF UTILITY

1. If the principle of utility be a right principle to be governed by, and that in all cases, it follows from what has been just observed, that whatever principle differs from it in any case must necessarily be a wrong one. To prove any other principle, therefore, to be a wrong one, there needs no more than just to show it to be what it is, a principle of which the dictates are in some point or other different from those of the principle of utility: to state it is to confute it.

2. A principle may be different from that of utility in two ways: 1. By being constantly opposed to it: this is the case with a principle which may be termed the principle of *asceticism*.[3] 2. By being sometimes opposed to it, and sometimes not, as it may happen: this is the case with another, which may be termed the principle of *sympathy* and *antipathy*.

3. By the principle of asceticism I mean that principle, which, like the principle of utility, approves or disapproves of any action, according to the tendency which it appears to have to augment or diminish the happiness of the party whose interest is in question; but in an inverse manner: approving of actions in as far as they tend to diminish his happiness; disapproving of them in as far as they tend to augment it.

---

[3] Ascetic is a term that has been sometimes applied to Monks. It comes from a Greek word which signifies *exercise*. The practices by which Monks sought to distinguish themselves from other men were called their Exercises. These exercises consisted in so many contrivances they had for tormenting themselves. By this they thought to ingratiate themselves with the Deity. For the Deity, said they, is a Being of infinite benevolence: now a Being of the most ordinary benevolence is pleased to see others make themselves as happy as they can: therefore to make ourselves as unhappy as we can is the way to please the Deity. If any body asked them, what motive they could find for doing all this? Oh! said they, you are not to imagine that we are punishing ourselves for nothing: we know very well what we are about. You are to know, that for every grain of pain it costs us now, we are to have a hundred grains of pleasure by and by. The case is, that God loves to see us torment ourselves at present: indeed he has as good as told us so. But this is done only to try us, in order just to see how we should behave: which it is plain he could not know, without making the experiment. Now then, from the satisfaction it gives him to see us make ourselves as unhappy as we can make ourselves in this present life, we have a sure proof of the satisfaction it will give him to see us as happy as he can make us in a life to come.

4. It is evident that any one who reprobates any the least particle of pleasure, as such, from whatever source derived, is *pro tanto* a partizan of the principle of asceticism. It is only upon that principle, and not from the principle of utility, that the most abominable pleasure which the vilest of malefactors ever reaped from his crime would be reprobated, if it stood alone. The case is, that it never does stand alone; but is necessarily followed by such a quantity of pain (or, what comes to the same thing, such a chance for a certain quantity of pain) that the pleasure in comparison of it, is as nothing: and this is the true and sole, but perfectly sufficient, reason for making it a ground for punishment.

5. There are two classes of men of very different complexions, by whom the principle of asceticism appears to have been embraced; the one a set of moralists, the other a set of religionists. Different accordingly have been the motives which appear to have recommended it to the notice of these different parties. Hope, that is the prospect of pleasure, seems to have animated the former: hope, the aliment of philosophic pride: the hope of honour and reputation at the hands of men. Fear, that is the prospect of pain, the latter: fear the offspring of superstitious fancy: the fear of future punishment at the hands of a splenetic and revengeful Deity. I say in this case fear: for of the invisible future, fear is more powerful than hope. These circumstances characterize the two different parties among the partizans of the principle of asceticism; the parties and their motives different, the principle the same.

6. The religious party, however, appear to have carried it farther than the philosophical: they have acted more consistently and less wisely. The philosophical party have scarcely gone farther than to reprobate pleasure: the religious party have frequently gone so far as to make it a matter of merit and of duty to court pain. The philosophical party have hardly gone farther than making pain a matter of indifference. It is no evil, they have said: they have not said, it is a good. They have not so much as reprobated all pleasure in the lump. They have discarded only what they have called the gross; that is, such as are organical, or of which the origin is easily traced up to such as are organical: they have even cherished and magnified the refined. Yet this, however, not under the name of pleasure: to cleanse itself from the sources of its impure original, it was necessary it should change its name: the honourable, the glorious, the reputable, the becoming, the *honestum,* the *decorum,* it was to be called: in short, any thing but pleasure.

7. From these two sources have flowed the doctrines from which the sentiments of the bulk of mankind have all along received a tincture of this principle; some from the philosophical, some from the religious, some from both. Men of education more frequently from the philosophical, as more suited to the elevation of their sentiments: the vulgar more frequently from the superstitious, as more suited to the narrowness of their intellect, undiluted by knowledge: and to the abjectness of their condition, continually open to the attacks of fear. The tinctures, however, derived from the two sources, would naturally intermingle, insomuch that a man would not always know by which of them he was most influenced: and they would often serve to corroborate and enliven one another. It was this conformity that made a kind of alliance between parties of a complexion otherwise so dissimilar: and disposed them to unite upon various occasions against the common enemy, the partizan of the principle of utility, whom they joined in branding with the odious name of Epicurean.

8. The principle of asceticism, however, with whatever warmth it may have been embraced by its partizans as a rule of private conduct, seems not to have been carried to any considerable length, when applied to the business of government. In a few instances it has been carried a little way by the philosophical party: witness the Spartan regimen. Though then, perhaps, it may be considered as having been a measure of security: and an application, though a precipitate and perverse application, of the principle of utility. Scarcely in any instances, to any considerable length, by the religious: for the various monastic orders, and the societies of the Quakers, Dumplers, Moravians, and other religionists, have been free societies, whose regimen no man has been astricted to without the intervention of his own consent. Whatever merit a man may

have thought there would be in making himself miserable, no such notion seems ever to have occurred to any of them, that it may be a merit, much less a duty, to make others miserable: although it should seem, that if a certain quantity of misery were a thing so desirable, it would not matter much whether it were brought by each man upon himself, or by one man upon another. It is true, that from the same source from whence, among the religionists, the attachment to the principle of asceticism took its rise, flowed other doctrines and practices, from which misery in abundance was produced in one man by the instrumentality of another: witness the holy wars, and the persecutions for religion. But the passion for producing misery in these cases proceeded upon some special ground: the exercise of it was confined to persons of particular descriptions: they were tormented, not as men, but as heretics and infidels. To have inflicted the same miseries of their fellow-believers and fellow-secretaries, would have been as blameable in the eyes even of these religionists, as in those of a partizan of the principle of utility. For a man to give himself a certain number of stripes was indeed meritorious: but to give the same number of stripes to another man, not consenting, would have been a sin. We read of saints, who for the good of their souls, and the mortification of their bodies, have voluntarily yielded themselves a prey to vermin: but though many persons of this class have wielded the reins of empire, we read of none who have set themselves to work, and made laws on purpose, with a view of stocking the body politic with the breed of highwaymen, housebreakers, or incendiaries. If at any time they have suffered the nation to be preyed upon by swarms of idle pensioners, or useless placemen, it has rather been from negligence and imbecility, than from any settled plan for oppressing and plundering of the people. If at any time they have sapped the sources of national wealth, by cramping commerce, and driving the inhabitants into emigration, it has been with other views, and in pursuit of other ends. If they have declaimed against the pursuit of pleasure, and the use of wealth, they have commonly stopped at declamation: they have not, like Lycurgus, made express ordinances

for the purpose of banishing the precious metals. If they have established idleness by a law, it has been not because idleness, the mother of vice and misery, is itself a virtue, but because idleness (say they) is the road to holiness. If under the notion of fasting, they have joined in the plan of confining their subjects to a diet, thought by some to be of the most nourishing and prolific nature, it has been not for the sake of making them tributaries to the nations by whom that diet was to be supplied, but for the sake of manifesting their own power, and exercising the obedience of the people. If they have established, or suffered to be established, punishments for the breach of celibacy, they have done no more than comply with the petitions of those deluded rigorists, who, dupes to the ambitious and deep-laid policy of their rulers, first laid themselves under that idle obligation by a vow.

9. The principle of asceticism seems originally to have been the reverie of certain hasty speculators, who having perceived, or fancied, that certain pleasures, when reaped in certain circumstances, have, at the long run, been attended with pains more than equivalent to them, took occasion to quarrel with every thing that offered itself under the name of pleasure. Having then got thus far, and having forgot the point which they set out from, they pushed on, and went so much further as to think it meritorious to fall in love with pain. Even this, we see, is at bottom but the principle of utility misapplied.

10. The principle of utility is capable of being consistently pursued; and it is but tautology to say, that the more consistently it is pursued, the better it must ever be for humankind. The principle of asceticism never was, nor ever can be, consistently pursued by any living creature. Let but one tenth part of the inhabitants of this earth pursue it consistently, and in a day's time they will have turned it into a hell.

11. Among principles adverse to that of utility, that which at this day seems to have most influence in matters of government, is what may be called the principle of sympathy and antipathy. By the principle of sympathy and antipathy, I mean that principle which approves or disapproves of certain actions, not on account of their tending to augment the happiness, nor yet on account of

their tending to diminish the happiness of the party whose interest is in question, but merely because a man finds himself disposed to approve or disapprove of them: holding up that approbation or disapprobation as a sufficient reason for itself, and disclaiming the necessity of looking out for any extrinsic ground. Thus far in the general department of morals: and in the particular department of politics, measuring out the quantum (as well as determining the ground) of punishment, by the degree of the disapprobation.

12. It is manifest, that this is rather a principle in name than in reality: it is not a positive principle of itself, so much as a term employed to signify the negation of all principle. What one expects to find in a principle is something that points out some external consideration, as a means of warranting and guiding the internal sentiments of approbation and disapprobation: this expectation is but ill fulfilled by a proposition, which does neither more nor less than hold up each of those sentiments as a ground and standard for itself.

13. In looking over the catalogue of human actions (says a partizan of this principle) in order to determine which of them are to be marked with the seal of disapprobation, you need but to take counsel of your own feelings: whatever you find in yourself a propensity to condemn, is wrong for that very reason. For the same reason it is also meet for punishment: in what proportion it is adverse to utility, or whether it be adverse to utility at all, is a matter that makes no difference. In that same *proportion* also is it meet for punishment: if you hate much, punish much: if you hate little, punish little: punish as you hate. If you hate not at all, punish not at all: the fine feelings of the soul are not to be overborne and tyrannized by the harsh and rugged dictates of political utility.

14. The various systems that have been formed concerning the standard of right and wrong, may all be reduced to the principle of sympathy and antipathy. One account may serve for all of them. They consist all of them in so many contrivances for avoiding the obligation of appealing to any external standard, and for prevailing upon the reader to accept of the author's sentiment or opinion as a reason for itself. The phrases are different, but the principle is the same.[4]

---

[4] It is curious enough to observe the variety of inventions men have hit upon, and the variety of phrases they have brought forward, in order to conceal from the world, and, if possible, from themselves, this very general and therefore very pardonable self-sufficiency.

1. One man says, he has a thing made on purpose to tell him what is right and what is wrong; and that it is called a *moral sense:* and then he goes to work at his ease, and says, such a thing is right, and such a thing is wrong—why? "because my moral sense tells me it is."

2. Another man comes and alters the phrase: leaving out *moral,* and putting in *common,* in the room of it. He then tells you, that his common sense teaches him what is right and wrong, as surely as the other's moral sense did: meaning by common sense, a sense of some kind or other, which, he says, is possessed by all mankind: the sense of those, whose sense is not the same as the author's being struck out of the account as not worth taking. This contrivance does better than the other; for a moral sense, being a new thing, a man may feel about him a good while without being able to find it out: but common sense is as old as the creation; and there is no man but would be ashamed to be thought not to have as much of it as his neighbours. It has another great advantage: by appearing to share power, it lessens envy: for when a man gets up upon this ground, in order to anathematize those who differ from him, it is not by a *sic volo sic jubeo,* but by a *velitis jubeatis.*

3. Another man comes, and says, that as to a moral sense indeed, he cannot find that he has any such thing: that however he has an *understanding,* which will do quite as well. This understanding, he says, is the standard of right and wrong: it tells him so and so. All good and wise men understand as he does: if other men's understandings differ in any point from his, so much the worse for them: it is a sure sign they are either defective or corrupt.

4. Another man says, that there is an eternal and immutable Rule of Right: that the rule of right dictates so and so: and then he begins giving you his sentiments upon any thing that comes uppermost: and these sentiments (you are to take for granted) are so many branches of the eternal rule of right.

5. Another man, or perhaps the same man (it's no matter) says, that there are certain practices conformable, and others repugnant, to the Fitness of Things; and then he tells you, at his

leisure, what practices are conformable and what repugnant: just as he happens to like a practice or dislike it.

6. A great multitude of people are continually talking of the Law of Nature; and then they go on giving you their sentiments about what is right and what is wrong: and these sentiments, you are to understand, are so many chapters and sections of the Law of Nature.

7. Instead of the phrase, Law of Nature, you have sometimes, Law of Reason, Right Reason, Natural Justice, Natural Equity, Good Order. Any of them will do equally well. This latter is most used in politics. The three last are much more tolerable than the others, because they do not very explicitly claim to be any thing more than phrases: they insist but feebly upon the being looked upon as so many positive standards of themselves, and seem content to be taken, upon occasion, for phrases expressive of the conformity of the thing in question to the proper standard, whatever that may be. On most occasions, however, it will be better to say *utility: utility* is clearer, as referring more explicitly to pain and pleasure.

8. We have one philosopher, who says, there is no harm in any thing in the world but in telling a lie: and that if, for example, you were to murder your own father, this would only be a particular way of saying, he was not your father. Of course, when this philosopher sees any thing that he does not like, he says, it is a particular way of telling a lie. It is saying, that the act ought to be done, or may be done, when, *in truth,* it ought not to be done.

9. The fairest and openest of them all is that sort of man who speaks out, and says, I am of the number of the Elect: now God himself takes care to inform the Elect what is right: and that with so good effect, and let them strive ever so, they cannot help not only knowing it but practising it. If therefore a man wants to know what is right and what is wrong, he has nothing to do but to come to me.

It is upon the principle of antipathy that such and such acts are often reprobated on the score of their being *unnatural:* the practice of exposing children, established among the Greeks and Romans, was an unnatural practice. Unnatural, when it means any thing, means unfrequent: and there it means something; although nothing to the present purpose. But here it means no such thing: for the frequency of such acts is perhaps the great complaint. It therefore means nothing; nothing, I mean which there is in the act itself. All it can serve to express is, the disposition of the person who is talking of it: the disposition he is in to be angry at the thoughts of it. Does it merit his anger? Very likely it may: but whether it does or not is a question, which, to be answered

rightly, can only be answered upon the principle of utility.

Unnatural, is as good a word as moral sense, or common sense; and would be as good a foundation for a system. Such an act is unnatural; that is, repugnant to nature: for I do not like to practice it: and, consequently, do not practice it. It is therefore repugnant to what ought to be the nature of every body else.

The mischief common to all these ways of thinking and arguing (which, in truth, as we have seen are but one and the same method, couched in different forms of words) is their serving as a cloak, and pretence, and aliment, to despotism: if not a despotism in practice, a despotism however in disposition: which is but too apt, when pretence and power offer, to show itself in practice. The consequence is, that with intentions very commonly of the purest kind, a man becomes a torment either to himself or his fellow-creatures. If he be of the melancholy cast, he sits in silent grief, bewailing their blindness and depravity: if of the irascible, he declaims with fury and virulence against all who differ from him; blowing up the coals of fanaticism, and branding with the charge of corruption and insincerity, every man who does not think, or profess to think, as he does.

If such a man happens to possess the advantages of style, his book may do a considerable deal of mischief before the nothingness of it is understood.

These principles, if such they can be called, it is more frequent to see applied to morals than to politics: but their influence extends itself to both. In politics, as well as morals, a man will be at least equally glad of a pretence for deciding any question in the manner that best pleases him, without the trouble of inquiry. If a man is an infallible judge of what is right and wrong in the actions of private individuals, why not in the measures to be observed by public men in the direction of those actions? accordingly (not to mention other chimeras) I have more than once known the pretended law of nature set up in legislative debates, in opposition to arguments derived from the principle of utility.

"But is it never, then, from any other considerations than those of utility, that we derive our notions of right and wrong?" I do not know: I do not care. Whether a moral sentiment can be originally conceived from any other source than a view of utility, is one question: whether upon examination and reflection it can, in point of fact, be actually persisted in and justified on any other ground, by a person reflecting within himself, is another: whether in point of right it can properly be justified on any other ground, by a person addressing himself to the community, is a third. The two first are questions of speculation:

15. It is manifest, that the dictates of this principle will frequently coincide with those of utility, though perhaps without intending any such thing. Probably more frequently than not: and hence it is that the business of penal justice is carried on upon that tolerable sort of footing upon which we see it carried on in common at this day. For

---

it matters not, comparatively speaking, how they are decided. The last is a question of practice: the decision of it is of as much importance as that of any can be.

"I feel in myself," (say you) "a disposition to approve of such or such an action in a moral view: but this is not owing to any notions I have of its being a useful one to the community. I do not pretend to know whether it be an useful one or not: it may be, for aught I know, a mischievous one." "But is it then," (say I) "a mischievous one? examine: and if you can make yourself sensible that it is so, then, if duty means any thing, that is, moral duty, it is your *duty* at least to abstain from it: and more than that, if it is what lies in your power, and can be done without too great a sacrifice, to endeavour to prevent it. It is not your cherishing the notion of it in your bosom, and giving it the name of virtue, that will excuse you."

"I feel in myself," (say you again) "a disposition to detest such or such an action in a moral view; but this is not owing to any notions I have of its being a mischievous one to the community. I do not pretend to know whether it be a mischievous one, or not: it may be not a mischievous one: it may be, for aught I know, an useful one."—"May it indeed," (say I) "be an useful one? but let me tell you then, that unless duty and right and wrong, be just what you please to make them, if it really be not a mischievous one, and any body has a mind to do it, it is no duty of yours, but, on the contrary, it would be very wrong in you, to take upon you to prevent him: detest it within yourself as much as you please; that it, may be a very good reason (unless it be also a useful one) for your not doing it yourself: but if you go about, by word or deed, to do any thing to hinder him, or make him suffer for it, it is you, and not be, that have done wrong: it is not your setting yourself to blame his conduct, or branding it with the name of vice, that will make him culpable, or you blameless. Therefore, if you can make yourself content that he shall be of one mind, and you of another, about this matter, and so continue, it is well: but if nothing will serve you, but that you and he must needs be of the same mind, I'll tell you what you have to do: it is for you to get the better of your antipathy, not for him to truckle to it."

what more natural or more general ground of hatred to a practice can there be, than the mischievousness of such practice? What all men are exposed to suffer by, all men will be disposed to hate. It is far yet, however, from being a constant ground: for when a man suffers, it is not always that he knows what it is he suffers by. A man may suffer grievously, for instance, by a new tax, without being able to trace up the cause of his sufferings to the injustice of some neighbour, who has eluded the payment of an old one.

16. The principle of sympathy and antipathy is most apt to err on the side of severity. It is for applying punishment in many cases which deserve none: in many cases which deserve some, it is for applying more than they deserve. There is no incident imaginable, be it ever so trivial, and so remote from mischief, from which this principle may not extract a ground of punishment: any difference in taste: any difference in opinion: upon one subject as well as upon another: no disagreement so trifling which perserverance and altercation will not render serious. Each becomes in the other's eyes an enemy, and, if laws permit, a criminal.[5] This is one of the circumstances by

---

[5] King James the First of England had conceived a violent antipathy against Arians: two of whom he burnt. This gratification he procured himself without much difficulty: the notions of the times were favourable to it. He . . . wrote a furious book called *A Counterblast to Tobacco,* against the use of that drug, which Sir Walter Raleigh had then lately introduced. Had the notions of the times co-operated with him, he would have burnt the Anabaptist and the smoke of tobacco in the same fire. However, he had the satisfaction of putting Raleigh to death afterwards, though for another crime. . . .

The ground of quarrel between the Bigendians and the Littleendians in the fable, was not more frivolous than many an one which has laid empires desolate. In Russia, it is said, there was a time when some thousands of persons lost their lives in a quarrel, in which the government had taken part, about the number of fingers to be used in making the sign of the cross. This was in days of yore: the ministers of Catherine II are better *instructed* than to take any other part in such disputes, than that of preventing the parties concerned from doing one another a mischief.

which the human race is distinguished (not much indeed to its advantage) from the brute creation.

17. It is not, however, by any means unexampled for this principle to err on the side of lenity. A near and perceptible mischief moves antipathy. A remote and imperceptible mischief, though no less real, has no effect. Instances in proof of this will occur in numbers in the course of the work. It would be breaking in upon the order of it to give them here.

18. It may be wondered, perhaps, that in all this while no mention has been made of the *theological* principle; meaning that principle which professes to recur for the standard of right and wrong to the will of God. But the case is, this is not in fact a distinct principle. It is never any thing more or less than one or other of the three before-mentioned principles presenting itself under another shape. The *will* of God here meant cannot be his revealed will, as contained in the sacred writings: for that is a system which nobody ever thinks of recurring to at this time of day, for the details of political administration: and even before it can be applied to the details of private conduct, it is universally allowed, by the most eminent divines of all persuasions, to stand in need of pretty ample interpretations; else to what use are the works of those divines? And for the guidance of these interpretations, it is also allowed, that some other standard must be assumed. The will then which is meant on this occasion, is that which may be called the *presumptive* will: that is to say, that which is presumed to be his will on account of the conformity of its dictates to those of some other principle. What then may be this other principle? it must be one or other of the three mentioned above: for there cannot, as we have seen, be any more. It is plain, therefore, that setting revelation out of the question, no light can ever be thrown upon the standard of right and wrong, by any thing that can be said upon the question, what is God's will. We may be perfectly sure, indeed, that whatever is right is conformable to the will of God: but so far is that from answering the purpose of showing us what is right, that it is necessary to know first whether a thing is right,

in order to know from thence whether it be conformable to the will of God.[6]

19. There are two things which are very apt to be confounded, but which it imports us carefully to distinguish:—the motive or cause, which, by operating on the mind of an individual, is productive of any act: and the ground or reason which warrants a legislator, or other bystander, in regarding that act with an eye of approbation. When the act happens, in the particular instance in question, to be productive of effects which we approve of, much more if we happen to observe that the same motive may frequently be productive, in other instances, of the like effects, we are apt to transfer our approbation to the motive itself, and to assume, as the just ground for the approbation we bestow on the act, the circumstance of its originating from that motive. It is in this way that the sentiment of antipathy has often been considered as a just ground of action. Antipathy, for instance, in such or such a case, is the cause of an action which is attended with good effects: but this does not make it a right ground of action in that case, any more than in any other. Still farther. Not only the effects are good, but the

---

[6] The principle of theology refers every thing to God's pleasure. But what is God's pleasure? God does not, he confessedly does not now, either speak or write to us. How then are we to know what is his pleasure? By observing what is our own pleasure, and pronouncing it to be his. Accordingly what is called the pleasure of God, is and must necessarily be (revelation apart) neither more nor less than the good pleasure of the person, whoever he be, who is pronouncing what he believes, or pretends, to be God's pleasure. How know you it to be God's pleasure that such or such an act should be abstained from? whence come you even to suppose as much? "Because the engaging in it would, I imagine, be prejudicial upon the whole to the happiness of mankind," says the partizan of the principle of utility: "Because the commission of it is attended with a gross and sensual, or at least with a trifling and transient satisfaction," says the partizan of the principle of asceticism: "Because I detest the thought of it; and I cannot, neither ought I to be called upon to tell why," says he who proceeds upon the principle of antipathy. In the words of one or other of these must that person necessarily answer (revelation apart) who professes to take for his standard the will of God.

agent sees beforehand that they will be so. This may make the action indeed a perfectly right action: but it does not make antipathy a right ground of action. For the same sentiment of antipathy, if implicitly deferred to, may be, and very frequently is, productive of the very worst effects. Antipathy, therefore, can never be a right ground of action. No more, therefore, can resentment, which, as will be seen more particularly hereafter, is but a modification of antipathy. The only right ground of action, that can possibly subsist, is, after all, the consideration of utility, which if it is a right principle of action, and of approbation, in any one case, is so in every other. Other principles in abundance, that is, other motives, may be the reasons why such and such an act *has* been done: that is, the reasons or causes of its being done: but it is this alone that can be the reason why it might or ought to have been done. Antipathy or resentment requires always to be regulated, to prevent its doing mischief to be regulated by what? always by the principle of utility. The principle of utility neither requires nor admits of any other regulator than itself.

OF THE FOUR SANCTIONS OR SOURCES OF PAIN AND PLEASURE

1. It has been shown that the happiness of the individuals, of whom a community is composed, that is their pleasures and their security, is the end and the sole end which the legislator ought to have in view: the sole standard, in conformity to which each individual ought, as far as depends upon the legislator, to be *made* to fashion his behaviour. But whether it be this or any thing else that is to be *done*, there is nothing by which a man can ultimately be *made* to do it, but either pain or pleasure. Having taken a general view of these two grand objects (*viz.,* pleasure, and what comes to the same thing, immunity from pain) in the character of *final* causes; it will be necessary to take a view of pleasure and pain itself, in the character of *efficient* causes or means.

2. There are four distinguishable sources from which pleasure and pain are in use to flow: considered separately, they may be termed the *physical,* the *political,* the *moral,* and the *religious:* and inasmuch as the pleasures and pains belonging to each of them are capable of giving a binding force to any law or rule of conduct, they may all of them be termed *sanctions.*

3. If it be in the present life, and from the ordinary course of nature, not purposely modified by the interposition of the will of any human being, nor by any extraordinary interposition of any superior invisible being, that the pleasure or the pain takes place or is expected, it may be said to issue from or to belong to the *physical sanction.*

4. If at the hands of a *particular* person or set of persons in the community, who under names correspondent to that of *judge,* are chosen for the particular purpose of dispensing it, according to the will of the sovereign or supreme ruling power in the state, it may be said to issue from the *political sanction.*

5. If at the hands of such *chance* persons in the community, as the party in question may happen in the course of his life to have concerns with, according to each man's spontaneous disposition, and not according to any settled or concerted rule, it may be said to issue from the *moral* or *popular sanction.*[7]

6. If from the immediate hand of a superior invisible being, either in the present life, or in a future, it may be said to issue from the *religious sanction.*

7. Pleasures or pains which may be expected to issue from the *physical, political,* or *moral* sanctions, must all of them be expected to be experienced, if ever, in the *present* life: those which may be expected to issue from the *religious* sanction, may be expected to be experienced either in the *present* life or in a *future.*

8. Those which can be experienced in the present life, can of course be no others

---

[7] Better termed *popular,* as more directly indicative of its constituent cause; as likewise of its relation to the more common phrase *public opinion,* in French *opinion publique,* the name there given to that tutelary power, of which of late so much is said, and by which so much is done. The latter appellation is however unhappy and inexpressive; since if *opinion* is material, it is only in virtue of the influence it exercises over action, through the medium of the affections and the will.

than such as human nature in the course of the present life is susceptible of: and from each of these sources may flow all the pleasures or pains of which, in the course of the present life, human nature is susceptible. With regard to these then (with which alone we have in this place any concern) those of them which belong to any one of those sanctions, differ not ultimately in kind from those which belong to any one of the other three: the only difference there is among them lies in the circumstances that accompany their production. A suffering which befalls a man in the natural and spontaneous course of things, shall be styled, for instance, a *calamity;* in which case, if it be supposed to befall him through any imprudence of his, it may be styled a punishment issuing from the physical sanction. Now this same suffering, if inflicted by the law, will be what is commonly called a *punishment;* if incurred for want of any friendly assistance, which the misconduct, or supposed misconduct, of the sufferer has occasioned to be withholden, a punishment issuing from the *moral* sanction; if through the immediate interposition of a particular providence, a punishment issuing from the *religious* sanction.

9. A man's goods, or his person, are consumed by fire. If this happened to him by what is called an accident, it was a calamity: if by reason of his own imprudence (for instance, from his neglecting to put his candle out) it may be styled a punishment of the physical sanction: if it happened to him by the sentence of the political magistrate, a punishment belonging to the political sanction; that is, what is commonly called a punishment: if for want of any assistance which his *neighbour* withheld from him out of some dislike to his *moral* character, a punishment of the *moral* sanction: if by an immediate act of *God's* displeasure, manifested an account of some *sin* committed by him, or through any distraction of mind, occasioned by the dread of such pleasure, a punishment of the *religious* sanction.[8]

---

[8] A suffering conceived to befall a man by the immediate act of God, as above, is often, for shortness' sake, called a *judgment:* instead of saying, a suffering inflicted on him in consequence of a special judgment formed, and resolution thereupon taken, by the Deity.

10. As to such of the pleasures and pains belonging to the religious sanction, as regard a future life, of what kind these may be we cannot know. These lie not open to our observation. During the present life they are matters only of expectation: and, whether that expectation be derived from natural or revealed religion, the particular kind of pleasure or pain, if it be different from all those which lie open to our observation, is what we can have no idea of. The best ideas we can obtain of such pains and pleasures are altogether unliquidated in point of quality. In what other respects our ideas of them *may* be liquidated will be considered in another place.

11. Of these four sanctions the physical is altogether, we may observe, the groundwork of the political and the moral, so is it also of the religious, in as far as the latter bears relation to the present life. It is included in each of those other three. This may operate in any case (that is, any of the pains or pleasures belonging to it may operate) independently of *them:* none of *them* can operate but by means of this. In a word, the powers of nature may operate of themselves; but neither the magistrate, nor men at large, *can* operate, nor is God in the case in question *supposed* to operate, but through the powers of nature.

12. For these four objects, which in their nature have so much in common, it seemed of use to find a common name. It seemed of use, in the first place, for the convenience of giving a name to certain pleasures and pains, for which a name equally characteristic could hardly otherwise have been found: in the second place, for the sake of holding up the efficacy of certain moral forces, the influence of which is apt not to be sufficiently attended to. Does the political sanction exert an influence over the conduct of mankind? The moral, the religious sanctions do so too. In every inch of his career are the operations of the political magistrate liable to be aided or impeded by these two foreign powers: who, one or other of them, or both, are sure to be either his rivals or his allies. Does it happen to him to leave them out of his calculations? he will be sure almost to find himself mistaken in the result. Of all this we shall find abundant proofs in the sequel of this work. It behoves him, therefore, to have them continually

before his eyes; and that under such a name as exhibits the relation they bear to his own purposes and designs.

VALUE OF A LOT OF PLEASURE OR PAIN, HOW TO BE MEASURED

1. Pleasures then, and the avoidance of pains, are the *ends* which the legislator has in view: it behoves him therefore to understand their *value*. Pleasures and pains are the *instruments* he has to work with: it behoves him therefore to understand their force, which is again, in other words, their value.

2. To a person considered *by himself,* the value of a pleasure or pain considered *by itself,* will be greater or less, according to the four following circumstances:[9]

    I. Its *intensity.*
    II. Its *duration.*
    III. Its *certainty* or *uncertainty.*
    IV. Its *propinquity* or *remoteness.*

3. These are the circumstances which are to be considered in estimating a pleasure or a pain considered each of them by itself. But when the value of any pleasure or pain is considered for the purpose of estimating the tendency of any *act* by which it is produced, there are two other circumstances to be taken into account; these are,

    V. Its *fecundity,* or the chance it has of being followed by sensations of the *same* kind: that is, pleasures, if it be a pleasure: pains, if it be a pain.

    VI. Its *purity,* or the chance it has of *not* being followed by sensations of the *opposite*

kind: that is, pains, if it be a pleasure: pleasures, if it be a pain.

These two last, however, are in strictness scarcely to be deemed properties of the pleasure or the pain itself; they are not, therefore, in strictness to be taken into the account of the value of that pleasure or that pain. They are in strictness to be deemed properties only of the act, or other event, by which such pleasure or pain has been produced; and accordingly are only to be taken into the account of the tendency of such act or such event.

4. To a *number* of persons, with reference to each of whom the value of a pleasure or a pain is considered, it will be greater or less, according to seven circumstances: to wit, the six preceeding ones; *viz.*

    I. Its *intensity.*
    II. Its *duration.*
    III. Its *certainty* or *uncertainty.*
    IV. Its *propinquity* or *remoteness.*
    V. Its *fecundity.*
    VI. Its *purity.*

And one other; to wit:

    VII. Its *extent;* that is, the number of persons to whom it *extends;* or (in other words) who are affected by it.

5. To take an exact account then of the general tendency of any act, by which the interests of a community are affected, proceed as follows. Begin with any one person of those whose interests seem most immediately to be affected by it: and take an account.

    I. Of the value of each distinguishable *pleasure* which appears to be produced by it in the *first* instance.

    II. Of the value of each *pain* which appears to be produced by it in the *first* instance.

    III. Of the value of each pleasure which appears to be produced by it *after* the first. This constitutes the *fecundity* of the first *pleasure* and the *impurity* of the first *pain.*

    IV. Of the value of each *pain* which appears to be produced by it after the first. This constitutes the *fecundity* of the first *pain,* and the *impurity* of the first *pleasure.*

    V. Sum up all the values of all the *pleasures* on the one side, and those of all the pains on the other. The balance, if it be on the side of pleasure, will give the *good* tendency of the act upon the whole, with respect to the interests of that *individual*

---

[9] These circumstances have since been denominated *elements* or *dimensions* of *value* in a pleasure or a pain.

Not long after the publication of the first edition, the following memoriter verses were framed, in the view of lodging more effectually, in the memory, these points, on which the whole fabric of morals and legislation may be seen to rest.

Intense, long, certain, speedy, fruitful, pure—
Such marks in *pleasures* and in *pains* endure.
Such pleasures seek if *private* be thy end:
If it be *public,* wide let them *extend.*
Such *pains* avoid, whichever be thy view:
If pains *must* come, let them *extend* to few.

person; if on the side of pain, the *bad* tendency of it upon the whole.

VI. Take an account of the *number* of persons whose interests appear to be concerned; and repeat the above process with respect to each. *Sum up* the numbers expressive of the degrees of *good* tendency, which the act has, with respect to each individual, in regard to whom the tendency of it is *good* upon the whole: do this again with respect to each individual, in regard to whom the tendency of it is *bad* upon the whole. Take the *balance;* which, if on the side of *pleasure,* will give the general *good tendency* of the act, with respect to the total number or community of individuals concerned; if on the side of pain, the general *evil tendency,* with respect to the same community.

6. It is not to be expected that this process should be strictly pursued previously to every moral judgment, or to every legislative or judicial operation. It may, however, be always kept in view: and as near as the process actually pursued on these occasions approaches to it, so near will such process approach to the character of an exact one.

7. The same process is alike applicable to pleasure and pain, in whatever shape they appear: and by whatever denomination they are distinguished: to pleasure, whether it be called *good* (which is properly the cause or instrument of pleasure) or *profit* (which is distant pleasure, or the cause or instrument of distant pleasure) or *convenience,* or *advantage, benefit, emolument, happiness,* and so forth: to pain, whether it be called *evil* (which corresponds to *good*) or *mischief,* or *inconvenience,* or *disadvantage,* or *loss,* or *unhappiness,* and so forth.

8. Nor is this a novel and unwarranted, any more than it is a useless theory. In all this there is nothing but what the practice of mankind, wheresoever they have a clear view of their own interest, is perfectly conformable to. An article of property, an estate in land, for instance, is valuable, on what account? On account of the pleasures of all kinds which it enables a man to produce, and what comes to the same thing the pains of all kinds which it enables him to avert. But the value of such an article of property is universally understood to rise or fall according to the length or shortness of the time which a man has in it: the certainty or uncertainty of its coming into possession: and the nearness or remoteness of the time at which, if at all, it is to come into possession. As to the *intensity* of the pleasures which a man may derive from it, this is never thought of, because it depends upon the use which each particular person may come to make of it: which cannot be estimated till the particular pleasures he may come to derive from it, or the particular pains he may come to exclude by means of it, are brought to view. For the same reason, neither does he think of the *fecundity* or *purity* of those pleasures.

CHAPTER TWENTY-SIX

TOCQUEVILLE

Every revolution contains a utopian element that inspires its makers and is indispensable to its success. The leaders of the English, American, and French revolutions in the seventeenth and eighteenth centuries looked upon democracy, not as a beginning, but as the end—the culmination of man's age-long struggle for freedom. As long as democracy was a dream, it was impossible to appraise it realistically, and the history of the discussions of democracy from Plato to Burke suffers from a sense of unreality and lack of sufficient experience. Defenders of democracy often saw in it a kind of paradise within the reach of man, whereas its opponents predicted that, if it were ever allowed to exist long enough, it would end in the destruction of society and the moral values that support it.

Various experiences in democracy had failed. The Puritan Revolution was democratic in inspiration, but it was unable to provide a true object lesson of democracy because it quickly turned into dictatorship. The Glorious Revolution of 1688, more successful than the Puritan Revolution in establishing itself as a lasting political regime, was liberal-conservative rather than radical-democratic. In the eighteenth century, England therefore attracted liberal aristocrats like Montesquieu but had little room for radical democrats like Tom Paine. The latter had to flee his native land to escape political persecution after he had vehemently defended the French Revolution in his controversy with Edmund Burke.

The French Revolution, too, which started with so little violence in 1789, ceased to be an experiment in democracy in 1799, when Napoleon set up a military dictatorship, and shortly thereafter his own brand of monarchy. Napoleon's regime was followed by the even less democratic restoration of the Bourbons, who attempted to go back to the prerevolutionary government of kingship by divine right, in alliance with the clergy and aristocracy. But the Bourbons, who had learned nothing and forgotten nothing, did not retain the throne for long. The Revolution of July, 1830, ousted King Charles X and established a constitutional monarchy in which the middle class was the predominant political and social element. The way was again open for experiments in popular government.

The first major democracy in the modern world is that of the United States; only after its establishment and success could the issue of democracy be brought down from the clouds of subjunctive and hypothetical speculation to the firm ground of positive and empirical observation. The political writer in the nineteenth century first to perceive that democracy was the "irresistible" new form of society and government, and that the United States was the world's key laboratory of democracy, was an aristocratic Frenchman, Alexis de Tocqueville (1805–1859).

Tocqueville's family belonged to the oldest Norman nobility, and one of his ancestors had fought at the Battle of Hastings. Tocqueville's interest in politics came to him naturally. His family had long been active in the magistracy and public administration, and his father was prefect, the highest government authority, in several departments of France. Tocqueville thus had ample opportunity to see the big and little problems of government from the inside. During the Revolution, Tocqueville's maternal grandmother and an aunt were executed, and his parents narrowly escaped the same fate. His father's hair turned white at the age of twenty-one as a result of harassing experiences and imprisonments.

Tocqueville studied the law, as was the tradition of his family, and at the age of twenty-one he embarked on a judicial career. From 1839 to 1848 he was a member of the Chamber of Deputies, where he voted, slightly Left of Center, with the constitutional opposition. In 1849 he was Foreign Minister for a few months. After Louis Napoleon set up his dictatorship, Tocqueville retired from public life, despite the former's repeated attempts to secure his collaboration. Tocqueville was not an outstanding parliamentarian, and he lacked the knack of the practical politician in dealing with people. But the rigorous and uncompromising standards that kept him from being a successful party leader and vote getter also prevented him from participating in the public affairs of a dictatorship. His retirement from active politics gave him time to write a penetrating analysis, *The Old Regime and the Revolution* (1856). He broke new ground by emphasizing the elements of continuity in the French Revolution rather than those of sudden change: "The despot fell; but the most substantial portion of his work remained; his administrative system survived his government."

Tocqueville's most famous book, and his most enduring contribution to political thought, is his *Democracy in America* (1835–1840). It is generally conceded to be the greatest work on the United States written by a foreign observer, and it would be difficult to find a work of similar depth and penetration written by an American on his own country. Nothing dates as quickly as books on other countries, yet *Democracy in America* has retained its original freshness and appeal. What is equally astonishing is that Tocqueville was able to grasp so much of American civilization after a stay of only nine months, and that the first part of *Democracy in America* was published when the author was barely thirty years old (the second part came out five years later). His ability to forecast the future—which is little different from the ability to interpret the present correctly—is illustrated by the statement that the time would come when North America would be inhabited by one hundred and fifty million people, and that Russia and the United States would each "sway the destinies of half the globe." There is some repetition in *Democracy in America,* which detracts from its readability and adds unnecessarily to its length, but its general impact is one of balance, reflection, sympathy, and—perhaps Tocqueville's most appealing quality—fairness.

Shortly after the July Revolution of 1830 introduced constitutional government into France, Tocqueville and a friend, Gustave de Beaumont, decided to visit America; officially, the purpose was to study the prison system in the United States, but in reality Tocqueville was eager to study democracy where he thought it was most firmly established. "I confess," Tocqueville says, "that in America I saw more than America; I sought the image of democracy itself, with its inclinations, its character, its prejudices, and its passions, in order to learn what we have to fear or to hope from its progress."

Tocqueville starts his introduction to *Democracy in America* with the very substance of his book: "Among the novel objects that attracted my attention during my stay in the

United States, nothing struck me more forcibly than the general equality of conditions." Whereas students of politics have, in the twentieth century, frequently separated the study of government from the folkways of a people, its way of life, its social, educational, economic, and religious institutions, Tocqueville realized that equality of conditions, the "fundamental fact" of American life, extended "far beyond the political character and the laws of the country, and that it has no less empire over civil society than over the Government; it creates opinions, engenders sentiments, suggests the ordinary practices of life, and modifies whatever it does not produce."

Tocqueville was one of the first European political writers to see that the age of European mastery and leadership in political inventiveness was passing away, and that the United States was destined to be the world's great experiment in democracy. Intellectually, the United States of the early nineteenth century was little more than a province or colony of England, and it was treated as such by most visiting English writers and lecturers. They were amused by the crudities and banalities of American life but failed to see that below the surface a new social and political principle was struggling for recognition and realization. By contrast, Tocqueville perceived that the United States, in the past a dependency of Europe, was going to play an active, independent, and decisive part in the future. What few Americans themselves would believe before the middle of the twentieth century, Tocqueville saw early in the nineteenth: that the United States would cease to be the pupil of Europe and become its teacher, and that the Americanization of the world—not in the sense of imperialist conquest, but of ever-increasing equality of conditions—was inevitable.

Tocqueville understood that the American and French revolutions, like the upheavals in other parts of Europe and the Americas, were not isolated events but parts of a *world revolution:* "It is evident to all alike that a great democratic revolution is going on among us." Tocqueville saw that the French Revolution was not an event but a continuous *process,* and that the Revolution of 1830, which he himself witnessed, was only one act of a drama the end of which he knew he was not to behold. He was convinced that the United States was the most advanced nation in the world revolution of equality, and, he said, "It appears to me beyond a doubt that sooner or later we shall arrive, like the Americans, at an almost complete equality of conditions."

In the preface to the twelfth edition of *Democracy in America* (1848), Toqueville writes that the principle of popular sovereignty, "enthroned in France but yesterday," had held undivided sway in the United States for sixty years in the most direct, unlimited, and absolute manner. While all the nations of Europe were devastated by war or torn by civil strife, the United States alone remained at peace, guaranteeing the rights of property and avoiding the pitfalls of both anarchy and despotism: "Where else could we find greater cause of hope, or more instructive lessons? Let us look to America, not in order to make a servile copy of the institutions that she has established, but to gain a clearer view of the polity that will be the best for us; let us look there less to find examples than instruction; let us borrow from her the principles, rather than the details, of her laws."

Tocqueville had no illusions about the future of his class. In a letter to Henry Reeve, the translator of *Democracy in America,* Tocqueville says (March 22, 1837) that aristocracy was dead when he was born, and that he could have no affection for it, since "one can be strongly attached only to the living." However, his realization that the age of government by privilege was gone did not lead him to embrace democracy unquestioningly and unhesitatingly. The real alternative was no longer between aristocracy and democracy, he felt. It was between "democracy without poetry and elevation indeed, but with order and morality, and an undisciplined and depraved democracy, subject to sudden frenzies, or to a yoke heavier than any that has galled mankind since the fall of the Roman Empire." Democracy—not only democratic government, but a way of life built on equality—was, Tocqueville saw, the "irresistible future."

What concerned him, however, was the difficulty of *reconciling individuality and liberty with democratic equality.* This is the central theme of *Democracy in America* and the major contribution of Tocqueville to modern political thought. He saw, more clearly than any of his contemporaries, that equality was not an invention of French and American revolutionary agitators, or of clever conspirators who managed to beguile the people and overthrow the established order of state and society. Approaching the issue of equality from an institutional rather than from a purely ideological viewpoint, Tocqueville found that the process of leveling and equalizing had been going on in Europe for seven hundred years, and that "absolute kings were the most efficient levellers of ranks among their subjects." The French and American Revolutions were not, Tocqueville thought, sharp breaks with the past as much as accelerations of trends that had already operated for centuries.

The human (as distinct from the administrative) problem of equality was nearer its solution in democracy than in monarchy and aristocracy, but the central issue of liberty still persisted. Whereas enthusiastic democrats assumed that liberty would cease to be a serious issue in democracy, Tocqueville pointed out that democracy, by the very fact of solving the issue of equality, created new problems of liberty that had not hitherto existed. Democracy demanded a "new science of politics indispensable to a new world," and the experience of the past could not sufficiently illuminate its difficulties, because there was no parallel to it in any age up to the "remotest antiquity."

Tocqueville saw—and his profound insight is still not fully grasped and acted upon in democratic societies—that the threat to liberty is potentially more real and menacing in a democracy than in a monarchy or an aristocracy: "The authority of a king is purely physical, and it controls the actions of the subject without subduing his private will; but the majority possesses a power which is physical and moral at the same time; it acts upon the will as well as upon the actions of men, and it represses not only all contest, but all controversy." Tocqueville saw that democratic despotism would work differently from the classical forms of one-man or class tyranny: "It would be more extensive and more mild; it would degrade men without tormenting them."

Tocqueville emphasizes, in particular, one kind of despotism in a democracy that is not easy to discern because it does not work openly, through political or legal sanctions: the *power of public opinion to suppress unpopular views.* Without being exposed "to the terrors of an auto-da-fé," the individual of unorthodox views may find his political career closed, be ostracized, shunned, spurned, and scorned by his fellow citizens, and abandoned by his friends who are most persuaded of his innocence, "lest they should be shunned in their turn." Nothing disturbed Tocqueville more in his study of democracy than the "quiet and gentle" kind of terror and intimidation that does not destroy, but prevents, existence; that does not tyrannize, but compresses, enervates, extinguishes, and stupefies people "till each nation is reduced to be nothing better than a flock of timid and industrious animals, of which the government is the shepherd."

The concept of the "tyranny of the majority" was not invented by Tocqueville. From Locke to Madison, leaders of liberal thought and statesmanship had wrestled with the problem of how to combine the principle of majority rule with that of individual liberty—a theme which also dominated the framers of the American Constitution. Yet, this classical liberal fear of the tyranny of the majority was focused on government and politics, and the remedies therefore for preventing it were also political and institutional: bicameralism, checks and balances, separation of powers, an independent judiciary, bills of rights, federalism—all these institutional safeguards were designed to protect individual liberty against the potential tyranny of the majority. The fear of the tyranny of the numerical majority was largely based on the realistic understanding of inherent conflicts in society, most pungently and frankly expressed by Madison, who considered "the various and unequal distribution of property" the "most common and durable source of factions" (*The Federalist,* No. 10).

Tocqueville was fully aware of the political and institutional aspects of the potential tyranny of the majority, and he thoroughly discusses these aspects in *Democracy in America.* Yet his main interest—and in this he broke new ground—was in democratic despotism of *society* rather than of government. Such despotism was the result—and here Tocqueville differs again sharply from the classical liberals from Locke to Madison—of too much agreement in society about basic moral issues, and not of too much social conflict, as the classical liberals from Locke to Madison had thought. The remedy for this tyranny of public opinion over the individual was much more difficult to find than in the case of political majority tyranny. Institutional devices would not do, since the oppression of the individual by public opinion was not institutional but mental, making itself felt through subtle social pressure rather than through overt acts of government. Moreover, a major difficulty in coping with the tyranny of public opinion was the fact that many individuals cheerfully submitted to that tyranny because they sincerely believed that public opinion was right.

Tocqueville in the end pins his hope on the education of man, so he can attain independence of character and rational knowledge, both of which will make him understand the invisible chains of the tyranny of society over his mind and conduct. However, Tocqueville was never sure that the mass of mankind had the ability to attain such levels of character and rationality. He had enough realism and common sense to grasp the importance of institutional devices in seeking to harmonize the principles of liberty and equality. Yet he also possessed the depth of insight which made him aware of the supreme importance of the moral and intellectual qualities of the individuals who make up a democratic society and government.

Tocqueville felt a kind of "religious dread" in contemplating "so irresistible a revolution" as the spread of democracy, and his attitude toward it was never free from ambivalence. He was keenly sensitive to the values of the individual, the unique, the lofty in man, and was distressed by the mediocrity, greed, and triviality in democracies: "When I survey this countless multitude of beings, shaped in each other's likeness, amidst whom nothing rises and nothing falls, the sight of such universal uniformity saddens and chills me, and I am tempted to regret that state of society which has ceased to be." Yet, despite his fears and apprehensions, Tocqueville concludes *Democracy in America* with a note of hope: "A state of equality is perhaps less elevated, but it is more just; and its justice constitutes its greatness and beauty."

Rejecting the view that man is a helpless prisoner of blind and fatal forces—history, race, soil, and climate—Tocqueville asserts man's freedom by virtue of his moral essence: "Providence has not created mankind entirely independent or entirely free. It is true that around every man a fatal circle is traced, beyond which he cannot pass; but within the wide verge of that circle he is powerful and free: as it is with man, so with communities. The nations of our time cannot prevent the conditions of men from becoming equal: but it depends upon themselves whether the principle of equality is to lead them to servitude or freedom, to knowledge or barbarism, to prosperity or to wretchedness."

In November, 1841, Tocqueville wrote a note to himself, entitled "My Instinct, My Opinions," which expresses more strongly—and perhaps more frankly because not meant for publication—his profound apprehension, and even a certain antipathy, with regard to democracy. "Intellectually," Tocqueville says in this note, "I have an inclination for democratic institutions, but I am an aristocrat by instinct—that is to say, I despise and fear the mob. I love passionately liberty, law, and respect for rights, but not democracy. There is the ultimate truth of my soul." As on so many other occasions, Tocqueville insisted that he was neither revolutionary nor conservative, yet "when all is said and done, I hold more by the latter than the former. For I differ from the latter more as to means than as to end, while I differ from the former both as to means and end. Liberty is my first passion. This is the truth."

Tocqueville's intellectual acceptance of democracy was rooted in two feelings: first, that it is irresistible, and that to oppose it with blind, sterile hatred would therefore be futile; second, he was skeptical enough to tolerate democracy without embracing it passionately. In his *Recollections* (written in 1850), he says that "what we call necessary institutions are often no more than institutions to which we have grown accustomed," this referring to traditional forms of social organization. Tocqueville's pragmatic attitude toward democracy was hesitant, fearful, and ambivalent, but he was willing to give it a fair chance.

This openness of mind, the attempt to build a political philosophy on empiricism and expediency, without the extremes of revolution and reaction, draws him into spiritual kinship with Bodin and Montesquieu. All three belong to the same spiritual family in France, though their backgrounds and ideas differed, and all three have contributed to an intellectual tradition of moderation, conciliation, and antifanaticism. In essence the tradition reflects a temper as much as a body of doctrine—the willingness to accept the second best rather than kill for the absolutely best.

One of the most prophetic passages in *Democracy in America* deals with the rise of an *aristocracy of manufacturers* in democratic societies. Tocqueville notes that democracy is favorable to the growth of industry for two reasons: first, there is the emphasis on material welfare for all, rather than for a small aristocratic class, so that the demand for goods is constantly increasing; second, equality of opportunity encourages talent to enter the field of business and industry and to acquire wealth without restrictions of birth, class, and caste. Inevitably, the expansion of manufacturing produces a new type of working class, highly specialized, and employed according to the principle of division of labor. But, while economically efficient, mass production has serious social effects because "in proportion as the workman improves, the man is degraded." The more the worker concentrates his effort and intelligence on a single detail, the more the employer has to survey an extensive whole, so that the mind of the latter is broadened in proportion as that of the former is narrowed. The *employer* resembles more and more the *administrator of a vast empire,* and the worker becomes more and more a brute. Between worker and employer there are frequent relations but "no real partnership." As industry becomes more settled, social relations become more rigid: the worker is continually dependent on the employer "and seems as much born to obey as that other is to command. What is that but aristocracy?"

As an aristocrat of preindustrial background, Tocqueville is keenly sensitive to the differences between the old landed and the new manufacturing aristocracy. In the first, the tie between the landlord and his men was one of shared experience rather than of weekly pay checks. In the age of manufacturing, the employer is not settled among those he employs, and his contact with them is confined to one aspect of life: he asks nothing of them but their labor, and they expect nothing but their wages. Between employer and workers there is thus no permanent tie of habit, duty, custom, or usage, whereas in the old landed aristocracy the master was obliged to protect, aid, and relieve his men, and they to defend and serve him. By contrast, the manufacturing aristocracy first impoverishes the men who serve it and then abandons them to public charity. It has no sense of public responsibility, and its aim is not to govern the population but to use it.

Because of its lack of responsibility the new industrial aristocracy is, Tocqueville predicts, the harshest that ever existed. He advises friends of democracy to "keep their eyes anxiously fixed in this direction; for if ever a permanent inequality of conditions and aristocracy again penetrate into the world, it may be predicted that this is the channel by which they will enter."

But Tocqueville did not think that the *discrepancy between political equality and economic inequality* would be indefinitely accepted by a democratic people. He saw that the first phase of the democratic world revolution, political in nature, would inevitably lead to a second phase, which would be primarily social and economic: "Those who believe that complete equality can be established in a permanent way in the political world without introducing at the same time a certain equality in civil society, seem to me to commit a dangerous error." The July Revolution of 1830 was the last purely political revolution in France, Tocqueville thought, and he foresaw that the next upheaval would result from economic grievances.

The February Revolution of 1848 was the first in which the industrial working class played a major role, and Tocqueville predicted before the Revolution on what issue the major battles of the future would be fought: "Before long, the political struggle will be restricted to those who have and those who have not; property will form the great field of battle." Only a few weeks before the outbreak of the February Revolution of 1848, Tocqueville said in a speech in the Chamber of Deputies that the passions of the working classes had turned from political to social questions, and that they were forming ideas and opinions destined "not only to upset this or that law, ministry, or even form of government, but society itself, until it totters upon the foundations on which it rests today."

The people are bound to discover, Tocqueville reflects in his *Recollections,* that, having destroyed all other obstacles to equality, the privilege of property remains the only obstacle. Yet he did not think that the people would necessarily use their legislative sovereignty to abolish altogether the institution of property, "the foundation of our social order." He hesitated to predict what specific form popular control of property in a democracy would eventually take because "in matters of social constitution the field of possibilities is much more extensive than men living in their various societies are ready to imagine."

Tocqueville was one of the first political thinkers in the nineteenth century to perceive the long-term pressure of economic inequality on political democracy. He understood, with consummate clarity, the paradoxical relation between democracy and the Industrial Revolution: on the one hand, democracy favors the growth of an industrial economy with its rising living standards for the people; and on the other hand, the process of industrialization creates new problems of inequality which in the past have threatened the foundations of democracy. The dilemma of democracy has been liberty or equality.

TOCQUEVILLE

*Democracy in America**

TYRANNY OF THE MAJORITY

I hold it to be an impious and an execrable maxim that, politically speaking, a people has a right to do whatsoever it pleases, and yet I have asserted that all authority originates in the will of the majority Am I, then, in contradiction with myself?

A general law—which bears the name of Justice—has been made and sanctioned, not only by it majority of this or that people, but by a majority of mankind. The rights of every people are consequently confined within the limits of what is just. A nation may be considered in the light of it jury which is empowered to represent society at large, and to apply the great and general law of Justice. Ought such a jury, which represents society, to have more power than the society in which the laws it applies originate?

When I refuse to obey an unjust law, I do not contest the right which the majority has of commanding, but I simply appeal from the sovereignty of the people to the sovereignty of mankind. It has been asserted that a people can never entirely outstep the boundaries of justice and of reason in those affairs which are more peculiarly its own; and that consequently full power may fearlessly be given to the majority by which it is represented. But this language is that of a slave.

A majority taken collectively may be regarded as a being whose opinions, and most frequently whose interests, are opposed to those of another being, which is styled a minority. If it be admitted that a man, possessing absolute power, may misuse that power by wronging his adversaries, why should a majority not be liable to the same reproach? Men are not apt to change their characters by agglomeration; nor does their patience in the presence of obstacles increase with the consciousness of their strength. And for these reasons I can never willingly invest any number of my fellow-creatures with that unlimited authority which I should refuse to any one of them.

I do not think that it is possible to combine several principles in the same government, so as at the same time to maintain freedom, and really to oppose them to one another. The form of government which is usually termed *mixed* has always appeared to me to be a mere chimera. Accurately speaking there is no such thing as a mixed government (with the meaning usually given to that word), because in all communities some one principle of action may be discovered, which preponderates over the others. England in the last century, which has been more especially cited as an example of this form of government, was in point of fact an essentially aristocratic state, although it comprised very powerful elements of democracy: for the laws and customs of the country were such, that the aristocracy could not but preponderate in the end, and subject the direction of public affairs to its own will. The error arose from too much attention being paid to the actual struggle which was going on between the nobles and the people, without considering the probable issue of the contest, which was in reality the important point. When a community really has a mixed government, that is to say, when it is equally divided between two adverse

---

*From Alexis de Tocqueville, *Democracy in America* (1835–1840; trans. Henry Reeve, 1835–1840).

principles, it must either pass through a revolution, or fall into complete dissolution.

I am therefore of opinion that some one social power must always be made to predominate over the others; but I think that liberty is endangered when this power is checked by no obstacles which may retard its course, and force it to moderate its own vehemence.

Unlimited power is in itself a bad and dangerous thing; human beings are not competent to exercise it with discretion; and God alone can be omnipotent, because his wisdom and his justice are always equal to his power. But no power upon earth is so worthy of honor for itself, or of reverential obedience to the rights which it represents, that I would consent to admit its uncontrolled and all-predominant authority. When I see that the right and the means of absolute command are conferred on a people or upon a king, upon an aristocracy or a democracy, a monarchy or a republic, I recognize the germ of tyranny, and I journey onwards to a land of more hopeful institutions.

In my opinion the main evil of the present democratic institutions of the United States does not arise, as is often asserted in Europe, from their weakness, but from their overpowering strength; and I am not so much alarmed at the excessive liberty which reigns in that country, as at the very inadequate securities which exist against tyranny.

When an individual or a party is wronged in the United States, to whom can he apply for redress? If to public opinion, public opinion constitutes the majority; if to the legislature, it represents the majority, and implicitly obeys its injunctions; if to the executive power, it is appointed by the majority and remains a passive tool in its hands; the public troops consist of the majority under arms; the jury is the majority invested with the right of hearing judicial cases; and in certain States even the judges are elected by the majority. However iniquitous or absurd the evil of which you complain may be, you must submit to it as well as you can.

If, on the other hand, a legislative power could be so constituted as to represent the majority without necessarily being the slave of its passions; an executive, so as to retain a certain degree of uncontrolled authority; and a judiciary, so as to remain independent of the two other powers; a government would be formed which would still be democratic, without incurring any risk of tyrannical abuse.

I do not say that tyrannical abuses frequently occur in America at the present day; but I maintain that no sure barrier is established against them, and that the causes which mitigate the government are to be found in the circumstances and the manners of the country more than in its laws.

POWER OF THE MAJORITY
OVER PUBLIC OPINION

It is in the examination of the display of public opinion in the United States, that we clearly perceive how far the power of the majority surpasses all the powers with which we are acquainted in Europe. Intellectual principles exercise an influence which is so invisible and often so inappreciable, that they baffle the toils of oppression. At the present time the most absolute monarchs in Europe are unable to prevent certain notions, which are opposed to their authority, from circulating in secret throughout their dominions, and even in their courts. Such is not the case in America; as long as the majority is still undecided, discussion is carried on; but as soon as its decision is irrevocably pronounced, a submissive silence is observed; and the friends, as well as the opponents of the measure, unite in assenting to its propriety. The reason of this is perfectly clear: no monarch is so absolute as to combine all the powers of society in his own hands, and to conquer all opposition, with the energy of a majority, which is invested with the right of making and of executing the laws.

The authority of a king is purely physical, and it controls the actions of the subject without subduing his private will; but the majority possesses a power which is physical and moral at the same time; it acts upon the will as well as upon the actions of men, and it represses not only all contest, but all controversy.

I know no country in which there is so little true independence of mind and freedom of discussion as in America. In any constitutional state in Europe every sort of religious and political theory may be advocated and propagated abroad; for there is no country in Europe so subdued by any single authority, as not to contain citizens who are ready to protect the man who raises his voice in the cause of truth, from the consequences of his hardihood. If he is unfortunate enough to live under an absolute government, the people is upon his side; if he inhabits a free country, he may find a shelter behind the authority of the throne, if he require one. The aristocratic part of society supports him in some countries, and the democracy in others. But in a nation where democratic institutions exist, organized like those of the United States, there is but one sole authority, one single element of strength and of success, with nothing beyond it.

In America, the majority arises very formidable barriers to the liberty of opinion: within these barriers an author may write whatever he pleases, but he will repent it if he ever step beyond them. Not that he is exposed to the terrors of an auto-da-fé, but he is tormented by the slights and persecutions of daily obloquy. His political career is closed for ever, since he has offended the only authority which is able to promote his success. Every sort of compensation, even that of celebrity, is refused to him. Before he published his opinions, he imagined that he held them in common with many others; but no sooner has he declared them openly than he is loudly censured by his overbearing opponents, whilst those who think, without having the courage to speak, like him, abandon him in silence. He yields at length, oppressed by the daily efforts he has been making, and he subsides into silence as if he was tormented by remorse for having spoken the truth.

Fetters and headsmen were the coarse instruments which tyranny formerly employed; but the civilization of our age has refined the arts of despotism, which seemed however to have been sufficiently perfected before. The excesses of monarchical power had devised a variety of physical means of oppression; the democratic republics of the present day have rendered it as entirely an affair of the mind, as that will which it is intended to coerce. Under the absolute sway of an individual despot, the body was attacked in order to subdue the soul; and the soul escaped the blows which were directed against it, and rose superior to the attempt; but such is not the course adopted by tyranny in democratic republics; there the body is left free, and the soul is enslaved. The sovereign can no longer say, "You shall think as I do on pain of death": but he says, "You are free to think differently from me, and to retain your life, your property, and all that you possess; but if such be your determination, you are henceforth an alien among your people. You may retain your civil rights, but they will be useless to you, for you will never be chosen by your fellow-citizens, if you solicit their suffrages; and they will affect to scorn you, if you solicit their esteem. You will remain among men, but you will be deprived of the rights of mankind. Your fellow-creatures will shun you like an impure being; and those who are most persuaded of your innocence will abandon you too, lest they should be shunned in their turn. Go in peace! I have given you your life, but it is an existence imcomparably worse than death."

Absolute monarchies have thrown an odium upon despotism; let us beware lest democratic republics should restore oppression, and should render it less odious and less degrading in the eyes of the many, by making it still more onerous to the few.

Works have been published in the proudest nations of the Old World, expressly intended to censure the vices and deride the follies of the time: Labruyère inhabited the palace of Louis XIV when he composed his chapter upon the Great, and Molière criticized the courtiers in the very pieces which were acted before the Court. But the ruling power in the United States is not to be made game of; the smallest reproach irritates its sensibility, and the slightest joke which has any foundation in truth renders it indignant; from the style of its language to the more solid virtues of its character, everything must be made the subject of encomium. No writer, whatever be his eminence, can escape from this tribute or adulation to his fellow-citizens. The majority lives in the perpetual practice of self-applause; and there are certain truths which the Americans can only learn from strangers or from experience.

If great writers have not at present existed in America, the reason is very simply given in these facts; there can be no literary genius without freedom of opinion, and freedom of opinion does not exist in America. The

Inquisition has never been able to prevent a vast number of antireligious books from circulating in Spain. The empire of the majority succeeds much better in the United States, since it actually removes the wish of publishing them. Unbelievers are to be met with in America, but, to say the truth, there is no public organ of infidelity. Attempts have been made by some governments to protect the morality of nations by prohibiting licentious books. In the United States no one is punished for this sort of works, but no one is induced to write them; not because all the citizens are immaculate in their manners, but because the majority of the community is decent and orderly.

In these cases the advantages derived from the exercise of this power are unquestionable; and I am simply discussing the nature of the power itself. This irresistible authority is a constant fact, and its judicial exercise is an accidental occurrence.

WHY DEMOCRATIC NATIONS LOVE EQUALITY MORE THAN LIBERTY

The first and most intense passion which is engendered by the equality of conditions is, I need hardly say, the love of that same equality. My readers will therefore not be surprised that I speak of it before all others.

Everybody has remarked, that in our time, and especially in France, this passion for equality is every day gaining ground in the human heart. It has been said a hundred times that our contemporaries are far more ardently and tenaciously attached to equality then to freedom; but, as I do not find that the causes of the fact have been sufficiently analyzed, I shall endeavour to point them out.

It is possible to imagine an extreme point at which freedom and equality would meet and be confounded together. Let us suppose that all the members of the community take a part in the government, and that each one of them has an equal right to take a part in it. As none is different from his fellows, none can exercise a tyrannical power: men will be perfectly free, because they will all be entirely equal; and they will all be perfectly equal, because they will be entirely free. To this ideal state democratic nations tend. Such is the completest form that

equality can assume upon earth; but there are a thousand others which, without being equally perfect, are not less cherished by those nations.

The principle of equality may be established in civil society, without prevailing in the political world. Equal rights may exist of indulging in the same pleasures, of entering the same professions, of frequenting the same places—in a word, of living in the same manner and seeking wealth by the same means, although all men do not take an equal share in the government.

A kind of equality may even be established in the political world, though there should be no political freedom there. A man may be the equal of all his countrymen save one, who is the master of all without distinction, and who selects equally from among them all the agents of his power.

Several other combinations might be easily imagined, by which very great equality would be united to institutions more or less free, or even to institutions wholly without freedom.

Although men cannot become absolutely equal unless they be entirely free, and consequently equality, pushed to its furthest extent, may be confounded with freedom, yet there is good reason for distinguishing the one from the other. The taste which men have for liberty, and that which they feel for equality, are, in fact, two different things; and I am not afraid to add, that, among democratic nations, they are two unequal things.

Upon close inspection, it will be seen that there is in every age some peculiar and preponderating fact with which all others are connected; this fact almost always gives birth to some pregnant idea or some ruling passion, which attracts to itself, and bears away in its course, all the feelings and opinions of the time: it is like a great stream, toward which each of the surrounding rivulets seems to flow.

Freedom has appeared in the world at different times and under various forms; it has not been exclusively bound to any social condition, and it is not confined to democracies. Freedom cannot, therefore, form the distinguishing characteristic of democratic ages. The peculiar and preponderating fact which marks those ages as its own is the equality of conditions; the ruling passion of men in those periods is the love of this equality. Ask not what singular charm the men of democratic ages find in being equal, or what special reasons they may have for clinging so tenaciously to equality rather than to the other advantages which society holds out to them: equality is the distinguishing characteristic of the age they live in; that, of itself, is enough to explain that they prefer it to all the rest.

But independently of this reason there are several others, which will at all times habitually lead men to prefer equality to freedom.

If a people could ever succeed in destroying, or even diminishing, the equality which prevails in its own body, this could only be accomplished by long and laborious efforts. Its social condition must be modified, its laws abolished, its opinions superseded, its habits changed, its manners corrupted. But political liberty is more easily lost; to neglect to hold it fast, is to allow it to escape.

Men therefore not only cling to equality because it is dear to them; they also adhere to it because they think it will last for ever.

That political freedom may compromise in its excesses the tranquillity, the property, the lives of individuals, is obvious to the narrowest and most unthinking minds. But, on the contrary, none but attentive and clearsighted men perceive the perils with which equality threatens us, and they commonly avoid pointing them out. They know that the calamities they apprehend are remote, and flatter themselves that they will only fall upon future generations, for which the present generation takes but little thought. The evils which freedom sometimes brings with it are immediate; they are apparent to all, and all are more or less affected by them. The evils which extreme equality may produce are slowly disclosed; they creep gradually into the social frame; they are only seen at intervals, and at the moment at which they become most violent, habit already causes them to be no longer felt.

The advantages which freedom brings are only shown by length of time; and it is always easy to mistake the cause in which they originate. The advantages of equality are instantaneous, and they may constantly be traced from their source.

Political liberty bestows exalted pleasures, from time to time, upon a certain number of citizens. Equality every day confers a number of small enjoyments on every man. The charms of equality are every instant felt, and are within the reach of all: the noblest hearts are not insensible to them, and the most vulgar souls exult in them. The passion which equality engenders must therefore be at once strong and general. Men cannot enjoy political liberty unpurchased by some sacrifices, and they never obtain it without great exertions. But the pleasures of equality are self-proffered: each of the petty incidents of life seems to occasion them, and in order to taste them nothing is required but to live.

Democratic nations are at all times fond of equality, but there are certain epochs at which the passion they entertain for it swells to the height of fury. This occurs at the moment when the old social system, long menaced, completes its own destruction after a last intestine struggle, and when the barriers of rank are at length thrown down. At such times men pounce upon equality as their booty, and they cling to it as to some precious treasure which they fear to lose. The passion for equality penetrates on every side into men's hearts, expands there, and fills them entirely. Tell them not that by this blind surrender of themselves to an exclusive passion, they risk their dearest interests: they are deaf. Show them not freedom escaping from their grasp, while they are looking another way: they are blind—or rather, they can discern but one sole object to be desired in the universe.

What I have said is applicable to all democratic nations: what I am about to say concerns the French alone. Among most modern nations, and especially among all those of the continent of Europe, the taste and the idea of freedom only began to exist and to extend itself at the time when social conditions were tending to equality, and as a consequence of that very equality. Absolute kings were the most efficient levellers of ranks among their subjects. Among these nations equality preceded freedom: equality was therefore a fact of some standing, when freedom was still a novelty: the one had already created customs, opinions, and laws belonging to it, when the other, alone and for the first time, came into actual existence. Thus the latter was till only recently an affair of opinion and of taste, while the former had already crept into the habits of the people, possessed itself of their manners, and given a particular turn to the smallest actions in their lives. Can it be wondered that the men of our own time prefer the one to the other?

I think that democratic communities have a natural taste for freedom: left to themselves, they will seek it, cherish it, and view any privation of it with regret. But for equality, their passion is ardent, insatiable, incessant, invincible: they call for equality in freedom; if they cannot obtain that, they still call for equality in slavery. They will endure poverty, servitude, barbarism—but they will not endure aristocracy.

This is true at all times, and especially true in our own. All men and all powers seeking to cope with this irresistible passion, will be overthrown and destroyed by it. In our age, freedom cannot be established without it, and despotism itself cannot reign without its support.

ARISTOCRACY OF MANUFACTURERS

I have shown that democracy is favourable to the growth of manufactures, and that it increases without limit the numbers of the manufacturing classes: we shall now see by what side-road manufactures may possibly in their turn bring men back to aristocracy.

It is acknowledged, that when a workman is engaged every day upon the same detail, the whole commodity is produced with greater ease, promptitude, and economy. It is likewise acknowledged, that the cost of the production of manufactured goods is diminished by the extent of the establishment in which they are made, and by the amount of capital employed or of credit. These truths had long been imperfectly discerned, but in our time they have been demonstrated. They have been already applied to many very important kinds of manufactures, and the humblest will gradually be governed by them. I know of nothing in politics which deserves to fix the attention of the legislator more closely than these two new axioms of the science of manufactures.

When a workman is unceasingly and exclusively engaged in the fabrication of one thing, he ultimately does his work with singular dexterity; but at the same time he loses the general faculty of applying his mind to the direction of the work. He every day becomes more adroit and less industrious; so that it may be said of him, that in proportion as the workman improves, the man is degraded. What can be expected of a man who has spent twenty years of his life in making heads for pins? And to what can that mighty human intelligence, which has so often stirred the world, be applied in him, except it be to investigate the best method of making pins' heads? When a workman has spent a considerable portion of his existence in this manner, his thoughts are for ever set upon the object of his daily toil; his body has contracted certain fixed habits, which it can never shake off: in a word, he no longer belongs to himself, but to the calling which be has chosen. It is in vain that laws and manners have been at pains to level all barriers round such a man, and to open to him on every side a thousand different paths to fortune; a theory of manufactures more powerful than manners and laws binds him to a craft, and frequently to a spot, which he cannot leave: it assigns to him a certain place in society, beyond which he cannot go: in the midst of universal movement, it has rendered him stationary.

In proportion as the principle of the division of labour is more extensively applied, the workman becomes more weak, more narrow-minded and more dependent. The art advances, the artisan recedes. On the other hand, in proportion as it becomes more manifest that the productions of manufactures are by so much the cheaper and better as the manufacture is larger and the amount of capital employed more considerable, wealthy and educated men come forward to embark in manufactures which were heretofore abandoned to poor or ignorant handicraftsmen. The magnitude of the efforts required, and the importance of the results to be obtained, attract them. Thus at the very time at which the science of manufactures lowers the class of workmen, it raises the class of masters.

Whereas the workman concentrates his faculties more and more upon the study of a single detail, the master surveys a more extensive whole, and the mind of the latter is enlarged in proportion as that of the former is narrowed. In a short time the one will require nothing but physical strength without intelligence; the other stands in need of science, and almost of genius, to ensure success. This man resembles more and more the administrator of a vast empire—that man, a brute.

The master and the workman have then here no similarity, and their differences increase every day. They are only connected as the two rings at the extremities of a long chain. Each of them fills the station which is made for him, and out of which he does not get: the one is continually, closely, and necessarily dependent upon the other, and seems as much born to obey as that other is to command. What is this but aristocracy?

As the conditions of men constituting the nation become more and more equal, the demand for manufactured commodities becomes more general and more extensive; and the cheapness which places these objects within the reach of slender fortunes becomes a great element of success. Hence there are every day more men of great opulence and education who devote their wealth and knowledge to manufactures; and who seek, by opening large establishments, and by a strict division of labour, to meet the fresh demands which are made on all sides. Thus, in proportion as the mass of the nation turns to democracy, that particular class which is engaged in manufactures becomes more aristocratic. Men grow more alike in the one—more different in the other; and inequality increases in the less numerous class, in the same ratio in which it decreases in the community.

Hence it would appear, on searching to the bottom, that aristocracy should naturally spring out of the bosom of democracy.

But this kind of aristocracy by no means resembles those kinds which preceded it. It will be observed at once, that, as it applies exclusively to manufactures and to some manufacturing callings, it is a monstrous exception in the general aspect of society. The small aristocratic societies which are formed by some manufacturers in the midst of the immense democracy of our age, contain, like the great aristocratic societies of former ages, some men who are very opulent, and a multitude who are wretchedly poor. The poor have few means of escaping from their condition and becoming rich; but the rich are constantly becoming poor, or they give up business when they have realized a fortune, Thus the elements of which

the class of the poor is composed, are fixed; but the elements of which the class of the rich is composed are not so. To say the truth, though there are rich men, the class of rich men does not exist; for these rich individuals have no feelings or purposes in common, no mutual traditions or mutual hopes: there are therefore members, but no body,

Not only are the rich not compactly united among themselves, but there is no real bond between them and the poor. Their relative position is not a permanent one; they are constantly drawn together or separated by their interests. The workman is generally dependent on the master, but not on any particular master; these two men meet in the factory, but know not each other elsewhere; and while they come into contact on one point, they stand very wide apart on all others. The manufacturer asks nothing of the workman but his labour; the workman expects nothing from him but his wages. The one contracts no obligation to protect, nor the other to defend; and they are not permanently connected either by habit or by duty.

The aristocracy created by business rarely settles in the midst of the manufacturing population which it directs: the object is not to govern that population, but to use it. An aristocracy thus constituted can have no great hold upon those whom it employs; and even if it succeed in retaining them at one moment, they escape the next: it knows not how to will, and it cannot act.

The territorial aristocracy of former ages was either bound by law, or thought itself bound by usage, to come to the relief of its serving-men, and to succour their distresses. But the manufacturing aristocracy of our age first impoverishes and debases the men who serve it, and then abandons them to be supported by the charity of the public. This is a natural consequence of what has been said before. Between the workman and the master there are frequent relations, but no real partnership.

I am of opinion, upon the whole, that the manufacturing aristocracy which is growing up under our eyes, is one of the harshest which ever existed in the world; but at the same time it is one of the most confined and least dangerous. Nevertheless the friends of democracy should keep their eyes anxiously fixed in this direction; for if ever a permanent inequality of conditions and aristocracy again penetrate into the world, it may be predicted that this is the channel by which they will enter.

EQUALITY AND FREE INSTITUTIONS

The principle of equality, which makes men independent of each other, gives them a habit and a taste for following, in their private actions, no other guide but their own will. This complete independence, which they constantly enjoy toward their equals and in the intercourse of private life, tends to make them look upon all authority with a jealous eye, and speedily suggests to them the notion and the love of political freedom. Men living at such times have a natural bias to free institutions. Take any one of them at a venture, and search if you can his most deep-seated instincts; you will find that of all governments he will soonest conceive and most highly value that government, whose head he has himself elected, and whose administration he may control.

Of all the political effects produced by the equality of conditions, this love of independence is the first to strike the observing, and to alarm the timid; nor can it be said that their alarm is wholly misplaced, for anarchy has a more formidable aspect in democratic countries than elsewhere. As the citizens have no direct influence on each other, as soon as the supreme power of the nations fails, which kept them all in their several stations, it would seem that disorder must instantly reach its utmost pitch, and that, every man drawing aside in a different direction, the fabric of society must at once crumble away. I am however persuaded that anarchy is not the principal evil which democratic ages have to fear, but the least. For the principle of equality begets two tendencies; the one leads men straight to independence, and may suddenly drive them into anarchy; the other conducts them by a longer, more secret, but more certain road, to servitude. Nations readily discern the former tendency, and are prepared to resist it; they are led away by the latter, without perceiving its drift; hence it is peculiarly important to point it out.

For myself, I am so far from urging as a reproach to the principle of equality that it renders men untractable, that this very circumstance principally calls forth my approbation. I admire to see how it deposits in the mind and heart of man the dim conception and instinctive love of political independence, thus preparing the remedy for the evil which it engenders: it is on this very account that I am attached to it.

CENTRALIZATION OF POLITICAL POWER

As in ages of equality no man is compelled to lend his assistance to his fellowmen, and none has any right to expect much support from them, every one is at once independent and powerless. These two conditions, which must never be either separately considered or confounded together, inspire the citizen of a democratic country with very contrary propensities. His independence fills him with self-reliance and pride among his equals; his debility makes him feel from time to time the want of some outward assistance, which he cannot expect from any of them, because they are all impotent and unsympathizing. In this predicament he naturally turns his eyes to that imposing power which alone rises above the level of universal depression. Of that power his wants and especially his desires continually remind him, until he ultimately views it as the sole and necessary support of his own weakness.

This may more completely explain what frequently takes place in democratic countries, where the very men who are so impatient of superiors patiently submit to a master, exhibiting at once their pride and their servility.

The hatred which men bear to privilege increases in proportion as privileges become more scarce and less considerable, so that democratic passions would seem to burn most fiercely at the very time when they have least fuel. I have already given the reason of this phenomenon. When all conditions are unequal, no inequality is so great as to offend the eye; whereas the slightest dissimilarity is odious in the midst of general uniformity: the more complete is this uniformity, the more insupportable does the sight of such a difference become. Hence it is natural that the love of equality should constantly increase together with equality itself, and that it should grow by what it feeds upon.

This never-dying, ever-kindling hatred, which sets a democratic people against the smallest privileges, is peculiarly favourable to the gradual concentration of all political rights in the hands of the representative of the state alone. The sovereign, being necessarily and incontestably above all the citizens, excites not their envy, and each of them thinks that he strips his equals of the prerogative which he concedes to the crown.

The man of a democratic age is extremely reluctant to obey his neighbour who is his equal; he refuses to acknowledge in such a person ability superior to his own; he mistrusts his justice, and is jealous of his power; he fears and he contemns him; and he loves continually to remind him of the common dependence in which both of them stand to the same master.

Every central power which follows its natural tendencies courts and encourages the principle of equality; for equality singularly facilitates, extends, and secures the influence of a central power.

In like manner it may be said that every central government worships uniformity: uniformity relieves it from inquiry into an infinite number of small details which must be attended to if rules were to be adapted to men, instead of indiscriminately subjecting men to rules: thus the government likes what the citizens like, and naturally hates what they hate. These common sentiments which, in democratic nations, constantly unite the sovereign and every member of the community in one and the same conviction, establish a secret and lasting sympathy between them. The faults of the government are pardoned for the sake of its tastes; public confidence is only reluctantly withdrawn in the midst even of its excesses and its errors, and it is restored at the first call. Democratic nations often hate those in whose hands the central power is vested; but they always love that power itself.

Thus, by two separate paths, I have reached the same conclusion. I have shown that the principle of equality suggests to men the notion of a sole, uniform, and strong government: I have now shown that the principle of equality imparts to them a taste for it. To governments of this kind the nations of our age are therefore tending. They are drawn thither by the natural inclination of mind and heart; and in order to reach that result, it is enough that they do not check themselves in their course.

I am of opinion, that, in the democratic ages which are opening upon us, individual independence and local liberties will ever be the produce of artificial contrivance; that centralization will be the natural form of government.[1]

DEMOCRACY AND DESPOTISM

I had remarked during my stay in the United States, that a democratic state of society, similar to that of the Americans, might offer singular facilities for the establishment of despotism; and I perceived, upon my return to Europe, how much use had already been made by most of our rulers, of the notions, the sentiments, and the wants engendered by this same social condition, for the purpose of extending the circle of their power. This led me to think that the nations of Christendom would perhaps eventually undergo some sort of oppression like that which hung over several of the nations of the ancient world.

A more accurate examination of the subject, and five years of further meditations, have not diminished my apprehensions, but they have changed the object of them.

No sovereign ever lived in former ages so absolute or so powerful as to undertake to administer by his own agency, and without the assistance of intermediate powers, all the parts of a great empire: none ever attempted to subject all his subjects indiscriminately to strict uniformity of regulation, and

---

[1] A democratic people is not only led by its own tastes to centralize its government, but the passions of all the men by whom it is governed constantly urge it in the same direction. It may easily be foreseen that almost all the able and ambitious members of a democratic community will labour without ceasing to extend the powers of government, because they all hope at some time or other to wield those powers. It is a waste of time to attempt to prove to them that extreme centralization may be injurious to the State, since they are centralizing for their own benefit. Among the public men of democracies there are hardly any but men of great disinterestedness or extreme mediocrity who seek to oppose the centralization of government: the former are scarce, the latter powerless.

personally to tutor and direct every member of the community. The notion of such an undertaking never occurred to the human mind; and if any man had conceived it, the want of information, the imperfection of the administrative system, and above all, the natural obstacles caused by the inequality of conditions, would speedily have checked the execution of so vast a design.

When the Roman emperors were at the height of their power, the different nations of the empire still preserved manners and customs of great diversity; although they were subject to the same monarch, most of the provinces were separately administered; they abounded in powerful and active municipalities; and although the whole government of the empire was centered in the hands of the emperor alone, and be always remained, upon occasions, the supreme arbiter in all matters, yet the details of social life and private occupations lay for the most part beyond his control. The emperors possessed, it is true, an immense and unchecked power, which allowed them to gratify all their whimsical tastes, and to employ for that purpose the whole strength of the State. They frequently abused that power arbitrarily to deprive their subjects of property or of life: their tyranny was extremely onerous to the few, but it did not reach the greater number; it was fixed to some few main objects, and neglected the rest; it was violent, but its range was limited.

But it would seem that if despotism were to be established among the democratic nations of our days, it might assume a different character; it would be more extensive and more mild; it would degrade men without tormenting them. I do not question, that in an age of instruction and equality like our own, sovereigns might more easily succeed in collecting all political power into their hands, and might interfere more habitually and decidedly within the circle of private interests, than any sovereign of antiquity could ever do. But this same principle of equality which facilitates despotism, tempers its rigour. We have seen how the manners of society become more humane and gentle in proportion as men become more equal and alike. When no member of the community has much power or much wealth, tyranny is, as it were, without opportunities and a field of action. As all fortunes are

scanty, the passions of men are naturally circumscribed—their imagination limited, their pleasures simple. This universal moderation moderates the sovereign himself, and checks within certain limits the inordinate stretch of his desires.

Independently of these reasons drawn from the nature of the state of society itself, I might add many others arising from causes beyond my subject; but I shall keep within the limits I have laid down to myself.

Democratic governments may become violent and even cruel at certain periods of extreme effervescence or of great danger; but these crises will be rare and brief. When I consider the petty passions of our contemporaries, the mildness of their manners, the extent of their education, the purity of their religion, the gentleness of their morality, their regular and industrious habits, and the restraint which they almost all observe in their vices no less than in their virtues, I have no fear that they will meet with tyrants in their rulers, but rather guardians.

I think then that the species of oppression by which democratic nations are menaced is unlike anything which ever before existed in the world: our contemporaries will find no prototype of it in their memories. I am trying myself to choose an expression which will accurately convey the whole of the idea I have formed of it, but in vain; the old words *despotism* and *tyranny* are inappropriate: the thing itself is new; and since I cannot name it, I must attempt to define it.

I seek to trace the novel features under which despotism may appear in the world. The first thing that strikes the observation is an innumerable multitude of men all equal and alike, incessantly endeavouring to procure the petty and paltry pleasures with which they glut their lives. Each of them, living apart, is as a stranger to the fate of all the rest—his children and his private friends constitute to him the whole of mankind; as for the rest of his fellow-citizens, he is close to them, but he sees them not;—he touches them, but he feels them not; he exists but in himself and for himself alone; and if his kindred still remain to him, he may be said at any rate to have lost his country.

Above this race of men stands an immense and tutelary power, which takes upon itself alone to secure their gratifications, and watch over their fate. That power is absolute, minute, regular, provident, and mild. It would be like the authority of a parent, if, like that authority, its object was to prepare men for manhood; but it seeks on the contrary to keep them in perpetual childhood: it is well content that the people should rejoice, provided they think of nothing but rejoicing. For their happiness such a government willingly labours, but it chooses to be the sole agent and the only arbiter of that happiness: it provides for their security, foresees and supplies their necessities, facilitates their pleasures, manages their principal concerns, directs their industry, regulates the descent of property, and subdivides their inheritances—what remains, but to spare them all the care of thinking and all the trouble of living?

Thus it every day renders the exercise of the free agency of man less useful and less frequent; it circumscribes the will within a narrower range, and gradually robs a man of all the uses of himself. The principle of equality has prepared men for these things: it has predisposed men to endure them, and oftentimes to look on them as benefits.

After having thus successively taken each member of the community in its powerful grasp, and fashioned them at will, the supreme power then extends its arm over the whole community. It covers the surface of society with a net-work of small complicated rules, minute and uniform, through which the most original minds and the most energetic characters cannot penetrate, to rise above the crowd. The will of man is not shattered, but softened, bent, and guided: men are seldom forced by it to act, but they are constantly restrained from acting: such a power does not destroy, but it prevents existence; it does not tyrannize, but it compresses, enervates, extinguishes, and stupefies a people, till each nation is reduced to be nothing better than a flock of timid and industrious animals, of which the government is the shepherd.

I have always thought that servitude of the regular, quiet, and gentle kind which I have just described, might be combined more easily than is commonly believed with some of the outward forms of freedom; and that it might even establish itself under the wing of the sovereignty of the people.

Our contemporaries are constantly excited by two conflicting passions; they want to be led, and they wish to remain free: as they cannot destroy either one or the other of these contrary propensities, they strive to satisfy them both at once. They devise a sole, tutelary, and all-powerful form of government, but elected by the people. They combine the principle of centralization and that of popular sovereignty; this gives them a respite: they console themselves for being in tutelage by the reflection that they have chosen their own guardians. Every man allows himself to be put in leading-strings, because he sees that it is not a person or a class of persons, but the people at large that hold the end of his chain.

By this system the people shake off their state of dependence just long enough to select their master, and then relapse into it again. A great many persons at the present day are quite contented with this sort of compromise between administrative despotism and the sovereignty of the people; and they think they have done enough for the protection of individual freedom when they have surrendered it to the power of the nation at large. This does not satisfy me: the nature of him I am to obey signifies less to me than the fact of extorted obedience.

I do not however deny that a constitution of this kind appears to me to be infinitely preferable to one, which, after having concentrated all the powers of government, should vest them in the hands of an irresponsible person or body of persons. Of all the forms which democratic despotism could assume, the latter would assuredly be the worst.

When the sovereign is elective, or narrowly watched by a legislature which is really elective and independent, the oppression which he exercises over individuals is sometimes greater, but it is always less degrading; because every man, when he is oppressed and disarmed, may still imagine, that while he yields obedience it is to himself he yields it, and that it is to one of his own inclinations that all the rest give way. In like manner I can understand that when the sovereign represents the nation, and is dependent upon the people, the rights and the power of which every citizen is deprived, not only serve the head of the state, but the state itself; and that private persons derive some return from the sacrifice of their independence which they have made to the public. To create a representation of the people in a very centralized country is, therefore, to diminish the evil which extreme centralization may produce, but not to get rid of it.

I admit that by this means room is left for the intervention of individuals in the more important affairs; but it is not the less suppressed in the smaller and more private ones. It must not be forgotten that it is especially dangerous to enslave men in the minor details of life. For my own part, I should be inclined to think freedom less necessary in great things than in little ones, if it were possible to be secure of the one without possessing the other.

Subjection in minor affairs breaks out every day, and is felt by the whole community indiscriminately. It does not drive men to resistance, but it crosses them at every turn, till they are led to surrender the exercise of their will. Thus their spirit is gradually broken and their character enervated; whereas that obedience, which is exacted on a few important but rare occasions, only exhibits servitude at certain intervals, and throws the burden of it upon a small number of men. It is vain to summon a people, which has been rendered so dependent on the central power, to choose from time to time the representatives of that power; this rare and brief exercise of their free choice, however important it may be, will not prevent them from gradually losing the faculties of thinking, feeling, and acting for themselves, and thus gradually failing below the level of humanity.[2]

I add that they will soon become incapable of exercising the great and only privilege which remains to them. The democratic nations which have introduced freedom into their political constitution, at the very time when they were augmenting the despotism of their administrative constitution, have been led into strange paradoxes. To manage those minor affairs in which good sense is all that is wanted—the people are held to be unequal to the task; but when the government of the country is at stake, the people are invested with immense powers; they are alternately made the playthings of their ruler, and his masters—more than kings, and less than men. After having exhausted all the different modes of election, without finding one to suit their purpose, they are still amazed, and still bent on seeking further; as if the evil they remark did not originate in the constitution of the country far more than in that of the electoral body.

It is, indeed, difficult to conceive how men who have entirely given up the habit of self-government should succeed in making a proper choice of those by whom they are to be governed; and no one will ever believe that a liberal, wise, and energetic government can spring from the suffrages of a subservient people.

A constitution, which should be republican in its head and ultra-monarchical in all its other parts, has ever appeared to me to be a short-lived monster. The vices of rulers and the ineptitude of the people would speedily bring about its ruin; and the nation, weary of its representatives and of itself, would create freer institutions, or soon return to stretch itself at the feet of a single master.

THE COMING ERA OF WORLD DEMOCRACY

Before I close for ever the theme that has detained me so long, I would fain take a

---

[2] It cannot be absolutely or generally affirmed that the greatest danger of the present age is license or tyranny, anarchy or despotism. Both are equally to be feared; and the one may as easily proceed as the other from the self-same cause, namely, that *general apathy,* which is the consequence of what I have termed Individualism: it is because this apathy exists, that the executive government, having mustered a few troops, is able to commit acts of oppression one day, and the next day a party, which has mustered some thirty men in its ranks, can also commit acts of oppression. Neither one nor the other can found anything to last; and the causes which enable

them to succeed easily, prevent them from succeeding long: they rise because nothing opposes them, and they sink because nothing supports them. The proper object therefore of our most strenuous resistance, is far less either anarchy or despotism, than that apathy which may almost indifferently beget either the one or the other.

parting survey of all the various characteristics of modern society, and appreciate at last the general influence to be exercised by the principle of equality upon the fate of mankind; but I am stopped by the difficulty of the task, and in presence of so great an object my sight is troubled, and my reason fails.

The society of the modern world which I have sought to delineate, and which I seek to judge, has but just come into existence. Time has not yet shaped it into perfect form: the great revolution by which it has been created is not yet over; and amid the occurrences of our time, it is almost impossible to discern what will pass away with the revolution itself, and what will survive its close. The world which is rising into existence is still half encumbered by the remains of the world which is waning into decay; and amid the vast perplexity of human affairs, none can say how much of ancient institutions and former manners will remain, or how much will completely disappear.

Although the revolution which is taking place in the social condition, the laws, the opinions and the feelings of men, is still very far from being terminated, yet its results already admit of no comparison with anything that the world has ever before witnessed. I go back from age to age up to the remotest antiquity: but I find no parallel to what is occurring before my eyes: as the past has ceased to throw its light upon the future, the mind of man wanders in obscurity.

Nevertheless, in the midst of a prospect so wide, so novel, and so confused, some of the more prominent characteristics may already be discerned and pointed out. The good things and the evils of life are more equally distributed in the world: great wealth tends to disappear, the number of small fortunes to increase; desires and gratifications are multiplied, but extraordinary prosperity and irremediable penury are alike unknown. The sentiment of ambition is universal, but the scope of ambition is seldom vast. Each individual stands apart in solitary weakness; but society at large is active, provident, and powerful: the performances of private persons are insignificant, those of the State immense.

There is little energy of character; but manners are mild, and laws humane. If there be few instances of exalted heroism or of virtues of the highest, brightest, and purest temper, men's habits are regular, violence is rare, and cruelty almost unknown. Human existence becomes longer, and property more secure: life is not adorned with brilliant trophies, but it is extremely easy and tranquil. Few pleasures are either very refined or very coarse; and highly polished manners are as uncommon as great brutality of tastes. Neither men of great learning, nor extremely ignorant communities, are to be met with; genius becomes more rare, information more diffused. The human mind is impelled by the small efforts of all mankind combined together, not by the strenuous activity of certain men. There is less perfection, but more abundance, in all the productions of the arts. The ties of race, of rank, and of country are relaxed; the great bond of humanity is strengthened.

If I endeavour to find out the most general and the most prominent of all these different characteristics, I shall have occasion to perceive, that what is taking place in men's fortunes manifests itself under a thousand other forms. Almost all extremes are softened or blunted: all that was most prominent is superseded by some mean term, at once less lofty and less low, less brilliant and less obscure, than what before existed in the world.

When I survey this countless multitude of beings, shaped in each other's likeness, amidst whom nothing rises and nothing falls, the sight of such universal uniformity saddens and chills me, and I am tempted to regret that state of society which has ceased to be. When the world was full of men of great importance and extreme insignificance, of great wealth and extreme poverty, of great learning and extreme ignorance, I turned aside from the latter to fix my observation on the former alone, who gratified my sympathies. But I admit that this gratification arose from my own weakness; it is because I am unable to see at once all that is around me, that I am allowed thus to select and separate the objects of my predilection from among so many others. Such is not the case with that Almighty and Eternal Being, whose gaze necessarily includes the whole of created things, and who surveys distinctly, though at once, mankind and man.

We may naturally believe that it is not the singular prosperity of the few, but the greater well-being of all, which is most pleasing in the sight of the Creator and Preserver of men. What appears to me to be man's decline, is to His eye advancement; what afflicts me is acceptable to Him. A state of equality is perhaps less elevated, but is more just; and its justice constitutes its greatness and its beauty. I would strive then to raise myself to this point of the Divine contemplation, and thence to view and to judge the concerns of men.

No man, upon the earth, can as yet affirm absolutely and generally, that the new state of the world is better than its former one; but it is already easy to perceive that this state is different. Some vices and some virtues were so inherent in the constitution of an aristocratic nation, and are so opposite to the character of a modern people, that they can never be infused into it; some good tendencies and some bad propensities which were unknown to the former, are natural to the latter; some ideas suggest themselves spontaneously to the imagination of the one, which are utterly repugnant to the mind of the other. They are like two distinct orders of human beings, each of which has its own merits and defects, its own advantages and its own evils. Care must therefore be taken not to judge the state of society, which is now coming into existence, by notions derived from a state of society which no longer exists; for as these states of society are exceedingly different in their structure, they cannot be submitted to a just or fair comparison.

It would be scarcely more reasonable to require of our own contemporaries the peculiar virtues which originated in the social condition of their forefathers, since that social condition is itself fallen, and has drawn into one promiscuous ruin the good and evil which belonged to it.

But as yet these things are imperfectly understood. I find that a great number of my contemporaries undertake to make a certain selection from among the institutions, the opinions, and the ideas which originated in the aristocratic constitution of society as it was: a portion of these elements they would willingly relinquish, but they would keep the remainder and transplant them into their new world. I apprehend that such men are wasting their time and their strength in virtuous but unprofitable efforts.

The object is not to retain the peculiar advantages which the inequality of conditions bestows upon mankind, but to secure the new benefits which equality may supply. We have not to seek to make ourselves like our progenitors, but to strive to work out that species of greatness and happiness which is our own.

For myself, who now look back from this extreme limit of my task, and discover from afar, but at once, the various objects which have attracted my more attentive investigation upon my way, I am full of apprehensions and of hopes. I perceive mighty dangers which it is possible to ward off—mighty evils which may be avoided or alleviated; and I cling with a firmer hold to the belief, that for democratic nations to be virtuous and prosperous they require but to will it.

I am aware that many of my contemporaries maintain that nations are never their own masters here below, and that they necessarily obey some insurmountable and unintelligent power, arising from anterior events, from their race, or from the soil and climate of their country. Such principles are false and cowardly; such principles can never produce aught but feeble men and pusillanimous nations. Providence has not created mankind entirely independent or entirely free. It is true that around every man a fatal circle is traced, beyond which he cannot pass; but within the wide verge of that circle he is powerful and free: as it is with man, so with communities. The nations of our time cannot prevent the conditions of men from becoming equal: but it depends upon themselves whether the principle of equality is to lead them to servitude or freedom, to knowledge or barbarism, to prosperity or to wretchedness.

CHAPTER TWENTY-SEVEN

MILL

Democracy in America, translated into English almost immediately after publication, aroused considerable attention on both sides of the Atlantic. One of the most enthusiastic English reviewers of the work was John Stuart Mill (1806–1873), who compared Tocqueville to Montesquieu and thought that nothing equally profound had yet been written on the subject of democracy. Tocqueville seemed to Mill to have "changed the face of political philosophy" by posing new questions that went to the core of democracy as a system of government and way of life.

Mill was impressed by the fact that the tendencies which Tocqueville had noted in America—the drive toward equality of conditions with its new problems and pressures—were also gradually permeating England. He shared Tocqueville's concern about the possibility of the tyranny of the majority in democracy, and he added that "it is not from the separate interests, real or imaginary, that minorities are in danger; but from its antipathies of religion, political party, or race." The more perfectly each knows himself the equal of any other individual, "the more helpless he feels against the aggregate mass; and the more incredible it appears to him that the opinions of all the world can possibly be erroneous."

In his *Autobiography,* too, Mill avows how much he owes to Tocqueville from whom he learned the specific virtues and defects of democracy. In turn, Tocqueville wrote to Mill that of all reviewers of *Democracy in America* he was the one who best understood the meaning of the work; the two met during Tocqueville's second visit to England in 1835, and their friendly association lasted until Tocqueville's death in 1859.

Mill's *Autobiography* (1873), one of the most fascinating autobiographies of a political philosopher, is remarkable for several reasons. It provides a lifelike, and occasionally intimate, account of the Benthamite circle, Mill's father, James, being the leading disciple of the master. The *Autobiography* also spans an important era of nineteenth-century intellectual history. Mill's interest was not confined to England, and he was particularly conversant with developments in France and the United States. Above all, the *Autobiography* is noteworthy for its account of the intellectual development of Mill himself.

For the generation of Bentham as for that of James Mill, democracy still was an objective to aim at, a goal to work for. John Stuart Mill, who belongs to the third generation of Utilitarianism, lived in a world in which middle-class reform had attained a high degree of realization and—gradually shedding the magic of the envisioned future—had begun to reveal its own shortcomings and imperfections. The heyday of middle-class

democracy heralded the first dawn of the next phase of social and political development, pointing toward socialism and the welfare state.

Mill typifies in his own life history the evolution of nineteenth-century liberalism.
Born and reared as an orthodox and uncontaminated Benthamite, he ended as a "qualified socialist." From a personal viewpoint, moreover, the *Autobiography* is a remarkable record of human endurance. James Mill had definite ideas on how to educate John
Stuart from the moment he was born. At the age of three, John began to learn Greek,
and Latin at the much later age of seven. By this time he already had acquired a solid
knowledge of Greek literature and philosophy, including Plato, Herodotus, and
Xenophon. He also learned arithmetic and ancient and modern history. When he came
to the American war, Mill recalls, he took the side of England, but he quickly was set
right by his father who, like all Philosophical Radicals, regarded the United States as
the advance guard of democracy and the model of future developments in England.

From his eighth year on, Mill went thoroughly through Latin literature and broadened his knowledge of Greek literature by reading Thucydides, Homer, Euripides,
Sophocles, and Polybius. At the same time, he delved into algebra, geometry, the differential calculus, and other portions of high mathematics. He also read books on experimental science and, at the age of twelve, began a course of study in logic from
Aristotle to Hobbes. At thirteen, Mill's primary study was political economy, particularly Smith and David Ricardo, the latter being a close friend of Mill's father. At fourteen Mill went to France for a year, spending part of his time with the family of General
Sir Samuel Bentham, Jeremy's brother. Mill fell in love with France, later returned
there for prolonged visits, and died in Avignon in 1873.

At the age of seventeen, Mill joined the staff of the East India Company as a clerk,
became head of his department in 1856, and retired two years later. Most of his immense literary output was accomplished while he held a full-time and absorbing job. In
1865 Mill was asked by a body of voters in Westminster to stand for Parliament. He was
convinced that no numerous or influential body of any constituency would wish to be
represented by a person of his opinions. He also held the fixed conviction that a candidate should neither incur election expenses nor canvass his constituency. He nevertheless won with a small majority over his Conservative opponent, but he stayed in the
House of Commons for only three years. In the election of 1868 he was defeated, but he
confesses in his *Autobiography* that he was less surprised by his defeat than by his having been elected the first time.

In his teens Mill wrote and published essays on various political and philosophical
topics and contributed to the *Westminster Review,* the official organ of Philosophical
Radicalism from its foundation in 1824. In 1834 he published the *System of Logic,* his
principal work on philosophy. In 1848 he brought out his *Political Economy,* next to
Adam Smith's *Wealth of Nations* the most authoritative work in its field for several
generations, and long the most popular textbook in economics in England and the
United States.

Yet Mill's claim to enduring fame derives from *On Liberty* (1859); he predicted that
of all his writings *On Liberty* was likely to survive longest, and his prediction has come
true. Mill says in the *Autobiography* that he wrote *On Liberty* at a time when there may
have seemed comparatively little need for it. But he foresaw that illiberal forces in modern society would gain in weight, and he hoped that men then would turn to the teachings
of *On Liberty*. Though Mill modestly disclaimed originality other than that which "every
thoughtful mind gives to its own mode of conceiving and expressing truths which
are common property," *On Liberty* long has been held to be, together with Milton's
Areopagitica, the finest and most moving essay on liberty in English, perhaps in any

language. As time goes on, *On Liberty* grows in stature and meaning because its predictions have come to life more realistically, and more tragically, than seemed possible in the middle of the nineteenth century, when belief in the progress of liberty was well-nigh universal.

Mill explodes the illusion that the evolution of government from tyranny to popular self-rule necessarily solves the problem of liberty. Like Tocqueville, he sees that *society* may practice a social tyranny more formidable than many kinds of political oppression, because social tyranny leaves fewer means of escape, "penetrating much more deeply into the details of life, and enslaving the soul itself." Protection against political tyranny therefore is not enough; there also must be protection against the tyranny of prevailing opinion and feeling. Unless *absolute freedom* of opinion and sentiment—scientific, moral, and theological—is guaranteed, a society is not completely free. Mill makes the point, seldom made in the optimistic nineteenth century, that the natural disposition of man is to impose his views, as ruler or fellow citizen, on others, and that want of power is often the cause of toleration of dissent.

The issue of liberty is one not only of power but of right and obligation, and it makes little difference how numerous the dissentient minority is: "If all mankind minus one, were of one opinion, and only one person were of the contrary opinion, mankind would be no more justified in silencing that one person, than he, if he had the power, would be justified in silencing mankind." Silencing an unorthodox opinion is not only wrong but harmful, because it robs mankind of an opportunity to become acquainted with ideas that may possibly be true, or partly true: "All silencing of discussion is an assumption of infallibility."

Mill recognizes that each individual can grasp no more than some aspects of truth, and that the imperfection of truth is due to the partial knowledge that man is able to attain in his limited experience of the world. Not only is society no infallible judge of truth, but even "ages are no more infallible than individuals." History is full of opinions held by one age to be the ultimate truth and considered by subsequent ages to be false and absurd.

Just as liberty is not complete unless it is absolute, so discussion must be completely unhampered, and free discussion must not be ruled out when "pushed to an extreme," because the arguments for a case are not good unless they are good for an extreme case. Mill is aware of the favorite argument that some opinions must be protected from public discussion and attack because of their usefulness to society, and he retorts that the "usefulness of an opinion is itself a matter of opinion."

Mill does not believe in the "pleasant falsehood" that truth inevitably triumphs over persecution; history "teems with instances of truth put down by persecution." He cites numerous examples of successful persecution in religion in support of his view that "persecution has always succeeded, save where the heretics were too strong a party to be effectually persecuted." The greatest harm of persecution is not done to those who are heretics but to those who are not, because the mental development of the latter is stifled by the fear of heresy. In an atmosphere of cowed conformity and slavish submission there may be a few exceptional great individual thinkers, but not an intellectually active people: "No one can be a great thinker who does not recognize, that as a thinker it is his first duty to follow his intellect to whatever conclusions it may lead."

Mill particularly warns against the blind acceptance of dead formulas as truth, without the challenge of discussion. For its own vitality and survival, truth needs to be "fully, frequently, and fearlessly" discussed, and Mill adds the not unimportant point that the opposing opinion be presented by someone who really believes in it. Only in the constant process of being challenged and assailed can truth grow and establish itself: "Both teachers and learners go to sleep at their post, as soon as there is no enemy in the field."

In summary, says Mill, the necessity of freedom of opinion, and freedom of expression, may be based upon three grounds. First, any opinion we silence may be true, and in silencing it we assume our own *infallibility.* Second, though the *silenced opinion* be on the whole erroneous, it may be *partly true,* and because the prevailing opinion on any subject is rarely the *complete truth,* "it is only by the collision of adverse opinions that the remainder of the truth has any chance of being supplied." Third, even if the prevailing opinion be the *complete truth,* it will inevitably become dogma, prejudice, and formula unless it is exposed to the *challenge of free discussion.*

In his *Autobiography,* Mill says that his father felt himself more indebted for his mental culture to Plato than to any other writer. He shares his father's high esteem for Plato, not because of any sympathy with Plato's specific political or social views, but because of his admiration for the Socratic method, "unsurpassed" in correcting errors and clearing up confusions through relentless exposure of generalities, the "perpetual testing of all general statements by particular instances." Long before instrumentalism made its formal contribution to philosophy, Mill was an instrumentalist in his approach to the problem of truth. He recognized that truth never is finished, certain, and timeless, but that it always is unfinished, tentative, and temporary, subject to new data and experiences; that the quest for truth is an endless road; and that the free debate between opposite viewpoints is more likely to result in an approximation of truth than is the one-sided assertion of dogma and creed which are beyond dispute. In this concept of truth as a dynamic process of colliding opposites, Mill sacrifices the certainty that is devoid of mental freedom to the uncertainty that is the pride of intellectual liberty.

In championing liberty, Mill has a broad goal in mind: the "Greek ideal of self-development." It is the privilege of every human being to use and interpret experience in his own way, and the act of choosing between alternatives brings man's moral faculties into play. A person who acts according to custom and tradition makes no choice, and he who lets others choose his plan of life for him has no need of any faculty other than ape-like imitation. Different persons should be permitted to lead different lives; and the plea for *variety* in *On Liberty* is as strong as that for *freedom.* The very progress of industrial civilization creates a uniformity of conditions that makes it difficult for persons to remain individuals, because "they now read the same things, listen to the same things, go to the same places, have their hopes and fears directed to the same objects, have the same rights and liberties, and the same means of asserting them." Moreover, Mill feels that "genius" is an absolutely indispensable ingredient in social progress: "there are but few persons, in comparison with the whole of mankind, whose experiments, if adopted by others, would be likely to be any improvement on established practice," and "genius can only breathe freely in an atmosphere of freedom." Liberty, therefore, is essential not just to individual advancement but to societal progression.

Mill reminds those who are willing to repress individual liberty for the sake of a strong state that the worth of a state is no more than the worth of the individuals composing it. The concluding words of *On Liberty* contain a message that always is timely: "A state which dwarfs its men, in order that they may be more docile instruments in its hands even for beneficial purposes—will find that with small men no great thing can really be accomplished; and that the perfection of machinery to which it has sacrificed everything, will in the end avail it nothing, for want of the vital power which, in order that the machine might work smoothly, it has preferred to banish."

Mill understood that the issue of liberty is closely related to the larger question of social power and organization. Bred as an orthodox economist, his faith in *laissez faire* was originally stronger than that of Bentham himself; but as time went on, Mill gradually abandoned what was reactionary in the economic philosophy of *laissez faire*. Although in the first edition of his *Political Economy* (1848) his general view of socialism was that it was neither desirable nor practicable, in subsequent editions he revised his attitude. As a utilitarian and pragmatist, Mill was unwilling to commit himself to any economic perspective without qualifications. He felt that the decision between capitalism and socialism ultimately would be based upon one chief consideration "which of the two systems is consistent with the greatest amount of human liberty and spontaneity." It would be rash to predict that socialism would be unable to realize a great part of its aspirations, and the best way to find out, Mill thought, was to give socialists an opportunity of trial.

With regard to individual property, Mill held that the aim of an enlightened social policy should be not to destroy it, but to improve it, and to enable every member of the community to own property. The ultimate form of ownership of the means of production would not be, Mill says in the *Political Economy,* that of capitalist chiefs, with the workers deprived of any voice in the management, but the "association of the laborers themselves on terms of equality, collectively owning the capital with which they carry on their operations, and working under managers elected and removable by themselves."

In 1869 Mill began a book on socialism but did not finish it. *Chapters on Socialism,* published in 1879 by his stepdaughter, contains further important additions to Mill's previously held ideas. Avoiding an extreme position, Mill asserts on the one hand, that the present system is "not hurrying us into a state of general indigence and slavery from which only socialism can save us." Though the evils and injustices of capitalism are great, they are not increasing but generally decreasing. On the other hand, Mill foresees that individual property is only of provisional existence, though it still has a long term before it, and that the nature of property would change in the course of time. Property denotes in every state of society the largest power of exclusive control over things, "and sometimes, unfortunately, over persons," but these powers vary greatly in accordance with the conceptions of right and justice held in different countries and times. In his *Autobiography,* Mill sums up most succinctly the problem of socialism as he saw it: how to "unite the greatest individual liberty of action with a common ownership in the raw material of the globe, and an equal participation of all in the benefits of combined labor."

In his analysis of socialist ideas and proposals, Mill does not mention Marx and Engels—probably because he was not familiar with their writings—and relies most heavily upon Robert Owen, Charles Fourier, Saint-Simon, and Louis Blanc. Mill foresaw that socialism would run into a dead end if it gave up its liberal heritage and embraced the philosophy of the all-powerful state. He therefore was solely interested in French and British socialists, who stressed the cooperative, individualist, and fraternal elements in socialism as a new way of life. He ignored the doctrines of revolution and dictatorship. He was an idealist, not scientific, socialist.

Mill felt that socialism was more than a legal problem of transferring productive property from private to public ownership and also more than a purely economic problem of organizing the economy on the foundations of new principles of the common good rather than entrepreneurial profits. He thought that socialism would demand a higher moral and intellectual level of the people than did capitalism. He therefore emphasized that socialist experiments along cooperative lines should be tried first among "elite groups" of workers before such experiments of a broader scope would be justified. In particular, he opposed wholesale transfer of private property to public ownership, because he seriously doubted whether in a collectivized economy "there would be any asylum left for individuality of character; whether public opinion would not be a tyrannical yoke; whether the absolute dependence of each on all, and surveillance of each by all, would not grind all down into a tame uniformity of thoughts, feelings, and actions."

Mill was aware that many democratic socialists of his time felt unconcerned about possible deleterious political effects of large-scale public ownership and operation of the economy by the state as long as the government would be elected by democratic procedures and as long as a free press would continue. Mill did not share this optimistic expectation, and argued that, under a fully collectivized economy, "not all the freedom of the press and popular constitution would make this or any other country free otherwise than in name." The abandonment of large-scale nationalization as a goal by socialist parties vindicates Mill's conviction that an economically all-powerful state cannot be politically liberal in relation to the individual. Mill favored cooperation within working places and competition between them.

Mill's other most enduring work, in addition to *On Liberty,* is *Utilitarianism* (1861), originally published in three parts in *Fraser's Magazine.* Mill mostly wrote *Utilitarianism* in 1854, slightly before *On Liberty,* though it was not published until after *On Liberty.* The subject of *Utilitarianism* is the *summum bonum,* or ultimate good. Following Bentham, Mill holds this to be happiness.

Mill's theory of utilitarianism generally is held to differ from Bentham's in Mill's introduction of quality of pleasures and pains. Mill states: "It is quite compatible with the principle of utility to recognize the fact, that some *kinds* of pleasure are more desirable and more valuable than others. It would be absurd that while, in estimating all other things, quality is considered as well as quantity, the estimation of pleasures should be supposed to depend on quantity alone."

Historically, the great objection to utilitarianism stems from its emphasis on pleasure and pain. Carlyle called utilitarianism "pig philosophy." Does the exaltation of pleasures and pains necessarily reduce humanity to swine? Mill responds this way: "When thus attacked, the Epicureans have always answered, that it is not they, but their accusers, who represent human nature in a degrading light; since the accusation supposes human beings to be capable of no pleasures except those of which swine are capable."

Mill holds in *Utilitarianism* that the highest form of pleasure is sympathetic affection. For individuals who are "tolerably fortunate in their outward lot" who do not find happiness, the "cause generally is . . . caring for nobody but themselves." Public and private affections provide much of life's joy. Mill believes in a "powerful natural sentiment" that can form the basis for utilitarian morality: "This firm foundation is . . . the social feelings of mankind; the desire to be in unity with our fellow creatures . . ."

Mill's most amazing claim for utilitarianism is contained in these lines: "In the golden rule of Jesus of Nazareth, we read the complete spirit of the ethics of utility. To do as you would be done by, and to love your neighbour as yourself, constitute the ideal perfection of utilitarian morality." How is Mill able to say this, as he believes pleasure and freedom from pain are the only desirable ends? How can the golden rule not only be reconcilable with the principle of utility but its "complete spirit"?

Mill's answer is found in his conception of pleasure and pain. He believes that pleasures and pains have both quality and quantity. He further believes that the highest quality pleasure—the most intense pleasure—is sympathetic affection, loving one's neighbors. Individuals experience their greatest, highest pleasure, according to Mill, when they help others to be happy. In this way, to love one's neighbor as oneself is not merely reconcilable with, but constitutes the "ideal perfection" of, utilitarian ethics.

Mill does not believe the happiest person necessarily is the one who is happiest for the greatest period of time. Indeed, he holds that one of two pleasures can have a "superiority in quality" so great compared to quantity as in comparison to render the latter of "small account." The quality of pleasures differs so markedly that an individual who experiences high quality pleasures even for a short period of time can be happier overall—can have a higher quotient of happiness—than an individual who experiences lower quality pleasures for a longer period of time.

Mill holds in *Utilitarianism* that the "utilitarian morality does recognize in human beings the power of sacrificing their own greatest good for the good of others." How is this possible? If one genuinely loves one's neighbor as oneself, there is no greater pleasure than loving others. Humans become happiest through the happiness of others.

It is unnecessary to postulate as Aristotle does in *Nichomachean Ethics* that the greatest happiness comes about through a single act of self-sacrifice. Aristotle writes "it is true of the good man . . . that he does many acts for the sake of his friends and country, and if necessary dies for them . . . since he would prefer a short period of intense pleasure to a long one of mild enjoyment, a twelve-month of noble life to many years of humdrum existence, and one great and noble action to many trivial ones." Rather, it is the spirit that enables self-sacrifice that is enjoined by utilitarian ethics. It is this spirit that is such great happiness, regardless of whether or how it is called upon to act or not.

The sublime quality of happiness that one receives in being able to make the ultimate sacrifice allows one to transcend the earthly and touch the ethereal. If one genuinely loves others, there is no greater happiness than sacrificing oneself for another. The only correction that should be made in Mill's statement for it really to be compatible with Christian ethics is that "the utilitarian morality does recognize in human beings the power of *realizing* their own greatest good in the good of others."

Mill is a great optimist. He writes in *Utilitarianism* that "no one whose opinion deserves a moment's consideration can doubt that most of the great positive evils of the world are in themselves removable, and will, if human affairs continue to improve, be in the end reduced within narrow limits. Poverty, in any sense implying suffering, may be completely extinguished by the wisdom of society . . . Even that most intractable of enemies, disease, may be indefinitely reduced in dimensions . . . And every advance in that direction relieves us from some, not only of the chances which cut short our own lives, but, what concerns us still more, which deprive us of those in whom our happiness is wrapt up . . . All the grand sources, in short, of human suffering are in a great degree, many of them almost entirely, conquerable by human care and effort."

Like other democrats and liberals, Mill's thought on the subject of political and economic liberty suffers from tensions and dilemmas that are not so much a result of personal inconsistencies as of deeper tensions between democracy and liberalism. In dealing with both political and economic liberty, Mill always tries to reconcile his emotional attachment for the negative conception of liberty (liberalism) with his intellectual acceptance of the positive conception of liberty (democracy). Despite the evolution of his thought through several phases of diverse emphases, his ultimate and decisive commitment was to the more difficult ideal of liberalism than the more appealing ideal of democracy. This is true of his concern with both political and economic liberty.

An area of great interest to Mill was women's rights. His interest in this area was furthered by his wife, the former Harriet Taylor. While it seems almost inconceivable in 2000, in 1900, women almost everywhere were denied the suffrage. In the fifth chapter of *Utilitarianism,* on justice, Mill prophetically writes that "the entire history of social improvement has been a series of transitions by which one custom or institution after another . . . has passed into the rank of a universally stigmatized injustice and tyranny. So it has been with the distinctions of slaves and freemen, nobles and serfs, patricians and plebeians; and so it will be, and in part already is, with the aristocracies of color, race, and sex."

Mill turned to the topic of women's rights in *The Subjection of Women* (1869). He here takes the position, exceedingly controversial for his time, that "the principle which regulates the existing social relations between the two sexes—the legal subordination of one sex to the other—is wrong in itself, and . . . ought to be replaced by a principle of perfect equality." He particularly is concerned with legal equality in marriage: "The moral regeneration of mankind will only really commence when the most fundamental of social relations is placed under the rule of equal justice."

Mill attempted to advance legal equality between the sexes while a member of Parliament. During debate on the Reform Bill of 1867, extending the right to vote, he moved that "man" should be replaced by "person," the first time the question of women's right to vote was heard in Parliament and a half-century before similar legislation passed. On this, as many other issues, he deeply felt and was ahead of his time.

Mill was the greatest philosophical liberal of the nineteenth century; William Gladstone, who called Mill the "saint of rationalism," was the greatest political liberal (and Liberal). Mill's thought forms a bridge between the classical liberals of the nineteenth century and democratic socialists and democratic interventionist welfare state capitalists of the twentieth—from Bentham to Fabianism and Keynesians.

On Liberty remains, moreover, the best libertarian statement. In putting forward in *On Liberty* his "one very simple principle . . . that the sole end for which mankind are warranted, individually or collectively, in interfering with the liberty of action of any of their number is self-protection," Mill exactly states libertarianism. As he continues, "the only purpose for which power can be rightfully exercised over any member of a civilised community, against his will, is to prevent harm to others." Unfortunately, Mill conflated the libertarian standard for coercive involvement in others' lives of doing no harm to others with the far more general standard merely of an individual not engaging in activity that "concerns" others, and he thus was not a consistent libertarian.

Mill was the first intellectual of major stature to adopt a sympathetic attitude toward socialism, without being dogmatic. He sought the greatest happiness for all. He prefaced *On Liberty* with this passage from Wilhem von Humboldt: "The grand, leading principle, towards which every argument unfolded in these pages directly converges, is the absolute and essential importance of human development in its richest diversity."

MILL

*On Liberty**

LIBERTY AND AUTHORITY

The subject of this Essay is not the so-called Liberty of the Will, so unfortunately opposed to the misnamed doctrine of Philosophical Necessity; but Civil, or Social Liberty: the nature and limits of the power which can be legitimately exercised by society over the individual. A question seldom stated, and hardly ever discussed, in general terms, but which profoundly influences the practical controversies of the age by its latent presence, and is likely soon to make itself recognized as the vital question of the future. It is so far from being new, that, in a certain sense, it has divided mankind, almost from the remotest ages; but in the stage of progress into which the more civilized portions of the species have now entered, it presents itself under new conditions, and requires a different and more fundamental treatment.

The struggle between Liberty and Authority is the most conspicuous feature in the portions of history with which we are earliest familiar, particularly in that of Greece, Rome, and England. But in old times this contest was between subjects, or some classes of subjects, and the Government. By liberty, was meant protection against the tyranny of the political rulers. The rulers were conceived (except in some of the popular governments of Greece) as in a necessarily antagonistic position to the people whom they ruled. They consisted of a governing One, or a governing tribe or caste, who derived their authority from inheritance or conquest, who, at all events, did not hold it at the pleasure of the governed, and whose

supremacy men did not venture, perhaps did not desire, to contest, whatever precautions might be taken against its oppressive exercise. Their power was regarded as necessary, but also as highly dangerous; as a weapon which they would attempt to use against their subjects, no less than against external enemies. To prevent the weaker members of the community from being preyed upon by innumerable vultures, it was needful that there should be an animal of prey stronger than the rest, commissioned to keep them down. But as the king of the vultures would be no less bent upon preying on the flock than any of the minor harpies, it was indispensable to be in a perpetual attitude of defense against his beak and claws. The aim, therefore, of patriots was to set limits to the power which the ruler should be suffered to exercise over the community; and this limitation was what they meant by liberty. It was attempted in two ways. First, by obtaining a recognition of certain immunities, called political liberties or rights, (which it was to be regarded as a breach of duty in the ruler to infringe, and which, if he did infringe, specific resistance, or general rebellion, was held to be justifiable). A second, and generally a later expedient, was the establishment of constitutional checks, (by which the consent of the community, or of a body of some sort, supposed to represent its interests, was made a necessary condition to some of the more important acts of the governing power). To the first of these modes of limitation, the ruling power, in most European countries, was compelled, more or less, to submit. It was not so with the second; and, to attain this, or when already in some degree possessed, to attain it more completely, became everywhere the principal

---

*From John Stuart Mill, *On Liberty* (1859).

object of the lovers of liberty. And so long as mankind were content to combat one enemy by another, and to be ruled by a master, on condition of being guaranteed more or less efficaciously against his tyranny, they did not carry their aspirations beyond this point.

A time, however, came, in the progress of human affairs, when men ceased to think it a necessity of nature that their governors should be an independent power, opposed in interest to themselves. It appeared to them much better that the various magistrates of the State should be their tenants or delegates, revocable at their pleasure. In that way alone, it seemed, could they have complete security that the powers of government would never be abused to their disadvantage. By degrees this new demand for elective and temporary rulers became the prominent object of the exertions of the popular party, wherever any such party existed; and superseded, to a considerable extent, the previous efforts to limit the power of rulers. As the struggle proceeded for making the ruling power emanate from the periodical choice of the ruled, some persons began to think that too much importance had been attached to the limitation of the power itself. *That* (it might seem) was a resource against rulers whose interests were habitually opposed to those of the people. What was now wanted was, that the rulers should be identified with the people; that their interest and will should be the interest and will of the nation. The nation did not need to be protected against its own will. There was no fear of tyrannizing over itself. Let the rulers be effectually responsible to it, promptly removable by it, and it could afford to trust them with power of which it could itself dictate the use to be made. Their power was but the nation's own power, concentrated, and in a form convenient for exercise. This mode of thought, or rather perhaps of feeling, was common among the last generation of European liberalism, in the Continental section of which it still apparently predominates. Those who admit any limit to what a government may do, except in the case of such governments as they think ought not to exist, stand out as brilliant exceptions among the political thinkers of the Continent. A similar tone of sentiment might by this time have been prevalent in our own country, if the circumstances which for a time encouraged it, had continued unaltered.

But, in political and philosophical theories, as well as in persons, success discloses faults and infirmities which failure might have concealed from observation. The notion, that the people have no need to limit their power over themselves, might seem axiomatic, when popular government was a thing only dreamed about, or read of as having existed at some distant period of the past. Neither was that notion necessarily disturbed by such temporary aberrations as those of the French Revolution, the worst of which were the work of an usurping few, and which, in any case, belonged, not to the permanent working of popular institutions, but to a sudden and convulsive outbreak against monarchical and aristocratic despotism. In time, however, a democratic republic came to occupy a large portion of the earth's surface, and made itself felt as one of the most powerful members of the community of nations; and elective and responsible government became subject to the observations and criticisms which wait upon a great existing fact. It was now perceived that such phrases as "self-government," and "the power of the people over themselves," do not express the true state of the case. The "people" who exercise the power are not always the same people with those over whom it is exercised; and the "self-government" spoken of is not the government of each by himself, but of each by all the rest. The will of the people, moreover, practically means the will of the most numerous or the most active *part* of the people: the majority, or those who succeed in making themselves accepted as the majority; the people, consequently, *may* desire to oppress a part of their number; and precautions are as much needed against this as against any other abuse of power. The limitation, therefore, of the power of government over individuals loses none of its importance when the holders of power are regularly accountable to the community, that is, to the strongest party therein. This view of things, recommending itself equally to the intelligence of thinkers and to the inclination of those important classes in European society to whose real or supposed interests democracy is adverse, has had no difficulty in establishing itself; and in political speculations "the tyranny of the majority" is now generally included among the evils against which society requires to be on its guard.

Like other tyrannies, the tyranny of the majority was at first, and is still vulgarly, held in dread, chiefly as operating through the acts of the public authorities. But reflecting persons perceived that when society is itself the tyrant—society collectively, over the separate individuals who compose it—its means of tyrannizing are not restricted to the acts which it may do by the hands of its political functionaries. Society can and does execute its own mandates: and if it issues wrong mandates instead of right, or any mandates at all in things with which it ought not to meddle, it practices a social tyranny more formidable than many kinds of political oppression, since, though not usually upheld by such extreme penalties, it leaves fewer means of escape, penetrating much more deeply into the details of life, and enslaving the soul itself. Protection, therefore, against the tyranny of the magistrate is not enough: there needs protection also against the tyranny of the prevailing opinion and feeling; against the tendency of society to impose, by other means than civil penalties, its own ideas and practices as rules of conduct on those who dissent from them; to fetter the development, and, if possible, prevent the formation, of any individuality not in harmony with its ways, and compel all characters to fashion themselves upon the model of its own. There is a limit to the legitimate interference of collective opinion with individual independence: and to find that limit, and maintain it against encroachment, is as indispensable to a good condition of human affairs, as protection against political despotism.

But though this proposition is not likely to be contested in general terms, the practical question, where to place the limit—how to make the fitting adjustment between individual independence and social control—is a subject on which nearly everything remains to be done.

The object of this Essay is to assert one very simple principle, as entitled to govern absolutely the dealings of society with the individual in the way of compulsion and control, whether the means used be physical force in the form of legal penalties, or the moral coercion of public opinion. That principle is, that the sole end for which mankind are warranted, individually or collectively, in interfering with the liberty of action of any of their number, is self-protection. That the only purpose for which power can be rightfully exercised over any member of a civilized community, against his will, is to prevent harm to others. His own good, either physical or moral, is not a sufficient warrant. He cannot rightfully be compelled to do or forbear because it will be better for him to do so, because it will make him happier, because, in the opinions of others, to do so would be wise, or even right. These are good reasons for remonstrating with him, or reasoning with him, or persuading him, or entreating him, but not for compelling him, or visiting him with any evil in case he do otherwise. To justify that, the conduct from which it is desired to deter him, must be calculated to produce evil to some one else. The only part of the conduct of any one, for which he is amenable to society, is that which concerns others. In the part which merely concerns himself, his independence is, of right, absolute. Over himself, over his own body and mind, the individual is sovereign.

It is, perhaps, hardly necessary to say that this doctrine is meant to apply only to human beings in the maturity of their faculties. We are not speaking of children, or of young persons below the age which the law may fix as that of manhood or womanhood. Those who are still in a state to require being taken care of by others, must be protected against their own actions as well as against external injury. For the same reason, we may leave out of consideration those backward states of society in which the race itself may be considered as in its nonage. The early difficulties in the way of spontaneous progress are so great, that there is seldom any choice of means for overcoming them; and a ruler full of the spirit of improvement is warranted in the use of any expedients that will attain an end, perhaps otherwise unattainable. Despotism is a legitimate mode of government in dealing with barbarians, provided the end be their improvement, and the means justified by actually effecting that end. Liberty, as a principle, has no application to any state of things anterior to the time when mankind have become capable of being improved by free and equal discussion. Until then, there is nothing for them but implicit obedience to an Akbar or a Charlemagne, if they are so fortunate as to find one. But as soon as mankind have attained the capacity of being guided to their own improvement by conviction or persuasion (a period long since reached in all nations with whom we need here concern ourselves), compulsion, either in the direct form or in that of pains and penalties for non-compliance, is no longer admissible as a means to their own good, and justifiable only for the security of others.

It is proper to state that I forego any advantage which could be derived to my argument from the idea of abstract right, as a thing independent of utility. I regard utility as the ultimate appeal on all ethical questions; but it must be utility in the largest sense, grounded on the permanent interests of man as a progressive being. Those interests, I contend, authorize the subjection of individual spontaneity to external control, only in respect to those actions of each, which concern the interest of other people. If any one does an act hurtful to others, there is a prima facie case for punishing him, by law, or, where legal penalties are not safely applicable, by general disapprobation. There are also many positive acts for the benefit of others, which he may rightfully be compelled to perform; such as, to give evidence in a court of justice; to bear his fair share in the common defense, or in any other joint work necessary to the interest of the society of which he enjoys the protection; and to perform certain acts of individual beneficence, such as saving a fellow creature's life, or interposing to protect the defenseless against ill-usage, things which whenever it is obviously a man's duty to do, he may rightfully be made responsible to society for not doing. A person may cause evil to others not only by his actions but by his inaction, and in either case he is justly accountable to them for the injury. The latter case, it is true, requires a much more cautious exercise of compulsion than the former. To make any one answerable for doing evil to others, is the rule; to make

him answerable for not preventing evil, is, comparatively speaking, the exception. Yet there are many cases clear enough and grave enough to justify that exception. In all things which regard the external relations of the individual, he is *de jure* amenable to those whose interests are concerned, and if need be, to society as their protector. There are often good reasons for not holding him to the responsibility; but these reasons must arise from the special expediencies of the case: either because it is a kind of case in which he is on the whole likely to act better, when left to his own discretion, than when controlled in any way in which society have it in their power to control him; or because the attempt to exercise control would produce other evils, greater than those which it would prevent. When such reasons as these preclude the enforcement of responsibility, the conscience of the agent himself should step into the vacant judgment-seat, and protect those interests of others which have no external protection; judging himself all the more rigidly, because the case does not admit of his being made accountable to the judgment of his fellow creatures.

But there is a sphere of action in which society, as distinguished from the individual, has, if any, only an indirect interest: comprehending all that portion of a person's life and conduct which affects only himself, or if it also affects others, only with their free, voluntary, and undeceived consent and participation. When I say only himself, I mean directly, and in the first instance: for whatever affects himself, may affect others through himself; and the objection which may be grounded on this contingency will receive consideration in the sequel. This, then, is the appropriate region of human liberty. It comprises, first, the inward domain of consciousness; demanding liberty of conscience, in the most comprehensive sense; liberty of thought and feeling; absolute freedom of opinion and sentiment on all subjects, practical or speculative, scientific, moral, or theological. The liberty of expressing and publishing opinions may seem to fall under a different principle, since it belongs to that part of the conduct of an individual which concerns other people; but, being almost of as much importance as the liberty of thought itself, and resting in great part on the same reasons, is practically inseparable from it. Secondly, the principle requires liberty of tastes and pursuits; of framing the plan of our life to suit our own character; of doing as we like, subject to such consequences as may follow: without impediment from our fellow creatures, so long as what we do does not harm them, even though they should think our conduct foolish, perverse, or wrong. Thirdly, from this liberty of each individual, follows the liberty, within the same limits, of combination among individuals; freedom to unite, for any purpose not involving harm to others: the persons combining being supposed to be of full age, and not forced or deceived.

No society in which these liberties are not, on the whole, respected, is free, whatever may be its form of government; and none is completely free in which they do not exist absolute and unqualified. The only freedom which deserves the name, is that of pursuing our own good in our own way, so long as we do not attempt to deprive others of theirs, or impede their efforts to obtain it. Each is the proper guardian of his own health, whether bodily, or mental and spiritual. Mankind are greater gainers by suffering each other to live as seems good to themselves, than by compelling each to live as seems good to the rest.

LIBERTY OF THOUGHT AND DISCUSSION

The time, it is to be hoped, is gone by, when any defense would be necessary of the "liberty of the press" as one of the securities against corrupt or tyrannical government. No argument, we may suppose, can now be needed, against permitting a legislature or an executive, not identified in interest with the people, to prescribe opinions to them, and determine what doctrines or what arguments they shall be allowed to hear. This aspect of the question, besides, has been so often and so triumphantly enforced by preceding writers, that it needs not be specially insisted on in this place. Though the law of England, on the subject of the press, is as servile to this day as it was in the time of the Tudors, there is little danger of its being actually put in force against political discussion, except during some temporary panic, when fear of insurrection drives ministers

and judges from their propriety;[1] and, speaking generally, it is not, in constitutional countries, to be apprehended, that the government, whether completely responsible to the people or not, will often attempt to control the expression of opinion, except when in doing so it makes itself the organ of the general intolerance of the public. Let us suppose, therefore, that the government is entirely at one with the people, and never thinks of exerting any power of coercion unless in agreement with what it conceives to be their voice. But I deny the right of the people to exercise such coercion, either by

---

[1] These words had scarcely been written, when, as if to give them an emphatic contradiction, occurred the Government Press Prosecutions of 1858. That ill-judged interference with the liberty of public discussion has not, however, induced me to alter a single word in the text, nor has it at all weakened my conviction that, moments of panic excepted, the era of pains and penalties for political discussion has, in our own country, passed away. For, in the first place, the prosecutions were not persisted in; and, in the second, they were never, properly speaking, political prosecutions. The offense charged was not that of criticizing institutions, or the acts or persons of rulers, but of circulating what was deemed an immoral doctrine, the lawfulness of Tyrannicide.

If the arguments of the present chapter are of any validity, there ought to exist the fullest liberty of professing and discussing, as a matter of ethical conviction, any doctrine, however immoral it may be considered. It would, therefore, be irrelevant and out of place to examine here, whether the doctrine of Tyrannicide deserves that title. I shall content myself with saying that the subject has been at all times one of the open questions of morals; that the act of a private citizen in striking down a criminal, who, by raising himself above the law, has placed himself beyond the reach of legal punishment or control, has been accounted by whole nations, and by some of the best and wisest of men, not a crime, but an act of exalted virtue; and that, right or wrong, it is not of the nature of assassination, but of civil war. As such, I hold that the instigation to it, in a specific case, may be a proper subject of punishment, but only if an overt act has followed, and at least a probable connection can be established between the act and the instigation. Even then, it is not a foreign government, but the very government assailed, which alone, in the exercise of self-defense, can legitimately punish attacks directed against its own existence.

themselves or by their government. The power itself is illegitimate. The best government has no more title to it than the worst. It is as noxious, or more noxious, when exerted in accordance with public opinion, than when in opposition to it. If all mankind minus one, were of one opinion, and only one person were of the contrary opinion, mankind would be no more justified in silencing that one person, than he, if he had the power, would be justified in silencing mankind. Were an opinion a personal possession of no value except to the owner; if to be obstructed in the enjoyment of it were simply a private injury, it would make some difference whether the injury was inflicted only on a few persons or on many. But the peculiar evil of silencing the expression of an opinion is, that it is robbing the human race; posterity as well as the existing generation; those who dissent from the opinion, still more than those who hold it. If the opinion is right, they are deprived of the opportunity of exchanging error for truth: if wrong, they lose, what is almost as great a benefit, the clearer perception and livelier impression of truth, produced by its collision with error.

It is necessary to consider separately these two hypotheses, each of which has a distinct branch of the argument corresponding to it. We can never be sure that the opinion we are endeavoring to stifle is a false opinion; and if we were sure, stifling it would be an evil still.

First: the opinion which it is attempted to suppress by authority may possibly be true. Those who desire to suppress it, of course deny its truth; but they are not infallible. They have no authority to decide the question for all mankind, and exclude every other person from the means of judging. To refuse a hearing to an opinion, because they are sure that it is false, is to assume that *their* certainty is the same thing as *absolute* certainty. All silencing of discussion is an assumption of infallibility. Its condemnation may be allowed to rest on this common argument, not the worse for being common.

Unfortunately for the good sense of mankind, the fact of their fallibility is far from carrying the weight in their practical judgment, which is always allowed to it in theory; for while every one well knows himself to be fallible, few think it necessary to take any precautions against their own fallibility, or admit the supposition that any opinion, of which they feel very certain, may be one of the examples of the error to which they acknowledge themselves to be liable. Absolute princes, or others who are accustomed to unlimited deference, usually feel this complete confidence in their own opinions on nearly all subjects. People more happily situated, who sometimes hear their opinions disputed, and are not wholly unused to be set right when they are wrong, place the same unbounded reliance only on such of their opinions as are shared by all who surround them, or to whom they habitually defer: for in proportion to a man's want of confidence in his own solitary judgment, does he usually repose, with implicit trust, on the infallibility of "the world" in general. And the world, to each individual, means the part of it with which he comes in contact; his party, his sect, his church, his class of society: the man may be called, by comparison, almost liberal and large-minded to whom it means anything so comprehensive as his own country or his own age. Nor is his faith in this collective authority at all shaken by his being aware that other ages, countries, sects, churches, classes, and parties have thought, and even now think, the exact reverse. He devolves upon his own world the responsibility of being in the right against the dissentient worlds of other people; and it never troubles him that mere accident has decided which of these numerous worlds is the object of his reliance, and that the same causes which make him a Churchman in London, would have made him a Buddhist or a Confucian in Pekin. Yet it is as evident in itself, as any amount of argument can make it, that ages are no more infallible than individuals; every age having held many opinions which subsequent ages have deemed not only false but absurd; and it is as certain that many opinions, now general, will be rejected by future ages, as it is that many, once general, are rejected by the present.

The objection likely to be made to this argument would probably take some such form as the following. There is no greater assumption of infallibility in forbidding the propagation of error, than in any other thing which is done by public authority on its own judgment and responsibility. Judgment is given to men that they may use it. Because it may be used erroneously, are men to be told that they ought not to use it at all? To prohibit what they think pernicious, is not claiming exemption from error, but fulfilling the duty incumbent on them, although fallible, of acting on their conscientious conviction. If we were never to act on our opinions, because those opinions may be wrong, we should leave all our interests uncared for, and all our duties unperformed. An objection which applies to all conduct, can be no valid objection to any conduct in particular. It is the duty of governments, and of individuals, to form the truest opinions they can; to form them carefully, and never impose them upon others unless they are quite sure of being right. But when they are sure (such reasoners may say), it is not conscientiousness but cowardice to shrink from acting on their opinions, and allow doctrines which they honestly think dangerous to the welfare of mankind, either in this life or in another, to be scattered abroad without restraint, because other people, in less enlightened times, have persecuted opinions now believed to be true. Let us take care, it may be said, not to make the same mistake: but governments and nations have made mistakes in other things, which are not denied to be fit subjects for the exercise of authority: they have laid on bad taxes, made unjust wars. Ought we therefore to lay on no taxes, and, under whatever provocation, make no wars? Men, and governments, must act to the best of their ability. There is no such thing as absolute certainty, but there is assurance sufficient for the purposes of human life. We may, and must, assume our opinion to be true for the guidance of our own conduct: and it is assuming no more when we forbid bad men to pervert society by the propagation of opinions which we regard as false and pernicious.

I answer, that it is assuming very much more. There is the greatest difference between presuming an opinion to be true, because, with every opportunity for contesting it, it has not been refuted, and assuming its truth for the purpose of not permitting its refutation. Complete liberty of contradicting and disproving our opinion, is the very condition which justifies us in assuming its truth for purposes of action; and on no other terms can a being with human faculties have any rational assurance of being right.

When we consider either the history of opinion, or the ordinary conduct of human life, to what is it to be ascribed that the one and the other are no worse than they are? Not certainly to the inherent force of the human understanding; for, on any matter not self-evident, there are ninety-nine persons totally incapable of judging of it, for one who is capable; and the capacity of the hundredth person is only comparative; for the majority of the eminent men of every past generation held many opinions now known to be erroneous, and did or approved numerous things which no one will now justify. Why is it, then, that there is on the whole a preponderance among mankind of rational opinions and rational conduct? If there really is this preponderance—which there must be unless human affairs are, and have always been, in an almost desperate state— it is owing to a quality of the human mind, the source of everything respectable in man either as an intellectual or as a moral being, namely, that his errors are corrigible. He is capable of rectifying his mistakes, by discussion and experience. Not by experience alone. There must be discussion, to show how experience is to be interpreted. Wrong opinions and practices gradually yield to fact and argument: but facts and arguments, to produce any effect on the mind, must be brought before it. Very few facts are able to tell their own story, without comments to bring out their meaning. The whole strength and value, then, of human judgment, depending on the one property, that it can be set right when it is wrong, reliance can be placed on it only when the means of setting it right are kept constantly at hand. In the case of any person whose judgment is really deserving of confidence, how has it become so? Because he has kept his mind open to criticism of his opinions and conduct. Because it has been his practice to listen to all that could be said against him; to profit by as much of it as was just, and expound to himself, and upon occasion to others, the fallacy of what was fallacious. Because he has felt, that the only way in which a human being can make some approach to knowing the whole of a subject, is by hearing what can be said about it by persons of every variety of opinion, and studying all modes in which it can be looked at by every character of mind. No wise man ever acquired his wisdom in any mode but this; nor is it in the nature of human intellect to become wise in any other manner. The steady habit of correcting and completing his own opinion by collating it with those of others, so far from causing doubt and hesitation in carrying it into practice, is the only stable foundation for a just reliance on it: for, being cognizant of all that can, at least obviously, be said against him, and having taken up his position against all gain-sayers—knowing that he has sought for objections and difficulties, instead of avoiding them, and has shut out no light which can be thrown upon the subject from any quarter—he has a right to think his judgment better than that of any person, or any multitude, who have not gone through a similar process.

It is not too much to require that what the wisest of mankind, those who are best entitled to trust their own judgment, find necessary to warrant their relying on it, should be submitted to by that miscellaneous collection of a few wise and many foolish individuals, called the public. The most intolerant of churches, the Roman Catholic Church, even at the canonization of a saint, admits, and listens patiently to, a "devil's advocate." The holiest of men, it appears, cannot be admitted to posthumous honors, until all that the devil could say against him is known and weighed. If even the Newtonian philosophy were not permitted to be questioned, mankind could not feel as complete assurance of its truth as they now do. The beliefs which we have most warrant for, have no safeguard to rest on, but a standing invitation to the whole world to prove them unfounded. If the challenge is not accepted, or is accepted and the attempt fails, we are far enough from certainty still; but we have done the best that the existing state of human reason admits of; we have neglected nothing that could give the truth a chance of reaching us: if the lists are kept open, we may hope that if there be a better truth, it will be found when the human mind is capable of receiving it; and in the meantime we may rely on having attained such approach to truth, as is possible in our own day. This is the amount of certainty attainable by a fallible being, and this the sole way of attaining it.

Strange it is, that men should admit the validity of the arguments for free discussion, but object to their being "pushed to an extreme"; not seeing that unless the reasons are good for an extreme case, they are not good for any case. Strange that they should imagine that they are not assuming infallibility, when they acknowledge that there should be free discussion on all subjects which can possibly be *doubtful,* but think that some particular principle or doctrine should be forbidden to be questioned because it is so *certain,* that is, because *they are certain* that it is certain. To call any proposition certain, while there is any one who would deny its certainty if permitted, but who is not permitted, is to assume that we ourselves, and those who agree with us, are the judges of certainty, and judges without hearing the other side.

In the present age—which has been described as "destitute of faith, but terrified at scepticism"—in which people feel sure, not so much that their opinions are true, as that they should not know what to do without them—the claims of an opinion to be protected from public attack are rested not so much on its truth, as on its importance to society. There are, it is alleged, certain beliefs, so useful, not to say indispensable to well-being, that it is as much the duty of governments to uphold those beliefs, as to protect any other of the interests of society. In a case of such necessity, and so directly in the line of their duty, something less than infallibility may, it is maintained, warrant, and even bind, governments, to act on their own opinion, confirmed by the general opinion of mankind. It is also often argued, and still oftener thought, that none but bad men would desire to weaken these salutary beliefs; and there can be nothing wrong, it is thought, in restraining bad men, and prohibiting what only such men would wish to practice. This mode of thinking makes the justification of restraints on discussion not a question of the truth of doctrines, but of their usefulness; and flatters itself by that means to escape the responsibility of claiming to be an infallible judge of opinions. But those who thus satisfy themselves, do not perceive that the assumption of infallibility is merely shifted from one point to another. The usefulness of an opinion is itself matter of opinion: as disputable, as open to discussion, and requiring discussion as much, as the opinion itself. There is the same need of an infallible judge of opinions to decide an opinion to be noxious, as to decide it to be false, unless the opinion condemned has full opportunity of defending itself. And it will not do to say that the heretic may be allowed to maintain the utility or harmlessness of his opinion, though forbidden to maintain its truth. The truth of an opinion is part of its utility. If we would know whether or not it is desirable that a proposition should be believed, is it possible to exclude the consideration of whether or not it is true? In the opinion, not of bad men, but of the best men, no belief which is contrary to truth can be really useful: and can you prevent such men from urging that plea, when they are charged with culpability for denying some doctrine which they are told is useful, but which they believe to be false? Those who are on the side of received opinions, never fail to take all possible advantage of this plea; you do not find *them* handling the question of utility as if it could be completely abstracted from that of truth: on the contrary, it is, above all, because their doctrine is the "truth," that the knowledge or the belief of it is held to be so indispensable. There can be no fair discussion of the question of usefulness, when an argument so vital may be employed on one side, but not on the other. And in point of fact, when law or public feeling do not permit the truth of an opinion to be disputed, they are just as little tolerant of a denial of its usefulness. The utmost they allow is an extenuation of its absolute necessity, or of the positive guilt of rejecting it.

In order more fully to illustrate the mischief of denying a hearing to opinions because we, in our own judgment, have condemned them, it will be desirable to fix down the discussion to a concrete case; and I choose, by preference, the cases which are least favorable to me—in which the argument against freedom of opinion, both on the score of truth and on that of utility, is considered the strongest. Let the opinions impugned be the belief in a God and in a future state, or any of the commonly received doctrines of morality. To fight the battle on such ground, gives a great advantage to an unfair antagonist; since he will be sure to say (and many who have no desire to be unfair will say it internally), Are these the doctrines which you do not deem sufficiently certain to be taken under the protection of law? Is the belief in a God one of the opinions, to feel sure of which, you hold to be assuming infallibility? But I must be permitted to observe, that it is not the feeling sure of a doctrine (be it what it may) which I call an assumption of infallibility. It is the undertaking to decide that question *for others,* without allowing them to hear what can be said on the contrary side. And I denounce and reprobate this pretension not the less, if put forth on the side of my most solemn convictions. However positive any one's persuasion may be, not only of the falsity but of the pernicious consequences—not only of the pernicious consequences, but (to adopt expressions which I altogether condemn) the immorality and impiety of an opinion; yet if, in pursuance of that private judgment, though backed by the public judgment of his country or his contemporaries, he prevents the opinion from being heard in its defense, he assumes infallibility. And so far from the assumption being less objectionable or less dangerous because the opinion is called immoral or impious, this is the case of all others in which it is most fatal. These are exactly the occasions on which the men of one generation commit those dreadful mistakes, which excite the astonishment and horror of posterity. It is among such that we find the instances memorable in history, when the arm of the law has been employed to root out the best men and the noblest doctrines; with deplorable success as to the men, though some of the doctrines have survived to be (as if in mockery) invoked, in defense of similar conduct towards those who dissent from *them,* or from their received interpretation.

Mankind can hardly be too often reminded, that there was once a man named Socrates, between whom and the legal authorities and public opinion of his time, there took place a memorable collision. Born in an age and country abounding in individual greatness, this man has been handed down to us by those who best knew both him and the age, as the most virtuous man in it; while *we* know him as the head and prototype of all subsequent teachers of virtue, the source equally of the lofty inspiration of Plato and the judicious utilitarianism of Aristotle, *i maestri di color che sanno,* the two headsprings of ethical as of all other philosophy. This acknowledged master of all the eminent thinkers who have since lived—whose fame, still growing after more than two thousand years, all but outweighs the whole remainder of the names which make his native city illustrious—was put to death by his countrymen, after a judicial conviction, for impiety and immorality. Impiety, in denying the gods recognized by the State; indeed his accuser asserted (see the *Apologia*) that he believed in no gods at all. Immorality, in being, by his doctrines and instructions, a "corruptor of youth." Of these charges the tribunal, there is every ground for believing, honestly found him guilty, and condemned the man who probably of all then born had deserved best of mankind, to be put to death as a criminal.

To pass from this to the only other instance of judicial iniquity, the mention of which, after the condemnation of Socrates, would not be an anti-climax: the event which took place on Calvary rather more than eighteen hundred years ago. The man who left on the memory of those who witnessed his life and conversation, such an impression of his moral grandeur, that eighteen subsequent centuries have done homage to him as the Almighty in person, was ignominiously put to death, as what? As a blasphemer. Men did not merely mistake their benefactor; they mistook him for the exact contrary of what he was, and treated him as that prodigy of impiety, which they themselves are now held to be, for their treatment of him. The feelings with which mankind now regard these lamentable transactions, especially the later of the two, render them extremely unjust in their judgment of the unhappy actors. These were, to all appearance, not bad men—not worse than men commonly are, but rather the contrary: men who possessed in a full, or somewhat more than a full measure, the religious, moral, and patriotic feelings of their time and people: the very kind of men who, in all times, our own included, have every chance of passing through life blameless and respected. The high-priest who rent his garments when the words were pronounced, which, according to all the ideas of his country, constituted the blackest guilt, was in all probability quite as sincere in his horror and indignation, as the generality of respectable and pious men now are in the religious and moral sentiments they profess; and most of those who now shudder at his conduct, if they had lived in his time, and been born Jews, would have acted precisely as he did. Orthodox Christians who are tempted to think that those who stoned to death the first martyrs must have been worse men than they themselves are, ought to remember that one of those persecutors was Saint Paul.

Let us add one more example, the most striking of all, if the impressiveness of an error is measured by the wisdom and virtue of him who falls into it. If ever any one, possessed of power, had grounds for thinking himself the best and most enlightened among his contemporaries, it was the Emperor Marcus Aurelius. Absolute monarch of the whole civilized world, he preserved through life not only the most unblemished justice, but what was less to be expected from his Stoical breeding, the tenderest heart. The few failings which are attributed to him, were all on the side of indulgence: while his writings, the highest ethical product of the ancient mind, differ scarcely perceptibly, if they differ at all, from the most characteristic teachings of Christ. This man, a better Christian in all but the dogmatic sense of the word, than almost any of the ostensibly Christian sovereigns who have since reigned, persecuted Christianity. Placed at the summit of all the previous attainments of humanity, with an open, unfettered intellect, and a character which led him of himself to embody in his moral writings the Christian ideal, he yet failed to see that Christianity was to be a good and not an evil to the world, with his duties to which he was so deeply penetrated. Existing society he knew to be in a deplorable state. But such as it was, he saw, or thought he saw, that it was held together, and prevented from being worse, by belief and reverence of the received divinities. As a ruler of mankind, he deemed it his duty not to suffer society to fall in pieces; and saw not how, if its existing ties were removed, any others could be formed which could again knit it together. The new religion openly aimed at dissolving these ties: unless, therefore, it was his duty to adopt that religion, it seemed to be his duty to put it down. Inasmuch then as the theology of Christianity did not appear to him true or of divine origin; inasmuch as this strange history of a crucified God was not credible to him, and a system which purported to rest entirely upon a foundation to him so wholly unbelievable, could not be foreseen by him to be that renovating agency which, after all abatements, it has in fact proved to be; the gentlest and most amiable of philosophers and rulers, under a solemn sense of duty, authorized the persecution of Christianity. To my mind this is one of the most tragical facts in all history. It is a bitter thought, how different a thing the Christianity of the world might have been, if the Christian faith had been adopted as the religion of the empire under the auspices of Marcus Aurelius instead of those of Constantine. But it would be equally unjust to him and false to truth, to deny, that no one plea which can be urged for punishing anti-Christian teaching, was wanting to Marcus Aurelius for punishing, as he did, the propagation of Christianity. No Christian more firmly believes that Atheism is false, and tends to the dissolution of society, than Marcus Aurelius believed the same things of Christianity; he who, of all men then living, might have been thought the most capable of appreciating it. Unless any one who approves of punishment for the promulgation of opinions, flatters himself that he is a wiser and better man than Marcus Aurelius—more deeply versed in the wisdom of his time, more elevated in his intellect above it—more earnest in his search for truth, or more singleminded in his devotion to it when found;—let him abstain from that assumption of the joint infallibility of himself and the multitude, which the great Antoninus made with so unfortunate a result.

Aware of the impossibility of defending the use of punishment for restraining irreligious opinions, by any argument which will not justify Marcus Antoninus, the enemies of religious freedom, when hard pressed, occasionally accept this consequence, and say, with Dr. Johnson, that the persecutors of Christianity were in the right; that persecution is an ordeal through which truth ought to pass, and always passes successfully, legal penalties being, in the end, powerless against truth, though sometimes beneficially effective against mischievous errors. This is a form of the argument for religious intolerance, sufficiently remarkable not to be passed without notice.

A theory which maintains that truth may justifiably be persecuted because persecution cannot possibly do it any harm, cannot be charged with being intentionally hostile to the reception of new truths; but we cannot commend the generosity of its dealing with the persons to whom mankind are indebted for them. To discover to the world something which deeply concerns it, and of which it was previously ignorant; to prove to it that it had been mistaken on some vital point of temporal or spiritual interest, is as important a service as a human being can render to his fellow creatures, and in certain cases, as in those of the early Christians and of the Reformers, those who think with Dr. Johnson believe it to have been the most precious gift which could be bestowed on mankind. That the authors of such splendid benefits should be requited by martyrdom; that their reward should be to be dealt with as the vilest of criminals, is not, upon this theory, a deplorable error and misfortune, for which humanity should mourn in sackcloth and ashes, but the normal and justifiable state of things. The propounder of a new truth, according to this doctrine, should stand, as stood, in the legislation of the Locrians, the proposer of a new law, with a halter round his neck, to be instantly tightened if the public assembly did not, on hearing his reasons, then and there adopt his proposition. People who defend this mode of treating benefactors, cannot be supposed to set much value on the benefit; and I believe this view of the subject is mostly confined to the sort of persons who think that new truths may have been desirable once, but that we have had enough of them now.

But, indeed, the dictum that truth always triumphs over persecution, is one of those pleasant falsehoods which men repeat after one another till they pass into commonplaces, but which all experience refutes. History teems with instances of truth put down by persecution. If not suppressed for ever, it may be thrown back for centuries. To speak only of religious opinions: the Reformation broke out at least twenty times before Luther, and was put down. Arnold of Brescia was put down. Fra Dolcino was put down. Savonarola was put down. The Albigeois were put down. The Vaudois were put down. The Lollards were put down. The Hussites were put down. Even after the era of Luther, wherever persecution was persisted in, it was successful. In Spain, Italy, Flanders, the Austrian empire, Protestantism was rooted out; and, most likely, would have been so in England, had Queen Mary lived, or Queen Elizabeth died. Persecution has always succeeded, save where the heretics were too strong a party to be effectually persecuted.

No reasonable person can doubt that Christianity might have been extirpated in the Roman Empire. It spread, and became predominant, because the persecutions were only occasional, lasting but a short time, and separated by long intervals of almost undisturbed propagandism. It is a piece of idle sentimentality that truth, merely as truth, has any inherent power denied to error, of prevailing against the dungeon and the stake. Men are not more zealous for truth than they often are for error, and a sufficient application of legal or even of social penalties will generally succeed in stopping the propagation of either. The real advantage which truth has, consists in this, that when an opinion is true, it may be extinguished once, twice, or many times, but in the course of ages there will generally be found persons to rediscover it, until some one of its reappearances falls on a time when from favorable circumstances it escapes persecution until it has made such head as to withstand all subsequent attempts to suppress it.

What is boasted of at the present time as the revival of religion, is always, in narrow and uncultivated minds, at least as much the revival of bigotry; and where there is the strong permanent leaven of intolerance in the feelings of a people, which at all times abides in the middle classes of this country, it needs but little to provoke them into actively persecuting those whom they have never ceased to think proper objects of persecution. For it is this—it is the opinions men entertain, and the feelings they cherish, respecting those who disown the beliefs they deem important, which makes this country not a place of mental freedom. For a long time past, the chief mischief of the legal penalties is that they strengthen the social stigma. It is that stigma which is really effective, and so effective is it, that the profession of opinions which are under the ban of society is much less common in England, than is, in many other countries, the avowal of those which incur risk of judicial punishment. In respect to all persons but those whose pecuniary circumstances make them independent of the goodwill of other people, opinion, on this subject, is as efficacious as law; men might as well be imprisoned, as excluded from the means of earning their bread. Those whose bread is already secured, and who desire no favors from men in power, or from bodies of men, or from the public, have nothing to fear from the open avowal of any opinions, but to be ill-thought of and ill-spoken of, and this it ought not to require a very heroic mold to enable them to bear. There is no room for any appeal *ad misericordiam* in behalf of such persons. But though we do not now inflict so much evil on those who think differently from us, as it was formerly our custom to do, it may be that we do ourselves as much evil as ever by our treatment of them. Socrates was put to death, but the Socratic philosophy rose like the sun in heaven, and spread its illumination over the whole intellectual firmament. Christians were cast to the lions, but the Christian church grew up a stately and spreading tree, overtopping the older and less vigorous growths, and stifling them by its shade. Our merely social intolerance kills no one, roots out no opinions, but induces men to disguise them, or to abstain from any active effort for their diffusion. With us, heretical opinions do not perceptibly gain, or even lose, ground in each decade or generation; they never blaze out far and wide, but continue to smolder in the narrow circles of thinking and studious persons among whom they originate, without ever lighting up the general affairs of mankind with either a true or a deceptive light. And thus is kept up a state of things very satisfactory to some minds, because, without the unpleasant process of fining or imprisoning anybody, it maintains all prevailing opinions outwardly undisturbed, while it does not absolutely interdict the exercise of reason by dissentients afflicted with the malady of thought. A convenient plan for having peace in the intellectual world, and keeping all things going on therein very much as they do already. But the price paid for this sort of intellectual pacification, is the sacrifice of the entire moral courage of the human mind. A state of things in which a large portion of the most active and inquiring intellects find it advisable to keep the general principles and grounds of their convictions within their own breasts, and attempt, in what they address to the public, to fit as much as they can of their own conclusions to premises which they have internally renounced, cannot send forth the open, fearless characters, and logical, consistent intellects who once adorned the thinking world. The sort of men who can be looked for under it, are either mere conformers to commonplace, or time-servers for truth, whose arguments on all great subjects are meant for their hearers, and are not those which have convinced themselves. Those who avoid this alternative, do so by narrowing their thoughts and interest to things which can be spoken of without venturing within the region of principles, that is, to small practical matters, which would come right of themselves, if but the minds of mankind were strengthened and enlarged, and which will never be made effectually right until then: while that which would strengthen and enlarge men's minds, free and daring speculation on the highest subjects, is abandoned.

Those in whose eyes this reticence on the part of heretics is no evil, should consider in the first place, that in consequence of it there is never any fair and thorough discussion of heretical opinions; and that such of them as could not stand such a discussion, though they may be prevented from spreading, do not disappear. But it is not the minds of heretics that are deteriorated most, by the ban placed on all inquiry which does not end in the orthodox conclusions. The greatest harm done is to those who are not heretics, and whose whole mental development is cramped, and their reason cowed, by the fear of heresy. Who can compute what the world loses in the multitude of promising intellects combined with timid characters, who dare not follow out any bold, vigorous, independent train of thought, lest it should land them in something which would admit of being considered irreligious or immoral? Among them we may occasionally see some man of deep conscientiousness, and subtle and refined understanding, who spends a life in sophisticating with an intellect which he cannot silence, and exhausts the resources of ingenuity in attempting to reconcile the promptings of his conscience and reason with orthodoxy, which yet he does not, perhaps, to the end succeed in doing. No one can be a great thinker who does not recognize, that as a thinker it is his first duty to follow his intellect to whatever conclusions it may lead. Truth gains more even by the errors of one who, with due study and preparation, thinks for himself, than by the true opinions of those who only hold them because they do not suffer themselves to think. Not that it is solely, or chiefly, to form great thinkers, that freedom of thinking is required. On the contrary, it is as much and even more indispensable, to enable average human beings to attain the mental stature which they are capable of. There have been, and may again be, great individual thinkers, in a general atmosphere of mental slavery. But there never has been, nor ever will be, in that atmosphere, an intellectually active people. When any people has made a temporary approach to such a character, it has been because the dread of heterodox speculation was for a time suspended. Where there is a tacit convention that principles are not to be disputed; where the discussion of the greatest questions which can occupy humanity is considered to be closed, we cannot hope to find that generally high scale of mental activity which has made some periods, of history so remarkable. Never when controversy avoided the subjects which are large and important enough to kindle enthusiasm, was the mind of a people stirred up from its foundations, and the impulse given which raised even persons of the most ordinary intellect to something of the dignity of thinking beings. Of such we have had an example in the condition of Europe during the times immediately following the Reformation; another, though limited to the Continent and to a more cultivated class, in the speculative movement of the latter half of the eighteenth century; and a third, of still briefer duration, in the intellectual fermentation of Germany during the Goethian and Fichtean period. These periods differed widely in the particular opinions which they developed; but were alike in this, that during all three the yoke of authority was broken. In each, an old mental despotism had been thrown off, and no new one had yet taken its place. The impulse given at these three periods has made Europe what it now is. Every single improvement which has taken place either in the human mind or in institutions, may be traced distinctly to one or other of them. Appearances have for some time indicated that all three impulses are wellnigh spent; and we can expect no fresh start, until we again assert our mental freedom.

Let us now pass to the second division of the argument, and dismissing the supposition that any of the received opinions may be false, let us assume them to be true, and examine into the worth of the manner in which they are likely to be held, when their truth is not freely and openly canvassed. However unwillingly a person who has a strong opinion may admit the possibility that his opinion may be false, he ought to be moved by the consideration that however true it may be, if it is not fully, frequently, and fearlessly discussed, it will be held as a dead dogma, not a living truth.

There is a class of persons (happily not quite so numerous as formerly) who think it enough if a person assents undoubtingly to what they think true, though he has no knowledge whatever of the grounds of the opinion, and could not make a tenable defense of it against the most superficial objections. Such persons, if they can once get their creed taught from authority, naturally think that no good, and some harm, comes of its being allowed to be questioned. Where their influence prevails, they make it nearly impossible for the received opinion to be rejected wisely and considerately, though it may still be rejected rashly and ignorantly; for to shut out discussion entirely is seldom possible and, when it once gets in, beliefs not grounded on conviction are apt to give way before the slightest semblance of an argument. Waiving, however, this possibility—assuming that the true opinion abides in the mind, but abides as a prejudice, a belief independent of, and proof against, argument—this is not the way in which truth ought to be held by a rational being. This is not knowing the truth. Truth, thus held, is but one superstition the more accidentally clinging to the words which enunciate a truth.

If the intellect and judgment of mankind ought to be cultivated, a thing which Protestants at least do not deny, on what can these faculties be more appropriately exercised by any one, than on the things which concern him so much that it is considered necessary for him to hold opinions on them? If the cultivation of the understanding consists in one thing more than in another, it is surely in learning the grounds of one's own opinions. Whatever people believe, on subjects on which it is of the first importance to believe rightly, they ought to be able to defend against at least the common objections. But, some one may say, "Let them be *taught* the grounds of their opinions. It does not follow that opinions must be merely parroted because they are never heard controverted. Persons who learn geometry do not simply commit the theorems to memory, but understand and learn likewise the demonstrations; and it would be absurd to say that they remain ignorant of the grounds of geometrical truths, because they never hear any one deny, and attempt to disprove them." Undoubtedly: and such teaching suffices on a subject like mathematics, where there is nothing at all to be said on the wrong side of the question. The peculiarity of the evidence of mathematical truths is, that all the argument is on one side. There are no objections, and no answers to objections. But on every subject on which difference of opinion is possible, the truth depends on a balance to be struck between two sets of conflicting reasons. Even in natural philosophy, there is always some other explanation possible of the same facts; some geocentric theory instead of heliocentric, some phlogiston instead of oxygen; and it has to be shown why that other theory cannot be the true one: and until this is shown, and until we know how it is shown, we do not understand the grounds of our opinion. But when we turn to subjects infinitely more complicated, to morals, religion, politics, social relations, and the business of life, three-fourths of the arguments for every disputed opinion consist in dispelling the appearances which favor some opinion different from it. The greatest orator, save one, of antiquity, has left it on record that he always studied his adversary's case with as great, if not with still greater, intensity than even his own. What Cicero practiced as the means of forensic success, requires to be imitated by all who study any subject in order to arrive at the truth. He who knows only his own side of the case, knows little of that. His reasons may be good, and no one may have been able to refute them. But if he is equally unable to refute the reasons on the opposite side; if he does not so much as know what they are, he has no ground for preferring either opinion. The rational position for him would be suspension of judgment, and unless he contents himself with that, he is either led by authority, or adopts, like the generality of the world, the side to which he feels most inclination. Nor is it enough that he should hear the arguments of adversaries from his own teachers, presented as they state them, and accompanied by what they offer as refutations. That is not the way to do justice to the arguments, or bring them into real contact with his own mind. He must be able to hear them from persons who actually believe them; who defend them in earnest, and do their very utmost for them. He must know them in their most plausible and persuasive form; he must feel the whole force of the difficulty which the true view of the subject has to encounter and dispose of; else he will never really possess himself of the portion of truth which meets and removes that difficulty. Ninety-nine in a hundred of what are called educated men are in this condition; even of those who can argue fluently for their opinions. Their conclusion may be true, but it might be false for anything they know: they have never thrown themselves into the mental position of those who think differently from them, and considered what such persons may have to say; and consequently they do not, in any proper sense of the word, know the doctrine which they themselves profess. They do not know those parts of it which explain and justify the remainder; the considerations which show that a fact which seemingly conflicts with another is reconcilable with it, or that, of two apparently strong reasons, one and not the other ought to be preferred. All that part of the truth which turns the scale, and decides the judgment of a completely informed mind, they are strangers to; nor is it ever really known, but to those who have attended equally and impartially to both sides, and endeavored to see the reasons of both in the strongest light. So essential is this discipline to a real understanding of moral and human subjects, that if opponents of all important truths do not exist, it is indispensable to imagine them, and supply them with the strongest arguments which the most skillful devil's advocate can conjure up.

To abate the force of these considerations, an enemy of free discussion may be supposed to say, that there is no necessity for mankind in general to know and understand all that can be said against or for their opinions by philosophers and theologians. That it is not needful for common men to be able to expose all the misstatements or fallacies of an ingenious opponent. That it is enough if there is always somebody capable of answering them, so that nothing likely to mislead uninstructed persons remains unrefuted. That simple minds, having been taught the obvious grounds of the truths inculcated on them, may trust to authority for the rest, and being aware that they have neither knowledge nor talent to resolve every difficulty which can be raised, may repose in the assurance that all those which have been raised have been or can be answered, by those who are specially trained to the task.

Conceding to this view of the subject the utmost that can be claimed for it by those most easily satisfied with the amount of understanding of truth which ought to accompany the belief of it; even so, the argument for free discussion is no way weakened. For even this doctrine acknowledges that mankind ought to have a rational assurance that all objections have been satisfactorily answered; and how are they to be answered if that which requires to be answered is not spoken? or how can the answer be known to be satisfactory, if the objectors have no opportunity of showing that it is unsatisfactory? If not the public, at least the philosophers and theologians who are to resolve the difficulties, must make themselves familiar with those difficulties in their most puzzling form; and this cannot be accomplished unless they are freely stated, and placed in the most advantageous light which they admit of. The Catholic Church has its own way of dealing with this embarrassing problem. It makes a broad separation between those who can be permitted to receive its doctrines on conviction, and those who must accept them on trust. Neither, indeed, are allowed any choice as to what they will accept; but the clergy, such at least can be fully confided in, may admissibly and meritoriously make themselves acquainted with the arguments of opponents, in order to answer them, and may, therefore, read heretical books; the laity, not unless by special permission, hard to be obtained. This discipline recognizes a knowledge of the enemy's case as beneficial to the teachers, but finds means, consistent with this, of denying it to the rest of the world: thus giving to the *élite* more mental culture, though not more mental freedom, than it allows to the mass. By this device it succeeds in obtaining the kind of mental superiority which its purposes require; for though culture without freedom never made a large and liberal mind, it can make a clever *nisi prius* advocate of a cause. But in countries professing Protestantism, this resource is denied; since Protestants hold, at least in theory, that the responsibility for the choice of a religion must be borne by each for himself, and cannot be thrown off upon teachers. Besides, in the present state of the world, it is practically impossible that writings which are read by the instructed can be kept from the uninstructed. If the teachers of mankind are to be cognizant of all that they ought to know, everything must be free to be written and published without restraint.

If, however, the mischievous operation of the absence of free discussion, when the received opinions are true, were confined to leaving men ignorant of the grounds of those opinions, it might be thought that this, if an intellectual, is no moral evil, and does not affect the worth of the opinions, regarded in their influence on the character. The fact, however, is, that not only the grounds of the opinion are forgotten in the absence of discussion, but too often the meaning of the opinion itself. The words which convey it, cease to suggest ideas, or suggest only a small portion of those they were originally employed to communicate. Instead of a vivid conception and a living belief, there remain only a few phrases retained by rote; or, if any part, the shell and husk only of the meaning is retained, the finer essence being lost. The great chapter in human history which this fact occupies and fills, cannot be too earnestly studied and meditated on.

It is illustrated in the experience of almost all ethical doctrines and religious creeds. They are all full of meaning and vitality to those who originate them, and to the direct disciples of the originators. Their meaning continues to be felt in undiminished strength, and is perhaps brought out into even fuller consciousness, so long as the struggle lasts to give the doctrine or creed an ascendancy over other creeds. At last it either prevails, and becomes the general opinion, or its progress stops; it keeps possession of the ground it has gained, but ceases to spread further. When either of these results has become apparent, controversy on the subject flags, and gradually dies away. The doctrine has taken its place, if not as a received opinion, as one of the admitted sects or divisions of opinion: those who hold it have generally inherited, not adopted it; and conversion from one of these doctrines to another, being now an exceptional fact, occupies little place in the thoughts of their professors. Instead of being, as at first, constantly on the alert either to defend themselves against the world, or to bring the world over to them, they have subsided into acquiescence, and neither listen, when they can help it, to arguments against their creed, nor trouble dissentients (if there be such) with arguments in its favor. From this time may usually be dated the decline in the living power of the doctrine. We often hear the teachers of all creeds lamenting the difficulty of keeping up in the minds of believers a lively apprehension of the truth which they nominally recognize, so that it may penetrate the feelings, and acquire a real mastery over the conduct. No such difficulty is complained of while the creed is still fighting for its existence: even the weaker combatants then know and feel what they are fighting for, and the difference between it and other doctrines; and in that period of every creed's existence, not a few persons may be found, who have realized its fundamental principles in all the forms of thought, have weighed and considered them in all their important bearings, and have experienced the full effect on the character, which belief in that creed ought to produce in a mind thoroughly imbued with it. But when it has come to be an hereditary creed, and to be received passively, not actively—when the mind is no longer compelled, in the same degree as at first, to exercise its vital powers on the questions which its belief presents to it, there is a progressive tendency to forget all of the belief except the formularies, or to give it a dull and torpid assent, as if accepting it on trust dispensed with the necessity of realizing it in consciousness, or testing it by personal experience; until it almost ceases to connect itself at all with the inner life of the human being. Then are seen the cases, so frequent in this age of the world as almost to form the majority, in which the creed remains as it were outside the mind, encrusting and petrifying it against all other influences addressed to the higher parts of our nature; manifesting its power by not suffering any fresh and living conviction to get in, but itself doing nothing for the mind or heart, except standing sentinel over them to keep them vacant.

To what an extent doctrines intrinsically fitted to make the deepest impression upon the mind may remain in it as dead beliefs, without being ever realized in the imagination, the feelings, or the understanding, is exemplified by the manner in which the majority of believers hold the doctrines of Christianity. By Christianity I here mean what is accounted such by all churches and sects—the maxims and precepts contained in the New Testament. These are considered sacred, and accepted as laws, by all professing Christians. Yet it is scarcely too much to say that not one Christian in a thousand guides or tests his individual conduct by reference to those laws. The standard to which he does refer it, is the custom of his nation, his class, or his religious profession. He has thus, on the one hand, a collection of ethical maxims, which he believes to have been vouchsafed to him by infallible wisdom as rules for his government; and on the other, a set of everyday judgments and practices, which go a certain length with some of those maxims, not so great a length with others, stand in direct opposition to some, and are, on the whole, a compromise between the Christian creed and the interests and suggestions of worldly life. To the first of these standards he gives his homage; to the other his real allegiance. All Christians believe that the blessed are the poor and humble, and those who are ill-used by the world; that it is easier for a camel to pass through the eye of a needle than for a rich man to enter the kingdom of heaven; that they should judge not, lest they be judged; that they should swear not at all; that they should love their neighbor as themselves; that if one take their cloak, they should give him their coat also; that they should take no thought for the morrow; that if they would be perfect, they should sell all that they have and give it to the poor. They are not insincere when they say that they believe these things. They do believe them, as people believe what they have always heard lauded and never discussed. But in the sense of that living belief which regulates conduct, they believe these doctrines just up to the point to which it is usual to act upon them. The doctrines in their integrity are serviceable to pelt adversaries with; and it is understood that they are to be put forward (when possible) as the reasons for whatever people do that they think laudable. But any one who reminded them that the maxims require an infinity of things which they never even think of doing, would gain nothing but to be classed among those very unpopular characters who affect to be better than other people. The doctrines have no hold on ordinary believers—are not a power in their minds. They have an habitual respect for the sound of them, but no feeling which spreads from the words of the things signified, and forces the mind to take *them* in, and make them conform to the formula. Whenever conduct is concerned, they look round for Mr. A and B to direct them how far to go in obeying Christ.

Now we may be well assured that the case was not thus, but far otherwise, with the early Christians. Had it been thus, Christianity never would have expanded from an obscure sect of the despised Hebrews into the religion of the Roman empire. When their enemies said, "See how these Christians love one another" (a remark not likely to be made by anybody now), they assuredly had a much livelier feeling of the meaning of their creed than they have ever had since. And to this cause, probably, it is chiefly owing that Christianity now makes so little progress in extending its domain, and after eighteen centuries, is still nearly confined to Europeans and the descendants of Europeans. Even with the strictly religious, who are much in earnest about their doctrines, and attach a greater amount of meaning to many of them than people in general, it commonly happens that the part which is thus comparatively active in their minds is that which was made by Calvin, or Knox, or some such person much nearer in character to themselves. The sayings of Christ co-exist passively in their minds, producing hardly any effect beyond what is caused by mere listening to words so amiable and bland. There are many reasons, doubtless, why doctrines which are the badge of a sect retain more of their vitality than those common to all recognized sects, and why more pains are taken by teachers to keep their meaning alive; but one reason certainly is, that the peculiar doctrines are more questioned, and have to be oftener defended against open gainsayers. Both teachers and learners go to sleep at their post, as soon as there is no enemy in the field.

The same thing holds true, generally speaking, of all traditional doctrines—those of prudence and knowledge of life, as well as morals or religion. All languages and literatures are full of general observations on life, both as to what it is, and how to conduct oneself in it; observations which everybody knows, which everybody repeats, or hears with acquiescence, which are received as truisms, yet of which most people first truly learn the meaning, when experience, generally of a painful kind, has made it a reality to them. How often, when smarting under some unforeseen misfortune or disappointment, does a person call to mind some proverb or common saying, familiar to him all his life, the meaning of which, if he had ever before felt it as he does now, would have saved him from the calamity. There are indeed reasons for this, other than the absence of discussion: there are many truths of which the full meaning *cannot* be realized, until personal experience has brought it home. But much more of the meaning even of these would have been understood, and what was understood would have been far more deeply impressed on the mind, if the man had been accustomed to hear it argued *pro* and *con* by people who did understand it. The fatal tendency of mankind to leave off thinking about a thing when it is no longer doubtful, is the cause of half their errors. A contemporary author has well spoken of "the deep slumber of a described opinion."

But what! (it may be asked) Is the absence of unanimity an indispensable condition of true knowledge? Is it necessary that some part of mankind should persist in error, to enable any to realize the truth? Does a belief cease to be real and vital as soon as it is generally received—and is a proposition never thoroughly understood and felt unless some doubt of it remains? As soon as mankind have unanimously accepted a truth, does the truth perish within them? The highest aim and best result of improved intelligence, it has hitherto been thought, is to unite mankind more and more in the acknowledgment of all important truths: and does the intelligence only last as long as it has not achieved its object? Do the fruits of conquest perish by the very completeness of the victory?

I affirm no such thing. As mankind improve, the number of doctrines which are no longer disputed or doubted will be constantly on the increase: and the well-being of mankind may almost be measured by the number and gravity of the truths which have reached the point of being uncontested. The cessation, on one question after another, of serious controversy, is one of the necessary incidents of the consolidation of opinion; a consolidation as salutary in the case of true opinions, as it is dangerous and noxious when the opinions are erroneous. But though this gradual narrowing of the bounds of diversity of opinion is necessary in both senses of the term, being at once inevitable and indispensable, we are not therefore obliged to conclude that all its consequences must be beneficial. The loss of so important an aid to the intelligent and living apprehension of a truth, as is afforded by the necessity of explaining it to, or defending it against, opponents, though not sufficient to outweigh, is no trifling drawback from, the benefit of its universal recognition. Where this advantage can no longer be had, I confess I should like to see the teachers of mankind endeavoring to provide a substitute for it; some contrivance for making the difficulties of the question as present to the learner's consciousness, as if they were pressed upon him by a dissentient champion, eager for his conversion.

But instead of seeking contrivances for this purpose, they have lost those they formerly had. The Socratic dialectics, so magnificently exemplified in the dialogues of Plato, were a contrivance of this description. They were essentially a negative discussion of the great questions of philosophy and life, directed with consummate skill to the purpose of convincing any one who had merely adopted the commonplaces of received opinion, that he did not understand the subject—that he as yet attached no definite meaning to the doctrines he professed; in order that, becoming aware of his ignorance, he might be put in the way to attain a stable belief, resting on a clear apprehension both of the meaning of doctrines and of their evidence. The school disputations of the Middle Ages had a somewhat similar object. They were intended to make sure that the pupil understood his own opinion, and (by necessary correlation) the opinion opposed to it, and could enforce the grounds of the one and confute those of the other. These last-mentioned contests had indeed the incurable defect, that the premises appealed to were taken from authority, not from reason; and, as a discipline to the mind, they were in every respect inferior to the powerful dialectics which formed the intellects of the "Socratici viri": but the modern mind owes far more to both than it is generally willing to admit, and the present modes of education contain nothing which in the smallest degree supplies the place either of the one or of the other. A person who derives all his instruction from teachers or books, even if he escape the besetting temptation of contenting himself with cram, is under no compulsion to hear both sides; accordingly it is far from a frequent accomplishment, even among thinkers, to know both sides; and the weakest part of what everybody says in defense of his opinion, is what he intends as a reply to antagonists. It is the fashion of the present time to disparage negative logic—that which points out weaknesses in theory or errors in practice, without establishing positive truths. Such negative criticism would indeed be poor enough as an ultimate result; but as a means to attaining any positive knowledge or conviction worthy the name, it cannot be valued too highly; and until people are again systematically trained to it, there will be few great thinkers, and a low general average of intellect, in any but the mathematical and physical departments of speculation. On any other subject no one's opinions deserve the name of knowledge, except so far as he has either had forced upon him by others, or gone through of himself, the same mental process which would have been required of him in carrying on an active controversy with opponents. That, therefore, which when absent, it is so indispensable, but so difficult, to create, how worse than absurd it is to forego, when spontaneously offering itself! If there are any persons who contest a received opinion, or who will do so if law or opinion will let them, let us thank them for it, open our minds to listen to them, and rejoice that there is some one to do for us what we otherwise ought, if we have any regard for either the certainty or the vitality of our convictions, to do with much greater labor for ourselves.

It still remains to speak of one of the principal causes which make diversity of opinion advantageous, and will continue to do so until mankind shall have entered a stage of intellectual advancement which at present seems at an incalculable distance. We have hitherto considered only two possibilities: that the received opinion may be false, and some other opinion, consequently, true; or that, the received opinion being true, a conflict with the opposite error is essential to a clear apprehension and deep feeling of its truth. But there is a commoner case than either of these; when the conflicting doctrines, instead of being one true and the other false, share the truth between them; and the nonconforming opinion is needed to supply the remainder of the truth, of which the received doctrine embodies only a part. Popular opinions, on subjects not palpable to sense, are often true, but seldom or never the whole truth. They are a part of the truth; sometimes a greater, sometimes a smaller part, but exaggerated, distorted, and disjoined from the truths by which they ought to be accompanied and limited. Heretical opinions, on the other hand, are generally some of these suppressed and neglected truths, bursting the bonds which kept them down, and either seeking reconciliation with the truth contained in the common opinion, or fronting it as enemies, and setting themselves up, with similar exclusiveness, as the whole truth. The latter case is hitherto the most frequent, as, in the human mind, one-sidedness has always been the rule, and many-sidedness the exception. Hence, even in revolutions of opinion, one part of the truth usually sets while another rises. Even progress, which ought to superadd, for the most part only substitutes, one partial and incomplete truth for another; improvement consisting chiefly in this, that the new fragment of truth is more wanted, more adapted to the needs of the time, than that which it displaces. Such being the partial character of prevailing opinions, even when resting on a true foundation, every opinion which embodies somewhat of the portion of truth which the common opinion omits, ought to be considered precious, with whatever amount of error and confusion that truth may be blended. No sober judge of human affairs will feel bound to be indignant because those who force on our notice truths which we should otherwise have overlooked, overlook some of those which we see. Rather, he will think that so long as popular truth is one-sided, it is more desirable than otherwise that unpopular truth should have one-sided asserters too; such being usually the most energetic, and the most likely to compel reluctant attention to the fragment of wisdom which they proclaim as if it were the whole.

Thus, in the eighteenth century, when nearly all the instructed, and all those of the uninstructed who were led by them, were lost in admiration of what is called civilization, and of the marvels of modern science, literature, and philosophy, and while greatly overrating the amount of unlikeness between the men of modern and those of ancient times, indulged the belief that the whole of the difference was in their own favor; with what a salutary shock did the paradoxes of Rousseau explode like bombshells in the midst, dislocating the compact mass of one-sided opinion, and forcing its elements to recombine in a better form and with additional ingredients. Not that the current opinions were on the whole farther from the truth than Rousseau's were; on the contrary, they were nearer to it; they contained more of positive truth, and very much less of error. Nevertheless there lay in Rousseau's doctrine, and has floated down the stream of opinion along with it, a considerable amount of exactly those truths which the popular opinion wanted; and these are the deposit which was left behind when the flood subsided. The superior worth of simplicity of life, the enervating and demoralizing effect of the trammels and hypocrisies of artificial society, are ideas which have never been entirely absent from cultivated minds since Rousseau wrote; and they will in time produce their due effect, though at present needing to be asserted as much as ever, and to be asserted by deeds, for words, on this subject, have nearly exhausted their power.

In politics, again, it is almost a commonplace, that a party of order or stability, and a party of progress or reform, are both necessary elements of a healthy state of political life; until the one or the other shall have so enlarged its mental grasp as to be a party equally of order and of progress, knowing and distinguishing what is fit to be preserved from what ought to be swept away. Each of these modes of thinking derives its utility from the deficiencies of the other; but it is in a great measure the opposition of the other that keeps each within the limits of reason and sanity. Unless opinions favorable to democracy and to aristocracy, to property and to equality, to co-operation and to competition, to luxury and to abstinence, to sociality and individuality, to liberty and discipline, and all the other standing antagonisms of practical life, are expressed with equal freedom, and enforced and defended with equal talent and energy, there is no chance of both elements obtaining their due; one scale is sure to go up, and the other down. Truth, in the great practical concerns of life, is so much a question of the reconciling and combining of opposites, that very few have minds sufficiently capacious and impartial to make the adjustment with an approach to correctness, and it has to be made by the rough process of a struggle between combatants fighting under hostile banners. On any of the great open questions just enumerated, if either of the two opinions has a better claim than the other, not merely to be tolerated, but to be encouraged and countenanced, it is the one which happens at the particular time and place to be in a minority. That is the opinion which, for the time being, represents the neglected interests, the side of human well-being which is in danger of obtaining less than its share. I am aware that there is not, in this country, any tolerance of differences of opinion on most of these topics. They are adduced to show, by admitted and multiplied examples, the universality of the fact, that only through diversity of opinion is there, in the existing state of human intellect, a chance of fair play to all sides of the truth. When there are persons to be found, who form an exception to the apparent unanimity of the world on any subject, even if the world is in the right, it is always probable that dissentients have something worth hearing to say for themselves, and that truth would lose something by their silence.

It may be objected, "But *some* received principles, especially on the highest and most vital subjects, are more than half-truths. The Christian morality, for instance, is the whole truth on that subject, and if any one teaches a morality which varies from it, he is wholly in error." As this is of all cases the most important in practice, none can be fitter to test the general maxim. But before pronouncing what Christian morality is or is not, it would be desirable to decide what is meant by Christian morality. If it means the morality of the New Testament, I wonder that any one who derives his knowledge of this from the book itself, can suppose that it was announced, or intended, as a complete doctrine of morals. The Gospel always refers to a pre-existing morality, and confines its precepts to the particulars in which that morality was to be corrected, or superseded by a wider and higher; expressing itself, moreover, in terms most general, often impossible to be interpreted literally, and possessing rather the impressiveness of poetry or eloquence than the precision of legislation. To extract from it a body of ethical doctrine, has never been possible without eking it out from the Old Testament, that is, from a system elaborate indeed, but in many respects barbarous, and intended only for a barbarous people. St. Paul, a declared enemy to this Judaical mode of interpreting the doctrine and filling up the scheme of his Master, equally assumes a pre-existing morality, namely that of the Greeks and Romans; and his advice to Christians is in a great measure a system of accommodation to that; even to the extent of giving an apparent sanction to slavery. What is called Christian, but should rather be termed theological, morality, was not the work of Christ or the Apostles, but is of much later origin, having been gradually built up by the Catholic Church of the first five centuries, and though not implicitly adopted by moderns and Protestants, has been much less modified by them than might have been expected. For the most part, indeed, they have contented themselves with cutting off the additions which had been made to it in the Middle Ages, each sect supplying the place by fresh additions, adopted to its own character and tendencies. That mankind owe a great debt to this morality, and to its early teachers, I should be the last person to deny; but I do not scruple to say of it, that it is, in many important points, incomplete and one-sided, and that unless ideas and feelings, not sanctioned by it, had contributed to the formation of European life and character, human affairs would have been in a worse condition than they now are. Christian morality (so called) has all the characters of a reaction; it is, in great part, a protest against Paganism. Its ideal is negative rather than positive; passive rather than active; innocence rather than Nobleness; Abstinence from Evil, rather than energetic Pursuit of Good: in its precepts (as has been well said) "thou shalt not" predominates unduly over "thou shalt." In its horror of sensuality, it made an idol of asceticism, which has been gradually compromised away into one of legality. It holds out the hope of heaven and the threat of hell, as the appointed and appropriate motives to a virtuous life: in this falling far below the best of the ancients, and doing what lies in it to give to human morality an essentially selfish character, by disconnecting each man's feelings of duty from the interests of his fellow-creatures, except so far as a self-interested inducement is offered to him for consulting them. It is essentially a doctrine of passive obedience; it inculcates submission to all authorities, found established; who indeed are not to be actively obeyed when they command what religion forbids, but who are not to be resisted, far less rebelled against, for any amount of wrong to ourselves. And while, in the morality of the best Pagan nations, duty to the State holds even a disproportionate place, infringing on the just liberty of the individual; in purely Christian ethics, that grand department of duty is scarcely noticed or acknowledged. It is in the Koran, not the New Testament, that we read the maxim—"A ruler who appoints any man to an office, when there is in his dominions another man better qualified for it, sins against God and against the State." What little recognition the idea of obligation to the public attains in modern morality, is derived from Greek and Roman sources, not from Christian; as, even in the morality of private life, whatever exists of magnanimity, high-mindedness, personal dignity, even the sense of honor, is derived from the purely human, not the religious part of our education, and never could have grown out of a standard of ethics in which the only worth, professedly recognized, is that of obedience.

I am as far as any one from pretending that these defects are necessarily inherent in the Christian ethics, in every manner in which it can be conceived, or that the many requisites of a complete moral doctrine which it does not contain, do not admit of being reconciled with it. Far less would I insinuate this of the doctrines and precepts of Christ himself. I believe that the sayings of Christ are all, that I can see any evidence of their having been intended to be; that they are irreconcilable with nothing which a comprehensive morality requires; that everything which is excellent in ethics may be brought within them, with no greater violence to their language than has been done to it by all who have attempted to deduce from them any practical system of conduct whatever. But it is quite consistent with this, to believe that they contain, and were meant to contain, only a part of the truth; that many essential elements of the highest morality are among the things which are not provided for, nor intended to be provided for, in the recorded deliverances of the Founder of Christianity, and which have been entirely thrown aside in the system of ethics erected on the basis of those deliverances by the Christian Church. And this being so, I think it a great error to persist in attempting to find in the Christian doctrine that complete rule for our guidance, which its author intended it to sanction and enforce, but only partially to provide. I believe, too, that this narrow theory is becoming a grave practical evil, detracting greatly from the value of the moral training and instruction, which so many well-meaning persons are now at length exerting themselves to promote. I much fear that by attempting to form the mind and feelings on an exclusively religious type, and discarding those secular standards (as for want of a better name they may be called) which heretofore co-existed with and supplemented the Christian ethics, receiving some of its spirit, and infusing into it some of theirs, there will result, and is even now resulting, a low, abject, servile type of character, which, submit itself as it may to what it deems the Supreme Will, is incapable of rising to or sympathizing in the conception of Supreme Goodness. I believe that other ethics than any which can be evolved from exclusively Christian sources, must exist side by side with Christian ethics to produce the moral regeneration of mankind; and that the Christian system is no exception to the rule, that in an imperfect state of the human mind, the interests of truth require a diversity of opinions. It is not necessary that in ceasing to ignore the moral truths not contained in Christianity, men should ignore any of those which it does contain. Such prejudice, or oversight, when it occurs, is altogether an evil; but it is one from which we cannot hope to be always exempt, and must be regarded as the price paid for an inestimable good. The exclusive pretension made by a part of the truth to be the whole, must and ought to be protested against; and if a reactionary impulse should make the protestors unjust in their turn, this one-sidedness, like the other, may be lamented, but must be tolerated. If Christians would teach infidels to be just to Christianity, they should themselves be just to infidelity. It can do truth no service to blink the fact, known to all who have the most ordinary acquaintance with literary history, that a large portion of the noblest and most valuable moral teaching has been the work, not only of men who did not know, but of men who knew and rejected, the Christian faith.

I do not pretend that the most unlimited use of the freedom of enunciating all possible opinions would put an end to the evils of religious or philosophical sectarianism. Every truth which men of narrow capacity are in earnest about, is sure to be asserted, inculcated, and in many ways even acted on, as if no other truth existed in the world, or at all events none that could limit or qualify the first. I acknowledge that the tendency of all opinions to become sectarian is not cured by the freest discussion, but is often heightened and exacerbated thereby; the truth which ought to have been, but was not, seen, being rejected all the more violently because proclaimed by persons regarded as opponents. But it is not on the impassioned partisan, it is on the calmer and more disinterested bystander, that this collision of opinions works its salutary effect. Not the violent conflict between parts of the truth, but the quiet suppression of half of it, is the formidable evil; there is always hope when people are forced to listen to both sides; it is when they attend only to one that errors harden into prejudices, and truth itself ceases to have the effect of truth, by being exaggerated into falsehood. And since there are few mental attributes more rare than that judicial faculty which can sit in intelligent judgment between two sides of a question, of which only one is represented by an advocate before it, truth has no chance but in proportion as every side of it, every opinion which embodies any fraction of the truth, not only finds advocates, but is so advocated as to be listened to.

We have now recognized the necessity to the mental well-being of mankind (on which all their other well-being depends) of freedom of opinion, and freedom of the expression of opinion, on four distinct grounds; which we will now briefly recapitulate.

First, if any opinion is compelled to silence, that opinion may, for aught we can certainly know, be true. To deny this is to assume our own infallibility.

Secondly, though the silenced opinion be an error, it may, and very commonly does, contain a portion of truth; and since the general or prevailing opinion on any subject is rarely or never the whole truth, it is only by the collision of adverse opinions that the remainder of the truth has any chance of being supplied.

Thirdly, even if the received opinion be not only true, but the whole truth; unless it is suffered to be, and actually is, vigorously and earnestly contested, it will, by most of those who receive it, be held in the manner of a prejudice, with little comprehension or feeling of its rational grounds. And not only this, but, fourthly, the meaning of the doctrine itself will be in danger of being lost, or enfeebled, and deprived of its vital effect on the character and conduct: the dogma becoming a mere formal profession, inefficacious for good, but cumbering the ground, and preventing the growth of any real and heartfelt conviction, from reason or personal experience.

INDIVIDUALITY AS ONE OF THE ELEMENTS OF WELL-BEING

Such being the reasons which make it imperative that human beings should be free to form opinions, and to express their opinions without reserve; and such the baneful consequences to the intellectual, and through that to the moral nature of man, unless this liberty is either conceded, or asserted in spite of prohibition; let us next examine whether the same reasons do not require that men should be free to act upon their opinions—to carry these out in their lives, without hindrance, either physical or moral,

from their fellow men, so long as it is at their own risk and peril. This last proviso is of course indispensable. No one pretends that actions should be as free as opinions. On the contrary, even opinions lose their immunity, when the circumstances in which they are expressed are such as to constitute their expression a positive instigation to some mischievous act. An opinion that corn-dealers are starvers of the poor, or that private property is robbery, ought to be unmolested when simply circulated through the press, but may justly incur punishment when delivered orally to an excited mob assembled before the house of a corn-dealer, or when handed about among the same mob in the form of a placard. Acts, of whatever kind, which, without justifiable cause, do harm to others, may be, and in the more important cases absolutely require to be, controlled by the unfavorable sentiments, and, when needful, by the active interference of mankind. The liberty of the individual must be thus far limited; he must not make himself a nuisance to other people. But if he refrains from molesting others in what concerns them, and merely acts according to his own inclination and judgment in things which concern himself, the same reasons which show that opinion should be free, prove also that he should be allowed, without molestation, to carry his opinions into practice at his own cost. That mankind are not infallible; that their truths, for the most part, are only half-truths; that unity of opinion, unless resulting from the fullest and freest comparison of opposite opinions, is not desirable, and diversity not an evil, but a good, until mankind are much more capable than at present of recognizing all sides of the truth, are principles applicable to men's modes of action, not less than to their opinions. As it is useful that mankind are imperfect there should be different opinions, so it is that there should be experiments of living; that free scope should be given to varieties of character, short of injury to others; and that the worth of different modes of life should be proved practically, when any one thinks fit to try them. It is desirable, in short, that in things which do not primarily concern others, individuality should assert itself. Where (not the person's own character) but the traditions or customs of other people are the rule of conduct, there is wanting one of the principal ingredients of human happiness, and quite the chief ingredient of individual and social progress.

In maintaining the principle, the greatest difficulty to be encountered does not lie in the appreciation of means towards an acknowledged end, but in the indifference of persons in general to the end itself. If it were felt that the free development of individuality is one of the leading essentials of well-being; that it is not only a co-ordinate element with all that is designated by the terms civilization, instruction, education, culture, but is itself a necessary part and condition of all those things; there would be no danger that liberty should be undervalued, and the adjustment of the boundaries between it and social control would present no extraordinary difficulty. But the evil is, that individual spontaneity is hardly recognized by the common modes of thinking, as having any intrinsic worth, or deserving any regard on its own account. The majority, being satisfied with the ways of mankind as they now are (for it is they who make them what they are), cannot comprehend why those ways should not be good enough for everybody; and what is more, spontaneity forms no part of the ideal of the majority of moral and social reformers, but is rather looked on with jealousy, as a troublesome and perhaps rebellious obstruction to the general acceptance of what these reformers, in their own judgment, think would be best for mankind. Few persons, out of Germany, even comprehend the meaning of the doctrine which Wilhelm von Humboldt, so eminent both as a savant and as a politican, made the text of a treatise—that "the end of man, or that which is prescribed by the eternal or immutable dictates of reason, and not suggested by vague and transient desires, is the highest and most harmonious development of his powers to a complete and consistent whole"; that, therefore, the object "towards which every human being must ceaselessly direct his efforts, and on which especially those who design to influence their fellow men must ever keep their eyes, is the individuality of power and development"; that for this there are two requisites, "freedom, and variety of situations"; and that from the union of these arise "individual vigor and manifold diversity," which combine themselves in "originality."

Little, however, as people are accustomed to a doctrine like that of von Humboldt, and surprising as it may be to them to find so high a value attached to individuality, the question, one must nevertheless think, can only be one of degree. No one's idea of excellence in conduct is that people should do absolutely nothing but copy one another. No one would assert that people ought not to put into their mode of life, and into the conduct of their concerns, any impress whatever of their own judgment, or of their own individual character. On the other hand, it would be absurd to pretend that people ought to live as if nothing whatever had been known in the world before they came into it; as if experience had as yet done nothing towards showing that one mode of existence, or of conduct, is preferable to another. Nobody denies that people should be so taught and trained in youth, as to know and benefit by the ascertained results of human experience. But it is the privilege and proper condition of a human being, arrived at the maturity of his faculties, to use and interpret experience in his own way. It is for him to find out what part of recorded experience is properly applicable to his own circumstances and character. The traditions and customs of other people are, to a certain extent, evidence of what their experience has taught *them;* presumptive evidence, and as such, have a claim to his deference: but, in the first place, their experience may be too narrow; or they may not have interpreted it rightly. Secondly, their interpretation of experience may be correct, but unsuitable to him. Customs are made for customary circumstances, and customary characters; and his circumstances or his character may be uncustomary. Thirdly, though the customs be both good as customs, and suitable to him, yet to conform to custom, merely *as* custom, does not educate or develop in him any of the qualities which are the distinctive endowment of a human being. The human facilities of perception, judgment, discriminative feeling, mental activity, and even moral preference, are exercised only in making a choice. He who does anything because it is the custom, makes no choice. He gains no practice either in discerning or in desiring what is best. The mental and moral, like the muscular powers, are improved only by being used. The faculties are called into no exercise by doing a thing merely because others do it, no more than by believing a thing only because others believe it. If the grounds of an opinion are not conclusive to the person's own reason, his reason cannot be strengthened, but is likely to be weakened, by his adopting it: and if the inducements to an act are not such as are consentaneous to his own feelings and character (where affection, or the rights of others, are not concerned) it is so much done towards rendering his feelings and character inert and torpid, instead of active and energetic.

He who lets the world, or his own portion of it, choose his plan of life for him, has no need of any other faculty than the ape-like one of imitation. He who chooses his plan for himself, employs all his faculties. He must use observation to see, reasoning and judgment to foresee, activity to gather materials for decision, discrimination to decide, and when he has decided, firmness and self-control to hold to his deliberate decision. And these qualities he requires and exercises exactly in proportion as the part of his conduct which he determines according to his own judgment and feelings is a large one. It is possible that he might be guided in some good path, and kept out of harm's way, without any of these things. But what will be his comparative worth as a human being? It really is of importance, not only what men do, but also what manner of men they are that do it. Among the works of man, which human life is rightly employed in perfecting and beautifying, the first in importance surely is man himself. Supposing it were possible to get houses built, corn grown, battles fought, causes tried, and even churches erected and prayers said, by machinery— by automatons in human form—it would be a considerable loss to exchange for these automatons even the men and women who at present inhabit the more civilized parts of the world, and who assuredly are but starved specimens of what nature can and will produce. Human nature is not a machine to be built after a model, and set to do exactly the work prescribed for it, but a tree, which requires to grow and develop itself on all sides, according to the tendency of the inward forces which make it a living thing.

It will probably be conceded that it is desirable people should exercise their understandings, and that an intelligent following of custom, or even occasionally an intelligent deviation from custom, is better than a blind and simply mechanical adhesion to it. To a certain extent it is admitted, that our understanding should be our own: but there is not the same willingness to admit that our desires and impulses should be our own likewise; or that to possess impulses of our own, and of any strength, is anything but a peril and a snare. Yet desires and impulses are as much a part of a perfect human being, as beliefs and restraints: and strong impulses are only perilous when not properly balanced; when one set of aims and inclinations is developed into strength, while others, which ought to co-exist with them, remain weak and inactive. It is not because men's desires are strong that they act ill; it is because their consciences are weak. There is no natural connection between strong impulses and a weak conscience. The natural connection is the other way. To say that one person's desires and feelings are stronger and more various than those of another, is merely to say that he has more of the raw material of human nature, and is therefore capable, perhaps of more evil, but certainly or more good. Strong impulses are but another name for energy. Energy may be turned to bad uses; but more good may always be made of an energetic nature, than of an indolent and impassive one. Those who have most natural feeling, are always those whose cultivated feelings may be made the strongest. The same strong susceptibilities which make the personal impulses vivid and powerful, are also the source from whence are generated the most passionate love of virtue, and the sternest self-control. It is through the cultivation of these, that society both does its duty and protects its interests: not by rejecting the stuff of which heroes are made, because it knows not how to make them. A person whose desires and impulses are his own—are the expression of his own nature, as it has been developed and modified by his own culture—is said to have a character. One whose desires and impulses are not his own, has no character, no more than a steam-engine has a character. If, in addition to being his own, his impulses are strong, and are under the government of a strong will, he has an energetic character. Whoever thinks that individuality of desires and impulses should not be encouraged to unfold itself, must maintain that society has no need of strong natures—is not the better for containing many persons who have much character—and that a high general average of energy is not desirable.

In some early states of society, these forces might be, and were, too much ahead of the power which society then possessed of disciplining and controlling them. There has been a time when the element of spontaneity and individuality was in excess, and the social principle had a hard struggle with it. The difficulty then was, to induce men of strong bodies or minds to pay obedience to any rules which required them to control their impulses. To overcome this difficulty, law and discipline, like the Popes struggling against the Emperors, asserted a power over the whole man, claiming to control all his life in order to control his character—which society had not found any other sufficient means of binding. But society has now fairly got the better of individuality; and the danger which threatens human nature is not the excess, but the deficiency, of personal impulses and preferences. Things are vastly changed, since the passions of those who were strong by station or by personal endowment were in a state of habitual rebellion against laws and ordinances, and required to be rigorously chained up to enable the persons within their reach to enjoy any particle of security. In our times, from the highest class of society down to the lowest, every one lives as under the eye of a hostile and dreaded censorship. Not only in what concerns others, but in what concerns only themselves, the individual or the family do not ask themselves—what do I prefer? or, what would suit my character and disposition? or, what would allow the best and highest in me to have fair play, and enable it to grow and thrive? They ask themselves, what is suitable to my position? what is usually done by persons of my station and pecuniary circumstances? or

(worse still) what is usually done by persons of a station and circumstances superior to mine? I do not mean that they choose what is customary, in preference to what suits their own inclination. It does not occur to them to have any inclination, except for what is customary. Thus the mind itself is bowed to the yoke: even in what people do for pleasure, conformity is the first thing thought of; they like in crowds; they exercise choice only among things commonly done: peculiarity of taste, eccentricity of conduct, are shunned equally with crimes: until by dint of not following their own nature, they have no nature to follow: their human capacities are withered and starved: they become incapable of any strong wishes or native pleasures, and are generally without either opinions or feelings of home growth, or properly their own. Now is this, or is it not, the desirable condition of human nature?

It is so, on the Calvinistic theory. According to that, the one great offense of man is self-will. All the good of which humanity is capable, is comprised in obedience. You have no choice; thus you must do, and no otherwise: "whatever is not a duty, is a sin." Human nature being radically corrupt, there is no redemption for any one until human nature is killed within him. To one holding this theory of life, crushing out any of the human faculties, capacities, and susceptibilities, is no evil: man needs no capacity, but that of surrendering himself to the will of God: and if he uses any of his faculties for any other purpose but to do that supposed will more effectually, he is better without them. This is the theory of Calvinism; and it is held, in a mitigated form, by many who do not consider themselves Calvinists; the mitigation consisting in giving a less ascetic interpretation to the alleged will of God; asserting it to be his will that mankind should gratify some of their inclinations; of course not in the manner they themselves prefer, but in the way of obedience, that is, in a way prescribed to them by authority; and, therefore, by the necessary conditions of the case, the same for all.

In some such insidious form there is at present a strong tendency to this narrow theory of life, and to the pinched and hide-bound type of human character which it patronizes. Many persons, no doubt, sincerely think that human beings thus cramped and dwarfed, are as their Maker designed them to be; just as many have thought that trees are a much finer thing when clipped into pollards, or cut out into figures of animals, than as nature made them. But if it be any part of religion to believe that man was made by a good Being, it is more consistent with that faith to believe, that this Being gave all human faculties that they might be cultivated and unfolded, not rooted out and consumed, and that he takes delight in every nearer approach made by his creatures to the ideal conception embodied in them, every increase in any of their capabilities of comprehension, of action, or of enjoyment. There is a different type of human excellence from the Calvinistic; a conception of humanity as having its nature bestowed on it for other purposes than merely to be abnegated. "Pagan self-assertion" is one of the elements of human worth, as well as "Christian self-denial." There is a Greek ideal of self-development, which the Platonic and Christian ideal of self-government blends with, but does not supersede. It may be better to be a John Knox than an Alcibiades, but it is better to be a Pericles than either; nor would a Pericles, if we had one in these days, be without anything good which belonged to John Knox.

It is not by wearing down into uniformity all that is individual in themselves, but by cultivating it and calling it forth, within the limits imposed by the rights and interests of others, that human beings become a noble and beautiful object of contemplation; and as the works partake the character of those who do them, by the same process human life also becomes rich, diversified, and animating, furnishing more abundant aliment to high thoughts and elevating feelings, and strengthening the tie which binds every individual to the race, by making the race infinitely better worth belonging to. In proportion to the development of his individuality, each person becomes more valuable to himself, and is therefore capable of being more valuable to others. There is a greater fullness of life about his own existence, and when there is more life in the units there is more in the mass which is composed of them. As much compression as is necessary to prevent the stronger specimens of human nature from encroaching on the rights of others, cannot be dispensed with; but for this there is ample compensation even in the point of view of human development. The means of development which the individual loses by being prevented from gratifying his inclinations to the injury of others, are chiefly obtained at the expense of the development of other people. And even to himself there is a full equivalent in the better development of the social part of his nature, rendered possible by the restraint put upon the selfish part. To be held to rigid rules of justice for the sake of others, develops the feelings and capacities which have the good of others for their object. But to be restrained in things not affecting their good, by their mere displeasure, develops nothing valuable, except such force of character as may unfold itself in resisting the restraint. If acquiesced in, it dulls and blunts the whole nature. To give any fair plan to the nature of each, it is essential that different persons should be allowed to lead different lives. In proportion as this latitude has been exercised in any age, has that age been noteworthy to posterity. Even despotism does not produce its worst effects, so long as individuality exists under it; and whatever crushes individuality is despotism, by whatever name it may be called, and whether it professes to be enforcing the will of God or the injunctions of men.

Having said that Individuality is the same thing with development, and that it is only the cultivation of individuality which produces, or can produce, well-developed human beings, I might here close the argument: for what more or better can be said of any condition of human affairs, than that it begins human beings themselves nearer to the best thing they can be? or what worse can be said of any obstruction to good, than that it prevents this? Doubtless, however, these considerations will not suffice to convince those who most need convincing; and it is necessary further to show, that these developed human beings arc of some use to the undeveloped—to point out to those who do not desire liberty, and would not avail themselves of it, that they may be in some intelligible manner rewarded for allowing other people to make use of it without hindrance.

In the first place, then, I would suggest that they might possibly learn something from them. It will not be denied by anybody, that originality is a valuable element in human affairs. There is always need of persons not only to discover new truths, and point out when what were once truths are true no longer, but also to commence new practices, and set the example of more enlightened conduct, and better taste and sense in human life. This cannot well be gainsaid by anybody who does not believe that the world has already attained perfection in all its ways and practices. It is true that this benefit is not capable of being rendered by everybody alike: there are but few persons, in comparison with the whole of mankind, whose experiments, if adopted by others, would be likely to be any improvement on established practice. But these few are the salt of the earth; without them, human life would become a stagnant pool. Not only is it they who introduce good things which did not before exist; it is they who keep the life in those which already existed. If there were nothing new to be done, would human intellect cease to be necessary? Would it be a reason why those who do the old things should forget why they are done, and do them like cattle, not like human beings? There is only too great a tendency in the best beliefs and practices to degenerate into the mechanical; and unless there were a succession of persons whose ever-recurring originality prevents the grounds of those beliefs and practices from becoming merely traditional, such dead matter would not resist the smallest shock from anything really alive, and there would be no reason why civilization should not die out, as in the Byzantine Empire. Persons of genius, it is true, are, and are always likely to be, a small minority; but in order to have them, it is necessary to preserve the soil in which they grow. Genius can only breathe freely in an *atmosphere* of freedom. Persons of genius are, *ex vi termini, more* individual than any other people—less capable, consequently, of fitting themselves, without hurtful compression, into any of the small number of molds which society provides in order to save its members the trouble of forming their own character. If from timidity they consent to be forced into one of these molds, and to let all that part of themselves which cannot

expand under the pressure remain unexpanded, society will be little the better for their genius. If they are of a strong character, and break their fetters, they become a mark for the society which has not succeeded in reducing them to commonplace, to point at with solemn warning as "wild," "erratic," and the like; much as if one should complain of the Niagara river for not flowing smoothly between its banks like a Dutch canal.

I insist thus emphatically on the importance of genius, and the necessity of allowing it to unfold itself freely both in thought and in practice, being well aware that no one will deny the position in theory, but knowing also that almost every one, in reality, is totally indifferent to it. People think genius a fine thing if it enables a man to write an exciting poem, or paint a picture. But in its true sense, that of originality in thought and action, though no one says that it is not a thing to be admired, nearly all, at heart, think that they can do very well without it. Unhappily this is too natural to be wondered at. Originality is the one thing which unoriginal minds cannot feel the use of. They cannot see what it is to do for them: how should they? If they could see what it would do for them, it would not be originality. The first service which originality has to render them, is that of opening their eyes: which being once fully done, they would have a chance of being themselves original. Meanwhile, recollecting that nothing was ever yet done which some one was not the first to do, and that all good things which exist are the fruits of originality, let them be modest enough to believe that there is something still left for it to accomplish, and assure themselves that they are more in need of originality, the less they are conscious of the want.

In sober truth, whatever homage may be professed, or even paid, to real or supposed mental superiority, the general tendency of things throughout the world is to render mediocrity the ascendant power among mankind. In ancient history, in the Middle Ages, and in a diminishing degree through the long transition from feudality to the present time, the individual was a power in himself; and if he had either great talents or a high social position, he was a considerable power. At present individuals are lost in the crowd. In politics it is almost a triviality to say that public opinion now rules the world. The only power deserving the name is that of masses, and of governments while they make themselves the organ of the tendencies and instincts of masses. This is as true in the moral and social relations of private life as in public transactions. Those whose opinions go by the name of public opinion, are not always the same sort of public: in America they are the whole white population; in England, chiefly the middle class. But they are always a mass, that is to say, collective mediocrity. And what is a still greater novelty, the mass do not now take their opinions from dignitaries in Church or State, from ostensible leaders, or from books. Their thinking is done for them by men much like themselves, addressing them or speaking in their name, on the spur of the moment, through the newspapers. I am not complaining of all this. I do not assert that anything better is compatible, as a general rule, with the present low state of the human mind. But that does not hinder the government of mediocrity from being mediocre government. No government by a democracy or numerous aristocracy, either in its political acts or in the opinions, qualifies, and tone of mind which it fosters, ever did or could rise above mediocrity, except in so far as the sovereign Many have let themselves be guided (which in their best times they always have done) by the counsels and influence of a more highly gifted and instructed One or Few. The initiation of all wise or noble things, comes and must come from individuals; generally at first from some one individual. The honor and glory of the average man is that he is capable of following that initiative; that he can respond internally to wise and noble things, and be led to them with his eyes open. I am not countenancing the sort of "hero-worship" which applauds the strong man of genius for forcibly seizing on the government of the world and making it do his bidding in spite of itself. All he can claim is, freedom to point out the way. The power of compelling others into it, is not only incon-

sistent with the freedom and development of all the rest, but corrupting to the strong man himself. It does seem, however, that when the opinions of masses of merely average men are everywhere become or becoming the dominant power, the counterpoise and corrective to that tendency would be, the more and more pronounced individuality of those who stand on the higher eminences of thought. It is in these circumstances most especially, that exceptional individuals, instead of being deterred, should be encouraged in acting differently from the mass. In other times there was no advantage in their doing so, unless they acted not only differently, but better. In this age, the mere example of nonconformity, the mere refusal to bend the knee to custom, is itself a service. Precisely because the tyranny of opinion is such as to make eccentricity a reproach, it is desirable, in order to break through that tyranny, that people should be eccentric. Eccentricity has always abounded when and where strength of character has abounded; and the amount of eccentricity in a society has generally been proportional to the amount of genius, mental vigor, and moral courage which it contained. That so few now dare to be eccentric, marks the chief danger of the time.

The worth of a State, in the long run, is the worth of the individuals composing it; and a State which postpones the interests of *their* mental expansion and elevation, to a little more of administrative skill, or of that semblance of it which practice gives, in the details of business; a State which dwarfs its men, in order that they may be more docile instruments in its hands even for beneficial purposes—will find that with small men no great thing can really be accomplished; and that the perfection of machinery to which it has sacrificed everything, will in the end avail it nothing, for want of the vital power which, in order that the machine might work more smoothly, it has preferred to banish.

*Utilitarianism**

The creed which accepts as the foundation of morals "utility" or the "greatest happiness principle" holds that actions are right in proportion as they tend to promote happiness; wrong as they tend to produce the reverse of happiness. By happiness is intended pleasure and the absence of pain; by unhappiness, pain and the privation of pleasure. To give a clear view of the moral standard set up by the theory, much more requires to be said; in particular, what things it includes in the ideas of pain and pleasure, and to what extent this is left an open question. But these supplementary explanations do not affect the theory of life on which this theory of morality is grounded—namely, that pleasure and freedom from pain are the only things desirable as ends; and that all desirable things (which are as numerous in the utilitarian as in any other scheme) are desirable either for pleasure inherent in themselves or as means to the promotion of pleasure and the prevention of pain.

Now such a theory of life excites in many minds, and among them in some of the most estimable in feeling and purpose, inveterate dislike. To suppose that life has (as they express it) no higher end than pleasure—no better and nobler object of desire and pursuit—they designate as utterly mean and groveling, as a doctrine worthy only of swine, to whom the following of Epicurus were, at a very early period, contemptuously likened; and modern holders of the doctrine are occasionally made the subject of equally polite

comparisons by its German, French, and English assailants.

When thus attacked, the Epicureans have always answered that it is not they, but their accusers, who represent human nature in a degrading light, since the accusation supposes human beings to be capable of no pleasures except those of which swine are capable. The comparison of the Epicurean life to that of beasts is felt as degrading, precisely because a beast's pleasures do not satisfy a human being's conceptions of happiness. Human beings have faculties more elevated than the animal appetites and, when once made conscious of them, do not regard anything as happiness which does not include their gratification. I do not, indeed, consider the Epicureans to have been by any means faultless in drawing out their scheme of consequences from the utilitarian principle. To do this in any sufficient manner, many Stoic, as well as Christian, elements require to be included. But there is no known Epicurean theory of life which does not assign to the pleasures of the intellect, of the feelings and imagination, and of the moral sentiments a much higher value as pleasures than to those of mere sensation. It must be admitted, however, that utilitarian writers in general have placed the superiority of mental over bodily pleasure chiefly in the greater permanency, safety, uncostliness, etc., of the former—that is, in their circumstantial advantages rather than in their intrinsic nature. And on all these points utilitarians have fully proved their case; but they might have taken the other and, as it may be called, higher ground with entire consistency. It is quite compatible with the

---

*From John Stuart Mill, *Utilitarianism* (1861).

principle of utility to recognize the fact that some kinds of pleasure are more desirable and more valuable than others. It would be absurd that, while in estimating all other things quality is considered as well as quantity, the estimation of pleasure should be supposed to depend on quantity alone. . . .

Now it is an unquestionable fact that those who are equally acquainted with and equally capable of appreciating and enjoying both do give a most marked preference to the manner of existence which employs their higher faculties. Few human creatures would consent to be changed into any of the lower animals for a promise of the fullest allowance of a beast's pleasures; no intelligent human being would consent to be a fool, no instructed person would be an ignoramus, no person of feeling and conscience would be selfish and base, even though they should be persuaded that the fool, the dunce, or the rascal is better satisfied with his lot than they are with theirs. They would not resign what they possess more than he for the most complete satisfaction of all the desires which they have in common with him. If they ever fancy they would, it is only in cases of unhappiness so extreme that to escape from it they would exchange their lot for almost any other, however undesirable in their own eyes. A being of higher faculties requires more to make him happy, is capable probably of more acute suffering, and certainly accessible to it at more points, than one of an inferior type; but in spite of these liabilities, he can never really wish to sink into what he feels to be a lower grade of existence. We may give what explanation we please of this unwillingness; we may attribute it to pride, a name which is given indiscriminately to some of the most and to some of the least estimable feelings of which mankind are capable; we may refer it to the love of liberty and personal independence, an appeal to which was with the Stoics one of the most effective means for the inculcation of it; to the love of power or to

the love of excitement, both of which do really enter into and contribute to it; but its most appropriate appellation is a sense of dignity, which all human beings possess in one form or other, and in some, though by no means in exact, proportion to their higher faculties, and which is so essential a part of the happiness of those in whom it is strong that nothing which conflicts with it could be otherwise than momentarily an object of desire to them. Whoever supposes that this preference takes place at a sacrifice of happiness—that the superior being, in anything like equal circumstances, is not happier than the inferior—confounds the two very different ideas of happiness and content . . .

It may be objected that many who are capable of the higher pleasures occasionally, under the influence of temptation, postpone them to the lower. But this is quite compatible with a full appreciation of the intrinsic superiority of the higher. Men often, from infirmity of character, make their election for the nearer good, though they know it to be the less valuable; and this no less when the choice is between two bodily pleasures than when it is between bodily and mental. They pursue sensual indulgences to the injury of health, though perfectly aware that health is the greater good. It may be further objected that many who begin with youthful enthusiasm for everything noble, as they advance in years, sink into indolence and selfishness. But I do not believe that those who undergo this very common change voluntarily choose the lower description of pleasures in preference to the higher. I believe that, before they devote themselves exclusively to the one, they have already become incapable of the other. Capacity for the nobler feelings is in most natures a very tender plant, easily killed, not only by hostile influences, but by mere want of sustenance; and in the majority of young persons it speedily dies away if the occupations to which their position in life has devoted them, and the society into which it has thrown them, are not favorable to keeping that higher capacity in exercise. Men lose their high aspirations as they lose their intellectual tastes, because they have not time or opportunity for indulging them; and they addict themselves to inferior pleasures, not because they deliberately prefer them, but because they are either the only ones to which they have access or the only ones which they are any longer capable of enjoying . . .

I must again repeat what the assailants of utilitarianism seldom have the justice to acknowledge, that the happiness which forms the utilitarian standard of what is right in conduct is not the agent's own happiness but that of all concerned. As between his own happiness and that of others, utilitarianism requires him to be as strictly impartial as a disinterested and benevolent spectator. In the golden rule of Jesus of Nazareth, we read the complete spirit of the ethics of utility. "To do as you would be done by," and "to love your neighbor as yourself," constitute the ideal perfection of utilitarian morality. As the means of making the nearest approach to this ideal, utility would enjoin, first, that laws and social arrangements should place the happiness or (as, speaking practically, it may be called) the interest of every individual as nearly as possible in harmony with the interest of the whole; and secondly, that education and opinion, which have so vast a power over human character, should so use that power as to establish in the mind of every individual an indissoluble association between his own happiness and the good of the whole, especially between his own happiness and the practice of such modes of conduct, negative and positive, as regard for the universal happiness prescribes: so that not only he may be unable to conceive the possibility of happiness to himself, consistently with conduct opposed to the general good, but also that a direct impulse to promote the general good may be in every individual one of the habitual motives of action, and the sentiments connected therewith may fill a large and prominent place in every human being's sentient existence.

The Subjection of Women*

THE OBJECT OF THIS ESSAY is to explain as clearly as I am able, the grounds of an opinion which I have held from the very earliest period when I had formed any opinions at all on social or political matters, and which, instead of being weakened or modified, has been constantly growing stronger by the progress of reflection and the experience of life: That the principle which regulates the existing social relations between the two sexes—the legal subordination of one sex to the other—is wrong in itself, and now one of the chief hindrances to human improvement; and that it ought to be replaced by a principle of perfect equality, admitting no power or privilege on the one side, nor disability on the other.

The generality of a practice is in some cases a strong presumption that it is, or at all events once was, conducive to laudable ends. This is the case, when the practice was first adopted, or afterwards kept up, as a means to such ends, and was grounded on experience of the mode in which they could be most effectually attained. If the authority of men over women, when first established, had been the result of a conscientious comparison between different modes of constituting the government of society; if, after trying various other modes of social organization—the government of women over men, equality between the two, and such mixed and divided modes of government as might be invented—it had been decided, on the testimony of experience, that the mode in which women are wholly under the rule of men, having no share at all in public concerns, and each in private being under the legal obligation of obedience to

the man with whom she has associated her destiny, was the arrangement most conducive to the happiness and well being of both; its general adoption might then be fairly thought to be some evidence that, at the time when it was adopted, it was the best: though even then the considerations which recommended it may, like so many other primeval social facts of the greatest importance, have subsequently, in the course of ages, ceased to exist. But the state of the case is in every respect the reverse of this. In the first place, the opinion in favor of the present system, which entirely subordinates the weaker sex to the stronger, rests upon theory only; for there never has been trial made of any other: so that experience, in the sense in which it is vulgarly opposed to theory, cannot be pretended to have pronounced any verdict. And in the second place, the adoption of this system of inequality never was the result of deliberation, or forethought, or any social ideas, or any notion whatever of what conduced to the benefit of humanity or the good order of society. It arose simply from the fact that from the very earliest twilight of human society, every woman (owing to the value attached to her by men, combined with her inferiority in muscular strength) was found in a state of bondage to some man. Laws and systems of polity always begin by recognizing the relations they find already existing between individuals. They convert what was a mere physical fact into a legal right, give it the sanction of society, and principally aim at the substitution of public and organized means of asserting and protecting these rights, instead of the irregular and lawless conflict of physical strength. Those who had already been compelled to obedience became in this manner legally bound to it. Slavery, from being a mere affair of force between the master and the slave, became regularized and a matter of compact among

---

*From John Stuart Mill, *The Subjection of Women* (1869).

the masters, who, binding themselves to one another for common protection, guaranteed by their collective strength the private possessions of each, including his slaves. In early times, the great majority of the male sex were slaves, as well as the whole of the female. And many ages elapsed, some of them ages of high cultivation, before any thinker was bold enough to question the rightfulness, and the absolute social necessity, either of the one slavery or of the other. By degrees such thinkers did arise: and (the general progress of society assisting) the slavery of the male sex has, in all the countries of Christian Europe at least (though, in one of them, only within the last few years) been at length abolished, and that of the female sex has been gradually changed into a milder form of dependence. But this dependence, as it exists at present, is not an original institution, taking a fresh start from considerations of justice and social expediency—it is the primitive state of slavery lasting on, through successive mitigations and modifications occasioned by the same causes which have softened the general manners, and brought all human relations more under the control of justice and the influence of humanity. It has not lost the taint of its brutal origin. No presumption in its favor, therefore, can be drawn from the fact of its existence. The only such presumption which it could be supposed to have, must be grounded on its having lasted till now, when so many other things which came down from the same odious source have been done away with. And this, indeed, is what makes it strange to ordinary ears, to hear it asserted that the inequality of rights between men and women has no other source than the law of the strongest.

That this statement should have the effect of a paradox, is in some respects creditable to the progress of civilization, and the improvement of the moral sentiments of mankind. We now live—that is to say, one or two of the most advanced nations of the world now live—in a state in which the law of the strongest seems to be entirely abandoned as the regulating principle of the world's affairs: nobody professes it, and, as regards most of the relations between human beings, nobody is permitted to practice it. When any one succeeds in doing so, it is under cover of some pretext which gives

him the semblance of having some general social interest on his side. This being the ostensible state of things, people flatter themselves that the rule of mere force is ended; that the law of the strongest cannot be the reason of existence of anything which has remained in full operation down to the present time. However any of our present institutions may have begun, it can only, they think, have been preserved to this period of advanced civilization by a well-grounded feeling of its adaptation to human nature, and conduciveness to the general good. They do not understand the great vitality and durability of institutions which place right on the side of might; how intensely they are clung to; how the good as well as the bad propensities and sentiments of those who have power in their hands, become identified with retaining it; how slowly these bad institutions give way, one at a time, the weakest first, beginning with those which are least interwoven with the daily habits of life; and how very rarely those who have obtained legal power because they first had physical, have ever lost their hold of it until the physical power had passed over to the other side. Such shifting of the physical force not having taken place in the case of women; this fact, combined with all the peculiar and characteristic features of the particular case, made it certain from the first that this branch of the system of right founded on might, though softened in its most atrocious features at an earlier period than several of the others, would be the very last to disappear. It was inevitable that this one case of a social relation grounded on force, would survive through generations of institutions grounded on equal justice, an almost solitary exception to the general character of their laws and customs; but which, so long as it does not proclaim its own origin, and as discussion has not brought out its true character, is not felt to jar with modern civilization, any more than domestic slavery among the Greeks jarred with their notion of themselves as a free people.

All causes, social and natural, combine to make it unlikely that women should be collectively rebellious to the power of men. They are so far in a position different from all other subject classes, that their masters require something more from them than actual service. Men do not want solely the obedience of women, they want their sentiments. All men, except the most brutish, desire to have, in the woman most nearly connected with them, not a forced slave but a willing one, not a slave merely, but a favorite. They have therefore put everything in practice to enslave their minds. The masters of all other slaves rely, for maintaining obedience, on fear; either fear of themselves, or religious fears. The masters of women wanted more than simple obedience, and they turned the whole force of education to effect their purpose. All women are brought up from the very earliest years in the belief that their ideal of character is the very opposite to that of men; not self-will, and government by self-control, but submission, and yielding to the control of others. All the moralities tell them that it is the duty of women, and all the current sentimentalities that it is their nature, to live for others; to make complete abnegation of themselves, and to have no life but in their affections. And by their affections are meant the only ones they are allowed to have—those to the men with whom they are connected, or to the children who constitute an additional and indefeasible tie between them and a man. When we put together three things—first, the natural attraction between opposite sexes; secondly, the wife's entire dependence on the husband, every privilege or pleasure she has being either his gift, or depending entirely on his will; and lastly, that the principal object of human pursuit, consideration, and all objects of social ambition, can in general be sought or obtained by her only through him, it would be a miracle if the object of being attractive to men had not become the polar star of feminine education and formation of character. And, this great means of influence over the minds of women having been acquired, an instinct of selfishness made men avail themselves of it to the utmost as a means of holding women in subjection, by representing to them meekness, submissiveness, and resignation of all individual will into the hands of a man, as an essential part of sexual attractiveness. Can it be doubted that any of the other yokes which mankind have succeeded in breaking, would have

subsisted till now if the same means had existed, and had been as sedulously used, to bow down their minds to it? If it had been made the object of the life of every young plebeian to find personal favor in the eyes of some patrician, of every young serf with some seigneur; if domestication with him, and a share of his personal affections, had been held out as the prize which they all should look out for, the most gifted and aspiring being able to reckon on the most desirable prizes; and if, when this prize had been obtained, they had been shut out by a wall of brass from all interests not centering in him, all feelings and desires but those which he shared or inculcated; would not serfs and seigneurs, plebeians and patricians, have been as broadly distinguished at this day as men and women are? and would not all but a thinker here and there, have believed the distinction to be a fundamental and unalterable fact in human nature?

I am far from pretending that wives are in general no better treated than slaves; but no slave is a slave to the same lengths, and in so full a sense of the word, as a wife is. Hardly any slave, except one immediately attached to the master's person, is a slave at all hours and all minutes; in general he has, like a soldier, his fixed task, and when it is done, or when he is off duty, he disposes, within certain limits, of his own time, and has a family life into which the master rarely intrudes. "Uncle Tom" under his first master had his own life in his "cabin," almost as much as any man whose work takes him away from home, is able to have in his own family. But it cannot be so with the wife. Above all, a female slave has (in Christian countries) an admitted right, and is considered under a moral obligation, to refuse to her master the last familiarity. Not so the wife: however brutal a tyrant she may unfortunately be chained to—though she may know that he hates her, though it may be his daily pleasure to torture her, and though she may feel it impossible not to loathe him—he can claim from her and enforce the lowest degradation of a human being, that of being made the instrument of an animal function contrary to her inclinations. While she is held in this worst description of slavery as to her own person, what is her position in regard to the children in whom she and her master have a joint interest? They are by law *his* children. He alone has any legal rights over them. Not one act can she do towards or in relation to them, except by delegation from him. Even after he is dead she is not their legal guardian, unless he by will has made her so. He could even send them away from her, and deprive her of the means of seeing or corresponding with them, until this power was in some degree restricted by Serjeant Talfourd's Act. This is her legal state. And from this state she has no means of withdrawing herself. If she leaves her husband, she can take nothing with her, neither her children nor anything which is rightfully her own. If he chooses, he can compel her to return, by law, or by physical force; or he may content himself with seizing for his own use anything which she may earn, or which may be given to her by her relations. It is only legal separation by a decree of a court of justice, which entitles her to live apart, without being forced back into the custody of an exasperated jailer—or which empowers her to apply any earnings to her own use, without fear that a man whom perhaps she has not seen for twenty years will pounce upon her some day and carry all off. This legal separation, until lately, the courts of justice would only give at an expense which made it inaccessible to any one out of the higher ranks. Even now it is only given in cases of desertion, or of the extreme of cruelty; and yet complaints are made every day that it is granted too easily. Surely, if a woman is denied any lot in life but that of being the personal body-servant of a despot, and is dependent for everything upon the chance of finding one who may be disposed to make a favorite of her instead of merely a drudge, it is a very cruel aggravation of her fate that she should be allowed to try this chance only once. The natural sequel and corollary from this state of things would be, that since her all in life depends upon obtaining a good master, she should be allowed to change again and again until she finds one. I am not saying that she ought to be allowed this privilege. That is a totally different consideration. The question of divorce, in the sense involving liberty of remarriage, is one into which it is foreign to my purpose to enter. All I now say is, that to those to whom nothing but servitude is allowed, the free choice of servitude is the only, though a most insufficient, alleviation. Its refusal completes the assimilation of the wife to the slave—and the slave under not the mildest form of slavery: for in some slave codes the slave could, under certain circumstances of ill usage, legally compel the master to sell him. But no amount of ill usage, without adultery superadded, will in England free a wife from her tormentor.

When we consider how vast is the number of men, in any great country, who are little higher than brutes, and that this never prevents them from being able, through the law of marriage, to obtain a victim, the breadth and depth of human misery caused in this shape alone by the abuse of the institution swells to something appalling. Yet these are only the extreme cases. They are the lowest abysses, but there is a sad succession of depth after depth before reaching them. In domestic as in political tyranny, the case of absolute monsters chiefly illustrates the institution by showing that there is scarcely any horror which may not occur under it if the despot pleases, and thus setting in a strong light what must be the terrible frequency of things only a little less atrocious.

The equality of married persons before the law, is not only the sole mode in which that particular relation can be made consistent with justice to both sides, and conducive to the happiness of both, but it is the only means of rendering the daily life of mankind, in any high sense, a school of moral cultivation. Though the truth may not be felt or generally acknowledged for generations to come, the only school of genuine moral sentiment is society between equals. The moral education of mankind has hitherto emanated chiefly from the law of force, and is adapted almost solely to the relations which force creates. In the less advanced states of society, people hardly recognize any relation with their equals. To be an equal is to be an enemy. Society, from its highest place to its lowest, is one long chain, or rather ladder, where every individual is either above or below his nearest neighbor, and wherever he does not command he must obey. Existing moralities, accordingly, are mainly fitted to a relation of command and obedience. Yet command and obedience are but unfortunate necessities of human life: society in equality is its normal state. Already in modern life, and more and more as it progressively improves, command and obedience become exceptional facts in life, equal association its general rule. The morality of the first ages rested on the obligation to submit to power; that of the ages next following, on the right of the weak to the forbearance and protection of the strong. How much longer is one form of society and life to content itself with the morality made for another? We have had the morality of submission, and the morality of chivalry and generosity; the time is now come for the morality of justice. Whenever, in former ages, any approach has been made to society in equality, Justice has asserted its claims as the foundation of virtue. It was thus in the free republics of antiquity. But even in the best of these, the equals were limited to the free male citizens; slaves, women, and the unenfranchised residents were under the law of force. The joint influence of Roman civilization and of Christianity obliterated these distinctions, and in theory (if only partially in practice) declared the claims of the human being, as such, to be paramount to those of sex, class, or social position. The barriers which had begun to be levelled were raised again by the northern conquests; and the whole of modern history consists of the slow process by which they have since been wearing away. We are entering into an order of things in which justice will again be the primary virtue; grounded as before on equal, but now also on sympathetic association; having its root no longer in the instinct of equals for self-protection, but in a cultivated sympathy between them; and no one being now left out, but an equal measure being extended to all. It is no novelty that mankind do not distinctly foresee their own changes, and that their sentiments are adapted to past, not to coming ages. To see the futurity of the species has always been the privilege of the intellectual élite, or of those who have learnt from them; to have the feelings of that futurity has been the distinction, and usually the martyrdom, of a still rarer élite. Institutions, books, education, society, all go on training human

beings for the old, long after the new has come; much more when it is only coming. But the true virtue of human beings is fitness to live together as equals; claiming nothing for themselves but what they as freely concede to every one else; regarding command of any kind as an exceptional necessity, and in all cases a temporary one; and preferring, whenever possible, the society of those with whom leading and following can be alternate and reciprocal. To these virtues, nothing in life as at present constituted gives cultivation by exercise. The family is a school of despotism, in which the virtues of despotism, but also its vices, are largely nourished. Citizenship, in free countries, is partly a school of society in equality; but citizenship fills only a small place in modern life, and does not come near the daily habits or inmost sentiments. The family, justly constituted, would be the real school of the virtues of freedom. It is sure to be a sufficient one of everything else. It will always be a school of obedience for the children, of command for the parents. What is needed is, that it should be a school of sympathy in equality, of living together in love, without power on one side or obedience on the other. This it ought to be between the parents. It would then be an exercise of those virtues which each requires to fit them for all other association, and a model to the children of the feelings and conduct which their temporary training by means of obedience is designed to render habitual, and therefore natural, to them. The moral training of mankind will never be adapted to the conditions of the life for which all other human progress is a preparation, until they practice in the family the same moral rule which is adapted to the normal constitution of human society.

The moral regeneration of mankind will only really commence, when the most fundamental of the social relations is placed under the rule of equal justice, and when human beings learn to cultivate their strongest sympathy with an equal in rights and in cultivation.

Thus far, the benefits which it has appeared that the world would gain by ceasing to make sex a disqualification for privileges and a badge of subjection, are social rather than individual; consisting in an increase of the general fund of thinking and acting power, and an improvement in the general conditions of the association of men with women. But it would be a grievous understatement of the case to omit the most direct benefit of all, the unspeakable gain in private happiness to the liberated half of the species; the difference to them between a life of subjection to the will of others, and a life of rational freedom. After the primary necessities of food and raiment, freedom is the first and strongest want of human nature. While mankind are lawless, their desire is for lawless freedom. When they have learnt to understand the meaning of duty and the value of reason, they incline more and more to be guided and restrained by these in the exercise of their freedom; but they do not therefore desire freedom less; they do not become disposed to accept the will of other people as the representative and interpreter of those guiding principles. On the contrary, the communities in which the reason has been most cultivated, and in which the idea of social duty has been most powerful, are those which have most strongly asserted the freedom of action of the individual—the liberty of each to govern his conduct by his own feelings of duty, and by such laws and social restraints as his own conscience can subscribe to.

He who would rightly appreciate the worth of personal independence as an element of happiness, should consider the value he himself puts upon it as an ingredient of his own.

Every restraint on the freedom of conduct of any of their human fellow creatures, (otherwise than by making them responsible for any evil actually caused by it), dries up *pro tanto* the principal fountain of human happiness, and leaves the species less rich, to an inappreciable degree, in all that makes life valuable to the individual human being.

CHAPTER TWENTY-EIGHT

HEGEL

The French Revolution accentuated political and intellectual divisions in Europe. It made democrats more democratic and conservatives more conservative. In England, the French Revolution delayed reform for more than a generation, but in the end could not forestall advances of democracy, liberalism, and freedom. English liberalism derived its vitality from the twin roots of the Puritan and Glorious Revolutions through which monarchical absolutism was overthrown and parliament became supreme over a century before the French Revolution. Long having made peace with constitutionalism, English ruling classes were more afraid of Napoleon's militarism than Rousseau's political philosophy.

By contrast, the philosophy of French egalitarianism and the Rights of Man—more than French power—initially appeared to threaten the foundations of Continental societies. Napoleon's armies at first brought to other people of the Continent relief from political and social oppression of their own, native ruling classes. French armies at first were welcomed as bearers of a new order in which liberty, equality, fraternity, and reason would replace outmoded and discredited institutions and governing individuals. As time proceeded, however, the French struggle with England for world domination turned the whole Continent into a battlefield, the cost and burden of which were borne by Continental countries. The French objective of conquering England led to the collapse of the European economy and to the control of European nations by what evolved into a French regime of tyranny.

The Napoleonic wars had especially disastrous consequences in Germany. In England and France, democracy and liberalism arose as national movements against internal oppression and exploitation. In addition, democracy in both nations as in the United States proved successful because it promoted material welfare at home and enhanced national power and prestige abroad. By contrast, Germans first learned of democracy through invasion of French revolutionary armies. Enthusiasm for the French Revolution—and later for Napoleon—was sincere and exuberant in many parts of Germany, especially among the middle classes and peasants. If the victorious Napoleonic armies had followed the destruction of the feudal order in Germany with creation of a free German republic rather than a dictatorial vassal state, the history of Europe could have taken a much different turn with the Oder (separating Germany and Poland) instead of the Rhine (separating Germany and France) becoming the frontier of democracy.

As it was, the initial destruction of feudalism and absolutism in Germany was followed by a French regime of military and economic control in pursuit of Napoleon's vainglorious dreams of world empire. While French armies entered

Germany as torchbearers of liberty and human brotherhood, they left it as the enemies of the German people. German ruling classes thus discredited "the West"—a
geographical as well as political concept. Democracy, liberty, parliamentarism, and
self-government became identified in much of the German collective mind as symbols
of defeat, oppression, and Germany's national enemy. This tragic heritage bore bitter
fruit in the First and Second World Wars.

In the German intellectual tradition, the philosophy of G. W. F. Hegel (1770–1831)
towers over the rest. Hegel's system encompasses philosophy, metaphysics, religion, art,
ethics, aesthetics, history, and politics. In its range alone, his work is impressive and of
a truly encyclopedic character. His intellectual position in Germany was so commanding that all subsequent German thinkers, whether they agreed with him or not, had to
take his work into consideration. His ideas have been considered by most Germans
themselves as the most typically representative, more German than those of any other
major philosopher, not barring Kant. So commanding was Hegel's position in German
thought that even the most ferocious challenge to orthodox German philosopher, that of
Karl Marx, largely sprang from Hegelian assumptions.

Hegel primarily was a philosopher and his political thought emanates from his philosophy. Trained in theology, he always was a believing, if heterodox, Christian. He saw
history as the unfolding of God's purpose in the world, and the state as God's instrument for moving the world. The state is, in his famous phrase, "the Divine Idea as it
exists on Earth." The state is "the way of God in the world." The state is the actually
existing, realized moral life, and "all the worth which the human being possesses—all
spiritual reality—he possesses only through the State." The individual only has moral
value because he is part of a state.

In the Judeo-Christian tradition, the Earthly City never can take the place of the
City of God, and no human-made law or institution therefore can command the complete allegiance of humanity. According to this tradition, humanity's spiritual
essence—based upon reason, nature, and God—is prior and superior to law and the
state. Human law and state at best merely are means of serving the fulfillment of
human moral aspirations.

Hegel believed that human moral purpose only can be discovered in and through a
community, and that individual progress without collective progress is illusory.
Through the Earthly City never can reach the City of God, it ever more closely can approximate it. Though it always will be fallible men rather than the infallible God who
reign in the Earthly City, they are capable—through reason—dialectically of advancing
the Earthly City toward the City of God. Hegel denied the most fundamental philosophical principle of Judeo-Christian monotheism: that there is a sphere of conscience in
each human being that is exempt from the claims of political authority, and that the
state should not absorb the spiritual self of the individual.

Hegel possessed an idealist rather than empirical conception of reason, and this influences both his thought and its understanding. In the British tradition, reason is the
empirical method. Truth is the observation and accumulation of evidence, resulting in
the proposal of tentative hypotheses subject to testing, confirmation, disconfirmation,
and further—always tentative—hypotheses. Truth never is known; it always is merely
hypothesized. The universal invariability of the natural world and its laws cannot be
proven. It is the ultimate hypothesis upon which science is built. For the empirical
method, the fatal sin is to presume that absolute truth ever may be obtained by the
human mind.

Germanic idealism conceives knowledge and reason differently than British
empiricists such as Locke and Hume. Focus is directed not so much to the world as to

human perception of the world. This perhaps is most prevalent in Kant's philosophy, emphasizing the *Ding an sich* ("thing in itself") existing on the other side of perception, timeless, and without sensory characteristics of space—of which an individual never absolutely can know, but only can presume exists. What is important is not what is, but what individuals think to be so. As Goethe famously wrote, "all that is factual is already theory." Hegel firmly is located within the Germanic idealist tradition.

Hegel's philosophy is also deeply influenced by the Greeks, who played such a large role in the German philosophical heritage. The Germans saw themselves as inheritors of the ancient world through the Holy Roman Empire—which during the Middle Ages comprised most of what now is Germany and Austria—in the Germanic mind, successor of the ancient Roman Empire and the spirit of Greece. The Holy Roman Empire played a much larger role in the German intellectual heritage than it has in the Anglo-American tradition. Hegel's account of the development of human progress and order through the state should be considered within his philosophical and historical context. When he put forward the German Prussian state as the historically existent manifestation of God's will on earth, he did so with a different historical and philosophical background than Anglo-American thinkers and writers.

After finishing studies in theology, Hegel, like so many thinkers and writers of his day, intellectually moved to the intellectualworlds of ancient Greece and Rome. His thought is an amalgam of Christianity, Greece, and the unique challenges of his time and place. He followed his predecessor Herder in the beliefs that human culture is evolving and each historical period is singular. Hegel's thought was not static; it is dynamic, and its dynamism reflected his concept of an orderly world moving toward the ultimate in accordance with God's purpose. He as well is influenced by Fichte's concept of the nation as a manifestation of divine order.

The specific political context within which Hegel wrote was informed by disunity among the German states. Following the disastrous Thirty Years' War (from 1618 to 1648)—during which the German population was decimated and the Catholic emperor in Vienna lost power within much of what now is Germany to Protestant princes, during which almost the entire European continent was a massive field of operations, and during which German–French enmity grew and England and Russia managed to remain apart from European battles—the German political world was shattered into countless political sub-jurisdictions, while retaining the concept, furthered by a common culture and language, of the German people or *Volk*.

The great desire of the German people or *nation*, as distinct from German *state*, during the eighteenth and nineteenth centuries was to unify, and Hegel's political thought reflects this desire. The best statement of his political ideas is found in *Philosophy of Law* (1821). It expresses his conception of freedom, natural and social, which provides the key to an understanding of his political thought. Hegel starts with the thesis that in the physical world nature as it is, as understood by the human mind, is the proper subject of investigation, and the object of knowledge and philosophy.

What knowledge has to investigate in nature, he argues, is its "eternal harmony" and "inherent rationality." Proceeding from nature to ethics, he argues against those who put forward that the ethical world, actualized in the state, should be considered in a different manner than nature. Just as reason becomes "actual" in nature, so it becomes actual in the state. In both, the observer cannot make laws expressing reason but merely can understand them, the purpose of philosophy. There is no "chance and caprice" in rationality in either the physical world, or the ethical world of the state. Hegel transfers the ojectivity and determinateness of the physical world to the ethical world through the state.

In both *Philosophy of Law* and *Philosophy of History,* Hegel takes up the question of who ought to determine the laws. He attacks the doctrine that all should participate in the business of the state as a "ridiculous notion." To permit all persons to share in public decisions because affairs of state are the concern of all its members is "tantamount to a proposal to put the democratic element without any rational form into the organism of the state." He puts forward the *corporate* organization of the state by his emphasis that the individual should be politically articulate only as a member of a social group or class, and not just as a citizen *qua* citizen as in democracies. The advantage of the monarchical form of government lies in the fact that leadership always is clearly present in it, whereas in aristocracy, and even more in democracy, leaders only may rise to the top.

Shortly before Hegel died, he wrote a detailed analysis on the *English Reform Bill* (1831). He found that England was behind the "glorious and fortunate" progress of Germany because it lacked the "great sense of princes" and because its monarchical power was weak and powerless against the "thoughtless mob," which was given too much influence. He predicted that the Reform Bill, if enacted, would amount to revolution rather than reform. He penetratingly observed that in unreformed England, new governments reflected the same class interests of the old, but that after the broadening of the suffrage, new governments would represent new interests. He concluded that enactment of the Reform Bill might threaten the stability of English political order.

The doctrine that democracy is the first step toward anarchy is the staple argument of all authoritarian political thinkers, from Plato to latter-day opponents of democracy, and Hegel shared the classical authoritarian doctrine that society requires a strong monarch as a balancing element among contending economic and political interests. Democratic theory, on the other hand, denies that there is one individual or class who from an olympic height of absolute justice and disinterestedness can view conflicts of human values and interests. Democratic theory teaches that societal conflicts peacefully may be resolved through discussion, participation, and persuasion.

In the democratic tradition of political thought, society means choice and alternatives, not submission and will. According to Hegel, society is a man-made copy of nature with its laws of necessity, in which liberty can be found only by voluntary submission: "In duty the individual finds his liberation." When "the subjective will of man submits to laws, the contradiction between Liberty and Necessity vanishes." By contrast, the democratic tradition accepts necessity in physical nature, *but not in human relations.* The reasoning of democrats is that, although one must accept the validity of the law of gravity, one may challenge the validity of any man-made law. Submission to laws of physical nature but potential defiance of human controls is the distinction democratic political philosophy carefully draws.

Hegel rejects social revolution, just as, he thought, there is no revolution in nature—while democrats, though accepting evolution as the main process of change in nature, nevertheless accept the possibility, and in some instances even the desirability, of revolution as a method of social change. In the Hegelian approach to this problem, the physical conception of necessity is transferred from the mechanism of nature to the organization of society. The political effects of this transfer are fundamental: Just as we relatively are free in nature by knowing, and voluntarily submitting to, the laws of nature rather than uselessly trying to change them, we are free in society, the Hegelian argument holds, if we willingly accept the laws imposed upon us.

The fundamental law of the state is the constitution. Hegel opposes the democratic idea of the constitution as an instrument of government, a charter and compact consciously framed for desired ends. The constitution, he maintains, "should not be regarded as something made, even though it has come into being in time. It must be treated rather as something simply existent in and by itself, as divine therefore, and constant, and so exalted above the sphere of things that are made." He identifies morality with the power of the state both domestically and internationally.

The Jewish-Stoic-Christian tradition affirms there is a far higher law than commands of the state. The antidemocratic theory of politics maintains, in contrast, that social conflict should not be decided by the haphazard and approximate methods of a system in which the "thoughtless mob" is the final source of authority, but only by those who know what absolute justice is. Because they know, they must be obeyed.

As early as 1802, Hegel wrote in his *Constitution of Germany* that in their naive concern for freedom of conscience and political liberty, men are foolish enough to overlook the "truth which lies in power." Power is of the "higher justice of nature and truth" and therefore may forcibly bring men and women under its sway, despite their inner convictions and theories.

In his posthumously-published *Philosophy of History* (1837), Hegel inquires into the progress of humanity from ancient times to the present. Starting with the premise that "Freedom is the sole Truth of Spirit," he believes he demonstrates the history of the world "is none other than the progress of the consciousness of Freedom." The Oriental concept was very narrow indeed: "They only knew that one is free." In the practice of government, this meant despotism, because if only one is free, all others are unfree. The Greeks and Romans made some advance over Orientals, because they knew some were free. Their concept of liberty was tied to slavery, though, which was unfreedom of many. But the fulfillment of freedom for "man, as man" came with the German states of his time, Hegel believes.

Hegel's societal philosophy is vitally influenced by the eighteenth century from which he emerged. The split, particularly in the Germanic world, of science and philosophy was not complete, and his goal was to achieve the same degree of precision and determinacy in ethical philosophy as is possible in science. He strongly believes in the power of reason, but it is a different conception of reason than what has become accepted since his time. He sees reason as being able to achieve in society what it already had begun to achieve in explaining nature. His idea is that just as there may be scientific understanding of nature, there may be scientific understanding of society.

His conception of society, moreover, encompasses more than government. He considers society as all of the interlocking web of relationships and activities that comprise a community's life, including art, religion, and philosophy, as well as government. Within this comprehensive view of society, he does not maximize the role of government. In the tradition of Kant, he favors limited government and a relatively competitive market order incorporating private property.

Hegel's view of society is not atomistic. He vehemently disagrees with Bentham that "the community is a fictitious *body,* composed of the individual persons who are considered as constituting as it were its *members.*" The interest of the community then is, what?—the sum of the interest of the several members who compose it." In Hegel's conception, the community is all, and individual fulfillment is found only in and through it. Freedom—inner spiritual realization—is achieved through individual conformity within an ethical society, and an ethical society is an outward manifestation of a free and rational, moral human being. In *Philosophy of History,* Hegel defines the state as the "realization of freedom."

Perhaps Hegel's most famous metaphor is, "the owl of Minerva spreads its wings only with the falling of dusk." The place of philosophy is not so much to understand the future as to conceptualize previous experience very different interpretations of Hegel's thought have been made. His thought paved the way for Marx, for just as Hegel saw inexorable laws of state, Marx saw inexorable laws of society and class.

HEGEL

I *Philosophy of Law**

FREEDOM IN NATURE
AND SOCIETY

At the present time, the idea that freedom of thought, and of mind generally, evinces itself only in divergence from, indeed in hostility to, what is publicly recognized, might seem to be most firmly rooted in connection with the state, and it is chiefly for this reason that a philosophy of the state might seem essentially to have the task of discovering and promulgating still another theory, and a special and original one at that. In examining this idea and the activity in conformity with it, we might suppose that no state or constitution had ever existed in the world at all or was even in being at the present time, but that nowadays—and this "nowadays" lasts for ever—we had to start all over again from the beginning, and that the ethical world had just been waiting for such present-day projects, proofs, and investigations. So far as nature is concerned, people grant that it is nature as it is which philosophy has to bring within its ken, that the philosopher's stone lies concealed somewhere within nature itself, that nature is inherently rational and that what knowledge has to investigate and grasp in concepts is this actual reason present in it; not the formations and accidents evident to the superficial observer, but nature's eternal harmony, its harmony however, in the sense of the law and essence immanent within it. The ethical world, on the other hand, the state (i.e. reason as it actualizes itself in the element of self-consciousness), is not allowed

to enjoy the good fortune which springs from the fact that it is reason which has achieved power and mastery within that element and which maintains itself and has its home there. The universe of mind is supposed rather to be left to the mercy of chance and caprice, to be God-forsaken, and the result is that if the ethical world is Godless, truth lies outside it, and at the same time, since even so reason is supposed to be in it as well, truth becomes nothing but a problem. But it is this also that is to authorize, nay to oblige, every thinker to take his own road, though not in search of the philosopher's stone, for he is saved this search by the philosophizing of our contemporaries, and everyone nowadays is assured that he has this stone in his grasp as his birthright. Now admittedly it is the case that those who live their lives in the state as it actually exists here and now and find satisfaction there for their knowledge and volition (and of these there are many, more in fact than think or know it, because ultimately this is the position of everybody), or those at any rate who *consciously* find their satisfaction in the state, laugh at these operations and affirmations and regard them as an empty game, sometimes rather funny, sometimes rather serious, now amusing, now dangerous. Thus this restless activity of empty reflection, together with its popularity and the welcome it has received, would be a thing on its own, developing in privacy in its own way, were it not that it is philosophy itself which has earned all kinds of scorn and discredit by its indulgence in this occupation. The worst of these kinds of scorn is this, that, as I said just now, everyone is convinced that his mere birthright puts him in a position to pass judgment on

*From G.W.F. Hegel, *Philosophy of Law* (1821; trans. T.M. Knox as *Philosophy of Right*, Oxford University Press, 1942). By permission.

philosophy in general and to condemn it. No other art or science is subjected to this last degree of scorn, to the supposition that we are masters of it without ado.

What is rational is actual and what is actual is rational. On this conviction the plain man like the philosopher takes his stand, and from it philosophy starts in its study of the universe of mind as will as the universe of nature. If reflection, feeling, or whatever form subjective consciousness may take, looks upon the present as something vacuous and looks beyond it with the eyes of superior wisdom, it finds itself in a vacuum, and because it is actual only in the present, it is itself mere vacuity. If on the other hand the Idea passes for "only an Idea," for something represented in an opinion, philosophy rejects such a view and shows that nothing is actual except the Idea. Once that is granted, the great thing is to apprehend in the show of the temporal and transient the substance which is immanent and the eternal which is present. For since rationality (which is synonomous with the Idea) enters upon external existence simultaneously with its actualization, it emerges with an infinite wealth of forms, shapes and appearances. Around its heart it throws a motley covering with which consciousness is at home to begin with, a covering which the concept has first to penetrate before it can find the inward pulse and feel it still beating in the outward appearances. But the infinite variety of circumstance which is developed in this externality by the light of the essence glinting in it—this endless material and its organization—this is not the subject matter of philosophy.

It is the fact that the ethical order is the system of these specific determinations of the Idea which constitutes rationality. Hence the ethical order is freedom or the absolute will as what is objective, a circle of necessity whose moments are the ethical powers which regulate the life of individuals. To these powers individuals are related as accidents to substance, and it is in individuals that these powers are represented, have the shape of appearance, and become actualized.

The bond of duty can appear as a restriction only on indeterminate subjectivity or abstract freedom, and on the impulses either of the natural will or of the moral will which determines its indeterminate good arbitrarily. The truth is, however, that in duty the individual finds his liberation; first, liberation from dependence on mere natural impulse and from the depression which as a particular subject he cannot escape in his moral reflections on what ought to be and what might be; secondly, liberation from the indeterminate subjectivity which, never reaching reality or the objective determinacy of action, remains self-enclosed and devoid of actuality. In duty the individual acquires his substantive freedom.

Virtue is the ethical order reflected in the individual character so far as that character is determined by its natural endowment. When virtue displays itself solely as the individual's simple conformity with the duties of the station to which he belongs, it is rectitude.

The state is the actuality of concrete freedom. But concrete freedom consists in this, that personal individuality and its particular interests not only achieve their complete development and gain explicit recognition for their right (as they do in the sphere of the family and civil society) but, for one thing, they also pass over of their own accord into the interest of the universal, and, for another thing, they know and will the universal; they even recognize it as their own substantive mind; they take it as their end and aim and are active in its pursuit. The result is that the universal does not prevail or achieve completion except along with particular interests and through the cooperation of particular knowing and willing; and individuals likewise do not live as private persons for their own ends alone, but in the very act of willing these they will the universal in the light of the universal and their activity is consciously aimed at none but the universal end. The principle of modern states has prodigious strength and depth because it allows the principle of subjectivity to progress to its culmination in the extreme of self-subsistent personal particularity, and yet at the same time bring it back to the substantive unity and so maintains this unity in the principle of subjectivity itself.

In contrast with the spheres of private rights and private welfare (the family and civil society), the state is from one point of view an external necessity and their higher authority; its nature is such that their laws and interests are subordinate to it and dependent on it. On the other hand, however, it is the end immanent within them, and its strength lies in the unity of its own universal end and aim with the particular interest of individuals, in the fact that individuals have duties to the state in proportion as they have rights against it.

To hold that every single person should share in deliberating and deciding on political matters of general concern on the ground that all individuals are members of the state, that its concerns are their concerns, and that it is their right that what is done should be done with their knowledge and volition, is tantamount to a proposal to put the democratic element without any rational form into the organism of the state, although it is only in virtue of the possession of such a form that the state is an organism at all. This idea comes readily to mind because it does not go beyond the abstraction of "being a member of the state," and it is superficial thinking which clings to abstractions. The rational consideration of a topic, the consciousness of the Idea, is concrete and to that extent coincides with a genuine practical sense. Such a sense is itself nothing but the sense of rationality or the Idea, though it is not to be confused with mere business routine or the horizon of a restricted sphere. The concrete state is the whole, articulated into its particular groups. The member of a state is a member of such a group, i.e. of a social class, and it is only as characterized in this objective way that he comes under consideration when we are dealing with the state. His mere character as universal implies that he is at one and the same time both a private person and also a thinking consciousness, a will which wills the universal. This consciousness and will, however, lose their emptiness and acquire a content and a living actuality only when they are filled with particularity, and particularity means determinacy as particular and a particular class-status; or to put the matter otherwise, abstract individuality is a generic essence, but has its immanent universal actuality as the generic essence next higher in the scale. Hence the single person

attains his actual and living destiny for universality only when he becomes a member of a Corporation, a society, &c., and thereby it becomes open to him on the strength of his skill, to enter any class for which he is qualified, the class of civil servants included.

Another presupposition of the idea that all should participate in the business of the state is that everyone is at home in this business—a ridiculous notion, however commonly we may hear it sponsored. Still, in public opinion a field is open to everyone where he can express his purely personal political opinions and make them count.

Since the laws and institutions of the ethical order make up the concept of freedom, they are the substance or universal essence of individuals, who are thus related to them as accidents only. Whether the individual exists or not is all one to the objective ethical order. It alone is permanent and is the power regulating the life of individuals. Thus the ethical order has been represented by mankind as eternal justice, as gods absolutely existent, in contrast with which the empty business of individuals is only a game of see-saw.

Duty is a restriction only on the self-will of subjectivity. It stands in the way only of that abstract good to which subjectivity adheres. When we say: "We want to be free," the primary meaning of the words is simply: "We want abstract freedom," and every institution and every organ of the state passes as a restriction on freedom of that kind. Thus duty is not a restriction on freedom, but only on freedom in the abstract, i.e. on unfreedom. Duty is the attainment of our essence, the winning of positive freedom.

The intrinsic worth of courage as a disposition of mind is to be found in the genuine, absolute, final end, the sovereignty of the state. The work of courage is to actualize this final end, and the means to this end is the sacrifice of personal actuality. This form of experience thus contains the harshness of extreme contradictions: a self-sacrifice which yet is the real existence of one's freedom; the maximum self-subsistence of individuality, yet only as a cog playing its part in the mechanism of an external organization; absolute obedience, renunciation of personal opinions and reasonings, in fact complete *absence* of mind, coupled with the most intense and comprehensive *presence* of mind and decision in the moment of acting; the most hostile and so most personal action against individuals, coupled with an attitude of complete indifference or even liking towards them as individuals.

MONARCHICAL VERSUS POPULAR GOVERNMENT

The state in and by itself is the ethical whole, the actualization of freedom; and it is an absolute end of reason that freedom should be actual. The state is mind on earth and consciously realizing itself there. In nature, on the other hand, mind actualizes itself only as its own other, as mind asleep. Only when it is present in consciousness, when it knows itself as a really existent object, is it the state. In considering freedom, the starting-point must be not individuality, the single self consciousness, but only the essence of self-consciousness; for whether man knows it or not, this essence is externally realized as a self-subsistent power in which single individuals are only moments. The march of God in the world, that is what the state is. The basis of the state is the power of reason actualizing itself as will. In considering the Idea of the state, we must not have our eyes on particular states or on particular institutions. Instead we must consider the Idea, this actual God, by itself. On some principle or other, any state may be shown to be bad, this or that defect may be found in it; and yet, at any rate if one of the mature states of our epoch is in question, it has in it the moments essential to the existence of the state. But since it is easier to find defects than to understand the affirmative, we may readily fall into the mistake of looking at isolated aspects of the state and so forgetting its inward organic life. The state is no ideal work of art; it stands on earth and so in the sphere of caprice, chance, and error, and bad behavior may disfigure it in many respects. But the ugliest of men, or a criminal, or an invalid, or a cripple, is still always a living man. The affirmative, life, subsists despite his defects, and it is this affirmative factor which is our theme here.

We should desire to have in the state nothing except what is an expression of rationality. The state is the world which mind has made for itself; its march, therefore, is on lines that are fixed and absolute. How often we talk of the wisdom of God in nature! But we are not to assume for that reason that the physical world of nature is a loftier thing than the world of mind. As high as mind stands above nature, so high does the state stand above physical life. Man must therefore venerate the state as a secular deity, and observe that if it is difficult to comprehend nature, it is infinitely harder to understand the state. It is a fact of the highest importance that nowadays we have gained a clearcut intuition into the state in general and have been so much engaged in discussing and making constitutions. But by getting so far we have not yet settled everything. In addition, it is necessary to bring to bear on a rational topic the reason underlying intuition, to know what the essence of the matter is and to realize that the obvious is not always the essential.

Another question readily presents itself here: "Who is to frame the constitution?" This question seems clear, but closer inspection shows at once that it is meaningless, for it presupposes that there is no constitution there, but only an agglomeration of atomic individuals. How an agglomeration of individuals could acquire a constitution, whether automatically or by someone's aid, whether as a present or by force or by thought, it would have to be allowed to settle for itself, since with an agglomeration the concept has nothing to do. But if the question presupposes an already existent constitution, then it is not about framing, but only about altering the constitution and the very presupposition of a constitution directly implies that its alteration may come about only by constitutional means. In any case, however, it is absolutely essential that the constitution should not be regarded as something made, even though it has come into being in time. It must be treated rather as something simply existent in and by itself, as divine therefore, and constant, and so as exalted above the sphere of things that are made.

The conception of the monarch is therefore of all conceptions the hardest of ratiocination, i.e. for the method of reflection employed by the Understanding. This method refuses to move beyond isolated categories and hence here again knows only *raisonnement,* finite points of view, and deductive argumentation. Consequently it exhibits the dignity of the monarch as something deduced, not only in its form, but in its essence. The truth is, however, that to be something not deduced but purely self-originating is precisely the conception of monarchy. Akin, then, to this reasoning is the idea of treating the monarch's right as grounded in the authority of God, since it is in its divinity that its unconditional character is contained. We are familiar, however, with the misunderstandings connected with this idea, and it is precisely this "divine" element which it is the task of a philosophic treatment to comprehend.

We may speak of the "sovereignty of the people" in the sense that any people whatever is self-subsistent *vis-à-vis* other peoples, and constitutes a state of its own, like the British people for instance. But the peoples of England, Scotland, or Ireland, or the peoples of Venice, Genoa, Ceylon, &c., are not sovereign peoples at all now that they have ceased to have rulers or supreme governments of their own.

We may also speak of sovereignty in home affairs residing in the people, provided that we are speaking generally about the whole state and meaning only what was shown above, namely, that it is to the state that sovereignty belongs.

The usual sense, however, in which men have recently begun to speak of the "sovereignty of the people" is that it is something opposed to the sovereignty existent in the monarch. So opposed to the sovereignty of the monarch, the sovereignty of the people is one of the confused notions based on the wild idea of the "people." Taken without its monarch and the articulation of the whole which is the indispensable and direct concomitant of monarchy, the people is a formless mass and no longer a state. It lacks every one of those determinate characteristics—sovereignty, government, judges, magistrates, class-divisions, &c.,—which are to be found only in a whole which is inwardly organized. By the very emergence into a people's life of moments of this kind which have a bearing on an organization, on political

life, a people ceases to be that indeterminate abstraction which, when represented in a quite general way, is called the "people."

At the stage at which constitutions are divided, as above mentioned, into democracy, aristocracy, and monarchy, the point of view taken is that of a still substantial unity, abiding in itself, without having yet embarked on its infinite differentiation and the plumbing of its own depths. At that stage, the moment of the final, self-determining, decision of the will does not come on the scene explicitly in its own proper actuality as an organic moment immanent in the state. None the less, even in those comparatively immature constitutional forms, there must always be individuals at the head. Leaders must either be available already, as they are in monarchies of that type, or, as happens in aristocracies, but more particularly in democracies, they may rise to the top, as statesmen or generals, by chance and in accordance with the particular needs of the hour. This must happen since everything done and everything actual is inaugurated and brought to completion by the single decisive act of a leader.

It is often alleged against monarchy that it makes the welfare of the state dependent on chance, for, it is urged, the monarch may be ill educated, he may perhaps be unworthy of the highest position in the state, and it is senseless that such a state of affairs should exist because it is supposed to be rational. But all this rests on a presupposition which is nugatory, namely that everything depends on the monarch's *particular* character. In a completely organized state, it is only a question of the culminating point of formal decision (and a natural bulwark against passion). It is wrong therefore to demand objective qualities in a monarch; he has only to say "yes" and dot the "i," because the throne should be such that the significant thing in its holder is not his particular make up. (Monarchy in this sense is rational because it corresponds with the concept, but since this is hard to grasp, we often fail to notice the rationality of monarchy.) Monarchy must be inherently stable and whatever else the monarch may have in addition to this power of final decision is part and parcel of his private character and should be of no consequence. Of course there may be circumstances in which it is this private character alone which has prominence, but in that event the state is either not fully developed, or else is badly constructed. In a well-organized monarchy, the objective aspect belongs to law alone, and the monarch's part is merely to set to the law the subjective "I will."

If we are to grasp the Idea of the monarch, we cannot be content with saying that God has appointed kings to rule over us, since God has made everything, even the worst of things. The point of view of utility does not get us very far either, and it is always possible to point out counter-balancing disadvantages. Still less does it help to regard monarchy as a *positive* right. That I should hold property is necessary, but my holding of this particular property is contingent; and in the same way, the right that there must be one man at the head of affairs seems contingent too if it is treated as abstract and as posited. This right, however, is inevitably present both as a felt want and as a requirement of the situation. Monarchs are not exactly distinguished for bodily prowess or intellectual gifts, and yet millions submit to their rule. Now to say that men allow themselves to be ruled counter to their own interests, ends, and intentions is preposterous. Men are not so stupid. It is their need, it is the inner might of the Idea, which, even against what they appear to think, constrains them to obedience and keeps them in that relation.

To define freedom of the press as freedom to say and write whatever we please is parallel to the assertion that freedom as such means freedom to do as we please. Talk of this kind is due to wholly uneducated, crude, and superficial ideas. Moreover, it is in the very nature of the thing that abstract thinking should nowhere be so stubborn, so unintelligent, as in this matter of free speech, because what it is considering is the most fleeting, the most contingent, and the most personal side of opinion in its infinite diversity of content and tergiversation. Beyond the direct incitation to theft, murder, rebellion, &c., there lies its artfully constructed expression—an expression which seems in itself quite general and vague, while all the time it conceals a meaning anything but vague, or else is compatible with inferences which are not actually expressed, and it is impossible to determine whether they rightly follow from it, or whether they were meant to be inferred from it. This vagueness of matter and form precludes laws on these topics from attaining the requisite determinacy of law, and since the trespass, wrong, and injury here are so extremely personal and subjective in form, judgement on them is reduced equally to a wholly subjective verdict. Such an injury is directed against the thoughts, opinions, and wills of others, but apart from that, these form the element in which alone it is actually anything. But this element is the sphere of the freedom of others, and it therefore depends on them whether the injurious expression of opinion is or is not actually an effective act.

PEACE AND WAR

War is not to be regarded as an absolute evil and as a purely external accident, which itself therefore has some accidental cause, be it injustices, the passions of nations or the holders of power, &c., or in short, something or other which ought not to be. It is to what is by nature accidental that accidents happen, and the fate whereby they happen is thus a necessity. Here as elsewhere, the point of view from which things seem pure accidents vanishes if we look at them in the light of the concept and philosophy, because philosophy knows accident for a show and sees in it its essence, necessity. It is necessary that the finite—property and life—should be definitely established as accidental, because accidentality is the concept of the finite. From one point of view this necessity appears in the form of the power of nature, and everything is mortal and transient. But in the ethical substance, the state, nature is robbed of this power, and the necessity is exalted to be the work of freedom, to be something ethical. The transience of the finite becomes a willed passing away, and the negativity lying at the roots of the finite becomes the substantive individuality proper to the ethical substance.

War is the state of affairs which deals in earnest with the vanity of temporal goods and concerns—a vanity at other times a common theme of edifying sermonizing. This is what makes it the moment in which the ideality of the particular attains its right and is actualized. War has the higher significance that by its agency, as I have remarked elsewhere, "the ethical health of peoples is preserved in their indifference to the stabilization of finite institutions; just as the blowing of the winds preserves the sea from the foulness which would be the result of a prolonged calm, so also corruption in nations would be the product of prolonged, let alone 'perpetual,' peace." This, however, is said to be only a philosophic idea, or, to use another common expression, a "justification of Providence," and it is maintained that actual wars require some other justification.

The ideality which is in evidence in war, i.e. in an accidental relation of a state to a foreign state, is the same as the ideality in accordance with which the domestic powers of the state are organic moments in a whole. This fact appears in history in various forms, e.g. successful wars have checked domestic unrest and consolidated the power of the state at home. Other phenomena illustrate the same point: e.g. peoples unwilling or afraid to tolerate sovereignty at home have been subjugated from abroad, and they have struggled for their independence with the less glory and success the less they have been able previously to organize the powers of the state in home affairs—their freedom has died from the fear of dying; states whose autonomy has been guaranteed not by their armed forces but in other ways (e.g. by their disproportionate smallness in comparison with their neighbours) have been able to subsist with a constitution of their own which by itself would not have assured peace in either home or foreign affairs.

In peace civil life continually expands; all its departments wall themselves in, and in the long run men stagnate. Their idiosyncrasies become continually more fixed and ossified. But for health the unity of the body is required, and if its parts harden themselves into exclusiveness, that is death. Perpetual peace is often advocated as an ideal towards which humanity should strive. With that end in view, Kant proposed a league of monarchs to adjust differences between states, and the Holy Alliance was meant to be a league of much the same kind. But the state is an individual, and individuality essentially implies negation. Hence even if a number of states make themselves into a family, this group as an individual must engender an opposite and create an enemy. As a result of war, nations are strengthened, but peoples involved in civil strife also acquire peace at home through making wars abroad. To be sure, war produces insecurity of property, but this insecurity of things is nothing but their transience—which is inevitable. We hear plenty of sermons from the pulpit about the insecurity, vanity, and instability of temporal things, but everyone thinks, however much he is moved by what he hears, that he at least will be able to retain his own. But if this insecurity now comes on the scene in the form of hussars with shining sabres and they actualize in real earnest what the preachers have said, then the moving and edifying discourses which foretold all these events turn into curses against the invader. Be that as it may, the fact remains that wars occur when the necessity of the case requires. The seeds burgeon once more, and harangues are silenced by the solemn cycles of history.

States are not private persons but completely autonomous totalities in themselves, and so the relation between them differs from a moral relation and a relation involving private rights. Attempts have often been made to regard the state as a person with the rights of persons and as a moral entity. But the position with private persons is that they are under the jurisdiction of a court which gives effect to what is right in principle. Now a relation between states ought also to be right in principle, but in mundane affairs a principle ought also to have power. Now since there is no power in existence which decides in face of the state what is right in principle and actualizes this decision, it follows that so far as international relations are concerned we can never get beyond an "ought." The relation between states is a relation between autonomous entities which make mutual stipulations but which at the same time are superior to these stipulations.

The nation-state is mind in its substantive rationality and immediate actuality and is therefore the absolute power on earth. It follows that every state is sovereign and autonomous against its neighbours. It is entitled in the first place and without qualification to be sovereign from their point of view, i.e. to be recognized by them as sovereign. At the same time, however, this title is purely formal, and the demand for this recognition of the state, merely on the ground that it is a state, is abstract. Whether a state is in fact something absolute depends on its content, i.e. on its constitution and general situation; and recognition, implying as it does an identity of both form and content, is conditional on the neighbouring state's judgement and will.

If states disagree and their particular wills cannot be harmonized, the matter can only be settled by war. A state through its subjects has widespread connexions and many-sided interests, and these may be readily and considerably injured; but it remains inherently indeterminable which of these injuries is to be regarded as a specific breach of treaty or as an injury to the honour and autonomy of the state. The reason for this is that a state may regard its infinity and honour as a stake in each of its concerns, however minute, and it is all the more inclined to susceptibility to injury the more its strong individuality is impelled as a result of long domestic peace to seek and create a sphere of activity abroad.

Apart from this, the state is in essence mind and therefore cannot be prepared to stop at just taking notice of an injury *after* it has actually occurred. On the contrary, there arises in addition as a cause of strife the *idea* of such an injury as the idea of a danger *threatening* from another state, together with calculations of degrees of probability on this side and that, guessing at intentions, &c., &c.

At one time the opposition between morals and politics, and the demand that the latter should conform to the former, were much canvassed. On this point only a general remark is required here. The welfare of a state has claims to recognition totally different from those of the welfare of the individual. The ethical substance, the state, has its determinate being, i.e. its right, directly embodied in something existent, something not abstract but concrete, and the principle of its conduct and behaviour can only be this concrete existent and not one of the many universal thoughts supposed to be moral commands. When politics is alleged to clash with morals and so to be always wrong, the doctrine propounded rests on superficial ideas about morality, the nature of the state, and the state's relation to the moral point of view.

II   *Philosophy of History**

THE GERMANS—THE CLIMAX OF WORLD HISTORY AND WORLD SPIRIT

The nature of Spirit may be understood by a glance at its direct opposite—*Matter*. As the essence of Matter is Gravity, so, on the other hand, we may affirm that the substance, the essence of Spirit is Freedom. All will readily assent to the doctrine that Spirit, among other properties, is also endowed with Freedom; but philosophy teaches that all the qualities of Spirit exist only through Freedom; that all are but means for attaining Freedom; that all seek and produce this and this alone. It is a result of speculative Philosophy, that Freedom is the sole truth of Spirit. Matter possesses gravity in virtue of its tendency towards a central point. It is essentially composite; consisting of parts that *exclude* each other. It seeks its Unity; and therefore exhibits itself as self-destructive, as verging towards its opposite (an indivisible point). It if could attain this, it would be Matter no longer, it would have perished. It strives after the realization of its Idea; for in Unity it exists *ideally*. Spirit, on the contrary, may be defined as that which has its centre in itself. It has not a unity outside itself, but has already found it; it exists *in* and *with itself.* Matter has its essence out of itself; Spirit is *self-contained existence (Bei-sich-selbst-sein).* Now this is Freedom, exactly. For if I am dependent, my being is referred to something else which I am not: I cannot exist independently of something external. I am free, on the contrary, when my existence depends upon myself. This self-contained existence of Spirit is none other than self-consciousness—consciousness of one's own being. Two things must be distinguished in consciousness; first, the fact *that I know;* secondly, *what I know.* In *self* consciousness these are merged in one; for Spirit *knows itself.* It involves an appreciation of its own nature, as also an energy enabling it to realise itself; to make itself *actually* that which it is *potentially.* According to this abstract definition it may be said of Universal History, that it is the exhibition of Spirit in the process of working out the knowledge of that which it is potentially. And as the germ bears in itself the whole nature of the tree, and the taste and form of its fruits, so do the first traces of Spirit virtually contain the whole of that History. The Orientals have not attained the knowledge of that Spirit—Man *as such*—is free; and because they do not know this, they are not free. They only know that *one is free.* But on this very account, the freedom of that one is only caprice; ferocity—brutal recklessness of passion, or a mildness and tameness of the desires, which is itself only an accident of Nature—mere caprice like the former.—That *one* is therefore only a Despot; not a *free man.* The consciousness of Freedom first arose among the Greeks, and therefore they were free; but they, and the Romans likewise, knew only that *some* are free,—not man as such. Even Plato and Aristotle did not know this. The Greeks, therefore, had slaves; and their whole life and the maintenance of their splendid liberty, was implicated with the institution of slavery: a fact moreover, which made that liberty on the one hand only an accidental, transient, and limited growth; on the other hand, constituted it a rigorous thraldom of our common nature—of the Human. The German nations, under the influence of Christianity, were the first to attain the consciousness,

---

*From G. W. F. Hegel, *Philosophy of History* (1837; translated by J. Sibree, Willey Book Co., 1900).

that man, as man, is free: that it is the *freedom* of Spirit which constitutes its essence.

The general statement given above, of the various grades in the consciousness of Freedom—and which we applied in the first instance to the fact that the Eastern nations knew only that *one* is free; the Greek and Roman world only that *some* are free; whilst *we* know that all men absolutely (man *as man*) are free,—supplies us with the natural division of Universal History, and suggests the model of its discussion.

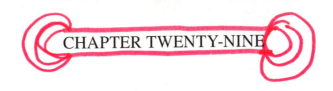

CHAPTER TWENTY-NINE

REVOLUTIONARY
COMMUNISM

In the nineteenth century, democracy seemed the goal toward which the whole world was inevitably moving. In some countries it was more cheerfully welcomed and more faithfully practiced than in others, but even politically backward states like Russia and Germany had to pay homage to political virtue by gradually broadening, in form, though not always in substance, the range of self-government. In the twentieth century, political hypocrisy, like other expressions of nineteenth-century politeness and formality, became no longer obligatory, and attacks upon democracy were carried out in the open, without the protective facade of apparent concessions to the principle of democracy. During the two decades between World Wars I and II, fascism (merged with the imperial ambitions of Germany, Japan, and Italy), was the main challenge to the democratic way of life for a time, it was so successful that it was openly hailed even in democratic states as "the wave of the future" by its sympathizers, or by those who felt that democracy was done for in a vain attempt to stem the tide of fascism.

World War II destroyed the military ambitions of the fascist Axis. The strains and stresses of war revealed the hollowness of fascism's claim to have inaugurated a new way of life that combined scientific and industrial efficiency with youthful and dynamic heroism. Yet World War II was hardly over when communism emerged as the new threat to democracy. At the end of World War I, when Russia was the only communist state in the world, and when its industrial and military power seemed to be low, communism was interpreted as a specifically Russian phenomenon without much practical applicability elsewhere. But the defeat of Nazi Germany by Russian armies in World War II revealed the extent to which the strength of Communist Russia had been underrated. When the war was over, Russia was the dominant military power in eastern Europe, and it quickly communized Poland, Rumania, Bulgaria, Hungary, Czechoslovakia, and East Germany.

Though the Russian armies were the principal instrument in spreading communism, the force of communist ideology was of vital significance. Whereas fascism did not possess a single creative or constructive idea that went beyond crass national egotism and lust for power, communism—unhampered, in particular, by the deadly burden of fascist racism—addressed itself to the world as the true heir of the libertarian, egalitarian democratic tradition. Also, whereas fascism proudly proclaimed its "pagan" character in relation to the democratic way of life, which it rejected *in toto,* communism is more "heretical" in terms of the democratic tradition: it accepts the democratic ideals of liberty, equality, and fraternity, and its charge against democracy is not, as was the charge of fascism, that democracy is too faithful to its ideals, but that it has, in fact, betrayed them. Just as in religion paganism generally has been less ruinous than heresy, because the former rejects the perceived truth in its entirety, whereas the latter mingles the true with the false, so communism, in the long run, proved more dangerous than fascism, precisely because communism contains important elements of the democratic tradition, distorted as they may be in practice.

In Europe, communism represented itself with considerable success, even in the eyes of many conservatives, as the authentic fighter against social and economic injustice. In Asia, communism was hunger become articulate, longing for faith and action. Whereas the western democracies taught Asia the right to be happy, without giving it the means to achieve happiness, communism promised the masses of landless, destitute, and forgotten Asians a new life of equality and abundance.

The greatest single influence in the development of revolutionary communism was Karl Marx (1818–1883). He was born in the Rhineland, which more than any other part of Germany had been strongly permeated with democratic ideas by the French Revolution. Marx attended the University of Berlin for several years, where he studied jurisprudence, philosophy, and history. But he quickly became engaged in political activities and in 1842 joined the staff of the *Rheinische Zeitung,* a democratic newspaper in Cologne. In the following year the paper was suppressed by the Prussian Government, and Marx went to Paris, then the European headquarters of radical movements.

In Paris, Marx met Proudhon, the leading French socialist thinker, Bakunin, the Russian anarchist, and Friedrich Engels (1820–1895), a Rhinelander like Marx, and soon to become his lifelong companion and close collaborator. Engels was the son of a German textile manufacturer with business interests in Germany and England, and he was sent by his father to Manchester in 1842. His *Condition of the Working Class in England* (1844) was a remarkably penetrating study of squalor, drabness, and poverty in the midst of luxurious wealth, and Engels was the first to draw Marx's attention to England as a laboratory in which industrial capitalism could be most accurately observed.

In 1845 Marx was expelled from France through the intervention of the Prussian Government, and he went to Brussels, another center of political refugees from all over Europe. There Marx composed, with the aid of Engels, the *Communist Manifesto* (1848), the most influential of all his writings, a pamphlet that has made history, inspired devotion and hatred, and divided mankind as profoundly as any other political document. Marx participated in the revolutions of 1848 in France and Germany, and early in 1849 he again was expelled by the Prussian Government, forbidden to return to his native land.

He went to London in the late summer of 1849, soon followed by Engels. Marx had planned to stay in England for only a few weeks, but he stayed there until his death in 1883. He spent most of his time in the British Museum, digging up obscure sources throwing light on the history and working of industrial capitalism. The first volume of *Das Kapital,* his monumental analysis of the capitalist system, was published in 1867; the second and third volumes appeared posthumously in 1885–1895, edited by Engels.

Marx's writings show little penetration of English *political* ideas and ways of thought, and his lack of insight into the forces and motivations of English politics would have been little better or worse had he stayed in Germany all his life. By contrast, his writings demonstrate a profound knowledge of the English *economic* system, based on detailed and painstaking research. Marx was one of the first social scientists to use neglected government reports and statistical materials as a basic tool of research in the study of social and economic problems. Yet it never occurred to him that the self-analysis of English capitalism, to which he owed the documentary sources of his grand indictment, might eventually evolve into peaceful self-improvement and change.

Marx's analysis of the capitalist system has influenced the making of history even more than the writing of history. Regardless of what one accepts or rejects of Marx's social, economic, political, and philosophical ideas, it is impossible to bypass him. He said of himself that he was not a "Marxist," and those who insist on all or nothing in relation to his ideas, betray Marx in his own painful and long search for a philosophy that he did not receive ready-made from any master but gathered, and added to his own life experience, from diverse sources: German philosophy, French revolutionary politics, and English economics.

In German philosophy, it was above all Hegel who greatly influenced Marx. Although Marx very early criticized Hegel, he never abandoned the basic categories of Hegel's thought. Like Hegel, Marx felt that history had meaning, and that it moved in a set pattern toward a known goal. In a rationalized version of the religious conception of history, in which history derives meaning from God and moves toward the kingdom of God, Hegel replaced God with the concept of Spirit or Reason, and history was seen by Hegel as the progressive unfolding of Reason. Marx held that history had both a meaning and a goal, and the historical process was dominated by the struggles between social classes; each phase of the struggle, as in Hegel, represented a higher phase of human evolution than the preceding one. The goal of history was predetermined for Marx: the classless society, leading to full human freedom.

This philosophy of history has, in Hegel, a conscious religious connotation, and in Marx, too, there is a quasi-religious element. As in religion, Hegel and Marx both view history as a perpetual struggle between lower and higher forces; however, the outcome of the struggle is predetermined. In religion, God triumphs when mankind finally turns toward him and abandons the false idols of lust and greed. In Hegel, the outcome is certain: the final victory of Reason and Spirit over enslavement to caprice and passion. In Marx, the outcome is the abolition of capitalism, and the destruction of all forms of injustice and exploitation in a new society based on freedom and fraternal cooperation. Many who embrace Marxism come from the ranks of persons who have lost faith in traditional forms of supernatural religion, but who still need the psychic support often derived from religious beliefs. Marxists find comfort in the feeling that man is not alone in this world, that there is meaning in the cosmos and in human history, and that mankind is inexorably moving toward a noble goal, compared with which one's temporary and individual sufferings and frustrations are not too important.

Thus, while Marx was personally a convinced atheist and insisted that his thought was guided by strictly scientific criteria, the historical influence of Marxism was not so much in the realm of scientific analysis as in its popular appeal as a *new religion* of the dispossessed and oppressed. The devout follower of the Marxian faith has an unshakable conviction that he knows what the meaning of history is, the goal toward which it is moving, that he has joined the forces that in the end must win, and that opposing the coming of communism is not only wrong but also futile, since "the march of history" cannot be stopped by any "reactionary" individual or group. In underdeveloped countries in particular, in which literacy is low, the spread of Marxism was overwhelmingly a quasi-religious phenomenon rather than a sign of expanding science.

French *revolutionary politics* was another important source for Marx's intellectual development. With his instinct of genius, Marx realized that, if revolution was the principal method of destroying a capitalist society, France and her revolutionary experience served as the best laboratory. France was among the most advanced major western nations because its revolutions were most clearly based on social antagonisms. Marx fully understood that the English Puritan revolution in the 1640s was a war between the middle class and the existing order based on landed property, but this social aspect of the Puritan revolution was too commingled with religious and political issues to serve as a pure, or almost pure, case of a social revolution. Moreover, the Puritan revolution was finally brought to a conclusion by the moderate settlement of the Glorious (and bloodless) Revolution of 1688, a conclusion which had little appeal for Marx. Similarly, the American Revolution was not the perfect case of a class war that Marx looked for. In Marx's mind, the American Revolution was a class war between the rising bourgeoisie and the aristocratic order in the American colonies. Yet the political issue of independence befuddled the class issue, and once the revolutionary struggle was won, the United States seemed to show few symptoms of intense conflict between its social classes.

In France, Marx felt, the historical development was different. The French Revolution of 1789 was by common agreement a purely social revolution of the peasants and urban middle classes against the aristocratic order. However, whereas revolutionary activity came to an end in England in 1688 and in the United States in the 1780s, the French Revolution of 1789 was merely the beginning of a series of revolutionary upheavals the end of which was not in sight. France experienced major revolutionary upheavals in 1830 and 1848, experiences which both England and the United States were spared. Finally, France was the scene of the short-lived proletarian dictatorship of the Paris Commune in 1871, the first of its kind in modern history. For Marx, both England and the United States had become too conservative after their successful revolutions; on the European continent, there was no other major nation in which social revolution was as much an integral part of the national experience as was France. As to Germany, Marx considered it intellectually and politically provincial, held back by feudal anachronisms and national disunity; Italy was economically backward and politically disunited, and until these two issues were resolved, there was little chance for a social revolution. Russia seemed to Marx more Asian than European, and although he sensed that Russia was a sleeping giant, he nevertheless shared the prejudices of many Germans that Russia, and Slavdom in general, was not culturally, socially, and economically in the same league with the more advanced nations of the West.

Finally, Marx perceptively saw that industrial capitalism and economic science could best be studied in England. Since Marx viewed economic forces as the main driving force in history, and since he felt that industrial civilization was irresistibly spreading throughout the whole world, he was convinced that England was the country to live in if one wanted to study industrial capitalism firsthand, and that English (and Scottish) economic analysis was the most advanced of any country. While Marx had no doubt that English economic doctrines were no more than a rationalization and justification of the capitalist system, they nevertheless supplied him with the basic concepts and tools of economic analysis which could also be used in demonstrating that capitalism was both wasteful and exploitative.

Above all, Marx shares with English classical economics basic presuppositions and tacit assumptions which are as important as his explicit rejection of specific doctrines of its leading representatives. For example, Marx looks upon *work* as man's most creative and noblest form of personal self-fulfillment. His quarrel with English classical economic theory and capitalist practice is not that they, too, take such a high view of work, but that under capitalism work becomes a mechanism of exploitation, degrading the worker to a soulless robot, enslaved to the "fetishism of commodities."

In Marx's thought, the classless communist society of the future was by no means to abolish the duty to work. The first stage of communism, Marx argued, would be guided by the principle of "from each according to his ability, to each according to his work." In the second, and higher, phase of communism, the principle of "from each according to his ability, to each according to his needs" would prevail. Most students of Marx concentrate on the difference of awards for work in the second as compared with the first stage of communism, but they often overlook that even in the second stage man is still expected to contribute to the best of his ability, that is, to perform socially useful work. Even in the second stage of communism, when the new man of communist society has become cooperative and has lost the competitive and acquisitive vices of capitalism and when production creates abundance, work is still, Marx says, "the primary necessity of life."

This Marxian worship of work is strictly adhered to by communists today. Communist states, for example, have not provided monetary relief for the unemployed, since an unemployed person is expected to work in any job he can find, regardless of pay, skill, or location. Interestingly, in noncommunist countries the religion of work has been greatly weakened in recent years, and liberal thinkers have attacked the idea of work as the main channel of personal self-fulfillment. In communist countries the duty to work is still an article of faith that must not be challenged. Though they rarely quote from the Bible, on this particular issue communists like to cite the Biblical injunction that "he who does not work, neither shall he eat"—although in communist literature this is often called a "socialist principle."

Marx's conception of *property* is closely related to that held by classical English liberal thinkers from Locke on. Locke and later English economists assumed that private property was a *relation of man to things,* and not a power relation between men—provided government does not meddle in the economy, thus injecting an element of compulsion into the property relation. Marx retains the basic concept of English classical economics of property as a relation of man to things, but according to Marx such property without power can exist only under public ownership, whereas private property is by definition a power relation. Marx thought that he completely rejected classical economic thought on property, since he reversed the roles of public and private property as viewed by the classical economists. Yet he still shares with them the belief—or illusion—that *any* form of productive property (private in the case of the classical economists, public in the case of Marx) can be interpreted as being a purely technical relationship between man and things, or as the "administration of things," as Marx referred to public ownership in a communist society.

The three major sources of Marx's intellectual development—German philosophy, French revolutionary politics, English political economy—nourished his thought from his youth to his old age. Early in his life, however, Marx was influenced by another powerful movement that was particularly strong in Germany: *romanticism.* From a purely literary viewpoint, romanticism was a movement of protest against the classical literary traditions of reason, order, measure, and form, as represented above all by the great age of French cultural predominance in the eighteenth century. In its social outlook, romanticism was a protest against the rising industrialization. The romantics felt that industrial civilization was destroying the natural and organic bonds of life that characterized preindustrial Europe, and that, as a result, man in an industrial society was becoming estranged or "alienated" from his fellow men, from nature, and—most important of all—from himself. The romantics had no positive program to cope with the evils of industrialism. Some romantics felt that the only solution was to abandon industrialism altogether and to return to the agrarian life of the preindustrial age—a highly impractical program quickly overtaken by events, since masses of propertyless farm workers kept on streaming into the cities. Other romantics withdrew from the ugly world of industrialism into a philosophy of extreme individualism—a solution which was purely literary rather than social, and which could only be adopted by a few individuals, but which provided no answer to problems affecting society as a whole.

In his *Economic and Philosophical Manuscripts,* written by Marx in 1844, at the age of twenty-six, Marx reflects the romantics' concern about alienation, but under a different perspective. Whereas the romantics saw the evil in industrialism as a new way of life, Marx perceived alienation as the result of *capitalist* industrialism. Under capitalism, Marx said in his *Economic and Philosophical Manuscripts,* man is alienated from his work, the objects he produces, his employers, other workers, nature, and from himself. Under capitalism, Marx argues, the worker does not work in order to fulfill himself as a person, for his work "is not voluntary but imposed, *forced* labor." His work does not satisfy his own needs, but is merely a means to satisfy the needs of others, the capitalist employers who use the worker as an instrument of profit making. The worker thus "sinks to the level of a commodity," producing palaces for the rich, but hovels for the poor. The worker is also alienated from the capitalist employer, who appropriates the products of labor and enjoys pleasures and privileges denied to the worker. Being alienated from the product of his labor, the worker is also alienated from other men. Marx vehemently attacks the role of money in the new capitalist economy. Money is the "highest good, and so its possessor is good." Money is the "visible deity" of capitalist industrialism, transforming all natural human relations into monetary relations. Since in a capitalist society everything can be bought with money, Marx affirms the need for a society in which man is related to his fellow men as an individual human being, in which love cannot be bought, but can "only be exchanged for love."

Marx showed in his *Economic and Philosophical Manuscripts* that man's predicament had economic, as well as ethical and psychological facets. However, in a crucial change of outlook Marx quickly abandoned the ethical element in his conception of communism, and in *The German Ideology,* written jointly with Frederick Engels in 1846, the Left Hegelians were subjected to a strong attack for talking of "human nature, of Man in general" rather than of man as a member of a particular class. The individualistic leanings of the *Manuscripts* were replaced by the concept of class, to which Marx adhered for the rest of his life, and the ideal of love and fellowship was replaced by that of class struggle and hatred. In the *Communist Manifesto* he specifically ridicules and attacks philosophical socialists who talk about the "alienation of humanity" or about the "philosophical foundation of socialism." Marx also attacks ethically oriented socialists as "utopians," because they reject revolutionary action and "wish to attain their ends by peaceful means, and endeavor, by small experiments, necessarily doomed to failure, and by the force of example, to pave the way for the new social gospel."

Since Marx himself had expressed, in the *Economic and Philosophical Manuscripts* of 1844, ideas which were akin to those of the philosophical and ethical socialists, he decided not to publish what he later considered a juvenile aberration. In fact, the *Manuscripts* were not published during his lifetime, and even after his death Engels, his literary executor, refrained from publishing them. In 1932, the *Manuscripts* were finally published for the first time in German, followed by translation into English nearly three decades later. Since then, the *Manuscripts*—with their fashionable doctrine of "human alienation"—have been used in communist and noncommunist countries for diverse purposes. In communist countries, particularly in Eastern Europe, the *Manuscripts* served as a weapon used by *liberal* elements who sought to discredit totalitarian attitudes and ideas of orthodox communism. While more liberally minded thinkers in Eastern Europe could not propagate liberalism by name, they could advocate some of its substance under the protective shield of the "Young Marx." In noncommunist countries, by contrast, the *Manuscripts* have served the opposite goal of making *Marxism* respectable, since Marx has been presented as a humanist socialist and liberal individualist primarily concerned with man's need for self-fulfillment through love and free cooperation. Whatever the merits of these two *political* efforts in communist and noncommunist countries—to make liberalism respectable in the former and Marxism in the latter— from the purely analytical and historical viewpoint the middle-aged and mature Marx cannot be turned into a liberal humanist, since from *The German Ideology* on, he saw in the liberal, humanist brand of socialism the most dangerous enemy of communism. This attitude of Marx was later faithfully emulated by communists, who consistently considered democratic socialists of the British Labor party type as more dangerous and damaging to the cause of communism than the openly conservative parties of a capitalist society.

As Marx became involved in practical political activities in his early life, he criticized the philosophical socialists, and philosophers in general, for analyzing society rather than actively trying to change it. Marx believed as he expressed it in one of his early writings (*Theses on Feuerbach,* 1845), "in practice man must prove the truth"; thus the easier method of discovering truth through revelation and authority, whether based on Marx or any other god or prophet, is excluded. The *Theses on Feuerbach* were written by Marx when he was only twenty-seven, and his conception of the task of philosophy is clearly indicated by his charge that "the philosophers have only *interpreted* the world, the point however is to *change* it." This activist approach to philosophy is distinctly un-Hegelian, and Marx's life was dedicated to the anti-Hegelian proposition that the actual was far from rational, and that the rational would finally be imposed upon actuality, not by a mystical world spirit, but by the new social class that was the heir of bourgeois science and rationalism: the proletariat.

Marx's philosophy of history and politics has to be gathered from many incidental remarks and comments in his writings and letters, as he never wrote a systematic statement on the basic assumptions of his thought. In the preface to his *Critique of Political Economy* (1859), Marx briefly states his general philosophy of history, based on the thesis that "the anatomy of civil society is to be found in political economy." Pre-Marxian social analysis had emphasized law and politics as the determining factors in society and social change. Marx reverses the scale of importance and considers the "productive forces" of society as the basis, whereas legal relations and forms of government are the "superstructure." Marx puts it in this fashion: "The mode of production of the material means of existence conditions the whole process of social, political, and intellectual life."

One of Marx's most famous sayings is that *men's social existence determines their consciousness,* and not, as had been generally accepted before Marx, that the "consciousness of men determines their existence." What Marx stresses here is that men's ideas are not accidental and haphazard, or freely left to their choice. Thus the legal, political, and religious ideas of a pastoral civilization will fundamentally differ from those of an agricultural, feudal society, and both will have little in common with the social, political, religious, and intellectual outlook of modern capitalist society.

Turning to the question of what causes historical change, Marx renounces the study of monarchs and their relations with court ladies and fellow dynasts, and he is equally dissatisfied with the study of history as a long list of battles and wars. Instead, Marx attempts to find the deeper causes of historical change in forces that go beyond the power of individual rulers and victorious war leaders: "At a certain stage of their development the material productive forces of society come into contradiction with the existing productive relationships, or, what is but a legal expression for these, with the property relationships within which they have moved before. From forms of development of the productive forces these relationships are transformed into their fetters. Then an epoch of social revolution opens. With the change in the economic foundation the whole vast superstructure is more or less rapidly transformed." Thus, when new *productive forces* developed within the *productive relationships* of the feudal system, social revolution was, according to Marx, inevitable, because the productive relationships of the feudal system (property relations, market controls, internal customs and tariffs, monetary instability) did not permit the utilization of the newly developing productive forces of industrial capitalism. What has doomed all historically known economic systems is the fact, according to Marx, that when new productive forces develop, the existing productive relationships stand in the way of their proper utilization. Each system thus becomes eventually wasteful in terms of the potentialities that have developed in its womb but that are not permitted to be born and to grow.

The capitalist system, too, shows the same tendency, according to Marx, and is due to undergo the same fate when the *productive forces* (the capacity to produce) have *outstripped* the *productive relationships* (law of property, production for private profit). The capitalist system as a system of social, economic, and legal relations thus eventually stands in the way of the scientific resources and technological know-how that are not permitted to be fully utilized. Only the public ownership of the means of production will, according to Marx, bring into existence a new system of productive relationships (production for common use rather than private profit) that will match the tremendous forces of production actually or potentially existent and known to man.

In the *Communist Manifesto,* Marx and Engels explain how social change through revolution actually occurs. When the forces of production begin to outstrip the methods of production (or productive relationships), the owners of the means of production do not step aside and thus accelerate the inevitable course of history. Bound by the limitations of their ideology (which, in turn, reflects the existing modes of production), they sincerely believe that the existing system is economically the most efficient, socially the most equitable, and generally in harmony with the laws of nature and the will of whatever god they venerate. It is not a question of the greed of the individual feudal landowner (who obstructs the birth of the more productive capitalist system) or of the selfishness of the individual capitalist (who impedes the nationalization of the means of production). The owners of the means of production will utilize all the instruments of the legal, political, and ideological superstructure to block the growth of the forces that represent the potentially more progressive economic system. For this reason Marx and Engels state early in the *Communist Manifesto* that the "history of all hitherto existing society is the history of class struggles." In the nineteenth century, the bourgeoisie liked to think of itself as conservative, law-abiding, and antirevolutionary—once it had won its class struggle. Yet Marx and Engels remind the bourgeoisie that, historically, it "has played a most revolutionary part."

The end of capitalism will be brought about, according to the *Communist Manifesto,* not by "subversive" conspiracies of professional agitators and revolutionaries, but by the same inexorable laws of social change that destroyed previous systems. Just as feudalism, for example, prepared its own grave by developing these forces—the urban bourgeoisie—which eventually destroyed it, capitalism does the same thing: "The essential condition for the existence and for the sway of the bourgeois class is the formation and augmentation of capital; the condition for capital is wage-labor. Wage-labor rests exclusively on competition between the laborers. The advance of industry, whose involuntary promoter is the bourgeoisie, replaces the isolation of the laborers, due to competition, by their revolutionary combinations, due to association. The development of modern industry, therefore, cuts from under its feet the very foundation on which the bourgeoisie produces and appropriates products. What the bourgeoisie therefore produces, above all, are its own grave-diggers. Its fall and the victory of the proletariat are equally inevitable."

As Marx and Engels look at history, they can find no instance where a major social and economic system has freely abdicated to its successor. Therefore the communists "openly declare that their ends can be attained only by the forcible overthrow of all existing social conditions." This is one of the crucial tenets of Marxist revolutionary communism, and the one that most clearly opposed it irreconcilably to democracy, be it capitalist or socialist democracy.

Marx had no clear-cut theory as to how the political transformation from capitalist to proletarian rule could come about. Though in the *Communist Manifesto* he believed in the need for revolution, he was less dogmatic later. Speaking in 1872 at a public meeting in Amsterdam following the Congress of the International, Marx declared that the means of attaining power for the working class are not everywhere the same: "We know that we must take into consideration the institutions, the habits and customs of different regions, and we do not deny that there are countries like America, England, and—if I knew your institutions better I would perhaps add Holland—where the workers can attain their objective by peaceful means. But such is not the case in all other countries."

Marx never fully pursued the implications of this distinction, and the generally accepted doctrine of communist Marxism is the impossibility of fundamental social and economic change except by class war, violence, and revolution. If Marx had accorded the political factor its due weight, if he had studied the implications of the Reform Act of 1832—a bloodless revolution in which the governing class peacefully ceded its position to the new middle class—he might have foreseen that socialism, too, might be accomplished without violence in countries whose democratic tradition was strong enough to absorb far-reaching social and economic changes without civil war.

A full recognition of the cultural and political factors in the equation of social change would have amounted to a virtual abandonment, however, of the central position of Marx: that history is the history of class wars, and that ruling classes defend their position to the last, not because of selfish greed, but because their ideological framework, the superstructure of the economic system, compels them to identify their privileged position with that of the whole community. Conversely, the proletariat attacks the capitalist system, and finally overthrows it, according to Marx, not because of some abstract ideals of justice, but because the inevitable evolution of capitalism puts the proletariat in a position of misery and exploitation, while men, knowledge, and resources lie idle.

In Hegel, *war between nations* is the vehicle of historical decision and progress, and the World Spirit assigns to different nations special missions at particular times. In Marx, social change and progress are attained by *war between classes,* and in each historical epoch one particular class is assigned the mission of representing the idea of progress. For Hegel, world history culminates in the Germanic peoples, which embody the finest flowering of freedom and spirit. For Marx, history culminates in the proletariat, which embodies the highest social principles of progress and rational ordering of society. Just as Hegel assumed that the process of the fulfillment of spirit and freedom was consummated in Prussianized Germany, Marx assumed that the process of history, the record of class wars, would be consummated in the final victory of the proletariat, after which the dynamics of class war would be followed by the *statics of the classless society.*

No one before Marx saw as clearly as he did the *intimate relationship between private property and power.* In particular, Marx demonstrated that the link between power and property was heightened to its extreme in the capitalist system, inasmuch as its scientific, technological, and managerial forces made possible an accumulation of economic power in the hands of the few, such as would have been impossible before the Industrial Revolution. Yet, realistic as Marx was in his appraisal of *private* property as a system of private government and power of man over man, he was utopian in assuming that property lost the character of power merely by being collectivized. The Marx-Engels doctrine of the "withering away of the state" in the classless society is based on the hypothesis that property in a socialist or communist society ceases to be a system of power when owned by the whole community. Whereas private ownership of the means of production under capitalism, Marx and Engels argue, entails the domination of man over man, public ownership of the means of production under socialism or communism will lead to the "administration of things," so that the state (in its historical meaning as a system of force) would wither away by itself, as there would no longer be any need for it.

The *administration of things* is a matter of technical *knowledge* and not of political *will.* Government as an agency of settling disputes between men by force would be replaced in the classless society by administration as a scientific method of using resources in the best way in accordance with verifiable procedures of science and technology. Locke was the first modern writer to define property as a relationship of man to things, inasmuch as he saw the origin of property in the admixture of human effort to natural resources. Marx's concept of *publicly owned property as a relationship between man and things* closely follows Locke's concept of private property.

The ideal of classical liberalism and that of Marx-Engels have a common utopian element: both assume that human nature can be so improved and perfected by the right kind of institutional changes that government as a mechanism of force becomes superfluous. In the classical doctrine of liberal democracy, the equitable distribution of private property seemed to point to such a state of harmony; in the doctrine of Marx-Engels, the transformation of individual work into collective work in the capitalist factory pointed to the practical conclusion that collective ownership of the means of production would assure a basic equality of men that would make government in the traditional sense unnecessary. Both classical democracy and Marxism suffer from an excessive optimism with regard to the perfectibility of man, and both wrongly assume that any system of society can be devised that can achieve perfect harmony of interests. Nevertheless, the liberal doctrine of "the less government, the better" and the Marxian doctrine of the "withering away of the state" can be valuable as permanent reminders that the state exists for man, and not man for the state. Whereas a society without force and government is humanly unattainable, the ideal at least of a civilized community should be that of the lowest possible amount of force and compulsion in human relations.

The main difference between the theory of classical democracy and that of Marx-Engels is that the former envisaged a free, harmoniously ordered society as the result of peaceful, gradual growth, whereas Marx-Engels saw in revolution, civil war, and the dictatorship of the proletariat the preparatory stages of peace and harmony. Experience has shown since Marx-Engels that revolution and dictatorship are less likely to induce the state to wither away, or even decrease the use of force and violence, than the slower and more difficult methods of peaceful persuasion and consent. The failure to see the fatal relationship between means and ends is one of the most striking philosophical and practical weaknesses of Marxism, and the one that fundamentally separates it from liberal democracy.

There were two major countries in the nineteenth century in which the ideas of Marx and Engels became important ideological and political forces: Germany and Russia. Despite the facade of the legislative Reichstag, Germany was in fact a political autocracy that did not permit the development of genuine representative government. Philosophically, Marxism may be Hegelianism put upside down (as Marx claimed), but Hegel upside down is still Hegel, and the fixed determinism and closed system of Marxism appealed to much that was deeply rooted in the German philosophical tradition. Just as Hegel had asserted that the *state* was an *objective reality,* and its laws, like those of nature, beyond the whim and caprice of the individual, Marx now claimed that the *laws of society* followed an inexorable course, possessing the same *scientific validity* that Hegel had claimed for the laws of the state. By contrast, the liberal philosophical tradition of the West has always rejected the Hegel-Marx conception that human reason can only *understand* the laws of the state or society, and has affirmed the possibility of rational control and creative change of social and political institutions. The experience of free government forms the psychological foundation of the western conceptions of state and society, just as the experience of autocratic government in Germany provides the psychological background for the determinism of Hegel and Marx.

In actual practice, the original extremism of Marxism was gradually transformed into more evolutionary views in the German labor movement, because the Second Reich (1871–1918) provided some measure of legal political activity, supplemented by a considerable amount of paternalistic social-welfare legislation. In phraseology, however, German Marxism continued revolutionary and "scientific," disdainful of the "utopian," that is, ethical and peaceful outlook of western socialists. It is particularly striking that anarchism, the extreme ideal of individualism, never took root in the German labor movement, because Marxism expressed more satisfactorily the need for strong collective action and discipline. In one sense, the political theory of Marx was a form of inverted Prussianism: before the revolution, the Junkers and capitalists sit on top, and rule with an iron hand over the masses of the people. Come the revolution, the roles are reversed: The people control the state through customary authoritarian methods, and the erstwhile oppressors and exploiters are put in their place.

The other major country in which Marx's and Engels' ideas were widely accepted by radical thinkers and political action groups was czarist Russia. In Russia the conditions for the acceptance of Marx were even more favorable than in imperial Germany. Whereas Germany made the pretense of bowing to democracy and parliamentary government, czarism long recoiled from committing itself even to the formalities of liberalism and democracy, on the ground that pretenses, if practiced long enough, might too easily develop into reality. Of all major European states, czarist Russia was first in illiteracy, economic backwardness, religious obscurantism, oppression of minorities, political despotism, and social inequality. Marx's ideas, particularly the prospect of inevitable liberation of the working classes from bondage and oppression through revolutionary action, made a strong impression on Russian radicals, and Russian was the language into which *Das Kapital* was first translated. The Russian censorship permitted the publication of the work on the ground that it would not be read by many because of its difficult style and its scholarly method of argumentation.

The spread of Marxist ideas in Russia supplied a new focus of ideology for the disunited anticzarist opposition. It ranged from extreme terrorists, who saw in individual acts of assassination and destruction the road to Russia's liberation, to dedicated populists, who "went to the people," that is, lived and worked with the peasants, hoping that Russia would pass from serfdom to a free and modern peasant community without having to go through the painful process of capitalist industrialization and all its accompanying evils.

In the last quarter of the nineteenth century, industry in Russia made rapid headway, often with the aid of foreign engineers and financiers, and an urban proletariat began to fill the big factory towns. A sense of acute class consciousness developed in the new proletariat, which was without political protection, without hope of social equality, and which was working at a wage level below the bare necessities of life.

The class consciousness of the Russian proletariat was, however, not only a product of oppression and degradation. Because industry came so late to Russia, it skipped the stage of the small workshop and the small factory and adopted the latest methods of technology, which meant large enterprises from the outset. Though the absolute size of the industrial proletariat in Russia was much smaller than that in England, Germany, or the United States, the proportion of workers employed in enterprises of more than one thousand employees was considerably higher in Russia before World War I than even in the United States, not to speak of Germany, France, and England. In cities like Petersburg and Moscow, about half of all industrial workers were concentrated in large factories of more than one thousand employees, a fact that made it easy to awaken in the workers a sense of solidarity and the need for united action.

Because industry was so concentrated in Russia, it lacked a strong intermediary social class between capitalist and worker. In Western Europe and the United States, capitalism had largely grown out of already existing middle classes, and their liberal tradition reduced the inevitable tensions between capital and labor. Because such a middle class was largely lacking in Russia, the gulf between employer and employee was well-nigh unbridgeable. Marxism appealed to the rank and file of Russian labor as well as to its leaders, because it seemed an answer to the misery and degradation of the proletariat, inasmuch as the czarist autocracy provided no alternative for revolutionary change.

The man who made of Marxism a political reality in Russia was Vladimir Ilyich Ulyanov, or Lenin, as he later called himself (1870–1924). Lenin came from a middleclass family, both his father and mother having been teachers with progressive views. Their five surviving children became revolutionaries, and Lenin's eldest brother, Alexander, was hanged at the age of nineteen for complicity in an amateurish and abortive plot against Czar Alexander III. Lenin had a typical middle-class education, first attending the secondary school at Simbirsk, and then the law school of the University of Kazan. Because of his early political activities and the circumstances of his brother's execution, Lenin found himself under constant police supervision. However, the czarist police was not nearly so efficient as the later Soviet police, and Lenin managed to maintain political contacts and join illegal groups.

In December, 1895, Lenin was arrested in Petersburg and spent fourteen months in prison. From his prison cell he guided a revolutionary organization he had formed, and he also found the time and means to write letters and pamphlets that he managed to smuggle out of prison. He was able to obtain the books and magazines he needed, and he began in prison to work on *The Development of Capitalism in Russia*. Although in January, 1897, he was sentenced to three years' exile in Siberia, he continued his political and philosophical studies there, received illegal literature, and maintained contacts with illegal revolutionary groups. In 1898 Lenin married Nadezhda Krupskaya, a fellow revolutionary, in his Siberian exile, and their home became the headquarters for the political exiles in that territory. Lenin also found time for recreation, hunting, ice skating, hiking, and chess. His exile provided him with a new name, "Lenin," derived from the river Lena, which flowed through the region of Siberia where he was exiled.

After his release from Siberia in 1900, Lenin went abroad; he spent the next seventeen years with but few interruptions in various European countries, organizing from abroad the illegal revolutionary movement in Russia that was to culminate in the seizure of power in 1917. He returned to Russia after the first Revolution in the spring of 1917, and it was a liberal government that permitted him to return. In seven months he managed to overthrow the Kerensky government, the only free government Russia had known in its history to that time.

Lenin's most important contribution to the theory of Marxism is the doctrine of the *professional revolutionary,* as first developed in *What Is to Be Done?* (1902). Lenin drew a distinction between an organization of workers and an organization of revolutionaries. The former must be essentially trade-union in character, as large as possible, and as public as political conditions will allow. By contrast, the organization of revolutionaries must consist exclusively of professional revolutionaries, must be small, and "as secret as possible."

Whereas Marx had assumed that the working class would inevitably develop its class consciousness in the daily struggle for its economic existence, Lenin had much less confidence in the ability of the workers to develop politically by their own effort and experience: "Class political consciousness can be brought to the workers *only from without,* that is, only outside of the economic struggle, outside of the sphere of relations between workers and employers." Lenin did not care whether the professional revolutionaries destined to lead the proletariat were of working-class origin or not (he, like Marx and Engels, was middle class), as long as the professional revolutionary did his job well. But because of the difficulties of the work to be done, Lenin insisted that the professional revolutionary must be "no less professionally trained than the police," and, like the police, the organization of professional revolutionaries must be highly centralized and able to supervise and control the open organizations of workers that are legally permitted.

Lenin's views of the extreme concentration of power in the hands of a few leaders of professional revolutionaries led Trotsky in 1904 to assert that Lenin's doctrine of the dictatorship of the proletariat really meant the *dictatorship over the proletariat,* and the struggle of centralism versus democracy became one of the major issues of communist party organization before and after 1917. Trotsky also predicted in 1904 that if Lenin ever took power, "the leonine head of Marx would be the first to fall under the guillotine."

Lenin's most influential political work is *State and Revolution* (1918), written in the late summer of 1917; Lenin was hiding near the Finnish border part of the time, as the Kerensky government had issued an order for his arrest. *State and Revolution* consists of six chapters; as Lenin explains in a postscript (dated December 13, 1917), he planned to add a seventh chapter on the Russian revolutions of 1905 and 1917, but was "interrupted" by the November revolution of 1917, and, as he puts it: "It is more pleasant and useful to go through the 'experience of revolution' than to write about it."

In the literature of Marxism and communism, *State and Revolution* is of immense importance. Where Marx and Engels (in typically nineteenth-century liberal fashion) neglected the factor of *political power,* Lenin, the master strategist of one of the half-dozen great revolutions in history, was keenly interested in the anatomy of the state.

Lenin fully accepts the Marxian thesis that the transitional state between capitalism and communism "can be only the revolutionary dictatorship of the proletariat." He denies that capitalism and democracy are compatible, and affirms that under capitalism democracy always remains "a democracy for the minority, only for the possessing classes, only for the rich." Lenin then describes the techniques that the capitalist state employs in order to maintain itself in power. In the words of the *Communist Manifesto,* the "executive of the modern State is but a committee for managing the common affairs of the whole bourgeoisie."

Behind the formalities of *capitalist democracy,* Lenin sees, in effect, the *dictatorship of the bourgeoisie.* He also denies that the transition from capitalism to communism can be accomplished simply, smoothly, and directly, "as the liberal professors and petty-bourgeois opportunists would have us believe. No, development—toward communism— proceeds through the dictatorship of the proletariat; it cannot be otherwise, for the *resistance* of the capitalist exploiters cannot be *broken* by anyone else or in any other way." Whereas Marx had left open the possibility for peaceful social change from capitalism to socialism in politically advanced countries like England, the United States, and the Netherlands, Lenin claims that, by 1917, "this exception made by Marx is no longer valid," because England and the United States had developed bureaucratic institutions "to which everything is subordinated and which trample everything under foot." Far from admitting that both England and the United States had moved steadily in the direction of social reform since Marx, Lenin maintains that both countries had become more repressive, authoritarian, and plutocratic in the meantime. In 1884, Sir William Harcourt, a Liberal leader in the British Parliament, made the statement, "We are all socialists now," indicating the general acceptance of far-reaching social and economic reform by all parties. Yet, according to Lenin, Sir William should have said, "We are all bloodthirsty militaristic capitalists now."

In the transitional stage between capitalism and communism the state will continue to exist, Lenin holds, because machinery for the suppression of the capitalist exploiters will still be required in the dictatorship of the proletariat. But Lenin points out that in this phase the state is already beginning to "wither away," because the task of the majority (the victorious proletariat) in suppressing the minority (the defeated capitalists) is different, in quantitative and qualitative terms, from the previous capitalist state, in which a minority (of capitalists) suppressed the majority (of the exploited). Finally, once communism is fully established, the state becomes "absolutely unnecessary, for there is *no one* to be suppressed—'no one' in the sense of a *class,* in the sense of a systematic struggle against a definite section of the population." With the causes of exploitation of class by class removed, with the abolition of classes, the state will therefore inevitably "wither away." There will be true freedom for all, and "when freedom exists, there will be no state."

Lenin cautiously adds that he leaves the question of length of time, or of "the concrete withering away, quite open." Without indicating the time it will take to transform the "lower phase" of communist society (the dictatorship of the proletariat) into the "higher phase" (the withering away of the state), Lenin describes the conditions of such transformation: "The state will be able to wither away completely when society can apply the rule: 'From each according to his ability, to each according to his needs,' that is, when people have become so accustomed to observing the fundamental rules of social life and when their labor is so productive that they will voluntarily work *according to their ability.*" Lenin, like Marx, denies that the vision of a society without a machinery of force and power ("the state") is utopian. Yet Marxism shares with religion, pacifism, and anarchy the faith that man is so perfectible that one day he will no longer need the corrective force of government. In religion, the trouble is the Adam in man; in Marx and Lenin, the Adam is capitalism.

In comparing Lenin with Marx, one is struck by the differences of temperament, background, and outlook. Marx was above all the scholar and thinker, whereas Lenin was primarily the master organizer and practical politician and leader. Marx sought to change the whole world by his new ideas, whereas Lenin had one fixed, and more limited, goal: to seize power in his own country, Russia, and remake it according to the principles of communism. Yet the most important difference between the two men is not based on fundamental doctrine but on the fact that both reflected the inarticulate and implicit premises of their times. Marx was the product of the nineteenth century, and though he tried to envision, and help create, the society of the future, he always retained elements of the typically nineteenth-century world view. By contrast, Lenin, though born in the nineteenth century, developed to maturity and stature in the twentieth century, and his deepest attitudes were typical of the twentieth rather than of the nineteenth century.

Marx's belief in the *primacy of economics over politics* was not only the result of his economic interpretation of history, but also reflected a nineteenth-century prejudice. The dominant view in the nineteenth century was one of almost infinite faith in economic forces as the main engines of social and political progress. Thus, liberals in the nineteenth century confidently expected that the right economic policies would ensure domestic stability and progress, solve the problem of poverty, and lead to universal peace. Free trade within and between nations was the magic economic formula that would lead to a world without force and oppression. While Marx's economic formula was different from that of his liberal contemporaries, it was nevertheless an economic formula.

By contrast, Lenin believed, in typically twentieth-century fashion, in the *primacy of politics over economics,* although in explicit terms of pure doctrine he considered himself a faithful follower of Marx's economic interpretation of history. Because of his deep belief in the overriding importance of politics, Lenin spent most of his revolutionary energy in building up an organizational apparatus in czarist Russia. Although he spent seventeen years before the revolution abroad, mostly in Switzerland, he kept in close touch with the day-to-day activities of the Bolshevik group in Russia of which he was the undisputed leader.

Because Marx was so committed to nineteenth-century economic thinking, he thought that the communist revolution would first occur after capitalism had matured in the advanced countries of Western Europe. Marx took it for granted that the laws of economic development could not be interfered with, and that each country had to go through the various stages of capitalism before it was ripe for communist revolution. By contrast, Lenin looked at the problem of communist revolution from a more political viewpoint. The task of the communist leadership, Lenin thought, was to attack and destroy the existing social and political system where it was weakest—in the economically undeveloped areas of Europe, Asia, and Africa.

As a Russian, Lenin had a profound insight into the basic weakness of backward nations, their lack of strong social forces. In economically underdeveloped countries, the mass of the population consists of poor peasants, living in isolated villages, with inadequate means of communication. There are few or no independent labor unions and only a small urban middle class—the backbone of anticommunist resistance in developed countries. Where society lacks this kind of social cohesion, Lenin's concept of the professional revolutionary is crucial in the communist goal of seizure of power. In his country, Russia, Lenin noticed that a comparatively small force of army a could keep control over a vast—but unorganized—mass of people. Lenin therefore believed that with a relatively small, but highly disciplined and well organized counterforce power could be wrested from the apparatus of the existing system, and the success of his revolution in November of 1917 proved him to be right.

Closely related to Lenin's concept of the professional revolutionary and the primacy of politics over economics was his deep understanding of the importance of the underdeveloped areas in the balance of world power. Marx had the common European prejudice of the nineteenth century that Europe was the center of the world and that the underdeveloped areas were mere colonial appendages of the leading European imperial powers. As a Russian, with more than one foot therefore also in Asia, Lenin had none of this European conceit. He was the first important political figure who saw early in the twentieth century that the world was more than Europe, and that, above all, the underdeveloped (or "colonial") areas would increasingly become a decisive factor in world affairs. Since many people still do not fully realize the importance of the underdeveloped countries, it is remarkable that Lenin—with his genius for political analysis and political action—saw at such an early date that communism would first be established in Asia, Africa, and Latin America before the hard core of anticommunist resistance—Western Europe and North America—could be tackled. A master strategist, Lenin also hoped that, once the "soft underbelly" of world capitalism would be conquered by communism, the Western European and North American citadels of capitalism might not put up too much resistance, seeing the irresistible force of communism.

The different approaches of Marx and Lenin can also be seen in their views of the communist proletarian revolution. Marx expected that a communist revolution would lead to the *dictatorship of the proletariat,* an essentially economic entity, *over the bourgeoisie,* also a basically economic category. Marx even hoped that in such a temporary dictatorship of the proletariat there would be a variety of parties and groups, all united in the common goal of destroying the last remnants of capitalism but differing on lesser issues. By contrast, Lenin's concept of proletarian dictatorship meant, in more political terms, the *dictatorship of the Communist party over the proletariat,* since he had no faith that the proletariat had the political understanding or ability to secure the existence and expansion of a communist state.

Both Marx and Lenin believed in the inevitable triumph of communism throughout the world. Yet, here too, there are important differences. Marx believed that communism in each country would be preceded by internal economic crises, and that each country would develop its own revolutionary movements and forces when the condition would be "objectively ripe." By contrast, Lenin took a more activist, and worldwide, view. He saw, after the victory of communism in Russia, that it would become the base and nerve center from which communist revolutions in other countries could be instigated and engineered.

Whereas Marx believed in—and often enjoyed—vigorous polemics with communist, socialist, and anarchist groups with whom he disagreed, Lenin's strategy was different. He believed in infiltrating other political parties, labor unions, and local authorities. In 1917, for example, Lenin's Bolshevik followers infiltrated disrupted the Social Revolutionaries, Russia's largest political party, political democracy and socialist economic reform. The same technique was again used by communist parties during and after World War take over socialist parties through infiltration in a number of the communists did not fully succeed in that objective, they ten the local socialist party, as in Czechoslovakia before the communist takeover in 1948, so that there was little or no effective socialist resistance to communist seizure of power.

Finally, Marx and Lenin viewed international politics under different perspectives. In nineteenth-century fashion, Marx took comparatively little interest in international politics, since economic forces and tendencies were presumed to determine domestic as well as world politics. By contrast, Lenin saw every problem in its global perspective, both before he seized power in Russia and after he had become its ruler. Even while Russia was still reeling under the devastating impact of military defeat, revolution, and civil war, while millions of Russians were starving, Lenin devoted much of his thought and political activity to organizing centers of communist activity and infiltration throughout the world, particularly in Asia, Latin America, and Africa. Lenin agreed with Marx that, in the long run, the internal economic contradictions of capitalism would bring about its doom in every country. But unlike Marx, Lenin felt that communism, particularly after the establishment of the Soviet Union as the base of worldwide revolutionary activity, could shorten the long run by hastening the demise of noncommunist social and political systems through the strategies and tactics which he planned and put into practice.

The collapse of communism in the former Soviet Union, Eastern Europe, and elsewhere indicates the bankruptcy of Leninist—but also of Marxist—thought. History has not moved, and is not moving, in the direction foretold by Marx; outside of China and a few other states, no country today is willing to organize a society along Leninist principles. As has happened with other revolutionary systems over time, it is probable that what is of value particularly in Marx will be incorporated into strands of thought more capable simultaneously of containing divergent views. Lenin, on the other hand, is more likely to be consigned to "the dustbin of history."

I MARX

*Economic and Philosophical Manuscripts**

ALIENATED LABOUR

We have begun from the presuppositions of political economy. We have accepted its terminology and its laws. We presupposed private property; the separation of labour, capital and land, as also of wages, profit and rent; the division of labour; competition; the concept of exchange value, etc. From political economy itself, in its own words, we have shown that the worker sinks to the level of a commodity, and to a most miserable commodity; that the misery of the worker increases with the power and volume of his production; that the necessary result of competition is the accumulation of capital in a few hands, and thus a restoration of monopoly in a more terrible form; and finally that the distinction between capitalist and landlord, and between agricultural labourer and industrial worker, must disappear, and the whole of society divide into the two classes of property *owners* and *propertyless* workers.

Political economy begins with the fact of private property; it does not explain it. It conceives the *material* process of private property, as this occurs in reality, in general and abstract formulas which serve it as laws. It does not *comprehend* these laws; that is, it does not show how they arise out of the nature of private property. Political economy provides no explanation of the basis for the distinction of labour from capital, of capital from land. When, for example, the relation of wages to profits is defined, this is explained in terms of the

interests of capitalists; in other words, what should be explained is assumed. Similarly, competition is referred to at every point and is explained in terms of external conditions. Political economy tells us nothing about the extent to which these external and apparently accidental conditions are simply the expression of a necessary development. We have seen how exchange itself seems an accidental fact. The only motive forces which political economy recognizes are *avarice* and the *war between the avaricious, competition.*

Just because political economy fails to understand the interconnexions within this movement it was possible to oppose the doctrine of competition to that of monopoly, the doctrine of freedom of the crafts to that of the guilds, the doctrine of the division of landed property to that of the great estates; for competition, freedom of crafts, and the division of landed property were conceived only as accidental consequences brought about by will and force, rather than as necessary, inevitable and natural consequences of monopoly, the guild system and feudal property.

Thus we have now to grasp the real connexion between this whole system of alienation—private property, acquisitiveness, the separation of labour, capital and land, exchange and competition, value and the devaluation of man, monopoly and competition—and the system of *money*.

Let us not begin our explanation, as does the economist, from a legendary primordial condition. Such a primordial condition does not explain anything; it merely removes the question into a grey and nebulous distance. It asserts as a fact or event what it should deduce, namely, the necessary relation

*From *Karl Marx: Early Writings* (translated and edited by T. B. Bottomore. © T. B. Bottomore, 1963). By permission of McGraw-Hill Book Company and C. A. Watts & Co., Ltd.

between two things; for example, between the division of labour and exchange. In the same way theology explains the origin of evil by the fall of man; that is, it asserts as a historical fact what it should explain.

We shall begin from a *contemporary* economic fact. The worker becomes poorer the more wealth he produces and the more his production increases in power and extent. The worker becomes an ever cheaper commodity the more goods he creates. The *devaluation* of the human world increases in direct relation with the *increase in value* of the world of things. Labour does not only create goods; it also produces itself and the worker as a *commodity,* and indeed in the same proportion as it produces goods.

This fact simply implies that the object produced by labour, its product, now stands opposed to it as an *alien* being, as a *power independent* of the producer. The product of labour is labour which has been embodied in an object and turned into a physical thing; this product is an *objectification* of labour. The performance of work is at the same time its objectification. The performance of work appears in the sphere of political economy as a vitiation of the worker, objectification as a *loss* and as *servitude to the object,* and appropriation as *alienation.*

So much does the performance of work appear as vitiation that the worker is vitiated to the point of starvation. So much does objectification appear as loss of the object that the worker is deprived of the most essential things not only of life but also of work. Labour itself becomes an object which he can acquire only by the greatest effort and with unpredictable interruptions. So much does the appropriation of the object appear as alienation that the more objects the worker produces the fewer he can possess and the more he falls under the domination of his product, of capital.

All these consequences follow from the fact that the worker is related to the *product of his labour* as to an *alien* object. For it is clear on this presupposition that the more the worker expends himself in work the more powerful becomes the world of objects which he creates in face of himself, the poorer he becomes in his inner life, and the less he belongs to himself. It is just the same as in religion. The more of himself man attributes to God the less he has left in himself. The

worker puts his life into the object, and his life then belongs no longer to himself but to the object. The greater his activity, therefore, the less he possesses. What is embodied in the product of his labour is no longer his own. The greater this product is, therefore, the more he is diminished. The *alienation* of the worker in his product means not only that his labour becomes an object, assumes an *external existence,* but that it exists independently, *outside himself,* and alien to him, and that it stands opposed to him as an autonomous power. The life which he has given to the object sets itself against him as an alien and hostile force.

Let us now examine more closely the phenomenon of *objectification;* the worker's production and the *alienation* and *loss* of the object it produces, which is involved in it. The worker can create nothing without *nature,* without the *sensuous external world.* The latter is the material in which his labour is realized, in which it is active, out of which and through which it produces things.

But just as nature affords the *means of existence* of labour, in the sense that labour cannot *live* without objects upon which it can be exercised, so also it provides the *means of existence* in a narrower sense; namely the means of physical existence for the *worker* himself. Thus, the more the worker *appropriates* the external world of sensuous nature by his labour the more he deprives himself of *means of existence,* in two respects: first, that the sensuous external world becomes progressively less an object belonging to his labour or a means of existence of his labour, and secondly, that it becomes progressively less a means of existence in the direct sense, a means for the physical subsistence of the worker.

In both respects, therefore, the worker becomes a slave of the object; first, in that he receives an *object of work,* i.e. receives *work,* and secondly, in that he receives *means of subsistence.* Thus the object enables him to exist, first as a *worker* and secondly, as a *physical subject.* The culmination of this enslavement is that he can only maintain himself as a *physical subject* so far as he is a *worker,* and that it is only as a *physical subject* that he is a worker.

(The alienation of the worker in his object is expressed as follows in the laws of political economy: the more the worker produces the less he has to consume; the more value he creates the more worthless he becomes; the more refined his product the more crude and misshapen the worker; the more civilized the product the more barbarous the worker; the more powerful the work the more feeble the worker; the more the work manifests intelligence the more the worker declines in intelligence and becomes a slave of nature.

Political economy conceals the alienation in the nature of labour in so far as it does not examine the direct relationship between the worker (work) and production. Labour certainly produces marvels for the rich but it produces privation for the worker. It produces palaces, but hovels for the worker. It produces beauty, but deformity for the worker. It replaces labour by machinery, but it casts some of the workers back into a barbarous kind of work and turns the others into machines. It produces intelligence, but also stupidity and cretinism for the workers.

The direct relationship of labour to its products is the relationship of the worker to the objects of his production. The relationship of property owners to the objects of production and to production itself is merely a *consequence* of this first relationship and confirms it. We shall consider this second aspect later.

Thus, when we ask what is the important relationship of labour, we are concerned with the relationship of the *worker* to production.

So far we have considered the alienation of the worker only from one aspect; namely, *his relationship with the products of his labour.* However, alienation appears not merely in the result but also in the *process* of *production,* within *productive activity* itself. How could the worker stand in an alien relationship to the product of his activity if he did not alienate himself in the act of production itself? The product is indeed only the *résumé* of activity, of production. Consequently, if the product of labour is alienation, production itself must be active alienation—the alienation of activity and the activity of alienation. The alienation of the object of labour merely summarizes the alienation in the work activity itself.

What constitutes the alienation of labour? First, that the work is *external* to the worker,

that it is not part of his nature; and that, consequently, he does not fulfil himself in his work but denies himself, has a feeling of misery rather than well-being, does not develop freely his mental and physical energies but is physically exhausted and mentally debased. The worker, therefore, feels himself at home only during his leisure time, whereas at work he feels homeless. His work is not voluntary but imposed, *forced labour.* It is not the satisfaction of a need, but only a *means* for satisfying other needs. Its alien character is clearly shown by the fact that as soon as there is no physical or other compulsion it is avoided like the plague. External labour, labour in which man alienates himself, is a labour of self-sacrifice, of mortification. Finally, the external character of work for the worker is shown by the fact that it is not his own work but work for someone else, that in work he does not belong to himself but to another person.

Just as in religion the spontaneous activity of human fantasy, of the human brain and heart, reacts independently as an alien activity of gods or devils upon the individual, so the activity of the worker is not his own spontaneous activity. It is another's activity and a loss of his own spontaneity.

We arrive at the result that man (the worker) feels himself to be freely active only in his animal functions—eating, drinking and procreating, or at most also in his dwelling and in personal adornment—while in his human functions he is reduced to an animal. The animal becomes human and the human becomes animal.

Eating, drinking and procreating are of course also genuine human functions. But abstractly considered, apart from the environment of human activities, and turned into final and sole ends, they are animal functions.

We have now considered the act of alienation of practical human activity, labour, from two aspects: (1) the relationship of the worker to the *product of labour* as an alien object which dominates him. This relationship is at the same time the relationship to the sensuous external world, to natural objects, as an alien and hostile world; (2) the relationship of labour to the *act of production* within *labour.* This is the relationship of the worker to his own activity as something alien and not belonging to him, activity as suffering (passivity), strength as power-lessness, creation as emasculation, the *personal* physical and mental energy of the worker, his personal life (for what is life but activity?), as an activity which is directed against himself, independent of him and not belonging to him. This is *self-alienation* as against the above-mentioned alienation of the *thing*.

We have now to infer a third characteristic of *alienated labour* from the two we have considered.

Man is a species-being not only in the sense that he makes the community (his own as well as those of other things) his object both practically and theoretically, but also (and this is simply another expression for the same thing) in the sense that he treats himself as the present, living species, as a *universal* and consequently free being.

Species-life, for man as for animals, has its physical basis in the fact that man (like animals) lives from inorganic nature, and since man is more universal than an animal so the range of inorganic nature from which he fives is more universal. Plants, animals, minerals, air, light, etc. constitute, from the theoretical aspect, a part of human consciousness as objects of natural science and art; they are man's spiritual inorganic nature, his intellectual means of life, which he must first prepare for enjoyment and perpetuation. So also, from the practical aspect, they form a part of human life and activity. In practice man lives only from these natural products, whether in the form of food, heating, clothing, housing, etc. The universality of man appears in practice in the universality which makes the whole of nature into his inorganic body: (1) as a direct means of life; and equally (2) as the material object and instrument of his life activity. Nature is the inorganic body of man; that is to say nature, excluding the human body itself. To say that man *lives* from nature means that nature is his *body* with which he must remain in a continuous interchange in order not to die. The statement that the physical and mental life of man, the nature, are interdependent means simply that nature is interdependent with itself, for man is a part of nature.

Since alienated labour: (1) alienates nature from man; and (2) alienates man from himself, from his own active function, his life activity; so it alienates him from the species. It makes *species-life* into a means of individual life. In the first place it alienates species-life and individual life, and secondly, it turns the latter, as an abstraction, into the purpose of the former, also in its abstract and alienated form.

For labour, *life activity, productive life,* now appear to man only as *means* for the satisfaction of a need, the need to maintain his physical existence. Productive life is, however, species-life. It is life creating life. In this type of life activity resides the whole character of a species, its species-character; and free, conscious activity is the species-character of human beings. Life itself appears only as a *means of life.*

The animal is one with its life activity. It does not distinguish the activity from itself. It is *its activity*. But man makes his life activity itself an object of his will and consciousness. He has a conscious life activity. It is not a determination with which he is completely identified. Conscious life activity distinguishes man from the life activity of animals. Only for this reason is he a species-being. Or rather, he is only a self-conscious being, i.e. his own life is an object for him, because he is a species-being. Only for this reason is his activity free activity. Alienated labour reverses the relationship, in that man because he is a self-conscious being makes his life activity, his *being,* only a means for his *existence.*

The practical construction of an *objective world,* the *manipulation* of inorganic nature, is the confirmation of man as a conscious species-being, i.e. a being who treats the species as his own being or himself as a species-being. Of course, animals also produce. They construct nests, dwellings, as in the case of bees, beavers, ants, etc. But they only produce what is strictly necessary for themselves or their young. They produce only in a single direction, while man produces universally. They produce only under the compulsion of direct physical needs, while man produces when he is free from physical need and only truly produces in freedom from such need. Animals produce only themselves, while man reproduces the whole of nature. The products of animal production belong directly to their physical bodies, while man is free in face of his product. Animals construct only in accordance with the standards and needs of the species to which they belong, while man knows how to produce in accordance with the standards of every species and knows how to apply the appropriate standard to the object. Thus man constructs also in accordance with the laws of beauty.

It is just in his work upon the objective world that man really proves himself as a *species-being*. This production is his active species-life. By means of it nature appears as *his* work and his reality. The object of labour is, therefore, the *objectification of man's species-life;* for he no longer reproduces himself merely intellectually, as in consciousness, but actively and in a real sense, and he sees his own reflection in a world which he has constructed. While, therefore, alienated labour takes away the object of production from man, it also takes away his *species-life,* his real objectivity as a species-being, and changes his advantage over animals into a disadvantage in so far as his inorganic body, nature, is taken from him.

Just as alienated labour transforms free and self-directed activity into a means, so it transforms the species-life of man into a means of physical existence.

Consciousness, which man has from his species, is transformed through alienation so that species-life becomes only a means for him. (3) Thus alienated labour turns the *species-life of man,* and also nature as his mental species-property, into an *alien* being and into a *means* for his *individual existence.* It alienates from man his own body, external nature, his mental life and his *human* life. (4) A direct consequence of the alienation of man from the product of his labour, from his life activity and from his species-life, is that *man is alienated* from other *men.* When man confronts himself he also confronts *other* men. What is true of man's relationship to his work, to the product of his work and to himself, is also true of his relationship to other men, to their labour and to the objects of their labour.

In general, the statement that man is alienated from his species-life means that each man is alienated from others, and that each of the others is likewise alienated from human life.

Human alienation, and above all the relation of man to himself, is first realized and expressed in the relationship between each man and other men. Thus in the relationship of alienated labour every man regards other men according to the standards and relationships in which he finds himself placed as a worker.

We began with an economic fact, the alienation of the worker and his production. We have expressed this fact in conceptual terms as *alienated labour,* and in analysing the concept we have merely analysed an economic fact.

Let us now examine further how this concept of alienated labour must express and reveal itself in reality. If the product of labour is alien to me and confronts me as an alien power, to whom does it belong? If my own activity does not belong to me but is an alien, forced activity, to whom does it belong? To a being *other* than myself. And who is this being? The *gods?* It is apparent in the earliest stages of advanced production, e.g. temple building, etc. in Egypt, India, Mexico, and in the service rendered to gods, that the product belonged to the gods. But the gods alone were never the lords of labour. And no more was *nature.* What a contradiction it would be if the more man subjugates nature by his labour, and the more the marvels of the gods are rendered superfluous by the marvels of industry, the more he should abstain from his joy in producing and his enjoyment of the product for love of these powers.

The *alien* being to whom labour and the product of labour belong, to whose service labour is devoted, and to whose enjoyment the product of labour goes, can only be *man* himself. If the product of labour does not belong to the worker, but confronts him as an alien power, this can only be because it belongs to *a man other than the worker.* If his activity is a torment to him it must be a source of *enjoyment* and pleasure to another. Not the gods, nor nature, but only man himself can be this alien power over men.

Consider the earlier statement that the relation of man to himself is first *realized, objectified,* through his relation to other men. If he is related to the product of his labour, his objectified labour, as to an *alien,* hostile, powerful and independent object, he is related in such a way that another alien, hostile, powerful and independent man is the lord of this object. If he is related to his own activity as to unfree activity, then he is related to it as activity in the service, and under the domination, coercion and yoke, of another man.

Every self-alienation of man, from himself and from nature, appears in the relation which he postulates between other men and himself and nature. Thus religious self-alienation is necessarily exemplified in the relation between laity and priest, or, since it is here a question of the spiritual world, between the laity and a mediator. In the real world of practice this self-alienation can only be expressed in the real, practical relation of man to his fellow men. The medium through which alienation occurs is itself a *practical* one. Through alienated labour, therefore, man not only produces his relation to the object and to the process of production as to alien and hostile men; he also produces the relation of other men to his production and his product, and the relation between himself and other men. Just as he creates his own production as a vitiation, a punishment, and his own product as a loss, as a product which does not belong to him, so he creates the domination of the non-producer over production and its product. As he alienates his own activity, so he bestows upon the stranger an activity which is not his own.

We have so far considered this relation only from the side of the worker, and later on we shall consider it also from the side of the non-worker.

Thus, through alienated labour the worker creates the relation of another man, who does not work and is outside the work process, to this labour. The relation of the worker to work also produces the relation of the capitalist (or whatever one likes to call the lord of labour) to work. *Private property* is, therefore, the product, the necessary result, of *alienated labour,* of the external relation of the worker to nature and to himself.

Private property is thus derived from the analysis of the concept of *alienated labour;* that is, alienated man, alienated labour, alienated life, and estranged man.

We have, of course, derived the concept of *alienated labour (alienated life)* from political economy, from an analysis of the *movement of private property.* But the analysis of this concept shows that

although private property appears to be the basis and cause of alienated labour, it is rather a consequence of the latter, just as the gods are *fundamentally* not the cause but the product of confusions of human reason. At a later stage, however, there is a reciprocal influence.

Only in the final stage of the development of private property is its secret revealed, namely, that it is on one hand the *product* of alienated labour, and on the other hand the *means* by which labour is alienated, *the realization of this alienation.*

This elucidation throws light upon several unresolved controversies—

1. Political economy begins with labour as the real soul of production and then goes on to attribute nothing to labour and everything to private property. Proudhon, faced by this contradiction, has decided in favour of labour against private property. We perceive, however, that this apparent contradiction is the contradiction of *alienated labour* with itself and that political economy has merely formulated the laws of alienated labour.

We also observe, therefore, that *wages* and *private property* are identical, for wages, like the product or object of labour, labour itself remunerated, are only a necessary consequence of the alienation of labour. In the wage system labour appears not as an end in itself but as the servant of wages. We shall develop this point later on and here only bring out some of the consequences.

An enforced *increase in wages* (disregarding the other difficulties, and especially that such an anomaly could only be maintained by force) would be nothing more than a *better remuneration of slaves,* and would not restore, either to the worker or to the work, their human significance and worth.

Even the *equality of incomes* which Proudhon demands would only change the relation of the present-day worker to his work into a relation of all men to work. Society would then be conceived as an abstract capitalist.

2. From the relation of alienated labour to private property it also follows that the emancipation of society from private property, from servitude, takes the political form of the *emancipation of the workers;* not in the sense that only the latter's emancipation is

involved, but because this emancipation includes the emancipation of humanity as a whole. For all human servitude is involved in the relation of the worker to production, and all the types of servitude are only modifications or consequences of this relation.

As we have discovered the concept of *private property* by an *analysis* of the concept of *alienated labour,* so with the aid of these two factors we can evolve all the *categories* of political economy, and in every category, e.g. trade, competition, capital, money, we shall discover only a particular and developed expression of these fundamental elements.

However, before considering this structure let us attempt to solve two problems.

1. To determine the general nature of *private property* as it has resulted from alienated labour, in its relation to *genuine human and social property.*

2. We have taken as a fact and analysed the *alienation of labour.* How does it happen, we may ask, that *man alienates his labour?* How is this alienation founded in the nature of human development? We have already done much to solve the problem in so far as we have *transformed* the question concerning the *origin of private property* into a question about the relation between *alienated labour* and the process of development of mankind. For in speaking of private property one believes oneself to be dealing with something external to mankind. But in speaking of labour one deals directly with mankind itself. This new formulation of the problem already contains its solution.

ad (1) *The general nature of private property and its relation to genuine human property.*

We have resolved alienated labour into two parts, which mutually determine each other, or rather, which constitute two different expressions of one and the same relation. *Appropriation* appears as *alienation* and *alienation* as *appropriation,* alienation as genuine acceptance in the community.

We have considered one aspect, *alienated* labour, in its bearing upon the *worker* himself, i.e. *the relation of alienated labour to itself.* And we have found as the necessary consequence of this relation the *property relation* of the *non-worker* to the *worker* and to labour. *Private property* as the material, summarized expression of alienated labour includes both relations; *the relation of the worker to labour, to the product of his labour and to the non-worker,* and the relation of the *non-worker to the worker and to the product of the latter's labour.*

We have already seen that in relation to the worker, who *appropriates* nature by his labour, appropriation appears as alienation, self-activity as activity for another and of another, living as the sacrifice of life, and production of the object as loss of the object to an alien power, an alien man. Let us now consider the relation of this *alien* man to the worker, to labour, and to the object of labour.

It should be noted first that everything which appears to the worker as an *activity of alienation,* appears to the non-worker as a *condition of alienation.* Secondly, the *real, practical* attitude (as a state of mind) of the worker in production and to the product appears to the non-worker who confronts him as a *theoretical* attitude.

Thirdly, the non-worker does everything against the worker which the latter does against himself, but he does not do against himself what he does against the worker.

II MARX AND ENGELS

*The Communist Manifesto**

A spectre is haunting Europe—the spectre of Communism. All the powers of old Europe have entered into a holy alliance to exorcise this spectre: Pope and Czar, Metternich and Guizot, French Radicals and German police-spies.

Where is the party in opposition that has not been decried as communistic by its opponents in power? Where the Opposition that has not hurled back the branding reproach of Communism, against the more advanced opposition parties, as well as against its reactionary adversaries?

Two things result from this fact:

I. Communism is already acknowledged by all European powers to be itself a power.

II. It is high time that Communists should openly, in the face of the whole world, publish their views, their aims, their tendencies, and meet this nursery tale of the spectre of Communism with a manifesto of the party itself.

To this end, Communists of various nationalities have assembled in London, and sketched the following manifesto, to be published in the English, French, German, Italian, Flemish and Danish languages.

BOURGEOIS AND PROLETARIANS

The history of all hitherto existing society is the history of class struggles.

Freeman and slave, patrician and plebeian, lord and serf, guild-master and journeyman, in a word, oppressor and oppressed, stood in constant opposition to one another, carried on an uninterrupted, now hidden,

now open fight, a fight that each time ended, either in a revolutionary reconstitution of society at large, or in the common ruin of the contending classes.

In the earlier epochs of history, we find almost everywhere a complicated arrangement of society into various orders, a manifold gradation of social rank. In ancient Rome we have patricians, knights, plebeians, slaves; in the Middle Ages, feudal lords, vassals, guildmasters, journeymen, apprentices, serfs; in almost all of these classes, again, subordinate gradations.

The modern bourgeois society that has sprouted from the ruins of feudal society, has not done away with class antagonisms. It has but established new classes, new conditions of oppression, new forms of struggle in place of the old ones.

Our epoch, the epoch of the bourgeoisie, possesses, however, this distinctive feature: It has simplified the class antagonisms. Society as a whole is more and more splitting up into two great hostile camps, into two great classes directly facing each other—bourgeoisie and proletariat.

From the serfs of the Middle Ages sprang the chartered burghers of the earliest towns. From these burgesses the first elements of the bourgeoisie were developed.

The discovery of America, the rounding of the Cape, opened up fresh ground for the rising bourgeoisie. The East-Indian and Chinese markets, the colonisation of America, trade with the colonies, the increase in the means of exchange and in commodities generally, gave to commerce, to navigation, to industry, an impulse never before known, and thereby, to the revolutionary element in the tottering feudal society at rapid development.

---

*(1848; English trans. of 1888, ed. Friedrich Engels.)

The feudal system of industry, in which industrial production was monopolised by closed guilds, now no longer sufficed for the growing wants of the new markets. The manufacturing system took its place. The guild-masters were pushed aside by the manufacturing middle class; division of labour between the different corporate guilds vanished in the face of division of labour in each single workshop.

Meantime the markets kept ever growing, the demand ever rising. Even manufacture no longer sufficed. Thereupon, steam and machinery revolutionised industrial production. The place of manufacture was taken by the giant, modern industry, the place of the industrial middle class, by industrial millionaires—the leaders of whole industrial armies, the modern bourgeoisie.

Modern industry has established the world market, for which the discovery of America paved the way. This market has given an immense development to commerce, to navigation, to communication by land. This development has, in its turn, reacted on the extension of industry; and in proportion as industry, commerce, navigation, railways extended, in the same proportion the bourgeoisie developed, increased its capital, and pushed into the background every class handed down from the Middle Ages.

We see, therefore, how the modern bourgeoisie is itself the product of a long course of development, of a series of revolutions in the modes of production and of exchange.

Each step in the development of the bourgeoisie was accompanied by a corresponding political advance of that class. An oppressed class under the sway of the feudal nobility, it became an armed and self-governing association in the mediæval commune; here independent urban republic (as in Italy and Germany), there taxable "third estate" of the monarchy (as in France); afterwards, in the period of manufacture proper, serving either the semi-feudal or the absolute monarchy as a counterpoise against the nobility, and, in fact, cornerstone of the great monarchies in general—the bourgeoisie has at last, since the establishment of modern industry and of the world market, conquered for itself, in the modern representative state, exclusive political sway. The executive of the modern state is but a committee for managing the common affairs of the whole bourgeoisie.

The bourgeoisie has played a most revolutionary rôle in history.

The bourgeoisie, wherever it has got the upper hand, has put an end to all feudal, patriarchal, idyllic relations. It has pitilessly torn asunder the motley feudal ties that bound man to his "natural superiors," and has left no other bond between man and man than naked self-interest, than callous "cash payment." It has drowned the most heavenly ecstasies of religious fervour, of chivalrous enthusiasm, of philistine sentimentalism, in the icy water of egotistical calculation. It has resolved personal worth into exchange value, and in place of the numberless indefeasible chartered freedoms, has set up that single, unconscionable freedom—Free Trade. In one word, for exploitation, veiled by religious and political illusions, it has substituted naked, shameless, direct, brutal exploitation.

The bourgeoisie has stripped of its halo every occupation hitherto honoured and looked up to with reverent awe. It has converted the physician, the lawyer, the priest, the poet, the man of science, into its paid wage-labourers.

The bourgeoisie has torn away from the family its sentimental veil, and has reduced the family relation to a mere money relation.

The bourgeoisie has disclosed how it came to pass that the brutal display of vigour in the Middle Ages, which reactionaries so much admire, found its fitting complement in the most slothful indolence. It has been the first to show what man's activity can bring about. It has accomplished wonders far surpassing Egyptian pyramids, Roman aqueducts, and Gothic cathedrals; it has conducted expeditions that put in the shade all former migrations of nations and crusades.

The bourgeoisie cannot exist without constantly revolutionising the instruments of production, and thereby the relations of production, and with them the whole relations of society. Conservation of the old modes of production in unaltered form, was, on the contrary, the first condition of existence for all earlier industrial classes. Constant revolutionising of production, uninterrupted disturbance of all social conditions, everlasting uncertainty and agitation distinguish the bourgeois epoch from all earlier ones. All fixed, fast-frozen relations, with their train of ancient and venerable prejudices and opinions, are swept away, all new-formed ones become antiquated before they can ossify. All that is solid melts into air, all that is holy is profaned, and man is at last compelled to face with sober senses his real conditions of life and his relations with his kind.

The need of a constantly expanding market for its products chases the bourgeoisie over the whole surface of the globe. It must nestle everywhere, settle everywhere, establish connections everywhere.

The bourgeoisie has through its exploitation of the world market given a cosmopolitan character to production and consumption in every country. To the great chagrin of reactionaries, it has drawn from under the feet of industry the national ground on which it stood. All old-established national industries have been destroyed or are daily being destroyed. They are dislodged by new industries, whose introduction becomes a life and death question for all civilised nations, by industries that no longer work up indigenous raw material, but raw material drawn from the remotest zones; industries whose products are consumed, not only at home, but in every quarter of the globe. In place of the old wants, satisfied by the production of the country, we find new wants, requiring for their satisfaction the products of distant lands and climes. In place of the old local and national seclusion and self-sufficiency, we have intercourse in every direction, universal inter-dependence of nations. And as in material, so also in intellectual production. The intellectual creations of individual nations become common property. National one-sidedness and narrow-mindedness become more and more impossible, and from the numerous national and local literatures there arises a world literature.

The bourgeoisie, by the rapid improvement of all instruments of production, by the immensely facilitated means of communication, draws all nations, even the most barbarian, into civilisation. The cheap prices of its commodities are the heavy artillery with which it batters down all Chinese walls, with which it forces the barbarians' intensely obstinate hatred of foreigners to capitulate. It compels all nations, on pain of extinction, to adopt the bourgeois mode of production; it compels them to introduce what it calls civilisation into their midst, *i.e.,* to become bourgeois themselves. In a word, it creates a world after its own image.

The bourgeoisie has subjected the country to the rule of the towns. It has created enormous cities, has greatly increased the urban population as compared with the rural, and has thus rescued a considerable part of the population from the idiocy of rural life. Just as it has made the country dependent on the towns, so it has made barbarian and semi-barbarian countries dependent on the civilised ones, nations of peasants on nations of bourgeois, the East on the West.

The bourgeoisie keeps more and more doing away with the scattered state of the population, of the means of production, and of property. It has agglomerated population, centralised means of production, and has concentrated property in a few hands. The necessary consequence of this was political centralisation. Independent, or but loosely connected provinces, with separate interests, laws, governments and systems of taxation, became lumped together into one nation, with one government, one code of laws, one national class interest, one frontier and one customs tariff.

The bourgeoisie, during its rule of scarce one hundred years, has created more massive and more colossal productive forces than have all preceding generations together. Subjection of nature's forces to man, machinery, application of chemistry to industry and agriculture, steam-navigation, railways, electric telegraphs, clearing of whole continents for cultivation, canalisation of rivers, whole populations conjured out of the ground—what earlier century had even a presentiment that such productive forces slumbered in the lap of social labour?

We see then that the means of production and of exchange, which served as the foundation for the growth of the bourgeoisie, were generated in feudal society. At a certain stage in the development of these means of production and of exchange, the conditions under which feudal society produced and exchanged, the feudal organisation of agriculture and manufacturing industry, in a word, the feudal relations of property became no longer compatible with the already developed productive forces; they became so many fetters. They had to be burst asunder; they were burst asunder.

Into their place stepped free competition, accompanied by a social and political constitution adapted to it, and by the economic and political sway of the bourgeois class.

A similar movement is going on before our own eyes. Modern bourgeois society with its relations of production, of exchange and of property, a society that has conjured up such gigantic means of production and of exchange, is like the sorcerer who is no longer able to control the powers of the nether world whom he has called up by his spells. For many a decade past the history of industry and commerce is but the history of the revolt of modern productive forces against modern conditions of production, against the property relations that are the conditions for the existence of the bourgeoisie and of its rule. It is enough to mention the commercial crises that by their periodical return put the existence of the entire bourgeois society on trial, each time more threateningly. In these crises a great part not only of the existing products, but also of the previously created productive forces, are periodically destroyed. In these crises there breaks out an epidemic that, in all earlier epochs, would have seemed an absurdity—the epidemic of over-production. Society suddenly finds itself put back into a state of momentary barbarism; it appears as if a famine, a universal war of devastation had cut off the supply of every means of subsistence; industry and commerce seem to be destroyed. And why? Because there is too much civilization, too much means of subsistence, too much industry, too much commerce. The productive forces at the disposal of society no longer tend to further the development of the conditions of bourgeois property; on the contrary, they have become too powerful for these conditions, by which they are fettered, and no sooner do they overcome these fetters than they bring disorder into the whole of bourgeois society, endanger the existence of bourgeois property. The conditions of bourgeois society are too narrow to comprise the wealth created by them. And how does the bourgeoisie get over these crises? On the one hand by enforced destruction of

a mass of productive forces; on the other, by the conquest of new markets, and by the more thorough exploitation of the old ones. That is to say, by paving the way for more extensive and more destructive crises, and by diminishing the means whereby crises are prevented.

The weapons with which the bourgeoisie felled feudalism to the ground are now turned against the bourgeoisie itself.

But not only has the bourgeoisie forged the weapons that bring death to itself; it has also called into existence the men who are to wield those weapons—the modern working class—the proletarians.

In proportion as the bourgeoisie, *i.e.,* capital, is developed, in the same proportion is the proletariat, the modern working class, developed—a class of labourers, who live only so long as they find work, and who find work only so long as their labour increases capital. These labourers, who must sell themselves piecemeal, are a commodity, like every other article of commerce, and are consequently exposed to all the vicissitudes of competition, to all the fluctuations of the market.

Owing to the extensive use of machinery and to division of labour, the work of the proletarians has lost all individual character, and, consequently, all charm for the workman. He becomes an appendage of the machine, and it is only the most simple, most monotonous, and most easily acquired knack, that is required of him. Hence, the cost of production of a workman is restricted, almost entirely, to the means of subsistence that he requires for his maintenance, and for the propagation of his race. But the price of a commodity, and therefore also of labour, is equal to its cost of production. In proportion, therefore, as the repulsiveness of the work increases, the wage decreases. Nay more, in proportion as the use of machinery and division of labour increases, in the same proportion the burden of toil also increases, whether by prolongation of the working hours, by increase of the work exacted in a given time, or by increased speed of the machinery, etc.

Modern industry has converted the little workshop of the patriarchal master into the great factory of the industrial capitalist. Masses of labourers, crowded into the factory, are organised like soldiers. As privates of the industrial army they are placed under the command of a perfect hierarchy of officers and sergeants. Not only are they slaves of the bourgeois class, and of the bourgeois state; they are daily and hourly enslaved by the machine, by the overseer, and, above all, by the individual bourgeois manufacturer himself. The more openly this despotism proclaims gain to be its end and aim, the more petty, the more hateful and the more embittering it is.

The less the skill and exertion of strength implied in manual labour, in other words, the more modern industry develops, the more is the labour of men superseded by that of women. Differences of age and sex have no longer any distinctive social validity for the working class. All are instruments of labour, more or less expensive to use, according to their age and sex.

No sooner has the labourer received his wages in cash, for the moment escaping exploitation by the manufacturer, than he is set upon by the other portions of the bourgeoisie, the landlord, the shopkeeper, the pawnbroker, etc.

The lower strata of the middle class—the small tradespeople, shopkeepers, and retired tradesman generally, the handicraftsmen and peasants—all these sink gradually into the proletariat, partly because their diminutive capital does not suffice for the scale on which modern industry is carried on, and is swamped in the competition with the large capitalists, partly because their specialised skill is rendered worthless by new methods of production. Thus the proletariat is recruited from all classes of the population.

The proletariat goes through various stages of development. With its birth begins its struggle with the bourgeoisie. At first the contest is carried on by individual labourers, then by the work people of a factory, then by the operatives of one trade, in one locality, against the individual bourgeois who directly exploits them. They direct their attacks not against the bourgeois conditions of production, but against the instruments of production themselves; they destroy imported wares that compete with their labour, they smash machinery to pieces, they set factories ablaze, they seek to restore by force the vanished status of the workman of the Middle Ages.

At this stage the labourers still form an incoherent mass scattered over the whole country, and broken up by their mutual competition. If anywhere they unite to form more compact bodies, this is not yet the consequence of their own active union, but of the union of the bourgeoisie, which class, in order to attain its own political ends, is compelled to set the whole proletariat in motion, and is moreover still able to do so for a time. At this stage, therefore, the proletarians do not fight their enemies, but the enemies of their enemies, the remnants of absolute monarchy, the landowners, the nonindustrial bourgeois, the petty bourgeoisie. Thus the whole historical movement is concentrated in the hands of the bourgeoisie; every victory so obtained is a victory for the bourgeoisie.

But with the development of industry the proletariat not only increases in number; it becomes concentrated in greater masses, its strength grows, and it feels that strength more. The various interests and conditions of life within the ranks of the proletariat are more and more equalised, in proportion as machinery obliterates all distinctions of labour and nearly everywhere reduces wages to the same low level. The growing competition among the bourgeois, and the resulting commercial crises, makes the wages of the workers ever more fluctuating. The unceasing improvement of machinery, ever more rapidly developing, makes their livelihood more and more precarious; the collisions between individual workmen and individual bourgeois take more and more the character of collisions between two classes. Thereupon the workers begin to form combinations (trade unions) against the bourgeoisie; they club together in order to keep up the rate of wages; they found permanent associations in order to make provision beforehand for these occasional revolts. Here and there the contest breaks out into riots.

Now and then the workers are victorious, but only for a time. The real fruit of their battles lies, not in the immediate result, but in the ever expanding union of the workers. This union is furthered by the improved means of communication which are created by modern industry, and which place the workers of different localities in contact with one another. It was just this contact that was needed to centralise the numerous local struggles, all of the same character, into one national struggle between classes. But every class struggle is a political struggle. And that union, to attain which the burghers of the Middle Ages, with their miserable highways, required centuries, the modern proletarians, thanks to railways, achieve in a few years.

This organisation of the proletarians into a class, and consequently into a political party, is continually being upset again by the competition between the workers themselves. But it ever rises up again, stronger, firmer, mightier. It compels legislative recognition of particular interests of the workers, by taking advantage of the divisions among the bourgeoisie itself. Thus the ten-hour bill in England was carried.

Altogether, collisions between the classes of the old society further the course of development of the proletariat in many ways. The bourgeoisie finds itself involved in a constant battle. At first with the aristocracy; later on, with those portions of the bourgeoisie itself whose interests have become antagonistic to the progress of industry; at all times with the bourgeoisie of foreign countries. In all these battles it sees itself compelled to appeal to the proletariat, to ask for its help, and thus, to drag it into the political arena. The bourgeoisie itself, therefore, supplies the proletariat with its own elements of political and general education, in other words, it furnishes the proletariat with weapons for fighting the bourgeoisie.

Further, as we have already seen, entire sections of the ruling classes are, by the advance of industry, precipitated into the proletariat, or are at least threatened in their conditions of existence. These also supply the proletariat with fresh elements of enlightenment and progress.

Finally, in times when the class struggle nears the decisive hour, the process of dissolution going on within the ruling class, in fact within the whole range of old society, assumes such a violent, glaring character, that a small section of the ruling class cuts itself adrift, and joins the revolutionary class, the class that holds the future in its hands. Just as, therefore, at an earlier period,

a section of the nobility went over to the bourgeoisie, so now a portion of the bourgeoisie goes over to the proletariat, and in particular, a portion of the bourgeois ideologists, who have raised themselves to the level of comprehending theoretically the historical movement as a whole.

Of all the classes that stand face to face with the bourgeoisie today, the proletariat alone is a really revolutionary class. The other classes decay and finally disappear in the face of modern industry: the proletariat is its special and essential product.

The lower middle class, the small manufacturer, the shopkeeper, the artisan, the peasant, all these fight against the bourgeoisie, to save from extinction their existence as fractions of the middle class. They are therefore not revolutionary but conservative. Nay more, they are reactionary, for they try to roll back the wheel of history. If by chance they are revolutionary, they are so only in view of their impending transfer into the proletariat; they thus defend not their present, but their future interests; they desert their own standpoint to adopt that of the proletariat.

The "dangerous class," the social scum (Lumpenproletariat), that passively rotting mass thrown off by the lowest layers of old society, may, here and there, be swept into the movement by a proletarian revolution; its conditions of life, however, prepare it far more for the part of a bribed tool of reactionary intrigue.

The social conditions of the old society no longer exist for the proletariat. The proletarian is without property; his relation to his wife and children has no longer anything in common with bourgeois family relations; modern industrial labour, modern subjection to capital, the same in England as in France, in America as in Germany, has stripped him of every trace of national character. Law, morality, religion, are to him so many bourgeois prejudices, behind which lurk in ambush just as many bourgeois interests.

All the preceding classes that got the upper hand, sought to fortify their already acquired status by subjecting society at large to their conditions of appropriation. The proletarians cannot become masters of the productive forces of society, except by abolishing their own previous mode of appropriation, and thereby also every other previous mode of appropriation. They have nothing of their own to secure and to fortify; their mission is to destroy all previous securities for, and insurances of, individual property.

All previous historical movements were movements of minorities, or in the interest of minorities. The proletarian movement is the self-conscious, independent movement of the immense majority, in the interest of the immense majority. The proletariat, the lowest stratum of our present society, cannot stir, cannot raise itself up, without the whole super-incumbent strata of official society being sprung into the air.

Though not in substance, yet in form, the struggle of the proletariat with the bourgeoisie is at first a national struggle. The proletariat of each country must, of course, first of all settle matters with its own bourgeoisie.

In depicting the most general phases of the development of the proletariat, we traced the more or less veiled civil war, raging within existing society, up to the point where that war breaks out into open revolution, and where the violent overthrow of the bourgeoisie lays the foundation for the sway of the proletariat.

Hitherto, every form of society has been based, as we have already seen, on the antagonism of oppressing and oppressed classes. But in order to oppress a class, certain conditions must be assured to it under which it can, at least, continue its slavish existence. The serf, in the period of serfdom, raised himself to membership in the commune, just as the petty bourgeois, under the yoke of feudal absolutism, managed to develop into a bourgeois. The modern labourer, on the contrary, instead of rising with the progress of industry, sinks deeper and deeper below the conditions of existence of his own class. He becomes a pauper, and pauperism develops more rapidly than population and wealth. And here it becomes evident, that the bourgeoisie is unfit any longer to be the ruling class in society, and to impose its conditions of existence upon society as an over-riding law. It is unfit to rule because it is incompetent to assure an existence to its slave within his slavery, because it cannot help letting him sink into such a state, that it has to feed him, instead of being fed by him. Society can no longer live under this bourgeoisie, in other words, its existence is no longer compatible with society.

The essential condition for the existence and sway of the bourgeois class, is the formation and augmentation of capital; the condition for capital is wage-labour. Wage-labour rests exclusively on competition between the labourers. The advance of industry, whose involuntary promoter is the bourgeoisie, replaces the isolation of the labourers, due to cornpetition, by their revolutionary combination, due to association. The development of modern industry, therefore, cuts from under its feet the very foundation on which the bourgeoisie produces and appropriates products. What the bourgeoisie therefore produces, above all, are its own grave-diggers. Its fall and the victory of the proletariat are equally inevitable.

PROLETARIANS AND COMMUNISTS

In what relation do the Communists stand to the proletarians as a whole?

The Communists do not form a separate party opposed to other working class parties.

They have no interests separate and apart from those of the proletariat as a whole.

They do not set up any sectarian principles of their own, by which to shape and mould the proletarian movement.

The Communists are distinguished from the other working class parties by this only: 1. In the national struggles of the proletarians of the different countries, they point out and bring to the front the common interests of the entire proletariat, independently of all nationality. 2. In the various stages of development which the struggle of the working class against the bourgeoisie has to pass through, they always and everywhere represent the interests of the movement as a whole.

The Communists, therefore, are on the one hand, practically, the most advanced and resolute section of the working class parties of every country, that section which pushes forward all others; on the other hand, theoretically, they have over the great mass of the proletariat the advantage of clearly understanding the line of march, the conditions, and the ultimate general results of the proletarian movement.

The immediate aim of the Communists is the same as that of all the other proletarian parties: Formation of the proletariat into a class, overthrow of bourgeois supremacy, conquest of political power by the proletariat.

The theoretical conclusions of the Communists are in no way based on ideas or principles that have been invented, or discovered, by this or that would-be universal reformer.

They merely express, in general terms, actual relations springing from an existing class struggle, from a historical movement going on under our very eyes. The abolition of existing property relations is not at all a distinctive feature of Communism.

All property relations in the past have continually been subject to historical change consequent upon the change in historical conditions.

The French Revolution, for example, abolished feudal property in favour of bourgeois property.

The distinguishing feature of Communism is not the abolition of property generally, but the abolition of bourgeois property. But modern bourgeois private property is the final and most complete expression of the system of producing and appropriating products that is based on class antagonisms, on the exploitation of the many by the few.

In this sense, the theory of the Communists may be summed up in the single sentence: Abolition of private property.

We Communists have been reproached with the desire of abolishing the right of personally acquiring property as the fruit of a man's own labour, which property is alleged to be the groundwork of all personal freedom, activity and independence.

Hard-won, self-acquired, self-earned property! Do you mean the property of the petty artisan and of the small peasant, a form of property that preceded the bourgeois form? There is no need to abolish that; the development of industry has to a great extent already destroyed it, and is still destroying it daily.

Or do you mean modern bourgeois private property?

But does wage-labour create any property for the labourer? Not a bit. It creates capital, *i.e.,* that kind of property which exploits wage-labour, and which cannot increase except upon condition of begetting a new supply of wage-labour for fresh exploitation. Property, in its present form, is based on the antagonism of capital and wage-labour. Let us examine both sides of this antagonism.

To be a capitalist, is to have not only a purely personal, but a social *status* in production. Capital is a collective product, and only by the united action of many members, nay, in the last resort, only by the united action of all members of society, can it be set in motion.

Capital is therefore not a personal, it is a social, power.

When, therefore, capital is converted into common property, into the property of all members of society, personal property is not thereby transformed into social property. It is only the social character of the property that is changed. It loses its class character.

Let us now take wage-labour.

The average price of wage-labour is the minimum wage, *i.e.,* that quantum of the means of subsistence which is absolutely requisite to keep the labourer in bare existence as a labourer. What, therefore, the wage-labourer appropriates by means of his labour, merely suffices to prolong and reproduce a bare existence. We by no means intend to abolish this personal appropriation of the products of labour, an appropriation that is made for the maintenance and reproduction of human life, and that leaves no surplus wherewith to command the labour of others. All that we want to do away with is the miserable character of this appropriation, under which the labourer lives merely to increase capital, and is allowed to live only insofar as the interest of the ruling class requires it.

In bourgeois society, living labour is but a means to increase accumulated labour. In Communist society, accumulated labour is but a means to widen, to enrich, to promote the existence of the labourer.

In bourgeois society, therefore, the past dominates the present; in Communist society, the present dominates the past. In bourgeois society capital is independent and has individuality, while the living person is dependent and has no individuality.

And the abolition of this state of things is called by the bourgeois, abolition of individuality and freedom! And rightly so. The abolition of bourgeois individuality, bourgeois independence, and bourgeois freedom is undoubtedly aimed at.

By freedom is meant, under the present bourgeois conditions of production, free trade, free selling and buying.

But if selling and buying disappears, free selling and buying disappears also. This talk about free selling and buying, and all the other "brave words" of our bourgeoisie about freedom in general, have a meaning, if any, only in contrast with restricted selling and buying, with the fettered traders of the Middle Ages, but have no meaning when opposed to the Communist abolition of buying and selling, of the bourgeois condition of production, and of the bourgeoisie itself.

You are horrified at our intending to do away with private property. But in your existing society, private property is already done away with for nine-tenths of the population; its existence for the few is solely due to its non-existence in the hands of those nine-tenths. You reproach us, therefore, with intending to do away with a form of property, the necessary condition for whose existence is the non-existence of any property for the immense majority of society.

In a word, you reproach us with intending to do away with your property. Precisely so; that is just what we intend.

From the moment when labour can no longer be converted into capital, money, or rent, into a social power capable of being monopolised, *i.e.,* from the moment when individual property can no longer be transformed into bourgeois property, into capital, from that moment, you say, individuality vanishes.

You must, therefore, confess that by "individual" you mean no other person than the bourgeois, than the middle class owner of property. This person must, indeed, be swept out of the way, and made impossible.

Communism deprives no man of the power to appropriate the products of society; all that it does is to deprive him of the power to subjugate the labour of others by means of such appropriation.

It has been objected, that upon the abolition of private property all work will cease, and universal laziness will overtake us.

According to this, bourgeois society ought long ago to have gone to the dogs through sheer idleness; for those of its members who work, acquire nothing, and those who acquire anything, do not work. The whole of this objection is but another expression of the tautology: There can no longer be any wage-labour when there is no longer any capital.

All objections urged against the Communist mode of producing and appropriating material products, have, in the same way, been urged against the Communist modes of producing and appropriating intellectual products. Just as, to the bourgeois, the disappearance of class property is the disappearance of production itself, so the disappearance of class culture is to him identical with the disappearance of all culture.

That culture, the loss of which he laments, is, for the enormous majority, a mere training to act as a machine.

But don't wrangle with us so long as you apply, to our intended abolition of bourgeois property, the standard of your bourgeois notions of freedom, culture, law, etc. Your very ideas are but the outgrowth of the conditions of your bourgeois production and bourgeois property, just as your jurisprudence is but the will of your class made into a law for all, a will whose essential character and direction are determined by the economic conditions of existence of your class.

The selfish misconception that induces you to transform into eternal laws of nature and of reason, the social forms springing from your present mode of production and form of property—historical relations that rise and disappear in the progress of production—this misconception you share with every ruling class that has preceded you. What you see clearly in the case of ancient property, what you admit in the case of feudal property, you are of course forbidden to admit in the case of your own bourgeois form of property.

Abolition of the family! Even the most radical flare up at this infamous proposal of the Communists.

On what foundation is the present family, the bourgeois family, based? On capital, on private gain. In its completely developed form this family exists only among the bourgeoisie. But this state of things finds its complement in the practical absence of the family among the proletarians, and in public prostitution.

The bourgeois family will vanish as a matter of course when its complement vanishes, and both will vanish with the vanishing of capital.

Do you charge us with wanting to stop the exploitation of children by their parents? To this crime we plead guilty.

But, you will say, we destroy the most hallowed of relations, when we replace home education by social.

And your education! Is not that also social, and determined by the social conditions under which you educate, by the intervention of society, direct or indirect, by means of schools, etc.? The Communists have not invented the intervention of society in education; they do but seek to alter the character of that intervention, and to rescue education from the influence of the ruling class.

The bourgeois claptrap about the family and education, about the hallowed co-relation of parent and child, becomes all the more disgusting, the more, by the action of modern industry, all family ties among the proletarians are torn asunder, and their children transformed into simple articles of commerce and instruments of labour.

But you Communists would introduce community of women, screams the whole bourgeoisie in chorus.

The bourgeois sees in his wife a mere instrument of production. He hears that the instruments of production are to be exploited in common, and, naturally, can come to no other conclusion than that the lot of being common to all will likewise fall to the women.

He has not even a suspicion that the real point aimed at is to do away with the status of women as mere instruments of production.

For the rest, nothing is more ridiculous than the virtuous indignation of our bourgeois at the community of women which, they pretend, is to be openly and officially established by the Communists. The Communists have no need to introduce community of women; it has existed almost from time immemorial.

Our bourgeois, not content with having the wives and daughters of their proletarians at their disposal, not to speak of common prostitutes, take the greatest pleasure in seducing each other's wives.

Bourgeois marriage is in reality a system of wives in common and thus, at the most, what the Communists might possibly be reproached with is that they desire to introduce, in substitution for a hypocritically concealed, an openly legalised community of women. For the rest, it is self-evident, that the abolition of the present system of production must bring with it the abolition of the community of women springing from that system, *i.e.*, of prostitution both public and private.

The Communists are further reproached with desiring to abolish countries and nationality.

The workingmen have no country. We cannot take from them what they have not got. Since the proletariat must first of all acquire political supremacy, must rise to be the leading class of the nation, must constitute itself *the* nation, it is, so far, itself national, though not in the bourgeois sense of the word.

National differences and antagonisms between peoples are vanishing gradually from day to day, owing to the development of the bourgeoisie, to freedom of commerce, to the world market, to uniformity in the mode of production and in the conditions of life corresponding thereto.

The supremacy of the proletariat will cause them to vanish still faster. United action, of the leading civilised countries at least, is one of the first conditions for the emancipation of the proletariat.

In proportion as the exploitation of one individual by another is put an end to, the exploitation of one nation by another will also be put an end to. In proportion as the antagonism between classes within the nation vanishes, the hostility of one nation to another will come to an end.

The charges against Communism made from a religious, a philosophical, and, generally, from an ideological standpoint, are not deserving of serious examination.

Does it require deep intuition to comprehend that man's ideas, views, and conceptions, in one word, man's consciousness, changes with every change in the conditions of his material existence, in his social relations and in his social life?

What else does the history of ideas prove, than that intellectual production changes its character in proportion as material production is changed? The ruling ideas of each age have ever been the ideas of its ruling class.

When people speak of ideas that revolutionise society, they do but express the fact that within the old society the elements of a new one have been created, and that the dissolution of the old ideas keeps even pace with the dissolution of the old conditions of existence.

When the ancient world was in its last throes, the ancient religions were overcome by Christianity. When Christian ideas succumbed in the 18th century to rationalist ideas, feudal society fought its death-battle with the then revolutionary bourgeoisie. The ideas of religious liberty and freedom of conscience, merely gave expression to the sway of free competition within the domain of knowledge.

"Undoubtedly," it will be said, "religion, moral, philosophical and juridical ideas have been modified in the course of historical development. But religion, morality, philosophy, political science, and law, constantly survived this change."

"There are, besides, eternal truths, such as Freedom, Justice, etc., that are common to all states of society. But Communism abolishes eternal truths, it abolishes all religion, and all morality, instead of constituting them on a new basis; it therefore acts in contradiction to all past historical experience."

What does this accusation reduce itself to? The history of all past society has consisted in the development of class antagonisms, antagonisms that assumed different forms at different epochs.

But whatever form they may have taken, one fact is common to all past ages, viz., the exploitation of one part of society by the other. No wonder, then, that the social consciousness of past ages, despite all the multiplicity and variety it displays, moves within certain common forms, or general ideas, which cannot completely vanish except with the total disappearance of class antagonisms.

The Communist revolution is the most radical rupture with traditional property relations; no wonder that its development involves the most radical rupture with traditional ideas,

But let us have done with the bourgeois objections to Communism.

We have seen above, that the first step in the revolution by the working class, is to raise the proletariat to the position of ruling class, to establish democracy.

The proletariat will use its political supremacy to wrest, by degrees, all capital from the bourgeoisie, to centralise all instruments of production in the hands of the state, *i.e.,* of the proletariat organised as the ruling class; and to increase the total of productive forces as rapidly as possible.

Of course, in the beginning, this cannot be effected except by means of despotic inroads on the rights of property, and on the conditions of bourgeois production; by means of measures, therefore, which appear economically insufficient and untenable, but which, in the course of the movement, outstrip themselves, necessitate further inroads upon the old social order, and are unavoidable as a means of entirely revolutionising the mode of production.

These measures will of course be different in different countries.

Nevertheless in the most advanced countries, the following will be pretty generally applicable.

1. Abolition of property in land and application of all rents of land to public purposes.

2. A heavy progressive or graduated income tax.

3. Abolition of all right of inheritance.

4. Confiscation of the property of all emigrants and rebels.

5. Centralisation of credit in the hands of the state, by means of a national bank with state capital and an exclusive monopoly.

6. Centralisation of the means of communication and transport in the hands of the state.

7. Extension of factories and instruments of production owned by the state; the bringing into cultivation of waste lands, and the improvement of the soil generally in accordance with a common plan.

8. Equal obligation of all to work. Establishment of industrial armies, especially for agriculture.

9. Combination of agriculture with manufacturing industries; gradual abolition of the distinction between town and country, by a more equable distribution of the population over the country.

10. Free education for all children in public schools. Abolition of child factory labour in its present form. Combination of education with industrial production, etc.

When, in the course of development, class distinctions have disappeared, and all production has been concentrated in the hands of a vast association of the whole nation, the public power will lose its political character. Political power, properly so called, is merely the organised power of one class for oppressing another. If the proletariat during its contest with the bourgeoisie is compelled, by the force of circumstances, to organise itself as a class; if, by means of a revolution, it makes itself the ruling class, and, as such sweeps away by force the old conditions of production, then it will, along with these conditions, have swept away the conditions for the existence of class antagonisms, and of classes generally, and will thereby have abolished its own supremacy as a class.

In place of the old bourgeois society, with its classes and class antagonisms, we shall have an association, in which the free development of each is the condition for the free development of all.

SOCIALIST AND COMMUNIST LITERATURE

REACTIONARY SOCIALISM

Feudal Socialism Owing to their historical position, it became the vocation of the aristocracies of France and England to write pamphlets against modern bourgeois society. In the French revolution of July, 1830, and in the English reform agitation, these aristocracies again succumbed to the hateful upstart. Thenceforth, a serious political struggle was altogether out of the question. A literary battle alone remained possible. But even in the domain of literature the old cries of the restoration period had become impossible.

In order to arouse sympathy, the aristocracy was obliged to lose sight, apparently, of its own interests, and to formulate its indictment against the bourgeoisie in the interest of the exploited working class alone. Thus the aristocracy took its revenge by singing lampoons against its new master, and whispering in his ears sinister prophecies of coming catastrophe.

In this way arose Feudal Socialism: Half lamentation, half lampoon; half echo of the past, half menace of the future; at times, by its bitter, witty and incisive criticism, striking the bourgeoisie to the very heart's core, but always ludicrous in its effect through total incapacity to comprehend the march of modern history.

The aristocracy, in order to rally the people to them, waved the proletarian almsbag in front for a banner. But the people, as often as it joined them, saw on their hindquarters the old feudal coats of arms, and deserted with loud and irreverent laughter.

One section of the French Legitimists, and "Young England," exhibited this spectacle.

In pointing out that their mode of exploitation was different from that of the bourgeoisie, the feudalists forget that they exploited under circumstances and conditions that were quite different, and that are now antiquated. In showing that, under their rule, the modern proletariat never existed, they forget that the modern bourgeoisie is the necessary offspring of their own form of society.

For the rest, so little do they conceal the reactionary character of their criticism, that their chief accusation against the bourgeoisie amounts to this, that under the bourgeois regime a class is being developed, which is destined to cut up root and branch the old order of society.

What they upbraid the bourgeoisie with is not so much that it creates a proletariat, as that it creates a *revolutionary* proletariat.

In political practice, therefore, they join in all coercive measures against the working class; and in ordinary life, despite their high-falutin phrases, they stoop to pick up the golden apples dropped from the tree of industry, and to barter truth, love, and honour for traffic in wool, beetroot-sugar, and potato spirits.

As the parson has ever gone hand in hand with the landlord, so has Clerical Socialism with Feudal Socialism.

Nothing is easier than to give Christian asceticism a Socialist tinge. Has not Christianity declaimed against private property, against marriage, against the state? Has it not preached in the place of these, charity and poverty, celibacy and mortification of the flesh, monastic life and Mother Church? Christian Socialism is but the holy water with which the priest consecrates the heart-burnings of the aristocrat.

Petty Bourgeois Socialism   The feudal aristocracy was not the only class that was ruined by the bourgeoisie, not the only class whose conditions of existence pined and perished in the atmosphere of modern bourgeois society. The mediæval burgesses and the small peasant proprietors were the precursors of the modern bourgeoisie. In those countries which are but little developed, industrially and commercially, these two classes still vegetate side by side with the rising bourgeoisie.

In countries where modern civilisation has become fully developed, a new class of petty bourgeois has been formed, fluctuating between proletariat and bourgeoisie, and ever renewing itself as a supplementary part of bourgeois society. The individual members of this class, however, are being constantly hurled down into the proletariat by the action of competition, and, as modern industry develops, they even see the moment approaching when they will completely disappear as an independent section of modern society, to be replaced, in manufactures, agriculture and commerce, by overseers, bailiffs and shopmen.

In countries, like France, where the peasants constitute far more than half of the population, it was natural that writers who sided with the proletariat against the bourgeoisie, should use, in their criticism of the bourgeois regime, the standard of the peasant and petty bourgeois, and from the standpoint of these intermediate classes should take up the cudgels for the working class. Thus arose petty bourgeois Socialism. Sismondi was the head of this school, not only in France but also in England.

This school of Socialism dissected with great acuteness the contradictions in the conditions of modern production. It laid bare the hypocritical apologies of economists. It proved, incontrovertibly, the disastrous effects of machinery and division of labour; the concentration of capital and land in a few hands; overproduction and crises; it pointed out the inevitable ruin of the petty bourgeois and peasant, the misery of the proletariat, the anarchy in production, the crying inequalities in the distribution of wealth, the industrial war of extermination between nations, the dissolution of old moral bonds, of the old family relations, of the old nationalities.

In its positive aims, however, this form of Socialism aspires either to restoring the old means of production and of exchange, and with them the old property relations, and the old society, or to cramping the modern means of production and of exchange within the framework of the old property relations that have been, and were bound to be, exploded by those means. In either case, it is both reactionary and utopian.

Its last words are: Corporate guilds for manufacture; patriarchal relations in agriculture.

Ultimately, when stubborn historical facts had dispersed all intoxicating effects of self-deception, this form of Socialism ended in a miserable fit of the blues.

German or "True" Socialism   The Socialist and Communist literature of France, a literature that originated under the pressure of a bourgeoisie in power, and that was the expression of the struggle against this power, was introduced into Germany at a time when the bourgeoisie, in that country, had just begun its contest with feudal absolutism.

German philosophers, would-be philosophers, and men of letters eagerly seized on this literature, only forgetting that when these writings immigrated from France into Germany, French social conditions had not immigrated along with them. In contact with German social conditions, this French literature lost all its immediate practical significance, and assumed a purely literary aspect. Thus, to the German philosophers of the 18th century, the demands of the first French Revolution were nothing more than the demands of "Practical Reason" in general, and the utterance of the will of the revolutionary French bourgeoisie signified in their eyes the laws of pure will, of will as it was bound to be, of true human will generally.

The work of the German *literati* consisted solely in bringing the new French ideas into harmony with their ancient philosophical conscience, or rather, in annexing the French ideas without deserting their own philosophic point of view.

This annexation took place in the same way in which a foreign language is appropriated, namely by translation.

It is well known how the monks wrote silly lives of Catholic saints *over* the manuscripts on which the classical works of ancient heathendom had been written. The German *literati* reversed this process with the profane French literature. They wrote their philosophical nonsense beneath the French original. For instance, beneath the French criticism of the economic functions of money, they wrote "alienation of humanity," and beneath the French criticism of the bourgeois state, they wrote, "dethronement of the category of the general," and so forth.

The introduction of these philosophical phrases at the back of the French historical criticisms they dubbed "Philosophy of Action," "True Socialism," "German Science of Socialism," "Philosophical Foundation of Socialism," and so on.

The French Socialist and Communist literature was thus completely emasculated. And, since it ceased in the hands of the German to express the struggle of one class with the other, he felt conscious of having overcome "French one-sidedness" and of representing, not true requirements, but the requirements of truth; not the interests of the proletariat, but the interests of human nature, of man in general, who belongs to no class, has no reality, who exists only in the misty realm of philosophical phantasy.

This German Socialism, which took its school-boy task so seriously and solemnly, and extolled its poor stock-in-trade in such mountebank fashion, meanwhile gradually lost its pedantic innocence.

The fight of the German and especially of the Prussian bourgeoisie against feudal aristocracy and absolute monarchy, in other words, the liberal movement, became more earnest.

By this, the long-wished-for opportunity was offered to "True" Socialism of confronting the political movement with the Socialist demands, of hurling the traditional anathemas against liberalism, against representative government, against bourgeois competition, bourgeois freedom of the press, bourgeois legislation, bourgeois liberty and equality, and of preaching to the masses that they had nothing to gain, and everything to lose, by this bourgeois movement. German Socialism forgot, in the nick of time, that the French criticism, whose silly echo it was, presupposed the existence of modern bourgeois society, with its corresponding economic conditions of existence, and the political constitution adapted thereto, the very things whose attainment was the object of the pending struggle in Germany.

To the absolute governments, with their following of parsons, professors, country squires and officials, it served as a welcome scarecrow against the threatening bourgeoisie.

It was a sweet finish after the bitter pills of floggings and bullets, with which these same governments, just at that time, dosed the risings of the German working class.

While this "True" Socialism thus served the governments as a weapon for fighting the German bourgeoisie, it, at the same time, directly represented a reactionary interest, the interest of the German Philistines. In Germany the petty bourgeois class, a relic of the 16th century, and since then constantly cropping up again under various forms, is the real social basis of the existing state of things.

To preserve this class, is to preserve the existing state of things in Germany. The industrial and political supremacy of the bourgeoisie threatens it with certain destruction—on the one hand, from the concentration of capital; on the other, from the rise of a revolutionary proletariat. "True" Socialism appeared to kill these two birds with one stone. It spread like an epidemic.

The robe of speculative cobwebs, embroidered with flowers of rhetoric, steeped in the dew of sickly sentiment, this transcendental robe in which the German Socialists wrapped their sorry "eternal truths," all skin and bone, served to increase wonderfully the sale of their goods amongst such a public.

And on its part, German Socialism recognised, more and more, its own calling as the bombastic representative of the petty bourgeois Philistine.

It proclaimed the German nation to be the model nation, and the German petty Philistine to be the typical man. To every villainous meanness of this model man it gave a hidden, higher, socialistic interpretation, the exact contrary of his real character. It went to the extreme length of directly opposing the "brutally destructive" tendency of Communism, and of proclaiming its supreme and impartial contempt of all class struggles. With very few exceptions, all the so-called Socialist and Communist publications that now (1847) circulate in Germany belong to the domain of this foul and enervating literature.

CONSERVATIVE OR BOURGEOIS SOCIALISM

A part of the bourgeoisie is desirous of redressing social grievances, in order to secure the continued existence of bourgeois society.

To this section belong economists, philanthropists, humanitarians, improvers of the condition of the working class, organisers of charity, members of societies for the prevention of cruelty to animals, temperance fanatics, hole-and-corner reformers of every imaginable kind. This form of Socialism has, moreover, been worked out into complete systems.

We may cite Proudhon's *Philosophy of Poverty* as an example of this form.

The socialistic bourgeois want all the advantages of modern social conditions without the struggles and dangers necessarily resulting therefrom. They desire the existing state of society minus its revolutionary and disintegrating elements. They wish for a bourgeoisie without a proletariat. The bourgeoisie naturally conceives the world in which it is supreme to be the best; and bourgeois Socialism develops this comfortable conception into various more or less complete systems. In requiring the proletariat to carry out such a system, and thereby to march straightway into the social New Jerusalem, it but requires in reality, that the proletariat should remain within the bounds of existing society, but should cast away all its hateful ideas concerning the bourgeoisie.

A second and more practical, but less systematic, form of this Socialism sought to depreciate every revolutionary movement in the eyes of the working class, by showing that no mere political reform, but only a change in the material conditions of existence, in economic relations, could be of any advantage to them. By changes in the material conditions of existence, this form of Socialism, however, by no means understands abolition of the bourgeois relations of production, an abolition that can be effected only by a revolution, but administrative reforms, based on the continued existence of these relations; reforms, therefore, that in no respect affect the relations between capital and labour, but at the best, lessen the cost, and simplify the administrative work of bourgeois government.

Bourgeois Socialism attains adequate expression, when, and only when, it becomes a mere figure of speech.

Free trade: For the benefit of the working class. Protective duties: For the benefit of the working class. Prison reform: For the benefit of the working class. These are the last words and the only seriously meant words of bourgeois Socialism.

It is summed up in the phrase: the bourgeois are bourgeois—for the benefit of the working class.

CRITICAL-UTOPIAN SOCIALISM AND COMMUNISM

We do not here refer to that literature which, in every great modern revolution, has always given voice to the demands of the proletariat, such as the writings of Babeuf and others.

The first direct attempts of the proletariat to attain its own ends—made in times of universal excitement, when feudal society was being overthrown—necessarily failed, owing to the then undeveloped state of the proletariat, as well as to the absence of the economic conditions for its emancipation, conditions that had yet to be produced, and could be produced by the impending bourgeois epoch alone. The revolutionary literature that accompanied these first movements of the proletariat had necessarily a reactionary character. It inculcated universal asceticism and social levelling in its crudest form.

The Socialist and Communist systems properly so called, those of St. Simon, Fourier, Owen and others, spring into existence in the early undeveloped period, described above, of the struggle between proletariat and bourgeoisie (see Section 1. Bourgeois and Proletarians).

The founders of these systems see, indeed, the class antagonisms, as well as the action of the decomposing elements in the prevailing form of society. But the proletariat, as yet in its infancy, offers to them the spectacle of a class without any historical initiative or any independent political movement.

Since the development of class antagonism keeps even pace with the development of industry, the economic situation, as such Socialists find it, does not as yet offer to them the material conditions for the emancipation of the proletariat. They therefore search after a new social science, after new social laws, that are to create these conditions.

Historical action is to yield to their personal inventive action; historically created conditions of emancipation to phantastic ones; and the gradual, spontaneous class organisation of the proletariat to an organisation of society specially contrived by these inventors. Future history resolves itself, in their eyes, into the propaganda and the practical carrying out of their social plans.

In the formulation of their plans they are conscious of caring chiefly for the interests of the working class, as being the most suffering class. Only from the point of view of being the most suffering class does the proletariat exist for them.

The undeveloped state of the class struggle, as well as their own surroundings, causes Socialists of this kind to consider themselves far superior to all class antagonisms. They want to improve the condition of every member of society, even that of the most favoured. Hence, they habitually appeal to society at large, without distinction of class; nay, by preference, to the ruling class. For how can people, when once they understand their system, fail to see in it the best possible plan of the best possible state of society?

Hence, they reject all political, and especially all revolutionary action; they wish to attain their ends by peaceful means, and endeavour, by small experiments, necessarily doomed to failure, and by the force of example, to pave the way for the new social gospel.

Such phantastic pictures of future society, painted at a time when the proletariat is still in a very undeveloped state and has but a phantastic conception of its own position, correspond with the first instinctive yearnings of that class for a general reconstruction of society.

But these Socialist and Communist writings contain also a critical element. They attack every principle of existing society. Hence they are full of the most valuable materials for the enlightenment of the working class. The practical measures proposed in them—such as the abolition of the distinction between town and country; abolition of the family, of private gain and of the wage-system; the proclamation of social harmony; the conversion of the functions of the state into a mere superintendence of production—all these proposals point solely to the disappearance of class antagonisms which were, at that time, only just cropping up, and which, in these publications, are recognised in their earliest, indistinct and undefined forms only. These proposals, therefore, are of a purely utopian character.

The significance of Critical-Utopian Socialism and Communism bears an inverse relation to historical development. In proportion as the modern class struggle develops and takes definite shape, this phantastic standing apart from the contest, these phantastic attacks on it, lose all practical value and all theoretical justification. Therefore, although the originators of these systems were, in many respects, revolutionary, their disciples have, in every case, formed mere reactionary sects. They hold fast by the original views of their masters, in opposition to the progressive historical development of the proletariat. They, therefore, endeavour, and that consistently, to deaden the class struggle and to reconcile the class antagonisms. They still dream of experimental realisation of their social utopias, of founding isolated *phalanstères*, of establishing "Home Colonies," or setting up a "Little Icaria"—pocket editions of the New Jerusalem—and to realise all these castles in the air, they are compelled to appeal to the feelings and purses of the bourgeois. By degrees they sink into the category of the reactionary conservative Socialists depicted above, differing from these only by more systematic pedantry, and by their fanatical and superstitious belief in the miraculous effects of their social science.

They, therefore, violently oppose all political action on the part of the working class; such action, according to them, can only result from blind unbelief in the new gospel.

The Owenites in England, and the Fourierists in France, respectively, oppose the Chartists and the *Réformistes*.

POSITION OF THE COMMUNISTS IN RELATION TO THE VARIOUS EXISTING OPPOSITION PARTIES

Section 2 has made clear the relations of the Communists to the existing working class parties, such as the Chartists in England and the Agrarian Reformers in America.

The Communists fight for the attainment of the immediate aims, for the enforcement of the momentary interests of the working class; but in the movement of the present, they also represent and take care of the future of that movement. In France the Communists ally themselves with the Social-Democrats, against the conservative and radical bourgeoisie, reserving, however, the right to take up a critical position in regard to phrases and illusions traditionally handed down from the great Revolution.

In Switzerland they support the Radicals, without losing sight of the fact that this party consists of antagonistic elements, partly of Democratic Socialists, in the French sense, partly of radical bourgeois.

In Poland they support the party that insists on an agrarian revolution as the prime condition for national emancipation, that party which fomented the insurrection of Cracow in 1846.

In Germany they fight with the bourgeoisie whenever it acts in a revolutionary way, against the absolute monarchy, the feudal squirearchy, and the petty bourgeoisie.

But they never cease, for a single instant, to instil into the working class the clearest possible recognition of the hostile antagonism between bourgeoisie and proletariat, in order that the German workers may straightway use, as so many weapons against the bourgeoisie, the social and political conditions that the bourgeoisie must necessarily introduce along with its supremacy, and in order that, after the fall of the reactionary classes in Germany, the fight against the bourgeoisie itself may immediately begin.

The Communists turn their attention chiefly to Germany, because that country is on the eve of a bourgeois revolution that is bound to be carried out under more advanced conditions of European civilisation and with a much more developed proletariat than what existed in England in the 17th and in France in the 18th century, and because the bourgeois revolution in Germany will be but the prelude to an immediately following proletarian revolution.

In short, the Communists everywhere support every revolutionary movement against the existing social and political order of things.

In all these movements they bring to the front, as the leading question in each case, the property question, no matter what its degree of development at the time.

Finally, they labour everywhere for the union and agreement of the democratic parties of all countries.

The Communists disdain to conceal their views and aims. They openly declare that their ends can be attained only by the forcible overthrow of all existing social conditions. Let the ruling classes tremble at a Communist revolution. The proletarians have nothing to lose but their chains. They have a world to win.

Workingmen of all countries, unite!

III LENIN

Selected Works

PROFESSIONAL REVOLUTIONARIES*

I assert: (1) that no movement can be durable without a stable organisation of leaders to maintain continuity; (2) that the more widely the masses are spontaneously drawn into the struggle and form the basis of the movement and participate in it, the more necessary is it to have such an organisation, and the more stable must it be (for it is much easier for demagogues to side-track the more backward sections of the masses); (3) that the organisation must consist chiefly of persons engaged in revolutionary activities as a profession; (4) that in a country with an autocratic government, the more we restrict the membership of this organisation to persons who are engaged in revolutionary activities as a profession and who have been professionally trained in the art of combating the political police, the more difficult will it be to catch the organisation, and (5) the *wider* will be the circle of men and women of the working class or of other classes of society able to join the movement and perform active work in it.

We can never give a mass organisation that degree of secrecy which is essential for the persistent and continuous struggle against the government. But to concentrate all secret functions in the hands of as small

a number of professional revolutionaries as possible does not mean that the latter will "do the thinking for all" and that the crowd will not take an active part in the *movement*. On the contrary, the crowd will advance from its ranks increasing numbers of professional revolutionaries, for it will know that it is not enough for a few students and working-men, waging economic war, to gather together and form a "committee," but that it takes years to train professional revolutionaries; the crowd will "think" not of primitive ways but of training professional revolutionaries. The centralisation of the secret functions of the *organisation* does not mean the centralisation of all the functions of the movement. The active participation of the broad masses in the dissemination of illegal literature will not diminish because a dozen professional revolutionaries centralise the secret part of the work; on the contrary, it will *increase tenfold*. Only in this way will the reading of illegal literature, the contribution to illegal literature and to some extent even the distribution of illegal literature *almost cease to be secret work,* for the police will soon come to realise the folly and futility of setting the whole judicial and administrative machine into motion to intercept every copy of a publication that is being broadcast in thousands. This applies not only to the press, but to every function of the movement, even to demonstrations. The active and widespread participation of the masses will not suffer; on the contrary, it will benefit by the fact that a "dozen" experienced revolutionaries, no less professionally trained

*From V. I. Lenin, *What Is to Be Done?* (1902) from *Selected Works,* Vol. II, pp. 138–140, 146–148. Reprinted by permission of International Publishers Co. Copyright © 1936.

than the police, will centralise all the secret side of the work—prepare leaflets, work out approximate plans and appoint bodies of leaders for each urban district, for each factory district and for each educational institution, etc. (I know that exception will be taken to my "undemocratic" views, but I shall reply to this altogether unintelligent objection later on.) The centralisation of the more secret functions in an organisation of revolutionaries will not diminish, but rather increase the extent and the quality of the activity of a large number of other organisations intended for wide membership and which, therefore, can be as loose and as public as possible, for example, trade unions, workers' circles for self-education and the reading of illegal literature, and socialist and also democratic circles for *all other sections of the population,* etc., etc.

In order to be fully prepared for his task, the working class revolutionary must also become a professional revolutionary. Hence B—v is wrong when he says that as the worker is engaged for eleven and a half hours a day in the factory, therefore, the brunt of all the other revolutionary functions (apart from agitation) *"must necessarily* fall mainly upon the shoulders of an extremely small intellectual force." It need not "necessarily" be so. It is so because we are backward, because we do not recognise our duty to assist every capable worker to become a *professional* agitator, organiser, propagandist, literature distributor, etc. In this respect, we waste our strength in a positively shameful manner; we lack the ability to husband that which should be tended and reared with special care. Look at the Germans: they have a hundred times more forces than we have. But they understand perfectly well that the "average" does not too frequently promote really capable agitators, etc., from its ranks.

Hence they immediately try to place every capable workingman in such conditions as will enable him to develop and apply his abilities to the utmost: he is made a professional agitator, he is encouraged to widen the field of his activity, to spread it from one factory to the whole of his trade, from one locality to the whole country. He acquires experience and dexterity in his profession, his outlook becomes wider, his knowledge increases, he observes the prominent political leaders from other localities and other parties, he strives to rise to their level and combine within himself the knowledge of working class environment and freshness of socialist convictions with professional skill, without which the proletariat *cannot* carry on a stubborn struggle with the excellently trained enemy. Only in this way can men of the stamp of Bebel and Auer be promoted from the ranks of the working class. But what takes place very largely automatically in a politically free country must in Russia be done deliberately and systematically by our organisations. A workingman agitator who is at all talented and "promising" *must not be left* to work eleven hours day in a factory. We must arrange that he be maintained by the Party, that he may in due time go underground, that he change the place of his activity, otherwise he will not enlarge his experience, he will not widen his outlook, and will not be able to stay in the fight against the gendarmes for at least a few years. As the spontaneous rise of the working class masses becomes wider and deeper, they not only promote from their ranks an increasing number of talented agitators, but also of talented organisers, propagandists and "practical workers" in the best sense of the term (of whom there are so few among our intelligentsia who, in the majority of cases, are somewhat careless and sluggish in their habits, so characteristic of Russians). When we have detachments of specially trained working class revolutionaries who have gone through long years of preparation (and, of course, revolutionaries "of all arms"), no political police in the world will be able to contend against them, for these detachments of men absolutely devoted and loyal to the revolution will themselves enjoy the absolute confidence and devotion of the broad masses of the workers. The *sin* we commit is that we do not sufficiently "stimulate" the workers to take this path, "common" to them and to the "intellectuals," of professional revolutionary training, and that we too frequently drag them back by our silly speeches about what "can be understood" by the masses of the workers, by the "average workers," etc.

CLASS SOCIETY
AND THE STATE*

The "Withering Away" of the
State and Violent Revolution

Engels' words regarding the "withering away" of the state enjoy such popularity, they are so often quoted, and they show so clearly the essence of the usual adulteration by means of which Marxism is made to look like opportunism, that we must dwell on them in detail. Let us quote the whole passage from which they are taken.

The proletariat seizes state power, and then transforms the means of production into state property. But in doing this, it puts an end to itself as the proletariat, it puts an end to all class differences and class antagonisms, it puts an end also to the state as the state. Former society, moving in class antagonisms, had need of the state, that is, an organisation of the exploiting class at each period for the maintenance of its external conditions of production; therefore, in particular, for the forcible holding down of the exploited class in the conditions of oppression (slavery, bondage or serfdom, wage-labour) determined by the existing mode of production. The state was the official representative of society as a whole, its embodiment in a visible corporate body; but it was this only in so far as it was the state of that class which itself, in its epoch, represented society as a whole: in ancient times, the state of the slave-owning citizens; in the Middle Ages, of the feudal nobility; in our epoch, of the bourgeoisie. When ultimately it becomes really representative of society as a whole, it makes itself superfluous. As soon as there is no longer any class of society to be held in subjection; as soon as, along with class domination and the struggle for individual existence based on the former anarchy of production, the collisions and excesses arising from these have also been abolished, there is nothing more to be repressed, and a special repressive force, a state, is no longer necessary. The first act in which the state really comes forward as the

representative of society as a whole—the seizure of the means of production in the name of society—is at the same time its last independent act as a state. The interference of a state power in social relations becomes superfluous in one sphere after another, and then becomes dormant of itself. Government over persons is replaced by the administration of things and the direction of the processes of production. The state is not "abolished," *it withers away*. It is from this standpoint that we must appraise the phrase "people's free state"—both its justification at times for agitational purposes, and its ultimate scientific inadequacy—and also the demand of the so-called Anarchists that the state should be abolished overnight.[1]

Without fear of committing an error, it may be said that of this argument by Engels so singularly rich in ideas, only one point has become an integral part of Socialist thought among modern Socialist parties, namely, that, unlike the Anarchist doctrine of the "abolition" of the state, according to Marx the state "withers away." To emasculate Marxism in such a manner is to reduce it to opportunism, for such an "interpretation" only leaves the hazy conception of a slow, even, gradual change, free from leaps and storms, free from revolution. The current popular conception, if one may say so, of the "withering away" of the state undoubtedly means a slurring over, if not a negation, of revolution.

Yet, such an "interpretation" is the crudest distortion of Marxism, which is advantageous only to the bourgeoisie; in point of theory, it is based on a disregard for the most important circumstances and considerations pointed out in the very passage summarising Engels' ideas, which we have just quoted in full.

In the first place, Engels at the very outset of his argument says that, in assuming state power, the proletariat by that very act "puts an end to the state as the state." One is "not accustomed" to reflect on what this really means. Generally, it is either ignored altogether, or it is considered as a piece of

---

*From V. I. Lenin, *State and Revolution* (1917). Reprinted by permission of International Publishers Co. Copyright © 1936.

---

[1] Fredrich Engels, *Anti-Dühring,* London and New York, 1933.

"Hegelian weakness" on Engels' part. As a matter of fact, however, these words express succinctly the experience of one of the greatest proletarian revolutions—the Paris Commune of 1871, of which we shall speak in greater detail in its proper place. As a matter of fact, Engels speaks here of the destruction of the bourgeois state by the proletarian revolution, while the words about its withering away refer to the remains of *proletarian* statehood *after* the Socialist revolution. The bourgeois state does not "wither away," according to Engels, but is "put an end to" by the proletariat in the course of the revolution. What withers away after the revolution is the proletarian state or semi-state.

Secondly, the state is a "special repressive force." This splendid and extremely profound definition of Engels' is given by him here with complete lucidity. It follows from this that the "special repressive force" of the bourgeoisie for the suppression of the proletariat, of the millions of workers by a handful of the rich, must be replaced by a "special repressive force" of the proletariat for the suppression of the bourgeoisie (the dictatorship of the proletariat). It is just this that constitutes the destruction of "the state as the state." It is just this that constitutes the "act" of "the seizure of the means of production in the name of society." And it is obvious that such a substitution of one (proletarian) "special repressive force" for another (bourgeois) "special repressive force" can in no way take place in the form of a "withering away."

Thirdly, as to the "withering away" or, more expressively and colourfully, as to the state "becoming dormant," Engels refers quite clearly and definitely to the period *after* "the seizure of the means of production [by the state] in the name of society," that is, *after* the Socialist revolution. We all know that the political form of the "state" at that time is complete democracy. But it never enters the head of any of the opportunists who shamelessly distort Marx that when Engels speaks here of the state "withering away," or "becoming dormant," he speaks of *democracy*. At first sight this seems very strange. But it is "unintelligible" only to one who has not reflected on the fact that democracy is *also* a state and that, consequently, democracy will *also* disappear when the state disappears. The bourgeois state can only be "put an end to" by a revolution. The state in general, *i.e.,* most complete democracy, can only "wither away."

Fourthly, having formulated his famous proposition that "the state withers away," Engels at once explains concretely that this proposition is directed equally against the opportunists and the Anarchists. In doing this, however, Engels puts in the first place that conclusion from his proposition about the "withering away" of the state which is directed against the opportunists. . . .

Fifthly, in the same work of Engels, from which every one remembers his argument on the "withering away" of the state, there is also a disquisition on the significance of a violent revolution. The historical analysis of its rôle becomes, with Engels, a veritable panegyric on violent revolution. This, of course, "no one remembers"; to talk or even to think of the importance of this idea is not considered good form by contemporary Socialist parties, and in the daily propaganda and agitation among the masses it plays no part whatever. Yet it is indissolubly bound up with the "withering away" of the state in one harmonious whole.

Here is Engels' argument:

> . . . That force, however, plays another rôle (other than that of a diabolical power) in history, a revolutionary rôle; that, in the words of Marx, it is the midwife of every old society which is pregnant with the new; that it is the instrument with whose aid social movement forces its way through and shatters the dead, fossilised political forms—of this there is not a word in Herr Dühring. It is only with sighs and groans that he admits the possibility that force will perhaps be necessary for the overthrow of the economic system of exploitation—unfortunately! because all use of force, forsooth, demoralises the person who uses it. And this in spite of the immense moral and spiritual impetus which has resulted from every victorious revolution! And this in Germany, where a violent collision—which indeed may be forced on the people—would at least have the advantage of wiping out the servility which has permeated the national consciousness as a result of the humiliation of the

Thirty Years' War. And this parson's mode of thought—lifeless, insipid and impotent—claims to impose itself on the most revolutionary party which history has known?[2]

How can this panegyric on violent revolution, which Engels insistently brought to the attention of the German Social-Democrats between 1878 and 1894, *i.e.,* right to the time of his death, be combined with the theory of the "withering away" of the state to form one doctrine? . . .

The replacement of the bourgeois by the proletarian state is impossible without a violent revolution. The abolition of the proletarian state, *i.e.,* of all states, is only possible through "withering away."

BOURGEOIS DEMOCRACY AND PROLETARIAN DICTATORSHIP*

History teaches that not a single oppressed class has ever come into power, or could come into power, without passing through the period of dictatorship, *i.e.,* the conquest of political power and the violent suppression of the desperate, furious and unscrupulous resistance which the exploiters always put up. The bourgeoisie, whose rule the Socialists who oppose "dictatorship in general" and who bow down before "democracy in general" now defend, achieved power in the advanced countries by means of a number of rebellions, by civil wars, by the violent suppression of kings, feudal barons and slave-owners, and their attempts at restoration. In their books and pamphlets, in the resolutions of their congresses and in their agitational speeches, the Socialists of all countries have explained to the people the class character of these bourgeois revolutions, of this bourgeois dictatorship, a thousand and a million times. Hence, the present defence of bourgeois democracy cloaked in speeches about "democracy in general" and the present howling and shouting against the dictatorship

of the proletariat cloaked by cries about "dictatorship in general" are a downright betrayal of socialism, the practical desertion to the side of the bourgeoisie, the denial of the right of the proletariat to make its own proletarian revolution, and defence of bourgeois reformism at the very historical moment when bourgeois reformism is bankrupt all over the world, and when the war has created a revolutionary situation.

In explaining the class character of bourgeois civilisation, of bourgeois democracy and of bourgeois parliamentarism, all Socialists express the idea which was most scientifically expressed by Marx and Engels when they said that even the most democratic bourgeois republic is nothing more than a machine for the suppression of the working class by the bourgeoisie, of the masses of the toilers by a handful of capitalists. Every one of the revolutionaries, every one of the Marxists who is now shouting against dictatorship and for democracy has sworn and assured the workers that he recognises this fundamental truth of socialism; but now, when the revolutionary proletariat is in a state of ferment and motion, which are directed towards the destruction of this machine of oppression and towards the achievement of the proletarian dictatorship, these traitors to socialism try to make it appear that the bourgeoisie granted the toilers "pure democracy," that the bourgeoisie has ceased to resist and is prepared to submit to the majority of the toilers, and that no state machine for the suppression of labour by capital exists, or has ever existed, in a democratic republic.

"The right of assembly" may be taken as an example of the demands of "pure democracy." Every class conscious worker who has not broken connections with his class will understand at once that it would be absurd to promise the right of assembly to the exploiters in the period and in the circumstances in which the exploiters are resisting their overthrow and are defending their privileges. . . .

"Freedom of the press" is another of the principal slogans of "pure democracy." Here, too, the workers know, and the Socialists of all countries have admitted a million times, that this freedom is a sham as long as the best printing plants and the huge stocks of paper are in the possession of the

---

[2] Engels, *Anti-Dühring.*

*From V. I. Lenin, *Theses and Report on Bourgeois Democracy and the Dictatorship of the Proletariat* (Submitted to the First Congress of the Communist International, March 4, 1919) from *Selected Works,* Vol. VII, pp. 223–231. Reprinted by permission of International Publishers Co. Copyright © 1937.

capitalists, and as long as the press is ruled by capital—which rule manifests itself the more strikingly, more sharply and more cynically, the more democracy and the republican system are developed, as for example in America. . . .

The dictatorship of the proletariat is similar to the dictatorship of other classes in that, like all dictatorships, it was called forth by the necessity of suppressing the violent resistance of the class that was being deprived of political rule. The fundamental difference between the dictatorship of the proletariat and the dictatorship of other classes—the dictatorship of the landlords in the Middle Ages, the dictatorship of the bourgeoisie in all civilised capitalist countries—is that the dictatorship of the landlords and of the bourgeoisie meant the violent suppression of the resistance of the overwhelming majority of the population, *viz.,* the toilers. The dictatorship of the proletariat, on the contrary, means the violent suppression of the resistance of the exploiters, *i.e.,* the insignificant minority of the population, the landlords and capitalists.

Hence, it follows from this that the dictatorship of the proletariat must inevitably lead, not only to a change in the forms and institutions of democracy, speaking generally, but to such a change as will lead to the extension of the actual enjoyment of democracy to those who are oppressed by capitalism, to the toiling classes, to a degree hitherto unprecedented in world history.

COMMUNIST MINORITY DICTATORSHIP AND ILLEGAL WORK*

The victory of Socialism (as the first stage of Communism) over capitalism requires that the proletariat, as the only really revolutionary class, shall fulfil the three following tasks. First,—overthrow the exploiters, primarily the bourgeoisie as the principal economic and politic representatives of the

---

*From V. I. Lenin, *Theses on the Fundamental Tasks of the Second Congress of the Communist International* (July 4, 1920) from *Selected Works,* Vol. X, pp. 163–165, 169–170, 172–174. Reprinted by permission of International Publishers Co. Copyright © 1938.

latter; utterly rout them; suppress their resistance; make it utterly impossible for them to attempt to restore the yoke of capital and wage slavery. Second—win over and bring under the leadership of the revolutionary vanguard of the proletariat, of its Communist Party, not only the whole of the proletariat, or the overwhelming, the enormous majority of the latter, but also the whole mass of toilers and those exploited by capital; educate, organise, train and discipline them in the very process of the supremely bold and ruthlessly firm struggle against the exploiters; tear this overwhelming majority of the population in all capitalist countries from its dependence on the bourgeoisie; imbue it by means of its practical experience with confidence in the leading role of the proletariat and of its revolutionary vanguard. Third—neutralise, or render harmless, the inevitable vacillation between the bourgeoisie and the proletariat, between bourgeois democracy and Soviet power, of the class of small proprietors in agriculture, industry and commerce—which is still fairly numerous in nearly all advanced countries, although it comprises the minority of the population—as well as the stratum of intellectuals, office employees, etc., which corresponds to this class.

The first and second tasks are independent tasks, each requiring its own special methods of action toward the exploiters and toward the exploited. The third task emerges from the first two and merely requires the skilful, timely and flexible combination of the first and second types of method in accordance with the concrete circumstances in each separate case of vacillation.

In the concrete situation which has been created by militarism, imperialism, all over the world, and most of all in the most advanced, powerful, most enlightened and free capitalist countries, the strangulation of colonies and weak countries, the world imperialist butchery and the Versailles "Peace"—the very thought of peacefully subordinating the capitalists to the will of the majority of the exploited, of the peaceful, reformist transition to Socialism is not only extreme philistine stupidity, but also downright deception of the workers, the embellishment of capitalist wage slavery, concealment of the truth. The truth is that the bourgeoisie, even the most educated and democratic, now no longer hesitates to resort to any fraud or crime, to massacre millions of workers and peasants in order to save the private ownership of the means of production. Only the violent overthrow of the bourgeoisie, the confiscation of its property, the destruction of the whole of the bourgeois state apparatus from top to bottom—parliamentary, judicial, military, bureaucratic, administrative, municipal, etc., right up to the very wholesale deportation or internment of the most dangerous and stubborn exploiters—putting them under strict surveillance in order to combat inevitable attempts to resist and to restore capitalist slavery—only such measures can ensure the real subordination of the whole class of exploiters. . . .

The victory over capitalism requires a proper correlation between the leading, Communist, Party, the revolutionary class—the proletariat—and the masses, *i.e.,* all the toilers and exploited. The Communist Party alone, if it is really the vanguard of the revolutionary class, if it really contains all its best representatives, if it consists of fully conscious and loyal Communists who have been educated and hardened by the experience of the persistent revolutionary struggle, if this Party has succeeded in linking itself inseparably with the whole life of its class, and through it, with the whole mass of exploited, and if it has succeeded in completely winning the confidence of this class and this mass—such a Party alone is capable of leading the proletariat in the most ruthless, decisive and final struggle against all the forces of capitalism. On the other hand, only under the leadership of such a Party can the proletariat display the full force of its revolutionary onslaught and neutralise the inevitable apathy and sometimes resistance of the small minority of the aristocracy of labour, the old trade union and co-operative leaders, etc., who have been corrupted by capitalism—only then will it be able to display its whole might, which is immeasurably greater than the proportion of the population it represents owing to the very economic structure of capitalist society. Finally, only after they have been actually emancipated from the yoke of the bourgeoisie and of the bourgeois state apparatus, only after they have obtained the opportunity of organising

in their Soviets in a really free (from the exploiters) manner, can the masses, *i.e.,* all the toilers and the exploited, for the first time in history, display all the initiative and energy of tens of millions of people who have been crushed by capitalism. Only when the Soviets have become the sole state apparatus is it possible really to secure the participation in the work of administration of the whole mass of exploited, ninety-nine hundredths of whom even under the most enlightened and free bourgeois democracy were actually debarred from taking part in the work of administration. Only in the Soviets do the masses of exploited really begin to learn, not from booklets, but from their own practical experience, the work of Socialist construction, of creating a new social discipline, a free union of free workers.

The dictatorship of the proletariat is the exercise of the fullest leadership of all the toilers and exploited, who are oppressed, downtrodden, crushed, intimidated, disunited and deceived by the capitalist class, by the only class that has been trained by the whole history of capitalism for such a leading role. Hence, preparation for the dictatorship of the proletariat must be started everywhere and immediately with the following method among others.

In all organisations without exception—unions and associations, primarily proletarian, and also organisations of the non-proletarian, toiling and exploited masses (political, industrial, military, cooperative, educational, sports, etc., etc.), groups or nuclei of Communists should be formed—mainly open groups, but also secret groups, which should be obligatory in every case when their suppression, or the arrest or deportation of their members by the bourgeoisie may be expected—and these nuclei, closely connected with each other and with the Party centre, interchanging their experiences, carrying on work of agitation, propaganda and organisation, adapting themselves to absolutely all spheres of public life, absolutely to all varieties and subdivisions of the toiling masses, must systematically train themselves, and the Party, and the class, and the masses, by means of this diversified work.

In this it is extremely important to work out in a practical manner the various necessary methods of work, on the one hand, in relation to the "leaders" or to the "responsible representatives," who, very often, are hopelessly corrupted by petty-bourgeois and imperialist prejudices; these "leaders" must be ruthlessly exposed and driven out of the working class movement; and on the other hand, in relation to the masses, who, particularly after the imperialist slaughter, are for the most part inclined to pay heed to and assimilate the doctrine that the leadership of the proletariat is necessary as the only way out of capitalist slavery; we must learn to approach the masses with special patience and caution in order to be able to understand the specific and peculiar features of the psychology of every stratum, profession, etc., of these masses.

CHAPTER THIRTY

NIETZSCHE

The western traditions of rationalism, faith, and love never have in the past, and now are not, consistently or completely enunciated. At any point in time, western civilization seems a rich kaleidoscope of motley colors, shapes, and figures. First one root of western culture and thought, and then another, plays a more dominant role.

Almost all modern political theorists have emphasized aspects of the western tradition, and in so doing have helped to guide and configure it for future generations. Utilitarianism, for example, is certainly a rationalist philosophy, and its emphasis on the greatest happiness of the greatest number reflects the Christian love ethic. Further, utilitarianism's emphasis on individuals' equality ultimately is based upon Jewish monotheism to the extent the fatherhood of God makes all men and women equal brothers and sisters.

Marxism, too, draws much from the western tradition. Like utilitarianism, Marxism emphasizes equality, although—also like utilitarianism—it no longer bases this equality in a religious outlook of the world. Marxism has, further, emphasized reason; indeed, it claims to be "scientific." And, Marxism even draws from the Christian conception of love, to the extent that the ideal society of Marxian thinkers were able to be realized, though it must be admitted that in practice Marxist activists have appeared to be as much motivated by hatred of the bourgeoisie as love of their fellowman.

It is unusual, then, for the western traditions to be completely absent from a thinker's or school's work. It is even more unusual for them to be renounced. Yet, particularly during the last part of the nineteenth, and first part of the twentieth, centuries, thinkers arose who repudiated all western traditions.

The tangled thought of Friedrich Nietzsche (1844–1900) is perhaps best unravelled starting from his famous statement, "God is dead." Nietzsche saw western society at a full stop and sought the "revaluation of all values"—a new moral order. What had come before was worthless, partially because of Darwinian theories showing man's descent not from Adam, but from animals. What was required were new moral concepts to fill the gap left by the departure of the old. Nietzsche tried to fill the gap.

It is important when approaching Nietzsche to separate the myths that have sprung up about him from his actual thought though it is the myths that have had the most practical significance. He was born in Prussia and named after King Friedrich Wilhelm IV of Prussia, because he was born on the same birthday. Nietzsche was raised in a pious Protestant background as the only male in a home comprised of his grandmother, mother, two aunts, and sister, as well as himself, his father having gone insane and then died in 1849. Nietzsche was a brilliant student. As a young man at school away from his family, he became an atheist. At the University of Bonn and then at Leipzig, he studied philology—in his case, emphasizing ancient Greek literature. Though as a philologist he was a lover of words, he was no philogynist—that is, lover of women.

In 1869, before he had even received his doctorate, Nietzsche was appointed a professor of classical philology at the University of Basel. He served in this position for ten years, before ill health forced him to resign. For much of his tortured existence, he suffered from migraine headaches and vomiting, and used drugs (including opium) to relieve the pain. In 1889, he went insane—most probably from syphilis—while watching a horse being flogged, though he had shown signs of significant mental instability for some time before this. He pitifully lasted eleven years before dying.

Nietzsche's attitude toward the great German composer Richard Wagner indicates his outlook on life as well as unstable personality. At first, Nietzsche thought Wagner was the salvation of German culture and became an intimate friend of his. Later, he thought Wagner had become corrupted by fame, and in opposition to proclaiming the will to power of the true, atheistic aristocrat, settled for the approbation of the world through more Christian, renunciative, decadent, and romantic work. Nietzsche ended the relationship.

Nietzsche myths were started in part by Nietzsche himself. While he sought a new sort of aristocracy of supermen or above-men who were better than others, not by birth, but by their being, he found it necessary himself to attempt to identify with the older aristocracy. He (untruly) claimed descent from Polish nobility, and even his great, handle-bar mustache has been held to be an affectation of his desire to elevate his origins, presumably emphasizing a Polish and noble appearance.

The Nietzsche legend was started in earnest following his insanity, primarily by his sister. Elisabeth Forster-Nietzsche had been married to a virulent anti-Semite, and she edited and arranged her brother's substantial unpublished work in line with the philosophy of her late husband. In her compilation of Nietzsche's notes which were published as *The Will to Power* (1906, second edition), Elisabeth chose, for example, a four-line draft to organize the writings that included a heading referring, to "Breeding," though her brother had discarded this draft.

All philosophers are subject to interpretation, and Nietzsche more than most. He was a superb writing stylist and sometimes chose form over content. Much of his writing is in aphorisms, and these, too, conceal as much as reveal his thought. Moreover, Nietzsche considered himself to have had three stages in his thought, and he wrote on a wide variety of topics—from ancient Greece to Richard Wagner to the revaluation of all values. Finally, his last works were written when he was approaching insanity, and their reliability is therefore sometimes questioned. His intellectual autobiography—*Ecce Homo* (1908), itself a reference to Pilate's introduction of Christ—for example, written in his final sane months, contains chapter headings "Why I Am So Wise," "Why I Am So Clever," and "Why I Write Such Excellent Books," surely indicating impending collapse.

Three core Nietzschean concepts based on the proposition that God is dead are *eternal recurrence,* the *superman or above-man,* and the *will to power.* By eternal recurrence, Nietzsche meant that—as the energy in the universe is finite—every possible configuration of reality must have been experienced in the past and will be experienced again in the future. Life is, thus, part of a cosmic drama that will be played over and over again. In a way, eternal recurrence is Nietzsche's substitute for the death of God and the closing of heaven's gates. Although humans may not live forever, they do gain a measure of immortality through time's endless cycles. The influence of eastern thought, transmitted to Nietzsche through Arthur Schopenhauer, is evident here.

The superman or above-man is the ultimate goal of civilized existence. The term "superman" or "above-man" is a translation of the German "übermensch," which can have several meanings, including the ruling man, overman, and higher man. Nietzsche also means by *übermensch* the man who overcomes the insignificant man within himself. The sources for the superman or above-man were several. Darwin's theory of evolution suggested to Nietzsche the idea of humanity as an evolving species, although Nietzsche emphatically rejected the superman or above-man as the end result of a biological process, but rather of a civilizing one. Another source for the superman or above-man was the traditional aristocratic ideal. A final source was Nietzsche's focus on the individual, albeit a focus on only a very few individuals—the superior beings. In a sense, the superman or above-man is a spiritualized form of Darwinism, where the focus is not biological.

Supermen or above-men are worth incomparably more than the mass of mere insignificant men. Indeed, the difference between the superman or above-man and the ordinary man is greater than the difference between ordinary men and animals. Because of this gap, there is no morality that can, should, or will bind the superman or above-man. Nietzsche is scornful of religions or philosophies that posit human equality—rather, humanity is inherently absolutely unequal. He thus despised Christianity (though not necessarily Christ), and considered the utilitarian formula of the greatest happiness for the greatest number to be ridiculous, implying that the interests of all should be considered equally. John Stuart Mill received his special wrath; Nietzsche called him, "that blockhead." The superman or above-man does not hesitate to look reality straight in the eye, and to separate the chaff of common-place opinion from the wheat of truth.

"Wherever I found a living thing, there found I the Will of Power." This is a strong statement, if not a true one, and follows from the death of God and the existence of superior beings. In a universe bereft of absolute moral purpose, inhabited by supermen or above-men, what transitory goal can there be, other than the imposition of the will of the higher ones over the lesser ones? Will is what gives such a universe purpose. This may not be most people's ethical value, but it was Nietzsche's.

Nietzsche was against most preceding thinkers. He opposed Kant and Hegel, because, in his opinion, they perverted reason to attempt to reconcile it with Christian principles, which Nietzsche thought impossible as well as undesirable. He opposed Rousseau and the entire romantic movement because of their emphasis on the nobility of the brute: Nietzsche believed right culture was essential to producing the superman or above-man—the one who justifies humanity and life.

In the early twentieth century, Nietzsche was used, whether fairly or not, as a spiritual progenitor of "the children of darkness" (in Reinhold Niebuhr's famous title). Nietzsche's criticism is directed against not just this or that detail of his age, but against the assumptions and values of rationalism and liberalism in whatever form they appeared—politics, religion, economics, philosophy. As such, it is important to consider his practical impact. Nietzsche disdained the human race in general, whom he contemptuously called "slaves," "herd," or "mass." In democracy (mere majority rule), in particular, he sees nothing but the triumph of slave morality, which had started with the Jews and was transmitted to the modern world through Christianity.

Democracy is, according to Nietzsche, the destruction of the aristocratic values of power, beauty, and authority through a mass conspiracy of moralizing weaklings who erect a new, and contrary, set of values—that "the poor, the weak, the lowly, are alone the good." This contempt for democracy, however, should not be interpreted as support for a conservative status quo, for he as much opposes a conservative order that panders to the masses or stifles the individuality of superior men as a democracy that smothers supermen or above-men.

Nietzsche's *Genealogy of Morals* (1887) contains a famous description of the kind of men whom he provisionally admired as the true aristocrats. In dealing with each other, these individuals display consideration, loyalty, self-control, delicacy, and friendship. Outside of their own country, however, they behave "not much better than beasts of prey which have been let loose. They enjoy their freedom from all social control, they feel that in the wilderness they can give vent with impunity to that tension which is produced by the enclosure and imprisonment in the peace of society, they *revert* to the innocence of the beast-of-prey conscience, like jubilant monsters, who perhaps come from a ghostly bout of murder, arson, rape, and torture, with bravado and a moral equanimity, as though merely some wild student's prank had been played, perfectly convinced that the poets have now an ample theme to sing and celebrate. It is impossible not to recognize at the core of all these aristocratic races the beast of prey; the magnificent *blond beast,* avidly rampant for spoil and victory."

The "decline of humanity" is seen by Nietzsche in the attempt to tame and civilize the beast of prey in those men in whom the beast exists. Democracy is the rule of the slaves over the masters, and is the political consummation of the disease which destroys those who "still say 'yes' to life," and elevates those who constantly say "nay" to life—the low, the weak, the cunning. Nietzsche's exaltation of the beast of prey should not be taken as support for the "natural man," as Rousseau's noble savage lacks the civilized qualities which are necessary for the true aristocrat. In Nietzsche's terms, both the Dionysian (natural) and Apollonian (civilized) elements in human nature are required.

Nietzsche's political philosophy is essentially anarchical. He opposes any rule of law, whether imposed by many or few, which constrains the will of the chosen few. At the same time, he primarily vents his spleen against rule by the many, for rule by the few has at least the possibility of being on the right track (though it rarely is in practice). Although he was no German nationalist, and in fact considered himself a "good European," Nietzsche thought that of all German social groups, the Prussian officer was the least affected by the infiltrating poisons of Christianity, democracy, rationalism, liberalism, and socialism. "The future of German culture rests with the sons of Prussian officers," he held.

The influence of Nietzsche on the Nazis is disputed, and it is undoubtedly the case that his influence was as much indirect as direct, and fostered more by others (particularly his sister) than by what he intended himself. Nonetheless, a work of his that cultivated the growth of the Nazi mentality in Germany was *The Antichrist* (1902). Nietzsche's attack on Christianity was the first in modern times to aim at the morals of Christianity rather than its religion and theology, as had been done by so many opponents of Christianity. Unlike many modern thinkers who were opposed, or indifferent, to religious faith in Christianity—yet fully accepted its moral teachings—Nietzsche was relatively indifferent to the religious aspects of Christianity and concentrated all his opposition on Christian ethics and morals. Of all the creeds that have sought to undermine the natural order (the few strong ruling the many weak), none has had, according to Nietzsche, such disastrous effects as Christianity. "The weak and the failures shall perish: first principle of *our* love of man": This Nietzschean ethic is completely antithetical to Christian ethics. He sought an ethic that is, as he stated in the title of another of his books, "beyond good and evil," that is, beyond traditional good and evil.

While he was not especially or consistently a racist from a biological perspective (he called anti-Semitism the "German disease"), what aroused Nietzsche's ire about Christianity above all was that it was able to corrupt the most aristocratic of races, the peoples of northern Europe. Nietzsche could not forgive the Nordics that they were unable to resist Christian monotheism, "this hybrid creature of decay, nonentity, concept and contradiction, in which all the instincts of decadence, all the cowardices and languors of the soul find their sanction." Earlier, the Christians ("bloodsuckers," "parasites") had succeeded in demolishing another great race and empire, the Roman Empire. In both cases, Nietzsche claimed, Christianity merely destroyed, without showing a capacity to build anything new.

All of these sentiments were incorporated into the process of moral disintegration that raged through Germany during the first half of the twentieth century. Nazi propagandists integrally accepted the Nietzschean interpretation of Christianity as a revolt of what is low and unlovely in the herd against the aristocratic virtues of power, honor, and war. Nietzsche also supplied German anti-Christianism with a new argument: Christianity was in fact a Jewish conspiracy to dominate the world through the doctrines of monotheism, immortality of the soul, and equality before God. St. Paul particularly attracted Nietzsche's wrath; he was the "eternal Jew," who recognized how, by the help of Christianity, a "universal conflagration could be kindled." In the Middle Ages, Jews were persecuted because they rejected Christianity. Though not an anti-Semite, Nietzsche established in Germany the tradition of anti-Jewish persecution on the grounds that the Jews had created Christianity.

In Nietzsche's most famous work—*Thus Spake Zarathustra* (1883–1885)— he developed the concept of superman or above-man as the new type. Without giving a very exact picture of this new breed of man who was to surpass the man hitherto known, Nietzsche makes it clear that his coming would make a clean slate of all the traditional values of the herd men. Supermen or above-men would form a new class of masters who would rule over the lowly herd.

The conception of superman or above-man was intended partially by Nietzsche to indicate the need for more individuality and personality in the face of increasing standardization. There is value in the Nietzschean ideal of someone who becomes supremely himself by overcoming what is weak or low in himself. Yet, to the average German of his time and for some time afterward, the Nietzschean view of superior beings heralded the coming of the German master race—the new race of superior beings—to world power. Nietzsche himself would no doubt have abhorred the mass of any nation, perhaps especially the Germans, collectively aggrandizing themselves. But he who preached the revaluation of all values could hardly have complained if some who came after him revalued his master man into the master race.

In the sense of helping to create an attitude, Nietzsche more than any other single German thinker aided the preparation of the era of nihilism in which the code of the beast of prey was to prevail over the morality of the west. Twice within fifty years of his death, Germany went to war against the world, and the second time almost succeeded. German soldiers took Nietzsche's books to war with them as an American or British soldier might have taken the Bible. During the Nazi era, a huge (and hideous) museum was built in his honor, and Hitler for a number of years had his picture taken with a bust of Nietzsche in the background. Nietzsche's sister lived to know Hitler, and his insanity was seen by some Nazis as a kind of apotheosis.

Nietzsche's writings are mostly non-political, though of immense political consequence. He was essentially a moralist, though a perverse one (indeed, he called himself an "immoralist"). The superman or above-man was *not* a political leader or hero. One of Nietzsche's few goals that could be termed political was a united Europe. Prophetically, he suggested that Europe would experience the bloodiest wars before it obtained a united form. His prophecy of European wars added to his appeal among militarists, as well as cultivated the mystique that grew up around him. He held that wars were inevitable because of the loss of values that accompany the death of God. Neither liberal nor conservative, Nietzsche's political thought might best be characterized as Machiavellian. Some of the Nazis' glombing on to Nietzsche was the result of their desire to establish intellectual credibility for their program. Few other philosophers could do.

Nietzsche wrote in brilliant poetic imagery enriched by years of suffering and struggle. This gave his work a force and vigor that makes it appeal to readers sheerly as literature. He had substantial impact on psychoanalysis and existentialism, and continues to exert huge impact on recent (especially French) postmodernist and poststructuralist thought. One of his books—*The Twilight of the Idols* (1889)—was subtitled *How One Philosophizes with a Hammer*. Ultimately, Nietzsche was more of a destroyer than builder.

I *Thus Spake Zarathustra**

WHEN Zarathustra was thirty years old, he left his home and the lake of his home, and went into the mountains. There he enjoyed his spirit and his solitude, and for ten years did not weary of it. But at last his heart changed,—and rising one morning with the rosy dawn, he went before the sun, and spake thus unto it:

Thou great star! What would be thy happiness if thou hadst not those for whom thou shinest!

For ten years hast thou climbed hither unto my cave: thou wouldst have wearied of thy light and of the journey, had it not been for me, mine eagle, and my serpent.

But we awaited thee every morning, took from thee thine overflow, and blessed thee for it.

Lo! I am weary of my wisdom, like the bee that hath gathered too much honey; I need hands outstretched to take it.

I would fain bestow and distribute, until the wise have once more become joyous in their folly, and the poor happy in their riches.

Therefore must I descend into the deep: as thou doest in the evening, when thou goest behind the sea, and givest light also to the nether-world, thou exuberant star!

Like thee must I *go down,* as men say, to whom I shall descend.

Bless me, then, thou tranquil eye, that canst behold even the greatest happiness without envy!

Bless the cup that is about to overflow, that the water may flow golden out of it, and carry everywhere the reflection of thy bliss!

Lo! This cup is again going to empty itself, and Zarathustra is again going to be a man.

Thus began Zarathustra's down-going.

Zarathustra went down the mountain alone, no one meeting him. When he entered the forest, however, there suddenly stood before him an old man, who had left his holy cot to seek roots. And thus spake the old man to Zarathustra:

"No stranger to me is this wanderer: many years ago passed he by. Zarathustra he was called; but he hath altered.

Then thou carriedst thine ashes into the mountains: wilt thou now carry thy fire into the valleys? Fearest thou not the incendiary's doom?

Yea, I recognize Zarathustra. Pure is his eye, and no loathing lurketh about his mouth. Goeth he not along like a dancer?

Altered is Zarathustra; a child hath Zarathustra become; an awakened one is Zarathustra: what will thou do in the land of the sleepers?

As in the sea hast thou lived in solitude, and it hath borne thee up. Alas, wilt thou now go ashore? Alas, wilt thou again drag thy body thyself?"

Zarathustra answered: "I love mankind."

"Why," said the saint, "did I go into the forest and the desert? Was it not because I loved men far too well?

Now I love God: Men, I do not love. Man is a thing too imperfect for me. Love to man would be fatal to me."

Zarathustra answered: "What spake I of love! I am bringing gifts unto men."

"Give them nothing," said the saint. "Take rather part of their load, and carry it along with them—that will be most agreeable unto them: if only it be agreeable unto thee!

---

*From Friedrich Nietzsche, *Thus Spake Zarathustra* (1883; trans. Thomas Common, The Modern Library, 1941). By permission.

If, however, thou wilt give unto them, give them no more than an alms, and let them also beg for it!"

"No," replied Zarathustra, "I give no alms. I am not poor enough for that."

The saint laughed at Zarathustra, and spake thus: "Then see to it that they accept thy treasures! They are distrustful of anchorites, and do not believe that we come with gifts.

The fall of our footsteps ringeth too hollow through their streets. And just as at night, when they are in bed and hear a man abroad long before sunrise, so they ask themselves concerning us: Where goeth the thief?

Go not to men, but stay in the forest! Go rather to the animals! Why not be like me—a bear amongst bears, a bird amongst birds?"

"And what doeth the saint in the forest?" asked Zarathustra.

The saint answered: "I make hymns and sing them; and in making hymns I laugh and weep and mumble: thus do I praise God.

With singing, weeping, laughing, and mumbling do I praise the God who is my God. But what dost thou bring us as a gift?"

When Zarathustra had heard these words, he bowed to the saint and said: "What should I have to give thee! Let me rather hurry hence lest I take aught away from thee!"—And thus they parted from one another, the old man and Zarathustra, laughing like schoolboys.

When Zarathustra was alone, however, he said to his heart: "Could it be possible! This old saint in the forest hath not yet heard of it, that *God is dead!"*

When Zarathustra arrived at the nearest town which adjoineth the forest, he found many people assembled in the market-place; for it had been announced that a rope-dancer would give a performance. And Zarathustra spake thus unto the people:

I teach you the Superman. Man is something that is to be surpassed. What have ye done to surpass man?

All beings hitherto have created something beyond themselves: and ye want to be the ebb of that great tide, and would rather go back to the beast than surpass man?

What is the ape to man? A laughing-stock, a thing of shame. And just the same shall man be to the Superman: a laughing-stock, a thing of shame.

Ye have made your way from the worm to man, and much within you is still worm. Once were ye apes, and even yet man is more of an ape than any of the apes.

Even the wisest among you is only a disharmony and hybrid of plant and phantom. But do I bid you become phantoms or plants?

Lo, I teach you the Superman!

The Superman is the meaning of the earth. Let your will say: The Superman *shall be* the meaning of the earth!

I conjure you, my brethren, *remain true to the earth,* and believe not those who speak unto you of superearthly hopes! Poisoners are they, whether they know it or not.

Despisers of life are they, decaying ones and poisoned ones themselves, of whom the earth is weary: so away with them!

Once blasphemy against God was the greatest blasphemy; but God died, and therewith also those blasphemers. To blaspheme the earth is now the dreadfulest sin, and to rate the heart of the unknowable higher than the meaning of the earth!

Once the soul looked contemptuously on the body, and then that contempt was the supreme thing—the soul wished the body meagre, ghastly, and famished. Thus it thought to escape from the body and the earth.

Oh, that soul was itself meagre, ghastly, and famished; and cruelty was the delight of that soul!

But ye, also, my brethren, tell me: What doth your body say about your soul? Is your soul not poverty and pollution and wretched self-complacency?

Verily, a polluted stream is man. One must be a sea, to receive a polluted stream without becoming impure.

Lo, I teach you the Superman: he is that sea; in him can your great contempt be submerged.

What is the greatest thing ye can experience? It is the hour of great contempt. The hour in which even your happiness becometh loathsome unto you, and so also your reason and virtue.

The hour when ye say: "What good is my happiness! It is poverty and pollution and wretched self-complacency. But my happiness should justify existence itself!"

The hour when ye say: "What good is my reason! Doth it long for knowledge as the lion for his food? It is poverty and pollution and wretched self-complacency!"

The hour when ye say: "What good is my virtue! As yet it hath not made me passionate. How weary I am of my good and my bad! It is all poverty and pollution and wretched self-complacency!"

The hour when ye say: "What good is my justice! I do not see that I am fervor and fuel. The just, however, are fervor and fuel!"

The hour when we say: "What good is my pity! Is not pity the cross on which he is nailed who loveth man? But my pity is not a crucifixion."

Have ye ever spoken thus? Have ye ever cried thus? Ah! would that I had heard you crying thus!

It is not your sin—it is your self-satisfaction that crieth unto heaven; your very sparingness in sin crieth unto heaven!

Where is the lightning to lick you with its tongue? Where is the frenzy with which ye should be inoculated?

Lo, I teach you the Superman: He is that lightning, he is that frenzy!—

When Zarathustra had thus spoken, one of the people called out: "We have now heard enough of the rope-dancer; it is time now for us to see him!" And all the people laughed at Zarathustra. But the rope-dancer, who thought the words applied to him, began his performance.

Zarathustra, however, looked at the people and wondered. Then he spake thus:

Man is a rope stretched between the animal and the Superman—a rope over an abyss.

A dangerous crossing, a dangerous wayfaring, a dangerous looking-back, a dangerous trembling and halting.

What is great in man is that he is a bridge and not a goal: what is lovable in man is that he is an *over-going* and a *down-going*.

I love those that know not how to live except as down-goers, for they are the over-goers.

I love the great despisers, because they are the great adorers, and arrows of longing for the other shore.

I love those who do not first seek a reason beyond the stars for going down and being sacrifices, but sacrifice themselves to the earth, that the earth of the Superman may hereafter arrive.

I love him who liveth in order to know, and seeketh to know in order that the Superman may hereafter live. Thus seeketh he his own down-going.

I love him who laboreth and inventeth, that he may build the house for the Superman, and prepare for him earth, animal, and plant: for thus seeketh he his own down-going.

I love him who loveth his virtue: for virtue is the will to down-going, and an arrow of longing.

I love him who reserveth no share of spirit for himself, but wanteth to be wholly the spirit of his virtue: thus walketh he as spirit over the bridge.

I love him who maketh his virtue his inclination and destiny: thus, for the sake of his virtue, he is willing to live on, or live no more.

I love him who desireth not too many virtues. One virtue is more of a virtue than two, because it is more of a knot for one's destiny to cling to.

I love him whose soul is lavish, who wanteth no thanks and doth not give back: for he always bestoweth, and desireth not to keep for himself.

I love him who is ashamed when the dice fall in his favor, and who then asketh: "Am I a dishonest player?"—for he is willing to succumb.

I love him who scattereth golden words in advance of his deeds, and always doeth more than he promiseth: for he seeketh his own down-going.

I love him who justifieth the future ones, and redeemeth the past ones: for he is willing to succumb through the present ones.

I love him who chasteneth his God, because he loveth his God: for he must succumb through the wrath of his God.

I love him whose soul is deep even in the wounding, and may succumb through a small matter: thus goeth he willingly over the bridge.

I love him whose soul is so overfull that he forgetteth himself, and all things are in him: Thus all things become his down-going.

I love him who is of a free spirit and a free heart: thus is his head only the bowels of his heart; his heart, however, causeth his down-going.

I love all who are like heavy drops falling one by one out of the dark cloud that lowereth over man: They herald the coming of the lightning, and succumb as heralds.

Lo, I am a herald of the lightning, and a heavy drop out of the cloud: the lightning, however, is the *Superman*.—

When Zarathustra had spoken these words, he again looked at the people, and was silent. "There they stand," said he to his heart; "there they laugh: they understand me not; I am not the mouth for these ears.

Must one first batter their ears, that they may learn to hear with their eyes? Must one clatter like kettledrums and penitential preachers? Or do they only believe the stammerer?

They have something whereof they are proud. What do they call it, that which maketh them proud? Culture, they call it; it distinguisheth them from the goatherds.

They dislike, therefore, to hear of 'contempt' of themselves. So I will appeal to their pride.

I will speak unto them of the most contemptible thing that, however, is *the last man!*"

And thus spake Zarathustra unto the people:

It is time for man to fix his goal. It is time for man to plant the germ of his highest hope.

Still is his soil rich enough for it. But that soil will one day be poor and exhausted, and no lofty tree will any longer be able to grow thereon.

Alas! there cometh the time when man will no longer launch the arrow of his longing beyond man—and the string of his bow will have unlearned to whizz!

I tell you: one must still have chaos in one, to give birth to a dancing star. I tell you: ye have still chaos in you.

Alas! There cometh the time when man will no longer give birth to any star. Alas! There cometh the time of the most despicable man, who can no longer despise himself.

Lo! I show you *the last man*.

"What is love? What is creation? What is longing? What is a star?"—so asketh the last man and blinketh.

The earth hath then become small, and on it there hoppeth the last man who maketh everything small. His species is ineradicable like that of the ground-flea; the last man liveth longest.

"We have discovered happiness"—say the last men, and blink thereby.

They have left the regions where it is hard to live; for they need warmth. One still loveth one's neighbour and rubbeth against him; for one needeth warmth.

Turning ill and being distrustful, they consider sinful: they walk warily. He is a fool who still stumbleth over stones or men!

A little poison now and then: that maketh pleasant dreams. And much poison at last for a pleasant death.

One still worketh, for work is a pastime. But one is careful lest the pastime should hurt one.

One no longer becometh poor or rich; both are too burdensome. Who still wanteth to rule? Who still wanteth to obey? Both are too burdensome.

No shepherd, and one herd! Every one wanteth the same; every one is equal: he who hath other sentiments goeth voluntarily into the madhouse.

"Formerly all the world, was insane,"—say the subtlest of them and blink thereby.

They are clever, and know all that hath happened: so, there is no end to their raillery. People still fall out, but are soon reconciled—otherwise it spoileth their stomachs.

They have their little pleasures for the day, and their little pleasures for the night: but they have a regard for health.

"We have discovered happiness,"—say the last men, and blink thereby.—

And here ended the first discourse of Zarathustra, which is also called "The Prologue": for at this point the shouting and mirth of the multitude interrupted him. "Give us this last man, O Zarathustra,"—they called out—"make us into these last men! Then will we make thee a present of the Superman!" And all the people exulted and smacked their lips. Zarathustra, however, turned sad, and said to his heart:

"They understand me not: I am not the mouth for these ears.

Too long, perhaps, have I lived in the mountains; too much have I hearkened unto the brooks and trees: now do I speak unto them as unto the goarherds.

Calm is my soul, and clear, like the mountains in the morning. But they think me cold, and a mocker with terrible jests.

And now do they look at me and laugh: and while they laugh they hate me too. There is ice in their laughter."

II   *The Antichrist**

REVALUATION OF ALL VALUES

This book belongs to the very few. Perhaps not one of them is even living yet. Maybe they will be the readers who understand my *Zarathustra:* How *could* I mistake myself for one of those for whom there are ears even now? Only the day after tomorrow belongs to me. Some are born posthumously.

The conditions under which I am understood, and then of *necessity*—I know them only too well. One must be honest in matters of the spirit to the point of hardness before one can even endure my seriousness and my passion. One must be skilled in living on mountains—seeing the wretched ephemeral babble of politics and national self-seeking *beneath* oneself. One must have become indifferent; one must never ask if the truth is useful or if it may prove our undoing. The predilection of strength for questions for which no one today has the courage; the courage for the *forbidden;* the predestination to the labyrinth. An experience of seven solitudes. New ears for new music. New eyes for what is most distant. A new conscience for truths that have so far remained mute. *And* the will to the economy of the great style: keeping our strength, our *enthusiasm* in harness. Reverence for oneself; love of oneself; unconditional freedom before oneself.

Well then! Such men alone are my readers, my right readers, my predestined readers: what matter the *rest?* The rest—that is merely mankind. One must be above mankind in strength, in *loftiness* of soul—in contempt.

ATTEMPT AT A CRITIQUE OF CHRISTIANITY

Let us face ourselves. We are Hyperboreans; we know very well how far off we live. "Neither by land nor by sea will you find the way to the Hyperboreans"—Pindar already knew this about us. Beyond the north, ice, and death—*our* life, *our* happiness. We have discovered happiness, we know the way, we have found the exit out of the labyrinth of thousands of years. Who *else* has found it? Modern man perhaps? "I have got lost; I am everything that has got lost," sighs modern man.

This modernity was our sickness: lazy peace, cowardly compromise, the whole virtuous uncleanliness of the modern Yes and No. This tolerance and *largeur* of the heart, which "forgives" all because it "understands" all, is *sirocco* for us. Rather live in the ice than among modern virtues and other south winds!

We were intrepid enough, we spared neither ourselves nor others; but for a long time we did not know where to turn with our intrepidity. We became gloomy, we were called fatalists. *Our fatum*—the abundance, the tension, the damming of strength. We thirsted for lightning and deeds and were most remote from the happiness of the weakling, "resignation." In our atmosphere was a thunderstorm; the nature we are became dark—*for we saw no way.* Formula for our happiness: a Yes, a No, a straight line, a goal.

What is good? Everything that heightens the feeling of power in man, the will to power, power itself.

What is bad? Everything that is born of weakness.

What is happiness? The feeling that power is *growing,* that resistance is overcome.

---

*From Friedrich Nietzsche, *The Antichrist* (1895; trans. Walter Kaufman in *The Portable Nietzsche,* Viking Penguin, 1982). By permission.

Not contentedness but more power; not peace but war; not virtue but fitness (Renaissance virtue, *virtù,* virtue that is moraline-free).

The weak and the failures shall perish: first principle of *our* love of man. And they shall even be given every possible assistance.

What is more harmful than any vice? Active pity for all the failures and all the weak: Christianity.

The problem I thus pose is not what shall succeed mankind in the sequence of living beings (man is an *end*), but what type of man shall be *bred,* shall be *willed,* for being higher in value, worthier of life, more certain of a future.

Even in the past this higher type has appeared often—but as a fortunate accident, as an exception, never as something *willed.* In fact, this has been the type most dreaded—almost *the* dreadful—and from dread the opposite type was willed, bred, and *attained:* the domestic animal, the herd animal, the sick human animal—the Christian.

Mankind does *not* represent a development toward something better or stronger or higher in the sense accepted today. "Progress" is merely a modern idea, that is, a false idea. The European of today is vastly inferior in value to the European of the Renaissance: further development is altogether *not* according to any necessity in the direction of elevation, enhancement, or strength.

In another sense, success in individual cases is constantly encountered in the most widely different places and cultures: Here we really do find a *higher type,* which is, in relation to mankind as a whole, a kind of overman. Such fortunate accidents of great success have always been possible and *will* perhaps always be possible. And even whole families, tribes, or peoples may occasionally represent such a *bull's eye.*

Christianity should not be beautified and embellished: It has waged deadly war against this higher type of man; it has placed all the basic instincts of this type under the ban; and out of these instincts it has distilled evil and the Evil One: The strong man as the typically reprehensible man, the "reprobate." Christianity has sided with all that is weak and base, with all failures; it has made

an ideal of whatever *contradicts* the instinct of the strong life to preserve itself; it has corrupted the reason even of those strongest in spirit by teaching men to consider the supreme values of the spirit as something sinful, as something that leads into error—as temptations. The most pitiful example: The corruption of Pascal, who believed in the corruption of his reason through original sin when it had in fact been corrupted only by his Christianity.

It is a painful, horrible spectacle that has dawned on me: I have drawn back the curtain from the *corruption* of man. In my mouth, this word is at least free from one suspicion: that it might involve a moral accusation of man. It is meant—let me emphasize this once more—*moraline-free.* So much so that I experience this corruption most strongly precisely where men have so far aspired most deliberately to "virtue" and "godliness." I understand corruption, as you will guess, in the sense of decadence: it is my contention that all the values in which mankind now sums up its supreme desiderata are *decadence-values.*

I call an animal, a species, or an individual corrupt when it loses its instincts, when it chooses, when it prefers, what is disadvantageous for it. A history of "lofty sentiments," of the "ideals of mankind"—and it is possible that I shall have to write it—would almost explain too *why* man is so corrupt. Life itself is to my mind the instinct for growth, for durability, for an accumulation of forces, for *power:* Where the will to power is lacking there is decline. It is my contention that all the supreme values of mankind *lack* this will—that the values which are symptomatic of decline, *nihilistic* values, are lording it under the holiest names.

It is necessary to say whom we consider our antithesis: It is the theologians and whatever has theologians' blood in its veins—and that includes our whole philosophy.

Whoever has seen this catastrophe at close range or, better yet, been subjected to it and almost perished of it, will no longer consider it a joking matter (the free-thinking of our honorable natural scientists and physiologists is, to my mind, a joke: They lack passion in these matters, they do not suffer them as their passion and martyrdom). This poisoning is much more extensive than is generally supposed: I have found the theologians' instinctive arrogance wherever anyone today considers himself an "idealist"—wherever a right is assumed, on the basis of some higher origin, to look at reality from a superior and foreign vantage point.

The idealist, exactly like the priest, holds all the great concepts in his hand (and not only in his hand!); he plays them out with a benevolent contempt for the "understanding," the "senses," "honors," "good living," and "science"; he considers all that *beneath* him, as so many harmful and seductive forces over which "the spirit" hovers in a state of pure foritselfness—as if humility, chastity, poverty, or, in one word, *holiness,* had not harmed life immeasurably more than any horrors or vices. The pure spirit is the pure lie.

As long as the priest is considered a *higher* type of man—this *professional* negator, slanderer, and poisoner of life—there is no answer to the question: What *is* truth? For truth has been stood on its head when the conscious advocate of nothingness and negation is accepted as the representative of "truth."

Against this theologians' instinct I wage war: I have found its traces everywhere. Whoever has theologians' blood in his veins, sees all things in a distorted and dishonest perspective to begin with. The pathos which develops out of this condition calls itself *faith:* Closing one's eyes to oneself once and for all, lest one suffer the sight of incurable falsehood. This faulty perspective on all things is elevated into a morality, a virtue, a holiness; the good conscience is tied to faulty vision; and no *other* perspective is conceded any further value once one's own has been made sacrosanct with the names of "God," "redemption," and "eternity." I have dug up the theologians' instinct everywhere: It is the most widespread, really *subterranean,* form of falsehood found on earth.

Whatever a theologian feels to be true *must* be false: This is almost a criterion of truth. His most basic instinct of self-preservation forbids him to respect reality at any point or even to let it get a word in. Wherever the theologians' instinct extends, *value judgments* have been stood on their heads and the concepts of "true" and "false" are of necessity reversed: Whatever is most harmful to life is called "true"; whatever elevates it, enhances, affirms, justifies it, and makes it triumphant, is called "false." When theologians reach out for *power* through the "conscience" of princes (*or* of peoples), we need never doubt what really happens at bottom: the will to the end, the *nihilistic* will, wants power.

A critique of the *Christian conception of God* forces us to the same conclusion. A people that still believes in itself retains its own god. In him it reveres the conditions which let it prevail, its virtues: It projects its pleasure in itself, its feeling of power, into a being to whom one may offer thanks. Whoever is rich wants to give of his riches; a proud people needs a god: it wants to *sacrifice.* Under such conditions, religion is a form of thankfulness. Being thankful for himself, man needs a god. Such a god must be able to help and to harm, to be friend and enemy—he is admired whether good or destructive. The *anti-natural* castration of a god, to make him a god of the good alone, would here be contrary to everything desirable. The evil god is needed no less than the good god: After all, we do not owe our own existence to tolerance and humanitarianism.

What would be the point of a god who knew nothing of wrath, revenge, envy, scorn, cunning, and violence? who had perhaps never experienced the delightful *ardeurs* of victory and annihilation? No one would understand such a god: Why have him then?

To be sure, when a people is perishing, when it feels how its faith in the future and its hope of freedom are waning irrevocably, when submission begins to appear to it as the prime necessity and it becomes aware of the virtues of the subjugated as the conditions of self-preservation, then its god *has to* change too. Now he becomes a sneak, timid and modest; he counsels "peace of soul," hate-no-more, forbearance, even "love" of friend and enemy. He moralizes constantly, he crawls into the cave of every private virtue, he becomes god for everyman, he becomes a private person, a cosmopolitan.

Formerly, he represented a people, the strength of a people, everything aggressive and power-thirsty in the soul of a people; now he is merely the good god.

Indeed, there is no other alternative for gods: *either* they are the will to power, and they remain a people's gods, *or* the *incapacity* for power, and then they necessarily become *good*.

Wherever the will to power declines in any form, there is invariably also a physiological retrogression, decadence. The deity of decadence, gelded in his most virile virtues and instincts, becomes of necessity the god of the physiologically retrograde, of the weak. Of course, they do not *call* themselves the weak; they call themselves "the good."

No further hint is required to indicate the moments in history at which the dualistic fiction of a good and an evil god first became possible. The same instinct which prompts the subjugated to reduce their god to the "good-in-itself" also prompts them to eliminate all the good qualities from the god of their conquerors; they take revenge on their masters by turning their god into the *devil*. The *good* god and the devil—both abortions of decadence.

How can anyone today still submit to the simplicity of Christian theologians to the point of insisting with them that the development of the conception of God from the "God of Israel," the god of a people, to the Christian God, the quintessence of everything good, represents *progress?* Yet even Renan does this. As if Renan had the right to be simple-minded! After all, the opposite stares you in the face. When the presuppositions of *ascending* life, when everything strong, brave, masterful, and proud is eliminated from the conception of God; when he degenerates step by step into a mere symbol, a staff for the weary, a sheet-anchor for the drowning; when he becomes the god of the poor, the sinners, and the sick par excellence, and the attribute "Savior" or "Redeemer" remains in the end as the one essential attribute of divinity—just *what* does such a transformation signify? what, such a *reduction* of the divine?

To be sure, "the kingdom of God" has thus been enlarged. Formerly he had only his people, his "chosen" people. Then he, like his people, became a wanderer and went into foreign lands; and ever since, he has not settled down anywhere—until he finally came to feel at home anywhere, this great cosmopolitan—until "the great numbers" and half the earth were on his side. Nevertheless, the god of "the great numbers," the democrat among the gods, did not become a proud pagan god: He remained a Jew, he remained a god of nooks, the god of all the dark corners and places, of all the unhealthy quarters the world over!

His world-wide kingdom is, as ever, an underworld kingdom, a hospital, a *souterrain* kingdom, a ghetto kingdom. And he himself. So pale, so weak, so decadent. Even the palest of the pale were able to master him: our honorable metaphysicians those concept-albinos. They spun their webs around him until, hypnotized by their motions, he himself became a spider, another metaphysician. Now he, in turn, spun the world out of himself—*sub specie Spinozae*. Now he transfigured himself into something ever thinner and paler; he became an "ideal," he became "pure spirit," the "Absolute," the "thing-in-itself." The deterioration of a god: God became the "thing-in-itself."

The Christian conception of God—God as god of the sick, God as a spider, God as spirit—is one of the most corrupt conceptions of the divine ever attained on earth. It may even represent the low-water mark in the descending development of divine types. God degenerated into the *contradiction* of life, instead of being its transfiguration and eternal Yes! God as the declaration of war against life, against nature, against the will to live! God—the formula for every slander against "this world," for every lie about the "beyond"! God—the deification of nothingness, the will to nothingness pronounced holy!

That the strong races of northern Europe did not reject the Christian God certainly does no credit to their religious genius—not to speak of their taste. There is no excuse whatever for their failure to dispose of such a sickly and senile product of decadence. But a curse lies upon them for this failure: They have absorbed sickness, old age, and contradiction into all their instincts—and since then they have not *created* another god. Almost two thousand years—and not a single new god! But still, as if his existence were justified, as if he represented the ultimate and the maximum of the god-creating power, of the *creator spiritus* in man, this pitiful god of Christian monotono-theism! This hybrid product of decay, this mixture of zero, concept, and contradiction, in which all the instincts of decadence, all cowardices and wearinesses of the soul, find their sanction!

Here I merely touch on the problem of the *genesis* of Christianity. The *first* principle for its solution is: Christianity can be understood only in terms of the soil out of which it grew—it is *not* a counter-movement to the Jewish instinct, it is its very consequence, one inference more in its awe-inspiring logic. In the formula of the Redeemer: "Salvation is of the Jews." The *second* principle is: The psychological type of the Galilean is still recognizable; but only in its complete degeneration (which is at the same time a mutilation and an overloading with alien features) could it serve as that for which it has been used—as the type of a redeemer of mankind.

The Jews are the strangest people in world history because, confronted with the question whether to be or not to be, they chose, with a perfectly uncanny deliberateness, to be *at any price:* this price was the radical *falsification* of all nature, all naturalness, all reality, of the whole inner world as well as the outer. They defined themselves sharply *against* all the conditions under which a people had hitherto been able to live, been *allowed* to live; out of themselves they created a counterconcept to *natural* conditions: they turned religion, cult, morality, history, psychology, one after the other, into an incurable *contradiction to their natural values.* We encounter this same phenomenon once again and in immeasurably enlarged proportions, yet merely as a copy: The Christian church cannot make the slightest claim to originality when compared with the "holy people." That precisely is why the Jews are the *most catastrophic* people of world history: By their aftereffect they have made mankind so thoroughly false that even today the Christian can feel anti-Jewish without realizing that he himself is *the ultimate Jewish consequence.*

One should not be deceived: Great spirits are skeptics. Zarathustra is a skeptic.

Strength, *freedom* which is born of the strength and overstrength of the spirit, proves itself by skepticism. Men of conviction are not worthy of the least consideration in fundamental questions of value and disvalue. Convictions are prisons. Such men do not look far enough, they do not look *beneath* themselves: but to be permitted to join in the discussion of value and disvalue, one must see five hundred convictions *beneath* oneself—*behind* oneself.

A spirit who wants great things, who also wants the means to them, is necessarily a skeptic. Freedom from all kinds of convictions, to be able to see freely, is part of strength. Great passion, the ground and the power of his existence, even more enlightened, even more despotic than he is himself, employs his whole intellect; it makes him unhesitating; it gives him courage even for unholy means; under certain circumstances it does not begrudge him convictions. Conviction as a *means:* many things are attained only by means of a conviction. Great passion uses and uses up convictions, it does not succumb to them—it knows itself sovereign.

Conversely: The need for faith, for some kind of unconditional Yes and No, this Carlylism, if one will forgive me this word, is a need born of *weakness.* The man of faith, the "believer" of every kind, is necessarily a dependent man—one who cannot posit *himself* as an end, one who cannot posit any end at all by himself. The "believer" does not belong to *himself* he can only be a means, he must be *used up,* he requires somebody to use him up. His instinct gives the highest honor to a morality of self-abnegation; everything persuades him in this direction: his prudence, his experience, his vanity. Every kind of faith is itself an expression of self-abnegation, of self-alienation.

If one considers how necessary most people find something regulatory, which will bind them from without and tie them down; how compulsion, *slavery* in a higher sense, is the sole and ultimate condition under which the more weak-willed human being, woman in particular, can prosper—then one will also understand conviction, "faith." The man of conviction has his backbone in it. *Not* to see many things, to be impartial at no point, to be party through and through, to have a strict and necessary perspective in all questions of value—this alone makes it possible for this kind of human being to exist at all. But with this they are the opposite, the antagonists, of what is truthful—of truth.

The believer is not free to have any conscience at all for questions of "true" and "untrue": To have integrity on *this* point would at once destroy him. The pathological condition of his perspective turns the convinced into fanatics—Savonarola, Luther, Rousseau, Robespierre, Saint-Simon: the opposition-type of the strong spirit who has *become* free. Yet, the grand pose of these *sick* spirits, these epileptics of the concept, makes an impression on the great mass: the fanatics are picturesque; mankind prefers to see gestures rather than to hear *reasons*.

III *Genealogy of Morals**

The really great haters in the history of the world have always been priests, who are also the cleverest haters—in comparison with the cleverness of priestly revenge, every other piece of cleverness is practically negligible. Human history would be too fatuous for anything were it not for the cleverness imported into it by the weak—take at once the most important instance. All the world's efforts against the "aristocrats," the "mighty," the "masters," the "holders of power," are negligible by comparison with what has been accomplished against those classes by *the Jews*—the Jews, that priestly nation which eventually realized that the one method of effecting satisfaction on its enemies and tyrants was by means of a radical transvaluation of values, which was at the same time an act of the *cleverest revenge*. Yet, the method was only appropriate to a nation of priests, to a nation of the most jealously nursed priestly revengefulness. It was the Jews who, in opposition to the aristocratic equation (good = aristocratic = beautiful = happy = loved by the gods), dared with a terrifying logic to suggest the contrary equation, and indeed to maintain with the teeth of the most profound hatred (the hatred of weakness) this contrary equation, namely, "the wretched are alone the good; the poor, the weak, the lowly, are alone the good; the suffering, the needy, the sick, the loathsome, are the only ones who are pious, the only ones who are blessed, for them alone is salvation—but you, on the other hand, you aristocrats, you men of power, you are to all eternity the evil, the horrible, the covetous, the insatiate, the godless; eternally also shall you be the unblessed, the cursed, the damned!" We know who it was who reaped the heritage of

this Jewish transvaluation. In the context of the monstrous and inordinately fateful initiative which the Jews have exhibited in connection with this most fundamental of all declarations of war, I remember the passage which came to my pen on another occasion (*Beyond Good and Evil*, Aph. 195)—that it was, in fact, with the Jews that the *revolt of the slaves* begins in the sphere *of morals;* that revolt which has behind it a history of two millennia, and which at the present day has only moved out of our sight, because it—has achieved victory.

While the aristocratic man lived in confidence and openness with himself the resentful man, on the other hand, is neither sincere nor naive, nor honest and candid with himself. His soul *squints;* his mind loves hidden crannies, tortuous paths and backdoors, everything secret appeals to him as *his* world, *his* safety, *his* balm; he is past master in silence, in not forgetting, in waiting, in provisional self-depreciation and self-abasement. A race of such *resentful* men will of necessity eventually prove more *prudent* than any aristocratic race, it will honour prudence on quite a distinct scale, as, in fact, a paramount condition of existence, while prudence among aristocratic men is apt to be tinged with a delicate flavor of luxury and refinement; so among them it plays nothing like so integral a part as that complete certainty of function of the governing *unconscious* instincts, or as indeed a certain lack of prudence, such as a vehement and valiant charge, whether against danger or the enemy, or as those ecstatic bursts of rage, love, reverence, gratitude, by which at all times noble souls have recognized each other. When the resentment of the aristocratic man manifests itself, it fulfills and exhausts itself in an immediate reaction, and consequently instills no *venom:* on the other hand, it never manifests itself at all

---

*From Friedrich Nietzsche, *Genealogy of Morals* (1887; trans. Oscar Levy, 1910).

in countless instances, when in the case of the feeble and weak it would be inevitable. An inability to take seriously for any length of time their enemies, their disasters, their *misdeeds*—that is the sign of the full strong natures who possess a superfluity of moulding plastic force, that heals completely and produces forgetfulness: a good example of this in the modern world is Mirabeau, who had no memory for any insults and meannesses which were practiced on him, and who was only incapable of forgiving because he forgot. Such a man indeed shakes off with a shrug many a worm which would have buried itself in another; it is only in characters like these that we see the possibility (supposing, of course, that there is such a possibility in the world) of the real *"love of one's enemies."* What respect for his enemies is found, forsooth, in an aristocratic man—and such a reverence is already a bridge to love! He insists on having his enemy to himself as his distinction. He tolerates no other enemy but a man in whose character there is nothing to despise and *much* to honor! On the other hand, imagine the "enemy" as the resentful man conceives him—and it is here exactly that we see his work, his creativeness; he has conceived "the evil enemy," the "evil one," and indeed that is the root idea from which he now evolves as a contrasting and corresponding figure a "good one," himself—his very self!

The method of this man is quite contrary to that of the aristocratic man, who conceives the root idea "good" spontaneously and straight away, that is to say, out of himself, and from that material then creates for himself a concept of "bad"! This "bad" of aristocratic origin and that "evil" out of the cauldron of unsatisfied hatred—the former an imitation, an "extra," an additional nuance; the latter, on the other hand, the original, the beginning, the essential act in the conception of a slave morality—these two words "bad" and "evil," how great a difference do they mark, in spite of the fact that they have an identical contrary in the idea "good." But the idea "good" is *not* the same: much rather let the question be asked, "Who is really evil according to the meaning of the morality of resentment?" In all sternness let it be answered thus:—*just* the good man of the other morality, just the aristocrat, the powerful one, the one who rules, but who is

distorted by the venomous eye of resentfulness, into a new colour, a new signification, a new appearance. This particular point we would be the last to deny: the man who learnt to know those "good" ones only as enemies, learnt at the same time not to know them only as *"evil enemies,"* and the same men who *inter pares* were kept so rigorously in bounds through convention, respect, custom, and gratitude, though much more through mutual vigilance and jealousy *inter pares,* these men who in their relations with each other find so many new ways of manifesting consideration, self-control, delicacy, loyalty, pride, and friendship, these men are in reference to what is outside their circle (where the foreign element, a *foreign* country, begins), not much better than beasts of prey, which have been let loose. They enjoy there freedom from all social control, they feel that in the wilderness they can give vent with impunity to that tension which is produced by enclosure and imprisonment in the peace of society, they *revert* to the innocence of the beast-of-prey conscience, like jubilant monsters, who perhaps come from a ghostly bout of murder, arson, rape, and torture, with bravado and a moral equanimity, as though merely some wild student's prank had been played, perfectly convinced that the poets have now an ample theme to sing and celebrate. It is impossible not to recognize at the core of all these aristocratic races the beast of prey; the *magnificent blond beast,* avidly rampant for spoil and victory; this hidden core needed an outlet from time to time, the beast must get loose again, must return into the wilderness—the Roman, Arabic, German, and Japanese nobility, the Homeric heroes, the Scandinavian Vikings, are all alike in this need. It is the aristocratic races who have left the idea "Barbarian" on all the tracks in which they have marched; nay, a consciousness of this very barbarianism, and even a pride in it, manifests itself even in their highest civilization (for example, when Pericles says to his Athenians in that celebrated funeral oration, "Our audacity has forced a way over every land and sea, rearing everywhere imperishable memorials of itself for *good* and for *evil*").

Granted the truth of the theory now believed to be true, that the very *essence of all civilization* is to *train* out of man, the beast of prey, a tame and civilized animal, a domesticated animal, it follows indubitably that we must regard as the real *tools of civilization* all those instincts of reaction and resentment, by the help of which the aristocratic races, together with their ideals, were finally degraded and overpowered; though that has not yet come to be synonymous with saying that the bearers of those tools also *represented* the civilization. It is rather the contrary that is not only probable—nay, it is *palpable* today; these bearers of vindictive instincts that have to be bottled up, these descendants of all European and non-European slavery, especially of the pre-Aryan population—these people, I say, represent the *decline* of humanity! These "tools of civilization" are a disgrace to humanity, and constitute in reality more of an argument against civilization, more of a reason why civilization should be suspected. One may be perfectly justified in being always afraid of the blond beast that lies at the core of all aristocratic races, and in being on one's guard: but who would not a hundred times prefer to be afraid, when one at the same time admires, than to be immune from fear, at the cost of being perpetually obsessed with the loathsome spectacle of the distorted, the dwarfed, the stunted, the envenomed? And is that not our fate? What produces today our repulsion towards "man"?—for we *suffer* from "man," there is no doubt about it. It is not fear; it is rather that we have nothing more to fear from men; it is that the worm "man" is in the foreground and pullulates; it is that the "tame man," the wretched mediocre and unedifying creature, has learnt to consider himself a goal and a pinnacle, an inner meaning, an historic principle, a "higher man"; yes, it is that he has a certain right so to consider himself, in so far as he feels that in contrast to that excess of deformity, disease, exhaustion, and effeteness whose odor is beginning to pollute present-day Europe, he at any rate has achieved a relative success; he at any rate still says "yes" to life.

The future of German culture rests with the sons of Prussian officers.

Parliaments may be very useful to a strong and versatile statesman: He has something there to rely upon (every such thing must, however, be able to resist!)—upon which he can throw a great deal of responsibility. On the whole, however, I could wish that the counting mania and the superstitious belief in majorities were not established in Germany, as with the Latin races, and that one could finally invent something new even in politics! It is senseless and dangerous to let the custom of universal suffrage—which is still but a short time under cultivation, and could easily be uprooted—take a deeper root: whilst, of course, its introduction was merely an expedient to steer clear of temporary difficulties.

CHAPTER THIRTY-ONE

FASCISM

The expansion of democracy in the nineteenth and twentieth centuries intensified the antidemocratic reaction of conservative authoritarianism. Starting first in Italy as an antidemocratic and antisocialist movement after World War I, *fascism* is in essence the twentieth-century version of age-old tendencies in politics. Like democracy, it is a universal phenomenon, and it appeared in different forms and varieties in accordance with national traditions and circumstances.

Unlike the authoritarianism of the seventeenth and eighteenth centuries, fascism is a *postdemocratic* political system and cannot be understood except as a reaction to democracy. Fascism is not possible in countries with no democratic experience at all: in such countries dictatorship may be based on the army, bureaucracy, and church, but it will lack the element of mass enthusiasm and participation characteristic of fascism. Conversely, fascism never succeeded in a country whose democratic experience had been prolonged and generally shared by the people. Fascism learned from democracy the value of popular support for national policies, and it sought to manufacture popular consent by a mixture of propaganda and terror.

In its social background, fascism particularly appealed to two groups: first, a numerically small group of industrialists and landowners who were willing to finance fascist parties in the hope of thereby getting rid of free labor unions and radical political movements; second, the numerically much more important lower middle classes who dreaded the prospect of proletarianization and looked to fascism for the salvation of their status and prestige in society. Typically, it was the employee rather than industrial worker who was susceptible to fascism, and the small marginal businessman who was afraid of Big Business and Big Labor. In times of depression, fascism appealed to the unemployed, hopeless, cheerless—the forgotten of society: by putting them into uniforms, and incorporating them into an organized movement, fascism made them feel that they "belonged," that they were not outcasts, as existing society may have seemed to consider them.

There is no Locke, Marx, or Lenin in the theory of fascism; it cannot be gathered from one systematic treatise but must be culled from various sources that express thought and opinion as much as political philosophy. One of the most authoritative brief statements of fascist theory is Mussolini's *Doctrine of Fascism* (1932), which he contributed, with the aid of the Italian philosopher Giovanni Gentile, to the *Italian Encyclopedia* in his capacity as *Duce* of fascism and of Italy.

Benito Mussolini (1883–1945) started his political career as a journalist; for some time he edited the socialist daily, *Avanti.* When World War I broke out, the majority of the Socialist party favored neutrality. Mussolini, who had previously belonged to the revolutionary, syndicalist wing of the Socialist party, suddenly reversed his stand and favored intervention on the side of the Allies, for which he was expelled from the party in November, 1914. In the same month he started his own paper, *Popolo d'Italia,* later to become the official organ of Italian fascism. In March, 1919, Mussolini and his interventionist friends and associates formed "combat groups" *(Fasci di Combattimento),* the program of which was a mixture of ultrarevolutionary and ultranationalist slogans. At first, Mussolini tried to woo the working classes away from the Socialist party, but he soon had to admit failure. He then steadily courted political support from the middle classes and financial support from big landowners and industrialists. Realizing the futility of achieving power by legal means, the Fascists began to terrorize opponents, not refraining from arson and assassination. A new feature of Fascist methods emerged in "punitive expeditions" against numerous communities, in which the police allowed the Fascists to terrorize and virtually take over whole towns.

In the national elections of 1921, the Fascists obtained only 35 of 535 seats in Parliament, and Mussolini became more determined than ever to seize the government by force. On October 28, 1922, the Fascists converged on Rome from all parts of Italy, and the following day Mussolini was asked by the King to form a new administration. Mussolini quickly consolidated his power by ruthless persecution of his opponents; the assassination in 1924 of Giacomo Matteotti, a Socialist Deputy, showed that murder was an officially sanctioned weapon of the new regime.

Until 1933, Mussolini was comparatively isolated; but with the advent of the Nazi regime in Germany, a new fascist international was gradually being formed, later joined by Japan and lesser powers. His hatred of democracy and the democratic nations drove Mussolini—all his life anti-German—into the arms of Hitler, and he entered the war on the side of Nazi Germany in June, 1940, when the war, after the defeat of France, seemed to be over. Yet the long years of preparation for war were of no avail, and the military weakness of the Fascist regime became evident from the first operations. Even after Italy surrendered in September, 1943, Mussolini continued to head a German puppet regime in northern Italy. In April, 1945, seeing that all was lost, he sought to escape to Switzerland, where he had spent several years in his youth as a penniless worker and agitator. On his way to the border he was captured by Italian partisans operating behind enemy lines, sentenced to death by an improvised partisan court, and executed. His dead body was publicly hung from a lamppost in Milan—the city in which the Fascist movement was born. Only a few days later, Hitler committed suicide in the Reich Chancellery in Berlin.

The most characteristic feature of the fascist temper and outlook is *irrationalism,* the distrust of reason, and the stress on the irrational, sentimental, uncontrollable parts of man. Fascism opposes the whole western tradition of rationalism that stems from Greece. The psychological mood of fascism is fanaticism, not skeptical reflection. Because of its basic irrationalism, fascism has "taboo issues" (such as race, the dogma of the party, or the personality of the "leader") that must not be critically discussed. During the Fascist regime in Italy, Mussolini's picture was in all schoolrooms, and it had the caption, "Mussolini is always right."

Fascism denies in principle the basic human equality of the western tradition, and not only accepts *inequality* as a fact but affirms it as an ideal. Though democratic societies do not always live up to their ideal of human equality, they at least accept it as a long-term goal of public policy.

The code of fascist behavior affirms the values of *violence* and the *lie*. Because it distrusts reason and rejects universally valid standards of conduct, fascism does not hesitate to use any means in pursuing its aims. For the same reason, fascism is ready to sacrifice the individual to the state: in the fascist view, the *state* is the *end* and the *individual* the *means*—the exact opposite of the democratic philosophy. "For the Fascist," Mussolini says, "everything is in the State, and nothing human or spiritual exists, much less has value, outside the State." Mussolini therefore also candidly admits that the fascist state is necessarily *totalitarian,* allowing no competing values or social associations besides itself. By contrast, the democratic state is pluralistic: it must recognize the fact that in a free society the loyalty of the individual to the state may conflict with his loyalties to the family, church, or his own conscience as a free person.

The fascist acceptance of inequality and violence naturally results in the theory and practice of government by an *elite:* Some men are born to rule, and others to obey. Fascist regimes are undemocratic, not because they always lack the support of the people (in some instances this support may be wholehearted), but because they rule *independently* of popular consent, without a free party system, and without free elections and a free press. The leadership principle is the extreme form of the fascist elite concept, and it fully expresses the irrational character of fascist politics: The leader is considered infallible, endowed with mystical gifts and insight, and he personifies the nation. In a conflict of opinion between leader and people, the will of the leader prevails, because his is the General Will, whereas that of the people is only the Will of All.

The fascist emphasis on leadership collides with the simultaneous enforcement of orthodoxy and conformity—the totalitarian uniformity of fascist society. Leaders of fascism like Mussolini and Hitler were formed in nonfascist societies with considerable free competition. The relatively short duration of the main fascist regimes in Italy and Germany has made it impossible for the student of comparative political systems and philosophies to appraise the leadership qualities of a generation born and bred under conditions of fascist uniformity and orthodoxy.

Because fascism is not only a political system but a way of life, it employs *authority* rather than discussion in all spheres of social activity, including the nonpolitical ones. Fascism is typically antifeminist in public life and also supports strong paternal authority in the family, over both wife and children. The father is the "leader of the family." In the schools, discipline is the supreme value inculcated into the minds and hearts of children, and the educational program is little more than a prelude to military training and indoctrination. In industry, authority takes the place of free bargaining between capital and labor. Officially, the fascist state is impartial between capitalists and workers; yet the cemeteries of fascist countries are filled with victimized bodies of trade-unionists rather than bankers and industrialists. Relying on authority and obedience, fascism attracts not only those who want to command but also those who long to obey. In every society there are those who would rather follow and obey than think for themselves and assume responsibilities, and the "escape from freedom" is one of the chief psychological conditions of the spread of fascism.

The *corporate state* is another feature of fascism that expresses its lack of faith in the people: in the corporate system, the economy is organized in state-controlled associations of capital and labor, all working harmoniously for the common good, with the aid and guidance of the dictatorial one-party state. The underlying assumption of corporatism is that man (except for the elite in power) should not be politically articulate in his capacity as a citizen, but as a member of a social or economic group; general political issues are too complicated for him, whereas he is familiar with his work and profession.

In the international field, racism and imperialism express the two fundamental fascist principles of inequality and violence. Just as, within the nation, the elite is superior to the rest and may impose its will by violence, so between nations the "elite nation" is considered superior to the others and entitled to rule them by force. As a result, fascism is opposed to international organization and world peace: It "believes neither in the possibility nor in the utility of perpetual peace," Mussolini says, because "war alone brings up to their highest tension all human energies and puts the stamp of nobility upon the peoples who have the courage to meet it." Moreover, fascism is opposed to international organizations for two other reasons: they recognize in some measure the principle of equality among nations, and, second, they seek to institute government by discussion on an international plane. Neither aim is compatible with a fascist theory of politics.

MUSSOLINI

*The Doctrine of Fascism**

FUNDAMENTAL IDEAS

1. Like every sound political conception, Fascism is both practice and thought; action in which a doctrine is immanent, and a doctrine which, arising out of a given system of historical forces, remains embedded in them and works there from within. Hence it has a form correlative to the contingencies of place and time, but it has also a content of thought which raises it to a formula of truth in the higher level of the history of thought. In the world one does not act spiritually as a human will dominating other wills without a conception of the transient and particular reality under which it is necessary to act, and of the permanent and universal reality in which the first has its being and its life. In order to know men it is necessary to know man; and in order to know man it is necessary to know reality and its laws. There is no concept of the State which is not fundamentally a concept of life: philosophy or intuition, a system of ideas which develops logically or is gathered up into a vision or into a faith, but which is always, at least virtually, an organic conception of the world.

2. Thus Fascism could not be understood in many of its practical manifestations as a party organization, as a system of education, as a discipline, if it were not always looked at in the light of its whole way of conceiving life, a spiritualized way. The world seen through Fascism is not this material world which appears on the surface, in which man is an individual separated from all others and standing by himself, and in which he is governed by a natural law that makes him instinctively live a life of selfish and momentary pleasure. The man of Fascism is an individual who is nation and fatherland, which is a moral law, binding together individuals and the generations into a tradition and a mission, suppressing the instinct for a life enclosed within the brief round of pleasure in order to restore within duty a higher life free from the limits of time and space: a life in which the individual, through the denial of himself, through the sacrifice of his own private interests, through death itself, realizes that completely spiritual existence in which his value as a man lies.

3. Therefore it is a spiritualized conception, itself the result of the general reaction of modern times against the flabby materialistic positivism of the nineteenth century. Anti-positivistic, but positive: not sceptical, nor agnostic, nor pessimistic, nor passively optimistic, as are, in general, the doctrines (all negative) that put the centre of life outside man, who with his free will can and must create his own world. Fascism desires an active man, one engaged in activity with all his energies: it desires a man virilely conscious of the difficulties that exist in action and ready to face them. It conceives of life as a struggle, considering that it behoves man to conquer for himself that life truly worthy of him, creating first of all in himself the instrument (physical, moral, intellectual) in order to construct it. Thus for the single individual, thus for the nation, thus for humanity. Hence the high value of culture in all its forms (art, religion, science), and the enormous importance of education. Hence also the essential value of work, with

---

*From Michael Oakeshott, *The Social and Political Doctrines of Contemporary Europe* (Cambridge Univ. Press, 1939). By permission.

which man conquers nature and creates the human world (economic, political, moral, intellectual).

4. This positive conception of life is clearly an ethical conception. It covers the whole of reality, not merely the human activity which controls it. No action can be divorced from moral judgement; there is nothing in the world which can be deprived of the value which belongs to everything in its relation to moral ends. Life, therefore, as conceived by the Fascist, is serious, austere, religious: the whole of it is poised in a world supported by the moral and responsible forces of the spirit. The Fascist disdains the "comfortable" life.

5. Fascism is a religious conception in which man is seen in his immanent relationship with a superior law and with an objective Will that transcends the particular individual and raises him to conscious membership of a spiritual society. Whoever has seen in the religious politics of the Fascist regime nothing but mere opportunism has not understood that Fascism besides being a system of government is also, and above all, a system of thought.

6. Fascism is an historical conception, in which man is what he is only in so far as he works with the spiritual process in which he finds himself, in the family or social group, in the nation and in the history in which all nations collaborate. From this follows the great value of tradition, in memories, in language, in customs, in the standards of social life. Outside history man is nothing. Consequently Fascism is opposed to all the individualistic abstractions of a materialistic nature like those of the eighteenth century; and it is opposed to all Jacobin utopias and innovations. It does not consider that "happiness" is possible upon earth, as it appeared to be in the desire of the economic literature of the eighteenth century, and hence it rejects all teleological theories according to which mankind would reach a definitive stabilized condition at a certain period in history. This implies putting oneself outside history and life, which is a continual change and coming to be. Politically, Fascism wishes to be a realistic doctrine; practically, it aspires to solve only the problems which arise historically of themselves and that of themselves find or suggest their own solution. To act among men, as to act in

the natural world, it is necessary to enter into the process of reality and to master the already operating forces.

7. Against individualism, the Fascist conception is for the State; and it is for the individual in so far as he coincides with the State, which is the conscience and universal will of man in his historical existence. It is opposed to classical Liberalism, which arose from the necessity of reacting against absolutism, and which brought its historical purpose to an end when the State was transformed into the conscience and will of the people. Liberalism denied the State in the interests of the particular individual; Fascism reaffirms the State as the true reality of the individual. And if liberty is to be the attribute of the real man, and not of that abstract puppet envisaged by individualistic Liberalism, Fascism is for liberty. And for the only liberty which can be a real thing, the liberty of the State and of the individual within the State. Therefore, for the Fascist, everything is in the State, and nothing human or spiritual exists, much less has value, outside the State. In this sense Fascism is totalitarian, and the Fascist State, the synthesis and unity of all values, interprets, develops and gives strength to the whole life of the people.

8. Outside the State there can be neither individuals nor groups (political parties, associations, syndicates, classes). Therefore Fascism is opposed to Socialism, which confines the movement of history within the class struggle and ignores the unity of classes established in one economic and moral reality in the State; and analogously it is opposed to class syndicalism. Fascism recognizes the real exigencies for which the socialist and syndicalist movement arose, but while recognizing them wishes to bring them under the control of the State and give them a purpose within the corporative system of interests reconciled within the unity of the State.

9. Individuals form classes according to the similarity of their interests, they form syndicates according to differentiated economic activities within these interests; but they form first, and above all, the State, which is not to be thought of numerically as the sum-total of individuals forming the majority of a nation. And consequently Fascism is opposed to Democracy, which equates the nation to the majority, lowering

it to the level of that majority; nevertheless it is the purest form of democracy if the nation is conceived, as it should be, qualitatively and not quantitatively, as the most powerful idea (most powerful because most moral, most coherent, most true) which acts within the nation as the conscience and the will of a few, even of One, which ideal tends to become active within the conscience and the will of all—that is to say, of all those who rightly constitute a nation by reason of nature, history or race, and have set out upon the same line of development and spiritual formation as one conscience and one sole will. Not a race,[1] nor a geographically determined region, but as a community historically perpetuating itself, a multitude unified by a single idea, which is the will to existence and to power: consciousness of itself, personality.

10. This higher personality is truly the nation in so far as it is the State. It is not the nation that generates the State, as according to the old naturalistic concept which served as the basis of the political theories of the national States of the nineteenth century. Rather the nation is created by the State, which gives to the people, conscious of its own moral unity, a will and therefore an effective existence. The right of a nation to independence derives not from a literary and ideal consciousness of its own being, still less from a more or less unconscious and inert acceptance of a *de facto* situation, but from an active consciousness, from a political will in action and ready to demonstrate its own rights: that is to say, from a state already coming into being. The State, in fact, as the universal ethical will, is the creator of right.

11. The nation as the State is an ethical reality which exists and lives in so far as it develops. To arrest its development is to kill it. Therefore the State is not only the authority which governs and gives the form of laws and the value of spiritual life to the wills of individuals, but it is also a power that makes its will felt abroad, making it known and respected, in other words, demonstrating the fact of its universality in all the necessary directions of its development. It is

consequently organization and expansion, at least virtually. Thus it can be likened to the human will which knows no limits to its development and realizes itself in testing its own limitlessness.

12. The Fascist State, the highest and most powerful form of personality, is a force, but a spiritual force, which takes over all the forms of the moral and intellectual life of man. It cannot therefore confine itself simply to the functions of order and supervision as Liberalism desired. It is not simply a mechanism which limits the sphere of the supposed liberties of the individual. It is the form, the inner standard and the discipline of the whole person; it saturates the will as well as the intelligence. Its principle, the central inspiration of the human personality living in the civil community, pierces into the depths and makes its home in the heart of the man of action as well as of the thinker, of the artist as well as of the scientist: it is the soul of the soul.

13. Fascism, in short, is not only the giver of laws and the founder of institutions, but the educator and promoter of spiritual life. It wants to remake, not the forms of human life, but its content, man, character, faith. And to this end it requires discipline and authority that can enter into the spirits of men and there govern unopposed. Its sign, therefore, is the Lictors' rods, the symbol of unity, of strength and justice.

POLITICAL AND SOCIAL DOCTRINE

1. When in the now distant March of 1919 I summoned to Milan, through the columns of the *Popolo d' Italia,* my surviving supporters who had followed me since the constitution of the Fasces of Revolutionary Action, founded in January 1915, there was no specific doctrinal plan in my mind. I had known and lived through only one doctrine, that of the Socialism of 1903–4 up to the winter of 1914, almost ten years. My experience in this had been that of a follower and of a leader, but not that of a theoretician. My doctrine, even in that period, had been a doctrine of action. An unequivocal Socialism, universally accepted, did not exist after 1905, when the Revisionist Movement began in Germany under Bernstein and there was formed in opposition to

---

[1] "Race; it is an emotion, not a reality; ninety-five per cent of it is emotion." Mussolini.

that, in the see-saw of tendencies, an extreme revolutionary movement, which in Italy never emerged from the condition of mere words, whilst in Russian Socialism it was the prelude to Bolshevism. Reform, Revolution, Centralization—even the echoes of the terminology are now spent; whilst in the great river of Fascism are to be found the streams which had their source in Sorel, Peguy, in the Lagardelle of the *Mouvement Socialiste* and the groups of Italian Syndicalists, who between 1904 and 1914 brought a note of novelty into Italian Socialism, which by that time had been devitalized and drugged by fornication with Giolitti, in *Pagine Libere* of Olivetti, *La Lupa* of Orano and *Divenire Sociale* of Enrico Leone.

In 1919, at the end of the War, Socialism as a doctrine was already dead: it existed only as hatred, it had still only one possibility, especially in Italy, that of revenge against those who had wished for the War and who should be made to expiate it. The *Popolo d' Italia* expressed it in its subtitle—"The Newspaper of Combatants and Producers." The word "producers" was already the expression of a tendency. Fascism was not given out to the wet nurse of a doctrine elaborated beforehand round a table: it was born of the need for action; it was not a party, but in its first two years it was a movement against all parties. The name which I gave to the organization defined its characteristics. Nevertheless, whoever rereads, in the now crumpled pages of the time, the account of the constituent assembly of the *Fasci italiani di Combattimento* will not find a doctrine, but a series of suggestions, of anticipations, of admonitions, which when freed from the inevitable vein of contingency, were destined later, after a few years, to develop into a series of doctrinal attitudes which made of Fascism a self-sufficient political doctrine able to face all others, both past and present. "If the bourgeoisie," I said at that time, "thinks to find in us a lightning-conductor, it is mistaken. We must go forward in opposition to Labour. . . . We want to accustom the working classes to being under a leader, to convince them also that it is not easy to direct an industry or a commercial undertaking successfully. . . . We shall fight against technical and spiritual retrogression. . . . The successors of the present regime still

being undecided, we must not be unwilling to fight for it. We must hasten; when the present regime is superseded, we must be the ones to take its place. The right of succession belongs to us because we pushed the country into the War and we led it to victory. The present method of political representation cannot be sufficient for us, we wish for a direct representation of individual interests. . . . It might be said against this programme that it is a return to the corporations. It doesn't matter! . . . I should like, nevertheless, the Assembly to accept the claims of national syndicalism from the point of view of economics. . . . "

Is it not surprising that from the first day in the Piazza San Sepolcro there should resound the word "Corporation" which was destined in the course of the revolution to signify one of the legislative and social creations at the base of the regime?

2. The years preceding the March on Rome were years during which the necessity of action did not tolerate enquiries or complete elaborations of doctrine. Battles were being fought in the cities and villages. There were discussions, but—and this is more sacred and important—there were deaths. People knew how to die. The doctrine—beautiful, well-formed, divided into chapters and paragraphs and surrounded by a commentary—might be missing; but there was present something more decisive to supplant it—Faith. Nevertheless, he who recalls the past with the aid of books, articles, votes in Parliament, the major and the minor speeches, he who knows how to investigate and weigh evidence, will find that the foundations of the doctrine were laid while the battle was raging. It was precisely in these years that Fascist thought armed itself, refined itself, moving towards one organization of its own. The problems of the individual and the State; the problems of authority and liberty; political and social problems and those more specifically national, the struggle against liberal, democratic, socialist, Masonic, demagogic doctrines was carried on at the same time as the "punitive expeditions." But since the "system" was lacking, adversaries ingenuously denied that Fascism had any power to make a doctrine of its own, while the doctrine rose up, even though tumultuously, at first under the aspect of a violent and dogmatic negation, as

happens to all ideas that break new ground, then under the positive aspect of a constructive policy which, during the years 1926, 1927, 1928, was realized in the laws and institutions of the regime.

Fascism is to-day clearly defined not only as a regime but as a doctrine. And I mean by this that Fascism to-day, self-critical as well as critical of other movements, has an unequivocal point of view of its own, a criterion, and hence an aim, in the face of all the material and intellectual problems which oppress the people of the world.

3. Above all, Fascism, in so far as it considers and observes the future and the development of humanity quite apart from the political considerations of the moment, believes neither in the possibility nor in the utility of perpetual peace. It thus repudiates the doctrine of Pacifism—born of a renunciation of the struggle and an act of cowardice in the face of sacrifice. War alone brings up to their highest tension all human energies and puts the stamp of nobility upon the peoples who have the courage to meet it. All other trials are substitutes, which never really put a man in front of himself in the alternative of life and death. A doctrine, therefore, which begins with a prejudice in favour of peace is foreign to Fascism; as are foreign to the spirit of Fascism, even though acceptable by reason of the utility which they might have in given political situations, all internationalistic and socialistic systems which, as history proves, can be blown to the winds when emotional, idealistic and practical movements storm the hearts of peoples. Fascism carries over this antipacifist spirit even into the lives of individuals. The proud motto of the *Squadrista,* "Me ne frego," written on the bandages of a wound is an act of philosophy which is not only stoical, it is the epitome of a doctrine that is not only political: it is education for combat, the acceptance of the risks which it brings: it is a new way of life for Italy. Thus the Fascist accepts and loves life, he knows nothing of suicide and despises it; he looks on life as duty, ascent, conquest: life which must be noble and full: lived for oneself but above all for those others near and far away, present and future.

4. The "demographic" policy of the regime follows from these premises. Even the Fascist does in fact love his neighbour, but this "neighbour" is not for him a vague and ill-defined concept; love for one's neighbour does not exclude necessary educational severities, and still less differentiations and distances. Fascism rejects universal concord, and, since it lives in the community of civilized peoples, it keeps them vigilantly and suspiciously before its eyes, it follows their states of mind and the changes in their interests and its does not let itself be deceived by temporary and fallacious appearances.

5. Such a conception of life makes Fascism the precise negation of that doctrine which formed the basis of the so-called Scientific or Marxian Socialism: the doctrine of historical Materialism according to which the history of human civilizations can be explained only as the struggle of interest between the different social groups and as arising out of change in the means and instruments of production. That economic improvements—discoveries of raw materials, new methods of work, scientific inventions—should have an importance of their own, no one denies, but that they should suffice to explain human history to the exclusion of all other factors is absurd: Fascism believes, now and always, in holiness and in heroism, that is in acts in which no economic motive—remote or immediate—plays a part. With this negation of historical materialism, according to which men would be only by-products of history, who appear and disappear on the surface of the waves while in the depths the real directive forces are at work, there is also denied the immutable and irreparable "class struggle" which is the natural product of this economic conception of history, and above all it is denied that the class struggle can be the primary agent of social changes. Socialism, being thus wounded in these two primary tenets of its doctrine, nothing of it is left save the sentimental aspiration—old as humanity—towards a social order in which the sufferings and the pains of the humblest folk could be alleviated. But here Fascism rejects the concept of an economic "happiness" which would be realized socialistically and almost automatically at a given moment of economic evolution by assuring to all a maximum prosperity. Fascism denies the possibility of the materialistic conception of "happiness" and leaves it to the

economists of the first half of the eighteenth century; it denies, that is, the equation of prosperity with happiness, which would transform men into animals with one sole preoccupation: that of being well-fed and fat, degraded in consequence to a merely physical existence.

6. After Socialism, Fascism attacks the whole complex of democratic ideologies and rejects them both in their theoretical premises and in their applications or practical manifestations. Fascism denies that the majority, through the mere fact of being a majority, can rule human societies; it denies that this majority can govern by means of a periodical consultation; it affirms the irremediable, fruitful and beneficent inequality of men, who cannot be levelled by such a mechanical and extrinsic fact as universal suffrage. By democratic regimes we mean those in which from time to time the people is given the illusion of being sovereign, while true effective sovereignty lies in other, perhaps irresponsible and secret, forces. Democracy is a regime without a king, but with very many kings, perhaps more exclusive, tyrannical and violent than one king even though a tyrant. This explains why Fascism, although before 1922 for reasons of expediency it made a gesture of republicanism, renounced it before the March on Rome, convinced that the question of the political forms of a State is not preeminent today, and that studying past and present monarchies, past and present Republics, it becomes clear that monarchy and republic are not to be judged *sub specie aeternitatis,* but represent forms in which the political evolution, the history, the tradition, the psychology of a given country are manifested. Now Fascism overcomes the antithesis between monarchy and republic which retarded the movements of democracy, burdening the former with every defect and defending the latter as the regime of perfection. Now it has been seen that there are inherently reactionary and absolutistic republics, and monarchies that welcome the most daring political and social innovations.

7. "Reason, Science," said Renan (who was inspired before Fascism existed) in one of his philosophical Meditations, "are products of humanity, but to expect reason directly from the people and through the people is a chimera. It is not necessary for the existence of reason that everybody should know it. In any case, if such an initiation should be made, it would not be made by means of base democracy, which apparently must lead to the extinction of every difficult culture, and every higher discipline. The principle that society exists only for the prosperity and the liberty of the individuals who compose it does not seem to conform with the plans of nature, plans in which the species alone is taken into consideration and the individual seems to be sacrificed. It is strongly to be feared lest the last word of democracy thus understood (I hasten to say that it can also be understood in other ways) would be a social state in which a degenerate mass would have no other care than to enjoy the ignoble pleasures of vulgar men."

Thus far Renan. Fascism rejects in democracy the absurd conventional lie of political equalitarianism clothed in the dress of collective irresponsibility and the myth of happiness and indefinite progress. But if democracy can be understood in other ways, that is, if democracy means not to relegate the people to the periphery of the State, then Fascism could be defined as an "organized, centralized, authoritarian democracy."

8. In face of Liberal doctrines, Fascism takes up an attitude of absolute opposition both in the field of politics and in that of economics. It is not necessary to exaggerate—merely for the purpose of present controversies—the importance of Liberalism in the past century, and to make of that which was one of the numerous doctrines sketched in that century a religion of humanity for all times, present and future. Liberalism flourished for no more than some fifteen years. It was born in 1830, as a reaction against the Holy Alliance that wished to drag Europe back to what it had been before 1789, and it had its year of splendour in 1848 when even Pius IX was a Liberal. Immediately afterwards the decay set in. If 1848 was a year of light and of poetry, 1849 was a year of darkness and of tragedy. The Republic of Rome was destroyed by another Republic, that of France. In the same year Marx launched the gospel of the religion of Socialism with the famous *Communist Manifesto.* In 1851 Napoleon III carried out his unliberal *coup d'état* and ruled over France until 1870, when he was dethroned by a popular revolt,

but as a consequence of a military defeat which ranks among the most resounding that history can relate. The victor was Bismarck, who never knew the home of the religion of liberty or who were its prophets. It is symptomatic that a people of high culture like the Germans should have been completely ignorant of the religion of liberty during the whole of the nineteenth century. It was, there, no more than a parenthesis, represented by what has been called the "ridiculous Parliament of Frankfort" which lasted only a season. Germany has achieved her national unity outside the doctrines of Liberalism, against Liberalism, a doctrine which seems foreign to the German soul, a soul essentially monarchical, whilst Liberalism is the historical and logical beginning of anarchism. The stages of German unity are the three wars of 1864, 1866 and 1870, conducted by "Liberals" like Moltke and Bismarck. As for Italian unity, Liberalism has had in it a part absolutely inferior to the share of Mazzini and of Garibaldi, who were not Liberals. Without the intervention of the unliberal Napoleon we should not have gained Lombardy, and without the help of the unliberal Bismarck at Sadowa and Sedan, very probably we should not have gained Venice in 1866; and in 1870 we should not have entered Rome. From 1870–1915 there occurs the period in which the very priests of the new creed had to confess the twilight of their religion: defeated as it was by decadence in literature, by activism in practice. Activism: that is to say, Nationalism, Futurism, Fascism. The "Liberal" century, after having accumulated an infinity of Gordian knots, tried to untie them by the hecatomb of the World War. Never before has any religion imposed such a cruel sacrifice. Were the gods of Liberalism thirsty for blood? Now Liberalism is about to close the doors of its deserted temples because the peoples feel that its agnosticism in economics, its indifferentism in politics and in morals, would lead, as they have led, the States to certain ruin. In this way one can understand why all the political experiences of the contemporary world are anti-Liberal, and it is supremely ridiculous to wish on that account to class them outside of history; as if history were a hunting ground reserved to Liberalism and its professors, as if Liberalism were the

definitive and no longer surpassable message of civilization.

9. But the Fascist repudiations of Socialism, Democracy, Liberalism must not make one think that Fascism wishes to make the world return to what it was before 1789, the year which has been indicated as the year of the beginning of the liberal-democratic age. One does not go backwards. The Fascist doctrine has not chosen De Maistre as its prophet. Monarchical absolutism is a thing of the past and so also is every theocracy. So also feudal privileges and division into impenetrable and isolated castes have had their day. The theory of Fascist authority has nothing to with the police State. A party that governs a nation in a totalitarian way is a new fact in history. References and comparisons are not possible. Fascism takes over from the ruins of Liberal Socialistic democratic doctrines those elements which still have a living value. It preserves those that can be called the established facts of history, it rejects all the rest, that is to say the idea of a doctrine which holds good for all times and all peoples. If it is admitted that the nineteenth century has been the century of Socialism, Liberalism, and Democracy, it does not follow that the twentieth must also be the century of Liberalism, Socialism, and Democracy. Political doctrines pass; peoples remain. It is to be expected that this century may be that of authority, a century of the "Right," a Fascist century. If the nineteenth was the century of the individual (Liberalism means individualism) it may be expected that this one may be the century of "collectivism" and therefore the century of the State. That a new doctrine should use the still vital elements of other doctrines is perfectly logical. No doctrine is born quite new, shining, never before seen. No doctrine can boast of an absolute "originality." It is bound, even if only historically, to other doctrines that have been, and to develop into other doctrines that will be. Thus the scientific socialism of Marx is bound to the Utopian Socialism of the Fouriers the Owens and the Saint-Simons; thus the Liberalism of the nineteenth century is connected with the whole "Enlightenment" of the eighteenth century. Thus the doctrines of democracy are bound to the *Encyclopédie*. Every doctrine tends to direct the activity of men

towards a determined objective; but the activity of man reacts upon the doctrine, transforms it, adapts it to new necessities or transcends it. The doctrine itself, therefore, must be, not words, but an act of life. Hence, the pragmatic veins in Fascism, its will to power, its will to be, its attitude in the face of the fact of "violence" and of its own courage.

10. The keystone of Fascist doctrine is the conception of the State, of its essence, of its tasks, of its ends. For Fascism the State is an absolute before which individuals and groups are relative. Individuals and groups are "thinkable" in so far as they are within the State. The Liberal State does not direct the interplay and the material and spiritual development of the groups, but limits itself to registering the results; the Fascist State has a consciousness of its own, a will of its own, on this account it is called an "ethical" State. In 1929, at the first quinquennial assembly of the regime, I said:

> For Fascism, the State is not the night-watchman who is concerned only with the personal security of the citizens; nor is it an organization for purely material ends, such as that of guaranteeing a certain degree of prosperity and a relatively peaceful social order, to achieve which a council of administration would be sufficient, nor is it a creation of mere politics with no contact with the material and complex reality of the lives of individuals and the life of peoples. The State, as conceived by Fascism and as it acts, is a spiritual and moral fact because it makes concrete the political, juridical, economic organization of the nation and such an organization is, in its origin and in its development, a manifestation of the spirit. The State is the guarantor of internal and external security, but it is also the guardian and the transmitter of the spirit of the people as it has been elaborated through the centuries in language, custom, faith. The State is not only present, it is also past, and above all future. It is the State which, transcending the brief limit of individual lives, represents the immanent conscience of the nation. The forms in which States express themselves change, but the necessity of the State remains. It is the State which educates citizens for civic virtue, makes them conscious of their mission, calls them to unity; harmonizes their interests in justice; hands on the achievements of thought in the sciences, the arts, in law, in human solidarity; it carries men from the elementary life of the tribe to the highest human expression of power which is Empire; it entrusts to the ages the names of those who died for its integrity or in obedience to its laws; it puts forward as an example and recommends to the generations that are to come the leaders who increased its territory and the men of genius who gave it glory. When the sense of the State declines and the disintegrating and centrifugal tendencies of individuals and groups prevail, national societies move to their decline.

11. From 1929 up to the present day these doctrinal positions have been strengthened by the whole economico-political evolution of the world. It is the State alone that grows in size, in power. It is the State alone that can solve the dramatic contradictions of capitalism. What is called the crisis cannot be overcome except by the State, within the State. Where are the shades of the Jules Simons who, at the dawn of Liberalism, proclaimed that "the State must strive to render itself unnecessary and to prepare for its demise"; of the MacCullochs who, in the second half of the last century, affirmed that the State must abstain from too much governing? And faced with the continual, necessary and inevitable interventions of the State in economic affairs what would the Englishman Bentham now say, according to whom industry should have asked of the State only to be left in peace? Or the German Humboldt, according to whom the "idle" State must be considered the best? It is true that the second generation of Liberal economists was less extremist than the first, and already Smith himself opened, even though cautiously, the door to State intervention in economics. But when one says Liberalism, one says the individual; when one says Fascism, one says the State. But the Fascist State is unique; it is an original creation. It is not reactionary, but revolutionary in that it anticipates the solutions of certain universal problems. These problems are no longer seen in the same light: in the sphere of politics they are removed from party rivalries, from the supreme power of parliament, from the irresponsiblity of assemblies; in the sphere of economics they are removed from the

sphere of the syndicates' activities—activities that were ever widening their scope and increasing their power both on the workers' side and on the employers'—removed from their struggles and their designs; in the moral sphere they are divorced from ideas of the need for order, discipline, and obedience, and lifted into the plane of the moral commandments of the fatherland. Fascism desires the State to be strong, organic and at the same time founded on a wide popular basis. The Fascist State has also claimed for itself the field of economics and, through the corporative, social, and educational institutions which it has created, the meaning of the State reaches out to and includes the farthest offshoots; and within the State, framed in their respective organizations, there revolve all the political, economic and spiritual forces of the nation. A State founded on millions of individuals who recognize it, feel it, are ready to serve it, is not the tyrannical State of the medieval lord. It has nothing in common with the absolutist States that existed either before or after 1789. In the Fascist State the individual is not suppressed, but rather multiplied, just as in a regiment a soldier is not weakened but multiplied by the number of his comrades. The Fascist State organizes the nation, but it leaves sufficient scope to individuals; it has limited useless or harmful liberties and has preserved those that are essential. It cannot be the individual who decides in this matter, but only the State.

12. The Fascist State does not remain indifferent to the fact of religion in general and to that particular positive religion which is Italian Catholicism. The State has no theology, but it has an ethic. In the Fascist State religion is looked upon as one of the deepest manifestations of the spirit; it is, therefore, not only respected, but defended and protected. The Fascist State does not create a "God" of its own, as Robespierre once, at the height of the Convention's foolishness, wished to do; nor does it vainly seek, like Bolshevism, to expel religion from the minds of men; Fascism respects the God of the as-cetics, of the saints, of the heroes, and also God as seen and prayed to by the simple and primitive heart of the people.

13. The Fascist State is a will to power and to government. In it the tradition of Rome is an idea that has force. In the doctrine of Fascism Empire is not only a territorial, military, or mercantile expression, but spiritual or moral. One can think of an empire, that is to say a nation that directly or indirectly leads other nations, without needing to conquer a single square kilometre of territory. For Fascism the tendency to Empire, that is to say, to the expansion of nations, is a manifestation of vitality; its opposite, staying at home, is a sign of decadence: peoples who rise or re-rise are imperialist, peoples who die are renunciatory. Fascism is the doctrine that is most fitted to represent the aims, the states of mind, of a people, like the Italian people, rising again after many centuries of abandonment or slavery to foreigners. But Empire calls for discipline, co-ordination of forces, duty, and sacrifice; this explains many aspects of the practical working of the regime and the direction of many of the forces of the State and the necessary severity shown to those who would wish to oppose this spontaneous and destined impulse of the Italy of the twentieth century, to oppose it in the name of the superseded ideologies of the nineteenth, repudiated wherever great experiments of political and social transformation, have been courageously attempted: especially where, as now, peoples thirst for authority, for leadership, for order. If every age has its own doctrine, it is apparent from a thousand signs that the doctrine of the present age is Fascism. That it is a doctrine of life is shown by the fact that it has resuscitated a faith. That this faith has conquered minds is proved by the fact that Fascism has had its dead and its martyrs.

Fascism henceforward has in the world the universality of all those doctrines which, by fulfilling themselves, have significance in the history of the human spirit.

CHAPTER THIRTY-TWO

FREUD

One of the main causes of Plato's lasting influence is that his theory of the state is based on a *theory of man*. Although his conception of the nature of man may seem out of date, in some respects it shows a remarkable understanding of the complexity of human personality. His psychological hypotheses are weakest where his aristocratic, antidemocratic political outlook blocks his objective appraisal of reality, and where the antiscientific, mythical elements in his philosophy are reflected in his views on the nature of man. Yet, despite these psychological imperfections, his political theory gained immensely from his realization that no study of state and society can be fruitful unless it is based on a systematic conception of man's nature and motivations. In particular, Plato's sense of the complexity of social and political issues is anchored in the realization that they cannot be dealt with in isolation, and that they are ultimately human problems, infused with all the contradictory and irrational elements of man's nature and existence. This psychological element in Plato's political theory has always been one of the most suggestive aspects, regardless of whether one follows or rejects the conclusions of political Platonism.

In modern political theory, Rousseau was perhaps the last writer who was keenly interested in the totality of man rather than in his political behavior alone. Like Plato, Rousseau was intensely concerned with education as a process of taming man's irrational forces and transmuting them into socially desirable activities from which the state could derive strength and cohesion. After Rousseau, political speculation increasingly abandoned the older tradition of Platonic and medieval thought in which the nature of the state was related to the nature of man. The classical political doctrines since the late eighteenth century generally have assumed an oversimplified rationalistic conception of man without subjecting it carefully to empirical analysis, and have proceeded to build a theory of state and society on the basis of such an assumption. Facts that do not seem to fit into the framework of theory have been dismissed as extraordinary, abnormal, irregular, or contrary to reason. The intellectual failure to account for the causes and existence of irrational, aggressive, and destructive facts in human relations was later reflected in the practical weakness of coping with such tendencies on the larger international scale.

A new dimension of understanding human behavior has been added by the work of Sigmund Freud (1856–1939). Freud started as a practicing physician in Vienna, and his psychological theories evolved out of his experience as a neurologist and psychiatrist, and not from any preconceived ideas. His pioneering contributions to medicine, psychology, and psychiatry are related to his discoveries of the processes and mechanisms of the *unconscious* in man's mind. Whereas pre-Freudian psychology virtually identified mental with conscious processes, Freud maintains (in his *General Introduction to Psychoanalysis,* 1916–1917) that "mental processes are essentially unconscious, and that those which are conscious are merely isolated acts and parts of the whole psychic entity."

Starting his clinical work with the treatment of the repressions and conflicts of neurotics, Freud soon saw that such conflicts were not peculiar to neurotics but were also found in mentally healthy persons, and the neuroses were not diseases in the traditional meaning of the word but ineffective and distorted ways of dealing with psychological stresses and strains. In his *Psychopathology of Everyday Life* (1904), one of his earliest major works, Freud had already shown that the ordinary slips of the tongue, forgetting of familiar names or events, and other faulty actions of normal persons in everyday life were not the product of accident but repressed thoughts of the unconscious that come to the surface despite the attempt to conceal and repress them. The study of the unconscious led Freud to examine the nature of dreams and of wit and humor as expressions of thoughts that cannot be tolerated in the conscious layers of the mind.

Freud's emphasis on the vital role of repressed sexual impulses at first aroused a great deal of opposition. Later that opposition died down when it was understood that the scientific analysis of the unconscious, irrational forces in man has the effect of lessening their damaging effect: the more we progress in understanding the mechanisms and processes of these irrational forces, the more we may eventually succeed in rationally controlling them.

Firmly believing that psychological phenomena are embedded, like all other phenomena of nature, in the stream of causality, Freud pursued the origin of neurotic conflicts in adults to their childhood experiences, repressions, and conflicts. He found striking similarities between the mental processes of neurotics and children, and between these and the mental processes of primitive peoples. Pathological behavior of neurotics is essentially regression to earlier, infantile stages in the development of normal functions, and the myths of primitive peoples show a striking resemblance to the phantasies of some classes of mentally ill in the western world. Particularly as he grew older, Freud became increasingly absorbed in the study of archaeology, ethnology, anthropology, religion, folklore, and mythology, and he drew attention to the remarkable similarities in the mental development of the individual and that of the human race as a whole.

One of Freud's most general works is his *Civilization and Its Discontents* (1930). Freud analyzes modern civilization in terms of two basic types of man's instinctual life: on the one hand, man has an impulse to love and cooperate, and, on the other, man has the impulse to attack and destroy. The first impulse is called by Freud (as by Plato in his *Symposium*) Eros, of which sexual love is only one manifestation. The purpose of the erotic impulse is to tie together, to establish ever greater unities, whereas the purpose of the second, the *death* instinct, is to attack, dissolve, destroy, and, finally, to reduce living things to an inorganic death. Freud shows that civilization owes its existence to the possibility of sublimating love for one's family into the wider friendship and loyalty for the group, society, and, lastly, the state.

Yet the very act of this transformation and sublimation of love creates tensions and frustrations that strengthen the aggressive impulses in man. The progress of civilization is thus a constant struggle between the cooperative and aggressive impulses in man, whose frustrations and conflicts turn into aggressive attitudes toward himself or others.

Writing in 1930, when the world seemed to be relatively safe and stable, Freud says in *Civilization and Its Discontents* that "civilized society is perpetually menaced with disintegration through this primary hostility of men towards one another." Freud argues against the communist thesis that the abolition of private property would eliminate personal and collective aggressions. Without taking sides with regard to the economic desirability of private property, Freud predicted in 1930 that the abolition of private property would not inaugurate a reign of love and cooperation in the Soviet Union. On the contrary, Freud warned that persecution in the Soviet Union would not come to an end once the bourgeois class was liquidated, and he predicted that the Russian Communists would eventually direct their aggressive tendencies against the outside world.

The emotional, "libidinal" ties that bind men together in furthering the progress of civilization are thus constantly menaced by the "natural instinct of aggressiveness in man, the hostility of each one against all and of all against each one." The meaning of the evolution of culture is therefore to be found in the constant struggle between "Eros and Death." Freud refused to prophesy whether cooperation would ultimately triumph over aggression and destruction, and he was perturbed by a new source of tension: men have learned to subdue the forces of nature to such an extent that the extermination of the whole human race has become a distinct possibility, and Freud ascribes to this fact (intensified a thousand times by the subsequent development of the atom and hydrogen bombs) an increased state of unrest, dejection, and apprehension that will lead to still more hostility and aggression.

In 1932, the League of Nations and the International Institute of Intellectual Cooperation asked Albert Einstein, the greatest physicist since Newton, to choose a significant issue of the time, and to discuss it with a person to be selected by him. Einstein chose the problem: "Is there a way of delivering mankind from the menace of war?" as the most important issue of humanity, and he selected Freud as the person most qualified to illuminate its cause and cure. This exchange of letters was published by the League of Nations under the title of *Why War?* in 1933. By that time the establishment of the Nazi regime in Germany had made the question one of tragic timeliness.

Applying his two basic concepts of erotic and destructive impulses, Freud came to the conclusion in his correspondence with Einstein that "there is no likelihood of our being able to suppress humanity's aggressive tendencies." The problem of eliminating war, Freud argues, cannot be tackled directly by seeking to abolish the aggressive impulses in man, but must be tackled indirectly, by diverting these impulses into channels other than warfare and strengthening the emotional ties that bring men together in common efforts and enjoyments. Freud also holds that the organization of society along rational principles rather than the traditional pattern of authoritarian leadership would indirectly strengthen the forces of peace. All such indirect methods, however, he is bound to admit, "conjure up an ugly picture of mills that grind so slowly that, before the flour is ready, men are dead of hunger."

Yet, owing to two facts, Freud is not wholly pessimistic about the possibility of eliminating war: first, man's progressive ability to master intellectually his instinctual life, and, second, "a well-founded dread of the form that future wars will take." Civilization is essentially the process of taming and domesticating man's instincts, and Freud does not know how the next phase of that process will come about. But he ends with the not altogether hopeless note that "meanwhile we may rest on the assurance that whatever makes for cultural development is working also against war."

Freud did most of his life's work in a period of optimistic, rationalistic liberalism. He was one of the few scientists and thinkers of his era who realized how fragile were the foundations of rationalism and optimism, always menaced by the dark and little-known forces of demonic irrationality lurking in the unconscious of man. If the progress of civilization consists in advancing into the frontiers of the unknown, in conquering more and more ignorance and suffering, Freud's contribution to the tradition of scientific humanism is immense. Freud himself resolutely denied that psychoanalysis is in itself a comprehensive philosophy of life, a *Weltanschauung,* and insisted (in the last of his *New Introductory Lectures on Psycho-Analysis,* 1933) that psychoanalysis shares, as a specialized science and branch of psychology, in the general philosophical orientation of all science: "It asserts that there is no other source of knowledge of the universe but the systematic intellectual analysis of carefully verified observations—in fact, what is called research—and that no knowledge can be obtained from revelation, intuition, or divination.

Although Freud well understood that scientific thought is "still in its infancy," and that there are still many problems with which science has been unable to cope, he did not regard reason as an end in itself. In the great tradition of western humanism, he postulated the value of increasing man's happiness and decreasing his suffering as a worthwhile practical goal, with reason as the only means to that end.

Whereas Plato saw in vision the supreme act of knowing truth, and in irrational myths the basis of authoritarian leadership, Freud regards verifiable experience as the only source of knowledge, and the rational organization of society—without the Platonic pattern of thought control and aristocratic domination—as the only means to a life of freedom and happiness. Wherever the adversaries of objective science have gained power, Freud's name has been considered dangerous and subversive. Wherever, on the other hand, thought is free and science unfettered, Freud's illumination of the dark recesses of the human mind—the unconscious—and his strengthening of the scientific tradition has been considered a milestone of humanist rationalism.

FREUD

*Civilization and Its Discontents**

THE LOVE IMPULSE

What are the influences to which the evolution of culture owes its origin, how did it arise and what determined its course?

This task seems too big a one; one may well confess oneself diffident. Here follows what little I have been able to elicit about it.

Once primitive man had made the discovery that it lay in his own hands—speaking literally—to improve his lot on earth by working, it cannot have been a matter of indifference to him whether another man worked with him or against him. The other acquired the value of a fellow-worker, and it was advantageous to live with him. Even earlier, in his apelike prehistory, man had adopted the habit of forming families: his first helpers were probably the members of his family. One may suppose that the founding of families was in some way connected with the period when the need for genital satisfaction, no longer appearing like an occasional guest who turns up suddenly and then vanishes without letting one hear anything of him for long intervals, had settled down with each man like a permanent lodger. When this happened, the male acquired a motive for keeping the female, or rather, his sexual objects, near him; while the female, who wanted not to be separated from her helpless young, in their interests, too, had to stay by the stronger male. In this primitive family one essential feature of culture is lacking: the will of the father, the head of it, was unfettered. I have

endeavoured in *Totem and Taboo* to show how the way led from this family-life to the succeeding phase of communal existence in the form of a band of brothers. By overpowering the father, the sons had discovered that several men united can be stronger than a single man. The totemic stage of culture is founded upon the restrictions that the band were obliged to impose on one another in order to maintain the new system. These taboos were the first "Right" or law. The life of human beings in common therefore had a twofold foundation, *i.e.* the compulsion to work, created by external necessity, and the power of love, causing the male to wish to keep his sexual object, the female, near him, and the female to keep near her that part of herself which has become detached from her, her child. Eros and Ananke were the parents of human culture, too. The first result of culture was that a larger number of human beings could then live together in common. And since the two great powers were here cooperating together, one might have expected that further cultural evolution would have proceeded smoothly towards ever greater mastery over the external world, as well as towards greater extension in the numbers of men sharing the life in common. Nor is it easy to understand how this culture can be felt as anything but satisfying by those who partake of it.

Before we go on to enquire where the disturbances in it arise, we will let ourselves digress from the point that love was one of the founders of culture and so fill a gap left in our previous discussion. We said that man, having found by experience that sexual (genital) love afforded him his greatest gratification, so that it became in effect a prototype of all happiness to him, must have

*From Sigmund Freud, *Civilization and Its Discontents* (Hogarth Press, 1930). By permission of Hogarth Press, Ltd., London, and W.W. Norton and Company, Inc., New York.

been thereby impelled to seek his happiness further along the path of sexual relations, to make genital erotism the central point of his life. We went on to say that in so doing he becomes to a very dangerous degree dependent on a part of the outer world, namely, on his chosen love-object, and this exposes him to most painful sufferings if he is rejected by it or loses it through death or defection. The wise men of all ages have consequently warned us emphatically against this way of life; but in spite of all it retains its attraction for a great number of people.

A small minority are enabled by their constitution nevertheless to find happiness along the path of love; but far-reaching mental transformations of the erotic function are necessary before this is possible. These people make themselves independent of their object's acquiescence by transferring the main value from the fact of being loved to their own act of loving; they protect themselves against loss of it by attaching their love not to individual objects but to all men equally, and they avoid the uncertainties and disappointments of genital love by turning away from its sexual aim and modifying the instinct into an impulse with an *inhibited aim.* The state which they induce in themselves by this process—an unchangeable, undeviating, tender attitude— has little superficial likeness to the stormy vicissitudes of genital love, from which it is nevertheless derived. It seems that Saint Francis of Assisi may have carried this method of using love to produce an inner feeling of happiness as far as anyone; what we are thus characterizing as one of the procedures by which the pleasure-principle fulfils itself has in fact been linked up in many ways with religion; the connection between them may lie in those remote fastnesses of the mind where the distinctions between the ego and objects and between the various objects become matters of indifference. From one ethical standpoint, the deeper motivation of which will later become clear to us, this inclination towards an all-embracing love of others and of the world at large is regarded as the highest state of mind of which man is capable. Even at this early stage in the discussion I will not withhold the two principal objections we have to raise against this view. A love that does not discriminate seems to us to lose some of its own value, since it does an injustice to its object. And secondly, not all men are worthy of love.

The love that instituted the family still retains its power; in its original form it does not stop short of direct sexual satisfaction, and in its modified form as aim-inhibited friendliness it influences our civilization. In both these forms it carries on its task of binding men and women to one another, and it does this with greater intensity than can be achieved through the interest of work in common. The casual and undifferentiated way in which the word "love" is employed by language has its genetic justification. In general usage the relation between a man and a woman whose genital desires have led them to found a family is called love; but the positive attitude of feeling between parents and children, between brothers and sisters in a family, is also called love, although to us this relation merits the description of aim-inhibited love or affection. Love with an inhibited aim was indeed originally full sensual love and in men's unconscious minds is so still. Both of them, the sensual and the aim-inhibited forms, reach out beyond the family and create new bonds with others who before were strangers. Genital love leads to the forming of new families; aim-inhibited love to "friendships," which are valuable culturally because they do not entail many of the limitations of genital love—for instance, its exclusiveness. But the interrelations between love and culture lose their simplicity as development proceeds. On the one hand, love opposes the interests of culture; on the other, culture menaces love with grievous restrictions.

This rift between them seems inevitable; the cause of it is not immediately recognizable. It expresses itself first in a conflict between the family and the larger community to which the individual belongs. We have seen already that one of culture's principal endeavours is to cement men and women together into larger units. But the family will not give up the individual. The closer the attachment between the members of it, the more they often tend to remain aloof from others, and the harder it is for them to enter into the wider circle of the world at large. That form of life in common which is phylogenetically older, and is in childhood its only form, resists being displaced by the type that becomes acquired later with culture. Detachment from the family has become a task that awaits every adolescent, and often society helps him through it with pubertal and initiatory rites. One gets the impression that these difficulties form an integral part of every process of mental evolution—and indeed, at bottom, of every organic development, too.

The next discord is caused by women, who soon become antithetical to cultural trends and spread around them their conservative influence—the women who at the beginning laid the foundations of culture by the appeal of their love. Women represent the interests of the family and sexual life; the work of civilization has become more and more men's business; it confronts them with ever harder tasks, compels them to sublimations of instinct which women are not easily able to achieve. Since man has not an unlimited amount of mental energy at his disposal, he must accomplish his tasks by distributing his libido to the best advantage. What he employs for cultural purposes he withdraws to a great extent from women and his sexual life; his constant association with men and his dependence on his relations with them even estrange him from his duties as husband and father. Woman finds herself thus forced into the background by the claims of culture and she adopts an inimical attitude towards it.

The tendency of culture to set restrictions upon sexual life is no less evident than its other aim of widening its sphere of operations. Even the earliest phase of it, the totemic, brought in its train the prohibition against incestuous object-choice, perhaps the most maiming wound ever inflicted throughout the ages on the erotic life of man. Further limitations are laid on it by taboos, laws and customs, which touch men as well as women. Various types of culture differ in the lengths to which they carry this; and the material structure of the social fabric also affects the measure of sexual freedom that remains. We have seen that culture obeys the laws of psychological economic necessity in making the restrictions, for it obtains a great part of the mental energy it needs by subtracting it from sexuality. Culture behaves towards sexuality in this respect like a tribe or a section of the population which has gained the upper hand and is exploiting the rest to its own advantage. Fear of a revolt among the oppressed then becomes a motive for even stricter regulations. A high-water mark in this type of development has been reached in our Western European civilization. Psychologically it is fully justified in beginning by censuring any manifestations of the sexual life of children, for there would be no prospect of curbing the sexual desires of adults if the ground had not been prepared for it in childhood. Nevertheless there is no sort of justification for the lengths beyond this to which civilized society goes in actually denying the existence of these manifestations, which are not merely demonstrable but positively glaring. Where sexually mature persons are concerned, object-choice is further narrowed down to the opposite sex and most of the extra-genital forms of satisfaction are interdicted as perversions. The standard which declares itself in these prohibitions is that of a sexual life identical for all; it pays no heed to the disparities in the inborn and acquired sexual constitutions of individuals and cuts off a considerable number of them from sexual enjoyment, thus becoming a cause of grievous injustice. The effect of these restrictive measures might presumably be that all the sexual interest of those who are normal and not constitutionally handicapped could flow without further forfeiture into the channel left open to it. But the only outlet not thus censured, heterosexual genital love, is further circumscribed by the barriers of legitimacy and monogamy. Present-day civilization gives us plainly to understand that sexual relations are permitted only on the basis of a final, indissoluble bond between a man and woman; that sexuality as a source of enjoyment for its own sake is unacceptable to it, and that its intention is to tolerate it only as the hitherto irreplaceable means of multiplying the human race.

This, of course, represents an extreme. Everyone knows that it has proved impossible to put it into execution, even for short periods. Only the weaklings have submitted to such comprehensive interference with their sexual freedom, and stronger natures have done so only under one compensatory condition, of which mention may be made later. Civilized society has seen itself obliged to pass over in silence many transgressions which by its own ordinances it ought to have penalized. This does not justify anyone, however, in leaning towards the other side and assuming that, because it does not achieve all it aims at, such an attitude on the part of society is altogether harmless. The sexual life of civilized man is seriously disabled, whatever we may say; it sometimes makes an impression of being a function in process of becoming atrophied, just as organs like our teeth and our hair seem to be. One is probably right in supposing that the importance of sexuality as, a source of pleasurable sensations, *i.e.* as a means of fulfilling the purpose of life, has perceptibly decreased. Sometimes one imagines one perceives that it is not only the oppression of culture, but something in the nature of the function itself, that denies us full satisfaction and urges us in other directions. This may be an error; it is hard to decide.

THE AGGRESSIVE IMPULSE

Psycho-analytic work has shown that these frustrations in respect of sexual life are especially unendurable to the so-called neurotics among us. These persons manufacture substitute-gratifications for themselves in their symptoms, which, however, are either painful in themselves or become the cause of suffering owing to the difficulties they create with the person's environment and society at large. It is easy to understand the latter fact, but the former presents us with a new problem. But culture demands other sacrifices besides that of sexual gratifications.

We have regarded the difficulties in the development of civilization as part of the general difficulty accompanying all evolution, for we have traced them to the inertia of libido, its disinclination to relinquish an old position in favour of a new one. It is much the same thing if we say that the conflict between civilization and sexuality is caused by the circumstance that sexual love is a relationship between two people, in which a third can only be superfluous or disturbing, whereas civilization is founded on relations between larger groups of persons. When a love-relationship is at its height no room is left for any interest in the surrounding world; the pair of lovers are sufficient unto themselves, do not even need the child they have in common to make them

happy. In no other case does Eros so plainly betray the core of his being, his aim of making one out of many; but when he has achieved it in the proverbial way through the love of two human beings, he is not willing to go further.

From all this we might well imagine that a civilized community could consist of pairs of individuals such as this, libidinally satisfied in each other, and linked to all the others by work and common interests. If this were so, culture would not need to levy energy from sexuality. But such a desirable state of things does not exist and never has existed; in actuality culture is not content with such limited ties as these; we see that it endeavours to bind the members of the community to one another by libidinal ties as well, that it makes use of every means and favours every avenue by which powerful identifications can be created among them, and that it exacts a heavy toll of aim-inhibited libido in order to strengthen communities by bonds of friendship between the members. Restrictions upon sexual life are unavoidable if this object is to be attained. But we cannot see the necessity that forces culture along this path and gives rise to its antagonism to sexuality. It must be due to some disturbing influence not yet detected by us.

We may find the clue in one of the so-called ideal standards of civilized society. It runs: "Thou shalt love thy neighbour as thyself." It is world-renowned, undoubtedly older than Christianity which parades it as its proudest profession, yet certainly not very old; in historical times men still knew nothing of it. We will adopt a naïve attitude towards it, as if we were meeting it for the first time. Thereupon we find ourselves unable to suppress a feeling of astonishment, as at something unnatural. Why should we do this? What good is it to us? Above all, how can we do such a thing? How could it possibly be done? My love seems to me a valuable thing that I have no right to throw away without reflection. It imposes obligations on me which I must be prepared to make sacrifices to fulfil. If I love someone, he must be worthy of it in some way or other. (I am leaving out of account now the use he may be to me, as well as his possible significance to me as a sexual object; neither of these two kinds of relationship between us come into question where the injunction to love my neighbour is concerned.) He will be worthy of it if he is so like me in important respects that I can love myself in him; worthy of it if he is so much more perfect than I that I can love my ideal of myself in him; I must love him if he is the son of my friend, since the pain my friend would feel if anything untoward happened to him would be my pain—I should have to share it. But if he is a stranger to me and cannot attract me by any value he has in himself or any significance he may have already acquired in my emotional life, it will be hard for me to love him. I shall even be doing wrong if I do, for my love is valued as a privilege by all those belonging to me; it is an injustice to them if I put a stranger on a level with them. But if I am to love him (with that kind of universal love) simply because he, too, is a denizen of the earth, like an insect or an earthworm or a grass-snake, then I fear that but a small modicum of love will fall to his lot and it would be impossible for me to give him as much as by all the laws of reason I am entitled to retain for myself. What is the point of an injunction promulgated with such solemnity, if reason does not recommend it to us?

When I look more closely I find still further difficulties. Not merely is this stranger on the whole not worthy of love, but, to be honest, I must confess be has more claim to my hostility, even to my hatred. He does not seem to have the least trace of love for me, does not show me the slightest consideration. If it will do him any good, he has no hesitation in injuring me, never even asking himself whether the amount of advantage he gains by it bears any proportion to the amount of wrong done to me. What is more, he does not even need to get an advantage from it; if he can merely get a little pleasure out of it, he thinks nothing of jeering at me, insulting me, slandering me, showing his power over me; and the more secure he feels himself, or the more helpless I am, with so much more certainty can I expect this behaviour from him towards me. If he behaved differently, if he showed me consideration and did not molest me, I should in any case, without the aforesaid commandment, be willing to treat him similarly. If the high-sounding ordinance had run, "Love thy neighbour as thy neighbour loves thee," I should not take objection to it. And there is a second commandment that seems to me even more incomprehensible, and arouses still stronger opposition in me. It is: "Love thine enemies." When I think it over, however, I am wrong in treating it as a greater imposition. It is at bottom the same thing.[1]

I imagine now I hear a voice gravely adjuring me: "Just because thy neighbour is not worthy of thy love, is probably full of enmity towards thee, thou shouldst love him as thyself." I then perceive the case to be like that of *Credo quia absurdum.*

Now it is, of course, very probable that my neighbour, when he is commanded to love me as himself, will answer exactly as I have done and reject me for the same reasons. I hope he will not have the same objective grounds for doing so, but he will hope so as well. Even so, there are variations in men's behaviour which ethics, disregarding the fact that they are determined, classifies as "good" and "evil." As long as these undeniable variations have not been abolished, conformity to the highest ethical standards constitutes a betrayal of the interests of culture, for it puts a direct premium on wickedness. One is irresistibly reminded here of an incident in the French Chamber when capital punishment was being discussed; the speech of a member who had passionately supported its abolition was being applauded with loud acclamation, when suddenly a voice was heard calling out from the back of the room, *"Que messieurs les assassins commencent!"*

The bit of truth behind all this—one so eagerly denied—is that men are not gentle, friendly creatures wishing for love, who

---

[1] A great poet may permit himself, at least in jest, to give utterance to psychological truths that are heavily censured. Thus Heine: "Mine is the most peaceable disposition. My wishes are a humble dwelling with a thatched roof, but a good bed, good food, milk and butter of the freshest, flowers at my windows, some fine tall trees before my door; and if the good God wants to make me completely happy, he will grant me the joy of seeing some six or seven of my enemies hanging from these trees. With my heart full of deep emotion I shall forgive them before they die all the wrong they did me in their lifetime—true, one must forgive one's enemies, but not until they are brought to execution." (Heine, *Gedanken und Einfälle.*)

simply defend themselves if they are attacked, but that a powerful measure of desire for aggression has to be reckoned as part of their instinctual endowment. The result is that their neighbour is to them not only a possible helper or sexual object, but also a temptation to them to gratify their aggressiveness on him, to exploit his capacity for work without recompense, to use him sexually without his consent, to seize his possessions, to humiliate him, to cause him pain, to torture and to kill him. *Homo homini lupus;* who has the courage to dispute it in the face of all the evidence in his own life and in history? This aggressive cruelty usually lies in wait for some provocation, or else it steps into the service of some other purpose, the aim of which might as well have been achieved by milder measures. In circumstances that favour it, when those forces in the mind which ordinarily inhibit it cease to operate, it also manifests itself spontaneously and reveals men as savage beasts to whom the thought of sparing their own kind is alien. Anyone who calls to mind the atrocities of the early migrations, of the invasion by the Huns or by the so-called Mongols under Jenghiz Khan and Tamurlane, of the sack of Jerusalem by the pious Crusaders, even indeed the horrors of the last world-war, will have to bow his head humbly before the truth of this view of man.

The existence of this tendency to aggression which we can detect in ourselves and rightly presume to be present in others is the factor that disturbs our relations with our neighbours and makes it necessary for culture to institute its high demands. Civilized society is perpetually menaced with disintegration through this primary hostility of men towards one another. Their interests in their common work would not hold them together; the passions of instinct are stronger than reasoned interests. Culture has to call up every possible reinforcement in order to erect barriers against the aggressive instincts of men and hold their manifestations in check by reaction-formations in men's minds. Hence its system of methods by which mankind is to be driven to identifications and aim-inhibited love-relationships; hence the restrictions on sexual life; and hence, too, its ideal command to love one's neighbour as oneself, which is really justified by the fact that nothing is so completely at variance with original human nature as this. With all its striving, this endeavour of culture's has so far not achieved very much. Civilization expects to prevent the worst atrocities of brutal violence by taking upon itself the right to employ violence against criminals, but the law is not able to lay hands on the more discreet and subtle forms in which human aggressions are expressed. The time comes when every one of us has to abandon the illusory anticipations with which in our youth we regarded our fellow-men and when we realize how much hardship and suffering we have been caused in life through their ill-will. It would be unfair, however, to reproach culture with trying to eliminate all disputes and competition from human concerns. These things are undoubtedly indispensable; but opposition is not necessarily enmity, only it may be misused to make an opening for it.

The Communists believe they have found a way of delivering us from this evil. Man is whole-heartedly good and friendly to his neighbour, they say, but the system of private property has corrupted his nature. The possession of private property gives power to the individual and thence the temptation arises to ill-treat his neighbour; the man who is excluded from the possession of property is obliged to rebel in hostility against the oppressor. If private property were abolished, all valuables held in common and all allowed to share in the enjoyment of them, ill-will and enmity would disappear from among men. Since all needs would be satisfied, none would have any reason to regard another as an enemy; all would willingly undertake the work which is necessary. I have no concern with any economic criticisms of the communistic system; I cannot enquire into whether the abolition of private property is advantageous and expedient.[2] But I am able to recognize that

---

[2] Anyone who has been through the misery of poverty in his youth, and has endured the indifference and arrogance of those who have possessions, should be exempt from the suspicion that he has no understanding of or goodwill towards the endeavours made to fight the economic inequality of men and all that it leads to. To be sure, if an attempt is made to base this fight upon an abstract demand for equality for all in

psychologically it is founded on an untenable illusion. By abolishing private property one deprives the human love of aggression of one of its instruments, a strong one undoubtedly, but assuredly not the strongest. It in no way alters the individual differences in power and influence which are turned by aggressiveness to its own use, nor does it change the nature of the instinct in any way. This instinct did not arise as the result of property; it reigned almost supreme in primitive times when possessions were still extremely scanty; it shows itself already in the nursery when possessions have hardly grown out of their original anal shape; it is at the bottom of all the relations of affection and love between human beings—possibly with the single exception of that of a mother to her male child. Suppose that personal rights to material goods are done away with, there still remain prerogatives in sexual relationships, which must arouse the strongest rancour and most violent enmity among men and women who are otherwise equal. Let us suppose this were also to be removed by instituting complete liberty in sexual life, so that the family, the germ-life of culture, ceased to exist; one could not, it is true, foresee the new paths on which cultural development might then proceed, but one thing one would be bound to expect, and that is that the ineffaceable feature of human nature would follow wherever it led.

Men clearly do not find it easy to do without satisfaction of this tendency to aggression that is in them; when deprived of satisfaction of it they are ill at ease. There is an advantage, not to be undervalued, in the existence of smaller communities, through which the aggressive instinct can find an outlet in enmity towards those outside the group. It is always possible to unite considerable numbers of men in love towards one another, so long as there are still some remaining as objects for aggressive manifestations. I once interested myself in the peculiar fact that peoples whose territories are adjacent, and are otherwise closely

related, are always at feud with and ridiculing each other, as, for instance, the Spaniards and the Portuguese, the North and South Germans, the English and the Scotch, and so on. I gave it the name of "narcissism in respect of minor differences," which does not do much to explain it. One can now see that it is a convenient and relatively harmless form of satisfaction for aggressive tendencies, through which cohesion amongst the members of a group is made easier. The Jewish people, scattered in all directions as they are, have in this way rendered services which deserve recognition to the development of culture in the countries where they settled; but unfortunately not all the massacres of Jews in the Middle Ages sufficed to procure peace and security for their Christian contemporaries. Once the apostle Paul had laid down universal love between all men as the foundation of his Christian community, the inevitable consequence in Christianity was the utmost intolerance towards all who remained outside of it; the Romans, who had not founded their state on love, were not given to lack of religious toleration, although religion was a concern of the state, and the state was permeated through and through with it. Neither was it an unaccountable chance that the dream of a German world-dominion evoked a complementary movement towards anti-semitism; and it is quite intelligible that the attempt to establish a new communistic type of culture in Russia should find psychological support in the persecution of the bourgeois. One only wonders, with some concern, however, how the Soviets will manage when they have exterminated their bourgeois entirely.

If civilization requires such sacrifices, not only of sexuality but also of the aggressive tendencies in mankind, we can better understand why it should be so hard for men to feel happy in it. In actual fact primitive man was better off in this respect, for he knew nothing of any restrictions on his instincts. As a set-off against this, his prospects of enjoying his happiness for any length of time were very slight. Civilized man has exchanged some part of his chances of happiness for a measure of security. We will not forget, however, that in the primal family only the head of it enjoyed this instinctual freedom; the other members lived in slavish thraldom. The antithesis between

---

the name of justice, there is a very obvious objection to be made, namely, that nature began the injustice by the highly unequal way in which she endows individuals physically and mentally, for which there is no help.

a minority enjoying cultural advantages and a majority who are robbed of them was therefore most extreme in that primeval period of culture. With regard to the primitive human types living at the present time, careful investigation has revealed that their instinctual life is by no means to be envied on account of its freedom; it is subject to restrictions of a different kind but perhaps even more rigorous than is that of modern civilized man.

In rightly finding fault, as we thus do, with our present state of civilization for so inadequately providing us with what we require to make us happy in life, and for the amount of suffering of a probably avoidable nature it lays us open to—in doing our utmost to lay bare the roots of its deficiencies by our unsparing criticisms, we are undoubtedly exercising our just rights and not showing ourselves enemies of culture. We may expect that in the course of time changes will be carried out in our civilization so that it becomes more satisfying to our needs and no longer open to the reproaches we have made against it. But perhaps we shall also accustom ourselves to the idea that there are certain difficulties inherent in the very nature of culture which will not yield to any efforts at reform. Over and above the obligations of putting restrictions upon our instincts, which we see to be inevitable, we are imminently threatened with the dangers of a state one may call *"la misère psychologique"* of groups. This danger is most menacing where the social forces of cohesion consist predominantly of identifications of the individuals in the group with one another, whilst leading personalities fail to acquire the significance that should fall to them in the process of group-formation. The state of civilization in America at the present day offers a good opportunity for studying this injurious effect of civilization which we have reason to dread. But I will resist the temptation to enter upon a criticism of American culture; I have no desire to give the impression that I would employ American methods myself.

THE STRUGGLE BETWEEN EROS AND DEATH

Never before in any of my previous writings have I had the feeling so strongly as I have now that what I am describing is common knowledge, that I am requisitioning paper and ink, and in due course the labour of compositors and printers, in order to expound things that in themselves are obvious. For this reason, if it should appear that the recognition of a special independent instinct of aggression would entail a modification of the psychoanalytical theory of instincts, I should be glad enough to seize upon the idea.

We shall see that this is not so, that it is merely a matter of coming to closer quarters with a conclusion to which we long ago committed ourselves and following it out to its logical consequences. The whole of analytic theory has evolved gradually enough, but the theory of instincts has groped its way forward under greater difficulties than any other part of it. And yet a theory of instincts was so indispensable for the rest that something had to be adopted in place of it. In my utter perplexity at the beginning, I took as my starting-point the poet-philosopher Schiller's aphorism, that hunger and love make the world go round. Hunger would serve to represent those instincts which aim at preservation of the individual; love seeks for objects; its chief function, which is favoured in every way by nature, is preservation of the species. Thus first arose the contrast between ego instincts and object instincts. For the energy of the latter instincts and exclusively for them I introduced the term libido; an antithesis was thus formed between the ego instincts and the libidinal instincts directed towards objects, *i.e.* love in its widest sense. One of these object instincts, the sadistic, certainly stood out from the rest in that its aim was so very unloving; moreover, it clearly allied itself in many of its aspects with the ego instincts, and its close kinship with instincts of mastery without any libidinal purpose could not be concealed, but these ambiguities could be overcome; in spite of them, sadism plainly belonged to sexual life—the game of cruelty could take the place of the game of love. Neurosis appeared as the outcome of a struggle between the interests of self-preservation and the claims of libido, a struggle in which the ego was victorious, but at the price of great suffering and renunciations.

Every analyst will admit that none of this even now reads like a statement long since recognized as erroneous. All the same, modifications had to be made as our researches advanced from the repressed to the repressing, from the object instincts to the ego. A cardinal point in this advance was the introduction of the concept of narcissism; *i.e.* the idea that libido cathects the ego itself, that its first dwelling-place was in the ego, and that the latter remains to some extent its permanent headquarters. This narcissistic libido turns in the direction of objects, thus becoming object-libido, and can transform itself back into narcissistic libido. The concept of narcissism made it possible to consider the traumatic neuroses, as well as many diseases bordering on the psychoses, and also the latter themselves, from the psycho-analytic angle. It was not necessary to abandon the view that the transference-neuroses are attempts on the part of the ego to guard itself against sexuality, but the concept of the libido was jeopardized. Since the ego-instincts were found to be libidinal as well, it seemed for a time inevitable that libido should become synonymous with instinctual energy in general, as C.G. Jung had previously advocated. Yet there still remained in me a kind of conviction, for which as yet there were no grounds, that the instincts could not all be of the same nature. I made the next step in *Beyond the Pleasure Principle* (1920), when the repetition-compulsion and the conservative character of instinctual life first struck me. On the basis of speculations concerning the origin of life and of biological parallels, I drew the conclusion that, beside the instinct preserving the organic substance and binding it into ever larger units,[3] there must exist another in antithesis to this, which would seek to dissolve these units and reinstate their antecedent inorganic state; that is to say, a death instinct as well as Eros; the phenomena of life would then be explicable from the interplay of the two and their counteracting effects on each other. It was not

easy, however, to demonstrate the working of this hypothetical death instinct. The manifestations of Eros were conspicuous and audible enough; one might assume that the death instinct worked silently within the organism towards its disintegration, but that, of course, was no proof. The idea that part of the instinct became directed towards the outer world and then showed itself as an instinct of aggression and destruction carried us a step further. The instinct would thus itself have been pressed into the service of Eros, in that the organism would be destroying something animate or inanimate outside itself instead of itself. Conversely, any cessation of this flow outwards must have the effect of intensifying the self-destruction which in any case would always be going on within. From this example one could then surmise that the two kinds of instincts seldom—perhaps never—appear in isolation, but always mingle with each other in different, very varying proportions, and so make themselves unrecognizable to us. Sadism, long since known to us as a component-instinct of sexuality, would represent a particularly strong admixture of the instinct of destruction into the love impulse; while its counterpart, masochism, would be an alliance between sexuality and the destruction at work within the self, in consequence of which the otherwise imperceptible destructive trend became directly evident and palpable.

The assumption of the existence of a death instinct or a destruction instinct has aroused opposition even in analytical circles; I know that there is a great tendency to ascribe all that is dangerous and hostile in love rather to a fundamental bipolarity in its own nature. The conceptions I have summarized here I first put forward only tentatively, but in the course of time they have won such a hold over me that I can no longer think in any other way. To my mind they are theoretically far more fruitful than any others it is possible to employ; they provide us with that simplification, without either ignoring or doing violence to the facts, which is what we strive after in scientific work. I know that we have always had before our eyes manifestations of the destruction instinct fused with erotism, directed outwards and inwards in sadism and masochism; but I can no longer understand how we could have

---

[3] The contradiction between the tireless tendency of Eros to spread ever further and the general conservative nature of the instincts here becomes very noticeable; it would serve as the starting-point of enquiries into further problems.

overlooked the universality of nonerotic aggression and destruction, and could have omitted to give it its due significance in our interpretation of life. (It is true that the destructive trend that is directed inwards, when it is not erotically tinged, usually eludes our perceptions.) I can remember my own defensive attitude when the idea of an instinct of destruction first made its appearance in psychoanalytical literature and how long it took until I became accessible to it. That others should have shown the same resistance, and still show it, surprises me less. Those who love fairy tales do not like it when people speak of the innate tendencies in mankind towards aggression, destruction and, in addition, cruelty. For God has made them in his own image, with his own perfections; no one wants to be reminded how hard it is to reconcile the undeniable existence— in spite of all the protestations of Christian Science—of evil with his omnipotence and supreme goodness. The devil is, in fact, the best way out in acquittal of God; he can be used to play the same economic rôle of outlet as Jews in the world of Aryan ideals. But even so, one can just as well hold God responsible for the existence of the devil as for the evil he personifies. In view of these difficulties, it is expedient for every man to make humble obeisance on suitable occasions in honour of the high-minded nature of men; it will assist him to become universally beloved and much shall be forgiven unto him on account of it.[4]

The name libido can again be used to denote the manifestations of the power of Eros in contradistinction to the energy of the death instinct.[5] We must confess that it is more difficult for us to detect the latter, and to a great extent we can merely conjecture its existence as a background to Eros, also that it eludes us wherever it is not betrayed by a fusion with Eros. In sadism, where it bends the erotic aim to its own will and yet at the same time gratifies the sexual craving completely, we can obtain the clearest insight into its nature and its relation to Eros. But even where it shows itself without any sexual purpose, even in the blindest frenzy of destructiveness, one cannot ignore the fact that satisfaction of it is accompanied by an extraordinarily intense narcissistic enjoyment, due to the fulfilment it brings to the ego of its oldest omnipotence-wishes. The instinct of destruction, when tempered and harnessed (as it were, inhibited in its aim) and directed towards objects, is compelled to provide the ego with satisfaction of its needs and with power over nature. Since the assumption of its existence is based essentially on theoretical grounds, it must be confessed that it is not entirely proof against theoretical objections. But this is how things appear to us now in the present state of our knowledge; future research and reflection will undoubtedly bring further light which will decide the question.

In all that follows I take up the standpoint that the tendency to aggression is an innate, independent, instinctual disposition in man, and I come back now to the statement that it constitutes the most powerful obstacle to culture. At one point in the course of this discussion the idea took possession of us that culture was a peculiar process passing over human life and we are still under the influence of this idea. We may add to this that the process proves to be in the service of Eros, which aims at binding together single human individuals, then families, then tribes, races, nations, into one great unity, that of humanity. Why this has to be done we do not know; it is simply the

---

[4] In Goethe's Mephistopheles we have a quite exceptionally striking identification of the principle of evil with the instinct of destruction:

All entities that be
Deserve their end—nonentity.
　　• • • • •
So all that you name sin, destruction—
Wickedness, briefly—proves to be
The native element for me.

As his adversary, the devil himself cites not what is holy and good, but the power in nature working towards the creation and renewal of life—that is, Eros.

From air, from water, germs in thousands,
As from the soil, break forth, break free,
Dry, wet, warm, cold—a pullulation!
Had I not laid on flame a reservation,
Nothing were set apart for me.

---

[5] Our present point of view ran be roughly expressed in the statement that libido participates in every instinctual manifestation, but that not everything in that manifestation is libido.

work of Eros. These masses of men must be bound to one another libidinally; necessity alone, the advantages of common work, would not hold them together. The natural instinct of aggressiveness in man, the hostility of each one against all and of all against each one, opposes this programme of civilization. This instinct of aggression is the derivative and main representative of the death instinct we have found alongside of Eros, sharing his rule over the earth. And now, it seems to me, the meaning of the evolution of culture is no longer a riddle to us. It must present to us the struggle between Eros and Death, between the instincts of life and the instincts of destruction, as it works itself out in the human species. This struggle is what all life essentially consists of and so the evolution of civilization may be simply described as the struggle of the human species for existence. And it is this battle of the Titans that our nurses and governesses try to compose with their lullaby-song of Heaven!

For various reasons, it is very far from my intention to express any opinion concerning the value of human civilization. I have endeavoured to guard myself against the enthusiastic partiality which believes our civilization to be the most precious thing that we possess or could acquire, and thinks it must inevitably lead us to undreamt-of heights of perfection. I can at any rate listen without taking umbrage to those critics who aver that when one surveys the aims of civilization and the means it employs, one is bound to conclude that the whole thing is not worth the effort and that in the end it can only produce a state of things which no individual will be able to bear. My impartiality is all the easier to me since I know very little about these things and am sure only of one thing, that the judgments of value made by mankind are immediately determined by their desires for happiness; in other words, that those judgments are attempts to prop up their illusions with arguments. I could understand it very well if anyone were to point to the inevitable nature of the process of cultural development and say, for instance, that the tendency to institute restrictions upon sexual life or to carry humanitarian ideals into effect at the cost of natural selection is a developmental trend which it is impossible to avert or divert, and to which it is best for us to submit as though they were natural necessities. I know, too, the objection that can be raised against this: that tendencies such as these, which are believed to have insuperable power behind them, have often in the history of man been thrown aside and replaced by others. My courage fails me, therefore, at the thought of rising up as a prophet before my fellow-men, and I bow to their reproach that I have no consolation to offer them; for at bottom this is what they all demand—the frenzied revolutionary as passionately as the most pious believer.

The fateful question of the human species seems to me to be whether and to what extent the cultural process developed in it will succeed in mastering the derangements of communal life caused by the human instinct of aggression and self-destruction. In this connection, perhaps the phase through which we are at this moment passing deserves special interest. Men have brought their powers of subduing the forces of nature to such a pitch that by using them they could now very easily exterminate one another to the last man. They know this—hence arises a great part of their current unrest, their dejection, their mood of apprehension. And now it may be expected that the other of the two "heavenly forces," eternal Eros, will put forth his strength so as to maintain himself alongside of his equally immortal adversary.

CHAPTER THIRTY-THREE

GANDHI

More than for most social thinkers, the work of Mohandas Gandhi (1869–1948) (also called Mahatma, or "great-soul") is best understood through his actions. It is, further, necessary to have some background of the circumstances within which Gandhi lived, because this helps to explain his ideas and actions. Strictly in terms of people, the components of former British India (India, Pakistan, and Bangladesh) today have a population almost twice that of Europe, and have a physical area comparable in size to Europe. Culturally, India's history extends back 4,000 years. The story of India is one of a vast conglomeration of peoples, religions, languages, and castes. There are, broadly speaking, four classes within the Hindu varna system which, while related, is different than the caste system. Hinduism is based on the concept of reincarnation and transmigration, in which all living beings, from plant life to gods, are part of an everlasting cycle. As the result of how they have lived in a prior life, individuals are born (or reborn) into different positions. The three twice-born castes are brahmins (priests), kshatriyas (warriors), and vaisha (merchants). In addition, there is the sudra caste (peasants). Apart from these four—which comprise the varna system—are the outcastes, or untouchables. The caste system, then, is the more particular and localized social structure, which generally also determines a person's occupation (again, by birth). In one linguistic area, there may be as many as 50–200 castes with as many as 500–2,000 subcastes.

Gandhi was born a member of the modh bania caste, a grocer's caste. In his home region, the merchant vaisha castes had thrown off traditional deference to brahmins through their absorption of Jainism, a sect which split off from Hinduism in the sixth century B.C. Jainism stresses non-violence and the absence of caste distinctions, and strongly affected Gandhi. His father was the chief minister of one of the numerous small Indian princely states. In not untypical Indian fashion, Gandhi had an arranged marriage at age 13.

Formative influences on Gandhi included Hinduism and his mother, "the outstanding impression" of whom on him, he states in his autobiography (titled, *The Story of My Experiments with Truth*), was "saintliness." She belonged to a Hindu sect especially opposed to idolatry, one which sought a connection between Hinduism and Islam, and had sympathy for Jainism. Gandhi attended an English secondary school where all lessons were taught in English and cricket was played. To ensure future career opportunities, his family determined it was necessary for him to attend college in England. This was a monumental decision which led to ostracism by his local caste community, which by some was never withdrawn.

Gandhi studied law in England, and took classes in other academic areas as well. He joined the London Vegetarian Society and became involved with members of the Theosophical Society who, paradoxically, introduced him in depth to the Hindu *Bhagavad Gita (The Song Celestial),* which Gandhi considered his greatest debt to the west, and which deepened his love of his faith. He also read the works of Leo Tolstoy and John Ruskin.

Later, from reading Tolstoy's *The Kingdom of God Is Within You,* Gandhi greatly was impressed with the power of non-violence, and along the lines of Tolstoy's argument—that no one has a monopoly on truth, and this should lead individuals to be wary of using force. Gandhi was also sympathetic to Tolstoy's opposition to modern life and preference for agrarian living. Ruskin's *Unto this Last* "brought about an instantaneous and practical transformation in my life." Ruskin highly valued work (particularly of the common laborer), criticized nineteenth century economics, and may have planted the seed of the concept in Gandhi's mind that property is, or should be, held for the benefit of all.

On returning to India, Gandhi learned that his father had died, which prevented him from eventually succeeding him in governmental service. After less than two years of practicing law in India, Gandhi was hired by Indian Moslem merchants to settle a legal dispute in South Africa. While he is above all associated with India, it is vital to remember that Gandhi spent most of a period of over twenty years in South Africa—from 1893 to 1914—during his formative adult years.

The Indian community was and remains a small minority in South Africa, outnumbered both by Africans and Europeans, and occupied an intermediate place between them in the social order. In South Africa, Gandhi first experienced virulent racism. Immediately on arriving, he was subjected to discrimination in his travel and accommodations. He commented as follows: "The hardship to which I was subjected was superficial—only a symptom of the deep disease of color prejudice. I should try, if possible, to root out the disease and suffer hardships in the process. Redress for wrongs I should seek only to the extent that would be necessary for the removal of color prejudice." This passage indicates Gandhi's approach to social issues—problems are generally deep-rooted and may require fundamental change to be solved. An individual must be prepared to suffer himself to right social wrongs. Such suffering must be other-directed; it cannot be aimed simply at relieving one's own situation.

Gandhi became leader of the Indian community in South Africa. He started a political association to advocate for the rights of Indians, published a weekly newspaper, began his campaigns of non-violent resistance, organized his first *ashram* (spiritual community). At one point, he wrote a brochure, popularly called "The Green Pamphlet," which caused him to be mobbed by thousands of white South Africans following his return from a trip to India to bring back his wife and children.

In 1906, the white South African government proposed an ordinance that would require all Indians to register with the authorities and carry a certificate at all times. Called the "Black Act," Gandhi believed it would spell disaster for the Indian community. During the course of an Indian mass meeting, the proposal to pass a resolution to refuse submission to the ordinance, with God as a witness, was made. Gandhi was struck by the oath portion of the resolution, and his reaction indicates the religious character of his thought: "A man who makes an ordinary resolution is not ashamed of himself when he deviates from it, but a man who violates an oath administered to him is not only ashamed of himself, but is also looked upon by society as a sinner." Later he wrote, "Politics, divorced from religion, has absolutely no meaning."

Gandhi's Hinduism was essential to his philosophy, and he always considered Hinduism the superior religion, while valuing other religions. Given the religious character of India, and that in Hindu India it was religion that served as the unifying thread of the polyglottal social system, it was vital that he stress religious themes in order to be able to communicate with the Indian people. He sought, however, a broader reconciliation, and in his comments on the occasion of the Black Act, noted to the mixed Hindu-Moslem audience, "We all believe in one and the same God, the differences of nomenclature in Hinduism and Islam notwithstanding."

Gandhi at first used the term "passive resistance" for the fledgling South African movement, but quickly realized that the struggle could hardly be known only by an English name, and came later to dislike the term passive resistance, indicating, he thought, a method of the weak. Therefore, the Hindi term *satyagraha* was coined, combining the words *satya* (truth) and *agraha* (firmness of force). *Satya* also implies love, and therefore *satyagraha* is "the Force which is born of Truth and Love or non-violence." The concept of non-violence is paramount in Gandhi's thought, and, as well as being implied in *satya,* is found directly in the word *ahimsa* (literally, "non-injury"), another key Gandhian term. By *non-injury,* Gandhi meant not just restraint in using physical force, but restraint in the use of any hurtful method, whether of words or even thoughts. Moreover, *ahimsa* enjoins positive actions. The link between *satya* and *ahimsa* is that *ahimsa* lies at the heart of *satya:* Since our notions of truth are incomplete, one may not impose his fragmentary views on others.

Satyagraha is a method for bringing about social change through the persuasion of one's antagonist that he is wrong. There can be no physical force used in this process; the goal is to convince one's adversary, not subjugate him. Violence has no part in this process for, according to Gandhi, the use of violence can only temporarily suppress evil at the cost of having it arise later with redoubled vigor. Non-violence, on the other hand, puts an end to evil by converting the evildoer.

Gandhi considered *satyagraha* to be a method of the strong. Its practitioner—a *satyagrahi*—is an individual who comes up against evil in the world, which he must resist. He will submit to any punishment in order to attain the end he seeks. This is why *satyagraha* enjoins *satyagrahis* willingly to accept legal penalties for their "illegal" (in the eyes of authority) actions. The aim is change through persuasion, not compulsion; the latter can never lead to true change. *Satyagraha* demands absolute self-control and other-directedness. It may take the form of non-cooperation with authority in general, as well as active disobedience to particular edicts. Fasting may also be undertaken but only as a last resort when all other means of *satyagraha* have failed to enable an opponent to see the error of his ways.

Gandhi left South Africa in 1914 for good, returning to India a national hero as the result of the publicity his campaigns in South Africa received. He then became leader of the Indian home rule movement. British India was the exemplar of colonialism, and Gandhi gradually felt his way to the position of complete Indian independence from Britain. In 1909, Gandhi had written *Hind Swaraj,* or *Indian Home Rule.* Despite its title, he did not demand instantaneous departure of the British Empire from India in this book; rather, he advocated that governance of the colony should be in India's interest and by Indian precepts.

Swaraj can be translated "self-rule" as well as "home rule." It is somewhat inaccurate to place western concepts of national organization onto the Indian scene both because they are (or were) somewhat inapplicable there, and they are not the concepts of organization that are intrinsic to the inhabitants. What Gandhi had in mind by *swaraj* was as much how India was governed as who governed it. Whether by Indian or foreigner: "What others get for me is not Home Rule but foreign rule."

Gandhi was opposed to modern western civilization and industrialism. He had an aversion to machinery and preferred goods produced by hand. He looked forward not to a material, but a spiritual, civilization. He thought competition, on which modern western economies are based, to be a tragic waste. He believed that social ills such as alcoholism and prostitution are the inevitable result of materialistic values. His goal was a revitalized rural India, not a westernized one. He favored decentralization.

In all of these views, Gandhi bespoke a radically different outlook than the one to which we are usually accustomed and one which has had less success than his ideas on methods of social change. His ideas on ultimate social order were as far from materialistic communism as from materialistic capitalism. He quite frankly looked backwards concerning industrialism, not—as Marx—desiring to harness it for the good of humanity but wanting to discard it altogether. Unlike most modern preoccupation with affluence, Gandhi believed: "A man is not necessarily happy because he is rich, or unhappy because he is poor."

Three of the lodestars of Gandhi's day-to-day social program were anti-untouchability, Hindu–Moslem reconciliation, and self-sufficiency in economic production (swadeshi). He considered untouchability "an ineffaceable blot that Hinduism today carries." Some castes practiced that even the shadow of an untouchable should not fall upon a brahmin. Gandhi's ideal was that untouchables should be absorbed within the sudra (peasant) caste. He admitted untouchables to his *ashrams,* though this caused problems with some of the other participants, and preached against discrimination directed toward untouchables.

Gandhi was viscerally opposed to Hindu–Moslem partition of India (although this was the plan ultimately adopted), and he believed that, in its diversity, India gained strength. He strove mightily to bring the two communities together. This goal dovetailed with that of anti-untouchability, because the majority of Indian Moslems were the descendants of converts from untouchables. In British India, one-quarter of the population was Moslem and one-fifth untouchables. Regarding Hindu–Moslem partition, Gandhi stated: "I find no parallel in history for a body of converts . . . claiming to be a nation apart from the parent stock."

Swadeshi, or the consumption of goods made in one's country, was the practical application of Gandhi's economic ideas. Gandhi strongly supported laboring with one's hands. He thought each person, each village, and each nation should be as self-sufficient as possible. He recommended that every person take up the art of spinning and wear nothing but homespun garments. He presided over bonfires which consumed piles of western clothes. When he met the King and Queen of England, he wore a homespun garment and no shoes. Gandhi aptly described his ideal economic and social order, giving also his conception of the role of the individual: "Life will not be a pyramid with the apex sustained by the bottom. But it will be an oceanic circle whose center will be the individual always ready to perish for the village, the latter ready to perish for the circle of villages till at last the whole becomes one life composed of individuals, never aggressive in their arrogance, but ever humble, sharing the majesty of the oceanic circle of which they are integral units. Therefore, the outermost circumference will not wield power to crush the inner circle, but will give strength to all within and will derive its own strength from it."

Gandhi led three major civil disobedience movements in India, at roughly ten-year intervals in the early 1920s, 1930s, and 1940s ("non-violent" and "civil" were interchangeable prefixes to describe the disobedience he had in mind). He felt it was essential that the people should be morally and spiritually ready for a campaign of civil disobedience before it commenced, as otherwise it might be counterproductive. On more than one occasion, he called off a campaign of non-violent disobedience because the movement got out of hand and turned violent. While there is some question to what extent Gandhi later in his life countenanced some violence if it truly were inescapable, it remains a fact that, in his words, non-violence was the "first" and "last article of my creed."

The Indian National Congress Party, of which Gandhi was the guiding spirit, resolved in 1928 that unless Britain agreed to allow India a constitution and dominion status (held, for example, by Canada and Australia) within one year, another nation-wide civil disobedience movement would be started. When these terms were not met, the Congress Party announced that its goal was full independence and authorized Gandhi to start the new campaign.

Brilliantly, he chose to attack the government's monopoly on the manufacture of salt, an action that would not alienate moderates and yet would generate a mass following among those whom the current salt law required to pay tax, and which was consistent with his economic ideals. Gandhi began a twenty-six day trek to the sea, which garnered great publicity, to boil salt. The next action on the part of the Indian people was insurrection without arms. Many villagers on India's long coastline also went to the sea to make salt. Following Gandhi's decision to invade a salt works, he was arrested, as were tens of thousands of others, and the number of Indian political prisoners grew to over 100,000.

Gandhi was released after eight months in jail. Subsequently, other political prisoners were released, Gandhi ceased the disobedience campaign, and the Congress Party sent representatives, including Gandhi, to forthcoming talks in London on a constitution for India. While the talks themselves were unsuccessful, he considered his real dialogue to have been with the British people. His stay there did much to enlist popular British sympathy for the Indian cause.

One of the controversial aspects of Gandhi's practice of *satyagraha* was his willingness to respond to an opponent's proposal of compromise. Seeing the purpose of *satyagraha* as to persuade one's adversary, he would leave no stone unturned in his quest to accommodate his opponent's view as long as progress was being made. Another tool of *satyagraha* was the *hartal,* or temporary strike.

The importance of India in Indians' and Gandhi's eyes is and was immense. Understanding this helps to explain why, for example, he supported a "Quit India" policy to the British government during the midst of World War II, for which he was arrested and imprisoned (he spent at different times a total of over six years in jail). Gandhi believed that, as important as World War II was to Europeans, India and its people's needs had at least equally valid claims to attention. This outlook asserts the equality of all peoples, wherever they may live in the world.

Gandhi's influence has been far-reaching. Of him, Albert Einstein said: "Generations to come will scarce believe that such a one as this ever in flesh and blood walked upon this earth." Gandhi's method of non-violent disobedience was not only used in the struggle to achieve Indian independence but also influenced later social movements. According to Martin Luther King, Jr.: "As I delved deeper into the philosophy of Gandhi . . . I came to see for the first time its potency in the area of social reform. Prior to reading Gandhi . . . I had about concluded that the ethics of Jesus were only effective in individual relationships. . . . But after reading Gandhi, I saw how utterly mistaken I was. Gandhi was probably the first person in history to lift the love ethic of Jesus above mere interaction between individuals to a powerful and effective social force on a large scale."

Gandhi believed that the follower of *satyagraha* had to be willing to die for the movement; in fact, "nothing better can happen to a *Satyagrahi* than meeting death unsought in the very act of *Satyagraha,* i.e., pursuing Truth." His concept of *satyagraha* is egalitarian, because "there are no leaders and hence no followers." He believed political and social change were more the product of internal changes in people than the result of external changes in their circumstances. Ultimately, a people's government is as good (or bad) as its people.

In his statement that what Indians wanted was not the "bread made of wheat, but . . . the bread of liberty," Gandhi expressed a sentiment that fired the entire developing world. The fall of colonialism in India sent a signal around the globe that helped lead to the dissolution of European empires following World War II. Gandhi rejected colonialism and its mentality, and, in so doing, furthered the rights and equality of all peoples. His emphasis on the intolerability of racism and the right of indigenous peoples to live according to their own culture and speak in their own language(s) has left a legacy that continues to this day.

Gandhi's goal for humanity was not a modernistic, socialist one. He explicitly rejected this end, as he did the methods of other nineteenth and twentieth century revolutionaries. Unlike those who saw earthly paradise as being able to be constructed through the use of the most abhorrent means, Gandhi saw an inextricable link between ends and means: "The means may be likened to a seed, the end to a tree; and there is just the same inviolable connection between the seed and the tree."

Gandhi's non-violent methods are what his ultimate impact rely upon. His propositions that non-cooperation with evil is as much a duty as cooperation with good, and that non-violence is the best and ultimately only effective way to achieve positive social change, are enduring contributions to world political thought. His emphases on non-materialism, spirituality, and human equality were vital, as well. Ironically, Gandhi—a man of non-violence—perished in an act of violence, by assassination at the hands of a Hindu extremist. His tragic death paradoxically contributed, however, to bringing a measure of peace to battling communal factions, for it demonstrated the evilness of physical force.

GANDHI

Selected Writings

SATYAGRAHA, CIVIL DISOBEDIENCE, PASSIVE RESISTANCE, NON-COOPERATION*

Satyagraha is literally holding on to Truth and it means, therefore, Truth-force. Truth is soul or spirit. It is, therefore, known as soul-force. It excludes the use of violence because man is not capable of knowing the absolute truth and, therefore, not competent to punish. The word was coined in South Africa to distinguish the non-violent resistance of the Indians of South Africa from the contemporary 'passive resistance' of the suffragettes and others. It is not conceived as a weapon of the weak.

Passive resistance is used in the orthodox English sense and covers the suffragette movement as well as the resistance of the Non-conformists. Passive resistance has been conceived and is regarded as a weapon of the weak. Whilst it avoids violence, being not open to the weak, it does not exclude its use if, in the opinion of a passive resister, the occasion demands it. However, it has always been distinguished from armed resistance and its application was at one time confined to Christian martyrs.

Civil Disobedience is civil breach of unmoral statutory enactments. The expression was, so far as I am aware, coined by Thoreau to signify his own resistance to the laws of a slave State. He has left a masterly treatise on the duty of Civil Disobedience. But Thoreau was not perhaps an out and out champion of non-violence. Probably, also, Thoreau limited his breach of statutory laws to the revenue law, i.e. payment of taxes. Whereas the term Civil Disobedience as

practiced in 1919 covered a breach of any statutory and unmoral law. It signified the resister's outlawry in a civil, i.e., non-violent manner. He invoked the sanctions of the law and cheerfully suffered imprisonment. It is a branch of *Satyagraha*.

Non-cooperation predominantly implies withdrawing of cooperation from the State that in the non-cooperator's view has become corrupt and excludes Civil Disobedience of the fierce type described above. By its very nature, non-cooperation is even open to children of understanding and can be safely practiced by the masses. Civil Disobedience presupposes the habit of willing obedience to laws without fear of their sanctions. It can, therefore, be practiced only as a last resort and by a select few in the first instance at any rate. Non-cooperation, too, like Civil Disobedience is a branch of *Satyagraha* which includes all non-violent resistance for the vindication of Truth.

THE THEORY AND PRACTICE OF SATYAGRAHA*

Carried out to its utmost limit, *Satyagraha* is independent of pecuniary or other material assistance; certainly, even in its elementary form, of physical force or violence. Indeed, violence is the negation of this great spiritual force, which can only be cultivated or wielded by those who will entirely eschew violence. It is a force that may be used by individuals as well as by communities. It may be used as well in political as in domestic affairs. Its universal applicability is a demonstration of its permanence

---

* *Young India*, 23–2–'21.

* *Young India*, 3–11–'27.

and invincibility. It can be used alike by men, women and children. It is totally untrue to say that it is a force to be used only by the weak so long as they are not capable of meeting violence by violence. This superstition arises from the incompleteness of the English expression, *passive resistance.* It is impossible for those who consider themselves to be weak to apply this force. Only those who realize that there is something in man which is superior to the brute nature in him and that the latter always yields to it, can effectively be *Satyagrahis.* This force is to violence, and, therefore, to all tyranny, all injustice, what light is to darkness. In politics, its use is based upon the immutable maxim, that government of the people is possible only so long as they consent either consciously or unconsciously to be governed. We did not want to be governed by the Asiatic Act of 1907 of the Transvaal, and it had to go before this mighty force. Two courses were open to us: to use violence when we were called upon to submit to the Act, or to suffer the penalties prescribed under the Act, and thus to draw out and exhibit the force of the soul within us for a period long enough to appeal to the sympathetic chord in the governors or the law-makers. We have taken long to achieve what we set about striving for. That was because our *Satyagraha* was not of the most complete type. All *Satyagrahis* do not understand the full value of the force, nor have we men who always from conviction refrain from violence. The use of this force requires the adoption of poverty, in the sense that we must be indifferent whether we have the wherewithal to feed or clothe ourselves. During the past struggle, all *Satyagrahis,* if any at all, were not prepared to go that length. Some again were only *Satyagrahis* so called. They came without any conviction, often with mixed motives, less often with impure motives. Some even, whilst engaged in the struggle, would gladly have resorted to violence but for most vigilant supervision. Thus it was that the struggle became prolonged; for the exercise of the purest soul-force, in its perfect form, brings about instantaneous relief. For this exercise, prolonged training of the individual soul is an absolute necessity, so that a perfect *Satyagrahi* has to be almost, if not entirely, a perfect man. We cannot all suddenly become

such men, but if my proposition is correct— as I know it to be correct—the greater the spirit of *Satyagraha* in us, the better men will we become. Its use, therefore, is, I think, indisputable, and it is a force, which, if it became universal, would revolutionize social ideals and do away with despotisms and the ever-growing militarism under which the nations of the west are groaning and are being almost crushed to death, and which fairly promises to overwhelm even the nations of the east. If the past struggle has produced even a few Indians who would dedicate themselves to the task of becoming *Satyagrahis* as nearly perfect as possible, they would not only have served themselves in the truest sense of the term, they would also have served humanity at large. Thus viewed, *Satyagraha* is the noblest and best education. It should come, not after the ordinary education in letters, of children, but it should precede it. It will not be denied, that a child, before it begins to write its alphabet and to gain worldly knowledge, should know what the soul is, what truth is, what love is, what powers are latent in the soul. It should be an essential of real education that a child should learn, that in the struggle of life, it can easily conquer hate by love, untruth by truth, violence by self-suffering.

CONDITIONS FOR SUCCESSFUL SATYAGRAHA*

There can be no *Satyagraha* in an unjust cause. *Satyagraha* in a just cause is vain, if the men espousing it are not determined and capable of fighting and suffering to the end; and the slightest use of violence often defeats a just cause. *Satyagraha* excludes the use of violence in any shape or form, whether in thought, speech, or deed. Given a just cause, capacity for endless suffering and avoidance of violence, victory is a certainty.

NON-RETALIATION†

Victory is impossible until we are able to keep our temper under the gravest provocation. Calmness under fire is a soldier's

---

* *Young India,* 27–4–'21.
† *Young India,* 25–8–'21.

indispensable quality. A non-cooperator is nothing if he cannot remain calm and unperturbed under a fierce fire of provocation.

There should be no mistake. There is no civil disobedience possible, until the crowds behave like disciplined soldiers. And we cannot resort to civil disobedience, unless we can assure every Englishman that he is as safe in India as he is in his own home. It is not enough that we give the assurance. Every Englishman and Englishwoman must feel safe, not by reason of the bayonet at their disposal but by reason of our living creed of non-violence. That is the condition not only of success but our own ability to carry on the movement in its present form. There is no other way of conducting the campaign of non-cooperation.

SATYAGRAHI PRISONER'S CONDUCT *

Whether all of us realize or not the method of non-cooperation is a process of touching the heart and appealing to reason, not one of frightening by rowdyism. Rowdyism has no place in a non-violent movement.

I have often likened *Satyagrahi* prisoners to prisoners of war. Once caught by the enemy, prisoners of war act towards the enemy as friends. It will be considered dishonorable on the part of a soldier as a prisoner of war to deceive the enemy. It does not affect my argument that the Government does not regard *Satyagrahi* prisoners as prisoners of war. If we act as such, we shall soon command respect. We must make the prison a neutral institution in which we may, nay, must cooperate to a certain extent.

We would be highly inconsistent and hardly self-respecting if on the one hand we deliberately break prison rules and in the same breath complain of punishment and strictness. We may not, for instance, resist and complain of search and at the same time conceal prohibited things in our blankets or our clothes. There is nothing in *Satyagraha* that I know whereby we may under certain circumstances tell untruths or practice other deception.

When we say that if we make the lives of prison officials uncomfortable, the

Government will be obliged to sue for peace, we either pay them a subtle compliment or regard them as simpletons. We pay a subtle compliment when we consider that even though we may make prison officials' lives uncomfortable, the Government will look on in silence and hesitate to award us condign punishment so as utterly to break our spirit. That is to say we regard the administrators to be so considerate and humane that they will not severely punish us even though we give them sufficient cause. As a matter of fact, they will not and do not hesitate to throw over-board all idea of decency and award not only authorized but even unauthorized punishments on given occasions.

But it is my deliberate conviction that had we but acted with uniform honesty and dignity, behoving *Satyagrahis,* we would have disarmed all opposition on the part of the Government and such strictly honorable behavior on the part of so many prisoners would have at least shamed the Government into confessing their error in imprisoning so many honorable and innocent men. For is it not their case that our non-violence is but a cloak for our violence? Do we not therefore play into their hands every time we are rowdy?

In my opinion therefore as *Satyagrahis* we are bound, when we become prisoners,

1. to act with the most scrupulous honesty;
2. to cooperate with the prison officials in their administration;
3. to set by our obedience to all reasonable discipline an example to co-prisoners;
4. to ask for no favors and claim no privileges which the meanest of prisoners do not get and which we do not need strictly for reasons of health;
5. not to fail to ask what we do so need and not to get irritated if we do not obtain it;
6. to do all the tasks allotted, to the utmost of our ability.

It is such conduct which will make the Government position uncomfortable and untenable. It is difficult for them to meet honesty with honesty for their want of faith and unpreparedness for such a rare eventuality.

---

* *Young India,* 5–6–'24.

Rowdyism they expect and meet with a double dose of it. They were able to deal with anarchical crime but they have not yet found out any way of dealing with non-violence save by yielding to it.

The idea behind the imprisonment of *Satyagrahis* is that he expects relief through humble submission to suffering. He believes that meek suffering for a just cause has a virtue all its own and infinitely greater than the virtue of the sword. This does not mean that we may not resist when the treatment touches our self-respect. Thus for instance we must resist to the point of death the use of abusive language by officials or if they were to throw our food at us which is often done. Insult and abuse are no part of an official's duty, Therefore we must resist them. But we may not resist search because it is part of prison regulations.

Nor are my remarks about mute suffering to be construed to mean that there should be no agitation against putting innocent prisoners like *Satyagrahis* in the same class as confirmed criminals. Only as prisoners we may not ask for favors. We must be content to live with the confirmed criminals and even welcome the opportunity of working moral reform in them. It is however expected of a government that calls itself civilized to recognize the most natural divisions.

FASTING*

Fasting is a potent weapon in the *Satyagraha* armory. It cannot be taken by every one. Mere physical capacity to take it is no qualification for it. It is of no use without a living faith in God. It should never be a mechanical effort nor a mere imitation. It must come from the depth of one's soul. It is therefore always rare. I seem to be made for it. It is noteworthy that not one of my colleagues on the political field has felt the call to fast. And I am thankful to be able to say that they have never resented my fasts. Nor have fellow-members of the Ashram felt the call except on rare occasions. They have even accepted the restriction that they may not take penitential fasts without my permission, no matter how urgent the inner call may seem to be.

Thus fasting, though a very potent weapon, has necessarily very strict limitations and is to be taken only by those who have undergone previous training. And, judged by my standard, the majority of fasts do not at all come under the category of *Satyagraha* fasts and are, as they are popularly called, hunger-strikes undertaken without previous preparation and adequate thought. If the process is repeated too often, these hunger-strikes will lose what little efficacy they may possess and will become objects of ridicule.

SOME RULES
OF SATYAGRAHA *

Satyagraha literally means insistence on truth. This insistence arms the votary with matchless power. This power or force is connoted by the word *Satyagraha. Satyagraha,* to be genuine, may be offered against one's wife or one's children, against rulers, against fellow citizens, even against the whole world.

Such a universal force necessarily makes no distinction between kinsmen and strangers, young and old, man and woman, friend and foe. The force to be so applied can never be physical. There is in it no room for violence. The only force of universal application can, therefore, be that of *ahimsa* or love. In other words it is soul-force.

Love does not burn others, it burns itself. Therefore, a *Satyagrahi,* i.e. a civil resister, will joyfully suffer even unto death.

It follows, therefore, that a civil resister, whilst he will strain every nerve to compass the end of the existing rule, will do no intentional injury in thought, word or deed to the person of a single Englishman. This necessarily brief explanation of *Satyagraha* will perhaps enable the reader to understand and appreciate the following rules:

As an Individual

1. A *Satyagrahi,* i.e., a civil resister will harbor no anger.
2. He will suffer the anger of the opponent.
3. In so doing he will put up with assaults from the opponent, never

---

* *Harijan,* 18–3–'39.

* *Young India,* 27–2–'30.

retaliate; but he will not submit, out of fear of punishment or the like, to any order given in anger.

4. When any person in authority seeks to arrest a civil resister, he will voluntarily submit to the arrest, and he will not resist the attachment or removal of his own property, if any, when it is sought to be confiscated by the authorities.

5. If a civil resister has any property in his possession as a trustee, he will refuse to surrender it, even though in defending it he might lose his life. He will however, never retaliate.

6. Non-retaliation excludes swearing and cursing.

7. Therefore a civil resister will never insult his opponent, and therefore also not take part in many of the newly coined cries which are contrary to the spirit of *ahimsa.*

8. A civil resister will not salute the Union Jack, nor will he insult it or officials, English or Indian.

9. In the course of the struggle if any one insults an official or commits an assault upon him, a civil resister will protect such official or officials from the insult or attack even at the risk of his life.

As a Prisoner

10. As a prisoner, a civil resister, will behave courteously towards prison officials, and will observe all such discipline of the prison as is not contrary to self-respect; as for instance, whilst he will *salaam* officials in the usual manner, he will not perform any humiliating gyrations and refuse to shout 'Victory to *Sarkar*' or the like. He will take cleanly cooked and cleanly served food, which is not contrary to his religion, and will refuse to take food insultingly served or served in unclean vessels.

11. A civil resister will make no distinction between an ordinary prisoner and himself, will in no way regard himself as superior to the rest, nor will he ask for any conveniences that may not be necessary for keeping his body in good health and condition.

He is entitled to ask for such conveniences as may be required for his physical or spiritual well-being.

12. A civil resister may not fast for want of conveniences whose deprivation does not involve any injury to one's self-respect.

As a Unit

13. A civil resister will joyfully obey all the orders issued by the leader of the corps, whether they please him or not.

14. He will carry out orders in the first instance even though they appear to him insulting, inimical or foolish, and then appeal to higher authority. He is free before joining to determine the fitness of the corps to satisfy him, but after he has joined it, it becomes a duty to submit to its discipline irksome or otherwise. If the sum total of the energy of the corps appears to a member to be improper or immoral, he has a right to sever his connection, but being within it, he has no right to commit a breach of its discipline.

15. No civil resister is to expect maintenance for his dependents. It would be an accident if any such provision is made. A civil resister entrusts his dependents to the care of God. Even in ordinary warfare wherein hundreds of thousands give themselves up to it, they are able to make no previous provision. How much more, then, should such be the case in *Satyagraha?* It is the universal experience that in such times hardly anybody is left to starve.

In Communal Fights

16. No civil resister will intentionally become a cause of communal quarrels.

17. In the event of any such outbreak, he will not take sides, but he will assist only that party which is demonstrably in the right. Being a Hindu he will be generous towards Mussalmans and others, and will sacrifice himself in the attempt to save non-Hindus from a Hindu attack. And if the attack is from the other side, he will not participate

in any retaliation but will give his life in protecting Hindus.

18. He will, to the best of his ability, avoid every occasion that may give rise to communal quarrels.

19. If there is a procession of *Satyagrahis* they will do nothing that would wound the religious susceptibilities of any community, and they will not take part in any other processions that are likely to wound such susceptibilities.

QUALIFICATIONS FOR SATYAGRAHA*

Satyagraha presupposes self-discipline, self-control, self-purification, and a recognized social status in the person offering it. A *Satyagrahi* must never forget the distinction between evil and the evil-doer. He must not harbor ill-will or bitterness against the latter. He may not even employ needlessly offensive language against the evil person, however unrelieved his evil might be. For it should be an article of faith with every *Satyagrahi* that there is none so fallen in this world but can be converted by love. A *Satyagrahi* will always try to overcome evil by good, anger by love, untruth by truth, *himsa* by *ahimsa*. There is no other way of purging the world of evil. Therefore a person who claims to be a *Satyagrahi* always tries by close and prayerful self-introspection and self-analysis to find out whether he is himself completely free from the taint of anger, ill-will and such other human infirmities, whether he is not himself capable of those very evils against which he is out to lead a crusade. In self-purification and penance lies half the victory of a *Satyagrahi*. A *Satyagrahi* has faith that the silent and undemonstrative action of truth and love produces far more permanent and abiding results than speeches or such other showy performances.

But although *Satyagraha* can operate silently, it requires a certain amount of action on the part of a *Satyagrahi*. A *Satyagrahi*, for instance, must first mobilize public opinion against the evil which he is out to eradicate, by means of a wide and intensive agitation. When public opinion is sufficiently roused against a social abuse

even the tallest will not dare to practice or openly to lend support to it. An awakened and intelligent public opinion is the most potent weapon of a *Satyagrahi*. When a person supports a social evil in total disregard of unanimous public opinion, it indicates a clear justification for his social ostracism. But the object of social ostracism should never be to do injury to the person against whom it is directed. Social ostracism means complete non-cooperation on the part of society with the offending individual; nothing more, nothing less, the idea being that a person who deliberately sets himself to flout society has no right to be served by society. For all practical purposes this should be enough. Of course, special action may be indicated in special cases and the practice may have to be varied to suit the peculiar features of each individual case.

SATYAGRAHA ASHRAM VOWS*

IMPORTANCE OF VOWS

Taking vows is not a sign of weakness, but of strength. To do at any cost something that one ought to do constitutes a vow. It becomes a bulwark of strength. A man who says that he will do something 'as far as possible', betrays either his pride or his weakness. I have noticed in my own case, as well as in the case of others, that the limitation 'as far as possible' provides a fatal loophole. To do something 'as far as possible' is to succumb to the very first temptation. There is no sense in saying that one would observe truth 'as far as possible'. Even as no businessman will look at a note in which a man promises to pay a certain amount on a certain date 'as far as possible', so will God refuse to accept a promissory note drawn by a man, who will observe truth as far as possible.

God is the very image of the vow. God would cease to be God if He swerved from His own laws even by a hair's breadth. The sun is a greater keeper of observances; hence the possibility of measuring time and publishing almanacs. All business depends upon men fulfilling their promises. Are such promises less necessary in character building or self-realization? We should therefore never doubt the necessity of vows

---

* *Young India,* 8–8–'29.

* From Yeravda Mandir, ch.s 1–3, 6.

for the purpose of self-purification and self-realization.

TRUTH

I deal with Truth first of all, as the *Satyagraha Ashram* owes its very existence to the pursuit and the attempted practice of Truth.

The word *Satya* (Truth) is derived from *Sat*, which means 'being'. Nothing is or exists in reality except Truth. That is why *Sat* or Truth is perhaps the most important name of God. In fact it is more correct to say that Truth is God, than to say that God is Truth. But as we cannot do without a ruler or a general, names of God such as 'King of Kings' or 'the Almighty' are and will remain generally current. On deeper thinking, however, it will be realized, that *Sat* or *Satya* is the only correct and fully significant name for God.

And where there is Truth, there also is knowledge which is true. Where there is no Truth, there can be no true knowledge. That is why the word *Chit* or knowledge is associated with the name of God. And where there is true knowledge, there is always bliss *(Ananda)*. Sorrow has no place there. And even as Truth is eternal, so is the bliss derived from it. Hence we know God as *Sat-chit-ananda,* One who combines in Himself Truth, Knowledge and Bliss.

Devotion to this Truth is the sole justification for our existence. All our activities should be centred in Truth. Truth should be the very breath of our life. When once this stage in the pilgrim's progress is reached, all other rules of correct living will come without effort, and obedience to them will be instinctive. But without Truth it would be impossible to observe any principles or rules in life.

Generally speaking, observation of the law of Truth is understood merely to mean that we must speak the truth. But we in the Ashram should understand the word *Satya* or Truth in a much wider sense. There should be Truth in thought, Truth in speech, and Truth in action. To the man who has realized this Truth in its fulness, nothing else remains to be known, because all knowledge is necessarily included in it. What is not included in it is not Truth, and so not true knowledge; and there can be no inward peace without true knowledge. If we once

learn how to apply this never-failing test of Truth, we will at once be able to find out what is worth doing, what is worth seeing, what is worth reading.

But how is one to realize this Truth, which may be likened to the philosopher's stone or the cow of plenty? By single-minded devotion *(abhyasa)* and indifference to all other interests in life *(vairagya)*—replies the *Bhagavadgita*. In spite, however, of such devotion, what may appear as truth to one person will often appear as untruth to another person. But that need not worry the seeker. Where there is honest effort, it will be realized that what appear to be different truths are like the countless and apparently different leaves of the same tree. Does not God Himself appear to different individuals in different aspects? Yet we know that He is one. But Truth is the right designation of God. Hence there is nothing wrong in every man following Truth according to his lights. Indeed it is his duty to do so. Then if there is a mistake on the part of any one so following Truth, it will be automatically set right. For the quest of Truth involves *tapas*—self-suffering, sometimes even unto death. There can be no place in it for even a trace of self-interest. In such selfless search for Truth nobody can lose his bearings for long. Directly he takes to the wrong path he stumbles, and is thus redirected to the right path. Therefore the pursuit of Truth is truth *bhakti* (devotion). It is the path that leads to God. There is no place in it for cowardice, no place for defeat. It is the talisman by which death itself becomes the portal to life eternal.

In this connection it would be well to ponder over the lives and examples of Harishchandra, Prahlad, Ramachandra, Imam Hasan and Imam Husain, the Christian saints, etc. How beautiful it would be, if all of us, young and old, men and women, devoted ourselves wholly to Truth in all that we might do in our waking hours, whether working, eating, drinking or playing, till dissolution of the body makes us one with Truth? God as Truth has been for me a treasure beyond price; may He be so to every one of us.

AHIMSA OR LOVE

We saw last week how the path of Truth is as narrow as it is straight. Even so is that of *ahimsa*. It is like balancing oneself on the edge of a sword. By concentration an acrobat can walk on a rope. But the concentration required to tread the path of Truth and *ahimsa* is far greater. The slightest inattention brings one tumbling to the ground. One can realize Truth and *ahimsa* only by ceaseless striving.

But it is impossible for us to realize perfect Truth so long as we are imprisoned in this mortal frame. We can only visualize it in our imagination. We cannot, through the instrumentality of this ephemeral body, see face to face Truth which is eternal. That is why in the last resort one must depend on faith.

It appears that the impossibility of full realization of Truth in this mortal body led some ancient seeker after Truth to the appreciation of *ahimsa*. The question which confronted him was: "Shall I bear with those who create difficulties for me, or shall I destroy them?" The seeker realized that he who went on destroying others did not make headway but simply stayed where he was, while the man who suffered those who created difficulties marched ahead, and at times even took the others with him. The first act of destruction taught him that the Truth which was the object of his quest was not outside himself but within. Hence the more he took to violence, the more he receded from Truth. For in fighting the imagined enemy without, he neglected the enemy within.

We punish thieves, because we think they harass us. They may leave us alone; but they will only transfer their attentions to another victim. This other victim however is also a human being, ourselves in a different form, and so we are caught in a vicious circle. The trouble from thieves continues to increase, as they think it is their business to steal. In the end we see that it is better to endure the thieves than to punish them. The forbearance may even bring them to their senses. By enduring them we realize that thieves are not different from ourselves, they are our brethren, our friends, and may not be punished. But whilst we may bear with the thieves, we may not endure the infliction. That would only induce cowardice. So we realize a further duty. Since we regard the thieves as our kith and kin, they must be made to realize the kinship. And so we must take pains to devise ways and means of winning them over. This is the path of *ahimsa*. It may entail continuous suffering and the cultivating of endless patience. Given these two conditions, the thief is bound in the end to turn away from his evil ways. Thus step by step we learn how to make friends with all the world; we realize the greatness of God—of Truth. Our peace of mind increases in spite of suffering; we become braver and more enterprising; we understand more clearly the difference between what is everlasting and what is not; we learn how to distinguish between what is our duty and what is not. Our pride melts away, and we become humble. Our worldly attachments diminish, and the evil within us diminishes from day to day.

Ahimsa is not the crude thing it has been made to appear. Not to hurt any living thing is no doubt a part of *ahimsa*. But it is its least expression. The principle of *ahimsa* is hurt by every evil thought, by undue haste, by lying, by hatred, by wishing ill to anybody. It is also violated by our holding on to what the world needs. But the world needs even what we eat day by day. In the place where we stand there are millions of microorganisms to whom the place belongs, and who are hurt by our presence there. What should we do then? Should we commit suicide? Even that is no solution, if we believe, as we do, that so long as the spirit is attached to the flesh, on every destruction of the body it weaves for itself another. The body will cease to be only when we give up all attachment to it. This freedom from all attachment is the realization of God as Truth. Such realization cannot be attained in a hurry. The body does not belong to us. While it lasts, we must use it as a trust handed over to our charge. Treating in this way, the things of the flesh, we may one day expect to become free from the burden of the body. Realizing the limitations of the flesh, we must strive day by day towards the ideal with what strength we have in us.

It is perhaps clear from the foregoing, that without *ahimsa* it is not possible to seek and find Truth. *Ahimsa* and Truth are so intertwined that it is practically impossible to disentangle and separate them. They are like the two sides of a coin, or rather of a smooth unstamped metallic disc. Who can say, which is the obverse, and which is the reverse? Nevertheless *ahimsa* is the means; Truth is the end. Means to be means must always be within our reach, and so *ahimsa* is our supreme duty. If we take care of the means, we are bound to reach the end sooner or later. When once we have grasped this point, final victory is beyond question. Whatever difficulties we encounter, whatever apparent reverses we sustain, we may not give up the quest for Truth which alone is, being God Himself.

BRAHMACHARYA OR CHASTITY

The third among our observances is *brahmacharya*. As a matter of fact all observances are deducible from Truth, and are meant to subserve it. The man, who is wedded to Truth and worships Truth alone, proves unfaithful to her, if he applies his talents to anything else. How then can he minister to the senses? A man, whose activities are wholly consecrated to the realization of Truth, which requires utter selflessness, can have no time for the selfish purpose of begetting children and running a household. Realization of Truth through self-gratification should, after what has been said before, appear a contradiction in terms.

If we look at it from the standpoint of *ahimsa* (nonviolence), we find that the fulfilment of *ahimsa* is impossible without utter selflessness. *Ahimsa* means Universal Love. If a man gives his love to one woman, or a woman to one man, what is there left for all the world besides? It simply means, "We two first, and the devil take all the rest of them." As a faithful wife must be prepared to sacrifice her all for the sake of her husband, and a faithful husband for the sake of his wife, it is clear that such persons cannot rise to the height of Universal Love, or look upon all mankind as kith and kin. For they have created a boundary wall round their love. The larger their family, the farther are they from Universal Love. Hence one who would obey the law of *ahimsa* cannot marry, not to speak of gratification outside the marital bond.

Then what about people who are already married? Will they never be able to realize Truth? Can they never offer up their all at the altar of humanity? There is a way out for them. They can behave as if they were not married. Those who have enjoyed this happy condition will be able to bear me out. Many have to my knowledge successfully tried the experiment. If the married couple can think of each other as brother and sister, they are freed for universal service. The very thought that all the women in the world are his sisters, mothers or daughters will at once ennoble a man and snap his chains. The husband and wife do not lose any thing here, but only add to their resources and even to their family. Their love becomes free from the impurity of lust and so grows stronger. With the disappearance of this impurity, they can serve each other better, and the occasions for quarrelling become fewer. There are more occasions for quarrelling where the love is selfish and bounded.

If the foregoing argument is appreciated, a consideration of the physical benefits of chastity becomes a matter of secondary importance. How foolish it is intentionally to dissipate vital energy in sensual enjoyment! It is a grave misuse to fritter away for physical gratification that which is given to man and woman for the full development of their bodily and mental powers. Such misuse is the root cause of many a disease.

Brahmacharya, like all other observances, must be observed in thought, word and deed. We are told in the *Gita,* and experience will corroborate the statement, that the foolish man, who appears to control his body, but is nursing evil thoughts in his mind, makes a vain effort. It may be harmful to suppress the body, if the mind is at the same time allowed to go astray. Where the mind wanders, the body must follow sooner or later.

It is necessary here to appreciate a distinction. It is one thing to allow the mind to harbor impure thoughts; it is a different thing altogether if it strays among them in spite of ourselves. Victory will be ours in the end, if we non-cooperate with the mind in its evil wanderings.

We experience every moment of our lives, that often while the body is subject to our control, the mind is not. This physical control should never be relaxed, and in addition we must put forth a constant endeavour to bring the mind under control. We can do nothing more, nothing less. If we give way to the mind, the body and the mind will put different ways, and we shall be false to ourselves. Body and mind may be said to go together, so long as we continue to resist the approach of every evil thought.

The observance of *brahmacharya* has been believed to be very difficult, almost impossible. In trying to find a reason for this belief, we see that the term *brahmacharya* has been taken in a narrow sense. Mere control of animal passion has been thought to be tantamount to observing *brahmacharya*. I feel, that this conception is incomplete and wrong. *Brahmacharya* means control of all the organs of sense. He, who attempts to control only one organ, and allows all the others free play, is bound to find his effort futile. To hear suggestive stories with the ears, to see suggestive sights with the eyes, to taste stimulating food with the tongue, to touch exciting things with the hands, and then at the same time expect to control the only remaining organ is like putting one's hands in the fire, and expecting to escape being burnt. He therefore who is resolved to control the one must be likewise determined to control the rest. I have always felt, that much harm has been done by the narrow definition of *brahmacharya*. If we practice simultaneous self-control in all directions, the attempt will be scientific and possible of success. Perhaps the palate is the chief sinner. That is why in the *Ashram* we have assigned to control of the palate a separate place among our observances.

Let us remember the root meaning of *brahmacharya*. *Charya* means course of conduct; *brahma-charya* conduct adapted to the search of *Brahma*, i.e., Truth. From this etymological meaning arises the special meaning, viz., control of all the senses. We must entirely forget the incomplete definition which restricts itself to the sexual aspect only.

NON-POSSESSION

Possession implies provision for the future. A seeker after Truth, a follower of the law of Love cannot hold anything against tomorrow. God never stores for the morrow; He never creates more than what is strictly needed for the moment. If therefore we repose faith in His providence, we should rest assured that He will give us every day our daily bread, meaning everything that we require. Saints and devotees, who have lived in such faith, have always derived a justification for it from their experience. Our ignorance or negligence of the Divine Law, which gives to man from day to day his daily bread and no more, has given rise to inequalities with all the miseries attendant upon them. The rich have a superfluous store of things which they do not need, and which are therefore neglected and wasted; while millions are starved to death for want of sustenance. If each retained possession only of what he needed, no one would be in want, and all would live in contentment. As it is, the rich are discontented no less than the poor. The poor man would fain become a millionaire, and the millionaire a multimillionaire. The rich should take the initiative in dispossession with a view to a universal diffusion of the spirit of contentment. If only they keep their own property within moderate limits, the starving will be easily fed, and will learn the lesson of contentment along with the rich.

Perfect fulfilment of the ideal of Nonpossession requires, that man should, like the birds, have no roof over his head, no clothing and no stock of food for the morrow. He will indeed need his daily bread, but it will be God's business, and not his, to provide it. Only the fewest possible, if any at all, can reach this ideal. We ordinary seekers may not be repelled by the seeming impossibility. But we must keep the ideal constantly in view, and in the light thereof, critically examine our possessions, and try to reduce them. Civilization, in the real sense of the term, consists not in the multiplication, but in the deliberate and voluntary reduction of wants. This alone promotes real happiness and contentment, and increases the capacity for service. Judging by this criterion, we find that in the Ashram we possess many things, the necessity for which cannot be proved, and we thus tempt our neighbors to thieve.

From the standpoint of pure Truth, the body too is a possession. It has been truly said that desire for enjoyment creates bodies for the soul. When this desire vanishes, there remains no further need for the body, and man is free from the vicious cycle of births and deaths. The soul is omnipresent; why should she care to be confined within the cagelike body, or do evil and even kill for the sake of that cage? We thus arrive at the ideal of total renunciation, and learn to use the body for the purposes of service so long as it exists, so much so that service, and not bread, becomes with us the staff of life. We eat and drink, sleep and wake, for service alone. Such an attitude of mind brings us real happiness, and the beatific vision in the fulness of time. Let us all examine ourselves from this standpoint.

We should remember, that Non-possession is a principle applicable to thoughts, as well as to things. A man who fills his brain with useless knowledge violates that inestimable principle. Thoughts, which turn us away from God, or do not turn us towards Him, constitute impediments in our way.

SATYAGRAHA OR PASSIVE RESISTANCE*

Reader: Is there any historical evidence as to the success of what you have called soul-force or truth-force? No instance seems to have happened of any nation having risen through soul-force. I still think that the evil-doers will not cease doing evil without physical punishment.

Editor: The poet Tulsidas has said: "Of religion, pity, or love, is the root, as egotism of the body. Therefore, we should not abandon pity so long as we are alive." This appears to me to be a scientific truth. I believe in it as much as I believe in two and two being four. The force of love is the same as the force of the soul or truth. We have evidence of its working at every step. The universe would disappear without the existence of that force. But you ask for historical evidence. It is, therefore, necessary to know what history means. The Gujarati equivalent means: "It so happened." If that is the meaning of history, it is possible to give copious evidence. But, if it means the doings of kings and emperors, there can be no evidence of soul-force or passive resistance in such history. You cannot expect silver ore in a tin mine. History, as we know it, is a record of the wars of the world, and so there is a proverb among Englishmen that a nation which has no history, that is, no wars, is a happy nation. How kings played, how they became enemies of one another, how they

murdered one another, is found accurately recorded in history, and if this were all that had happened in the world, it would have been ended long ago. If the story of the universe had commenced with wars, not a man would have been found alive today. Those people who have been warred against have disappeared as, for instance, the natives of Australia of whom hardly a man was left alive by the intruders. Mark, please, that these natives did not use soul-force in self-defense, and it does not require much foresight to know that the Australians will share the same fate as their victims. "Those that take the sword shall perish by the Sword." With us the proverb is that professional swimmers will find a watery grave.

The fact that there are so many men still alive in the world shows that it is based not on the force of arms but on the force of truth or love. Therefore, the greatest and most unimpeachable evidence of the success of this force is to be found in the fact that, in spite of the wars of the world, it still lives on.

Thousands, indeed tens of thousands, depend for their existence on a very active working of this force. Little quarrels of millions of families in their daily lives disappear before the exercise of this force. Hundreds of nations live in peace. History does not and cannot take note of this fact. History is really a record of every interruption of the even working of the force of love or of the soul. Two brothers quarrel; one of them repents and re-awakens the love that was lying dormant in him; the two again begin to live in peace; nobody takes note of this. But if the two brothers, through the intervention of solicitors or some other reason, take up arms or go to law—which is another form of the exhibition of brute force—their doing would be immediately noticed in the press, they would be the talk of their neighbors and would probably go down to history. And what is true of families and communities is true of nations. There is no reason to believe that there is one law for families and another for nations. History, then, is a record of an interruption of the course of nature. Soul-force, being natural, is not noted in history.

Reader: According to what you say, it is plain that instances of this kind of passive resistance are not to be found in history. It is

---

Hind Swaraj or Indian Home Rule, ch. 17.

necessary to understand this passive resistance more fully. It will be better, therefore, if you enlarge upon it.

Editor: Passive resistance is a method of securing rights by personal suffering: It is the reverse of resistance by arms. When I refuse to do a thing that is repugnant to my conscience, I use soul-force. For instance, the Government of the day has passed a law which is applicable to me. I do not like it. If by using violence I force the Government to repeal the law, I am employing what may be termed body-force. If I do not obey the law and accept the penalty for its breach, I use soul-force. It involves sacrifice of self.

Everybody admits that sacrifice of self is infinitely superior to sacrifice of others. Moreover, if this kind of force is used in a cause that is unjust, only the person using it suffers. He does not make others suffer for his mistakes. Men have before now done many things which were subsequently found to have been wrong. No man can claim that he is absolutely in the right or that a particular thing is wrong because he thinks so, but it is wrong for him so long as that is his deliberate judgment. It is therefore meet that he should not do that which he knows to be wrong, and suffer the consequence whatever it may be. This is the key to the use of soul-force.

Reader: You would then disregard laws—this is rank disloyalty. We have always been considered a law-abiding nation. You seem to be going even beyond the extremists. They say that we must obey the laws that have been passed, but that if the laws be bad, we must drive out the lawgivers even by force.

Editor: Whether I go beyond them or whether I do not is a matter of no consequence to either of us. We simply want to find out what is right and to act accordingly. The real meaning of the statement that we are a law-abiding nation is that we are passive resisters. When we do not like certain laws, we do not break the heads of lawgivers but we suffer and do not submit to the laws. That we should obey laws whether good or bad is a newfangled notion. There was no such thing in former days. The people disregarded those laws they did not like and suffered the penalties for their breach. It is contrary to our manhood if we obey laws repugnant to our conscience. Such teaching is opposed to religion and means slavery. If the Government were to ask us to go about without any clothing, should we do so? If I were a passive resister, I would say to them that I would have nothing to do with their law. But we have so forgotten ourselves and become so compliant that we do not mind any degrading law.

A man who has realized his manhood, who fears only God, will fear no one else. Man-made laws are not necessarily binding on him. Even the Government does not expect any such thing from us. They do not say: "You must do such and such a thing," but they say: "If you do not do it, we will punish you." We are sunk so low that we fancy that it is our duty and our religion to do what the law lays down. If man will only realize that it is unmanly to obey laws that are unjust, no man's tyranny will enslave him. This is the key to self-rule or home-rule.

It is a superstition and ungodly thing to believe that an act of a majority binds a minority. Many examples can be given in which acts of majorities will be found to have been wrong and those of minorities to have been right. All reforms owe their origin to the initiation of minorities in opposition to majorities. If among a band of robbers a knowledge of robbing is obligatory, is a pious man to accept the obligation? So long as the superstition that men should obey unjust laws exists, so long will their slavery exist. And a passive resister alone can remove such a superstition.

To use brute-force, to use gunpowder, is contrary to passive resistance, for it means that we want our opponent to do by force that which we desire but he does not. And, if such a use of force is justifiable, surely he is entitled to do likewise by us. And so we should never come to an agreement. We may simply fancy, like the blind horse moving in a circle round a mill, that we are making progress. Those who believe that they are not bound to obey laws which are repugnant to their conscience have only the remedy of passive resistance open to them. Any other must lead to disaster.

CHAPTER THIRTY-FOUR

FROM CLASSICAL LIBERALISM TO DEMOCRATIC SOCIALISM

As the nineteenth century turned into the twentieth, the ideas and ideals that inspired and characterized an earlier time no longer proved adequate. During the first half of the nineteenth century, the essential challenge was to reduce the role of government and tradition in national economies. Smith wrote in *The Wealth of Nations* in 1776 that "to expect, indeed, that freedom of trade should ever be entirely restored in Great Britain is as absurd as to expect an Oceana or Utopia should ever be established in it." Yet, within seventy years, in part as a result of his work, free trade was established.

Individualistic societies are associated with rationalism and industrialism. The rationalist root of individualism presupposes a basic equality of all men and women on the ground that every human being is endowed with reason: rationalism stresses the value of the individual rather than that of superindividual, collective, institutional forces that are not rational in origin but the product of custom, sentiment, and belief. Modern industrialism largely was the product of a revolt of the individual against obsolete and obstructionist state and societal regulation of economic life.

The individual element of the pioneering phase of the Industrial Revolution was enhanced by the entrepreneur's personal responsibility and willingness to take risks. The spirit of individualism permeated all spheres of life and thought: agnosticism in religion, empiricism in philosophy, utilitarianism in ethics, *laissez faire* in economics, anti-authoritarianism in politics, pacifism, anti-imperialism and free trade in international relations, equality for all regardless of sex, class, religion, or race—these expressions of individualism were characteristic of the classical period of liberalism.

Having first experienced the impact of the Industrial Revolution, England developed the earliest and most advanced forms of individualist, classical liberalism. Locke was the first great European liberal in modern times; his philosophy was based on experience; his politics, on individual liberty and collective consent; his religion, on toleration of diversity. When the factory replaced the village as the dominant social institution in the nineteenth century, when science increasingly challenged the authority of custom and faith, individualism reached its peak in speculative and practical politics.

The most extreme reflection of nineteenth-century individualism is to be found in the encyclopedic system of Herbert Spencer (1820–1903). Both his paternal and maternal ancestors were of a long line of English and French nonconformists, dissenters and rebels, and Spencer traces in his *Autobiography* (1904) his "conspicuous disregard" of political, religious, and social authority to the tradition of independence and dissent so long cherished by his family. Spencer's education was informal, unconventional, and highly deficient in the more traditional studies of literature and history. His father encouraged his interest in science and technology, and Spencer became an engineer. However, he practiced his profession for but a few years, because he became increasingly interested in political economy, sociology, biology, and philosophy. He was a subeditor of *The Economist* from 1848 to 1853, and then ventured into a full-time career as a freelance author.

As early as 1842 Spencer contributed to the *Nonconformist* a series of letters called *The Proper Sphere of Government,* his first major publication. It contains his political philosophy of extreme individualism and *laissez faire,* which was little, if at all, modified in his writings of the subsequent sixty years. Spencer expresses in *The Proper Sphere of Government* his belief that "everything in nature has its laws," organic as well as inorganic matter. Man is subject to laws both in his physical and spiritual essence, and "as with man individually, so with man socially." Concerning the evils of society, Spencer postulates a "self-adjusting principle" under which evils rectify themselves, provided that no one interferes with the inherent law of society.

In discussing the functions of the state, Spencer is concerned with what the state should not do, rather than what it should do. Maintenance of order and administration of justice are the only two proper realms of government activity, and their purpose is "simply to defend the natural rights of man—to protect person and property." The state has no business to promote religion, regulate trade and commerce, encourage colonization, aid the poor, or enforce sanitary laws. Spencer went even so far as to deny the state the right to wage war; but, as he says in his *Autobiography,* his "youthful enthusiasm of two-and twenty" had carried him too far in this respect.

Spencer's next major publication was *Social Statics* (1851). In it he repeats the catalogue of functions the state should not exercise, and he adds the two novel proposals that the state abstain from regulating the currency and that it drop the postal business. Both functions could be carried on more efficiently, he held, by private competitive enterprise. Like Bentham, he considered the greatest happiness of the greatest number the ultimate standard for measuring contrasting social policies. Unlike Bentham, who was willing to use the machinery of Parliament and administration for the active promotion of reform and improvement, Spencer firmly believes that active interference with the natural laws of society would do much harm and little good.

Spencer introduced the concept of *evolution* into his political and social speculations and held that the same basic law of growth and evolution pervaded the physical, animal, and human worlds. The *advance from the simple to the complex* is the cardinal principle that Spencer sees exemplified in the origin and development of the earth, its flora and fauna, and, finally, in the evolution of human society. Progress consists essentially in the "transformation of the homogeneous into the heterogeneous." Because it pervades all nature, animate and inanimate, progress is, therefore, "not an accident, but a necessity."

Translating the newly developing concepts of biology into social-science terms, Spencer defines evil as the result of the "non-adaptation of constitution to conditions." The shrub that dwindles in poor soil or dies when removed to a cold climate is no different, in principle, from the suffering of man who is incapable of adapting himself to his environment by means of the faculties he possesses: "Pervading all nature we must see at work a stern discipline, which is a little cruel that it may be very kind." The aged and weak animal is rightly killed by some beast of prey, and such death creates three kinds of happiness: the old animal is spared the suffering of slow and painful starvation, the younger generation can enjoy itself more fully by ridding itself of the burdensome old, and the beasts of prey derive happiness from their activity of killing off the weak and infirm animals. The happiness of humanity is "secured by that same beneficent, though severe discipline, to which the animate creation at large is subject: a discipline which is pitiless in the working out of good: a felicity-pursuing law which never swerves for the avoidance of partial and temporary suffering."

Spencer warns against interference with suffering for sentimental reasons, because this distorts the operation of social laws even more grievously. Nature remedies incompetence and ignorance by "inconvenience, suffering, and death." If such penalties seem harsh, Spencer suggests that in reality they produce happiness, because society as a whole benefits from the elimination of the unfit, and the "survival of the fittest" (a phrase coined by Spencer and adopted by Darwin) ensures a constant improvement of the quality of the human race. To relax or suspend the stern discipline of nature slows the progress of society toward the stage in which it will be composed only of those who are well adjusted to their environment, in which the overall equilibrium between man and his surroundings will be one of static repose. Those who are ill-adapted to their conditions of existence are on trial: "If they are sufficiently complete to live, they *do* live, and it is well they should live. If they are not sufficiently complete to live, they die, and it is best they should die."

Viewing the nature of the state in evolutionary terms, Spencer is little interested in forms of government, such as the traditional distinctions of monarchies, aristocracies, and democracies. The two main forms of state and society, according to Spencer, are the *military state* and the *industrial state*. The military state is the early form of social organization, primitive, barbarian, and geared to permanent readiness for war. The individual is no more than a means to an end set by the state: victory in war. Society is rigidly organized, and every individual occupies the place assigned to him by the exigencies of militarism and authoritarian government. *Status* is the characteristic principle of the military society, and there is little mobility between classes and groups. Spencer defines the military state as one in which "the army is the nation mobilized while the nation is the quiescent army."

Showing unusual foresight long before total war was a reality, Spencer understood the impact of war on society as a whole; although his analysis of the military state refers to an early stage of society, it anticipates with remarkable accuracy developments of the twentieth century. In the military state, Spencer says, the military chief is likely to be the political leader, and he keenly perceived the inner relations between militarism and despotism. Chauvinism, nationalism, and imperialism are the ideological inspiration of the military state, and the task of its ecclesiastical body is to teach obedience and discipline as primary civic virtues. The economic activities of the industrial classes are subordinated to the military needs of the state, and the purpose of the economy is not to increase personal happiness through greater material welfare but to enhance collective power through successful conquests. There is considerable cooperation in a military state, but it is enforced and involuntary. Because the security of the state is the primary objective of all public action, there is little room for individual liberty, unorthodoxy, or experimentation.

As the military state expands its territory and achieves peace and stability over a long period of time, it gradually evolves into the industrial type of state and society.

The latter is in every respect the opposite of the military state. *Contract* rather than status determines the position of the individual in society, as well as his opportunity to move upward or downward. The way of life in the industrial state and society is based on voluntary cooperation, and the tendency is toward the gradual elimination of coercion in all its forms. Spontaneity, diversity, variety, and nonconformity characterize the industrial society with its emphasis on the value of the individual as the supreme end of government. The purpose of the industrial society is to assure the maximum liberty and happiness of its members, whereas the purpose of the military society is to increase its power by rigid regimentation at home and imperialist conquest abroad. In relation to other nations, the industrial society is pacific, eager to exchange the products of labor rather than to acquire wealth by force. Members of the industrial society are therefore antimilitarist, anti-imperialist, cosmopolitan, and humanitarian. Free trade within and between nations is the formula of the industrial society, whereas economic nationalism is the ideal of the military state.

The progress from the military to the industrial society meant for Spencer a simultaneous progressive diminution of government, because government is no more than "proof of still-existing barbarism." The more men learn to cooperate on a peaceful, voluntary basis, the closer they approximate the ideal of the industrial state and the less they need government, which will eventually wither away.

Even when Spencer's idealization of industrialism is allowed for, his insight into the fundamental difference between the military and industrial state is of lasting importance. His basic distinction throws a great deal of light on the political behavior of nations. The intimate relation between the internal structure of a state and its foreign aims and policies were amply demonstrated in the twentieth century by aggressive wars waged by totalitarian states. Where the production of wealth has been the predominant objective of a nation, its record as a member of the world community has, on the whole, been less aggressive and rapacious than that of nations whose internal organization has been thoroughly militarized and regimented for the attainment of power and glory. Spencer thought that private enterprise without interference from the state is the best guarantee of internal and international peace and security.

In 1884 Spencer published four essays in the *Contemporary Review,* subsequently assembled in book form under the title, *The Man versus the State.* It is his most famous work on politics and still the most influential statement of the philosophy of implacable *laissez faire.* In the first essay, "The New Tories," he attacks the English Liberals for abandoning their historical individualism in favor of social reform and state-provided services. According to Spencer, English Conservatives, like conservatives generally, are the historical descendants of the principles of militancy and status, whereas the English Liberals, like liberals generally, stem from individualism and contract. Spencer also noticed that economic individualism, abandoned by Liberals, was more and more adopted by Conservatives, so that the roles of both parties came to be the opposite of what they originally had been. Spencer thus foresaw that the British Conservatives would become the party of economic individualism and free enterprise, whereas the Liberals would increasingly accept public control of the economy.

The second essay of *The Man versus the State* is "The Coming Slavery." In it, he reiterates his belief that the laws of society must not be interfered with by artificial political measures, that it is both futile and harmful to interfere with the beneficent process of the survival of the fittest, and that interference with natural selection lowers the standards of society as a whole. He specifically states that all human suffering ought not to be prevented, because "much of the suffering is curative, and prevention of it is prevention of a remedy." He stresses the tendency of officialdom and official regulations to increase in a geometrical ratio to the power of resistance of the regulated citizens. People get more and more accustomed to the idea that government will take care of them, and thus lose the spirit of initiative and enterprise. The growth of popular suffrage represents a danger, according to Spencer, inasmuch as the various parties, in order to capture the popular vote, find they have to outbid each other in promises of more social welfare.

Spencer predicted that social welfare programs would eventually lead to socialization of the means of production, and "all socialism is slavery." He defines a slave as a person who "labors under coercion to satisfy another's desires." Under socialism or communism the individual would be enslaved to the whole community rather than to a particular master, and "it matters not whether his master is a single person or a society." Spencer says that the existence of democratic government would not prevent the despotic character of socialism, and he maintains that officialism will always work differently from the way it may be intended to work. The concentration of great economic power in the hands of the bureaucracy will inevitably lead to political despotism.

His basic objection to socialism is his feeling that institutional changes cannot abolish the difficulties created by the nature of man, and he attacks the view that "by due skill an ill-working humanity may be framed into well-working institutions. It is a delusion. The defective natures of citizens will show themselves in the bad acting of whatever social structure they are arranged into. There is no political alchemy by which you can get golden conduct out of leaden instincts."

In his third essay, "The Sins of Legislators," he deplores the spread of government activity in social and economic areas. Progress is the result of the desire to "increase personal welfare," and not the product of governmental regulation: "It is not to the State that we owe the multitudinous useful inventions from the spade to the telephone; it was not the State which made possible extended navigation by a developed astronomy; it was not the State which made the discoveries in physics, chemistry, and the rest, which guide modern manufacturers; it was not the State which devised the machinery for producing fabrics of every kind, for transferring men and things from place to place, and for ministering in a thousand ways to our comforts."

Legislators must understand the laws of society before they meddle with them, and Spencer particularly charges legislators with confusing *family ethics* with *state ethics*. In the family, generosity is the guiding principle, and benefits received have little or no relation to merit. In the state, Spencer maintains, the ruling principle ought to be justice, according to which there is a proportioning of benefits to merits, "as throughout the animal world." The intrusion of family ethics into state ethics is a dangerous interference with the laws of nature and society, and is slowly followed by "fatal results." The poverty of the incapable, the sufferings of the imprudent, and the shoulderings aside of the weak by the strong are the decrees of a farseeing benevolence, and Spencer sees his doctrine of society confirmed by Darwin's principle of "natural selection." He defines government as "begotten of aggression and by aggression," reminiscent of St. Augustine's description of kingdoms as "great robberies," and Spencer writes that government continually betrays its aggressive nature, even if it apparently seeks to mitigate suffering, because in the end such relief of suffering is cruelty rather than kindness: "For is it not cruel to increase the sufferings of the better that the sufferings of the worse may be decreased?"

The last essay of *The Man versus the State* is "The Great Political Superstition." In the past, Spencer says, the great political superstition was the divine right of kings. In the present it is the "divine right of parliaments." Spencer attacks the doctrine of sovereignty as propounded by Hobbes and rejects the claim of popular majorities for unlimited authority as being inconsistent with the inalienable rights of the individual. Spencer also rejects the Benthamite doctrine that *individual rights* are created by the state and reverts to the Lockean notion that they *precede the state*. In particular, Spencer emphasizes that "property was well recognized before law existed." The state does not create rights but merely formally sanctions and better defines "those assertions of claims and recognitions of claims which naturally originate from the individual desires of men who have to live in presence of one another." Far from being created by the state, rights stand in inverse relation to it. As the state grows, status and slavery grow with it. The recognition of rights begins when "militancy ceases to be chronic and governmental power declines."

Spencer concludes *The Man versus the State* with the final reminder that government is not a divine institution but a committee of management, and that it has no intrinsic authority beyond the sanction bestowed on it by the free consent of the citizens: "The function of Liberalism in the past was that of putting a limit to the powers of kings. The function of true Liberalism in the future will be that of putting a limit to the powers of parliaments."

Spencer's political ideas hardly changed between 1842, when he published his *Proper Sphere of Government,* and 1903, the year of his death. The constancy of his political thought in the face of a rapidly changing social and economic scene explains why the same ideas that were the last word in radical individualism in the 1840s had become the *ne plus ultra* of orthodox conservatism by 1900. Although Spencer's influence declined in England, it steadily grew in the United States. Just as John Locke dominated American political thought in the eighteenth century by supplying the rationale of government based on consent, Spencer dominated American social philosophy of the latter part of the nineteenth century by supplying the rationale of *laissez faire.*

The period was one of tremendous industrial expansion in the United States, and Spencer's ideas of *laissez faire* and the survival of the fittest by natural selection appealed to businessmen and industrial entrepreneurs who themselves had gone through the hard school of ruthless competition, in which no quarter was asked or given. Spencer supplied businessmen with the comforting thought that the survival of the fittest was not only a principle of political or economic conservatism but a universal law that pervaded nature as well as human society. By linking economic *laissez faire* with progress, he assured the wealthy classes that competitive capitalism was not only in harmony with universal laws but also was in the interest of the general welfare. Business found in Spencer's biological and scientific system a substitute for the lost religious inspiration, and Spencerism became a total view of life rather than a mere social or political theory. With the aid of Spencerism, opposition to social reform appeared not as class egotism but as defense of the true principles of social evolution and progress.

When Spencer visited the United States in 1882, he was immensely impressed by its industrial power, and in his *Autobiography* he records his conviction that "the United States will very soon be by far the most powerful nation in the world." One of Spencer's closest American friends was Andrew Carnegie, the steel magnate, and during his triumphal tour of the country, Spencer saw many other successful businessmen and leaders of conservative thought. Yet the restlessness and strain of American life perturbed him, and before he departed for England he declared that the future "has in store a new ideal, differing as much from the present ideal of industrialization as that ideal differs from the past ideal of militancy." His earlier dream that industrialism was the utopia now gave way to the dawning realization that the human cost of industrialism was perhaps higher than he had thought.

The early parts of the Industrial Age witnessed the concentration of capital and—even more significantly—control of business. Monopolies, trusts, and gigantic enterprises created a sense of frustration and protest among the millions whose livelihood depended upon their new employers, and were considered incompatible with the democratic yearnings of the common man. As Tocqueville had predicted, the "new aristocracy of manufacturers" was as anxious to exploit the people as the old aristocracy of birth had been, without, however, any feeling of obligation to those who worked for them. The second change that, later, undermined the general faith in the validity of *laissez faire* was unemployment. When, during the Great Depression, millions remained out of work for years and great productive resources lay idle, men and women began to doubt that a national economy, left to its own laws and harmonies, naturally produces the maximum common good.

Capitalism and liberalism originally developed as affirmations of individual rights and opportunities against the power of the state, customs, and tradition. As corporate and monopolistic business created vast power aggregates, the individual turned to government for protection. True liberalism, from Locke to the present, always insists that government is no more and no less than an instrument of the people. Where nineteenth century liberalism differed from twentieth century liberalism was in the former's view that once the dominion of the state is removed, the problem of power as such is also removed—the state would be replaced by society as a free association of equals, without rulers or ruled. By contrast, twentieth century liberals emphasized that private economic power, and destitute living conditions, can impinge as directly on the lives and liberties of people as political and social power did in the past, and that there will always be a major role for government to play.

Liberals then found themselves in the unusual position of looking to government, their historical enemy, for help against new forms of economic and financial power. Yet this paradox was more apparent than real. All liberalism—whether nineteenth or twentieth century—*is about curbing power,* whether power manifests in politics or economics. Throughout the eighteenth and early nineteenth centuries, liberals therefore acted consistently by invoking *laissez faire* and individual economic authority as a counteracting force against the power of the state. From the late nineteenth century on, private economic power became perceived in Britain and the United States as the main source threatening the individual. Liberals therefore acted consistently by invoking the power of government against large, private, corporate business. Throughout its career, liberalism has thus remained constant in its core objective of curbing power; all that has changed are the means used in attaining this objective. Strengthening the power of government would have been illiberal policy in the nineteenth century because government had too much power. Similarly, advocating *laissez faire* became illiberal during the first seventy years of the twentieth century, since the goal became to curb economic power that was perceived to exist excessively in private corporations.

A contrast to Spencer's atomistic individualism was provided by Thomas Hill Green (1836–1882), an Oxford don who put forward different views in philosophy and politics. In philosophy, Green was an idealist in the tradition of Plato, Kant, and Hegel, and thus outside mainstream British empiricist thought. Nonetheless, for a period of several decades from the 1870s to the early years of the twentieth century, his thought dominated Oxford and other British intellectual circles—until the work of Bertrand Russell and Ludwig Wittgenstein again refocused British philosophy on the material world and logical analysis.

Green's thought harkens back to the ancient Greek *polis* in his emphasis on community. Just as Aristotle believed that man is a social animal, Green wrote that "The self is a social self." To conceive of an individual living in isolation was, he thought, unrealistic and fruitless. The appropriate role of politics is to integrate individuals within a community. Unless humanity are conceived primarily in social terms, no understanding of either individual or community is possible.

Green died at forty-five and had not published much to this time. His major work that appeared during his lifetime was a several hundred pages' introduction to Hume's *Treatise of Human Nature,* in which he opposed Hume's empiricism. Green's essential philosophical view was spiritual, not materialistic. He believed a spiritual, moral force permeates and animates the universe. This belief undergirded much of his political thought. To separate politics from morality is, he thought, inconceivable. What politics is precisely about is the best human order that produces the best human beings. He was Professor of Moral Philosophy at Oxford.

During the years he developed his political thought, changes in public opinion and law were occurring. Industrialization and urbanization created new issues in social order that had not been confronted before. Moreover, more wealth was created than ever. Green was a Christian, and on his deathbed he requested that the eighth chapter of *Romans* be read to him, which includes: "To be carnally minded is death; but to be spiritually minded is life and peace." Despite its emphasis on a higher material standard of living for all, socialism ultimately is not of this world. Its goal is to bring about better men and women in whom Christian virtues of love and other-centeredness are central. In its British idealist variant, socialism was not about hatred of the bourgeoisie, but love of the common and all men, and wanting the best life for all.

Industrialization had the effects of ravaging countryside and initiating an urban underclass living in squalor adjacent to rapidly growing middle and upper classes. It became virtually impossible for caring and intelligent individuals not to recognize that the new conditions required new ways of looking at government. It fell to government not merely to clear away medieval and traditional restraints on trade and occupation (the political agenda of the first half of the nineteenth century), and to maintain order (government's universal role), but also to lead a society into a better way of life. This required considerable positive legislation to restrict child and women's labor, to require schooling and some form of public charity, and to establish standards of safety and health, among other efforts. All of these functions of government, and many others, have of course greatly expanded during the twentieth century.

Green was not only an academic, but he actively involved himself in Oxford municipal affairs. He served on both the Oxford town council and school board and participated in the temperance movement. He was, according to historian of political thought Sir Ernest Barker, as much a "sober realist" as "soaring idealist." In contrast to more recent views that consider such problems as illiteracy and alcoholism to be a function of poverty or social conditions, Green considered such issues from the perspective of individual virtue. Raising the material standard of living was not government's only or even primary goal. Improving men and women is. He was especially interested in education.

Green argued against Spencer and the earlier Mill that the state has a considerable positive role to play. While he always remained a Liberal, he was a Liberal who pointed the way from the nineteenth to twentieth century meaning of the term. He did not conceive of freedom only as "freedom from" governmental interference. He saw freedom in largest part as "freedom to" engage in certain activities, to be a certain person. He enunciated a positive conception of freedom. He essentially was egalitarian and demo-cratic in his political views.

Though egalitarian, he did not favor expropriation of the expropriators in a Marx-ist sense. Particularly before the Russian Revolution of 1917, Marx never really entered the British political or philosophical consciousness. There was a socialist ideal in Britain before the Marxist one overwhelmed it on the world stage, and this preexisting British socialist ideal is important in itself, as well as for light it sheds on subsequent political development in Britain and America. Green's view of socialism was of a moral community of equals living as well as the conditions of this world allow. It was more akin to St. Augustine's City of God than to Marx and Lenin's City of Man.

The transcendent quality of British idealist socialism separates it greatly from the temporal quality of Marx's emphasis on matter rather than spirit. Method as well as outcome is central to British idealist socialism, and Green saw the method by which so-ciety is conducted and improved as vitally influencing and being a constituent part of its outcomes. He emphasized social means as well as ends, saw these two as integrally tied, and considered the means of social improvement as incorporated within its ends. The best society is not so much a destination as a process. He endeavored, his biogra-pher R. L. Nettleship wrote, "to awaken a consciousness of what man actually is and does in certain functions of his everyday life, this being, as he conceived, the true way to awaken the further consciousness of what he ought to be and do . . ."

The philosophical idea of community stems from the belief that humanity are inex-tricably located within a social context, and that principles of justice and fairness should reign within a group. It is neither right nor fair that some should profit at the ex-pense and to the detriment of others, at least not as long as the harm experienced by others is not in some way necessary for a greater common good. Green rejected utilitar-ianism in its hedonistic form of the greatest pleasure and the least pain. He endorsed utilitarianism, however, in the form of seeking the greatest good, which he defined as maximum individual moral development. As a society becomes more typified by a higher moral standard—to which adequate housing, nutrition, education, and health care contribute, though they are by no means the same thing as—individuals will accept that in order to have the best life for all, some restraints should be placed on individ-uals, and that—on a more practical level—there will be a substantial role for gov-ernment. Furthermore, as society develops in a materially progressive direction, individuals will choose this role for government. Justice and fairness do not rule when they are imposed from without, but when they are realized within. Social organization through government can further this end.

Green, in the British, pre-Marxian tradition of socialism, did not at all put forward that government should be all-encompassing. He was close to a *laissez faire* position, though it was arrived at from different premises than previous British economists. He considered morality to exist independently of government and law. There is a consider-able place for voluntary and private expressions of community independent of the gov-ernment of realm. He was opposed to centralized government authority. Following in the British tradition of individualism and protest, he held that it is dangerous for gov-ernment to become too large. He would have reacted in horror to a society in which gov-ernment owned and controlled all land and industry and employed all workers. He considered the state "a society of societies."

Following his premature death, a number of Green's writings and lectures were pub-lished, most prominently *Lectures on the Principles of Political Obligation* (1882) and

Prolegomena to Ethics (1883). In 1906 appeared the three-volume *Works of Thomas Hill Green.*

His influence was as much or more through his students and colleagues as directly by his writings, and one of his most distinguished students was Bernard Bonsanquet, who in his 1899 *The Philosophical Theory of the State* well expressed a considerable aspect of the notion of government, society, and the individual that informed Green's view, though from a somewhat more Hegelian perspective:

> To apprehend the State as the realisation of freedom was the aim of Hegel's *Philosophy of Right* . . . [W]e treat the analysis of a Modern State as a chapter in the *Philosophy of Mind.* For Hegel's *Philosophy of Right* (or of *Law*) . . . is essentially an expansion of . . . one subdivision of his *Philosophy of Mind . . .*
>
> The position of the analysis of a State in the *Philosophy of Mind* may be briefly indicated as follows. When we embark on the study of ordinary Psychology, we take the individual human being as we find him to-day. We accept him as a formed individual, distinguishing himself from external things, and possessing what we call a will—a capacity of seeking his own satisfaction . . .
>
> Here, however, the problem can no longer be deferred. The 'free mind' does not explain itself and cannot stand alone. Its impulses cannot be ordered, or, in other words, its purposes cannot be made determinate, except in an actual system of selves. Except by expressing itself in relation to an ordered life, which implies others, it cannot exist. And, therefore, not something additional and parallel to it, which might or might not exist, but a necessary form of its own action as real and determinate, is the actual fabric in which it utters itself as Society and the State. . . . A particular society stands in time, and is open to criticism and to destruction. Beyond it lies the reality, continuous with mind as known in the State, but eternal as the former is perishable, which as Absolute Mind is open to human experience in Art, Religion, and Philosophy.

Bosanquet appropriately called attention to the tie between Hegel's conception and that of Plato, who saw ideal forms generally and an ideal state in the *Republic* conforming to eternal properties in the soul. Green emphasized the soul as the overarching concern in political life. The self does not and cannot exist independently of a community.

In the development of British democratic socialism during the last decades of the nineteenth and first half of the twentieth centuries, no one figure really stands out. The process of developing democratic socialism was cooperative as the society it envisioned was to be. Of the central figures, though, Harold Laski (1893–1950) was the most internationally prominent. During the 1930s and 1940s, he was the most well-known democratic socialist in the world. Notwithstanding the relative eclipse into which he has gone since his demise an obituarist of his wrote that "the future historian may talk of the period between 1920 and 1950 as the 'Age of Laski.'"

British socialism traces its roots to Robert Owen, who coined the term "socialist" and who, in *A New View of Society* (1813), advocated "progressive repeal and modification" of unjust and inhumane laws and conditions, though he strongly rejected revolutionary change. Far from being a revolutionary, in fact, Owen dedicated his book to His Royal Highness, the Prince Regent of the British Empire. Owen considered drink an incentive to crime and a main source of human misery. His list of virtues and vices would appeal to any current social conservative. He venerated the British constitution and placed his hope in reason and education. He considered human nature "universally plastic," supported reduction in child labor, opposed the dole (cash relief to the unemployed), and saw socialism as being realized through voluntary cooperatives.

The place of John Stuart Mill in the development of British socialism and the welfare state is immense. He was the towering intellectual figure in progressive political reform during the second half of the nineteenth century. Though in his earlier writings and the first edition of *Principles of Political Economy* (1848) he supported a more or less consistent *laissez faire* position, in subsequent editions he moved toward a British (as distinct from Marxian) socialist view. Hayek wrote that Mill "probably led more intellectuals into socialism than any other single person . . ." Mill favored voluntary workers' cooperatives, believing in cooperation within the working place and competition between working places.

British democratic socialism, as it developed, drew its nourishment not only from political economists, but from religious leaders, artists, and literary figures. Clement Attlee, first Labour prime minister of a majority Labour government in Great Britain (1945–51), believed that "the first place in the influences that built up the Socialist movement must be given to religion. England in the nineteenth century was still a nation of Bible leaders. To put the Bible into the hands of an Englishman is to do a very dangerous thing. He will find there material which may send him out as a preacher of some religious, social, or economic doctrine." According to George Lansbury, Attlee's predecessor as Labour Party leader, "Socialism, which means love, cooperation, and brotherhood in every department of human affairs, is the . . . outward expression of a Christian's faith."

Ethical and aesthetic idealism was another source of British democratic socialism. Expressed by poets like John Ruskin and William Morris, ethical idealism was not a political or economic program, but a revolt against squalor, drabness, and poverty in early industrial capitalism. Perhaps because capitalism first developed in England, it was the first place to have clean air and water industrially polluted, the first to have the beauty of countryside lost to industrial development, the first to have graceful old towns and villages disfigured by slums and factory centers. Morris in particular felt intensely that the arts should be brought into the lives of ordinary men and women.

The Fabian Society was founded in England in 1884 to introduce socialism peacefully and gradually through a process of slow permeation into British life. Early and influential members included Sidney and Beatrice Webb, George Bernard Shaw, and Graham Wallas. The Fabians rejected violent revolutionary change. The Webbs were more technocratic and authoritarian than other, earlier British socialists. Leading Fabian historians Norman and Jeanne MacKenzie characterize the Webbs' goal as "something very like a Positivist state inspired by a Religion of Humanity and governed by a disinterested élite." Sidney played a leading role in drafting Labour's 1918 party constitution calling for nationalization of industry in Great Britain.

Among Sidney Webb's greatest accomplishment was the founding of the London School of Economics and Political Science (LSE) in 1895. Crucial among the Webbs' and other Fabians' beliefs was that socialism would be best attained through rational persuasion. They genuinely believed that socialism in its form of nationalizing an economy's means of production would be more materially productive than the "anarchy" of free enterprise. Margaret Cole, wife of socialist professor G. D. H. Cole at Oxford, said that "one of the most important parts of the Fabian creed" is that "no reasonable person *who knows the facts* can fail to become a Socialist, or, at the very least, to be converted to Socialist policy." Beatrice Webb rhetorically asked: "Do we want to organise the unthinking persons into Socialistic Societies, or to make the thinking persons socialistic? We believe in the latter process."

LSE was an outgrowth of the belief in rational persuasion. Its motto is *"Rerum cognoscere causas"*—"to know the causes of things"—and the school has been a font from which many leading political theorists, economists, and philosophers have emerged and worked, including Laski, Wallas, Richard Tawney, Beveridge, Hayek, Ronald Coase, and Karl Popper. Wallas was the first Professor of Political Science at LSE. He was more a traditional British, humanistic socialist than a technocratic or scientific socialist. He placed particular hope in the transformation of society through education: "If this generation were wise, it would spend on education not only more than any other generation has ever spent before, but more than any generation would ever need to spend again. It would fill the school buildings with the means not only of comfort, but even of the higher luxury; it would serve the [students] meals on tables spread with flowers, in halls surrounded with beautiful pictures, or even . . . filled with the sound of music . . ." He meant it. His perspective was by no means shared by all. Philosopher G. E. Moore at Cambridge, Keynes's idol, wrote of him: "A beastly fool . . . [E]verything is to subserve his wretched utility—serving the masses! Educating them for what? He cannot tell you. He is the blind leader of the blind."

Tawney was another great democratic socialist at LSE. He was a professor in economic history and wrote several well-known books, including *The Acquisitive Society* (1920), *Religion and the Rise of Capitalism* (1926), and *Equality* (1931). The most famous (or notorious) professor at the school, though, who more than anyone else gave it an undeserved reputation as being a haven solely for leftwingers, was Laski, who came to LSE, following a stint in America at Harvard, in 1920. Like Green, it was as a teacher that Laski may have had his greatest influence. Daniel Patrick Moynihan, who studied at LSE, wrote when he was American ambassador to the United Nations that the school was "the most important institution of higher education in Asia and Africa," and that "Harold Laski once molded the minds of so many future leaders of the new majority." John Kenneth Galbraith, a former American ambassador to India and LSE postgraduate student, has said that "the centre of [first Indian Prime Minister Jawaharlal] Nehru's thinking was Laski," and that "India [was] the country most influenced by Laski's ideas." Another Laski student is former Canadian prime minister Pierre Trudeau. When Laski taught at LSE, from 1920 to 1950, it still was when the sun never set on the British Empire. He made a great mark as a teacher in the British political world as well. Of the 393 Labour members of parliament elected in Labour's 1945 landslide victory, sixty-seven had, in one form or another, studied under him.

The times of the 1920s and 1930s naturally greatly influenced the content and course of political and economic discussion. World War I destroyed the great liberal dream of the nineteenth century of a peaceful and harmonious world united by commerce and free trade. The Great War appeared to demonstrate that, left to themselves, humanity will not necessarily develop in a positive direction. There is, instead, a great role for government to play. The destruction the war engendered, societal collapse across Europe it caused, and truly substantial expansion of government it furthered led to new conceptions of the appropriate and feasible roles of government. Furthermore, the example of Soviet Russia appeared to indicate that wholesale social reconfiguration of a society by government is possible and desirable. The *laissez faire* liberalism of the nineteenth century was dead, or, at the very least, in a state of suspended animation.

Economic conditions in Britain and the United States were different during the 1920s, and it is important to be clear about this in order to understand subsequent political and economic discussion and activity, which so significantly reflected and informed developments in political and economic theory in both. While, following readjustment after World War I, the 1920s were the prosperous "roaring 20s" in America, this was not so in Britain, which experienced high unemployment and low economic growth throughout the decade. Then, when the Great Depression struck during the early 1930s, the economies of both the United States and Great Britain were pummeled.

The difference in economic conditions between the two nations during the 1920s helps to explain why socialism—especially socialism of an increasingly nationalization-type—gained ground in Britain during the decade. Bad economic conditions prompt reflection on how an economic system should change. Conversely, in good economic times, relatively little thought is given to fundamental alteration. Moreover, the example of Soviet Russia was geographically and culturally closer to Britain than the United States.

Laski's major scholarly work was *The Grammar of Politics* (1925), a general treatise. It was his most ambitious volume and is a classic in the field of political literature. In the tradition of humanistic liberalism, he opened his analysis with the definition of liberty as "the eager maintenance of that atmosphere in which men have the opportunity to be their best selves." This was not socialism of a Marxian or Leninist sort. The "life of spiritual enrichment" was the sole test which determines when restraint is justified.

After examining the "safeguards of liberty," he discusses the central problem of the relationship between liberty and equality. He rejected the view of two outstanding classical liberals of the nineteenth century, Tocqueville and Lord Acton, that liberty and equality are "antithetic," and ascribes this erroneous conclusion to the mistaken conception of equality as "identity of treatment." Laski did not find equal outcomes incompatible with human differences: "The meaning, ultimately, of equality surely lies in the fact that the very differences in the nature of men require mechanisms for the expression of their wills that give to each its due hearing." Absence of special privileges, still prevalent in Britain during the 1920s, and meaningful opportunities open to all were the two primary conditions he saw for social equality. In particular, he stressed educational opportunity—its lack inflicts not only cruel injustice on individuals, but causes waste of talent and loss of ability, to the detriment of society as a whole.

Laski argued that, in the context of modem civilization, social and economic inequality are the most serious obstacles to freedom: "There are men in every community whose power is built upon not what they are or do, but upon the possessions they embody." Analyzing the influence of wealth in government, education, communication of information and ideas, and religion, he arrived at the conclusion, enunciated by thinkers as diverse as Aristotle and Madison, that "political equality . . . is never real unless it is accompanied by virtual economic equality." To Laski, equality in economic power means not only approximate equality of wealth; he was even more concerned about the power of private enterprise over the individual, and believed that as political power was controlled by law, so should economic power be. Political democracy is not enough. There must also be economic democracy.

Laski vigorously reaffirmed the Lockean-Jeffersonian theory of revolution. During the 1930s—when Nazism and fascism grew stronger and stronger, democracies throughout the world were weak and divided, England had suffered from poor economic conditions for almost two decades, and the new system in the Soviet Union beckoned—Laski, like many democratic socialists, became intellectually moody and a bit pessimistic as to the ability of traditional democracies to survive. In this period, he accepted some of the points of the Marxian analysis of history; his *State in Theory and Practice* (1935) is the book that best represents this phase of his thought. But even here, the main assumptions of his political theory are set in the grand framework established by Locke, not Marx's deviation: "The roots of valid law are, and can only be, with the individual conscience." This was pure Locke. To the charge that such a view, "by justifying refusal to obey, opens the door to anarchy," he further held, "the answer is that the accusation is true." This, again, was a leading idea expressed by Laski in words that can almost identically be found in Locke.

Indeed, Laski outdid Locke: Where Locke restricted the right to rebel to an injured majority, Laski went further. He saw many examples in history of minorities and even single individuals revolting against intolerable inequities and conditions, and was driven to the conclusion that, in the final analysis, the individual must decide for himself whether he will bow to established law and order, or whether he will feel compelled, by an inner impulse of irrepressible intensity, to rebel.

Throughout the 1930s and 1940s, Laski's irrepressible nature brought him to not infrequent public attention, usually in support of one leftwing cause or another. He was always very sympathetic to the Soviet Union; he supported the Republicans over the Francoists in the Spanish Civil War; he encouraged colonial subjects to seek independence from British rule; he strongly favored nationalization of industry; he railed against big business and capitalism; he was always on hand to give a speech, write an article, or attend a rally in support of some radical leftist effort. If it cannot be said that the direction in which socialism moved in Great Britain entirely or even mostly was the result of his influence, he represented democratic socialism's new direction—away from voluntary cooperation and toward state initiative and control.

I SPENCER

Social Statics and
The Man Versus the State

THE SURVIVAL OF
THE FITTEST*

Pervading all nature we may see at work a stern discipline, which is a little cruel that it may be very kind. That state of universal warfare maintained throughout the lower creation, to the great perplexity of many worthy people, is at bottom the most merciful provision which the circumstances admit of. It is much better that the ruminant animal, when deprived by age of the vigour which made its existence a pleasure, should be killed by some beast of prey, than that it should linger out a life made painful by infirmities, and eventually die of starvation. By the destruction of all such, not only is existence ended before it becomes burdensome, but room is made for a younger generation capable of the fullest enjoyment; and, moreover, out of the very act of substitution happiness is derived for a tribe of predatory creatures. Note further, that their carnivorous enemies not only remove from herbivorous herds individuals past their prime, but also weed out the sickly, the malformed, and the least fleet or powerful. By the aid of which purifying process, as well as by the fighting, so universal in the pairing season, all vitiation of the race through the multiplication of its inferior samples is prevented; and the maintenance of a constitution completely adapted to surrounding conditions, and therefore most productive of happiness, is ensured.

_____

*From Herbert Spencer, *Social Statics* (1851).

The development of the higher creation is a progress towards a form of being capable of a happiness undiminished by these drawbacks. It is in the human race that the consummation is to be accomplished. Civilization is the last stage of its accomplishment. And the ideal man is the man in whom all the conditions of that accomplishment are fulfilled. Meanwhile the well-being of existing humanity, and the unfolding of it into this ultimate perfection, are both secured by that same beneficent, though severe discipline, to which the animate creation at large is subject: a discipline which is pitiless in the working out of good: a felicity-pursuing law which never swerves for the avoidance of partial and temporary suffering. The poverty of the incapable, the distresses that come upon the imprudent, the starvation of the idle, and those shoulderings aside of the weak by the strong, which leave so many "in shallows and in miseries," are the decrees of a large, far-seeing benevolence. It seems hard that an unskilfulness which with all his efforts he cannot overcome, should entail hunger upon the artisan. It seems hard that a labourer incapacitated by sickness from competing with his stronger fellows, should have to bear the resulting privations. It seems hard that widows and orphans should be left to struggle for life or death. Nevertheless, when regarded not separately, but in connection with the interests of universal humanity, these harsh fatalities are seen to be full of the highest beneficence—the same beneficence which brings to early graves the children of diseased parents, and singles out the low-spirited, the intemperate, and the debilitated as the victims of an epidemic.

There are many very amiable people—people over whom in so far as their feelings are concerned we may fitly rejoice—who have not the nerve to look this matter fairly in the face. Disabled as they are by their sympathies with present suffering, from duly regarding ultimate consequences, they pursue a course which is very injudicious, and in the end even cruel. We do not consider it true kindness in a mother to gratify her child with sweetmeats that are certain to make it ill. We should think it a very foolish sort of benevolence which led a surgeon to let his patient's disease progress to a fatal issue, rather than inflict pain by an operation. Similarly, we must call those spurious philanthropists, who, to prevent present misery, would entail greater misery upon future generations. All defenders of a poor-law must, however, be classed amongst such. That rigorous necessity which, when allowed to act on them, becomes so sharp a spur to the lazy, and so strong a bridle to the random, these paupers' friends would repeal, because of the wailings it here and there produces. Blind to the fact, that under the natural order of things society is constantly excreting its unhealthy, imbecile, slow, vacillating, faithless members, these unthinking, though well-meaning, men advocate an interference which not only stops the purifying process, but even increases the vitiation—absolutely encourages the multiplication of the reckless and incompetent by offering them an unfailing provision, and *discourages* the multiplication of the competent and provident by heightening the prospective difficulty of maintaining a family. And thus, in their eagerness to prevent the really salutary sufferings that surround us, these sigh-wise and groan-foolish people bequeath to posterity a continually increasing curse.

Returning again to the highest point of view, we find that there is a second and still more injurious mode in which law-enforced charity checks the process of adaptation. To become fit for the social state, man has not only to lose his savageness, but he has to acquire the capacities needful for civilized life. Power of application must be developed; such modification of the intellect as shall qualify it for its new tasks must take place;

and, above all, there must be gained the ability to sacrifice a small immediate gratification for a future great one. The state of transition will of course be an unhappy state. Misery inevitably results from incongruity between constitution and conditions. All these evils, which afflict us, and seem to the uninitiated the obvious consequences of this or that removable cause, are unavoidable attendants on the adaptation now in progress. Humanity is being pressed against the inexorable necessities of its new position—is being moulded into harmony with them, and has to bear the resulting unhappiness as best it can. The process *must* be undergone, and the sufferings *must* be endured. No power on earth, no cunningly-devised laws of statesmen, no world-rectifying schemes of the humane, no communist panaceas, no reforms that men ever did broach or ever will broach, can diminish them one jot. Intensified they may be, and are; and in preventing their intensification, the philanthropic will find ample scope for exertion. But there is bound up with the change a *normal* amount of suffering, which cannot be lessened without altering the very laws of life. Every attempt at mitigation of this eventuates in exacerbation of it. All that a poor-law, or any kindred institution can do, is to partially suspend the transition—to take off for awhile, from certain members of society, the painful pressure which is effecting their transformation. At best this is merely to postpone what must ultimately be borne. But it is more than this: it is to undo what has already been done. For the circumstances to which adaptation is taking place cannot be superseded without causing a retrogression—a partial loss of the adaptation previously effected; and as the whole process must some time or other be passed through, the lost ground must be gone over again, and the attendant pain borne afresh. Thus, besides retarding adaptation, a poor-law adds to the distresses inevitably attending it.

At first sight these considerations seem conclusive against *all* relief to the poor—voluntary as well as compulsory; and it is no doubt true that they imply a condemnation of whatever private charity enables the recipients to elude the necessities of our social existence. With this condemnation, however, no rational man will quarrel. That careless squandering of pence which has fostered into perfection a system of organized begging—which has made skilful mendicancy more profitable than ordinary manual labour—which induces the simulation of palsy, epilepsy, cholera, and no end of diseases and deformities—which has called into existence warehouses for the sale and hire of impostor's dresses—which has given to pity-inspiring babes a market value of 9 d. per day—the unthinking benevolence which has generated all this, cannot but be disapproved by every one. Now it is only against this injudicious charity that the foregoing argument tells. To that charity which may be described as helping men to help themselves, it makes no objection—countenances it rather. And in helping men to help themselves, there remains abundant scope for the exercise of a people's sympathies. Accidents will still supply victims on whom generosity may be legitimately expended. Men thrown upon their backs by unforeseen events, men who have failed for want of knowledge inaccessible to them, men ruined by the dishonesty of others, and men in whom hope long delayed has made the heart sick, may, with advantage to all parties, be assisted. Even the prodigal, after severe hardship has branded his memory with the unbending conditions of social life to which he must submit, may properly have another trial afforded him. And, although by these ameliorations the process of adaptation must be remotely interfered with, yet in the majority of cases, it will not be so much retarded in one direction as it will be advanced in another.

Objectionable as we find a poor-law to be, even under the supposition that it does what it is intended to do—diminish present suffering—how shall we regard it on finding that in reality it does no such thing—cannot do any such thing? Yet, paradoxical as the assertion looks, this is absolutely the fact. Let but the observer cease to contemplate so fixedly one side of the phenomenon—pauperism and its relief—and begin to examine the other side—rates and the *ultimate* contributors of them—and he will discover that to suppose the sum-total of distress diminishable by act-of-parliament bounty is a delusion. A statement of the case in terms of labour and produce will quickly make this clear.

Here, at any specified period, is a given quantity of food and things exchangeable for food, in the hands or at the command of the middle and upper classes. A certain portion of this food is needed by these classes themselves, and is consumed by them at the same rate, or very near it, be there scarcity or abundance. Whatever variation occurs in the sum-total of food and its equivalents must therefore affect the remaining portion, not used by these classes for personal sustenance. This remaining portion is given by them to the people in return for their labour, which is partly expended in the production of a further supply of necessaries, and partly in the production of luxuries. Hence, by how much this portion is deficient, by so much must the people come short. Manifestly a redistribution by legislative or other agency cannot make that sufficient for them which was probably insufficient. It can do nothing but change the parties by whom the insufficiency is felt. If it gives enough to some who else would not have enough, it must inevitably reduce certain others to the condition of not having enough. And thus, to the extent that a poor-law mitigates distress in one place, it unavoidably produces distress in another.

THE COMING SLAVERY*

The kinship of pity to love is shown among other ways in this, that it idealizes its object. Sympathy with one in suffering suppresses, for the time being, re-feeling which vents itself in "poor felmembrance of his trangressions. The low!" on seeing one in agony, excludes the thought of "bad fellow," which might at another time arise. Naturally, then, if the wretched are unknown or but vaguely known, all the demerits they may have are ignored; and thus it happens that when, as just now, the miseries of the poor are depicted, they are thought of as the miseries of the deserving poor, instead of being thought of, as in large measure they should be, as the miseries of the undeserving poor. Those whose hardships are set forth in pamphlets and proclaimed in sermons and speeches which echo throughout society, are assumed to be all worthy souls, grievously wronged; and none of them are

---

Contemporary Review, XLV (April, 1884). Reprinted in Herbert Spencer, *The Man versus the State* (1884).

thought of as bearing the penalties of their own misdeeds.

On hailing a cab in a London street, it is surprising how generally the door is officiously opened by one who expects to get something for his trouble. The surprise lessens after counting the many loungers about tavern-doors, or after observing the quickness with which a street-performance, or procession, draws from neighbouring slums and stable-yards a group of idlers. Seeing how numerous they are in every small area, it becomes manifest that tens of thousands of such swarm through London. "They have no work," you say. Say rather that they either refuse work or quickly turn themselves out of it. They are simply good-for-nothings, who in one way or other live on the good-for-somethings—vagrants and sots, criminals and those on the way to crime, youths who are burdens on hard-worked parents, men who appropriate the wages of their wives, fellows who share the gains of prostitutes; and then, less visible and less numerous, there is a corresponding class of women.

Is it natural that happiness should be the lot of such? or is it natural that they should bring unhappiness on themselves and those connected with them? Is it not manifest that there must exist in our midst an immense amount of misery which is a normal result of misconduct, and ought not to be dissociated from it? There is a notion, always more or less prevalent and just now vociferously expressed, that all social suffering is removable, and that it is the duty of somebody or other to remove it. Both these beliefs are false. To separate pain from ill-doing is to fight against the constitution of things, and will be followed by far more pain. Saving men from the natural penalties of dissolute living, eventually necessitates the infliction of artificial penalties in solitary cells, on tread-wheels, and by the lash. I suppose a dictum, on which the current creed and the creed of science are at one, may be considered to have as high an authority as can be found. Well, the command "if any would not work neither should he eat," is simply a Christian enunciation of that universal law of Nature under which life has reached its present height—the law that a creature not energetic enough to maintain itself must die: the sole difference being that the law

which in the one case is to be artificially enforced, is, in the other case, a natural necessity. And yet this particular tenet of their religion which science so manifestly justifies, is the one which Christians seem least inclined to accept. The current assumption is that there should be no suffering, and that society is to blame for that which exists.

"But surely we are not without responsibilities, even when the suffering is that of the unworthy?"

If the meaning of the word "we" be so expanded as to include with ourselves our ancestors, and especially our ancestral legislators, I agree. I admit that those who made, and modified, and administered, the old Poor Law, were responsible for producing an appalling amount of demoralization, which it will take more than one generation to remove. I admit, too, the partial responsibility of recent and present lawmakers for regulations which have brought into being a permanent body of tramps, who ramble from union to union; and also their responsibility for maintaining a constant supply of felons by sending back convicts into society under such conditions that they are almost compelled again to commit crimes. Moreover, I admit that the philanthropic are not without their share of responsibility; since, that they may aid the offspring of the unworthy, they disadvantage the offspring of the worthy through burdening their parents by increased local rates. Nay, I even admit that these swarms of good-for-nothings, fostered and multiplied by public and private agencies, have, by sundry mischievous meddlings, been made to suffer more than they would otherwise have suffered. Are these the responsibilities meant? I suspect not.

But now, leaving the question of responsibilities, however conceived, and considering only the evil itself, what shall we say of its treatment? Let me begin with a fact.

A late uncle of mine, the Rev. Thomas Spencer, for some twenty years incumbent of Hinton Charterhouse, near Bath, no sooner entered on his parish duties than he proved himself anxious for the welfare of the poor, by establishing a school, a library, a clothing club, and land-allotments, besides building some model cottages. Moreover, up to 1833 he was a pauper's friend—always for the pauper against the overseer.

There presently came, however, the debates on the Poor Law, which impressed him with the evils of the system then in force. Though an ardent philanthropist he was not a timid sentimentalist. The result was that, immediately the new Poor Law was passed, he proceeded to carry out its provisions in his parish. Almost universal opposition was encountered by him: not the poor only being his opponents, but even the farmers on whom came the burden of heavy poor-rates. For, strange to say, their interests had become apparently identified with the maintenance of this system which taxed them so largely. The explanation is that there had grown up the practice of paying out of the rates a part of the wages of each farm-servant—"make-wages," as the sum was called. And though the farmers contributed most of the fund from which "make-wages" were paid, yet, since all other ratepayers contributed, the farmers seemed to gain by the arrangement. My uncle, however, not easily deterred, faced all this opposition and enforced the law. The result was that in two years the rates were reduced from £700 a year to £200 a year; while the condition of the parish was greatly improved. "Those who had hitherto loitered at the corners of the streets, or at the doors of the beer-shops, had something else to do, and one after another they obtained employment"; so that out of a population of 800, only 15 had to be sent as incapable paupers to the Bath Union (when that was formed), in place of the 100 who received out-door relief a short time before. If it be said that the £25 telescope which, a few years after, his parishioners presented to my uncle, marked only the gratitude of the ratepayers; then my reply is the fact that when, some years later still, having killed himself by overwork in pursuit of popular welfare, he was taken to Hinton to be buried, the procession which followed him to the grave included not the well-to-do only but the poor.

Several motives have prompted this brief narrative. One is the wish to prove that sympathy with the people and self-sacrificing efforts on their behalf, do not necessarily imply approval of gratuitous aids. Another is the desire to show that benefit may result, not from multiplication of artificial appliances to mitigate distress, but, contrariwise, from diminution of them. And a further

purpose I have in view is that of preparing the way for an analogy.

Under another form and in a different sphere, we are now yearly extending a system which is identical in nature with the system of "make-wages" under the old Poor Law. Little as politicians recognize the fact, it is nevertheless demonstrable that these various public appliances for working-class comfort, which they are supplying at the cost of ratepayers, are intrinsically of the same nature as those which, in past times, treated the farmer's man as half-labourer and half-pauper. In either case the worker receives in return for what he does, money wherewith to buy certain of the things he wants; while, to procure the rest of them for him, money is furnished out of a common fund raised by taxes. What matters it whether the things supplied by ratepayers for nothing, instead of by the employer in payment, are of this kind or that kind? the principle is the same. For sums received let us substitute the commodities and benefits purchased; and then see how the matter stands. In old Poor-Law times, the farmer gave for work done the equivalent, say of house-rent, bread, clothes, and fire; while the ratepayers practically supplied the man and his family with their shoes, tea, sugar, candles, a little bacon, &c. The division is, of course, arbitrary; but unquestionably the farmer and the ratepayers furnished these things between them. At the present time the artisan receives from his employer in wages, the equivalent of the consumable commodities he wants; while from the public comes satisfaction for others of his needs and desires. At the cost of rate payers he has in some cases, and will presently have in more, a house at less than its commercial value; for of course when, as in Liverpool, a municipality spends nearly £200,000 in pulling down and reconstructing low-class dwellings, and is about to spend as much again, the implication is that in some way the ratepayers supply the poor with more accommodation than the rents they pay would otherwise have brought. The artisan further receives from them, in schooling for his children, much more than he pays for; and there is every probability that he will presently receive it from them gratis. The ratepayers also satisfy what desire he may have for books and newspapers, and comfortable places to read them in. In some cases too, as in Manchester, gymnasia for his children of both sexes, as well as recreation grounds, are provided. That is to say, he obtains from a fund raised by local taxes, certain benefits beyond those which the sum received for his labour enables him to purchase. The sole difference, then, between this system and the old system of "make-wages," is between the kinds of satisfactions obtained; and this difference does not in the least affect the nature of the arrangement.

Moreover, the two are pervaded by substantially the same illusion. In the one case, as in the other, what looks like a gratis benefit is not a gratis benefit. The amount which, under the old Poor Law, the half-pauperized labourer received from the parish to eke out his weekly income, was not really, as it appeared, a bonus; for it was accompanied by a substantially-equivalent decrease of his wages, as was quickly proved when the system was abolished and the wages rose. Just so is it with these seeming boons received by working people in towns. I do not refer only to the fact that they unawares pay in part through the raised rents of their dwellings (when they are not actual ratepayers); but I refer to the fact the wages received by them are, like the wages of the farm-labourer, diminished by these public burdens falling on employers. Read the accounts coming of late from Lancashire concerning the cotton-strike, containing proofs, given by artisans themselves, that the margin of profit is so narrow that the less skilful manufacturers, as well as those with deficient capital, fail, and that the companies of co-operators who compete with them can rarely hold their own; and then consider what is the implication respecting wages. Among the costs of production have to be reckoned taxes, general and local. If, as in our large towns, the local rates now amount to one-third of the rental or more— if the employer has to pay this, not on his private dwelling only, but on his business-premises, factories, warehouses, or the like; it results that the interest on his capital must be diminished by that amount, or the amount must be taken from the wages-fund, or partly one and partly the other. And if competition among capitalists in the same business, and in other businesses, has the effect of so keeping down interest that while some gain, others lose, and not a few are ruined—if capital, not getting adequate interest, flows elsewhere and leaves labour unemployed; then it is manifest that the choice for the artisan under such conditions, lies between diminished amount of work or diminished rate of payment for it. Moreover, for kindred reasons these local burdens raise the costs of the things he consumes. The charges made by distributors, too, are, on the average, determined by the current rates of interest on capital used in distributing businesses; and the extra costs of carrying on such businesses have to be paid for by extra prices. So that as in the past the rural worker lost in one way what he gained in another, so in the present does the urban worker: there being, too, in both cases, the loss entailed on him by the cost of administration and the waste accompanying it.

"But what has all this to do with 'the coming slavery'?" will perhaps be asked. Nothing directly, but a good deal indirectly, as we shall see after yet another preliminary section.

It is said that when railways were first opened in Spain, peasants standing on the tracks were not unfrequently run over; and that the blame fell on the engine-drivers for not stopping: rural experiences having yielded no conception of the momentum of a large mass moving at a high velocity. The incident is recalled to me on contemplating the ideas of the so-called "practical" politician, into whose mind there enters no thought of such a thing as political momentum, still less of a political momentum which, instead of diminishing or remaining constant, increases. The theory on which he daily proceeds is that the change caused by his measure will stop where he intends it to stop. He contemplates intently the things his act will achieve, but thinks little of the remoter issues of the movement his act sets up, and still less its collateral issues. When, in war-time, "food for powder" was to be provided by encouraging population—when Mr. Pitt said, "Let us make relief in cases where there are a number of children a matter of right and honour, instead of a ground for opprobrium and contempt;" it was not expected that the poor-rates would be quadrupled in fifty years, that women with many bastards would be preferred as wives to modest women, because of their incomes from the parish, and that hosts of ratepayers would be pulled down into the ranks of pauperism. Legislators who in 1833 voted £20,000 a year to aid in building schoolhouses, never supposed that the step they then took would lead to forced contributions, local and general, now amounting to £6,000,000; they did not intend to establish the principle that A should be made responsible for educating B's offspring; they did not dream of a compulsion which should deprive poor widows of the help of their elder children; and still less did they dream that their successors, by requiring impoverished parents to apply to Boards of Guardians to pay the fees which School Boards would not remit, would initiate a habit of applying to Boards of Guardians and so cause pauperization. Neither did those who in 1834 passed an Act regulating the labour of women and children in certain factories, imagine that the system they were beginning would end in the restriction and inspection of labour in all kinds of producing establishments where more than fifty people are employed; nor did they conceive that the inspection provided would grow to the extent of requiring that before a "young person" is employed in a factory, authority must be given by a certifying surgeon, who, by personal examination (to which no limit is placed) has satisfied himself that there is no incapacitating disease or bodily infirmity: his verdict determining whether the "young person" shall earn wages or not. Even less, as I say, does the politician who plumes himself on the practicalness of his aims, conceive the indirect results that will follow the direct results of his measures. Thus, to take a case connected with one named above, it was not intended through the system of "payment by results," to do anything more than give teachers an efficient stimulus: it was not supposed that in numerous cases their health would give way under the stimulus; it was not expected that they would be led to adopt a cramming system and to put undue pressure on dull and weak children, often to their great injury; it was not foreseen that in many cases a bodily enfeeblement would be caused which no amount of grammar and geography can compensate for. The licensing of public-houses

was simply for maintaining public order: those who devised it never imagined that there would result an organized interest powerfully influencing elections in an unwholesome way. Nor did it occur to the "practical" politicians who provided a compulsory load-line for merchant vessels, that the pressure of ship-owners' interests would habitually cause the putting of the load-line at the very highest limit, and that from precedent to precedent, tending ever in the same direction, the load-line would gradually rise in the better class of ships; as from good authority I learn that it has already done. Legislators who, some forty years ago, by Act of Parliament compelled railway-companies to supply cheap locomotion, would have ridiculed the belief, had it been expressed, that eventually their Act would punish the companies which improved the supply; and yet this was the result to companies which began to carry third-class passengers by fast trains, since a penalty to the amount of the passenger-duty was inflicted on them for every third-class passenger so carried. To which instance concerning railways, add a far more striking one disclosed by comparing the railway policies of England and France. The law-makers who provided for the ultimate lapsing of French railways to the State, never conceived the possibility that inferior travelling facilities would result—did not foresee that reluctance to depreciate the value of property eventually coming to the State, would negative the authorization of competing lines, and that in the absence of competing lines locomotion would be relatively costly, slow, and infrequent; for, as Sir Thomas Farrer has shown, the traveller in England has great advantages over the French traveller in the economy, swiftness, and frequency with which his journeys can be made.

But the "practical" politician who, in spite of such experiences repeated generation after generation, goes on thinking only of proximate results, naturally never thinks of results still more remote, still more general, and still more important than those just exemplified. To repeat the metaphor used above—he never asks whether the political momentum set up by his measure, in some cases decreasing but in other cases greatly increasing, will or will not have the same general direction with other such momenta; and whether it may not join them in presently producing an aggregate energy working changes never thought of. Dwelling only on the effects of his particular stream of legislation, and not observing how such other streams already existing, and still other streams which will follow his initiative, pursue the same average course, it never occurs to him that they may presently unite into a voluminous flood utterly changing the face of things. Or to leave figures for a more literal statement, he is unconscious of the truth that he is helping to form a certain type of social organization, and that kindred measures, effecting kindred changes of organization, tend with ever-increasing force to make that type general; until, passing a certain point, the proclivity towards it becomes irresistible. Just as each society aims when possible to produce in other societies a structure akin to its own—just as among the Greeks, the Spartans and the Athenians struggled to spread their respective political institutions, or as, at the time of the French Revolution, the European absolute monarchies aimed to re-establish absolute monarchy in France while the Republic encouraged the formation of other republics; so within every society, each species of structure tends to propagate itself. Just as the system of voluntary co-operation by companies, associations, unions, to achieve business ends and other ends, spreads throughout a community; so does the antagonistic system of compulsory co-operation under State-agencies spread; and the larger becomes its extension the more power of spreading it gets. The question of questions for the politician should ever be—"What type of social structure am I tending to produce?" But this is a question he never entertains.

Here we will entertain it for him. Let us now observe the general course of recent changes, with the accompanying current of ideas, and see whither they are carrying us.

The blank form of a question daily asked is—"We have already done this; why should we not do that?" And the regard for precedent suggested by it, is ever pushing on regulative legislation. Having had brought within their sphere of operation more and more numerous businesses, the Acts restricting hours of employment and dictating the treatment of workers are now to be made applicable to shops. From inspecting lodging-houses to limit the numbers of occupants and enforce sanitary conditions, we have passed to inspecting all houses below a certain rent in which there are members of more than one family, and are now passing to a kindred inspection of all small houses. The buying and working of telegraphs by the State is made a reason for urging that the State should buy and work the railways. Supplying children with food for their minds by public agency is being followed in some cases by supplying food for their bodies; and after the practice has been made gradually more general, we may anticipate that the supply, now proposed to be made gratis in the one case, will eventually be proposed to be made gratis in the other: the argument that good bodies as well as good minds are needful to make good citizens, being logically urged as a reason for the extension.[1] And then, avowedly proceeding on the precedents furnished by the church, the school, and the reading-room, all publicly provided, it is contended that "pleasure, in the sense it is now generally admitted, needs legislating for and organizing at least as much as work."

Not precedent only prompts this spread, but also the necessity which arises for supplementing ineffective measures, and for dealing with the artificial evils continually caused. Failure does not destroy faith in the agencies employed, but merely suggests more stringent use of such agencies or wider ramifications of them. Laws to check intemperance, beginning in early times and coming down to our own times, when further restraints on the sale of intoxicating liquors occupy nights every session, not having done what was expected, there come demands for more thorough-going laws, locally preventing the sale altogether; and here, as in America, these will doubtless be

---

[1] Verification comes more promptly than I expected. This article has been standing in type since January 30, and in the interval, namely on March 13, the London School Board resolved to apply for authority to use local charitable funds for supplying gratis meals and clothing to indigent children. Presently the definition of "indigent" will be widened; more children will be included, and more funds asked for.

followed by demands that prevention shall be made universal. All the many appliances for "stamping out" epidemic diseases not having succeeded in preventing outbreaks of smallpox, fevers, and the like, a further remedy is applied for in the shape of police-power to search houses for diseased persons, and authority for medical officers to examine any one they think fit, to see whether he or she is suffering from an infectious or contagious malady. Habits of improvidence having for generations been cultivated by the Poor-Law, and the improvident enabled to multiply, the evils produced by compulsory charity are now proposed to be met by compulsory insurance.

The extension of this policy, causing extension of corresponding ideas, fosters everywhere the tacit assumption that Government should step in whenever anything is not going right. "Surely you would not have this misery continue!" exclaims some one, if you hint a demurrer to much that is now being said and done. Observe what is implied by this exclamation. It takes for granted, first, that all suffering ought to be prevented, which is not true: much suffering is curative, and prevention of it is prevention of a remedy. In the second place, it takes for granted that every evil can be removed: the truth being that, with the existing defects of human nature, many evils can only be thrust out of one place or form into another place or form—often being increased by the change. The exclamation also implied the unhesitating belief, here especially concerning us, that evils of all kinds should be dealt with by the State. There does not occur the inquiry whether there are at work other agencies capable of dealing with evils, and whether the evils in question may not be among those which are best dealt with by these other agencies. And obviously, the more numerous governmental interventions become, the more confirmed does this habit of thought grow, and the more loud and perpetual the demands for intervention.

Every extension of the regulative policy involves an addition to the regulative agents—a further growth of officialism and an increasing power of the organization formed of officials. Take a pair of scales with many shot in the one and a few in the other. Lift shot after shot out of the loaded scale and put it into the unloaded scale. Presently you will produce a balance; and if you go on, the position of the scales will be reversed. Suppose the beam to be unequally divided, and let the lightly loaded scale be at the end of a very long arm; then the transfer of each shot, producing a much greater effect, will far sooner bring about a change of position. I use the figure to illustrate what results from transferring one individual after another from the regulated mass of the community to the regulating structures. The transfer weakens the one and strengthens the other in a far greater degree than is implied by the relative change of numbers. A comparatively small body of officials, coherent, having common interests, and acting under central authority, has an immense advantage over an incoherent public which has no settled policy, and can be brought to act unitedly only under strong provocation. Hence an organization of officials, once passing a certain stage of growth, becomes less and less resistible; as we see in the bureaucracies of the Continent.

Not only does the power of resistance of the regulated part decrease in a geometrical ratio as the regulating part increases, but the private interests of many in the regulated part itself, make the change of ratio still more rapid. In every circle conversations show that now, when the passing of competitive examinations renders them eligible for the public service, youths are being educated in such ways that they may pass them and get employment under Government. One consequence is that men who might otherwise reprobate some further growth of officialism, are led to look on it with tolerance, if not favourably, as offering possible careers for those dependent on them and those related to them. Any one who remembers the numbers of upper-class and middle-class families anxious to place their children, will see that no small encouragement to the spread of legislative control is now coming from those who, but for the personal interests thus arising, would be hostile to it. . . .

The diffusion of education has worked, and will work still more, in the same direction. "We must educate our masters," is the well-known saying of a Liberal who opposed the last extension of the franchise. Yes, if the education were worthy to be so called, and were relevant to the political enlightenment needed, much might be hoped from it. But knowing rules of syntax, being able to add up correctly, having geographical information, and a memory stocked with the dates of kings' accessions and generals' victories, no more implies fitness to form political conclusions than acquirement of skill in drawing implies expertness in telegraphing, or than ability to play cricket implies proficiency on the violin. "Surely," rejoins some one, "facility in reading opens the way to political knowledge." Doubtless; but will the way be followed? Table-talk proves that nine out of ten people read what amuses them or interests them rather than what instructs them; and that the last thing they read is something which tells them disagreeable truths or dispels groundless hopes. That popular education results in an extensive reading of publications which foster pleasant illusions rather than of those which insist on hard realities, is beyond question. Says "A Mechanic," writing in the *Pall Mall Gazette* of December 3, 1883:—

> Improved education instils the desire for culture—culture instils the desire for many things as yet quite beyond working men's reach . . . . in the furious competition to which the present age is given up they are utterly impossible to the poorer classes; hence they are discontented with things as they are, and the more educated the more discontented. Hence, too, Mr. Ruskin and Mr. Morris are regarded as true prophets by many of us.

And that the connection of cause and effect here alleged is a real one, we may see clearly enough in the present state of Germany.

Being possessed of electoral power, as are now the mass of those who are thus led to nurture sanguine anticipations of benefits to be obtained by social reorganization, it results that whoever seeks their votes must at least refrain from exposing their mistaken beliefs, even if he does not yield to the temptation to express agreement with them. Every candidate for Parliament is prompted to propose or support some new piece of *ad captandum* legislation. Nay, even the chiefs of parties—these anxious to retain office and those to wrest it from them—severally aim to get adherents by outbidding one another. Each seeks popularity by promising more than his opponent has promised, as we have lately seen. And then, as divisions in Parliament show us, the traditional loyalty to leaders overrides questions concerning the intrinsic propriety of proposed measures. Representatives are unconscientious enough to vote for Bills which they regard as essentially wrong in principle, because party-needs and regard for the next election demand it. And thus a vicious policy is strengthened even by those who see its viciousness. . . .

The policy initiated by the Industrial Dwellings Acts admits of development, and will develop. Where municipal bodies turn house-builders, they inevitably lower the value of houses otherwise built, and check the supply of more. Every dictation respecting modes of building and conveniences to be provided, diminishes the builder's profit, and prompts him to use his capital where the profit is not thus diminished. So, too, the owner, already finding that small houses entail much labour and many losses—already subject to troubles of inspection and interference, and to consequent costs, and having his property daily rendered a more undesirable investment, is prompted to sell; and as buyers are for like reasons deterred, he has to sell at a loss. And now these still-multiplying regulations, ending, it may be, as Lord Grey proposes, in one requiring the owner to maintain the salubrity of his houses by evicting dirty tenants, and thus adding to his other responsibilities that of inspector of nuisances, must further prompt sales and further deter purchasers—so necessitating greater depreciation. What must happen? The multiplication of houses, and especially small houses, being increasingly checked, there must come an increasing demand upon the local authority to make up for the deficient supply. More and more the municipal or kindred body will have to build houses, or to purchase houses rendered unsaleable to private persons in the way shown—houses which, greatly lowered in value as they must become, it will, in many cases, pay to buy rather than to build new ones. Nay, this process must work in a double way; since every entailed increase of local taxation still further depreciates property.[2] And then, when in towns this process has gone so far as to make the local authority the chief owner of houses, there will be a good precedent for publicly providing houses for the rural population, as proposed in the Radical programme, and as urged by the Democratic Federation; which insists on "the compulsory construction of healthy artisans' and agricultural labourers' dwellings in proportion to the population." Manifestly, the tendency of that which has been done, is being done, and is presently to be done, is to approach the socialistic ideal in which the community is sole house-proprietor.

Then, again, comes State-ownership of railways. Already this exists to a large extent on the Continent. Already we have had here a few years ago loud advocacy of it. And now the cry, which was raised by sundry politicians and publicists, is taken up afresh by the Democratic Federation, which proposes "State-appropriation of railways, with or without compensation." Evidently, pressure from above joined by pressure from below, is likely to effect this change dictated by the policy everywhere spreading; and with it must come many attendant changes. For railway-proprietors, at first owners and workers of railways only, have become masters of numerous businesses directly or indirectly connected with railways; and these will have to be purchased by Government when the railways are purchased. Already exclusive carrier of letters, exclusive transmitter of telegrams, and on the way to become exclusive carrier of parcels, the State will not only

---

[2] If any one thinks such fears are goundless, let him contemplate the fact that from 1867–8 to 1880–1, our annual local expenditure for the United Kingdom has grown from £36,132,834 to £63,276,283; and that during the same 13 years, the municipal expenditure in England and Wales alone, has grown from 13 millions to 30 millions a year! How the increase of public burdens will join with other causes in bringing about public ownership, is shown by a statement made by Mr. W. Rathbone, M.P., to which my attention has been drawn since the above paragraph was in type. He says, "within my own experience, local taxation in New York has risen from 12s. 6d. per cent. to £2 12s. 6d. per cent. on the capital of its citizens—a charge which would more than absorb the whole income of an average English landlord."—*Nineteenth Century,* February, 1883.

be exclusive carrier of passengers, goods, and minerals, but will add to its present various trades many other trades. Even now, besides erecting its naval and military establishments and building harbours, docks, breakwaters, &c., it does the work of shipbuilder, cannon-founder, small-arms maker, manufacturer of ammunition, army-clothier and boot-maker; and when the railways have been appropriated "with or without compensation," as the Democratic Federationists say, it will have to become locomotive-engine-builder, carriage-maker tarpaulin and grease manufacturer, passenger-vessel owner, coal-miner, stone-quarrier, omnibus proprietor, &c. Meanwhile its local lieutenants, the municipal governments, already in many places suppliers of water, gas-makers, owners and workers of tramways, proprietors of baths, will doubtless have undertaken various other businesses. And when the State, directly or by proxy, has thus come into possession of, or has established, numerous concerns for wholesale production and for wholesale distribution, there will be good precedents for extending its function to retail distribution: following such an example, say, as is offered by the French Government, which has long been a retail tobacconist.

Evidently then, the changes made, the changes in progress, and the changes urged, are carrying us not only towards State-ownership of land and dwellings and means of communication, all to be administered and worked by State-agents, but towards State-usurpation of all industries the private forms of which, disadvantaged more and more in competition with the State, which can arrange everything for its own convenience, will more and more die away; just as many voluntary schools have, in presence of Board-schools. And so will be brought about the desired ideal of the socialists. . . .

"But we shall be on our guard against all that—we shall take precautions to ward off such disasters," will doubtless say the enthusiasts. Be they "practical" politicians with their new regulative measures, or communists with their schemes for re-organizing labour, the answer is ever the same:—"It is true that plans of kindred nature have, from unforeseen causes and adverse accidents, or the misdeeds of those concerned, been brought to failure; but this time we shall profit by past experiences and succeed." There seems no getting people to accept the truth, which nevertheless is conspicuous enough, that the welfare of a society and the justice of its arrangements are at bottom dependent on the characters of its members; and that improvement in neither can take place without that improvement in character which results from carrying on peaceful industry under the restraints imposed by an orderly social life. The belief, not only of the socialists but also of those so-called Liberals who are diligently preparing the way for them, is that by due skill an ill-working humanity may be framed into well-working institutions. It is a delusion. The defective natures of citizens will show themselves in the bad acting of whatever social structure they are arranged into. There is no political alchemy by which you can get golden conduct out of leaden instincts.

II GREEN

Prolegomena to Ethics

THE THEORY OF THE GOOD AS HUMAN PERFECTION

According to the doctrine of this treatise, as we have previously endeavoured to state it, there is a principle of self-development in man, independent of the excitement of new desires by those new imaginations, which presuppose new experiences, of pleasure. In virtue of this principle he anticipates experience. In a certain sense he makes it, instead of merely waiting to be made by it. He is capable of being moved by an idea of himself, as becoming that which he has it in him to be—an idea which does not represent previous experience, but gradually brings an experience into being, gradually creates a filling for itself, in the shape of arts, laws, institutions and habits of living, which, so far as they go, exhibit the capabilities of man, define the idea of his end, afford a positive answer to the otherwise unanswerable question, what in particular it is that man has it in him to become. The action of such an idea in the individual accounts for two things which, upon the Hedonistic supposition, are equally unaccountable. It accounts for the possibility of the question, Why should I trouble about making myself or my neighbours other than we are? and, given the question, it accounts for an answer being rendered to it, in the shape of a real initiation of effort for the improvement of human life.

The supposition, therefore, of a free or self-objectifying spiritual agency in human history is one to which a fair analysis of human history inevitably leads us. But it remains to be asked by what rule the effort is to be guided, which we suppose the idea of a possible human perfection thus to initiate.

That idea, according to our view, is primarily in man unfilled and unrealised; and within the experience of men it is never fully realised, never acquires a content adequate to its capacity. There are arts and institutions and rules of life, in which the human spirit has so far incompletely realised its idea of a possible Best; and the individual in whom the idea is at work will derive from it a general injunction to further these arts, to maintain and, so far as he can, improve these institutions. It is when this general injunction has to be translated into particulars that the difficulty arises. How is the essential to be distinguished from the unessential and obstructive, in the processes through which an effort after the perfection of man may be traced? How are the arts to become a more thorough realisation of the ideal which has imperfectly expressed itself in them? How are the institutions of social life, and the rules of conventional morality, to be cleared of the alien growths which they owe to the constant co-operation of selfish passions with interest in common good, and which render them so imperfectly organic to the development of the human spirit? Above all, how is this or that individual—circumstanced as he is, and endowed, physically and mentally, as he is—to take part in the work? When he is called upon to decide between adherence to some established rule of morality and service to a particular person, or to face some new combination of circumstances to which recognised rules of conduct do not seem to apply, how is he to find guidance in an idea which merely moves him to aim at the best and highest in conduct? In short, as we put the difficulty after first stating the doctrine which finds the basis of morality in such an idea—'So far as it can be translated into practice at all, must not its effect be either a dead conformity to the code of customary morality, anywhere and at any time established, without effort to reform or expand it, or else unlimited licence in departing from it at the prompting of any impulse which the individual may be pleased to consider a higher law?'

Unless these questions can be satisfactorily answered, it would seem that our theory of the basis of morality, though its adoption might save some speculative persons from that distrust of their own conscience to which Hedonism would naturally lead them, can be of no further practical value. It may still serve to dispel the notion that the inclination to take one's ease and let the world have its way is justified by philosophy. It may still have an important bearing on that examination by the individual of his own walk and conduct, in which the question of motive should hold the first place; for it recognises, as the one motive which should be supreme, a desire which the Hedonist must ignore. But it will have no guidance to offer to the impulse which it explains, and of which it asserts the importance. In those cases in which, as we have previously pointed out, the question, Ought this or that to be done? has to be answered irrespectively of motive and with reference merely to the effects of actions, it will be of no avail. For that purpose we need some conception of a 'Summum Bonum' or ultimate good, definite enough to enable us to enquire whether the effects of a particular action contribute to that end or no. But if the idea of a possible perfection of life cannot be translated into any definite conceptions of what contributes to the attainment of that life, except such as are derived from existing usage and law, it cannot afford such a criterion as we want of the value of possible actions, when we are in doubt which of them should be done; for we want a criterion that shall be independent of law and usage, while at the same time it shall be other than the casual conviction of the individual.

Now, as we have more than once admitted, we can form no positive conception of what the ultimate perfection of the human spirit would be; what its life would be when all its capabilities were fully realised. We can no more do this than we can form a pos-

itive conception of what the nature of God in itself is. All the notions that we can form of human excellences or virtues are in some way relative to present imperfections. We may say perhaps, with the Apostle, that Faith, Hope and Charity *'abide;'* that they are not merely passing phases of a life which may come to enter on conditions in which they would cease to be possible; and there may be a sense in which this is true. But when we come to speak of the functions in which those virtues manifest themselves, we find that we are speaking of functions essentially relative to a state of society in which it is impossible to suppose that the human spirit has reached its full development. 'Charity beareth all things, believeth all things, hopeth all things;' but if all men had come to be what they should be, what would there be for Charity to bear, to hope, and to believe?

Though the idea of an absolutely perfect life, however, cannot be more to us than the idea that there must be such a life, as distinct from an idea of what it is—and we may admit this while holding that this idea is in a supreme sense formative and influential—it does not follow that there is any difficulty in conceiving very definitely a life of the individual and of society more perfect, because more completely fulfilling the vocation of individual and society, than any which is being lived. There may have been a period in the history of our race when the idea of a possible perfection was a blindly moving influence; when it had not yet taken sufficient effect in the ordering of life and the formation of virtues for reflection on these to enable men to say what it would be to be more perfect. But we are certainly not in that state now. We all recognise, and perhaps in some fragmentary way practise, virtues which both carry in themselves unfulfilled possibilities, and at the same time plainly point out the direction in which their own further development is to be sought for. It has already been sought in this treatise to trace the ideal of the cardinal virtues, as recognised by the conscience of Christendom. In none of these would the man who came nearest the ideal, 'count himself to have attained,' nor would he have any difficulty in defining the path of his further attainment. No one is eager *enough* to know what is true or make what is beautiful; no one ready *enough* to endure pain and forgo pleasure in the service of his fellows; no one impartial *enough* in treating the claims of another exactly as his own. Thus to have more 'intellectual excellence;' to be more brave, temperate and just, in the sense in which any one capable of enquiring what it is to be more perfect would now understand these virtues, is a sufficient object for him to set before himself by way of answer to the question, so far as it concerns him individually; while a state of society in which these virtues shall be more generally attainable and attained, is a sufficient account of the more perfect life considered as a social good.

It would seem then that, though statements at once positive and instructive as to the absolutely Best life may be beyond our reach, yet, by help of mere honest reflection on the evidence of its true vocation which the human spirit has so far yielded in arts and sciences, in moral and political achievement, we can know enough of a better life than our own, of a better social order than any that now is, to have an available criterion of what is good or bad in law and usage, and in the tendencies of men's actions. The working theory of the end, which we derive from the doctrine that the ultimate good for man must be some full development of the human spirit in character and conduct, may be represented by some such question as the following: Does this or that law or usage, this or that course of action—directly or indirectly, positively or as a preventive of the opposite—contribute to the better-being of society, as measured by the more general establishment of conditions favourable to the attainment of the recognised excellences and virtues, by the more general attainment of those excellences in some degree, or by their attainment on the part of some persons in higher degree without detraction from the opportunities of others? In order to put this question we must, no doubt, have a definite notion of the direction in which the 'Summum Bonum' is to be sought, but not of what its full attainment would actually be; and this, it will be found, is all that we need or can obtain for our guidance in estimating the value of laws and institutions, actions and usages, by their effects. It will do nothing indeed to help us in ascertaining what the effects of any institution or action really are. No theory whatever of the 'Summum Bonum,' Hedonistic or other, can avail for the settlement of this question, which requires analysis of facts and circumstances, not consideration of ends. But it will sufficiently direct us in regard to the kind of effects we should look out for in our analysis, and to the value we should put upon them when ascertained.

III LASKI

A Grammar of Politics

LIBERTY AND GOVERNMENT

This view of liberty and equality lays cardinal importance upon the powers of government and the mechanisms by which they may be made to respond to the wills of those affected. I do not argue that the action of legislation can make men free and equal; but unless some such conditions exist as those here urged, it is certain enough that the effect of legislation will be to keep the majority unfree and unequal. To make the personality of the ordinary man creative, it is necessary to build the conditions within which creativeness is possible. That can only happen when ordinary men are made to feel significant, and this, in the absence of liberty and equality, we cannot hope to achieve. Where there is in a community the absence of those factors which make the interests of men so differently considered, there is likely to be the means at hand for the development of personality. The enforcement of equality by the State has the great merit of promoting freedom by preventing the private person from the exercise of force for his own ends. By force I do not necessarily mean physical violence, but the use of a differential advantage to hinder another from the opportunity to be the best he can.

But it is also important to remember that whatever adds to the power of government is always attended by contingent danger. The individual in the modem State tends to feel impotent before the vast administrative machine by which he is confronted. It seems to have absorbed all initiative towards a single centre and to have deprived him of the power to make, or to share in making, responsible decisions. That is a real difficulty.

In relieving the individual from the power of his fellow, we may well seem to subject him to a collective power under which he seems hardly more free than before. That was the danger which made Rousseau insistent that liberty is the product of the small State only, and to find in a modern Athens the area within which alone democratic initiative is possible.

We cannot adopt that view because the nature of modern economic organisation makes it impossible to return to the city-State. But in States of the modern size the mere achievement of equality would be harmful without the maximum decentralization. That is the solution to the paradox by which Rousseau was, haunted. It solves the dread of constraint by making men in wider numbers the authors of the power to which they are subjected, and, through that authority, the utilisation of power to liberate the creative energy which is in them. Ultimately, at least, any laws save those which men make for themselves are devoid of meaning. But to make laws for themselves at all adequately, they must have the instruction to judge what laws they ought to make and the character to operate those laws. Someone, doubtless, they will have to trust; the artist will have no desire to scrutinise each act of the policeman. But they must be so intimately a part of the system as to know that they can trust with safety or, if there is abuse of confidence, to be able to apply pressure to its correction. In that sense, liberty is the organisation of resistance to abuse; and the chief safeguard against the emergence of abuse is such a wide distribution of power as makes certain and effective the onset of refusal to obey.

But the utmost that the action of government can achieve will be worthless save in so far as its action is paralleled by effort on the part of individual men. Ultimately, each one of us has sufficient of the Athanasius in him to make it certain that the true liberty we build is for ourselves. The State is built so certainly upon the character of men that they can only mould it to their desire by consistent devotion to its activities. If men are indifferent or careless, if they are satisfied to withdraw from the arena, not the most ingenious mechanisms can ultimately prevent abuse of power. That was the meaning of Thoreau's great sentence that "under a government which imprisons any unjustly, the true place for a just man is also prison."[1] Men must learn that the actions of the State are their own. They must learn that they will realise justice only to the degree that they bend their efforts to the making of justice. Every man is essential to the State if he has a mind and will. Every man can make that State responsive to the things he needs only by making his knowledge of life accessible as a basis for its actions. He can be free, ultimately, only by willing to be free. No State will be governed by that reason which alone guarantees him significance save as he makes his mind a part of its possessions.

But if the individual is thus, in concert with his fellows, the author of his own freedom, he cannot exert himself to build it save as he is prepared for that constructiveness. He must know what it means to find himself before he seeks the adventure. That is no easy task in a world encumbered by its traditions. There is never likely to be an enlightened State until there is respect for individuality; but, also, there will not be respect for individuality until there is an enlightened State. It is only the emphasis upon equality which will break this vicious circle. When the source of power is found outside of property, authority is balanced upon a principle which bases prestige on service. At that stage, the effort of statesmanship is the elevation of the common man. A society which seeks to protect acquisition is replaced by a society which seeks to protect the spiritual heritage of the race. We cannot assure ourselves of an entrance to that heritage, but at least we can discover the pathway to the goal.

---

[1] Thoreau, *On the Duty of Civil Disobedience.*

CHAPTER THIRTY-FIVE

THE WELFARE STATE

When socialism as an organized political force first made its appearance in the late nineteenth and early twentieth centuries, many students of government were concerned that democracy would be unable to stand the strain of conflict between two diametrically opposed economic philosophies. On the one hand, there was the philosophy of socialism, ultimately aiming at nationalization of the means of production, exchange, and distribution within a society. On the other hand, both Liberal and Conservative parties held that, without private property, enterprise, and exchange, democracy would decay and disappear. Since democracy can only exist if there is general agreement on fundamentals, it was felt by many that disagreement over one such fundamental—the question of property and the relation of government to the economy—would undermine the vitality and very existence of democracy.

Yet experience has proven otherwise. As is often the case in democratic politics, apparently irreconcilable positions are eventually reconciled by compromise in which each contending side has to make important concessions to the other. Capitalism has moved in the direction of socialism with respect to government provision of services and macro-management of the economy, because the democratic ideal of human dignity is incompatible with personal insecurity, substantial social inequality, economic want, and human suffering where the means are available to remedy such conditions. On the other side, socialists moved in the direction of classical political economy on the issue of private ownership of an economy's means of production, because public ownership of productive resources through nationalization proved inefficient and, more importantly, because the democratic values of power's diffusion and personal liberty are incompatible with total ownership and management of a nation's economy by the state.

As social discourse developed during the twentieth century, there was increasing focus on economic as opposed to strictly political issues. In a way, this was progress. At one time, core political questions were the best form of government and who should vote. Now, these issues are largely resolved. Other than a genuinely small minority in democratic nations, almost no one today contests that all adult members in a society— men and women of all races and religions—should have the right politically to participate in society's governance through voting. This consensus existed almost nowhere in the world at the beginning of the twentieth century, and even as recently as the 1970s, democracy was restricted mainly to the nations of Western Europe, the United States and Canada, and Japan.

There are at least two aspects of the welfare state that has emerged in industrial democracies during the twentieth century: provision of social welfare, and national economic management or intervention. Both are vital. While the phrase the "welfare state" perhaps most often is associated with such government activities as social security, education, health care, and the like, it actually involves much more. From the start, the new view of government that evolved particularly in response to the Great Depression of the 1930s considered a key task of the state to be promoting maximum economic growth. Indeed, in industrial democracies today, economic macro-management as distinct from provision of government social welfare services may well be the greatest criterion for political success or failure.

In developing the new view of government comprising both significantly expanded public services and national economic intervention, British economist John Maynard Keynes (1883–1946) played a leading role. Keynes was an elitist. He was by no means a socialist. Once, when attacking Marxism, he rhetorically asked: "How can I adopt a creed which, preferring the mud to the fish, exalts the boorish proletariat above the bourgeois and intelligentsia who, with whatever faults, are the quality of life and surely carry the seeds of all human advancement?" On another occasion, he wrote to George Bernard Shaw: "I've made another shot at old K[arl] M[arx] last week, reading the Marx-Engels correspondence just published, without making much progress. . . . I can see they invented a certain method of carrying on and a vile manner of writing, both of which their successors have maintained with fidelity. But if you tell me that they discovered a clue to the economic riddle, still I am beaten—I can discover nothing but out-of-date controversialising."

Keynes's position was not that government should control the economy in a socialist or communist sense of managing all businesses, owning all land, and employing all workers. His position was rather that government should manage the economic conditions within which private enterprise takes place. He nowhere expressed this idea more clearly than in his *magnum opus, The General Theory of Employment, Interest, and Money,* whose February 1936 publication was an epochal event in the history of economic thought. Writing in the midst of the Great Depression, he held:

> I see no reason to suppose that the existing system seriously misemploys the factors of production which are in use. . . . When 9,000,000 men are employed out of 10,000,000 willing and able to work, there is no evidence that the labour of these 9,000,000 is misdirected. The complaint against the present system is not that these 9,000,000 men ought to be employed on different tasks, but that tasks should be available for the remaining 1,000,000 men. It is in determining the volume, not the direction, of actual employment that the existing system has broken down.
>
> . . . I agree . . . that the result of filling in the gaps in the classical theory is not to dispose of the 'Manchester System,' but to indicate the nature of the environment which the free play of economic forces requires if it is to realise the full potentialities of production.

He noted here as well that "the traditional advantages of individualism" include that it "is the best safeguard of personal liberty . . ."

Keynes first burst onto the scene with his 1919 *The Economic Consequences of the Peace*—a blistering attack on the economic aspects of the Versailles Peace Treaty and the makers of the treaty. He possessed unsurpassed influence in British academic economic thought. From 1911 to 1945, he was editor of the *Economic Journal,* the leading periodical in British economics. He was secretary of the Royal Economic Society.

Cambridge, from which he graduated and at which he taught, was the center of economic scholarship in England, though LSE attempted to challenge its place. Moreover, in addition to more strictly scholarly avenues of suasion, he was a very prominent member of society. He served on committees and commissions advising governments, and was chairman of the British *Nation,* a popular magazine of opinion and news. He wrote articles and opinion pieces for newspapers and magazines around the world. According to his magnificent biographer, Robert Skidelsky, he "was not just a man of establishments; Robert Skidelsky, but part of the elite of each establishment of which he was a member. There was scarcely a time in his life when he did not look down at the rest of England, and much of the world, from a great height."

Keynes's next major work, following *The Economic Consequences of the Peace,* was *A Tract on Monetary Reform* (1923), which Friedman calls his "best book." *A Tract on Monetary Reform* was for the most part a collection of articles and lectures he wrote and gave during the previous three years. His great concern at this time was that domestic prices should be stabilized from either inflation or deflation, rather than that the primary goal of monetary policy should be fixed inter-currency exchange rates. Under the gold standard system of monetary thinking that characterized national and international monetary policy during this period, the crucial variable over which national monetary authorities were to exercise control was the exchange rate. The intention was to keep these rates fixed. National money supplies were to be adjusted to keep the price of currencies constant in relation to a certain amount of gold and each other. In the case of Great Britain and the United States, for example, the goal of monetary policy was to keep the ratio of dollars to pounds fixed at $4.86 to £1, the rate that prevailed before World War I.

Keynes challenged the prevalent thinking. His conception was that national monetary authorities should focus on stable domestic prices rather than stable exchange rates. Stable domestic prices were not guaranteed under the gold standard system of monetary policy for, if the value of a nation's currency were threatening to decline on international exchanges, it was to reduce its internal supply of money—thus deflating its economy—and thereby right the balance. Conversely, if its currency value were impending to increase internationally, a nation was to inflate its domestic economy, thereby reducing the value of its money at home and abroad. Keynes's objection to the gold standard was that it could be very upsetting to a nation's economy. He thought that as an economy becomes advanced, as he held Britain's was, it is characterized by "stickiness of social and business arrangements." While internal wages and prices might react harmoniously in theory with changes in money supply occasioned by maintaining fixed international exchange rates, in practice this is not so. It is hard to force prices and wages down following diminution of the money supply without economic contraction, unemployment, and recession or depression.

Basic to Keynes's conception of the influence of monetary policy on prices was the relative stress he placed on the speed at which money changes hands (its velocity) compared to the amount of money in an economy (its supply) in establishing at least short–run prices. He subscribed to the fundamental monetary equation $MV = PQ$, where M is the supply of money in an economy, V is the velocity at which it changes hands, P is the general price level, and Q is the amount of goods and services in an economy. Typically, more emphasis is placed on M (money) and P (prices) in this equation than on V and Q, on the assumption that velocity and the amount of goods and services do not change as much, or vary in relative proportion to one another. Conventional anaysis is, in other words, more that changes in money supply *(M)* lead to changes in prices *(P)*. Keynes believed, on the other hand, that, at least in the short run, prices do not necessarily vary with changes in the money supply. Instead, velocity of money may shift, and thus a change in the supply of money may not be equilibrated with a comparable shift in general price level. Especially during times of economic downturn—when producers are not expanding and consumers are not spending—a given increase in the money supply may have relatively little impact on aggregate prices. He granted that, in the long run, it is "probably true" that prices vary with the quantity of money. But, in his most famous words, he continued: "This *long run* is a misleading guide to current affairs. *In the long run* we are all dead. Economists set themselves too easy, too useless a task if in tempestuous seasons they can only tell us that when the storm is long past the ocean is flat again." His goal was stable domestic prices and thereby stable business conditions. Government should control money supply so as to level economic expansion and contraction, not to react to changes in currency exchange rates.

Keynes believed a breakthrough in monetary management was achieved in *A Tract on Monetary Reform.* Key basics of the Keynesian Revolution in economics were present in embryo form: relative bifurcation of money supply from prices, stress on immediate financial circumstances in setting policy, a prominent role for government in managing—though not directing the details of—a nation's economy. Following publication of *A Tract on Monetary Reform,* Keynes waged an unsuccessful effort to prevent Britain from returning to the gold standard at prewar parity (during World War I the gold standard was suspended). He considered a policy of returning to gold at prewar parity to be madness. During the period leading up to restoration, the pound possessed a value somewhere in the vicinity of 10 percent less than the dollar at prewar parity. To close the gap would require deflationary policies in Britain, further depressing an economy that already suffered from significant unemployment.

Following the return to the gold standard at prewar parity, he wrote an attack on it, "The Economic Consequences of Mr. Churchill," who at the time was Chancellor of the Exchequer. In 1926, Keynes wrote *The End of Laissez Faire* (reproduced here in its entirety), where by *"laissez faire"* he meant the idea that government does not have a large role to play in managing the conditions of a nation's economy. The upshot of British economic policies during the 1920s was that Britain experienced a decade of poor economic times even before the decade-long international depression that began in 1929. Thus, economic conditions appeared worse in Britain than they did in America at the beginning of the 1930s. Consequently, more extreme, in the sense of socialist, measures were proposed and eventually implemented (particularly following World War II) in Britain than in America. The United States never embarked on the program of nationalization of key industries that Great Britain did.

Between 1900 and 1920, unemployment in Great Britain averaged 3.4 percent a year. Between 1921 and 1940, on the other hand, unemployment averaged 13.7 percent—over 10 percentage points higher—for a generation. During the whole period between 1921 and 1939, unemployment nudged beneath 10 percent only once, to 9.7 percent in 1927. Clearly something had gone awry. What? Keynes's answer was that the nation had become a stultified and rigid beast. It was no longer a growing and vibrant organism: "The forces of the nineteenth century have run their course and are exhausted."

As the Great Depression became an even greater catastrophe than the weak 1920s in Britain, monetary policy became ineffective. In a deflationary circumstance, monetary policy is a weak tool. When prices are decreasing—deflation—people experience the purchasing power of their money going up simply by holding onto it. Moreover, if banks are going out of business right and left, as occurred during the depression, there will be little incentive to deposit funds in banks. In a depression, there is little borrowing and because of deflation and financial uncertainty, interest rates will be only 1–2 percent.

Interest rates cannot be pushed to less than this amount through government action, so monetary policy became relatively ineffective during the 1930s.

In monetary policy's place, Keynes recommended fiscal policy. Now, it was the responsibility of government to prime the pump, to get the economy moving again. Government should employ people, perform public works, provide social security, require unemployment insurance, and maintain high spending among the people of a society. This was undoubtedly the best philosophy and policy during the 1930s, once the Great Depression had started. Essentially, Keynes the monetarist became Keynes the fiscalist as the 1920s evolved into the 1930s in Britain, and economic conditions changed. An active national government fiscal policy thus became the final aspect of Keynesianism.

Keynes's goal was not to destroy capitalism but to save it. He rendered his final service to his country by negotiating the American loan in 1945 and 1946, and he was one of the principal authors of the two new agencies for international monetary and economic cooperation and coordination following the war, the International Monetary Fund and the International Bank for Reconstruction and Development (now World Bank). He never ceased to be a Liberal, in party and in spirit.

As a result of the exigencies of modern life, with fantastically large economies, there has been little apparent alternative to some macro-management of economies at the national level. The goal, since Keynes, has been to structure national economies so that they will result in the greatest economic growth each year. This has required considerable intervention by national governments, but is very different than state socialism planning and managing every detail of economic activity.

Keynes attacked the idea that national economies are self-righting systems which with no involvement or "interference" by government will naturally result in the greatest material production and highest standard of living. In addition to appropriate monetary policies that will result in stable prices and low interest rates, there is, he thought, a very considerable role for government to play in evening out the vagaries of a business cycle. In depressed or recessionary times in particular, there is a need for government stimulation of economic production through increased spending. Furthermore, one of the economic, as distinct from social, benefits of government programs such as social security and generally significant government participation in a nation's economy is that this maintains a floor of activity that is to an economy's benefit. In a national economy that is over 90 percent private, as many national economies were early in the twentieth century, if the private economy goes belly up, there can be a cumulative impact that leads to real economic contraction. When, on the other hand, government spends 30–50 percent or so of national income, as currently is the case in most industrial democracies, it is more difficult for a real depression to get started. Since the Great Depression, there has been no downturn comparable to it.

Keynes was a renaissance man. In the years between World Wars I and II, he concentrated on his scholarly activities at Cambridge, but did not lose touch with practical affairs. In addition to his heavy duties of writing, editing, and teaching, he found time to serve as chairman of a major insurance company, run an investment company, organize a distinguished ballet, and build a new theater. He enthusiastically supported bringing art to the people—he became chairman of the Council for the Encouragement of Music and the Arts. He was given his peerage in 1942.

Sir (later Lord) William Beveridge (1879–1963) was one of the leading exponents of the welfare state during the twentieth century. Director of the London School of Economics from 1919 to 1937, he presided over the school's greatest period of advance to date. He achieved greatest renown as the primary author in 1942 of the *Report on Social Insurance and Allied Services*—the celebrated "Beveridge Report"—and, in 1944, for *Full Employment in a Free Society*. Like Keynes, he was a member of the British Liberal Party, not, like Laski, Labour.

Following World War II, Britain, as a number of western industrialized nations—though not the United States—nationalized considerable portions of its economy. The Bank of England, the coal industry, civil aviation, railways, electricity, gas, and steel all were nationalized by 1951. Beveridge was not necessarily opposed to this trend, but his policy thrust was in a different direction. The 1942 Beveridge Report focused on the provision of social welfare services to all citizens.

The idea of the welfare state has probably been more sustained by reasons of fairness, decency, equity, and charity than by arguments about its national macroeonomic advantages. As a society becomes more wealthy, it has more resources to distribute. Moreover, as a society becomes more technologically advanced, it becomes practically easier to provide programs and services. The welfare state could develop only after industrialization.

Beveridge was born in Bengal; his father was a member of the Indian Civil Service. He was a free trader; when Keynes temporarily deviated on this issue, Beveridge and young LSE economists wrote a book opposing protection and defending free international trade. He was essentially pragmatic in his governmental outlook like many twentieth century political reformers, he was guided more by exigencies of the day than fixed principles.

Beveridge's 1942 *Report on Social Insurance and Allied Services* was a landmark because it called for a comprehensive approach to social services in Great Britain. As in most western nations, these had expanded in haphazard and piecemeal fashion since the last years of the nineteenth century. Beveridge now recommended a system. In the same way that Keynes saw a gap in *laissez faire* in its inability necessarily to reach full production without government involvement, Beveridge saw another deficiency in a purely free market society—the failure to provide all protection against "interrupted earnings."

Beveridge used graphic language to describe his goal. He sought a social system that would slay the five "giants" of Want, Sickness, Squalor, Idleness (through involuntary unemployment), and Ignorance. His core idea was that all working individuals should pay the same percentage of their income into a National Insurance Fund that would provide the same cash benefits to all for "the principal forms of cessation of earnings—unemployment, disability, retirements." In addition, there should be a government safety net for those who fall "out of benefit"—that is, those unable to pay the national insurance.

Within its service, as opposed to economic macro-management, functions, the welfare state therefore is composed of at least two elements—some form of national "insurance," in which benefits are in some way tied to taxation, and outright public assistance, regardless of whether a person has paid into the system. These functions were implemented in all western industrial nations in the decades surrounding the Beveridge Report. Social Security began in the United States, for example, in 1935.

National social insurance programs have not been very actuarial. There often is little correlation between what a person pays in taxes and what he receives in benefits. The systems initially worked to redistribute income from those with higher incomes to those with lower, and more recently from the young to the old.

Once social insurance programs were implemented, they proved capable of great expansion. In the United States, Social Security initially applied to retired workers in industrial and commercial occupations. Benefits were extended over time to include survivors of workers, individuals with disabilities, and health insurance. Those covered by Social Security have increased to farm and domestic workers, many self-employed individuals, and employees of state and local government and non-profit organizations.

Expansion has similarly been the case regarding payments, services, and programs for individuals whose benefits in no way are tied to taxes they have paid. Aid to Families with Dependent Children (AFDC) started in the United States during, like Social Security, Franklin Roosevelt's New Deal. It originally was intended for widows with small children. Over time it grew to include mostly unmarried women with children and was supplemented by various other benefits in such areas as nutrition, housing, and medical services.

The welfare state was a new way of organizing a society. No longer were the poor, elderly, unemployed, and infirm to rely upon voluntary, private charity; rather, they have a legal right to support from the national government. The degree of national government involvement that the welfare state has fostered in economies has been unprecedented. National governments have redistributed significant portions of national income and created vast panoplies of services, programs, and activities. Once government permeated as deeply into nations' lives as more traditional welfare state functions allowed it, national governmental activity was capable of even greater expansion. There became virtually no societal problem in which government could not legitimately be involved, and so national, as well as more local, governments grew in size and scope.

During the 1950s and 1960s, there was still considerable emphasis in most western welfare states on equalization of income and wealth. Redistribution is, of course, not necessarily from the rich to the poor, and though government transfers income through such programs as Social Security, it is not necessarily the case that the net impact of government taxation and expenditure is to reallocate wealth from the better off to the less well off. In the immediate postwar period, though, this was more a specifically desired outcome of the welfare state. Not only were social services directed this way, but there were high marginal rates of taxation and greater inheritance taxation.

The final aspect of the postwar welfare state—in addition to expanding government services, redistributing income and wealth from rich to poor, sharply progressive income taxation, and inheritance taxes—was support for organized labor, again largely in response to the Great Depression. Unions were strongly supported legally and in tolerating petty infractions by them of civil authority.

Beveridge's second major work, following his 1942 report, was the 1944 *Full Employment in a Free Society*. In the immediate post-Great Depression environment, there remained considerable concern and fear that once again truly substantial unemployment might grip national economies, where a third or more of able-bodied men, including married men with children, would be unable to find work because of economic conditions. It was at this time held that full employment was certainly possible in an unfree, command economy, such as the Soviet Union's, which could dictate to people what to do and where and what to work at. The important question was whether full employment were possible in a free society, and the conditions to realize this goal. Ensuring full employment, or at least not mass unemployment, was seen as vital to preserving and improving democracy.

In the years since the Great Depression, there has not been an economic downturn comparable to it, when unemployment was so rife and national incomes dropped by a third or more. Moreover, not only during the Great Depression were material living standards very considerably lower than they now are, the work force did not include many who now participate. There is little meaningful comparison between economic conditions at the turn of the twenty-first century and during the 1920s. There was real material poverty that existed among intact families with children. This has largely been eliminated, as, for the most part, has poverty among those over sixty or sixty-five. The welfare state has accomplished much.

Sweden was among the pioneers of the welfare state as a social concept such that government spending was as much as 60 percent of a society's income. Gunnar Myrdal (1898–1987) brought an unusual combination of experiences to the analysis of the welfare state. First, he was not only a socialist by conviction, but was a leader of the Swedish Social Democratic Party, serving for many years as a member of the Swedish Senate and for several years as Minister of Trade and Commerce. Since the Swedish Social Democrats had the longest record of any Socialist party in governing a nation— they continuously held office from 1932 to 1976—Myrdal was intimately familiar with the practical problems of politics. Secondly, Myrdal was a political economist of the first rank. In addition to many economic writings of a more professional nature, he authored two major works. In 1938–1943, he was asked to do a study of the place of African Americans in American society. The study took five years, and was published in 1944 under the title, *An American Dilemma: The Negro Problem and Modern Democracy.* This massive work was an immediate, even sensational, success. It is considered a classic in its field, particularly since events have proven Myrdal's primary proposition to be true, that the status of African Americans in the United States is the great American dilemma, the solution of which may well determine the future of the nation. After working ten years for the United Nations, Myrdal began a study on the problem of economic underdevelopment in South Asia, which was published in 1968 under the title, *Asian Drama: An Inquiry into the Poverty of Nations.*

In *Beyond the Welfare State* Myrdal makes the important point that economic planning was not the result of a master plan or ideology favoring government intervention in the economy, but that the relation between the two was the reverse: *ad hoc* government interventions, caused either by domestic economic crises or by international disturbances, came first, and, as such governmental interventions in the economy multiplied, the need arose to coordinate them: "Coordination leads to planning or, rather, it *is* planning." Improved statistical data and more sophisticated economic analysis make it possible for governments to make short-term and long-term forecasts of the economy, and to plan in accordance with such forecasts. In particular, Myrdal stresses that welfare state policies—originally adopted mainly for reasons of social justice— have had a considerable impact on national economies by raising productivity and redirecting the distribution of a large share of national income.

Full employment was considered by Myrdal the biggest commitment of western nations to economic planning. The days are gone when workers are satisfied with relief during unemployment: what they now insist on is that government take positive measures which will maintain an effective demand for labor. Before 1914, public revenues and expenditures were too small to have a significant impact on the whole economy. Since World War I, and particularly since the Great Depression, the share of government expenditures in relation to the national income increased consistently, and now amounts to about 30 to 50 percent in most developed nations. In commanding such a large share of the national income, governments now possess a powerful lever to influence the level of economic activity: "The expansionist theory of spending one's way out of a depression is now on the way to becoming orthodox, even in the more conservative sections of the business world." Differences of degree may, nevertheless, spell success or failure. Thus, Myrdal noted that vigorous "pump priming" by the Social Democratic government in Sweden during the early years of the Great Depression was successful, whereas similar policies in the United States and other countries were less successful, because their non-socialist governments did not spend enough, because large budget deficits were considered incompatible with traditional precepts of capitalist economic orthodoxy. The determination to maintain full employment is "the crowning accomplishment of the democratic Welfare State."

Concerning the question of *nationalization,* Myrdal observed that Socialist parties, when small and without much influence, propose the nationalization of industries and financial institutions. But as they gain popular support and run the government, they tend to play down the issue of nationalization and concentrate on comprehensive welfare policies. For tactical reasons, some Socialist parties kept nationalization as part of their program, but, he accurately foresaw, "I would expect that sooner or later nationalization will disappear from the program, too."

I KEYNES

The End of Laissez-Faire*

THE ORIGINS OF INDIVIDUALISM

The disposition towards public affairs, which we conveniently sum up as Individualism and *laissez-faire,* drew its sustenance from many different rivulets of thought and springs of feeling. For more than a hundred years our philosophers ruled us, because, by a miracle, they nearly all agreed, or seemed to agree, on this one thing. We do not dance even yet to a new tune. But a change is in the air. We hear but indistinctly what were once the clearest and most distinguishable voices which have ever instructed political mankind. The orchestra of diverse instruments, the chorus of articulate sound, is receding at last into the distance.

At the end of the seventeenth century the divine right of monarchs gave place to Natural Liberty and to the Compact, and the divine right of the Church to the principle of Toleration, and to the view that a church is "a voluntary society of men," coming together, in a way which is "absolutely free and spontaneous."[1] Fifty years later the divine origin and absolute voice of duty gave place to the calculations of Utility. In the hands of Locke and Hume these doctrines founded Individualism. The Compact presumed rights in the individual; the new ethics, being no more than a scientific study of the consequences of rational self-love, placed the individual at the centre. "The sole trouble Virtue demands," said Hume, "is that of just Calculation, and a

steady preference of the greater Happiness."[2] These ideas accorded with the practical notions of conservatives and of lawyers. They furnished a satisfactory intellectual foundation to the rights of property and to the liberty of the individual in possession to do what he liked with himself and with his own. This was one of the contributions of the eighteenth century to the air we still breathe.

The purpose of promoting the Individual was to depose the Monarch and the Church; the effect—through the new ethical significance attributed to Contract—was to buttress Property and Prescription. But it was not long before the claims of Society raised themselves anew against the individual. Paley and Bentham accepted utilitarian hedonism[3] from the hands of Hume and his predecessors, but enlarged it into social utility. Rousseau took the Social Contract from Locke and drew out of it the General Will. In each case the transition was made by virtue of the new emphasis laid on Equality. "Locke applies his Social Contract to modify the natural equality of mankind, so far as that phrase implies equality of property or even of privilege, in consideration of general

---

*From John Maynard Keynes, *Laissez-Faire and Communism* (New Republic, 1926), Part I, pp. 5–73.
[1] Locke, *A Letter Concerning Toleration.*

---

[2] *An Enquiry Concerning the Principles of Morals,* section 1x.

[3] "I omit," says Archdeacon Paley, "much usual declamation upon the dignity and capacity of our nature, the superiority of the soul to the body, of the rational to the animal part of our constitution; upon the worthiness, refinement, and delicacy of some satisfactions, and the meanness, grossness, and sensuality of others: because I hold that pleasures differ in nothing but in continuance and intensity."—*Principles of Moral and Political Philosophy,* Bk. I, chap. 6.

security. In Rousseau's version equality is not only the starting point but the goal."[4]

Paley and Bentham reached the same destination, but by different routes. Paley avoided an egoistic conclusion to his hedonism by a God from the machine. "Virtue," he says, "is the doing good to mankind, in obedience to the will of God, and for the sake of everlasting happiness"—in this way bringing back *I* and *others* to a parity. Bentham reached the same result by pure reason. There is no rational ground, he argued, for preferring the happiness of one individual, even oneself, to that of any other. Hence the greatest happiness of the greatest number is the sole rational object of conduct—taking Utility from Hume, but forgetting that sage man's cynical corollary: "'Tis not contrary to reason to prefer the destruction of the whole world to the scratching of my finger. 'Tis not contrary to reason for me to choose my total ruin to prevent the least uneasiness of an Indian, or person totally unknown to me. . . . Reason is and ought only to be the slave of the passions, and can never pretend to any other office than to serve and obey them."

Rousseau derived equality from the State of Nature, Paley from the Will of God, Bentham from a mathematical law of Indifference. Equality and altruism had thus entered political philosophy, and from Rousseau and Bentham in conjunction sprang both Democracy and Utilitarian Socialism.

This is the second current—sprung from long-dead controversies, and carried on its way by long-exploded sophistries—which still permeates our atmosphere of thought. But it did not drive out the former current. It mixed with it. The early nineteenth century performed the miraculous union. It harmonised the conservative individualism of Locke, Hume, Johnson, and Burke with the Socialism and democratic egalitarianism of Rousseau, Paley, Bentham, and Godwin.[5]

Nevertheless that age would have been hard put to it to achieve this harmony of opposites if it had not been for the *economists,* who sprang into prominence just at the right moment. The idea of a divine harmony between private advantage and the public good is already apparent in Paley. But it was the economists who gave the notion a good scientific basis. Suppose that by the working of natural laws individuals pursuing their own interests with enlightenment in conditions of freedom always tend to promote the general interest at the same time! Our philosophical difficulties are resolved—at least for the practical man, who can then concentrate his efforts on securing the necessary conditions of freedom. To the philosophical doctrine that Government has no right to interfere, and the divine miracle that it has no need to interfere, there is added a scientific proof that its interference is inexpedient. This is the third current of thought, just discoverable in Adam Smith, who was ready in the main to allow the public good to rest on "the natural effort of every individual to better his own condition," but not fully and self-consciously developed until the nineteenth century begins. The principle of *laissez-faire* had arrived to harmonise Individualism and Socialism, and to make at one Hume's Egoism with the Greatest Good of the Greatest Number. The political philosopher could retire in favour of the business man—for the latter could attain the philosopher's *summum bonum* by just pursuing his own private profit.

Yet some other ingredients were needed to complete the pudding. First the corruption and incompetence of eighteenth-century government, many legacies of which survived into the nineteenth. The Individualism of the political philosophers pointed to *laissez-faire.* The divine or scientific harmony (as the case might be) between private interest and public advantage pointed to *laissez-faire.* But above all, the ineptitude of public administrators strongly prejudiced the practical man in favour of *laissez-faire*—a sentiment which has by no means disappeared. Almost everything which the State did in the eighteenth

---

[4] Leslie Stephen, *English Thought in the Eighteenth Century,* ii, 192.

[5] Godwin carried *laissez-faire* so far that he thought *all* government an evil, in which Bentham almost agreed with him. The doctrine of equality becomes with him one of extreme individualism, verging on anarchy. "The universal exercise of private judgment," he says, "is a doctrine so unspeakably beautiful that the true

---

politician will certainly feel infinite reluctance in admitting the idea of interfering with it."—*Vide* Leslie Stephen, *op. cit.,* ii, 277.

century in excess of its minimum functions was, or seemed, injurious or unsuccessful.

On the other hand, material progress between 1750 and 1850 came from individual initiative, and owed almost nothing to the directive influence of organised society as a whole. Thus practical experience reinforced *a priori* reasonings. The philosophers and the economists told us that for sundry deep reasons unfettered private enterprise would promote the greatest good of the whole. What could suit the business man better? And could a practical observer, looking about him, deny that the blessings of improvement which distinguished the age he lived in were traceable to the activities of individuals "on the make"? Thus the ground was fertile for a doctrine that, whether on divine, natural, or scientific grounds, State Action should be narrowly confined and economic life left, unregulated so far as may be, to the skill and good sense of individual citizens actuated by the admirable motive of trying to get on in the world.

By the time that the influence of Paley and his like was waning, the innovations of Darwin were shaking the foundations of belief. Nothing could seem more opposed than the old doctrine and the new—the doctrine which looked on the world as the work of the divine Watchmaker and the doctrine which seemed to draw all things out of Chance, Chaos, and Old Time. But at this one point the new ideas bolstered up the old. The economists were teaching that wealth, commerce, and machinery were the children of free competition—that free competition built London. But the Darwinians could go one better than that—free competition had built Man. The human eye was no longer the demonstration of Design, miraculously contriving all things for the best; it was the supreme achievement of Chance, operating under conditions of free competition and *laissez-faire*. The principle of the Survival of the Fittest could be regarded as a vast generalisation of the Ricardian economics. Socialistic interferences became, in the light of this grander synthesis, not merely inexpedient, but impious, as calculated to retard the onward movement of the mighty process by which we ourselves had risen like Aphrodite out of the primeval slime of Ocean.

Therefore I trace the peculiar unity of the everyday political philosophy of the nineteenth century to the success with which it harmonised diversified and warring schools and united all good things to a single end. Hume and Paley, Burke and Rousseau, Godwin and Malthus, Cobbett and Huskisson, Bentham and Coleridge, Darwin and the Bishop of Oxford, were all, it was discovered, preaching practically the same thing— Individualism and *laissez-faire*. This was the Church of England and those her apostles, whilst the company of the economists were there to prove that the least deviation into impiety involved financial ruin.

These reasons and this atmosphere are the explanations, whether we know it or not—and most of us in these degenerate days are largely ignorant in the matter—why we feel such a strong bias in favour of *laissez-faire*, and why State action to regulate the value of money, or the course of investment, or the population, provoke such passionate suspicions in many upright breasts. We have not read these authors; we should consider their arguments preposterous if they were to fall into our hands. Nevertheless we should not I fancy, think as we do, if Hobbes, Locke, Hume, Rousseau, Paley, Adam Smith, Bentham, and Miss Martineau had not thought and written as they did. A study of the history of opinion is a necessary preliminary to the emancipation of the mind. I do not know which makes a man more conservative—to know nothing but the present, or nothing but the past.

LAISSEZ-FAIRE AND THE ECONOMISTS

I have said that it was the economists who furnished the scientific pretext by which the practical man could solve the contradiction between egoism and socialism which emerged out of the philosophising of the eighteenth century and the decay of revealed religion. But having said this for shortness' sake, I hasten to qualify it. This is what the economists are *supposed* to have said. No such doctrine is really to be found in the writings of the greatest authorities. It is what the popularisers and the vulgarisers said. It is what the Utilitarians, who admitted Hume's egoism and Bentham's egalitarianism at the same time, were *driven* to believe in, if they were to effect a synthesis.[6] The language of the economists lent itself to the *laissez-faire* interpretation. But the popularity of the doctrine must be laid at the door of the political philosophers of the day, whom it happened to suit, rather than of the political economists.

The maxim *laissez-nous faire* is traditionally attributed to the merchant Legendre addressing Colbert sometime towards the end of the seventeenth century.[7] But there is no doubt that the first writer to use the phrase, and to use it in clear association with the doctrine, is the Marquis d'Argenson about 1751.[8] The Marquis was the first man to wax passionate on the economic advantages of Governments leaving trade alone. To govern better, he said, one must govern less.[9] The true cause of the decline of our manufactures, he declared, is the protection we have given to them.[10] "Laissez-faire, telle devrait être la devise de toute puissance publique, depuis que le monde est civilisé." "Detestable principe que celui de ne vouloir notre grandeur que par l'abaissement de nos voisins! Il n'y a que la méchanceté et la malignité du cœur de satisfaites dans ce principe, et l'intérêt y est opposé. Laissez faire morbleu! Laissez faire!!"

Here we have the economic doctrine of *laissez-faire,* with its most fervent expression in Free Trade, fully clothed. The phrases and the idea must have passed current in Paris from that time on. But they were slow to establish themselves in Literature; and the tradition associating with them the Physiocrats, and particularly de Gournay and Quesnay, finds little support in the writings of this school, though they were, of course, proponents of the essential harmony of social and individual interests. The phrase *laissez-faire* is not to be found in the works of Adam Smith, of Ricardo, or of Malthus. Even the idea is not present in a dogmatic form in any of these authors. Adam Smith, of course, was a Free Trader and an opponent of many eighteenth-century restrictions on trade. But his attitude towards the Navigation Acts and the Usury laws shows that he was not dogmatic. Even his famous passage about "the invisible hand" reflects the philosophy which we associate with Paley rather than the economic dogma of *laissez-faire.* As Sidgwick and Cliff Leslie have pointed out, Adam Smith's advocacy of the "obvious and simple system of natural liberty" is derived from his theistic and optimistic view of the order of the world, as set forth in his *Theory of Moral Sentiments,* rather than from any proposition of Political Economy proper."[11] The phrase *laissez-faire* was, I think, first brought into popular usage in England by a well-known passage of Dr Franklin's.[12] It is not, indeed, until we come to the later works of Bentham—who was not an economist at all—that we discover the rule of *laissez-faire,* in the shape in which our grandfathers knew it, adopted into the service of the Utilitarian philosophy. For example, in *A Manual of Political Economy,*[13] he writes: "The general rule is that nothing ought to be done or attempted by government; the motto or watchword of government, on these

---

[6] One can sympathise with the view of Coleridge, as summarised by Leslie Stephen, that "the Utilitarians destroyed every element of cohesion, made Society a struggle of selfish interests, and struck at the very roots of all order, patriotism, poetry, and religion."

[7] "Que faut-il faire pour vous aider?" asked Colbert. "Nous laisser faire," answered Legendre.

[8] For the history of the phrase, *vide* Oncken, "Die Maxime *Laissez-faire* et laissez passer," from whom most of the following quotations are taken. The claims of the Marquis d'Argenson were overlooked until Oncken put them forward, partly because the relevant passages published during his lifetime were anonymous (*Journal Œconomique,* 1751), and partly because his works were not published in full (though probably passed privately from hand to hand during his lifetime) until 1858 (*Mémoires et Journal inédit du Marquis d'Argenson*).

[9] "Pour gouverner mieux, il faudrait gouverner moins."

[10] "On ne peut dire autant de nos fabriques: la vraie cause de leur declin, c'est la protection outrée qu'on leur accorde."

---

[11] Sidgwick, *Principles of Political Economy,* p. 20.

[12] Bentham uses the expression *"laissez-nous faire,"* *Works,* p. 440.

[13] Written in 1793, a chapter published in the *Bibliothèque Britannique* in 1798, and the whole first printed in Bowring's edition of his *Works* (1843).

occasions, ought to be—*Be quiet.* . . . The request which agriculture, manufacturers, and commerce present to governments is as modest and reasonable as that which Diogenes made to Alexander: Stand out of my sunshine."

From this time on it was the political campaign for Free Trade, the influence of the so-called Manchester School and of the Benthamite Utilitarians, the utterances of secondary economic authorities, and the educational stories of Miss Martineau and Mrs. Marcet, that fixed *laissez-faire* in the popular mind as the practical conclusion of orthodox Political Economy—with this great difference, that the Malthusian view of Population having been accepted in the meantime by this same school of thought, the optimistic *laissez-faire* of the last half of the eighteenth century gives place to the pessimistic *laissez-faire* of the first half of the nineteenth century.[14]

In Mrs. Marcet's *Conversations on Political Economy* (1817) Caroline stands out as long as she can in favour of controlling the expenditure of the rich. But by page 418 she has to admit defeat:

> *Caroline.*—The more I learn upon this subject, the more I feel convinced that the interests of nations, as well as those of individuals, so far from being opposed to each other, are in the most perfect unison.
>
> *Mrs. B.*—Liberal and enlarged views will always lead to similar conclusions, and teach us to cherish sentiments of universal benevolence towards each other; hence the superiority of science over mere practical knowledge.

By 1850 the *Easy Lessons for the Use of Young People,* by Archbishop Whately, which the Society for Promoting Christian Knowledge was distributing wholesale, do not admit even of those doubts which Mrs B. allowed Caroline occasionally to entertain.

---

[14] See Sidgwick (*op. cit.,* p. 22): "Even those economists, who adhered in the main to Adam Smith's limitations of the sphere of government, enforced these limitations sadly rather than triumphantly; not as admirers of the social order at present resulting from 'natural liberty,' but as convinced that it is at least preferable to any artificial order that government might be able to substitute for it."

More harm than good is likely to be done, the little book concludes,

> by almost any interference of Government with men's money transactions, whether letting and leasing, or buying and selling of any kind.

True liberty is

> that every man should be left free to dispose of his own property, his own time, and strength, and skill, in whatever way he himself may think fit, provided he does no wrong to his neighbours.

In short, the dogma had got hold of the educational machine; it had become a copybook maxim. The Political Philosophy, which the seventeenth and eighteenth centuries had forged in order to throw down Kings and Prelates, had been made milk for babes, and had literally entered the nursery.

Finally, in the works of Bastiat we reach the most extravagant and rhapsodical expression of the Political Economist's religion. In his *Harmonies Economiques,*

> I undertake [he says] to demonstrate the Harmony of those laws of Providence which govern human society. What makes these laws harmonious and not discordant is, that all principles, all motives, all springs of action, all interests, co-operate towards a grand final result. . . . And that result is, the indefinite approximation of all classes towards a level, which is always rising; in other words, the equalisation of individuals in the general amelioration.

And when, like other priests, he drafts his Credo, it runs as follows:

> I believe that He who has arranged the material universe has not withheld His regard from the arrangements of the social world. I believe that He has combined and caused to move in harmony free agents as well as inert molecules. . . . I believe that the invincible social tendency is a constant approximation of men towards a common moral, intellectual, and physical level, with, at the same time, a progressive and indefinite elevation of that level. I believe that all that is necessary to the gradual and peaceful development of humanity is

that its tendencies should not be disturbed, nor have the liberty of their movements destroyed.

From the time of John Stuart Mill, economists of authority have been in strong reaction against all such ideas. "Scarcely a single English economist of repute," as Professor Carman has expressed it, "will join in a frontal attack upon Socialism in general," though, as he also adds. "nearly every economist, whether of repute or not, is always ready to pick holes in most socialistic proposals."[15] Economists no longer have any link with the theological or political philosophies out of which the dogma of Social Harmony was born, and their scientific analysis leads them to no such conclusions.

Cairnes, in the Introductory Lecture on "Political Economy and *Laissez-Faire*," which he delivered at University College, London, in 1870, was perhaps the first orthodox economist to deliver a frontal attack upon *laissez-faire* in general. "The maxim of *laissez-faire*," he declared, "has no scientific basis whatever, but is at best a mere handy rule of practice."[16] This, for fifty years past, has been the view of all leading economists. Some of the most important work of Alfred Marshall—to take one instance—was directed to the elucidation of the leading cases in which private interest and social interest are *not* harmonious. Nevertheless the guarded and undogmatic attitude of the best economists has not prevailed against the general opinion that an individualistic *laissez-faire* is both what they ought to teach and what in fact they do teach.

THE ASSUMPTIONS OF ECONOMIC INDIVIDUALISM

Economists, like other scientists, have chosen the hypothesis from which they set out, and which they offer to beginners, because it is the simplest, and not because it is the nearest to the facts. Partly for this reason, but partly, I admit, because they have been biassed by the traditions of the subject, they have begun by assuming a state of affairs where the ideal distribution of productive resources can be brought about through individuals acting independently by the method of trial and error in such a way that those individuals who move in the right direction will destroy by competition those who move in the wrong direction. This implies that there must be no mercy or protection for those who embark their capital or their labour in the wrong direction. It is a method of bringing the most successful profit-makers to the top by a ruthless struggle for survival, which selects the most efficient by the bankruptcy of the less efficient. It does not count the cost of the struggle, but looks only to the benefits of the final result which are assumed to be permanent. The object of life being to crop the leaves off the branches up to the greatest possible height, the likeliest way of achieving this end is to leave the giraffes with the longest necks to starve out those whose necks are shorter.

Corresponding to this method of attaining the ideal distribution of the instruments of production between different purposes, there is a similar assumption as to how to attain the ideal distribution of what is available for consumption. In the first place, each individual will discover what amongst the possible objects of consumption *he* wants most by the method of trial and error "at the margin," and in this way not only will each consumer come to distribute his consumption most advantageously, but each object of consumption will find its way into the mouth of the consumer whose relish for it is greatest compared with that of the others, because that consumer will outbid the rest. Thus, if only we leave the giraffes to themselves, (1) the maximum quantity of

---

[15] *Theories of Production and Distribution,* p. 494.

[16] Cairnes well described the "prevailing notion" in the following passage from the same lecture: "The prevailing notion is that P.E. undertakes to show that wealth may be most rapidly accumulated and most fairly distributed; that is to say, that human well-being may be most effectually promoted, by the simple process of leaving people to themselves; leaving individuals, that is to say, to follow the promptings of self-interest, unrestrained either by the State or by public opinion, so long as they abstain from force and fraud. This is the doctrine commonly known as *laissez-faire;* and accordingly political economy is, I think, very generally regarded as a sort of scientific rendering of this maxim—a vindication of freedom of individual enterprise and of contract as the one and sufficient solution of all industrial problems."

leaves will be cropped because the giraffes with the longest necks will, by dint of starving out the others, get nearest to the trees; (2) each giraffe will make for the leaves which he finds most succulent amongst those in reach; and (3) the giraffes whose relish for a given leaf is greatest will crane most to reach it. In this way more and juicier leaves will be swallowed, and each individual leaf will reach the throat which thinks it deserves most effort.

This assumption, however, of conditions where unhindered natural selection leads to progress, is only one of the two provisional assumptions which, taken as literal truth, have become the twin buttresses of *laissez-faire.* The other one is the efficacy, and, indeed, the necessity, of the opportunity for unlimited private money-making as an *incentive* to maximum effort. Profit accrues, under *laissez-faire,* to the individual who, whether by skill or good fortune, is found with his productive resources in the right place at the right time. A system which allows the skilful or fortunate individual to reap the whole fruits of this conjuncture evidently offers an immense incentive to the practice of the art of being in the right place at the right time. Thus one of the most powerful of human motives, namely, the love of money, is harnessed to the task of distributing economic resources in the way best calculated to increase wealth.

The parallelism between economic *laissez-faire* and Darwinianism, already briefly noted, is now seen, as Herbert Spencer was foremost to recognise, to be very close indeed. Just as Darwin invoked sexual love, acting through sexual selection, as an adjutant to Natural Selection by competition, to direct evolution along lines which should be desirable as well as effective, so the individualist invokes the love of money, acting through the pursuit of profit, as an adjutant to Natural Selection, to bring about the production on the greatest possible scale of what is most strongly desired as measured by exchange value.

The beauty and the simplicity of such a theory are so great that it is easy to forget that it follows not from the actual facts, but from an incomplete hypothesis introduced for the sake of simplicity. Apart from other objections to be mentioned later, the conclusion

that individuals acting independently for their own advantage will produce the greatest aggregate of wealth, depends on a variety of unreal assumptions to the effect that the processes of production and consumption are in no way organic, that there exists a sufficient foreknowledge of conditions and requirements, and that there are adequate opportunities of obtaining this foreknowledge. For economists generally reserve for a later stage of their argument the complications which arise—(1) when the efficient units of production are large relatively to the units of consumption, (2) when overhead costs or joint costs are present, (3) when internal economies tend to the aggregation of production, (4) when the time required for adjustments is long, (5) when ignorance prevails over knowledge, and (6) when monopolies and combinations interfere with equality in bargaining—they reserve, that is to say, for a later stage their analysis of the actual facts. Moreover, many of those who recognise that the simplified hypothesis does not accurately correspond to fact conclude nevertheless that it does represent what is "natural" and therefore ideal. They regard the simplified hypothesis as health, and the further complications as disease.

Yet, besides this question of fact, there are other considerations, familiar enough, which rightly bring into the calculation the cost and character of the competitive struggle itself, and the tendency for wealth to be distributed where it is not appreciated most. If we have the welfare of the giraffes at heart, we must not overlook the suffering of the shorter necks who are starved out, or the sweet leaves which fall to the ground and are trampled underfoot in the struggle, or the overfeeding of the long-necked ones, or the evil look of anxiety or struggling greediness which overcasts the mild faces of the herd.

But the principles of *laissez-faire* have had other allies besides economic textbooks. It must be admitted that they have been confirmed in the minds of sound thinkers and the reasonable public by the poor quality of the opponent proposals—Protectionism on one hand, and Marxian Socialism on the other. Yet these doctrines are both characterised, not only or chiefly by their infringing the general presumption in favour of *laissez-faire,* but by *mere* logical fallacy. Both are examples of poor thinking, of inability to analyse a process and follow it out to its conclusion. The arguments against them, though reinforced by the principle of *laissez-faire,* do not strictly require it. Of the two, Protectionism is at least plausible, and the forces making for its popularity are nothing to wonder at. But Marxian Socialism must always remain a portent to the historians of Opinion—how a doctrine so illogical and so dull can have exercised so powerful and enduring an influence over the minds of men, and, through them, the events of history. At any rate, the obvious scientific deficiencies of these two schools greatly contributed to the prestige and authority of nineteenth-century *laissez-faire.*

Nor has the most notable divergence into centralised social action on a great scale—the conduct of the late war—encouraged reformers or dispelled old-fashioned prejudices. There is much to be said, it is true, on both sides. War experience in the organisation of socialised production has left some near observers optimistically anxious to repeat it in peace conditions. War socialism unquestionably achieved a production of wealth on a scale far greater than we ever knew in Peace, for though the goods and services delivered were destined for immediate and fruitless extinction, none the less they were wealth. Nevertheless the dissipation of effort was also prodigious, and the atmosphere of waste and not counting the cost was disgusting to any thrifty or provident spirit.

Finally. Individualism and *laissez-faire* could not, in spite of their deep roots in the political and moral philosophies of the late eighteenth and early nineteenth centuries, have secured their lasting hold over the conduct of public affairs, if it had not been for their conformity with the needs and wishes of the business world of the day. They gave full scope to our erstwhile heroes, the great business men. "At least one-half of the best ability in the Western world," Marshall used to say, "is engaged in business." A great part of "the higher imagination" of the age was thus employed. It was on the activities of these men that our hopes of Progress were centred.

"Men of this class," Marshall wrote,

live in constantly shifting visions, fashioned in their own brains, of various routes to their desired end; of the difficulties which Nature will oppose to them on each route, and of the contrivances by which they hope to get the better of her opposition. This imagination gains little credit with the people, because it is not allowed to run riot; its strength is disciplined by a stronger will; and its highest glory is to have attained great ends by means so simple that no one will know, and none but experts will even guess, how a dozen other expedients, each suggesting as much brilliancy to the hasty observer, were set aside in favour of it. The imagination of such a man is employed, like that of the master chess-player, in forecasting the obstacles which may be opposed to the successful issue of his far-reaching projects, and constantly rejecting brilliant suggestions because he has pictured to himself the counter-strokes to them. His strong nervous force is at the opposite extreme of human nature from that nervous irresponsibility which conceives hasty Utopian schemes, and which is rather to be compared to the bold facility of a weak player, who will speedily solve the most difficult chess problem by taking on himself to move the black men as well as the white.[17]

This is a fine picture of the great Captain of Industry, the Master-Individualist, who serves us in serving himself, just as any other artist does. Yet this one, in his turn, is becoming a tarnished idol. We grow more doubtful whether it is he who will lead us into Paradise by the hand.

These many elements have contributed to the current intellectual bias, the mental make-up, the orthodoxy of the day. The compelling force of many of the original reasons has disappeared, but, as usual, the vitality of the conclusions outlasts them. To suggest social action for the public good to the City of London is like discussing the *Origin of Species* with a Bishop sixty years ago. The first reaction is not intellectual, but moral. An orthodoxy is in question, and

---

[17] "The Social Possibilities of Economic Chivalry," *Economic Journal* (1907), xvii, p. 9.

the more persuasive the arguments the graver the offence. Nevertheless, venturing into the den of the lethargic monster, at any rate I have traced his claims and pedigree so as to show that he has ruled over us rather by hereditary right than by personal merit.

THE FUTURE ORGANIZATION
OF SOCIETY

Let us clear from the ground the metaphysical or general principles upon which, from time to time, *laissez-faire* has been founded. It is *not* true that individuals possess a prescriptive "natural liberty" in their economic activities. There is *no* "compact" conferring perpetual rights on those who Have or on those who Acquire. The world is *not* so governed from above that private and social interest always coincide. It is *not* so managed here below that in practice they coincide. It is *not* a correct deduction from the Principles of Economics that enlightened self-interest always operates in the public interest. Nor is it true that self-interest generally *is* enlightened; more often individuals acting separately to promote their own ends are too ignorant or too weak to attain even these. Experience does *not* show that individuals, when they make up a social unit, are always less clear-sighted than when they act separately.

We cannot therefore settle on abstract grounds, but must handle on its merits in detail what Burke termed "one of the finest problems in legislation, namely, to determine what the State ought to take upon itself to direct by the public wisdom, and what it ought to leave, with as little interference as possible, to individual exertion."[18] We have to discriminate between what Bentham, in his forgotten but useful nomenclature, used to term *Agenda* and *Non-Agenda,* and to do this without Bentham's prior presumption that interference is, at the same time, "generally needless" and "generally pernicious."[19] Perhaps the chief task of economists at this hour is to distinguish afresh the *Agenda* of Government from the

Non-Agenda; and the companion task of Politics is to devise forms of Government within a Democracy which shall be capable of accomplishing the *Agenda.* I will illustrate what I have in mind by two examples.

1. I believe that in many cases the ideal size for the unit of control and organisation lies somewhere between the individual and the modern State. I suggest, therefore, that progress lies in the growth and the recognition of semi-autonomous bodies within the State—bodies whose criterion of action within their own field is solely the public good as they understand it, and from whose deliberations motives of private advantage are excluded, though some place it may still be necessary to leave, until the ambit of men's altruism grows wider, to the separate advantage of particular groups, classes, or faculties—bodies which in the ordinary course of affairs are mainly autonomous within their prescribed limitations, but are subject in the last resort to the sovereignty of the democracy expressed through Parliament.

I propose a return, it may be said, towards mediæval conceptions of separate autonomies. But, in England at any rate, corporations are a mode of government which has never ceased to be important and is sympathetic to our institutions. It is easy to give examples, from what already exists, of separate autonomies which have attained or are approaching the mode I designate—the Universities, the Bank of England, the Port of London Authority, even perhaps the Railway Companies. In Germany there are doubtless analogous instances.

But more interesting than these is the trend of Joint Stock Institutions, when they have reached a certain age and size, to approximate to the status of public corporations rather than that of individualistic private enterprise. One of the most interesting and unnoticed developments of recent decades has been the tendency of big enterprise to socialise itself. A point arrives in the growth of a big institution—particularly a big railway or big public utility enterprise, but also a big bank or a big insurance company—at which the owners of the capital, *i.e.* the shareholders, are almost entirely dissociated from the management, with the result that the direct personal interest of the latter in the making of great profit becomes quite

---

[18] Quoted by M'Culloch in his *Principles of Political Economy.*

[19] Bentham's *Manual of Political Economy,* published posthumously, in Bowring's edition (1843).

secondary. When this stage is reached, the general stability and reputation of the institution are more considered by the management than the maximum of profit for the shareholders. The shareholders must be satisfied by conventionally adequate dividends; but once this is secured, the direct interest of the management often consists in avoiding criticism from the public and from the customers of the concern. This is particularly the case if their great size or semi-monopolistic position renders them conspicuous in the public eye and vulnerable to public attack. The extreme instance, perhaps, of this tendency in the case of an institution, theoretically the unrestricted property of private persons, is the Bank of England. It is almost true to say that there is no class of persons in the Kingdom of whom the Governor of the Bank of England thinks less when he decides on his policy than of his shareholders. Their rights, in excess of their conventional dividend, have already sunk to the neighbourhood of zero. But the same thing is partly true of many other big institutions. They are, as time goes on, socialising themselves.

Not that this is unmixed gain. The same causes promote conservatism and a waning of enterprise. In fact, we already have in these cases many of the faults as well as the advantages of State Socialism. Nevertheless we see here, I think, a natural line of evolution. The battle of Socialism against unlimited private profit is being won in detail hour by hour. In these particular fields—it remains acute elsewhere—this is no longer the pressing problem. There is, for instance, no so-called important political question so really unimportant, so irrelevant to the re-organisation of the economic life of Great Britain, as the Nationalisation of the Railways.

It is true that many big undertakings, particularly Public Utility enterprises and other business requiring a large fixed capital, still need to be semi-socialised. But we must keep our minds flexible regarding the forms of this semi-socialism. We must take full advantage of the natural tendencies of the day, and we must probably prefer semi-autonomous corporations to organs of the Central Government for which Ministers of State are directly responsible.

I criticise doctrinaire State Socialism, not because it seeks to engage men's altruistic impulses in the service of Society, or because it departs from *laissez-faire,* or because it takes away from man's natural liberty to make a million, or because it has courage for bold experiments. All these things I applaud. I criticise it because it misses the significance of what is actually happening; because it is, in fact, little better than a dusty survival of a plan to meet the problems of fifty years ago, based on a misunderstanding of what someone said a hundred years ago. Nineteenth-century State Socialism sprang from Bentham, free competition, etc., and is in some respects a clearer, in some respects a more muddled version of just the same philosophy as underlies nineteenth-century individualism. Both equally laid all their stress on freedom, the one negatively to avoid limitations on existing freedom, the other positively to destroy natural or acquired monopolies. They are different reactions to the same intellectual atmosphere.

2. I come next to a criterion of *Agenda* which is particularly relevant to what it is urgent and desirable to do in the near future. We must aim at separating those services which are *technically social* from those which are *technically individual.* The most important *Agenda* of the State relate not to those activities which private individuals are already fulfilling, but to those functions which fall outside the sphere of the individual, to those decisions which are made by *no one* if the State does not make them. The important thing for Government is not to do things which individuals are doing already, and to do them a little better or a little worse; but to do those things which at present are not done at all.

It is not within the scope of my purpose on this occasion to develop practical policies. I limit myself, therefore, to naming some instances of what I mean from amongst those problems about which I happen to have thought most.

Many of the greatest economic evils of our time are the fruits of risk, uncertainty, and ignorance. It is because particular individuals, fortunate in situation or in abilities, are able to take advantage of uncertainty and ignorance, and also because for the same reason big business is often a lottery, that great inequalities of wealth come about; and these same factors are also the cause of the Unemployment of Labour, or the disappointment of reasonable business expectations and of the impairment of efficiency and production. Yet the cure lies outside the operations of individuals; it may even be to the interest of individuals to aggravate the disease. I believe that the cure for these things is partly to be sought in the deliberate control of the currency and of credit by a central institution, and partly in the collection and dissemination on a great scale of data relating to the business situation, including the full publicity, by law if necessary, of all business facts which it is useful to know. These measures would involve Society in exercising directive intelligence through some appropriate organ of action over many of the inner intricacies of private business, yet it would leave private initiative and enterprise unhindered. Even if these measures prove insufficient, nevertheless they will furnish us with better knowledge than we have now for taking the next step.

My second example relates to Savings and Investment. I believe that some coordinated act of intelligent judgment is required as to the scale on which it is desirable that the community as a whole should save, the scale on which these savings should go abroad in the form of foreign investments, and whether the present organisation of the investment market distributes savings along the most nationally productive channels. I do not think that these matters should be left entirely to the chances of private judgment and private profits, as they are at present.

My third example concerns Population. The time has already come when each country needs a considered national policy about what size of Population, whether larger or smaller than at present or the same, is most expedient. And having settled this policy, we must take steps to carry it into operation. The time may arrive a little later when the community as a whole must pay attention to the innate quality as well as to the mere numbers of its future members.

THE MONEY-MOTIVE

These reflections have been directed towards possible improvements in the technique of modern Capitalism by the agency of collective action. There is nothing in them which is seriously incompatible with what seems to me to be the essential characteristic of Capitalism, namely the dependence upon an intense appeal to the money-making and money-loving instincts of individuals as the main motive force of the economic machine. Nor must I, so near to my end, stray towards other fields. Nevertheless I may do well to remind you, in conclusion, that the fiercest contests and the most deeply felt divisions of opinion are likely to be waged in the coming years not round technical questions, where the arguments on either side are mainly economic, but round those which, for want of better words, may be called psychological or, perhaps, moral.

In Europe, or at least in some parts of Europe—but not, I think, in the United States of America—there is a latent reaction, somewhat widespread, against basing Society to the extent that we do upon fostering, encouraging, and protecting the money-motives of individuals. A preference for arranging our affairs in such a way as to appeal to the money-motive as little as possible, rather than as much as possible, need not be entirely *a priori,* but may be based on the comparison of experiences. Different persons, according to their choice of profession, find the money-motive playing a large or a small part in their daily lives, and historians can tell us about other phases of social organisation in which this motive has played a much smaller part than it does now. Most religions and most philosophies deprecate, to say the least of it, a way of life mainly influenced by considerations of personal money profit. On the other hand, most men to-day reject ascetic notions and do not doubt the real advantages of wealth. Moreover, it seems obvious to them that one cannot do without the money-motive, and that, apart from certain admitted abuses, it does its job well. In the result the average man averts his attention from the problem and has no clear idea what he really thinks and feels about the whole confounded matter.

Confusion of thought and feeling leads to confusion of speech. Many people, who are really objecting to Capitalism as a way of life, argue as though they were objecting to it on the ground of its inefficiency in attaining its own objects. Contrariwise, devotees of Capitalism are often unduly conservative, and reject reforms in its technique, which might really strengthen and preserve it, for fear that they may prove to be first steps away from Capitalism itself. Nevertheless a time may be coming when we shall get clearer than at present as to when we are talking about Capitalism as an efficient or inefficient technique, and when we are talking about it as desirable or objectionable in itself. For my part, I think that Capitalism, wisely managed, can probably be made more efficient for attaining economic ends than any alternative system yet in sight, but that in itself it is in many ways extremely objectionable. Our problem is to work out a social organisation which shall be as efficient as possible without offending our notions of a satisfactory way of life.

The next step forward must come, not from political agitation or premature experiments, but from thought. We need by an effort of the mind to elucidate our own feelings. At present our sympathy and our judgment are liable to be on different sides, which is a painful and paralysing state of mind. In the field of action reformers will not be successful until they can steadily pursue a clear and definite object with their intellects and their feelings in tune. There is no party in the world at present which appears to me to be pursuing right aims by right methods. Material Poverty provides the incentive to change precisely in situations where there is very little margin for experiments. Material Prosperity removes the incentive just when it might be safe to take a chance. Europe lacks the means, America the will, to make a move. We need a new set of convictions which spring naturally from a candid examination of our own inner feelings in relation to the outside facts.

II BEVERIDGE

Report on Social Insurance and *Allied Services*

THREE GUIDING PRINCIPLES
OF RECOMMENDATIONS

In proceeding from this first comprehensive survey of social insurance to the next task—of making recommendations—three guiding principles may be laid down at the outset.

The first principle is that any proposals for the future, while they should use to the full the experience gathered in the past, should not be restricted by consideration of sectional interests established in the obtaining of that experience. Now, when the war is abolishing landmarks of every kind, is the opportunity for using experience in a clear field. A revolutionary moment in the world's history is a time for revolutions, not for patching.

The second principle is that organisation of social insurance should be treated as one part only of a comprehensive policy of social progress. Social insurance fully developed may provide income security; it is an attack upon Want. But Want is one only of five giants on the road of reconstruction and in some ways the easiest to attack. The others are Disease, Ignorance, Squalor and Idleness.

The third principle is that social security must be achieved by co-operation between the State and the individual. The State should offer security for service and contribution. The State in organising security should not stifle incentive, opportunity, responsibility; in establishing a national minimum, it should leave room and encouragement for voluntary action by each individual to provide more than that minimum for himself and his family.

The Plan for Social Security set out in this Report is built upon these principles. It uses experience but is not tied by experience. It is put forward as a limited contribution to a wider social policy, though as something that could be achieved now without waiting for the whole of that policy. It is, first and foremost, a plan of insurance—of giving in return for contributions benefits up to subsistence level, as of right and without means test, so that individuals may build freely upon it. . . .

PLANNING FOR
PEACE IN WAR

Freedom from want cannot be forced on a democracy or given to a democracy. It must be won by them. Winning it needs courage and faith and a sense of national unity: courage to face facts and difficulties and overcome them; faith in our future and in the ideals of fair-play and freedom for which century after century our forefathers were prepared to die; a sense of national unity overriding the interests of any class or section. The Plan for Social Security in this Report is submitted by one who believes that in this supreme crisis the British people will not be found wanting, of courage and faith and national unity, of material and spiritual power to play their part in achieving both social security and the victory of justice among nations upon which security depends.

III MYRDAL

*Beyond the Welfare State**

THE HISTORICAL AND CAUSAL ORDER

In the last half century, the state, in all the rich countries in the Western world, has become a democratic "Welfare State," with fairly explicit commitments to the broad goals of economic development, full employment, equality of opportunity for the young, social security, and protected minimum standards as regards not only income, but nutrition, housing, health, and education for people of all regions and social groups. The Welfare State is nowhere, as yet, an accomplishment; it is continually in the process of coming into being. In no country was it originally planned in advance—certainly not as a structure of its present imposing ramifications and importance for the individual citizens. In all countries, even in those where the building of the Welfare State is most advanced, the architects are continually laboring with the tasks of simplification, coordination, rationalization and achievement of efficiency. Indeed, this planning becomes pressing as the edifice of the Welfare State rises.

That this must be so, should be clear from the analysis I have given of the forces behind the trend towards planning in the Western countries. The historical and causal order has been that acts of intervention in the play of market forces came first, and that planning then became a necessity. In a process of cumulative causation, the secular

increase in the volume of intervention has been spurred on by the sequence of violent international crises since World War I, the increasing rationality of people's attitudes, the democratization of political power, and the growth of provincial and municipal self-government and of large-scale enterprises and interest organizations in all markets. Thus, as public and private intervention became more frequent and more far-reacing and closely related to the other constituents of this mighty process of social change, so there arose situations of growing complexity, contradiction, and confusion. With ever greater impact, the need for a rationalizing coordination of them all was pressed upon the state as the central organ for the public will.

Coordination leads to planning or, rather, it *is* planning, as this term has come to be understood in the Western world. Coordination of measures of intervention implies a reconsideration of them all from the point of view of how they combine to serve the development goals of the entire national community, as these goals become determined by the political process that provides the basis for power. The need for this coordination arose because the individual acts of intervention, the total volume of which was growing, had not been considered in this way when they were initiated originally.

As the state is increasingly involved in coordinating and regulating the national economy, it becomes compelled to make short-term and long-term forecasts, and to try to modify its policies for commerce, finance, development, and social reform in the light of what these forecasts show. A very much improved basis of statistical and other information is also becoming available to the

---

*From Gunnar Myrdal, *Beyond the Welfare State: Economic Planning and Its International Implications* (1960). By permission of Yale University Press and Gerald Duckworth.

governments. This coordination of policies, and their continued modification in order to remain appropriate in the setting of factual trends revealed by the forecasts, does not take the shape of a rigid, all-embracing plan. Nevertheless, it constitutes a steadily developing approach to planning, which tends to become firmer and more embracing as present tendencies work themselves out.

FROM INTERVENTION TO PLANNING

As regards the activities of the big enterprises and the organizations in the infrastructure beneath the formal constitutional structure, it is, of course, clear at the outset that they were not from the beginning part of a rationally coordinated national plan. They regularly represented special interests, not the general and common interests of the nation. But, as a matter of fact, the lack of coordination is equally apparent in public policies as they were initially motivated and decided upon. The history of economic policies in every country, as regards, for instance, tariffs and taxes, gives abundant proof of this thesis.

There is further proof in the records of how the huge structures for primary and higher education and for public health were built up, and also in the big redistributional reforms, such as the social security schemes and other measures for the care of the sick, the disabled, the unemployed, the aged, and the children. All these complexes of economic and social intervention, as they now exist, have been the end product of a long process of piecemeal, gradually induced changes, which in the different fields have been pressed forward, at first as independent and unrelated policy measures, motivated on their own merits or undertaken in response to group pressures.

It is, for instance, remarkable that the social security schemes, which are becoming increasingly expensive, were initially supported only by arguments of social justice and welfare for specific groups of people in need; and such arguments remained predominant for a long time. When the opponents of these schemes, who argued all the time that they would ruin the economy of

the country, were again and again proved wrong this was largely the result of the effect of these reforms in raising the productivity of the mass of the people—an effect which had never played an important part in their motivation. As considerations of these wider effects and interrelations gradually come to the fore in public discussion, the explanation is mainly that these policy measures have by now become so numerous and important, and that they re-direct the distribution of such a very large portion of the national product, that they simply must be coordinated with one another, and with the development of the entire national economy. Thus we arrive at planning in the modern sense.

Public intervention in the field of housing and construction of new houses, affords another example. Since the scanty and diffuse beginnings of a few decades ago, it has been increasing tremendously in all Western countries. The state now finds itself responsible for influencing decisively—directly through its legislation and administration and that of the provincial and municipal authorities, or indirectly through the organizations in the infrastructure that operate under the state's indulgence and sanction—the conditions under which people can find houses to live in, and under which some people can make it a business to provide homes. This involved complex of intervention concerns the level of rents, the availability and price of building and mortgage credits, the conditions on the several labor markets and the markets for building materials, and, indeed, every aspect of the entire economic process by which houses are built, owned or rented, and inhabited. The future number and the age composition of families and other factors determining both human need and effective demand for housing, must be predicted and allowed for, as must the effects of building activity upon trends of general business activity, in the short and long run. The latter effects are so important that the level of building activity has to be watched carefully, even from the point of view of general economic policy. As the cities grow, and as more public investment becomes involved in preparing for such growth, town planning becomes ever more necessary, as does the general public preoccupation with planning and directing the location of industry.

In the same way, the rapid development of higher and professional education now absorbs so much money, and concerns so many young people in all these countries, that it is gradually becoming realized that this activity cannot continue as an independent process of dispersed public policies. Instead, it has to be planned carefully on the basis of calculations of future demand for, and supply of, labor trained in different ways. This necessarily involves a forecast and a plan for the whole national economy. Again, the converse also applies; no long-range forecast or plan for the national economy can any longer be made without including policies for education and training.

Sweden is now inaugurating, as a final effort to complete the edifice of social security, a compulsory provident and pension scheme, aimed at eradicating what are almost the last remnants of class distinction between manual workers and other employees of public and private enterprises. It is probably taking the lead in a reform movement which other Western countries will soon join. All old people will, by legislation, be guaranteed an income corresponding to two-thirds of their earnings during the best fifteen years of their working life. It is clear that a redistributional reform of this huge magnitude must be founded on the most careful forecast of the development of the entire national economy for a long period ahead, and must be integrated into the whole system of public policies influencing this development. Otherwise it would represent the most reckless gambling with the future economy of the country, risking the frustration of national efforts in all fields. This is more evidently the case as the social security payments to the old are being guaranteed in real terms. It is characteristic of the situation Western countries have now reached in regard to planning that a main criticism raised in Sweden against this reform is that the calculations of its effects on the total economic development of the country are not complete and tight enough. This preoccupation with planning is not least prominent in the minds of the conservatives, who oppose the reform.

"FULL EMPLOYMENT"

In a sense, the biggest commitment to economic planning in the Welfare State of the Western countries is that they are all now pledged to preserving "full employment," though the definition, as well as the form, of the commitment varies. The political process by which governments have gradually reached this situation illuminates this trend towards planning.

Not many decades ago the periodic appearance of mass unemployment was accepted as a more or less natural consequence of necessary market adjustments to changing business conditions, about which not much could be done. As, however, the political power of the workers increased in the process of democratization, to which I have referred, and as the social conscience became more alert to the sufferings of the unemployed and their families—two changes which, of course, are closely related—measures of financial aid to the unemployed were instituted in one country after another.

At first, these policy measures were all of a compensatory nature, aimed merely at providing the unemployed workers with some of the incomes they had lost by becoming unemployed. It was the symptom, not the cause, of unemployment that was being dealt with. Unemployment insurance, which now forms an integral part of the social security system in all Western countries, represents the consummation of this line of social policy. But soon the demand was raised that the state should take positive measures in order to create additional work opportunities for the unemployed. In the twenties, and still more during the Great Depression, public works policies spread in all Western countries. At the same time, the workers began to press for full wages even in these public works.

These developments represented only steps towards demanding that the state should so direct all its financial and economic policies as to create demand for labor sufficient to liquidate mass unemployment and to keep the national economy uninterruptedly in high gear. Economic theory now responded to the ideological needs of the time by placing the responsibility for economic depressions and unemployment on an imbalance between aggregate demand and supply, opening up a rational way for the state to raise investment and production and to create employment simply by raising its expenditure while keeping down taxation. In Sweden, which amongst the Western countries was the first, both theoretically and practically, to adopt this policy, "pump priming" worked fairly well even in the early years of the Great Depression, as it happened to be supplemented by other simultaneous changes in general business conditions which were favorable to a recovery but not part of intentional policy. Similar policies in the United States and many other countries were less successful, the main explanation being that the over-spending was too small to have much effect.

After World War II, we have all become accustomed to much bigger budgets and also to taking huge budget deficits less seriously. The expansionist theory of spending one's way out of a depression is now on the way to becoming orthodox, even in the more conservative sections of the business world. It has, as yet, not been put to much of a test, however, as first the urgent reconstruction needs and the pent-up demands immediately after the war, and later the immense armament expenditures and other financial consequences of the cold war, have contributed in mighty fashion to sustain total demand. Inflation and not deflation has been the continuous worry. But, whatever the explanation, it is in any case a fact that on the whole all the Western countries have enjoyed full employment, not only during but also after the war. Now only a dwindling minority of workers in these countries have any personal experience of mass unemployment or any recollection of the situation some few decades ago, when even in boom years the fear of unemployment was a sinister cloud on the horizon for every working-class family. It is safe to predict that in none of the Western countries will a period of severe unemployment ever again be tolerated by the people.

In a sense, this determination to preserve full employment is the crowning accomplishment of the democratic Welfare State. It is generally understood and accepted that this implies a preparedness to use even radical policy measures, when needed, in order to keep the entire labor force employed, and

also that this assumes is most careful watch on the entire economic development and a planned coordination of all economic policies.

CONVERGING POLITICAL ATTITUDES

One interesting aspect of this gradual perfection of the modern democratic Welfare State is that many divisions of opinion, once of burning importance, now tend to fade away, or to change character and thereby to become much less important.

This is, for instance, to a large extent true of the discussion of redistributional reform. Nobody nowadays gets very excited about the issue of whether or not there should be progressive taxation. The disagreement between participants in public debate, and between political parties, no longer concerns this issue of principle, but to what extent and by what devices taxation should be used to influence the distribution of wealth and income. Similarly, the discussion about whether there should be a system of social security has ended. The practical problem is now only how much money should be devoted to this purpose, who should pay it, and how it should be used. Reforms that have been carried through in a country generally win quick and sincere acceptance from the whole population. Even the continuation of this policy is accepted, and more redistributional reforms are becoming an almost automatic consequence of economic progress. We tend to arrive at a situation where there is a large measure of agreement among all the political parties. They sometimes even compete in propagating new and constantly more sweeping redistributional reforms as levels of income rise. In any case, we have seen very few examples, if any, where the coming into power of a more conservative political party has meant a substantial retraction of reforms previously carried through by a party which was further left.

This implies a gradual retreat from their earlier positions by the conservatives. In the opposite direction, we can also witness a coolness on the left towards many ideas of radical reform which were propounded by the Social Democrats when they were a small minority party without influence.

Their demand for public ownership of banks, insurance companies, and industries, for instance, did not begin to take hold, and thus never built up any cumulative force. I have already referred in the Introduction to the inherited aversion, in the Western countries, to a "planned economy," of which large-scale nationalization, of course, is an extreme variant. That this aversion was supported and exploited by the business interests—whose power over the communications industry is everywhere strong—is obvious. It is apparent that, as the Social Democrats gradually won popular support and achieved political influence, they generally tended to play down the nationalization issue—with a longer or shorter ideological lag in the different countries. It now plays an ever decreasing role in all Western countries, and may be on the way to disappearing altogether from the political scene.

There was, however, a more logical reason for this adjustment on the part of the Social Democrats. Nationalization could only be a means to reaching the basic aims of their policy. As the Welfare State developed, these were, however, largely attained by other means, and nationalization was no longer necessary, or even very desirable.

Private banks and insurance companies, for instance, are now closely regulated by legislative and administrative controls, initiated primarily to safeguard the interests of the depositors and policyholders, but increasingly used to serve wider social ends. In the advanced Welfare State, these enterprises become increasingly involved in regular cooperation, both among themselves and with the central bank and the treasury, in order to preserve the balance in the money and capital markets. This cooperation can be made more efficient, and the leadership of the state authorities, as the guardians of the public interest, can be asserted, by an extension of such controls—without nationalization. Moreover, state and cooperative enterprises enter as competitors, establishing standards in their markets. Last but not least, the enterprises are legally bound to subject more and more of their activities to public scrutiny. They are followed in detail by an increasingly vigilant public and in particular by a whole array of private power groups, each with its own facilities for research. When all these

things have happened, these enterprises are not very private any more. Usually nothing much could be attained by their being taken over by the state.

Or consider even the private industrial concern. Its activities in the market are as a participant in industrial associations. For most of its labor relations, it has to abide by agreements reached between the employers' association, of which it is a member, and the trade union system. It is legally bound to disclose periodically its complete accounts and also to discuss these and all major policy decisions with representatives of the workers. All profits from it are heavily taxed, as a matter of fact twice, according to steeply graduated rates, when they are distributed as incomes to the shareholders. Its decisions on the disposal of profits and internal consolidation are becoming increasingly regulated by law, and are open to state intervention when considerations of general economic policy make this desirable. In all these respects public control can be tightened, without resort to nationalization.

The industrial firm is a participant in a national community which is developing rapidly in the direction of the democratic Welfare State of equity and solidarity. Whether it is a family affair or a more impersonal concern, it is already, in essential respects, "socialized." Moreover, all its operations are constantly influenced by the knowledge, on the part of its owners as well as its managers, that each year it has to justify its existence as a private undertaking on pain of becoming more closely controlled and, perhaps, nationalized.

I may be exaggerating slightly. It is anyhow a fact that during the time, over a quarter of a century, that Sweden has been ruled by the Social-Democratic Labor Party—in fact longer, i.e., since that party in the 'twenties started to become a rising political force—while in all respects the development towards the Welfare State has been exceedingly rapid, there has, in that country, been no major move towards nationalization, although the party is committed to such a line by its formal program, which it has conservatively left unaltered. I would expect that sooner or later nationalization will disappear from the program, too.

In judging this development, it should, of course, be remembered that the Swedish state, as a legacy from long ago—and usually very long ago, in many cases from the era preceding even the liberal one—disposes of large domains of land, forests, and ore deposits, and, together with the municipalities, most water power; and that the state runs the railways and, together with the municipalities, has always owned almost all other public utility industries. That the nationalization issue, at least until recently, has played a more important role in English politics is very much due, I believe, to a difference in the initial situation, as well as to the Jag in rationalization and efficiency in many private enterprises and to the relative lack of effective social control of private business, particularly through taxation.

It is possible that, in the Welfare State of the future, public ownership and public management will come to play a somewhat larger role, perhaps in the very long run a much larger one. But the change will in any case not come suddenly over the whole field. Whether or not to nationalize a particular industry will stand out less and less as a question of political principle and will be more and more a matter of practical expediency.

And in the individual case the change will not usually be of great importance. New state enterprises cannot now be run very differently from any other enterprise, state or private. They will not be "freer" towards other partners in the markets where they sell their products. In the labor markets they will have to negotiate the wages of their workers with the trade unions, as other enterprises do. The profits will go to the state, but through taxation some, and in some countries most, profits of private enterprises are going that way already, and the taxation screw can be further tightened, if that is desirable. The power relations in the national community will be changed by nationalization. But these are being changed anyway, by all the other changes in this process I have been analyzing, which has not nearly reached its end in any country and which in some countries is still far from the democratic ideal. As a matter of fact, all private enterprises in the advanced Welfare State are already in essential respects publicly controlled or are becoming so—without any nationalization of formal ownership.

A "CREATED HARMONY"

The examples I have given of a trend towards convergence of attitudes and ideologies—in regard to the now largely undisputed, and consequently almost automatic, progress of further redistributional reforms, to which could be added educational and health reforms, etc., and the virtual disappearance of the nationalization issue—point to the increasing political harmony that has come to exist much more generally between all the citizen groups in the advanced Welfare State. The internal political debate in those countries is becoming increasingly technical in character, ever more concerned with detailed arrangements, and less involved with broad issues, since those are slowly disappearing.

To some extent, this harmony of interests and opinions is often spirited away and concealed by the professionals in the political parties and in the interest organizations. They have all a vested interest of self-preservation in making their flocks so much dissatisfied with existing conditions and trends that they can keep up active participation and retain momentum in their organizations. When they then occasionally mobilize the old armory of slogans from the time when people were still basically divided on broad issues of principle—liberalism, socialism, and capitalism; free enterprise and planned economy; private property and nationalization; individualism and collectivism, etc.—it can add emotional stimulus to a public debate otherwise tending to become colorless and bickering, because it arouses the associations still lingering in the old battle cries from a time when there were wider divisions of interest and wider disagreements on major issues as to bow the national community should be organized. To the simpleminded it can almost give a feeling of intellectual elevation.

But these slogans are actually becoming rather shallow, and are generally felt to be so, when applied to the practical problems of the day in a functioning Welfare State. When instead the professionals restrict themselves merely to bickering in order to, stimulate popular backing for their strivings on behalf of political parties and interest organizations, they are more in tune with how people really feel in a Welfare

State—or can easily be brought to feel by propaganda.

The professionals' interests are divided, however. They seek, at the same time, to give the people to whom they appeal a feeling of satisfaction, and to associate this with an appreciation of what they have attained through participation in the organizations. When, in the advanced Welfare States, complete participation in the ordinary interest organizations, like the trade unions, is becoming the established pattern, this more positive interest in keeping people satisfied is becoming the stronger one. Even in such a state, political parties naturally still mostly have to take up a fighting position—at least at election times when they have to stimulate the lazy and undecided voters to vote, and to vote for them. All professionals, including the politicians, have, however, an interest in preserving favorable conditions for the normal day-to-day cooperation and collective bargaining among them all.

All things considered, it is my feeling that in the most advanced Welfare States the professionals, except for special occasions such as elections or strikes, tend to do their best to keep people happy and tone down their dissatisfactions. There are, of course, always plenty of frustrated querulants, and they play a not altogether insignificant role in every Western country. But the general mood of the ordinary citizens in the advanced Welfare State can be observed to be one of quiet satisfaction—although combined with a ubiquitous urge, but also a reasonable hope, to get more and more of the good things of life.

Behind this attitude is the reality that in the Welfare State a higher degree of harmony of interests actually becomes attained through cooperation and collective bargaining. When in recent years the Social Democrats in Sweden sponsored, and had a decisive influence in inaugurating, social security legislation affording insurance payments rising with a person's income up to a very high level—in unemployment, sickness, and old age insurance—this was an indication, among many others, that the present income distribution, including the expectation of how it is going to change, is widely accepted in that country as just and fair, even by those who are in the relatively lower income brackets.

CHAPTER THIRTY-SIX

LIBERTARIANISM

The encounter between capitalism and socialism has led, through the slow working of the democratic political process, to an economy which is neither capitalist, if capitalism means unrestricted *laissez-faire* and rugged individualism, nor socialist, if socialism means an economy that is owned and operated by the state. The mixed economy welfare state seeks to combine the best of capitalism and socialism—the predominantly private energy in private property with predominantly public responsibility in economic macromanagement and social welfare. The relative strength of these two elements always is in flux.

Development of the welfare state was bound to cause a reaction. In the United States, for example, the national government share of gross national product has increased eight-fold since 1929, from 2.5 percent to over 20 percent. There is more spending at state and local levels, as well. To consider the expansion of government in the United States from another perspective, government at all levels spent less than $2 billion per year early in the century, but by the end of the century, this figure had increased one-thousand-fold. The scope of government, as well as its size, also has enormously increased.

Libertarianism—the movement toward less government—is not, at least according to its best proponents, a conservative reaction to the welfare state and general growth of government, but a liberal or even radical one. Friedrich Hayek (1899–1992), perhaps the foremost philosopher of libertarianism during the twentieth century, summed up differences between conservatism and "true liberalism" (or libertarianism) best in his 1956 foreword to his most well-known book, *The Road to Serfdom* (1944): "Conservatism, though a necessary element in any stable society, is not a social program; in its paternalistic, nationalistic, and power-adoring tendencies it is often closer to socialism than true liberalism; and with its traditionalistic, anti-intellectual, and often mystical propensities it will never, except in short periods of disillusionment, appeal to the young and all those who believe that change is desirable if this world is to become a better place."

Trained as an economist in the Austrian tradition, Hayek emerged at the London School of Economics in 1931 as an opponent of Keynes and rival of Laski. At Chicago, he was a colleague of Friedman. In 1974, he received the Nobel Prize in Economics with Myrdal. Educated at the University of Vienna and intellectually brought to maturity as an assistant to Austrian economist Ludwig von Mises, Hayek was, with Friedman, the leading academic proponent of less government during the twentieth century.

814

The historical Austrian school of economics can be traced to the nineteenth century Viennese economist Carl Menger, who, in Hayek's view, was the writer after Smith who most explored the idea, as Smith put it, that man in society "constantly promotes ends which are not part of his intention." For Menger, the question "how it is possible that institutions which serve the common welfare and are most important for its advancement can arise without a common will aiming at their creation" is "the significant, perhaps the most significant, problem of the social sciences."

Mises's contribution to libertarian thought and Hayek's work was fundamental. Mises inaugurated the long-lasting and influential "socialist calculation debate," which raised the question of how production in a socialist economy would be determined. Mises stated the main point beautifully: "The [socialist] director wants to build a house. Now, there are many methods that can be resorted to. Each of them offers . . . certain advantages and disadvantages with regard to the utilization of the future building, and results in a different duration of the building's serviceableness; each of them requires . . . [differing] expenditures of building materials and labor . . . Which method should the director choose? He cannot reduce to a common denominator the items of various materials and various kinds of labor to be expended. Therefore, he cannot compare them."

Mises's argument was that prices, private property, private management, and private exchange are vital to economic productivity. He wrote in the prescient 1920 "Economic Planning in the Socialist Commonwealth": "There are many socialists who have never come to grips in any way with the problems of economics, and who have made no attempt at all to form for themselves any clear conception of the conditions which determine the character of human society. . . . They have criticized freely enough the economic structure of 'free' society, but have consistently neglected to apply to the economics of the disputed socialist state the same caustic acumen . . . Economics, as such, figures all too sparsely in the glamorous pictures painted by the Utopians. They invariably explain how, in the cloud-cuckoo lands of their fancy, roast pigeons will in some way fly into the mouths of the comrades, but they omit to show how this miracle is to take place." How should production practically be organized in a socialist economy? It is not enough to point to deficiencies in capitalism.

Hayek was born in the pre–World War I Austro-Hungarian Empire and imbibed much from the society in which he grew up. He emphasized order in his thought. The first requisite for a society is safety and order. Without these, no satisfactory life is possible. He also emphasized hierarchy and class. He took it for granted that some will have more and others less in every society—this is a fact of life. He also may have acquired some of his relative disdain for democracy from his Viennese roots. Finally, he adopted a conception of federation as offering the best form of government for resolving many intersocietal issues. Austria-Hungary was a federation.

World War I was an even greater event at the time than it became in retrospect because the worse horrors and convulsions of World War II made the first world war lose some of its centrality. But for central Europeans who experienced it, such as Hayek, World War I was the defining conflagration in their lives. The world that died with the First World War was the nineteenth century, classical liberal world. Keynes perhaps said it best in *The Economic Consequences of the Peace:* "What an extraordinary episode in the economic progress of man that age was which came to an end in August, 1914! The greater part of the population, it is true, worked hard and lived at a low standard of comfort, yet were, to all appearances, reasonably contented with this lot. But escape was possible, for any man of capacity or character at all exceeding the average, into the middle and upper classes, for whom life offered, at a low cost and with the least trouble, conveniences, comforts, and amenities beyond the compass of the richest and most powerful monarchs of other ages. The inhabitant of London could order by telephone, sipping his morning tea in bed, the various products of the whole earth, in such quantity as he might see fit, and reasonably expect their early delivery upon his doorstep . . . [H]e regarded this state of affairs as normal, certain, and permanent . . . The projects and politics of militarism and imperialism, of racial and cultural rivalries . . . were little more than the amusements of his daily newspaper, and appeared to exercise almost no influence at all on the ordinary course of social and economic life, the internationalization of which was nearly complete in practice." It was always Hayek's goal in many respects to return to the pre–World War I world—which he thought would be progress, not retrogression.

During the 1920s in Vienna under Mises, Hayek focused on monetary theory, industrial fluctuations, and the economics of socialism. His work in monetary theory and a business cycle is disregarded in mainstream economics today. Far more significant was his participation in the socialist calculation debate, beginning in 1935, and his enunciation in the 1937 "Economics and Knowledge" article of "the division of knowledge." The idea he presents in "Economics and Knowledge" is that knowledge is divided:

> There is . . . a problem of the *division of knowledge* which is quite analogous to, and at least as important as, the problem of the division of labor. But, while the latter has been one of the main subjects of investigation ever since the beginning of our science, the former has been as completely neglected, although it seems to me to be the really central problem of economics as a social science. . . .
>
> [E]conomics has come closer than any other social science to an answer to that central question of all social sciences: How can the combination of fragments of knowledge existing in different minds bring about results which, if they were to be brought about deliberately, would require a knowledge on the part of the directing mind which no single person can possess? . . . [T]he spontaneous actions of individuals will, under conditions which we can define, bring about a distribution of resources which can be understood as if it were made according to a single plan, although nobody has planned it. . . .

He added in a later essay, "The Use of Information in Society": "We must look at the price system as . . . a mechanism for communicating information . . . "

Hayek is most well known for the 1944 anti-planning book *The Road to Serfdom*. He was concerned that, following World War II, Britain might move headlong into wholesale socialist reconstruction of its society, wherein government would own and run all of the means of production. He insightfully argued that not only is a socialist economy inherently unproductive, it is intrinsically despotic: "Whoever controls all economic activity controls the means for all our ends, and must therefore decide which are to be satisfied and which not. This is really the crux of the matter. Economic control is not merely control of a sector of human life which can be separated from the rest; it is the control of the means for all our ends."

Hayek's essential argument against socialism is not that humanity are not good enough for socialism—that we are not benevolent or other-directed enough—but that we are not intelligent enough. Even in a community of saints, a private market and freely-fluctuating prices would be necessary effectively to direct production because of limitations in individual human knowledge.

His next major work following *The Road to Serfdom* was *The Constitution of Liberty* (1960), dedicated to "the unknown civilization that is growing in America." In 1950, Hayek left the London School of Economics for the University of Chicago, where he joined Friedman and others, though Hayek was not a member of the economics department at Chicago (he was on the Committee on Social Thought). *The Constitution of Liberty,* conceived as his *magnum opus,* attempted to flesh out arguments made in only a negative and truncated form in *The Road to Serfdom.* Particularly in the first part of *The Constitution of Liberty,* "The Creative Powers of a Free Civilization," he sought to rebut a century of socialist argument: "As a statement of fact, it just is not true that 'all men are born equal.' . . . From the fact that people are very different it follows that, if we treat them equally, the result must be inequality in their actual position, and that the only way to place them in an equal position would be to treat them differently. Equality before the law and material equality are therefore not only different but are in conflict with each other; and we can achieve either the one or the other, but not both at the same time." Hayek chose equality before the law over material equality.

He applied the same standard to relations between nations as he did within them: "There can be little doubt that the prospect of the poorer, 'undeveloped' countries reaching the present level of the West is very much better than it would have been, had the West not pulled so far ahead. Furthermore, it is better than it would have been, had some world authority . . . seen to it that no part pulled too far ahead of the rest and made sure at each step that the material benefits were distributed evenly throughout the world. If today some nations can in a few decades acquire a level of material comfort that took the West hundreds or thousands of years to achieve, is it not evident that their path has been made easier by the fact that the West was not forced to share its material achievements with the rest—that it was not held back but was able to move far in advance of the others?" He was both a domestic and international inegalitarian.

Among the most difficult concepts Hayek put forward is "spontaneous order." As initially developed in his "Economics and Knowledge" article, the idea of a spontaneous order is in largest part that government cannot so much direct every action—economic or otherwise—in a society, but that the goal of government should be to construct certain framework laws or rules that enable a society's members cooperatively to interact. The goal should be not to tell people what to do, but to create opportunities for them to do what they choose to do. He used as an example in *The Road to Serfdom* the difference between government telling people where to travel and providing roads and traffic rules to allow transportation effectively to occur.

Hayek was not opposed to law—he was not an anarchist. He held, in fact, following Locke, that law creates liberty. Hayek quoted Locke: "The end of the law is, not to abolish or restrain, but to preserve and enlarge freedom. For in all the states of created beings capable of laws, where there is no law there is no freedom. For liberty is to be free from restraint and violence from others; which cannot be where there is no law: and it is not, as we are told, a liberty for every man to do what he lists [wishes]. (For who could be free when every other man's humour might domineer over him?) But a liberty to dispose, and order as he lists, his person, actions, possessions, and his whole property, within the allowance of those laws under which he is, and therein not to be the subject of the arbitrary will of another, but freely follow his own."

Law is the crucial constituent of a freedom. Where there is no law, there can be no freedom. Law creates liberty. Law is not inconsistent with liberty, but is its embodiment.

Hayek sanctioned a considerable positive role for government. He allowed many welfare state provisions of social services by government, including in education, health care, unemployment and retirement insurance, and public charity, among many others. In the area of government provision of social welfare services, his primary concern was that government should not have a monopoly in these areas—that if, for example, there is a government retirement program, there should also be able to be private retirement programs—and that government services should be privatized to the greatest extent possible. He also thought that public charity should be as minimal as possible, and largely restricted to the elderly, infirm, and widows with children. He hoped that most societal welfare functions would be provided voluntarily. While he theoretically allowed a significant welfare state, his practical views were more limited.

He opposed a progressive income tax, though he sanctioned some inheritance taxes. In regard to his opposition to a progressive income tax, he felt that it is both unjust and uneconomical. No individual should have to pay more than the same percentage of his income in taxes than anyone else, and taxing at a greater proportion those who earn more discourages initiative. He greatly was opposed to inflation, and thought inflation perhaps is the most ruinous financial condition that can befall a national economy. He was not, though, a Chicago monetarist of Friedman's school.

Law, Legislation and Liberty (1973–79) was mostly written during the 1960s, but completed during the later 1970s, when Hayek was in his seventies. He enjoyed a resurgence in his later years after he was awarded the Nobel Prize in Economics. *Law, Legislation and Liberty* is a more scholarly presentation of many of the ideas in *The Constitution of Liberty*. He emphasized the importance of law as distinct from governmental direction and moral compulsion, though he did not deemphasize the latter as much as he came later to feel that Mill did. For Hayek, cultural norms in addition to law are completely appropriate, indeed an essential part of an effective society.

In *The Fatal Conceit: The Errors of Socialism* (1988), his final work, Hayek returned to the socialist calculation debate. He was now more concerned to attempt to demonstrate that socialism necessarily is unproductive economically than to provide a case for the beneficial operation of democratic interventionist welfare state capitalism: "The main point of my argument is . . . that the conflict between, on one hand, advocates of the spontaneous extended human order created by a competitive market, and on the other hand those who demand a deliberate arrangement of human interaction by central authority based on collective command over available resources is due to a factual error by the latter about how knowledge of these resources is and can be generated and utilised." It is not that socialism would be ethically undesirable; it is that it factually is not possible: "To follow socialist morality would destroy much of present humankind and impoverish much of the rest." He ultimately was a completely materialist philosopher. The best society and best world is the one in which the material standard of living for all people everywhere is as high as it technologically can be. Libertarianism is a rational philosophy. Hayek concluded *The Constitution of Liberty* with a postscript, "Why I Am Not a Conservative": "Personally, I find that the most objectionable feature of the conservative attitude is its propensity to reject well-substantiated new knowledge because it dislikes some of the consequences which seem to follow from it. . . . "

Hayek emphasized the roles of prices and profits. He remarked in one of the last pieces that he himself prepared for publication, "The Moral Imperative of the Market" (1986): "In 1936 . . . , I suddenly saw . . . that my previous work in different branches of economics had a common root. This insight was that the price system was really an instrument which enabled millions of people to adjust their efforts to events, demands and conditions, of which they had no concrete, direct knowledge . . . Here my thinking was inspired largely by Ludwig von Mises' conception of the problem of ordering a planned economy. . . . [T]he whole economic order rested on the fact that by using prices as a guide, or as signals, we were led to serve the demands and enlist the powers and capacities of people of whom we knew nothing. . . . Basically, the insight that prices were signals bringing about the . . . co-ordination of . . . efforts . . . became the leading idea behind my work." He held in *The Fatal Conceit:* "Profits are all that most producers need to be able to serve more effectively the needs of men they do not know"; "in the evolution of . . . human activities, profitability works as a signal that guides selection towards what makes man more fruitful . . . "

During his later years, Hayek was an intellectual inspirer for many in the Reagan and Thatcher governments. He soundly believed Keynes's famous closing lines to *The General Theory:* "The ideas of economists and political philosophers, both when they are right and when they are wrong, are more powerful than is commonly understood. Indeed the world is ruled by little else." To the extent this is true, Hayek's own influence may be evaluated.

Hayek's ultimate goal (beyond a world federation of free nations) was of a world of universal law: "It is only by extending the rules of just conduct to the relations with all other men, and at the same time depriving of their obligatory character those rules which cannot be universally applied, that we can approach a universal order of peace which might integrate all mankind into a single society."

In the emergence of libertarian thought during the twentieth century, a number of names stand out in addition to Hayek, Friedman, and Mises—Ayn Rand, Frank Knight, Edwin Cannan, Walter Eucken, Ronald Coase, James Buchanan, Brent Bozell (ghostwriter of Barry Goldwater's *The Conscience of a Conservative*), Thomas Sowell, Arthur Seldon, Charles Murray, and, among journalists, William F. Buckley, R. Emmett Tyrrell, and George Will. Within academia, there have been four main centers of libertarian thought—the University of Vienna, the London School of Economics, the University of Freiburg, and the University of Chicago. Milton Friedman (1912–   ) is the dominating influence in the Chicago school of economics, and, together with Keynes, the most influential economist of the twentieth century.

Friedman's parents were poor Jewish immigrants to the United States. Friedman's father (who died when Milton was 15) was a petty trader; his mother ran a family-owned clothing sweatshop. He entered Rutgers University in New Jersey at 16 in 1928, having won a state scholarship. He recalled of his circumstances at the time that "we never had a family income that by today's standards would have put us above the poverty level. . . . However, thanks to the state scholarship plus the usual combination of such jobs as waiting on tables, clerking in stores, and working in the summer, I was well able to pay my own way through college—and indeed ended up with a small nest egg that helped meet the expenses of my first year of graduate study."

From Rutgers, Friedman first went to the University of Chicago for graduate work. He was, at this time, undecided between mathematics and economics, but decided to pursue economics, because "the United States was at the bottom of the deepest depression in its history before or since. The dominant problem of our time was economics. How to get out of the depression? How to reduce unemployment? What explained the paradox of great need on the one hand and unused resources on the other?"

The Great Depression was the defining twentieth century economic event for academicians and others who experienced it. The Great Depression seemed to confirm Marx's prophecy that capitalism is inherently unstable and prone to collapse. When millions were unemployed throughout the western world, preexisting economic belief in *laissez-faire* appeared outdated and irresponsible. Among Friedman's most significant accomplishments is to have reconceptualized the cause of the Great Depression.

At the time, during the 1930s, there was not a universally accepted explanation of what caused the worldwide depression. The United States stock market crash of October 1929 was considered a trigger. This often was held at the time, and subsequently, to represent the intrinsic weakness of unfettered *laissez-faire* capitalism. Stock market speculators purchasing securities on excessive credit created a financial house of cards, a pyramid scheme, that all came crashing down, taking many smaller and hardworking investors with them and wreaking havoc on the economy—this sort of analysis became the accepted opinion. The gold standard also was criticized. Certainly in Britain, its restoration in 1925 coincided with continuing bad economic times. The Smoot-Hawley tariff, enacted by Congress in 1930, was blamed. It led to retaliatory tariffs by a number of foreign countries, and international trade—and portions of domestic economies based on international trade—declined. Finally, there were deflation and bank failures. Prices dropped by about one-third in the United States between 1929 and 1933, and about two in five banks disappeared through failure, liquidation, or merger.

When millions were destitute and unemployed, democratic government had to respond. The basic theme of the day was to get the economy moving again. It was necessary for government to "prime the pump" of economic activity through work programs and deficit budgets. In time (though not initially), monetary policy also was loosened. The view became general that unregulated free enterprise is economically unsustainable, and that there is a significant place for government in macromanaging a nation's economy.

Friedman agrees that there is a substantial role for government in establishing the parameters of a nation's economy. Where he disagrees, and where he has had such influence, is in his reinterpretation of the cause of the Great Depression. In a letter to Hayekian economist Mark Skousen, Friedman (in an article published in 1995) "reiterated what he and Anna Schwartz concluded in *A Monetary History of the United States*: the 1920s was the 'high tide' of Federal Reserve policy, inflation was virtually non-existent, and economic growth was reasonably rapid. Monetarists even deny that the stock market was overvalued in 1929! In short, 'everything going on in the 1920s was fine.' The problem, according to Friedman, was not the 1920s, but the 1930s, when the Federal Reserve permitted the 'Great Contraction' of the money supply and drove the economy into the worst depression."

Friedman's position is not at all that the Great Depression represented some sort of Marxian collapse of capitalism, or even the Keynesian thesis that "the forces of the nineteenth century have run their course and are exhausted." Instead, Friedman puts forward that the depression simply was a result of national monetary mismanagement by the United States Federal Reserve Board. Prices were stable in the United States during most of the 1920s. Then, between July 1929 and March 1933, money supply fell by over one-third. Non-expansionary monetary conditions prevailed in the United States from mid-1928. While the American stock market crash in October 1929 usually is seen as the start of the Great Depression, business activity actually peaked two months earlier. The market crash combined with diminishing business activity to result in an even greater economic crimp. Instead of expanding money supply, as in past downturns, the Federal Reserve allowed money supply to contract. Until 1932, the Federal Reserve refrained from increasing money supply, when, under strong pressure from Congress, it engaged in large open market purchases of government bonds. This program was discontinued when Congress adjourned, allowing money supply to resume its downward course. Concomitant with deflation and the continuing decline of the stock market (which by 1933 was one-sixth the level it had been four years before) came the run on the nation's banks. In 1931, the Federal Reserve disastrously raised the discount rate (the rate of interest charged to banks) in response to Britain's departure from the gold standard, tightening monetary policy during what already was a significant economic downturn. Most of the decline in United States money supply, as well as most bank failures, took place after the discount rate was raised.

Friedman's analysis—that the Great Depression was caused by national monetary mismanagement that easily could have been corrected—has become the mainstream view within academic economics. It was, however, not accepted for many years. During the 1940s through the 1960s, the basic macroeconomic policies that most national governments followed in the western world were nearly balanced budgets (and greatly surplus capital budgets) and stable prices. This was a primary source of prosperity during these decades, not economic fiddling or "fine-tuning" called Keynesian.

By the late 1960s or so, most western nations were confronted by nascent inflation which, during the early 1970s, accelerated into double digits. This inflation often was accompanied by high unemployment, so-called "stagflation" (economic stagnation and inflation). Standard Keynesian analysis could not account for stagflation. There should, according to Keynesian analysis, be a trade-off between economic activity and inflation. A loose monetary policy, resulting in inflation, should result in more economic activity, not less. Something was wrong in the Keynesian analysis. What?

Friedman's response was several-fold. In the first place, more than anyone else, he established or reestablished the tie in the popular and academic minds between the amount of money in an economy and the general price level. "Inflation is always and everywhere a monetary phenomenon," he preaches. He effectively argues against views that see inflation as having other than a monetary cause, whether that cause supposedly is labor or business. It now almost is hard to recall that as recently as three decades ago, perhaps most mainstream economists did not see the most significant source of inflation as excessive monetary growth.

Secondly, Friedman vigorously argues against large government. While there is no necessary correlation between his positions in monetary theory and his general opposition to government, he emphasizes the latter as he does the former. His essential position is that a free market almost invariably will provide better services cheaper than government, and that the best thing government can do for an economy often is to stay out of the way. He is consistent in his opposition to government. Unlike many economic conservatives who favor government keeping out of people's pocketbooks, but who favor government intervention in a wide variety of other areas, Friedman supports legalization of drugs, legal pornography, legal abortion, legalized suicide, legalized prostitution, and an all-volunteer army, among other areas in which he thinks that personal freedom should be dominant. He also has championed flexible international exchange rates, stable prices, balanced government budgets, and school vouchers.

From the 1960s through the 1990s, Friedman was the leading popular and academic exponent of libertarianism. His 1962 *Capitalism and Freedom* was a best-seller; he served as president of the American Economics Association in 1966; he wrote a regular *Newsweek* column from 1966–1984; he was an adviser to presidential candidate Goldwater and Presidents Nixon and Reagan (one former Reagan official calls him "guru" of the administration); and, in 1979, with his wife, Rose, he published the best-selling *Free to Choose,* which was the number one national non-fiction best-seller in the United States that year, as well as an international best-seller, accompanied by the popular *Free to Choose* television series. Friedman has also expressed his views as a teacher and in innumerable speeches, interviews, and other formats. His most famous statement in general parlance is: "There is no such thing as a free lunch."

Friedman's methodology is empirical-factual. He states his method best in "The Methodology of Positive Economics" (1953), one of the most cited articles in the history of professional economic thought. He distinguishes here between "normative" and "positive" economics. The former refers to the way things ought to be; the latter, to how economics actually works. He gives minimum wage laws as an example: "I venture the judgment . . . that currently in the Western world, and especially in the United States, differences about economic policy among disinterested citizens derive predominantly from different predictions about the economic consequences of taking action—differences that in principle can be eliminated by the progress of positive economics—rather than from fundamental differences in basic values . . . An obvious and not unimportant example is minimum-wage legislation. Underneath the welter of arguments offered for and against such legislation there is an underlying consensus on the objective of achieving a 'living wage' for all . . . The difference of opinion is largely grounded on an implicit or explicit difference in predictions about the efficacy of this particular means in furthering the agreed-on end. Proponents believe (predict) that legal minimum wages diminish poverty by raising the wages of those receiving less than the minimum wage . . . Opponents believe (predict) that legal minimum wages increase poverty by increasing the number of people who are unemployed . . . " In theory, at least, facts should be able to be separated from values.

Among the areas that Friedman emphasizes are also included Hong Kong and school vouchers. Hong Kong is probably the place most influenced by his thought, and when, in 1998, he spoke out against reforms there in response to the People's Republic of China's ascension, the Hong Kong stock market tumbled. In the area of school vouchers, Friedman's influence is paramount. He virtually introduced this concept, which is playing a prominent role in discussion of American education's future.

Friedman, like Hayek, does not possess a clear view of where to draw the line of government. Libertarianism, is again, not anarchism—it is not the absence of law. Rather, libertarianism recognizes that law creates liberty. Friedman says along these lines: "The paternalistic ground for governmental activity is in many ways the most troublesome to a [classical] liberal; for it involves the acceptance of a principle—that some shall decide for others—which he finds objectionable . . . Yet there is no use pretending that problems are simpler than in fact they are. . . . As Dicey wrote in 1914, . . . "The Mental Deficiency Act is the first step along a path on which no sane man can decline to enter, but which, if too far pursued, will bring statesmen across difficulties hard to meet without considerable interference with individual liberty. There is no formula that can tell us where to stop. We must rely on our fallible judgment and, having reached a judgment, on our ability to persuade our fellow men that it is a correct judgment, or their ability to persuade us to modify our views. We must put our faith, here as elsewhere, in a consensus reached by imperfect and biased men through free discussion and trial and error." Friedman, unlike Hayek, is optimistic and a full-hearted supporter of democracy. He frequently endorses state ballot measures.

The welfare state originated in a number of European countries starting in the last decades of the nineteenth century. The *laissez-faire* creed of government nonintervention broke down under the stresses of industrialization. It was not just that individuals who are ignorant, ill-nourished, uneducated, and sick are less productive than those who are not, but that social unity is threatened when gaps between classes became as large as they did, particularly when those at the bottom were genuinely impoverished materially. For this reason came greater government expenditures in education, social insurance, and sanitary and other health measures. Full employment became the goal after the Great Depression.

Keynes presciently wrote in a letter to Hayek after receiving *The Road to Serfdom:* "My dear Hayek, The voyage has given me the chance to read your book properly. In my opinion it is a grand book. We all have the greatest reason to be grateful to you for saying so well what needs so much to be said. . . . I come . . . to what is really my only serious criticism of the book. You admit here and there that it is a question of knowing where to draw the line. You agree that the line has to be drawn somewhere, and the logical extreme is not possible. But you give us no guidance whatever as to where to draw it. . . . It is true that you and I would probably draw it in different places. I should guess that according to my ideas you greatly underestimate the practicability of the middle course. But as soon as you admit that the extreme is not possible, and that a line has to be drawn, you are, on your own argument, done . . ." Where to draw the line of government?

The world has moved decisively in the direction of democratic interventionist welfare state capitalism during recent decades. Classical socialism in the sense of government ownership and management of all of a society's productive resources has been practically refuted.

The twentieth century has witnessed the greatest increase in material living standards ever. In the United States, 15 percent of families had flush toilets in 1900; 99 percent did seventy years later. Twenty-four percent of families had running water in 1900; 92 percent did seventy years later; 3 percent of families had electricity in 1900 and 99 percent in 1970, and so it goes. From automobiles to refrigeration, to central heating, to radio, to television, to computers and biotechnology, more people have more than ever before, increasingly around the world.

A surprisingly significant portion of Friedman's platform for practical political reform has been implemented during recent decades. In 1973, in part upon the recommendation of a federal commission on which he served, conscription ended in the United States. The high inflation of the 1970s has been brought down to low levels, almost entirely following Friedmanian prescriptions and diagnosis. The United States federal budget now is in surplus. International exchange rates now are flexible. International trade is freer and more extensive than ever. There has been some privatization of welfare state functions. Even, in the United States, the federal government share of Gross National Product is declining, from 23 percent in Reagan's first term to 21 percent twelve years later during Clinton's first term.

Democratic productive welfare state capitalism has been the most successful, freest, and most materially, prosperous form of human organization ever. Libertarians have always been somewhat unclear as to what exactly they would change in the welfare state—other than reducing it in size and making it more competitive—and how they would change it, what incremental steps would be taken. In a world of potential global environmental damage and nuclear weapons, it can be anticipated that, in some form or other, government is here to stay. Libertarians would appear to be happy if the size and regulatory scope of government were lessened, as reflected by total government share of GNP from the 30–50 percent now prevalent in most developed nations to less than half these figures. This might not be the ultimate Hayekian "universal order of peace," but many philosophical libertarians probably would consider it to be a significant step.

Once in power, even democratic socialist parties have come to emphasize welfare state, rather than state socialism, policies. A good example of a socialist party doing a U-turn once in power was provided by the government of Francois Mitterand in France following his election as president in 1981. After initially following a more classically socialist path of moving toward greater state ownership and control of industry and finance, Mitterand shifted to a more free market policy, because the French economy and financial markets reacted negatively to his socialist reforms. Similarly, under Margaret

Thatcher in Great Britain during the 1980s, considerable success was experienced in curbing the power of labor unions and in selling off most nationalized British industries, but relatively little success, from Thatcher's perspective, was experienced in reducing or privatizing social welfare services.

The welfare state has corresponded with the greatest economic production ever: elimination of much real deprivation, particularly among intact families and the elderly, and a significant, but not all-encompassing government role, combined with very significant wealth creation, direction, and ownership by private individuals. The purpose of the welfare state, however poorly it has at times been implemented, is both to better people's conditions and to produce economic growth. *(These it has accomplished and is accomplishing.)* If democratic interventionist welfare state capitalism is to be supplanted by libertarianism or any other "ism," it can only be so because some other system actually is positively better than it, not because it now is miserably failing—or, at least, so it now appears.

I HAYEK

*The Road to Serfdom**

THE ABANDONED ROAD

A programme whose basic thesis is, not that the system of free enterprise for profit has failed in this generation, but that it has not yet been tried.

F. D. Roosevelt.

WHEN the course of civilization takes an unexpected turn, when instead of the continuous progress which we have come to expect, we find ourselves threatened by evils associated by us with past ages of barbarism, we blame naturally anything but ourselves. Have we not all striven according to our best lights, and have not many of our finest minds incessantly worked to make this a better world? Have not all our efforts and hopes been directed towards greater freedom, justice, and prosperity? If the outcome is so different from our aims, if, instead of freedom and prosperity, bondage and misery stare us in the face, is it not clear that sinister forces must have foiled our intentions, that we are the victims of some evil power which must be conquered before we can resume the road to better things? However much we may differ when we name the culprit, whether it is the wicked capitalist or the vicious spirit of a particular nation, the stupidity of our elders, or a social system not yet, although we have struggled against it for half a century, fully overthrown—we all are, or at least were until recently, certain of one thing: that the leading ideas which during the last generation have become common to most

people of goodwill and have determined the major changes in our social life cannot have been wrong. We are ready to accept almost any explanation of the present crisis of our civilization except one: that the present state of the world may be the result of genuine error on our own part, and that the pursuit of some of our most cherished ideals have apparently produced results utterly different from those which we expected.

While all our energies are directed to bringing this war to a victorious conclusion, it is sometimes difficult to remember that even before the war the values for which we are now fighting were threatened here and destroyed elsewhere. Though for the time being the different ideals are represented by hostile nations fighting for their existence, we must not forget that this conflict has grown out of a struggle of ideas within what, not so long ago, was a common European civilization; and that the tendencies which have culminated in the creation of the totalitarian systems were not confined to the countries which have succumbed to them. Though the first task must now be to win the war, to win it will only gain us another opportunity to face the basic problems and to find a way of averting the fate which has overtaken kindred civilizations.

Now, it is somewhat difficult to think of Germany and Italy, or of Russia, not as different worlds, but as products of a development of thought in which we have shared; it is, at least so far as our enemies are concerned, easier and more comforting to think that they are entirely different from us and that what happened there cannot happen here. Yet, the history of these countries in the years before the rise of the totalitarian system showed few features with which

* From Friedrich Hayek, *The Road to Serfdom* (1944). By permission.

we are not familiar. The external conflict is a result of a transformation of European thought in which others have moved so much faster as to bring them into irreconcilable conflict with our ideals, but which has not left us unaffected.

That a change of ideas, and the force of human will, have made the world what it is now, though men did not foresee the results, and that no spontaneous change in the facts obliged us thus to adapt our thought, is perhaps particularly difficult for the English to see, just because in this development the English have, fortunately for them, lagged behind most of the European peoples. We still think of the ideals which guide us and have guided us for the past generation, as ideals only to be realized in the future, and are not aware how far in the last twenty-five years they have already transformed, not only the world, but also this country. We still believe that until quite recently we were governed by what are vaguely called nineteenth-century ideas or the principle of *laissez-faire*. Compared with some other countries, and from the point of view of those impatient to speed up the change, there may be some justification for such belief. But although till 1931 this country had followed only slowly on the path on which others had led, even by then we had moved so far that only those whose memory goes back to the years before the last war know what a liberal world has been like.

The crucial point of which people here are still so little aware is, however, not merely the magnitude of the changes which have taken place during the last generation, but the fact that they mean a complete change in the direction of the evolution of our ideas and social order. For at least twenty-five years before the spectre of totalitarianism became a real threat, we had progressively been moving away from the basic ideas on which European civilization has been built. That this movement on which we have entered with such high hopes and ambitions should have brought us face to face with the totalitarian horror has come as a profound shock to this generation, which still refuses to connect the two facts. Yet this development merely confirms the warnings of the fathers of the liberal philosophy which we still profess. We have progressively abandoned that freedom in

economic affairs without which personal and political freedom has never existed in the past. Although we had been warned by some of the greatest political thinkers of the nineteenth century, by de Tocqueville and Lord Acton, that socialism means slavery, we have steadily moved in the direction of socialism. And now that we have seen a new form of slavery arise before our eyes, we have so completely forgotten the warning, that it scarcely occurs to us that the two things may be connected.

How sharp a break not only with the recent past but with the whole evolution of western civilization the modern trend towards socialism means, becomes clear if we consider it not merely against the background of the nineteenth century, but in a longer historical perspective. We are rapidly abandoning not the views merely of Cobden and Bright, of Adam Smith and Hume, or even of Locke and Milton, but one of the salient characteristics of western civilization as it has grown from the foundations laid by Christianity and the Greeks and Romans. Not merely nineteenth- and eighteenth-century liberalism, but the basic individualism inherited by us from Erasmus and Montaigne, from Cicero and Tacitus, Pericles and Thucydides is progressively relinquished.

The Nazi leader who described the National-Socialist revolution as a counter-Renaissance spoke more truly than he probably knew. It was the decisive step in the destruction of that civilization which modern man had built up from the age of the Renaissance and which was above all an individualist civilization. Individualism has a bad name today and the term has come to be connected with egotism and selfishness. But the individualism of which we speak in contrast to socialism and all other forms of collectivism has no necessary connection with these. Only gradually in the course of this book shall we be able to make clear the contrast between the two opposing principles. But the essential features of that individualism which, from elements provided by Christianity and the philosophy of classical antiquity, was first fully developed during the Renaissance and has since grown and spread into what we know as western European civilization—the respect for the individual man *qua* man, that is the recognition of his own views and tastes as supreme in his own sphere, however narrowly that may be circumscribed, and the belief that it is desirable that men should develop their own individual gifts and bents. "Freedom" and "liberty" are now words so worn with use and abuse that one must hesitate to employ them to express the ideals for which they stood during that period. Tolerance is, perhaps, the only word which still preserves the full meaning of the principle which during the whole of this period was in the ascendant and which only in recent times has again been in decline, to disappear completely with the rise of the totalitarian state.

The gradual transformation of a rigidly organized hierarchic system into one where men could at least attempt to shape their own life, where man gained the opportunity of knowing and choosing between different forms of life, is closely associated with the growth of commerce. From the commercial cities of Northern Italy the new view of life spread with commerce to the west and north, through France and the southwest of Germany to the Low Countries and the British Isles, taking firm root wherever there was no despotic political power to stifle it. In the Low Countries and Britain it for a long time enjoyed its fullest development and for the first time had an opportunity to grow freely and to become the foundation of the social and political life of these countries. And it was from there that in the late seventeenth and eighteenth centuries it again began to spread in a more fully developed form to the west and east, to the New World and the centre of the European continent where devastating wars and political oppression had largely submerged the earlier beginnings of a similar growth.

During the whole of this modern period of European history the general direction of social development was one of freeing the individual from the ties which had bound him to the customary or prescribed ways in the pursuit of his ordinary activities. The conscious realization that the spontaneous and uncontrolled efforts of individuals were capable of producing a complex order of economic activities could come only after this development had made some progress. The subsequent elaboration of a consistent argument in favor of economic freedom was the outcome of a free growth of economic activity which had been the undesigned and unforeseen by-products of political freedom.

Perhaps the greatest result of the unchaining of individual energies was the marvellous growth of science which followed the march of individual liberty from Italy to England and beyond. That the inventive faculty of man had been no less in earlier periods is shown by the many highly ingenious automatic toys and other mechanical contrivances constructed while industrial technique still remained stationary, and by the development in some industries which, like mining or watchmaking, were not subject to restrictive controls. But the few attempts towards a more extended industrial use of mechanical inventions, some extraordinarily advanced, were promptly suppressed, and the desire for knowledge was stifled, so long as the dominant views were held to be binding for all: the beliefs of the great majority on what was right and proper were allowed to bar the way of the individual innovator. Only since industrial freedom opened the path to the free use of new knowledge, only since everything could be tried—if somebody could be found to back it at his own risk—and, it should be added, as often as not from outside the authorities officially entrusted with the cultivation of learning, has science made the great strides which in the last hundred and fifty years have changed the face of the world.

As is so often true, the nature of our civilization has been seen more clearly by its enemies than by most of its friends: "the perennial western malady, the revolt of the individual against the species," as that nineteenth-century totalitarian, Auguste Comte, has described it, was indeed the force which built our civilization. What the nineteenth century added to the individualism of the preceding period was merely to make all classes conscious of freedom, to develop systematically and continuously what had grown in a haphazard and patchy manner and to spread it from England and Holland over most of the European Continent.

The result of this growth surpassed all expectations. Wherever the barriers to the free exercise of human ingenuity were removed man became rapidly able to satisfy ever-widening ranges of desire. And while the rising standard soon led to the discovery of very dark spots in society, spots which men were no longer willing to tolerate, there was probably no class that did not substantially benefit from the general advance. We cannot do justice to this astonishing growth if we measure it by our present standards, which themselves result from this growth and now make many defects obvious. To appreciate what it meant to those who took part in it we must measure it by the hopes and wishes men held when it began: and there can be no doubt that its success surpassed man's wildest dreams, that by the beginning of the twentieth century the working man in the western world had reached a degree of material comfort, security, and personal independence which a hundred years before had seemed scarcely possible.

What in the future will probably appear the most significant and far-reaching effect of this success is the new sense of power over their own fate, the belief in the unbounded possibilities of improving their own lot, which the success already achieved created among men. With the success grew ambition—and man had every right to be ambitious. What had been an inspiring promise seemed no longer enough, the rate of progress far too slow; and the principles which had made this progress possible in the past came to be regarded more as obstacles to speedier progress, impatiently to be brushed away, than as the conditions for the preservation and development of what had already been achieved.

THE GREAT UTOPIA

What has always made the state a hell on earth has been precisely that man has tried to make it his heaven.

F. Hoelderlin.

THAT socialism has displaced liberalism as the doctrine held by the great majority of progressives does not simply mean that people had forgotten the warnings of the great liberal thinkers of the past about the consequences of collectivism. It has happened because they were persuaded of the very opposite of what these men had predicted. The extraordinary thing is that the same socialism that was not only early recognized as the gravest threat to freedom, but quite openly began as a reaction against the liberalism of

the French Revolution, gained general acceptance under the flag of liberty. It is rarely remembered now that socialism in its beginnings was frankly authoritarian. The French writers who laid the foundations of modern socialism had no doubt that their ideas could be put into practice only by a strong dictatorial government. To them socialism meant an attempt to "terminate the revolution" by a deliberate reorganization of society on hierarchical lines, and the imposition of a coercive "spiritual power." Where freedom was concerned, the founders of socialism made no bones about their intentions. Freedom of thought they regarded as the root-evil of nineteenth-century society, and the first of modern planners, Saint-Simon even predicted that those who did not obey his proposed planning boards would be "treated as cattle."

Only under the influence of the strong democratic currents preceding the revolution of 1848 did socialism begin to ally itself with the forces of freedom. But it took the new "democratic socialism" a long time to live down the suspicions aroused by its antecedents. Nobody saw more clearly than de Tocqueville that democracy as an essentially individualist institution stood in an irreconcilable conflict with socialism:

Democracy extends the sphere of individual freedom [he said in 1848], socialism restricts it. Democracy attaches all possible value to each man; socialism makes each man a mere agent, a mere number. Democracy and socialism have nothing in common but one word: equality. But notice the difference: while democracy seeks equality in liberty, socialism seeks equality in restraint and servitude.

To allay these suspicions and to harness to its cart the strongest of all political motives, the craving for freedom, socialism began increasingly to make use of the promise of a "new freedom." The coming of socialism was to be the leap from the realm of necessity to the realm of freedom. It was to bring "economic freedom," without which the political freedom already gained was "not worth having." Only socialism was capable of effecting the consummation of the agelong struggle for freedom in which the attainment of political freedom was but a first step.

The subtle change in meaning to which the word freedom was subjected in order that this argument should sound plausible is important. To the great apostles of political freedom the word had meant freedom from coercion, freedom from the arbitrary power of other men, release from the ties which left the individual no choice but obedience to the orders of a superior to whom he was attached. The new freedom promised, however, was to be freedom from necessity, release from the compulsion of the circumstances which inevitably limit the range of choice of all of us, although for some very much more than for others. Before man could be truly free, the "despotism of physical want" had to be broken, the "restraints of the economic system" relaxed.

Freedom in this sense is, of course, merely another name for power or wealth. Yet, although the promises of this new freedom were often coupled with irresponsible promises of a great increase in material wealth in a socialist society, it was not from such an absolute conquest of the niggardliness of nature that economic freedom was expected. What the promise really amounted to was that the great existing disparities in the range of choice of different people were to disappear. The demand for the new freedom was thus only another name for the old demand for an equal distribution of wealth. But the new name gave the socialists another word in common with the liberals and they exploited it to the full. And although the word was used in a different sense by the two groups, few people noticed this and still fewer asked themselves whether the two kinds of freedom promised really could be combined.

There can be no doubt that the promise of greater freedom has become one of the most effective weapons of socialist propaganda and that the belief that socialism would bring freedom is genuine and sincere. But this would only heighten the tragedy if it should prove that what was promised to us as the Road to Freedom was in fact the High Road to Servitude. Unquestionably the promise of more freedom was responsible for luring more and more liberals along the socialist road, for blinding them to the conflict which exists between the basic principles of socialism and liberalism, and for often enabling socialists

to usurp the very name of the old party of freedom. Socialism was embraced by the greater part of the intelligentsia as the apparent heir of the liberal tradition: therefore it is not surprising that to them the idea should appear inconceivable of socialism leading to the opposite of liberty.

INDIVIDUALISM AND COLLECTIVISM

> The socialists believe in two things which are absolutely different and perhaps even contradictory: freedom and organization.
>
> *Elie Halévy.*

BEFORE we can progress with our main problem, an obstacle has yet to be surmounted. A confusion largely responsible for the way in which we are drifting into things which nobody wants must be cleared up.

This confusion concerns nothing less than the concept of socialism itself. It may mean, and is often used to describe, merely the ideals of social justice, greater equality and security which are the ultimate aims of socialism. But it means also the particular method by which most socialists hope to attain these ends and which many competent people regard as the only methods by which they can be fully and quickly attained. In this sense socialism means the abolition of private enterprise, of private ownership of the means of production, and the creation of a system of "planned economy" in which the entrepreneur working for profit is replaced by a central planning body.

There are many people who call themselves socialists although they care only about the first, who fervently believe in those ultimate aims of socialism but neither care nor understand how they can be achieved, and who are merely certain that they must be achieved, whatever the cost. But to nearly all those to whom socialism is not merely a hope but an object of practical politics, the characteristic methods of modern socialism are as essential as the ends themselves. Many people, on the other hand, who value the ultimate ends of socialism no less than the socialists, refuse to support socialism because of the dangers to other values they see in the methods proposed by the socialists. The dispute about socialism has thus become largely a dispute about means and not about ends—although the question whether the different ends of socialism can be simultaneously achieved is also involved.

This would be enough to create confusion. And the confusion has been further increased by the common practice of denying that those who repudiate the means value the ends. But this is not all. The situation is still more complicated by the fact that the same means, the "economic planning" which is the prime instrument of socialist reform, can be used for many other purposes. We must centrally direct economic activity if we want to make the distribution of income conform to current ideas of social justice. "Planning," therefore, is wanted by all those who demand that "production for use" be substituted for production for profit. But such planning is no less indispensable if the distribution of incomes is to be regulated in a way which to us appears to be the opposite of just. Whether we should wish that more of the good things of this world should go to some racial élite, the Nordic men, or the members of a party or an aristocracy, the methods which we shall have to employ are the same as those which could ensure an equalitarian distribution.

It may, perhaps, seem unfair to use the term socialism to describe its methods rather than its aims, to use for a particular method a term which for many people stands for an ultimate ideal. It is probably preferable to describe the methods which can be used for a great variety of ends as collectivism and to regard socialism as a species of that genus. Yet, although to most socialists only one species of collectivism will represent true socialism, it must always be remembered that socialism is a species of collectivism and that therefore everything which is true of collectivism as such must apply also to socialism. Nearly all the points which are disputed between socialists and liberals concern the methods common to all forms of collectivism and not the particular ends for which socialists want to use them; and all the consequences with which we shall be concerned in this book follow from the methods of collectivism irrespective of the ends for which they are used. It must also not be forgotten that socialism is not only by far the most important species of collectivism or "planning"; but that it is socialism which has persuaded liberal-minded people to submit once more to that regimentation of economic life which they had overthrown because, in the words of Adam Smith, it puts governments in a position where "to support themselves they are obliged to be oppressive and tyrannical."

HAYEK

*The Constitution of Liberty**

THE DECLINE OF SOCIALISM AND THE RISE OF THE WELFARE STATE

Experience should teach us to be most on our guard to protect liberty when the Government's purposes are beneficent. Men born to freedom are naturally alert to repel invasion of their liberty by evil-minded rulers. The greatest dangers to liberty lurk in insidious encroachment by men of zeal, well meaning but without understanding.

L. Brandeis.

Efforts toward social reform, for something like a century, have been inspired mainly by the ideals of socialism—during part of this period even in countries like the United States which never has had a socialist party of importance. Over the course of these hundred years socialism captured a large part of the intellectual leaders and came to be widely regarded as the ultimate goal toward which society was inevitably moving. This development reached its peak after the second World War, when Britain plunged into her socialist experiment. This seems to have marked the high tide of the socialist advance. Future historians will probably regard the period from the revolution of 1848 to about 1948 as the century of European socialism.

During this period socialism had a fairly precise meaning and a definite program. The common aim of all socialist movements was the nationalization of the "means of produc-

tion, distribution, and exchange," so that all economic activity might be directed according to a comprehensive plan toward some ideal of social justice. The various socialist schools differed mainly in the political methods by which they intended to bring about the reorganization of society. Marxism and Fabianism differed in that the former was revolutionary and the latter gradualist; but their conceptions of the new society they hoped to create were basically the same. Socialism meant the common ownership of the means of production and their "employment for use, not for profit."

The great change that has occurred during the last decade is that socialism in this strict sense of a particular method of achieving social justice has collapsed. It has not merely lost its intellectual appeal; it has also been abandoned by the masses so unmistakably that socialist parties everywhere are searching for a new program that will insure the active support of their followers. They have not abandoned their ultimate aim, their ideal of social justice. But the methods by which they had hoped to achieve this and for which the name "socialism" had been coined have been discredited. No doubt the name will be transferred to whatever new program the existing socialist parties will adopt. But socialism in the old definite sense is now dead in the western world.

Though such a sweeping statement will still cause some surprise, a survey of the stream of disillusionist literature from socialist sources in all countries and the discussions inside the socialist parties amply confirm it. To those who watch merely the developments inside a single country, the

---

**From Friedrich Hayek, *The Constitution of Liberty* (1960). By permission.

decline of socialism may still seem no more than a temporary setback, the reaction to political defeat. But the international character and the similarity of the developments in the different countries leave no doubt that it is more than that. If, fifteen years ago, doctrinaire socialism appeared as the main danger to liberty, today it would be tilting at windmills to direct one's argument against it. Most of the arguments that were directed at socialism proper can now be heard from within the socialist movements as arguments for a change of program.

Unlike socialism, the conception of the welfare state has no precise meaning. The phrase is sometimes used to describe any state that "concerns" itself in any manner with problems other than those of the maintenance of law and order. But, though a few theorists have demanded that the activities of government should be limited to the maintenance of law and order, such a stand cannot be justified by the principle of liberty. Only the coercive measures of government need be strictly limited. We have already seen that there is undeniably a wide field for non-coercive activities of government and that there is a clear need for financing them by taxation.

Indeed, no government in modern times has ever confined itself to the "individualist minimum" which has occasionally been described, nor has such confinement of governmental activity been advocated by the "orthodox" classical economists. All modern governments have made provision for the indigent, unfortunate, and disabled and have concerned themselves with questions of health and the dissemination of knowledge. There is no reason why the volume of these pure service activities should not increase with the general growth of wealth. There are common needs that can be satisfied only by collective action and which can be thus provided for without restricting individual liberty. It can hardly be denied that, as we grow richer, that minimum of sustenance which the community has always provided for those not able to look after themselves, and which can be provided outside the market, will gradually rise, or that government may, usefully and without doing any harm, assist or even lead in such endeavors. There is little reason

why the government should not also play some role, or even take the initiative, in such areas as social insurance and education, or temporarily subsidize certain experimental developments. Our problem here is not so much the aims as the methods of government action.

References are often made to those modest and innocent aims of governmental activity to show how unreasonable is any opposition to the welfare state as such. But, once the rigid position that government should not concern itself at all with such matters is abandoned—a position which is defensible but has little to do with freedom—the defenders of liberty commonly discover that the program of the welfare state comprises a great deal more that is represented as equally legitimate and unobjectionable. If, for instance, they admit that they have no objection to pure-food laws, this is taken to imply that they should not object to any government activity directed toward a desirable end. Those who attempt to delimit the functions of government in terms of aims rather than methods thus regularly find themselves in the position of having to oppose state action which appears to have only desirable consequences or of having to admit that they have no general rule on which to base their objections to measures which, though effective for particular purposes, would in their aggregate effect destroy a free society. Though the position that the state should have nothing to do with matters not related to the maintenance of law and order may seem logical so long as we think of the state solely as a coercive apparatus, we must recognize that, as a service agency, it may assist without harm in the achievement of desirable aims which perhaps could not be achieved otherwise. The reason why many of the new welfare activities of government are a threat to freedom, then, is that, though they are presented as mere service activities, they really constitute an exercise of the coercive powers of government and rest on its claiming exclusive rights in certain fields.

The current situation has greatly altered the task of the defender of liberty and made it much more difficult. So long as the danger came from socialism of the frankly collectivist kind, it was possible to argue that the tenets of the socialists were simply false: that socialism would not achieve what the socialists wanted and that it would produce other consequences which they would not like. We cannot argue similarly against the welfare state, for this term does not designate a definite system. What goes under that name is a conglomerate of so many diverse and even contradictory elements that, while some of them may make a free society more attractive, others are incompatible with it or may at least constitute potential threats to its existence.

We shall see that some of the aims of the welfare state can be realized without detriment to individual liberty, though not necessarily by the methods which seem the most obvious and are therefore most popular; that others can be similarly achieved to a certain extent, though only at a cost much greater than people imagine or would be willing to bear, or only slowly and gradually as wealth increases; and that, finally, there are others—and they are those particularly dear to the hearts of the socialists—that cannot be realized in a society that wants to preserve personal freedom.

There are all kinds of public amenities which it may be in the interest of all members of the community to provide by common effort, such as parks and museums, theaters and facilities for sports—though there are strong reasons why they should be provided by local rather than national authorities. There is then the important issue of security, of protection against risks common to all, where government can often either reduce these risks or assist people to provide against them. Here, however, an important distinction has to be drawn between two conceptions of security: a limited security which can be achieved for all and which is, therefore, no privilege, and absolute security, which in a free society cannot be achieved for all. The first of these is security against severe physical privation, the assurance of a given minimum of sustenance for all; and the second is the assurance of a given standard of life, which is determined by comparing the standard enjoyed by a person or a group with that of others. The distinction, then, is that between the security of an equal minimum income for all and the security of a particular income that a person is thought to deserve. The latter is closely related to the third main ambition that inspires the welfare state: the desire to use the powers of government to insure a more even or more just distribution of goods. Insofar as this means that the coercive powers of government are to be used to insure that particular people get particular things, it requires a kind of discrimination between, and an unequal treatment of, different people which is irreconcilable with a free society. This is the kind of welfare state that aims at "social justice" and becomes "primarily a redistributor of income." It is bound to lead back to socialism and its coercive and essentially arbitrary methods.

TAXATION

Those who advocated progressive taxation during the latter part of the nineteenth century generally stressed that their aim was only to achieve equality of sacrifice and not a redistribution of income; also they generally held that this aim could justify only a "moderate" degree of progression and that its "excessive" use (as in fifteenth-century Florence, where rates had been pushed up to 50 per cent) was, of course, to be condemned. Though all attempts to supply an objective standard for an appropriate rate of progression failed and though no answer was offered when it was objected that, once the principle was accepted, there would be no assignable limit beyond which progression might not be carried with equal justification, the discussion moved entirely in a context of contemplated rates which made any effect on the distribution of income appear negligible. The suggestion that rates would not stay within these limits was treated as a malicious distortion of the argument, betraying a reprehensible lack of confidence in the wisdom of democratic government.

It was in Germany, then the leader in "social reform," that the advocates of progressive taxation first overcame the resistance and its modern evolution began. In 1891, Prussia introduced a progressive income tax rising from 0.67 to 4 per cent. In vain did Rudolf von Geist, the venerable leader of the then recently consummated movement for the *Rechtsstaat,* protest in the Diet that this meant the abandonment of the fundamental principle of equality before the law, "of the most sacred principle of equality," which provided the only barrier against encroachment on property. The very smallness of the burden involved in the new schemes made ineffective any attempt to oppose it as a matter of principle.

Though some other Continental countries soon followed Prussia, it took nearly twenty years for the movement to reach the great Anglo-Saxon powers. It was only in 1910 and 1913 that Great Britain and the United States adopted graduated income taxes rising to the then spectacular figures of $8\frac{1}{4}$ and 7 per cent, respectively. Yet within thirty years these figures had risen to $97\frac{1}{2}$ and 91 per cent.

Thus in the space of a single generation what nearly all the supporters of progressive taxation had for half a century asserted could not happen came to pass. This change in the absolute rates, of course, completely changed the character of the problem, making it different not merely in degree but in kind. All attempt to justify these rates on the basis of capacity to pay was, in consequence, soon abandoned, and the supporters reverted to the original, but long avoided, justification of progression as a means of bringing about a more just distribution of income. It has come to be generally accepted once more that the only ground on which a progressive scale of overall taxation can be defended is the desirability of changing the distribution of income and that this defense cannot be based on any scientific argument but must be recognized as a frankly political

postulate, that is, as an attempt to impose upon society a pattern of distribution determined by majority decision.

An explanation of this development that is usually offered is that the great increase in public expenditure in the last forty years could not have been met without resort to steep progression, or at least that, without it, an intolerable burden would have had to be placed on the poor and that, once the necessity of relieving the poor was admitted, some degree of progression was inevitable. On examination, however, the explanation dissolves into pure myth. Not only is the revenue derived from the high rates levied on large incomes, particularly in the highest brackets, so small compared with the total revenue as to make hardly any difference to the burden borne by the rest; but for a long time after the introduction of progression it was not the poorest who benefited from it but entirely the better-off working class and the lower strata of the middle class who provided the largest number of voters. It would probably be true, on the other hand, to say that the illusion that by means of progressive taxation the burden can be shifted substantially onto the shoulders of the wealthy has been the chief reason why taxation has increased as fast as it has done and that, under the influence of this illusion, the masses have come to accept a much heavier load than they would have done otherwise. The only major result of the policy has been the severe limitation of the incomes that could be earned by the most successful and thereby gratification of the envy of the less-well-off.

Law, Legislation and Liberty*

CONSTRUCTION AND EVOLUTION

There are two way of looking at the pattern of human activities which lead to very different conclusions concerning both its explanation and the possibilities of deliberately altering it. Of these, one is based on conceptions which are demonstrably false, yet are so pleasing to human vanity that they have gained great influence and are constantly employed even by people who know that they rest on a fiction, but believe that fiction to be innocuous. The other, although few people will question its basic contentions if they are stated abstractly, leads in some respects to conclusions so unwelcome that few are willing to follow it through to the end.

The first gives us a sense of unlimited power to realize our wishes, while the second leads to the insight that there are limitations to what we can deliberately bring about, and to the recognition that some of our present hopes are delusions. Yet the effect of allowing ourselves to be deluded by the first view has always been that man has actually limited the scope of what he can achieve. For it has always been the recognition of the limits of the possible which has enabled man to make full use of his powers.

The first view holds that human institutions will serve human purposes only if they have been deliberately designed for these purposes, often also that the fact that an institution exists is evidence of its having been created for a purpose, and always that we should so re-design society and its institutions that all our actions will be wholly guided by known purposes. To most people

these propositions seem almost self-evident and to constitute an attitude alone worthy of a thinking being. Yet the belief underlying them, that we owe all beneficial institutions to design, and that only such design has made or can make them useful for our purposes, is largely false.

This view is rooted originally in a deeply ingrained propensity of primitive thought to interpret all regularity to be found in phenomena anthropomorphically, as the result of the design of a thinking mind. But just when man was well on the way to emancipating himself from this naïve conception, it was revived by the support of a powerful philosophy with which the aim of freeing the human mind from false prejudices has become closely associated, and which became the dominant conception of the Age of Reason.

The other view, which has slowly and gradually advanced since antiquity but for a time was almost entirely overwhelmed by the more glamorous constructivist view, was that that orderliness of society which greatly increased the effectiveness of individual action was not due solely to institutions and practices which had been invented or designed for that purpose, but was largely due to a process described at first as 'growth' and later as 'evolution', a process in which practices which had first been adopted for other reasons, or even purely accidentally, were preserved because they enabled the group in which they had arisen to prevail over others. Since its first systematic development in the eighteenth century this view had to struggle not only against the anthropomorphism of primitive thinking but even more against the reinforcement these naïve views had received from the new rationalist philosophy. It was indeed the challenge which this philosophy provided that led to the explicit formulation of the evolutionary view.

---

*From Friedrich Hayek, *Law, Legislation and Liberty* (1973–79). By permission.

THE PERMANENT LIMITATIONS OF OUR FACTUAL KNOWLEDGE

The constructivist approach leads to false conclusions because man's actions are largely successful, not merely in the primitive stage but perhaps even more so in civilization, because they are adapted both to the particular facts which he knows and to a great many other facts he does not and cannot know. And this adaptation to the general circumstances that surround him is brought about by his observance of rules which he has not designed and often does not even know explicitly, although he is able to honour them in action. Or, to put this differently, our adaptation to our environment does not consist only, and perhaps not even chiefly, in an insight into the relations between cause and effect, but also in our actions being governed by rules adapted to the kind of world in which we live, that is, to circumstances which we are not aware of and which yet determine the pattern of our successful actions. . . .

What we must ask the reader to keep constantly in mind throughout this book, then, is the fact of the necessary and irremediable ignorance on everyone's part of most of the particular facts which determine the actions of all the several members of human society. This may at first seem to be a fact so obvious and incontestable as hardly to deserve mention, and still less to require proof. Yet the result of not constantly stressing it is that it is only too readily forgotten. This is so mainly because it is a very inconvenient fact which makes both our attempts to explain and our attempts to influence intelligently the processes of society very much more difficult, and which places severe limits on what we can say or do about them. There exists therefore a great temptation, as a first approximation, to begin with the assumption that we know everything needed for full explanation or control. This provisional assumption is often treated as something of little consequence which can later be dropped without much effect on the conclusions. Yet this necessary ignorance of most of the particulars which enter the order of a Great Society is the source of the central problem of all social order and the false assumption by which it is provisionally put aside is mostly never explicitly abandoned but merely conveniently forgotten. The argument then proceeds as if that ignorance did not matter.

THE CONCEPT OF ORDER

The central concept around which the discussion of this book will turn is that of order, and particularly the distinction between two kinds of order which we will provisionally call 'made' and 'grown' orders. Order is an indispensable concept for the discussion of all complex phenomena, in which it must largely play the role the concept of law plays in the analysis of simpler phenomena. There is no adequate term other than "order' by which we can describe it, although 'system', 'structure' or 'pattern' may occasionally serve instead. The term 'order' has, of course, a long history in the social sciences, but in recent times it has generally been avoided, largely because of the ambiguity of its meaning and its frequent association with authoritarian views. We cannot do without it, however, and shall have to guard against misinterpretation by sharply defining the general sense in which we shall employ it and then clearly distinguishing between the two different ways in which such order can originate.

By 'order' we shall throughout describe *a state of affairs in which a multiplicity of elements of various kinds are so related to each other that we may learn from our acquaintance with some spatial or temporal part of the whole to form correct expectations concerning the rest, or at least expectations which have a good chance of proving correct.* It is clear that every society must in this sense possess an order and that such an order will often exist without having been deliberately created. As has been said by a distinguished social anthropologist, 'that there is some order, consistency and constancy in social life, is obvious. If there were not, none of us would be able to go about our affairs or satisfy our most elementary needs.'

Living as members of society and dependent for the satisfaction of most of our needs on various forms of co-operation with others, we depend for the effective pursuit of our aims clearly on the correspondence of the expectations concerning the actions of others on which our plans are based with what they will really do. This matching of the intentions and expectations that determine the actions of different individuals is the form in which order manifests itself in social life; and it will be the question of how such an order does come about that will be our immediate concern. The first answer to which our anthropomorphic habits of thought almost inevitably lead us is that it must be due to the design of some thinking mind. And because order has been generally interpreted as such a deliberate *arrangement* by somebody, the concept has become unpopular among most friends of liberty and has been favoured mainly by authoritarians. According to this interpretation order in society must rest on a relation of command and obedience, or a hierarchical structure of the whole of society in which the will of superiors, and ultimately of some single supreme authority, determines what each individual must do.

*The Fatal Conceit**

WAS SOCIALISM A MISTAKE?

The idea of Socialism is at once grandiose and simple. . . . We may say, in fact, that it is one of the most ambitious creations of the human spirit, . . . so magnificent, so daring, that it has rightly aroused the greatest admiration. If we wish to save the world from barbarism we have to refute Socialism, but we cannot thrust it carelessly aside.

Ludwig von Mises.

This book argues that our civilization depends, not only for its origin but also for its preservation, on what can be precisely described only as the extended order of human cooperation, an order more commonly, if somewhat misleadingly, known as capitalism. To understand our civilization, one must appreciate that the extended order resulted not from human design or intention but spontaneously: it arose from unintentionally conforming to certain traditional and largely *moral* practices, many of which men tend to dislike, whose significance they usually fail to understand, whose validity they cannot prove, and which have nonetheless fairly rapidly spread by means of an evolutionary selection—the comparative increase of population and wealth—of those groups that happened to follow them. The unwitting, reluctant, even painful adoption of these practices kept these groups together, increased their access to valuable information of all sorts, and enabled them to be 'fruitful, and multiply, and replenish the earth, and subdue it' (*Genesis* 1:28). This process is perhaps the least appreciated facet of human evolution.

Socialists take a different view of these matters. They not only differ in their conclusions, they see the facts differently. That

socialists are wrong *about the facts* is crucial to my argument, as it will unfold in the pages that follow. I am prepared to admit that if socialist analyses of the operation of the existing economic order, and of possible alternatives, were factually correct, we might be obliged to ensure that the distribution of incomes conform to certain moral principles, and that this distribution might be possible only by giving a central authority the power to direct the use of available resources, and might presuppose the abolition of individual ownership of means of production. If it were for instance true that central direction of the means of production could effect a collective product of at least the same magnitude as that which we now produce, it would indeed prove a grave moral problem how this could be done justly. This, however, is not the position in which we find ourselves. For there is no known way, other than by the distribution of products in a competitive market, to inform individuals in what direction their several efforts must aim so as to contribute as much as possible to the total product.

The main point of my argument is, then, that the conflict between, on one hand, advocates of the spontaneous extended human order created by a competitive market, and on the other hand those who demand a deliberate arrangement of human interaction by central authority based on collective command over available resources is due to a factual error by the latter about how knowledge of these resources is and can be generated and utilized. As a question of fact, this conflict must be settled by scientific study. Such study shows that, by following the spontaneously generated moral traditions underlying the competitive market order (traditions which do not satisfy the canons or norms of rationality embraced by most socialists), we generate and garner greater knowledge and wealth than could

---

*From Friedrich Hayek, *The Fatal Conceit* (1988). By permission.

ever be obtained or utilized in a centrally-directed economy whose adherents claim to proceed strictly in accordance with 'reason'. Thus socialist aims and programmes are factually impossible to achieve or execute; and they also happen, into the bargain as it were, to be logically impossible.

This is why, contrary to what is often maintained, these matters are not merely ones of differing interests or value judgements. Indeed, the question of how men came to adopt certain values or norms, and what effect these had on the evolution of their civilization, is itself above all a factual one, one that lies at the heart of the present book. The demands of socialism are not moral conclusions derived from the traditions that formed the extended order that made civilization possible. They endeavor to overthrow these traditions by a rationally designed moral system whose appeal depends on the instinctual appeal of its promised consequences. They assume that, since people had been able to *generate* some system of rules coordinating their efforts, they must also be able to *design* an even better and more gratifying system. But if humankind owes its very existence to one particular rule-guided form of conduct of proven effectiveness, it simply does not have the option of choosing another merely for the sake of the apparent pleasantness of its immediately visible effects. The dispute between the market order and socialism is no less than a matter of survival. To follow socialist morality would destroy much of present humankind and impoverish much of the rest.

II FRIEDMAN

*Capitalism and Freedom**

THE ROLE OF GOVERNMENT
IN A FREE SOCIETY

A common objection to totalitarian societies is that they regard the end as justifying the means. Taken literally, this objection is clearly illogical. If the end does not justify the means, what does? But this easy answer does not dispose of the objection; it simply shows that the objection is not well put. To deny that the end justifies the means is indirectly to assert that the end in question is not the ultimate end, that the ultimate end is itself the use of the proper means. Desirable or not, any end that can be attained only by the use of bad means must give way to the more basic end of the use of acceptable means.

To the liberal, the appropriate means are free discussion and voluntary co-operation, which implies that any form of coercion is inappropriate. The ideal is unanimity among responsible individuals achieved on the basis of free and full discussion. . . .

From this standpoint, the role of the market . . . is that it permits unanimity without conformity; that it is a system of effectively proportional representation. On the other hand, the characteristic feature of action through explicitly political channels is that it tends to require or to enforce substantial conformity. The typical issue must be decided "yes" or "no"; at most, provision can be made for a fairly limited number of alternatives. Even the use of proportional representation in its explicitly political form does

not alter this conclusion. The number of separate groups that can in fact be represented is narrowly limited, enormously so by comparison with the proportional representation of the market. More important, the fact that the final outcome generally must be a law applicable to all groups, rather than separate legislative enactments for each "party" represented, means that proportional representation in its political version, far from permitting unanimity without conformity, tends toward ineffectiveness and fragmentation. It thereby operates to destroy any consensus on which unanimity with conformity can rest.

There are clearly some matters with respect to which effective proportional representation is impossible. I cannot get the amount of national defense I want and you, a different amount. With respect to such indivisible matters we can discuss, and argue, and vote. But having decided, we must conform. It is precisely the existence of such indivisible matters—protection of the individual and the nation from coercion are clearly the most basic—that prevents exclusive reliance on individual action through the market. If we are to use some of our resources for such indivisible items, we must employ political channels to reconcile differences.

The use of political channels, while inevitable, tends to strain the social cohesion essential for a stable society. The strain is least if agreement for joint action need be reached only on a limited range of issues on which people in any event have common views. Every extension of the range of issues for which explicit agreement is sought strains further the delicate threads that hold society together. If it goes so far as to touch

---

* From Milton Friedman, *Capitalism and Freedom* (1962, 1982). By permission.

an issue on which men feel deeply yet differently, it may well disrupt the society. Fundamental differences in basic values can seldom if ever be resolved at the ballot box; ultimately they can only be decided, though not resolved, by conflict. The religious and civil wars of history are a bloody testament to this judgment.

The widespread use of the market reduces the strain on the social fabric by rendering conformity unnecessary with respect to any activities it encompasses. The wider the range of activities covered by the market, the fewer are the issues on which explicitly political decisions are required and hence on which it is necessary to achieve agreement. In turn, the fewer the issues on which agreement is necessary, the greater is the likelihood of getting agreement while maintaining a free society.

Unanimity is, of course, an ideal. In practice, we can afford neither the time nor the effort that would be required to achieve complete unanimity on every issue. We must perforce accept something less. We are thus led to accept majority rule in one form or another as an expedient. That majority rule is an expedient rather than itself a basic principle is clearly shown by the fact that our willingness to resort to majority rule, and the size of the majority we require, themselves depend on the seriousness of the issue involved. If the matter is of little moment and the minority has no strong feelings about being overruled, a bare plurality will suffice. One the other hand, is the minority feels strongly about the issue involved, even a bare majority will not do. Few of us would be willing to have issues of free speech, for example, decided by a bare majority. Our legal structure is full of such distinctions among kinds of issues that require different kinds of majorities. At the extreme are those issues embodied in the Constitution. These are the principles that are so important that we are willing to make minimal concessions to expediency. Something like essential consensus was achieved initially in accepting them, and we require something like essential consensus for a change in them.

The self-denying ordinance to refrain from majority rule on certain kinds of issues that is embodied in our Constitution and in similar written or unwritten constitutions elsewhere, and the specific provisions in these constitutions or their equivalents prohibiting coercion of individuals, are themselves to be regarded as reached by free discussion and as reflecting essential unanimity about means.

I turn now to consider more specifically, though still in very broad terms, what the areas are that cannot be handled through the market at all, or can be handled only at so great a cost that the use of political channels may be preferable.

GOVERNMENT AS RULE-MAKER AND UMPIRE

It is important to distinguish the day-to-day activities of people from the general customary and legal framework within which these take place. The day-to-day activities are like the actions of the participants in a game when they are playing it; the framework, like the rules of the game they play. And just as a good game requires acceptance by the players both of the rules and of the umpire to interpret and enforce them, so a good society requires that its members agree on the general conditions that will govern relations among them, on some means of arbitrating different interpretations of these conditions, and on some device for enforcing compliance with the generally accepted rules. As in games, so also in society, most of the general conditions are the unintended outcome of custom, accepted unthinkingly. At most, we consider explicitly only minor modifications in them, though the cumulative effect of a series of minor modifications may be a drastic alteration in the character of the game or of the society. In both games and society also, no set of rules can prevail unless most participants most of the time conform to them without external sanctions; unless that is, there is a broad underlying social consensus. But we cannot rely on custom or on this consensus alone to interpret and to enforce the rules; we need an umpire. These then are the basic roles of government in a free society: to provide a means whereby we can modify the rules, to mediate differences among us on the meaning of the rules, and to enforce compliance with the rules on the part of those few who would otherwise not play the game.

The need for government in these respects arises because absolute freedom is impossible. However attractive anarchy may be as a philosophy, it is not feasible in a world of imperfect men. Men's freedoms can conflict, and when they do, one man's freedom must be limited to preserve another's—as a Supreme Court Justice once put it, "My freedom to move my fist must be limited by the proximity of your chin."

The major problem in deciding the appropriate activities of government is how to resolve such conflicts among the freedoms of different individuals. In some cases, the answer is easy. There is little difficulty in attaining near unanimity to the proposition that one man's freedom to murder his neighbor must be sacrificed to preserve the freedom of the other man to live. In other cases, the answer is difficult. In the economic area, a major problem arises in respect of the conflict between freedom to combine and freedom to compete. What meaning is to be attributed to "free" as modifying "enterprise"? In the United States, "free" has been understood to mean that anyone is free to set up an enterprise, which means that existing enterprises are not free to keep out competitors except by selling a better product at the same price or the same product at a lower price. In the continental tradition, on the other hand, the meaning has generally been that enterprises are free to do what they want, including the fixing of prices, division of markets, and the adoption of other techniques to keep out potential competitors. Perhaps the most difficult specific problem in this area arises with respect to combinations among laborers, where the problem of freedom to combine and freedom to compete is particularly acute.

A still more basic economic area in which the answer is both difficult and important is the definition of property rights. The notion of property, as it has developed over centuries and as it is embodied in our legal codes, has become so much a part of us that we tend to take it for granted, and fail to recognize the extent to which just what constitutes property and what rights the ownership of property confers are complex social creations rather than self-evident propositions. Does my having title to land, for example, and my freedom to use my property as I wish, permit me to deny to someone else the right to fly over my land in his airplane?

Or does his right to use his airplane take precedence? Or does this depend on how high he flies? Or how much noise he makes? Does voluntary exchange require that he pay me for the privilege of flying over my land? Or that I must pay him to refrain from flying over it? The mere mention of royalties, copyrights, patents; shares of stock in corporations; riparian rights, and the like, may perhaps emphasize the role of generally accepted social rules in the very definition of property. It may suggest also that, in many cases, the existence of a well specified and generally accepted definition of property is far more important than just what the definition is.

Another economic area that arises particularly difficult problems is the monetary system. Government responsibility for the monetary system has long been recognized. It is explicitly provided for in the constitutional provision which gives Congress the power "to coin money, regulate the value thereof, and of foreign coin." There is probably no other area of economic activity with respect to which government action has been so uniformly accepted. This habitual and by now almost unthinking acceptance of governmental responsibility makes thorough understanding of the grounds for such responsibility all the more necessary, since it enhances the danger that the scope of government will spread from activities that are, to those that are not, appropriate in a free society, from providing a monetary framework to determining the allocation of resources among individuals. . . .

In summary, the organization of voluntary exchange presumes that we have provided, through government, for the maintenance of law and order to prevent coercion of one individual by another, the enforcement of contracts voluntarily entered into, the definition of the meaning of property rights, the interpretation and enforcement of such rights, and the provision of a monetary framework.

MONOPOLY AND NEIGHBORHOOD EFFECTS

The role of government just considered is to do something that the market cannot do for itself, namely, to determine, arbitrate and enforce the rules of the game. We may also want to do through government some things that might conceivably be done through the market but that technical or similar conditions render it difficult to do in that way. These all reduce to cases in which strictly voluntary exchange is either exceedingly costly or practically impossible. There are two general classes of such cases: monopoly and similar market imperfections, and neighborhood effects.

Exchange is truly voluntary only when nearly equivalent alternatives exist. Monopoly implies the absence of alternatives and thereby inhibits effective freedom of exchange. In practice, monopoly frequently, if not generally, arises from government support or from collusive agreements among individuals. With respect to these, the problem is either to avoid governmental fostering of monopoly or to stimulate the effective enforcement of rules such as those embodied in our anti-trust laws. However, monopoly may also arise because it is technically efficient to have a single producer or enterprise. I venture to suggest that such cases are more limited than is supposed but they unquestionably do arise. A simply example is perhaps the provision of telephone services within a community. I shall refer to such cases as "technical" monopoly.

When technical conditions make a monopoly the natural outcome of competitive market forces, there are only three alternatives that seem available: private monopoly, public monopoly, or public regulation. All three are bad so we must choose among evils. Henry Simons, observing public regulation of monopoly in the United States, found the results so distasteful that he concluded public monopoly would be a lesser evil. Walter Eucken, a noted German liberal, observing public monopoly in German railroads, found the results so distasteful that he concluded public regulation would be a lesser evil. Having learned from both, I reluctantly conclude that, if tolerable, private monopoly may be the least of the evils.

If society were static so that the conditions which give rise to a technical monopoly were sure to remain, I would have little confidence in this solution. In a rapidly changing society, however, the conditions making for technical monopoly frequently change and I suspect that both public regulation and public monopoly are likely to be less responsive to such changes in condi-

tions, to be less readily capable of elimination, than private monopoly.

Railroads in the United States are an excellent example. A large degree of monopoly in railroads was perhaps inevitable on technical grounds in the nineteenth century. This was the justification for the Interstate Commerce Commission. But conditions have changed. The emergence of road and air transport has reduced the monopoly element in railroads to negligible proportions. Yet we have not eliminated the ICC. On the contrary, the ICC, which started out as an agency to protect the public from exploitation by the railroads, has become an agency to protect railroads from competition by trucks and other means of transport, and more recently even to protect existing truck companies from competition by new entrants. Similarly, in England, when the railroads were nationalized, trucking was at first brought into the state monopoly. If railroads had never been subjected to regulation in the United States, it is nearly certain that by now transportation, including railroads, would be a highly competitive industry with little or no remaining monopoly elements.

The choice between the evils of private monopoly, public monopoly, and public regulation cannot, however, be made once and for all, independently of the factual circumstances. If the technical monopoly is of a service of commodity that is regarded as essential and if its monopoly power is sizable, even the short-run effects of private unregulated monopoly may not be tolerable, and either public regulation or ownership may be a lesser evil.

Technical monopoly may on occasion justify a *de facto* public monopoly. It cannot by itself justify a public monopoly achieved by making it illegal for anyone else to compete. For example, there is no way to justify our present public monopoly of the post office. It may be argued that the carrying of mail is a technical monopoly and that a government monopoly is the least of evils. Along these lines, one could perhaps justify a government post office but not the present law, which makes it illegal for anybody else to carry mail. If the delivery of mail is a technical monopoly, no one will be able to succeed in competition with the government. If it is not, there is no reason why the government should be engaged in it. The only way to find out is to leave other people free to enter.

The historical reason why we have a post office monopoly is because the Pony Express did such a good job of carrying the mail across the continent that, when the government introduced transcontinental service, it couldn't compete effectively and lost money. The result was a law making it illegal for anybody else to carry the mail. That is why the Adams Express Company is an investment trust today instead of an operating company. I conjecture that if entry into the mail-carrying business were open to all, there would be a large number of firms entering it and this archaic industry would become revolutionized in short order.

A second general class of cases in which strictly voluntary exchange is impossible arises when actions of individuals have effects on other individuals for which it is not feasible to charge or recompense them. This is the problem of "neighborhood effects." An obvious example is the pollution of a stream. The man who pollutes a stream is in effect forcing others to exchange good water for bad. These others might be willing to make the exchange at a price. But it is not feasible for them, acting individually, to avoid the exchange or to enforce appropriate compensation.

A less obvious example is the provision of highways. In this case, it is technically possible to identify and hence charge individuals for their use of the roads and so to have private operation. However, for general access roads, involving many points of entry and exit, the costs of collection would be extremely high if a charge were to be made for the specific services received by each individual, because of the necessity of establishing toll booths or the equivalent at all entrances. The gasoline tax is a much cheaper method of charging individuals roughly in proportion to their use of the roads. This method, however, is one in which the particular payment cannot be identified closely with the particular use. Hence, it is hardly feasible to have private enterprise provide the service and collect the charge without establishing extensive private monopoly.

These considerations do not apply to long-distance turnpikes with high density of traffic and limited access. For these, the costs of collection are small and in many cases are now being paid, and there are often numerous alternatives, so that there is no serious monopoly problem. Hence, there is every reason why these should be privately owned and operated. If so owned and operated, the enterprise running the highway should receive the gasoline taxes paid on account of travel on it.

Parks are an interesting example because they illustrate the difference between cases that can and cases that cannot be justified by neighborhood effects, and because almost everyone at first sight regards the conduct of National Parks as obviously a valid function of government. In fact, however, neighborhood effects may justify a city park; they do not justify a national park, like Yellowstone National Park or the Grand Canyon. What is the fundamental difference between the two? For the city park, it is extremely difficult to identify the people who benefit from it and to charge them for the benefits which they receive. If there is a park in the middle of the city, the houses on all sides get the benefit of the open space, and people who walk through it or by it also benefit. To maintain toll collectors at the gates or to impose annual charges per window overlooking the park would be very expensive and difficult. The entrances to a national park like Yellowstone, on the other hand, are few; most of the people who come stay for a considerable period of time and it is perfectly feasible to set up toll gates and collect admission charges. This is indeed now done, though the charges do not cover the whole costs. If the public wants this kind of an activity enough to pay for it, private enterprises will have every incentive to provide such parks. And, of course, there are many private enterprises of this nature now in existence. I cannot myself conjure up any neighborhood effects or important monopoly effects that would justify governmental activity in this area.

Considerations like those I have treated under the heading of neighborhood effects have been used to rationalize almost every conceivable intervention. In many instances, however, this rationalization is special pleading rather than a legitimate application of the concept of neighborhood effects.

Neighborhood effects cut both ways. They can be a reason for limiting the activities of government as well as for expanding them. Neighborhood effects impede voluntary exchange because it is difficult to identify the effects on third parties and to measure their magnitude; but this difficulty is present in governmental activity as well. It is hard to know when neighborhood effects are sufficiently large to justify particular costs in overcoming them and even harder to distribute the costs in an appropriate fashion. Consequently, when government engages in activities to overcome neighborhood effects, it will in part introduce an additional set of neighborhood effects by failing to charge or to compensate individuals properly. Whether the original or the new neighborhood effects are the more serious can only be judged by the facts of the individual case, and even then, only very approximately. Furthermore, the use of government to overcome neighborhood effects itself has an extremely important neighborhood effect which is unrelated to the particular occasion for government action. Every act of government intervention limits the area of individual freedom directly and threatens the preservation of freedom indirectly. . . .

Our principles offer no hard and fast line how far it is appropriate to use government to accomplish jointly what it is difficult or impossible for us to accomplish separately through strictly voluntary exchange. In any particular case of proposed intervention, we must make up a balance sheet, listing separately the advantages and disadvantages. Our principles tell us what items to put on the one side and what items on the other and they give us some basis for attaching importance to the different items. In particular, we shall always want to enter on the liability side of any proposed government intervention, its neighborhood effect in threatening freedom, and give this effect considerable weight. Just how much weight to give to it, as to other items, depends upon the circumstances. If, for example, existing government intervention is minor, we shall attach a smaller weight to the negative effects of additional government intervention. This is an important reason why many earlier liberals, like Henry Simons, writing at a time when government was small by today's standards,

were willing to have government undertake activities that today's liberals would not accept now that government has become so overgrown.

ACTION THROUGH GOVERNMENT ON PATERNALISTIC GROUNDS

Freedom is a tenable objective only for responsible individuals. We do not believe in freedom for madmen or children. The necessity of drawing a line between responsible individuals and others is inescapable, yet it means that there is an essential ambiguity in our ultimate objective of freedom. Paternalism is inescapable for those whom we designate as not responsible.

The clearest case, perhaps, is that of madmen. We are willing neither to permit them freedom nor to shoot them. It would be nice if we could rely on voluntary activities of individuals to house and care for the madmen. But I think we cannot rule out the possibility that such charitable activities will be inadequate, if only because of the neighborhood effect involved in the fact that I benefit if another man contributes to the care of the insane. For this reason, we may be willing to arrange for their care through government.

Children offer a more difficult case. The ultimate operative unit in our society is the family, not the individual. Yet the acceptance of the family as the unit rests in considerable part on expediency rather than principle. We believe that parents are generally best able to protect their children and to provide for their development into responsible individuals for whom freedom is appropriate. But we do not believe in the freedom of parents to do what they will with other people. The children are responsible individuals in embryo, and a believer in freedom believes in protecting their ultimate rights.

To put this in a different and what may seem a more callous way, children are at one and the same time consumer goods and potentially responsible members of society. The freedom of individuals to use their economic resources as they want includes the freedom to use them to have children—to buy, as it were, the services of children as a particular form of consumption. But once this choice is exercised, the children have a value in and of themselves and have a freedom of their own that is not simply an extension of the freedom of the parents.

The paternalistic ground for governmental activity is in many ways the most troublesome to a liberal; for it involves the acceptance of a principle—that some shall decide for others—which he finds objectionable in most applications and which he rightly regards as a hallmark of his chief intellectual opponents, the proponents of collectivism in one or another of its guises, whether it be communism, socialism, or a welfare state. Yet there is no use pretending that problems are simpler than in fact they are. There is no avoiding the need for some measure of paternalism. As Dicey wrote in 1914 about an act for the protection of mental defectives, "The Mental Deficiency Act is the first step along a path on which no sane man can decline to enter, but which, if too far pursued, will bring statesmen across difficulties hard to meet without considerable interference with individual liberty."[1] There is no formula that can tell us where to stop. We must rely on our fallible judgment and, having reached a judgment, on our ability to persuade our fellow men that it is a correct judgment, or their ability to persuade us to modify our views. We must put our faith, here as elsewhere, in a consensus reached by imperfect and biased men through free discussion and trial and error.

CONCLUSION

A government which maintained law and order, defined property rights, served as a means whereby we could modify property rights and other rules of the economic game, adjudicated disputes about the interpretation of the rules, enforced contracts, promoted competition, provided a monetary framework, engaged in activities to counter technical monopolies and to overcome neighborhood effects widely regarded as sufficiently important to justify government intervention, and which supplemented private charity and the private

---

[1] A. V. Dicey, *Lectures on the Relation between Law and Public Opinion in England during the Nineteenth Century* (2d. ed.; London: Macmillan & Co., 1914), p. li.

family in protecting the irresponsible, whether madman or child—such a government would clearly have important functions to perform. The consistent liberal is not an anarchist.

Yet it is also true that such a government would have clearly limited functions and would refrain from a host of activities that are now undertaken by federal and state governments in the United States, and their counterparts in other Western countries. Succeeding chapters will deal in some detail with some of these activities, and a few have been discussed above, but it may help to give a sense of proportion about the role that a liberal would assign government simply to list, in closing this chapter, some activities currently undertaken by government in the U.S., that cannot, so far as I can see, validly be justified in terms of the principles outlined above:

1. Parity price support programs for agriculture.
2. Tariffs on imports or restrictions on exports, such as current oil import quotas, sugar quotas, etc.
3. Governmental control of output, such as through the farm program, or through pro-rationing of oil as is done by the Texas Railroad Commission.
4. Rent control, such as is still practiced in New York, or more general price and wage controls such as were imposed during and just after World War II.
5. Legal minimum wage rates, or legal maximum prices, such as the legal maximum of zero on the rate of interest that can be paid on demand deposits by commercial banks, or the legally fixed maximum rates that can be paid on savings and time deposits.
6. Detailed regulation of industries, such as the regulation of transportation by the Interstate Commerce Commission. This had some justification on technical monopoly grounds when initially introduced for railroads; it has none now for any means of transport. Another example is detailed regulation of banking.
7. A similar example, but one which deserves special mention because of its implicit censorship and violation of free speech, is the control of radio and television by the Federal Communications Commission.

8. Present social security programs, especially the old-age and retirement programs compelling people in effect (*a*) to spend a specified fraction of their income on the purchase of retirement annuity, (*b*) to buy the annuity from a publicly operated enterprise.

9. Licensure provisions in various cities and states which restrict particular enterprises or occupations or professions to people who have a license, where the license is more than a receipt for a tax which anyone who wishes to enter the activity may pay.

10. So-called "public-housing" and the host of other subsidy programs directed at fostering residential construction such as F.H.A. and V.A. guarantee of mortgage, and the like.

11. Conscription to man the military services in peacetime. The appropriate free market arrangement is volunteer military forces; which is to say, hiring men to serve. There is no justification for not paying whatever price is necessary to attract the required number of men. Present arrangements are inequitable and arbitrary, seriously interfere with the freedom of young men to shape their lives, and probably are even more costly than the market alternative. (Universal military training to provide a reserve for war time is a different problem and may be justified on liberal grounds.)

12. National parks, as noted above.

13. The legal prohibition on the carrying of mail for profit.

14. Publicly owned and operated toll roads, as noted above.

This list is far from comprehensive.

CHAPTER THIRTY-SEVEN

BERLIN

Almost a century after Mill's *On Liberty* came "Two Concepts of Liberty," by Sir Isaiah Berlin (1909–1997). A twentieth century classic in the language of liberty, and much shorter than *On Liberty,* Berlin's essay examines one of a free society's continuing issues—the proper boundaries between the discretion and freedom of the individual and the needs and demands of society particularly in social and economic matters. Berlin was one of the twentieth century's greatest essayists. Born in Latvia, he emigrated to Great Britain in 1921. He was accomplished in philosophy, history, literature, and Russian thought, and was a great conversationalist. After moving to England, he became a student at Oxford, where he remained almost the rest of his life.

The work for which he is and will be most remembered is the 1958 lecture "Two Concepts of Liberty." Berlin forcefully defines these two perspectives: the first, the negative concept that political freedom is the absence in a political society of the arbitrary will of another; the second, the positive concept that political freedom is a certain standard of living and the opportunity to maximize one's lifetime opportunities and accomplishments.

To some, the question of political liberty thus merely is a semantic question—more a philosopher's quibble than a real, live issue. Political liberty in a negative sense is desirable, and a high standard of living and "self-actualization" are desirable. If they are separate ends, simply call them such and be done with it. The issue of liberty is much more important than mere definition, however. The varying concepts of political liberty enlighten whole outlooks of the ways societies do and should run.

Berlin often has been misconstrued as a partisan of negative liberty, which he was not. He believes in a plurality of diverse social ends which are not necessarily reconcilable. In "Two Concepts of Liberty," he remarks against "the natural tendency of all but a very few thinkers to believe that all the things they hold good must be intimately connected, or at least compatible, with one another." He is for negative liberty, but he also favors positive liberty and thinks there is tension between the two. He does not look forward to a political utopia within which all of humanity's issues might be resolved, but—to the extent he was interested in practical political outcomes—he sought the most workable systems for producing varieties of ends. He was within the broad stream of twentieth century democratic interventionist welfare state capitalism.

He occasionally took umbrage at being mistaken for a partisan of negative liberty or libertarianism, and in part because he was not especially interested in non-academic affairs and never wrote a sustained treatise of his ideas, he often is misunderstood on the basis of "Two Concepts of Liberty." This work's greatness stems from the crystalline presentation of the two perspectives, and from his presentation it often is assumed that Berlin gave his allegiance to negative freedom. This is not so. He wrote in 1969 in introducing republication of the work: "Belief in negative freedom is compatible with, and (so far as ideas influence conduct) has played its part in, generating great and lasting social evils. . . . The bloodstained story of economic individualism and unrestrained capitalist competition does not, I should have thought, today need stressing." He added in 1992: "The only reason for which I have been suspected of defending negative liberty against positive and saying that it is more civilized is that I do think that the concept of positive liberty, which is of course essential to a decent existence, has been more often abused or perverted than that of negative liberty. . . . Certainly the weak must be protected against the strong. . . . Negative liberty must be curtailed if positive liberty is to be sufficiently realized; there must be a balance between the two, about which no clear principles can be enunciated."

Negative liberty, in Berlin's terminology, is "freedom from." It is freedom from others' coercive involvement in one's life. Positive freedom, on the other hand, is "freedom to." It is the meaningful ability to become one's highest and best self. A problem arises when these two senses of freedom are conflated, a question Berlin really does not address. When political freedom becomes defined as self-actualization or self-realization, then the freedom-maximizing political regime has considerable discretion. By contrast, a political system emphasizing negative liberty places more considerable restraints upon government actions. As Berlin notes in "Two Concepts of Liberty," a positive conception of freedom "renders it easy for me to conceive of myself as coercing others for their own sake, in their, not my, interest. I am then claiming that I know what they truly need better than they know it themselves. . . . But I may go on to claim a good deal more than this. I may declare that they are actually aiming at what in their benighted state they consciously resist . . ."

Berlin does not explicitly consider the welfare state in "Two Concepts of Liberty." One usually is uncertain in his work what the practical outcomes of his ideas would be, or what he intended these to be. At the same time, his pluralistic liberalism provides a basis for policies that have characterized most developed democratic nations during the postwar era.

Certainly a principal idea among most democratic nations during the past half-century is the vital importance of freedom of speech. This freedom largely separated western nations from the Soviet Union during the Cold War. The negative concept of liberty inextricably is tied to free speech, for if the essential idea of negative liberty is that individuals should be able to do as they wish as long as they do no harm to others—if this does not apply to speech, to what else can it pertain? What intrinsically is less harmful than sounds in the air or marks on paper? If people are not permitted to disseminate ideas, they hardly can be said to be free of others' coercive interference.

Berlin's idea of a multiplicity of desirable social ends that are not necessarily reconcilable is compatible with an idea of modern government that does not see it as optimal for government to be controlled by one philosophical or ideological system. It instead is desirable that there are many competing interests and views within a society, and that none of these becomes all-dominating. The result may be a society that is less philosophically tidy, but more desirable in which to live. Pluralism was a defining idea in American political ideology especially during the 1950s and 1960s, and to some extent has evolved into the current emphasis upon diversity. The idea of pluralism includes that there is and should be sub-groups within a community that only are quasi-governmental, if governmental at all. Pluralism is a factual and normative way of regarding human communities.

Berlin was at his best when in "Two Concepts of Liberty" he defined negative and positive liberty:

> I am normally said to be free to the degree to which no man or body of men interferes with my activity. Political liberty in this sense is simply the area within which a man can act unobstructed by others. . . . You lack political liberty or freedom only if you are prevented from attaining a goal by human beings. Mere incapacity to attain a goal is not lack of political freedom. . . .
>
> The 'positive' sense of the word 'liberty' derives from the wish on the part of the individual to be his own master. I wish my life and decisions to depend on myself . . . I wish to be the instrument of my own . . . acts of will. . . . I wish to be . . . a doer—deciding, . . . self-directed.

The positive conception of liberty often has provided a philosophical justification for expansion of government. It is by educating people, by providing housing, jobs, medical care, and so forth that individuals can become autonomous human beings. Until the material basics are met, talk of humanity reaching higher levels is just this—talk. Berlin sagely observes in "Two Concepts of Liberty," however, that the notion of positive liberty often has been misused "to justify the coercion of some men by others in order to raise them to a 'higher' level of freedom . . .

Democracy, Winston Churchill thought, is "the worst form of government excepting all the others." As long as democracy characterizes political systems, there will be Berlinian multiplicity of ends and logically irreconcilable government services and activities. Another essay for which Berlin is well-known is "The Hedgehog and the Fox" (1953). He here discusses the distinction drawn by the Greek poet Archilochus between the fox who knows many things and the hedgehog who knows one big thing. Berlin saw himself as a philosophical fox, recognizing multiplicity of social ends and values, and unfavorably compares the hedgehog-like philosopher believing in the unity of knowledge to the fox. His writings are suggestive and stimulating, and require and inform considerable background in democratic liberalism.

BERLIN

Two Concepts of Liberty

I

To coerce a man is to deprive him of freedom—freedom from what? Almost every moralist in human history has praised freedom. Like happiness and goodness, like nature and reality, it is a term whose meaning is so porous that there is little interpretation that it seems able to resist. I do not propose to discuss either the history of this protean word or the more than two hundred senses of it recorded by historians of ideas. I propose to examine no more than two of these senses—but they are central ones, with a great deal of human history behind them, and, I dare say, still to come. The first of these political senses of freedom or liberty (I shall use both words to mean the same), which (following much precedent) I shall call the 'negative' sense, is involved in the answer to the question 'What is the area within which the subject—a person or group of persons—is or should be left to do or be what he is able to do or be, without interference by other persons?' The second, which I shall call the 'positive' sense, is involved in the answer to the question 'What, or who, is the source of control or interference that can determine someone to do, or be, this rather than that?' The two questions are clearly different, even though the answers to them may overlap.

THE NOTION OF NEGATIVE FREEDOM

I am normally said to be free to the degree to which no man or body of men interferes with my activity. Political liberty in this sense is simply the area within which a man can act unobstructed by others. If I am prevented by others from doing what I could otherwise do, I am to that degree unfree; and if this area is contracted by other men beyond a certain minimum, I can be described as being coerced, or, it may be, enslaved. Coercion is not, however, a term that covers every form of inability. If I say that I am unable to jump more than ten feet in the air, or cannot read because I am blind, or cannot understand the darker pages of Hegel, it would be eccentric to say that I am to that degree enslaved or coerced. Coercion implies the deliberate interference of other human beings within the area in which I could otherwise act. You lack political liberty or freedom only if you are prevented from attaining a goal by human beings.[1] Mere incapacity to attain a goal is not lack of political freedom.[2] This is brought out by the use of such modern expressions as 'economic freedom' and its counterpart, 'economic slavery'. It is argued, very plausibly, that if a man is too poor to afford something on which there is no legal ban—a loaf of bread, a journey round the world, recourse to the law courts—he is as little free to have it as he would be if it were forbidden him by law. If my poverty were a kind of disease which prevented me from buying bread, or paying for the journey round the world or getting my case heard, as lameness prevents me from running, this inability would not naturally be described as a lack of freedom,

---

[1] I do not, of course, mean to imply the truth of the converse.

[2] Helvétius made this point very clearly: 'The free man is the man who is not in irons, not imprisoned in a gaol, nor terrorised like a slave by the fear of punishment.' It is not lack of freedom not to fly like an eagle or swim like a whale. *De l'esprit*, first discourse, chapter 4.

least of all political freedom. It is only because I believe that my inability to get a given thing is due to the fact that other human beings have made arrangements whereby I am, whereas others are not, prevented from having enough money with which to pay for it, that I think myself a victim of coercion or slavery. In other words, this use of the term depends on a particular social and economic theory about the causes of my poverty or weakness. If my lack of material means is due to my lack of mental or physical capacity, then I begin to speak of being deprived of freedom (and not simply about poverty) only if I accept the theory.[3] If, in addition, I believe that I am being kept in want by a specific arrangement which I consider unjust or unfair, I speak of economic slavery or oppression. The nature of things does not madden us, only ill will does, said Rousseau.[4] The criterion of oppression is the part that I believe to be played by other human beings, directly or indirectly, with or without the intention of doing so, in frustrating my wishes. By being free in this sense I mean not being interfered with by others. The wider the area of non-interference the wider my freedom.

This is what the classical English political philosophers meant when they used this word.[5] They disagreed about how wide the area could or should be. They supposed that it could not, as things were, be unlimited, because if it were, it would entail a state in which all men could boundlessly interfere with all other men; and this kind of 'natural' freedom would lead to social chaos in which men's minimum needs would not be satisfied; or else the liberties of the weak would be suppressed by the strong. Because they perceived that human purposes and activities do not automatically harmonise with one another, and because (whatever their official doctrines) they put high value on other goals, such as justice, or happiness, or culture, or security, or varying degrees of equality, they were prepared to curtail freedom in the interests of other values and, indeed, of freedom itself. For, without this, it was impossible to create the kind of association that they thought desirable. Consequently, it is assumed by these thinkers that the area of men's free action must be limited by law. But equally it is assumed, especially by such libertarians as Locke and Mill in England, and Constant and Tocqueville in France, that there ought to exist a certain minimum area of personal freedom which must on no account be violated; for if it is overstepped, the individual will find himself in an area too narrow for even that minimum development of his natural faculties which alone makes it possible to pursue, and even to conceive, the various ends which men hold good or right or sacred. It follows that a frontier must be drawn between the area of private life and that of public authority. Where it is to be drawn is a matter of argument, indeed of haggling. Men are largely interdependent, and no man's activity is so completely private as never to obstruct the lives of others in any way. 'Freedom for the pike is death for the minnows';[6] the liberty of some must depend on the restraint of others. Freedom for an Oxford don, others have been known to add, is a very different thing from freedom for an Egyptian peasant.

This proposition derives its force from something that is both true and important, but the phrase itself remains a piece of political claptrap. It is true that to offer political rights, or safeguards against intervention by the State, to men who are half-naked, illiterate, underfed and diseased is to mock their condition; they need medical help or education before they can understand, or make use of, an increase in

---

[3] The Marxist conception of social laws is, of course, the best-known version of this theory, but it forms a large element in some Christian and utilitarian, and all socialist, doctrines.

[4] *Émile*, book 2: p. 320 in *Oeuvres complètes*, ed. Bernard Gagnebin and others (Paris, 1959–   ). vol. 4.

[5] 'A free man', said Hobbes, 'is he that . . . is not hindered to do what he has a will to.' *Leviathan*, chapter 21: p. 146 in Richard Tuck's edition (Cambridge, 1991). Law is always a fetter, even if it protects you from being bound in chains that are heavier than those of the law, say some more repressive law or custom, or arbitrary despotism or chaos. Bentham says much the same.

[6] R. H. Tawney, *Equality* (1931), 3rd ed. (London, 1938), chapter 5, section 2, 'Equality and Liberty', p. 208 (not in previous editions).

their freedom. What is freedom to those who cannot make use of it? Without adequate conditions for the use of freedom, what is the value of freedom? First things come first: there are situations in which—to use a saying satirically attributed to the nihilists by Dostoevsky—boots are superior to Pushkin; individual freedom is not everyone's primary need. For freedom is not the mere absence of frustration of whatever kind; this would inflate the meaning of the word until it meant too much or too little. The Egyptian peasant needs clothes or medicine before, and more than, personal liberty, but the minimum freedom that he needs today, and the greater degree of freedom that he may need tomorrow, is not some species of freedom peculiar to him, but identical with that of professors, artists and millionaires.

What troubles the consciences of Western liberals is, I think, the belief, not that the freedom that men seek differs according to their social or economic conditions, but that the minority who possess it have gained it by exploiting, or, at least, averting their gaze from, the vast majority who do not. They believe, with good reason, that if individual liberty is an ultimate end for human beings, none should be deprived of it by others; least of all that some should enjoy it at the expense of others. Equality of liberty; not to treat others as I should not wish them to treat me; repayment of my debt to those who alone have made possible my liberty or prosperity or enlightenment; justice, in its simplest and most universal sense—these are the foundations of liberal morality. Liberty is not the only goal of men. I can, like the Russian critic Belinsky, say that if others are to be deprived of it—if my brothers are to remain in poverty, squalor and chains—then I do not want it for myself, I reject it with both hands and infinitely prefer to share their fate. But nothing is gained by a confusion of terms. To avoid glaring inequality or widespread misery I am ready to sacrifice some, or all, of my freedom: I may do so willingly and freely; but it is freedom that I am giving up for the sake of justice or equality or the love of my fellow men. I should be guilt-stricken, and rightly so, if I were not, in some circumstances, ready to make this sacrifice. But a sacrifice is not an increase in what is being sacrificed, namely freedom, however great the moral need or the compensation for it. Everything is what it is: liberty is liberty, not equality or fairness or justice or culture, or human happiness or a quiet conscience. If the liberty of myself or my class or nation depends on the misery of a number of other human beings, the system which promotes this is unjust and immoral. But if I curtail or lose my freedom in order to lessen the shame of such inequality, and do not thereby materially increase the individual liberty of others, an absolute loss of liberty occurs. This may be compensated for by a gain in justice or in happiness or in peace, but the loss remains, and it is a confusion of values to say that although my 'liberal', individual freedom may go by the board, some other kind of freedom—'social' or 'economic'—is increased. Yet it remains true that the freedom of some must at times be curtailed to secure the freedom of others. Upon what principle should this be done? If freedom is a sacred, untouchable value, there can be no such principle. One or other of these conflicting rules or principles must, at any rate in practice, yield: not always for reasons which can be clearly stated, let alone generalised into rules or universal maxims. Still, a practical compromise has to be found.

Philosophers with an optimistic view of human nature and a belief in the possibility of harmonising human interests, such as Locke or Adam Smith or, in some moods, Mill, believed that social harmony and progress were compatible with reserving a large area for private life over which neither the State nor any other authority must be allowed to trespass. Hobbes, and those who agreed with him, especially conservative or reactionary thinkers, argued that if men were to be prevented from destroying one another and making social life a jungle or a wilderness, greater safeguards must be instituted to keep them in their places; he wished correspondingly to increase the area of centralised control and decrease that of the individual. But both sides agreed that some portion of human existence must remain independent of the sphere of social control. To invade that preserve, however small, would be despotism. The most eloquent of all defenders of freedom and privacy, Benjamin Constant, who had not forgotten the Jacobin dictatorship, declared that at the very least the liberty of religion, opinion, expression, property must be guaranteed against arbitrary invasion. Jefferson, Burke, Paine, Mill compiled different catalogues of individual liberties, but the argument for keeping authority at bay is always substantially the same. We must preserve a minimum area of personal freedom if we are not to 'degrade or deny our nature'.[7] We cannot remain absolutely free, and must give up some of our liberty to preserve the rest. But total self-surrender is self-defeating. What then must the minimum be? That which a man cannot give up without offending against the essence of his human nature. What is this essence? What are the standards which it entails? This has been, and perhaps always will be, a matter of infinite debate. But whatever the principle in terms of which the area of non-interference is to be drawn, whether it is that of natural law or natural rights, or of utility, or the pronouncements of a categorical imperative, or the sanctity of the social contract, or any other concept with which men have sought to clarify and justify their convictions, liberty in this sense means liberty *from;* absence of interference beyond the shifting, but always recognisable, frontier. 'The only freedom which deserves the name, is that of pursuing our own good in our own way', said the most celebrated of its champions.[8] If this is so, is compulsion ever justified? Mill had no doubt that it was. Since justice demands that all individuals be entitled to a minimum of freedom, all other individuals were of necessity to be restrained, if need be by force, from depriving anyone of it. Indeed, the whole function of law was the prevention of just such collisions: the State was reduced to what Lassalle contemptuously described as the functions of a night-watchman or traffic policeman.

What made the protection of individual liberty so sacred to Mill? In his famous essay he declares that, unless the individual is left to live as he wishes in the 'the part [of his conduct] which merely concerns himself',[9] civilisation cannot advance; the truth will not, for lack of a free market in ideas, come to light; there will be no scope for spontaneity, originality, genius, for mental energy, for moral courage. Society will be crushed by the weight of 'collective mediocrity'.[10] Whatever is rich and diversified will be crushed by the weight of custom, by men's constant tendency to conformity, which breeds only 'withered' capacities, 'pinched and hidebound', 'cramped and dwarfed' human beings. 'Pagan self-assertion' is as worthy as 'Christian self-denial'.[11] 'All errors which [a man] is likely to commit against advice and warning, are far outweighed by the evil of allowing others to constrain him to what they deem his good.'[12] The defence of liberty consists in the 'negative' goal of warding off interference. To threaten a man with persecution unless he submits to a life in which he exercises no choices of his goals; to block before him every door but one, no matter how noble the prospect upon which it opens, or how benevolent the motives of those who arrange this, is to sin against the truth that he is a man, a being with a life of his own to live. This is liberty as it has been conceived by liberals in the modern world from the days of Erasmus (some would say of Occam) to our own. Every plea for civil liberties and individual rights, every protest against exploitation and humiliation, against the encroachment of public authority, or the mass hypnosis of custom or organised propaganda, springs from this individualistic, and much disputed, conception of man.

Three facts about this position may be noted. In the first place Mill confuses two distinct notions. One is that all coercion is, in so far as it frustrates human desires, bad as such, although it may have to be applied to prevent other, greater evils; while non-interference, which is the opposite of coercion, is good as such, although it is not the only good. This is the 'negative' conception of liberty in its classical form. The other is

---

[7] Constant, *Principes de politique,* chapter 1: p. 275 in Benjamin Constant, *De la liberté chez les modernes: écrits politiques,* ed. Marcel Gauchet ([Paris], 1980).

[8] J. S. Mill, *On Liberty,* chapter 1: p. 226 in *Collected Works of John Stuart Mill,* ed. J. M. Robson (Toronto/London, 1981–   ), vol. 18.

[9] ibid., p. 224.

[10] ibid., chapter 3, p. 268.

[11] ibid., pp. 265–6.

[12] ibid., chapter 4, p. 277.

that men should seek to discover the truth, or to develop a certain type of character of which Mill approved—critical, original, imaginative, independent, non-conforming to the point of eccentricity, and so on—and that truth can be found, and such character can be bred, only in conditions of freedom. Both these are liberal views, but they are not identical, and the connection between them is, at best, empirical. No one would argue that truth or freedom of self-expression could flourish where dogma crushes all thought. But the evidence of history tends to show (as, indeed, was argued by James Stephen in his formidable attack on Mill in his *Liberty, Equality, Fraternity*) that integrity, love of truth and fiery individualism grow at least as often in severely disciplined communities, among, for example, the puritan Calvinists of Scotland or New England, or under military discipline, as in more tolerant or indifferent societies; and if this is so, Mill's argument for liberty as a necessary condition for the growth of human genius falls to the ground. If his two goals proved incompatible, Mill would be faced with a cruel dilemma, quite apart from the further difficulties created by the inconsistency of his doctrines with strict utilitarianism, even in his own humane version of it.[13]

In the second place, the doctrine is comparatively modern. There seems to be scarcely any discussion of individual liberty as a conscious political ideal (as opposed to its actual existence) in the ancient world. Condorcet had already remarked that the notion of individual rights was absent from the legal conceptions of the Romans and Greeks; this seems to hold equally of the Jewish, Chinese and all other ancient civilisations that have since come to light.[14] The domination of this ideal has been the exception rather than the rule, even in the recent history of the West. Nor has liberty in this sense often formed a rallying cry for the great masses of mankind. The desire not to be impinged upon, to be left to oneself, has been a mark of high civilisation on the part of both individuals and communities. The sense of privacy itself, of the area of personal relationships as something sacred in its own right, derives from a conception of freedom which, for all its religious roots, is scarcely older, in its developed state, than the Renaissance or the Reformation.[15] Yet its decline would mark the death of a civilisation, of an entire moral outlook.

The third characteristic of this notion of liberty is of greater importance. It is that liberty in this sense is not incompatible with some kinds of autocracy, or at any rate with the absence of self-government. Liberty in this sense is principally concerned with the area of control, not with its source. Just as a democracy may, in fact, deprive the individual citizen of a great many liberties which he might have in some other form of society, so it is perfectly conceivable that a liberal-minded despot would allow his subjects a large measure of personal freedom. The despot who leaves his subjects a wide area of liberty may be unjust, or encourage the wildest inequalities, care little for order, or virtue, or knowledge; but provided he does not curb their liberty, or at least curbs it less than many other regimes, he meets with Mill's specification.[16] Freedom in this sense is not, at any rate logically, connected

---

[13] This is but another illustration of the natural tendency of all but a very few thinkers to believe that all the things they hold good must be intimately connected, or at least compatible, with one another. The history of thought, like the history of nations, is strewn with examples of inconsistent, or at least disparate, elements artificially yoked together in a despotic system, or held together by the danger of some common enemy. In due course the danger passes, and conflicts between the allies arise, which often disrupt the system, sometimes to the great benefit of mankind.

[14] See the valuable discussion of this in Michel Villey, *Leçons d'histoire de la philosophie du droit* (Paris, 1957), which traces the embryo of the notion of subjective rights to Occam.

[15] Christian (and Jewish or Muslim) belief in the absolute authority of divine or natural laws, or in the equality of all men in the sight of God, is very different from belief in freedom to live as one prefers.

[16] Indeed, it is arguable that in the Prussia of Frederick the Great or in the Austria of Joseph II men of imagination, originality and creative genius, and, indeed, minorities of all kinds, were less persecuted and felt the pressure, both of institutions and custom, less heavy upon them than in many an earlier or later democracy.

with democracy or self-government. Self-government may, on the whole, provide a better guarantee of the preservation of civil liberties than other regimes, and has been defended as such by libertarians. But there is no necessary connection between individual liberty and democratic rule. The answer to the question 'Who governs me?' is logically distinct from the question 'How far does government interfere with me?' It is in this difference that the great contrast between the two concepts of negative and positive liberty, in the end, consists.[17] For the

'positive' sense of liberty comes to light if we try to answer the question, not 'What am I free to do or be?', but 'By whom am I ruled?' or 'Who is to say what I am, and what I am not, to be or do?' The connection between democracy and individual liberty is a good deal more tenuous than it seemed to many advocates of both. The desire to be governed by myself, or at any rate to participate in the process by which my life is to be controlled, may be as deep a wish as that for a free area for action, and perhaps historically older. But it is not a desire for the same thing. So different is it, indeed, as to have led in the end to the great clash of ideologies that dominates our world. For it is this, the 'positive' conception of liberty, not freedom from, but freedom to—to lead one prescribed form of life—which the adherents of the 'negative' notion represent as being, at times, no better than a specious disguise for brutal tyranny.

II

The Notion of Positive Freedom

The 'positive' sense of the word 'liberty' derives from the wish on the part of the individual to be his own master. I wish my life and decisions to depend on myself, not on external forces of whatever kind. I wish to be the instrument of my own, not of other men's, acts of will. I wish to be a subject, not an object; to be moved by reasons, by conscious purposes, which are my own, not by causes which affect me, as it were, from outside. I wish to be somebody, not nobody; a doer—deciding, not being decided for, self-directed and not acted upon by external nature or by other men as if I were a thing, or an animal, or a slave incapable of playing a human role, that is, of conceiving goals and policies of my own and realising them.

---

[17] 'Negative liberty' is something the extent of which, in a given case, it is difficult to estimate. It might, *prima facie,* seem to depend simply on the power to choose between at any rate two alternatives. Nevertheless, not all choices are equally free, or free at all. If in a totalitarian State I betray my friend under threat of torture, perhaps even if I act from fear of losing my job, I can reasonably say that I did not act freely. Nevertheless, I did, of course, make a choice, and could, at any rate in theory, have chosen to be killed or tortured or imprisoned. The mere existence of alternatives is not, therefore, enough to make my action free (although it may be voluntary) in the normal sense of the word. The extent of my freedom seems to depend on (*a*) how many possibilities are open to me (although the method of counting these can never be more than impressionistic; possibilities of action are not discrete entities like apples, which can be exhaustively enumerated); (*b*) how easy or difficult each of these possibilities is to actualise; (*c*) how important in my plan of life, given my character and circumstances, these possibilities are when compared with each other; (*d*) how far they are closed and opened by deliberate human acts; (*e*) what value not merely the agent, but the general sentiment of the society in which he lives, puts on the various possibilities. All these magnitudes must be 'integrated', and a conclusion, necessarily not precise, or indisputable, drawn from this process. It may well be that there are many incommensurable kinds and degrees of freedom, and that they cannot be drawn up on any single scale of magnitude. Moreover, in the case of societies, we are faced by such (logically absurd) questions as 'Would arrangement X increase the liberty of Mr. A more than it would that of Messrs B, C and D between them, added together?' The same difficulties arise in applying utilitarian criteria. Nevertheless, provided we do not demand precise measurement, we can give valid reasons for saying that the average subject of the King of Sweden is, on the whole, a

---

good deal freer today [1958] than the average citizen of Spain or Albania. Total patterns of life must be compared directly as wholes, although the method by which we make the comparison, and the truth of the conclusions, are difficult or impossible to demonstrate. But the vagueness of the concepts, and the multiplicity of the criteria involved, are attributes of the subject-matter itself, not of our imperfect methods of measurement, or of incapacity for precise thought.

This is at least part of what I mean when I say that I am rational, and that it is my reason that distinguishes me as a human being from the rest of the world. I wish, above all, to be conscious of myself as a thinking, willing, active being, bearing responsibility for my choices and able to explain them by reference to my own ideas and purposes. I feel free to the degree that I believe this to be true, and enslaved to the degree that I am made to realise that it is not.

The freedom which consists in being one's own master, and the freedom which consists in not being prevented from choosing as I do by other men, may, on the face of it, seem concepts at no great logical distance from each other—no more than negative and positive ways of saying much the same thing. Yet the 'positive' and 'negative' notions of freedom historically developed in divergent directions, not always by logically reputable steps, until, in the end, they came into direct conflict with each other.

One way of making this clear is in terms of the independent momentum which the, initially perhaps quite harmless, metaphor of self-mastery acquired. 'I am my own master'; 'I am slave to no man'; but may I not (as Platonists or Hegelians tend to say) be a slave to nature? Or to my own 'unbridled' passions? Are these not so many species of the identical genus 'slave'—some political or legal, others moral or spiritual? Have not men had the experience of liberating themselves from spiritual slavery, or slavery to nature, and do they not in the course of it become aware, on the one hand, of a self which dominates, and, on the other, of something in them which is brought to heel? This dominant self is then variously identified with reason, with my 'higher nature', with the self which calculates and aims at what will satisfy it in the long run, with my 'real', or 'ideal', or 'autonomous' self, or with my self 'at its best'; which is then contrasted with irrational impulse, uncontrolled desires, my 'lower' nature, the pursuit of immediate pleasures, my empirical' or 'heteronomous' self, swept by every gust of desire and passion, needing to be rigidly disciplined if it is ever to rise to the full height of its 'real' nature. Presently the two selves may be represented as divided by an even larger gap; the real self may be conceived as something wider than the individual (as the term is normally understood), as a social 'whole' of which the individual is an element or aspect: a tribe, a race, a Church, a State, the great society of the living and the dead and the yet unborn. This entity is then identified as being the 'true' self which, by imposing its collective, or 'organic', single will upon its recalcitrant 'members', achieves its own, and therefore their, 'higher' freedom. The perils of using organic metaphors to justify the coercion of some men by others in order to raise them to a 'higher' level of freedom have often been pointed out. But what gives such plausibility as it has to this kind of language is that we recognise that it is possible, and at times justifiable, to coerce men in the name of some goal (let us say, justice or public health) which they would, if they were more enlightened, themselves pursue, but do not, because they are blind or ignorant or corrupt. This renders it easy for me to conceive of myself as coercing others for their own sake, in their, not my, interest. I am then claiming that I know what they truly need better than they know it themselves. What, at most, this entails is that they would not resist me if they were rational and as wise as I and understood their interests as I do. But I may go on to claim a good deal more than this. I may declare that they are actually aiming at what in their benighted state they consciously resist, because there exists within them an occult entity—their latent rational will, or their 'true' purpose—and that this entity, although it is belied by all that they overtly feel and do and say, is their 'real' self, of which the poor empirical self in space and time may know nothing or little; and that this inner spirit is the only self that deserves to have its wishes taken into account.[18] Once I take this view, I am in a

---

[18] 'The ideal of true freedom is the maximum of power for all members of human society alike to make the best of themselves', said T. H. Green in 1881. *Lecture on Liberal Legislation and Freedom of Contract:* p. 200 in T. H. Green, *Lectures on the Principles of Political Obligation and Other Writings,* eds. Paul Harris and John Morrow (Cambridge, 1986). Apart from the confusion of freedom with equality, this entails that if a man chose some immediate pleasure—which (in whose view?) would not enable him to make the best of himself (what self?)—what he was

position to ignore the actual wishes of men or societies, to bully, oppress, torture them in the name, and on behalf, of their 'real' selves, in the secure knowledge that whatever is the true goal of man (happiness, performance of duty, wisdom, a just society, self-fulfilment) must be identical with his freedom—the free choice of his 'true', albeit often submerged and inarticulate, self.

This paradox has been often exposed. It is one thing to say that I know what is good for X, while he himself does not; and even to ignore his wishes for its—and his—sake; and a very different one to say that he has *eo ipso* chosen it, not indeed consciously, not as he seems in everyday life, but in his role as a rational self which his empirical self may not know—the 'real' self which discerns the good, and cannot help choosing it once it is revealed. This monstrous impersonation, which consists in equating what X would choose if he were something he is not, or at least not yet, with what X actually seeks and chooses, is at the heart of all political theories of self-realisation. It is one thing to say that I may be coerced for my own good, which I am too blind to see: this may, on occasion, be for my benefit; indeed it may enlarge the scope of my liberty. It is another to say that if it is my good, then I am not being coerced, for I have willed it, whether I know this or not, and am free (or 'truly' free) even while my poor earthly body and foolish mind bitterly reject it, and struggle with the greatest desperation against those who seek, however benevolently, to impose it.

---

exercising was not 'true' freedom: and if deprived of it, he would not lose anything that mattered. Green was a genuine liberal: but many a tyrant could use this formula to justify his worst acts of oppression.

This magical transformation, or sleight of hand (for which William James so justly mocked the Hegelians), can no doubt be perpetrated just as easily with the 'negative' concept of freedom, where the self that should not be interfered with is no longer the individual with his actual wishes and needs as they are normally conceived, but the 'real' man within, identified with the pursuit of sonic ideal purpose not dreamed of by his empirical self. And, as in the case of the 'positively' free self, this entity may be inflated into some super-personal entity—a State, a class, a nation, or the march of history itself, regarded as a more 'real' subject of attributes than the empirical self. But the 'positive' conception of freedom as self-mastery, with its suggestion of a man divided against himself, has in fact, and as a matter of history, of doctrine and of practice, lent itself more easily to this splitting of personality into two: the transcendent, dominant controller, and the empirical bundle of desires and passions to be disciplined and brought to heel. It is this historical fact that has been influential. This demonstrates (if demonstration of so obvious a truth is needed) that conceptions of freedom directly derive from views of what constitutes a self, a person, a man. Enough manipulation of the definition of man, and freedom can be made to mean whatever the manipulator wishes. Recent history has made it only too clear that the issue is not merely academic.

The consequences of distinguishing between two selves will become even clearer if one considers the two major forms which the desire to be self-directed—directed by one's 'true' self—has historically taken: the first, that of self-abnegation in order to attain independence; the second, that of self-realisation, or total self-identification with a specific principle or ideal in order to attain the selfsame end.

CHAPTER THIRTY-EIGHT

RAWLS

The rise of democratic interventionist welfare state capitalism proved in the end the greatest movement in government during the twentieth century. Advances of fascism, communism, and socialism, which to many for a time seemed waves of the future, in the end proved ephemeral. In 1900, full-scale democracy as in most of the world now exists—the ability of all adults to vote for governmental leaders—nowhere existed. Government on the scale it now exists nowhere existed. Government intervention in nations' economies as it now exists nowhere existed.

Among twentieth century postwar political thinkers, John Rawls (1921–   ) attained renown for *A Theory of Justice* (1971), the development of a series of papers written over the previous dozen years. *A Theory of Justice* received great attention when it was published. It received rave reviews in many journals, both for its positive message and importance. The *New York Times Book Review* designated *A Theory of Justice* one of the five most important books of the year on the grounds that "its political implications may change our lives."

Notwithstanding the attention *A Theory of Justice* received upon publication, it has not weathered well. The first critical response to the work was from political theorists of the left, who considered it potentially to allow too many concessions to capitalism, and it never really has been considered by those upon the right.

A Theory of Justice is an abstract work with little discussion of practical political issues. Rawls seeks to reintroduce a social contract theory of the origination of societal justice, building upon the legacy of Locke, Rousseau, and especially Kant. In their final form, Rawls' two principles of societal justice to regulate a community's basic institutions of government, economic system, and family are:

First Principle
Each person is to have an equal right to the most extensive total system of equal basic liberties compatible with a similar system of liberty for all.

Second Principle
Social and economic inequalities are to be arranged so that they are both:
    a)   to the greatest benefit of the least advantaged, consistent with the just savings principle, and
    b)   attached to offices and positions open to all under conditions of fair equality of opportunity.

Rawls' principles of justice are in lexical or serial order, meaning that the first principle is more important than the second and, more importantly, that equal basic liberties cannot be sacrificed for greater social or economic benefits. Rawls values rights such as freedom of speech and expression, and political participation rights, above economic opportunities.

Within his work, Rawls' second principle of justice has attracted the most attention. Also in part by him referred to as the "difference principle" or "maximin" (maximizing the minimum) rule, the idea can be, and has been, interpreted both in egalitarian and non-egalitarian manners. From an egalitarian perspective, the requirement that social and economic institutions should be to the greatest advantage of the least fortunate might seem to indicate a society in which the goods of social interaction equally are shared.

On the other hand, the more conventional interpretation of Rawls, particularly from Marxians, is that the difference principle legitimizes highly inegalitarian societies if the ruling classes claim that an inegalitarian social order is to the benefit of the least well off, which they almost always have.

Unfortunately, it is difficult to know where Rawls stands on this crucial issue. At one point in the section "The Tendency to Equality" of the first chapter of *A Theory of Justice,* he remarks:

> We may observe that the difference principle gives some weight to the consideration singled out by the principle of redress. This is the principle that undeserved inequalities call for redress; and since inequalities of birth and natural endowment are undeserved, these inequalities are to be somehow compensated for. Thus the principle holds that in order to treat all persons equally, to provide genuine equality of opportunity, society must give more attention to those with fewer native assets and to those born into the less favorable social positions.

He also says, though, in the very next paragraph:

> But the difference principle would allocate resources in education, say, so as to improve the long-term expectation of the least favored. If this end is attained by giving more attention to the better endowed, it is permissible; otherwise not.

The strength of the difference principle is that it is non-contentual. Rawls' position is that the best society is the one in which the least fortunate, over time, have the most, regardless of how this goal is achieved—socialism or capitalism.

Rawls is wrong in *A Theory of Justice* when he maintains that utilitarianism values equality only to "break ties." Utilitarianism's core idea is the moral equality of all humanity—in Bentham's words, "everybody to count for one, nobody for more than one." Mill remarked in his own *Utilitarianism*'s closing chapter, on justice, that the principle of utility "is a mere form of words without rational signification, unless one person's happiness, supposed equal in degree . . . , is counted for exactly as much as another's."

Moreover, utilitarianism is highly egalitarian in its conception of the declining marginal utility of most economic goods. Mill wrote in *Principles of Political Economy:* "The difference to the happiness of the possessor between a moderate independence and five times as much, is insignificant when weighed against the enjoyment that might be given . . . by some other disposal of the four-fifths." One of the great strengths of democratic interventionist welfare state capitalism is the emphasis—though not, of course, total emphasis—it places upon equality. It is important that all have some. There is no natural order within which a small minority should have most while the great masses starve.

The human condition is evolving as the "scarce means of satisfaction" that Rawls assumes as one of the bedrock circumstances of humanity is changing. While some may always have more and others will have less, the real privation that characterized the conditions of so many in even western industrial nations during much of the twentieth century may over time become as uncommon around the globe as it is becoming in western industrial nations. This may influence the ethical force of the difference principle, for it is one thing to advocate for those with less when they genuinely have little than when they have access to a decent material standard of living.

Rawls is also incorrect when he suggests of utilitarianism that "since each desires to protect his interests, . . . no one has a reason to acquiesce in an enduring loss for himself in order to bring about a greater net balance of satisfaction. In the absence of strong and lasting benevolent impulses, a rational man would not accept a basic structure merely because it maximized the algebraic sum of advantages irrespective of its permanent effects on his own . . . interests." There are at least two errors here. First, utilitarianism assumes potentially strong and lasting benevolent impulses; its ethical objective is the greatest happiness of all. Second, in determining the basic institutions of society, individuals do not know, according to Rawls, their place in a society. It is not the case, therefore, that individuals would potentially be choosing to sacrifice their own interests in a utilitarian society for others. All they would know is that in a utilitarian society, there would be the greatest happiness.

Perhaps the most unrealistic aspect of Rawls' conception of the practical world, as distinct from his theoretical vision, are his comments on the family. He holds that the "monogamous family" is a "major social institution," coming, therefore, under the jurisdiction of his two principles of justice. He states that "the principle of fair opportunity can be only imperfectly carried out, at least as long as the institution of the family exists. . . . Is the family to be abolished then? Taken by itself and given a certain primacy, the idea of equality of opportunity inclines in this direction. But within the context of the theory of justice as a whole, there is much less urgency to take this course. . . . We are more ready to dwell upon our good fortune now that . . . differences are made to work to our advantage, rather than to be downcast by how much better off we might have been had we had an equal chance along with others if only all social barriers had been removed."

Rawls briefly considers the possibility of genetic manipulation in *A Theory of Justice:* "I should mention one further question. I have assumed so far that the distribution of natural assets is a fact of nature and that no attempt is made to change it. . . . But to some extent this distribution is bound to be affected by the social system . . . [I]t is possible to adopt eugenic policies, more or less explicit . . . It is . . . in the interest of each to have greater natural assets. This enables him to pursue a preferred plan of life. . . . [P]arties want to ensure for their descendants the best genetic endowment . . . [O]ver time a society is to take steps at least to preserve the general level of natural abilities and to prevent the diffusion of serious defects . . ."

The primary driving force during the twentieth century has been the growth of scientific knowledge. Humanity's fantastically increasing ability to tame nature, to shape it to our purposes, defines the twentieth century. Particularly in the area of genetic knowledge, the possibilities of purposeful human direction and control of DNA will lead to a new human condition, whatever decisions are made. Knowledge itself creates new circumstances that before have not existed. Having once eaten of the tree of knowledge, humanity cannot remain in the Eden of ignorance. We are entering a new age. As humanity gains the knowledge to mold the further development of life, one must hope that the heritage of Hebrew monotheism, Greek rationalism, and Christian love will guide us.

A Theory of Justice is a rich and compelling work and goes into many topics that here have not been touched upon, including Rawls' highly creative attempt to revive the social contract theory of basic governmental institutions through a philosophical "veil of ignorance." He writes within the current of European political philosophy. The extent to which his own work will become a tributary to this mighty river remains to be seen.

In his later work *Political Liberalism* (1993), Rawls discusses diversity, and the circumstance where a "well-ordered society" does not reflect a democratic polity, an assumption of *A Theory of Justice.* In *Political Liberalism,* he offers one of his few specific examples of a concrete application of his ideas (in this case of political pluralism) when he remarks in an illustrative footnote of the proposition in the main text that "the only comprehensive doctrines that run afoul of public reason are those that cannot support a reasonable balance of political values": "Consider the troubled question of abortion. Suppose first that the society in question is well-ordered and that we are dealing with the normal case of mature adult women. . . . Suppose further that we consider the question in terms of these three important political values: the due respect for human life, the ordered reproduction of political society over time . . . , and finally the equality of women as citizens. . . . Now I believe any reasonable balance of these three values will give a woman a duly qualified right to decide whether or not to end her pregnancy during the first trimester . . . [A]ny comprehensive doctrine that leads to a balance of political values excluding the duly qualified right in the first trimester is to that extent unreasonable . . ."

One may agree or disagree with Rawls' position on abortion, but this is not the present point, which is that his position is that it objectively is unreasonable to have a position other than his on abortion, and therefore impermissible, even in a diverse, pluralistic polity, to restrict abortion beyond the position he presents. This outlook of objective reason echoes sentiments he expresses within *A Theory of Justice* upon "generally recognized ways of reasoning" and "ways of reasoning acceptable to all." This conception of reason, and sentiment, is different than that of Hume, who holds in *A Treatise of Human Nature* that "reason is, and ought only to be the slave of the passions," and that "the rules of morality are not the conclusions of our reason"; of Mill, who maintains in *On Liberty* that "if all mankind minus one were of one opinion, and only one person were of the contrary opinion, mankind would be no more justified in silencing that one person, than he, if he had the power, would be justified in silencing mankind"; or of Hayek in *The Constitution of Liberty:* "The freedom that will be used by only one man in a million may be more important to society and more beneficial to the majority than any freedom that we all use."

The essence of a truly liberal position is promotion of genuine diversity. Free speech, the moral equality of all people, the factual diversity of humankind, democracy, the right to rebel, a competitive economic order, and internationalism also characterize the liberal view. As humanity enters a new age, the wisdom as well as errors of great political thinkers undoubtedly will continue to influence and reflect societal institutions and government. From Plato to the present, the roots of the west—Greek rationalism, Hebrew monotheism, and Christian love—have defined at its best western political thought.

RAWLS

*A Theory of Justice**

THE ROLE OF JUSTICE

Justice is the first virtue of social institutions, as truth is of systems of thought. A theory however elegant and economical must be rejected or revised if it is untrue; likewise laws and institutions no matter how efficient and well-arranged must be reformed or abolished if they are unjust. Each person possesses an inviolability founded on justice that even the welfare of society as a whole cannot override. For this reason justice denies that the loss of freedom for some is made right by a greater good shared by others. It does not allow that the sacrifices imposed on a few are outweighed by the larger sum of advantages enjoyed by many. Therefore in a just society the liberties of equal citizenship are taken as settled; the rights secured by justice are not subject to political bargaining or to the calculus of social interests. The only thing that permits us to acquiesce in an erroneous theory is the lack of a better one; analogously, an injustice is tolerable only when it is necessary to avoid an even greater injustice. Being first virtues of human activities, truth and justice are uncompromising.

These propositions seem to express our intuitive conviction of the primacy of justice. No doubt they are expressed too strongly. In any event I wish to inquire whether these contentions or others similar to them are sound, and if so how they can be accounted for. To this end it is necessary to work out a theory of justice in the light of which these assertions can be interpreted and assessed. I shall begin by considering the role of the principles of justice. Let us assume, to fix ideas, that a society is a more or less self-sufficient association of persons who in their relations to one another recognize certain rules of conduct as binding and who for the most part act in accordance with them. Suppose further that these rules specify a system of cooperation designed to advance the good of those taking part in it. Then, although a society is a cooperative venture for mutual advantage, it is typically marked by a conflict as well as by an identity of interests. There is an identity of interests since social cooperation makes possible a better life for all than any would have if each were to live solely by his own efforts. There is a conflict of interests since persons are not indifferent as to how the greater benefits produced by their collaboration are distributed, for in order to pursue their ends they each prefer a larger to a lesser share. A set of principles is required for choosing among the various social arrangements which determine this division of advantages and for underwriting an agreement on the proper distributive shares. These principles are the principles of social justice: They provide a way of assigning rights and duties in the basic institutions of society and they define the appropriate distribution of the benefits and burdens of social cooperation.

Now let us say that a society is well-ordered when it is not only designed to advance the good of its members but when it is also effectively regulated by a public conception of justice. That is, it is a society in which (1) everyone accepts and knows that the others accept the same principles of

*Reprinted by permission of the publishers from *A Theory of Justice* by John Rawls, Cambridge, Mass.: The Belknap Press of Harvard University Press. Copyright © 1971 by the President and Fellows of Harvard College.

justice, and (2) the basic social institutions generally satisfy and are generally known to satisfy these principles. In this case while men may put forth excessive demands on one another, they nevertheless acknowledge a common point of view from which their claims may be adjudicated. If men's inclination to self-interest makes their vigilance against one another necessary, their public sense of justice makes their secure association together possible. Among individuals with disparate aims and purposes a shared conception of justice establishes the bonds of civic friendship; the general desire for justice limits the pursuit of other ends. One may think of a public conception of justice as constituting the fundamental charter of a well-ordered human association.

THE SUBJECT OF JUSTICE

Many different kinds of things are said to be just and unjust: not only laws, institutions, and social systems, but also particular actions of many kinds, including decisions, judgments, and imputations. We also call the attitudes and dispositions of persons, and persons themselves, just and unjust. Our topic, however, is that of social justice. For us the primary subject of justice is the basic structure of society, or more exactly, the way in which the major social institutions distribute fundamental rights and duties and determine the division of advantages from social cooperation. By major institutions I understand the political constitution and the principal economic and social arrangements. Thus the legal protection of freedom of thought and liberty of conscience, competitive markets, private property in the means of production, and the monogamous family are examples of major social institutions. Taken together as one scheme, the major institutions define men's rights and duties and influence their life-prospects, what they can expect to be and how well they can hope to do. The basic structure is the primary subject of justice because its effects are so profound and present from the start. The intuitive notion here is that this structure contains various social positions and that men born into different positions have different expectations of life determined, in part, by the political system as well as by economic and social circumstances. In this way

the institutions of society favor certain starting places over others. These are especially deep inequalities. Not only are they pervasive, but they affect men's initial chances in life; yet they cannot possibly be justified by an appeal to the notions of merit or desert. It is these inequalities, presumably inevitable in the basic structure of any society, to which the principles of social justice must in the first instance apply. These principles, then, regulate the choice of a political constitution and the main elements of the economic and social system. The justice of a social scheme depends essentially on how fundamental rights and duties are assigned and on the economic opportunities and social conditions in the various sectors of society.

THE MAIN IDEA OF THE THEORY OF JUSTICE

My aim is to present a conception of justice which generalizes and carries to a higher level of abstraction the familiar theory of the social contract as found, say, in Locke, Rousseau, and Kant. In order to do this we are not to think of the original contract as one to enter a particular society or to set up a particular form of government. Rather, the guiding idea is that the principles of justice for the basic structure of society are the object of the original agreement. They are the principles that free and rational persons concerned to further their own interests would accept in an initial position of equality as defining the fundamental terms of their association. These principles are to regulate all further agreements; they specify the kinds of social cooperation that can be entered into and the forms of government that can be established. This way of regarding the principles of justice I shall call justice as fairness.

Thus we are to imagine that those who engage in social cooperation choose together, in one joint act, the principles which are to assign basic rights and duties and to determine the division of social benefits. Men are to decide in advance how they are to regulate their claims against one another and what is to be the foundation charter of their society. Just as each person must decide by rational reflection what constitutes his good, that is, the system of ends which it is rational for him to pursue, so a group of persons must decide once and for all what is to count among them as just and unjust. The choice which rational men would make in this hypothetical situation of equal liberty, assuming for the present that this choice problem has a solution, determines the principles of justice.

In justice as fairness the original position of equality corresponds to the state of nature in the traditional theory of the social contract. This original position is not, of course, thought of as an actual historical state of affairs, much less as a primitive condition of culture. It is understood as a purely hypothetical situation characterized so as to lead to a certain conception of justice. Among the essential features of this situation is that no one knows his place in society, his class position or social status, nor does any one know his fortune in the distribution of natural assets and abilities, his intelligence, strength, and the like. I shall even assume that the parties do not know their conceptions of the good or their special psychological propensities. The principles of justice are chosen behind a veil of ignorance. This ensures that no one is advantaged or disadvantaged in the choice of principles by the outcome of natural chance or the contingency of social circumstances. Since all are similarly situated and no one is able to design principles to favor his particular condition, the principles of justice are the result of a fair agreement or bargain. For given the circumstances of the original position, the symmetry of everyone's relations to each other, this initial situation is fair between individuals as moral persons, that is, as rational beings with their own ends and capable, I shall assume, of a sense of justice. The original position is, one might say, the appropriate initial status quo, and thus the fundamental agreements reached in it are fair. This explains the propriety of the name "justice as fairness": it conveys the idea that the principles of justice are agreed to in an initial situation that is fair. The name does not mean that the concepts of justice and fairness are the same, any more than the phrase "poetry as metaphor" means that the concepts of poetry and metaphor are the same.

Justice as fairness begins, as I have said, with one of the most general of all choices which persons might make together, namely, with the choice of the first principles of a conception of justice which is to regulate all subsequent criticism and reform of institutions. Then, having chosen a conception of justice, we can suppose that they are to choose a constitution and a legislature to enact laws, and so on, all in accordance with the principles of justice initially agreed upon. Our social situation is just if it is such that by this sequence of hypothetical agreements we would have contracted into the general system of rules which defines it. Moreover, assuming that the original position does determine a set of principles (that is, that a particular conception of justice would be chosen), it will then be true that whenever social institutions satisfy these principles those engaged in them can say to one another that they are cooperating on terms to which they would agree if they were free and equal persons whose relations with respect to one another were fair. They could all view their arrangements as meeting the stipulations which they would acknowledge in an initial situation that embodies widely accepted and reasonable constraints on the choice of principles. The general recognition of this fact would provide the basis for a public acceptance of the corresponding principles of justice. No society can, of course, be a scheme of cooperation which men enter voluntarily in a literal sense; each person finds himself placed at birth in some particular position in some particular society, and the nature of this position materially affects his life prospects. Yet a society satisfying the principles of justice as fairness comes as close as a society can to being a voluntary scheme, for it meets the principles which free and equal persons would assent to under circumstances that are fair. In this sense its members are autonomous and the obligations they recognize self-imposed.

One feature of justice as fairness is to think of the parties in the initial situation as rational and mutually disinterested. This does not mean that the parties are egoists, that is, individuals with only certain kinds of interests, say in wealth, prestige, and domination. But they are conceived as not taking an interest in one another's interests. They are to presume that even their spiritual aims may be opposed, in the way that the aims of those of different religions may be opposed. Moreover, the concept of rationality must be interpreted as far as possible in the narrow sense, standard in economic theory, of taking the most effective means to given ends. I shall modify this concept to some extent, but one must try to avoid introducing into it any controversial ethical elements. The initial situation must be characterized by stipulations that are widely accepted.

In working out the conception of justice as fairness one main task clearly is to determine which principles of justice would be chosen in the original position. To do this we must describe this situation in some detail and formulate with care the problem of choice which it presents. These matters I shall take up in the immediately succeeding chapters. It may be observed, however, that once the principles of justice are thought of as arising from an original agreement in a situation of equality, it is an open question whether the principle of utility would be acknowledged. Offhand it hardly seems likely that persons who view themselves as equals, entitled to press their claims upon one another, would agree to a principle which may require lesser life prospects for some simply for the sake of a greater sum of advantages enjoyed by others. Since each desires to protect his interests, his capacity to advance his conception of the good, no one has a reason to acquiesce in an enduring loss for himself in order to bring about a greater net balance of satisfaction. In the absence of strong and lasting benevolent impulses, a rational man would not accept a basic structure merely because it maximized the algebraic sum of advantages irrespective of its permanent effects on his own basic rights and interests. Thus it seems that the principle of utility is incompatible with the conception of social cooperation among equals for mutual advantage. It appears to be inconsistent with the idea of reciprocity implicit in the notion of a well-ordered society. Or, at any rate, so I shall argue.

I shall maintain instead that the persons in the initial situation would choose two rather different principles: the first requires equality in the assignment of basic rights and duties, while the second holds that social and economic inequalities, for example inequalities of wealth and authority, are just only if they result in compensating benefits for everyone, and in particular for the least advantaged members of society. These principles rule out justifying institutions on the grounds that the hardships of some are offset by a greater good in the aggregate. It may be expedient but it is not just that some should have less in order that others may prosper. But there is no injustice in the greater benefits earned by a few provided that the situation of persons not so fortunate is thereby improved. The intuitive idea is that since everyone's well-being depends upon a scheme of cooperation without which no one could have a satisfactory life, the division of advantages should be such as to draw forth the willing cooperation of everyone taking part in it, including those less well situated. Yet this can be expected only if reasonable terms are proposed. The two principles mentioned seem to be a fair agreement on the basis of which those better endowed, or more fortunate in their social position, neither of which we can be said to deserve, could expect the willing cooperation of others when some workable scheme is a necessary condition of the welfare of all. Once we decide to look for a conception of justice that nullifies the accidents of natural endowment and the contingencies of social circumstance as counters in quest for political and economic advantage, we are led to these principles. They express the result of leaving aside those aspects of the social world that seem arbitrary from a moral point of view.

Justice as fairness is an example of what I have called a contract theory. Now there may be an objection to the term "contract" and related expressions, but I think it will serve reasonably well. Many words have misleading connotations which at first are likely to confuse. The terms "utility" and "utilitarianism" are surely no exception. They too have unfortunate suggestions which hostile critics have been willing to exploit; yet they are clear enough for those prepared to study utilitarian doctrine. The same should be true of the term "contract" applied to moral theories. As I have mentioned, to understand it one has to keep in mind that it implies a certain level of abstraction. In particular, the content of the relevant agreement is not to enter a given society or to adopt a given form of government, but to accept certain moral principles. Moreover, the undertakings referred to are purely hypothetical: a contract view holds that certain principles would be accepted in a well-defined initial situation.

THE ORIGINAL POSITION AND JUSTIFICATION

I have said that the original position is the appropriate initial status quo which insures that the fundamental agreements reached in it are fair. This fact yields the name "justice as fairness." It is clear, then, that I want to say that one conception of justice is more reasonable than another, or justifiable with respect to it, if rational persons in the initial situation would choose its principles over those of the other for the role of justice. Conceptions of justice are to be ranked by their acceptability to persons so circumstanced. Understood in this way the question of justification is settled by working out a problem of deliberation: we have to ascertain which principles it would be rational to adopt given the contractual situation. This connects the theory of justice with the theory of rational choice.

If this view of the problem of justification is to succeed, we must, of course, describe in some detail the nature of this choice problem. A problem of rational decision has a definite answer only if we know the beliefs and interests of the parties, their relations with respect to one another, the alternatives between which they are to choose, the procedure whereby they make up their minds, and so on. As the circumstances are presented in different ways, correspondingly different principles are accepted. The concept of the original position, as I shall refer to it, is that of the most philosophically favored interpretation of this initial choice situation for the purposes of a theory of justice.

But how are we to decide what is the most favored interpretation? I assume, for one thing, that there is a broad measure of agreement that principles of justice should be chosen under certain conditions. To justify a particular description of the initial situation one shows that it incorporates these commonly shared presumptions. One argues from widely accepted but weak premises to more specific conclusions. Each of the presumptions should by itself be natural and plausible; some of them may seem innocuous or even trivial. The aim of the contract approach is to establish that taken together they impose significant bounds on acceptable principles of justice. The ideal outcome would be that these conditions determine a unique set of principles; but I shall be satisfied if they suffice to rank the main traditional conceptions of social justice.

One should not be misled, then, by the somewhat unusual conditions which characterize the original position. The idea here is simply to make vivid to ourselves the restrictions that it seems reasonable to impose on arguments for principles of justice, and therefore on these principles themselves. Thus it seems reasonable and generally acceptable that no one should be advantaged or disadvantaged by natural fortune or social circumstances in the choice of principles. It also seems widely agreed that it should be impossible to tailor principles to the circumstances of one's own case. We should insure further that particular inclinations and aspirations, and persons' conceptions of their good do not affect the principles adopted. The aim is to rule out those principles that it would be rational to propose for acceptance, however little the chance of success, only if one knew certain things that are irrelevant from the standpoint of justice. For example, if a man knew that he was wealthy, he might find it rational to advance the principle that various taxes for welfare measures be counted unjust; if he knew that he was poor, he would most likely propose the contrary principle. To represent the desired restrictions one imagines a situation in which everyone is deprived of this sort of information. One excludes the knowledge of those contingencies which sets men at odds and allows them to be guided by their prejudices. In this manner the veil of ignorance is arrived at in a natural way. This concept should cause no difficulty if we keep in mind the constraints on arguments that it is meant to express. At any time we can enter the original position, so to speak, simply by following a certain procedure, namely, by arguing for principles of justice in accordance with these restrictions.

It seems reasonable to suppose that the parties in the original position are equal. That is, all have the same rights in the procedure for choosing principles; each can make proposals, submit reasons for their acceptance, and so on. Obviously the purpose of these conditions is to represent equality between human beings as moral persons, as creatures having a conception of their good and capable of a sense of justice. The basis of equality is taken to be similarity in these two respects. Systems of ends are not ranked in value; and each man is presumed to have the requisite ability to understand and to act upon whatever principles are adopted. Together with the veil of ignorance, these conditions define the principles of justice as those which rational persons concerned to advance their interests would consent to as equals when none are known to be advantaged or disadvantaged by social and natural contingencies.

There is, however, another side to justifying a particular description of the original position. This is to see if the principles which would be chosen match our considered convictions of justice or extend them in an acceptable way. We can note whether applying these principles would lead us to make the same judgments about the basic structure of society which we now make intuitively and in which we have the greatest confidence; or whether, in cases where our present judgments are in doubt and given with hesitation, these principles offer a resolution which we can affirm on reflection. There are questions which we feel sure must be answered in a certain way. For example, we are confident that religious intolerance and racial discrimination are unjust. We think that we have examined these things with care and have reached what we believe is an impartial judgment not likely to be distorted by an excessive attention to our own interests. These convictions are provisional fixed points which we presume any conception of justice must fit. But we have much less assurance as to what is the correct distribution of wealth and authority. Here we may be looking for a way to remove our doubts. We can check an interpretation of the initial situation, then, by the capacity of its principles to accommodate our firmest convictions and to provide guidance where guidance is needed.

THE DIFFERENCE PRINCIPLE

To illustrate the difference principle, consider the distribution of income among social classes. Let us suppose that the various income groups correlate with representative individuals by reference to whose expectations we can judge the distribution. Now those starting out as members of the entrepreneurial class in property-owning democracy, say, have a better prospect than those who begin in the class of unskilled laborers. It seems likely that this will be true even when the social injustices which now exist are removed. What, then, can possibly justify this kind of initial inequality in life prospects? According to the difference principle, it is justifiable only if the difference in expectation is to the advantage of the representative man who is worse off, in this case the representative unskilled worker. The inequality in expectation is permissible only if lowering it would make the working class even more worse off. Supposedly, given the rider in the second principle concerning open positions, and the principle of liberty generally, the greater expectations allowed to entrepreneurs encourages them to do things which raise the long-term prospects of laboring class. Their better prospects act as incentives so that the economic process is more efficient, innovation proceeds at a faster pace, and so on. Eventually the resulting material benefits spread throughout the system and to the least advantaged. I shall not consider how far these things are true. The point is that something of this kind must be argued if these inequalities are to be just by the difference principle.

I shall now make a few remarks about this principle. First of all, in applying it, one should distinguish between two cases. The first case is that in which the expectations of the least advantaged are indeed maximized (subject, of course, to the mentioned constraints). No changes in the expectations of those better off can improve the situation of those worst off. The best arrangement obtains, what I shall call a perfectly just scheme. The second case is that in which the expectations of all those better off at least contribute to the welfare of the more unfortunate. That is, if their expectations were decreased, the prospects of the least advantaged would likewise fall. Yet the maximum is not yet achieved. Even higher expectations for the more advantaged would raise the expectations of those in the lowest position. Such a scheme is, I shall say, just throughout, but not the best just arrangement. A scheme is unjust when the higher expectations, one or more of them, are excessive. If these expectations were decreased, the situation of the least favored would be improved. How unjust an arrangement is depends on how excessive the higher expectations are and to what extent they depend upon the violation of the other principles of justice, for example, fair equality of opportunity; but I shall not attempt to measure in any exact way the degrees of injustice. The point to note here is that while the difference principle is, strictly speaking, a maximizing principle, there is a significant distinction between the cases that fall short of the best arrangement. A society should try to avoid the region where the marginal contributions of those better off are negative, since, other things equal, this seems a greater fault than falling short of the best scheme when these contributions are positive. The even larger difference between rich and poor makes the latter even worse off, and this violates the principle of mutual advantage as well as democratic equality.

A further point is this. We saw that the system of natural liberty and the liberal conception attempt to go beyond the principle of efficiency by moderating its scope of operation, by constraining it by certain background institutions and leaving the rest to pure procedural justice. The democratic conception holds that while pure procedural justice may be invoked to some extent at least, the way previous interpretations do, this still leaves too much to social and natural contingency. But it should be noted that the difference principle is compatible with the principle of efficiency. For when the former is fully satisfied, it is indeed impossible to make any one representative man better off without making another worse off, namely, the least advantaged representative man whose expectations we are to maximize. Thus justice is defined so that it is consistent with efficiency, at least when the two principles are perfectly fulfilled. Of course, if the basic structure is unjust, these principles will authorize changes that may lower the expectations of some of those better off, and therefore the democratic conception is not consistent with the principle of efficiency if this principle is taken to mean that only changes which improve everyone's prospects are allowed. Justice is prior to efficiency and requires some changes that are not efficient in this sense. Consistency obtains only in the sense that a perfectly just scheme is also efficient.

Next, we may consider a certain complication regarding the meaning of the difference principle. It has been taken for granted that if the principle is satisfied, everyone is benefited. One obvious sense in which this is so is that each man's position is improved with respect to the initial arrangement of equality. But it is clear that nothing depends upon being able to identify this initial arrangement; indeed, how well off men are in this situation plays no essential role in applying the difference principle. We simply maximize the expectations of the least favored position subject to the required constraints. As long as doing this is an improvement for everyone, as we assume it is, the estimated gains from the situation of hypothetical equality are irrelevant, if not largely impossible to ascertain anyway. There may be, however, a further sense in which everyone is advantaged when the difference principle is satisfied, at least if we make certain natural assumptions. Let us suppose that inequalities in expectations are chain-connected: that is, if an advantage has the effect of raising the expectations of the lowest position, it raises the expectations of all positions in between. For example, if the greater expectations for entrepreneurs benefit the unskilled worker, they also benefit the semiskilled. Notice that chain connection says nothing about the case where the least advantaged do not gain, so that it does not mean that all effects move together. Assume further that expectations are close-knit: that is, it is impossible to raise or lower the expectation of any representative man without raising or lowering the expectation of every other representative man, especially that of the least advantaged. There is no loose-jointedness, so to speak, in the way expectations hang together. Now with these assumptions there is a sense in which everyone benefits when the difference principle is satisfied. For the representative man who is better off in any two-way comparison gains by the advantages offered him, and the man who is worse off gains from the contributions which these inequalities make. Of course, these conditions may not hold. But in this case those who are better off should not have a veto over the benefits available for the least favored. We are still to maximize the expectations of those most disadvantaged.

FAIR EQUALITY
OF OPPORTUNITY

I should now like to comment upon the second part of the second principle, henceforth to be understood as the liberal principle of fair equality of opportunity. It must not then be confused with the notion of careers open to talents; nor must one forget that since it is tied in with the difference principle its consequences are quite distance from the liberal interpretation of the two principles taken together. In particular, I shall try to show further on that this principle is not subject to the objection that it leads to a meritocratic society. Here I wish to consider a few other points, especially its relation to the idea of pure procedural justice.

First, though, I should note that the reasons for requiring open positions are not solely, or even primarily, those of efficiency. I have not maintained that offices must be open if in fact everyone is to benefit from an arrangement. For it may be possible to improve everyone's situation by assigning certain powers and benefits to positions despite the fact that certain groups are excluded from them. Although access is restricted, perhaps these offices can still attract superior talent and encourage better performance. But the principle of open positions forbids this. It expresses the conviction that if some places were not open on a basis fair to all, those kept out would be right in feeling unjustly treated even though they benefited from the greater efforts of those who were allowed to hold them. They would be justified in their complaint not only because they were excluded from certain external rewards of office such as wealth and privilege, but because they were debarred from experiencing the realization

of self which comes from a skillful and devoted exercise of social duties. They would be deprived of one of the main forms of human good.

Now I have said that the basic structure is the primary subject of justice. This means, as we have seen, that the first distributive problem is the assignment of fundamental rights and duties and the regulation of social and economic inequalities and of the legitimate expectations founded on these. Of course, any ethical theory recognizes the importance of the basic structure as a subject of justice, but not all theories regard its importance in the same way. In justice as fairness society is interpreted as a cooperative venture for mutual advantage. The basic structure is a public system of rules defining a scheme of activities that leads men to act together so as to produce a greater sum of benefits and assigns to each certain recognized claims to a share in the proceeds. What a person does depends upon what the public rules say he will be entitled to, and what a person is entitled to depends on what he does. The distribution which results is arrived at by honoring the claims determined by what persons undertake to do in the light of these legitimate expectations.

THE TENDENCY
TO EQUALITY

I wish to conclude this discussion of the two principles by explaining the sense in which they express an egalitarian conception of justice. Also I should like to forestall the objection to the principle of fair opportunity that it leads to a callous meritocratic society. In order to prepare the way for doing this, I note several aspects of the conception of justice that I have set out.

First we may observe that the difference principle gives some weight to the considerations singled out by the principle of redress. This is the principle that undeserved inequalities call for redress; and since inequalities of birth and natural endowment are undeserved, these inequalities are to be somehow compensated for. Thus the principle holds that in order to treat all persons equally, to provide genuine equality of opportunity, society must give more attention to those with fewer native assets and to those born into the less favorable social positions. The idea is to redress the bias of contingencies in the direction of equality. In pursuit of this principle greater resources might be spent on the education of the less rather than the more intelligent, at least over a certain time of life, say the earlier years of school.

Now the principle of redress has not to my knowledge been proposed as the sole criterion of justice, as the single aim of the social order. It is plausible as most such principles are only as a prima facie principle, one that is to be weighed in the balance with others. For example, we are to weigh it against the principle to improve the average standard of life, or to advance the common good. But whatever other principles we hold, the claims of redress are to be taken into account. It is thought to represent one of the elements in our conception of justice. Now the difference principle is not of course the principle of redress. It does not require society to try to even out handicaps as if all were expected to compete on a fair basis in the same race. But the difference principle would allocate resources in education, say, so as to improve the long-term expectation of the least favored. If this end is attained by giving more attention to the better endowed, it is permissible; otherwise not. And in making this decision, the value of education should not be assessed solely in terms of economic efficiency and social welfare. Equally if not more important is the role of education in enabling a person to enjoy the culture of his society and to take part in its affairs, and in this way to provide for each individual a secure sense of his own worth.

Thus although the difference principle is not the same as that of redress, it does achieve some of the intent of the latter principle. It transforms the aims of the basic structure so that the total scheme of institutions no longer emphasizes social efficiency and technocratic values. We see then that the difference principle represents, in effect, an agreement to regard the distribution of natural talents as a common asset and to share in the benefits of this distribution whatever it turns out to be. Those who have been favored by nature, whoever they are, may gain from their good fortune only on terms that improve the situation of those who have lost out. The naturally advantaged are not to gain merely because they are more gifted, but only to cover the costs of training and education and for using their endowments in ways that help the less fortunate as well. No one deserves his greater natural capacity nor merits a more favorable starting place in society. But it does not follow that one should eliminate these distinctions. There is another way to deal with them. The basic structure can be arranged so that these contingencies work for the good of the least fortunate. Thus we are led to the difference principle if we wish to set up the social system so that no one gains or loses from his arbitrary place in the distribution of natural assets or his initial position in society without giving or receiving compensating advantages in return.

In view of these remarks we may reject the contention that the ordering of institutions is always defective because the distribution of natural talents and the contingencies of social circumstance are unjust, and this injustice must inevitably carry over to human arrangements. Occasionally this reflection is offered as an excuse for ignoring injustice, as if the refusal to acquiesce in injustice is on a par with being unable to accept death. The natural distribution is neither just nor unjust; nor is it unjust that persons are born into society at some particular position. These are simply natural facts. What is just and unjust is the way that institutions deal with these facts. Aristocratic and caste societies are unjust because they make these contingencies the ascriptive basis for belonging to more or less enclosed and privileged social classes. The basic structure of these societies incorporates the arbitrariness found in nature. But there is no necessity for men to resign themselves to these contingencies. The social system is not an unchangeable order beyond human control but a pattern of human action. In justice as fairness men agree to share one another's fate. In designing institutions they undertake to avail themselves of the accidents of nature and social circumstance only when doing so is for the common benefit. The two principles are a fair way of meeting the arbitrariness of fortune; and while no doubt imperfect in other ways, the institutions which satisfy these principles are just.

THE PRIORITY OF LIBERTY

Aristotle remarks that it is a peculiarity of men that they possess a sense of the just and the unjust and that their sharing a common understanding of justice makes a polis. Analogously one might say, in view of our discussion, that a common understanding of justice as fairness makes a constitutional democracy. For I have tried to show, after presenting further arguments for the first principle, that the basic liberties of a democratic regime are most firmly secured by this conception of justice. In each case the conclusions reached are familiar. My aim has been to indicate not only that the principles of justice fit our considered judgments but also that they provide the strongest arguments for freedom. By contrast ideological principles permit at best uncertain grounds for liberty, or at least for equal liberty. And liberty of conscience and freedom of thought should not be founded on philosophical or ethical skepticism, nor on indifference to religious and moral interests. The principles of justice define an appropriate path between dogmatism and intolerance on the one side, and a reductionism which regards religion and morality as mere preferences on the other. And since the theory of justice relies upon weak and widely held presumptions, it may win quite general acceptance. Surely our liberties are most firmly based when they are derived from principles that persons fairly situated with respect to one another can agree to if they can agree to anything at all.

I now wish to examine more carefully the meaning of the priority of liberty. I shall not argue here for this priority; instead I wish to clarify its sense in view of the preceding examples, among others. There are several priorities to be distinguished. By the priority of liberty I mean the precedence of the principle of equal liberty over the second principle of justice. The two principles are in lexical order, and therefore the claims of liberty are to be satisfied first. Until this is achieved no other principle comes into play. The priority of the right over the good, or of fair opportunity over the difference principle, is not presently our concern.

As all the previous examples illustrate, the precedence of liberty means that liberty can be restricted only for the sake of liberty itself. There are two sorts of cases. The basic liberties may either be less extensive though still equal, or they may be unequal. If liberty is less extensive, the representative citizen must find this a gain for his freedom on balance; and if liberty is unequal, the freedom of those with the lesser liberty must be better secured. In both instances the justification proceeds by reference to the whole system of the equal liberties. These priority rules have already been noted on a number of occasions.

There is, however, a further distinction that must be made between two kinds of circumstances that justify or excuse a restriction of liberty. First a restriction can derive from the natural limitations and accidents of human life, or from historical and social contingencies. The question of the justice of these constraints does not arise. For example, even in a well-ordered society under favorable circumstances, liberty of thought and conscience is subject to reasonable regulations and the principle of participation is restricted in extent. These constraints issue from the more or less permanent conditions of political life; others are adjustments to the natural features of the human situation, as with the lesser liberty of children. In these cases the problem is to discover the just way to meet certain given limitations.

In the second kind of case, injustice already exists, either in social arrangements or in the conduct of individuals. The question here is what is the just way to answer injustice. This injustice may, of course, have many explanations, and those who act unjustly often do so with the conviction that they pursue a higher cause. The examples of intolerant and of rival sects illustrate this possibility. But men's propensity to injustice is not a permanent aspect of community life; it is greater or less depending in large part on social institutions, and in particular on whether these are just or unjust. A well-ordered society tends to eliminate or at least to control men's inclinations to injustice, and therefore warring and intolerant sects, say, are much less likely to exist, or to be a danger, once such a society is established. How justice requires us to meet injustice is a very different problem from how best to cope with the inevitable limitations and contingencies of human life.

These two kinds of cases raise several questions. It will be recalled that strict compliance is one of the stipulations of the original position; the principles of justice are chosen on the supposition that they will be generally complied with. Any failures are discounted as exceptions. By putting these principles in lexical order, the parties are choosing a conception of justice suitable for favorable conditions and assuming that a just society can in due course be achieved. Arranged in this order, the principles define then a perfectly just scheme; they belong to ideal theory and set up an aim to guide the course of social reform. But even granting the soundness of these principles for this purpose, we must still ask how well they apply to institutions under less than favorable conditions, and whether they provide any guidance for instances of injustice. The principles and their lexical order were not acknowledged with these situations in mind and so it is possible that they no longer hold.

I shall not attempt to give a systematic answer to these questions. The intuitive idea is to split the theory of justice into two parts. The first or ideal part assumes strict compliance and works out the principles that characterize a well-ordered society under favorable circumstances. It develops the conception of a perfectly just basic structure and the corresponding duties and obligations of persons under the fixed constraints of human life. My main concern is with this part of the theory. Nonideal theory, the second part, is worked out after an ideal conception of justice has been chosen; only then do the parties ask which principles to adopt under less happy conditions. This division of the theory has, as I have indicated, two rather different subparts. One consists of the principles for governing adjustments to natural limitations and historical contingencies, and the other of principles for meeting injustice.

Viewing the theory of justice as a whole, the ideal part presents a conception of a just society that we are to achieve if we can. Existing institutions are to be judged in the light of this conception and held to be unjust to the extent that they depart from it without sufficient reason. The lexical ranking of the principles specifies which elements of the ideal are relatively more urgent, and the priority rules this ordering suggests are to be applied to nonideal cases as well. Thus as far as circumstances permit, we have a natural duty to remove any injustices, beginning with the most grievous as identified by the extent of the deviation from perfect justice. Of course, this idea is extremely rough. The measure of departures from the ideal is left importantly to intuition. Still our judgment is guided by the priority indicated by the lexical ordering. If we have a reasonably clear picture of what is just, our considered convictions of justice may fall more closely into line even though we cannot formulate precisely how this greater convergence comes about. Thus while the principles of justice belong to the theory of an ideal state of affairs, they are generally relevant.

The several parts of nonideal theory may be illustrated by various examples, some of which we have discussed. One type of situation is that involving a less extensive liberty. Since there are no inequalities, but all are to have a narrower rather than a wider freedom, the question can be assessed from the perspective of the representative equal citizen. To appeal to the interests of this representative man in applying the principles of justice is to invoke the principle of the common interest. (The common good I think of as certain general conditions that are in an appropriate sense equally to everyone's advantage.) Several of the preceding examples involve a less extensive liberty: the regulation of liberty of conscience and freedom of thought in ways consistent with public order, and the limitation on the scope of majority rule belong to this category. These constraints arise from the permanent conditions of human life and therefore these cases belong to that part of nonideal theory which deals with natural limitations. The two examples of curbing the liberties of the intolerant and of restraining the violence of contending sects, since they involve injustice, belong to the partial compliance part of nonideal theory. In each of these four cases, however, the argument proceeds from the viewpoint of the representative citizen. Following the idea of the lexical ordering, the limitations upon the extent of liberty are for the sake of liberty itself and result in a lesser but still equal freedom.

The second kind of case is that of an unequal liberty. If some have more votes than others, political liberty is unequal, and the same is true if the votes of some are weighted much more heavily, or if a segment of society is without the franchise altogether. In many historical situations a lesser political liberty may have been justified. Perhaps Burke's unrealistic account of representation had an element of validity in the context of eighteenth century society. If so, it reflects the fact that the various liberties are not all on a par, for while at that time unequal political liberty might conceivably have been a permissible adjustment to historical limitations, serfdom and slavery, and religious intolerance, certainly were not. These constraints do not justify the loss of liberty of conscience and the rights defining the integrity of the person. The case for certain political liberties and the rights of fair equality of opportunity is less compelling. As I noted before, it may be reasonable to forgo part of these freedoms when the long-run benefits are great enough to transform a less fortunate society into one where the equal liberties can be fully enjoyed. This is especially true when circumstances are not conducive to the exercise of these rights in any case. Under certain conditions that cannot be at present removed, the value of some liberties may not be so high as to rule out the possibility of compensation to those less fortunate. To accept the lexical ordering of the two principles we are not required to deny that the value of liberty depends upon circumstances. But it does have to be shown that as the general conception of justice is followed social conditions are eventually brought about under which a lesser than equal liberty would no longer be accepted. Unequal liberty is then no longer justified. The lexical order is, so to speak, the inherent long-run equilibrium of a just system. Once the tendency to equality has worked itself out, if not long before, the two principles are to be serially ranked.

In these remarks I have assumed that it is always those with the lesser liberty who must be compensated. We are always to appraise the situation from their point of view (as seen from the constitutional convention or the legislature). Now it is this restriction that makes it practically certain that slavery and serfdom, in their familiar forms anyway, are tolerable only when they relieve even worse injustices. There may be transition cases where enslavement is better

than current practice. For example, suppose that city-states that previously have not taken prisoners of war but have always put captives to death agree by treaty to hold prisoners as slaves instead. Although we cannot allow the institution of slavery on the grounds that the greater gains of some outweigh the losses to others, it may be that under these conditions, since all run the risk of capture in war, this form of slavery is less unjust than present custom. At least the servitude envisaged is not hereditary (let us suppose) and it is accepted by the free citizens of more or less equal city-states. The arrangement seems defensible as an advance on established institutions, if slaves are not treated too severely. In time it will presumably be abandoned altogether, since the exchange of prisoners of war is a still more desirable arrangement, the return of the captured members of the community being preferable to the services of slaves. But none of these considerations, however fanciful, tend in any way to justify hereditary slavery or serfdom by citing natural or historical limitations. Moreover, one cannot at this point appeal to the necessity or at least to the great advantage of these servile arrangements for the higher forms of culture.

The problem of paternalism deserves some discussion here, since it has been mentioned in the argument for equal liberty, and concerns a lesser freedom. In the original position the parties assume that in society they are rational and able to manage their own affairs. Therefore they do not acknowledge any duties to self, since this is unnecessary to further their good. But once the ideal conception is chosen, they will want to insure themselves against the possibility that their powers are undeveloped and they cannot rationally advance their interests, as in the case of children; or that through some misfortune or accident they are unable to make decisions for their good, as in the case of those seriously injured or mentally disturbed. It is also rational for them to protect themselves against their own irrational inclinations by consenting to a scheme of penalties that may give them a sufficient motive to avoid foolish actions and by accepting certain impositions designed to undo the unfortunate consequences of their imprudent behavior. For these cases the parties adopt principles stipulating when others are authorized to act in their behalf and to override their present wishes if necessary; and this they do recognizing that sometimes their capacity to act rationally for their good may fail, or be lacking altogether.

Thus the principles of paternalism are those that the parties would acknowledge in the original position to protect themselves against the weakness and infirmities of their reason and will in society. Others are authorized and sometimes required to act on our behalf and to do what we would do for ourselves if we were rational, this authorization coming into effect only when we cannot look after our own good. Paternalistic decisions are to be guided by the individual's own settled preferences and interests insofar as they are not irrational, or failing a knowledge of these, by the theory of primary goods. As we know less and less about a person, we act for him as we would act for ourselves from the standpoint of the original position. We try to get for him the things he presumably wants whatever else he wants. We must be able to argue that with the development or the recovery of his rational powers the individual in question will accept our decision on his behalf and agree with us that we did the best thing for him.

BIBLIOGRAPHICAL NOTES

Among the general histories of ideas, Bertrand Russell's, *A History of Western Philosophy: And Its Connection with Political and Social Circumstances from the Earliest Times to the Present Day* (New York, 1945), holds a special place. It is written by a distinguished philosopher, and it has three outstanding qualities: first, it is a source of pleasure from a purely literary viewpoint (Russell received the Nobel Prize in literature) and thus demonstrates that there need be no drudgery in science and philosophy; second, Russell's discussion of political ideas is constantly related to the main issues of general philosophy; third, unlike some writers of histories of political theory who identify themselves in each chapter with the thinker they discuss, Russell writes from a definite and clearly stated point of view. Thus his work has direction and consistency. Another work of merit from a general philosophical perspective is Frederick Copleston's nine-volume *A History of Philosophy* (Westminster, Maryland, 1946–1974).

The following histories of political philosophy will be found useful: Crane Brinton, *Ideas and Men: The Story of Western Thought* (New York, 1950); George Catlin, *The Story of the Political Philosophers* (New York–London, 1939); William Elliott and Neil McDonald, *Western Political Heritage* (New York, 1949); Andrew Hacker, *Political Theory: Philosophy, Ideology, Science* (New York, 1961); Lee McDonald, *(Western Political Theory* New York, 1968); Robert Nisbet, *The Social Philosophers* (New York, 1973); Gerald Runkle, *A History of Western Political Theory* (New York, 1968); George H. Sabine and Thomas Thorson, *A History of Political Theory,* 4th ed. (New York, 1973); Mulford Sibley, *Political Ideas and Ideologies; A History of Political Thought* (New York, 1970); and Leo Strauss and Joseph Cropsey (eds.), *History of Political Philosophy,* 3rd ed. (Chicago, 1987).

Other works by William Ebenstein in the area of the history of political theory include *Modern Political Thought; The Great Issues,* 2nd ed. (New York, 1960), which includes introductory essays and readings on a wide variety of modern political issues; and *Political Thought in Perspective* (New York, 1957), which features essays on great political thinkers by other leading thinkers or political figures. The eleventh edition of *Today's Isms: Socialism, Capitalism, Fascism, Communism, Libertarianism* (North Brunswick, N. J., 2000), provides interesting and valuable interpretation and historical information.

I. ANCIENT AND MEDIEVAL

CHAPTER ONE

ROOTS OF THE WEST

(See Bibliographical Notes to Chapter Two, "The Greek Discovery of Reason in Nature," and Chapter Eight, "The Jewish Belief in One God, and Christian Love.")

CHAPTER TWO

THE GREEK DISCOVERY OF REASON IN NATURE

• BURCKHARDT, JACOB, *History of Greek Culture* (New York, 1963). This abridged translation of a classic work by the great nineteenth-century Swiss historian contains interesting analyses of Greek government and politics.

• CALHOUN, GEORGE M., *Introduction to Greek Legal Science* (Oxford, 1944). Contains considerable material of interest to the student of politics; Chap. III, "Legal Thought in the Aristocracies" (pp. 15–21), and V, "The Athenian Democracy" (pp. 30–49), are particularly relevant.

• DODDS, E. R., *The Greeks and the Irrational* (Berkeley, 1951). In probing into the place of irrationality in Greek life and thought, the author explores much territory hitherto unknown or neglected. Chap. VII (pp. 207–235) deals with the irrational, theological, and mystical elements in Plato's thought. Plato's place in the "mystical tradition" (as distinct from the scientific) of classical Greece is also examined in F. M. Cornford, *From Religion to Philosophy* (Harper Torchbooks, 1957), particularly pp. 242–263, and in M. B. Foster, *Mystery and Philosophy* (London, 1957), pp. 31–37. A comprehensive and systematic survey of the evolution and vicissitudes of Greek rationalism from its beginnings in the sixth century B.C. to its "final capitulation" in the third century A.D. will be found in George Boas, *Rationalism in Greek Philosophy* (Baltimore, 1961).

• FARRAR, CYNTHIA, *The Origins of Democratic Thinking* (Cambridge, 1988). A study on the development of politics in ancient Athens, with special attention on Protagoras, Thucydides, and Democritus.

• FREEMAN, KATHLEEN, *The Pre-Socratic Philosophers* (Oxford, 1946), and *Ancilla to the Pre-Socratic Philosophers* (Oxford, 1948). The first is a companion to H. Diels, *Fragmente der Vorsokratiker,* 5th ed. (Berlin, 1934–1938), the foremost collection (in Greek) of pre-Socratic Greek philosophy. The second work by Kathleen Freeman is a complete English translation of the fragments in Diels's collection.

Plato and Aristotle were not, as is often thought, the beginning of Greek philosophy but its peak, or, as some think, the beginning of its decay. One of the main reasons for the pervasive influence of Plato and Aristotle is that their most important writings have been preserved. By contrast, most of the pre-Socratic philosophical writings have either been lost or preserved in small bits and fragments. Thus the *Ancilla to the Pre-Socratic Philosophers,* which contains the complete translation of the fragments in the Diels collection, is only 162 pages long, though referring to ninety sources; in numerous instances, not a single line of important thinkers is preserved.

For a detailed history of pre-Socratic Greek philosophy, see J. Burnet, *Early Greek Philosophy* (London–Edinburgh, 1892), and Theodor Gomperz, *Greek Thinkers* (London–New York, 1901, reprinted 1964), Vol. I. See also Léon Robin, *Greek Thought and the Origins of the Scientific Spirit* (London–New York, 1928), pp. 1–147; F. M. Cornford, *Before and after Socrates* (Cambridge, 1932), pp. 1–32; Milton C. Nahm (ed.), *Selections from Early Greek Philosophy,* 2nd ed. (New York, 1944); and Felix M. Cleve, *The Giants of Pre-Sophistic Greek Philosophy: An Attempt to Reconstruct Their Thought,* 2 vols. (The Hague, 1965).

Mario Untersteiner, *The Sophists* (translated from the Italian by Kathleen Freeman, Oxford, 1954), is the best introduction to the lives and ideas of the most important sophists, and corrects many traditional misunderstandings and distortions first expressed in Plato's writings. To the sophists we owe the concept, Untersteiner writes, that man has "the right to a human life, human speech, and human thought" (p. xvi).

• FRENCH, A., *The Growth of the Athenian Economy* (London, 1964). Tracing the economic development of Athens from Solon to the Persian wars, French considers both internal factors of economic growth as well as external factors of war and diplomacy which made Athens the cultural and economic center of Greece and Europe. Of particular interest is Chap. VIII (pp. 135–162) on the "social consequences" of rising wealth on the Athenian class structure and political ideas and practices. For a more general study, see also H. Mitchell, *The Economics of Ancient Greece* (Cambridge, 1940). Both French and Mitchell have extensive bibliographical data. The problem of slavery, both in its economic and noneconomic aspects, is dealt with in M. I. Finley (ed.), *Slavery in Classical Antiquity* (Cambridge, 1960), and Victoria Cuffel, "The Classical Greek Concept of Slavery," *Journal of the History of Ideas,* XXVII (July–September, 1966), 323–342.

• GUTHRIE, W. K. C., *A History of Greek Philosophy,* 6 vols. (Cambridge, 1962–1981). The first volume covers *The Earlier Presocratics and the Pythagoreans;* the second, *The Presocratic Tradition from Parmenides to Democritus;* the third, *The Fifth-Century Enlightenment;* the fourth, *Plato; The Man and His Dialogues: Earlier Period;* the fifth, *The Later Plato and the Academy;* and the sixth, *Aristotle: An Encounter.* This is the most detailed account of Greek thought in the English language and a landmark of classical scholarship.

• HUXLEY, G. L., *The Early Ionians* (London, 1966). Provides a historical and social background of the early Ionians, and discusses the birth of natural philosophy and the contributions of its major figures. See also Giorgio de Santillana, *The Origins of Scientific Thought* (New York, 1961).

• JAEGER, WERNER, *Paideia: The Ideals of Greek Culture,* 3 vols. (New York, 1939–1944). This ambitious work is comprehensive in scope, though lacking somewhat in novelty of interpretation. Vols. II and III deal mainly with Plato, and the *Republic* is analyzed in Vol. II (pp. 198–370).

• JONES, A. H. M., *Sparta* (Cambridge, Mass., 1967). Briefly presents Sparta's political institutions and its evolution from its origins to its final subjection to Roman rule. In Chap. IX ("The Discipline"), the author describes the training of Sparta's youth as follows: "The training was mainly athletic and military, but there was singing of traditional songs, and no doubt Homer and the Spartan poets were read. The boys lived very hard—they slept in dormitories on rushes which they had to cut themselves without knives, received one garment a year, and very meager rations. They were not allowed baths (of course they could bathe in the river, but the Eurotas is very cold in winter). To supplement their meager diet they were encouraged to steal food and punished if they were caught for being so clumsy. Contemporary Greeks found this funny and quizzed Spartans about it. Girls received a similar athletic and musical training and like the boys held public competition; other Greeks were shocked at girls appearing naked in public. Some of the tests to which the boys were put were very brutal. Notorious was the game of stealing cheeses from the altar of Artemis Orthia; the boys had to run a gauntlet of flogging under which not a few died" (p. 35).

Victor Ehrenberg, *Aspects of the Ancient World* (Oxford, 1946), deals in Chap. VII, "A Totalitarian State" (pp. 94–104), with Sparta and shows how "this first and greatest of all authoritarian and totalitarian states" became, after its victory over Athens, "the starting-point and center of political theory. The development, which reached its culmination, though by no means its end, in Plato's imposing and bewildering picture of an ideal state in the *Republic,* led far away from reality." The educational system and communal life of the Spartan ruling class closely resembled those of the guardians in the *Republic,* although they were by no means identical.

E. N. Tigerstedt, *The Legend of Sparta in Classical Antiquity,* Vol. I (Stockholm, 1965), discusses the relations of Plato to Sparta's thought and institutions in detail (pp. 244–276), and concludes that Plato played an important role in fostering the legend of Sparta, for example, its glorification as a moral, political, and social ideal. Although conceding that Plato at times sharply criticized some of Sparta's practices and institutions, the author points to the numerous affinities which Plato's "contemporaries and posterity were bound to find between the political ideal as proposed by Plato and the historical Lacedaemon. Which other state in Greece could at one and the same time show the same division of the inhabitants into a small ruling minority and a great majority of politically disenfranchised, the same—at least outwardly professed—disregard for wealth, the same equality between its members, the same freedom for women, the same state education for youth, the same moral and political order and surveillance of citizens?" (p. 274). Tigerstedt also adds that "Plato's criticism of Sparta, even where it is most outspoken, does not have the scornful and contemptuous bitterness which characterizes his pronouncements on Athens, the Athens of democracy. Plato takes Sparta seriously, as he never does Athens. It would be quite unthinkable that he should subject Athenian democracy to a similar searching inquiry as Spartan timocracy. The folly of

democracy and its worthlessness is for him a self-evident fact. To the extent to which Athens is identified with democracy, to the same extent Sparta indirectly profits from Plato's loathing of democracy" *(ibid.).* See also John H. Randall, "Plato's Treatment of the Theme of the Good Life and His Criticism of the Spartan Ideal," *Journal of the History of Ideas,* XXVIII (July–September 1967), 307–324.

• KRAUT, RICHARD, *Socrates and the State* (Princeton, 1984). Chapters VII and VIII deal with Socrates's opinions on democracy generally and Athens particularly. Kraut's conclusion is that Socrates was a critic of democracy.

• LIVINGSTONE, R. W. (ed.), *The Legacy of Greece* (Oxford, 1921). One of the best general introductions to Greek civilization, with contributions by Gilbert Murray ("The value of Greece to the Future of the World"), J. Burnet ("Philosophy"), D'Arcy W. Thompson ("Natural Science"), Arnold Toynbee ("History"), A. E. Zimmern ("Political Thought"), and others on such varied topics as religion, mathematics and astronomy, biology, medicine, literature, and art.

In *The Greek Genius and Its Meaning to Us* (London, 1912), Livingstone interprets Greek genius in terms of the following principal qualities: beauty, freedom, directness, humanism, sanity, and manysidedness. He stresses that the "main stream of Hellenism" was characterized by these qualities, but there was a "subordinate current of thought" in Greek life that reflected the absence or even opposite of these qualities, and "the one great extant writer who fully represents" this "unhellenic spirit" is Plato (3rd imp., 1924, p. 182). Livingstone refers particularly to Plato's theories of poetry and love, his hostility to liberty and humanism, and his tendencies toward asceticism and otherworldliness.

In the introduction to his *Plato: Selected Passages* (London–New York–Toronto, 1940), Livingstone states that the "gravest criticisms against Plato are that he imposes goodness forcibly, that his methods would fail in practice, and that at best they could only produce a mechanical virtue and a static and stereotyped humanity," and that the "authoritarians of all ages are his children—all who from natural pessimism or bitter experience have held that the masses must be saved from themselves by a governing elite" (p. xxi). Livingstone arrives at this critical view of Plato although he starts his appraisal with the words: "Perhaps no thinker has had as deep and permanent an influence on European thought as Plato, and many people meet him there without recognizing him" (p. vii).

• MURRAY, GILBERT, *Five Stages of Greek Religion* (Thinker's Library, London, 1946). Chap. IV, "The Failure of Nerve" (pp. 123–172), is the most famous of the book. See also Murray's *Greek Studies* (New York, 1946). Greek religious conceptions are also discussed in Kathleen Freeman, *God, Man, and State: Greek Concepts* (London, 1952); Werner Jaeger, *The Theology of the Early Greek Philosophers* (Oxford, 1947); Carl Kerenyi, *The Gods of the Greeks* (Penguin Books, Baltimore, 1958); and Martin P. Nilsson, *Cults, Myths, Oracles, and Politics in Ancient Greece* (Lund, 1951).

• OBER, JOSIAH, *Mass and Elite in Democratic Athens* (Princeton, 1989). A detailed examination of the ancient city-state. See also Ellen Wood, *Peasant-Citizen and State* (London, 1988) and R. K. Sinclair, *Democracy and Participation in Athens* (Cambridge, 1988).

• SCHRÖDINGER, ERWIN, *Nature and the Greeks* (Cambridge, 1954). The birth of Greek science, as seen by one of the greatest physicists of the twentieth century. See also George Sarton, *Ancient Science and Modern Civilization* (New York, 1959).

• STONE, I. F., *The Trial of Socrates* (New York, 1988). A work which attempts to explain Socrates's rejection of Athens, as well as its rejection of him.

• STRAUSS, LEO, *Xenophon's Socrates* (Ithaca, NY, 1972). A textual analysis of the only major non-Platonic sources of information about Socrates—Xenophon's *Memorabilia, Apology of Socrates,* and *Symposium.*

• TAYLOR, ALFRED EDWARD, *Socrates* (Doubleday Anchor Books, New York, 1957). An excellent brief introduction into the life and thought of Socrates. The best portrait of Socrates appears in the pages of Plato's dialogues *Apology* and *Crito.* See also John D. Montgomery, *The State versus Socrates: A Case Study in Civic Freedom* (Boston, 1954), an anthology of writings on Socrates by many authors, including Friedrich Wilhelm Nietzsche, John Stuart Mill, George Grote,

Vilfredo Pareto, A. E. Taylor, Werner Jaeger, Karl R. Popper, Arnold J. Toynbee, and others. Similarly, Herbert Spiegelberg (ed.), *The Socratic Enigma: A Collection of Testimonies through Twenty-Four Centuries* (Indianapolis–New York, 1964), presents a variety of viewpoints on Socrates from antiquity to the present. The bulk of the collection is taken from the modern period and is organized according to major countries and languages. See also Michael J. O'Brien, *The Socratic Paradoxes and the Greek Mind* (Chapel Hill, 1967), focusing on the main ethical paradoxes of Socrates: that "no one does wrong willingly; no one wishes evil; virtue can be taught; virtue is an art like medicine or carpentry; virtue is knowledge; vice is ignorance" (p. 16). Alexander Eliot, *Socrates* (New York, 1967), presents a brief and popular portrait of Socrates as a man and prophet, with special emphasis on his relevance to our contemporary world.

• TOYNBEE, ARNOLD J., *Hellenism: The History of a Civilization* (New York, 1959). The author sees in "man-worship or Humanism" (p. 10) the distinctive mark of Greek civilization. While humanism flourished at other times and places (such as the Italian Renaissance and the French Age of Reason), the Hellenic experiment in Humanism "was the most whole-hearted and uncompromising practice of man-worship that is on record up to date. This is the distinctive mark of Hellenic history, and it raises an interesting question: What was the connexion between the Hellenes' worship of man and Hellenism's rise, achievements, breakdown, and eventual fall? That is the subject of this book" (*ibid.*). The failure of the Greeks to unite politically, the author concludes, rendered the collapse of their civilization inevitable. Today we see again the revival of the Greek worship of idolized local states: "The Modern World must exorcise this demon resolutely if it is to save itself from meeting with its Hellenic predecessor's fate" (p. 253).

• VLASTOS, GREGORY, "The Historical Socrates and Athenian Democracy," *Political Theory* (November 1983), 495–516. Presents the opinion that Socrates was much more inclined toward democracy than generally is held. For a response, see Ellen Wood and Neal Wood, "Socrates and Democracy," *Political Theory* (February 1986), 55–82.

• ZIMMERN, ALFRED, *The Greek Common-wealth: Politics and Economics in Fifth-Century Athens,* 5th ed. (Oxford, 1931). The best book on the subject. See also André Bonnard, *Greek Civilization,* 3 vols. (New York, 1958–1961); C. M. Bowra, *The Greek Experience* (New York, 1958); H. D. F. Kitto, *The Greeks* (Penguin Books, Baltimore,

1951); Moses Hadas, *Humanism: The Greek Ideal and Its Survival* (New York, 1960); M. I. Finley, *The Ancient Greeks: An Introduction to Their Life and Thought* (New York, 1964); Hugh Lloyd-Jones (ed.), *The Greek World* (London–Baltimore, 1965); and Victor Ehrenberg, *The Greek State* (New York, 1960).

CHAPTER THREE

PLATO

• ANNAS, JULIA, *An Introduction to Plato's Republic,* (Oxford, 1981). Annas holds that Plato's authoritarianism is partially the result of "an expansive theory of justice" which sees justice more broadly than modern conceptions do. Good "Further Reading" sections at the end of each chapter.

• AVERROES, *Averroes on Plato's* Republic (trans. Ralph Lerner, with an introduction and notes, Ithaca, NY, 1974). The twelfth century philosopher's commentary.

• BAMBROUGH, RENFORD (ed.), *Plato, Popper and Politics: Some Contributions to a Modern Controversy* (Cambridge, 1967). A collection of essays separately published elsewhere for and against Plato.

• BARKER, ERNEST, *Greek Political Theory: Plato and His Predecessors,* 2nd ed. (London, 1925). The first four chapters on pre-Platonic political thought (pp. 1–85) are especially valuable, as is the Appendix, "The Later History of Plato's Political Theory" (pp. 383–392). The analysis of the *Republic* forms the core of the book (pp. 145–270).

• BARROW, ROBIN, *Plato, Utilitarianism and Education* (London, 1975). Argues that the ethical, social, and educational systems of the *Republic* are essentially utilitarian, with each class performing the role for which it is particularly suited.

• BOSANQUET, BERNARD, *A Companion to Plato's Republic* (New York, 1895). Preceded by an introduction (pp. 1–35), the commentary follows the text of the *Republic* book by book.

• BRUMBAUGH, ROBERT S., *Plato for the Modern Age* (New York, 1964). Traces the main stages of Plato's life and thought in a succinct and simple manner, and appraises the relevance of Plato's key ideas to the modern world. Brumbaugh notes that "there has been, in the Western world, a tremendous increase in our intuitive ethical sensitivity since Plato's times" (p. 214), but he points out that many later developments are causally related to Plato's philosophy. In his brief analysis of the *Republic* (pp. 85–103), Brumbaugh stresses Plato's conception of the good and takes up the question of whether he should be regarded as a mystic: "In the sense that his system recognizes a direct intellectual vision of some highest form of being, Plato is surely a mystic. In the sense that such a vision is different from and totally unlike all other experience, so that it is disconnected from reason and experiment, Plato equally surely is not" (p. 102). On Plato's mysticism, see also Paul Friedländer, *Plato,* Vol. I (New York, 1958), pp. 72–80.

• CAVARNOS, CONSTANTINE, *Plato's View of Man* (Belmont, Mass., 1975). A brief (95 pages) work. Two Bowen Prize essays on the problems of the destiny of man and the individual life, together with selected passages from Plato on the soul.

• CRAIG, LEON H., *The War Lover: A Study of Plato's Republic* (Toronto, 1994). This fascinating exploration of Plato's political psychology seeks to defend the philosophic life against those who would condemn it as a "soft, indolent, pacifistic, irreverent, politically useless, effeminizing corrupter of young men" (p. 13). Craig's goal of bringing together the "lover of war" with the "lover of wisdom" is only partially successful, but remains a useful and enriching resource.

• CROMBIE, I. M., *An Examination of Plato's Doctrines*, 2 vols. (London–New York, 1962–1963). The first volume is devoted to Plato's life and writings and the development of his thought, including a discussion of the relation of Plato to Socrates. Then follows a detailed interpretation of Plato's politics, ethics, esthetics, and religion. The second volume examines Plato's theory of knowledge, cosmology, metaphysics, and logic. Written from the viewpoint of modern philosophical scholarship and analysis, rather than from that of classical or historical scholarship, Crombie's work is a major contribution to a better understanding of Plato's thought. Crombie is sympathetic to what Plato tried to do without turning him into an idol, and at the same time he is critical where criticism is valid, without cutting down Plato to the size of a pigmy. In fairness, clarity, and depth Crombie's work ranks with the best in any language written in the last several generations. In *Plato: The Midwife's Apprentice* (London, 1964), Crombie summarizes the major findings and conclusions of his larger work, but without providing the supporting arguments in detail. In less than 200 pages, the short volume covers the major themes and problems of Plato's thought, and is therefore particularly useful for the beginning student of Plato. Morris Stockhammer (ed.), *Plato Dictionary* (New York, 1963) presents the important concepts and ideas of Plato through appropriate passages from his various works. The arrangement is in alphabetical order in dictionary form.

• CROPSEY, JOSEPH, *Plato's World: Man's Place in the Cosmos* (Chicago, 1995). The author's scholarly reputation recommends this work. This deeply respectful analysis of eight of Plato's dialogues enlightens and intellectually engages in Cropsey's reading of Plato.

• CROSS, R. C., and A. D. WOOZLEY, *Plato's Republic: A Philosophical Commentary* (New York, 1964). A highly successful attempt to present the main problems of philosophy through a systematic examination of the main philosophical themes in the *Republic*. The subjects covered follow, in general, the sequence of the *Republic*. In dealing with the key conceptions of the *Republic,* as of Greek thought in general, the authors repeatedly go into considerable detail in showing the difficulties of translating Greek terms into English. This aspect of the book is of special value to the reader who has no (or only little) knowledge of Greek. See also William Boyd, *An Introduction to the Republic of Plato* (New York, 1963); Alexander Sesonske (ed.), *Plato's Republic: Interpretation and Criticism* (Belmont, Cal., 1966); Neville R. Murphy, *The Interpretation of Plato's Republic* (New York, 1960); and Noah E. Fehl, *A Guide to the Study of Plato's Republic* (Hong Kong, 1962).

• DEMOS, RAPHAEL, *The Philosophy of Plato* (New York, 1939). "Man," the fourth and last part (pp. 303–399), is divided into four chapters: "Human Nature"; "Degeneration in the Individual and in the Society"; "The Ideal of Reason"; "Portrait of the Philosopher." Though many interpretive works on Plato deal with his dialogues, which are treated individually, Demos organizes his analysis according to topics; his discussion of Plato's political ideas is therefore drawn from many Platonic sources and thus gains in interest and perspective. Demos arrives at the conclusion that Plato's ideal state "combines the features both of aristocracy and of what we know as democracy." As to the former, the aristocracy "is of the benevolent kind. The rulers will not exploit the masses but will guide them to the fullest realization of their possibilities." As to the democratic aspect, "the state will be democratic in that the energies of the state will be used for the service of the interests, not of the few, but of all" (p. 357).

Demos seems to be insufficiently aware that government *of* the people and *by* the people is indispensable to democracy, and that government *for* the people is perfectly compatible with undemocratic forms of rule. Demos arrives at his position, so similar to that of Plato himself, from the assumption that today reason is "a disintegrating factor," and that since the Reformation the "modern world is broken up into a multiplicity of sects. This is not reason but the chaos in the receptacle" (p. 378). One of the main purposes of the *Republic* was a unified social system, dominated by a hierarchy of values and persons. Modern Platonists, too, dread the diversity and pluralism of the nonhierarchical and egalitarian society, and yearn for the absolute and universal Good that all men will accept.

• FERGUSON, JOHN, *Utopias of the Classical World* (Ithaca, N.Y., 1975). Includes an excellent chapter on Plato's thought from the *Republic* to the *Laws,* with reference to other dialogues.

• FIELD, G. C. *Plato and His Contemporaries,* 2nd ed. (London, 1948). An excellent survey of Plato's life and work against the background of his contemporaries.

• FINDLAY, JOHN, *Plato: The Written and Unwritten Doctrines* (New York, 1974). Presents the view that Plato's political philosophy is based on his larger cosmology: "political life derives from the metaphysical Ultimates of the Universe." Findlay's conclusion is "Plato is best regarded as having constructed an imaginary Pythagorean commune." See also Findlay's *Plato and Platonism: An Introduction* (New York, 1978).

• FOSTER, M. B., *The Political Philosophies of Plato and Hegel* (Oxford, 1935). The first two chapters (pp. 1–71) are on Plato and rank among the most brilliant contributions to Platonic studies. Indispensable to an understanding of Plato's political philosophy.

• GROTE, GEORGE, *Plato and the Other Companions of Sokrates,* 3 vols. (London, 1865). Despite its age, still one of the best analyses and interpretations of Platonic and Socratic doctrines. Grote's considerable classical scholarship was buttressed by extensive experience in business and government, including ten years as a Member of Parliament, and his comments on the *Republic* (Vol. III, Chaps. XXXIII–XXXV, pp. 27–242) deserve special attention.

Socrates, the central figure in the *Republic,* seems to Grote to have been portrayed by Plato in a distorted fashion. The "real Socrates," as depicted by Plato himself in the *Apology* and other, earlier, dialogues, was a dissenter from the established order, confessing his own ignorance and his inability to teach anything. But in the *Republic,* Plato presents Socrates as "passing to the opposite pole; taking up the orthodox, conservative, point of view," and Socrates "now expects every individual to fall into place, and contract the opinions, prescribed by

authority; including among those opinions deliberate ethical and political fictions, such as that about the gold and silver earthborn men. Free-thinking minds, who take views of their own, and enquire into the evidence of these beliefs, become inconvenient and dangerous" (III, 240). Grote's general estimate of the *Republic* was that "we must look upon Plato as a preacher—inculcating a belief which he thinks useful to be diffused; rather than as philosopher, announcing truths of human nature, and laying down a consistent, scientific, theory of Ethics" (*ibid.,* p. 156). See also Vols. II and III of Theodor Gomperz, *Greek Thinkers* (London–New York, 1905, reprinted 1964), a classic in the field.

• GULLEY, NORMAN, *Plato's Theory of Knowledge* (London, 1962). Examines Plato's views on truth, knowledge, belief, perception, and sensation. F. M. Cornford, *Plato's Theory of Knowledge* (London, 1955), contains translations of Plato's *Theaetetus* and *Sophist,* with running commentaries and an introduction by the translator. See also William D. Ross, *Plato's Theory of Ideas* (Oxford, 1951), and Robert E. Cushman, *Therapeia: Plato's Conception of Philosophy* (Chapel Hill, 1958). For analyses of the role of mathematical concepts in Plato's thought, see Gulley, *op. cit.,* pp. 169–187; F. Lasserre, *The Birth of Mathematics in the Age of Plato* (New York, 1964); Robert S. Brumbaugh, *Plato's Mathematical Imagination* (Bloomington, 1954); Anders E. O. Wedberg, *Plato's Philosophy of Mathematics* (Stockholm, 1955); and R. M. Hare, "Plato and the Mathematicians," in Renford Bambrough (ed.), *New Essays on Plato and Aristotle* (New York, 1965), pp. 21–38.

• HAVELOCK, ERIC A., *The Liberal Temper in Greek Politics* (New Haven, 1957). The author of this pioneering work strongly objects to the fact that in most conventional histories of Greek political thought "the naturalists and the materialists, the sophists and the democrats, are treated only as faint and futile voices protesting off-stage," while the undemocratic or antidemocratic views of Plato and Aristotle occupy the center of the stage (p. 19). By contrast, Havelock documents in detail his main thesis that liberalism was a part of the intellectual history of classic Greece, growing outside the walls of Plato's idealism and Aristotle's teleology. Throughout his book Havelock deals fully and fairly with Plato's political thought, presenting many points in a new light.

• ———, *Preface to Plato* (Cambridge, Mass., 1963). Plato's attack on poetry in the *Republic* has generally been condemned or defended by students of Platonic thought on political grounds. Havelock places the whole issue into a much broader perspective. In Plato's time, and even more so before his time, poetry in Greece did not mean poetry or even literature in the modern sense, but the orally transmitted sum total of all existing knowledge—history, politics, ethics, and technology. Oral transmission depended on emphasizing the concrete and the emotional aspects of happenings, using colorful images as vehicles of communication. Plato's attack against poetry, Havelock argues, was therefore not a side issue, but central in his attempt to develop conceptual and abstract thinking: "Platonism at bottom is an appeal to substitute a conceptual discourse for an imagistic one" (p. 261). Plato's theory of Forms dramatized this split between "the image-thinking of poetry and the abstract thinking of philosophy" (p. 266), and thus turned Greek, and European, thought into a new direction.

• KELSEN, HANS, *What Is Justice: Justice, Law, and Politics in the Mirror of Science* (Berkeley and Los Angeles, 1957). Chap. III (pp. 82–109) is on "Platonic Justice." Originally published in *KantStudien*, XXXVIII, Nos. 1–2 (1933), pp. 91–117, this is one of the most penetrating studies of Plato and basic to an understanding of his political ideas in the light of his general philosophy and metaphysics. Kelsen writes incisively on the irrational and mystical elements in Plato's philosophy that lead to politically dangerous consequences: "Plato's mysticism, this most complete expression of irrationalism, is the justification of his antidemocratic politics; it is the ideology of every autocracy." Concerning the problem of justice, Kelsen concludes that "rational science can never give an answer to the question concerning the nature of justice, that it cannot solve that problem, but only resolve it. The final position rational science will take in all its different forms is this: there is no such thing as absolute justice, which cannot be defined conceptually. Such

an ideal is an illusion. There are only interests and conflicts of interests, which are resolved either by struggle or compromise. In the sphere of rationality, the idea of peace inevitably replaces the ideal of justice" (pp. 116–117 of the original German version, from which this translation is made directly).

• ———, "Platonic Love," *American Imago*, III (April 1942), pp. 1–112, originally published (in German) in *Imago*, XIX, Nos. 1–2 (1933), pp. 34–98, 225–255, and reprinted in his *Aufsaetze zur Ideologiekritik* (Neuwied am Rhein-Berlin, 1964), pp. 114–197. A detailed critical analysis of Plato's defense of homosexuality and its reflection in his philosophical and political ideas. Contrary to common belief, homosexuality was not widespread in ancient Greece but practiced by only a thin layer of the aristocratic class; the general reaction to boy love was condemnatory and punitive in both social mores and actual penal legislation. Most of those inclined toward homosexuality were married and raised families, and their love of boys was in addition to their heterosexual lives; Plato was—even by the standards of these men—more extreme, because he confined himself to an erotic world in which there was no room for marriage or family, or any intimate personal relation with a woman. It was inevitable that the profound conflict between himself and society should pervade all his thinking and writing. Kelsen brilliantly traces the inner relation between Plato's personal life, full of love and affection as well as guilt and shame, and his schemes for political reform. A short critical discussion, "Platonic Love," will also be found in Warner Fite, *The Platonic Legend* (New York, 1934), Chap. VIII (pp. 153–179).

The views of Plato on love and sex are defended against Kelsen and Fite by Ronald B. Levinson, *In Defense of Plato* (Cambridge, Mass., 1953), Chap. VI (pp. 81–138). Highly sympathetic to Plato's views on love is also Thomas Gould, *Platonic Love* (London, 1963). Gould does not confine himself to the *Symposium* and the *Phaedrus*, the two main Platonic dialogues that deal directly with the subject of love, but also examines Platonic statements in other dialogues, including the *Republic*. Comparing Plato's conception of love with the Christian, Romantic, and Freudian concepts, Gould finds that "only

Plato and Freud have worked out the philosophical implications" of the idea of love as the key to everything in life. But "compared to Plato, Freud hardly got going" (p. 17). See also the following: Stanley Rosen, *Plato's Symposium* (New Haven, 1968); Douglas N. Morgan, *Love: Plato, the Bible and Freud* (Englewood Cliffs, N.J., 1964); Josef Pieper, *Love and Inspiration: A Study of Plato's Phaedrus* (New York, 1964); Herman L. Sinaiko, *Love, Knowledge, and Discourse in Plato: Dialogue and Dialectic in Phaedrus, Republic, Parmenides* (Chicago, 1965); and H. D. Rankin, *Plato and the Individual* (London, 1964); Chap. V, "Man, Woman, and Eros" (pp. 77–100).

• KLOSKO, GEORGE, *The Development of Plato's Political Theory* (New York, 1986). A valuable addition to the Platonic literature. Klosko attempts a comprehensive treatment of Plato's political theory, discussing both the scholarly literature and the relevant dialogues. Klosko also discusses Plato within the social and political context of his times.

• LEVINSON, RONALD B., "The *Republic* Revisited," *Yale Review*, XXIX (Autumn 1939), 153–166. Interprets Plato as "the moralist and poet of the spiritual life" and, though admitting, "without argument or reservation, that Plato was not a democrat," denies that the *Republic* is an "anticipatory confirmation of the contemporary dictatorships." Later, Levinson elaborated his approach in a larger work, *In Defense of Plato* (Cambridge, Mass., 1953). For further studies in defense of Plato, see John Wild, *Plato's Theory of Man* (Cambridge, Mass., 1946), and *Plato's Modern Enemies and the Theory of Natural Law* (Chicago, 1953); Rupert C. Lodge, *The Philosophy of Plato* (London, 1956); and Paul Friedländer, *Plato,* 3 vols. (New York–Princeton, 1958–1969).

• MARA, GERALD, *Socrates' Discursive Democracy: Logos and Ergon in Platonic Political Philosophy* (Albany, 1997). Mara seeks to present Plato's Socrates as a democratic philosopher. This work will be valuable for those wishing to engage modern and postmodern debates on this subject.

• MORE, PAUL ELMER, *Platonism* (Princeton, 1917). Of particular importance is Chap. VI, "The Doctrine of Ideas" (pp. 162–203).

• MORROW, GLENN, *Plato's Cretan City* (Princeton, 1960). Argues that the social order described in the *Laws* is much influenced by contemporary Athenian practice and the "ancestral" Athenian constitution.

• NETTLESHIP, RICHARD LEWIS, *Lectures on the Republic of Plato* (London, 1937). Unlike most commentaries that analyze the *Republic* topically, Nettleship's *Lectures* follows the *Republic* from beginning to end in its own order of themes. For the reader who approaches the *Republic* for the first time, Nettleship's commentary is perhaps the most useful guide, because it follows the text of the *Republic* closely and sympathetically. See also Nettleship's *The Theory of Education in Plato's Republic* (Oxford, 1935) for a brief exposition of Plato's system of education, in many respects the heart of the *Republic*.

A fuller treatment of Plato's educational philosophy will be found in Sir Richard Livingstone, *Plato and Modern Education* (Cambridge–New York, 1944) and Rupert C. Lodge, *Plato's Theory of Education* (London, 1947). These works present systematic analyses of Plato's educational philosophy based on the *Republic* as well as on several other major dialogues.

• PANGLE, THOMAS, *The Roots of Political Philosophy* (Ithaca, N.Y., 1987). Literal translations of and interpretive essays on ten little-known Platonic dialogues from a Straussian perspective.

• PLATO, *The Republic of Plato* (trans. with notes and an interpretive essay by Alan Bloom, New York, 1968). The most literal translation in English of the *Republic*.

• POPPER, KARL R., *The Open Society and Its Enemies* (Princeton, 1950). Part I, "The Spell of Plato" (pp. 11–195), is a scathing critique of Plato's political philosophy and its destructive impact on Western civilization. Popper views Plato's proposal to reconstruct the natural harmony of society as follows: "The more we try to return to the heroic age of tribalism, the more surely do we arrive at the Inquisition, at the Secret Police, and at a romanticized gangsterism. Beginning with the suppression of reason and truth, we must end with the most brutal and violent destruction of all that is human. *There is no return to a harmonious state of nature. If we turn back, then we must go the whole way—we must return to the beasts"* (p. 195). For a critical examination, from the viewpoint of logical positivism, of Plato's analogy of government and politics with arts, crafts, and specialized skills, leading to the Platonic justification of rule by the few, see Renford Bambrough, "Plato's Political Analogies," in Peter Laslett (ed.), *Philosophy, Politics, and Society* (Oxford, 1956), pp. 98–115.

• RAVEN, J. E., *Plato's Thought in the Making: A Study of the Development of His Metaphysics* (Cambridge, 1965). After two introductory chapters on the sources of Plato's thought and his early life, Raven analyzes the development of Plato's key metaphysical conceptions. Plato's central concept of the Good is defined by Raven as follows: "The Good, for Plato, is first and most obviously the end or aim of life, the supreme object of all desire and all aspiration. Second, and more surprisingly, it is the condition of knowledge, that which makes the world intelligible and the mind intelligent. And third and last and most important, it is the creative and sustaining cause of the whole world and all its contents, that which gives to everything else its very existence" (p. 130). Similarly, Christopher Morris, *Western Political Thought,* Vol. I: *Plato to Augustine* (New York, 1967), writes: "Plato's 'good' is, in the last analysis, an intellectual thing. It is what the philosopher knows and sees and contemplates, what he has discovered by venturing outside the Cave. It has something in common with the Beatific Vision but it is neither closely nor clearly connected with most of what we now call goodness. It is related far more closely to what a man understands than to what he is or to what he does" (p. 47). A variety of viewpoints on basic problems of Plato's metaphysics is presented in the symposium, R. E. Allen (ed.) *Studies in Plato's Metaphysics* (New York, 1965).

• REEVE, C. D. C., *Philosopher-Kings: The Argument of Plato's Republic* (Princeton, 1988). An avowedly "to some extent . . . revisionist work," *Philosopher-Kings* attempts to explode various "myths" about the *Republic*—that it contains the doctrine of the forms, that it is not a unified work, that it teaches a form of proto-totalitarianism, and that Plato does not make his case for justice. Chapter four is specifically on politics.

• RITTER, CONSTANTIN, *The Essence of Plato's Philosophy* (New York, 1933). A portion of the book deals with Plato's political

ideas (pp. 319–356). Ritter was one of Germany's leading authorities on Plato.

• RYLE, GILBERT, *Plato's Progress* (Cambridge, 1966). Examines the evolution of Plato's thought in a fresh and unorthodox manner. In Chap. VII (pp. 216–300) the author gives a "Timetable" of Plato's dialogues. The problems of the dates of composition of the different parts of the *Republic* are discussed on pp. 244–250. Ryle frequently discusses the relations of Aristotle's thought to Plato, and there are also interesting sidelights on writing, publishing, selling, and reading books in Plato's time.

• SEUNG, T. K., *Plato Rediscovered: Human Value and Social Order* (Lanham, 1996). This dense and intricate presentation of Plato both provides classical interpretations and original reinterpretations. It will be most appreciated by more advanced students and scholars.

• SHOREY, PAUL, *Platonism: Ancient and Modern* (Berkeley, 1938). Analyzes the impact of Plato on antiquity, Christianity, the Middle Ages, the Renaissance, and French and English thought. See also Gilbert Murray, *Hellenism and the Modern World* (London, 1953).

• STALLEY, R. F., *An Introduction to Plato's Laws* (Oxford, 1983). The only recent book devoted exclusively to Plato's last and longest work.

• STRAUSS, LEO, *The Argument and the Action of Plato's Laws* (Chicago, 1975). Strauss's last book; a demanding work that requires close attention to both itself and the *Laws.* Those who disagree with Strauss's approach may find it of little value.

• ———, *The City and Man* (Chicago, 1964). Includes an extensive examination of Plato's conceptions of the city and justice in government (Chap. II, pp. 50–138).

• ———, *Studies in Platonic Political Philosophy,* with an introduction by Thomas Pangle and a foreword by Joseph Cropsey (Chicago, 1983). A collection of Strauss pieces on Platonic themes. Pangle's introduction places the essays in the context of Strauss's other writings.

• TAYLOR, ALFRED EDWARD, *Plato: The Man and His Work,* 6th ed. (London, 1949). Chap. I (pp. 1–9) briefly describes Plato's life, and the subsequent chapters analyze his writings. The *Republic* is dealt with in Chap. XI (pp. 263–298). Taylor's *Plato,*

generally written from the orthodox viewpoint, ranks as one of the standard works in
the field. Accounts of Plato's excursions into
practical politics in his earlier years will be
found in Gertrude R. Levy, *Plato in Sicily*
(London, 1956), and Ludwig Marcuse, *Plato
and Dionysius* (New York, 1947).
• VLASTOS, GREGORY, *Platonic Studies,* 2nd
printing (Princeton, 1981). A collection of
essays by one of the great contemporary
Plato scholars. Part I is on "Morals, Politics,
Metaphysics."
• WHITE, NICHOLAS, *A Companion to
Plato's Republic* (Oxford, 1979). Consists
for the most part of a book-by-book exposition of the *Republic,* preceded by an introduction emphasizing the centrality of the
search of justice to the totality of the
Republic.
• WINSPEAR, ALBAN DEWES, *The Genesis of
Plato's Thought* (New York, 1940). The first
systematic analysis, in English, of Plato's
political ideas from a Marxist viewpoint. As
Winspear was a good scholar, as well as a
good Marxist, his book will be found suggestive, although overdrawn in part. For
a Marxist interpretation of Socrates, see
Alban D. Winspear and Tom Silverberg,
Who Was Socrates?, 2nd ed. (New York,
1960). Of related interest, and equally writ-

ten from a strict Marxian angle, are George
Thomson's *Aeschylus and Athens* (London,
1941), and *Studies in Ancient Greek Society,*
2 vols. (London, 1954–1961); the first volume is on *The Prehistoric Aegean,* and the
second, on *The First Philosophers.* Thomson
summarizes his appraisal of Plato (*The First
Philosophers,* p. 328) as follows: "Granted
that in his theory of Ideas Plato made important contributions to epistemology, and that
all his writings (except the *Laws*) are presented with superb literary skill, his philosophy expresses the reactionary outlook of a
selfish oligarchy clinging blindly to its privileges at a time when their social and economic basis was crumbling away. It is a
philosophy founded on the denial of motion
and change and hence of life itself." Plato's
attitude to natural science is discussed in
Benjamin Farrington, *Science and Politics in
the Ancient World* (New York, 1932), Chaps.
VIII (pp. 87–106) and XI (pp. 130–147),
and *Greek Science* (London, 1944), Chap.
VII (pp. 81–101).
    F. M. Cornford, *The Unwritten Philosophy:
And Other Essays* (Cambridge Paperbacks,
1967), includes a critical examination,
"The Marxist View of Ancient Philosophy"
(pp. 117–137), directed particularly against
Farrington and Thomson.

CHAPTER FOUR

ARISTOTLE

• ACKRILL, J. L., *Aristotle the Philosopher*
(Oxford, 1981). A brief work on Aristotle's comprehensive philosophy; Ackrill regards Aristotle from the perspective that
Aristotle's system is "open," as opposed to
a closed set of doctrines. Another brief, recent work on Aristotle's comprehensive
philosophy is Jonathan Barnes (a contemporary translator), *Aristotle* (Oxford,
1982), which is part of the "Past Masters"
series.
• AMBER, WAYNE, "Aristotle on Nature and
Politics: The Case of Slavery," *Political*

Theory (August 1987), pp. 390–410. A reinterpretation of Aristotle's views on slavery
suggesting that his views reflect a tension
between what human nature provides and
what the city needs.
• BALDRY, H. C., *The Unity of Mankind in
Greek Thought* (Cambridge, 1965). In tracing
the awareness of the Greeks of the problem
of human unity from Homer to the Stoics, the
author points to the interesting fact that no
single Greek work deals with that subject as
a whole. Throughout his study, the author
concentrates on several main aspects of

Greek attitudes toward human unity: the hostility of Greeks against non-Greeks—the latter being considered barbarians by definition, that is, by not being Greek. Within the Greek city-state, there was the conflict between the "high" and the "low" classes, a distinction based on birth or wealth; the assumed superiority of men over women; and, finally, the basic difference of status between the free and the slaves. Aristotle's views are discussed on all these topics (pp. 88–101). In general, Aristotle followed the opinions and prejudices of his fellow Greeks with respect to the inferior position of the barbarians in terms of rational endowment and cultural accomplishment. As to women, Aristotle felt that women possessed less reason than men, and he considered the female state as "a kind of deformity." As to Aristotle's defense of slavery as being derived from natural differences between men, Baldry observes: "Rarely, it may be said, has a great thinker so sadly mistaken a transitory man-made institution for one of nature's laws" (p. 96).

• BARKER, ERNEST, *The Political Thought of Plato and Aristotle* (London–New York, 1906). Chaps. V–XI (pp. 208–496) deal with Aristotle in a clear and sympathetic manner. An epilogue ("The Later History of the *Politics*") provides a brief survey of the impact of Aristotle's political ideas on later writers from the Stoics to Hegel. See also Barker's *The Politics of Aristotle* (Oxford, 1946), a translation of Aristotle's *Politics,* with an introduction, notes, and appendixes. The introduction (pp. xi–lxxvi) considers the historical and scientific background, the substance, argument, and vocabulary of the *Politics.*

• CHERNISS, HAROLD, *Aristotle's Criticism of Plato and the Academy* (Baltimore, 1944), Vol. I. Purports to "give a complete account and analysis of all that Aristotle says about Plato and about Plato's pupils and associates in the Academy," and is a standard work on the subject. A brief treatment of the relation of Aristotle and Plato will be found in K. V. Gajendragadkar, *Aristotle's Critique of Platonism* (Mysore, 1953), in which the author concludes that Aristotle "remains after all the greatest of the Platonists as also the greatest critics of Plato and his school" (pp. 77–78). See also I. Duering and G. E. L. Owen (eds.), *Plato*

and Aristotle in the Mid-Fourth Century (Goeteborg, 1960), a symposium of leading European and American scholars dealing, to a large extent, with the relationships of Aristotle and Plato.

• EDEL, ABRAHAM, *Aristotle and His Philosophy* (Chapel Hill, N.C., 1982). A comprehensive exploration of Aristotle's thought, from his own frame of reference.

• GROTE, GEORGE, *Aristotle,* 2 vols. (London, 1872). Grote died before the work was finished. Neither the *Ethics* nor the *Politics* is specifically dealt with, but most of the other works of Aristotle are carefully analyzed.

• GUMMERE, RICHARD M., *The American Colonial Mind and the Classical Tradition: Essays in Comparative Culture* (Cambridge, Mass., 1963). Filling an important gap in American intellectual history, the author traces the impact of Greek and Roman thought on American thinkers and political leaders from the earliest colonial days to the Constitutional Convention of 1787. The outstanding influence of Aristotle is particularly stressed in the making of the Constitution, and Gummere holds that "the theory of our Constitution derives from Aristotle" (p. 176). Aristotle's opposition to tyranny and mob rule particularly appealed to the delegates at the Convention, as did his belief in the mixed constitution and in the importance of a strong and prosperous middle class as the foundation of political stability. By contrast, Gummere points out, Plato "rarely appeared in colonial America as an authority on governmental matters" (p. 179).

• HAMBURGER, MAX, *Morals and Law: The Growth of Aristotle's Legal Theory,* new ed. (New York, 1965). Examines Aristotle's concepts of law and justice as set forth, primarily, in his *Ethics, Politics,* and *Rhetoric.* The author holds that Aristotle's legal and political theory went beyond that of his predecessors, including Plato, and that "it is with Aristotle that modern legal and political science really begins" (p. 182). He concludes as follows: "There is a perfect harmony between Aristotle's ethical, legal, and political theory—the theory of the right mean is the basis; philia, social sympathy, is the life force; equity, fairness, reasonableness, and humaneness the leitmotiv; and well-being, i.e., human happiness and perfection, the supreme end" (p. 183). A diametrically opposed view will be found in

Hans Kelsen, "Aristotle's Doctrine of Justice" (in his *What Is Justice: Justice, Law, and Politics in the Mirror of Science,* Berkeley and Los Angeles, 1957, pp. 110–136). Kelsen holds that the Aristotelian principle of giving everyone his due, or "to each his own," is a purely tautological formula, and that "it is so interesting because it shows the unlimited possibility of using this formula to any purpose whatever" (p. 136). See also W. von Leyden, "Aristotle and the Concept of Law," *Philosophy,* XLII (January 1967), 1–19. For an analysis of Aristotle's concept of justice from the standpoint of linguistic philosophy, see Renford Bambrough, "Aristotle on Justice: A Paradigm of Philosophy," in Renford Bambrough (ed.), *New Essays on Plato and Aristotle* (New York, 1965), pp. 159–174.

• JAEGER, WERNER, *Aristotle: Fundamentals of the History of His Development* (Oxford, 1934). A biography of Aristotle's intellectual development. The last chapter is on "Aristotle's Place in History" (pp. 368–406).

• JOHNSON, CURTIS N., *Aristotle's Theory of the State* (New York, 1990). This work contains valuable analysis of Aristotle's *Politics.* Johnson provides evidence for questioning the "developmental" view of the overall work of Aristotle.

• KELSEN, HANS, "The Philosophy of Aristotle and the Hellenic-Macedonian Policy," *Ethics,* XLVIII (October 1937), 1–64. This essay on Aristotle stresses the inner relation and resemblance between Plato and Aristotle, in philosophy as in political thought, and paints a vivid picture of the background of Aristotle's *Politics.* Kelsen is particularly interested in the impact of Macedonian policy on Aristotle's ideas.

• KIERNAN, THOMAS P. (ed.), *Aristotle Dictionary* (New York, 1962). The main ideas and concepts of Aristotle presented in dictionary form, documented by textual passages from Aristotle's writings.

• KRAUT, RICHARD, *Aristotle on the Human Good* (Princeton, 1989). The author engages the debate over the concept of "agency" within Aristotelian theory. One strength of this work is its scholarly engagement with rival interpretations.

• LEYDEN, WOLFGANG VON, *Aristotle on Equality and Justice: His Political Argument* (New York, 1985). Seeks to contribute both

to Aristotelian scholarship and modern discussions of equality and justice. Leyden finds that, as the result of Aristotle's inequalitarian views, Aristotle's argument on justice (particularly regarding the division of social goods) is that "fair shares need not always be equal."

• MILLER, FRED D., JR., *Nature, Justice, and Rights in Aristotle's* Politics (New York, 1995). Miller takes up the controversial topic of Aristotle's defense of "rights." A deeply analytical work providing a "Straussian" view of objective rightness, *Nature, Justice, and Rights in Aristotle's Politics* will aid those seeking ancient roots for natural rights.

• MORRALL, JOHN, *Aristotle* (London, 1977). Part of the "Political Thinkers" series. Gives a full, but brief, presentation of Aristotle's political theory, with particular attention to his historical context.

• MULGAN, R. G., *Aristotle's Political Theory* (Oxford, 1977). Subtitled "An Introduction for Students of Political Theory," this is an excellent place to start for a comprehensive, yet concise, examination of the *Politics.*

• MURE, G. R. G., *Aristotle* (London, 1932). Part I is called "The Heritage of Aristotle" (pp. 3–68), Part II, "The Philosophy of Aristotle" (pp. 71–230), and Part III, "The Verdict of History" (pp. 233–274), a stimulating survey of the impact of Aristotelianism from antiquity to the modern period. A volume in the Leaders of Philosophy series.

• MURPHY, BENARD, *The Moral Economy of Labor: Aristotelian Themes in Economic Theory* (New Haven, 1993). The return to the issue of linking morality and labor in Aristotelian thought is Murphy's topic. This book should have considerable appeal and provides much for both political theorist and political economist.

• NEWMAN, WILLIAM L., *The Politics of Aristotle,* 4 vols. (Oxford, 1887–1902). The first volume is a detailed and scholarly introduction to the *Politics;* the other three volumes contain the Greek text of the *Politics,* with notes and critical comments. Comparing the Aristotelian conception of the state with modern views, the author writes: "We look back to a succession of States which have helped to build up the fabric of European civilization, and the State which has not fought a Salamis, or done great things for religion or law or science, falls, in our view, behind the State which has. We regard the State not as living to itself and dying to itself, but as influencing for good or ill the destinies of mankind. Aristotle, on the contrary, knows nothing of the historical mission of States. He looks to the quality of the life, not to the results achieved—to the intrinsic nobility of the life lived, not to its fruitfulness in consequences" (I, 562–563).

• NICHOLS, MARY P., *Citizens and Statesmen: A Study of Aristotle's* Politics (Savage, 1991). Nichols's thorough handling of Aristotle seeks to widen the debate of the role of philosophy in political life. Her argument—that a certain kind of political life requires philosophical contemplation—is interesting and solid reading for those studying "the political."

• POPPER, KARL R., *The Open Society and Its Enemies* (Princeton. 1950). Chap. XI critically presents several aspects of Aristotelianism (pp. 199–222).

• RANDALL, JOHN H., JR., *Aristotle* (New York, 1960). In this general account of Aristotle's thought, the author stresses its empirical characteristic. In particular, Randall holds that the *Politics* is written less from the standpoint of the moral physician of the soul, and more from that of "the natural philosopher observing and analyzing nature's way with human governments, the natural processes of the generation and the destruction of organized human societies" (p. 256). In comparing the *Politics* with Plato's *Republic,* Randall writes: "There is in Aristotle none of the free play of the imagination to be found in the *Republic,* there is no talk of 'remolding human nature' in the light of a more perfect model than that used by God in creating man. There is a sense of the limits imposed by the encountered facts of experience, and of a bondage to them" (pp. 247–248). A more concise account of Aristotle's general philosophy will be found in Marjorie Grene, *A Portrait of Aristotle* (London, 1963).

• ROBIN, LÉON, *Aristotle* (Paris, 1944). A general account of Aristotle's scientific, philosophical, and political ideas. The author, a leading French student of Greek thought, concludes his analysis of Aristotle's political theory by doubting whether it is as profound as is commonly assumed. In particular, Robin is surprised that Aristotle saw in the old Greek city-state the normal form of political organization, at the very time when his close personal association with "Macedonian imperialism" should have shown him that the city-state was doomed. Robin concludes that "a somewhat narrow empiricism and a prematurely too broad systematization are the substance of Aristotelian thinking on politics" (p. 283). A succinct account of the *Politics* will also be found in Robin's *Greek Thought and the Origins of the Scientific Spirit* (London–New York, 1928), pp. 268–276. The main criticism there of Aristotle is that he failed to see properly "the great events which were happening or brewing before his eyes in the Greek world. His eyes, like Plato's, were turned on the past, on the small self-centered republic, and he sought its future, blindly, in a reinforcement of that concentration" (p. 276).

• ROSS, W. D., *Aristotle,* 2nd ed. (London, 1930). Chap. VIII deals with Aristotle's political thought (pp. 235–269).

• SALKEVER, STEPHEN G., *Finding the Mean: Theory and Practice in Aristotelian Political Philosophy* (Princeton, 1990). Salkever's reading of Aristotle is complex and may be a bit abstruse for many readers; however, the overall treatment of Aristotle's political philosophy contributes well to the debate.

• STEENBERGHEN, FERNAND VAN, *Aristotle in the West: The Origins of Latin Aristotelianism* (Louvain, 1955). Aims to show "how the union between Aristotelianism and traditional Christian thought came about" (p. 5). The emphasis is on the role of Paris and Oxford Universities in the introduction of Aristotelianism in the thirteenth century. See also Ingemar Duering, *Aristotle in the Ancient Biographical Tradition* (Goeteborg, 1957).

• SWANSON, JUDITH A., *The Public and the Private in Aristotle's Political Philosophy* (Ithaca, 1992). This work is a deft and thorough examination of the philosophical life and the drawbacks of the public political life.

• TESSITORE, ARISTIDE, *Reading Aristotle's* Ethics: *Virtue, Rhetoric, and Political Philosophy* (Albany, 1996). Tessitore's astute explication of Aristotle's *Nicomachean Ethics* is a valuable resource for those seeking to understand *Ethics* within the framework of Aristotle's comprehensive political philosophy.

• WINN, CYRIL, and MAURICE JACKS, *Aristotle: His Thought and Its Relevance Today* (London–New York, 1967). This brief volume in "The Library of Educational Thought" summarizes Aristotle's ideas on education and their relevance to educational programs and objectives today. See also William K. Farnkena, *Three Historical Philosophies of Education: Aristotle, Kant, Dewey* (Chicago, 1965).

• YACK, BERNARD, *The Problems of a Political Animal: Community, Justice, and Conflict in Aristotelian Political Thought* (Berkeley, 1993). Yack uses the tension between the individual and the community to explore Aristotelian political thought. His understanding of the inherent nature of conflict within political communities allows him to explore contemporary interpretive debates of political philosophy and to contribute an insightful and well-written book.

CHAPTER FIVE

POLYBIUS

• ABBOTT, EVELYN (ed.), *Hellenica: A Collection of Essays on Greek Poetry, Philosophy, History and Religion* (Oxford and Cambridge, 1880). The essay, "Polybius" (pp. 387–424), is by James Leigh Strachan-Davidson; it provides the background of Polybius' deportation to Rome and critically examines the character of his political and historical views.

• BALDRY, H. C., *The Unity of Mankind in Greek Thought* (Cambridge, 1965). In his account of Polybius with regard to the problem of the unity of mankind (pp. 171–176), Baldry stresses Polybius' moving away from a narrow national historical perspective toward a broader transnational conception: "The main part of Polybius' work is indeed an embodiment of the idea of human affairs, springing directly from the rise of Roman power to balance the intellectual leadership of Greece" (p. 176). Yet Baldry also correctly points out that Polybius, while transcending national frontiers, continued to accept the traditional divisions of class and status, including the institution of slavery.

• CHINARD, GILBERT, "Polybius and the American Constitution," *Journal of the History of Ideas*, I (January 1940), 38–58. Illuminating on the role and use of Polybius' ideas in the making of the American Constitution. The author gives a brief account of

the classical background and education of the revolutionary leaders and then shows specifically, without overstressing his case, to what extent Polybius was a conscious intellectual influence at that time.

• FRITZ, KURT VON, *The Theory of the Mixed Constitution in Antiquity: A Critical Analysis of Polybius' Political Ideas* (New York, 1954). Presents, in a masterly fashion, the historical and analytical background of the theory of the mixed constitution, the most influential of Polybius' doctrines in antiquity as well as in the modern age, particularly in the formative stage of the United States.

• GLOVER, T. R., *Springs of Hellas* (Cambridge, 1945). Chap. VI, "Polybius at Rome" (pp. 109–130), is one of the best short summaries of the main events in Polybius's life and his leading political and historical ideas.

• USHER, S., "Polybius," *History Today*, XIII (April 1963), 267–274. In dealing with the political ambiguity of Polybius' views, the author writes that "the task that Polybius set himself was not one likely to promote his work's popularity among his countrymen: for he proposed to prove to them that Rome was irresistible, and that any people, Greeks included, who opposed her would be courting national disaster" (p. 270).

• WALBANK, F. W., *A Historical Commentary on Polybius* (Oxford, 1957). The most detailed commentary in English on Polybius' *Histories,* preceded by a detailed bibliography (pp. xiii–xxvii) and a lengthy Introduction on the life and thought of Polybius (pp. 1–37). See also Walbank's "Polemic in Polybius," *Journal of Roman Studies,* LII (1962), pp. 1–12.

• ——, *Polybius* (Berkeley, CA, 1972). Originally delivered as the Sather classical lectures. A general work on Polybius including a bibliography. See, further, Walbank's *Selected Papers: Studies in Greek and Roman History and Historiography* (Cambridge, Engl., 1985), which includes a number of papers about Polybius.

CHAPTER SIX

CICERO

• BAILEY, CYRIL (ed.), *The Legacy of Rome* (Oxford, 1923). Contains chapters on empire, administration, communications and commerce, law, family and social life, religion and philosophy, science, literature, art, engineering, and agriculture, written by authorities in their respective fields. Profusely illustrated, this volume is ideally suited as an introduction to Roman thought and civilization. See also R. H. Barrows, *The Romans* (Pelican Books, Harmondsworth, 1949), and Paul MacKendrick, *The Roman Mind at Work* (Anvil Books, Princeton, 1958).

• BAILEY, D. R. SHACKLETON, *Cicero* (New York, 1971). A life of Cicero largely through his letters.

• BARKER, ERNEST, *Church, State, and Study: Essays* (London, 1930). Chap. I (pp. 1–43) is "The Roman Conception of Empire," and Chap. VII (pp. 171–192) "The 'Rule of the Law.'"

• BUCKLAND, W. W., and ARNOLD D. MCNAIR, *Roman Law and Common Law: A Comparison in Outline,* 2nd ed. (Cambridge, 1965). The authors stress the point that, while the theoretical conceptions of the Roman law and common law are different, "the practical rules of the two systems show an astonishing amount of similarity" (p. xx). Chap. I, "The Sources" (pp. 1–20), is most relevant to the study of the history of political thought.

• CARLYLE, R. W., and A. J. CARLYLE, *A History of Medieval Political Theory in the West,* 3rd ed. (Edinburgh–London, 1930), Vol. I. The first chapter, "The Political Theory of Cicero" (pp. 1–18), is built around the thesis there "is no change in political theory so startling in its completeness as the change from the theory of Aristotle to the later philosophical view represented by Cicero and Seneca. Over against Aristotle's view of the natural inequality of human nature we find set out the theory of the natural equality of human nature" (p. 8).

• CHINARD, GILBERT, "Polybius and the American Constitution," *Journal of 'the History of Ideas,* I (January 1940), 38–58. The author points out that "most of the men who made a name for themselves during the revolutionary era were no mean classical scholars. That they read Locke and later Montesquieu cannot be disputed; but at all times they studied and memorized Cicero and some of the Greek historians. It was from Cicero particularly, among the ancients, that they derived their ideals of liberty and government" (p. 40). See also Richard M. Gummere, *The American Colonial Mind and the Classical Tradition* (Cambridge, Mass., 1963), pp. 176 ff. This article as well illuminates the role and use of Polybius' ideas in the making of the American constitution.

• CICERO, MARCUS TULLIUS, *Brutus: On the Nature of the Gods: On Divination: On Duties* (Chicago, 1950). With an excellent "Introduction to the Philosophy of Cicero" (pp. 1–65) by Richard McKeon.

• ———, *On the Commonwealth* (trans., with Notes and Introduction, by George H. Sabine and Stanley B. Smith, Columbus, Ohio, 1929). Chap. III of the Introduction deals with Cicero's political theory (pp. 39–67), and there is a useful bibliography (pp. 100–102). The text of the *Republic* (called by the translators *On the Commonwealth*) is profusely annotated.

• CROOK, JOHN, *Law and Life of Rome* (Ithaca, N.Y., 1967). Analyzes Roman law, not as a body of legal rules and concepts, but as a reflection of Roman society and as an influence on it. The first, introductory chapter (pp. 7–35) surveys the sources of Roman law, the relation of law to custom, the development of legal practice and jurisprudence, and the processes by which law was created. Chap. II (pp. 36–67) deals with "The Law of Status," and covers such subjects as citizenship, free status, and slavery. Chap. III (pp. 68–97) deals with "The Machinery of the Law," and shows the slow evolution of the judicial process. Chaps. IV–VII take up substantive law in the areas of the family, property, labor, and commerce, and are greatly enriched by numerous illustrative cases of Roman social and economic life. The final chapter (pp. 250–285) analyzes the relations of "The Citizen and the State" (pp. 250–285), both the citizen's rights and duties toward the state.

• DOREY, T. A. (ed.), *Cicero* (New York, 1965). This symposium by eminent classical scholars presents Cicero as a man, thinker, writer, and leading statesman, and also provides illuminating insights into Roman political values and attitudes. See also: R. E. Smith, *Cicero the Statesman* (Cambridge, 1966); Torsten Peterson, *Cicero: A Biography* (New York, 1963); and F. R. Cowell, *Cicero and the Roman Republic*, 2nd ed. (Baltimore, 1962). Edith Hamilton, *The Roman Way to Western Civilization* (Mentor Books, New York, 1957), devotes three chapters (pp. 42–75) to Cicero, depicting him as a man and politician, and drawing copiously on Cicero's letters, since he was one of the great letter-writers in world literature. John Dickinson, *Death of a Republic: Politics and Political Thought at Rome, 59–44 B.C.* (New York, 1963), presents a detailed analysis of Cicero's political thought and career in Chap. VI (pp. 257–323). Dickinson concludes that Cicero's "conception of mixed government leaves room for the ultimate supremacy of the people and for the leadership of an eminent individual. Likewise, his emphasis on the importance of laws and institutions is combined with recognition of the necessity and value of the noninstitutional element in a nation's life—the spirit and temper of the people, their character as individuals, and above all the personal character and qualifications of their leaders. In other words, the striking quality of Cicero's thought is that there was nothing mechanical or doctrinaire about it—he was not, in Napoleon's phrase, an ideologue" (p. 322).

• EARL, DONALD, *The Moral and Political Tradition of Rome* (Ithaca, N.Y., 1967). Seeks to show how the ideas and ideals of the Roman nobility became the traditional dominant outlook of the governing classes and later of all educated Romans. Chap. I, "Morality and Politics" (pp. 11–43), is the longest in the book and the most pertinent to the student of political thought. The two outstanding virtues expected of the Roman aristocrat, the author says, were courage and wisdom. However, wisdom did not mean "a rarefied philosophic detachment or an intellectual enquiry into first causes and the nature of things. It meant practical political judgment" (p. 33). See also F. E. Adcock, *Roman Political Ideas and Practice* (Ann Arbor Paperbacks, Ann Arbor, 1964), and M. L. Clarke, *The Roman Mind: Studies in the History of Thought from Cicero to Marcus Aurelius* (Cambridge, Mass., 1960).

• GRANT, MICHAEL, *The World of Rome* (Mentor Books, New York, 1961). Profusely illustrated, this is one of the most successful compact accounts of Roman civilization as a whole, treating government and law, philosophy and religion, and literature and the arts. Also has a useful bibliography (pp. 336–339). See also A. H. McDonald, *Republican Rome* (New York, 1966); Harold Mattingly, *Roman Imperial Civilization* (Anchor Books, Garden City, N.Y., 1959); and Jérôme Carcopino, *Daily Life in Ancient Rome* (Penguin Books, Harmondsworth, 1962). For straight histories, see M. Rostovtzeff, *Rome* (Galaxy Books, New York, 1960), and Donald R. Dudley, *The Civilization of Rome* (Mentor Books, New York, 1960).

• HASKELL, H. J., *This Was Cicero: Modern Politics in a Roman Toga* (New York, 1942). Fresh, readable, and written with a keen sense of human drama. The author, a newspaperman with a thorough knowledge of politics in Kansas City and Washington, justified his biography on the ground that it takes into account "factors that have escaped the attention of biographers who were not familiar with politics in action," and his work successfully conveys the political atmosphere in Rome during Cicero's lifetime. Extensive bibliographical notes will be found (pp. 368–406). See also G. C. Richards, *Cicero: A Study* (London, 1935), an account of Cicero's life and thought. The author concludes that "Cicero's position in Rome was one of great influence, because in the total absence of the Press, the Pulpit and the University, he in his single person supplied something of all three" (p. 282). *Eternal Lawyer: A Legal Biography of Cicero,* by (Judge) Robert N. Wilkin (New York, 1947), is a stimulating study of Cicero's career and ideas from the viewpoint of a lawyer with wide interests. The author points out that Cicero "was the first to use the word 'constitution' in its modern sense of public law of the state or law by which government itself was limited," and he stresses Cicero's impact on the makers of the American Constitution (pp. 217 ff.).

• LACEY, WALTER, *Cicero and the End of the Roman Republic* (London, 1978). A biography that places Cicero in his context, briefly discusses his impact, and contains a useful bibliography.

• LEE, R. W., *The Elements of Roman Law: With a Translation of the Institutes of Justinian* (London, 1944). The introduction (pp. 1–43) is a general survey of the Roman law, of interest to the student of law as well as the student of political thought. The remainder of the book is a translation of the *Institutes* of Justinian. Thomas Collett Sandars, *The Institutes of Justinian* (London–New York, 1903), contains the text of the *Institutes* in Latin and English, with detailed notes and commentaries. Whereas the *Institutes* are brief and elementary, the extensive code of Justinian is the *Digest,* a translation of which will be found in *The Digest of Justinian* (trans. Charles H. Monro, 2 vols., Cambridge, 1909). The beginning of the first volume contains the sections on the nature and types of law that are of most general interest. Paul Vinogradoff, *Roman Law in Mediaeval Europe* (Oxford, 1929), traces the spread of Roman law throughout Europe in the Middle Ages and its adaptation to local customs and needs. England remained the only country in Europe which did not "receive" Roman law as its general system of law in the late medieval and early modern periods, developing its own system of Common Law as the only other law in the Western world. Why did England not receive the Roman law when all other European nations eagerly turned to it? The answer is to be found in a famous lecture of Frederic William Maitland, *English Law and the Renaissance* (Cambridge, 1901).

• MITCHELL, THOMAS, *Cicero: The Ascending Years* (New Haven, Conn., 1979). Concentrates on the first two-thirds of Cicero's life and the political heritage that shaped his ideas, also tracing the way his political ideas affected his practical politics.

• NEDERMAN, CARY, "The Ciceronian Tradition in Medieval Political Thought," *Journal of the History of Ideas* (January–March 1988). Tracks Cicero's later political influence, noting: "Cicero was the only political thinker of pagan antiquity whose writings continued to be accessible to the Christian West following the collapse of Roman domination."

• RAND, E. K., *Cicero in the Courtroom of St. Thomas Aquinas* (Milwaukee, 1946). A study of Cicero's influence on St. Thomas Aquinas from a general philosophical and literary viewpoint. Cicero was one of the three ancient Latin authors most frequently referred to by St. Thomas Aquinas, the other two being Seneca and Boethius.

• RAWSON, ELIZABETH, *Cicero* (London, 1975). The best recent biography.

• ROLFE, JOHN C., *Cicero and His Influence* (Boston, 1923). A volume in the Our Debt to Greece and Rome series, which defends Cicero against his critics, and traces his influence from antiquity to modern times. See also Tenney Frank, *Cicero* (Annual Lecture on a Master Mind, in *Proceedings of the British Academy,* London, 1932, pp. 111–134), who summarizes Cicero's influence on the Middle Ages and Renaissance: "To the thinkers of the Middle Ages, who did not have access to the earlier sources, Cicero's philosophical dialogues were full of illumination and suggestion, and they played a decided role in humanizing philosophy in the fifteenth and sixteenth centuries. Without them the western world would not have been ready to comprehend the libraries of Greek thought that came westward during the renaissance. Even Copernicus confessed that it was from a citation found in Cicero that he formed the idea of the earth's revolutions. Furthermore, these essays are our only source for much of the lost post-Aristotelian work. But apart from our gratitude, the works themselves are of considerable interest because we can discover from them the spirit in which a cultivated Roman of the Republic approached the problems they discuss" (p. 127). An illuminating study, full of interesting historical detail, on Cicero's literary sources of inspiration and his love of books will be found in T. R. Glover, *Springs of Hellas and Other Essays* (Cambridge, 1945), pp. 131–159 ("Cicero among His Books").

• SHERWIN-WHITE, A. N., *The Roman Citizenship,* 2nd ed. (Oxford, 1973). A comprehensive investigation of Roman citizenship from the times of the republic to those of the empire.

• TAYLOR, HANNIS, *Cicero: A Sketch of His Life and Works* (Chicago, 1918). A comprehensive work, whose usefulness is enhanced by a bibliography (pp. xxxvii–xliv), and an appendix, "The Sayings of Cicero" (pp. 459–603), an anthology of about a thousand extracts selected from Cicero's writings and correspondence. Cicero's correspondence, an unusually rich source for the study of his temper and personality, ranks among the great examples of letter writing in world literature. See also Harold A. K. Hunt, *The Humanism of Cicero* (Melbourne, 1954).

• WIRSZUBSKI, CH., *Libertas as a Political Idea at Rome During the Late Republic and Early Principate* (Cambridge, 1960). Examines the corrosion of the concept and practice of political liberty in the two centuries between the Gracchi and Trajan. See also Ramsay MacMullen, *Enemies of the Roman Order: Treason, Unrest, and Alienation in the Empire* (Cambridge, Mass., 1966) for a uniquely valuable inquiry into the main philosophical, social, and political movements of dissent and revolt, particularly as republican institutions were increasingly replaced by a highly centralized, and ultimately autocratic, monarchy. An extensive bibliography (pp. 269–292) greatly enhances the usefulness of the pioneering work.

• WOOD, NEAL, *Cicero's Social and Political Thought* (Berkeley, 1988). The major work on this subject in decades. Wood's thesis is that Cicero is an important political philosopher, and that anticipations of much of what came later in political theory are found in his writings.

CHAPTER SEVEN

STOICISM AND EPICUREANISM: TWO HELLENISTIC PHILOSOPHIES

• ARNOLD, E. VERNON, *Roman Stoicism* (Cambridge, 1911). Includes and extensive bibliography (pp. 437–450). The last chapter stresses the profound impact of Stoicism on Christianity (pp. 408–436).

• ASMIS, ELIZABETH, *Epicurus' Scientific Method* (Ithaca, N.Y., 1984). A comprehensive study of Epicurus' scientific thought.

• BAILEY, CYRIL, *The Greek Atomists and Epicurus* (Oxford, 1928). A dated study on Epicurus' system, and the influence of the Greek atomic philosophers on him.

• BARKER, ERNEST, *From Alexander to Constantine: Passages and Documents Illustrating the History of Social and Political Ideas 336 B.C.–A.D. 337* (New York, 1956). The best sourcebook on the political thought of the Hellenistic period, including many less well-known materials.

• BEVAN, EDWYN, *Stoics and Sceptics* (Cambridge, 1959). The author sees the main beneficial impact of Stoicism in the fact that it "did nerve innumerable men for centuries to brave action and brave endurance in a world where brute force and cruelty had dreadful scope" (p. 76). Yet the Stoic ideal of inner tranquillity and detachment is also seen as its main weakness, and Bevan draws some interesting comparisons between this ideal and that of ancient Hindu philosophy and religion: "In India also complete detachment from the world of Fear and Desire has been for multitudes the supreme goal of wisdom, and Buddhism has carried from India the ideal of Detachment to the great nations which it has penetrated farther East. The Bhagavad-gita and the Buddhist scriptures present strange harmonies of language with the Stoic teaching; here, too, we find a great deal about good action, with the proviso that such action must be unaccompanied with desire; a great deal about benevolence, provided that there be no love. I think it is important to realize that mankind has two different ideals before it; and I do not see how the ideal of Detachment is compatible with the ideal of Love" (pp. 68–69).

• BIRLEY, ANTHONY, *Marcus Aurelius* (Boston, 1966). In this highly readable biography, the author shows how Marcus Aurelius managed to keep his Stoic serenity throughout his whole life, in spite of the many persistent difficulties and tribulations he had to face as an emperor as well as a husband and father. Chap. X (pp. 289–304) is on the *Meditations*. In Appendix IV (pp. 328–331) the author deals with the persecutions of Christians under the reign of Marcus Aurelius. Profusely illustrated, the volume has a detailed bibliography (pp. 332–339).

• CHRISTENSEN, JOHNNY, *An Essay on the Unity of Stoic Philosophy* (Copenhagen, 1962). The author concludes that "the identification of the supreme moral law with the all-determining law of Nature is the crowning achievement of the Stoic quest for unity. If the rationality of man, fully expanded in its scope, is the same rationality that governs Nature, man's striving for freedom is no longer senseless" (p. 73).

• CLAY, DISKIN, *Lucretius and Epicurus* (Ithaca, N.Y., 1983). A Straussian approach; this book concentrates more on Lucretius than on Epicurus.

• DE WITT, NORMAN, *Epicurus and His Philosophy* (Minneapolis, 1954). The most accessible work on Epicurus.

• EDELSTEIN, LUDWIG, *The Meaning of Stoicism* (Cambridge, Mass., 1966). In one hundred pages, the author manages to present the main ideas of Stoicism in a sympathetic, and yet not uncritical, manner. With respect to Stoic economic philosophy, the author holds that the Stoics accepted private property, but felt that the inequalities of a private property system cannot be resolved either by statism or *laissez faire*. They considered wealth as a trust rather than as absolute ownership, and they "asked the individual to learn that it is necessary for him to live for others and that he is born for human society at large, of which he must always feel himself to be a member rather than a fragment separated off" (p. 79). In politics, the Stoics were indifferent to the various forms of government, and the "judgment passed upon them depends on the spirit in which those in power govern" (p. 86). This disregard of institutions is considered by Edelstein one of the most vulnerable points in Stoic thought, since they "put the whole responsibility on the individual and underestimated the importance of institutions" (p. 96). Finally, the author criticizes the Stoic view of reason according to which "evil is nothing but misunderstanding and that enlightenment and change of conditions can restore man to his original good nature. We have learned to our dismay that if there is coolness of moral action and help without sympathy or love, there is also passionless crime, crime for the sake of crime, abetted and supported by reason" (p. 97). Yet, despite such criticisms, the author concludes that Stoicism is "the creed of all freedom-loving men" (p. 98). Throughout, the author also shows the impact of Stoicism on later ages, including the framers of the American Constitution.

• ERSKINE, ANDREW, *The Hellenistic Stoa: Political Thought and Action* (Ithaca, 1990). Erskine provides a thorough discussion of the origins of the first Stoics. His assertion of the pre-Socratic origins of much of political philosophy, which others derive from Plato and Aristotle, goes too far. This work remains, however, an addition to the field.

• FARQUHARSON, A. S. L., *The Meditations of the Emperor Marcus Antoninus*, 2 vols. (Oxford, 1944). The first volume contains a long introduction, the Greek text and English translation of the *Meditations*, the story of Marcus Aurelius' life, and a detailed commentary on the *Meditations,* book by book, and chapter by chapter. The second volume comments on the Greek text. All in all, this is the most scholarly edition of the *Meditations* and indispensable to the study of Marcus Aurelius and Stoic thought. See also Farquharson's biography, *Marcus Aurelius: His Life and His World,* 2nd ed. (Oxford, 1952), the last chapter of which (pp. 122–141) is on "The Religion of Stoicism." In an Appendix (pp. 142–148), the author deals with "The Christian Churches Under Marcus." Farquharson points out that atheism was "the charge most often in men's mouths about the Christians. It was part of the burden and dislike they inherited from the Jews. It means that they scorned the divinities of the pagan world" (p. 143).

• FARRINGTON, BENJAMIN, *The Faith of Epicurus* (New York, 1967). A sympathetic and brief presentation of Epicurus' thought. Chapter six is "Political Religion."

• HAHM, DAVID, *The Origins of Stoic Cosmology* (Columbus, Ohio, 1977). A relatively technical work concentrating on Stoic physics and its beginnings.

• HAYWARD, F. H., *Marcus Aurelius: A Saviour of Men* (London, 1935). See also the following biographies: C. Clayton Dove, *Marcus Aurelius Antoninus: His Life and Times* (London, 1930); John C. Joy, *The Emperor Marcus Aurelius: A Study in Ideals* (Dublin, 1913); Henry Dwight Sedgwick, *Marcus Aurelius* (New Haven, 1921); and Paul Barron Watson, *Marcus Aurelius Antoninus* (New York, 1884).

• HIBLER, RICHARD, *Happiness Through Tranquility: The School of Epicurus* (Lanham, Maryland, 1984). A very brief study on Epicurus, concentrating on his ethical thought.

• INWOOD, BRAD, *Ethics and Human Action in Early Stoicism* (Oxford, 1985). A book about the Stoic conception of human nature and how, in this conception, humans differ from animals.

• MITSIS, PHILLIP, *Epicurus' Ethical Theory* (Ithaca, N.Y., 1989). A scholarly investigation. Chapter two is "Justice and the Virtues."

• MURRAY, GILBERT, *The Stoic Philosophy* (Conway Memorial Lecture, New York–London, 1915). One of the outstanding essays in the vast literature on Stoicism. Reprinted in Murray's *Stoic, Christian, and Humanist*

(London, 1940), pp. 89–118. See also Margaret E. Reesor, *The Political Theory of the Old and Middle Stoa* (New York, 1951).

• NICHOLS, JAMES, *Epicurean Political Philosophy* (Ithaca, N.Y., 1976). A study of *On the Nature of Things* by Lucretius. Nichols's thesis is there is an Epicurean political philosophy, although there is no surviving specifically Epicurean political work.

• REESOR, MARGARET, *The Nature of Man in Early Stoic Philosophy* (London, 1989). A study of Stoic philosophers from 312 to 129 B.C.

• RENAN, ERNEST, *Marcus Aurelius* (trans. Walter G. Hutchinson, Camelot Series, London–Newcastle-on-Tyne, n.d.). One of the finest appreciations of Marcus Aurelius. Speaking of the worship that followed the emperor's death, Renen says: "Never was worship more legitimate, and it remains our own today. Yes, every one of us wears mourning in his heart for Marcus Aurelius, as though he died but yesterday" (p. 242). The main theme of the volume, the seventh and last of Renan's *Origines du Christianisme,* is the development of Christianity under Marcus Aurelius and the relation of Christianity ("the great principle which has effected moral reformation by faith in the supernatural") and of Stoicism ("the finest effort of the lay school of virtue which the world has up till now ever known").

• RIST, JOHN, *Stoic Philosophy* (London, 1968). A study not on Stoic philosophers, but, as its title states, on Stoic philosophy. Later, Rist wrote *Epicurus* (Cambridge, Eng., 1972), a comprehensive but brief introduction to Epicurus.

• ROSTOVTZEFF, M., *The Stoic and Economic History of the Hellenistic World,* 3 vols. (Oxford, 1941). Indispensable to an understanding of the background of Stoicism and of the whole period of Hellenistic civilization. See also his *Social and Economic History of the Roman Empire* (Oxford, 1926), in the last chapter of which the author examines the problem of decay of ancient civilization, and concludes as follows: "The evolution of the ancient world has a lesson and a warning for us. Our civilization will not last unless it be a civilization not of one class, but of the masses" (pp. 486–487).

• SANDBACH, F., *The Stoics* (New York, 1975). A good brief introduction to Stoicism and leading Stoics. Contains a short, but useful, bibliography.

• STOZIER, ROBERT, *Epicurus and Hellenistic Philosophy* (Lanham, Maryland, 1985). A work on the differences between Lucretius and Epicurus.

• TARN, W. W., *Hellenistic Civilization,* 3rd ed. (Meridian Books, Cleveland–New York, 1961). Much briefer than Rostovtzeff, it is organized analytically rather than historically, and covers the major social, economic, political, philosophical, and literary aspects of Hellenistic civilization. At the end of his work, the author seeks to explain how Hellenistic philosophy and religion paved the way for the spread of Christianity.

He writes that "of all the Hellenistic creeds, none was based on love of humanity; none had any message for the poor and the wretched, the publican and the sinner. Stoicism came nearest; it did transvaluate some earthly values, and Zeno, at least, gave offense by not repelling the poor and the squalid who came to him; but it had no place for love, and it scarcely met the misery of the world to tell the slave in the mines that if he would only think aright he would be happy. Those who labored and were heavy laden were to welcome a different hope from any which Hellenism could offer" (p. 360).

CHAPTER EIGHT

THE JEWISH BELIEF IN ONE GOD, AND CHRISTIAN LOVE

• AYERS, ROBERT, *Judaism and Christianity* (Lanham, Maryland, 1983). An introduction to the major beliefs, perspectives, and traditions of Judaism and Christianity. The first six chapters are on ancient Judaism and early Christianity.

• BOMAN, THORLEIF, *Hebrew Thought Compared With Greek* (London, 1960): Throughout the ages, the comparative study of early Christianity has often probed into the Hebrew and Greek elements that went into its making. Boman's pioneering work provides a more original approach to the problem. He does not seek to compare the contents of Hebrew and Greek ideas and values, but to discover what differences and similarities there are between the Hebrew *style of thought* as compared with the Greek, comparing "the intellectual world of the Old Testament with the intellectual world of the Greek, principally that of the philosophers, and particularly that of Plato" (p. 20). According to Boman, "the Greeks describe reality as *being,* the Hebrews as *movement*"

(p. 208), yet this distinction is not absolute but expresses two possible and equally necessary reactions to reality, mutually complementing each other. In *Culture and Anarchy* (London, 1869), an analysis of the basic forces and tensions in modern culture, Matthew Arnold extensively dealt with some aspects of the problem (particularly in the Preface and pp. 142–197). Arnold sees in Hebraism and Hellenism the two basic forces: "between these two points of influence moves our world" (p. 143). The "uppermost idea" in Hebraism is "right acting," whereas in Hellenism it is "right thinking." Arnold assigned to right acting the priority over right thinking, and he called Puritanism—one of the most powerful forces in shaping modern England—"a reaction of Hebraism against Hellenism" (p. 163). Reinhold Niebuhr, the most influential religious thinker of the twentieth century, deals with the issue of Hebrew and Greek elements in Christianity in many of his works (see, for example, his *The Self and the Dramas of History,* New York, 1955, pp. 75–88): "The basic fallacy of the Greek philosophers was to regard the rational faculty as the source of virtue. This error was partly due to their failure to recognize the ability of the self to use its reason for its own ends" (p. 84). By contrast, the Hebrew conception of man, Niebuhr argues, is more empirical than the Greek, for it understands the unity of man's body, mind, and soul: "The self is not related to God by sharing its reason with God and finding a point of identity with the divine through the rational faculty. The self is related to God in repentance, faith, and commitment." See also Martin Buber, *Pointing the Way* (New York, 1963), pp. 182–191; Norman Bentwich, *Hellenism* (Philadelphia, 1943); Dom Gregory Dix, *Jew and Greek: A Study in the Primitive Church* (London, 1953); and C. H. Dodd, *The Bible and the Greeks* (London, 1935); and G. H. C. Macgregor and A. C. Purdy, *Jew and Greek: Tutors unto Christ* (Edinburgh, 1959).

• BONSIRVEN, JOSEPH, *Palestinian Judaism in the Time of Jesus Christ* (trans. William Wolf, New York, 1964). A brief work on the beliefs of Jews in Palestine at the time of Jesus.

• BOX, GEORGE, *Early Christianity and Its Rivals* (New York, 1929). This book is about the conflict between religions in the early Roman Empire.

• BULTMANN, RUDOLF, *Primitive Christianity* (trans. R. H. Fuller, New York, 1956). Contains sections on "The Old Testament Heritage," "Judaism," "The Greek Heritage," "Hellenism," and "Primitive Christianity."

• DAVIES, JOHN, *The Early Christian Church* (New York, 1965). A detailed examination of the development of early Christianity. For a more social historical approach, see Davies' *Daily Life in the Early Church* (London, 1952).

• DAVIES, W. D., and LOUIS FINKELSTEIN, (eds.), *The Cambridge History of Judaism,* 2 vols. (Cambridge, Eng., 1984–1989). A major recent scholarly addition to works available on Jewish history. Volume I is on the Persian period; volume II, on the Hellenistic. Two more volumes, on later Jewish history, are planned.

• GOWAN, DONALD, *Bridge Between the Testaments,* 3rd ed. (Allison Park, Penn., 1986). A history of Judaism between the fall of Jerusalem in 587 B.C. and the failure of the second revolt against Rome in A.D. 135.

• GUIGNEBERT, CH., *The Jewish World in the Time of Jesus* (trans. S. H. Hooke, London, 1939). A comprehensive history and description.

• HALLIDAY, WILLIAM, *The Pagan Background of Early Christianity* (Liverpool, Eng., 1925). An extensive discussion of Greco-Roman elements in Christianity.

• HATCH, EDWIN, *The Influence of Greek Ideas on Christianity* (New York, 1957). As an introduction into the subject, this is a standard work. The influence of Plato and Platonism on Christian thought and theology is stressed (see particularly pp. 238–240). The following may also be consulted: A. H. Armstrong and R. A. Markus, *Christian Faith and Greek Philosophy* (London, 1960); E. R. Dodds, *Pagan and Christian in an Age of Anxiety* (Cambridge, 1965); William Fairweather, *Jesus and the Greeks* (Edinburgh, 1924); John Ferguson, *Moral Values in the Ancient World* (London, 1958); and James K. Feibleman, *Religious Platonism: The Influence of Religion on Plato and the Influence of Plato on Religion* (New York, 1959).

• HYDE, WALTER, *Paganism to Christianity in the Roman Empire* (New York, 1970). A comprehensive presentation of the rise of Christianity.

• JAEGER, WERNER, *Early Christianity and Greek Paideia* (Cambridge, Mass., 1961). Lectures, with extensive notes, on the movement of Hellenism into Christianity.

• JOHNSON, PAUL, *A History of Christianity* (London, 1976). The most popular history of recent years. See also Johnson's *A History of the Jews* (New York, 1987).

• MCNEILL, JOHN, ed., *Environmental Factors in Christian History* (Port Washington, N.Y., 1970). A collection of essays on early Christian topics.

• NASH, RONALD, *Christianity and the Hellenistic World* (Grand Rapids, Mich., 1984). This book, written from a Christian perspective, disputes the viewpoint that early Christianity was heavily influenced by Hellenistic philosophies.

• NEUSNER, JACOB, *Invitation to the Talmud,* 2nd ed. (New York, 1984). Subtitled *A Teaching Book,* this text is the most accessible entry to Talmudic writings.

• RAPHAEL, CHAIM, *The Springs of Jewish Life* (New York, 1982). A book for the general reader, with most chapters on the period of Judaism covered in *Great Political Thinkers*.

• RANDALL, JOHN, *Hellenistic Ways of Deliverance and the Making of the Christian Synthesis* (New York, 1970). A comprehensive presentation of the background and development of early Christianity.

• SNIDER, NANCY L., "The Political and Social Teachings of the Early Christian Church" (1964). Unpublished manuscript upon which the Christianity section in the fifth edition of *Great Political Thinkers* predominantly was based.

• SORDI, MARTA, *The Christians and the Roman Empire* (trans. Annabel Bedini, London, 1983). A brief and useful introduction to the changing relationships between Christians and political power, and Christians and the Roman Empire, to Constantine.

• TINDER, GLENN, *The Political Meaning of Christianity* (Baton Rouge, La., 1989). A contemporary political theorist, who also is a Christian, presents his view of Christianity's political significance.

• TYSON, JOSEPH, *The New Testament and Early Christianity* (New York, 1984). A study on the inter-relationship between the New Testament and early Christianity. This book does not consider Hellenism, and discusses all of the books of the New Testament.

• WALKER, WILLISTON, et al., *A History of the Christian Church,* 4th ed. (New York, 1985). Originally written by Walker and published in 1918, this excellent work has been revised every twenty years or so by a new generation of scholars.

CHAPTER NINE

ST. AUGUSTINE

• AUGUSTINE, ST., *The City of God* (trans. John Healey, London–New York, 1931). The introduction (pp. vii–lx) by Ernest Barker greatly adds to the value of this abridged reissue of an early seventeenth-century translation of the *City of God*. Concerning the relations between church and state, Barker suggests that this question "hardly enters into St. Augustine's thought, in the form in which it presented itself to the Middle Ages, or presents itself to us today" (p. xxxi). Granting this premise, Barker nevertheless says that "there is a sense in which the doctrine of the *City of God* is inimical to the State, and even subversive of its existence. St. Augustine shifts the centre of gravity. The men of the ancient world had thought in terms of the *Civitas Romana* as the one and only society; they had defied the Roman Emperor as its living incarnation. . . . The ultimate effect of the *City of God* is the elimination of the State: it is the enthronement of the Church. . . . " (p. xxxii).

• BATHORY, PETER, *Political Theory as Public Confession* (New Brunswick, N.J.,

1981). Subtitled *The Social and Political Thought of St. Augustine of Hippo,* this valuable work attempts to place Augustine and his political thought within his context—that of a practicing preacher within a church that was much more decentralized than it later became.

• BEVAN, EDWYN, *Hellenism and Christianity* (London, 1921). Chap. VII ("The Prophet of Personality") is a vivid study of Augustine, "the first modern man," as he is sometimes called, because of his searching self-analysis and psychological insights (pp. 136–144). The whole volume, a collection of essays on the formative period of Christianity and its impact on the Hellenistic world, is rewarding reading.

• BLOCH, MARC, *Feudal Society* (London, 1961). The best single volume on the subject, with a detailed Bibliography (pp. 453–481). The clarity of thought and style comes through successfully in the English version of the French original. For a much briefer account, see F. L. Ganshoff, *Feudalism* (Harper Torchbooks, New York, 1961).

- BROWN, P. R. L., "Saint Augustine," in Beryl Smalley (ed.), *Trends in Medieval Political Thought* (Oxford, 1965), pp. 1–21. The author asserts that St. Augustine is more relevant to our age than such classics of modern political thought as Hobbes, Locke, and Rousseau. "The central problem of Augustine's thought," he writes, "is one which we all have to face: to what extent is it possible to treat man as having a measure of rational control over his political environment? The discovery that the extent of this control is limited has revolutionized political theory. Half the world is committed to some form of Marxist determinism; and the other half, far from rallying to Hobbes, Locke, and Rousseau, studies Freud, the social psychologists, and the sociologists" (p. 3).
- BURLEIGH, JOHN H. S., *The City of God: A Study of St. Augustine's Philosophy* (London, 1949). Interpreting St. Augustine sympathetically from a Protestant viewpoint, the author suggests that "the City of God is none other than the Invisible Church of Wycliffe and Hus, Luther and Calvin" (p. 182).
- BUTLER, DOM CUTHBERT, *Western Mysticism,* 2nd ed. (Harper Torchbooks, New York, 1966). Much of the discussion is centered on St. Augustine's mysticism. In examining the Platonic element in St. Augustine's mysticism ("Mysticism or Platonism?" pp. 40–50), the author concedes that St. Augustine "to the end continued a convinced and devoted Platonist" (p. 41). Yet he concludes that St. Augustine's "contemplations" were "fully religious experiences," and not Platonism (p. 50).
- CARLYLE, R. W., and A. J. CARLYLE, *A History of Medieval Political Theory in the West,* 6 vols. (Edinburgh and London, 1903–1936). The most important work, in any language, on medieval political theory. The first volume discusses St. Augustine's doctrine of the state (pp. 164–170), property (pp. 139–142), and slavery (pp. 118–121).
- CHABANNES, JACQUES, *St. Augustine* (Garden City, N.Y., 1962). In this biography, written with deep sympathy and admiration for its subject, the author constantly shows how St. Augustine's life is linked with his thought. In conclusion, the author writes: "His work is made up of a surprising juxtaposition of opposites from which the truth springs forth as though by interaction. He turned everything into account—his

sensuality he changed into a yearning for things divine, his taste for enjoyment into peace, his human love into Christian charity" (p. 211). For a short biographical study, see Henri Marrou, *St. Augustine and His Influence Through the Ages* (Harper Torchbooks, New York, 1957). John J. O'Meara, *The Young Augustine: The Growth of St. Augustine's Mind Up to His Conversion* (Staten Island, N.Y., 1965), covers St. Augustine's personal and doctrinal development from his birth in 354 to his conversion in 387.
- CHADWICK, HENRY, *Augustine* (Oxford, 1986). A brief introduction to Augustine's thought, as opposed to his life and times. Part of the "Past Masters" series.
- COULBORN, RUSHTON (ed.), *Feudalism in History* (Princeton, 1956). Written by leading American scholars in the field, this symposium is a unique contribution to the comparative study of feudalism. In addition to Western Europe, the work deals with Russia, the Byzantine Empire, China, Japan, India, and other areas often neglected.
- COULTON, G. G., *Studies in Medieval Thought* (London, 1940). This is the best short introduction to medieval political ideas, by a leading authority on the Middle Ages. Chaps. II and III deal with Augustine and the *City of God* (pp. 24–47). Coulton stresses St. Augustine's acceptance of the state "as a real and necessary factor in human progress since the Fall." The Church "must render unto Caesar the things that are Caesar's. The City of God, being inextricably mixed up with the State—the Churchman being a citizen quite as really as he is a Churchman—therefore the City of God must obey the laws which are promulgated by the Earthly City" (p. 44). See also C. V. Wedgwood, *Velvet Studies* (London, 1946), pp. 74–79 ("The City of God").
- CULLMANN, OSCAR, *The State in the New Testament* (New York, 1956). The author, a leading Protestant theologian in the field of New Testament and early church history, seeks to demonstrate that "the apparent contradictions in the primitive Christian interpretations of the State are in reality not contradictions" (p. 87). The consistency of the New Testament with regard to the State is rooted, the author argues, in the essential Christian tension between the present and the future. A radically different view is presented by Hans Kelsen in his essay on

"Justice in the Holy Scriptures," included in his *What Is Justice? Justice, Law, and Politics in the Mirror of Science* (Berkeley and Los Angeles, 1957), pp. 25–81. Kelsen concludes that the Christian theology of justice, based on Paul's teaching, can be summed up as follows: "There is a relative, human, justice which is identical with the positive law, and an absolute, divine, justice which is the secret of faith. Hence, there is in this theology no answer to the question as to what is justice, as a question of human reason referring to an ideal which is not necessarily identical with every positive law and which can be realized in this world" (p. 81). See also Adolf Harnack, *What Is Christianity?* (Harper Torchbooks, New York, 1957), pp. 75–151, for an analysis of the relation of the Gospel to the main political, social, and economic issues of Western civilization.

• D'ARCY, M. C. (ed.), *Saint Augustine* (Meridian Books, New York, 1957). A symposium on Augustine's background, life, thought, and impact, written by leading Catholic theologians and philosophers, including Jacques Maritain, Étienne Gilson, Christopher Dawson, and Maurice Blondel. Roy W. Battenhouse (ed.), *A Companion to the Study of St. Augustine* (New York, 1955), is a symposium written from a sympathetic Protestant standpoint, with contributions from American and British students of religious philosophy. Chap. X (pp. 257–283) is on *The City of God.*

• DEANE, HERBERT A., *The Political and Social Ideas of St. Augustine* (New York, 1966). The author feels that the *City of God* is not sufficient for an adequate understanding of St. Augustine's political thought, and he therefore draws on his other works as well. Inquiring into the renewed interest in St. Augustine in our own age, Deane writes in his concluding chapter: "Both his theological beliefs and his experience and observation of men's actions in an age of disorder enforced upon him an attitude of pessimistic realism, which would not allow him to sentimentalize or evade the darker aspects of social and political life. In our own century, when, once more, men have been compelled to recognize the almost incredible brutalities of which human beings are capable, especially when they struggle for political power and military domination, it is no accident that Augustinian pessimism and realism have enjoyed a considerable revival among both theologians and secular thinkers" (pp. 241–242). See also H. Hohensee, *The Augustinian Concept of Authority* (New York, 1954), and R. S. Hartigan, "Saint Augustine on War and Killing: The Problem of the Innocent," *Journal of the History of Ideas,* XXVII (April–June 1966), 195–204.

• EARL, DONALD, *The Moral and Political Tradition of Rome* (Ithaca, N.Y., 1967). In the Epilogue, the author looks at St. Augustine from the perspective of the late Roman political experience rather than from that of early Christian history. Earl argues that St. Augustine, in working out his concepts, heavily drew on Roman social and political models and terminology. Specifically, "in the *De Civitate Dei* the speculations of the pagan philosophers and the moral and political traditions of Rome were fused with and transmuted by the teachings of the Scriptures and the doctrines of the early Fathers to serve the ideal of the Church and the glory of God" (p. 131).

• ELSHTAIN, JEAN B. *Augustine and the Limits of Politics* (Notre Dame, 1996). This thoughtful reading of Augustine seeks to redeem him from harsher presentations and to portray his eminence as a more moderate, deliberate, and balanced figure than usually is the case. This work is not an introductory text and is recommended to those familiar with the topic.

• FIGGIS, JOHN NEVILLE, *The Political Aspects of St. Augustine's "City of God"* (London, 1921). One of the most incisive analyses, in English, of St. Augustine's thought; the last two chapters trace his influence in the Middle Ages and the modern period (pp. 81–117), and the important literature on the *City of God* is briefly summarized in a "Bibliography" (pp. 118–122). Figgis stresses that the conflict between the heavenly and earthly cities is "not primarily between two policies" but represents a deeper antagonism "between the other-worldly and the this-worldly reference to all institutions" (p. 114).

• FRIBERG, HANS DANIEL, *Love and Justice in Political Theory: A Study of Augustine's Definition of the Commonwealth* (Chicago, 1944). A comparison between Cicero's conception of the state in terms of law and justice, and St. Augustine's stress on love as the bond of political organization: "Whereas Cicero denies the existence—at any time, including the future—of an absolutely perfect commonwealth, Augustine recognizes its existence now in full reality in heaven, also now by faith among the believers, and finally in full reality also among them who now believe" (p. 73).

• GILSON, ÉTIENNE, *The Christian Philosophy of Saint Augustine* (New York, 1960). The author, one of the world's foremost students of medieval Christian thought, provides here a comprehensive analysis of St. Augustine's philosophical, religious, moral, and political ideas. Concerning the divergent interpretations of St. Augustine's conception of the relations of state and church, the author holds that he "can neither be considered to have defined the medieval ideal of a civil society subject to the primacy of the Church, nor to have condemned such a conception in advance. What does remain strictly and absolutely true is that under no circumstances can the earthly city, much less the City of God, be identified with any form of the State whatsoever" (p. 182). An extensive Bibliography (pp. 367–383) is included.

• HEARNSHAW, F. J. C. (ed.), *Medieval Contributions to Modern Civilization* (New York, 1922). A collection of essays, by distinguished authorities, on religion, philosophy, science, art, literature, education, social relations, economics, and politics. The chapter on politics is by J. W. Allen (pp. 225–267), who concludes as follows: "I suggest not merely that any separation of politics from ethics is fatal, but that a society which has lost belief in the validity of its own moral intuitions rests on rotting foundations. I suggest, further, that the idea that government must be directed to a recognized, common, and ultimate end, and refer to a standard of absolute values or be radically purposeless, is perfectly sound. The end, perhaps, need not transcend this world. It may be possible to find a purpose referring only to this world that will satisfy the soul of man. But I suggest that no such end has yet been found. We can strip from the medieval system of ideas that I have tried to define in outline all that is not essential to it. We can eliminate the Church altogether, and it will still stand logically coherent. It is a question—it is perhaps

the question—whether we can also eliminate God" (pp. 267–268).

• ——, (ed.), *The Social and Political Ideas of Some Great Medieval Thinkers* (London, 1923). Chap. I is an excellent introduction to the main political ideas and issues of the Middle Ages, by Ernest Barker; Chap. II, "St. Augustine and the City of God," is by A. J. Carlyle (pp. 34–52). Concerning the influence of St. Augustine's political theory in his own time and in the Middle Ages, Carlyle says that "so far as it was different from the normal traditions of the Stoic philosophers and of the Christian Fathers it had no importance and no significance, but that so far as it corresponded with these, so far as in his own way and under his own terms he re-stated the traditional view of the Stoics and of the Christian Fathers, it may well be said that St. Augustine had much influence" (pp. 51–52).

• KIRWAN, CHRISTOPHER, *Augustine* (London, 1989). A philosophical approach to Augustine. Chapter XI is on Christian society.

• MORRALL, JOHN B., *Political Thought in Medieval Times* (London, 1958). Provides a brief introduction into the subject, emphasizing the main themes of medieval civilization. See also Gordon Leff, *Medieval Thought from Saint Augustine to Ockham* (Penguin Books, Baltimore, 1958), for a more general survey of medieval philosophy. Chap. II (pp. 32–54) deals with Augustine and his successors.

• MOSS, H. ST. L. B., *The Birth of the Middle Ages, 395–814* (London, 1935). Part I, "Romans and Barbarians," deals with the period that is fundamental to a full appreciation of St. Augustine (pp. 1–78). The following will also be found useful: R. W. Southern, *The Making of the Middle Ages* (Yale Paperbacks, New Haven, 1960), for the period of the late tenth to the early thirteenth century; Friedrich Heer, *The Medieval World: Europe 1100–1350* (Mentor Books, New York, 1963); and J. Huizinga, *The Waning of the Middle Ages* (Anchor Books, Garden City, N.Y., 1954), covering the period of the fourteenth and fifteenth centuries in France and the Netherlands.

• NIEBUHR, REINHOLD, *Christian Realism and Political Problems* (New York, 1953). Chap. IX (pp. 119–146) is on "Augustine's Political Realism" (also reprinted in William Ebenstein, *Political Thought in Perspective* [New York, 1957], pp. 109–124). Niebuhr holds that Augustine is, with regard to basic political problems "a more reliable guide than any known thinker" (p. 146). Augustine helps us, Niebuhr argues, to avoid the pitfalls of the three representative approaches to political problems. The "realists" understand the power of collective self-interest, but not its blindness; the pragmatists perceive the futility of fixed and detailed norms, but do not grasp that love must be the final norm; lastly, modern liberal Christians recognize that love is the supreme norm for man, but often fall into sentimentality by failing to appreciate the persisting power of self-love. Niebuhr stresses that Augustine's thought, avoiding these various pitfalls, is particularly pertinent to the problem of the growing world community today.

• POPE, HUGH, *Saint Augustine of Hippo: Essays dealing with his Life and Times and Some Features of His Work* (Westminster,

Md., 1949). The first two chapters on Roman Africa and its Christianization (pp. 1–77) are particularly interesting. The third chapter (pp. 78–138) tells the story of St. Augustine's life. The remaining six chapters (pp. 139–361) deal with his thought, stressing particularly his theology.

• TROELTSCH, ERNST, *The Social Teaching of the Christian Churches,* 2 vols. (London–New York, 1931). A standard work on the subject.

• ULLMANN, WALTER, *A History of Political Thought: The Middle Ages* (Penguin Books, Baltimore, 1965). Highly useful as a first introduction into the subject. See also his *Principles of Government and Politics in the Middle Ages* (New York, 1961), investigating the problem of medieval authority in relation to the papacy, kingship, and popular government.

CHAPTER TEN

JOHN OF SALISBURY

• CARLYLE, R. W., and A. J. CARLYLE, *A History of Medieval Political Theory in the West,* 2nd imp. (Edinburgh–London, 1932), Vol. IV. Chap. II of Part II deals with John of Salisbury's views on the relations of church and state (pp. 330–341). See also *op. cit.* (Edinburgh–London, 1928), Vol. III, Part II, Chap. V, which discusses John of Salisbury's distinction of kingship and tyranny in relation to other medieval doctrines on the subject (pp. 125–146), and G. G. Coulton, *Studies in Medieval Thought* (London, 1940), Chap. VII (pp. 87–95).

• KNOWLES, DAVID, *The Evolution of Medieval Thought* (Baltimore, 1962). Chapter XI (pp. 131–140) is on "The School of Chartres and John of Salisbury." The author calls John of Salisbury "the Erasmus, the Johnson of the twelfth century" and considers him "the most accomplished scholar and stylist of his age" (p. 135). See also M. Anthony Brown, "John of Salisbury," *Franciscan Studies,* XIX (September–December, 1959), pp. 241–297.

• LIEBESCHÜTZ, HANS, *Medieval Humanism in the Life and Writings of John of Salisbury* (London, 1950). An original contribution, portraying the life and thought of John of Salisbury against his own medieval background rather than against modern political ideas. A systematic survey of the literature on John in Chap. I (pp. 1–7) adds to the usefulness of the work. See also Johan Huizinga, "John of Salisbury: A Pre-Gothic Mind," in his *Men and Ideas: History, the Middle Ages, the Renaissance* (Meridian Books, New York, 1959), pp. 159–177.

• PIKE, JOSEPH B., *Frivolities of Courtiers and Footprints of Philosophers* (Minneapolis, 1938). A translation of the First, Second, and Third Books, and selections from the Seventh and Eighth Books of John of Salisbury's *Statesman's Book*. It thus supplements the translation of the *Statesman's Book* by John Dickinson (New York, 1928), which contains the Fourth, Fifth, and Sixth Books, and selections from the Seventh and Eighth Books. The Dickinson translation is preceded by a long and excellent introduction (pp. xvii–lxxxii). See also *John of Salisbury's Memoirs of the Papal Court* (trans. from the Latin with Introduction and Notes by Marjorie Chibnall, New York, 1956), and *The Letters of John of Salisbury* (ed. by W. J. Miller and H. E. Butler, revised by C. N. L. Brooke, New York, 1955), both with lengthy introductory essays on the life and thought of John of Salisbury.

• POOLE, REGINALD LANE, *Illustrations of the History of Medieval Thought and Learning,* 2nd ed. (New York, 1960). Chap. VII (pp. 176–197) is on John of Salisbury, and is one of the most useful short summaries of his life and thought. The distinctive mark of John's *Statesman's Book,* Poole says, "is a humanism which seems to remove it from medieval associations" (p. 191). See also Poole's "The Masters of the Schools at Paris and Chartres in John of Salisbury's Time," *English Historical Review,* XXXV (July 1920), 321–342.

• ULLMANN, WALTER, *Medieval Papalism: The Political Theories of the Medieval Canonists* (London, 1949). A scholarly study of papalist political theories, based on original sources, Medieval Papalism is an important and original contribution to a much neglected field. See also Ullmann's article, "The Influence of John of Salisbury on Medieval Italian Jurists," *English Historical Review,* LIX (September 1944), 384–392, in which he maintains that "recent researches into fourteenth-century jurisprudence have shown that the *Policraticus* was one of the most quoted and perused treatises written by a medieval philosopher" (p. 384). For a broader treatment of this subject, see Gaines Post, *Studies in Medieval Legal Thought: Public Law and the State, 1100–1322* (Princeton, 1964), pp. 259 ff., 514 ff., and 558 ff.

• WEBB, CLEMENT C. J., *John of Salisbury* (reprinted, New York, 1971). The author sees in John of Salisbury "a typical Englishman. He is a strong 'party man,' yet ready to be, so far as possible, on friendly terms with his opponents; he has a instinctive aversion to extremes, and distaste alike for rhetorical display and *doctrinaire* rigidity; with a constant disposition to seek means of accommodation and even of compromise, if they can be had without abandonment of a few principles which he regards as fundamental" (pp. 176–177). Indispensable as an introduction into the life and work of John of Salisbury.

• WULF, MAURICE DE, *History of Medieval Philosophy,* 2 vols., 3rd ed. (London–New York, 1935–1938). A short discussion of John of Salisbury is in the first volume (pp. 226–232). The *Statesman's Book* is called "the most complete philosophy of the State produced in the first period of the Middle Ages" (p. 231).

CHAPTER ELEVEN

ST. THOMAS AQUINAS

• BETTENSON, HENRY (ed.), *Documents of the Christian Church* (New York, 1947). The most easily accessible documentary source book of its kind, containing both official and unofficial statements.

• BLYTHE, JAMES, "The Mixed Constitution in the Work of Thomas Aquinas," *Journal of the History of Ideas* (October–December 1986). Blythe's position is that Aquinas always supported a mixed constitution and achieved a "truly original synthesis of Greek political theory and medieval political thought."

• BORRESEN, KARI, *Subordination and Equivalence: The Nature and Role of Women in Augustine and Thomas Aquinas* (trans. Charles Talbot, Washington, D.C., 1981). Discusses the status of women in these two great theologians.

• BOURKE, VERNON J., *Aquinas' Search for Wisdom* (Milwaukee, 1964). Firmly anchored in the most advanced Thomistic scholarship, this work combines a full biography of the life of St. Thomas Aquinas with a clear exposition of his doctrinal development. The biographical part does away with some of the legends and fictions that have surrounded traditional Thomistic lore. In the discussion of Thomistic doctrine, the author presents a fair and balanced picture within the faithfully accepted framework of Thomism, and concludes as follows: "What made St. Thomas' wisdom golden was not the philosophical, or even the theological, detail of his thought. He left an example of what can be done by a Christian scholar who is willing and able to learn from any source of information. His mind was open to the insights of pagan philosophers, of Mohammedan and Jewish sages, of the long tradition of Greek and Latin Christian Fathers. Thomas was able to admit his own limitations: there were things that he never understood; there were times when he could only resort to prayer. The myth of an Aquinas who knew all the answers is a false construction of overzealous followers. Yet Thomas was always optimistic and hopeful in his quest for truth; with God's help, he approached every problem in a spirit of confidence. Neither pessimism nor skepticism held any virtue for him. He did not pretend that he had solved all the riddles of reality and life; he kept looking for ever better answers; and he enjoyed the challenge of his search" (pp. 229–230). For a much briefer biographical and doctrinal account of St. Thomas, see L. H. Petitot, *The Life and Spirit of Thomas Aquinas* (Chicago, 1966).

• BRACTON, HENRY DE, *On the Laws and Customs of England* (written before 1256). The most systematic expression of the typically medieval doctrine that law derives from custom, that the king, though not subject to man, ought to be subject to "God and to the law, for the law makes the king," and that "there is no king where the will and not the law has dominion" (*On the Laws and Customs of England,* ed. Travers Twiss, London, 1878, I, 39). About two hundred years later, John Fortescue emphasized again the medieval principle that the king "is not able himself to change the laws without the assent of his subjects nor to burden an unwilling people with strange imposts" (*De laudibus legum Angliae [In Praise of the Laws of England],* written about 1470, edited and translated, with introduction and notes, by S. B. Chrimes, Cambridge, 1942, p. 25). The concept of the supremacy of law played a major political part in the struggles of Parliament against the Stuarts in the seventeenth century, and Bracton, in particular, was appealed to by Sir Edward Coke, the lawyer and leader of the parliamentary party. Walter Ullmann's *The Medieval Idea of Law* (London, 1946) is focused on the fourteenth century and illuminates hitherto neglected aspects of medieval legal thought and scholarship.

• BRENNAN, ROBERT EDWARD, *Thomistic Psychology* (New York, 1941). A "philosophic analysis of the nature of man," with an introduction by Mortimer J. Adler.

• CARLYLE, R. W., and A. J. CARLYLE, *A History of Medieval Political Theory in the West,* 2nd ed. (1938), Vol.V. The whole volume is devoted to the political theory of the thirteenth century, including detailed analyses of St. Thomas Aquinas.

• CASSIRER, ERNST, *The Myth of the State* (New Haven, 1946). Chaps. VII–IX deal with medieval political philosophy (pp. 78–115).

• CHENU, M. D., *Toward Understanding Saint Thomas* (New York, 1964). In the first half of the work, the author, a leading French Thomist scholar, provides a highly interesting background of the time and environment in which St. Thomas Aquinas grew up. He than analyzes St. Thomas' language and methods of documentation, throwing a good deal of light on the methods of medieval scholarship, philosophy, and theology. In the second half of the book, Chenu comments on the individual major works of St. Thomas. In all, this is one of the outstanding contributions to Thomistic literature.

• CHESTERTON, G. K., *St. Thomas Aquinas* (New York, 1933). A vivid and colorful biographical sketch, stressing the rational element in St. Thomas' thought. Chesterton calls him "one of the great liberators of the human intellect" (p. 19), and says that it was "the very life of Thomist teaching that Reason can be trusted; it was the very life of the Lutheran teaching that Reason is utterly untrustworthy" (p. 21). The Protestant Reformation of the sixteenth century was, according to Chesterton, "a belated revolt of the thirteenth-century pessimists" and "a backwash of the old Augustinian Puritanism against the Aristotelian liberality" (p. x).

• COPLESTON, F. C., *Aquinas* (Penguin Books, Baltimore, 1955). Chap. V (pp. 192–234) deals with the social and political thought of St. Thomas. Copleston, a leading English Jesuit historian of western ideas, holds that St. Thomas "favored constitutional monarchy" (p. 233). As to the controversial issue of St. Thomas' attitude on tyranny and resistance to tyranny, Copleston argues that according to St. Thomas tyrants "can legitimately be deposed on the ground that they are guilty of abusing their position and power unless, indeed, there is a reason for thinking that rebellion would result in as bad a state of affairs as the one which it was designed to remedy" (p. 232).

• CRANSTON, MAURICE, "St. Thomas Aquinas as a Political Philosopher," *History Today,* XIV (May 1964), 313–317. The author rejects Lord Acton's view of St. Thomas as "the first Whig" on several grounds: "Aquinas believed, assuredly, in freedom and natural rights and government by consent; but there is no clear evidence that he thought men had a right to rebellion; he explicitly rejected the theory of the social contract; and as for the 'natural right' that interested Whig theorists most—the right to property—Aquinas denied that it was, strictly speaking, a natural right at all" (pp. 313–314). Yet Cranston also rejects the notion that St. Thomas merely revived Aristotle's political thinking: "For he improved on Aristotle's notion of the state as a natural institution by incorporating an idea that, though not Christian in origin, has become a crucial notion in Christian thinking: that of Natural Law. His point here is not difficult to follow. It is natural for men to live under government; but governments do not fully conform to nature unless they are just: and the criterion of justice is something laid down by the Creator, and visible to the eye of reason in all men" (p. 315). Since natural law is closely linked to divine law, about which the Church claimed to speak with authority, St. Thomas' argument thus leads logically to the conception of the superiority of the Church over the state.

• D'ARCY, MARTIN C., *Thomas Aquinas* (Boston, 1930). A volume in the Leaders of Philosophy series. The first chapter (pp. 3–31) gives an illuminating account of the historical and philosophical background of the period, with special emphasis on Aristotelianism and scholasticism. The last chapter (pp. 251–275) deals with the impact of Thomism on modern thought, and the author stresses the lack of uniformity in Thomism: "There is a left wing and a right wing of Thomism, there are conservatives and liberals. For this reason one will find no agreement about what are the philosophical weaknesses in St. Thomas which need to be remedied" (p. 271).

• D'ENTRÈVES, ALEXANDER PASSERIN, *The Medieval Contribution to Political Thought* (Oxford, 1939). The first, introductory, chapter deals with the general characteristics of medieval political ideas (pp. 1–18). Chap. II is on Thomas Aquinas (pp. 19–43). See also D'Entrèves (ed.), *Aquinas: Selected Political Writings* (Blackwell's Political Texts, Oxford, 1948), pp. vii–xxxiii (introduction).

• GILBY, THOMAS, *The Political Thought of Thomas Aquinas* (Chicago, 1958). The first part gives the intellectual and social background of the whole period in which Thomas Aquinas lived. The second, and much longer, part, traces the philosophical and theological development of St. Thomas, drawn against a broad European canvas. The author, a Dominican teacher and scholar like St. Thomas himself, emphasizes four points in the latter's political thought. First, the acceptance of the Aristotelian view that the state springs from the social appetite of man rather than from his corruption and sin, as had been maintained by St. Augustine and the patristic tradition, later to be resurrected by Martin Luther. Second, the author claims (less convincingly) that St. Thomas adhered to the Gelasian concept of the twin authorities, spiritual and temporal, each being supreme in its own sphere. Third, St. Thomas upheld the idea of the limited scope of governmental authority; as to tyrannicide, the author concedes that St. Thomas was rather conservative, and 'more prim" and "more hesitant" (p. 289) than John of Salisbury, for example. Fourth, St. Thomas stressed that government was more an art than a branch of ethics and science, a point to be developed more fully in modern political thought by Edmund Burke.

• GILSON, E'TIENNE, *The Christian Philosophy of St. Thomas Aquinas* (New York, 1956). An over-all synthesis by one of the leading Thomist philosophers of the twentieth century. Part III (pp. 251–378) deals with the moral, legal, social, and political doctrines of St. Thomas Aquinas. Conceding that for St. Thomas "monarchy is the best form of government" (p. 329), Gilson stresses that this preference does not include absolute monarchy: "The prince or king can only ensure the common good of the people when he is dependent upon them" *(ibid.)*. Concerning the general orientation of St. Thomas' thinking, Gilson concludes as follows: "If we grant that a philosophy is not to be defined from the elements it borrows but from the spirit which quickens it, we shall see here neither Platonism nor Aristotelianism, but, above all, Christianity" (p. 378). See also Gilson's *The Spirit of Medieval Philosophy* (New York, 1940).

• GOERNER, E. A., "Thomistic Natural Right," *Political Theory* (August 1983), 393–418. Puts forward the unconventional view that "Thomas's moral and political doctrine is not fundamentally a natural law teaching at all." See also Goerner's "On Thomistic Natural Law," *Political Theory* (February 1979), 101–122.

• GRENET, PAUL, *Thomism: An Introduction* (New York, 1967). In this brief volume the author concentrates on St. Thomas' philosophy of nature and metaphysics rather than on his theology or ethics. In the concluding chapter the author presents St. Thomas's view of "The Place and the Role of Man in the Universe" (pp. 122–125), and stresses that Thomism is more a philosophy of universalism than of personalism: "Beyond all question, man is at home in the universe because he is in the house of God, and because God is the total good of the universe of which man is but a part" (p. 125).

• HENLE, ROBERT J., *Saint Thomas and Platonism* (The Hague, 1956). Because of the immense impact of Aristotle on St. Thomas, the relations between Thomism and Platonism are often neglected or obscured. The author shows in detail the relations of Plato's writings to Thomistic thought. See also H. V. Jaffa, *Thomism and Aristotelianism: A Study*

of the *Commentary* by Thomas Aquinas on the *Nicomachean Ethics* (Chicago, 1952), and J. L. Stocks, *Aristotelianism* (Boston, 1925), pp. 119–134.

• KLOCKER, HARRY R., *Thomism and Modern Thought* (New York, 1962). A critical exposition and refutation of some major trends in modern philosophy—Kantian idealism, Hegelianism, pragmatism, logical positivism, existentialism, and dialectical materialism—from a strict Thomist standpoint. See also Ralph M. McInerny, *Thomism in an Age of Renewal* (Garden City, N.Y., 1966), which examines the challenges confronting Thomism in an open and fearless manner, strongly influenced by Pope John XXIII who, in the author's view, inaugurated "an age of renewal in the Church" (p. 8).

• LEA, H. C., *A History of the Inquisition of the Middle Ages,* 3 vols. (New York, 1887–1888). A standard work on the subject. A penetrating and brief discussion of "Freethought and Inquisition" will be found in G. G. Coulton, *Medieval Panorama* (Cambridge, 1938), Chap. XXXV (pp. 457–476). St. Thomas Aquinas' main discussion of heresy and unbelief is in *Summa Theologica,* II–II, QQ. 10–14.

• McILWAIN, CHARLES HOWARD, *The Growth of Political Theory in the West* (New York, 1932). Contrary to most writers on the subject, McIlwain holds that St. Thomas Aquinas was neither a believer in limited, constitutional monarchy, nor a "Whig" or democrat, but "the greatest of all contemporary exponents of pure monarchy" (p. 333).

• MALLOY, MICHAEL, *Civil Authority in Medieval Philosophy* (Lanham, Maryland, 1985). Part II is on Aquinas.

• MARGENAU, HENRY, *Thomas and the Physics of 1958: A Confrontation* (Milwaukee, 1958). The author, an American physicist and philosopher of science, examines St. Thomas' views on science in relation to contemporary physics, and finds a harmonious concordance between the two.

• MARITAIN, JACQUES, *St. Thomas Aquinas* (Meridian Books, New York, 1958). Maritain is the outstanding liberal Catholic writer since Lord Acton, and one of the leading modern Thomist philosophers. One of the main propositions of the book is that "St. Thomas wrote not for the thirteenth century but for our time" (p. 103), and that he is "preeminently the apostle and teacher of our time" (p. 115). Maritain's estimate of St. Thomas' position is as follows: "It is proper to remember that God in His most exalted works proceeds by way of privileges and exceptions and unique cases. He once sent His only begotten Son on earth, and gave Him a precursor. He once gave the law through Moses—is there anything surprising in that He should once have given His Church a Doctor *par excellence* in philosophical and theological wisdom?" (p. 155). Testimonies of popes on St. Thomas Aquinas and four of the most important official papal pronouncements on Thomism as the official doctrine of the Roman Catholic Church are contained in an appendix (pp. 167–266).

Maritain applies his interpretation of Thomism to modern social and political problems in two books that are most representative of his liberal, democratic, antitotalitarian philosophy: *True Humanism* (New York, 1938), and *Scholasticism and Politics* (New York, 1940). In both books he develops his concept of "personalist democracy," which is opposed both to the "atomistic and mechanistic type of bourgeois individualism, which suppresses the social organic totality" (*Scholasticism and Politics,* p. 82), and to the totalitarian doctrines of communism, nazism, and fascism, which "engulf the person" *(ibid.).* Maritain contrasts "democracy of the individual and humanism of the individual," which "arise from an anthropocentric inspiration," with his own conception of "democracy of the person and humanism of the person," which "spring forth from a theocentric inspiration" (pp. 84–85), and which are based on the idea of man as God's image, the common good, human rights, and concrete liberty. Maritain is particularly concerned about the rights of man: "If the human person is without rights, then rights and, consequently, authority exist nowhere" (p. 111). Maritain is also keenly aware that there can be no rebuilding of society without thoroughgoing social and economic reforms. He interprets socialism as the result, not so much of demands for improved living conditions (which could also be obtained under reformist or paternalist capitalism), but of the struggle for recognition "of an offended and humiliated human dignity" (*True Humanism,* p. 225), which has been distorted by Marxism into class consciousness and

class war. Trade-unionism "is at the moment the most considerable and the most promising force of social renovation" (p. 233), though the Christian idea of community is above class, as it is above race and nation: "Yet, precisely because man is at once carnal and spiritual, because every great historic and temporal undertaking has biologico-sociological material foundations, where the very animality of man and a whole irrational capital is at once borne along and exalted, it is natural that, in the transformation of a regime such as the capitalist system, the working classes should furnish this sociological basis: and in a sense one may speak of their historic mission, may hold that the destiny of humanity depends largely, in actual fact, on their attitude and action" (p. 230).

Concerning the question of property, Maritain recalls the Thomistic doctrine that recognizes, on the one hand, private property, but insists, on the other, that it should serve the good of all. The remedy of the evil of concentration of private property in the hands of the few under capitalism is not, according to Maritain, the abolition of the institution of property but its diffusion and distribution "in ways which can remain very diverse, and which do not exclude, where they are necessary, certain collectivizations" (p. 179). In industry, Maritain is opposed to both state ownership and communism, and prefers cooperative ownership by the workers themselves, because such copartnerships would better protect the freedom of the workers and also provide a better solution of the problem of incentive than is possible under state ownership of industry. Socialist theory in democratic states is likely to move in an analogous direction, stressing socialization (by municipalities, cooperatives, and other associations and corporations) rather than nationalization (by the state). A succinct summary of Maritain's philosophy of "personalist democracy" will be found in his short book, *The Person and the Common Good* (New York, 1947). The basic doctrine of "personalism" is that "the human being is caught between two poles, a material pole, which, in reality, does not concern the true person but rather the shadow of personality or what, in the strict sense, is called *individuality,* and a spiritual pole, which does concern *true personality*" (p. 23). A detailed analysis of the various aspects of Maritain's philosophy will be found in Joseph W. Evans (ed.), *Jacques Maritain: The Man and His Achievement* (New York, 1963).

• PEGIS, ANTON C. (ed.), *Basic Writings of Saint Thomas Aquinas,* 2 vols. (New York, 1945). Contains substantial portions of the *Summa Theologica* and the *Summa contra gentiles,* his second most important work. The editor's introduction (pp. xxxv–liii) deals with the background of St. Thomas' thought, particularly in relation to Plato, Aristotle, and Christian theology. The anti-Platonism of St. Thomas receives special consideration. See also Pegis' *At the Origins of the Thomistic Notion of Man* (New York, 1963) and *St. Thomas and Philosophy* (Milwaukee, 1964).

• PIEPER, JOSEF, *Guide to Thomas Aquinas* (New York, 1962). Brief introduction into St. Thomas' intellectual and theological development, as exemplified by the style of his thought rather than its contents. Pieper's *The Silence of St. Thomas: Three Essays* (New York, 1957), particularly the third essay on "The Timeliness of Thomism" (pp. 75–108), has some suggestive comparisons between Thomism and existentialism. See also Ralph M. McInerny, *Thomism in an Age of Renewal* (Garden City, N.Y., 1966).

• SMITH, GEORGE D. (ed.), *The Teaching of the Catholic Church: A Summary of Catholic Doctrine,* 2 vols. (New York, 1949). A monumental work, with contributions from many distinguished scholars, all members of the clergy. See, in particular, Chap. I, "Faith and Revealed Truth," 1–37, and Chap. XX, "The Church on Earth," II, 691–732. There are more references to St. Thomas Aquinas than to any other source of doctrine (see Index, pp. 1313–1314).

• STOCKHAMMER, MORRIS (ed.), *Thomas Aquinas Dictionary* (New York, 1965). Presents, in alphabetical order, the principal concepts and ideas of St. Thomas, based on excerpts culled from his writings.

• STUBBS, WILLIAM, *Seventeen Lectures on the Study of Medieval and Modern History* (Oxford, 1886). Concerning medieval scholastic philosophers, Bishop Stubbs says that they "ticketed every portion of man's moral anatomy, found a rule for every possible choice, a reason and a reward for every virtue, and a punishment for every conceivable crime; they turned generalizations into laws, and deduced from them as laws the very facts from which they had generalized. They benefited mankind by exercising and training subtle wits, and they reduced dialectics, almost, we might say, logic itself, to absurdity. I do not undervalue them, because the great men among them were so great that even such a method did not destroy them: in reading Thomas Aquinas, for instance, one is constantly provoked to say, What could not such a mind have done if it had not been fettered by such a method?" (p. 90). For critical summaries of scholastic philosophy, see also G. G. Coulton, *Studies in Medieval Thought* (London–New York, 1940), pp. 130–150. How heresy and free thought continued to exist under scholasticism—albeit under precarious conditions—is described in J. M. Robertson, *A History of Freethought,* 4th ed. (London, 1936), I, 304–401.

• TAYLOR, A. E., *St. Thomas Aquinas as a Philosopher* (Oxford, 1924). St. Thomas is presented as a philosopher who appeared as a most audacious innovator to his contemporaries; in particular, the "substitution of Aristotelianism for Platonism as the basis of a specifically Christian philosophy was a revolution and a rather paradoxical revolution" (p. 10). Aristotle had two main tendencies: one directed toward naturalism, and another deeply embedded in the thought of Plato, and "it is Aristotle the Platonist rather than Aristotle the positivist who influences the thought of Thomas" (p. 25). See also John Frederick Piefer, *The Concept in Thomism* (New York, 1952).

• TRACY, DAVID (ed.), *Celebrating the Medieval Heritage* (Chicago, 1978). A collection of essays on Aquinas and Bonaventure. Part 3 is "Ethics and Political Thought."

• WULF, MAURICE DE, *History of Medieval Philosophy,* 2 vols., 3rd ed. (London–New York, 1935–1938). The first volume of this standard work, indispensable for reference purposes, deals with medieval philosophy to the end of the twelfth century, the second with the thirteenth century, including a study of St. Thomas Aquinas (pp. 116–151). Detailed bibliographies greatly enhance the value of the work. Concerning scholasticism—which he accepts enthusiastically—the author makes the point that, when scholastic philosophy is called "a religious philosophy, the qualification is correct if by it is meant that on the one hand revealed doctrine governed the choice of certain special problems, and that on the other hand, dogma served as a regulating principle and as an indirect control of philosophical research. But it ought to be understood that, speaking formally and in strict terms, a philosophy in the degree in which it is distinct from theology, is not susceptible of the adjective Christian, and hence, the expression Christian philosophy is an unsuitable one" (I, 280). To the extent that a philosophy is different from theology, it is not Christian (according to de Wulf), and to the extent that it is not different from theology, it is not philosophy. This extreme (though perhaps logically consistent) position is rejected by another neo-Thomist, Étienne Gilson, who admits the possibility of Christian philosophy in the acceptance of Christian revelation as "an indis-

pensable auxiliary to reason" (*The Spirit of Medieval Philosophy,* p. 37), and in the selection of those philosophical problems that affect the conduct of religious life. See also de Wulf's *Medieval Philosophy: Illustrated from the System of Thomas Aquinas* (Cambridge, Mass., 1922), a short account of St. Thomas' philosophy, including his theory of the state (pp. 117–128), and D. J. Kennedy, *St. Thomas Aquinas and Medieval Philosophy* (New York, 1919), which includes a detailed exposition of the three functions assigned to reason by St. Thomas: "(1) to prepare for faith, (2) to explain the truths of faith, (3) to defend the truths of faith" (pp. 82 ff.). A more critical approach will be found in Philip H. Wicksteed, *The Reactions between Dogma and Philosophy Illustrated from the Works of S. Thomas Aquinas* (Hibbert Lectures, Second Series, London, 1920).

CHAPTER TWELVE

DANTE

• BARBI, MICHELE, *The Life of Dante* (translated and edited by Paul G. Ruggiers, Berkeley and Los Angeles, 1954). Brief introduction into Dante's life and work by a leading Italian Dante specialist. Discussing Dante's *De monarchia,* Barbi writes that "the whole treatise is directed against all those who, for one reason or another, do not recognize the legitimacy of the Roman monarchy and its direct derivation from God. If on the whole it tends to confute the claims of the Church, that is because the Church has more authority and there is more harm in her usurpations" (p. 59). As an Italian patriot and nationalist, Barbi deeply sympathizes with Dante's praise of the Roman empire: "By exalting and defending the Empire he exalted and defended an Italian glory. Even if historical contingencies or divine justice had temporarily granted the imperial crown to foreign rulers, they were still imperial rulers. The Empire was Roman in every way, and

Rome had to be the seat of it; and Italy, 'queen of the peoples,' *(domina gentium),* thus had the honor of ruling the world" (pp. 63–64).
• BERGIN. THOMAS G., *Dante* (New York, 1965). The first four chapters cover Dante's Europe, Dante's Florence, Dante's life, and Dante's reading (pp. 1–66). Chap. X (pp. 177–194) analyzes *De monarchia.* While generally sympathetic to Dante's political reasoning, Bergin finds Dante's argument less convincing that Roman imperial power was sanctioned by God's will: "This section makes fascinating, if hardly very convincing, reading for a twentieth-century reader, who may find the comments of St. Augustine more appropriate. For Augustine, in the *City of God* (III, 17–19), has some very anti-Roman comments to make on the 'heroes' of the early republic, whom he saw as motivated purely by lust of glory. It seems as though Dante had very often fallen into the error he had

feared: that of identifying right with might" (p. 188).

• BRYCE, JAMES, *The Holy Roman Empire,* 7th ed. (New York, 1877). Chap. XV (pp. 239–269) provides a discussion of Dante against the political and intellectual currents of his age.

• BURNHAM, JAMES, *The Machiavellians: Defenders of Freedom* (New York, 1943). Part I is called "Dante: Politics as Wish" (pp. 3–26). Burnham considers *De monarchia* as the prototype of ninetenths of all writing on politics, whose general method consists in concealing the "real meaning" of the argument behind its "formal meaning," the latter being expressed "in terms of the fictional world of religion, metaphysics, miracles, and pseudo-history" (p. 9). Applying this distinction of formal and real meaning to *De monarchia,* Burnham writes: "We think we are debating universal peace, salvation, a unified world government, and the relations between Church and State, when what is really at issue is whether the Florentine Republic is to be run by its own citizens or submitted to the exploitation of a reactionary foreign monarch" (p. 24). Burnham also argues that Dante was a traitor to his country because he supported the imperial cause against Florence, and that "his sociological allegiance was reactionary" (p. 22) because he did not support the cause of the cities, at that time the most progressive elements in politics and culture, but sided with the great nobles and the imperial party, the Ghibellines, who "wanted to stop history short" *(ibid.). De monarchia* is, according to Burnham, no more than a "Ghibelline Party Platform," and its "vicious and reactionary" objectives are the "aims of an embittered and incompetent set of traitors" (p. 20). Burnham's severe critique of Dante is provocative, but debunking, too, can go too far.

• CHUBB, THOMAS CALDECOT, *Dante and His World* (Boston, 1966). A massive biography of Dante, written for the general reader and stressing Dante the man rather than the poet or political polemicist. Chap. XXII (pp. 653–674), which discusses *De monarchia,* contains the interesting statistical fact that of its 207 quotations 97 were from classical Latin and Greek authors, 65 from the New Testament, 28 from the Old

Testament, nine from the Church fathers, and eight from various sources (p. 659).

• CHURCH, R. W., *Dante and Other Essays* (London, 1888). The first essay is on Dante (pp. 1–191).

• DAVIS, CHARLES T., "Dante and Italian Nationalism," in William De Sua and Gino Rizzo (eds.), *A Dante Symposium: In Commemoration of the 700th Anniversary of the Poet's Birth (1265–1965)* (Chapel Hill, 1965), pp. 199–213. The author holds that Dante's "firm belief in the universality of Roman Power made any exclusive theory of nationalism impossible" (p. 202), and he concludes that during the liberal era of the Risorgimento Dante was a "political prophet for the whole nation" whereas during the fascist period "his voice reflected mainly the shrillness of official diatribes" (p. 213).

• ———, *Dante's Italy, and Other Essays* (Philadelphia, 1984). The main topics in this book are Dante's historical and political views, and the context from which they emerged. See also Davis's *Dante and the Idea of Rome* (Oxford, 1957).

• D'ENTRÈVES, A. P., *Dante as a Political Thinker* (Oxford, 1952). Interpreting Dante's political thought on the basis of the *Divine Comedy* as well as *De monarchia,* the author finds that there are important discrepancies between the two; specifically, *De monarchia* seems to be "characterized by a temporary forgetfulness, on Dante's side, of the fundamental Christian idea, that from within and not from without, must mankind be redeemed and saved" (p. 51). This viewpoint, the author argues, is recanted by Dante in the *Divine Comedy.* Extensive bibliographical notes (pp. 98–113) enhance the value of this provocative study by a leading authority in the field of Italian thought and letters.

• FARNELL, STEWART, *The Political Ideas of the Divine Comedy* (Lanham, Maryland, 1985). A brief introduction to this subject. Farnell states, "The threads of Dante's political thinking are essential parts of the splendid tapestry of *The Divine Comedy.*" A longer work on the same subject is Joan Ferrante, *The Political Vision of* The Divine Comedy (Princeton, 1984).

• FERGUSSON, FRANCIS, *Dante* (New York, 1966). Skillfully weaves together Dante's life, his intellectual sources, the political struggles in which Dante was involved, and his writings. The author's analyses are greatly enriched by his frequent analogies and comparisons, putting Dante's thought into a broader temporal and spatial context. Concerning *De monarchia,* Fergusson argues that, although Dante's idea of a Roman monarch of all mankind had no future, his idea of history as divine providence played an important role in forging the modern monarchies of national states, such as Spain, France, and England: "Book II of *De monarchia,* where Dante discusses the will of God in history, may be used to gloss Shakespeare's plays about the English monarchy, with their dramatic interplay between reason and religious loyalty to the anointed King; their more or less ritual ordeals by combat; their assumption that God's will in history is the ultimate arbiter of political conflict" (p. 78). Annotated Bibliographical Notes (pp. 201–208) are included.

• GILSON, ÉTIENNE, *Dante and Philosophy* (Harper Torchbooks, New York, 1963). Written from a neo-Thomist viewpoint, this is one of the most brilliant studies of Dante and essential to an understanding of his political philosophy, treated in Part III (pp. 162–224). Gilson is satisfied that Dante was completely loyal to his faith, religion, and church. Yet on the basic issues of the relation of ecclesiastical and temporal powers, and of philosophy and theology, "this alleged Thomist struck a mortal blow at the doctrine of St. Thomas Aquinas" (p. 212).

• HENRY, AURELIA, *The De Monarchia of Dante Alighieri* (Boston–New York, 1904). This translation of *De monarchia* contains a long introduction (pp. xvii–li) and numerous notes and cross references of considerable value and usefulness. A translation of *De monarchia* (by Philip H. Wicksteed) will also be found in *The Latin Works of Dante: Translated into English* (Temple Classics, London, 1904), pp. 127–280, accompanied by interpretative comments and explanations. The volume includes Dante's *Letters* (*Epistolae,* pp. 295–368) in an annotated translation; they are one of the principal sources of Dante's political ideas. A convenient edition of the Latin text is Dante, *De monarchia* (the Oxford Text edited by E. Moore, with an introduction on the political theory of Dante, by W. H. V. Reade, Oxford, 1916).

• LENKEITH, NANCY, *Dante and the Legend of Rome* (London, 1952). Dante's humanism, the glorification of the classical culture and heritage, had a decidedly political character: "It was a yearning for a new life which was to be a restoration of the ancient Roman way of being, of an entire civilization which would put to shame the barbarians across the Alps" (p. vii). While Dante was not the first Italian to revive the worship of ancient Rome, "he took the old 'patriotism' of the Italians, their half-poetical half-mythological love of their Roman origins, and attempted to give it a philosophical foundation" (p. 176). For a more recent study of Dante's conception of Rome, see Charles T. Davis, *Dante and the Idea of Rome* (Oxford, 1957).

• LIMENTANI, U. (ed.), *The Mind of Dante* (Cambridge, 1965). A symposium of essays by several British and Italian Dante scholars, mostly addressed to the general reader. In the essay on "Religion and Philosophy in Dante" by Kenelm Foster (pp. 47–78), the author, in comparing *De Monarchia* with the *Divine Comedy,* writes: "There may be no difference in principle between the *Monarchia* and the *Comedy;* but a difference of 'slant,' emphasis, perspective, there undoubtedly is: enough to repeat that one work looks wholly to temporal existence, the other to eternal. It does not follow, of course, that the *Monarchia* is simply an irreligious work, if by religion one means only a general reverence towards a felt 'divinity' in things; for there is certainly *that* in the *Monarchia.* But, more strictly, religion can mean trying to get as close as possible to that 'divinity,' whatever it may be; it means seeking God, in short; and to see Dante really seeking God we have to turn to the *Comedy*" (pp. 74–75). In his chapter on "Dante's Political Thought" (pp. 113–137), the editor concludes that Dante's general outlook can be summarized as "internationalism rather than nationalism, laicism rather than theocracy, in the arrangement of human affairs" (p. 137).

• MANCUSI-UNGARO, DONNA, *Dante and the Empire* (New York, 1987). A short book on Dante's political philosophy. The author attempts to understand and explain "Dante's view of man, mankind, and the political structure of a world-city."

• OZANAM, FRÉDÉRIC, *Dante and Catholic Philosophy in the Thirteenth Century* (New York, 1897). The author, a French scholar, finds that Dante's religious orthodoxy is well established; he calls him the "St. Thomas of poetry" in the Middle Ages (p. 357). An equally sympathetic interpretation will be found in Auguste Valensin, *Le christianisme de Dante* (Paris, 1954). The author, a French Jesuit theologian, warmly defends Dante's religious faith. In this, he follows the official view of the Roman Catholic Church of the last hundred years, as expressed by Pope Benedict XIV in 1914: "Alighierius noster est" ("Dante belongs to us"). Earlier, the Catholic attitude toward Dante was hostile.

A divergent view on Dante's religious thought is expressed by John Jay Chapman, *Dante* (Boston, 1927): "To speak of Dante as a Protestant would be so historically inexact as to be offensive. But Dante represents the spirit that was at the bottom of Protestantism, the impulse of a man to decide the religious question for himself, and to accept as much or as little as he sees fit" (p. 84). On Dante's relation to the papacy, Chapman writes that neither Luther, Calvin, nor John Knox ever "conceived of such supernal opposition to the Papacy as was Dante's bread and meat for many years. All that those northern reformers wanted was to be let alone. But Dante invades and browbeats the Roman Pontiff. He taught the Italians to hate the Vatican, and his influence it was which, more than any other one thing, led to the triumph of the Risorgimento and the unification of Italy in the last century" (p. 85). By contrast, Luigi Sturzo, a learned priest and scholar, writes as follows: "For man and Christian the *Divine Comedy* remains the book of art nearest to our spirit and faith" (*Church and State,* New York, 1939, p. 124).

• PAGE, THOMAS NELSON, *Dante and His Influence* (New York, 1922). Dante's political views are mainly discussed in Chap. III (pp. 89–116).

• PAPINI, GIOVANNI, *Dante Vivo* (English trans., New York, 1935). Dante's separation of the political from the religious power "was a first step in progressive anti-clericalism: the State ought to be independent of the Church; the State has a right to supervise and direct the Church; the State transfers to itself the greater part of the offices of the Church:

the State ignores the Church; the State ought to suppress the Church" (pp. 243–244). It is doubtful whether this kind of logic either proves or disproves Dante's basic position on the issue.

• PIRENNE, HENRI, *Economic and Social History of Medieval Europe* (London, 1936). Describes concisely and accurately the revival and growth of urban life, commerce, and trade in the Middle Ages, and provides the elementary social and economic data for an understanding of Dante's time. One of the best short books in the field.

• ROLBIECKI, JOHN JOSEPH, *The Political Philosophy of Dante Alighieri* (Washington, 1921). Stresses Dante's historical role as an advocate of international institutions for the regulation of the common interests of all mankind. The exposition of Dante's political ideas (pp. 15–150) is followed by a bibliography (pp. 151–156).

• SAYERS, DOROTHY L., *Introductory Papers on Dante* (London, 1954). Attempts to bring Dante to life for the modern reader, on the assumption that he was intended to be read by the common man and woman. The author doubts that *De monarchia* was Dante's "last word on the subject" (p. 211). Specifically, she claims that the two main theses of *De monarchia*—the complete emancipation of philosophy from faith and the establishment of a secular monarchy—were errors, and rectified by Dante himself in the *Divine Comedy.* While the author is primarily interested in Dante as an artist and poet, she has much to say that is relevant to a deeper understanding of Dante's general outlook and philosophy. See also her *Further Papers on Dante* (New York, 1957).

• TOYNBEE, PAGET, *Dante Alighieri: His Life and Works,* 4th ed. (Harper Torchbooks, New York, 1965). The emphasis is on the political background of Dante's time, particularly in Florence, and on his life and personal characteristics. Dante's Latin works, including *De monarchia,* are briefly analyzed in the last chapter (pp. 231–261). See also C. H. Grandgent, *Dante* (New York, 1916); Lonsdale Ragg, *Dante and His Italy* (New York, 1907); Paolo Milano (ed.), *The Portable Dante* (The Viking Portable Library, New York, 1948); and Karl Vossler, *Medieval Culture: An Introduction to Dante and His Times,* 2 vols. (New York, 1929).

• WICKSTEED, PHILIP H., *Dante and Aquinas* (London–New York, 1913). In this searching analysis of one of the crucial aspects of Dante's philosophy, the author concludes that "while Dante habitually moved within the circle of scholastic ideas, he did not allow it to confine him when his own thought or his poetic vision broke away from its limitations. In this respect his attitude towards it differed from his attitude towards Christian dogma, which he accepted without question, however grievous a strain it put upon his conscience or his affections" (p. 147). The book also includes illuminating analyses of the relations of medieval thought and Greek philosophy (pp. 1–26), Neoplatonism (pp. 27–43), and the migration of Aristotle and the transformations of Aristotelianism (pp. 44–85). Dante's relation to Virgil, his favorite poet, just as Aristotle was his favorite philosopher, is the main subject of J. H. Whitfield, *Dante and Virgil* (Oxford, 1949).

CHAPTER THIRTEEN

MARSILIO OF PADUA

• ALLEN, J. W., "Marsilio of Padua and Medieval Secularism," in *The Social and Political Ideas of Some Great Medieval Thinkers* (ed. F. J. C. Hearnshaw, London, 1923), pp. 167–191. The author is not sure whether Marsilio "was a Christian in any sense at all, in spite of the display of scriptural texts in the *Defensor*. We all know that the devil himself can quote Scripture" (p. 171). As to the meaning of Marsilio's concept of the "weightier part" of the citizenry, Allen suggests that normally it would mean the "numerical majority" (p. 182).

• BOASE, T. S. R., *Boniface VIII* (London, 1933). Includes, in the last chapter, a brief account of Boniface's successors, Benedict XI and Clement V.

• COULTON G. G., *Studies in Medieval Thought* (London, 1940). Chap. XIV is called "The Lay Revolt" (pp. 181–193). See also his *Medieval Panorama* (Cambridge, 1938), Chaps. XXXVI, "The Papal Schism" (pp. 477–484), and LII, "The Bursting of the Dykes" (pp. 720–731).

• D'ENTRÈVES, ALEXANDER PASSERIN, *The Medieval Contribution to Political Thought* (London, 1939). Chaps. III and IV are on Marsilio (pp. 44–87). Interprets Marsilio's political theory as a medieval revival of Aristotle's conception of the state.

• EMERTON, EPHRAIM, *The* Defensor Pacis *of Marsiglio of Padua* (Harvard Theological Studies, VIII, Cambridge, Mass., 1920). At the outset the author writes as follows: "Marsiglio is the herald of a new world, the prophet of a new social order, acutely conscious of his modernness and not afraid to confess it. His book has often been called the most remarkable literary product of the Middle Ages, and I am inclined to accept this verdict" (p. 1). This balanced study is excellent in both exposition and criticism.

• FIGGIS, JOHN NEVILLE, *The Divine Right of Kings* (Cambridge, 1934). Chap. III, "The Holy Roman Empire and the Papacy" (pp. 38–65), gives both the history and theory of the conflict, including brief accounts of Pope Boniface VIII, King Philip IV, and Marsilio of Padua.

• GEWIRTH, ALAN, "John of Jandun and the *Defensor Pacis*," *Speculum,* XXIII (April 1948), 267–272. On the basis of a careful comparison of Marsilio's works with those of John of Jandun, the author concludes that "no substantial part of the *Defensor Pacis* was written by John of Jandun. From the external evidence of his close association in friendship and in political activities with Marsilius, it is highly probable that John contributed advice and assistance. But the actual composition and doctrine of the entire treatise are the product of one man, Marsilius of Padua" (p. 272). See also Gewirth's

Marsilius of Padua and Medieval Political Philosophy (New York, 1951).

- GIERKE, OTTO, *Political Theories of the Middle Age* (trans., with an introduction, by Frederick William Maitland, Cambridge, 1938). Chaps. VI, "The Idea of Popular Sovereignty" (pp. 37–61), and X, "The Beginnings of the Modern State" (pp. 87–100), are particularly pertinent. Maitland's introduction (pp. xii–xlv) is a classic within a classic.
- HENDERSON, ERNEST F. (ed.), *Select Historical Documents of the Middle Ages* (London, 1903). Pope Boniface VIII's two bulls, *Clericis Laicos* (1296) and *Unam Sanctam* (1302), are reprinted (pp. 432–437).
- HOLMES, OLIVER WENDELL, "The Path of the Law," *Harvard Law Review,* X (No. 8, 1897), 457–478. The definition of the law is given as "the prophecies of what the courts will do in fact, and nothing more pretentious" (pp. 460–461). For Hans Kelsen's view of coercion as an essential element in law, see his *General Theory of Law and State* (Cambridge, Mass., 1945), pp. 18 ff., 122 ff., 391 ff.
- LEWIS, EWART, "The 'Positivism' of Marsiglio of Padua," *Speculum,* XXXVIII (October 1963), 541–582. The author challenges the dominant interpretation of Marsilio's concept of law, according to which he broke with the medieval view that reason was the essence of law, substituting for it the new concept that the essence of law was its coerciveness. "It seems clear that, far from basing the validity of laws on the coercive authority of a certain legislator," the author states, "Marsiglio is actually trying to base the valid authority of a certain legislator on the necessary characteristics of laws; and that, in this attempt, he is rather more concerned with the substantive requisites of laws than with their necessary coerciveness. And although, in common with all medieval theory of legislation, his theory assumes that an authoritative decision, an act of will, is essential to the minting of mere reason into law, he nowhere suggests that what is just and beneficial is itself determined by that act of will" (pp. 570–571).
- MCILWAIN, CHARLES HOWARD, *The Growth of Political Thought in the West* (New York, 1932). In his analysis of Marsilio's political ideas (pp. 295–315) the author rejects the accepted democratic interpretation of the doctrine of the "weightier part" of the citizens, and holds that it is "in much closer correspondence with the anti-democratic ideas of Aristotle than with the political conceptions of our modern time" (p. 304). McIlwain calls *The Defender of Peace* "one of the real landmarks" in the development of political thought (p. 313), because it is the first book that "denies to the clergy coercive authority of any kind whatsoever, spiritual or temporal, direct or indirect" *(ibid.).*
- MARSILIO OF PADUA, *The Defender of the Peace* (trans. out of Latin into English by William Marshall, London, 1535). Until the publication of Alan Gewith's translation in 1956, the Marshall translation was the only one. Published in 1535, at the height of Henry VIII's reign, it is noteworthy for the omission of passages in *The Defender of Peace* that treat of the correction of rulers who abuse their powers. For a study of the influence of Marsilio on Thomas Starkey, chaplain to Henry VIII, and author of an important political work, the *Dialogue between Cardinal Pole and Thomas Lupset,* see Franklin Le Van Baumer, "Thomas Starkey and Marsilius of Padua," *Politica,* II (November 1936), 188–205.
- POOLE, REGINALD LANE, *Illustrations of the History of Medieval Thought and Learning,* 2nd ed. (New York, 1960). In discussing *The Defender of Peace* (pp. 230–241), Poole stresses that it contains "the whole essence of the religious and political theory which separates modern times from the middle ages. The significance of the reformation, putting theological details aside, lay in the substitution of a ministry serving the church, the congregation of Christian men, for a hierarchical class. The significance of the later political revolution, even now far from universally realized, lay in the recognition of the people as the source of government, as the sovereign power in the state. Both these ideas Marsiglio appropriated. He had not only a glimpse of them as from afar off; he thought them out, defined them, stated them with the clearest precision, so that the modern constitutional statesman, the modern Protestant, has nothing to alter in their principle, has only to develop them and fill in their outline" (p. 240).
- POWICKE, F. M., *The Christian Life in the Middle Ages* (Oxford, 1935). Chap. III is on "Pope Boniface VIII" (pp. 47–73). See also

the author's *Ways of Medieval Life and Thought* (London 1950), Chap. VII: "Reflections on the Medieval State" (pp. 130–148).

• PREVITÉ-ORTON, C. W., *Marsilius of Padua* (Annual Italian Lecture of the British Academy, London, 1935). The best short introduction, in English, to Marsilio's main ideas. The author stresses the impact of republican Padua on Marsilio, and emphasizes the democratic aspects of his political theory. See also Previté-Orton's introduction to his edition of the Latin text of *The* Defensor Pacis *of Marsilio of Padua* (Cambridge, 1928), pp. ix–xliii; "Marsiglio of Padua," *English Historical Review*, XXXVIII (January 1923), pp. 1–18; and "The Authors Cited in the *Defensor Pacis*," in *Essays in History Presented to Reginald Lane Poole* (ed. by H. W. C. Davis, Oxford, 1927), pp. 405–420.

• REEVES, MARJORIE, "Marsiglio of Padua and Dante Alighieri," in Beryl Smalley (ed.), *Trends in Medieval Political Thought* (Oxford, 1965), pp. 86–104. The author of this perceptive comparative analysis notes striking parallels between the experiences of Marsilio and Dante, but she is even more impressed with the substantial difference of their ideas: "Both have an Italian civic background and it is noteworthy that only one incorporates it into his idea of peace. This sharp contrast perhaps gives us the most central point of divergence between Dante and Marsiglio, for whereas Dante's aspiration to achieve the possible intellect leads him straightforward to the single monarch as the only means to this end, Marsiglio's spread of varying civic values without distinction of grade is the basis of his republicanism. The qualities of his sufficient life are minimal enough to be desired and attained by a large proportion of the people, whereas a hierarchy of ends presupposes that only an elite will reach the highest" (p. 96).

• SIGMUND, PAUL E., "The Influence of Marsilius of Padua on Fifteenth-Century Conciliarism," *Journal of the History of Ideas*, XXIII (July–September 1962), pp. 392–402. Although The *Defender of Peace* was burned at the University of Paris in 1324 and Marsilio himself was condemned as a heretic in 1327, the author shows that Marsilio exercised a considerable influence on numerous writers in the fifteenth century who sought to circumscribe absolute papal power through the conciliar movement. On Marsilio and conciliarism, see also Michael Wilks, *The Problem of Sovereignty in the Middle Ages* (Cambridge, 1963), pp. 477 ff.

II. SIXTEENTH THROUGH EIGHTEENTH CENTURIES

CHAPTER FOURTEEN

MACHIAVELLI

• ACTON, LORD, *The History of Freedom and Other Essays* (London, 1907). Chap. VII (pp. 212–231), on Machiavelli, includes many comments on *The Prince* by famous writers and statesmen. Lord Acton concludes his observations as follows: "Machiavelli is the earliest conscious and articulate exponent of certain living forces in the present world. Religion, progressive enlightenment, the perpetual vigilance of public opinion, have not reduced his empire, or disproved the justice of his conception of mankind. He obtains a new lease of life from causes that are still prevailing, and from doctrines that are apparent in politics, philosophy, and science. Without sparing censure, or employing for comparison the grosser symptoms of the age, we find him near our common level, and perceive that he is not a vanishing type, but a constant and contemporary influence" (p. 231).

• CASSIRER, ERNST, *The Myth of the State* (New Haven, 1946). Chaps. X–XII (pp. 116–162) place Machiavelli in the philosophical and scientific background of his time and interpret his political thought in a fresh and penetrating manner. See also Cassirer's "Some Remarks on the Originality of the Renaissance," *Journal of the History of Ideas*, IV (January 1943), pp. 49–56. The entire issue is devoted to a symposium on the Renaissance.

• CHABOD, FEDERICO, *Machiavelli and the Renaissance* (trans. into English, Cambridge, Mass., 1958). Like most Italian students of Machiavelli, the author emphasizes the context of Italian history and civilization which provide the clue for a proper understanding of Machiavelli's thought. In the same tradition of Italian scholarship, Chabod con-centrates on *The Prince* as the core of Machiavelli's ideas, and assigns to *The Discourses* a much less important role than is customary among non-Italian scholars. The author arrives at this relative evaluation of the two works on grounds not only of intrinsic merit and analysis, but also of chronology: contrary to the commonly held view, according to which *The Discourses* was written much later than *The Prince,* Chabod argues that "it may be regarded as certain that at the time when Machiavelli started work on *The Prince* the first book of *The Discourses* was already largely complete" (p. 31). An extensive bibliography (pp. 201–247) examines the literature on the concept and meaning of the Renaissance. See also Chabod's *Scritti su Machiavelli* (Turin, 1964), a collection of his writings on Machiavelli over a period of three decades.

• CROCE, BENEDETTO, *Politics and Morals* (New York, 1945). Defends Machiavelli in the light of Italian politics and traditions: "The art and science of politics, of pure politics, brought to maturity by the Italians, were to him a source of pride" (p. 63). The last chapter is "Historical Pessimism" (pp. 200–204).

• DONALDSON, PETER S., *Machiavelli and Mystery of State* (New York, 1988). Donaldson explores widely divergent interpretations of Machiavelli by six Renaissance thinkers.

• FIGGIS, JOHN NEVILLE, *Studies of Political Thought from Gerson to Grotius, 1414–1625,* 2nd ed. (Cambridge, 1931). In his appraisal of Machiavelli (pp. 72–93), Figgis stresses the absence of the concept of natural law in Machiavelli and draws suggestive comparisons between Machiavelli and Nietzsche.

• FLEISHER, MARTIN (ed.), *Machiavelli and the Nature of Political Thought* (New York, 1972). Papers from the first Conference for the Study of Political Thought.

• GARVER, EUGENE, *Machiavelli and the History of Prudence* (Madison, Wisc., 1987). An essay on prudence or practical wisdom in which the place of Machiavelli is assessed.

• HEARNSHAW, F. J. C. (ed.), *The Social and Political Ideals of Some Great Thinkers of the Renaissance and the Reformation* (London, 1925), Chap. IV, by the editor, is on Machiavelli (pp. 87–121). The author reaches this conclusion: "I hold that both the conscience of mankind and the verdict of history have declared themselves decisively against Machiavellism. The one says that it is theoretically indefensible, the other that it is practically unsound" (p. 118). Numerous illustrations from history are cited to show that the application of Machiavellian principles does not pay—quite apart from the question of their ethical character.

• HULLIUNG, MARK, *Citizen Machiavelli* (Princeton, N.J., 1984). Hulliung holds the traditional view of Machiavelli, namely, that his moral and political thought is "scandal[ous]." Hulliung's view is not that Machiavelli was a misguided or misinterpreted humanist, but that he deliberately and intentionally put forth a political teaching different than his predecessors'.

• JENSEN, DE LAMAR (ed.), *Machiavelli: Cynic, Patriot, or Political Scientist?* (Boston, 1960). A useful brief symposium of excerpts from the writings of students of Machiavelli, giving the pros and cons on each of the major issues treated. Has "Suggestions for Additional Reading" (pp. 109–111).

• LANDI, ERNESTO, "The Political Philosophy of Machiavelli," *History Today,* XIV (August 1964), pp. 550–555. In this brief analysis, addressed to the general reader, the author writes: "Machiavelli was certainly a devious man; and much of what he says is literally shocking. What is perhaps the most audacious, and also the most original suggestion in his theory, is that there is not one morality, as all previous philosophers had taught, but two moralities—political morality and private morality" (p. 554). Yet the author recognizes that "there have been surprisingly few takers" for this basic concept of Machiavelli, "possibly because it entails too radical a break with that Christian

and Hellenistic tradition by which the European mind has been shaped" (p. 555).

• LASKI, HAROLD J., *The Dangers of Obedience and Other Essays* (New York, 1930). Chap. IX, "Machiavelli and the Present Time" (pp. 238–263), is a critical study of Machiavelli in the light of political philosophy and historical experience. Machiavelli's doctrine is called a "gospel of death" (p. 262).

• LEWIS, WYNDHAM, *The Lion and the Fox* (New York–London, n.d.). A suggestive study of the impact of Machiavelli on English literature, with particular reference to Shakespeare.

• MANSFIELD, HARVEY, *Machiavelli's New Modes and Orders: A Study of the Discourses on Livy* (Ithaca, N.Y., 1979). An interpretive and detailed commentary of the *Discourses* on a chapter-by-chapter basis, from a Straussian perspective.

• ———, *Machiavelli's Virtue* (Chicago, 1996). Twenty-five-plus years of writing on Machiavelli are combined within this single volume to create an essential work for Machiavelli scholars. His controversial Straussian interpretation of Machiavellian thought challenges accepted notions and is provocative.

• MATTINGLY, GARRETT, "Machiavelli's *Prince:* Political Science or Political Satire?" *The American Scholar,* XXVII (Autumn 1958), pp. 482–491. Puts forward the thesis that *The Prince* should be read as a parody or satirical version of "Mirrors of Princes," handbooks of advice to princes frequently written before and during Machiavelli's time: "In some ways, Machiavelli's little treatise was just like all the other 'Mirrors of Princes'; in other ways it was a diabolical burlesque of all of them, like a political Black Mass" (p. 487). The author finds supporting evidence for his thesis both in Machiavelli's life and thought, and even if his reappraisal is ultimately not fully convincing it deserves careful attention.

• MEINECKE, FRIEDRICH, *Machiavellism: The Doctrine of Raison d'État and Its Place in Modern History* (New Haven, 1957). The classic study of the concept and evolution of the reason of state by the foremost German historian of the twentieth century. The introduction (pp. 1–22) analyzes the essence of the reason of state, and Chap. I (pp. 25–48) is on Machiavelli. See also Gerhard Ritter,

The Corrupting Influence of Power (Hadleigh, Essex, 1952); Chap. II is on Machiavelli as the "Path-Finder of Continental Power Politics" (pp. 17–45). The principal theme of Ritter's book is the contrast between Machiavelli and Thomas More, the "Ideologist of the Island Welfare State" (pp. 46–89), and the historical consequences of this contrast in modern European history (pp. 90–197).

• MUIR, D. ERSKINE, *Machiavelli and His Times* (London, 1936). The author sees the clue to Machiavelli's political theory in his "burning indignation at the state of Italy and the decadence of Italians, and a hard ruthless determination to point to the only remedies in which he believed" (p. 251). Attractive illustrations are included in the book.

• OLSCHKI, LEONARDO, *Machiavelli the Scientist* (Berkeley, 1945). A brief and illuminating essay, stressing the relation of Machiavelli's ideas to the new scientific tendencies of his time. Olschki characterizes Machiavelli "as one of the greatest exponents of the laical genius of Italy that sought clarity, knowledge, and wisdom as manifestations of a free human judgment and of autonomous intellectual experiences" (p. 56).

• PITKIN, HANNA, *Fortune Is a Woman* (Berkeley, 1984). Subtitled *Gender and Politics in the Thought of Niccolò Machiavelli,* this book is a sustained investigation of Machiavelli's thought, in which the focus is made to be the role of masculinity in his thought.

• PREZZOLINI, GIUSEPPE, *Machiavelli* (New York, 1967). The main value of the book lies in the survey of Machiavelli's influence in the major European countries and the United States, taking up about half of the whole work. In the discussion of Machiavelli's political thought, the author stresses its atheistic and anti-Christian character.

• RAAB, FELIX, *The English Face of Machiavelli: A Changing Interpretation, 1500–1700* (London, 1964). Shows how Machiavelli's ideas found adherents and opponents during the Tudor and early Stuart periods, both among publicists and men in public affairs. See also J. G. A. Pocock, "Machiavelli, Harrington, and English Political Ideologies in the Eighteenth Century," *William and Mary Quarterly,* 3rd Series, XXII (October, 1965), 549–583.

• RIDOLFI, ROBERTO, *The Life of Niccolò Machiavelli* (Chicago, 1963). An outstanding biography of Machiavelli, stressing his character, life, and career rather than his thought, viewed perceptively and sympathetically by a Florentine historian. For a brief biographical introduction, see also J. R. Hale, *Machiavelli and Renaissance Italy* (London, 1961).

• STRAUSS, LEO, *Thoughts on Machiavelli* (Glencoe, Ill., 1958). Seeks to establish the unity of Machiavelli's thought in *The Prince* and *The Discourses,* contrary to the more accepted view that there is a real distinction of outlook between the two works. In trying to fathom the meaning of Machiavelli's doctrines, the author does not relate Machiavelli to his time and historical environment, but dissects the text of Machiavelli's writings in minute detail, including the frequency of some key concepts (or their absence). Strauss rejects the newer interpretations of Machiavelli as a patriot or scientific student of politics, and accepts the older view of Machiavelli as a "teacher of evil" (p. 9). The symbol of Machiavelli's new philosophy "is the Beast Man as opposed to the God Man: it understands man in the light of the subhuman rather than that of the super-human" (pp. 296–297). Despite its self-imposed limitations of approach, this work is indispensable to the study of Machiavelli.

• SULLIVAN, VICKIE B., *Machiavelli's Three Romes: Religion, Liberty, and Politics Reformed* (DeKalb, 1996). Sullivan's treatment of the role of religion as politics or belief within Machiavelli's texts provides the reader with an original and valuable look at this topic. Her engagement of scholars such as Skinner, Pocock, and Strauss make this an excellent resource.

• VILLARI, PASQUALE, *The Life and Times of Niccolò Machiavelli* (New York, 1898). First published in Italian in 1877, this is still a useful source of Machiavellian studies, though perhaps too apologetic in tendency. The massive work contains detailed accounts of the background of the whole period as well as of Machiavelli's life and thought. Numerous illustrations are included.

• WHITFIELD, JOHN H., *Machiavelli* (Oxford, 1947). Chap. IV (pp. 60–82) of this scholarly and searching work is on *The Prince.* A short bibliography is added (pp. 161–163).

• WOOD, NEAL, "Machiavelli's Concept of *Virtù* Reconsidered," *Political Studies*, XV (June 1967), 159–172. Machiavelli himself used the term "virtù" in many ways, and there has been ceaseless controversy as to whether the many specific meanings used by Machiavelli have a common core. After examining the concept of "virtù" in various works of Machiavelli, the author makes a good case for defining the core meaning of "virtù" as "a set of qualities, or a pattern of behavior most distinctively exhibited under what may be described as battlefield conditions, whether actual war or politics provide the context. Machiavelli's politico is cast in the mould of the warrior, and the standard of excellence of one is not so different from that of the other" (p. 171). For a different interpretation, see Joseph Anthony Mazzeo, *Renaissance and Seventeenth Century Studies* (New York, 1964), where "virtù" is defined as "sheer ability, prudence in the sense of practical insight and the power to act on it, without any ethical meaning attached. It involves an acute understanding of the real nature of things and circumstances as well as the ability to act on that understanding" (p. 156).

CHAPTER FIFTEEN

THE PROTESTANT REFORMATION

• ACTON, LORD, *The History of Freedom and Other Essays* (London, 1907). Chap. IV is called "The Massacre of St. Bartholomew" (pp. 101–149). The royal orders required the public authorities "to collect the Huguenots in some prison or other safe place, where they could be got at by hired bands of volunteer assassins. To screen the King it was desirable that his officers should not superintend the work themselves. Mandelot, the Governor of Lyons, having locked the gates of Lyons, and shut up the Huguenots together, took himself out of the way while the Huguenots were butchered" (p. 119). Lord Acton, a devout Catholic, describes the subsequent attempts to whitewash the massacre as follows: "A time came when the Catholics, having long relied on force, were compelled to appeal to opinion. That which had been defiantly acknowledged and defended required to be ingeniously explained away. The same motive which had justified the murder now prompted the lie. Men shrank from the conviction that the rulers and restorers of their Church had been murderers and abetters of murder, and that so much infamy had been coupled with so much zeal. They feared to say that the most monstrous of crimes had been solemnly approved at Rome, lest they should devote the Papacy to the execra-tion of mankind" (p. 148). See also Chap. V, "The Protestant Theory of Persecution" (pp. 150–187), in which Lord Acton deals, in particular, with doctrines and practices of persecution in Lutheranism and Calvinism, and his conclusion is summarized in one brief sentence: "Those who—in agreement with the principle of the early Church, that men are free in matters of conscience—condemn all intolerance, will censure Catholics and Protestants alike" (p. 186).

• ALLEN, J. W., *The History of Political Thought in the Sixteenth Century* (London, 1928). Sees the originality of the *Vindiciae* not in the idea of contract, but in the stress on the rights of municipalities, thus foreshadowing the concept of a federal system; the latter had little impact in France and England but influenced the internal political organization of Holland (pp. 320–331).

• ARMSTRONG, E., "The Political Theory of the Huguenots," *English Historical Review*, IV (January 1889), pp. 13–40. Emphasizes the immense practical impact of the *Vindiciae*, particularly in England, and less in France.

• BAINTON, ROLAND H., *The Reformation of the Sixteenth Century* (Beacon Paperbacks, Boston, 1956). While stressing the religious ideas and issues in the rise of Protestantism, the author gives due attention to its social, economic, and political background. Unlike most other writers, Bainton does not accept the "common generalization that Lutheranism made for totalitarianism and Calvinism for democracy" (p. 233), nor does he favor the view that Protestantism and Catholicism can be clearly juxtaposed in terms of their political impact: "Just as the Catholic Church will make a concordat with any regime that allows freedom to administer the sacraments, freedom to propagate the faith, freedom to hold property, and freedom for the monastic orders, so Protestantism has been willing to tolerate any form of government which accords religious liberty to Protestantism" (p. 234). Interesting comparisons between Catholic and Protestant attitudes on religious toleration from the fifteenth to the seventeenth centuries will be found in Bainton's *The Travails of Religious Liberty* (Harper Torchbooks, New York, 1958) and *The Age of the Reformation* (Anvil Books, Princeton, 1956).

• BARKER, ERNEST, *Church, State and Study* (London, 1930). Chap. III, "A Huguenot Theory of Politics," deals primarily with the *Vindiciae contra tyrannos* (pp. 72–108), and is one of the most instructive analyses of the work. Of special interest is Barker's detailed evidence of the striking similarity between the *Vindiciae* and Locke's *Second Treatise of Government* (pp. 98–99, pp. 106–108). The question of the authorship of the *Vindiciae* is examined by Barker in "The Authorship of the *Vindiciae contra tyrannos*," *Cambridge Historical Journal*, III (No. 2, 1930), pp. 164–181. A searching examination of the available facts leads Barker to support the traditional acceptance of Hubert Languet as the author of the *Vindiciae*, whereas the evidence against Duplessis-Mornay seems "absolutely conclusive" (p. 174).

• ———, *Traditions of Civility* (Cambridge, 1948). Chap. IV, "The Connection of the Renaissance and the Reformation" (pp. 74–123), is an illuminating interpretation of an age "from which we are sprung, and to which we must always return to understand what we are" (p. 123). The essay is admirably suited for a first introduction to the whole subject of Renaissance and Reformation.

• BORNKAMM, HEINRICH, *Luther's World of Thought* (St. Louis, 1958). The author, a German church historian and fervent

Lutheran, deals not only with Luther's religious doctrines, but also with his political ideas and their impact on German political development. Bornkamm argues that Luther was primarily a religious reformer rather than a political thinker or practical statesman. The main point in Luther's concept of the state is his rejection of the Aristotelian thesis that the state is the product of man's social impulses. Luther follows here—as in so many other issues—the doctrine of Augustine according to which the state is the result of, and remedy for, man's sinfulness. While not denying that the German Protestant rulers used the Lutheran churches as instruments of political absolutism, the author defends Luther on that point by arguing that such developments ran counter to Luther's intentions and expectations.

• BOUWSMA, WILLIAM, *John Calvin; A Sixteenth-Century Portrait* (Oxford, 1988). The most important recent biography on Calvin. This work much discusses Calvin's ideas (not so much his theology) and is therefore particularly valuable. Includes chapters on "Society" and "Polity."

• BREEN, QUIRINUS, *John Calvin: A Study in French Humanism* (Archon Books, U.S.A., 1968). This book concentrates on the early life of Calvin, which, in Breen's view, "reveals a cross-section in miniature of French humanism."

• CHADWICK, OWEN, *The Reformation* (Penguin Books, Baltimore, 1964). A useful overall introduction into the background, nature, and effects of the Reformation. For studies in depth, stressing particularly the social and economic underpinnings of the Reformation, see Arthur G. Dickens, *Reformation and Society in Sixteenth-Century Europe* (New York, 1966), and Guy E. Swanson, *Religion and Regime: A Sociological Account of the Reformation* (Ann Arbor, 1967).

• COLLINS, ROSS, *Calvin and the Libertines of Geneva* (Toronto, 1968). A brief biography of Calvin that defends him from the views that he was either a political tyrant or Protestant Pope in Geneva.

• DEFENCE OF LIBERTY AGAINST TYRANTS (A Translation of the *Vindiciae contra tyrannos* by Junius Brutus, with an Historical Introduction by Harold J. Laski, London, 1924). Laski's introduction is detailed and penetrating, providing a background of Huguenot political thought as well as a minute analysis of the chief ideas of the *Vindiciae* (pp. 1–60).

• FIGGIS, JOHN NEVILLE, *Studies of Political Thought from Gerson to Grotius, 1414–1625* (Cambridge, 1931). The first part of Lecture III, "Luther and Machiavelli," deals with the impact of Luther on politics (pp. 55–72). For a brief account of the *Vindiciae,* see pp. 134ff., and Figgis' *The Divine Right of Kings* (Cambridge, 1934), pp. 113–118.

• FOSDICK, HARRY EMERSON (ed.), *Great Voices of the Reformation* (Modern Library Giants, New York, 1954). An anthology of writers of the Reformation, from John Wycliffe to John Wesley, including brief excerpts from less well-known sources. The same subject is also covered in a much briefer anthology of Reformation writings by Lewis W. Spitz (ed.), *The Protestant Reformation* (Englewood Cliffs, N.J., 1966).

• GREEN, V. H. H., *Luther and the Reformation* (New York, 1964). In 200 pages the author, combining solid scholarship with fair judgment, succeeds in giving both a vivid portrait of Luther's personality and thought and an incisive account of the world in which he lived. Concerning Luther's attacks against the peasants during the peasant uprising, Green notes that "nothing can justify the shrill and savage tone" of Luther's condemnation of the peasants, but argues that Luther believed "the Evangelical Reformation was itself imperilled by the ravaging bands" (p. 153). In his conclusion, Green compares Luther with Calvin: "His mind was perhaps less incisive and his administrative genius less marked than that of John Calvin, and his general outlook more old-fashioned. In the long run Calvinism exerted greater influence over the future history of the world, but conservative revolutionary as he may well have been, Luther more than any other person fractured the unity of medieval Christendom and challenged the authority of the Church" (p. 197).

• GRISAR, HARTMANN, *Martin Luther: His Life and Work* (St. Louis, 1935). The leading Catholic biography of Luther. See also Jacques Maritain, *Three Reformers: Luther, Descartes, Rousseau* (New York, 1929), for a Catholic interpretation of Luther and his relation to Descartes and Rousseau from the viewpoint of metaphysics and social philosophy. The specific problem of toleration

of dissenting religious beliefs during the Reformation period is treated, in a critical yet scholarly manner, by Joseph Lecler, *Toleration and the Reformation,* 2 vols. (New York, 1960).

• HARBISON, E. HARRIS, *The Age of Reformation* (Ithaca, 1955). An outstanding brief survey of the period, skillfully relating the new religious movements to the underlying intellectual and social forces throughout Europe. See also Harbison's *The Christian Scholar in the Age of the Reformation* (New York, 1956), and *Christianity and History* (Princeton, 1964).

• HUNT, GEORGE L. (ed.), *Calvinism and the Political Order* (Philadelphia, 1965). A symposium of ten essays, five of which deal with American topics, such as the influence of the Puritan ethic on American democracy, Lincoln, and Woodrow Wilson. See also Jacob T. Hoogstra (ed.), *American Calvinism: A Survey* (Grand Rapids, 1957), and Roy F. Nichols, *Religion and American Democracy* (Baton Rouge, 1959).

• HUNTER, A. MITCHELL, *The Teaching of Calvin: A Modern Interpretation* (London, 1950). Stresses the impact of Calvinism on the rise of modern democracy: "It was principally because Calvin was such an outright uncompromising exponent of essential democracy in Church and State that his influence so quickly eclipsed that of Luther in the extent of its spread and the constructive and directive idealism he infused into the political systems of modern civilization. Calvinism in fact became the most powerful ferment of civil liberty which has ever worked in the world's heart" (p. 304).

• MACKINNON, JAMES, *Luther and the Reformation,* 4 vols. (New York, 1925–1930). Covers extensively the background, life, thought, and impact of Luther. The best short biography of Luther is Roland H. Bainton, *Here I Stand: A Life of Martin Luther* (New York, 1950). Older, but still useful, is Preserved Smith, *The Life and Letters of Martin Luther* (Boston–New York, 1911). See also Heinrich Boehmer, *Luther and the Reformation in the Light of Modern Research* (London, 1930); Edgar M. Carlson, *The Reinterpretation of Luther* (Philadelphia, 1948); and Robert M. Fife, *The Revolt of Martin Luther* (New York, 1957).

• MCNEILL, JOHN T., *The History and Character of Calvinism* (New York, 1954). The first half deals with the origins of Calvinism and the Geneva experiment under Calvin himself; the second half traces the spread of Calvinism to the rest of Europe and North America, and examines the relation of Calvinism to modern issues. With regard to the issue of slavery in the United States, the author writes that, when the civil war came in 1861, "most of the churches upheld the cause espoused by the states in which they were located" (p. 424). See also George L. Mosse, *Calvinism: Authoritarian or Democratic?* (New York, 1957) and Charles Davis Cremeans, *The Reception of Calvinistic Thought in England* (Urbana, 1949).

• NIEBUHR, REINHOLD, *The Nature and Destiny of Man: A Christian Interpretation,* 2 vols. in 1 (New York, 1949). This is the main work by Niebuhr, generally recognized as the most influential Protestant religious thinker of the twentieth century and considered by some as the foremost American political philosopher of his time. In his treatment of the Reformation (II, pp. 184–212), Niebuhr emphasizes that Luther "took a complacent attitude towards the social inequalities of feudalism and observed that on earth there will always be masters and slaves. Luther added an element of perversity to this social ethic by enlarging upon the distinction between an 'inner' and an 'outer' kingdom so that it became, in effect, a distinction between public and private morality. The rulers, as custodians of public morality, were advised to 'hit, stab, kill' when dealing with rebels. . . . The peasants on the other hand, as private citizens, were admonished to live in accordance with the ethic of the Sermon on the Mount. . . . The inevitable consequence of such an ethic is to encourage tyranny; for resistance to government is as important a principle of justice as maintenance of government" (II, pp. 193–195). Niebuhr also adds that Luther's "inordinate fear of anarchy" and his "corresponding indifference to the injustice of tyranny" *(ibid.)* were "not unrelated" to the subsequent history of Germany and to German Nazism. By contrast with Lutheranism, Niebuhr holds, both Calvinism and Catholicism "have a lively sense of the individual's responsibility for the whole of his common life" (*Faith and History,* New York, 1949, p. 200). See also the following works by Niebuhr: *The Children of Light and the Children of Darkness* (New York, 1944), *Moral Man and Immoral Society* (New York, 1960), *The Self and the Dramas of History* (New York, 1955), and *Pious and Secular America* (New York, 1958).

• PARKER, THOMAS, *John Calvin: A Biography* (London, 1975). When it appeared, the first full-length biography on Calvin in English for 40 years.

• PLASS, EWALD M. (ed.), *What Luther Says: An Anthology,* 3 vols. (St. Louis, 1959). Presents all aspects of Luther's thought—theological, philosophical, social, political, and economic—in his own words. The entries are in alphabetical order. Since Luther was a prolific writer, and had strong views on many and sundry subjects, this anthology is immensely useful as a quick reference guide to his thought. Luther's writings on the peasant rebellion will be found in Vol. 46 of *Luther's Works* (ed. by Robert C. Schultz, Philadelphia, 1967), pp. 3–85.

• REID, W. STANFORD (ed.), *John Calvin: His Influence in the Western World* (Grand Rapids, Mich., 1982). A collection of essays on various Calvinist subjects, mostly his influence on a country-by-country basis.

• RITTER, GERHARD, *Luther: His Life and Work* (New York, 1963). The author, a liberal German historian, views Luther in the perspective of both German and European history, and the last chapter, "Luther's Historical Importance" (pp. 210–247), is particularly valuable to the student of political ideas. Concerning the German peasant rebellion, Ritter writes: "The catastrophe of the Peasants' Revolt did not prevent the continuance of the Reformation, and perhaps did not seriously hold it up; but it gave the movement another character. It did away for ever with the confidence that one could achieve a reform of spiritual and secular life at once, The nation as a whole lost not only its hope in this transformation, but also its chance of internal participation in public life—that tempting prospect in which they had followed and applauded the breaking away of the Church from Rome as the beginning of a better period for the Germans. From now on the future of Germany was left entirely in the hands of the victors and oppressors, the German princes and their advisers" (p. 173).

• THOMPSON, CARGILL, *The Political Thought of Martin Luther,* ed. Philip Broadhead

(Brighton, Eng., 1984). A brief introduction to the subject.

• TROELTSCH, ERNST, *The Social Teaching of the Christian Churches,* trans. from the German, 2 vols. (New York, 1931). The second volume of this monumental study is devoted to Protestantism. In the treatment of Lutheranism (II, pp. 515–576) Troeltsch brings out the basic authoritarianism in Luther: "All along Luther is opposed to revolutionary schemes which are based on an individualistic point of view, and he is in favor of an authority which controls, conditions, and gradually molds them, even in case of necessity achieving its end by force. In this glorification of authority there were certain resemblances to the doctrine of Machiavelli, which early Lutherans had already noted" (p. 532). Concerning the Lutheran concept of the state, Troeltsch says that it is "the same 'police' and utilitarian idea of State as in Catholicism, only now, in accordance with the circumstances, there is a greater emphasis upon unity of authority" (p. 548).

The discussion of Calvinism (II, pp. 576–691) starts out with the observation that Calvinism rather than Lutheranism "is the chief force in the Protestant world today" (p. 576). The deeper reason for this lies, according to Troeltsch, in the "active character" of Calvinism, as contrasted with the acquiescence of Lutheranism in existing social and political conditions: "From the political and social point of view the significance of Lutheranism for the modern history of civilization lies in its connection with the reactionary parties" (II, p. 577). The "Democratic Tendency of Primitive Calvinism" is discussed (II, pp. 628–630). See also Troeltsch's *Protestantism and Progress: A Historical Study of the Relation of Protestantism to the Modern World* (Beacon Paperbacks, Boston, 1958).

• WALLACE, RONALD, *Calvin, Geneva and the Reformation* (Edinburgh, 1988). Not a biography of Calvin, but a collection of essays on different aspects of his life. Part I is "The Reformer and his City."

• WARFIELD, BENJAMIN B., *Calvin and Augustine* (Philadelphia, 1956). From Luther onward, Protestant thinkers have felt intense spiritual kinship with Augustine. The author, a distinguished Protestant theologian, states that "it is Augustine who gave us the Reformation" (p. 322).

• WEBER, MAX, *The Protestant Ethic and the Spirit of Capitalism* (London, 1930). Weber, the greatest German sociologist of the twentieth century, attacks the study of capitalism from the religious angle, and stresses the role of Calvinism and Puritanism in the growth of the capitalist spirit. A similar approach will be found in R. H. Tawney, *Religion and the Rise of Capitalism* (Mentor Books, New York, 1947). Weber's view is challenged by H. M. Robertson in his *Aspects of the Rise of Capitalism: A Criticism of Max Weber and His School* (Cambridge, 1933), in which he tries to prove that capitalism first started in Catholic countries like Italy and France. The answer to Robertson will be found in the work of a Jesuit writer, J. Broderick, *The Economic Morals of the Jesuits: An Answer to Dr. H. M. Robertson* (London, 1934). Excerpts from some of these and other related writings will be found in Robert W. Green (ed.), *Protestantism and Capitalism: The Weber Thesis and Its Critics* (Boston, 1959).

• WHALE, J. S., *The Protestant Tradition* (Cambridge, 1955). The first part deals with Luther, Calvin, and the later sectarian movements; the second part takes up the attitudes of the Protestant churches on modern issues, such as religious toleration, church and state, totalitarianism and democracy, and social reform. A brief survey of the history of Protestantism and its relation to modern intellectual and political issues will also be found in W. R. Inge, *Protestantism* (New York, 1935). Henry Townsend, *The Claims of Free Churches* (London, 1949), examines the crucial role of the nonconformist sects and churches in British history: "The idea and experience of freedom, which gave birth to the Free Church gave birth also to the Free State" (p. 193). For the impact of Puritanism on Britain and the United States, see also John Brown, *The English Puritans* (Cambridge, 1912); John S. Flynn, *The Influence of Puritanism on the Political and Religious Thought of the English* (London, 1920); and Ralph Barton Perry, *Puritanism and Democracy* (New York, 1944).

• WOLIN, SHELDON S., "Politics and Religion: Luther's Simplistic Imperative," *American Political Science Review,* L (March 1956), pp. 24–42. The author seeks to resolve the fundamental paradox in Luther's thought: the libertarian implications of his religious doctrines as contrasted with the absolutistic impact of his political writings. Whereas many students of Luther seek to resolve this contradiction in Luther by transforming him into a consistent libertarian or authoritarian in both religion and politics, Wolin argues that there is a common denominator between Luther's religious individualism and his political authoritarianism: his "simplistic imperative," or the tendency to oversimplify, and, above all, Luther's "failure to appreciate institutions" (p. 40). In religion, this simplistic imperative is shown in Luther's insistence on faith, the purely spiritual relation between man and God, in which churches, laws, ministers, and traditions play a subordinate role. In politics, too, Luther holds the notion that rules and regulations are not important; what matters is the wisdom of the rulers and the unquestioning obedience of the subjects: "In both instances the quest is for personal identification: the believer with his God, the citizen with his government" (p. 42). See also Wolin's "Calvin and the Reformation: The Political Education of Protestantism," *American Political Science Review,* LI (June 1957), pp. 428–453.

CHAPTER SIXTEEN

BODIN

• ALLEN, J. W., *A History of Political Thought in the Sixteenth Century* (London, 1928). Part III, Chap. VIII, "Jean Bodin" (pp. 394–444), greatly contributes to an understanding of Bodin. The author states that the originality of Bodin's theory of sovereignty consisted essentially "in the fact that he did not connect it specifically and directly with the will of God," and of the various elements that went into Bodin's theory, "the only one that is new is the conception of political society as absolutely and necessarily associated with the existence of the family and of private property and the conception of a consequent limitation of political authority" (p. 423). See also Allen's "Jean Bodin," in F. J. C. Hearnshaw (ed.), *The Social and Political Ideas of Some Great Thinkers of the Sixteenth and Seventeenth Centuries* (London, 1926), Chap. II (pp. 42–62).

• BODIN, JEAN, *The Six Bookes of a Commonweale* (edited with an Introduction by Kenneth Douglas McRae, Cambridge, Mass., 1962). This is a facsimile reprint of the English translation of *Les Six livres de la République* by Richard Knolles of 1606, the only English version of the complete work. The Knolles translation is based on the French and Latin texts of the treatise. In this edition, the text of Bodin's work is preceded by McRae's Introduction (pp. A3–A90), a detailed synopsis (pp. A91–A103), and the text itself is followed by a detailed critical apparatus of Notes (pp. A105–A172). See also the translation (in abridged form) by M. J. Tooley (Blackwell's Political Texts, Oxford–New York, 1955).

• CARLYLE, R. W., and A. J. CARLYLE, *A History of Medieval Political Theory in the West,* Vol. VI: *Political Theory from 1300 to 1600* (London, 1936). Includes an account of Bodin (pp. 417–429), particularly in relation to the theory of absolute monarchy.

• CHURCH, WILLIAM FARR, *Constitutional Thought in Sixteenth-Century France* (Cambridge, Mass., 1941). Includes a detailed analysis of Bodin in relation to his predecessors and contemporaries (pp. 194–242). Concerning Bodin's influence on his followers, the author writes that "it was not Bodin's thought as a whole which was adopted by his followers but rather certain salient features which were appropriated because of their immediate value or appeal to contemporary writers. And in the process of adoption by others, those portions of Bodin's system undergoing such treatment could but be distorted because of their removal from their original context. Certain important concepts were seized upon, torn from their immediate milieu, and, through association with other ideas, were attributed meanings entirely lacking to Bodin. Such was the fate of his most important contribution, his theory of sovereignty" (p. 244). A detailed bibliography is on pp. 339–350.

• DICKINSON, JOHN, "A Working Theory of Sovereignty," *Political Science Quarterly,* XLII (December 1927), pp. 524–548, and XLIII (March 1928), pp. 32–63. Defines sovereignty in the legal sense, following Bodin's juristic conception, as "nothing more nor less than a logical postulate or presupposition of any system of order according to law," because if there is to be uniformity of legal rules in a community, "then there must be a single final source of law" that all inferior tribunals and officials recognize as the ultimate authority (p. 525). If competing authorities exist side by side, subject to no common superior, the result is anarchy (p. 526). Dickinson's views are directed against those who confuse the legal concept of sovereignty with the psychological concept of power, as well as against those who, like the pluralists (Harold J. Laski, G. D. H. Cole), deny the usefulness and validity of the doctrine of sovereignty altogether.

The ablest juristic and analytic treatment of the problem of sovereignty will be found in Hans Kelsen, *General Theory of Law and State* (Cambridge, Mass., 1945) and *Principles of International Law,* 2nd ed. (New York, 1966). Dickinson's interpretation of the concept of sovereignty as a logical postulate or presupposition of a system of law is based on Kelsen's view that sovereignty is not a social fact but an hypothesis, the expression of the unity of a legal system. For accounts of Kelsen's legal theory, see William Ebenstein, *The Pure Theory of Law* (Madison, Wis., 1945), and "Kelsen, Hans," *International Encyclopedia of the Social Sciences,* Vol. VIII (New York, 1968), pp. 360–366.

• FIGGIS, J. N., *The Divine Right of Kings* (Cambridge, 1934). For a brief analysis of Bodin, see pp. 126–130; *Studies of Political Thought from Gerson to Grotius, 1414–1625* (Cambridge, 1931), pp. 110 ff; and "Political Thought in the Sixteenth Century," in *Cambridge Modern History* (Cambridge, 1904), Vol. III, Chap. XXII (pp. 736–769). See also, in the same volume, Chap. I, "The Wars of Religion in France," by A. J. Butler (pp. 1–52).

• FRANKLIN, JULIAN H., *Jean Bodin and the Rise of Absolutist Theory* (London, 1973). Development of Bodin's thoughts on sovereignty, presenting the position that his position shifted from one of limited to absolute sovereignty. Develops the influence of his historical context on Bodin. The central thesis of this book is that Bodin's later absolutism "was as unprecedented as the doctrine it opposed," namely, the constitutionalism of the Huguenots.

• ⸻, *Jean Bodin and the Sixteenth-Century Revolution in the Methodology of Law and History* (New York, 1963). Examines Bodin's pioneering role in introducing the historical and comparative methods into the study of public law and government. See also Constance I. Smith, "Jean Bodin and Comparative Law," *Journal of the History of Ideas,* XXV (July–September 1964), pp. 417–422.

• GREENLEAF, W. H., *Order, Empiricism and Politics: Two Traditions of English Political Thought, 1500–1700* (New York, 1964). English political thought of 1500–1700 is characterized, the author argues, by two main philosophies: the political theory of order, politically linked to absolute monarchy, and the political theory of empiricism, politically linked to theories of mixed government and limited monarchy. Chap. VII (pp. 125–141) is devoted to Bodin, the only non-English thinker to receive such special coverage, because he was one of the most frequently cited authors in England, particularly in the first half of the seventeenth century. In his general social philosophy, Bodin eulogized order and abhorred disorder, and in the specific sphere of politics Bodin advocated the doctrine of unlimited sovereignty and hereditary monarchy. After Bodin's political theory of order came under fire from the middle of the seventeenth century on, his "works seemed to lose much of their previous significance and they lapsed into an undeserved obscurity" (p. 126).

• KING, PRESTON, *The Ideology of Order: A Comparative Analysis of Jean Bodin and Thomas Hobbes* (New York, 1974). A critique of the politics of order. Part III is on Bodin.

• LASKI, HAROLD J., *A Grammar of Politics,* 2nd ed. (London, 1930). Chap. II, "Sovereignty" (pp. 44–88), rejects the validity and usefulness of the concept of sovereignty from the viewpoint of legal theory and political philosophy, and seeks to demonstrate that sovereignty does not satisfactorily describe the conduct and goals of the state in its domestic or foreign relations. A more detailed exposition of Laski's theory of pluralism, which replaces the traditional monistic concept of the sovereignty of the state with the concept of associations as the basis of the state, will be found in *Studies in the Problem of Sovereignty* (New Haven, 1917), *Authority in the Modern State* (New Haven, 1919), and *The Foundation of Sovereignty and Other Essays* (New Haven, 1921). Laski's theory of political pluralism stresses individualism and voluntarism: "The will of the State obtains preeminence over the wills of other groups exactly to the point where it is interpreted with sufficient wisdom to obtain general acceptance, and no further. It is a will to some extent competing with other wills, and, Darwinwise, surviving only by its ability to cope with its environment. Should it venture into dangerous places it pays the penalty of its audacity. It finds its sovereignty by consent transformed into impotence by disagreement. But, it may be objected, in such a view sovereignty means no more than the ability to secure assent. I can only reply to the objection by admitting it. There is no sanction for law other than the human mind. It is sheer illusion to imagine that the authority of the State has any other safeguard than the wills of its members" (*Studies in the Problem of Sovereignty,* p. 14).

See also Jacques Maritain, "The Concept of Sovereignty," *American Political Science Review,* XLIV (June 1950), pp. 343–357, who fully concurs with Laski, though writing from a different philosophical starting point. Maritain, basing his discussion of sovereignty on Bodin, Hobbes, and Rousseau, concludes that the concept of sovereignty be discarded altogether: "The two concepts of Sovereignty and Absolutism have been forged together on the same anvil. They must be scrapped together" (p. 357).

• MCILWAIN, CHARLES H., "Sovereignty Again," *Economica,* VI (November 1926), pp. 253–268, reprinted in his *Constitutionalism and the Changing World* (New York, 1939), Chap. II (pp. 26–46). Chap. III, "A Fragment on Sovereignty" (pp. 47–60), is mainly devoted to Bodin. McIlwain hails Bodin as the first author of the theory of the *Rechtsstaat,* the state based on the rule of law, and says that Bodin's analysis "is a sounder foundation on which to build than either the assertions of Hobbes or the negations of the modern Pluralists" (p. 60). The moderate and antidespotic position of Bodin is emphasized by McIlwain in *The Growth of Political Thought in the West* (New York, 1932), pp. 364–394. Concerning the later abuse of Bodin's doctrine of sovereignty for the justification of despotic government, McIlwain writes: "The more liberal parts of Bodin's conception of kingship are a heritage of the middle ages; the development of the absolute monarchy into an arbitrary one is a modern achievement" (p. 388). See also McIlwain's "Sovereignty in the World Today," *Measure,* I (Spring 1950), pp. 109–117.

• MURRAY, R. H., *The Political Consequences of the Reformation: Studies in Sixteenth-Century Political Thought* (New York, 1960). Chap. IV (pp. 129–168) is on "Bodin and the Theory of Sovereignty."

• SALMON, J. H. M., *The French Religious Wars in English Political Thought* (Oxford, 1959). In the late sixteenth and seventeenth centuries, French political experience and thought had a considerable influence in England, whereas from the eighteenth century onward English political philosophy had a strong appeal in France. Salmon's study shows in detail the impact of French political thought in the late sixteenth and seventeenth centuries on English political theory and practice. In particular, the influence of Bodin on England is analyzed, including his personal links with prominent English publicists and politicians.

CHAPTER SEVENTEEN

HOBBES

• Bowle, John, *Hobbes and His Critics* (London, 1951). Hobbes was a highly controversial figure in his own time, and this is the only full account of his contemporary critics—liberal, conservative, religious, and secular. The author not only contributes to a better understanding of Hobbes in the context of his own period, but also shows how some of the main arguments of Hobbes' contemporary critics became the dominant ideas in English political thought from Locke onward. See also Samuel I. Mintz, *The Hunting of Leviathan: Seventeenth-Century Reactions to the Materialism and Moral Philosophy of Thomas Hobbes* (Cambridge, 1962). This volume supplements the study by Bowle, since it concentrates on contemporary attacks on Hobbes' moral and religious opinions, whereas Bowle is largely concerned with political criticisms of Hobbes. The Mintz volume has extensive bibliographical data (pp. 157–183).

• Brown, Keith C. (ed.), *Hobbes Studies* (Oxford, 1965). Twelve essays on Hobbes' views on politics, ethics, law, and religion, written by scholars in Great Britain, the United States, Canada, and Italy. The period following World War II saw a remarkable resurgence of Hobbes studies, and this symposium provides a representative sampling of some of the more important essays.

• Carritt, E. F., *Morals and Politics* (London, 1935). Chap. III is on Hobbes (pp. 25–39). See also W. R. Sorley, *A History of English Philosophy* (Cambridge, 1937), pp. 47–74; R. H. S. Crossman, *Government and the Governed* (London, 1939), pp. 43–69; C. E. Vaughan, *Studies in the History of Political Philosophy before and after Rousseau* (Manchester, 1939), Vol. I, pp. 17–61; and J. W. Gough, *The Social Contract* (Oxford, 1936), pp. 100–107.

• Catlin, George E. G., "Thomas Hobbes and Contemporary Political Theory," *Political Science Quarterly* LXXXII (March 1967), pp. 1–13. Examines the relevance of Hobbes' political theory in the perspective of the world's most urgent problem in the atomic age: peace. The author writes that "the central contribution of Hobbes to political science is his theory of power, more developed and sophisticated than that which we owe, implicitly, to Machiavelli. Nothing, incidentally, can be more topical in our atomic age than the role which Hobbes assigned to the political factor of terror" (p. 5). The author concludes that the issue of world peace "has been the prime preoccupation of applied political theory since 1914, just as the comparable problem of local civil wars preoccupied Thomas Hobbes in the middle of the disturbed seventeenth century" (p. 13).

• Coleman, Frank, *Hobbes and America* (Toronto, 1977). Puts forward the thesis that Hobbes is the intellectual precursor of the American constitution.

• Cooke, Paul D., *Hobbes and Christianity: Reassessing the Bible in Leviathan* (Lanham, 1996). This Christian critique of *Leviathan* commences with an excellent review of Hobbes's argument. The work's strength lies in its comparison of the Bible and *Leviathan,* letting the reader decide on interpretation.

• Gauthier, David, *The Logic of Leviathan* (Oxford, 1969). Subtitled *The Moral and Political Theory of Thomas Hobbes,* this brief but comprehensive book was conceived in part as a response to Howard Warrender's *The Political Philosophy of Hobbes* (see below). Gauthier's conclusion is that Hobbes's theory, although illuminating, and profitable to study, is "a failure."

• Gert, Bernard, "Hobbes and Psychological Egoism," *Journal of the History of Ideas,* XXVIII (October–December 1967), pp. 503–520. The idea is widely held that Hobbes was a follower of the doctrine of psychological egoism, and that his political theory is necessarily linked to it. The author of this provocative study challenges this almost universal view and seeks to show that Hobbes did not adhere to psychological egoism and that his political theory not only does not require an egoistic psychology but is incompatible with it. Assembling his evidence from various works of Hobbes, the author concludes that "Hobbes believed that human nature was malleable, that one could train, educate, and discipline people into good citizens. Granted this conditioning must take into account the strong passions of natural man, still through such training man could become quite different from what he was originally" (p. 519).

• GOLDSMITH, M. M., *Hobbes's Science of Politics* (New York, 1966). The author examines Hobbes' thought in terms of his own intention to create a unified system encompassing both natural and civil philosophy. The first four chapters (pp. 1–128) deal with philosophy, natural philosophy, human nature, and the natural condition. In the last three chapters (pp. 129–242), Hobbes' concepts of constructing a social order as well as his theories of government and sovereignty are elaborated. The volume has a detailed bibliography (pp. 253–262).

• GOOCH, G. P., *Hobbes* (Annual Lecture on a Master Mind, British Academy, London, 1939). Presents Hobbes in the perspective of English history and his later influence at home and abroad. Gooch concludes that it "is one of the ironies of history that the disciples whom the author of *Leviathan* failed to find in his own country and his own time are crowding the continental stage after the lapse of three hundred years" (p. 42). See also Gooch's *Political Thought in England: From Bacon to Halifax* (Home University Library, London, 1937), Chap. II, "Hobbes" (pp. 35–57).

• HOOD, F. C., *The Divine Politics of Thomas Hobbes: An Interpretation of* Leviathan (Oxford, 1964). The author makes the bold attempt to interpret Hobbes as a "sincere Christian thinker," and to show how his views on ethics, natural law, and government reflect a basically Christian outlook. Even those who will not be persuaded by Hood's central argument will find much in the volume that is provocative and that forces the reader to reexamine accepted ideas about Hobbes.

• JAMES, DAVID G., *The Life of Reason: Hobbes, Locke, Bolingbroke* (New York, 1949). Chap. I. "The Proud Mind" (pp. 1–62), is on Hobbes. The author sees in the combination of rationalism and materialism in Hobbes a "hopeless contradiction" (p. 268).

• JOUVENEL, BERTRAND DE, *Sovereignty* (Cambridge, 1957). Chap. XIV is on "The Political Consequences of Hobbes" (pp. 231–246). The author rejects the interpretation of Hobbes as a forerunner of totalitarianism: "It is psychologically necessary to successful totalitarianism that each man feels himself a mere part, whereas Hobbesian man feels himself most vividly a whole" (p. 239). Far from being the "father of totalitarianism," Hobbes is "an individualist and progressive, who would like each man to develop his faculties in striving to fulfill his desires, as these are successively aroused. Only, men so employed may do each other harm. The State exists to stop the mischief which the intersection of their appetites may do them" *(ibid.)*.

• KRAUS, JODY S., *The Limits of Hobbesian Contractarianism* (Cambridge, 1993). This book is most useful in its in-depth presentation of three previous works on Hobbes: Gregory Kavka's *Hobbesian Moral and Political Theory* (1986), Hampton's *Hobbes and the Social Contract Tradition* (1986), and Gauthier's *Morals by Agreement* (1986).

• KRAYNAK, ROBERT P., *History and Modernity in the Thought of Thomas Hobbes* (Ithaca, 1990). Kraynak uses the concept of "civil history" to challenge the conventional wisdom on Hobbes. His project is less than successful, but his attempt at linking history and theory is instructive.

• LEMOS, RAMON, *Hobbes and Locke; Power and Consent* (Athens, Ga., 1978). A study of natural right, natural law, and social contract approaches in Hobbes and Locke.

• LLOYD, S. A., *Ideals as Interests in Hobbes's* Leviathan: *The Power of Mind over Matter* (New York, 1992). Lloyd's highly controversial contention that Hobbes's political theory holds a place for transcendent interests conflicts with much of the scholarly work on the subject. Her argument is difficult to sustain and, in the end, appears unsuccessful.

• MACPHERSON, C. B., *The Political Theory of Possessive Individualism: Hobbes to Locke* (Oxford, 1962). Hobbes is treated in Chap. II, "Hobbes: The Political Obligation of the Market" (pp. 9–106). Essentially Marxian in its approach, this reexamination of English political thought from Hobbes to Locke stresses the "possessive" quality of English individualism during that period. According to Macpherson, seventeenth-century England had become a "possessive market society" (p. 62), and Hobbes drew the logical conclusions from this type of society, "where all values are reduced to market values, justice itself is reduced to a market concept. And in demanding that a market concept of justice should replace the customary concept, he seems both to be claiming that a fully market society is here to stay, and to be acknowledging that it has only recently come" (p. 64). In an essay on "Hobbes's Bourgeois Man" (in Keith C. Brown, ed., *Hobbes Studies,* Oxford, 1965, pp. 169–183), Macpherson also writes that "Hobbes's morality is the morality of the bourgeois world and that his state is the bourgeois state. There is his attitude towards the poor, his view of thrift and extravagance, his insistence that the state should institute private property and provide freedom for individual enrichment, his expectation that the sovereign will provide for equality before the law" (p. 175). For critical examination of Macpherson's central thesis, see Sir Isaiah Berlin, "Hobbes, Locke and Professor Macpherson," *Political Quarterly,* XXXV (October–December 1964), pp. 444–468; Bertram Morris, "Possessive Individualism and Political Realities," *Ethics,* LXXV (April 1965), pp. 207–214; C. Williamson, "A Contradiction in Hobbes' Analysis of Sovereignty," *Canadian Journal of Economics and Political Science,* XXXII (May 1966), pp. 202–219; and Alan Ryan, "Locke and the Dictatorship of the Bourgeoisie," *Political Studies,* XIII (June 1965), pp. 219–230.

• MARTINICH, A. P., *The Two Gods of* Leviathan: *Thomas Hobbes on Religion and Politics* (New York, 1992). Martinich provides a deep and historically rich elucidation of Hobbes's religious thought. This work is essential for those who seek to engage the contemporary debate over Hobbesian religious theory.

• OAKESHOTT, MICHAEL, *Hobbes on Civil Association* (Berkeley, 1975). Oakeshott's famous introduction to the Blackwell's edition of *Leviathan,* and three other essays.

• PARSONS, TALCOTT, *The Structure of Social Action* (Glencoe, Ill., 1949). In his discussion of "Hobbes and the Problem of Order" Parsons says that "Hobbes' system of social theory is almost a pure case of utilitarianism" (p. 90), and that he "saw the problem with a clarity which has never been surpassed" (p. 93). On "Hobbes and the Utilitarians," see also John Plamenatz, *The English Utilitarians* (Oxford, 1949), pp. 10–16.

• PETERS, RICHARD, *Hobbes* (Penguin Books, Baltimore, 1956). A volume in the Pelican Philosophy Series. After an introductory chapter on the life of Hobbes in the context of his turbulent era, the author examines the major point of Hobbesian thought on government and politics as well as on logic, psychology, ethics, and religion.

• ROSS, RALPH, et al. (eds.), *Thomas Hobbes in His Time* (Minneapolis, 1975). Six essays, including John Dewey's 1918 "The Motivation of Hobbes's Political Philosophy," wherein sovereignty is presented as a solution to the conflict between church and state in Hobbes's time, not as a solution to the more subsequent conflict between personal freedom and state control.

• SHULMAN, GEORGE, "Hobbes, Puritans, and Promethean Politics," *Political Theory* (August 1989). This analysis presents Hobbes's project as directing Puritan rebellion away from grounding political power in the people and toward grounding it in the state. "It is on the grave of a defeated but assimilated Puritanism that Hobbes stands as the first great modernizer and state builder."

• SKINNER, QUENTIN, *Reason and Rhetoric in the Philosophy of Hobbes* (Cambridge, 1996). Skinner's larger project of attempting to "situate Hobbes's theory and practice of civil science within the intellectual context in which it was formed" continues within this historical approach (p. 6). His analysis of English humanist thought is thorough and instructive. His discussion of the changes in Hobbes's thought on reason and rhetoric in insightful and valuable.

• ———, "Thomas Hobbes and His Disciples in France and England," *Comparative Studies in Society and History,* VIII (January

1966), pp. 153–167. During his self-imposed exile in Paris from 1640 to 1651 Hobbes maintained close relations with some of the leading scientists and philosophers in France. After his return to England in 1651 Hobbes kept corresponding with his French friends; much of Skinner's investigation is based on previously unpublished letters from and to Hobbes' French correspondents. In Skinner's judgment, "Hobbes was widely denounced in England, but he seems to have been widely accepted abroad. . . . At least some of his followers recognized and sympathized with his most ambitious hopes for a Science of Politics. And at least some of this enthusiasm seems to have been conveyed back even to England" (pp. 163–164). For a more detailed examination of contemporary attitudes toward Hobbes, particularly in England, see also Skinner's article, "The Ideological Context of Hobbes's Political Thought," *Historical Journal,* IX, No. 3 (1966), pp. 286–317.

• STEPHEN, LESLIE, *Hobbes* (Ann Arbor Paperbacks, Ann Arbor, 1961). One of the best short books on Hobbes. Chap. I (pp. 1–69) is on his life, IV (pp. 173–236) on his political theory. See also George Croom Robertson, *Hobbes* (Edinburgh–London, 1886), and A. E. Taylor, *Hobbes* (London, 1908).

• STRAUSS, LEO, *The Political Philosophy of Hobbes: Its Basis and Its Genesis* (Oxford, 1936, reprinted Chicago, 1952). In this pioneering study, the author seeks to demonstrate that Hobbes' "new moral attitude" preceded his interest in modern science, and that his break with tradition and his original contribution were due rather to that new moral attitude than to his (later) contact with science. Specifically, Strauss argues that however much "Hobbes personally esteemed the aristocracy, and esteemed the specific qualities of the aristocracy, his political philosophy is directed against the aristocratic rules of life in the name of bourgeois rules of life. His morality is the morality of the bourgeois world" (pp. 120–121). The genesis of Hobbes' political philosophy is "nothing other than the progressive supplanting of aristocratic virtue by bourgeois virtue" (p. 126). In an earlier study on Hobbes, Strauss had already written that all the characteristic premises and affirmations of liberalism can be found in Hobbes, and that "the absolutism of Hobbes is nothing but militant liberalism *in statu nascendi,* that is, liberalism in its most radical form. Hobbes is thus the true founder of liberalism, and therefore in looking for a radical critique or justification of liberalism, one has to go back to him." Strauss emphasizes that Hobbes— though a founder of liberalism—was not a Liberal in the proper sense of the term.

• WARRENDER, HOWARD, *The Political Philosophy of Hobbes: His Theory of Obligation* (Oxford, 1957). Contrary to the traditional interpretation of Hobbes as a positivist sharply opposed to natural law, Warrender argues that Hobbes is "essentially a natural-law philosopher" (p. 323), because his "theory of political society is based upon a theory of duty, and his theory of duty belongs essentially to the natural-law tradition" (p. 322). Although its main conclusions will not be universally accepted, the book is an original and provocative contribution to the study of Hobbes.

• WATKINS, J. W. N., *Hobbes's System of Ideas* (London, 1965). The author seeks to show that Hobbes' political ideas are closely related to his general philosophical ideas and his views about nature and man. Avoiding excessive generalization and abstraction, Watkins sticks to essentials and draws his evidence from numerous works of Hobbes. In criticizing Hobbes' concept of sovereignty, the author makes this interesting comment: "He knew of only one political calamity (external wars excepted) besides which others pale into insignificance. We know of two: civil war *and totalitarianism.* And the question is whether his drastic remedy for civil war—an all-powerful sovereign upon whom there is no constitutional check—is not likely to lead to a situation as grim as the one it replaces" (p. 172).

• WILLEY, BASIL, *The Seventeenth Century Background: Studies in the Thought of the Age in Relation to Poetry and Religion* (Anchor Books, New York, 1953). In the section on Hobbes (pp. 99–124), the author stresses the "radical incompatibility between the principles of Hobbes's philosophy and those of any sort of Christianity, if not of any sort of religion" (p. 115).

CHAPTER EIGHTEEN

LOCKE

• AARON, R. I., *John Locke,* 2nd ed. (Oxford, 1963). Locke's political, moral, religious, and educational views are examined in Part III (pp. 256–308). A useful bibliography is included (pp. 313–320).

• ASHCROFT, RICHARD, *Revolutionary Politics and Locke's Two Treatises of Government* (Princeton, 1986). A very comprehensive work on the meaning and content of Locke's political views and politics.

• BROGAN, A. P., "John Locke and Utilitarianism," *Ethics,* LXIX (January 1959), pp. 79–93. The author shows that Locke not only dominated the intellectual climate which later produced the full-fledged utilitarian doctrines of Bentham and his followers, but that he directly formulated the main elements of utilitarian ethics.

• COX, RICHARD H., *Locke on Peace and War* (New York, 1960). Although Locke developed no systematic theory of international relations, his political ideas and observations have significant implications for such a theory. Specifically, Locke clearly saw that peace within the political community is not a natural condition, but can only be attained through the deliberately created mechanisms of positive law, impartial third-party adjudication, and effective enforcement of the law. From Locke's own premises, peace between states is also not natural, but would require the creation of the same three mechanisms, and there is "no suggestion in Locke that the attempt to *partially* introduce the techniques and institutions of civil government into relations among governments would be of decisive importance. So long as each state retains its power to judge its own case, and the force to back up that judgment, Locke's principles suggest that no intermediary arrangement can be successful" (pp. 189–190). Yet Locke did not draw the conclusions from his own premises with respect to the problem of peace among nations, and, in fact, was pessimistic about its possibility. In the concluding pages of his study, the author tries to explain the factors in Locke's pessimism on this issue (pp. 190–195). See also R. D. Masters, "The Lockean Tradition in American Foreign Policy," *Journal of International Affairs,* XXI, No. 2 (1967), pp. 253–277.

• CRANSTON, MAURICE, *John Locke: A Biography* (New York, 1957). The definitive biography of Locke, superseding previous accounts of his life. Utilizing a large collection of Locke's personal papers previously inaccessible to scholars, the author presents not only Locke as a man in a new light, but also corrects numerous misconceptions about his intellectual development. Indispensable to the study of Locke and his time.

• CROSSMAN, R. H. S., *Government and the Governed,* 4th ed. (London, 1958). Chap. III, "The English Revolution" (pp. 43–80), deals with the background of the age, the contrasting personalities of Hobbes and Locke, and with the latter's political theory. Crossman concludes that "we should not blame Locke for the faults of his successors. In his own day, he was a sane progressive, whose writings tempered the arrogance of the social oligarchy and taught it the discipline of representative institutions, And, if later he was to inspire Burke's conservatism, he inspired Paine and Rousseau—and even Karl Marx as well" (p. 80). See also Willmoore Kendall, *John Locke and the Doctrine of Majority Rule* (Illinois Studies in the Social Sciences, Vol. XXVI, No. 2, Urbana, Ill., 1941).

• DEWHURST, KENNETH, *John Locke (1632–1704), Physician and Philosopher: A Medical Biography* (London, 1963). Based on previously inaccessible papers, this medical biography of Locke has much that is of interest to anyone who desires to find out more about Locke's life and thought. Locke

had a life-long devotion to medicine, both its theory and practice, and distinguished British and Continental physicians were among his friends. The narrative part of the volume has many fascinating data that are not strictly medical, and even Locke's medical notes, reproduced in their entirety, illuminate Locke's character and personality.
• DUNN, JOHN, *Locke* (Oxford, 1984). Very brief, part of the "Past Masters" series. See also Dunn's *The Political Thought of John Locke; An Historical Account of the Argument of the* Two Treatises of Government (London, 1969).
• DWORETZ, STEVEN M., *The Unvarnished Doctrine: Locke, Liberalism, and the American Revolution* (Durham, 1990). Dworetz answers those who seek to rewrite America's founding theory from its Lockean roots to one of civic republicanism. His critique yields a notion of "liberal republicanism," which succeeds in melding both Lockean and republican thought in the American Revolution.
• GOUGH, J. W., *John Locke's Political Philosophy* (Oxford, 1950). Eight studies on the following topics: the law of nature; the rights of the individual; government by consent; theory of property; separation of powers and sovereignty; Locke and the Revolution of 1688; political trusteeship; and Locke's belief in toleration. Succinct and essential to the study of Locke. Gough's *The Social Contract,* 2nd ed. (Oxford, 1957), traces the development of the social-contract theory from antiquity to the nineteenth century, and has a chapter on Locke (IX, pp. 126–146). See also his introduction to John Locke, *The Second Treatise of Governemnt, and A Letter Concerning Toleration* (Blackwell's Political Texts, Oxford, 1946), pp. vii–xxxvi, and Ernest Barker's introduction to *Social Contract: Essays by Locke, Hume, and Rousseau* (New York, 1948), a considerable portion of which is on Locke (pp. xv–xxxvii).
• GRANT, RUTH W., *John Locke's Liberalism* (Chicago, 1987). This book (which stems from an award-winning dissertation) is thoughtful, well written, and thorough in its examination of Locke's major works. This volume provides much for both student and advanced scholar. Grant sees the central issue in Locke as "justifying both a duty to obey and a right to resist."

• HAMILTON, WALTON H., "Property—According to Locke," *Yale Law Journal* XLI (April 1931), pp. 864–880. Protects Locke against his own defenders, especially the zealots who have read into Locke's theory of property more than he himself meant. See also Paschal Larkin, *Property in the Eighteenth Century: with Special Reference to England and Locke* (Dublin, 1930), and Harold J. Laski, *The Rise of European Liberalism* (London, 1936). Laski writes that Locke's state "is nothing so much as a contract between a group of business men who form a limited liability company whose memorandum of association forbids to the directors all those practices of which the Stuarts had, until this time, been guilty" (p. 116). See also H. Moulds, "Private Property in John Locke's State of Nature," *American Journal of Economics and Sociology,* XXIII (April 1964), pp. 179–188; J. P. Day, "Locke on Property," *Philosophical Quarterly,* XVI (July 1966), pp. 207–220; and Max Milam, "The Epistemological Basis of Locke's Idea of Property," *Western Political Quarterly,* XX (March 1967), pp. 16–30. Critics of Locke have often pointed to the alleged discrepancy between Locke's empirical theory of knowledge (or epistemology) and his nonempirical, rationalist political and economic doctrines. Addressing himself specifically to the problem of property, Milam concludes that there is "no basis for the charge of inconsistency" between Locke's theory of knowledge and his idea of property (p. 28), at least as Locke understood empiricism—a term coined and substantively developed and refined by modern empiricists long after Locke.
• HARRISON, JOHN, and PETER LASLETT, *The Library of John Locke* (Oxford, 1965). Locke was an avid reader and buyer of books, and his collection included about four thousand books and pamphlets. In Part I (pp. 1–61), the authors describe his collection, how he built it up and what happened to it after his death, and in Part II (pp. 67–267) the individual items are listed with the appropriate bibliographical data. Some of the findings of the authors' analysis of the library are of more than biographical or bibliographical interest. As to the main subject categories, 24 percent of Locke's books were on theology, 11 percent on medicine, 11 percent on politics and law, and 7 percent on philosophy, to list but a few

major fields. In political philosophy, Locke had only three works by Hobbes, but ten volumes by Machiavelli. In religion, his library holdings suggest a stronger interest in, and sympathy for, Unitarianism than his public statements on religion and his communication in the Church of England indicated. Aficionados of Locke who can never read enough firsthand material about him will find this volume exceptionally rewarding and entertaining.

• HUYLER, JEROME, *Locke in America: The Moral Philsophy of the Founding Era* (Lawrence, 1995). The author engages the ongoing debate over revisionist theories of the role of Locke in the American founding. Huyler neither accepts republican reinterpretations nor sides with the post-revisionist centrality of Locke in the founding, but rather attempts to carve out a middle position. The outcome is a rich and informative analysis of Locke and the current debate over his role in the founding of American liberalism.

• KRAMER, MATTHEW H., *John Locke and the Origins of Private Property: Philosophical Explorations of Individualism, Community, and Equality* (New York, 1997). Kramer seeks to explore concepts of communitarian thought within Locke's works. This effort is only partially successful, but does produce interesting insights into Lockean conceptions of the individual, community, and equality.

• LASKI, HAROLE J., *Political Thought in England: From Locke to Bentham* (London, 1920), pp. 22–61. Laski gives a sympathetic account of Locke's relation to the Revolution of 1688 and his influence on subsequent English thought, as well as his contribution to French and American political ideas and institutions. He emphasizes that Locke was the first English political thinker whose argument was mainly secular, and that Locke rejected a purely legal theory as a sufficient basis of political society.

• LASLETT, PETER, "The English Revolution and John Locke's *Two Treatises of Government,*" *Cambridge Historical Journal* (1956), pp. 40–55. The definitive article on the origins and purposes of the *Two Treatises.*

• LOCKE, JOHN, *Essays on the Law of Nature* (trans. from the Latin and ed. by W. von Leyden, Oxford, 1954). Contains both the original Latin text and the English translation,

published in this volume for the first time. A long introduction (pp. 1–92) by von Leyden gives new information on Locke's early life during which his essays on the law of nature were written, and also relates these early essays to his later chief philosophical and political writings. See also Leo Strauss, "Locke's Doctrine of Natural Law," *American Political Science Review,* LII (June 1958), pp. 490–501; John W. Yolton, "Locke on the Law of Nature," *Philosophical Review,* LXVII (October 1958), pp. 477–498; R. Singh, "John Locke and the Theory of Natural Law," *Political Studies,* IX (June 1961), pp. 105–118; and M. Seliger, "Locke's Natural Law and the Foundation of Politics," *Journal of the History of Ideas* XXIV (July–September 1963), pp. 337–354.

• ———, *Two Tracts on Government* (edited with an Introduction, Notes and Translations by Philip Abrams, Cambridge, 1967). More generally known as the essays *On the Civil Magistrate,* these two essays (one in English and the other in Latin) were written by Locke in 1660–1661; but they remained inaccessible to the public until 1947, when Oxford University bought the Lovelace Collection of Locke's papers and journals. Locke himself provided no titles for the two essays, but the English essay starts with this introductory heading: "Questions: Whether the Civil Magistrate may lawfully impose and determine the use of indifferent things in reference to Religious Worship." The Latin essay has a similar introductory heading. The two essays are more related to Locke's lifelong interest in religious toleration than to his more general interest in the foundations of government. When Locke composed these two essays, he was still under thirty, and his outlook, as expressed in the essays, was more traditionalist and authoritarian than it was later. Only a few years after writing (but not publishing) the two essays, Locke was closely befriended by leading Whig politicians, and the brief youthful phase of traditionalist and authoritarian leanings in state-church relations was quickly, and permanently, overshadowed by his growing and deep commitment to the cause of liberalism in religion and politics.

• ———, *Two Treatises of Government* (a critical edition with an Introduction and Apparatus Criticus by Peter Laslett), 2nd ed. (Cambridge, 1967). Laslett's Introduction (pp. 3–120) and appended materials (pp. 121–152) are a book within a book. On the basis of previously inaccessible Locke papers, Laslett establishes conclusively that the *Two Treatises of Government* was written in 1779–1781, with changes and revisions added in later years. Laslett also discusses Locke as a man and writer, Locke and Hobbes, the relation of the *Two Treatises of Government* to the Revolution of 1688, and the social and political theory of the *Two Treatises of Government*. In addition, the text of the *Two Treatises of Government* is accompanied by many useful notes. This is likely to remain the most scholarly edition of Locke's classic.

• LOUGH, JOHN (ed.), *Locke's Travels in France, 1675–1679* (Cambridge, 1953). Taken from his diaries, letters, and other papers, Locke's extensive travels in France reveal not only his character and personality, but also contribute to a better understanding of his intellectual growth. For a more detailed study of Locke's intellectual relations with France, see Gabriel D. Bonno, *Les relations intellectuelles de Locke avec la France* (Berkeley, 1955).

• MARSHALL, JOHN, *John Locke: Resistance, Religion, and Responsibility* (Cambridge, 1994). The author provides an eclectic approach to the development of Locke's moral and political views. Some previously unpublished manuscripts are included.

• MCCLURE, KIRSTIE M., *Judging Rights: Lockean Politics and the Limits of Consent* (Ithaca, 1996). McClure joins the ranks of Lockean scholars who warn that to characterize Locke as strictly a liberal—leaving out the "theistic resonance" in his work—is simply to project contemporary values onto historical texts. This work is an excellent resource on Locke's political philosophy and an able reply to overliberalization of his writings.

• MEHTA, UDAY SINGH, *The Anxiety of Freedom: Imagination and Individuality in Locke's Political Thought* (Ithaca, 1992). Mehta explores the cognitive dimensions of Locke's political writings. Her argument that Locke is "concerned not merely with individuals' interests but also with their subjective identities" (pp. 3–4) is difficult to make and only marginally successful.

• PANGLE, THOMAS, *The Spirit of Modern Republicanism* (Chicago, 1988). Explores the philosophies of and relationship between Locke and America's founders. Pangle conceives this book as in part a completion of his earlier *Montesquieu's Philosophy of Liberalism*.

• RUSSELL, BERTRAND, *Philosophy and Politics* (London, 1947). Russell considers empiricism the only philosophy that can be a theoretical justification of democracy: "Locke, who may be regarded, so far as the modern world is concerned, as the founder of empiricism, makes it clear how closely this is connected with his views on liberty and toleration and with his opposition to absolute monarchy" (p. 20). Russell concludes that, "in our own day as in the time of Locke, empiricist Liberalism (which is not incompatible with *democratic socialism*) is the only philosophy that can be adopted by a man who, on the one hand, demands some scientific evidence for his beliefs, and, on the other hand, desires human happiness more than the prevalence of this or that party or creed" (p. 27).

• SCHOULS, PETER A., *Reasoned Freedom: John Locke and Enlightenment* (Ithaca, 1992). Schouls takes up the subject of reason and moral freedom as extracted from several of Locke's texts, and presents a view of Lockean freedom that is decidedly libertarian. This is not a new interpretation of Locke's work, but it provides a rich and informative account of several of his works.

• SELIGER, M., *The Liberal Politics of John Locke* (New York, 1969). A reassessment of Locke's thought, based partially on the notion that Locke was less democratic than he is often considered.

• SIMMONS, JOHN A., *The Lockean Theory of Rights* (Princeton, 1992). This work, which provides excellent scholarship and insightful analysis of many of Locke's writings, also provides a rare and welcome treatment of Locke's *First Treatise*. Simmons's arguments on a Lockean theory of rights are deft and sophisticated.

• ———, *On the Edge of Anarchy: Locke, Consent, and the Limits of Society* (Princeton, 1993). Simmons seeks to improve upon the understanding of Locke's theory of consent, and as such, enters the debate over the political/historical/contextual meanings of the idea of consent.

• SREENIVASAN, GOPAL, *The Limits of Lockean Rights in Property* (New York, 1995).

Sreenivasan's presentation is succinct and focused. His rather mainstream treatment of Lockean property rights is thorough and clear, and valuable to those new to the subject.

• WISHY, BERNARD, "John Locke and the Spirit of '76," *Political Science Quarterly,* LXXIII (September 1958), pp. 413–425. Examining the relations between Lockean ideas and the Declaration of Independence, the author agrees with the accepted view that the Declaration was a statement of Lockean principles, but doubts that this alone makes it necessarily a "liberal-individualistic" document. Wishy notes that Locke failed to deal with majority rule "as realistically and as fully as he dealt with divine right," and that he allowed only for revolution by the people against unjust rulers, but not for individual rebellion against the majority. The main problem of the Declaration as a Lockean statement of principles is therefore seen by Wishy as follows: "Does the Declaration assert fully and unambiguously a doctrine of human rights that amounts to supremacy of the individual conscience or does it establish a doctrine of popular sovereignty?" (p. 419). Wishy's conclusion is that the claim that "the Declaration of Independence did proclaim a theory of human rights effectively superior to the commands of any government seems strongly open to doubt" (p. 425). See also S. Gerald Sandler, "Lockean Ideas in Thomas Jefferson's *Bill For Establishing Religious Freedom," Journal of the History of Ideas,* XXI (January–March 1960), pp. 110–116, and Martin Seliger, "Locke's Theory of Revolutionary Action," *Western Political Quarterly,* XVI (September 1963), pp. 548–568.

• WOOD, NEAL, *The Politics of Locke's Philosophy* (Berkeley, 1983). This book's purpose is to find the political philosophy in Locke's *Essay Concerning Human Understanding.* Wood believes that this work was intended by Locke to be an "instrument for effecting social change," and reflects "bourgeois attitudes and ideals."

• YOLTON, JOHN M. (ed.), *John Locke: Problems and Perspectives* (Cambridge, 1969). A collection of essays on all aspects of Locke's thought, including political.

• ———, *John Locke and the Way of Ideas* (London, 1956). Analyzes Locke's theory of knowledge and its impact on ethics and religion in the seventeenth and eighteenth centuries. See also Douglas Odegard, "Locke as an Empiricist," *Philosophy,* XL (July 1965), pp. 185–196.

CHAPTER NINETEEN

MONTESQUIEU

• CABEEN, DAVID C., *Montesquieu: A Bibliography* (New York, 1947). An annotated bibliography of books and articles (87 pp.).

• CARRITHERS, DAVID, "Montesquieu's Philosophy of History," *Journal of the History of Ideas* (January–March 1986). An exploration of a critical element of Montesquieu's thought: how social and natural circumstances shape history.

• COHLER, ANNE M., *Montesquieu's Comparative Politics and the Spirit of American Constitutionalism* (Lawrence, 1988). This thoughtful and comprehensive examination of Montiequieu's *Spirit of the Laws* contributes to the growing debate over the influence of the work upon the American founders.

• COLLINS, J. CHURTON, *Voltaire, Montesquieu and Rousseau in England* (London, 1908). The section on Montesquieu's stay in England is on pp. 117–181. In England Montesquieu "perceived and understood what liberty meant, intellectually, morally, politically, socially. He saw it in its ugliness, he saw it in its beauty" (p. 178).

• COURTNEY, C. P., *Montesquieu and Burke* (Oxford, 1963). The author observes at the outset that "no French writer was more highly esteemed or more influential in England in the eighteenth century than Montesquieu" (p. 1). Burke called Montesquieu, in one of his earlier writings, "the greatest genius which has enlightened this age," and he continued to admire Montesquieu throughout his life, the only contemporary French writer for whom he harbored such sentiments. During the period of the French Revolution many revolutionaries considered the British constitution a product of superstitution and ignorance, in sharp contrast to Montesquieu who had earlier viewed it as the greatest monument to liberty—a fact which greatly enhanced Burke's admiration for Montesquieu. The specific impact of Montesquieu's *Spirit of the Laws* on English thought is also discussed (pp. 13–26).

• DEVLETOGLU, NICOS E., "Montesquieu and the Wealth of Nations," *Canadian Journal of Economics and Political Science,* XXIX (February 1963), pp. 1–25. Having secured for himself during his lifetime a place of enduring eminence in the study of political ideas, Montesquieu was later hailed as one of the founders, perhaps the founder, of modern sociology, and finally attracted the attention of economists. In his pioneering investigation, the author analyzes Montesquieu's views on agriculture, industry, enterprise, money, international trade, and population as well as on the relations of economic welfare to social and political institutions. Since this last point has attracted the attention of political economists so intensely in our own age, Montesquieu's insistence that "the social framework must be liberal" is termed by the author as "perhaps Montesquieu's most brilliant insight into the social and political roots of economic welfare" (p. 25).

• DURKHEIM, EMILE, *Montesquieu and Rousseau: Forerunners of Sociology* (Ann Arbor, 1960). Durkheim, one of the leaders of modern sociology, holds that "it is Montesquieu who first laid down the fundamental principles of social science" (p. 61). Montesquieu's classification of political systems is discussed (pp. 24–35). See also W. Stark, *Montesquieu: Pioneer of the Sociology of Knowledge* (London, 1960).

• FLETCHER, F. T. H., *Montesquieu and English Politics (1750–1800)* (London, 1939).

Unlike most studies on Montesquieu, which stress his indebtedness to England, the author traces the influence of Montesquieu on English political thought, particularly in the half century following the publication of the *Spirit of the Laws.* The end of this period is filled with the drama of the French Revolution, and the author notes that Montesquieu was used more by British conservative writers who opposed the French Revolution than by radical and liberal writers.

• HOLDSWORTH, W. S., "The Conventions of the Eighteenth Century Constitution," *Iowa Law Review,* XVII (January 1932), pp. 161–180. In this important study the author points out that the "conventions of the eighteenth century were directed to secure the maintenance of a system of divided powers and of checks and balances. The conventions of the nineteenth and twentieth centuries are directed to secure the political predominance of the House of Commons" (p. 163). King, Lords, and Commons were independent of one another, and it was from this constitution that Montesquieu deduced his view of English politics and of the doctrine of separation of powers. It must therefore be admitted "that there is an element of truth in Montesquieu's analysis. Independent benches of judges did administer a supreme law. The units of government were divided. Each had its independent autonomous powers that it could use freely, subject only to the supreme law administered by the independent benches of judges. The main faults of Montesquieu's theory were that it exaggerated the sharpness of the separation" (p. 165).

• HULLIUNG, MARK, *Montesquieu and the Old Regime* (Berkeley, 1976). A presentation of the unorthodox view that Montesquieu was a radical critic of the old regime and a convinced democrat, not an enlightened aristocrat.

• LEVIN, LAWRENCE MEYER, *The Political Doctrine of Montesquieu's Ésprit des Lois: Its Classical Background* (New York, 1936). Contains an extensive bibliography (pp. 331–359). See also Gilbert Chinard, "Montesquieu's Historical Pessimism," in *Studies in the History of Culture* (Menasha, Wis., 1942), pp. 161–172; Franz Neumann's Introduction to the *Spirit of the Laws* (Hafner Library of Classics, New York, 1949); and D. Lowenthal, "Book I of Montesquieu's *The Spirit of the Laws,*"

American Political Science Review, LIII (June 1959), 485–498. D. Kettler, "Montesquieu on Love: Notes on the *Persian Letters,*" *American Political Science Review,* LVIII (September 1964), pp. 658–661, briefly discusses Montesquieu's ideas on love in relation to social institutions, including government.

• MARTIN, KINGSLEY, *French Liberal Thought in the Eighteenth Century,* 2nd ed. (London, 1954). Chap. VI (pp. 147–169) is on Montesquieu. His "constitutional theory was based on Newtonian physics. In his early work he appears to have had a firmer grasp of the organic idea of the State than any other eighteenth-century writer, but his final political theory, in which each power is separate and related to the others only by a system of checks and balances, is entirely mechanical. The whole phraseology and conception is taken from mechanics: the State is a vast piece of engineering in which each joist is kept in place and made to do its work by an exact calculation of strains and stresses, held in place by a balance here, itself checking another joist, correctly attached and related to its neighbor. Since there is no animating principle, no directing head or organic life, the result would seem to be a motionless equilibrium" (p. 166). See also Harold J. Laski, "The Age of Reason," in F. J. C. Hearnshaw (ed.), *The Social and Political Ideas of Some Great French Thinkers of the Age of Reason* (London, 1930), pp. 9–38, and A. J. Grant, "Montesquieu," *ibid.,* pp. 114–135.

• MERRY, HENRY, *Montesquieu's System of Natural Government* (West Lafayette, Ind., 1970). Argues that particularly as Montesquieu wrote on the *spirit* of the laws and not their end, the best interpretation of his system is wholistically, not segmentally. Stresses the sociologic component of Montesquieu's thought. Downplays the philosophic nature of Montesquieu's writings. A comprehensive and sympathetic account.

• MORGAN, CHARLES, *The Liberty of Thought and the Separation of Powers* (The Zaharoff Lecture for 1948, Oxford, 1948). A reaffirmation of Montesquieu and the doctrine of the separation of powers. Democracy has not solved the issues with which Montesquieu was concerned: "Unchecked power is no less tyranny because someone has voted for it" (p. 17). See also Sir Courtenay Ilbert, *Montesquieu* (The Romanes Lecture 1904, Oxford, 1904), who writes on Montesquieu's central doctrine— the relativity of laws—as follows: "His doctrine of the relativity of laws, which is the foundation of enlightened conservatism, and has been used in defense of much conservatism which is not enlightened, is not a sufficient foundation for a constructive system, but was an admirable starting-point for a man whose primary interest lay in observing and comparing different institutions and drawing inferences from their similarities and diversities" (p. 27). The predominantly conservative influence of Montesquieu is more fully analyzed in C. E. Vaughan, *Studies in the History of Political Philosophy before and after Rousseau* (Manchester, 1939), Vol. I, pp. 253–302. See also John Plamenatz, *Man and Society: Political and Social Theory* (New York, 1963), Vol. I, pp. 253–298.

• PANGLE, THOMAS, *Montesquieu's Philosophy of Liberalism: A Commentary on "The Spirit of the Laws"* (Chicago, 1973). Pangle interprets Montesquieu as a liberal who favors commercial republics founded in the English experience, and who sees a connection between political and economic liberty. Pangle finds order in *The Spirit of the Laws,* which often is considered a disorganized work. Of the thinkers at the head of the liberal tradition, Pangle considers Montesquieu to be "the most helpful and relevant for us."

• SHACKLETON, ROBERT, *Montesquieu: A Critical Biography* (New York, 1961). In its scope, depth, and scholarship, this work supersedes all previous biographies of Montesquieu in English. As the author points out, Montesquieu's life was a life of ideas rather than of events, and this biography focuses therefore on the origins, development, and impact of Montesquieu's ideas. More than one third of the book is devoted to the *Spirit of the Laws.*

CHAPTER TWENTY

HUME

• AYER, A. J., *Hume* (Oxford, 1980). Part of the "Past Masters" series. The final chapter is on "Morals, Politics, and Religion."

• BOTWINICK, ARYEH, *Ethics, Politics and Epistemology: A Study in the Unity of Hume's Thought* (Lanham, Md., 1980). Botwinick sees an "utmost degree of coherence" in the various aspects of Hume's thought. The political conception of Hume's presented here is non-utilitarian, in contradistinction to that in *Great Political Thinkers.*

• CHAPPELL, V. C. (ed.), *Hume* (Garden City, N.Y., 1966). A collection of essays, mostly but not exclusively on philosophical subjects. Includes an essay, "The Legal and Political Philosophy of David Hume," by Friedrich Hayek.

• COLBOURN, TREVOR, (ed.), *Fame and the Founding Fathers* (New York, 1974). See the selections by Douglas Adair, particularly " 'That Politics May Be Reduced to a Science': David Hume, James Madison, and the Tenth Federalist," for the view that Hume significantly influenced Madison. For a somewhat different perspective, see James Conniff, "The Enlightenment and American Political Thought," *Political Theory* (August 1980), pp. 381–402.

• FORBES, DUNCAN, *Hume's Philosophical Politics* (Cambridge, 1975). A study of Hume's political theory, with emphasis on his political intentions and historical context.

• LAING, B. M., *David Hume* (New York, 1932, reprinted 1968). A single volume with three parts—on Hume's life, thought, and influence.

• MACKIE, J. L., *Hume's Moral Theory* (London, 1980). Particular attention is paid here to the practical virtues which sustain Hume's moral theory. For another

work on this subject, see Nicholas Capaldi, *Hume's Place in Moral Philosophy* (New York, 1989).

• MILLER, DAVID, *Philosophy and Ideology in Hume's Political Thought* (Oxford, 1981). A major recent work on Hume, though not a long book. Miller has three purposes: (1) to explain Hume's political theory, (2) to explicate the relationship between Hume's political theory and his philosophy, and (3) to clarify the ideological content of Hume's thought, which ideology Miller finds not to fit neatly into twentieth century categories. This book is more explanatory than critical.

• MORICE, G. P. (ed.), *David Hume; Bicentenary Papers* (Edinburgh, 1977). Papers presented on the 200th anniversary of Hume's death.

• MOSSNER, E. C., *The Life of David Hume* (Edinburgh, 1954). The definitive biography. Includes an interesting chapter on Hume's relationship with Rousseau.

• RUSSELL, PAUL, "Hume's *Treatise* and Hobbes's *The Elements of Law*," *Journal of the History of Ideas* (January–March 1985). The thesis is that Hume was much more influenced by Hobbes than has been thought previously, an influence which Hume concealed for prudential reasons.

• WHELAN, FREDERICK, *Order and Artifice in Hume's Political Philosophy* (Princeton, 1985). Concentrates on the philosophical presuppositions of Hume's political thought, with primary emphasis on the *Treatise of Human Nature*. Whelan holds that Hume's utilitarianism is distinct from Bentham's (contrary to the position put forward in *Great Political Thinkers*), and that Hume should be more considered a conservative than a liberal.

CHAPTER TWENTY-ONE

ROUSSEAU

• Babbitt, Irving, *Rousseau and Romanticism* (Meridian Books, New York, 1955). Originally published in 1919, this book has remained a highly useful introduction into the crucial conflict between classicism and romanticism, one of the main intellectual and cultural conflicts of the modern world. Babbitt sees in Rousseau the most typical and influential figure of the "great international movement" of romanticism, which is viewed by Babbitt as a profound threat to civilization. Chap. I, "The Terms Classic and Romantic" (pp. 16–38), is particularly helpful in tracing the origins, development, and meaning of classicism and romanticism. For a brief critical appraisal of romanticism, with particular reference to English letters, see Peter Quennell, "The Romantic Catastrophe," *Horizon,* I (May 1940), pp. 328–345. By contrast, a spirited defense of Rousseau and romanticism will be found in Jacques Barzun, *Classic, Romantic, and Modern* (Anchor Books, Garden City, N.Y., 1961). The work also includes an interesting collection of numerous samples of usage of the term "romantic" (pp. 155–168). While discussions of, and references to, Rousseau abound in Barzun's study, Chap. II (pp. 18–35) deals specifically with "Rousseau and Modern Tyranny."

• Broome, J. H., *Rousseau: A Study of His Thought* (London, 1963). In Chap. IV, "The Politics of Regeneration" (pp. 50–74), the author concentrates on the *Social Contract.* In dealing with the concept of the General Will, the author concedes its difficulties and complexities, and he suggests that it should be approached from a psychological viewpoint, since it "shows Rousseau's genuine insight into the psychology of the group" (p. 72). With respect to simple interpretations of Rousseau, Broome holds that "Rousseau's political theory cannot be reduced to liberalism or totalitarianism, as these terms have come to be used" (p. 68).

• Cassirer, Ernst, *The Question of Jean Jacques Rousseau* (translated and edited with an Introduction and Additional Notes by Peter Gay, Midland Books, Bloomington, Ind., 1963). This brief essay of less than one hundred pages is a landmark in the modern literature on Rousseau. The core problem of Rousseau's thought appears to Cassirer as follows: "How can we build a genuine and truly human community without falling in the process into the evils and depravity of conventional society? This is the question to which the *Contrat social* addresses itself. The return to the simplicity and happiness of the state of nature is barred to us, but the path of *freedom* lies open; it can and must be taken" (p. 54). Cassirer rejects the charge that Rousseau's political thought is either "atomistic-mechanistic" or totalitarian, and argues that two key conceptions stand out in Rousseau's mind: first, government by law, free from caprice and arbitrariness; and, second, the dignity of man, which seemed to him more important than happiness or utility. By assigning to reason, utility, and happiness comparatively less importance than was customary among the leaders of the Enlightenment at the time, Rousseau separated himself from them markedly. Yet, despite his deep religious feelings, Rousseau also alienated himself from both Protestant and Catholic theology, because he rejected the doctrine of original sin as the source of man's predicament and saw society as the source of man's evil condition. Society therefore has the responsibility of healing the wounds it has inflicted upon man, and Cassirer sees in this conception of the responsibility of society one of the chief legacies of Rousseau to posterity.

The value of the essay is greatly enhanced by Peter Gay's Introduction (pp. 3–30), in which he surveys the main interpretations of Rousseau in the nineteenth and twentieth centuries.

• CHAPMAN, JOHN W., *Rousseau—Totalitarian or Liberal?* (New York, 1956). The author strongly affirms the liberal character of Rousseau's thought. Yet Rousseau's liberalism is closer to modern than to classical liberalism, for "both Rousseau and the modern liberals repudiate the atomism of classical liberal democratic theory" (p. 143). For contrasting interpretations of Rousseau's political thought as totalitarian, see Sir Ernest Barker's Introduction to *Social Contract: Essays by Locke, Hume and Rousseau* (World's Classics, London, 1948), pp. xxxv–liv, and A. D. Lindsay, *The Modern Democratic State* (London, 1943), pp. 127–136.

• CHARVET, JOHN, *The Social Problem in the Philosophy of Rousseau* (Cambridge, 1974). Charvet defines and criticizes what he sees as the fundamental problem about society which Rousseau presents in the *Second Discourse, Social Contract,* and *Emile:* namely, that as individuals leave natural isolation and enter society, they lose their healthy egoism and acquire destructive vanity. Individuals forego natural desires and come to have social wants, which is the source of humanity's dilemma.

• COBBAN, ALFRED, *Rousseau and the Modern State,* 2nd ed. (London, 1964). The author argues that Rousseau should not be judged in terms of the twentieth-century sharp juxtaposition of individual versus the state, because he was primarily a moralist, a child of the Enlightenment, and "as such Rousseau's end is always the individual and his liberty," and that "his political theory starts with the individual and its ends with the individual" (p. 8). Concluding his investigation of Rousseau's political thought, Cobban writes that it "is not completely individualist, while at the same time it is equally not based on any glorification of society as distinct from the individuals of which it is composed" (p. 168). This tension and duality in Rousseau's political thought explains, the author holds, why Rousseau founded no school, and why he has been denounced by individualists as a collectivist, and by the authoritarians as an individualist.

See also Kingsley Martin, *French Liberal Thought in the Eighteenth Century,* 2nd ed. (London, 1954), pp. 192–219; F. J. C. Hearnshaw, "Rousseau," in the symposium volume edited by himself, *The Social and Political Ideas of Some Great French Thinkers of the Age of Reason* (London, 1930), pp. 168–193; and J. W. Gough, *The Social Contract,* 2nd ed. (Oxford, 1957), pp. 164–174.

• COLLINS, J. CHURTON, *Voltaire, Montesquieu and Rousseau in England* (London, 1908). Rousseau was a refugee in England between January 1766 and May 1767. Unlike Voltaire and Montesquieu, Rousseau felt thoroughly miserable in England, though treated with kindliness and consideration by his many friends and admirers there. He never learned the English language and developed little understanding for British institutions (pp. 182–271).

• CRANSTON, MAURICE, *Jean-Jacques: The Early Life and Work of Jean-Jacques Rousseau* (London, 1982). The first of a two-volume biography of Rousseau, which will undoubtedly become the standard in the field.

• ———, *The Noble Savage: Jean-Jacques Rousseau* (Chicago, 1991). This second volume of a three-part work extends the coverage of the first volume, and adds depth and richness to a narrative of Rousseau's life. Covering the *Discourse on Inequality, Julie, Emile,* and *The Social Contract,* this work gives insight into Rousseau's life and writings beyond the merely historical.

• EINAUDI, MARIO, *The Early Rousseau* (Ithaca, N.Y., 1967). Deals with Rousseau's earlier writings during the period of 1737–1756, with some attention to his personal life during those years. The author feels that "today Rousseau is increasingly seen as the most influential thinker of the eighteenth century" (p. v), and in Chap. I, "Rousseau Today" (pp. 1–25), he writes: "In the last fifty years in particular we have experienced, or have come very close to experiencing—in 1914, in 1929, in 1939, in 1945—many of the ultimate consequences of the phenomena of disintegration, loneliness, chaos, and selfishness, which are at the center of Rousseau's preoccupations" (p. 2).

• ELLENBURG, STEPHEN, *Rousseau's Political Philosophy: An Interpretation from Within* (Ithaca, N.Y., 1976). Sees greater unity in Rousseau's political thought than is generally considered the case. Ellenburg calls Rousseau a "nonindividualist" rather than a "collectivist."

• FERMON, NICOLE, *Domesticating Passions: Rousseau, Woman, and Nation* (London, 1997). The author provides a thorough work developing the importance of the concept of "sentiment" within Rousseau's writings. This decidedly feminist treatment of Rousseau concludes that women are, in fact, the agent and locus of "man's" reeducation.

• FRALIN, RICHARD, *Rousseau and Representation* (New York, 1978). An interpretation which portrays Rousseau as practically rather moderate in his political prescriptions. Traces the development of Rousseau's views on political institutions. Part 2 is on the *Social Contract.*

• GILDIN, HILAIL, *Rousseau's Social Contract* (Chicago, 1983). A Straussian perspective.

• GUÉHENNO, JEAN, *Jean-Jacques Rousseau,* 2 vols. (New York, 1966). An outstanding achievement by an eminent French writer, this story of Rousseau's life, "the drama of sincerity" (p. xv), is centered on Rousseau as a man rather than as a social or political thinker. The author seeks to relive Rousseau's life day by day, as felt and experienced by Rousseau himself rather than as interpreted by later critics and commentators. Yet with all his uniqueness, Rousseau seems to Guéhenno "extraordinarily representative of the state of man in the modern world, so that we see him formulating, and grappling with, a great many of the most serious problems with which we ourselves still have to contend. This explains why he cannot die, why he is still associated with all the controversies of our day" (p. xiii). See also Ronald Grimsley, *Jean-Jacques Rousseau: A Study in Self-Awareness* (Cardiff, 1961).

• HALL, JOHN, *Rousseau* (London, 1973). Part of the "Philosophers in Perspective" series. A brief introduction to Rousseau's political thinking. A good, though short, bibliography.

• HULLIUNG, MARK, *The Autocritique of Enlightenment: Rousseau and the Philosophes* (Cambridge, 1994). This deep and scholarly work explores the relationship of Rousseau to the Enlightenment movement. It presents Rousseau's "autocritique" of the Enlightenment in a manner both situating and revealing the ongoing dialectic within his work.

• KELLY, CHRISTOPHER, *Rousseau's Exemplary Life* (Ithaca, N.Y., 1987). Subtitled *The Confessions as Political Philosophy,* this book concentrates on that work not for what it shows about Rousseau's personality, but for what it tells about his politics.

• LASKI, HAROLD J., *The Danger of Disobedience and Other Essays* (New York, 1930). Chap. VII, "A Portrait of Jean Jacques Rousseau" (pp. 178–206), is an interpretation of Rousseau's main ideas and their impact on modern political theory. His influence was in the direction of both individualism and collectivism, but "the latter aspect has been the more enduring" (pp. 196–197). Laski notes Rousseau's impact on Hegel and Marx, with whom, as with their disciples, "Rousseauism has essentially meant the sacrifice of the individual to an end beyond himself" (p. 197). See also Laski's *Studies in Law and Politics* (London, 1932), Chap. I, "The Age of Reason" (pp. 13–37), and Chap. III, "The Socialist Tradition in the French Revolution" (pp. 66–103).

• LEMOS, RAMON, *Rousseau's Political Philosophy* (Atlanta, 1977). A comprehensive yet manageable interpretation of Rousseau's political theory. Lemos considers only the *Discourse on the Origin and Foundation of Inequality Among Men,* the *Discourse on Political Economy,* and the *Social Contract.*

• MASTERS, ROGER D., *The Political Philosophy of Rousseau* (Princeton, 1968). Highly unorthodox in approach, method of analysis, and interpretation. Part I deals with *Émile,* the *Second Discourse,* and the *First Discourse,* the three principal writings of Rousseau linked together by his key idea of "man's natural goodness." According to the author, Rousseau shows in all three of these writings how man's misery was created by the establishment of civil society, which condition cannot be fully remedied by any, even the best, political order. In Part II, called "The Possibilities of Politics," Masters concentrates on the *Social Contract* in both its original draft and its final version. In this concluding chapter, Masters explains why he considers Rousseau's *First Discourse* his most "defensible work" and the one which has the greatest relevance in our own time. This is a work which assumes considerable familiarity with Rousseau's thought and which makes heavy demands on the reader's attention, but which provides the student with a fresh perspective on Rousseau.

• McDonald, Joan, *Rousseau and the French Revolution* (London, 1965). The author of the study of this perennially interesting topic holds that "more than that of any of the great prerevolutionary writers, the memory of Rousseau captured the imagination of the revolutionary generation" (p. 161). However, his reputation and admiration rested on his appeal as a legendary figure, and on his pleas for social and moral regeneration in the *Nouvelle Héloise and Émile,* and not on his political theories of the *Social Contract.*

• Melzer, Arthur M., *The Natural Goodness of Man: On the System of Rousseau's Thought* (Chicago, 1990). Scholars inquiring into the history of political thought, as well as those seeking a comprehensive analysis of Rousseau's work, will find this excellent volume indispensable.

• Miller, Jim, *Rousseau: Dreamer of Democracy* (New Haven, Ct., 1984). Asserts the traditional view that Rousseau is among the most important of thinkers who fostered democratic ways of thought and action.

• Morgenstern, Mira, *Rousseau and the Politics of Ambiguity: Self, Culture, and Society* (University Park, Penn., 1996). Morgenstern gives a close reading to the work of Rousseau in this well-written work. Her feminist treatment of the material is deft and thoughtful, yielding many valuable insights.

• Noone, John, *Rousseau's Social Contract; A Conceptual Analysis* (Athens, Ga., 1980). An original interpretation of the *Social Contract,* purporting to find a system in it which others have failed to see, whose keystone is legitimacy.

• Perkins, Merle, *Jean-Jacques Rousseau on the Individual and Society* (Lexington, Ky., 1974). A detailed analysis of Rousseau's political viewpoints, with special reference to his views on international relations.

• Plattner, Marc, *Rousseau's State of Nature* (DeKalb, Ill., 1979). Subtitled *An Interpretation of the Discourse on Inequality,* this brief book is that, focusing on just one aspect of the *Discourse*–Rousseau's conception of the state of nature.

• Roche, Kennedy, *Rousseau; Stoic & Romantic* (London, 1974). An investigation into the Stoic influence on Rousseau.

• Roosevelt, Grace G., *Reading Rousseau in the Nuclear Age* (Philadelphia, 1990). Roosevelt includes a previously unpublished piece of Rousseau's discourse on the relationship between states to develop a deeper understanding of Rousseau's notion of innocence and human society. This is an excellent resource for both students and advanced Rousseau scholars.

• Rousseau, Jean Jacques, *Confessions* (1782–1789). Available in numerous English translations and indispensable to an appreciation of Rousseau's development and thought. The translation of the *Confessions* by J. M. Cohen (Penguin Books, Baltimore, 1953) is recommended.

• ———, *The Government of Poland* (trans. with an introduction by Willmoore Kendall, Indianapolis, 1972). A littleknown, but potentially significant, work of Rousseau's.

• ———, *The Social Contract, and Discourses* (Everyman's Library, London–New York, 1947). The value of the volume is greatly enhanced by the inclusion of the three *Discourses* on the *Arts and Sciences, Origin of Inequality,* and *Political Economy,* because Rousseau's political thought cannot be properly understood from the *Social Contract* alone. The Introduction by G. D. H. Cole (pp. v–xii) is a model of clarity and insight.

• Shklar, Judith, *Men and Citizens: A Study of Rousseau's Social Theory* (Cambridge, Mass., 1969). Shklar presents Rousseau as a pessimist, who believes that humanity possesses no happy past, but has no happy future, either. The human condition is irredeemably fallen: society is necessary; society engenders inequality; inequality leads to suffering.

• Simon, Julia, *Mass Enlightenment: Critical Studies in Rousseau and Diderot* (Albany, 1995). Simon extends the project of critical theorists in her treatment of Rousseau and Diderot. This work may not present much in the way of new interpretations, but it does provide some possible insights into future directions for critical theory and the work Rousseau.

• Talmon, J. L., *The Origins of Totalitarian Democracy* (London, 1952). The author's main thesis is that the eighteenth century saw the birth of two contradictory types of democracy: "empirical liberal democracy" and "Messianic totalitarian democracy." Rousseau is considered perhaps the most important single source of totalitarian democracy, particularly by marrying the concept of the general will with that of popular sovereignty (p. 43). For a similar juxtaposition of Rousseau's popular sovereignty and eighteenth-century English liberalism, see also Guido de Ruggiero, *The History of European Liberalism* (Beacon Paperbacks, Boston, 1959), particularly the Introduction on "The Eighteenth Century" (pp. 1–90). Ruggiero writes that the attributes of Rousseau's concept of sovereignty "are the exact opposite of the principles of guarantism as derived from the English Constitution" (p. 62).

• TRACHTENBERG, ZEV M., *Making Citizens: Rousseau's Political Theory of Culture* (New York, 1993). Trachtenberg brings to bear a powerful rationality in explicating Rousseau's theory of culture. The author's conclusion, that Rousseau's rational individual (via Mancur Olsen's *Logic of Collective Action*) will possess an agency that will undermine any attempt to achieve a "general will," is grounded within the rational choice school and contains the strengths and weaknesses of this approach.

• VIROLI, MAURIZIO, *Jean-Jacques Rousseau and the "Well-Ordered Society"* trans. Derek Hanson (Cambridge, Eng., 1988). An important work on Rousseau, founded in part on the notion that "Rousseau's political doctrine is based on the idea of a dual form of the artificial, rather than on the antithesis between nature and the artificial."

• WEISS, PENNY, "Rousseau, Antifeminism, and Woman's Nature," *Political Theory* (February 1987), pp. 81–98. Presentation of Rousseau's views on women, which, while antifeminist, are not found to include "natural sexual differentiation" as a basis for sexual inequality in society. This topic is also discussed in Joel Schwartz, *The Sexual Politics of Jean-Jacques Rousseau* (Chicago, 1985).

• WILLHOITE, FRED H., JR., "Rousseau's Political Religion," *Review of Politics,* XXVII (October 1965), pp. 501–515. The author writes that Rousseau's religion "is essentially social rather than theological; man, born into social sin yet capable of salvation only through society, is central, while a transcendent God, though present, is peripheral" (p. 501). Although Rousseau rejected reason and philosophy in favor of nature as

the ultimate source of knowledge, thus bringing himself into conflict with most leaders of the Enlightenment, he was still very much a child of the Enlightenment, because of his "agnostic attitude toward supernatural revelation" and his "acceptance of nature as a source of true knowledge" (p. 502). In conclusion, the author makes, from a theological viewpoint, the most serious charge, that of anthropocentricity: "Even in reacting against mechanistic rationalism, Rousseau remained committed to its basic anthropocentricity, its belief in man's ultimate omnicompetence. For Rousseau the perfect society is composed of atomistic, self-worshipping individuals, the sum of whose identical will produces a corporate, immanent, infallible guide force—the general will. The triumph of political society over transcendent religion is so complete that the state becomes the true church and the general will dictates true dogma" (p. 515). Christopher Dawson, "The Birth of Democracy," *Review of Politics,* XIX (January 1957), 48–61, also writing from a strongly religious viewpoint, offers a more sympathetic appraisal of Rousseau. Before Rousseau, the liberal ideas of the Enlightenment, the author holds, were restricted to a small, privileged class. If these liberal ideas were to penetrate broader classes of people, "they had to make an appeal to psychological forces that lay beneath the surface of rational consciousness. They had to be transformed from a philosophy into a religion: to cease to be mere ideas and to become articles of faith. This reinterpretation of liberalism in religious terms was the work of Jean Jacques Rousseau, who thus became the founder and prophet of a new faith—the religion of democracy" (p. 50).

• WOKLER, ROBERT, *Rousseau and Liberty* (Manchester, 1995). This edited edition contains thirteen traditional interpretations of Rousseau's writings. It covers a wide spectrum of the debate over contextual and interpretive aspects of his work.

• YALE FRENCH STUDIES, *Jean-Jacques Rousseau* (No. 28, Fall–Winter 1961–1962). The entire issue is on Rousseau, and contains contributions by distinguished French and American scholars on his life and personality as well as on his views on morals, politics, law, religion, and education.

CHAPTER TWENTY-TWO

KANT

• BENCIVENGA, ERMANNO, *Kant's Copernican Revolution* (New York, 1987). An attempt to understand the *Critique of Pure Reason*. For another relatively recent brief work on the same subject, see Robert Kahn, *Kant's Newtonian Revolution in Philosophy* (Carbondale, Ill., 1988).

• CASSIRER, ERNST, *Kant's Life and Thought* (trans. James Haden, New Haven, Ct., 1981). Originally published in German in 1918, this work is standard summation of Kant's career. For a more recent work, see Arsenij Gulyga, *Immanuel Kant; His Life and Thought* (trans. Marijan Despalatovic, Boston, 1987).

• GALLIE, W. B., *Philosophers of Peace and War* (New York, 1978). Chapter 1 is on Kant, and emphasizes the importance of Kant's new conception of international law in *Perpetual Peace*.

• GALSTON, WILLIAM, *Kant and the Problem of History* (Chicago, 1975). Includes a presentation of Kant's political philosophy.

• KANT, IMMANUEL, *Kant's Political Writings* (ed. with and introduction and notes by Hans Reiss, trans. H. B. Nisbet, Cambridge, Eng., 1970). See Reiss's introduction.

• ———, *The Philosophy of Kant* (ed. Carl Friedrich, New York, 1949). Subtitled *Immanuel Kant's Moral and Political Writings,* this book contains a number of Kant's writings on political subjects. See also Friedrich's introduction.

• MULHOLLAND, LESLIE, *Kant's System of Rights* (New York, 1990). A long work on the subject, including considerable discussion on political subjects and recent writers in political theory.

• PATON, H. J., *Kant's Metaphysic of Experience,* 2 vols. (London, 1936). A classic commentary on the first half of the *Critique of Pure Reason.*

• RABEL, GABRIELE, *Kant* (Oxford, 1963). A collection of snipets from each one of Kant's published works, with introductions.

• RAWLS, JOHN, *A Theory of Justice* (Cambridge, Mass., 1971). Much of Rawls's theory of justice is informed by Kant. Section 40 is "The Kantian Interpretation of Justice as Fairness." See also Rawls' "Kantian Constructivism in Moral Theory," *Journal of Philosophy* (September 1980).

• RILEY PATRICK, *Kant's Political Philosophy* (Totawa, N.J., 1983). Concentrates on the relationship between Kant's ethics and his political theory. Riley holds that Kant considers the state to be an imperfect (but necessary) realization of the good will. Very extensive quotations from Kant. This book is not a descriptive account of Kant's political theory, but an attempt to find the place of politics in Kant's comprehensive philosophy. See also Riley's "The 'Elements' of Kant's Practical Philosophy," *Political Theory* (November 1986), pp. 552–583, for a discussion of the *Groundwork of the Metaphysics of Morals* as the foundation for Kant's moral and political thought.

• ROSEN, ALLEN D., *Kant's Theory of Justice* (Ithaca, 1993). This rigorous but narrow reading of Kantian legal theory is a unique but limited view of the subject.

• SANER, HANS, *Kant's Political Thought* (trans. E. B. Ashton, Chicago, 1973). Saner argues that politics is intrinsic to Kant's thought, despite the relative paucity of explicit attention apparently paid to it, and that Kant's political thought "is one of the peaks" of the western political tradition.

• SCHELL, SUSAN M., *The Embodiment of Reason: Kant on Spirit, Generation, and Community* (Chicago, 1996). Schell provides an interesting contribution to the corpus of knowledge on Kantian philosophy. Besides provocative discussions of Kant's views on history, nature, and gender, the author includes a splendid elucidation of Kant's hypochondria. An impressive and valuable work describing Kant's world-view.

• SMITH, NORMAN, *A Commentary to Kant's Critique of Pure Reason,* 2nd ed. (London, 1923). A critical appraisal.

• SULLIVAN, ROGER, *Immanuel Kant's Moral Theory* (Cambridge, Eng., 1989). This book is an attempt to understand the parts of Kant's moral theory within the context of his larger moral conception.

• VELKLEY, RICHARD L., *Freedom and the End of Reason: On the Moral Foundations of Kant's Critical Philosophy* (Chicago, 1989). This ambitious and very successful treatment of Kant's critical philosophy challenges our understanding of Kantian reason, progress, and culture, among other concepts. Its endpoint is successful in encouraging a reappraisal of Kant's relationship with modernity.

• WERKMEISTER, W. H., *Kant; The Architectonic and Development of His Philosophy* (La Salle, Ill., 1980). An accessible introduction to the progression of Kant's thought.

• WILLIAMS, HOWARD, *Kant's Political Philosophy* (New York, 1983). A comprehensive survey and analysis of Kant's political thought, though this book is under 200 pages. The first half of the book concentrates on presenting Kant's political philosophy; the second, more on analyzing it, with interesting references to other authors. Williams finds: "Kant is, at heart, a republican with strong liberal sympathies."

CHAPTER TWENTY-THREE

SMITH

• CAMPBELL, R. H. and A. S., SKINNER *Adam Smith* (London, 1982). An accessible and brief biography which discusses Smith's academic work. See also Skinner's *A System of Social Science* (Oxford, 1979), a collection of essays published elsewhere on a variety of Smithian topics.

• CLARK, JOHN, et al., *Adam Smith, 1776–1926* (reprinted New York, 1966). A collection of general lectures on Smith on the occasion of the sesquicentennial of the publication of *The Wealth of Nations.*

• CROPSEY, JOSEPH, *Polity and Economy; An Interpretation of the Principles of Adam Smith* (The Hague, 1957). A useful examination of Smith's thought, including discussion of the *Theory of Moral Sentiments* as well as *The Wealth of Nations.* One premise of the book is that "capitalism is an embodiment of Smithian principles."

• FITZGIBBONS, ATHOL, *Adam Smith's System of Liberty, Wealth, and Virtue: The Moral and Political Foundations of The Wealth of Nations* (New York, 1995). This work, which benefits both the general public and scholars, seeks to explain, as Fitzgibbons puts it, "how Adam Smith set out to replace the Aristotelian Philosophy of Western Europe, which had become a hindrance to liberty and economic growth, with an equally comprehensive but more vital worldview" (p. v). The author makes a good argument, but leaves out much of contemporary literature on the subject. Nonetheless, this work is strongly recommended.

• FOLEY, VERNARD, *The Social Physics of Adam Smith* (West Lafayette, Ind., 1976). An idiosyncratic work advancing the thesis that "important elements of Adam Smith's thought were consciously, systematically, and secretly modeled after a system of physical, biological, and social evolution which he found in the writings of the ancients."

• GLAHE, FRED, ed., *Adam Smith and The Wealth of Nations; 1776–1976 Bicentennial Essays* (Boulder, Co., 1978). A collection of essays on a wide scope of Smithian positions and topics, including one by Milton Friedman on Smith's continuing relevance.

• HEILBRONER, ROBERT, *The Worldly Philosophers,* 6th ed. (New York, 1986). The most successful introduction to economic thinkers. Chapter III is on Smith. Also see chapter IV of Robert Lekachman's *A History of Economic Ideas* (New York, 1959).

• HOLLANDER, SAMUEL, *The Economics of Adam Smith* (Toronto, 1973). An excellent introduction to Smith's economic theories.

Not too difficult for the noneconomist. Includes two chapters on pre-Smithian economics. For another strictly economic view of Smith, see Maurice Brown, *Adam Smith's Economics* (London, 1988).

• MEEK, RONALD, *Smith, Marx, & After* (London, 1977). A collection of essays comparing and explaining Smith, Marx, and their influence.

• MULLER, JERRY Z., *Adam Smith: In His Time and Ours* (New York, 1993). Comprehensive, sympathetic account emphasizing the continuing relevance of Smith's "moral and political philosophy of capitalism" (p. 7). This work is highly recommended.

• MYERS, MILTON, *The Soul of Modern Economic Man* (Chicago, 1983). This book traces the place of self-interest in British political theorists from Hobbes to Smith. It argues that the *Wealth of Nations* can be seen as a reply to Hobbes's views on self-interest.

• O'DRISCOLL, GERALD, ed., *Adam Smith and Modern Political Economy: Bicentennial Essays on The Wealth of Nations* (Ames, Ia., 1979). Papers delivered at the University of California at Santa Barbara as the Harry Girvetz Memorial Lectures.

• RAE, JOHN, *Life of Adam Smith,* with an introduction by Jacob Viner (reprinted New York, 1965). Originally published in 1895, still contains much interesting and valuable information on Smith.

• REISMAN, DAVID, *Adam Smith's Sociological Economics* (London, 1976). A study that attempts to direct greater focus than usual on Smith's comprehensive Perspective on society rather than on his economics *per se.*

• ROSS, IAN SIMPSON, *The Life of Adam Smith* (Oxford, 1995). First comprehensive intellectual biography on Smith since Rae's *Life of Adam Smith* a century before. Ross' work is more for the professional academic; Rae's work remains more accessible to the student.

• SMITH, ADAM, *The Essential Adam Smith* (ed. and with introductory readings by Robert Heilbroner, New York, 1986). Probably the best abridgment available of Smith's comprehensive writings. Heilbroner's introduction, while brief, is interesting.

• TEICHGRAEBER, RICHARD, *"Free Trade" and Moral Philosophy* (Durham, N.C., 1986). A more comprehensive book arguing in part that the *Wealth of Nations* was conceived by Smith not just as an economic treatise, but as a description of the just political state. Teichgraeber traces Smith's philosophy to the Dutch jurist and statesman Hugo Grotius, who argued against distributive justice and in favor of private property. Because, under this view, liberty is essentially negative, politics plays a smaller role in societies.

• WEST, E. G., *Adam Smith: The Man and His Works* (Indianapolis, 1976). Brief, accessible account of Smith's life and thought.

• WINCH, DONALD, *Adam Smith's Politics: An Essay in Historiographic Revision* (Cambridge, 1978). Presents Smith as an eighteenth century political figure influenced by Montesquieu and Hume, and not as much influenced by Locke. Emphasis is on Smith's politics, not his economics.

CHAPTER TWENTY-FOUR

BURKE

• ARIS, REINHOLD, *History of Political Thought in Germany, 1789–1815* (London, 1936). Includes a succinct discussion of Burke's influence on German romanticism and conservatism (pp. 251–265). See also Frieda Braune, *Edmund Burke in Deutschland* (Heidelberg, 1917), which traces the contribution of Burke to the growth of German conservatism and political romanticism in the late eighteenth and early nineteenth centuries. Whereas Burke has been hailed in England not only by conservatives but also by liberals and socialists, his influence in Germany—and it was considerable—has been felt mainly in anti-democratic circles.

• BARKER, ERNEST, *Essays on Government* (Oxford, 1945). Chaps. VI and VII (pp. 155–235) are illuminating studies on "Burke and His Bristol Constituency," and "Burke and the French Revolution." See also C. E. Vaughan, *Studies in the History of Political Philosophy before and after Rousseau* (Manchester, 1939), II, pp. 1–63.

• BEVAN, RUTH, *Marx and Burke: A Revisionist View* (La Salle, Ill., 1973). The purpose of this book is to juxtapose a historical conservative (Burke) with a historical revolutionary (Marx) to gain a greater understanding of contemporary political issues.

• CANAVAN, FRANCIS P., *Edmund Burke: Prescription and Providence* (Durham, N.C., 1987). A Straussian interpretation of Burke, emphasizing religion.

• ———, *The Political Reason of Edmund Burke* (Durham, N.C., 1960). The author takes issue with interpreting Burke's political thought as a form of empiricism or utilitarianism. "The central idea in Burke's thought," the author writes, "was that of order" (p. 19). Yet, it is an order which is "the work of reason. The reason which creates order, however, is not solely nor even primarily human reason. In accordance with the intellectual tradition of Christian philosophy, Burke saw the entire universe as an intelligible whole, the product of Divine Reason. Within that universal order there was a natural moral order, derived from the structure and essential relationships of human nature as created by God" (p. 189). The author concedes that there was an element of pragmatism in Burke, but it was "principled pragmatism" with "absolutes" and "fixed stars" as provided by the moral law: "But within these limits, the realm of means and intermediate ends was the domain of prudence. In this area the mode of thought proper to the statesman was that of political reason, which was concerned with adapting means to ends in ever-changing circumstances, according to the norms of an intelligent and enlightened expediency" (pp. 26–27).

• CHAPMAN, GERALD W., *Edmund Burke: The Practical Imagination* (Cambridge, Mass., 1967). The book is organized around the five major critical issues in Burke's life: America, Ireland, Constitutional Reform, France, and India. Burke's thinking united, in the author's view, the two greatest achievements of English civilization, "its literary imagination, and its success in practical politics" (p. 2). The resultant concept of the "practical imagination" is defined by the author as the "power to experience a thing in its concrete complexity, to discriminate its relations, and to act upon or reverence its latent good" (p. 131). The complexity of Burke's own thought, defying any attempt to build a system out of it, is defined by the author as follows: "His thought is a master-solvent of antinomies—metaphysics and common sense, poetry and practicality, liberalism and conservatism, neoclassicism and romanticism, Christianity and pragmatism, to name but a few" (p. 2). Far from being an advocate of the status quo, Burke had, the author argues, a vivid sense of "things enduring, things changing, things changing in order to endure" (p. 33).

• COBBAN, ALFRED, *Edmund Burke and the Revolt against the Eighteenth Century,* 2nd ed. (London, 1960). Chaps. II–IV (pp. 37–132) are devoted to Burke. Cobban emphasizes Burke's originality in relation to the problem of nationality: "He saw, long before most of his contemporaries, the power and rights of that force of national sentiment which eighteenth-century theorists and politicians had conspired to ignore and trample on. The right of a subject nation to freedom just because it *was* a nation was a new idea in political thought. Though the fact had been there for centuries, Burke has the honor of first stating in definite form the theory of nationality" (p. 130).

• CONE, CARL B., *Burke and the Nature of Politics,* 2 vols. (Lexington, 1957–1964). The first major biography of Burke to make use of his papers, which became accessible to the public only in 1949. The first volume is on "The Age of the American Revolution," and the second is on "The Age of the French Revolution." In his final appraisal of Burke's place in the history of political philosophy, the author holds that Burke's utilitarian interpreters, particularly during the nineteenth century, put him in a "false position," and that he should more properly be placed in the "natural-law tradition," opposed to the "scientific materialism and the legal positivism of the Enlightenment" (II, pp. 510–511).

• FASEL, GEORGE, *Edmund Burke* (Boston, 1983). A good brief introduction to the major components of Burke's thought and writing.

• FAY, C. R., *Burke and Adam Smith* (Belfast, 1956). Analyzes the personal relations and intellectual affinities between Burke and Adam Smith. An ardent believer in custom, authority, and the organic conception in politics, Burke was an emphatic follower of *laissez faire* in economics. In fact, Fay writes that Burke's *Thoughts and Details on Scarcity* (1795) was even more effective than Adam Smith's *Wealth of Nations* (1776) in helping Cobden and the Anti-Corn Law League "in their fight for free food" (p. 25) in the first half of the nineteenth century.

• FENNESSY, R. R., *Burke, Paine, and the Rights of Man: A Difference of Political Opinion* (The Hague, 1963). Written from an avowedly pro-Burke viewpoint, the detailed account of the controversy between Burke and Paine—one of the great ideological debates in English—discusses the personal relations between the two as well as the basic reasons of their doctrinal disagreement. In the author's judgment, "Burke was no doubt a better thinker, and he offered an effective criticism of the kind of political theory that Paine believed in. But the society in which they lived was ripe for change; and when the time comes for great changes in political systems, a plain and intelligible political theory, however faulty, may serve the ends of the reformers better than one that is nearer the truth but more difficult to understand" (p. 254). With respect to Paine, the author makes the interesting comment that, while he failed to convert England to republicanism and thorough constitutional reform, Paine—particularly through the *Rights of Man*—had an enormous impact on the working class and the stirring working class movement (pp. 244–250).

• HART, JEFFREY, "Burke and Radical Freedom," *Review of Politics,* XXIX (April 1967), pp. 221–238. Noting a strong revival of interest in Burke, the author finds the explanation for it in the fact that Burke "was the first to recognize the deep moral division of the West, which was just then opening up, and which today, across the board, is decisive for our moral, political, and metaphysical opinions: and because Burke, having recognized the division and defined its doctrinal grounds, took sides" (pp. 221–222). Hart sees two opposing forces in the modern world: on the one hand, there is a force of perpetual dissatisfaction, "hatred of what *is*"; on the other hand, there is the older moral tradition of a "sense of being," of saying to the world: "Do not change: *Be*" (p. 238). Burke belongs to that older tradition that, according to the author, goes back to Plato, Aristotle, and Aquinas, and for this reason the concept of "tranquility" is central in Burke's thought: "On the one hand are the qualities to be desired in society: stability, public tranquility, peace, quiet, order, harmony, regularity, unity, decorum. Opposed to these are the symptoms of social disease: discord, contradiction, confusion, violence, excess, the need for coercion. The task of the statesman is to promote 'tranquility'" (p. 237).

• HAZLITT, WILLIAM, *Political Essays, with Sketches of Public Characters* (London, 1819). Hazlitt, a radical democrat and one of the leading English essayists of the early nineteenth century, devotes two essays to the "Character of Mr. Burke" (pp. 264–269 and pp. 361–377), the first written in 1807 and the second in 1817. Hazlitt concedes that Burke is "the most poetical of our prose writers" (p. 269), but argues that his theory of government is constructed "not on rational, but on picturesque and fanciful principles; as if a king's crown were a painted gewgaw, to be looked at on gala-days; titles an empty sound to please the ear; and the whole order of society a theatrical procession" (p. 267).

• KIRK, RUSSELL, *The Conservative Mind: From Burke to Santayana* (Chicago, 1953). Chap. II (pp. 11–61) is on Burke. The author states that "Burke's ideas provided the defenses of conservatism, on a great scale, that still stand and are not liable to fall in our time" (p. 61). As in the eighteenth century, "our age, too, seems to be groping for certain of the ideas which Burke's inspiration formed into a system of social preservation" (*ibid.*).

• KRAMNICK, ISAAC, "The Left and Edmund Burke," *Political Theory* (May 1983), pp. 189–214. A history of leftist critiques of Burke, which, surprisingly, have often been positive. See also Kramnick's *The Rage of Edmund Burke: Portrait of an Ambivalent*

Conservative (New York, 1977) for a recent biography which attempts to de-mythologize Burke.

• LASKI, HAROLD J., *Political Thought in England: from Locke to Bentham* (Home University Library, London, 1937). Chap. VI (pp. 165–215) is on Burke. Laski's conclusion is that "there is hardly a greater figure in the history of political thought in England" (p. 214). Similar, and even more lyrical, expressions are interesting evidence of the hold that the great conservative writer has over a socialist like Laski, and the whole chapter is highly revealing of the political and intellectual climate of England.

• MACCUNN JOHN, *The Political Philosophy of Burke* (London, 1913). A fair and well-balanced analysis of Burke's views on major issues of political philosophy, and one of the most useful works of its kind. In dealing with Burke's attitude on freedom of discussion and religious toleration (Chap. VII, pp. 104–121), the author says that "no man, it is safe to say, ever discussed politics as he did, none so persistently, none with such eloquence and penetration, none with more determination to go to the root of the matter" (p. 105). This did not prevent Burke from opposing untrammeled freedom in politics and religion: "Few great thinkers, indeed, have gone so far in using incomparable powers of discussion in proving that toleration, as well as discussion, ought to have its limits" (p. 111). See also F. J. C. Hearnshaw, "Edmund Burke," in the work edited by himself, *The Social and Political Ideas of Some Representative Thinkers of the Revolutionary Era* (London, 1931), pp. 72–99; Ivor Brown, *English Political Theory* (London, 1929), pp. 68–87; and R. H. S. Crossman, *Government and the Governed* (London, 1939), pp. 84–86, pp. 117–125. Both Crossman and Brown devote more space to Paine than to Burke in dealing with the English response to the French Revolution, and Crossman calls Paine the "ablest pamphleteer" (p. 117) of the French Revolution.

• MAGNUS, PHILIP, *Edmund Burke: A Life* (London, 1939). One of the best modern biographies, with illustrations and contemporary cartoons, and a Select Bibliography (pp. 351–355). The most frequently quoted British statesman, "Burke's political outlook was not shared by all Englishmen, but it was the outlook of the dominant and

most characteristic section of the English people. The instinctive political empiricism of the average Englishman now bears for all time the impress of the character and personality of Edmund Burke. It was Burke's genius which first gave shape and direction to what formerly had been little more than an inchoate mass of ideas, floating in the English mind. This was Burke's greatest achievement, and his legacy to his country" (p. 300).

• O'GORMAN, FRANK, *Edmund Burke: His Political Philosophy* (Bloomington, Ind., 1973). Places Burke's thought in historical perspective; uses the whole range of Burke's works. O'Gorman's thesis is that Burke's political theory should be evaluated from the perspective that it emerged from an active politician, not a scholarly philosopher.

• PARKIN, CHARLES, *The Moral Basis of Burke's Political Thought* (Cambridge, 1956). Starting from Burke's own thesis that "the principles of true politics are those of morality enlarged," the author examines the precise nature of Burke's moral principles. He concludes as follows: "The source of moral truth, for Burke, is an eternal moral order which is immanent in the historical process. His morality rests therefore on a religious perception. Man is by constitution a religious animal, and religion must be the foundation of civil society" (p. 131).

• ROSSITER, CLINTON, *Conservatism in America: The Thankless Persuasion*, 2nd ed. (Vintage Books, New York, 1962). Chap. VII, "The Conservative Minority, or With Edmund Burke in Darkest America" (pp. 197–234) is particularly important. The author delineates the different strands of conservatism in the United States, and he finds that, for more than a century, genuine and self-conscious American followers of Burkean conservatism have been but "an eccentric minority in the world of ideas, a misunderstood minority in the world of right-wing politics" (p. 234). Rossiter brilliantly summarizes the main similarities and differences between Burkean conservatism and the dominant (non-Burkean) American conservatism (pp. 198–201), and he identifies the principle of "the primacy of the community" as the most important area of difference between Burkean conservatism and individualistic American conservatism. "While our conservatives have occasionally gone abroad," Rossiter writes, "in search of philosophical support, they have gone to Spencer and Adam Smith rather than to Burke and Coleridge" (p. 198). As to the importance of Burke, Rossiter writes that Burke's *Reflections on the Revolution in France* (1790) "is rightly considered the first and greatest statement of consciously conservative principles" (p. 16).

• STANLIS, PETER J., *Edmund Burke and the Natural Law* (Ann Arbor Paperbacks, Ann Arbor, 1965). The thesis of the work is "that far from being an enemy of Natural Law, Burke was one of the most eloquent and profound defenders of Natural Law morality and politics in Western civilization" (p. ix). Emphasizing the religious roots of Burke's thought, the author calls Burke "the foremost modern Christian humanist in politics because he saw the world and the nature of man through the revelations of Christianity and the right reason of Natural Law" (p. 84). See also Leo Strauss, *Natural Right and History* (Chicago, 1953), pp. 294–323.

• STEPHEN, LESLIE, *History of English Thought in the Eighteenth Century*, 2 vols. (Harbinger Books, New York, 1962). This classic, first published in 1876, discusses Burke in Vol. II, Chap. X (pp. 185–214). The author, an emphatic Liberal, begins his analysis of Burke with these words: "No English writer has received, or has deserved, more splendid panegyrics than Burke" (II, 185). Stephen stresses in Burke's thought the concepts of experience and utility, in contrast to some recent writers who have attempted to interpret Burke as an adherent of natural law and metaphysics in politics and philosophy. Similarly, T. E. Utley, *Edmund Burke* (London–New York, 1957), considers the "principle of utility" the first and foremost principle in Burke's thought. This principle of utility means that "no consideration of abstract right can be a sufficient basis for just authority and just obedience, but that the proper end of government is the

happiness of its subjects, and that this should be the sovereign guide to its conduct, determining how far it shall press its authority in practice" (p. 24).

• WHITE, STEPHEN K., *Edmund Burke: Modernity, Politics, and Aesthetics*, Vol. 5 of *Modernity and Political Thought* (Cal, 1994). Zerilli seeks to revisit Burke in the aftermath of the end to the cold war. His deep and thoughtful analysis suggests he may be correct in asserting the value of such a return.

• WILKINS, BURLEIGH TAYLOR, *The Problem of Burke's Political Philosophy* (Oxford, 1967). The question of whether Burke should be interpreted as a natural law theorist or whether his outlook was essentially utilitarian is considered by the author *the* problem of Burke's political philosophy. Wilkins concedes that Burke used the vocabulary of utility ("utility," "expediency," "convenience") more frequently than the vocabulary of natural law ("justice," "equity," "law of nature," "natural right"), and that this was particularly the case at the height of his political and parliamentary career. Yet, looking at the whole context of Burke's thought, Wilkins writes: "Given Burke's organic conception of society, his traditionalism, his doctrine of virtual representation, and his ethical and religious beliefs, the resemblances between Burke and the utilitarians appear ultimately superficial" (p. 15). Conceding the many difficulties in interpreting Burke as a champion of natural law, Wilkins' position is a "qualified yes" (p. 88). Burke thought, the author concludes, that natural rights included the rights to life, liberty, and property, but not political rights, such as popular suffrage: "What this adds up to is that Burke's political philosophy was a conservative version of the natural law and not a denial of the natural law in the name of either history or utility" (p. 252).

III. NINETEENTH AND TWENTIETH CENTURIES

CHAPTER TWENTY-FIVE

BENTHAM

• BAUMGARDT, DAVID, *Bentham and the Ethics of Today: With Bentham Manuscripts Hitherto Unpublished* (Princeton, 1952). The author of this detailed analysis is, on the whole, sympathetic to Bentham's ethic, without uncritically accepting it as the last word on the subject. With respect to the common charge of egoism, Baumgardt writes: "Bentham's utilitarianism can in no way be considered a philosophy of egoism. On the contrary, it is the most consistent philosophy of altruism, provided that three critical limitations are not lost sight of. First, the disinterestedness of an action does not exclude all self-regarding interest of the same action. Second, it ought to be acknowledged that self-preference is, in the total life of nature, a far more necessary motive than disinterestedness. Third, neither the motive of self-regard nor that of disinterestedness is, ethically speaking, good or bad taken by itself; and it is in no wise lamentable that extra-regarding interests are much rarer than self-regarding ones" (p. 419).

• BENTHAM, JEREMY, *An Introduction to the Principles of Morals and Legislation* edited by J. H. Burns and H. L. A. Hart with a new introduction by F. Rosen (Oxford, 1996). Rosen's introduction is essential for further Bentham scholarship, as is Rosen's "Further Reading" section. Students of Bentham will want this particular edition of *An Introduction.*

• ———, *Bentham's Political Thought* (ed. Bhikhu Parekh, London, 1974). Includes previously unpublished or relatively inaccessible selections.

• BORALEVI, LEA, *Bentham and the Oppressed* (Berlin, 1984). Contains otherwise difficult to obtain writings of Bentham's on various subjects, such as his views on homosexuality.

• BURNS, J. H., "Bentham and the French Revolution," *Transactions of the Royal Historical Society,* Fifth Series, XVI (1966), pp. 95–114. Commentators on Bentham have frequently argued that his eventual conversion to radical democracy was, to some extent at least, caused by the French Revolution. Burns convincingly disproves this thesis. Although Bentham welcomed the French Revolution at an early stage, he became disenchanted with it within a few years, mainly on account of its revolutionary metaphysic and excessive fanaticism. "Radical as he might become," the author writes of Bentham, "in his advocacy of reform, utility as he understood it always drove a wedge between rational improvement and revolutionary Utopianism (p. 112).

• CRIMMINS, JAMES, "Bentham on Religion: Atheism and the Secular Society," *Journal of the History of Ideas* (January–March 1986). Demonstrates the extent to which Bentham intended a utilitarian society to be strictly secular, and his anti-religious feelings.

• ———, *Secular Utilitarianism: Social Science and the Critique of Religion in the Thought of Jeremy Bentham* (New York, 1990). Crimmins provides a compelling and original argument showing the importance of religion in Bentham's philosophy. His clear and insightful discussion of the suppression of Bentham's thoughts on religion by those who edited his work after his death is convincing and authoritative.

• DICEY, A. V., *Law and Public Opinion in England during the Nineteenth Century,* 2nd ed. (London, 1914). Lecture VI (pp. 126–210) is "The Period of Benthamism or Individualism" (1825–1870), and Lecture

IX (pp. 303–310), "The Debt of Collectivism to Benthamism." Dicey says that the debt of democratic socialism to Benthamism is three-fold: a legislative dogma—the principle of utility; a legislative instrument—the active use of parliamentary sovereignty; and a legislative tendency—the constant extension and improvement of the mechanism of government.

• DINWIDDY, JOHN, *Bentham* (Oxford, 1989). Accessible recent brief life and thought of Bentham. Part of the "Past Masters" series. Dinwiddy states that "Bentham had more influence than any other social theorist on the growth of government responsibility in the middle decades of the [nineteenth] century" (p. 118).

• EVERETT, CHARLES W., *Jeremy Bentham* (London, 1966). The author presents the essentials of Bentham's life and thought as well as his influence on social policy in many countries. In an earlier study, *The Education of Jeremy Bentham* (New York, 1931), Everett concentrated on Bentham's formative years, up to the publication of his *Principles of Morals and Legislation* in 1789.

• HALÉVY, ELIE, *The Growth of Philosophic Radicalism* (trans. Mary Morris, London, 1928). This is the most illuminating account of the Utilitarians, centered on Bentham. The author, the leading French authority on nineteenth-century England, has the advantage of looking at Utilitarianism from a broad European viewpoint, and he stresses the influence of French thought on Bentham, particularly in his youth. The volume contains a detailed bibliography of works by, and on, Bentham, compiled by C. W. Everett (pp. 522–546).

• HARRISON, ROSS, *Bentham* (London, 1983). A major recent philosophic work on Bentham.

• HART, H. L. A., "Bentham," *Proceedings of the British Academy, 1962*, XLVIII (London, 1963), pp. 297–320. In commenting on one of Bentham's most characteristic aspects of his thought, "the extraordinary combination in Bentham of a fly's-eye view of practical detail with boldness or even rashness in generalization," the author writes that Bentham "thought the criticism of existing institutions unaccompanied by demonstrably practical alternatives was worthless; and he believed this not only because criticism, like everything else, was to be judged by its Utility, but because hatred of anarchy and disorder was as strong a passion with him as hatred of blind custom and conservatism" (p. 301). The author also stresses Bentham's critique of language as one of his most outstanding and original contributions to philosophy and social thought, for its purpose "was no less than that of making men conscious of the seeds of deception and confusion buried in the very texture of human thought, and so to arm them against those who would use deception and confusion to cheat them of their happiness" (p. 311).

• ————, *Essays on Bentham* (Oxford, 1982). A collection of essays on Bentham by one who knew his thought well, and who was a leading legal scholar.

• HUME, L. J., *Bentham and Bureaucracy* (New York, 1982). A presentation of Bentham's views on the management and organization of government, with particular attention to the development of his thought on these matters.

• LETWIN, SHIRLEY ROBIN, *The Pursuit of Certainty: David Hume, Jeremy Bentham, John Stuart Mill, Beatrice Webb* (Cambridge, 1965). Part II (pp. 127–188) is on "Jeremy Bentham: Liberty and Logic." The author notes that the "moral foundation of Bentham's system was not the principle of utility but his conviction that to deny a normal adult the right to determine his own life was to treat him as a child and to derogate from his dignity as a rational being" (p. 138). Yet the author feels that Bentham failed in his supreme objective of turning political analysis and practical politics into an exact science, of replacing "practical wisdom with a technique" (p. 187).

• LONG, DOUGLAS, *Bentham on Liberty* (Toronto, 1977). A study in the development of Bentham's political views between the 1770s and first decade of the 1800s.

• MACK, MARY P., *Jeremy Bentham: An Odyssey of Ideas, 1748–1792* (New York, 1963). Using many of his unpublished manuscripts and notes, the author enthusiastically admires Bentham as a man and as a thinker. She particularly stresses the innovative genius of Bentham's philosophy and politics.

• MANNING, D. J., *The Mind of Jeremy Bentham* (New York, 1968). An unsympathetic account of Bentham in which his emphasis on rationality becomes tyrannical in creating a society of atomized individuals.

• MILL, JOHN STUART, "Bentham," in *Dissertations and Discussions* (New York, 1882), I, pp. 355–417, reprinted in F. R. Leavis (ed.), *Mill on Bentham and Coleridge* (Cambridge, Eng., 1980). Mill's testimony is particularly valuable, as he knew Bentham personally from early childhood, his father, James Mill, being one of Bentham's closest collaborators and disciples. Mill sees in Bentham, above all, "the great questioner of things established," who broke the yoke of authority by forcing every opinion received on tradition to give an account of itself: "Who, before Bentham (whatever controversies might exist on points of detail), dared to speak disrespectfully, in express terms, of the British Constitution or the English law?" (p. 357). Mill's main criticism of Bentham is want of imagination and failure to appreciate the role of feeling in human conduct: "Knowing so little of human feelings, he knew still less of the influences by which those feelings are formed: all the more subtle workings both of the mind upon itself, and of external things upon the mind, escaped him; and no one, probably, who, in a highly instructed age, ever attempted to give a rule to all human conduct, set out with a more limited conception either of the agencies by which human conduct *is,* or of those by which it *should* be, influenced" (p. 380). In his *Autobiography,* Mill discusses his views of Bentham and Benthamism in numerous passages.

• OGDEN, C. K., *Bentham's Theory of Fictions* (London–New York, 1932). Bentham is one of the founders of semantics, and his work is of direct relevance to the student of politics. The first part consists of Ogden's introduction (pp. ix–clii), the second is a collection of passages from Bentham's writings bearing on semantic problems (pp. 7–150). Ogden's introduction to his edition of Bentham's *Theory of Legislation* (London, 1931) succinctly summarizes the major points of Bentham's political thought (pp. ix–li). See also Ogden's *Jeremy Bentham: 1832–2032* (London, 1932), containing the Bentham Centenary Lecture, delivered at University College, London, on June 6, 1932, as well as ten appendixes on various topics, including Bentham's views on the United States (pp. 88–93). Despite

its brevity, Ogden's *Jeremy Bentham: 1832–2032* is one of the most brilliant appraisals of Bentham.

• PAREKH, BHIKHU, (ed.), *Jeremy Bentham: Ten Critical Essays* (London, 1974). Reactions to Bentham over time, including some nineteenth century essays.

• PLAMENATZ, JOHN, *The English Utilitarians* (London, 1949). Chap. IV (pp. 59–84) of this thoughtful study, valuable both for its philosophical and historical observations, is on Bentham. See also William L. Davidson, *Political Thought in England: The Utilitarians from Bentham to J. S. Mill* (Home University Library, London, 1935) and Ernest Albee, *A History of English Utilitarianism* (reprinted New York, 1962).

• POSTEMA, GERALD J., *Bentham and the Common Law Tradition* (Oxford, 1986). Significant work philosophically interpreting the debate between Bentham and classical Common Law theory emphasizing the writings of Sir Matthew Hale and Hume.

• ROSEN, FREDERICK, *Jeremy Bentham and Representative Democracy* (Oxford, 1983). Rosen is one of the leading scholars on Bentham in the world today, and general editor of the new collected works. In this incisive book, he traces the development of Bentham's views on democratic government, and indicates to just what an extent Bentham was ahead of his time.

• STEPHEN, LESLIE, *The English Utilitarians,* 3 vols. (London, 1900, reprinted, 1950). The first volume of this standard work is on Bentham. A "Note on Bentham's Writings" (pp. 319–326) gives a concise account of Bentham's literary career. The second volume of the *Utilitarians* is on James Mill, the third on John Stuart Mill.

• WILLEY, BASIL, *Nineteenth Century Studies* (London, 1949). Chap. V (pp. 132–140) deals with some aspects of Bentham's ethical and religious views. For different interpretations, See J. M. Robertson, *A History of Freethought in the Nineteenth Century* (London, 1929), pp. 86 ff., 200 ff., and Alfred William Benn, *The History of English Rationalism in the Nineteenth Century* (London–New York, 1906), I, pp. 285–325.

• WILLIAMSON, CHILTON, "Bentham Looks at America," *Political Science Quarterly,* LXX (December 1955), pp. 543–551. Contains interesting data on Bentham's relations with distinguished Americans, and illustrates his intense interest in, and admiration for, the American democratic system of government. See also D. P. Crook, "The United States in Bentham's Thought," *Australian Journal of Politics and History,* X (August 1964), pp. 196–204.

CHAPTER TWENTY-SIX

TOCQUEVILLE

• BOESCHE, ROGER, *The Strange Liberalism of Alexis de Tocqueville* (Ithaca, N.Y., 1987). Boesche attempts to place Tocqueville in the political ideologies of his time. Boesche argues that Tocqueville's conceptions do not fit neatly into twentieth century political frameworks. Contains an extensive bibliography.

• DRESCHER, SEYMOUR, *Tocqueville and England* (Cambridge, Mass., 1964). Since Tocqueville's fame is so closely connected with his *Democracy in America,* his personal, political, and literary ties with England have often received less than their due attention. Drescher's work fills an important gap in the literature on Tocqueville; it analyzes the influence of English ideas and institutions on Tocqueville's thought, follows him on his trips to England where he met with leading politicians and writers, and finally points to his influence on England, his "second country," as he called it. An excellent bibliography of works by, and on, Tocqueville is included (pp. 231–254).

• EISENSTADT, ABRAHAM (ed.), *Reconsidering Tocqueville's* Democracy in America (New Brunswick, N.J., 1988). A collection of essays by prominent authors and scholars.

• GARGAN, EDWARD T., *De Tocqueville* (London, 1965). This short essay of less than one hundred pages focuses on Tocqueville's main concern: the future of freedom in Western civilization. Tocqueville felt that the spread of democratic revolutions was inevitable, and the experience of England and the United States confirmed his hope that such revolutions "could lead to open rather than to closed societies" (p. 83). He had more doubts about the future of France and the rest of the Continent, but

these doubts did not turn him into a pessimist: "He learned throughout his life to live with both despair and hope and he did not reject an existence that included this condition" (pp. 83–84). See also Gargan's *Alexis de Tocqueville: The Critical Years, 1848–1851* (Washington, D.C., 1955), and "The Formation of Tocqueville's Historical Thought," *Review of Politics,* XXIV (January 1962), pp. 48–61.

• HARDARI, SAGUIV, A., *Theory in Practice: Tocqueville's New Science of Politics* (Stanford, 1989). Hardari presents a complex and detailed analysis of Tocqueville's methodology. This discussion requires significant understanding both of Tocqueville's works and contemporary theories in social science methodology.

• HERETH, MICHAEL, *Alexis de Tocqueville: Threats to Freedom in Democracy* (trans. George Bogardus, Durham, N.C., 1986). An attempt to make Tocqueville relevant to contemporary political issues. This book includes sections on Tocqueville's practical political career and his views on Algeria, as well as a discussion of the type of free republic he favored.

• HERR, RICHARD, *Tocqueville and the Old Regime* (Princeton, 1962). Focuses on Tocqueville's last major work, *The Old Regime and the French Revolution,* published three years before his death. While *The Old Regime* galvanized French thinking about France's past, showing that administrative centralism was not the product of the French Revolution but a legacy from the old regime of absolute monarchy, it is also of great interest to the student of political thought beyond the French frame of reference. Throughout his study, Herr relates *The Old*

Regime to Tocqueville's primary concern with the problem of liberty, particularly as exemplified by the different experience of France on the one hand and of England and the United States on the other. Despite their different settings, *Democracy in America* and *The Old Regime* deal, according to Herr, with the same problem: that without the guarantee of liberty, democracy could lead to despotism: "*Democracy in America* describes the danger of the tyranny acting through an uncontrolled political assembly. *Old Regime* is a response to the Caesarian democracy of the Second Empire. Events since Tocqueville's day have taught us that an unscrupulous minority can use either type of democratic tyranny to subvert a free people" (p. 127).

• HOROWITZ, MORTON J., "Tocqueville and the Tyranny of the Majority," *Review of Politics*, XXVIII (July 1966), pp. 293–307. The author, following Bryce, Laski, and others, suggests that *Democracy in America* can be understood only if one keeps in mind that Toequeville had two objectives in his book, intended primarily for Frenchmen: to describe and analyze the United States and at the same time to instruct and warn his own countrymen. Regarding the problem of the tyranny of the majority, the author argues that, when Tocqueville spoke of the potential political tyranny of the majority, he was thinking of France, in which political liberty was constantly under attack; however, when Tocqueville speaks of the potential tyranny of society and public opinion over the individual, the author holds, he was thinking of the United States. See also J. P. Mayer, "Tocqueville as a Political Sociologist," Political Studies, I (June 1953), pp. 132–142, in which the author states that *Democracy in America* is "the greatest contribution from political sociology in the nineteenth century or in our own time towards an interpretation of our civilization," which Mayer calls "the new society of the mass age" (p. 137).

• KORITANSKY, JOHN, *Alexis de Tocqueville and New Science of Politics* (Durham, N.C., 1986). An interpretive commentary on *Democracy in America*.

• LASKI, HAROLD J., "Alexis de Tocqueville and Democracy," in F. J. C. Hearnshaw (ed.), *The Social and Political Ideas of Some Representative Thinkers of the Victorian Age*

(London, 1933), Chap. V (pp. 100–115). Emphasizes Tocqueville as a precursor of Marx: "However different their ways of expression, however antagonistic the purposes they served, Toequeville would, I suspect, have subscribed to a good deal of what we call the Marxian interpretation of history. Many of his conclusions bear a striking resemblance to those of *The Communist Manifesto;* with, of course, the important difference that what for Marx represented victory for Tocqueville represented defeat" (pp. 113–114).

• LAWLER, PETER A., *The Restless Mind: Alexis de Tocqueville on the Origin and Perpetuation of Human Liberty* (Lanham, 1993). This Straussian reading of Tocqueville is interesting and thoughtful, but suffers from ignoring too much of Tocqueville's work in order to claim far too much from a limited text.

• LEROY, MAXIME, "Alexis de Tocqueville," *Politica*, I (August 1935), pp. 393–424, reprinted in William Ebenstein, *Political Thought in Perspective* (New York, 1957), pp. 472–500. One of the most trenchant critical analyses of Tocqueville's political ideas. On his liberalism, the author writes as follows: "What kind of liberal was he? He regarded himself as being one according to a particular and original fashion. He was mistaken in this point; for he was one in the conservative spirit as were a number of his liberal friends. Tocqueville does not say liberty without understanding by it liberty and property" (p. 401). Concerning Tocqueville's faith in free associations as a counterweight to the power of the state, Leroy says that they have, like business and labor organizations, developed a concentration of interest and power that may become a threat to individual liberty: "It is no longer the isolated individual, thinking in isolation, according to Tocqueville's wish, who affects society, but coalitions born of democracy. But do not these groups destroy it?" (p. 408). A forceful restatement of some of Tocqueville's main arguments will be found in Bertrand de Jouvenel, *On Power* (New York, 1949).

• MANET, PIERRE, *Tocqueville and the Nature of Democracry* (Lanham, 1996). This impressive work is a thorough and comprehensive treatment of Tocqueville's political philosophy. Manet covers such subjects as Tocqueville's liberalism, his thoughts on the future of political freedom, and Tocqueville's conception of the "Nature of Democracy." This work is an excellent resource for scholars.

• MATHEW, DAVID, *Acton: The Formative Years* (London, 1946). Chap. VI (pp. 86–98) analyzes the profound influence of Tocqueville on Lord Acton, one of the great liberal thinkers of the nineteenth century.

• MAYER, J. P., *Alexis de Tocqueville: A Biographical Essay in Political Science* (Harper Torchbooks, New York, 1960). Originally published in 1939, this edition has an added essay on "Tocqueville after a Century" (pp. 117–129). See also William J. Schlaerth (ed.), *Alexis de Tocqueville's Democracy in America: A Symposium* (Fordham University Studies, Burke Society Series, No. 1, New York, 1945).

• MITCHELL, JOSHUA, *The Fragility of Freedom: Tocqueville on Religion, Democracy, and the American Future* (Chicago, 1995). Mitchell attempts to reread Tocqueville as political theology in the tradition of Augustine. His argument is not compelling, but it may be useful to those who seek to explore Christian theology within the realm of political theory.

• PIERSON, GEORGE WILSON, *Tocqueville and Beaumont in America* (New York, 1938). The definitive work on the subject. The first eight parts of the book tell the story of Tocqueville's experiences in the United States. Part IX gives a summary of how *Democracy in America* was written, and also analyzes its defects and enduring qualities (pp. 681–777). A detailed bibliography is appended (pp. 825–833). There is an abridged version, *Tocqueville in America* (Anchor Books, New York, 1959).

• POPE, WHITNEY, *Alexis de Tocqueville: His Social and Political Theory* (Beverly Hills, Calif., 1986). A sociological interpretation of Tocqueville. Includes a section comparing him to Marx and Durkheim.

• PROBST, GEORGE E. (ed.), *The Happy Republic: A Reader in Tocqueville's America* (Harper Torchbooks, New York, 1962). Tocqueville's America, as reflected in the writings, essays, and speeches of contemporary Americans and foreign visitors. The readings are organized in line with Tocqueville's major themes in *Democracy in America.*

• SCHAPIRO, J. SALWYN, *Liberalism and the Challenge of Fascism: Social Forces in England and France (1815–1870)* (New York, 1949). In his discussion of "Alexis de Tocqueville, Pioneer of Democratic Liberalism in France" (pp. 290–307), the author concludes that Tocqueville was "an example of the tragedy of French liberalism, which since the French Revolution has waged unceasing war on two fronts: against reaction on the right and against revolution on the left" (p. 306). See also Guido de Ruggiero, *The History of European Liberalism* (Beacon Paperbacks, Boston, 1959), pp. 187–198, who calls Tocqueville "perhaps the greatest French writer of the nineteenth century" (p. 187), and James Bryce, *Studies in History and Jurisprudence* (Oxford, 1901), I, pp. 381–429, who describes *Democracy in America* as "one of the few treatises on the philosophy of politics which has risen to the rank of a classic" (p. 381).

• SCHLEIFER, JAMES, *The Making of Tocqueville's Democracy in America* (Chapel Hill, N.C., 1980). The definitive work on the composition of *Democracy in America,* which composition included much scholarly research as well as observation.

• TOCQUEVILLE, ALEXIS DE, *Democracy in America* (edited by J. P. Mayer and Max Lerner, with a new translation by George Lawrence, New York, 1966). This is the first new translation of *Democracy in America* since the translation by Henry Reeve (Vol. I in 1835 and Vol. II in 1840). It is prefaced by an introductory essay by Mayer on the reception and reputation of *Democracy in America* in Europe and by Lerner's essay on "Tocqueville and America" (pp. xi–lxxxiii). Seven Appendices containing a variety of materials related to *Democracy in America* further enhance the value of this edition. The Reeve translation is available in several editions, the best of which is *Democracy in America* (ed. Phillips Bradley, Vintage Books, New York, 1954). See also the following works of Tocqueville: *Recollections* (New York, 1949); *The Old Regime and the French Revolution* (Anchor Books, New York, 1955); *Journeys to England and Ireland* (New Haven, 1958); *The European Revolution and Correspondence with Gobineau* (Anchor Books, New York, 1959); and *Journey to America* (New York, 1971), a compilation of the notebooks Tocqueville kept during his journey through the United States and Canada.

• ZETTERBAUM, MARVIN, *Tocqueville and the Problem of Democracy* (Stanford, 1967). The author's thesis is that Tocqueville's central concern about democracy was how to reconcile demands of justice with those of excellence. Tocqueville's solution— "self-interest rightly understood" (p. 157)— does not solve the problem, Zetterbaum holds, because Tocqueville himself admitted that the majority of mankind is unable to attain the kind of "rational and independent conviction which true knowledge can produce out of the midst of doubt" *(ibid.).* The author therefore concludes that the core of

Tocqueville's teaching about democracy "is hardly hopeful" (p. 159). The main elements of Zetterbaum's thesis are briefly summarized in his article, "Tocqueville: Neutrality and the Use of History," *American Political Science Review,* LVIII (September 1964), pp. 611–621. For a fuller, and more balanced, treatment of Tocqueville's views on democracy, see Jack Lively, *The Social and Political Thought of Alexis de Tocqueville* (Oxford–New York, 1962), and Isaiah Berlin, "The Thought of De Tocqueville," *History* (June 1965), pp. 199–206.

CHAPTER TWENTY-SEVEN

MILL

• ANSCHUTZ, R. P., *The Philosophy of J. S. Mill* (Oxford, 1969). A brief review of Mill's thought, including several chapters on philosophical subjects.
• BAIN, ALEXANDER, *John Stuart Mill: A Criticism, with Personal Recollections* (London, 1882). A biography of Mill by one of his closest associates.
• BERGER, FRED, *Happiness, Justice, and Freedom; The Moral and Political Philosophy of John Stuart Mill* (Berkeley, 1984). Berger presents the view that Mill's theories are more consistent, and stronger, than often is thought.
• BERLIN, ISAIAH, *Four Essays on Liberty* (London, 1969). The fourth essay is "John Stuart Mill and the Ends of Life."
• BOUTON, CLARK W., "John Stuart Mill: On Liberty and History," *Western Political Quarterly,* XVIII (September 1965), pp. 569–578. The author argues that *On Liberty* "does not reveal a doctrinaire liberalism, but a teaching related to a certain historical situation and meant to be limited to certain conditions" (p. 574). Specifically, Bouton holds, the principles of *On Liberty* were meant by Mill to apply to the more advanced Western societies in Mill's own time, and

not to non-Western societies living in very different circumstances. Mill recognized that throughout history it was often necessary to curtail free speech and other basic freedoms, but "he was also able to envisage a future" (p. 576) in which such restrictions would no longer be necessary. Liberty for Mill, the author concludes, was not an ultimate abstract principle, but the highest principle on the basis of its utility, in relation to humanity's general improvement and progress.
• BRITTON, KARL, *John Stuart Mill* (Periguin Books, Baltimore, 1953). Presents the life of Mill and the main aspects of his logic, ethics, and political thought. See also Ruth Borchard, *John Stuart Mill: The Man* (London, 1957) and John C. Rees, *Mill and His Early Critics* (Leicester, 1956).
• BURNS, J. H., "J. S. Mill and Democracy, 1829–1861," *Political Studies,* V (June 1957), pp. 158–175, and (October 1957), pp. 281–294. A detailed analysis of Mill's views on democracy and representative government from 1829, when he began to depart from some orthodoxies of Philosophical Radicalism, to 1861, when he published *Considerations on Representative Government,* his most

systematic work on representative government. Other students of Mill have noticed that in his *Considerations on Representative Government* his fear of majority tyranny induced him to embrace ideas about voting and representation which are contrary to democratic principles as commonly understood and also contrary to his own earlier writings. Burns goes further and arrives at the provocative conclusion that a "consistent viewpoint unites Mill's political thought from start to finish; but it is not, in the strict sense he would himself have adopted, the viewpoint of a democrat" (p. 294). Even those who will not be entirely persuaded by the author's reasoning and interpretation of Mill's views on democracy will at least find ample material to ponder over regarding some basic differences between liberalism and democracy.

• CARR, ROBERT, "The Religious Thought of John Stuart Mill: A Study in Reluctant Scepticism," *Journal of the History of Ideas,* XXIII (October–December 1962), pp. 475–495. The author shows the development of Mill's religious views from his early years to his old age. The main source of Mill's difficulties derived from the relation of logic to morality, since he felt that "religion, if not intellectually sustainable, might nevertheless be morally useful" (p. 488). Mill feared anarchy more than rationally unprovable religious beliefs, and "good Victorian that he was, he longed for Christian ethics without Christian supernaturalism, but he feared he could not have the situation both ways" (p. 495). Carr's essay throws as much light on Mill the man as on Mill the thinker.

• COWLING, MAURICE, *Mill and Liberalism* (Cambridge, 1963). One of the most vehement criticisms of Mill in English. Cowling considers Mill "considerably less libertarian than is sometimes suggested," and he even goes so far as to charge him with "more than a touch of something resembling moral totalitarianism" (p. xii). *On Liberty,* Cowling states, "was not so much a plea for individual freedom, as a means of ensuring that Christianity would be superseded by that form of liberal, rationalistic utilitarianism which went by the name of the Religion of Humanity," and "Mill, no less than Marx, Nietzsche or Comte, claimed to replace Christianity by 'something better'" (p. xiii). The purpose of *On Liberty,* according to Cowling, was not

to offer safeguards for individuality, but to "propagate the individuality of the elevated by protecting *them* against the mediocrity of opinion as a whole" (p. 104). Mill's hostility to moral, philosophical, and religious dogmas does not necessarily prove his own avoidance of dogma, the author asserts, for there are "liberal dogmas as well as Christian ones, and Mill gives expression to them" (p. 114). For a rebuttal of Cowling's interpretation of Mill, see John Rees, "Was Mill for Liberty?" *Political Studies,* XIV (February 1966), pp. 72–77.

• CRANSTON, MAURICE, *John Stuart Mill* (Great Britain, 1958). An excellent introductory essay on Mill. See also Cranston's "J. S. Mill as a Political Philosopher," *Journal of the History of Ideas* (1958).

• EBENSTEIN, LANNY (ALAN), "Mill's Theory of Utility," *Philosophy* (October 1985), pp. 539–543. Presents the view that Mill's famous "quality–quantity" distinction is akin to the components of value in pleasures and pains that Bentham designates "intensity" and "duration."

• EBENSTEIN, WILLIAM, "John Stuart Mill: Democrat, Liberal, Socialism?," *Il Politico* (1974). Comments on the prescience of Mill on many political topics. Also see William Ebenstein, "John Stuart Mill: Political and Economic Liberty," in Carl J. Friedrich (ed.), *Liberty Nomos* IV, Yearbook of the American Society for Political and Legal Philosophy, (New York, 1962), pp. 89–109, where he concludes: "Mill always tried to reconcile his emotional preference for the negative conception of liberty (liberalism) with his intellectual acceptance of the positive conception of liberty (democracy). . . . Mill's ultimate and decisive commitment was to the more difficult ideal of liberalism than to the more appealing ideal of democracy. This is true of his concern with both political and economic liberty" (p. 109).

• GRAY, JOHN, *Mill on Liberty: A Defence* (London, 1983). Argues that Mill's principles of utility and liberty are consistent.

• HALLIDAY, R. J., *John Stuart Mill* (London, 1976). An introductory work. Halliday sees Mill as a pessimistic eclectic in his political thought.

• HAMBURGER, JOSEPH, *Intellectuals in Politics: John Stuart Mill and the Philosophic Radicals* (New Haven, 1965). The author starts from the premise that the Philosophical Radicals were, and considered themselves, both philosophers and politicians. Whereas most studies concentrate on their ideas, the author is primarily concerned with their political activities in and out of Parliament. However, the analysis of the political activities of the Philosophical Radicals also leads to a better understanding of their ideas. The author concludes that the Philosophical Radicals "did not hold abstract theories that discredited all the values and beliefs that upheld the established society, nor were they disposed to use philosophy as a means of justifying a new despotism; and their sectarian attitudes never brought them near to an affiliation with an organization that could even potentially have become a mass movement. Whereas other ideologies dreamed of benevolent despotism that would demand conformity to what they were sure was the fundamental order of reality, the Philosophic Radicals were doctrinaire politicians whose faith was revealed in nothing worse than dogmatism" (p. 295).

• HIMMELFARB, GERTRUDE, *On Liberty and Liberalism: The Strange Case of John Stuart Mill* (New York, 1974). Himmelfarb's thesis is that Mill's greatest work, *On Liberty,* is consistent with the rest of his work. Himmelfarb stresses the role of Harriet Taylor.

• MCCLOSKEY, H. J., *John Stuart Mill: A Critical Study* (Great Britain, 1971). Part of the "Philosophers in Perspective" series.

• MILL, JOHN STUART, "De Tocqueville on Democracy in America," *London Review,* XXVI (July 1835–January 1836), pp. 85–129, and *Edinburgh Review,* LXXII (October 1840–January 1841), pp. 1–47. In these reviews of the first and second volumes of *Democracy in America,* Mill came out enthusiastically for Tocqueville, comparing him to Montesquieu among French writers. The personal and intellectual relations between Mill and Tocqueville, an important chapter in the development of nineteenth-century European liberalism, still need to be fully explored. See T. H. Qualter, "John Stuart Mill, Disciple of De Tocqueville," *Western Political Quarterly,* XIII (December 1960), pp. 880–889, and H. O. Pappe, "Mill and Tocqueville," *Journal of the History of Ideas,* XXV (April–June 1964), pp. 217–234.

• MILLER, KENNETH E., "John Stuart Mill's Theory of International Relations," *Journal of the History of Ideas,* XXII (October–December 1961), pp. 493–514. The author discusses both Mill's thinking about world politics in general—a much neglected aspect of studies about Mill—as well as his ideas about major specific aspects of international relations. In Miller's view, John Stuart Mill was more realistic about problems of world politics than Bentham, Cobden, and most other liberals of the time. In particular, Mill's focus of emphasis was less on economics and more on national security, and he was less guided by abstract concepts such as the harmony of mankind. The author suggests that Mill's experience in the India Office provided him with a sense of realism and historical complexity in international relations that other liberals lacked.

• PACKE, MICHAEL ST. JOHN, *The Life of John Stuart Mill* (New York, 1954). The first full-length biography of Mill, utilizing important new sources previously inaccessible. His relation with Harriet Taylor, so crucial for Mill's personal and intellectual development, is analyzed in detail. See also F. A. Hayek, *John Stuart Mill and Harriet Taylor: Their Friendship and Subsequent Marriage* (Chicago, 1951). A contrary view of Harriet Taylor's influence on Mill will be found in H. O. Pappe, *John Stuart Mill and the Harriet Taylor Myth* (Parkville, Victoria, 1960).

• PLAMENATZ, JOHN, *The English Utilitarians,* 2nd ed. (Oxford, 1958). Chap. VIII (pp. 122–144) is on Mill.

• ROBBINS, LIONEL, *The Theory of Economic Policy in English Classical Political Economy* (London, 1952). Lecture V is on "The Classical Economists and Socialism: John Stuart Mill" (pp. 142–168).

• ROBSON, JOHN, *The Improvement of Mankind; The Social and Political Thought of John Stuart Mill* (Toronto, 1968). An outstanding work on Mill's comprehensive thought and its development by the editor of the masterful collected works of Mill published by the University of Toronto Press. Highly recommended.

• RUSSELL, BERTRAND, "John Stuart Mill," *Proceedings of the British Academy, 1955,* XLI (1956), 43–59. Russell does not consider Mill a great philosopher, like Descartes or Hume. Yet, "his influence was very great and very beneficent. He made rationalism and socialism respectable, though his socialism was of the pre-Marxist sort which did not involve an increase in the powers of the State. His advocacy of equality for women in the end won almost worldwide acceptance. His book *On Liberty* remains a classic: although it is easy to point out theoretical defects, its value increases as the world travels further and further from its teaching" (pp. 58–59).

• RYAN, ALAN, *J. S. Mill* (London, 1974). A book-by-book study of Mill's thought. For a more integrated approach, see Ryan's *The Philosophy of John Stuart Mill,* 2nd ed. (London, 1987).

• SCHNEEWIND, J. B. (ed.), *Mill: A Collection of Critical Essays* (Garden City, N.Y., 1968). A collection of essays on various subjects. See in particular that by J. O. Urmson, "The Interpretation of the Moral Philosophy of J. S. Mill," for the view that Mill was a rule- as opposed to an act-utilitarian.

• SEMMEL, BERNARD, *John Stuart Mill and the Pursuit of Virtue* (New Haven, Ct., 1984). This book is as much a discussion of the issues raised by Mill as it is a description of his particular positions. Semmel sees Mill as a follower of German transcendentalist positive freedom.

• SKORUPSKI, JOHN, *John Stuart Mill* (London, 1989). Focuses on Mill as a philosopher rather than political theorist or economist. Also see Skorupski's *The Cambridge Companion to Mill* (Cambridge, 1998) for a collection of essays on Mill by various scholars, and an exceptional bibliography.

• STEPHEN, LESLIE, *The English Utilitarians,* 3 vols. (London, 1900; reprinted by the London School of Economics and Political Science, 1950). Vol. III is on John Stuart Mill.

• SULLIVAN, EILEEN, "J. S. Mill's Defense of the British Empire," *Journal of the History of Ideas* (October–December 1985). An argument in support of a role for Mill in turning nineteenth century liberalism from anti-imperialism to support for imperialism.

• TEN, C. L., *Mill on Liberty* (Oxford, 1980). A sympathetic defense of Mill's *On Liberty.*

• THOMAS, WILLIAM, *The Philosophic Radicals* (Oxford, 1979). Nine essays on Bentham's circle; this book is as much about Mill's generation as it is about Bentham's.

• TULLOCH, GAIL, *Mill and Sexual Equality* (Boulder, 1989). Tulloch is only partially successful at explicating a Mill liberal feminist theory in her treatment of several of Mill's works. Her discussion of Mill's *The Subjection of Women* is perhaps the most valuable contribution within this volume.

• WARD, JOHN WILLIAM, "Mill, Marx, and Modern Individualism," *Virginia Quarterly Review,* XXXV (Autumn 1959), pp. 527–539. The author maintains that Marx' conception of individualism is "the complete negation" of Mill's. Whereas Mill saw the reality of the tensions between the individual and the group, Marx thought that in the classless, Communist society there is "no conflict between the individual and the collectivity, because the collective will is the will of the individual, rightly understood. One is to realize his individuality by participating in the will of the group. The idea is as old as Plato, of course, and individualism becomes an ideal of belonging, not an ideal of separateness" (p. 538). Ward summarizes the fundamental difference between Marx and Mill acutely by stating that for Marx freedom was to be won at the end of the unfolding of history, whereas for Mill "the free society was to be the premise of history, not its conclusion" (p. 534). See also Bernice Shoul, "Similarities in the Work of John Stuart Mill and Karl Marx," *Science and Society,* XXIX (Summer 1965), pp. 270–295, which compares the analyses of capitalism and its long-run tendencies in Mill and Marx.

CHAPTER TWENTY-EIGHT

HEGEL

• AVINERI, SHLOMO, *Hegel's Theory of the Modern State* (London, 1972). Avineri's thesis is that Hegel has been misunderstood continually. The *Philosophy of Right* was not just an attempt to justify the Prussian Restoration of 1815, but an effort to understand a new regime that had been changed inalterably from the old by the French Revolution and Napolean's reforms. Avineri traces the development of Hegel's political thought through all of his works, not only in the *Philosophy of Right,* and also attempts to integrate Hegel's political thought within his comprehensive philosophical outlook.

• BOSANQUET, BERNARD, *The Philosophical Theory of the State,* 3rd ed. (London, 1920). The ablest defense of Hegelian political philosophy, centering its analysis on the problem of the "Real Will." Because of its moderation, Bosanquet's book will appear to British and American readers more persuasive than original Hegelianism. An even more moderate expression of Hegelianism, considerably transmuted into, and adapted to, British liberal thought, will be found in Thomas Hill Green, *Principles of Political Obligation,* new imp. (London–New York, 1917).

• CARRITT, E. F., *Morals and Politics* (London, 1935). Chap. IX (pp. 105–127) deals with the moral foundations of Hegel's political thought, especially his approach to the problem of political obligation. For a discussion of the two chief exponents of Hegelian political philosophy in England, Green and Bosanquet, see pp. 128–157. John H. Muirhead, *The Platonic Tradition in Anglo-Saxon Philosophy* (London–New York, 1931), provides a brief account of Hegelian influences in England and America (pp. 147–218, pp. 315–323).

• COLLETTI, LUCIO, *Marxism and Hegel* (trans. Lawrence Garner, London, 1973). A

philosophic investigation into the theoretical relationship between Hegel and Marxism, from a Marxian perspective. More attention is paid to Hegel than Marx, as this book is only one part of the larger Italian work of the same title.

• CULLEN, BERNARD, *Hegel's Social and Political Thought* (London, 1979). A brief introductory book for those who are approaching Hegel for the first time. Cullen attempts to explain Hegel's social and political thought without simplifying it.

• DEWEY, JOHN, *German Philosophy and Politics* (New York, 1915). In his discussion of Hegel's political philosophy (pp. 107–120), Dewey emphasizes the elements of nationalism and militarism. See also George Santayana, *Egotism in German Philosophy,* new ed. (London, 1939), Chap. VIII (pp. 70–83). Santayana calls the servility of Hegel's moral philosophy "simply an apology for the established order of things and for the prejudices of his time and country" (p. 73). Hegel's philosophy sets up an "idol that feeds on blood, the Absolute State" (p. 83). Bertrand Russell, *A History of Western Philosophy* (New York, 1945), examines in Chap. XXII (pp. 730–746) Hegel's political theory in relation to his logic and metaphysics, and arrives at the conclusion that Hegel's doctrine of the state "justifies every internal tyranny and every external aggression" (p. 742).

• DICKEY, LAURENCE, *Hegel; Religion, Economics, and the Politics of Spirit* (Cambridge, Eng., 1987). Hegel's intellectual development to the publication of the *Phenomenology* in 1806.

• EASTON, LOYD D., *Hegel's First American Followers* (Athens, Ohio, 1966). Before the middle of the nineteenth century, Hegel's ideas found little sympathetic resonance in the United States. Easton describes how a group of four Ohioans (three of whom were born and raised in Germany) spread Hegelian ideas, both philosophical and political, around the middle of the nineteenth century, and thus formed the first American nucleus of Hegelianism. In Chap. I (pp. 1–27), Easton surveys briefly American writings on Hegel in the first half of the nineteenth century. The Appendix (pp. 229–330) contains selections from the writings of the four Ohio Hegelians: Peter Kaufmann, Moncure Conway, August Willich, and John B. Stallo. Although Easton's study is suffused with a measure of Ohio patriotism, it provides many interesting sidelights on American intellectual history in the nineteenth century.

• FINDLAY, JOHN N., *Hegel: A Reexamination* (London, 1958). A systematic presentation and analysis of the major aspects of Hegel's philosophy. Concerning Hegel's political philosophy, the author argues that Hegel described the Prussian state of his time as "the final fruits of the historic development of Spirit" (p. 327), and that Hegel's narrowness of view "is shown, above all, in his carping strictures on the political arrangements of France and England, the two great creative nations of his own time" *(ibid.).* Looking at Hegel's philosophy as a whole, the author calls him "the Aristotle of our post-Renaissance world, our synoptic thinker without peer" (p. 353). Despite Hegel's "later verging towards reaction, he remains the philosopher of Reformation 'inwardness,' of liberal humanism, of perpetual orderly revolution" (p. 354). See also W. T. Stace, *The Philosophy of Hegel: A Systematic Exposition* (New York, 1955), which includes a lucid statement of Hegel's views on state and society (pp. 404–438). Like Findlay, Stace defends Hegel against the charge of being an antiliberal statist and a forerunner of totalitarianism.

• FOSTER, M. B., *The Political Philosophies of Plato and Hegel* (Oxford, 1935). The second part on Hegel is nearly as brilliant as the first on Plato (pp. 72–204).

• FRIEDRICH, CARL J., "The Power of Negation: Hegel's Dialectic and Totalitarian Ideology," in D. C. Travis (ed.), *A Hegel Symposium* (Austin, 1962), pp. 13–35. Friedrich holds that Hegel's explicit (or "substantive") conception of the state has few, if any, links with totalitarian ideology of the fascist or communist type. However,

Friedrich argues, "totalitarian and more especially Marxist Communist ideology derives its peculiar flavor and significance from Hegel's dialectic" (pp. 30–31). Explanations and interpretations of Hegel's dialectic will be found in: G. R. G. Mure, *The Philosophy of Hegel* (Home University Library, London–New York, 1965), pp. 24–40; J. O. Wisdom, "Hegel's Dialectic in Historical Philosophy," *Philosophy,* XV (July 1940), pp. 243–268; Gustav E. Mueller, "The Hegel Legend of 'Thesis-Antithesis-Synthesis'," *Journal of the History of Ideas,* XIX (June 1958), pp. 411–414; and Sidney Hook, "Hegel and the Perspective of Liberalism," in D. C. Travis (ed.), *A Hegel Symposium* (Austin, 1962), pp. 44–53.

• GASCOIGNE, ROBERT, *Religion, Rationality and Community: Sacred and Secular in the Thought of Hegel and His Critics* (The Hague, 1985). While the focus of this book is on the relationships between religious belief and humanism in Hegel, Gascoigne also has much to say on the political relevance of Hegel's ideas. Includes discussions of Bauer, Schelling, and Kierkegaard

• HOBHOUSE, L. T., *The Metaphysical Theory of the State* (London, 1918). Still one of the best critiques of Hegelian political philosophy. See especially Chap. III, "The Real Will" (pp. 44–70), and Appendix I, "Hegel's Theory of the Will" (pp. 138–149).

• HOOK, SIDNEY, "Hegel Rehabilitated?" *Encounter,* XXIV (January 1965), pp. 53–58. The author, one of the leading American philosophers of the twentieth century, defends the commonly held interpretation of Hegel as a conservative against some revisionist attempts to turn Hegel into a liberal. Hook calls Hegel a "philosophical time-server of Metternichian reaction" (p. 57). Hook also shows that Hegel was an ardent nationalist from the beginning of his career, and not just after the fall of Napoleon, as is frequently alleged. In analyzing Hegel's relation to liberalism, Hook first defines the core of liberalism: "There is a family of traits which define the liberal temper, several of which must be present before we can justifiably classify a thinker as *liberal.* Among the things we look for in a liberal thinker are recognition of the moral primacy of the individual in appraising institutional life, acceptance of a free market of *ideas,* tolerance of political opposition, appreciation of diversity, openmindedness to alternatives, endorsement of the right to self-determination, national, social and personal, including the moral right to revolution if the demand for self-determination is persistently frustrated. And, underlying all, reliance on the methods of intelligence conceived not as Reason carrying out ends of which we are not aware, but as common sense fortified by relevant scientific knowledge. Liberalism is not so much a doctrine as an attitude towards political affairs which is aware of human finitude and the tentativeness of human judgment and yet is prepared to act vigorously in moments of crisis. When it is given to religious language, it regards the ascription of Perfection or Divinity to the State (which we find in Hegel), or to any other human institution, as blasphemous" (p. 58). If this is the liberal temper, Hegel is very far from it, and for "all his invocations to Reason, Hegel distrusted the critical and sceptical spirit of the Enlightenment, its striving for clarity, its exposure of theological and philosophical humbug" *(ibid)*. See also Hook's "Hegel and His Apologists," *Encounter,* XXVI (May 1966), pp. 84–91, and "Hegel and the Perspective of Liberalism," in D. C. Travis (ed.), *A Hegel Symposium* (Austin, 1962), pp. 39–62, where Hook spells out in greater detail why and how Hegel's philosophy was "markedly hostile" to the liberalism of his own days and also to its "perennial values" (p. 53).

• KAUFMANN, WALTER, *Hegel: Reinterpretation, Texts, and Commentary* (Garden City, N.Y., 1965). A work on Hegel's comprehensive thought and its development, though of manageable proportions, arguing that the traditional view of Hegel (as presented, for example, in *Great Political Thinkers*) is incorrect.

• KAUFMANN, WALTER (ed.), *Hegel's Political Philosophy* (New York, 1970). A collection of responsive essays from different perspectives on Hegel's political thought.

• KELLY, GEORGE, *Hegel's Retreat from Eleusis* (Princeton, 1978). This book traces the development of Hegel's political theories, with reference to present-day perspectives.

• KOJEVE, ALEXANDER, *Introduction to the Reading of Hegel* (Paris, 1973). An important work especially for elucidating the relationship between Hegel and Marx.

• LÖWITH, KARL, *From Hegel to Nietzsche: The Revolution in Nineteenth-Century Thought* (New York, 1964). The relations of Hegel and Hegelianism to the main currents and figures of nineteenth-century German thought, with some consideration of non-German thinkers, such as Kierkegaard, Tocqueville, and Sorel.

• MACGREGOR, DAVID, *The Communist Ideal in Hegel and Marx* (Toronto, 1984). An important work on the relation of Marx to Hegel. MacGregor sees Hegelian logic as ideally suited to Marx's purposes.

• MACINTYRE, ALASDAIR, ed., *Hegel: A Collection of Critical Essays* (Garden City, N.Y., 1972). Includes Walter Kaufmann's response to Popper's attack on Hegel in *The Open Society and Its Enemies.*

• MARCUSE, HERBERT, *Reason and Revolution: Hegel and the Rise of Social Theory* (Beacon Paperbacks, Boston, 1960). The most vigorous attempt to present Hegel as a liberal. The author argues that the "progressive ideas of liberalism" (p. 413) in Hegel's political thought are incompatible with fascist totalitarianism, and that German nazism was "anti-Hegelian in all its aims and principles" (pp. 418–419).

• MARX, KARL, *Critique of Hegel's "Philosophy of Right,"* ed. Joseph O'Malley (Cambridge, 1970). English translation of Marx's commentary on sections 261–313 of the *Philosophy of Right,* Marx's most comprehensive treatment of Hegel (though incomplete).

• PELCZYSKI, Z. A., *Hegel's Political Writings* (trans. T. M. Knox, with an Introductory Essay by Z. A. Pelczynski, Oxford, 1964). This admirable translation of the more important political writings of Hegel is an indispensable supplement to his *Philosophy of Law,* Hegel's major work in political philosophy. Hegel's writings are preceded by Pelczynski's introductory essay (pp. 5–137). Pelczynski seeks to expound Hegel's political thought and, more importantly, to defend him against charges of authoritarianism. However, he weakens his defense of Hegel by going to extremes; thus, he states in his conclusion that Hegel belongs to the main stream of Western political theory that favors "constitutionalism, democracy, and progress" (p. 134). Similarly, Pelczynski couples Hegel and Paine in his "Hegel Again," *Encounter,* XXVI (March 1966), pp. 47–50, as two liberals, making only the slight concession that

Paine belonged to the Left of liberalism whereas Hegel belonged to its Right wing. For other studies of Hegel, defending him against charges of nationalism, militarism, and authoritarianism, and portraying him, with varying degrees of intensity, as a cosmopolitan, pacifist, liberal humanist, see Shlomo Avineri, "The Problem of War in Hegel's Thought," *Journal of the History of Ideas,* XXII (October–December 1961), pp. 463–474, and "Hegel and Nationalism," *Review of Politics,* XXIV (October 1962), pp. 461–484; and Irving Louis Horowitz, "The Hegelian Concept of Political Freedom," *Journal of Politics,* XXVIII (February 1966), pp. 3–28. Horowitz concludes his essay with the astounding statement that Hegel, "no less than John Stuart Mill, set the terms of discourse for the nineteenth century struggle between liberal and conservative ideologies" (p. 28).

• PELCZYNSKI, Z. A., ed., *Hegel's Political Philosophy: Problems and Perspectives* (Cambridge, 1971). A collection of previously unpublished essays. More for the scholar than the student.

• PLANT, RAYMOND, *Hegel* (Bloomington, Ind., 1973). Hegel's political philosophy is presented as part of his larger, more general philosophy. The focus is on Hegel's central metaphysical doctrines.

• POPPER, K. R., *The Open Society and Its Enemies* (Princeton, 1950). Chap. XII, "Hegel and the New Tribalism," (pp. 223–273) contains a pungent point-by-point demonstration of the identity of Hegelianism with "the philosophy of modern totalitarianism" (p. 272).

• RÉGNIER, MARCEL, "Hegelianism and Marxism," *Social Research,* XXXIV (Spring 1967), pp. 31–46. For a more detailed analysis, see Sidney Hook, *From Hegel to Marx: Studies in the Intellectual Development of Karl Marx* (New York, 1950).

• RIEDEL, MANFRED, *Between Tradition and Revolution; The Hegelian Transformation of Political Philosophy* (trans. Walter Wright, Cambridge, 1984). Sees Hegel as having effectuated a conceptual revolution in political philosophy. Concentrates almost exclusively on the *Philosophy of Right.*

• SMITH, STEVEN B., *Hegel's Critique of Liberalism: Rights in Context* (Chicago, 1989). This contribution by the author is broad, deep, and deserving of attention by those considering Hegelian philosophy.

• SOLOMON, ROBERT C., *From Hegel to Existentialism* (Oxford, 1987). Considers Hegel within the context of existentialist philosophers and writers such as Camus.

• TAYLOR, CHARLES, *Hegel* (Cambridge, Eng., 1975). A comprehensive work on Hegel. Part IV is "History and Politics." Also see Taylor's *Hegel and Modern Society* (Cambridge, 1979).

• TUNICK, MARK, *Hegel's Political Philosophy: Interpreting the Practice of Legal Punishment* (Princeton, 1992). This is a fairly rigid and limited exploration of Hegel's ideas on the practice of legal punishment. The work contributes to this minor subject within Hegel's thought, but barely goes beyond it.

• WILKINS, BURLEIGH, *Hegel's Philosophy of History* (Ithaca, N.Y., 1974). A philosophical examination of Hegel's conception of history within the context of his overall system. Special reference to the *Science of Logic.*

CHAPTER TWENTY-NINE

REVOLUTIONARY COMMUNISM

• APPELBAUM, RICHARD, *Karl Marx* (Newbury Park, Calif., 1988). Part of the "Masters of Social Theory" series, this book is an excellent brief introduction to Marx's thought.

• AVINERI, SHLOMO, *The Social and Political Thought of Karl Marx* (Cambridge, 1968). A brief, yet useful, introduction to Marx for students and general readers. The focus is on Marx's theory as opposed to the practice that followed from it. Avineri does not here consider Engels. See also Avineri's collection of essays on Marx by various scholars, *Marx'x Socialism* (New York, 1973).

• BECKERMAN, GERARD, *Marx and Engles; A Conceptual Concordance* (trans. Terrell Carver, Oxford, 1983). A useful reference book for Marx and Engels' definition and depiction of various topics and subjects. For a similar work, but with fewer entries, see Terrell Carver, *A Marx Dictionary* (Cambridge, Eng., 1987).

• BERLIN, ISAIAH, *Karl Marx: His Life and Environment,* 3rd ed. (New York, 1963). Since its first publication in 1939, Berlin's account has established itself as the best brief biography of Marx's life and thought, vividly portrayed against the background of the intellectual and political currents of his time. A brilliant stylist, Berlin manages to combine broad coverage and treatment in depth. Includes a bibliography (pp. 285–289). For concise studies of Marx, see also Max Beer, *The Life and Teaching of Karl Marx* (London, 1925); Harold J. Laski, *Karl Marx: An Essay* (London, 1921), and *Marx and Today* (London, 1943); Robert Conquest, *Marxism Today* (London, 1964); and H. B. Acton, *What Marx Really Said* (New York, 1967).

• BERNSTEIN, SAMUEL (ed.), *A Centenary of Marxism* (New York, 1948). Published to commemorate the centenary of the *Communist Manifesto,* this volume represents a special issue of *Science and Society,* XII (Winter 1948), a leading Marxist quarterly. The first essay is "Marx and Engels on America" (pp. 3–21).

• BOTTOMORE, TOM, et al., (eds.), *A Dictionary of Marxist Thought* (Cambridge, Mass., 1983). A useful reference book for the definition and presentation of many Marxian terms and Marxist figures. Most contributors are from the United Kingdom or continental Europe,a nd are Marxists of one sort or another.

• COLE, G. D. H., *The Meaning of Marxism* (London, 1948). An excellent introduction to Marxism, this book is not so much a summary of Marx's ideas as a revaluation of his thought in relation to contemporary social and political developments. Cole successfully simplifies some of the complexities of Marx's essential doctrines without doing violence to them. In addition, he analyzes the social changes that have taken place

since Marx, and discusses their implications for democratic socialist movements. His discussion of the new class of white-collar workers and their political psychology is particularly noteworthy.

• COLLINS, HENRY, and CHIMEN ABRAMSKY, *Karl Marx and the British Labour Movement: Years of the First International* (New York, 1965). Marx lived in England from 1849 to his death in 1883, yet his influence on its labor movement was less than on that in any other European country. This book assesses one crucial aspect of this problem: the relation of the First International to British industrial and political forces of the time. A bibliography, the most comprehensive in this area, is included.

• CORNFORTH, MAURICE, *Dialectical Materialism: An Introduction,* 3 vols. (London, 1952–1954). Written from the orthodox Marxist-communist viewpoint. The author arrives at the conclusion that pragmatism, "particularly in the form which Dewey has given it, is the philosophy of American imperialism. It expresses the outlook and aspiration of American big business in philosophical form" (p. 214).

• CROCE, BENEDETTO, *Historical Materialism and the Economics of Karl Marx* (London, 1914). A critical interpretation by the greatest Italian philosopher of the twentieth century.

• DANIELS, ROBERT V., *The Nature of Communism* (Vintage Books, New York, 1963). Succinct survey of communist doctrines from Marx onward. The first four chapters deal with communism in relation to Marxist theory, communism and revolution, the communist party, and communism as a strategy of struggle. Chap. IX, the last, is on communism as a faith. Has bibliographical notes (pp. 376–388).

• DERRIDA, JACQUES, *Specters of Marx: The State of the Debt, the Work of Mourning, and the New International* (New York, 1994). This work is dense and eclectic. Derrida seeks to embrace an embedded notion of the "other" within Marxian theory. He stays away from formal theory and attempts to "open" a new discourse. Those interested in a postmodern response to the end of the cold war will find this book interesting; others will find it less so.

• DJILAS, MILOVAN, *The New Class* (Praeger Paperbacks, New York, 1959). Possibly the most important book on communism since the *Communist Manifesto.* The author, a former communist, shows the errors of communist totalitarianism by employing, to a large extent, Marxian concepts and techniques of analysis. See also his *Land Without Justice* (New York, 1958), *Anatomy of a Moral* (New York, 1959), and *Conversations With Stalin* (New York, 1962).

• DONHAM, DONALD L., *History, Power, Ideology: Central Issues in Marxism and Anthropology* (Cambridge, 1990). This deeply theoretical analysis of neo-classical economics and Marxist theory yields new insights into the relationship between history and ideology.

• DRACHKOVITCH, MILORAD M. (ed.), *Marxist Ideology in the Contemporary World: Its Appeals and Paradoxes* (New York, 1966). A symposium including essays on Marxism in the Western world, in communist countries, and in underdeveloped areas, on alienation in relation to student movements, and on Marxian economics. Among the contributors are Sidney Hook, Lewis S. Feuer, Daniel Bell, Gottfried Haberler, and others. See also Milorad M. Drachkovitch (ed.), *Marxism in the Modern World* (Stanford, Calif, 1965), in which leading European and American students of Marxism analyze the various forms of Marxism, from Leninism to Maoism and Castroism. The special issue of *Survey,* No. 62 (January 1967) on "Marxism Today" offers a variety of viewpoints on the impact of Marxism in communist and noncommunist countries.

• DRAPER, HAL, *Karl Marx's Theory of Revolution,* 2 vols. (New York, 1977). Written from a Marxian perspective, this work traces the development of and explains Marx's views. Vol. I is *State and Bureaucracy;* vol. II is *The Politics of Social Classes.*

• DUPRE, LOUIS, *The Philosophical Foundations of Marxism* (New York, 1966). After discussing the essentials of Hegel's philosophy, particularly its political and social aspects, the author traces the development and formation Marx's thought, and then discusses in detail Marx's philosophical writings, including the *Economic and Philosophical Manuscripts* of 1844 (pp. 120–137).

• EASTMAN, MAX, *Marx and Lenin: The Science of Revolution* (New York, 1927). Comparing Marx with Lenin, the author concludes as follows: "In Marx the Hegelian metaphysician was dominant over the practical scientific thinker; in Lenin the scientific thinker gained the victory. And that victory is the theoretical foundation of Bolshevism. Bolshevism is an unconscious, and therefore incomplete, substitution of a practical science of revolution for that revolutionary philosophy of the universe which Marx created" (p. 168).

• EASTON, LLOYD D., and KURT H. GUDDAT (trans. and eds.), *Writings of the Young Marx on Philosophy and Society* (Garden City, N.Y., 1967). The most comprehensive assemblage of Marx's early writings, from 1835 to 1847, in fresh translations. The collection begins with a piece on "Reflections of a Youth on Choosing an Occupation" (pp. 35–39), written by Marx before graduating from the Trier *Gymnasium,* and ends with his *Poverty of Philosophy,* written in 1847 (pp. 474–495). T. B. Bottomore (trans. and ed.), *Karl Marx: Early Writings* (New York, 1964), is a much shorter collection than that by Easton and Guddat, containing only the *Economic and Philosophical Manuscripts,* an essay on the Jewish question, and a critique of Hegel. For a concise analysis of Marx's early philosophical thought, see Bernard Delfgaauw, *The Young Marx* (Westminster, Md., 1967).

• ENGELS, FRIEDRICH, *On Historical Materialism* (New York, 1940). A brief essay, published first in 1892, and one of the most succinct statements of the meaning of historical materialism. It stresses the English roots of philosophical materialism, especially Bacon, Hobbes, and Locke, the "fathers of the brilliant French school of materialists" that made the eighteenth century a "preeminently French century" (p. 8).

• FELIX, DAVID, *Marx as Politician* (Carbondale, Ill., 1983). Felix concentrates on Marx as an active revolutionary. Felix believes that Marx's political goals help to explain his thought. Another book on Marx's practical political program is Alan Gilbert, *Marxist Politics* (New Brunswick, N.J., 1981).

• FEUER, LEWIS S. (ed.), *Marx and Engels: Basic Writings on Politics and Philosophy* (Anchor Books, Garden City, N.Y., 1959). Apart form a few excerpts from *Capital* bearing on economics, this anthology focuses on the writings and letters of Marx and Engels dealing with questions of philosophy, politics, ethics, and religion. T. B. Bottomore and Maximilien Rubel (eds.), *Karl Marx: Selected Writings in Sociology and Social Philosophy* (Penguin Books, Baltimore, 1963), is a briefer anthology, centered on Marx as a sociologist and social philosopher.

• FISCHER, LOUIS, *The Life of Lenin* (New York, 1964). One of the outstanding biographies of Lenin. The author, who served as an American correspondent in Moscow form 1922 to 1936, saw Lenin in action on many occasions, and has an intimate feeling for, and understanding of, the Russian people. See also Stefan T. Possony, *Lenin: The Compulsive Revolutionary* (Chicago, 1964); Adam B. Ulam, *The Bolsheviks: The Intellectual and Political History of the Triumph of Communism in Russia* (New York, 1965); and Leonard Schapiro and Peter Reddaway (eds.), *Lenin: The Man, the Theorist, the Leader* (New York, 1967).

• FROMM, ERICH, *Marx's Concept of Man* (New York, 1961). The bulk of the volume is made up of Marx's *Economic and Philosophical Manuscripts* and various other materials by, and on, Marx. Marx's writings are preceded by Fromm's introductory essay on "Marx's Concept of Man" (pp. 1–83), in which Fromm elaborates Marx's concept of alienation, arguing that it was not a passing phase of the young Marx, but that it provides the key to Marx's later work as well. Fromm's basic interpretation of Marx as a liberal humanist is critically examined by Sidney Hook, "Marx and Alienation," *The New Leader* (December 11, 1961), pp. 15–18, and Lewis Feuer, "What Is Alienation?," *New Politics,* I (Spring 1962), pp. 116–134. See also Daniel Bell, *The End of Ideology* (New York, 1960), Chap. 16, "Two Roads from Marx: The Themes of Alienation and Exploitation in Socialist Thought" (pp. 335–368), and "The Debate on Alienation," in Leopold Labedz (ed.), *Revisionism: Essays on the History of Marxist Ideas* (Praeger Paperbacks, New York, 1962), pp. 195–211.

• GORDON, DAVID, *Resurrecting Marx: The Analytical Marxists on Freedom, Exploitation, and Justice* (New Brunswick, 1990). This dismissal of Marxian theory is based upon a notion of justice born of laissez-faire economics. Gordon's approach is blunt and straight-forward, yet manages to make a number of substantial points.

• GRAY, ALEXANDER, *The Socialist Tradition: Moses to Lenin* (London, 1946). One of the few systematic historical treatments of the evolution of socialist thought from the ancients to the moderns; interesting on the Greek, Biblical, and medieval sources of socialist ethics. Chap. XII (pp. 297–351), called "Scientific Socialism," analyzes especially Marx and Engels, and Chap. XVIII (pp. 459–486) is on Lenin.

• HENRY, MICHAEL, *Marx; A Philosophy of Human Reality* (trans. Kathleen McLaughlin, Bloomington, Ind., 1983). A wholistic interpretation of Marx which portrays a unified philosophy between his earlier and later writings.

• HOOK, SIDNEY, *Towards the Understanding of Karl Marx* (New York, 1933). An illuminating interpretation of Marx's main ideas and their relation to basic problems of socialist theory. See also Hook's *From Hegel to Marx: Studies in the Intellectual Development of Karl Marx* (New York, 1950) and *Marx and the Marxists: The Ambiguous Legacy* (Anvil Books, Princeton, N.J., 1955).

• ——, *World Communism: Key Documentary Material* (Anvil Books, Princeton, N.J., 1962). Documents the theory and historical evolution of communism, with introductory comments by Hook on each selection. The source material is largely taken from official communist sources. For a brief survey of Soviet communism see also Robert H. McNeal, *The Bolshevik Tradition: Lenin, Stalin, Khrushchev* (Englewood Cliffs, N.J., 1963).

• HUNT, RICHARD, *The Political Ideas of Marx and Engels,* 2 vols. (Pittsburgh, Pa., 1974). A comprehensive work—vol. I considers Marx and Engels as totalitarian democrats; vol. II considers their mature thought.

• HUNT, R. N. CAREW, *Marxism: Past and Present* (New York, 1954). One of the best brief introductions into Marx's philosophy of dialectical materialism, his economic and political theories, and the doctrine of the dictatorship of the proletariat. See also H. Stuart Hughes, *Consciousness and Society: The Reorientation of European Social Thought, 1890–1930* (New York, 1958), particularly Chap. III on "The Critique of Marxism" (pp. 67–104).

• JAWORSKYJ, MICHAEL (ed.), *Soviet Political Thought: An Anthology* (Baltimore, 1968).

The most comprehensive collection of Soviet materials related to political thought, covering the period of 1917–1961, and expressing the views of Soviet political writers, economists, historians, and philosophers. The major sections of the anthology are prefaced by introductory essays of the editor.

• KAMENKA, EUGENE, *The Ethical Foundations of Marxism* (New York, 1962). The relation of Marx's thought to ethical philosophy is one of the most vexing, and rarely explored, problems in the study of Marx. Kamenka shows the development of Marx's ethical ideas from his earlier to his later stages of intellectual development. In Part V, "Communism and Ethics" (pp. 163–187), the author critically examines the ethical views and practices as officially expressed in the Soviet Union.

• KATZ, CLAUDIO J., *From Feudalism to Capitalism: Marxian Theories of Class Struggle and Social Change. Contributions in Political Science* no. 239, ed. Bernard K. Johnpoll (New York, 1989). Katz seeks to explicate Marx's conception of history by introducing the notion of qualitative transformations. This discussion, which relies heavily upon empirical historiography, surveys much of the contemporary literature and produces a compelling synthesis of Marxian thought and recent analysis.

• KELSEN, HANS, *The Political Theory of Bolshevism: A Critical Analysis* (Berkeley and Los Angeles, 1949). This short book of sixty pages is the best critical analysis of the political theory of Marx and Engels, and of its later development by Lenin and Stalin. The styles is clear and straightforward, and the documentation based largely on the original sources of Marx, Engels, Lenin, and Stalin. See also Leonard Schapiro, "Lenin's Contribution to Politics," *Political Quarterly,* XXXV (January–March 1964), pp. 9–22.

• KOESTLER, ARTHUR, *Darkness at Noon* (Signet Books, New York, 1948). This short novel supplies more insight into the working of totalitarian communism and its terroristic methods than many a ponderous work of nonfiction. The hero of the novel is an old revolutionary whose final fate—imprisonment, abject confession of crimes not committed, and execution—resembles that of the victims of the Moscow treason trials in the nineteen thirties, in which Stalin liquidated most of the remnants of the orig-

inal leaders of the revolution. See also George Orwell, *1984* (Signet Books, New York, 1950).

• KOLAKOWSKI, LESZEK, *Main Currents of Marxism: Its Rise, Growth, and Dissolution,* 3 vols. (trans. P. S. Falls, Oxford, 1978). The most important recent work in the field of the development of Marxist thought. Volume I is titled *The Founders,* and covers Marx and Engels, as well as some of their precursors and contemporaries. Volume II is *The Golden Age,* and deals with significant Marxists to the Russian Revolution. Volume III is *The Breakdown,* and covers Marxist theory from the Russian Revolution forward. Kolakowski's essential interpretation is that Marxism is a secular religion which—by raising the hope of an imminent secular millenium— paved the way for Stalinist totalitarianism, as any evil was sufferable to achieve this great good. For an older historical treatment which was unavailable in English for many years, see Karl Korsch, *Marxism and Philosophy* (trans. with an intro. by Fred Halliday, New York, 1970).

• LASKI, HAROLD J., *The Communist Manifesto* (New York, 1967). Contains the full text of the *Communist Manifesto,* with the prefaces to its several German, English, and Russian editions. The major feature of the volume is Laski's Introduction (pp. 3–105), a detailed critical examination in the light of historical experience.

• ———, *Communism: 1381–1927* (London, 1927). The materialist interpretation of history seems to Laski, "as general doctrine, undeniable." Yet he warns that "there is no justification for the resort to violence until the resources of reason have been exhausted" (p. 180). See, especially, Chap. IV, "The Communist Theory of the State" (pp. 123–182). Laski's conclusion is that the answer to "the new faith" of communism "is not the persecution of those who worship in its sanctuary, but the proof that those who do not share its convictions can scan an horizon not less splendid in the prospect it envisions nor less compelling in the allegiance it invokes" (pp. 250–251). See also Laski's *The Secret Battalion: An Examination of the Communist Attitude to the Labour Party* (London, 1946), a devastating critique of communist methods of political infiltration and deception.

• LEVIN, MICHAEL, *Marx, Engels, and Liberal Democracy* (New York, 1989). This work presents a fascinating discussion on the critical thought of Marx and Engels on liberal democracy. Liberal democracy was just emerging as a dominant form of popular governance in Marx and Engel's time, and there was much the two found attractive in it, despite their ultimate rejection of its basic tenets.

• LEWIS, JOHN, *The Life and Teaching of Karl Marx* (New York, 1965). One of the leading accounts of Marx written from a strictly orthodox Marxist-communist viewpoint.

• LICHTHEIM, GEORGE, *Marxism: An Historical and Critical Study,* 2nd ed. (Praeger Paperbacks, New York, 1965.) One of the most successful overall analyses of Marx and Marxism, in relation to philosophical and political ideas as well as to social and political movements. The author has no axe to grind, and his interpretations of ideas and events are fair and well balanced.

• LINDSAY, A. D., *Karl Marx's Capital: An Introductory Essay* (London, 1925). The first chapter (pp. 15–26) gives a brief outline of Marx and Hegel, emphasizing especially the influence of Hegelian dialectic on Marx. Chaps. II–IV (pp. 27–109) provide well-balanced introductions to economic determinism, the Marxian labor theory of value, and the meaning of surplus value. The final chapter (pp, 109–125) contains suggestive comparisons between Marx and Rousseau, each the father of a great revolution.

• LOBKOWICZ, NICHOLAS (ed.), *Marx and the Western World* (Notre Dame, Ind., 1967). One of the few international symposia on Marx, containing papers by scholars from noncommunist countries, such as the United States, Britain, France, and Germany, as well as by scholars from communist states, such as the Soviet Union, Poland, Yugoslavia, and Czechoslovakia. A variety of topics is covered: the foundations of Marx's political and ethical thought; the impact of Marx and Marxism on developed and underdeveloped countries; and the relations of Marxism to Christianity as seen by Catholic and Protestant thinkers. Some of the papers are followed by critical comments of fellow participants of the symposium. While the contributions are highly uneven in quality, the volume as a whole is stimulating in its breadth of scope and the confrontation of sharply contrasting viewpoints.

• LOHIA, RAMMANOHAR, *Marx, Gandhi, and Socialism* (Hyderabad, 1963). Essays, speeches, and articles by an Indian politician and publicist, whose sympathies lie with Gandhi and democratic socialism rather than with Marxism. The author is critical of both Soviet and American domestic and foreign policies, and his massive volume of six hundred pages provides implicit insights into Indian political thinking. His political ideal is "leftism from bottom" (p. xlvii), or unbureaucratic, democratic socialism with a high degree of governmental decentralization. See also Kalyan Chandra Gupta, *A Critical Examination of Marxist Philosophy* (Calcutta, 1962), for a briefer and more systematic treatment of Marxism.

• LOVELL, DAVID, *From Marx to Lenin: An Evaluation of Marx's Responsibility for Soviet Authoritarianism* (Cambridge, Eng., 1984). Lovell's study of this problem leads him to conclude that Soviet authoritarianism was not the only necessary practical outcome of Marxism.

• LUKES, STEVEN, *Marxism and Morality* (Oxford, 1985). This book is both about Marxian precepts and the degree to which Marxist practice followed from these precepts.

• MAGUIRE, JOHN, *Marx's Theory of Politics* (Cambridge, 1978). Focuses on the positive as opposed to normative aspect of Marx's political thought across his career and writings.

• MARX, KARL, *The Grundrisse* (ed. and trans. by David McLellan, New York, 1971). In many respects, *The Grundrisse* is the most complete exposition of Marx's entire political economy. While it was intended as the draft for a larger work (of which *Das Kapital* is only one of six projected parts), it is the only complete rendering of Marx's thought on political economy. This version of *The Grundrisse* amounts to about one-fifteenth of the original.

• MARX, KARL, and FRIEDRICH ENGELS, *Selected Correspondence* (New York, 1942). Over two hundred letters, written by Marx and Engels to each other or to leading socialist writers and publicists. These letters throw considerable light on the philosophies and personalities of Marx and Engels, and also contain succinctly formulated analyses that frequently make a point more clearly and convincingly than more ponderous treatments in their better-known works.

• ———, *Writings on the Paris Commune* (ed. Hal Draper, New York, 1971). Of interest more for the writings it brings together than for Draper's introduction.

• MAYER, GUSTAV, *Friedrich Engels* (New York, 1936). The standard biography of Engels. Concerning Engels' share in the *Communist Manifesto,* Mayer says that "although it was chiefly Marx who coined the gold, Engels had not been behind him in collecting the ore" (p. 88).

• MCLELLAN, DAVID, *Karl Marx: His Life and Thought,* 2 vols. (New York, 1973). The first full-scale biography on Marx written in the English language in decades. McLellan writes from a "sympathetically critical standpoint," and covers the major facets of Marx's life—personal, intellectual, and political.

• ———, *Marxism After Marx* (London, 1979). Chapter 7 is on Lenin. See also McLellan's extensive bibliographies.

• MCNALLY, DAVID, *Against the Market: Political Economy, Market Socialism and the Marxist Critique* (New York, 1993). This ambitious engagement of the theoretical forces of the free market is laudable but unfortunately incomplete. McNally provides a brilliant historical analysis of the emergence of Marxist socialism, but fails to deliver the coup-de-grace to modern capitalism by his return to Marxist labor theory without examining the difficulties inherent within that theory. His examination of the Mises-Hayek "calculation problem" is very informative and worthwhile reading for all scholars of political economy.

• MEISTER, ROBERT, *Political Identity: Thinking Through Marx* (Cambridge, 1990). Meister presents an argument that contemporary history parallels that of Western Europe during the late nineteenth century and that understanding Marxism as an institutional critique is essential to understanding our own political and economic time.

• ODAJNIK, WALTER, *Marxism and Existentialism* (Anchor Books, Garden City, N.Y., 1965). Of the various leaders of modern existentialism, Sartre has stood out in his attempt to reconcile it with Marxism. The author shows that Sartre has not succeeded in this attempt, sacrificing basic existentialist tenets of individual freedom to the collectivist assumptions of Marxism. See also Wilfrid Desan, *The Marxism of Jean-Paul Sartre* (Garden City, N.Y., 1965), likewise arriving at the conclusion that Sartre has failed to bring about the synthesis between existentialism and Marxism, but arguing that Sartre puts some basic elements of existentialist philosophy above Marxian materialism.

• OLLAMN, BERTELL, *Alienation: Marx's Conception of Man in Capitalist Society* (Cambridge, 1971). Develops the essential features of Marx's critique of modern society. Ollman argues that there is no philosophical break between the early and mature Marx, and that Marx's concept of human nature in his earlier works illuminates the larger analyses of the later works.

• PETROVIĆ, GAJO, *Marx in the Mid-Twentieth Century* (Anchor Books, Garden City, N.Y., 1967). The author, a professor of philosophy in communist Yugoslavia, vigorously rejects the Stalinist type of communist totalitarianism, and stresses Marx's humanist ideas, particularly as expressed in his early philosophical writings. In particular, he picks Marx's concept of alienation as the central idea of a humanist, antitotalitarian Marxian philosophy. However, Petrović sees no discontinuity between the ideas of the young and old Marx: "The theory of alienation is not only the central theme of Marx's 'early' writings; it is also the guiding idea of all his 'later' works" (p. 32). In one important respect, the author goes beyond most Marxists who consider the abolition of private property and its transfer to the state as the cure-all for the economic root of alienation. "The de-alienation of economic life," Petrović writes, "requires also the abolition of state property, its transformation into real social property; and this cannot be achieved without organizing the whole social life on the basis of the self-management of the immediate producers" (p. 153). Petrović thus takes the position that the important question with respect to productive property is, not who owns it, but by what methods it is managed. However, the author fails to follow up the broader ramifications of this issue, since this might lead to the issue of political democracy—still a touchy subject in Yugoslavia.

• POLAN, A. J., *Lenin and the Ends of Politics* (Berkeley, 1984). This book considers the influence of Lenin on politics and political theory, which is held to be almost entirely for the bad.

• POPPER, KARL, *The Open Society and its Enemies* (Princeton, 1950). The second part is on Hegel and Marx, and the author concentrates on Marx's claim to have formulated a "scientific" theory of society. In the literature on Marx, Popper's work is particularly illuminating, not only because it possesses analytical acumen and philosophical depth but because it places Marx in a tradition of the "enemies of the open society," starting with Plato. Popper's formulation of the concept of the open society is an important contribution to liberal-democratic thought in the twentieth century. See also H. B. Mayo, *Introduction to Marxist Theory* (New York, 1960), for a thoughtful confrontation of the basic tenets of democracy with Marxism.

• POSTONE, MOISHE, *Time, Labour, and Social Domination: A Reinterpretation of Marx's Critical Theory* (New York, 1993). The result of years of intense scholarship, as the literary result confirms, this is a major work. Postone seeks to rebuild Marx's critique of capitalism within a contemporary context. The mostly sociological treatment is aimed at the heart of Marxian thought, the relationship between labor and capital. This is a valuable contribution for anyone studying Marxian theory or Marxist politics.

• RUSSELL, BERTRAND, *Bolshevism: Practice and Theory* (New York, 1920). This remarkable book, based on a visit to Russia, is one of the few that have stood the test of time, and the author republished it, in an unchanged second edition, in 1949 (London and New York). Russell agreed with the economic objectives of public ownership of industry but disagreed with the political means of ruthlessness employed by communism for the attainment of its ends. Writing in 1920, Russell saw three possibilities of Soviet communist development: "The first is the ultimate defeat of Bolshevism by the forces of capitalism. The second is the victory of the Bolshevists accompanied by a complete loss of their ideals and a regime of Napoleonic imperialism. The third is a prolonged world-war, in which civilization will go under, and all its manifestations (including communism) will be forgotten" (p. 4).

• RYAZANOFF, D. (ed.), *Karl Marx: Man, Thinker, and Revolutionist* (New York, 1927). An interesting symposium on Marx, with personal reminiscences by Engels, his daughter Eleanor Marx, and his son-in-law Paul Lafargue, as well as sympathetic studies by Lenin, Mehring, Rosa Luxemburg, and others.

• SCHRAM, STUART R., *The Political Thought of Mao Tse-tung,* rev. ed. (Praeger University Paperbacks, New York, 1968). A collection of Mao's political writings, prefaced by a long introductory essay by Schram. See also Mao's biography by Schram, *Mao Tse-tung* (Penguin Books, 1966). John Wilson Lewis (ed.), *Major Doctrines of Communist China* (New York, 1964), and Anne Freemantle (ed.), *Mao Tse-tung: An Anthology of His Writings* (Mentor Books, New York, 1962), are useful compilations of the political ideas of Mao and the other former communist Chinese leadership.

• SCHUMPETER, JOSEPH A., *Ten Great Economists: From Marx to Keynes* (London, 1952). Schumpeter, one of the great economists of the twentieth century, devotes the longest chapter (pp. 3–73) to Marx. See also: Joan Robinson, *An Essay on Marxian Economics,* 2nd ed. (New York, 1966); Robert L. Heilbroner, *The Worldly Philosophers: The Lives, Times, and Ideas of the Great Economic Thinkers,* 6th ed. (New York, 1986), and Murray Wolfson, *A Reappraisal of Marxian Economics* (New York, 1966). For selections of Marx's own statements on economic issues, taken from *Capital* and some of his other writings, see Robert Freedman (ed.), *Marx on Economics* (Penguin Books, Baltimore, 1962).

• SCHWARZSCHILD, LEOPOLD, *The Red Prussian: The Life and Legend of Karl Marx* (London, 1948). A highly critical biography, written with verve and fire. The author "debunks" Marx as a man and thinker thoroughly and devastatingly, yet fails to explain why he exercised such a tremendous influence on history.

• SITTON, JOHN F., *Recent Marxian Theory: Class Formation and Social Conflict in Contemporary Capitalism* (New York, 1996). The author provides an extremely valuable tour of recent Marxian theory, at the end of which he concludes that "the proletariat is no longer a useful abstraction" (p. 247). His analysis relies upon rational choice assumptions of economic individuals, which may cause some to discount his conclusion, but the exercise is well performed.

• STOCKHAMMER, MORRIS, *Karl Marx Dictionary* (New York, 1965). Marxian key concepts and terms, taken from his writings, and alphabetically organized in dictionary form.

• STRVIK, DIRK (ed.), *Birth of the "Communist Manifesto"* (New York, 1971). A valuable collection of all of the prefaces by Marx and Engels to the *Manifesto,* together with early drafts by Engels and other supplementary materials, including Marx's and Engel's accounts of the history of the *Manifesto.*

• SWEEZY, PAUL M., *The Theory of Capitalist Development* (New York, 1942). Chaps. I–XII (pp. 11–236) contain one of the most authoritative statements of Marxian political economy, including such basic concepts as value, surplus value, capital accumulation, the law of the falling profit rate, and crises and depressions. Chap. XV (pp. 270–286) analyzes monopoly and its impact on the capitalist economy. See also Sweezy's *Socialism* (New York, 1949), and *The Present as History: Essays and Reviews on Capitalism and Socialism* (New York, 1953).

• TROTSKY, LEON, *The History of the Russian Revolution* (three vols, in one, New York, 1937, reprinted Ann Arbor, 1957). Of the prolific literary output of Trotsky, this is likely to remain his most enduring work, since he was not only one of the top leaders of the Russian Revolution in November 1917, but also a great historian and writer. See also his provocative theoretical contribution in *Permanent Revolution* (New York, 1931). *My Life* (New York, 1931) is one of the few great autobiographies ever written by a leading communist. An overall view of Trotsky's political ideas and personal experiences can be obtained from Irving Howe (ed.), *The Basic Writings of Trotsky* (New York, 1963), with a long introduction by the editor (pp. 3–39).

• ————, *Karl Marx* (The Living Thoughts Library, New York, 1939). Trotsky's introduction (pp. 1–45) is followed by selected passages from Marx's *Capital* (pp. 48–189). Writing for American readers, and illustrating his theoretical arguments with American materials, Trotsky comes to the conclusion that Marxism has a great future in the United States. For a scholarly examination of the influence of American communist ideas and experience on Marx, see Lewis S. Feuer, "The North American Origins of Marx's Socialism," *Western Political Quarterly,* XVI (March 1963), pp. 53–67, and "The Influence of the American Communist Colonies on Engels and Marx," *ibid.,* XIX (September 1966), pp. 456–474.

• TUCKER, ROBERT C., *Philosophy and Myth in Karl Marx* (Cambridge, 1961). In the light of the renewed interest in Marx's philosophy as stimulated, in particular, by the publication in English of his *Economic and Philosophical Manuscripts,* the author interprets Marxism essentially as a "religion of revolution" rather than as a system of social or economic science. Tucker also stresses the philosophical links between Marx and earlier German philosophers, particularly Kant, Hegel, and Feuerbach, The notion of Marxism as a scientific system is also refuted in Max Eastman, *Marxism: Is It Science?* (New York, 1940). By contrast, the scientific nature of Marxism is affirmed in Irving M. Zeitlin, *Marxism: A Re-Examination* (Princeton, N.J., 1967).

• WEYL, NATHANIEL, *Karl Marx: Racist* (New Rochelle, N.Y., 1979). A vitriolic attack on Marx for his allegedly holding racist views.

• WILSON, EDMUND, *To the Finland Station* (Anchor Books, New York, 1953). The bulk of the book (pp. 111–484) deals with Marx, Engels, Lenin, and Trotsky.

• WOLFE, BERTRAM D., *Marxism: One Hundred Years in the Life of a Doctrine* (Delta Paperbacks, New York, 1967). A comprehensive and critical analysis by a life-long student of Marxism and communism.

CHAPTER THIRTY

NIETZSCHE

• BERKOWITZ, PETER, *Nietzsche: The Ethics of an Immoralist* (Cambridge, 1995). Berkowitz presents a holistic approach to understanding Nietzsche. His argument that one should read Nietzsche within the context of the whole of his works is made credible, and even compelling, by the accomplished treatment he gives to six of Nietzsche's works. An excellent resource for Nietzsche scholars as well as students.

• DANNHAUSER, WERNER, *Nietzsche's View of Socrates* (Ithaca, N.Y., 1974). A work on the development of Nietzsche's views on Socrates, and of the former's challenge to the latter.

• DETWILER, BRUCE, *Nietzsche and the Politics of Aristocratic Radicalism* (Chicago, 1990). A comprehensive yet concise re-evaluation of Nietzsche's political views. Detwiler notes there have been many political interpretations of Nietzsche, and that Nietzsche has been considered both political and apolitical. Detwiler believes Nietzsche is politically significant, and his analysis of him is not unlike the one put forward in *Great Political Thinkers*. He puts forward the view that Nietzsche's politics were both radical and aristocratic.

• DUFFY, MICHAEL and WILLARD MITTELMAN, "Nietzsche's Attitudes Toward the Jews," *Journal of the History of Ideas* (April–June 1988). This article argues that Nietzsche had different attitudes toward Jews at different times in his life, and that he had different attitudes toward Judaism at different stages of its development.

• GILLESPIE, MICHAEL and TRACY STRONG (eds.), *Nietzsche's New Seas: Explorations in Philosophy, Aesthetics, and Politics* (Chicago, 1988). This collection of essays attempts to focus not on Nietzsche the theorist of nihilism, but rather as an aesthetic challenger to western culture. Strong's essay is excellent.

• HEIDEGGER, MARTIN, *Nietzsche,* 4 vols. (ed. David Krell, trans. David Krell et al., San Francisco, 1979–1987). Written from 1936 to 1946, and not published in German until 1961. Heidegger's reactions to and reflections on Nietzsche and Nietzschean subjects. Emphasis on nihilism and the death of God. In light of the presentation of Nietzsche in *Great Political Thinkers* it is not inappropriate to note Heidegger's flirtation with Nazism.

• HOLLINGDALE, R. J., *Nietzsche* (Baton Rouge, La., 1966). On Nietzsche's life and thought.

• KAUFMANN, WALTER, *Nietzsche; Philosopher, Psychologist, Antichrist,* 4th ed. (Princeton, 1974). Kaufman's reinterpretation and rehabilitation of Nietzsche (this book was originally published in 1950) was unquestionably the most influential in postwar Nietzschean scholarship. Kaufman saw Nietzsche as an important philosopher who was misused by the Nazis. This work is a comprehensive presentation of Nietzsche's life and work, and was refined by Kaufman over several decades. It includes an outstanding bibliography.

• KÖHLER, JOACHIM (Ronald Taylor, trans.), *Nietzsche and Wagner: A Study in Subjugation* (New Haven, 1999). Considers Nietzsche's evolving relationship with Richard and Cosima Wagner. Concludes with Nietzsche's words to the guardians at his mental asylum: "It was my wife Cosima Wagner who brought me here."

• LAMPERT, LAWRENCE, *Leo Strauss and Nietzsche* (Chicago, 1996). This work, which is aimed at the author's fellow Straussians, is provocative, well written, and deftly argued. For those outside this circle, the author provides an interesting example of Straussian self-critique.

• ———, *Nietzsche's Teaching: An Interpretation of* Thus Spoke Zarathustra (New

Haven, Conn., 1987). Nietzsche thought *Thus Spoke Zarathustra* was his central work. Lmapert's book attempts to decipher *Thus Spoke Zarathustra* and gives a sympathetic depiction of Nietzsche's philosophy (which is presented as mostly nonpolitical). Lampert ranks Nietzsche's philosophy with Plato's. This book is more valuable for its presentation of *Thus Spoke Zarathustra* than for its interpretation of it.

• Nocholas, Marius, *From Nietzsche Down to Hitler* (trans. E. G. Ecklin, Port Washington, N.Y., 1970). Investigates this Nietzschean issue.

• Pfeffer, Rose, *Nietzsche: Disciple of Dionysus* (Lewisburg, 1972). Focuses on Nietzsche's doctrine of eternal recurrence, which is presented as the most important portion of his thought and his solution to God's death.

• Strong, Tracy, *Friedrich Nietzsche and the Politics of Trnasfiguration,* expanded edition (Berkeley, Calif., 1988). With Kaufmann's work, another important book to study in order to understand Nietzsche. Strong considers various interpretations of Nietzsche. This book, like Kaufmann's, contains a useful bibliography.

• Warren, Mark, *Nietzsche and Political Thought* (Cambridge, 1988). This impressive work is a thorough and comprehensive treatment of Nietzsche's political thought. The author provides a clear and insightful analysis of Nietzsche's writings. This is an excellent resource for those seeking a deeper understanding of Nietzsche's nihilism.

• ———, *Nietzsche and Political Thought* (Cambridge, Mass., 1988). A postmodernist approach to Nietzsche.

CHAPTER THIRTY-ONE

FASCISM

• Allardyce, Gilbert, ed., *The Place of Fascism in European History* (Englewood Cliffs, N.J., 1971). A collection of essays by, among others, Erich Fromm, Peter Drucker, Hannah Arendt, and Seymour Martin Lipset.

• Arendt, Hannah, *The Origins of Totalitarianism,* 2nd ed. (New York, 1958). A classic in the field.

• Ashton, E. B., *The Fascist: His State and His Mind* (London, 1937). A general account of fascist theory and its application in economics, government, and international relations. See also William Ebenstein, *Fascist Italy* (New York, 1939, republished 1973), *The Nazi State* (New York, 1943, republished 1975), *The German Record: A Political Portrait* (New York, 1945), *Totalitarianism: New Perspectives* (New York, 1962), *Today's Isms: Communism, Fascism, Capitalism, Socialism,* 11th ed. (Englewood Cliffs, N.J., 2000), and "National Socialism," *International Encyclopedia of the Soviet Sciences,* Vol. XI (New York, 1968), pp. 45–50.

• Borgese, G. A., "The Intellectual Origins of Fascism," *Social Research,* I (November 1934), pp. 458–485. One of the best analyses of the literary and philosophical origins of fascism. Borgese's *Goliath: The March of Fascism* (New York, 1938) contains in Part I a lengthy account of the intellectual and historical background of Italian Fascism.

• Carsten, F. L., *The Rise of Fascism* (Berkeley–Los Angeles, 1967). In this major contribution to the literature on fascism, the author is primarily concerned with the period of fascist movements and parties before the seizure of power, thus showing the conditions and forces in non-fascist countries that enabled fascist movements to grow and win, as was the case in Italy and Germany. This analysis is particularly fruitful from the comparative viewpoint, since it is full of lessons for those countries in which fascist groups and parties exist but are unable to get control of the government. While the focus of the book is inevitably on Italy and Germany, the author also deals briefly with fascist groups in other European countries in the 1920s and 1930s. Other comparative accounts of fascism will be found in Hans Rogger and Eugen Weber (eds.), *The European Right: A Historical Profile* (Berkeley–Los Angeles, 1965); Eugen Weber, *Varieties of Fascism* (Anvil Books, Princeton, 1964); and Dennis Eisenberg, *The Re-Emergence of Fascism* (London, 1967). Vol. I, No. 1 (1966) of the *Journal of Contemporary History* is a special issue on "International Fascism, 1920–1945."

• COBBAN, ALFRED, *Dictatorship: Its History and Theory* (New York, 1939). See also Carl J. Friedrich (ed.), *Totalitarianism* (Universal Library Paperbacks, New York, 1964); Carl J. Friedrich and Zbigniew K. Brzezinski, *Totalitarian Dictatorship and Autocracy,* 2nd ed. (Cambridge, Mass., 1965); Sigmund Neumann, *Permanent Revolution,* 2nd ed. (Praeger Paperbacks, New York, 1965); and William S. Halperin, *Mussolini and Italian Fascism* (Anvil Books, Princeton, 1964).

• DRUCKER, PETER, *The End of Economic Man: The Origins of Totalitarianism* (New York, 1969). Drucker's interpretation is that fascism is the product of a general loss of faith in freedom and equality. Much to say about fascist economics.

• DUTT, R. PALME, *Fascism and Social Revolution* (New York, 1934). The most authoritative interpretation of fascism from the orthodox communist viewpoint. The subtitle of the book is "A Study of the Economics and Politics of the Extreme Stages of Capitalism in Decay." For other Marxist interpretations of fascism, see Paul Sweezy, *The Theory of Capitalist Development* (New York, 1942), pp. 329–347, and Daniel Guerin, *Fascism and Big Business* (New York, 1939).

• FROMM, ERICH, *Escape from Freedom* (New York, 1941). One of the most incisive interpretations of fascism from a psychological viewpoint. Indispensable to an understanding of fascism as a mass movement. See also Eric Hoffer, *The True Believer* (New York, 1951). A milestone in the empirical study of the psychology of fascism is T. W. Adorno and others, *The Authoritarian Personality* (New York, 1950). Its accomplishments and defects are analyzed in Richard Christie and Marie Jahoda (eds.), *Studies in the Scope and Method of "The Authoritarian Personality"* (Glencoe, 1954). See also Bruno Bettelheim, *The Informed Heart: The Human Condition in Modern Mass Society* (New York, 1960).

• GREGOR, A. JAMES, *Interpretations of Fascism* (Morristown, N.J., 1974). A systematic analysis of the major theoretical endeavors to interpret fascism from the 1920s forward.

• KEDWARD, H. RODERICK, *Fascism in Western Europe, 1900–1945* (New York, 1971). Brief accounts of a number of fascist movements.

• KIRKPATRICK, IVONE, *Mussolini: A Study in Power* (New York, 1964). The author of this massive study stresses Mussolini's impact on the world scene. Laura Fermi, *Mussolini* (Chicago, 1961), stresses Mussolini's personality and background, to which she devotes almost one half of her biography. Her account is greatly enriched by having experienced Italian fascism for sixteen years after the fascist seizure of power in 1922. See also Christopher Hibbert, *Il Duce: The Life of Benito Mussolini* (Boston, 1962).

• PUZZO, DANTE A., "Racism and the Western Tradition," *Journal of the History of Ideas,* XXV (October–December 1964), pp. 579–586. The author considers racism a modern conception, evolving from the sixteenth century on. He identifies the expansion of Europe overseas, the Protestant Reformation, the rise of the nation-state, and imperial struggles as the most important elements in this process. Since racism has been a decisive factor in fascism everywhere, Puzzo's brief study provides an illuminating historical background for fascist racism in the twentieth century.

• RADER, MELVIN, *No Compromise: The Conflict between Two Worlds* (New York, 1939). A philosophical analysis of the basic principles of fascism. See also C. E. M. Joad, *A Guide to the Philosophy of Politics and Morals* (London, 1938), pp. 605–663; Bertrand Russell, *In Praise of Idleness and Other Essays* (London, 1948), pp. 82–108; and Karl Mannheim, *Ideology and Utopia* (London–New York, 1940), pp. 119–134.

• REICH, WILHELM, *The Mass Psychology of Fascism* (New York, 1946). Interpreting fascism from the viewpoint of sexual and psychological maladjustments, the author writes that "fascist mysticism is orgastic longing under the conditions of mystification and inhibition of natural sexuality" (p. xvii). A suggestive book, which tries to harmonize the "depth psychology of Freud with the economic theory of Marx" (p. xix).

• SCHAPIRO, J. SALWYN, *Liberalism and the Challenge of Fascism* (New York, 1949). Chap. XV is entitled "Thomas Carlyle, Prophet of Fascism" (pp. 370–396).

CHAPTER THIRTY-TWO

FREUD

• ABRAMSON, JEFFREY, *Liberation and Its Limits: The Moral and Political Thought of Freud* (New York, 1984). Stresses the social implications of Freud's psychological theories, with particular emphasis on autonomy and individuality.

• ALEXANDER, FRANZ, *Fundamentals of Psychoanalysis* (New York, 1948). By one of the leading authorities on psychoanalysis. Each chapter of the book is followed by a bibliography. *The Scope of Analysis: Selected Papers, 1921–1961* (New York, 1961) contains a number of Alexander's papers on social and political problems (pp. 381–480). For presentations of the main theories of psychoanalysis see also David Stafford-Clark, *What Freud Really Said* (New York, 1965).

• BERLINER, ARTHUR, *Psychoanalysis and Society: The Social Thought of Sigmund Freud* (Washington, D.C., 1983). Explores the relationship between Freud's psychoanalytical and social views.

• BETTELHEIM, BRUNO, *The Informed Heart: The Human Condition in Modern Mass Society* (New York, 1960). The author, who was a practicing psychoanalyst in Vienna, spent a year (1938–1939) in the German concentration camps of Dachau and Buchenwald, and after his release went to the United States where he established himself as one of the leading psychologists, working particularly with children. In *The Informed Heart,* Bettelheim analyzes the disintegration of the human personality under conditions of extreme stress, and points out how his experiences modified his psychological and psychoanalytic thinking. See also a Dutch psychiatrist's experiences in German concentration camps, Elie A.

Cohen, *Human Behavior in the Concentration Camp* (New York, 1953).

• BIRNBACH, MARTIN, *Neo-Freudian Social Philosophy* (Stanford, Calif., 1961). After a brief discussion of Freudian thought and its implications for social and political philosophy, the author analyzes the neo-Freudian break with Freud by stressing the importance of society to the mental health of the individual. Specifically, he concentrates on Franz Alexander, Erich Fromm, Karen Horney, Abram Kardiner, Harry Stack Sullivan, and Harold D. Lasswell. See also J. A. C. Brown, *Freud and the Post-Freudians* (Penguin Books, Baltimore, 1961), and Edward Glover, "Freudian or Neofreudian?" *Psychoanalytic Quarterly,* XXXIII (Fall 1964), pp. 97–109.

• BOCOCK, ROBERT, *Sigmund Freud* (London, 1983). A brief work including discussion of Freud's political and social views.

• CANTRIL, HADLEY, *Human Nature and Political Systems* (New Brunswick, N.J., 1961). A leading American social psychologist examines the psychological requirements and patterns that underlie and condition particular political systems. In *The Politics of Despair* (Collier Books, New York, 1962), Cantril gives an account of an empirical study of people in France and Italy who voted Communist. See also his theoretical and comparative study, *The Pattern of Human Concerns* (New Brunswick, N.J., 1966), and *The Human Dimension: Experiences in Policy Research* (New Brunswick, N.J., 1967), describing the background and methods of his theoretical concepts and empirical researches in political philosophy.

• ERIKSON, ERIK H., *Insight and Responsibility: Lectures on the Ethical Implications of Psychoanalytic Thought* (New York, 1964). The author is a leading figure in American psychoanalytic research, with special emphasis on the field of human development. See also Heinz Hartmann, *Psychoanalysis and Moral Values* (New York, 1960); Lewis S. Feuer, *Psychoanalysis and Ethics* (Springfield, Ill., 1955); David H. Jones, "Freud's Theory of Moral Conscience," *Philosophy*, XLI (January 1966), pp. 34–57; R. N. Kaul, "Freud's Contribution to Ethical Theory," *Psychoanalytic Review*, LI (Winter 1964–1965), pp. 72–78; Anthony B. Gabriele, "The Principle of Irrational Loyalty," *Psychoanalytic Review*, LIII (Spring 1966), pp. 69–84; and Norman Kelman, "Psychoanalysis and Morality," *American Scholar*, XXIV (Spring 1955), pp. 158–170.

• EYSENCK, H. J., *The Psychology of Politics* (London, 1954). Empirical studies exploring the relations between personality and political ideology and behavior. About half of the material is derived from research and experiments in Britain, and the other half is based on work done mainly in the United States. See also R. E. Money-Kyrle, *Psychoanalysis and Politics* (London, 1951), and *Man's Picture of His World: A Psychoanalytic Study* (London, 1961), particularly Part II (pp. 105–190), in which the author correlates a person's "world-model" to his political ideas and attitudes.

• FODOR, NANDOR, and FRANK GAYNOR (eds.), *Freud: Dictionary of Psychoanalysis* (New York, 1950). Presents, in dictionary form, the main concepts of psychoanalysis in quotations from Freud's own writings. Useful for rapid reference.

• FREUD, SIGMUND, *A General Introduction to Psychoanalysis* (New York, 1920), and *New Introductory Lectures on Psycho-Analysis* (New York, 1933). These are the two basic introductory works. See also the following: *The Interpretation of Dreams*, 3rd ed. (New York, 1932); *The Psychopathology of Everyday Life* (New York, 1914); *Three Essays on the Theory of Sexuality* (New York, 1910); *Wit and Its Relation to the Unconscious* (New York, 1916); *Totem and Taboo* (New York, 1918); *Group Psychology and the Analysis of the Ego* (New York, 1922); *The Future of an Illusion* (New York, 1928); and *An Outline of Psycho-Analysis* (New York, 1949). *The Basic Writings of Sigmund Freud* (ed. A. A. Brill, Modern Library, New York, 1938), contains six of Freud's more important works. Freud's *Collected Papers*, 5 vols. (New York, 1959), contains papers contributed to journals and encyclopedias. Freud's personality is revealed in his letters, Ernst L. Freud (ed.), *Letters of Sigmund Freud* (New York, 1960), and Heinrich Meng and Ernst L. Freud (eds.), *Psychoanalysis and Faith: The Letters of Sigmund Freud and Oskar Pfister* (London–New York, 1963). For an informal portrait of Freud by his oldest son, see Martin Freud, *Sigmund Freud: Man and Father* (New York, 1958).

• FROMM, ERICH, *Escape from Freedom* (New York, 1941). One of the most successful applications of modified psychoanalytic methods and concepts to the analysis of modern totalitarianism. See also Fromm's *Beyond the Chains of Illusion: My Encounter with Marx and Freud* (New York, 1962), *Man for Himself: An Inquiry into the Psychology of Ethics* (New York, 1947), *Psychology and Religion* (New Haven, 1950), *The Sane Society* (New York, 1955), and *Sigmund Freud's Mission: An Analysis of His Personality and Influence* (New York, 1950).

• GREENSTEIN, FRED I., "The Impact of Personality on Politics: An Attempt to Clear Away Underbrush," *American Political Science Review*, LXI (September 1967), pp. 629–641. See also: Sol W. Ginsburg, *A Psychiatrist's Views on Social Issues* (New York, 1963); Max Mark, "What Image of Man for Political Science?" *Western Political Quarterly*, XV (December 1962), pp. 593–604; Jerome S. Bruner, "Freud and the Image of Man," *Partisan Review*, XXIII (Summer 1956), pp. 340–347; Morton Levitt, *Freud and Dewey on the Nature of Man* (New York, 1960); and Harold D. Lasswell, "Person, Personality, Group, Culture," *Psychiatry* (November 1939), pp. 539–561.

• HOOK, SIDNEY (ed.), *Psychoanalysis, Scientific Method, and Philosophy* (New York, 1959). See also Herbert Feigl (ed.), *The Foundations of Science and the Concepts of Psychology and Psychoanalysis* (Minneapolis, 1956).

• HORNEY, KAREN, *The Neurotic Personality of Our Time* (New York, 1937). One of the former leading American psychoanalysts, the author modified, or at least supplemented, Freud, by stressing more strongly the cultural and social pressures in the formation of neuroses and conflicts. See also the following of her works: *New Ways in Psychoanalysis* (New York, 1939) and *Our Inner Conflicts* (New York, 1945).

• JONES, ERNEST (ed.), *Social Aspects of Psycho-Analysis* (London, 1924). The most interesting essay is Chap. IV, "Politics" (pp. 128–168), by M. D. Eder. It suggests the potential resources of psychoanalysis that could be employed for a better understanding of politics. See also the following: Hendrick M. Ruitenbeek (ed.), *Psychoanalysis and Social Science* (Dutton Paperbacks, New York, 1962), with contributions by Harold D. Lasswell, Talcott Parsons, Erik H. Erikson, Heinz Hartmann, and other leading writers in the field; J. C. Flugel, *Man, Morals, and Society: A Psychoanalytical Study* (London, 1945); Ranyard West, *Conscience and Society: A Study of the Psychological Prerequisites of Law and Order* (London, 1942); Bruce Mazlish (ed.), *Psychoanalysis and History* (Englewood Cliffs, N.J., 1963); Fritz Schmidl, "Psychoanalysis and History," *Psychoanalytic Quarterly,* XXXI (No. 4, 1962), pp. 532–548; Ernest Becker, "Social Science and Psychiatry," *Antioch Review,* XXIII (Fall 1963), pp. 353–366; Walter A. Weisskopf, *The Psychology of Economics* (Chicago, 1955); Louis Schneider, *The Freudian Psychology and Veblen's Social Theory* (New York, 1948); and Howard P. Rome, "A Psychiatrist's View," in E. J. Faulkner (ed.), *Man's Quest for Security: A Symposium* (Lincoln, Neb., 1966), pp. 59–74.

• ———, *The Life and Work of Sigmund Freud,* 3 vols. (New York, 1953–1957). The most informative biography of Freud by one of his closest friends and collaborators, and likely to remain the standard source for a long time. See also Jones' *Sigmund Freud: Four Centenary Addresses* (New York, 1956).

• KELSEN, HANS, "The Conception of State and Social Psychology," *International Journal of Psycho-Analysis,* V (Part 1, 1924), pp. 1–38. Illuminating analysis of various conceptions of the state in social psychology, with particular reference to Freud's group theory.

• LASSWELL, HAROLD D., *World Politics and Personal Insecurity* (New York–London, 1935). Lasswell is the first political scientist who has successfully applied psychoanalytical research methods and experience to the empirical study of political processes. See also the following of his books: *Psychopathology and Politics* (Chicago, 1930); *Politics: Who Gets What, When, How* (New York–London, 1936); *The Analysis of Political Behaviour* (London, 1947); *Power and Personality* (Compass Paperbacks, New York, 1962); and, in coauthorship with Abraham Kaplan, *Power and Society: A Framework for Political Inquiry* (New Haven, 1950). *The Political Writings of Harold D. Lasswell* (Glencoe, Ill., 1951), contains *Psychopathology and Politics; Politics: Who Gets What, When, How,* and *Democratic Character,* summarizing Lasswell's thought.

• NELSON, BENJAMIN (ed.), *Freud and the 20th Century* (Meridian Books, New York, 1957). A collection of essays on various aspects of Freud's influence by distinguished writers, including Alfred Kazin, Gregory Zilboorg, Gardner Murphy, Jacques Maritain, and Reinhold Niebuhr. See also John D. Sutherland (ed.), *Psychoanalysis and Contemporary Thought* (London, 1958), and Hendrik M. Ruitenbeek (ed.), *Psychoanalysis and Contemporary American Culture* (Delta Paperbacks, New York, 1964).

• OSBORN, REUBEN, *Marxism and Psycho-Analysis* (London, 1965). Seeking to integrate Marxian and Freudian thought, the author writes: "Both Marxism and psychoanalysis, in their different ways, are studies of the irrational in man's life. Marxism studies the irrationalities of the social order that prevent men utilizing to the full the technical discoveries that science has given them. Psychoanalysis studies the irrational forces in men's minds that thwart their development into mature, rational beings able to use science for their well-being. An irrational world situation demands a scientific study of irrationalities, whether subjectively or objectively considered. This is the justification for both the Freudian and Marxian approach" (p. 126). The author concludes that Freudian and Marxian theory "provide important correctives for each other. Freudian theory makes us aware of the complexity of the subjective life but tends to look at it in isolation from the social background. Marxism calls attention to the social determinants of human behaviour but tends to ignore the subjective pressures that lead men to enter into relationship with the social environment. Without the insights of Freudian theory Marxism tends to be brutal and clumsy in its approach" (pp. 154–155).

• RIEFF, PHILIP, *Freud: The Mind of the Moralist* (New York, 1959). A social scientist looks at Freud's work as it bears on questions of ethics, politics, and philosophy. See also Paul Roazen, *Freud: Political and Social Thought* (New York, 1968); Jacob A. Arlow, *The Legacy of Freud* (New York, 1956); Gregory Zilboorg, *Sigmund Freud: His Exploration of the Mind of Man* (New York, 1951); Herbert Marcuse, *Eros and Civilization: An Inquiry into Sigmund Freud* (Boston, 1955); Lionel Trilling, *Freud and the Crisis of Our Culture* (Boston, 1955); and *Psychoanalysis and the Social Sciences,* 5 vols. (New York, 1947–1958), continued since 1960 as *The Psychoanalytic Study of Society.*

• ROAZEN, PAUL, *Freud: Political and Social Thought* (New York, 1968). Freud has an undoubted, though uncertain, place in political thought and science. Roazen believes that an understanding of Freud's clinical theories is essential to a complete understanding of his social theories. A complex work.

• SACHS, HANNS, *Freud: Master and Friend* (London, 1945). The author knew Freud from the early stages of psychoanalysis to his death. See also Marthe Robert, *The Psychoanalytic Revolution: Sigmund Freud's Life and Achievement* (New York, 1966); Reuben Fine, *Freud: A Critical Re-Evaluation of His Theories* (New York, 1962); Walter Hollitscher, *Sigmund Freud: An Introduction* (London, 1947); and Charles Rycroft (ed.), *Psychoanalysis Observed* (London, 1966).

• WAELDER, ROBERT, *Progress and Revolution: A Study of the Issues of Our Age* (New York, 1967). The author, a noted psychoanalyst who takes a special interest in social and political questions, discusses—in clear and simple language—the major issues that confront the modern world.

CHAPTER THIRTY-THREE

GANDHI

• ALEXANDER, HORACE, *Gandhi Through Western Eyes,* 2nd ed. (Philadelphia, 1984). A life of Gandhi by an English Quaker who knew him for twenty years.

• ANDREWS, C. F., *Mahatma Gandhi's Ideas* (London, 1929). One of the first books about Gandhi, and still a good introduction to his thought. See also Andrews's *Mahatma Gandhi: His Own Story* (New York, 1930) and *Mahatma Gandhi at Work* (New York, 1931).

• APPADORAI, A. (ed.), *Documents on Political Thought in Modern India,* vol. I (New York, 1974). From British assumption of direct rule in 1857 to Nehru's death in 1964. Many items from Gandhi; allows comparison and contrast with his predecessors, contemporaries, and successors.

• ASH, GEOFFREY, *Gandhi* (New York, 1968). An important biography.

• BAKSHI, S. R., *Gandhi and His Techniques of Satyagraha* (London, 1987). A detailed examination of the practices of non-violent change that Gandhi recommended.

• BOSE, NIRMAL and P. H. PATWARDHAN, *Gandhi in Indian Politics* (Bombay, India, 1967). Chapter two is "The Political Philosophy of Gandhi."

• BROWN, JUDITH, *Gandhi; Prisoner of Hope* (New Haven, Conn., 1989). The major recent biography. Includes a very brief, but useful, bibliography.

• CHATTERJEE, MARGARET, *Gandhi's Religious Thought* (Notre Dame, Ind., 1983). Gandhi's moral and political thought were intermeshed. This study attempts to elucidate the religious component in Gandhi's thought.

• COPLEY, ANTONY, *Gandhi; Against the Tide* (Oxford, 1987). A very brief and useful introduction to Gandhi.

• EDWARDES, MICHAEL, *The Myth of the Mahatma* (London, 1986). A revisionist account of the British Empire in India and of Gandhi's role in dismantling it.

• ERIKSON, ERIK, *Gandhi's Truth: On the Origins of Militant Nonviolence* (New York, 1969). Erikson presents the key event in Gandhi's life as the 1918 textile workers' strike. Gandhi was at this time almost 50, and, while well-known in India and abroad for his role in the South African civil rights movement, was not yet revered and despised. The textile workers' strike was a success for satyagraha, and was the first time the fast was used. According to Erikson, this paved the way for the following year's nationwide civil disobedience campaign. This book won the 1970 National Book Award.

• FISCHER, LOUIS, *The Life of Mahatma Gandhi* (New York, 1958). The first full-scale biography of Gandhi's whole life.

• GANDHI, MOHANDAS, *The Moral and Political Writings of Mahatma Gandhi*, 3 vols. (ed. Raghavan Iyer, Oxford, 1986–1987). This is the place to start when considering Gandhi's moral and political thought directly. Volume 1 is *Civilization, Politics, and Religion;* Volume 2 is *Truth and Non-Violence,* and Volume 3 is *Non-Violent Resistance and Social Transformation.* See also Iyer's introductions.

• GANGULI, BIRENDRANATH, *Gandhi's Social Philosophy* (Delhi, India, 1973). A very comprehensive work.

• GREEN, MARTIN, *The Challenge of the Mahatmas* (New York, 1978). A study in the thought of Gandhi and Tolstoy. See also Green's *The Origins of Nonviolence* (University Park, Pa., 1986) and, for Thoreau's influence on Gandhi, *Gandhi's Concept of Civil Disobedience* (New Delhi, India, 1986).

• JACK, HOMER (ed.), *The Gandhi Reader* (New York, 1961). Subtitled *A Source Book of His Life and Writings,* this book by a Unitarian minister is an invaluable reference for writings by, and about, Gandhi from 1869 to 1931.

• IYER, RAGHAVAN, *The Moral and Political Thought of Mahatma Gandhi* (New York, 1973). Iyer believes that "in order to grasp Gandhi's moral and political thought . . . it is necessary to accept his profound integrity as a thinker and as a seeker of truth."

• PANTHAM, THOMAS, "Thinking with Mahatma Gandhi," *Political Theory* (May 1983), pp. 165–188. Presents the view that Gandhi's ethics are necessary to replace contemporary liberal democracy.

• PRADHAN, BENUDHAR, *The Socialist Thought of Mahatma Gandhi,* 2 vols. (Delhi, India, 1980). Pradhan's thesis is not that Gandhi was exclusively a socialist, but that there is much that was socialistic in it.

• PURI, RASHMI-SUDHA, *Gandhi on War and Peace* (New York, 1987). The author points out that Gandhi was not only for non-violence, he was opposed to war.

• RANI, ASHA, *Gandhian Non-Violence and India's Freedom Struggle* (Delhi, India, 1981). A study in the historical development and practice of Gandhi's principle of non-violence.

• RAY, SIBNARAYAN (ed.), *Gandhi, India, and the World* (Philadelphia, 1970). A collection of essays on a variety of subjects.

• ROY, RAMASHRAY, *Gandhi: Soundings in Political Philosophy* (Delhi, India, 1984). The non-western character of Gandhi's thought is stressed.

• SHARMA, BISHAN, *Gandhi as Political Thinker* (New Delhi, India, 1956). A valuable study. Includes a chapter, "Gandhi and the English Liberal Tradition."

• SWAN, MAUREEN, *Gandhi; The South African Experience* (Johannesburg, S. Africa, 1985). Swan challenges the view that Gandhi was leader of the mass of Indians in South Africa; rather, he is presented as, for the most part, a representative for the highest strata of the South African Indian community.

• WOLFENSTEIN, E. VICTOR, *The Revolutionary Personality: Lenin, Trotsky, Gandhi* (Princeton, 1967). Includes a psychobiography of Gandhi in which his commitment to non-violence is found to be a combination of guilt and self-assertion.

CHAPTER THIRTY-FOUR

FROM CLASSICAL LIBERALISM
TO DEMOCRATIC SOCIALISM

• ALBEE, ERNEST, *A History of English Utilitarianism* (London–New York, 1902). Chaps. XIII–XV (pp. 268–357) are on Spencer. The author concludes that, "in order to do Mr. Spencer justice, one must regard him as the last great Individualist, in the eighteenth century sense of the word, rather than as the true exponent of Evolutional Ethics" (p. 356).

• BARKER, ERNEST, *Political Thought in England, 1848 to 1914* (Home University Library, London, 1932). Excellent work with ample coverage of Green, Spencer, and others. F. J. C. Hearnshaw, "Herbert Spencer and the Individualists," in Hearnshaw (ed.), *The Social and Political Ideas of Some Representative Thinkers of the Victorian Age* (London, 1933), pp. 53–83.

• BRINTON, CRANE, *English Political Thought in the Nineteenth Century* (London, 1933). Contains a section on Green: "No one, not even the Mill who wrote so sympathetically on Socialism in his later years, marks better than Thomas Hill Green the change which came over English Liberalism in the latter half of the nineteenth century" (p. 212).

• COLE, G. D. H., *A History of Socialist Thought, 1789–1939,* 5 vols. (New York, 1953–1960). The standard work on the subject, lucidly written, and very broad in coverage. See also the following of Cole's writings: *Social Theory* (London, 1920), *Guild Socialism Restated* (London, 1920), *Robert Owen* (London, 1925), *A Short History of the British Working Class Movement,* 1789–1947, rev. ed. (London, 1948), *Socialist Economics* (London, 1950), *Essays in Social Theory* (London, 1950), *Studies in Class Structure* (London, 1955), and *Socialism in Evolution* (London, 1938). In *Socialism and Evolution,* Cole was one of the first writers to point out the impact on the Socialist parties of the growth of white collar workers, the "salariat," while the proportion of the manual workers in the total labor force has been constantly declining.

• COLE, MARGARET, *The Story of Fabian Socialism* (Stanford, Calif., 1961). Like her husband G. D. H. Cole, who served as chairman and president of the Fabian Society for a number of years, Margaret Cole served the Fabian Society in various capacities for nearly four decades, including a term of office as chairman. Her story of the Fabian Society from its foundation in 1883 to 1960 thus encompasses part of her own life and that of her husband's, and her writing bears the stamp of authenticity and inside knowledge and feeling. Margaret Cole (ed.), *The Webbs and Their Work* (London, 1949), is the best introduction into the thought of the two great Fabians, Sidney and Beatrice Webb, and has contributions by Bernard Shaw, Lord Beveridge, G. D. H. Cole, and others. Chap. XVI, "Political Thought and the Webbs" (pp. 251–264), by Leonard Woolf, is an incisive and critical account of the political ideas of the Webbs. Margaret Cole is also the author of a biography, *Beatrice Webb* (New York, 1946). Beatrice Webb wrote two books about herself and her husband Sidney Webb that are important sources for the study of Fabianism and British socialism: *My Apprenticeship* (London, 1926), and *Our Partnership* (London, 1948).

• DEWEY, JOHN, *Characters and Events,* 2 vols. (New York, 1929). Includes a study of Spencer's philosophy (I, pp. 45–62).

• DUNCAN, DAVID, *Life and Letters of Herbert Spencer,* 2 vols. (New York, 1908). Supplements Spencer's *Autobiography,* 2 vols. (New York, 1904).

• ENSOR, R. C. K., *Some Reflections on Herbert Spencer's Doctrine That Progress Is Differentiation* (London, 1946). The

Herbert Spencer Lecture, delivered before the University of Oxford, May 28, 1946. Ensor brings out the lasting value of Spencer's doctrine that differentiation is progress, and he shows the dangers in modern civilization resulting from uniformity of mind and outlook, particularly in totalitarian states. Even in democracies, the press, radio, and cinema represent, according to Ensor, dangerous elements of uniformity: "It has been through choruses of enslaved minds that every dictatorship has shouted its way into power" (p. 27).

• GREEN, T. H., (R. L. Nettleship, ed.), *Works of Thomas Hill Green,* 3 volumes (London, 1889). Green's complete works. Volume 3 includes a memoir by Nettleship of Green.

• GREENGARTEN, I. M., *Thomas Hill Green and the Development of Liberal-Democratic Thought* (Toronto, 1981). Presentation of Green's political thought from the perspective of a modern liberal.

• HALL, PETER A. (ed.), *The Political Power of Economic Ideas: Keynesianism across Nations* (Princeton, 1989). This excellent edited edition explores the power and the weakness of the economic ideas of Keynes across several different nations and eras. This work is an attempt at explaining the spread of economic ideas. The end result, however, seems to fall short. Its value lies in the excellent historical data presented by the various contributors.

• HOFSTADTER, RICHARD, *Social Darwinism in American Thought,* rev. ed. (Beacon Paperbacks, Boston, 1955). Chap. II, "The Vogue of Spencer" (pp. 31–50), is the best brief analysis of the influence of Spencer's social and political philosophy on American thought. See also Edward L. Youmans, *Herbert Spencer on the Americans, and the Americans on Herbert Spencer* (New York, 1883), containing the text of an interview with Spencer, and a report of the speeches delivered at the farewell banquet given for Spencer before his return to England. Truxtun Beale (ed.), *The Man versus the State* (New York, 1916), contains the full text of *The Man versus the State,* with prefaces to each chapter by distinguished American leaders, such as William Howard Taft, Charles W. Eliot, Elihu Root, Henry Cabot Lodge, Nicholas Murray Butler, E H. Gary, and others.

• HOLLOWAY, HARRY, "Mill and Green on the Modern Welfare State," *Western Political Quarterly,* XIII (June 1960), pp. 389–405. The author starts out from the paradox that it was Green, "thorough Victorian and of conservative inclination" (p. 389), who helped lay the foundations of the modern welfare state, and not Mill, who had strong sympathies for socialism and even called himself a "qualified socialist." The author feels that Mill's "intense individualism and his antipathy to majority rule gave his defense of liberty a negative quality," and that his "individualism was fundamentally one of independence and self-sufficiency more akin to the position and aspirations of the middle classes than of the lower classes" (pp. 403–404). By contrast, Green emphasized, in his conception of freedom, the "opportunity to participate in the goods of society," and by stressing the worth and importance of the community, he "went far towards breaking the bonds of liberalism with an out-dated individualism. His conservatism carried with it the potentially radical principle of extensive government intervention" (p. 404).

• KRAMNICK, ISAAC and BARRY SHEERMAN, *Harold Laski: A Life on the Left* (London, 1993). The definitive biography, also a pleasure to read. *Harold Laski: A Life on the Left* captures the man, his times, his influence, and his thought.

• LEWIS, H. D., *Freedom and History* (London, 1962). A collection of essays, including several excellent ones on Green. "The clue to Green's treatment of political questions is to be found in the strictness of his adherence to the ethical teaching of Kant, and especially to the view that nothing has worth in itself besides the good will" (p. 60).

• MACPHERSON, HECTOR, *Spencer and Spencerism* (New York, 1900). A balanced appraisal of Spencer's social, economic, political, ethical, philosophical, and religious views. See also Josiah Royce, *Herbert Spencer: An Estimate and Review* (New York, 1904); William Henry Hudson, *Herbert Spencer* (London, 1908); and Alfred W. Tillett, *Spencer's Synthetic Philosophy: What It Is All About* (London, 1914).

• MUKHOPADHYAY, AMAL KUMAR, *The Ethics of Obedience: A Study of the Philosophy of T. H. Green* (Calcutta, 1967). Short but insightful work. Mukhopadhyay concludes that Green's "was a collectivism not for the sake of collectivism, but for the sake of individual freedom and welfare. Thus it was possible that at Green's hand collectivism never became a rigid dogma; it was basically an individualist creed flexible enough to meet the new needs of society" (p. 179).

• PAUL, ELLEN, "Herbert Spencer: The Historicist as a Failed Prophet," *Journal of the History of Ideas* (October–December 1983). Presents the view that Spencer's views were historicist, as they see evolution as following a necessary course. This prevented Spencer from being able to forecast the future accurately.

• PEEL, JOHN, *Herbert Spencer: The Evolution of a Sociologist* (New York, 1971). Concerns the origin, content, and influence of Spencer's sociology. The most extensive recent work on this subject.

• RICHTER, MELVIN, *The Politics of Conscience: T. H. Green and His Age* (Cambridge, Mass., 1964). The definitive biography on Green, placing him, and his thought, within historical context. Excellent work.

• ROUTH, D. A., "The Philosophy of International Relations: T. H. Green *versus* Hegel," *Politica,* III (September 1938), pp. 223–235. Interesting comparison and contrast between Hegel and Green with regard to the problem of international order.

• RUMNEY, J., *Herbert Spencer's Sociology* (London–New York, 1934, reprinted 1966). Chap. V (pp. 130–161) is on "Society, State, Government," and Chap. VI (pp. 162–186) on "Property and Economic Institutions." An extensive bibliography of writings by, and on, Spencer is appended (pp. 311–351). See also the Introduction by Talcott Parsons to Herbert Spencer, *The Study of Sociology* (Ann Arbor Paperbacks, Ann Arbor, 1961).

• SCHUMPETER, JOSEPH A., *Capitalism, Socialism, and Democracy,* 3rd ed. (New York, 1950). The bulk of this book, written by one of the great economists of the twentieth century, is on socialism. Whereas most students of socialism—whether sympathetic to it or not—relate the rise of socialism to the failures of capitalism, Schumpeter considers socialism primarily as the result of capitalist achievements and successes. Written in the early 1940s, Schumpeter's masterful analysis reflects the skeptical assumptions about the future of capitalism then common, but the value of the work is not thereby impaired. See also Henry Smith, *The Economics of Socialism Reconsidered* (London–New York, 1962).

• SHAW, BERNARD, and OTHERS, *Fabian Essays* (London, 1889). The most famous document on "Fabian Socialism." In addition to Shaw, the contributors are Sidney Webb, Graham Wallas, Sydney Olivier, William Clarke, Annie Besant, and Hubert Bland. It has sold many tens of thousands of copies since its first publication and has never ceased to be a steady seller in the field of socialist literature.

• TAWNEY, R. H., *Equality,* 4th ed. (New York, 1965). Originally published in 1931, the book is one of the classics of British socialist thought. Tawney, a social and economic historian of distinction, had a marked influence on British socialism, his chief sources of inspiration being moral and religious.

• THOMAS, GEOFFREY, *The Moral Philosophy of T. H. Green* (Oxford, 1987). Detailed examination of Green's philosophical work. Contains a useful bibliography.

• TURNER, JONATHAN, *Herbert Spencer: A Renewed Appreciation* (Beverly Hills, 1985). Concentrates on Spencer's sociology. Turner believes there is much useful still in it.

• ULAM, ADAM B., *Philosophical Foundations of English Socialism* (Cambridge, Mass., 1951). Shows, in particular, the impact of English philosophical idealism on the early English socialists.

• VINCENT, ANDREW (ed.), *The Philosophy of T. H. Green* (Aldershot, 1986). Collection of essays by different authors, including two essays on Green's religious views.

• WEBB, SIDNEY, and BEATRICE WEBB, *The Decay of Capitalist Civilization,* 3rd ed. (London, 1923). See also *The Consumers' Co-operative Movement* (London, 1921), and *A Constitution for the Socialist Commonwealth of Great Britain* (London, 1920).

• WILTSHIRE, DAVID, *The Social and Political Thought of Herbert Spencer* (Oxford, 1978). Contains both a biography/intellectual history of Spencer and an elucidation of his political concerns.

· CHAPTER THIRTY-FIVE

THE WELFARE STATE

· BEVERIDGE, WILLIAM H., *Full Employment in a Free Society* (London, 1944). Like Keynes' *General Theory of Employment, Interest, and Money,* Beveridge's *Full Employment in a Free Society* is a pioneering contribution to the solution of the problem of a free society without want and misery, and both works are the products of intellectual leaders of the Liberal party. The underlying principle of *Full Employment in a Free Society* is "to propose for the State only those things which the State alone can do or which it can do better than any local authority or than private citizens either singly or in association, and to leave to these other agencies that which, if they will, they can do as well as or better than the State" (p. 36).

· GIRVETZ, HARRY K., *The Evolution of Liberalism* (Collier Books, New York, 1966). The author of this clearly written and cogently argued work divides liberalism into two parts. Part I (pp. 23–149) deals with "Classical Liberalism," covering the period from the seventeenth to the nineteenth century. Part II (pp. 153–387) deals with "Contemporary Liberalism," as it has evolved in the twentieth century. Throughout, the author examines the psychological, philosophical, economic, and political assumptions and realities of liberalism. For an English approach to modern liberalism, see Kenneth R. Minogue, *The Liberal Mind* (Vintage Books, New York, 1968).

· HARRIS, SEYMOUR (ed.), *The New Economics: Keynes' Influence on Theory and Public Policy* (New York, 1947, reprinted 1965). Contains varied appraisals of Keynes' doctrines in relation to classical and Marxian political economy by distinguished American and European economists. Indispensable to an understanding of Keynes' impact on public policy in Britain and the United States. See also A. C. Pigou, *Keynes' General Theory* (London, 1950); Alvin H. Hansen, *A Guide to Keynes* (New York, 1953); and Joseph A. Schumpeter, *Ten Great Economists* (London, 1952), whose Chap. X is on Keynes (pp. 260–291).

· HARROD, R. F., *The Life of John Maynard Keynes* (New York, 1951). The first full-length biography of Keynes' life and thought, with particular reference to his economic and political views. In "Are We Really All Keynesians Now?" *Encounter,* XXII (January 1964, 46–50), Harrod argues that, at least as far as public policies in Britain and the United States are concerned, the influence of Keynes has not been nearly as great as is commonly alleged. Harrod refers particularly to the issues, all-important to Keynes, of low interest rates, budget deficits, full employment and economic growth, and international balance of payments and international monetary liquidity.

· HEILBRONER, ROBERT L., *The Worldly Philosophers: The Lives, Times, and Ideas of the Great Economic Thinkers,* 6th ed. (New York, 1986). Chap. IX of this popular book, addressed to the general reader, is on "The Sick World of John Maynard Keynes." The author stresses that Keynes was at heart a conservative, whose aim was to rescue capitalism, not to destroy it, to create "a capitalist economy in which unemployment—the single greatest and gravest threat to its continuance—would be forever eliminated."

· HUTT, W. H., *The Keynesian Episode: A Reassessment* (Indianapolis, 1979). A reworking of Hutt's 1963 *Keynesianism—Retrospect and Prospect* (Chicago). One of the most detailed and hostile criticisms of Keynes and Keynesianism.

· JOHNSON, ELIZABETH, *The Shadow of Keynes* (Oxford, 1978). A work on Keynes, his Cambridge environment, and Keynesianism.

· JOHNSON, HARRY G., "The *General Theory* after Twenty-Five Years," *American*

Economic Review (Papers and Proceedings), LI (May 1961), pp. 1–17. On the positive side, the author states, Keynes' *General Theory of Employment, Interest, and Money* "explained why the competitive capitalist economy does not automatically maintain a satisfactory level of employment and outlined the theory of remedial policy, thereby promoting a revolution in ideas on the responsibilities of government in such a system" (pp. 16–17). On the negative side "is the bias that the majority of Keynesians have drawn from the *General Theory* against allowing money, and consequently monetary policy, an important role in determining the level of activity of the economy. This bias has meant that Keynesian theory has proved a poor guide to the dominant postwar policy problem of inflation and that the Keynesian approach to this problem has tended to degenerate into a confused and often obstructive eclecticism" (p. 14).

• KAHN, RICHARD, *The Making of Keynes' General Theory* (Cambridge, 1984). Six lectures on the background and content of Keynes's economics, together with biographical matter on Keynes and an excellent bibliography.

• KEYNES, JOHN MAYNARD, *Two Memoirs* (London, 1949). The second memoir is on "My Early Beliefs" (written in 1938), which throws considerable light on Keynes' early intellectual development. See also Keynes' *Essays in Persuasion* (New York, 1932), particularly "Am I a Liberal?" (pp. 323–338), "Liberalism and Labour" (pp. 339–345), and "Economic Possibilities for Our Grandchildren" (pp. 358–373).

• KEYNES, MILO (ed.), *Essays on John Maynard Keynes* (London, 1975). A collection of mostly personal essays.

• LEKACHMAN, ROBERT, *The Age of Keynes* (Vintage Books, New York, 1968). Chaps. 1–7 (pp. 11–202) are on "Keynes and Keynesian Economics," and Chaps. 8–11 (pp. 205–301) on "The Keynesian Era." In the concluding "Epilogue" the author writes that Keynes' *General Theory* "was really a search for increased rationality in economic policy. In its contemporary applications, Keynesian economics is essentially a description of the ways in which an alert government, by taking thought, can tame the business cycle and alleviate the miseries of personal insecurity. If Keynes could be said to have possessed an ideology, it was a confidence born of the humane Locke-Hume-Mill tradition that intelligence in human affairs is both essential and possible" (p. 303). See also Lekachman's "John Maynard Keynes," *Encounter*, XXI (December 1963), pp. 34–43, and the symposium edited by him, *Keynes and the Classics* (Boston, 1964).

• MINSKY, HYMAN, *John Maynard Keynes* (New York, 1975). Concentrates almost exclusively on *The General Theory of Employment, Interest, and Money,* with little reference to Keynes's other, or to secondary, works. Minsky's thesis is that *The General Theory* has been misunderstood.

• Moggridge, Donald, *John Maynard Keynes* (New York, 1976). An introduction to Keynes and his thought. Part of the "Modern Masters" series.

• Ruggiero, Guido de, *The History of European Liberalism* (Beacon Paperbacks, Boston, 1959). The first part of the book deals with the evolution of liberalism in England, France, Germany, and Italy, while the second part inquires into the relations of liberalism and socialism, democracy, religion, and nationalism. A useful bibliography is included (pp. 445–463). See also Maurice Cranston, *Freedom: A New Analysis (* New York, 1953), which contains both a philosophical analysis of the concept of freedom and the historical varieties of liberalism in England, France, Germany, and the United States.

• Vicarelli, Fausto (ed.), *Keynes's Relevance Today* (Philadelphia, 1985). A collection of essays, mostly on economic topics. See also Vicarelli's *Keynes; The Instability of Capitalism* (trans. John Walker, Philadelphia, 1984).

CHAPTER THIRTY-SIX

LIBERTARIANISM

- BARRY, NORMAN, *Hayek's Social and Economic Philosophy* (London, 1979). Barry's work outlines and discusses the major ideas in philosophy, law, politics, and economics of Hayek.
- BERLIN, ISAIAH, *The Proper Study of Mankind: An Anthology of Essays* (New York, 1997). Definitive collection of all Berlin's major essays.
- BUTLER, EAMONN, *Hayek; His Contribution to the Political and Economic Thought of Our Time* (London, 1983). A good introduction to Hayek's comprehensive thought.
- CUNNINGHAM, ROBERT (ed.), *Liberty and the Rule of Law* (College Station, Tex., 1979). A collection of essays.
- FINER, HERMAN, *Road to Reaction* (Boston, Mass., 1945). Finer's preface gives the tone of this book, and of much early reaction to *The Road to Serfdom:* "Hayek's apparatus of learning is deficient, his reading incomplete; . . . his understanding of the economic process is bigoted, . . . his political science is almost non-existent."
- FRIEDMAN, MILTON, *Capitalism and Freedom* (Chicago, 1962). Friedman's policy recommendations for the American economy, and his presentation of how and why political and economic freedom are inter-related.
- GALEOTTI, ANNA, "Individualism, Social Rules, Tradition," *Political Theory* (May 1987), pp. 163–181. This article explores Hayek's conception of individualism, finding that it places very little importance on political citizenship, and concluding that his is a coherent perspective only when political citizenship is replaced by other social ties.
- GRAY, JOHN, *Hayek on Liberty* (Oxford, 1984). Emphasizes the naturalist character of Hayek's theory of justice, in that for him justice is what is naturally possible, not what would be ethically desirable. Includes an extensive bibliography.

- ————, *Isaiah Berlin* (Princeton, 1996). Book-length intellectual study emphasizing Berlin's pluralism. Somewhat like Berlin, Gray is highly erudite; his exegesis does not, however, match his elocution. Gray defines Berlin's position as "agnostic liberalism." Contains a good "Further Reading" section.
- HOY, CALVIN, *A Philosophy of Individual Freedom: The Political Thought of F. A. Hayek* (Westport, Conn., 1984). A thorough, though brief, investigation into the political thought of Hayek.
- IGNATIEFF, MICHAEL, *Isaiah Berlin: A Life* (New York, 1998). Highly favorable and intimate biography of Berlin by one who had dialogues with him for years. The picture of Berlin that emerges from Ignatieff's work is of a great conversationalist more than a great theoretician. Ignatieff covers all aspects of Berlin's life and thought. Ignatieff observes that "[b]y the early 1960s Berlin had a unique reputation, neither as a historian nor a philosopher, but as an idiosyncratic combination of the two" (p. 244).
- KOCIS, ROBERT, *A Critical Appraisal of Sir Isaiah Berlin's Political Philosophy* (Lewiston, N.Y., 1989). Comprehensive presentation.
- MACHLUP FRITZ (ed.), *Essays on Hayek* (New York, 1976). Essays by Hayek supporters, including Milton Friedman and William Buckley.
- PODHORETZ, NORMAN, "A Dissent on Isaiah Berlin," *Commentary* (February 1999). Podhoretz's view is well summarized in the synopsis of the article: "An extraordinary brilliant man was neither the great thinker nor the moral paragon his admirers have made him out to be." A useful corrective to excessively effusive views of Berlin.
- WALKER, GRAHAM, *The Ethics of F. A. Hayek* (Lanham, Maryland, 1986). A critique of the ethical underpinnings of Hayek's thought from a Christian perspective.

CHAPTER THIRTY-EIGHT

RAWLS

• *The American Political Science Review* (June 1975). Contains seven articles on *A Theory of Justice,* including one by Allan Bloom criticizing Rawls from the perspective of traditional political philosophy.

• BARRY, BRIAN, *The Liberal Theory of Justice* (Oxford, 1973). The first and in many ways still the best full-length refutation of Rawls. Barry's book subjects *A Theory of Justice* on a number of points to criticism.

• BLOCKER, H. G., et al. (eds.), *John Rawls' Theory of Social Justice: An Introduction* (Athens, Ohio, 1980). A collection of essays grouped under the headings "Fundamentals of the Rawlsian System of Justice," "Applications of the Rawlsian System of Justice," and "Rawls in Perspective."

• DANIELS, NORMAN (ed.), *Reading Rawls* (New York, 1980). An excellent collection of essays.

• DE CRESPIGNY, ANTHONY and KENNETH MINOGUE (eds.), *Contemporary Political Philosophers* (London, 1976). Includes a chapter by Samuel Gorovitz on Rawls.

• DI QUATTRO, ARTHUR, "Rawls and Left Criticism," *Political Theory* (February 1983), pp. 53–78. A defense of Rawls from left criticism, holding: "Rawls' theory of justice, though in need of some friendly amendments, is essentially compatible with socialist, including Marxist, ideas of social justice."

• ESQUITH, STEPHEN and RICHARD PETERSON, "The Original Position as Social Practice," *Political Theory* (May 1988), pp. 300–334. A Marxist critique of the original position and the ideology which the authors believe is inherent in it—"a kind of humanistic corporatism." Unsurprisingly, Rawls' division of political and economic spheres is criticized.

• KUKATHAS, CHANDRAN and PHILIP PETTIT, *Rawls:* A Theory of Justice *and its Critics*

(Stanford University Press: 1990). Includes consideration of Rawls from libertarian and communitarian perspectives.

• MARTIN, REX, *Rawls and Rights* (Lawrence, Kansas, 1985). Martin attempts to extend Rawls' principles in a way which he feels defends Rawls from some criticisms. Martin's emphasis is on the "basic structure rights" which he finds in Rawls, and which he considers of both a political and moral nature.

• NIELSEN, KAI and ROGER SHINER (eds.), *New Essays on Contract Theory* (Guleph, Canada, 1977). Most of the essays are on Rawls.

• POGGE, THOMAS, *Realizing Rawls* (Ithaca, N.Y., 1989). A defense and constructive critique of Rawls' work. Pogge focuses on the basic structure and the maximin principle.

• RAWLS, JOHN, "Some Reasons for the Maximin Criterion," *American Economic Review* (May 1974), pp. 141–146. A brief defense of the maximin criterion, holding in essence: "the maximin criterion is not meant to apply to small-scale situations . . . Maximin is a macro not a micro principle."

• SCHAEFER, DAVID, *Justice or Tyranny? A Critique of John Rawls'* A Theory of Justice (Washington, N.Y., 1979). The most strident criticism of Rawls, from a Straussian perspective.

• WELLBANK, J. H., et al., *John Rawls and His Critics: An Annotated Bibliography* (New York, 1982). Almost 700 pages and 2,500 entries. Includes all primary sources, and secondary sources by author, title, review, and concept.

• WOLFF, ROBERT, *Understanding Rawls: A Reconstruction and Critique of* A Theory of Justice (Princeton, 1977). Another criticism of Rawls, from a leftist viewpoint.

NAME INDEX

SUBJECT INDEX